PEARSON CUSTOM LIBRARY

MGMT 340 - Operations Management (Chapters from Heizer, Render, and Munson Operations Management Textbook) (Instructor: Randy Rosenberger)

PEARSON

Cover Art: Courtesy of EyeWire/Getty Images and PhotoDisc/Getty Images. Photodisc, "Globe surrounded by business people on computer monitors," courtesy of Photodisc/Getty Images. Dave Cutler (Artist), "Man Dropping Coins Into Glass Jar," courtesy of David Cutler/Images.com. Dave Cutler (Artist), "Three Coins in Glass Jar," courtesy of David Cutler/Images.com. Dean Turner, "Stock Vector: Global Finance" Courtesy of Dean Turner/iStockphoto. Hal Bergman, "Refinery Silhouette" Courtesy of Hal Bergman/iStockphoto. Dan Barnes, "Cargo Container Ship Aerial View" Courtesy of Dan Barnes/iStockphoto. Franc Podgorsek, "Stock Numbers" Courtesy of Franc Podgorsek/iStockphoto. "Customer in Line at Grocery Store" Courtesy of Digital Vision Photography/Veer Inc. Owaki-Kulla, "Pumping Gas" Courtesy of Flirt Photography/Veer Inc. Lynn Johnson, "Yunnan Province, People's Republic of China" Courtesy of Lynn Johnson/Getty Images, Inc. Thomas Bendy, "Student Typing" Courtesy of Thomas Bendy/iStockphoto. "Balance" courtesy of Denis Vorob´yev/iStockphoto; "Follow the leader" courtesy of Denis Vorob´yev/iStockphoto; "Office workers" courtesy of René Mansi/iStockphoto. "Shopping Mall 2" courtesy of Heng kong Chen/Fotolia. "Tokyo Pedestrian Crossing" courtesy of rigamondis/Fotolia. "Business adviser analyzing financial figures" courtesy of ty/Fotolia. "Internet shopping" courtesy of beawolf/Fotolia. Additional images courtesy of Photodisc, DigitalVision/Getty Images, Stockbyte/Getty Images, Photodisc/Getty Images, Eyewire/Getty Images, Digital Vision, Rubberball Productions/Getty Images, brandXpictures.

Pearson Learning Solutions, 501 Boylston Street, Suite 900, Boston, MA 02116
A Pearson Education Company
www.pearsoned.com

Printed in the United States of America
1 16

PEARSON

ISBN 10: 1-323-35826-9
ISBN 13: 978-1-323-35826-9

PEARSON

PEARSON CUSTOM LIBRARY

Table of Contents

Operations and Productivity

OUTLINE

10 OM STRATEGY DECISIONS

- Design of Goods and Services
- Managing Quality
- Process Strategy
- Location Strategies
- Layout Strategies
- Human Resources
- Supply-Chain Management
- Inventory Management
- Scheduling
- Maintenance

GLOBAL COMPANY PROFILE
Hard Rock Cafe

Operations Management at Hard Rock Cafe

Operations managers throughout the world are producing products every day to provide for the well-being of society. These products take on a multitude of forms. They may be washing machines at Whirlpool, motion pictures at DreamWorks, rides at Disney World, or food at Hard Rock Cafe. These firms produce thousands of complex products every day—to be delivered as the customer ordered them, when the customer wants them, and where the customer wants them. Hard Rock does this for over 35 million guests worldwide every year. This is a challenging task, and the operations manager's job, whether at Whirlpool, DreamWorks, Disney, or Hard Rock, is demanding.

Andre Jenny/Alamy

Hard Rock Cafe in Orlando, Florida, prepares over 3,500 meals each day. Seating more than 1,500 people, it is one of the largest restaurants in the world. But Hard Rock's operations managers serve the hot food hot and the cold food cold.

Demetrio Carrasco © Rough Guides

Operations managers are interested in the attractiveness of the layout, but they must be sure that the facility contributes to the efficient movement of people and material with the necessary controls to ensure that proper portions are served.

© Presselect/Alamy

Lots of work goes into designing, testing, and costing meals. Then suppliers deliver quality products on time, every time, for well-trained cooks to prepare quality meals. But none of that matters unless an enthusiastic wait staff, such as the one shown here, holding guitars previously owned by members of U2, is doing its job.

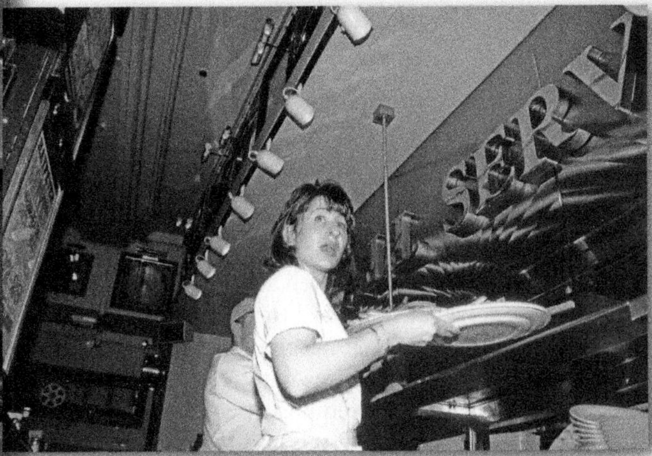

© Jack Picone/Alamy

Efficient kitchen layouts, motivated personnel, tight schedules, and the right ingredients at the right place at the right time are required to delight the customer.

Orlando-based Hard Rock Cafe opened its first restaurant in London in 1971, making it over 42 years old and the granddaddy of theme restaurants. Although other theme restaurants have come and gone, Hard Rock is still going strong, with 150 restaurants in more than 53 countries—and new restaurants opening each year. Hard Rock made its name with rock music memorabilia, having started when Eric Clapton, a regular customer, marked his favorite bar stool by hanging his guitar on the wall in the London cafe. Now Hard Rock has 70,000 items and millions of dollars invested in memorabilia. To keep customers coming back time and again, Hard Rock creates value in the form of good food and entertainment.

The operations managers at Hard Rock Cafe at Universal Studios in Orlando provide more than 3,500 custom products—in this case meals—every day. These products are designed, tested, and then analyzed for cost of ingredients, labor requirements, and customer satisfaction. On approval, menu items are put into production—and then only if the ingredients are available from qualified suppliers. The production process, from receiving, to cold storage, to grilling or baking or frying, and a dozen other steps, is designed and maintained to yield a quality meal. Operations managers, using the best people they can recruit and train, also prepare effective employee schedules and design efficient layouts.

Managers who successfully design and deliver goods and services throughout the world understand operations. In this text, we look not only at how Hard Rock's managers create value but also how operations managers in other services, as well as in manufacturing, do so. Operations management is demanding, challenging, and exciting. It affects our lives every day. Ultimately, operations managers determine how well we live.

LEARNING OBJECTIVES

- **LO1** *Define* operations management
- **LO2** *Explain* the distinction between goods and services
- **LO3** *Explain* the difference between production and productivity
- **LO4** *Compute* single-factor productivity
- **LO5** *Compute* multifactor productivity
- **LO6** *Identify* the critical variables in enhancing productivity

STUDENT TIP Let's begin by defining what this course is about.

What Is Operations Management?

LO1 *Define* operations management

Operations management (OM) is a discipline that applies to restaurants like Hard Rock Cafe as well as to factories like Ford and Whirlpool. The techniques of OM apply throughout the world to virtually all productive enterprises. It doesn't matter if the application is in an office, a hospital, a restaurant, a department store, or a factory—the production of goods and services requires operations management. And the *efficient* production of goods and services requires effective applications of the concepts, tools, and techniques of OM that we introduce in this text.

VIDEO 1 Operations Management at Hard Rock

VIDEO 2 Operations Management at Frito-Lay

As we progress through this text, we will discover how to manage operations in an economy in which both customers and suppliers are located throughout the world. An array of informative examples, charts, text discussions, and pictures illustrates concepts and provides information. We will see how operations managers create the goods and services that enrich our lives.

In this text, we first define *operations management*, explaining its heritage and exploring the exciting role operations managers play in a huge variety of organizations. Then we discuss production and productivity in both goods- and service-producing firms. This is followed by a discussion of operations in the service sector and the challenge of managing an effective and efficient production system.

Production The creation of goods and services.

Operations management (OM) Activities that relate to the creation of goods and services through the transformation of inputs to outputs.

Production is the creation of goods and services. **Operations management (OM)** is the set of activities that creates value in the form of goods and services by transforming inputs into outputs. Activities creating goods and services take place in all organizations. In manufacturing firms, the production activities that create goods are usually quite obvious. In them, we can see the creation of a tangible product such as a Sony TV or a Harley-Davidson motorcycle.

In an organization that does not create a tangible good or product, the production function may be less obvious. We often call these activities *services*. The services may be "hidden" from the public and even from the customer. The product may take such forms as the transfer of funds from a savings account to a checking account, the transplant of a liver, the filling of an empty seat on an airplane, or the education of a student. Regardless of whether the end product is a good or service, the production activities that go on in the organization are often referred to as operations, or *operations management*.

STUDENT TIP Operations is one of the three functions that every organization performs.

Organizing to Produce Goods and Services

To create goods and services, all organizations perform three functions (see Figure 1). These functions are the necessary ingredients not only for production but also for an organization's survival. They are:

1. *Marketing*, which generates the demand, or at least takes the order for a product or service (nothing happens until there is a sale).
2. *Production/operations*, which creates the product.
3. *Finance/accounting*, which tracks how well the organization is doing, pays the bills, and collects the money.

Universities, churches or synagogues, and businesses all perform these functions. Even a volunteer group such as the Boy Scouts of America is organized to perform these three basic

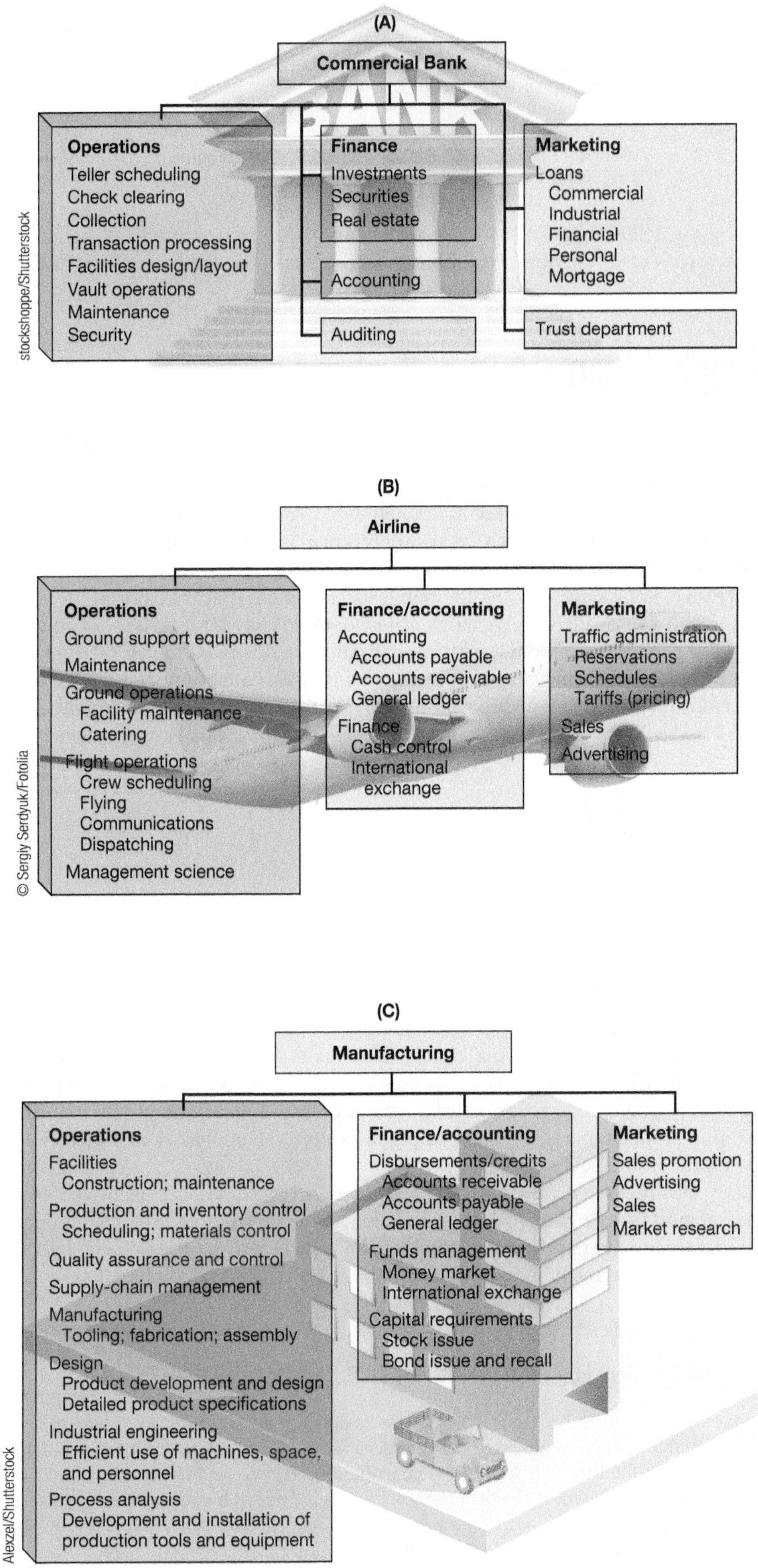

Figure 1

Organization Charts for Two Service Organizations and One Manufacturing Organization

(A) a bank, (B) an airline, and (C) a manufacturing organization. The blue areas are OM activities.

STUDENT TIP

The areas in blue indicate the significant role that OM plays in both manufacturing and service firms.

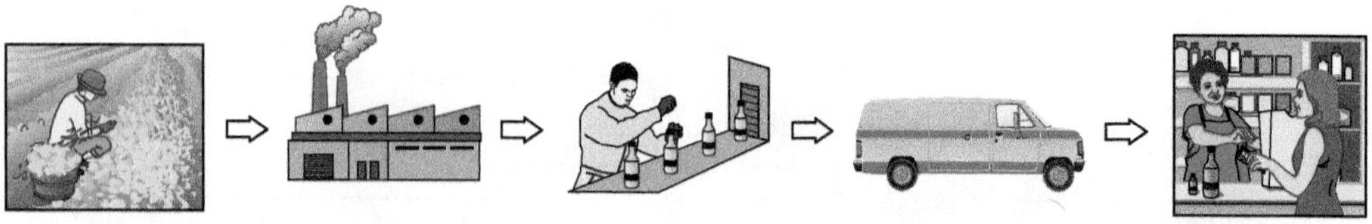

Figure 2
Soft Drink Supply Chain
A supply chain for a bottle of Coke requires a beet or sugar cane farmer, a syrup producer, a bottler, a distributor, and a retailer, each adding value to satisfy a customer. Only with collaborations between all members of the supply chain can efficiency and customer satisfaction be maximized. The supply chain, in general, starts with the provider of basic raw materials and continues all the way to the final customer at the retail store.

functions. Figure 1 shows how a bank, an airline, and a manufacturing firm organize themselves to perform these functions. The blue-shaded areas show the operations functions in these firms.

The Supply Chain

Through the three functions—marketing, operations, and finance—value for the customer is created. However, firms seldom create this value by themselves. Instead, they rely on a variety of suppliers who provide everything from raw materials to accounting services. These suppliers, when taken together, can be thought of as a *supply chain.* A supply chain (see Figure 2) is a global network of organizations and activities that supply a firm with goods and services.

Supply chain
A global network of organizations and activities that supplies a firm with goods and services.

As our society becomes more technologically oriented, we see increasing specialization. Specialized expert knowledge, instant communication, and cheaper transportation also foster specialization and worldwide supply chains. It just does not pay for a firm to try to do everything itself. The expertise that comes with specialization exists up and down the supply chain, adding value at each step. When members of the supply chain collaborate to achieve high levels of customer satisfaction, we have a tremendous force for efficiency and competitive advantage. Competition in the 21st century is no longer between companies; it is between *supply chains.*

Why Study OM?

STUDENT TIP Good OM managers are scarce and, as a result, career opportunities and pay are excellent.

We study OM for four reasons:

1. OM is one of the three major functions of any organization, and it is integrally related to all the other business functions. All organizations market (sell), finance (account), and produce (operate), and it is important to know how the OM activity functions. Therefore, we study *how people organize themselves for productive enterprise.*
2. We study OM because we want to know *how goods and services are produced.* The production function is the segment of our society that creates the products and services we use.
3. We study OM to *understand what operations managers do.* Regardless of your job in an organization, you can perform better if you understand what operations managers do. In addition, understanding OM will help you explore the numerous and lucrative career opportunities in the field.
4. We study OM *because it is such a costly part of an organization.* A large percentage of the revenue of most firms is spent in the OM function. Indeed, OM provides a major opportunity for an organization to improve its profitability and enhance its service to society. Example 1 considers how a firm might increase its profitability via the production function.

Example 1

EXAMINING THE OPTIONS FOR INCREASING CONTRIBUTION

Fisher Technologies is a small firm that must double its dollar contribution to fixed cost and profit in order to be profitable enough to purchase the next generation of production equipment. Management has determined that if the firm fails to increase contribution, its bank will not make the loan and the equipment cannot be purchased. If the firm cannot purchase the equipment, the limitations of the old equipment will force Fisher to go out of business and, in doing so, put its employees out of work and discontinue producing goods and services for its customers.

APPROACH ▶ Table 1 shows a simple profit-and-loss statement and three strategic options (marketing, finance/accounting, and operations) for the firm. The first option is a *marketing option*, where excellent marketing management may increase sales by 50%. By increasing sales by 50%, contribution will in turn increase 71%. But increasing sales 50% may be difficult; it may even be impossible.

TABLE 1 Options for Increasing Contribution

		MARKETING OPTION[a]	FINANCE/ ACCOUNTING OPTION[b]	OM OPTION[c]
	CURRENT	INCREASE SALES REVENUE 50%	REDUCE FINANCE COSTS 50%	REDUCE PRODUCTION COSTS 20%
Sales	$100,000	$150,000	$100,000	$100,000
Costs of goods	−80,000	−120,000	−80,000	−64,000
Gross margin	20,000	30,000	20,000	36,000
Finance costs	−6,000	−6,000	−3,000	−6,000
Subtotal	14,000	24,000	17,000	30,000
Taxes at 25%	−3,500	−6,000	−4,250	−7,500
Contribution[d]	$ 10,500	$ 18,000	$ 12,750	$ 22,500

[a] Increasing sales 50% increases contribution by $7,500, or 71% (7,500/10,500).
[b] Reducing finance costs 50% increases contribution by $2,250, or 21% (2,250/10,500).
[c] Reducing production costs 20% increases contribution by $12,000, or 114% (12,000/10,500).
[d] Contribution to fixed cost (excluding finance costs) and profit.

The second option is a *finance/accounting option*, where finance costs are cut in half through good financial management. But even a reduction of 50% is still inadequate for generating the necessary increase in contribution. Contribution is increased by only 21%.

The third option is an *OM option*, where management reduces production costs by 20% and increases contribution by 114%.

SOLUTION ▶ Given the conditions of our brief example, Fisher Technologies has increased contribution from $10,500 to $22,500. It may now have a bank willing to lend it additional funds.

INSIGHT ▶ The OM option not only yields the greatest improvement in contribution but also may be the only feasible option. Increasing sales by 50% and decreasing finance cost by 50% may both be virtually impossible. Reducing operations cost by 20% may be difficult but feasible.

LEARNING EXERCISE ▶ What is the impact of only a 15% decrease in costs in the OM option? [Answer: A $19,500 contribution; an 86% increase.]

Example 1 underscores the importance of the effective operations activity of a firm. Development of increasingly effective operations is the approach taken by many companies as they face growing global competition.

What Operations Managers Do

All good managers perform the basic functions of the management process. The management process consists of *planning*, *organizing*, *staffing*, *leading*, and *controlling*. Operations managers apply this management process to the decisions they make in the OM function. The 10 strategic OM decisions are introduced in Table 2. Successfully addressing each of these decisions requires planning, organizing, staffing, leading, and controlling.

10 Strategic OM Decisions
Design of goods and services
Managing quality
Process strategy
Location strategies
Layout strategies
Human resources
Supply-chain management
Inventory management
Scheduling
Maintenance

Where Are the OM Jobs? How does one get started on a career in operations? The 10 strategic OM decisions identified in Table 2 are made by individuals who work in the disciplines shown in the blue areas of Figure 1. Business students who know their accounting,

STUDENT TIP ☆
An operations manager must successfully address the 10 decisions around which this text is organized.

TABLE 2 Ten Strategic Operations Management Decisions

DECISION
1. *Design of goods and services:* Defines much of what is required of operations in each of the other OM decisions. For instance, product design usually determines the lower limits of cost and the upper limits of quality, as well as major implications for sustainability and the human resources required.
2. *Managing quality:* Determines the customer's quality expectations and establishes policies and procedures to identify and achieve that quality.
3. *Process and capacity design:* Determines how a good or service is produced (i.e., the process for production) and commits management to specific technology, quality, human resources, and capital investments that determine much of the firm's basic cost structure.
4. *Location strategy:* Requires judgments regarding nearness to customers, suppliers, and talent, while considering costs, infrastructure, logistics, and government.
5. *Layout strategy:* Requires integrating capacity needs, personnel levels, technology, and inventory requirements to determine the efficient flow of materials, people, and information.
6. *Human resources and job design:* Determines how to recruit, motivate, and retain personnel with the required talent and skills. People are an integral and expensive part of the total system design.
7. *Supply-chain management:* Decides how to integrate the supply chain into the firm's strategy, including decisions that determine what is to be purchased, from whom, and under what conditions.
8. *Inventory management:* Considers inventory ordering and holding decisions and how to optimize them as customer satisfaction, supplier capability, and production schedules are considered.
9. *Scheduling:* Determines and implements intermediate- and short-term schedules that effectively and efficiently utilize both personnel and facilities while meeting customer demands.
10. *Maintenance:* Requires decisions that consider facility capacity, production demands, and personnel necessary to maintain a reliable and stable process.

statistics, finance, and OM have an opportunity to assume entry-level positions in all of these areas. As you read this text, identify disciplines that can assist you in making these decisions. Then take courses in those areas. The more background an OM student has in accounting, statistics, information systems, and mathematics, the more job opportunities will be available. About 40% of *all* jobs are in OM.

The following professional organizations provide various certifications that may enhance your education and be of help in your career:

- APICS, the Association for Operations Management (www.apics.org)
- American Society for Quality (ASQ) (www.asq.org)
- Institute for Supply Management (ISM) (www.ism.ws)
- Project Management Institute (PMI) (www.pmi.org)
- Council of Supply Chain Management Professionals (www.cscmp.org)

Figure 3 shows some recent job opportunities.

The Heritage of Operations Management

The field of OM is relatively young, but its history is rich and interesting. Our lives and the OM discipline have been enhanced by the innovations and contributions of numerous individuals. We now introduce a few of these people, and we provide a summary of significant events in operations management in Figure 4.

Operations Management Positions

SEARCH JOBS

Date	Job Title
1/15	**Plant Manager** Division of Fortune 1000 company seeks plant manager for plant located in the upper Hudson Valley area. This plant manufactures loading dock equipment for commercial markets. The candidate must be experienced in plant management including expertise in production planning, purchasing, and inventory management. Good written and oral communication skills are a must, along with excellent application of skills in managing people.
2/23	**Operations Analyst** Expanding national coffee shop: top 10 "Best Places to Work" wants junior level systems analyst to join our excellent store improvement team. Business or I.E. degree, work methods, labor standards, ergonomics, cost accounting knowledge a plus. This is a hands-on job and excellent opportunity for a team player with good people skills. West Coast location. Some travel required.
3/18	**Quality Manager** Several openings exist in our small package processing facilities in the Northeast, Florida, and Southern California for quality managers. These highly visible positions require extensive use of statistical tools to monitor all aspects of service, timeliness, and workload measurement. The work involves (1) a combination of hands-on applications and detailed analysis using databases and spreadsheets, (2) processing of audits to identify areas for improvement and (3) management of implementation of changes. Positions involve night hours and weekends.
4/6	**Supply-Chain Manager and Planner** Responsibilities entail negotiating contracts and establishing long-term relationships with suppliers. We will rely on the selected candidate to maintain accuracy in the purchasing system, invoices, and product returns. A bachelor's degree and up to 2 years related experience are required. Working knowledge of MRP, ability to use feedback to master scheduling and suppliers and consolidate orders for best price and delivery are necessary. Proficiency in all PC Windows applications, particularly Excel and Word, is essential. Effective verbal and written communication skills are essential.
5/14	**Process Improvement Consultants** An expanding consulting firm is seeking consultants to design and implement lean production and cycle time reduction plans in both service and manufacturing processes. Our firm is currently working with an international bank to improve its back office operations, as well as with several manufacturing firms. A business degree required; APICS certification a plus.

Figure 3

Many Opportunities Exist for Operations Managers

Eli Whitney (1800) is credited for the early popularization of interchangeable parts, which was achieved through standardization and quality control. Through a contract he signed with the U.S. government for 10,000 muskets, he was able to command a premium price because of their interchangeable parts.

Frederick W. Taylor (1881), known as the father of scientific management, contributed to personnel selection, planning and scheduling, motion study, and the now popular field of ergonomics. One of his major contributions was his belief that management should be much more resourceful and aggressive in the improvement of work methods. Taylor and his colleagues, Henry L. Gantt and Frank and Lillian Gilbreth, were among the first to systematically seek the best way to produce.

Another of Taylor's contributions was the belief that management should assume more responsibility for:

1. Matching employees to the right job.
2. Providing the proper training.
3. Providing proper work methods and tools.
4. Establishing legitimate incentives for work to be accomplished.

From the collection of Henry Ford Museum & Greenfield Village

Cost Focus		Quality Focus	Customization Focus	Globalization Focus
Early Concepts 1776–1880 Labor Specialization (Smith, Babbage) Standardized Parts (Whitney) **Scientific Management Era 1880–1910** Gantt Charts (Gantt) Motion & Time Studies (Gilbreth) Process Analysis (Taylor) Queuing Theory (Erlang)	**Mass Production Era 1910–1980** Moving Assembly Line (Ford/Sorensen) Statistical Sampling (Shewhart) Economic Order Quantity (Harris) Linear Programming PERT/CPM (DuPont) Material Requirements Planning (MRP)	**Lean Production Era 1980–1995** Just-in-Time (JIT) Computer-Aided Design (CAD) Electronic Data Interchange (EDI) Total Quality Management (TQM) Baldrige Award Empowerment Kanbans	**Mass Customization Era 1995–2005** Internet/E-Commerce Enterprise Resource Planning International Quality Standards (ISO) Finite Scheduling Supply Chain Management Mass Customization Build-to-Order	**Globalization Era 2005–2020** Global Supply Chains Growth of Transnational Organizations Instant Communications Sustainability Ethics in a Global Workforce Logistics

Figure 4
Significant Events in Operations Management

By 1913, Henry Ford and Charles Sorensen combined what they knew about standardized parts with the quasi-assembly lines of the meatpacking and mail-order industries and added the revolutionary concept of the assembly line, where men stood still and material moved.

Quality control is another historically significant contribution to the field of OM. Walter Shewhart (1924) combined his knowledge of statistics with the need for quality control and provided the foundations for statistical sampling in quality control. W. Edwards Deming (1950) believed, as did Frederick Taylor, that management must do more to improve the work environment and processes so that quality can be improved.

Operations management will continue to progress with contributions from other disciplines, including *industrial engineering, statistics, management,* and *economics*, all improving decision making.

Innovations from the *physical sciences* (biology, anatomy, chemistry, physics) have also contributed to advances in OM. These innovations include new adhesives, faster integrated circuits, gamma rays to sanitize food products, and higher-quality glass for iPhones and plasma TVs. Innovation in products and processes often depends on advances in the physical sciences.

Especially important contributions to OM have come from *information technology*, which we define as the systematic processing of data to yield information. Information technology—with wireless links, Internet, and e-commerce—is reducing costs and accelerating communication.

Decisions in operations management require individuals who are well versed in analytical tools, in information technology, and often in one of the biological or physical sciences. In this text, we look at the diverse ways a student can prepare for a career in operations management.

Operations for Goods and Services

STUDENT TIP
Services are especially important because almost 80% of all jobs are in service firms.

Manufacturers produce a tangible product, while service products are often intangible. But many products are a combination of a good and a service, which complicates the definition of a service. Even the U.S. government has trouble generating a consistent definition. Because definitions vary, much of the data and statistics generated about the service sector are inconsistent. However, we define services as including repair and maintenance, government, food and lodging, transportation, insurance, trade, financial, real estate, education, legal, medical, entertainment, and other professional occupations.

Services
Economic activities that typically produce an intangible product (such as education, entertainment, lodging, government, financial, and health services).

The operation activities for both goods and services are often very similar. For instance, both have quality standards, are designed and produced on a schedule that meets customer demand, and are made in a facility where people are employed. However, some major differences *do* exist between goods and services. These are presented in Table 3.

LO2 *Explain* the distinction between goods and services

We should point out that in many cases, the distinction between goods and services is not clear-cut. In reality, almost all services and almost all goods are a mixture of a service and a tangible product. Even services such as consulting may require a tangible report. Similarly, the sale of most goods includes a service. For instance, many products have the service components of financing and delivery (e.g., automobile sales). Many also require after-sale training and maintenance (e.g., office copiers and machinery). "Service" activities may also be an integral part of production. Human resource activities, logistics, accounting, training, field service, and repair are all service activities, but they take place within a manufacturing organization. Very few services are "pure," meaning they have no tangible component. Counseling may be one of the exceptions.

Growth of Services

Services constitute the largest economic sector in postindustrial societies. Until about 1900, most Americans were employed in agriculture. Increased agricultural productivity allowed people to leave the farm and seek employment in the city. Similarly, manufacturing employment has decreased for the past 60 years. The changes in agriculture, manufacturing, and service employment as a percentage of the workforce are shown in Figure 5. Although the *number* of people employed in manufacturing has decreased since 1950, each person is now producing almost 20 times more than in 1950. Services became the dominant employer

TABLE 3 Differences Between Goods and Services

CHARACTERISTICS OF SERVICES	CHARACTERISTICS OF GOODS
Intangible: Ride in an airline seat	Tangible: The seat itself
Produced and consumed simultaneously: Beauty salon produces a haircut that is consumed as it is produced	Product can usually be kept in inventory (beauty care products)
Unique: Your investments and medical care are unique	Similar products produced (iPods)
High customer interaction: Often what the customer is paying for (consulting, education)	Limited customer involvement in production
Inconsistent product definition: Auto insurance changes with age and type of car	Product standardized (iPhone)
Often knowledge based: Legal, education, and medical services are hard to automate	Standard tangible product tends to make automation feasible
Services dispersed: Service may occur at retail store, local office, house call, or via internet.	Product typically produced at a fixed facility
Quality may be hard to evaluate: Consulting, education, and medical services	Many aspects of quality for tangible products are easy to evaluate (strength of a bolt)
Reselling is unusual: Musical concert or medical care	Product often has some residual value

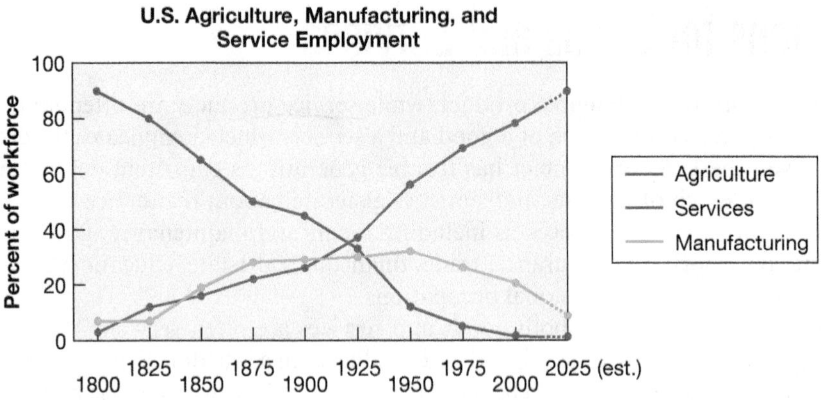

Figure 5
U.S. Agriculture, Manufacturing, and Service Employment
Sources: U.S. Bureau of Labor Statistics; and *Statistical Abstract of the United States* (2011).

in the early 1920s, with manufacturing employment peaking at about 32% in 1950. The huge productivity increases in agriculture and manufacturing have allowed more of our economic resources to be devoted to services. Consequently, much of the world can now enjoy the pleasures of education, health services, entertainment, and myriad other things that we call services. Examples of firms and percentage of employment in the U.S. service sector are shown in Table 4. Table 4 also provides employment percentages for the nonservice sectors of manufacturing, construction, agriculture, and mining on the bottom four lines.

Service sector
The segment of the economy that includes trade, financial, lodging, education, legal, medical, and other professional occupations.

Service Pay

Although there is a common perception that service industries are low paying, in fact, many service jobs pay very well. Operations managers in the maintenance facility of an airline are very well paid, as are the operations managers who supervise computer services to the financial community. About 42% of all service workers receive wages above the national average. However, the service-sector average is driven down because 14 of the U.S. Department of Commerce categories of the 33 service industries do indeed pay below the all-private industry average. Of these, retail trade, which pays only 61% of the national private industry average, is large. But even considering the retail sector, the average wage of all service workers is about 96% of the average of all private industries.

TABLE 4 **Examples of Organizations in Each Sector**

SECTOR	EXAMPLE	PERCENT OF ALL JOBS	
Service Sector			
Education, Legal, Medical, Other	San Diego Zoo, Arnold Palmer Hospital	13.2	85.9
Trade (retail, wholesale)	Walgreen's, Walmart, Nordstrom	13.8	
Utilities, Transportation	Pacific Gas & Electric, American Airlines	3.3	
Professional and Business Services	Snelling and Snelling, Waste Management, Inc.	10.1	
Finance, Information, Real Estate	Citicorp, American Express, Prudential, Aetna	21.0	
Food, Lodging, Entertainment	Olive Garden, Motel 6, Walt Disney	9.0	
Public Administration	U.S., State of Alabama, Cook County	15.5	
Manufacturing Sector	General Electric, Ford, U.S. Steel, Intel		8.2
Construction Sector	Bechtel, McDermott		4.1
Agriculture	King Ranch		1.4
Mining Sector	Homestake Mining		.4
Grand Total			100.0

Source: Statistical Abstract of the United States (2010), Table 625.

The Productivity Challenge

The creation of goods and services requires changing resources into goods and services. The more efficiently we make this change, the more productive we are and the more value is added to the good or service provided. Productivity is the ratio of outputs (goods and services) divided by the inputs (resources, such as labor and capital) (see Figure 6). The operations manager's job is to enhance (improve) this ratio of outputs to inputs. Improving productivity means improving efficiency.[1]

STUDENT TIP
Why is productivity important? Because it determines our standard of living.

Productivity
The ratio of outputs (goods and services) divided by one or more inputs (such as labor, capital, or management).

This improvement can be achieved in two ways: reducing inputs while keeping output constant or increasing output while keeping inputs constant. Both represent an improvement in productivity. In an economic sense, inputs are labor, capital, and management, which are integrated into a production system. Management creates this production system, which provides the conversion of inputs to outputs. Outputs are goods and services, including such diverse items as guns, butter, education, improved judicial systems, and ski resorts. *Production* is the making of goods and services. High production may imply only that more people are working and that employment levels are high (low unemployment), but it does not imply high *productivity*.

LO3 *Explain* the difference between production and productivity

Measurement of productivity is an excellent way to evaluate a country's ability to provide an improving standard of living for its people. *Only through increases in productivity can the standard of living improve.* Moreover, only through increases in productivity can labor, capital, and management receive additional payments. If returns to labor, capital, or management are increased without increased productivity, prices rise. On the other hand, downward pressure is placed on prices when productivity increases, because more is being produced with the same resources.

The benefits of increased productivity are illustrated in the *OM in Action* box "Improving Productivity at Starbucks."

For well over a century (from about 1869), the U.S. has been able to increase productivity at an average rate of almost 2.5% per year. Such growth has doubled U.S. wealth every 30 years. The manufacturing sector, although a decreasing portion of the U.S. economy, has on occasion seen annual productivity increases exceeding 4%, and service sector increases of almost 1%. However, U.S. annual productivity growth in the early part of the 21st century is slightly below the 2.5% range for the economy as a whole.[2]

In this text, we examine how to improve productivity through operations management. Productivity is a significant issue for the world and one that the operations manager is uniquely qualified to address.

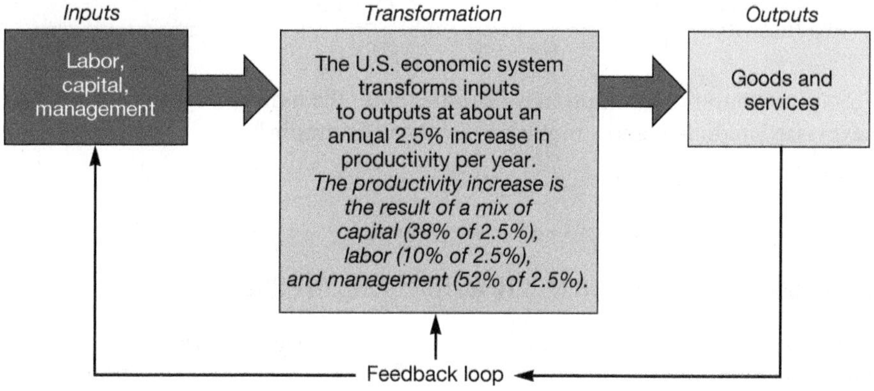
Inputs
Transformation
Outputs
Labor, capital, management
The U.S. economic system transforms inputs to outputs at about an annual 2.5% increase in productivity per year.
The productivity increase is the result of a mix of capital (38% of 2.5%), labor (10% of 2.5%), and management (52% of 2.5%).
Goods and services
Feedback loop

Figure 6
The Economic System Adds Value by Transforming Inputs to Outputs
An effective feedback loop evaluates performance against a strategy or standard. It also evaluates customer satisfaction and sends signals to managers controlling the inputs and transformation process.

[1]*Efficiency* means doing the job well—with a minimum of resources and waste. Note the distinction between being *efficient*, which implies doing the job well, and *effective*, which means doing the right thing. A job well done—say, by applying the 10 strategic decisions of operations management—helps us be *efficient*; developing and using the correct strategy helps us be *effective*.

[2]U.S. Dept. of Labor, 2011: www.bls.gov/lpc/

OM in Action Improving Productivity at Starbucks

"This is a game of seconds . . ." says Silva Peterson, whom Starbucks has put in charge of saving seconds. Her team of 10 analysts is constantly asking themselves: "How can we shave time off this?"

Peterson's analysis suggested that there were some obvious opportunities. First, stop requiring signatures on credit-card purchases under $25. This sliced 8 seconds off the transaction time at the cash register.

Then analysts noticed that Starbucks's largest cold beverage, the Venti size, required two bending and digging motions to scoop up enough ice. The scoop was too small. Redesign of the scoop provided the proper amount in one motion and cut 14 seconds off the average time of 1 minute.

Third were new espresso machines; with the push of a button, the machines grind coffee beans and brew. This allowed the server, called a "barista" in Starbucks's vocabulary, to do other things. The savings: about 12 seconds per espresso shot.

As a result, operations improvements at Starbucks outlets have increased the average yearly volume by $250,000, to about 1 million in the past 7 years. This is a 27% improvement in productivity—about 4.5% per year. In the service industry, a 4.5% per year increase is very tasty.

Sources: Fortune (November 17, 2011) and *The Wall Street Journal* (April 12, 2005 and August 4, 2009).

Productivity Measurement

LO4 *Compute* single-factor productivity

The measurement of productivity can be quite direct. Such is the case when productivity is measured by labor-hours per ton of a specific type of steel. Although labor-hours is a common measure of input, other measures such as capital (dollars invested), materials (tons of ore), or energy (kilowatts of electricity) can be used.[3] An example of this can be summarized in the following equation:

$$\text{Productivity} = \frac{\text{Units produced}}{\text{Input used}} \tag{1}$$

For example, if units produced = 1,000 and labor-hours used is 250, then:

$$\text{Productivity} = \frac{\text{Units produced}}{\text{Labor-hours used}} = \frac{1{,}000}{250} = 4 \text{ units per labor-hour}$$

Single-factor productivity
Indicates the ratio of one resource (input) to the goods and services produced (outputs).

Multifactor productivity
Indicates the ratio of many or all resources (inputs) to the goods and services produced (outputs).

The use of just one resource input to measure productivity, as shown in Equation (1), is known as single-factor productivity. However, a broader view of productivity is multifactor productivity, which includes all inputs (e.g., capital, labor, material, energy). Multifactor productivity is also known as *total factor productivity*. Multifactor productivity is calculated by combining the input units as shown here:

$$\text{Productivity} = \frac{\text{Output}}{\text{Labor} + \text{Material} + \text{Energy} + \text{Capital} + \text{Miscellaneous}} \tag{2}$$

To aid in the computation of multifactor productivity, the individual inputs (the denominator) can be expressed in dollars and summed as shown in Example 2.

Example 2

COMPUTING SINGLE-FACTOR AND MULTIFACTOR GAINS IN PRODUCTIVITY

Collins Title Insurance Ltd. wants to evaluate its labor and multifactor productivity with a new computerized title-search system. The company has a staff of four, each working 8 hours per day (for a payroll cost of $640/day) and overhead expenses of $400 per day. Collins processes and closes on 8 titles each day. The new computerized title-search system will allow the processing of 14 titles per day. Although the staff, their work hours, and pay are the same, the overhead expenses are now $800 per day.

APPROACH ▶ Collins uses Equation (1) to compute labor productivity and Equation (2) to compute multifactor productivity.

[3]The quality and time period are assumed to remain constant.

LO5 *Compute multifactor productivity*

SOLUTION ▶

$$\text{Labor productivity with the old system: } \frac{8 \text{ titles per day}}{32 \text{ labor-hours}} = .25 \text{ titles per labor-hour}$$

$$\text{Labor productivity with the new system: } \frac{14 \text{ titles per day}}{32 \text{ labor-hours}} = .4375 \text{ titles per labor-hour}$$

$$\text{Multifactor productivity with the old system: } \frac{8 \text{ titles per day}}{\$640 + 400} = .0077 \text{ titles per dollar}$$

$$\text{Multifactor productivity with the new system: } \frac{14 \text{ titles per day}}{\$640 + 800} = .0097 \text{ titles per dollar}$$

Labor productivity has increased from .25 to .4375. The change is $(.4375 - .25)/.25 = 0.75$, or a 75% increase in labor productivity. Multifactor productivity has increased from .0077 to .0097. This change is $(.0097 - .0077)/.0077 = 0.26$, or a 26% increase in multifactor productivity.

INSIGHT ▶ Both the labor (single-factor) and multifactor productivity measures show an increase in productivity. However, the multifactor measure provides a better picture of the increase because it includes all the costs connected with the increase in output.

LEARNING EXERCISE ▶ If the overhead goes to $960 (rather than $800), what is the multifactor productivity? [Answer: .00875.]

RELATED PROBLEMS ▶ 1, 2, 5, 6, 7, 8, 9, 11, 12, 14, 15

Use of productivity measures aids managers in determining how well they are doing. But results from the two measures can be expected to vary. If labor productivity growth is entirely the result of capital spending, measuring just labor distorts the results. Multifactor productivity is usually better, but more complicated. Labor productivity is the more popular measure. The multifactor-productivity measures provide better information about the trade-offs among factors, but substantial measurement problems remain. Some of these measurement problems are:

1. *Quality* may change while the quantity of inputs and outputs remains constant. Compare an HDTV of this decade with a black-and-white TV of the 1950s. Both are TVs, but few people would deny that the quality has improved. The unit of measure—a TV—is the same, but the quality has changed.
2. *External elements* may cause an increase or a decrease in productivity for which the system under study may not be directly responsible. A more reliable electric power service may greatly improve production, thereby improving the firm's productivity because of this support system rather than because of managerial decisions made within the firm.
3. *Precise units of measure* may be lacking. Not all automobiles require the same inputs: Some cars are subcompacts, others are 911 Turbo Porsches.

Productivity measurement is particularly difficult in the service sector, where the end product can be hard to define. For example, economic statistics ignore the quality of your haircut, the outcome of a court case, or service at a retail store. In some cases, adjustments are made for the quality of the product sold but *not* the quality of the sales presentation or the advantage of a broader product selection. Productivity measurements require specific inputs and outputs, but a free economy is producing worth—what people want—which includes convenience, speed, and safety. Traditional measures of outputs may be a very poor measure of these other measures of worth. Note the quality-measurement problems in a law office, where each case is different, altering the accuracy of the measure "cases per labor-hour" or "cases per employee."

Productivity Variables

As we saw in Figure 6, productivity increases are dependent on three **productivity variables**:

Productivity variables
The three factors critical to productivity improvement—labor, capital, and the art and science of management.

1. *Labor,* which contributes about 10% of the annual increase.
2. *Capital,* which contributes about 38% of the annual increase.
3. *Management,* which contributes about 52% of the annual increase.

These three factors are critical to improved productivity. They represent the broad areas in which managers can take action to improve productivity.

Figure 7

About Half of the 17-Year-Olds in the U.S. Cannot Correctly Answer Questions of this Type

6 yds

4 yds

What is the area of this rectangle?

______ 4 square yds
______ 6 square yds
______ 10 square yds
______ 20 square yds
______ 24 square yds

If $9y + 3 = 6y + 15$ then $y =$

______ 1 ______ 4
______ 2 ______ 6

Which of the following is true about 84% of 100?

______ It is greater than 100
______ It is less than 100
______ It is equal to 100

LO6 *Identify* the critical variables in enhancing productivity

Labor Improvement in the contribution of labor to productivity is the result of a healthier, better-educated, and better-nourished labor force. Some increase may also be attributed to a shorter workweek. Historically, about 10% of the annual improvement in productivity is attributed to improvement in the quality of labor. Three key variables for improved labor productivity are:

1. Basic education appropriate for an effective labor force.
2. Diet of the labor force.
3. Social overhead that makes labor available, such as transportation and sanitation.

Illiteracy and poor diets are a major impediment to productivity, costing countries up to 20% of their productivity. Infrastructure that yields clean drinking water and sanitation is also an opportunity for improved productivity, as well as an opportunity for better health, in much of the world.

In developed nations, the challenge becomes *maintaining and enhancing the skills of labor* in the midst of rapidly expanding technology and knowledge. Recent data suggest that the average American 17-year-old knows significantly less mathematics than the average Japanese at the same age, and about half cannot answer the questions in Figure 7. Moreover, about one-third of American job applicants tested for basic skills were deficient in reading, writing, or math.

Overcoming shortcomings in the quality of labor while other countries have a better labor force is a major challenge. Perhaps improvements can be found not only through increasing competence of labor but also via *better utilized labor with a stronger commitment*. Training, motivation, team building, human resource strategies, as well as improved education, may be among the many techniques that will contribute to increased labor productivity. Improvements in labor productivity are possible; however, they can be expected to be increasingly difficult and expensive.

Capital Human beings are tool-using animals. Capital investment provides those tools. Capital investment has increased in the U.S. every year except during a few very severe recession periods. Annual capital investment in the U.S. has increased at an annual rate of 1.5% after allowances for depreciation.

Inflation and taxes increase the cost of capital, making capital investment increasingly expensive. When the capital invested per employee drops, we can expect a drop in productivity. Using labor rather than capital may reduce unemployment in the short run, but it also makes economies less productive and therefore lowers wages in the long run. Capital investment is often a necessary, but seldom a sufficient, ingredient in the battle for increased productivity.

The trade-off between capital and labor is continually in flux. The higher the cost of capital or perceived risk, the more projects requiring capital are "squeezed out": they are not pursued because the potential return on investment for a given risk has been reduced. Managers adjust their investment plans to changes in capital cost and risk.

Management Management is a factor of production and an economic resource. Management is responsible for ensuring that labor and capital are effectively used to increase productivity. Management accounts for over half of the annual increase in productivity. This increase includes improvements made through the use of knowledge and the application of technology.

Using knowledge and technology is critical in postindustrial societies. Consequently, postindustrial societies are also known as knowledge societies. Knowledge societies are those in which much of the labor force has migrated from manual work to technical and information-processing

Knowledge society

A society in which much of the labor force has migrated from manual work to work based on knowledge.

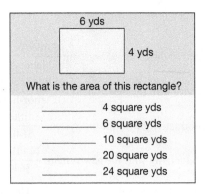

© Andrzej Thiel/Shutterstock

The effective use of capital often means finding the proper trade-off between investment in capital assets (automation, left) and human assets (a manual process, right). While there are risks connected with any investment, the cost of capital and physical investments is fairly clear-cut, but the cost of employees has many hidden costs including fringe benefits, social insurance, and legal constraints on hiring, employment, and termination.

tasks requiring ongoing education. The required education and training are important high-cost items that are the responsibility of operations managers as they build organizations and workforces. The expanding knowledge base of contemporary society requires that managers use *technology and knowledge effectively.*

More effective use of capital also contributes to productivity. It falls to the operations manager, as a productivity catalyst, to select the best new capital investments as well as to improve the productivity of existing investments.

The productivity challenge is difficult. A country cannot be a world-class competitor with second-class inputs. Poorly educated labor, inadequate capital, and dated technology are second-class inputs. High productivity and high-quality outputs require high-quality inputs, including good operations managers.

Productivity and the Service Sector

The service sector provides a special challenge to the accurate measurement of productivity and productivity improvement. The traditional analytical framework of economic theory is based primarily on goods-producing activities. Consequently, most published economic data relate to goods production. But the data do indicate that, as our contemporary service economy has increased in size, we have had slower growth in productivity.

Zick, Jochen/ZUMA Press/Newscom

Siemens, a multi-billion-dollar German conglomerate, has long been known for its apprentice programs in its home country. Because education is often the key to efficient operations in a technological society, Siemens has spread its apprentice-training programs to its U.S. plants. These programs are laying the foundation for the highly skilled workforce that is essential for global competitiveness.

OM in Action — Taco Bell Improves Productivity and Goes Green to Lower Costs

Founded in 1962 by Glenn Bell, Taco Bell seeks competitive advantage via low cost. Like many other services, Taco Bell relies on its operations management to improve productivity and reduce cost.

Its menu and meals are designed to be easy to prepare. Taco Bell has shifted a substantial portion of food preparation to suppliers who could perform food processing more efficiently than a stand-alone restaurant. Ground beef is precooked prior to arrival and then reheated, as are many dishes that arrive in plastic boil bags for easy sanitary reheating. Similarly, tortillas arrive already fried and onions prediced. Efficient layout and automation has cut to 8 seconds the time needed to prepare tacos and burritos and has cut time in the drive-through lines by 1 minute. These advances have been combined with training and empowerment to increase the span of management from one supervisor for 5 restaurants to one supervisor for 30 or more.

Operations managers at Taco Bell have cut in-store labor by 15 hours per day and reduced floor space by more than 50%. The result is a store that can average 164 seconds for each customer, from drive-up to pull-out.

In 2010, Taco Bell completed the rollout of its new Grill-to-Order kitchens by installing water- and energy-saving grills that conserve 300 million gallons of water and 200 million kilowatt hours of electricity each year. This "green"-inspired cooking method also saves the company's 5,800 restaurants $17 million per year.

Effective operations management has resulted in productivity increases that support Taco Bell's low-cost strategy. Taco Bell is now the fast-food low-cost leader with a 58% share of the Mexican fast-food market.

© Bob Pardue-Signs/Alamy

Sources: Business Week (May 5, 2011); *Harvard Business Review* (July/August 2008); and J. Hueter and W. Swart, *Interfaces* (January–February 1998).

Productivity of the service sector has proven difficult to improve because service-sector work is:

1. Typically labor intensive (e.g., counseling, teaching).
2. Frequently focused on unique individual attributes or desires (e.g., investment advice).
3. Often an intellectual task performed by professionals (e.g., medical diagnosis).
4. Often difficult to mechanize and automate (e.g., a haircut).
5. Often difficult to evaluate for quality (e.g., performance of a law firm).

The more intellectual and personal the task, the more difficult it is to achieve increases in productivity. Low-productivity improvement in the service sector is also attributable to the growth of low-productivity activities in the service sector. These include activities not previously a part of the measured economy, such as child care, food preparation, house cleaning, and laundry service. These activities have moved out of the home and into the measured economy as more and more women have joined the workforce. Inclusion of these activities has probably resulted in lower measured productivity for the service sector, although, in fact, actual productivity has probably increased because these activities are now more efficiently produced than previously.

However, in spite of the difficulty of improving productivity in the service sector, improvements are being made. And this text presents a multitude of ways to make these improvements. Indeed, what can be done when management pays attention to how work actually gets done is astonishing!

Although the evidence indicates that all industrialized countries have the same problem with service productivity, the U.S. remains the world leader in overall productivity *and* service productivity. Retailing is twice as productive in the U.S. as in Japan, where laws protect shopkeepers from discount chains. The U.S. telephone industry is at least twice as productive as Germany's. The U.S. banking system is also 33% more efficient than Germany's banking oligopolies. However, because productivity is central to the operations manager's job and because the service sector is so large, we take special note in this text of how to improve productivity in the service sector. (See, for instance, the *OM in Action* box "Taco Bell Improves Productivity and Goes Green to Lower Costs.")

STUDENT TIP One of the reasons OM is such an exciting discipline is that an operations manager is confronted with ever-changing issues, from technology, to global supply chains, to sustainability.

New Challenges in Operations Management

Operations managers work in an exciting and dynamic environment. This environment is the result of a variety of challenging forces, from globalization of world trade to the transfer of ideas, products, and money at electronic speeds. Let's look at some of these challenges:

- *Global focus:* The rapid decline in communication and transportation costs has made markets global. Similarly, resources in the form of capital, materials, talent, and labor are also now global. As a result, countries throughout the world are contributing to globalization as they vie for economic growth. Operations managers are rapidly seeking creative designs, efficient production, and high-quality goods via international collaboration.
- *Supply-chain partnering:* Shorter product life cycles, demanding customers, and fast changes in technology, materials, and processes require supply-chain partners to be in tune with the needs of end users. And because suppliers may be able to contribute unique expertise, operations managers are outsourcing and building long-term partnerships with critical players in the supply chain.
- *Sustainability:* Operations managers' continuing battle to improve productivity is concerned with designing products and processes that are ecologically sustainable. This means designing green products and packaging that minimize resource use, can be recycled or reused, and are generally environmentally friendly.
- *Rapid product development:* Technology combined with rapid international communication of news, entertainment, and lifestyles is dramatically chopping away at the life span of products. OM is answering with new management structures, enhanced collaboration, digital technology, and creative alliances that are more responsive and effective.
- *Mass customization:* Once managers recognize the *world* as the marketplace, the cultural and individual differences become quite obvious. In a world where consumers are increasingly aware of innovation and options, substantial pressure is placed on firms to respond in a creative way. And OM must rapidly respond with product designs and flexible production processes that cater to the individual whims of consumers. The goal is to produce customized products, whenever and wherever needed.
- *Just-in-time performance:* Inventory throughout the supply chain requires financial resources, hides quality issues, and constrains response to ever-shorter product life cycles. These forces push operations managers to work with their supply chains to viciously cut inventories at every level.
- *Empowered employees:* The knowledge explosion and a more technical workplace have combined to require more competence in the workplace. OM is responding by enriching jobs and moving more decision making to the individual contributor.

These trends are part of the exciting OM challenges currently facing operations managers.

Ethics, Social Responsibility, and Sustainability

The systems that operations managers build to convert resources into goods and services are complex. And they function in a world where the physical and social environment is evolving, as are laws and values. These dynamics present a variety of challenges that come from the conflicting perspectives of **stakeholders**, such as customers, distributors, suppliers, owners, lenders, employees, and community. Stakeholders, as well as government agencies at various levels, require constant monitoring and thoughtful responses.

Stakeholders
Those with a vested interest in an organization, including customers, distributors, suppliers, owners, lenders, employees, and community members.

Identifying ethical and socially responsible responses while developing sustainable processes that are also effective and efficient productive systems is not easy. Managers are also challenged to:

- Develop and produce safe, high-quality green products
- Train, retain, and motivate employees in a safe workplace
- Honor stakeholder commitments

Managers must do all this while meeting the demands of a very dynamic world marketplace. If operations managers have a *moral awareness and focus on increasing productivity in this system,* then many of the ethical challenges will be successfully addressed. The organization will use fewer resources, the employees will be committed, the market will be satisfied, and the ethical climate will be enhanced. Throughout this text, we note ways in which operations managers can take ethical and socially responsible actions while successfully addressing these challenges of the market. We also conclude with an *Ethical Dilemma* exercise.

Summary

Operations, marketing, and finance/accounting are the three functions basic to all organizations. The operations function creates goods and services. Much of the progress of operations management has been made in the twentieth century, but since the beginning of time, humankind has been attempting to improve its material well-being. Operations managers are key players in the battle to improve productivity.

As societies become increasingly affluent, more of their resources are devoted to services. In the U.S., more than 85% of the workforce is employed in the service sector. Productivity improvements and a sustainable environment are difficult to achieve, but operations managers are the primary vehicle for making improvements.

Key Terms

Production
Operations management (OM)
Supply chain
10 strategic OM decisions
Services
Service sector
Productivity
Single-factor productivity
Multifactor productivity
Productivity variables
Knowledge society
Stakeholders

Ethical Dilemma

The American car battery industry boasts that its recycling rate now exceeds 95%, the highest rate for any commodity. However, with changes brought about by specialization and globalization, parts of the recycling system are moving offshore. This is particularly true of automobile batteries, which contain lead. The Environmental Protection Agency (EPA) is contributing to the offshore flow with newly implemented standards that make domestic battery recycling increasingly difficult and expensive. The result is a major increase in used batteries going to Mexico, where environmental standards and control are less demanding than they are in the U.S. One in five batteries is now exported to Mexico. There is seldom difficulty finding buyers because lead is expensive and in worldwide demand. While U.S. recyclers operate in sealed, mechanized plants, with smokestacks equipped with scrubbers and plant surroundings monitored for traces of lead, this is not the case in most Mexican plants. The harm from lead is legendary, with long-run residual effects. Health issues include high blood pressure, kidney damage, detrimental effects on fetuses during pregnancy, neurological problems, and arrested development in children.
Given the two scenarios below, what action do you take?

a) You own an independent auto repair shop and are trying to safely dispose of a few old batteries each week. (Your battery supplier is an auto parts supplier who refuses to take your old batteries.)

b) You are manager of a large retailer responsible for disposal of thousands of used batteries each day.

Discussion Questions

1. Why should one study operations management?
2. Identify four people who have contributed to the theory and techniques of operations management.
3. Briefly describe the contributions of the four individuals identified in the preceding question.
4. Figure 1 outlines the operations, finance/accounting, and marketing functions of three organizations. Prepare a chart similar to Figure 1 outlining the same functions for one of the following:
   a. a newspaper
   b. a drugstore
   c. a college library
   d. a summer camp
   e. a small costume-jewelry factory
5. Answer Question 4 for some other organization, perhaps an organization where you have worked.
6. What are the three basic functions of a firm?
7. Identify the 10 strategic operations management decisions.
8. Name four areas that are significant to improving labor productivity.
9. The U.S., and indeed much of the rest of the world, has been described as a "knowledge society." How does this affect productivity measurement and the comparison of productivity between the U.S. and other countries?
10. What are the measurement problems that occur when one attempts to measure productivity?
11. Mass customization and rapid product development were identified as challenges to modern manufacturing operations. What is the relationship, if any, between these challenges? Can you cite any examples?
12. What are the five reasons productivity is difficult to improve in the service sector?
13. Describe some of the actions taken by Taco Bell to increase productivity that have resulted in Taco Bell's ability to serve "twice the volume with half the labor."

Solved Problems

Virtual Office Hours help is available at www.myomlab.com.

SOLVED PROBLEM 1

Productivity can be measured in a variety of ways, such as by labor, capital, energy, material usage, and so on. At Modern Lumber, Inc., Art Binley, president and producer of apple crates sold to growers, has been able, with his current equipment, to produce 240 crates per 100 logs. He currently purchases 100 logs per day, and each log requires 3 labor-hours to process. He believes that he can hire a professional buyer who can buy a better-quality log at the same cost. If this is the case, he can increase his production to 260 crates per 100 logs. His labor-hours will increase by 8 hours per day.

What will be the impact on productivity (measured in crates per labor-hour) if the buyer is hired?

SOLUTION

(a) $$\text{Current labor productivity} = \frac{240 \text{ crates}}{100 \text{ logs} \times 3 \text{ hours/log}} = \frac{240}{300} = .8 \text{ crates per labor-hour}$$

(b) $$\text{Labor productivity with buyer} = \frac{260 \text{ crates}}{(100 \text{ logs} \times 3 \text{ hours/log}) + 8 \text{ hours}} = \frac{260}{308} = .844 \text{ crates per labor-hour}$$

Using current productivity (.80 from [a]) as a base, the increase will be 5.5% (.844/.8 = 1.055, or a 5.5% increase).

SOLVED PROBLEM 2

Art Binley has decided to look at his productivity from a multifactor (total factor productivity) perspective (refer to Solved Problem 1). To do so, he has determined his labor, capital, energy, and material usage and decided to use dollars as the common denominator. His total labor-hours are now 300 per day and will increase to 308 per day. His capital and energy costs will remain constant at \$350 and \$150 per day, respectively. Material costs for the 100 logs per day are \$1,000 and will remain the same. Because he pays an average of \$10 per hour (with fringes), Binley determines his productivity increase as follows:

SOLUTION

CURRENT SYSTEM		
Labor:	300 hrs. @10 =	3,000
Material:	100 logs/day	1,000
Capital:		350
Energy:		150
Total Cost:		\$4,500

SYSTEM WITH PROFESSIONAL BUYER	
308 hrs. @10 =	\$3,080
	1,000
	350
	150
	\$4,580

Multifactor productivity of current system:
= 240 crates/\$4,500 = .0533 crates/dollar

Multifactor productivity of proposed system:
= 260 crates/\$4,580 = .0568 crates/dollar

Using current productivity (.0533) as a base, the increase will be .066. That is, .0568/.0533 = 1.066, or a 6.6% increase.

Problems

Note: Px means the problem may be solved with POM for Windows and/or Excel OM.

• **1** Chuck Sox makes wooden boxes in which to ship motorcycles. Chuck and his three employees invest a total of 40 hours per day making the 120 boxes.
a) What is their productivity?
b) Chuck and his employees have discussed redesigning the process to improve efficiency. If they can increase the rate to 125 per day, what will be their new productivity?
c) What will be their unit *increase* in productivity per hour?
d) What will be their percentage change in productivity? Px

• **2** Carbondale Casting produces cast bronze valves on a 10-person assembly line. On a recent day, 160 valves were produced during an 8-hour shift.
a) Calculate the labor productivity of the line.
b) John Goodale, the manager at Carbondale, changed the layout and was able to increase production to 180 units per 8-hour shift. What is the new labor productivity per labor-hour?
c) What is the percentage of productivity increase? Px

• **3** This year, Donnelly, Inc., will produce 57,600 hot water heaters at its plant in Delaware, in order to meet expected global demand. To accomplish this, each laborer at the plant will work 160 hours per month. If the labor productivity at the plant is 0.15 hot water heaters per labor-hour, how many laborers are employed at the plant?

• **4** As a library or Internet assignment, find the U.S. productivity rate (increase) last year for the (a) national economy, (b) manufacturing sector, and (c) service sector.

• **5** Lori Cook produces "Final Exam Care Packages" for resale by her sorority. She is currently working a total of 5 hours per day to produce 100 care packages.
a) What is Lori's productivity?
b) Lori thinks that by redesigning the package, she can increase her total productivity to 133 care packages per day. What will be her new productivity?
c) What will be the percentage increase in productivity if Lori makes the change? Px

•• **6** George Kyparisis makes bearing balls in his Miami plant. With recent increases in his costs, he has a newfound interest in efficiency. George is interested in determining the productivity of his organization. He would like to know if his organization is maintaining the manufacturing average of 3% increase in productivity per year? He has the following data representing a month from last year and an equivalent month this year:

	LAST YEAR	NOW
Units produced	1,000	1,000
Labor (hours)	300	275
Resin (pounds)	50	45
Capital invested ($)	10,000	11,000
Energy (BTU)	3,000	2,850

Show the productivity percentage change for each category and then determine the improvement for labor-hours, the typical standard for comparison. PX

•• **7** George Kyparisis (using data from Problem 6) determines his costs to be as follows:

- *Labor:* $10 per hour
- *Resin:* $5 per pound
- *Capital expense:* 1% per month of investment
- *Energy:* $.50 per BTU

Show the percent change in productivity for one month last year versus one month this year, on a multifactor basis with dollars as the common denominator. PX

• **8** Kleen Karpet cleaned 65 rugs in October, consuming the following resources:

Labor:	520 hours at $13 per hour
Solvent:	100 gallons at $5 per gallon
Machine rental:	20 days at $50 per day

a) What is the labor productivity per dollar?
b) What is the multifactor productivity? PX

•• **9** Lillian Fok is president of Lakefront Manufacturing, a producer of bicycle tires. Fok makes 1,000 tires per day with the following resources:

Labor:	400 hours per day @ $12.50 per hour
Raw material:	20,000 pounds per day @ $1 per pound
Energy:	$5,000 per day
Capital costs:	$10,000 per day

a) What is the labor productivity per labor-hour for these tires at Lakefront Manufacturing?
b) What is the multifactor productivity for these tires at Lakefront Manufacturing?
c) What is the percent change in multifactor productivity if Fok can reduce the energy bill by $1,000 per day without cutting production or changing any other inputs? PX

••• **10** Brown's, a local bakery, is worried about increased costs—particularly energy. Last year's records can provide a fairly good estimate of the parameters for this year. Wende Brown, the owner, does not believe things have changed much, but she did invest an additional $3,000 for modifications to the bakery's ovens to make them more energy efficient. The modifications were supposed to make the ovens at least 15% more efficient. Brown has asked you to check the energy savings of the new ovens and also to look over other measures of the bakery's productivity to see if the modifications were beneficial. You have the following data to work with:

	LAST YEAR	NOW
Production (dozen)	1,500	1,500
Labor (hours)	350	325
Capital investment ($)	15,000	18,000
Energy (BTU)	3,000	2,750

PX

•• **11** Munson Performance Auto, Inc., modifies 375 autos per year. The manager, Adam Munson, is interested in obtaining a measure of overall performance. He has asked you to provide him with a multifactor measure of last year's performance as a benchmark for future comparison. You have assembled the following data. Resource inputs were labor, 10,000 hours; 500 suspension and engine modification kits; and energy, 100,000 kilowatt-hours. Average labor cost last year was $20 per hour, kits cost $1,000 each, and energy costs were $3 per kilowatt-hour. What do you tell Mr. Munson? PX

•• **12** Lake Charles Seafood makes 500 wooden packing boxes for fresh seafood per day, working in two 10-hour shifts. Due to increased demand, plant managers have decided to operate three 8-hour shifts instead. The plant is now able to produce 650 boxes per day.

a) Calculate the company's productivity before the change in work rules and after the change.
b) What is the percentage increase in productivity?
c) If production is increased to 700 boxes per day, what is the new productivity? PX

••• **13** Charles Lackey operates a bakery in Idaho Falls, Idaho. Because of its excellent product and excellent location, demand has increased by 25% in the last year. On far too many occasions, customers have not been able to purchase the bread of their choice. Because of the size of the store, no new ovens can be added. At a staff meeting, one employee suggested ways to load the ovens differently so that more loaves of bread can be baked at one time. This new process will require that the ovens be loaded by hand, requiring additional manpower. This is the only thing to be changed. If the bakery makes 1,500 loaves per month with a labor productivity of 2.344 loaves per labor-hour, how many workers will Lackey need to add? (*Hint:* Each worker works 160 hours per month.)

•• **14** Refer to Problem 13. The pay will be $8 per hour for employees. Charles Lackey can also improve the yield by purchasing a new blender. The new blender will mean an increase in his investment. This added investment has a cost of $100 per month, but he will achieve the same output (an increase to 1,875) as the change in labor-hours. Which is the better decision?

a) Show the productivity change, in loaves per dollar, with an increase in labor cost (from 640 to 800 hours).
b) Show the new productivity, in loaves per dollar, with only an increase in investment ($100 per month more).
c) Show the percent productivity change for labor and investment.

••• **15** Refer to Problems 13 and 14. If Charles Lackey's utility costs remain constant at $500 per month, labor at $8 per hour, and cost of ingredients at $0.35 per loaf, but Charles does not purchase the blender suggested in Problem 14, what will the productivity of the bakery be? What will be the percent increase or decrease?

•• **16** In December, General Motors produced 6,600 customized vans at its plant in Detroit. The labor productivity at this plant is known to have been 0.10 vans per labor-hour during that month. 300 laborers were employed at the plant that month.

a) How many hours did the average laborer work that month?
b) If productivity can be increased to 0.11 vans per labor-hour, how many hours would the average laborer work that month?

•• **17** Susan Williams runs a small Flagstaff job shop where garments are made. The job shop employs eight workers. Each worker is paid $10 per hour. During the first week of March, each worker worked 45 hours. Together, they produced a batch of 132 garments. Of these garments, 52 were "seconds" (meaning that they were flawed). The seconds were sold for $90 each at a factory outlet store. The remaining 80 garments were sold to retail outlets at a price of $198 per garment. What was the labor productivity, in dollars per labor-hour, at this job shop during the first week of March?

Refer to MyOMLab for this additional homework problem: 18.

CASE STUDIES

National Air Express

National Air is a competitive air-express firm with offices around the country. Frank Smith, the Chattanooga, Tennessee, station manager, is preparing his quarterly budget report, which will be presented at the Southeast regional meeting next week. He is very concerned about adding capital expense to the operation when business has not increased appreciably. This has been the worst first quarter he can remember: snowstorms, earthquakes, and bitter cold. He has asked Martha Lewis, field services supervisor, to help him review the available data and offer possible solutions.

Service Methods

National Air offers door-to-door overnight air-express delivery within the U.S. Smith and Lewis manage a fleet of 24 trucks to handle freight in the Chattanooga area. Routes are assigned by area, usually delineated by zip code boundaries, major streets, or key geographical features, such as the Tennessee River. Pickups are generally handled between 3:00 P.M. and 6:00 P.M., Monday through Friday. Driver routes are a combination of regularly scheduled daily stops and pickups that the customer calls in as needed. These call-in pickups are dispatched by radio to the driver. Most call-in customers want as late a pickup as possible, just before closing (usually at 5:00 P.M.).

When the driver arrives at each pickup location, he or she provides supplies as necessary (an envelope or box if requested) and must receive a completed air waybill for each package. Because the industry is extremely competitive, a professional, courteous driver is essential to retaining customers. Therefore, Smith has always been concerned that drivers not rush a customer to complete his or her package and paperwork.

Budget Considerations

Smith and Lewis have found that they have been unable to meet their customers' requests for a scheduled pickup on many occasions in the past quarter. Although, on average, drivers are not handling any more business, they are unable on some days to arrive at each location on time. Smith does not think he can justify increasing costs by $1,200 per week for additional trucks and drivers while productivity (measured in shipments per truck/day) has remained flat. The company has established itself as the low-cost operator in the industry but has at the same time committed itself to offering quality service and value for its customers.

Discussion Questions

1. Is the productivity measure of shipments per day per truck still useful? Are there alternatives that might be effective?
2. What, if anything, can be done to reduce the daily variability in pickup call-ins? Can the driver be expected to be at several locations at once at 5:00 P.M.?
3. How should package pickup performance be measured? Are standards useful in an environment that is affected by the weather, traffic, and other random variables? Are other companies having similar problems?

Source: Adapted from a case by Phil Pugliese under the supervision of Professor Marilyn M. Helms, University of Tennessee at Chattanooga. Reprinted by permission.

Frito-Lay: Operations Management in Manufacturing

Video Case

Frito-Lay, the massive Dallas-based subsidiary of PepsiCo, has 38 plants and 48,000 employees in North America. Seven of Frito-Lay's 41 brands exceed $1 billion in sales: Fritos, Lay's Cheetos, Ruffles, Tostitos, Doritos, and Walker's Potato Chips. Operations is the focus of the firm—from designing products for new markets, to meeting changing consumer preferences, to adjusting to rising commodity costs, to subtle issues involving flavors and preservatives—OM is under constant cost, time, quality, and market pressure. Here is a look at how the 10 decisions of OM are applied at this food processor.

In the food industry, product development kitchens experiment with new products, submit them to focus groups, and perform test marketing. Once the product specifications have been set, processes capable of meeting those specifications and the necessary quality standards are created. At Frito-Lay, quality begins at the farm, with onsite inspection of the potatoes used in Ruffles and the corn used in Fritos. Quality continues throughout the manufacturing process, with visual inspections and with statistical process control of product variables such as oil, moisture, seasoning, salt, thickness, and weight.

Additional quality evaluations are conducted throughout shipment, receipt, production, packaging, and delivery.

The production process at Frito-Lay is designed for large volumes and small variety, using expensive special-purpose equipment, and with swift movement of material through the facility. Product-focused facilities, such as Frito-Lay's, typically have high capital costs, tight schedules, and rapid processing. Frito-Lay's facilities are located regionally to aid in the rapid delivery of products because freshness is a critical issue. Sanitary issues and necessarily fast processing of products put a premium on an efficient layout. Production lines are designed for balanced throughput and high utilization. Cross-trained workers, who handle a variety of production lines, have promotion paths identified for their particular skill set. The company rewards employees with medical, retirement, and education plans. Its turnover is very low.

The supply chain is integral to success in the food industry; vendors must be chosen with great care. Moreover, the finished food product is highly dependent on perishable raw materials. Consequently, the supply chain brings raw material (potatoes, corn, etc.) to the plant securely and rapidly to meet tight production schedules. For instance, from the time that potatoes are picked in St. Augustine, Florida, until they are unloaded at the Orlando plant, processed, packaged, and shipped from the plant is under 12 hours. The requirement for fresh product requires on-time, just-in-time deliveries combined with both low raw material and finished goods inventories. The continuous-flow nature of the specialized equipment in the production process permits little work-in-process inventory. The plants usually run 24/7. This means that there are four shifts of employees each week.

Tight scheduling to ensure the proper mix of fresh finished goods on automated equipment requires reliable systems and effective maintenance. Frito-Lay's workforce is trained to recognize problems early, and professional maintenance personnel are available on every shift. Downtime is very costly and can lead to late deliveries, making maintenance a high priority.

Discussion Questions*

1. From your knowledge of production processes and from the case and the video, identify how each of the 10 decisions of OM is applied at Frito-Lay.
2. How would you determine the productivity of the production process at Frito-Lay?
3. How are the 10 decisions of OM different when applied by the operations manager of a production process such as Frito-Lay versus a service organization such as Hard Rock Cafe (see the Hard Rock Cafe video case below)?

*You may wish to view the video that accompanies this case before addressing these questions.

Hard Rock Cafe: Operations Management in Services

Video Case

In its 42 years of existence, Hard Rock has grown from a modest London pub to a global power managing 150 cafes, 13 hotels/casinos, and live music venues. This puts Hard Rock firmly in the service industry—a sector that employs over 75% of the people in the U.S. Hard Rock moved its world headquarters to Orlando, Florida, in 1988 and has expanded to more than 40 locations throughout the U.S., serving over 100,000 meals each day. Hard Rock chefs are modifying the menu from classic American—burgers and chicken wings—to include higher-end items such as stuffed veal chops and lobster tails. Just as taste in music changes over time, so does Hard Rock Cafe, with new menus, layouts, memorabilia, services, and strategies.

At Orlando's Universal Studios, a traditional tourist destination, Hard Rock Cafe serves over 3,500 meals each day. The cafe employs about 400 people. Most are employed in the restaurant, but some work in the retail shop. Retail is now a standard and increasingly prominent feature in Hard Rock Cafes (since close to 48% of revenue comes from this source). Cafe employees include kitchen and wait staff, hostesses, and bartenders. Hard Rock employees are not only competent in their job skills but are also passionate about music and have engaging personalities. Cafe staff is scheduled down to 15-minute intervals to meet seasonal and daily demand changes in the tourist environment of Orlando. Surveys are done on a regular basis to evaluate quality of food and service at the cafe. Scores are rated on a 1-to-7 scale, and if the score is not a 7, the food or service is a failure.

Hard Rock is adding a new emphasis on live music and is redesigning its restaurants to accommodate the changing tastes. Since Eric Clapton hung his guitar on the wall to mark his favorite bar stool, Hard Rock has become the world's leading collector and exhibitor of rock 'n' roll memorabilia, with changing exhibits at its cafes throughout the world. The collection includes 70,000 pieces, valued at $40 million. In keeping with the times, Hard Rock also maintains a Web site, www.hardrock.com, which receives over 100,000 hits per week, and a weekly cable television program on VH1. Hard Rock's brand recognition, at 92%, is one of the highest in the world.

Discussion Questions*

1. From your knowledge of restaurants, from the video, from the *Global Company Profile* that opens this text, and from the case itself, identify how each of the 10 OM strategy decisions is applied at Hard Rock Cafe.
2. How would you determine the productivity of the kitchen staff and wait staff at Hard Rock?
3. How are the 10 OM strategy decisions different when applied to the operations manager of a service operation such as Hard Rock versus an automobile company such as Ford Motor Company?

*You may wish to view the video that accompanies this case before addressing these questions.

- **Additional Case Study:** Visit **www.myomlab.com** or **www.pearsonhighered.com/heizer** for this free case study: Zychol Chemicals Corp.: The production manager must prepare a productivity report, which includes multifactor analysis.

Bibliography

Broedner, P., S. Kinkel, and G. Lay. "Productivity Effects of Outsourcing." *International Journal of Operations and Production Management* 29, no. 2 (2009): 127.

Hounshell, D. A. *From the American System to Mass Production 1800–1932: The Development of Manufacturing.* Baltimore: Johns Hopkins University Press, 1985.

Lewis, William W. *The Power of Productivity.* Chicago: University of Chicago Press, 2005.

Malone, T. W., R J. Laubacher, and T Johns, "The Age of Hyperspecialization," *Harvard Business* 89, no.7 (July-August 2011): 56–65.

Maroto, A., and L. Rubalcaba. "Services Productivity Revisited." *The Service Industries Journal* 28, no. 3 (April 2008): 337.

Sahay, B. S. "Multi-factor Productivity Measurement Model for Service Organization." *International Journal of Productivity and Performance Management* 54, no. 1–2 (2005): 7–23.

San, G., T. Huang, and L. Huang. "Does Labor Quality Matter on Productivity Growth?" *Total Quality Management and Business Excellence* 19, no. 10 (October 2008): 1043.

Sprague, Linda G. "Evolution of the Field of Operations Management," *Journal of Operations Management* 25, no. 2 (March 2007): 219–238.

Tangen, S. "Demystifying Productivity and Performance." *International Journal of Productivity and Performance Measurement* 54, no. 1–2 (2005): 34–47.

Taylor, F. W. *The Principles of Scientific Management.* New York: Harper & Brothers, 1911.

van Biema, Michael, and Bruce Greenwald. "Managing Our Way to Higher Service-Sector Productivity." *Harvard Business Review* 75, no. 4 (July–August 1997): 87–95.

Wren, Daniel A. *The Evolution of Management Thought*, New York: Wiley, 1994.

APPENDIX

SOLUTIONS TO EVEN-NUMBERED PROBLEMS

2 **(a)** 2 valves/hr
(b) 2.25 valves/hr
(c) 12.5%

4 Varies by site and source.

6 Productivity of labor: 9.3%
Productivity of resin: 11.1%
Productivity of capital: −10.0%
Productivity of energy: 6.1%

8 **(a)** .0096 rugs/labor-dollar
(b) .00787 rugs/dollar

10 Productivity of capital dropped; labor and energy productivity increased.

12 **(a)** Before: 25 boxes/hr
After: 27.08 boxes/hr
(b) Increase: 8.3%
(c) 29.167 boxes/hr

14 **(a)** .293 loaves/dollar
(b) .359 loaves/dollar
(c) Labor change: 0%; Investment change: 22.5%

16 **(a)** 220 hours per laborer; 66,000 labor hours
(b) 200 hours per laborer

Rapid Review

Main Heading	Review Material	MyOMLab
WHAT IS OPERATIONS MANAGEMENT?	■ **Production**—The creation of goods and services ■ **Operations management (OM)**—Activities that relate to the creation of goods and services through the transformation of inputs to outputs	**VIDEOS 1 and 2** OM at Hard Rock OM at Frito-Lay
ORGANIZING TO PRODUCE GOODS AND SERVICES	All organizations perform three functions to create goods and services: 1. *Marketing*, which generates demand 2. *Production/operations,* which creates the product 3. *Finance/accounting,* which tracks how well the organization is doing, pays the bills, and collects the money	
THE SUPPLY CHAIN	**Supply chain**—A global network of organizations and activities that supply a firm with goods and services	
WHY STUDY OM?	We study OM for four reasons: 1. To learn how people organize themselves for productive enterprise 2. To learn how goods and services are produced 3. To understand what operations managers do 4. Because OM is a costly part of an organization	
WHAT OPERATIONS MANAGERS DO	Ten **OM strategic decisions** are required of operations managers: 1. Design of goods and services 2. Managing quality 3. Process strategy 4. Location strategies 5. Layout strategies 6. Human resources 7. Supply-chain management 8. Inventory management 9. Scheduling 10. Maintenance About 40% of *all* jobs are in OM. Operations managers possess job titles such as plant manager, quality manager, process improvement consultant, and operations analyst.	
THE HERITAGE OF OPERATIONS MANAGEMENT	Significant events in modern OM can be classified into six eras: 1. Early concepts (1776–1880)—Labor specialization (Smith, Babbage), standardized parts (Whitney) 2. Scientific management (1880–1910)—Gantt charts (Gantt), motion and time studies (Gilbreth), process analysis (Taylor), queuing theory (Erlang) 3. Mass production (1910–1980)—Assembly line (Ford/Sorensen), statistical sampling (Shewhart), economic order quantity (Harris), linear programming (Dantzig), PERT/CPM (DuPont), material requirements planning 4. Lean production (1980–1995)—Just-in-time, computer-aided design, electronic data interchange, total quality management, Baldrige Award, empowerment, kanbans 5. Mass customization (1995–2005)—Internet/e-commerce, enterprise resource planning, international quality standards, finite scheduling, supply-chain management, mass customization, build-to-order, sustainability 6. Globalization era (2005–2020)—Global supply chains, growth of transnational organizations, instant communications, sustainability, ethics in a global work force, logistics and shipping	
OPERATIONS FOR GOODS AND SERVICES	■ **Services**—Economic activities that typically produce an intangible product (such as education, entertainment, lodging, government, financial, and health services). Almost all services and almost all goods are a mixture of a service and a tangible product. ■ **Service sector**—The segment of the economy that includes trade, financial, lodging, education, legal, medical, and other professional occupations. Services now constitute the largest economic sector in postindustrial societies. The huge productivity increases in agriculture and manufacturing have allowed more of our economic resources to be devoted to services. Many service jobs pay very well.	

Rapid Review continued

Main Heading	Review Material	MyOMLab
THE PRODUCTIVITY CHALLENGE	■ **Productivity**—The ratio of outputs (goods and services) divided by one or more inputs (such as labor, capital, or management) High production means producing many units, while high productivity means producing units efficiently. Only through increases in productivity can the standard of living of a country improve. U.S. productivity has averaged a 2.5% increase per year for over a century. $$\text{Productivity} = \frac{\text{Units produced}}{\text{Input used}} \quad (1)$$ ■ **Single-factor productivity**—Indicates the ratio of one resource (input) to the goods and services produced (outputs). ■ **Multifactor productivity**—Indicates the ratio of many or all resources (inputs) to the goods and services produced (outputs). Multifactor productivity $$= \frac{\text{Output}}{\text{Labor} + \text{Material} + \text{Energy} + \text{Capital} + \text{Miscellaneous}} \quad (2)$$ Measurement problems with productivity include: (1) the quality may change, (2) external elements may interfere, and (3) precise units of measure may be lacking. ■ **Productivity variables**—The three factors critical to productivity improvement are labor (10%), capital (38%), and management (52%). ■ **Knowledge society**—A society in which much of the labor force has migrated from manual work to work based on knowledge	Problems: 1–17 Virtual Office Hours for Solved Problems: 1, 2
NEW CHALLENGES IN OPERATIONS MANAGEMENT	Some of the current challenges for operations managers include: ■ Global focus; international collaboration ■ Supply-chain partnering; joint ventures; alliances ■ Sustainability, green products; recycle, reuse ■ Rapid product development; design collaboration ■ Mass customization; customized products ■ Just-in-time performance; lean; continuous improvement ■ Empowered employees; enriched jobs	
ETHICS, SOCIAL RESPONSIBILITY, AND SUSTAINABILITY	Among the many ethical challenges facing operations managers are (1) efficiently developing and producing safe, quality products; (2) maintaining a clean environment; (3) providing a safe workplace; and (4) honoring stakeholder commitments. ■ **Stakeholders**—Those with a vested interest in an organization	

Self Test

■ **Before taking the self-test,** refer to the learning objectives listed at the beginning of the text and the key terms listed at the end of the text.

LO1. Productivity increases when:
- **a)** inputs increase while outputs remain the same.
- **b)** inputs decrease while outputs remain the same.
- **c)** outputs decrease while inputs remain the same.
- **d)** inputs and outputs increase proportionately.
- **e)** inputs increase at the same rate as outputs.

LO2. Services often:
- **a)** are tangible.
- **b)** are standardized.
- **c)** are knowledge based.
- **d)** are low in customer interaction.
- **e)** have consistent product definition.

LO3. Productivity:
- **a)** can use many factors as the numerator.
- **b)** is the same thing as production.
- **c)** increases at about 0.5% per year.
- **d)** is dependent upon labor, management, and capital.
- **e)** is the same thing as effectiveness.

LO4. Single-factor productivity:
- **a)** remains constant.
- **b)** is never constant.
- **c)** usually uses labor as a factor.
- **d)** seldom uses labor as a factor.
- **e)** uses management as a factor.

LO5. Multifactor productivity:
- **a)** remains constant.
- **b)** is never constant.
- **c)** usually uses substitutes as common variables for the factors of production.
- **d)** seldom uses labor as a factor.
- **e)** always uses management as a factor.

LO6. Productivity increases each year in the U.S. are a result of three factors:
- **a)** labor, capital, management
- **b)** engineering, labor, capital
- **c)** engineering, capital, quality control
- **d)** engineering, labor, data processing
- **e)** engineering, capital, data processing

Answers: LO1. b; LO2. c; LO3. d; LO4. c; LO5. c; LO6. a.

Decision-Making Tools

OUTLINE

LEARNING OBJECTIVES

LO1 ***Create*** a simple decision tree

LO2 ***Build*** a decision table

LO3 ***Explain*** when to use each of the three types of decision-making environments

LO4 ***Calculate*** an expected monetary value (EMV)

LO5 ***Compute*** the expected value of perfect information (EVPI)

LO6 ***Evaluate*** the nodes in a decision tree

LO7 ***Create*** a decision tree with sequential decisions

WOULD *YOU* GO ALL IN?

At the Legends of Poker tournament in Los Angeles, veteran T.J. Cloutier opens with a $60,000 bet. (Antes and required bets of $39,000 are already on the table.) Former Go2net CTO Paul Phillips ponders going "all in"—betting virtually all his chips. Using decision theory, here's how he decided.

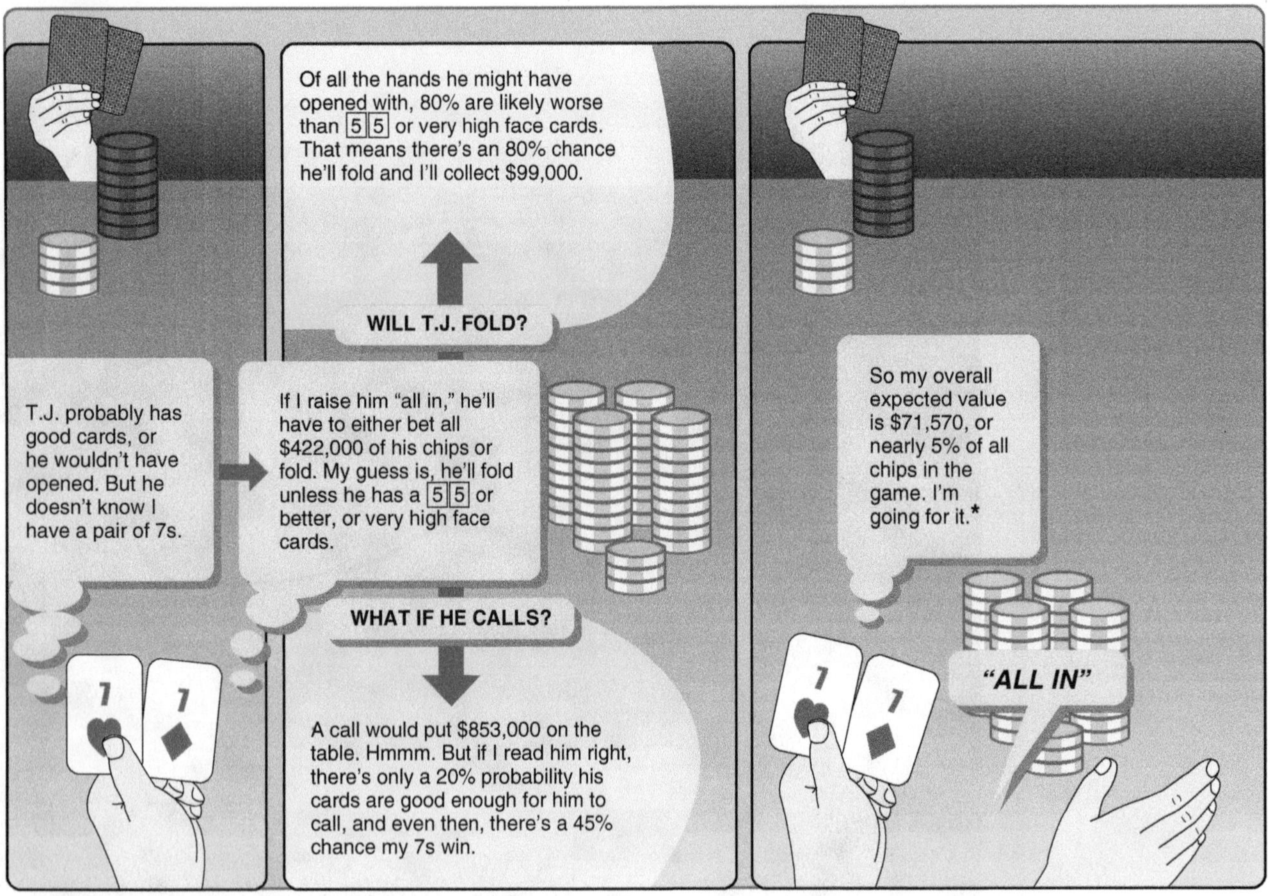

Source: Based on *Business 2.0* (November 2003): 128–134.

*To see the details of Phillips's decision, see Example 8.

The Decision Process in Operations

Operations managers are not gamblers. But they are decision makers. To achieve the goals of their organizations, managers must understand how decisions are made and know which decision-making tools to use. To a great extent, the success or failure of both people and companies depends on the quality of their decisions. Overcoming uncertainty is a manager's challenge.

What makes the difference between a good decision and a bad decision? A "good" decision—one that uses analytic decision making—is based on logic and considers all available data and possible alternatives. It also follows these six steps:

1. Clearly define the problem and the factors that influence it.
2. Develop specific and measurable objectives.
3. Develop a model—that is, a relationship between objectives and variables (which are measurable quantities).
4. Evaluate each alternative solution based on its merits and drawbacks.
5. Select the best alternative.
6. Implement and evaluate the decision and then set a timetable for completion.

Throughout this text, we have introduced a broad range of mathematical models and tools that help operations managers make better decisions. Effective operations depend on careful decision making. Fortunately, there are a whole variety of analytic tools to help make these decisions. This text introduces two of them—decision tables and decision trees. They are used in a wide number of OM situations, ranging from new-product analysis, to capacity planning, to location planning, to supply-chain disaster planning, to scheduling, and to maintenance planning.

Fundamentals of Decision Making

Regardless of the complexity of a decision or the sophistication of the technique used to analyze it, all decision makers are faced with alternatives and "states of nature." The following notation will be used in this text:

1. Terms:
   a. *Alternative*—A course of action or strategy that may be chosen by a decision maker (e.g., not carrying an umbrella tomorrow).
   b. *State of nature*—An occurrence or a situation over which the decision maker has little or no control (e.g., tomorrow's weather).
2. Symbols used in a decision tree:
   a. □—Decision node from which one of several alternatives may be selected.
   b. ○—A state-of-nature node out of which one state of nature will occur.

To present a manager's decision alternatives, we can develop *decision trees* using the above symbols. When constructing a decision tree, we must be sure that all alternatives and states of nature are in their correct and logical places and that we include *all* possible alternatives and states of nature.

Example 1

A SIMPLE DECISION TREE

Getz Products Company is investigating the possibility of producing and marketing backyard storage sheds. Undertaking this project would require the construction of either a large or a small manufacturing plant. The market for the product produced—storage sheds—could be either favorable or unfavorable. Getz, of course, has the option of not developing the new product line at all.

APPROACH ▶ Getz decides to build a decision tree.

SOLUTION ▶ Figure 1 illustrates Getz's decision tree.

LO1 *Create* a simple decision tree

INSIGHT ▶ We never want to overlook the option of "doing nothing," as that is usually a possible decision.

LEARNING EXERCISE ▶ Getz now considers constructing a medium-sized plant as a fourth option. Redraw the tree in Figure 1 to accommodate this. [Answer: Your tree will have a new node and branches between "Construct large plant" and "Construct small plant."]

RELATED PROBLEMS ▶ 2e, 8b, 14a, 15a, 17a, 18

Figure 1
Getz Products' Decision Tree

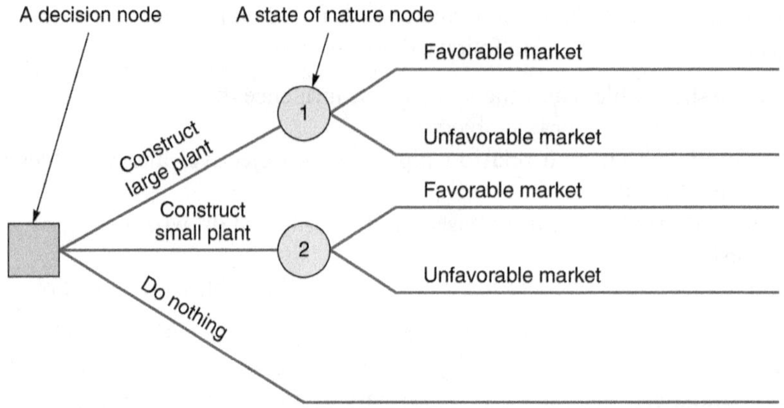

Decision Tables

Decision table
A tabular means of analyzing decision alternatives and states of nature.

We may also develop a decision or payoff table to help Getz Products define its alternatives. For any alternative and a particular state of nature, there is a *consequence* or *outcome*, which is usually expressed as a monetary value. This is called a *conditional value*. Note that all of the alternatives in Example 2 are listed down the left side of the table, that states of nature (outcomes) are listed across the top, and that conditional values (payoffs) are in the body of the **decision table**.

Example 2

A DECISION TABLE

Getz Products now wishes to organize the following information into a table. With a favorable market, a large facility will give Getz Products a net profit of $200,000. If the market is unfavorable, a $180,000 net loss will occur. A small plant will result in a net profit of $100,000 in a favorable market, but a net loss of $20,000 will be encountered if the market is unfavorable.

LO2 *Build* a decision table

APPROACH ▶ These numbers become conditional values in the decision table. We list alternatives in the left column and states of nature across the top of the table.

SOLUTION ▶ The completed table is shown in Table 1.

TABLE 1 Decision Table with Conditional Values for Getz Products

	STATES OF NATURE	
ALTERNATIVES	FAVORABLE MARKET	UNFAVORABLE MARKET
Construct large plant	$200,000	–$180,000
Construct small plant	$100,000	–$ 20,000
Do nothing	$ 0	$ 0

STUDENT TIP ☆
Decision tables force logic into decision making.

INSIGHT ▶ The toughest part of decision tables is obtaining the data to analyze.

LEARNING EXERCISE ▶ In Examples 3 and 4, we see how to use decision tables to make decisions.

Types of Decision-Making Environments

The types of decisions people make depend on how much knowledge or information they have about the situation. There are three decision-making environments:

- Decision making under uncertainty
- Decision making under risk
- Decision making under certainty

LO3 *Explain* when to use each of the three types of decision-making environments

Decision Making Under Uncertainty

When there is complete *uncertainty* as to which state of nature in a decision environment may occur (i.e., when we cannot even assess probabilities for each possible outcome), we rely on three decision methods:

1. **Maximax**: This method finds an alternative that *max*imizes the *max*imum outcome for every alternative. First, we find the maximum outcome within every alternative, and then we pick the alternative with the maximum number. Because this decision criterion locates the alternative with the *highest* possible *gain*, it has been called an "optimistic" decision criterion.
2. **Maximin**: This method finds the alternative that *max*imizes the *min*imum outcome for every alternative. First, we find the minimum outcome within every alternative, and then we pick the alternative with the maximum number. Because this decision criterion locates the alternative that has the *least* possible *loss*, it has been called a "pessimistic" decision criterion.
3. **Equally likely**: This method finds the alternative with the highest average outcome. First, we calculate the average outcome for every alternative, which is the sum of all outcomes divided by the number of outcomes. We then pick the alternative with the maximum number. The equally likely approach assumes that each state of nature is equally likely to occur.

Maximax
A criterion that finds an alternative that maximizes the maximum outcome.

Maximin
A criterion that finds an alternative that maximizes the minimum outcome.

Equally likely
A criterion that assigns equal probability to each state of nature.

Example 3

A DECISION TABLE ANALYSIS UNDER UNCERTAINTY

Getz Products Company would like to apply each of these three approaches now.

APPROACH ▶ Given Getz's decision table from Example 2, he determines the maximax, maximin, and equally likely decision criteria.

SOLUTION ▶ Table 2 provides the solution.

TABLE 2 Decision Table for Decision Making Under Uncertainty

	STATES OF NATURE				
ALTERNATIVES	FAVORABLE MARKET	UNFAVORABLE MARKET	MAXIMUM IN ROW	MINIMUM IN ROW	ROW AVERAGE
Construct large plant	$200,000	−$180,000	$200,000 ←	−180,000	$10,000
Construct small plant	$100,000	−$ 20,000	$100,000	−$20,000	$40,000 ←
Do nothing	$ 0	$ 0	$ 0	$ 0 ←	$ 0
			Maximax	Maximin	Equally likely

1. The maximax choice is to construct a large plant. This is the *max*imum of the *max*imum number within each row, or alternative.
2. The maximin choice is to do nothing. This is the *max*imum of the *min*imum number within each row, or alternative.

3. The equally likely choice is to construct a small plant. This is the maximum of the average outcome of each alternative. This approach assumes that all outcomes for any alternative are *equally likely*.

INSIGHT ▶ There are optimistic decision makers ("maximax") and pessimistic ones ("maximin"). Maximax and maximin present best case–worst case planning scenarios.

LEARNING EXERCISE ▶ Getz reestimates the outcome for constructing a large plant when the market is favorable and raises it to $250,000. What numbers change in Table 2? Do the decisions change? [Answer: The maximax is now $250,000, and the row average is $35,000 for large plant. No decision changes.]

RELATED PROBLEMS ▶ 1, 2b–d, 4, 6

Decision Making Under Risk

Expected monetary value (EMV)
The expected payout or value of a variable that has different possible states of nature, each with an associated probability.

Decision making under risk, a more common occurrence, relies on probabilities. Several possible states of nature may occur, each with an assumed probability. The states of nature must be mutually exclusive and collectively exhaustive and their probabilities must sum to 1.[1] Given a decision table with conditional values and probability assessments for all states of nature, we can determine the **expected monetary value (EMV)** for each alternative. This figure represents the expected value or *mean* return for each alternative *if we could repeat this decision (or similar types of decisions) a large number of times.*

The EMV for an alternative is the sum of all possible payoffs from the alternative, each weighted by the probability of that payoff occurring:

LO4 *Calculate* an expected monetary value (EMV)

$$\begin{aligned}\text{EMV(Alternative } i) = {} & \text{(Payoff of 1st state of nature)} \\ & \times \text{(Probability of 1st state of nature)} \\ & + \text{(Payoff of 2nd state of nature)} \\ & \times \text{(Probability of 2nd state of nature)} \\ & + \ldots + \text{(Payoff of last state of nature)} \\ & \times \text{(Probability of last state of nature)}\end{aligned}$$

Example 4 illustrates how to compute the maximum EMV.

Example 4

EXPECTED MONETARY VALUE

Getz would like to find the EMV for each alternative.

APPROACH ▶ Getz Products' operations manager believes that the probability of a favorable market is 0.6, and that of an unfavorable market is 0.4. He can now determine the EMV for each alternative (see Table 3).

SOLUTION ▶

1. EMV (A_1) = (0.6) ($200,000) + (0.4) (–$180,000) = $48,000
2. EMV (A_2) = (0.6) ($100,000) + (0.4) (–$20,000) = $52,000
3. EMV (A_3) = (0.6) ($0) + (0.4) ($0) = $0

[1]To review these other statistical terms, refer to Tutorial 1, "Statistical Review for Managers," at **www.pearsonhighered.com/heizer** or **www.myomlab.com.**

TABLE 3 Decision Table for Getz Products

	STATES OF NATURE	
ALTERNATIVES	FAVORABLE MARKET	UNFAVORABLE MARKET
Construct large plant (A_1)	\$200,000	−\$180,000
Construct small plant (A_2)	\$100,000	−\$ 20,000
Do nothing (A_3)	\$ 0	\$ 0
Probabilities	0.6	0.4

INSIGHT ▶ The maximum EMV is seen in alternative A_2. Thus, according to the EMV decision criterion, Getz would build the small facility.

LEARNING EXERCISE ▶ What happens to the three EMVs if Getz increases the conditional value on the "large plant/favorable market" result to \$250,000? [Answer: EMV (A_1) = \$78,000. A_1 is now the preferable decision.]

RELATED PROBLEMS ▶ 2e, 3a, 5a, 7a, 8, 9a, 10, 11, 12, 14a,b, 16a, 22

EXCEL OM Data File **ModAExA4.xls** can be found at **www.pearsonhighered.com/heizer**.

Decision Making Under Certainty

Now suppose that the Getz operations manager has been approached by a marketing research firm that proposes to help him make the decision about whether to build the plant to produce storage sheds. The marketing researchers claim that their technical analysis will tell Getz with certainty whether the market is favorable for the proposed product. In other words, it will change Getz's environment from one of decision making *under risk* to one of decision making *under certainty*. This information could prevent Getz from making a very expensive mistake. The marketing research firm would charge Getz \$65,000 for the information. What would you recommend? Should the operations manager hire the firm to make the study? Even if the information from the study is perfectly accurate, is it worth \$65,000? What might it be worth? Although some of these questions are difficult to answer, determining the value of such *perfect information* can be very useful. It places an upper bound on what you would be willing to spend on information, such as that being sold by a marketing consultant. This is the concept of the expected value of perfect information (EVPI), which we now introduce.

Expected Value of Perfect Information (EVPI)

LO5 *Compute* the expected value of perfect information (EVPI)

If a manager were able to determine which state of nature would occur, then he or she would know which decision to make. Once a manager knows which decision to make, the payoff increases because the payoff is now a certainty, not a probability. Because the payoff will increase with knowledge of which state of nature will occur, this knowledge has value. Therefore, we now look at how to determine the value of this information. We call this difference between the payoff under perfect information and the payoff under risk the **expected value of perfect information (EVPI)**.

Expected value of perfect information (EVPI)
The difference between the payoff under perfect information and the payoff under risk.

$$\text{EVPI} = \text{Expected value with perfect information} - \text{Maximum EMV}$$

To find the EVPI, we must first compute the **expected value *with* perfect information (EVwPI)**, which is the expected (average) return if we have perfect information before a decision has to be made. To calculate this value, we choose the best alternative for each state of nature and multiply its payoff times the probability of occurrence of that state of nature:

Expected value *with* perfect information (EVwPI)
The expected (average) return if perfect information is available.

Expected value *with* perfect information (EVwPI) = (Best outcome or consequence for 1st state of nature) × (Probability of 1st state of nature)
+ (Best outcome for 2nd state of nature) × (Probability of 2nd state of nature)
+ . . . + (Best outcome for last state of nature) × (Probability of last state of nature)

In Example 5 we use the data and decision table from Example 4 to examine the expected value of perfect information.

Example 5

EXPECTED VALUE OF PERFECT INFORMATION

The Getz operations manager would like to calculate the maximum that he would pay for information—that is, the expected value of perfect information, or EVPI.

APPROACH ▶ Referring to Table 3 in Example 4, he follows a two-stage process. First, the expected value *with* perfect information (EVwPI) is computed. Then, using this information, the EVPI is calculated.

SOLUTION ▶

1. The best outcome for the state of nature "favorable market" is "build a large facility" with a payoff of \$200,000. The best outcome for the state of nature "unfavorable market" is "do nothing" with a payoff of \$0. Expected value *with* perfect information = (\$200,000)(0.6) + (\$0)(0.4) = \$120,000. Thus, if we had perfect information, we would expect (on the average) \$120,000 if the decision could be repeated many times.
2. The maximum EMV is \$52,000 for A_2, which is the expected outcome without perfect information. Thus:

$$\text{EVPI} = \text{EVwPI} - \text{Maximum EMV}$$
$$= \$120{,}000 - \$52{,}000 = \$68{,}000$$

INSIGHT ▶ The *most* Getz should be willing to pay for perfect information is \$68,000. This conclusion, of course, is again based on the assumption that the probability of the first state of nature is 0.6 and the second is 0.4.

LEARNING EXERCISE ▶ How does the EVPI change if the "large plant/favorable market" conditional value is \$250,000? [Answer: EVPI = \$72,000.]

RELATED PROBLEMS ▶ 3b, 5b, 7, 9, 14, 16

STUDENT TIP ☆
EVPI places an upper limit on what you should pay for information.

Decision Trees

STUDENT TIP ☆
Decision trees can become complex, so we illustrate two of them in this section.

Decisions that lend themselves to display in a decision table also lend themselves to display in a decision tree. We will therefore analyze some decisions using decision trees. Although the use of a decision table is convenient in problems having one set of decisions and one set of states of nature, many problems include *sequential* decisions and states of nature.

When there are two or more sequential decisions, and later decisions are based on the outcome of prior ones, the decision tree approach becomes appropriate. A **decision tree** is a graphic display of the decision process that indicates decision alternatives, states of nature and their respective probabilities, and payoffs for each combination of decision alternative and state of nature.

Decision tree
A graphical means of analyzing decision alternatives and states of nature.

Expected monetary value (EMV) is the most commonly used criterion for decision tree analysis. One of the first steps in such analysis is to graph the decision tree and to specify the monetary consequences of all outcomes for a particular problem.

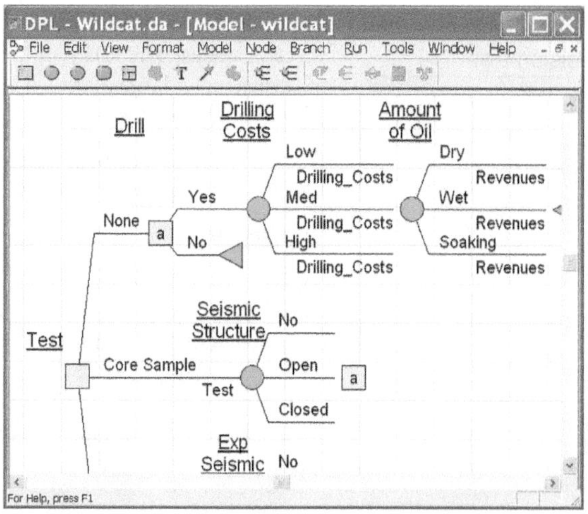

When Tomco Oil had to decide which of its new Kentucky lease areas to drill for oil, it turned to decision tree analysis. The 74 different factors, including geological, engineering, economic, and political factors, became much clearer. Decision tree software such as DPL (shown here), Tree Plan, and Supertree allow decision problems to be analyzed with less effort and greater depth than ever before.

Analyzing problems with *decision trees* involves five steps:

1. Define the problem.
2. Structure or draw the decision tree.
3. Assign probabilities to the states of nature.
4. Estimate payoffs for each possible combination of decision alternatives and states of nature.
5. Solve the problem by computing the expected monetary values (EMV) for each state-of-nature node. This is done by working *backward*—that is, by starting at the right of the tree and working back to decision nodes on the left.

Example 6

SOLVING A TREE FOR EMV

Getz wants to develop a completed and solved decision tree.

APPROACH ▶ The payoffs are placed at the right-hand side of each of the tree's branches (see Figure 2). The probabilities (first used by Getz in Example 4) are placed in parentheses next to each state of nature.

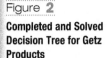

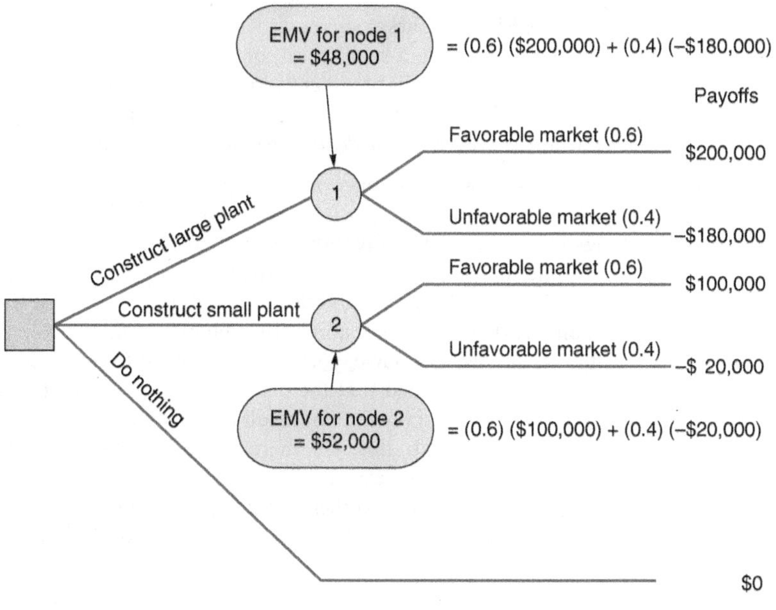

Figure 2
Completed and Solved Decision Tree for Getz Products

LO6 *Evaluate* the nodes in a decision tree

The expected monetary values for each state-of-nature node are then calculated and placed by their respective nodes. The EMV of the first node is $48,000. This represents the branch from the decision node to "construct a large plant." The EMV for node 2, to "construct a small plant," is $52,000. The option of "doing nothing" has, of course, a payoff of $0.

SOLUTION ▶ The branch leaving the decision node leading to the state-of-nature node with the highest EMV will be chosen. In Getz's case, a small plant should be built.

INSIGHT ▶ This graphical approach is an excellent way for managers to understand all the options in making a major decision. Visual models are often preferred over tables.

LEARNING EXERCISE ▶ Correct Figure 2 to reflect a $250,000 payoff for "construct large plant/favorable market." [Answer: Change one payoff and recompute the EMV for node 1.]

RELATED PROBLEMS ▶ 2e, 8b, 14a,b, 17, 18

EXCEL OM Data File **ModAExA6.xls** can be found at **www.pearsonhighered.com/heizer**.

A More Complex Decision Tree

When a *sequence* of decisions must be made, decision trees are much more powerful tools than are decision tables. Let's say that Getz Products has two decisions to make, with the second decision dependent on the outcome of the first. Before deciding about building a new plant, Getz has the option of conducting its own marketing research survey, at a cost of $10,000. The information from this survey could help it decide whether to build a large plant, to build a small plant, or not to build at all. Getz recognizes that although such a survey will not provide it with *perfect* information, it may be extremely helpful.

Getz's new decision tree is represented in Figure 3 of Example 7. Take a careful look at this more complex tree. Note that *all possible outcomes and alternatives* are included in their logical sequence. This procedure is one of the strengths of using decision trees. The manager is forced to examine all possible outcomes, including unfavorable ones. He or she is also forced to make decisions in a logical, sequential manner.

Example 7

A DECISION TREE WITH SEQUENTIAL DECISIONS

Getz Products wishes to develop the new tree for this sequential decision.

APPROACH ▶ Examining the tree in Figure 3, we see that Getz's first decision point is whether to conduct the $10,000 market survey. If it chooses not to do the study (the lower part of the tree), it can either build a large plant, a small plant, or no plant. This is Getz's second decision point. If the decision is to build, the market will be either favorable (0.6 probability) or unfavorable (0.4 probability). The payoffs for each of the possible consequences are listed along the right-hand side. As a matter of fact, this lower portion of Getz's tree is *identical* to the simpler decision tree shown in Figure 2.

SOLUTION ▶ The upper part of Figure 3 reflects the decision to conduct the market survey. State-of-nature node number 1 has 2 branches coming out of it. Let us say there is a 45% chance that the survey results will indicate a favorable market for the storage sheds. We also note that the probability is 0.55 that the survey results will be negative.

The rest of the probabilities shown in parentheses in Figure 3 are all *conditional* probabilities. For example, 0.78 is the probability of a favorable market for the sheds given a favorable result from the market survey. Of course, you would expect to find a high probability of a favorable market given that the research indicated that the market was good. Don't forget, though: There is a chance that Getz's $10,000 market survey did not result in perfect or even reliable information. Any market research study is subject to error. In this case, there remains a 22% chance that the market for sheds will be unfavorable given positive survey results.

Likewise, we note that there is a 27% chance that the market for sheds will be favorable given negative survey results. The probability is much higher, 0.73, that the market will actually be unfavorable given a negative survey.

Figure 3
Getz Products Decision Tree with Probabilities and EMVs Shown

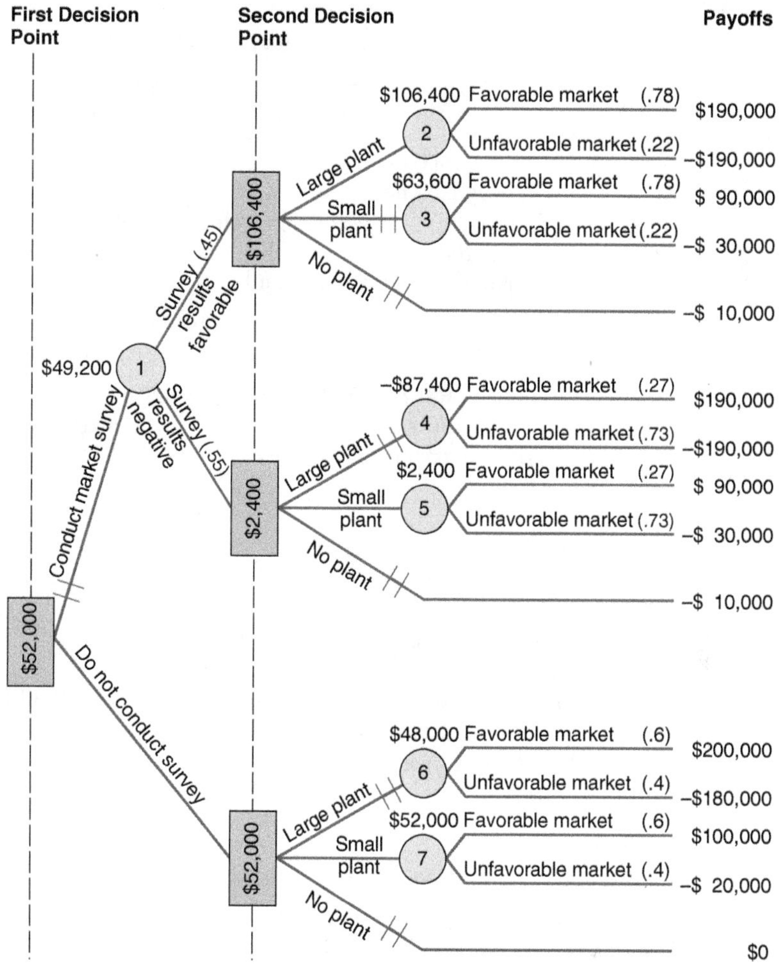

STUDENT TIP ☆
The short parallel lines mean "prune" that branch, as it is less favorable than another available option and may be dropped.

LO7 *Create* a decision tree with sequential decisions

Finally, when we look to the payoff column in Figure 3, we see that \$10,000—the cost of the marketing study—has been subtracted from each of the top 10 tree branches. Thus, a large plant constructed in a favorable market would normally net a \$200,000 profit. Yet because the market study was conducted, this figure is reduced by \$10,000. In the unfavorable case, the loss of \$180,000 would increase to \$190,000. Similarly, conducting the survey and building *no plant* now results in a –\$10,000 payoff.

With all probabilities and payoffs specified, we can start calculating the expected monetary value of each branch. We begin at the end or right-hand side of the decision tree and work back toward the origin. When we finish, the best decision will be known.

1. Given favorable survey results:

$$\text{EMV (node 2)} = (.78)(\$190{,}000) + (.22)(-\$190{,}000) = \$106{,}400$$
$$\text{EMV (node 3)} = (.78)(\$90{,}000) + (.22)(-\$30{,}000) = \$63{,}600$$

The EMV of no plant in this case is −\$10,000. Thus, if the survey results are favorable, a large plant should be built.

2. Given negative survey results:

$$\text{EMV (node 4)} = (.27)(\$190{,}000) + (.73)(-\$190{,}000) = -\$87{,}400$$
$$\text{EMV (node 5)} = (.27)(\$90{,}000) + (.73)(-\$30{,}000) = \$2{,}400$$

The EMV of no plant is again −\$10,000 for this branch. Thus, given a negative survey result, Getz should build a small plant with an expected value of \$2,400.

3. Continuing on the upper part of the tree and moving backward, we compute the expected value of conducting the market survey:

$$\text{EMV (node 1)} = (.45)(\$106{,}400) + (.55)(\$2{,}400) = \$49{,}200$$

4. If the market survey is *not* conducted:

$$\text{EMV (node 6)} = (.6)(\$200{,}000) + (.4)(-\$180{,}000) = \$48{,}000$$
$$\text{EMV (node 7)} = (.6)(\$100{,}000) + (.4)(-\$20{,}000) = \$52{,}000$$

The EMV of no plant is $0. Thus, building a small plant is the best choice, given the marketing research is not performed.

5. Because the expected monetary value of not conducting the survey is $52,000—vs. an EMV of $49,200 for conducting the study—the best choice is to *not seek marketing information*. Getz should build the small plant.

INSIGHT ▶ You can reduce complexity in a large decision tree by viewing and solving a number of smaller trees—start at the end branches of a large one. Take one decision at a time.

LEARNING EXERCISE ▶ Getz estimates that if he conducts a market survey, there is really only a 35% chance the results will indicate a favorable market for the sheds. How does the tree change? [Answer: The EMV of conducting the survey = $38,800, so Getz should still not do it.]

RELATED PROBLEMS ▶ 13, 18, 19, 20, 21, 23

The Poker Decision Process

We opened this text with ex-dot-commer Paul Phillips's decision to go "all in" at the Legends of Poker tournament in Los Angeles. Example 8 shows how he computed the expected value. Problem 24 gives you a chance to create a decision tree for this process.

Example 8

PHILLIPS'S POKER DECISION

As on the first page in this text, Paul Phillips is deciding whether to bet all his chips against poker star T.J. Cloutier. Phillips holds a pair of 7s. Phillips reasons that T.J. will fold (with 80% probability) if he does not have a pair of 5s or better, or very high cards like a jack, queen, king, or ace. But he also figures that a call would put $853,000 into the pot and surmises that even then, there is 45% chance his pair of 7s will win.

APPROACH ▶ Phillips does an expected monetary analysis.

SOLUTION ▶ If T.J. folds,

The amount of money already in the pot (↓ $99,000)

$$\text{EMV} = (.80)(\$99{,}000) = \$79{,}200$$

If T.J. calls,

the chance T.J. will call (↓ .20)

$$\begin{aligned}\text{EMV} &= .20[(.45)(\$853{,}000) - \text{Phillips's bet of } \$422{,}000] \\ &= .20\,[\$383{,}850 - \$422{,}000] \\ &= .20\,[-\$38{,}150] = -\$7{,}630\end{aligned}$$

Overall EMV = $79,200 − $7,630 = $71,570

INSIGHT ▶ The overall EMV of $71,570 indicates that if this decision were to be made many times, the average payoff would be large. So Phillips decides to bet almost all of his chips. As it turns out, T.J. was holding a pair of jacks. Even though Phillips's decision in this instance did not work out, his analysis and procedure was the correct one.

LEARNING EXERCISE ▶ What would happen if the amount of money already in the pot were only $39,000? [Answer: The overall EMV = $23,570.]

RELATED PROBLEM ▶ 24

Summary

This text examines two of the most widely used decision techniques—decision tables and decision trees. These techniques are especially useful for making decisions under risk. Many decisions in research and development, plant and equipment, and even new buildings and structures can be analyzed with these decision models. Problems in inventory control, aggregate planning, maintenance, scheduling, and production control also lend themselves to decision table and decision tree applications.

Key Terms

Decision table
Maximax
Maximin
Equally likely
Expected monetary value (EMV)
Expected value of perfect information (EVPI)
Expected value *with* perfect information (EVwPI)
Decision tree

Discussion Questions

1. Identify the six steps in the decision process.
2. Give an example of a good decision you made that resulted in a bad outcome. Also give an example of a bad decision you made that had a good outcome. Why was each decision good or bad?
3. What is the *equally likely* decision model?
4. Discuss the differences between decision making under certainty, under risk, and under uncertainty.
5. What is a decision tree?
6. Explain how decision trees might be used in several of the 10 OM decisions.
7. What is the expected value of perfect information (EVPI)?
8. What is the expected value *with* perfect information (EVwPI)?
9. Identify the five steps in analyzing a problem using a decision tree.
10. Why are the maximax and maximin strategies considered to be optimistic and pessimistic, respectively?
11. The expected value criterion is considered to be the rational criterion on which to base a decision. Is this true? Is it rational to consider risk?
12. When are decision trees most useful?

Using Software for Decision Models

Analyzing decision tables is straightforward with Excel, Excel OM, and POM for Windows. When decision trees are involved, Excel OM or commercial packages such as DPL, Tree Plan, and Supertree provide flexibility, power, and ease. POM for Windows will also analyze trees but does not have graphic capabilities.

USING EXCEL OM

Excel OM allows decision makers to evaluate decisions quickly and to perform sensitivity analysis on the results. Program 1 uses the Getz data to illustrate input, output, and selected formulas needed to compute the EMV and EVPI values.

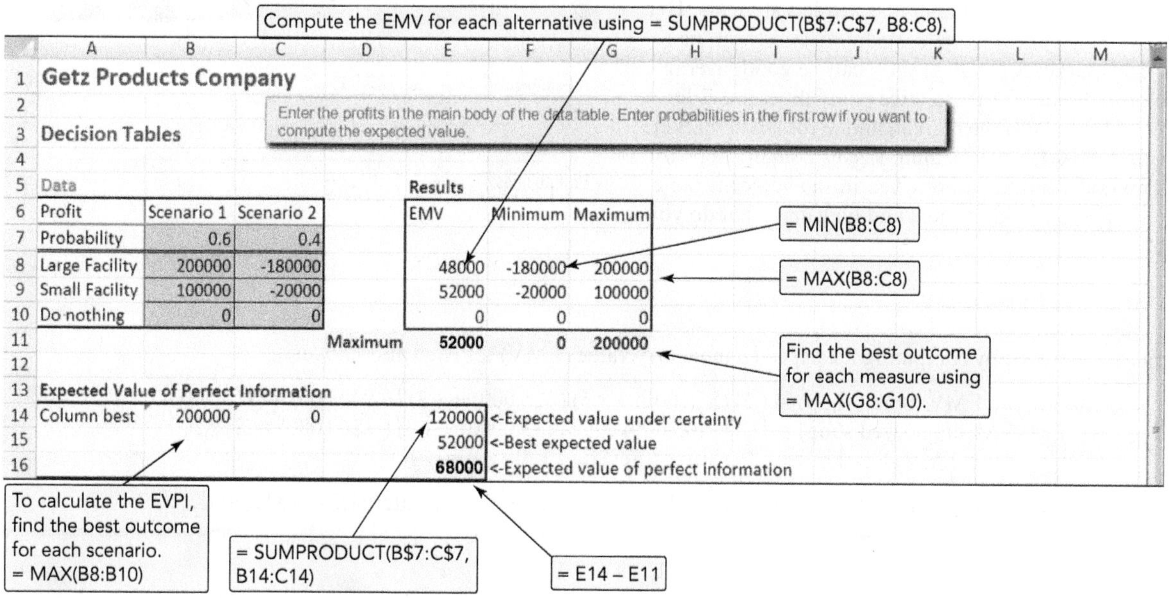

Program 1

Using Excel OM to Compute EMV and Other Measures for Getz

Program 2 uses Excel OM to create the decision tree for Getz Products shown earlier in Example 6. The tool to create the tree is seen in the window on the right.

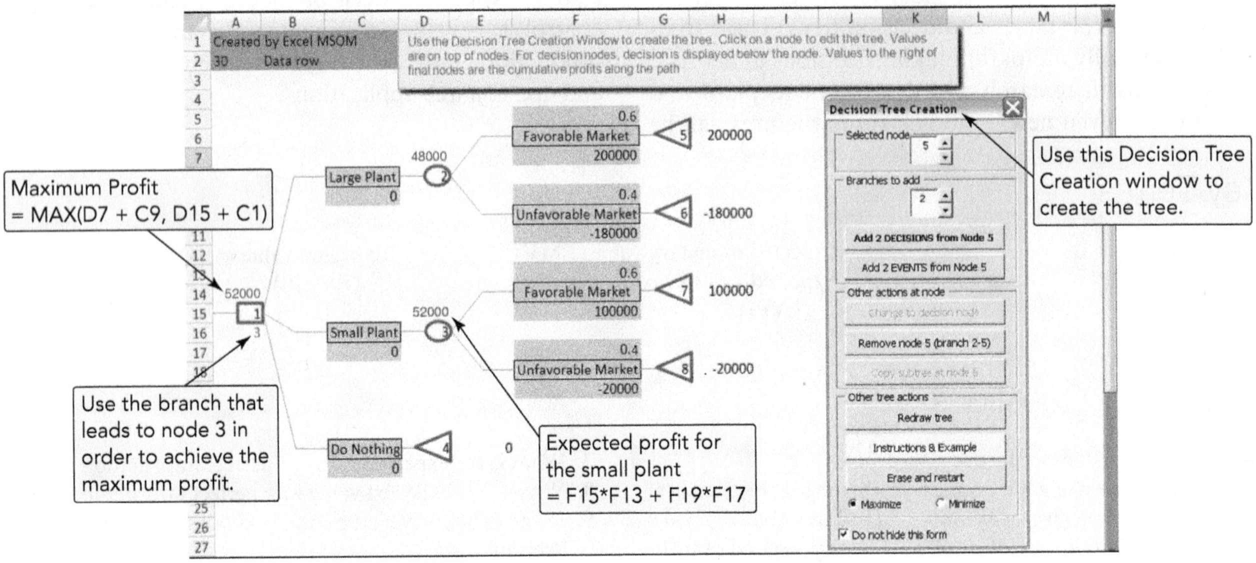

Program 2

Getz Products' Decision Tree Using Excel OM

P USING POM FOR WINDOWS

POM for Windows can be used to calculate all of the information described in the decision tables and decision trees in this text.

Solved Problems

Virtual Office Hours help is available at www.myomlab.com.

SOLVED PROBLEM 1

Stella Yan Hua is considering the possibility of opening a small dress shop on Fairbanks Avenue, a few blocks from the university. She has located a good mall that attracts students. Her options are to open a small shop, a medium-sized shop, or no shop at all. The market for a dress shop can be good, average, or bad. The probabilities for these three possibilities are .2 for a good market, .5 for an average market, and .3 for a bad market. The net profit or loss for the medium-sized or small shops for the various market conditions are given in the adjacent table. Building no shop at all yields no loss and no gain. What do you recommend?

	STATES OF NATURE		
ALTERNATIVES	GOOD MARKET ($)	AVERAGE MARKET ($)	BAD MARKET ($)
Small shop	75,000	25,000	−40,000
Medium-sized shop	100,000	35,000	−60,000
No shop	0	0	0
Probabilities	.20	.50	.30

SOLUTION

The problem can be solved by computing the expected monetary value (EMV) for each alternative:

$$\text{EMV (Small shop)} = (.2)(\$75{,}000) + (.5)(\$25{,}000) + (.3)(-\$40{,}000) = \$15{,}500$$
$$\text{EMV (Medium-sized shop)} = (.2)(\$100{,}000) + (.5)(\$35{,}000) + (.3)(-\$60{,}000) = \$19{,}500$$
$$\text{EMV (No shop)} = (.2)(\$0) + (.5)(\$0) + (.3)(\$0) = \$0$$

As you can see, the best decision is to build the medium-sized shop. The EMV for this alternative is $19,500.

SOLVED PROBLEM 2

T.S. Amer's Ski Shop in Nevada has a 100-day season. T.S. has established the probability of various store traffic, based on historical records of skiing conditions, as indicated in the table to the right. T.S. has four merchandising plans, each focusing on a popular name brand. Each plan yields a daily net profit as noted in the table. He also has a meteorologist friend who, for a small fee, will accurately tell tomorrow's weather so T.S. can implement one of his four merchandising plans.

a) What is the expected monetary value (EMV) under risk?
b) What is the expected value *with* perfect information (EVwPI)?
c) What is the expected value of perfect information (EVPI)?

	TRAFFIC IN STORE BECAUSE OF SKI CONDITIONS (STATES OF NATURE)			
DECISION ALTERNATIVES (MERCHANDISING PLAN FOCUSING ON:)	1	2	3	4
Patagonia	$40	92	20	48
North Face	50	84	10	52
Cloud Veil	35	80	40	64
Columbia	45	72	10	60
Probabilities	.20	.25	.30	.25

SOLUTION

a) The highest expected monetary value under risk is:

$$\text{EMV (Patagonia)} = .20(40) + .25(92) + .30(20) + .25(48) = \$49$$
$$\text{EMV (North Face)} = .20(50) + .25(84) + .30(10) + .25(52) = \$47$$
$$\text{EMV (Cloud Veil)} = .20(35) + .25(80) + .30(40) + .25(64) = \$55$$
$$\text{EMV (Columbia)} = .20(45) + .25(72) + .30(10) + .25(60) = \$45$$

So the maximum EMV = $55

b) The expected value *with* perfect information is:

$$\begin{aligned}\text{EVwPI} &= .20(50) + .25(92) + .30(40) + .25(64)\\ &= 10 + 23 + 12 + 16 = \$61\end{aligned}$$

c) The expected value of perfect information is:

$$\text{EVPI} = \text{EVwPI} - \text{Maximum EMV} = 61 - 55 = \$6$$

SOLVED PROBLEM 3

Daily demand for cases of Tidy Bowl cleaner at Ravinder Nath's Supermarket has always been 5, 6, or 7 cases. Develop a decision tree that illustrates her decision alternatives as to whether to stock 5, 6, or 7 cases.

SOLUTION

The decision tree is shown in Figure 4.

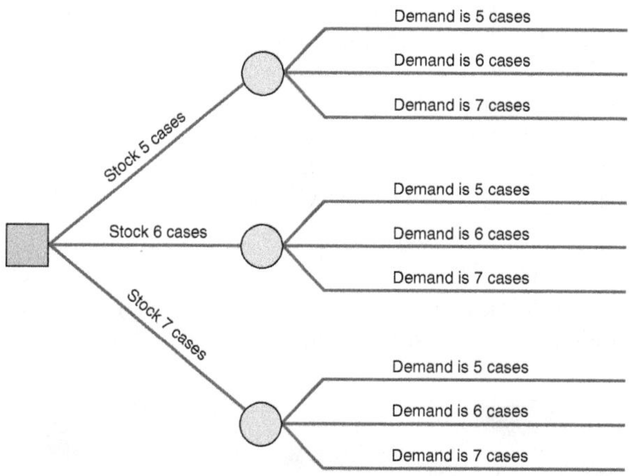

Figure 4

Demand at Ravinder Nath's Supermarket

Problems

Note: PX means the problem may be solved with POM for Windows and/or Excel OM.

• **1** Given the following conditional value table, determine the appropriate decision under uncertainty using:
a) Maximax
b) Maximin
c) Equally likely PX

	STATES OF NATURE		
ALTERNATIVES	VERY FAVORABLE MARKET	AVERAGE MARKET	UNFAVORABLE MARKET
Build new plant	$350,000	$240,000	–$300,000
Subcontract	$180,000	$ 90,000	–$ 20,000
Overtime	$110,000	$ 60,000	–$ 10,000
Do nothing	$ 0	$ 0	$ 0

••• **2** Even though independent gasoline stations have been having a difficult time, Ian Langella has been thinking about starting his own independent gasoline station. Ian's problem is to decide how large his station should be. The annual returns will depend on both the size of his station and a number of marketing factors related to the oil industry and demand for gasoline. After a careful analysis, Ian developed the following table:

SIZE OF FIRST STATION	GOOD MARKET ($)	FAIR MARKET ($)	POOR MARKET ($)
Small	50,000	20,000	–10,000
Medium	80,000	30,000	–20,000
Large	100,000	30,000	–40,000
Very large	300,000	25,000	–160,000

For example, if Ian constructs a small station and the market is good, he will realize a profit of $50,000.
a) Develop a decision table for this decision, like the one illustrated in Table 2 earlier.
b) What is the maximax decision?
c) What is the maximin decision?
d) What is the equally likely decision?
e) Develop a decision tree. Assume each outcome is equally likely, then find the highest EMV. PX

• **3** Andrew Thomas, a sandwich vendor at Hard Rock Cafe's annual Rockfest, created a table of conditional values for the various alternatives (stocking decision) and states of nature (size of crowd):

	STATES OF NATURE (DEMAND)		
ALTERNATIVES	BIG	AVERAGE	SMALL
Large stock	$22,000	$12,000	–$2,000
Average stock	$14,000	$10,000	$6,000
Small stock	$ 9,000	$ 8,000	$4,000

The probabilities associated with the states of nature are 0.3 for a big demand, 0.5 for an average demand, and 0.2 for a small demand.
a) Determine the alternative that provides Andrew the greatest expected monetary value (EMV).
b) Compute the expected value of perfect information (EVPI).

•• **4** Jeffrey Helm owns a health and fitness center called Bulk-Up in Harrisburg. He is considering adding more floor space to meet increasing demand. He will either add no floor space (N), a moderate area of floor space (M), a large area of floor space (L), or an area of floor space that doubles the size of the facility (D). Demand will either stay fixed, increase slightly, or increase greatly. The following are the changes in Bulk-Up's annual profits under each combination of expansion level and demand change level:

	EXPANSION LEVEL			
DEMAND CHANGE	N	M	L	D
Fixed	$ 0	–$4,000	–$10,000	–$50,000
Slight increase	$2,000	$8,000	$ 6,000	$ 4,000
Major increase	$3,000	$9,000	$20,000	$40,000

Jeffrey is risk averse and wishes to use the maximin criterion.
a) What are his decision alternatives and what are the states of nature?
b) What should he do? PX

• **5** Howard Weiss, Inc., is considering building a sensitive new radiation scanning device. His managers believe that there is a probability of 0.4 that the ATR Co. will come out with a competitive product. If Weiss adds an assembly line for the product and ATR Co. does not follow with a competitive product, Weiss's expected profit is $40,000; if Weiss adds an assembly line and ATR follows suit, Weiss still expects $10,000 profit. If Weiss adds a new plant addition and ATR does not produce a competitive product, Weiss expects a profit of $600,000; if ATR does compete for this market, Weiss expects a loss of $100,000.
a) Determine the EMV of each decision.
b) Compute the expected value of perfect information. PX

••• **6** Jerry Bildery's factory is considering three approaches for meeting an expected increase in demand. These three approaches are increasing capacity, using overtime, and buying more equipment. Demand will increase either slightly (S), moderately (M), or greatly (G). The profits for each approach under each possible scenario are as follows:

	DEMAND SCENARIO		
APPROACH	S	M	G
Increasing capacity	$700,000	$700,000	$ 700,000
Using overtime	$500,000	$600,000	$1,000,000
Buying equipment	$600,000	$800,000	$ 800,000

Since the goal is to maximize, and Jerry is risk-neutral, he decides to use the *equally likely* decision criterion to make the decision as to which approach to use. According to this criterion, which approach should be used?

• **7** The following payoff table provides profits based on various possible decision alternatives and various levels of demand at Robert Klassan's print shop:

	DEMAND	
	LOW	HIGH
Alternative 1	$10,000	$30,000
Alternative 2	$ 5,000	$40,000
Alternative 3	–$ 2,000	$50,000

The probability of low demand is 0.4, whereas the probability of high demand is 0.6.

a) What is the highest possible expected monetary value?
b) What is the expected value *with* perfect information (EVwPI)?
c) Calculate the expected value of perfect information for this situation. Px

• **8** Leah Johnson, director of Urgent Care of Brookline, wants to increase capacity to provide low-cost flu shots but must decide whether to do so by hiring another full-time nurse or by using part-time nurses. The table below shows the expected *costs* of the two options for three possible demand levels:

	STATES OF NATURE		
ALTERNATIVES	LOW DEMAND	MEDIUM DEMAND	HIGH DEMAND
Hire full-time	$300	$500	$ 700
Hire part-time	$ 0	$350	$1,000
Probabilities	.2	.5	.3

a) Using expected value, what should Ms. Johnson do?
b) Draw an appropriate decision tree showing payoffs and probabilities. Px

•• **9** Zhu Manufacturing is considering the introduction of a family of new products. Long-term demand for the product group is somewhat predictable, so the manufacturer must be concerned with the risk of choosing a process that is inappropriate. Faye Zhu is VP of operations. She can choose among batch manufacturing or custom manufacturing, or she can invest in group technology. Faye won't be able to forecast demand accurately until after she makes the process choice. Demand will be classified into four compartments: poor, fair, good, and excellent. The table below indicates the payoffs (profits) associated with each process/demand combination, as well as the probabilities of each long-term demand level:

	POOR	FAIR	GOOD	EXCELLENT
Probability	.1	.4	.3	.2
Batch	–$ 200,000	$1,000,000	$1,200,000	$1,300,000
Custom	$ 100,000	$ 300,000	$ 700,000	$ 800,000
Group technology	–$1,000,000	–$ 500,000	$ 500,000	$2,000,000

a) Based on expected value, what choice offers the greatest gain?
b) What would Faye Zhu be willing to pay for a forecast that would accurately determine the level of demand in the future? Px

•• **10** Consider the following decision table, which Joe Blackburn has developed for Vanderbilt Enterprises:

	STATES OF NATURE		
DECISION ALTERNATIVES	LOW	MEDIUM	HIGH
A	$40	$100	$60
B	$85	$ 60	$70
C	$60	$ 70	$70
D	$65	$75	$70
E	$70	$65	$80
Probability	.40	.20	.40

Which decision alternative maximizes the expected value of the payoff? Px

•• **11** The University of Miami bookstore stocks textbooks in preparation for sales each semester. It normally relies on departmental forecasts and preregistration records to determine how many copies of a text are needed. Preregistration shows 90 operations management students enrolled, but bookstore manager Vaidy Jayaraman has second thoughts, based on his intuition and some historical evidence. Vaidy believes that the distribution of sales may range from 70 to 90 units, according to the following probability model:

Demand	70	75	80	85	90
Probability	.15	.30	.30	.20	.05

This textbook costs the bookstore $82 and sells for $112. Any unsold copies can be returned to the publisher, less a restocking fee and shipping, for a net refund of $36.

a) Construct the table of conditional profits.
b) How many copies should the bookstore stock to achieve highest expected value? Px

•• **12** Palmer Jam Company is a small manufacturer of several different jam products. One product is an organic jam that has no preservatives, sold to retail outlets. Susan Palmer must decide how many cases of jam to manufacture each month. The probability that demand will be 6 cases is .1, for 7 cases it is .3, for 8 cases it is .5, and for 9 cases it is .1. The cost of every case is $45, and the price Susan gets for each case is $95. Unfortunately, any cases not sold by the end of the month are of no value as a result of spoilage. How many cases should Susan manufacture each month? Px

••• **13** Ronald Lau, chief engineer at South Dakota Electronics, has to decide whether to build a new state-of-the-art processing facility. If the new facility works, the company could realize a profit of $200,000. If it fails, South Dakota Electronics could lose $180,000. At this time, Lau estimates a 60% chance that the new process will fail.

The other option is to build a pilot plant and then decide whether to build a complete facility. The pilot plant would cost $10,000 to build. Lau estimates a 50–50 chance that the pilot plant will work. If the pilot plant works, there is a 90% probability that the complete plant, if it is built, will also work. If the pilot plant does not work, there is only a 20% chance that the complete project (if it is constructed) will work. Lau faces a dilemma. Should he build the plant? Should he build the pilot project and then make a decision? Help Lau by analyzing this problem. Px

•• **14** Dwayne Whitten, president of Whitten Industries, is considering whether to build a manufacturing plant in north Texas. His decision is summarized in the following table:

ALTERNATIVES	FAVORABLE MARKET	UNFAVORABLE MARKET
Build large plant	$400,000	–$300,000
Build small plant	$ 80,000	–$ 10,000
Don't build	$ 0	$ 0
Market probabilities	0.4	0.6

a) Construct a decision tree.
b) Determine the best strategy using expected monetary value (EMV).
c) What is the expected value of perfect information (EVPI)? Px

•• **15** Deborah Kellogg buys Breathalyzer test sets for the Winter Park Police Department. The quality of the test sets from her two suppliers is indicated in the following table:

PERCENT DEFECTIVE	PROBABILITY FOR WINTER PARK TECHNOLOGY	PROBABILITY FOR DAYTON ENTERPRISES
1	.70	.30
3	.20	.30
5	.10	.40

For example, the probability of getting a batch of tests that are 1% defective from Winter Park Technology is .70. Because Kellogg orders 10,000 tests per order, this would mean that there is a .70 probability of getting 100 defective tests out of the 10,000 tests if Winter Park Technology is used to fill the order. A defective Breathalyzer test set can be repaired for $0.50. Although the quality of the test sets of the second supplier, Dayton Enterprises, is lower, it will sell an order of 10,000 test sets for $37 less than Winter Park.

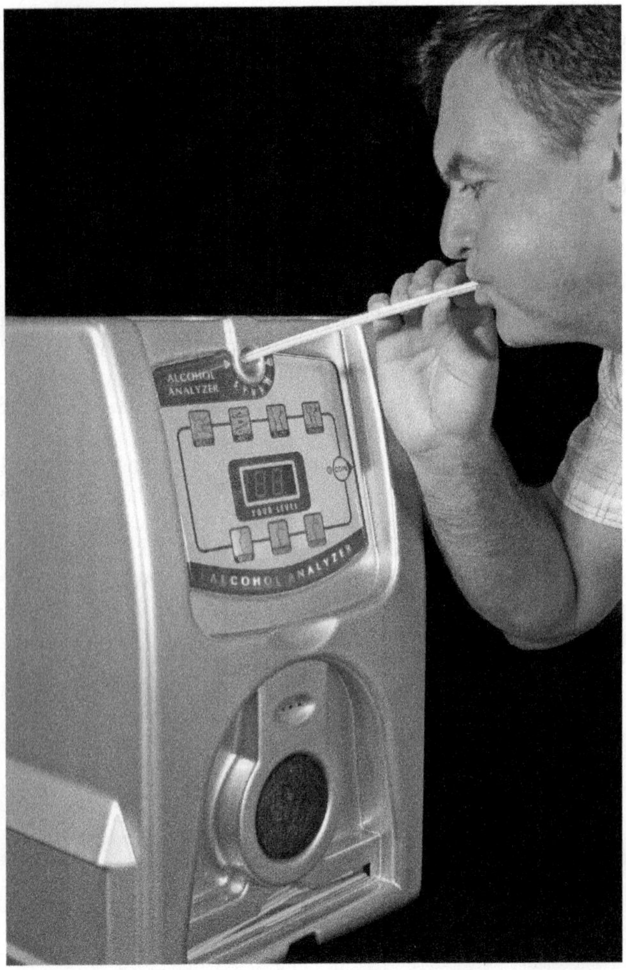

jabiru/Shutterstock

a) Develop a decision tree.
b) Which supplier should Kellogg use?

•• **16** Deborah Hollwager, a concessionaire for the Amway Center in Orlando, has developed a table of conditional values for the various alternatives (stocking decisions) and states of nature (size of crowd):

	STATES OF NATURE (SIZE OF CROWD)		
ALTERNATIVES	LARGE	AVERAGE	SMALL
Large inventory	$20,000	$10,000	−$2,000
Average inventory	$15,000	$12,000	$6,000
Small inventory	$ 9,000	$ 6,000	$5,000

If the probabilities associated with the states of nature are 0.3 for a large crowd, 0.5 for an average crowd, and 0.2 for a small crowd, determine:
a) The alternative that provides the greatest expected monetary value (EMV).
b) The expected value of perfect information (EVPI).

• **17** Joseph Biggs owns his own ice cream truck and lives 30 miles from a Florida beach resort. The sale of his products is highly dependent on his location and on the weather. At the resort, his profit will be $120 per day in fair weather, $10 per day in bad weather. At home, his profit will be $70 in fair weather and $55 in bad weather. Assume that on any particular day, the weather service suggests a 40% chance of foul weather.
a) Construct Joseph's decision tree.
b) What decision is recommended by the expected value criterion?

•• **18** Jonatan Jelen is considering opening a bicycle shop in New York City. Jonatan enjoys biking, but this is to be a business endeavor from which he expects to make a living. He can open a small shop, a large shop, or no shop at all. Because there will be a 5-year lease on the building that Jonatan is thinking about using, he wants to make sure he makes the correct decision. Jonatan is also thinking about hiring his old marketing professor to conduct a marketing research study to see if there is a market for his services. The results of such a study could be either favorable or unfavorable. Develop a decision tree for Jonatan.

•• **19** F. J. Brewerton Retailers, Inc., must decide whether to build a small or a large facility at a new location in Omaha. Demand at the location will either be low or high, with probabilities 0.4 and 0.6, respectively. If Brewerton builds a small facility and demand proves to be high, he then has the option of expanding the facility. If a small facility is built and demand proves to be high, and then the retailer expands the facility, the payoff is $270,000. If a small facility is built and demand proves to be high, but Brewerton then decides not to expand the facility, the payoff is $223,000.

If a small facility is built and demand proves to be low, then there is no option to expand and the payoff is $200,000. If a large facility is built and demand proves to be low, Brewerton then has the option of stimulating demand through local advertising. If he does not exercise this option, then the payoff is $40,000. If he does exercise the advertising option, then the response to advertising will either be modest or sizable, with probabilities of 0.3 and 0.7, respectively. If the response is modest, the payoff is $20,000. If it is sizable, the payoff is $220,000. Finally, if a large facility is built and demand proves to be high, then no advertising is needed and the payoff is $800,000.
a) What should Brewerton do to maximize his expected payoff?
b) What is the value of this expected payoff?

••• **20** Philip Musa can build either a large video rental section or a small one in his Birmingham drugstore. He can also gather additional information or simply do nothing. If he gathers additional information, the results could suggest either a favorable or an unfavorable market, but it would cost him $3,000 to gather the information. Musa believes that there is a 50–50 chance that the information will be favorable. If the rental market is favorable,

Musa will earn $15,000 with a large section or $5,000 with a small. With an unfavorable video-rental market, however, Musa could lose $20,000 with a large section or $10,000 with a small section. Without gathering additional information, Musa estimates that the probability of a favorable rental market is .7. A favorable report from the study would increase the probability of a favorable rental market to .9. Furthermore, an unfavorable report from the additional information would decrease the probability of a favorable rental market to .4. Of course, Musa could ignore these numbers and do nothing. What is your advice to Musa?

•••• **21** Jeff Kaufmann's machine shop sells a variety of machines for job shops. A customer wants to purchase a model XPO2 drilling machine from Jeff's store. The model XPO2 sells for $180,000, but Jeff is out of XPO2s. The customer says he will wait for Jeff to get a model XPO2 in stock. Jeff knows that there is a wholesale market for XPO2s from which he can purchase an XPO2. Jeff can buy an XPO2 today for $150,000, or he can wait a day and buy an XPO2 (if one is available) tomorrow for $125,000. If at least one XPO2 is still available tomorrow, Jeff can wait until the day after tomorrow and buy an XPO2 (if one is still available) for $110,000.

There is a 0.40 probability that there will be no model XPO2s available tomorrow. If there are model XPO2s available tomorrow, there is a 0.70 probability that by the day after tomorrow, there will be no model XPO2s available in the wholesale market. Three days from now, it is certain that no model XPO2s will be available on the wholesale market. What is the maximum expected profit that Jeff can achieve? What should Jeff do?

•••• **22** The city of Belgrade, Serbia, is contemplating building a second airport to relieve congestion at the main airport and is considering two potential sites, X and Y. Hard Rock Hotels would like to purchase land to build a hotel at the new airport. The value of land has been rising in anticipation and is expected to skyrocket once the city decides between sites X and Y. Consequently, Hard Rock would like to purchase land now. Hard Rock will sell the land if the city chooses not to locate the airport nearby. Hard Rock has four choices: (1) buy land at X, (2) buy land at Y, (3) buy land at both X and Y, or (4) do nothing. Hard Rock has collected the following data (which are in millions of euros):

	SITE X	SITE Y
Current purchase price	27	15
Profits if airport and hotel built at this site	45	30
Sale price if airport not built at this site	9	6

Hard Rock determines there is a 45% chance the airport will be built at X (hence, a 55% chance it will be built at Y).

a) Set up the decision table.
b) What should Hard Rock decide to do to maximize total net profit? Px

•••• **23** Louisiana is busy designing new lottery scratch-off games. In the latest game, Bayou Boondoggle, the player is instructed to scratch off one spot: A, B, or C. A can reveal "Loser," "Win $1," or "Win $50." B can reveal "Loser" or "Take a Second Chance." C can reveal "Loser" or "Win $500." On the second chance, the player is instructed to scratch off D or E. D can reveal "Loser" or "Win $1." E can reveal "Loser" or "Win $10." The probabilities at A are .9, .09, and .01. The probabilities at B are .8 and .2. The probabilities at C are .999 and .001. The probabilities at D are .5 and .5. Finally, the probabilities at E are .95 and .05. Draw the decision tree that represents this scenario. Use proper symbols and label all branches clearly. Calculate the expected value of this game.

•••• **24** On the opening page of this text and in Example 8, we follow the poker decision made by Paul Phillips against veteran T.J. Cloutier. Create a decision tree that corresponds with the decision made by Phillips. Px

MaxFX/Shutterstock

Refer to MyOMLab for these additional homework problems: 25–32

CASE STUDY

Warehouse Tenting at the Port of Miami

The Collector's Choice Inc. (CCI), a luxury car import company, has an old warehouse at the Port of Miami, Florida, where it temporarily stores expensive sports cars and automotive parts that arrive from Europe. This summer, CCI has noticed that the termite infestation in the warehouse has escalated to a point where tenting cannot be postponed anymore. (Tenting is the process of wrapping a building inside a huge tent that is subsequently filled with a poisonous gas capable of killing most forms of life inside, including insects, plants, pets, and human beings.) CCI's pest control company's contract specifies a to-do list of pre-tenting tasks, which include:

- Turning off all air-conditioning units and opening all windows of the warehouse
- Turning off all internal and external lights, including those operating on a timer
- Pruning all outdoor vegetation at least 18 away from the warehouse
- Soaking the soil around the warehouse on the first day of tenting

Halima Ahkdar/Shutterstock

The requirement of opening all windows is particularly worrisome to CCI because it means turning off the alarm system, leaving the warehouse vulnerable to burglary for 48 hours— the required amount of time for the poisonous gas to do its job. Therefore, Alex Ferrari, the warehouse manager, is thinking about hiring a security company to monitor the facility during that period. CCI's property insurance deductible is $25,000, and Alex is assuming that if thieves are willing to enter a building full of poisonous gas to steal something, they would certainly take more than $25,000 worth of parts— or even an entire car!

After making a few phone calls, Alex gets in touch with ProGuard, a trustworthy local security company that charges $150 per hour to have a security guard stationed outside their warehouse. The city of Miami police records indicate that about 30% of businesses that left their facilities unattended during tenting reported stolen property in the past 3 years. Although Alex thinks ProGuard's prices are reasonable, and having a guard outside the warehouse would certainly help, he is still not sure whether it is worth spending the extra money. After all, ProGuard's contract does not guarantee the protection it provides is infallible. In fact, an analysis of the company's records indicates that 3% of their clients were burglarized over the past 3 years. (Despite this figure, ProGuard is still the best security company in the area.)

Discussion Questions

1. Create a decision tree analysis to help decide whether Alex Ferrari should hire ProGuard's services.
2. Come up with a simple rule of thumb that can be applied to decisions of this nature, given any deductible amount d, extra surveillance cost c, and burglary probabilities p_1 (without surveillance) and p_2 (with surveillance).
3. Does your decision based on the tree guarantee success? Why or why not?

Source: Professor Tallys Yunes, University of Miami. Reprinted with permission.

- **Additional Case Studies:** Visit **www.myomlab.com** or **www.pearsonhighered.com/heizer** for these additional free case studies:
  Arctic, Inc.: A refrigeration company has several major options with regard to capacity and expansion.
  Ski Right Corp.: Which of four manufacturers should be selected to manufacture ski helmets?
  Tom Tucker's Liver Transplant: An executive must decide whether or not to opt for a dangerous surgery.

Bibliography

Balakrishnan, R., B. Render, and R. M. Stair Jr. *Managerial Decision Modeling with Spreadsheets*, 3rd ed. Upper Saddle River, NJ: Prentice Hall, 2012.

Buchannan, Leigh, and Andrew O'Connell. "A Brief History of Decision Making." *Harvard Business Review* 84, no. 1 (January, 2006): 32–41.

Hammond, J. S., R. L. Kenney, and H. Raiffa. "The Hidden Traps in Decision Making." *Harvard Business Review* 84, no. 1 (January 2006): 118–126.

Keefer, Donald L. "Balancing Drug Safety and Efficacy for a Go/No-Go Decision." *Interfaces* 34, no. 2 (March–April 2004): 113–116.

Miller, C. C., and R. D. Ireland. "Intuition in Strategic Decision Making." *Academy of Management Executive* 19, no. 1 (February 2005): 19.

Parmigiani, G., and L. Inoue. *Decision Theory: Principles and Approaches*. New York: Wiley, 2010.

Raiffa, H., and R. Schlaifer. *Applied Statistical Decision Theory*. New York: Wiley 2000.

Render, B., R. M. Stair Jr., and M. Hanna. *Quantitative Analysis for Management*, 11th ed. Upper Saddle River, NJ: Prentice Hall, 2012.

APPENDIX

SOLUTIONS TO EVEN-NUMBERED PROBLEMS

2 **(a)**

Size of First Station	Good Market ($)	Fair Market ($)	Poor Market ($)	EV Under Equally Likely
Small	50,000	20,000	−10,000	20,000
Medium	80,000	30,000	−20,000	30,000
Large	100,000	30,000	−40,000	30,000
Very large	300,000	25,000	−160,000	55,000

(b) Maximax: Build a very large station.
(c) Maximin: Build a small station.
(d) Equally likely: Build a very large station.
(e)

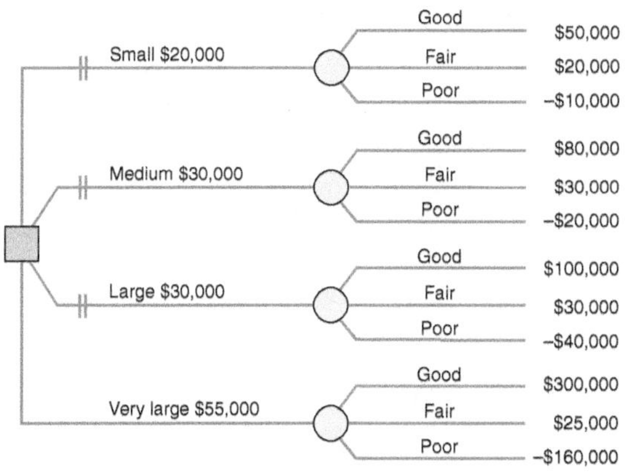

4 **(a)** Alternatives: N, M, L, D. States of nature: Fixed, Slight Increase, Major Increase
(b) Use maximin criterion. No floor space (N).

6 Buying equipment at $733,333

8 **(a)** E(cost full-time) = $520
(b) E(cost part-timers) = $475

10 Alternative B; 74

12 8 cases; EMV = $352.50

14 **(a)**
(b) Small plant with EMV = $26,000
(c) EVPI = $134,000

16 **(a)** Max EMV = $11,700
(b) EVPI = $13,200 − $11,700 = $1,500

18

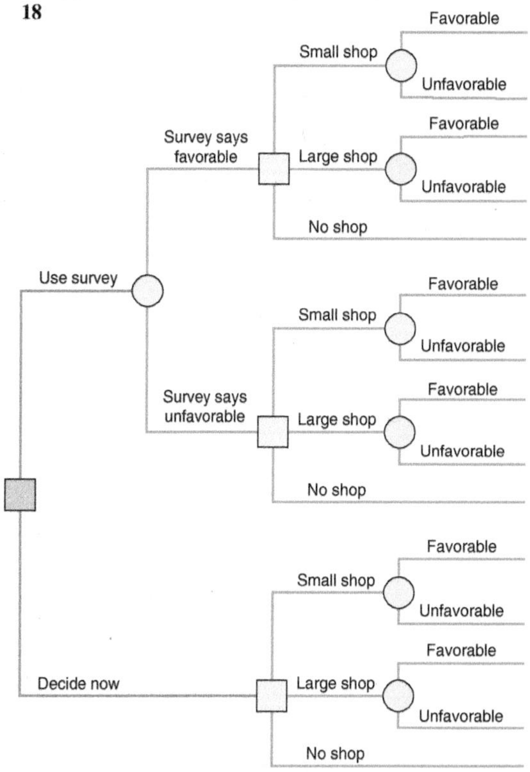

20 No information and build large; $4,500.

22 **(b)** EMV(Y) = 4.2, which is best

Rapid Review

Main Heading	Review Material	
THE DECISION PROCESS IN OPERATIONS	To achieve the goals of their organizations, managers must understand how decisions are made and know which decision-making tools to use. Overcoming uncertainty is a manager's mission. Decision tables and decision trees are used in a wide number of OM situations.	
FUNDAMENTALS OF DECISION MAKING	*Alternative*—A course of action or strategy that may be chosen by a decision maker. *State of nature*—An occurrence or a situation over which a decision maker has little or no control. Symbols used in a decision tree: 1. ☐ —A decision node from which one of several alternatives may be selected. 2. ◯ —A state-of-nature node out of which one state of nature will occur. When constructing a decision tree, we must be sure that all alternatives and states of nature are in their correct and logical places and that we include *all* possible alternatives and states of nature, usually including the "do nothing" option.	
DECISION TABLES	■ **Decision table**—A tabular means of analyzing decision alternatives and states of nature. A decision table is sometimes called a payoff table. For any alternative and a particular state of nature, there is a *consequence*, or an *outcome*, which is usually expressed as a monetary value; this is called the *conditional value*.	
TYPES OF DECISION-MAKING ENVIRONMENTS	There are three decision-making environments: (1) decision making under uncertainty, (2) decision making under risk, and (3) decision making under certainty. When there is complete *uncertainty* about which state of nature in a decision environment may occur (i.e., when we cannot even assess probabilities for each possible outcome), we rely on three decision methods: (1) maximax, (2) maximin, and (3) equally likely. ■ **Maximin**—A criterion that finds an alternative that maximizes the minimum outcome ■ **Maximin**—A criterion that finds an alternative that maximizes the minimum outcome ■ **Equally likely**—A criterion that assigns equal probability to each state of nature. Maximax is also called an "optimistic" decision criterion, while maximin is also called a "pessimistic" decision criterion. Maximax and maximin present best case/worst case planning scenarios. Decision making under risk relies on probabilities. The states of nature must be mutually exclusive and collectively exhaustive, and their probabilities must sum to 1. ■ **Expected monetary value (EMV)**—The expected payout or value of a variable that has different possible states of nature, each with an associated probability. The EMV represents the expected value or *mean* return for each alternative *if we could repeat this decision (or similar types of decisions) a large number of times*. The EMV for an alternative is the sum of all possible payoffs from the alternative, each weighted by the probability of that payoff occurring: EMV(Alternative i) = (Payoff of 1st state of nature) × (Probability of 1st of state of nature) + (Payoff of 2nd state of nature) × (Probability of 2nd state of nature) + . . . + (Payoff of last state of nature) × (Probability of last state of nature) ■ **Expected value of perfect information (EVPI)**—The difference between the payoff under perfect information and the payoff under risk. ■ **Expected value *with* perfect information (EVwPI)**—The expected (average) return if perfect information is available. EVPI represents an upper bound on what you would be willing to spend on state-of-nature information: EVPI = EVwPI − Maximum EMV EVwPI = (Best outcome for 1st state of nature) × (Probability of 1st state of nature) + (Best outcome for 2nd state of nature) × (Probability of 2nd state of nature) + . . . + (Best outcome for last state of nature) × (Probability of last state of nature)	Problems: 1–12, 14, 16 Virtual Office Hours for Solved Problems: 1, 2

Rapid Review *continued*

Main Heading	Review Material	MyOMLab
DECISION TREES	When there are two or more sequential decisions, and later decisions are based on the outcome of prior ones, the decision tree (as opposed to decision table) approach becomes appropriate.	Problems: 2, 8, 14, 17, 18, 19, 20, 21, 23, 24

- **Decision tree**—A graphical means of analyzing decision alternatives and states of nature.

Analyzing problems with *decision trees* involves five steps:

1. Define the problem.
2. Structure or draw the decision tree.
3. Assign probabilities to the states of nature.
4. Estimate payoffs for each possible combination of decision alternatives and states of nature.
5. Solve the problem by computing the expected monetary values (EMV) for each state-of-nature node. This is done by working *backward*—that is, by starting at the right of the tree and working back to decision nodes on the left:

Virtual Office Hours for Solved Problem: 3

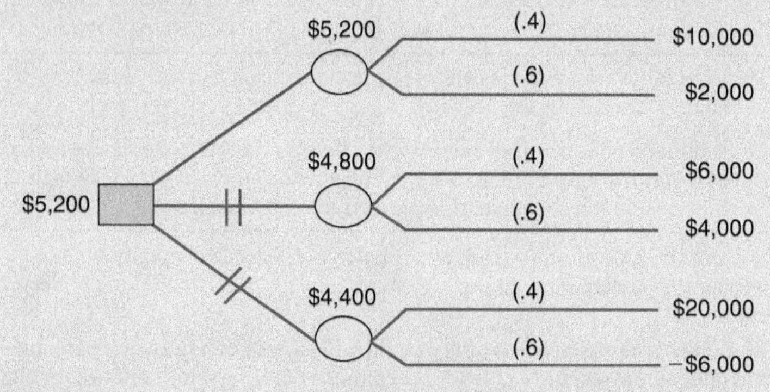

Decision trees force managers to examine all possible outcomes, including unfavorable ones. A manager is also forced to make decisions in a logical, sequential manner. Short parallel lines on a decision tree mean "prune" that branch, as it is less favorable than another available option and may be dropped.

Self Test

- **Before taking the self-test,** refer to the learning objectives listed at the beginning of the text and the key terms listed at the end of the text.

LO1. On a decision tree, at each state-of-nature node:
- **a)** the alternative with the greatest EMV is selected.
- **b)** an EMV is calculated.
- **c)** all probabilities are added together.
- **d)** the branch with the highest probability is selected.

LO2. In decision table terminology, a course of action or a strategy that may be chosen by a decision maker is called a(n):
- **a)** payoff. **b)** alternative.
- **c)** state of nature. **d)** all of the above.

LO3. If probabilities are available to the decision maker, then the decision-making environment is called:
- **a)** certainty. **b)** uncertainty.
- **c)** risk. **d)** none of the above.

LO4. What is the EMV for Alternative 1 in the following decision table?

	STATE OF NATURE	
Alternative	*S1*	*S2*
A1	$15,000	$20,000
A2	$10,000	$30,000
Probability	0.30	0.70

- **a)** $15,000 **b)** $17,000
- **c)** $17,500 **d)** $18,500
- **e)** $20,000

LO5. The most that a person should pay for perfect information is:
- **a)** the EVPI.
- **b)** the maximum EMV minus the minimum EMV.
- **c)** the minimum EMV.
- **d)** the maximum EMV.

LO6. On a decision tree, once the tree has been drawn and the payoffs and probabilities have been placed on the tree, the analysis (computing EMVs and selecting the best alternative):
- **a)** is done by working backward (starting on the right and moving to the left).
- **b)** is done by working forward (starting on the left and moving to the right).
- **c)** is done by starting at the top of the tree and moving down.
- **d)** is done by starting at the bottom of the tree and moving up.

LO7. A decision tree is preferable to a decision table when:
- **a)** a number of sequential decisions are to be made.
- **b)** probabilities are available.
- **c)** the maximax criterion is used.
- **d)** the objective is to maximize regret.

Answers: LO1. b; LO2. b; LO3. c; LO4. d; LO5. a; LO6. a; LO7. a.

Linear Programming

OUTLINE

LEARNING OBJECTIVES

LO1 ***Formulate*** linear programming models, including an objective function and constraints

LO2 ***Graphically*** solve an LP problem with the iso-profit line method

LO3 ***Graphically*** solve an LP problem with the corner-point method

LO4 ***Interpret*** sensitivity analysis and shadow prices

LO5 ***Construct*** and solve a minimization problem

LO6 ***Formulate*** production-mix, diet, and labor scheduling problems

The storm front closed in quickly on Chicago's O'Hare Airport, shutting it down without warning. The heavy thunderstorms, lightning, and poor visibility sent American Airlines passengers and ground crew scurrying. Because American Airlines uses linear programming (LP) to schedule flights, hotels, crews, and refueling, LP has a direct impact on profitability. If American gets a major weather disruption at one of its hubs, a lot of flights may get canceled, which means a lot of crews and airplanes in the wrong places. LP is the tool that helps airlines such as American unsnarl and cope with this weather mess.

Associated Press

Why Use Linear Programming?

Many operations management decisions involve trying to make the most effective use of an organization's resources. Resources typically include machinery (such as planes, in the case of an airline), labor (such as pilots), money, time, and raw materials (such as jet fuel). These resources may be used to produce products (such as machines, furniture, food, or clothing) or services (such as airline schedules, advertising policies, or investment decisions). Linear programming (LP) is a widely used mathematical technique designed to help operations managers plan and make the decisions necessary to allocate resources.

Linear programming (LP)
A mathematical technique designed to help operations managers plan and make decisions necessary to allocate resources.

A few examples of problems in which LP has been successfully applied in operations management are:

1. Scheduling school buses to *minimize* the total distance traveled when carrying students
2. Allocating police patrol units to high crime areas to *minimize* response time to 911 calls
3. Scheduling tellers at banks so that needs are met during each hour of the day while *minimizing* the total cost of labor

4. Selecting the product mix in a factory to make best use of machine- and labor-hours available while *maximizing* the firm's profit
5. Picking blends of raw materials in feed mills to produce finished feed combinations at *minimum* cost
6. Determining the distribution system that will *minimize* total shipping cost from several warehouses to various market locations
7. Developing a production schedule that will satisfy future demands for a firm's product and at the same time *minimize* total production and inventory costs
8. Allocating space for a tenant mix in a new shopping mall so as to *maximize* revenues to the leasing company

Requirements of a Linear Programming Problem

All LP problems have four requirements: an objective, constraints, alternatives, and linearity:

1. LP problems seek to *maximize* or *minimize* some quantity (usually profit or cost). We refer to this property as the objective function of an LP problem. The major objective of a typical firm is to maximize dollar profits in the long run. In the case of a trucking or airline distribution system, the objective might be to minimize shipping costs.
2. The presence of restrictions, or constraints, limits the degree to which we can pursue our objective. For example, deciding how many units of each product in a firm's product line to manufacture is restricted by available labor and machinery. We want, therefore, to maximize or minimize a quantity (the objective function) subject to limited resources (the constraints).
3. There must be *alternative courses of action* to choose from. For example, if a company produces three different products, management may use LP to decide how to allocate among them its limited production resources (of labor, machinery, and so on). If there were no alternatives to select from, we would not need LP.
4. The objective and constraints in linear programming problems must be expressed in terms of *linear equations* or inequalities. Linearity implies proportionality and additivity. If x_1 and x_2 are decision variables, there can be no products (e.g., x_1x_2) or powers (e.g., x_1^3) in the objective or constraints.

Objective function
A mathematical expression in linear programming that maximizes or minimizes some quantity (often profit or cost, but any goal may be used).

Constraints
Restrictions that limit the degree to which a manager can pursue an objective.

Formulating Linear Programming Problems

One of the most common linear programming applications is the *product-mix problem*. Two or more products are usually produced using limited resources. The company would like to determine how many units of each product it should produce to maximize overall profit given its limited resources. Let's look at an example.

STUDENT TIP
Here we set up an LP example that we will follow for most of this text.

Glickman Electronics Example

The Glickman Electronics Company in Washington, DC, produces two products: (1) the Glickman x-pod, a portable music player, and (2) the Glickman BlueBerry, an internet-connected color telephone. The production process for each product is similar in that both require a certain number of hours of electronic work and a certain number of labor-hours in the assembly department. Each x-pod takes 4 hours of electronic work and 2 hours in the assembly shop. Each BlueBerry requires 3 hours in electronics and 1 hour in assembly. During the current production period, 240 hours of electronic time are available, and 100 hours of assembly department time are available. Each x-pod sold yields a profit of $7; each BlueBerry produced may be sold for a $5 profit.

Glickman's problem is to determine the best possible combination of x-pods and BlueBerrys to manufacture to reach the maximum profit. This product-mix situation can be formulated as a linear programming problem.

ACTIVE MODEL 1
This example is further illustrated in Active Model B.1 at www.pearsonhighered.com/heizer.

We begin by summarizing the information needed to formulate and solve this problem (see Table 1). Further, let's introduce some simple notation for use in the objective function and constraints. Let:

$$X_1 = \text{number of x-pods to be produced}$$
$$X_2 = \text{number of BlueBerrys to be produced}$$

TABLE 1 Glickman Electronics Company Problem Data

	HOURS REQUIRED TO PRODUCE ONE UNIT		
DEPARTMENT	X-PODS (X_1)	BLUEBERRYS (X_2)	AVAILABLE HOURS THIS WEEK
Electronic	4	3	240
Assembly	2	1	100
Profit per unit	\$7	\$5	

Now we can create the LP *objective function* in terms of X_1 and X_2:

$$\text{Maximize profit} = \$7X_1 + \$5X_2$$

Our next step is to develop mathematical relationships to describe the two constraints in this problem. One general relationship is that the amount of a resource used is to be less than or equal to ($\leq$) the amount of resource *available*.

LO1 *Formulate* linear programming models, including an objective function and constraints

First constraint: Electronic time used is $\leq$ Electronic time available.

$$4X_1 + 3X_2 \leq 240 \text{ (hours of electronic time)}$$

Second constraint: Assembly time used is $\leq$ Assembly time available.

$$2X_1 + 1X_2 \leq 100 \text{ (hours of assembly time)}$$

Both these constraints represent production capacity restrictions and, of course, affect the total profit. For example, Glickman Electronics cannot produce 70 x-pods during the production period because if $X_1 = 70$, both constraints will be violated. It also cannot make $X_1 = 50$ x-pods and $X_2 = 10$ BlueBerrys. This constraint brings out another important aspect of linear programming; that is, certain interactions will exist between variables. The more units of one product that a firm produces, the fewer it can make of other products.

Graphical Solution to a Linear Programming Problem

The easiest way to solve a small LP problem such as that of the Glickman Electronics Company is the graphical solution approach. The graphical procedure can be used only when there are two decision variables (such as number of x-pods to produce, X_1, and number of BlueBerrys to produce, X_2). When there are more than two variables, it is *not* possible to plot the solution on a two-dimensional graph; we then must turn to more complex approaches described later in this text.

Graphical solution approach A means of plotting a solution to a two-variable problem on a graph.

Decision variables Choices available to a decision maker.

Graphical Representation of Constraints

To find the optimal solution to a linear programming problem, we must first identify a set, or region, of feasible solutions. The first step in doing so is to plot the problem's constraints on a graph.

The variable X_1 (x-pods, in our example) is usually plotted as the horizontal axis of the graph, and the variable X_2 (BlueBerrys) is plotted as the vertical axis. The complete problem may be restated as:

$$\text{Maximize profit} = \$7X_1 + \$5X_2$$

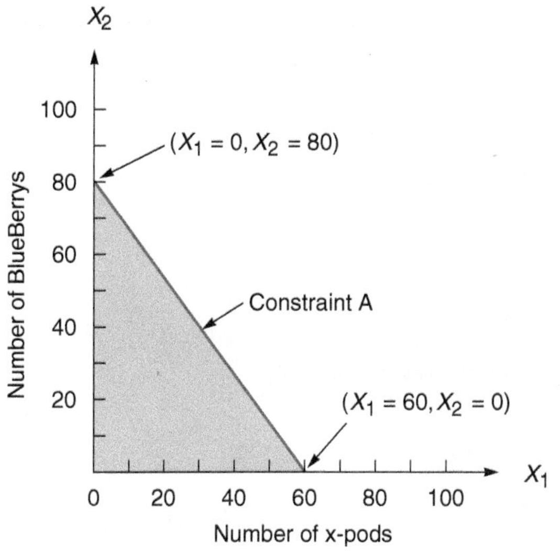

Figure 1
Constraint A

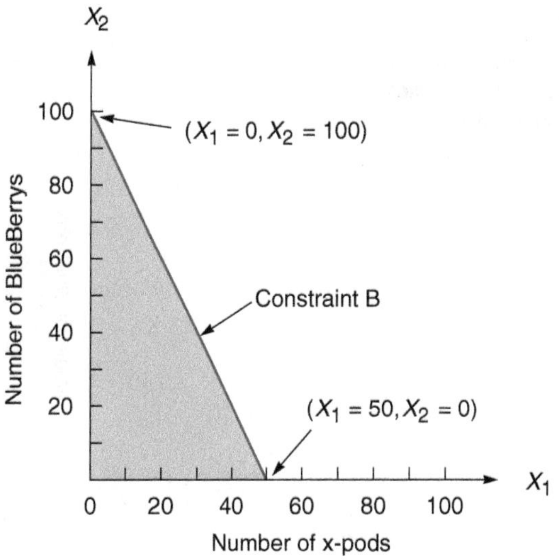

Figure 2
Constraint B

Subject to the constraints:

$$4X_1 + 3X_2 \leq 240 \text{ (\textit{electronics constraint})}$$
$$2X_1 + 1X_2 \leq 100 \text{ (\textit{assembly constraint})}$$
$$X_1 \geq 0 \text{ (\textit{number of x-pods produced is greater than or equal to} 0)}$$
$$X_2 \geq 0 \text{ (\textit{number of BlueBerrys produced is greater than or equal to} 0)}$$

(These last two constraints are also called *nonnegativity constraints*.)

The first step in graphing the constraints of the problem is to convert the constraint *inequalities* into *equalities* (or equations):

$$\text{Constraint A:} \quad 4X_1 + 3X_2 = 240$$
$$\text{Constraint B:} \quad 2X_1 + 1X_2 = 100$$

The equation for constraint A is plotted in Figure 1 and for constraint B in Figure 2.

To plot the line in Figure 1, all we need to do is to find the points at which the line $4X_1 + 3X_2 = 240$ intersects the X_1 and X_2 axes. When $X_1 = 0$ (the location where the line touches the X_2 axis), it implies that $3X_2 = 240$ and that $X_2 = 80$. Likewise, when $X_2 = 0$, we see that $4X_1 = 240$ and that $X_1 = 60$. Thus, constraint A is bounded by the line running from $(X_1 = 0, X_2 = 80)$ to $(X_1 = 60, X_2 = 0)$. The shaded area represents all points that satisfy the original *inequality*.

Constraint B is illustrated similarly in Figure 2. When $X_1 = 0$, then $X_2 = 100$; and when $X_2 = 0$, then $X_1 = 50$. Constraint B, then, is bounded by the line between $(X_1 = 0, X_2 = 100)$ and $(X_1 = 50, X_2 = 0)$. The shaded area represents the original inequality.

Figure 3 shows both constraints together. The shaded region is the part that satisfies both restrictions. The shaded region in Figure 3 is called the *area of feasible solutions*, or simply the **feasible region**. This region must satisfy *all* conditions specified by the program's constraints and is thus the region where all constraints overlap. Any point in the region would be a *feasible solution* to the Glickman Electronics Company problem. Any point outside the shaded area would represent an *infeasible solution*. Hence, it would be feasible to manufacture 30 x-pods and 20 BlueBerrys $(X_1 = 30, X_2 = 20)$, but it would violate the constraints to produce 70 x-pods and 40 BlueBerrys. This can be seen by plotting these points on the graph of Figure 3.

Feasible region
The set of all feasible combinations of decision variables.

Iso-Profit Line Solution Method

Now that the feasible region has been graphed, we can proceed to find the *optimal* solution to the problem. The optimal solution is the point lying in the feasible region that produces the highest profit.

Figure 3

Feasible Solution Region for the Glickman Electronics Company Problem

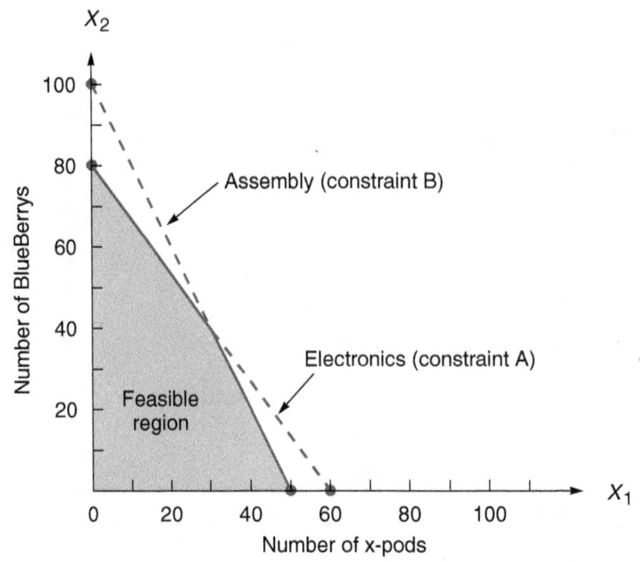

Iso-profit line method

An approach to solving a linear programming maximization problem graphically.

Once the feasible region has been established, several approaches can be taken in solving for the optimal solution. The speediest one to apply is called the iso-profit line method.[1]

We start by letting profits equal some arbitrary but small dollar amount. For the Glickman Electronics problem, we may choose a profit of \$210. This is a profit level that can easily be obtained without violating either of the two constraints. The objective function can be written as $\$210 = 7X_1 + 5X_2$.

This expression is just the equation of a line; we call it an *iso-profit line*. It represents all combinations (of X_1, X_2) that will yield a total profit of \$210. To plot the profit line, we proceed exactly as we did to plot a constraint line. First, let $X_1 = 0$ and solve for the point at which the line crosses the X_2 axis:

LO2 *Graphically* solve an LP problem with the iso-profit line method

$$\$210 = \$7(0) + \$5X_2$$
$$X_2 = 42 \text{ BlueBerrys}$$

Then let $X_2 = 0$ and solve for X_1:

$$\$210 = \$7X_1 + \$5(0)$$
$$X_1 = 30 \text{ x-pods}$$

We can now connect these two points with a straight line. This profit line is illustrated in Figure 4. All points on the line represent feasible solutions that produce a profit of \$210.

We see, however, that the iso-profit line for \$210 does not produce the highest possible profit to the firm. In Figure 5, we try graphing three more lines, each yielding a higher profit. The middle equation, $\$280 = \$7X_1 + \$5X_2$, was plotted in the same fashion as the lower line. When $X_1 = 0$:

$$\$280 = \$7(0) + \$5X_2$$
$$X_2 = 56 \text{ BlueBerrys}$$

When $X_2 = 0$:

$$\$280 = \$7X_1 + \$5(0)$$
$$X_1 = 40 \text{ x-pods}$$

Again, any combination of x-pods (X_1) and BlueBerrys (X_2) on this iso-profit line will produce a total profit of \$280.

[1]*Iso* means "equal" or "similar." Thus, an iso-profit line represents a line with all profits the same, in this case \$210.

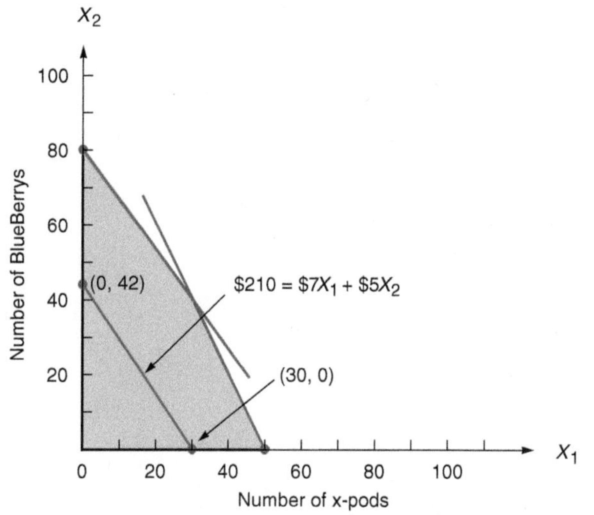

Figure 4
A Profit Line of $210 Plotted for the Glickman Electronics Company

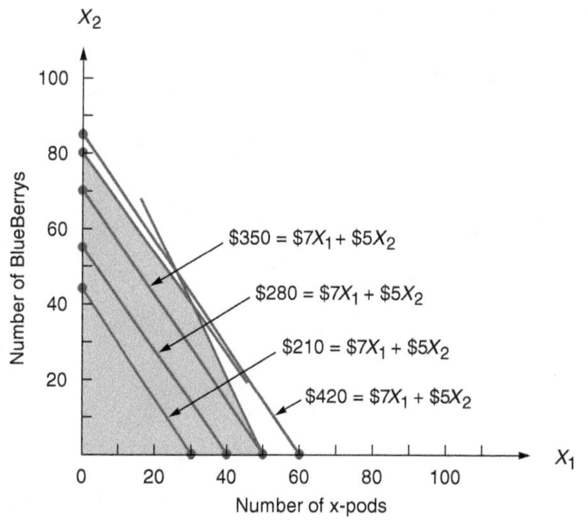

Figure 5
Four Iso-Profit Lines Plotted for the Glickman Electronics Company

Note that the third line generates a profit of $350, even more of an improvement. The farther we move from the 0 origin, the higher our profit will be. Another important point to note is that these iso-profit lines are parallel. We now have two clues as to how to find the optimal solution to the original problem. We can draw a series of parallel profit lines (by carefully moving our ruler in a plane parallel to the first profit line). The highest profit line that still touches some point of the feasible region will pinpoint the optimal solution. Notice that the fourth line ($420) is too high to count because it does not touch the feasible region.

The highest possible iso-profit line is illustrated in Figure 6. It touches the tip of the feasible region at the corner point ($X_1 = 30$, $X_2 = 40$) and yields a profit of $410.

Corner-Point Solution Method

A second approach to solving linear programming problems employs the corner-point method. This technique is simpler in concept than the iso-profit line approach, but it involves looking at the profit at every corner point of the feasible region.

Corner-point method
A method for solving graphical linear programming problems.

The mathematical theory behind linear programming states that an optimal solution to any problem (that is, the values of X_1, X_2 that yield the maximum profit) will lie at a *corner point*, or

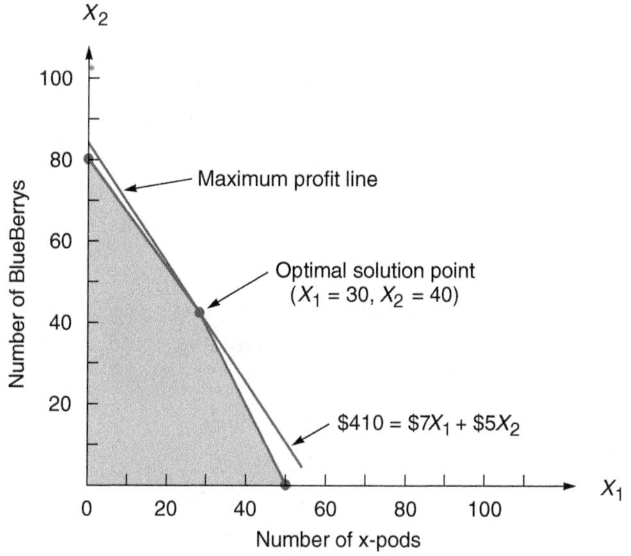

Figure 6
Optimal Solution for the Glickman Electronics Problem

Figure 7
The Four Corner Points of the Feasible Region

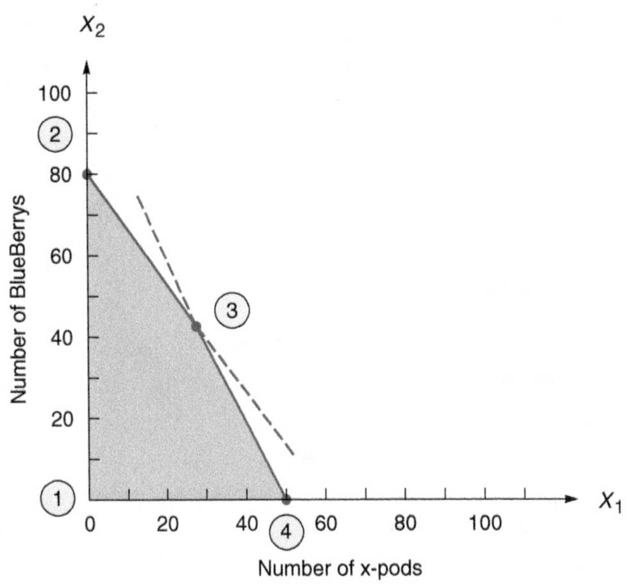

STUDENT TIP ☆
We named the decision variables X_1 and X_2 here, but any notations (e.g., *x-p* and *B* or *X* and *Y*) would do as well.

LO3 *Graphically* solve an LP problem with the corner-point method

extreme point, of the feasible region. Hence, it is necessary to find only the values of the variables at each corner; the maximum profit or optimal solution will lie at one (or more) of them.

Once again we can see (in Figure 7) that the feasible region for the Glickman Electronics Company problem is a four-sided polygon with four corner, or extreme, points. These points are labeled ①, ②, ③, and ④ on the graph. To find the (X_1, X_2) values producing the maximum profit, we find out what the coordinates of each corner point are, then determine and compare their profit levels:

$$\text{Point ①: } (X_1 = 0, X_2 = 0) \quad \text{Profit } \$7(0) + \$5(0) = \$0$$
$$\text{Point ②: } (X_1 = 0, X_2 = 80) \quad \text{Profit } \$7(0) + \$5(80) = \$400$$
$$\text{Point ④: } (X_1 = 50, X_2 = 0) \quad \text{Profit } \$7(50) + \$5(0) = \$350$$

We skipped corner point ③ momentarily because to find its coordinates *accurately*, we will have to solve for the intersection of the two constraint lines. As you may recall from algebra, we can apply the method of *simultaneous equations* to the two constraint equations:

$$4X_1 + 3X_2 = 240 \quad \textit{(electronics time)}$$
$$2X_1 + 1X_2 = 100 \quad \textit{(assembly time)}$$

To solve these equations simultaneously, we multiply the second equation by –2:

$$-2(2X_1 + 1X_2 = 100) = -4X_1 - 2X_2 = -200$$

and then add it to the first equation:

$$\begin{aligned} +4X_1 + 3X_2 &= 240 \\ -4X_1 - 2X_2 &= -200 \\ \hline +1X_2 &= 40 \end{aligned}$$

or:

$$X_2 = 40$$

Doing this has enabled us to eliminate one variable, X_1, and to solve for X_2. We can now substitute 40 for X_2 in either of the original constraint equations and solve for X_1. Let us use the first equation. When $X_2 = 40$, then:

$$\begin{aligned} 4X_1 + 3(40) &= 240 \\ 4X_1 + 120 &= 240 \\ 4X_1 &= 120 \\ X_1 &= 30 \end{aligned}$$

Thus, point ③ has the coordinates ($X_1 = 30$, $X_2 = 40$). We can compute its profit level to complete the analysis:

$$\text{Point ③: } (X_1 = 30, X_2 = 40) \quad \text{Profit} = \$7(30) + \$5(40) = \$410$$

Because point ③ produces the highest profit of any corner point, the product mix of $X_1 = 30$ x-pods and $X_2 = 40$ BlueBerrys is the optimal solution to the Glickman Electronics problem. This solution will yield a profit of $410 per production period; it is the same solution we obtained using the iso-profit line method.

Sensitivity Analysis

Operations managers are usually interested in more than the optimal solution to an LP problem. In addition to knowing the value of each decision variable (the X_is) and the value of the objective function, they want to know how sensitive these answers are to input parameter changes. For example, what happens if the coefficients of the objective function are not exact, or if they change by 10% or 15%? What happens if the right-hand-side values of the constraints change? Because solutions are based on the assumption that input parameters are constant, the subject of sensitivity analysis comes into play. Sensitivity analysis, or postoptimality analysis, is the study of how sensitive solutions are to parameter changes.

Parameter
Numerical value that is given in a model.

Sensitivity analysis
An analysis that projects how much a solution may change if there are changes in the variables or input data.

There are two approaches to determining just how sensitive an optimal solution is to changes. The first is simply a trial-and-error approach. This approach usually involves resolving the entire problem, preferably by computer, each time one input data item or parameter is changed. It can take a long time to test a series of possible changes in this way.

The approach we prefer is the analytic postoptimality method. After an LP problem has been solved, we determine a range of changes in problem parameters that will not affect the optimal solution or change the variables in the solution. This is done without resolving the whole problem. LP software, such as Excel's Solver or POM for Windows, has this capability. Let us examine several scenarios relating to the Glickman Electronics example.

Program 1 is part of the Excel Solver computer-generated output available to help a decision maker know whether a solution is relatively insensitive to reasonable changes in one or more of the parameters of the problem. (The complete computer run for these data, including input and full output, is illustrated in Programs 2 and 3 later in this text.)

☆ **STUDENT TIP**
Here we look at the sensitivity of the final answers to changing inputs.

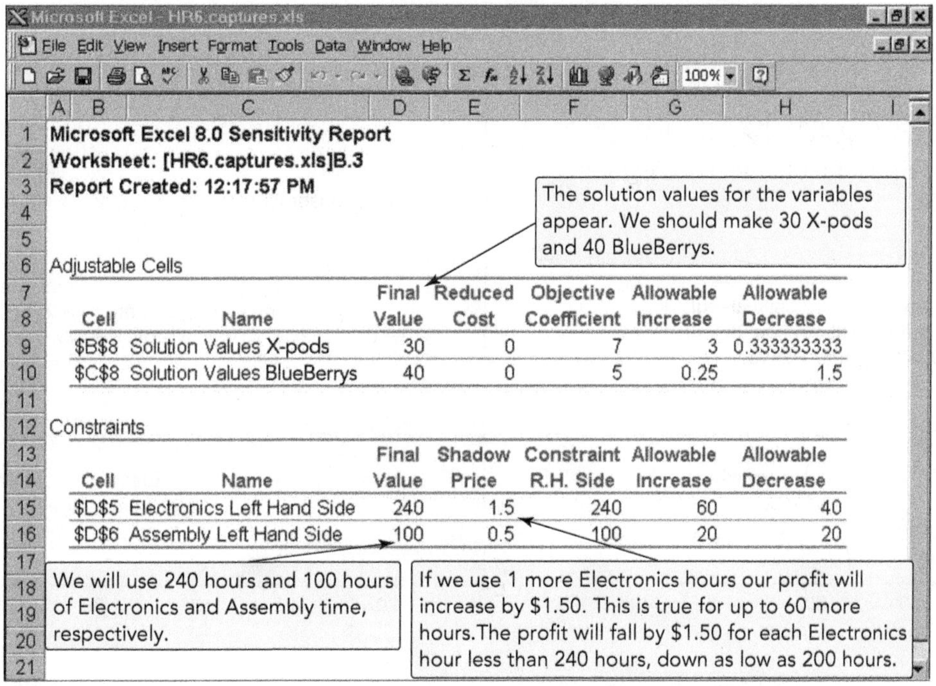
Microsoft Excel 8.0 Sensitivity Report
Worksheet: [HR6.captures.xls]B.3
Report Created: 12:17:57 PM

Adjustable Cells

Cell	Name	Final Value	Reduced Cost	Objective Coefficient	Allowable Increase	Allowable Decrease
$B$8	Solution Values X-pods	30	0	7	3	0.333333333
$C$8	Solution Values BlueBerrys	40	0	5	0.25	1.5

Constraints

Cell	Name	Final Value	Shadow Price	Constraint R.H. Side	Allowable Increase	Allowable Decrease
$D$5	Electronics Left Hand Side	240	1.5	240	60	40
$D$6	Assembly Left Hand Side	100	0.5	100	20	20

Program 1
Sensitivity Analysis for Glickman Electronics, Using Excel's Solver

LO4 *Interpret* sensitivity analysis and shadow prices

Sensitivity Report

The Excel *Sensitivity Report* for the Glickman Electronics example in Program 1 has two distinct components: (1) a table titled Adjustable Cells and (2) a table titled Constraints. These tables permit us to answer several what-if questions regarding the problem solution.

It is important to note that while using the information in the sensitivity report to answer what-if questions, we assume that we are considering a change to only a *single* input data value at a time. That is, the sensitivity information does not always apply to simultaneous changes in several input data values.

The *Adjustable Cells* table presents information regarding the impact of changes to the objective function coefficients (i.e., the unit profits of \$7 and \$5) on the optimal solution. The *Constraints* table presents information related to the impact of changes in constraint right-hand-side (RHS) values (i.e., the 240 hours and 100 hours) on the optimal solution. Although different LP software packages may format and present these tables differently, the programs all provide essentially the same information.

Changes in the Resources or Right-Hand-Side Values

The right-hand-side values of the constraints often represent resources available to the firm. The resources could be labor-hours or machine time or perhaps money or production materials available. In the Glickman Electronics example, the two resources are hours available of electronics time and hours of assembly time. If additional hours were available, a higher total profit could be realized. How much should the company be willing to pay for additional hours? Is it profitable to have some additional electronics hours? Should we be willing to pay for more assembly time? Sensitivity analysis about these resources will help us answer these questions.

If the right-hand side of a constraint is changed, the feasible region will change (unless the constraint is redundant), and often the optimal solution will change. In the Glickman example, there were 100 hours of assembly time available each week and the maximum possible profit was \$410. If the available assembly hours are *increased* to 110 hours, the new optimal solution seen in Figure 8(a) is (45,20) and the profit is \$415. Thus, the extra 10 hours of time resulted in an increase in profit of \$5 or \$0.50 per hour. If the hours are *decreased* to 90 hours as shown in Figure 8(b), the new optimal solution is (15,60) and the profit is \$405. Thus, reducing the hours by 10 results in a decrease in profit of \$5 or \$0.50 per hour. This \$0.50 per hour change in profit that resulted from a change in the hours available is called the shadow price, or dual value. The shadow price for a constraint is the improvement in the objective function value that results from a one-unit increase in the right-hand side of the constraint.

Shadow price (or dual value)
The value of one additional unit of a scarce resource in LP.

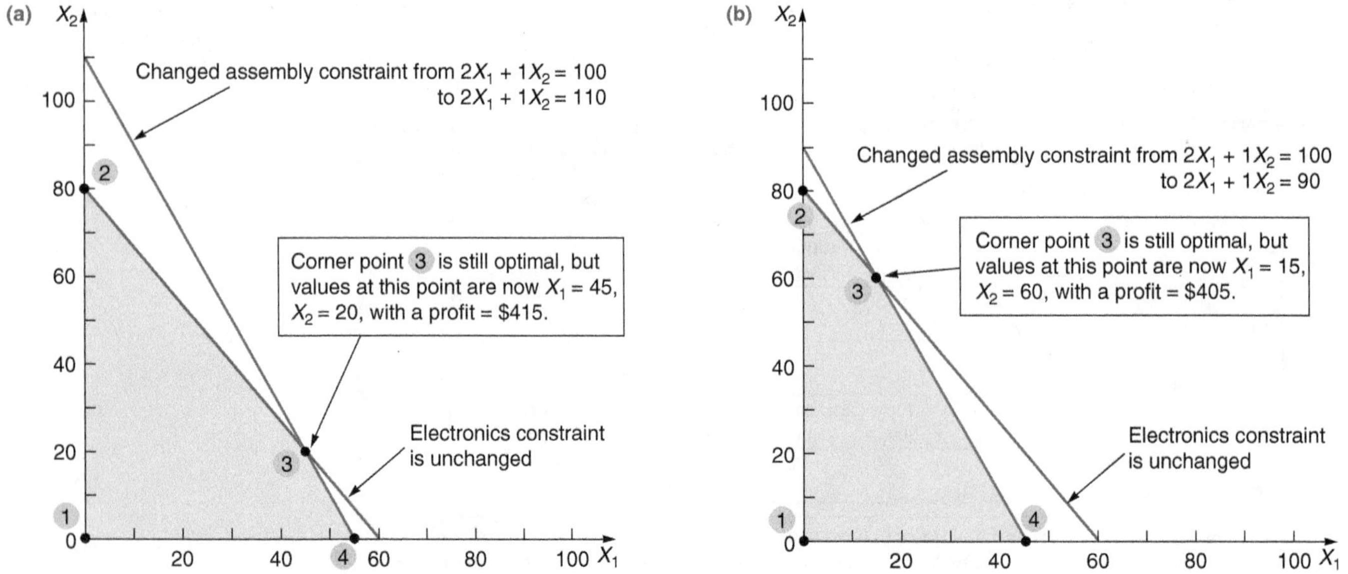

Figure 8
Glickman Electronics Sensitivity Analysis on Right-Hand-Side (RHS) Resources

Validity Range for the Shadow Price Given that Glickman Electronics' profit increases by $0.50 for each additional hour of assembly time, does it mean that Glickman can do this indefinitely, essentially earning infinite profit? Clearly, this is illogical. How far can Glickman increase its assembly time availability and still earn an extra $0.50 profit per hour? That is, for what level of increase in the RHS value of the assembly time constraint is the shadow price of $0.50 valid?

The shadow price of $0.50 is valid as long as the available assembly time stays in a range within which all current corner points continue to exist. The information to compute the upper and lower limits of this range is given by the entries labeled Allowable Increase and Allowable Decrease in the *Sensitivity Report* in Program 1. In Glickman's case, these values show that the shadow price of $0.50 for assembly time availability is valid for an increase of up to 20 hours from the current value and a decrease of up to 20 hours. That is, the available assembly time can range from a low of 80 (= 100 − 20) to a high of 120 (= 100 + 20) for the shadow price of $0.50 to be valid. Note that the allowable decrease implies that for each hour of assembly time that Glickman loses (up to 20 hours), its profit decreases by $0.50.

Changes in the Objective Function Coefficient

Let us now focus on the information provided in Program 1 titled Adjustable Cells. Each row in the Adjustable Cells table contains information regarding a decision variable (i.e., x-pods or BlueBerrys) in the LP model.

Allowable Ranges for Objective Function Coefficients As the unit profit contribution of either product changes, the slope of the iso-profit lines we saw earlier in Figure 5 changes. The size of the feasible region, however, remains the same. That is, the locations of the corner points do not change.

The limits to which the profit coefficient of x-pods or BlueBerrys can be changed without affecting the optimality of the current solution is revealed by the values in the Allowable Increase and Allowable Decrease columns of the *Sensitivity Report* in Program 1. The allowable increase in the objective function coefficient for BlueBerrys is only $0.25. In contrast, the allowable decrease is $1.50. Hence, if the unit profit of BlueBerrys drops to $4 (i.e., a decrease of $1 from the current value of $5), it is still optimal to produce 30 x-pods and 40 BlueBerrys. The total profit will drop to $370 (from $410) because each BlueBerry now yields less profit (of $1 per unit). However, if the unit profit drops below $3.50 per BlueBerry (i.e., a decrease of more than $1.50 from the current $5 profit), the current solution is no longer optimal. The LP problem will then have to be resolved using Solver, or other software, to find the new optimal corner point.

Solving Minimization Problems

☆ **STUDENT TIP**
LP problems can be structured to minimize costs as well as maximize profits.

Many linear programming problems involve *minimizing* an objective such as cost instead of maximizing a profit function. A restaurant, for example, may wish to develop a work schedule to meet staffing needs while minimizing the total number of employees. Also, a manufacturer may seek to distribute its products from several factories to its many regional warehouses in such a way as to minimize total shipping costs.

Minimization problems can be solved graphically by first setting up the feasible solution region and then using either the corner-point method or an iso-cost line approach (which is analogous to the iso-profit approach in maximization problems) to find the values of X_1 and X_2 that yield the minimum cost.

Iso-cost
An approach to solving a linear programming minimization problem graphically.

Example 1 shows how to solve a minimization problem.

Example 1

A MINIMIZATION PROBLEM WITH TWO VARIABLES

Cohen Chemicals, Inc., produces two types of photo-developing fluids. The first, a black-and-white picture chemical, costs Cohen $2,500 per ton to produce. The second, a color photo chemical, costs $3,000 per ton.

Based on an analysis of current inventory levels and outstanding orders, Cohen's production manager has specified that at least 30 tons of the black-and-white chemical and at least 20 tons of the color chemical must be produced during the next month. In addition, the manager notes that an existing inventory of a highly perishable raw material needed in both chemicals must be used within 30 days. To avoid wasting the expensive raw material, Cohen must produce a total of at least 60 tons of the photo chemicals in the next month.

APPROACH ▶ Formulate this information as a minimization LP problem.
Let:

X_1 = number of tons of black-and-white photo chemical produced
X_2 = number of tons of color photo chemical produced
Objective: Minimize cost = $\$2{,}500X_1 + \$3{,}000X_2$

Subject to:

$$X_1 \geq 30 \text{ tons of black-and-white chemical}$$
$$X_2 \geq 20 \text{ tons of color chemical}$$
$$X_1 + X_2 \geq 60 \text{ tons total}$$
$$X_1, X_2 \geq 0 \text{ nonnegativity requirements}$$

SOLUTION ▶ To solve the Cohen Chemicals problem graphically, we construct the problem's feasible region, shown in Figure 9.

Figure 9
Cohen Chemicals' Feasible Region

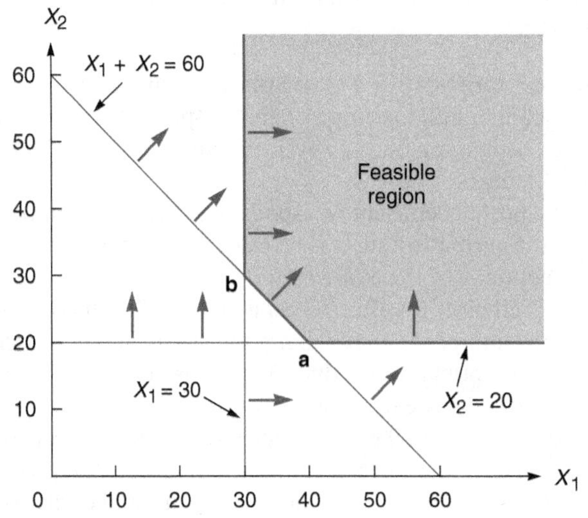

LO5 *Construct* and solve a minimization problem

Minimization problems are often unbounded outward (that is, on the right side and on the top), but this characteristic causes no problem in solving them. As long as they are bounded inward (on the left side and the bottom), we can establish corner points. The optimal solution will lie at one of the corners.

In this case, there are only two corner points, **a** and **b**, in Figure 9. It is easy to determine that at point **a**, $X_1 = 40$ and $X_2 = 20$, and that at point **b**, $X_1 = 30$ and $X_2 = 30$. The optimal solution is found at the point yielding the lowest total cost.

Thus:

$$\begin{aligned} \text{Total cost at } \mathbf{a} &= 2{,}500X_1 + 3{,}000X_2 \\ &= 2{,}500(40) + 3{,}000(20) \\ &= \$160{,}000 \\ \text{Total cost at } \mathbf{b} &= 2{,}500X_1 + 3{,}000X_2 \\ &= 2{,}500(30) + 3{,}000(30) \\ &= \$165{,}000 \end{aligned}$$

The lowest cost to Cohen Chemicals is at point **a**. Hence the operations manager should produce 40 tons of the black-and-white chemical and 20 tons of the color chemical.

INSIGHT ▶ The area is either not bounded to the right or above in a minimization problem (as it is in a maximization problem).

LEARNING EXERCISE ▶ Cohen's second constraint is recomputed and should be $X_2 \geq 15$. Does anything change in the answer? [Answer: Now $X_1 = 45$, $X_2 = 15$, and total cost = \$157,500.]

RELATED PROBLEMS ▶ 3, 5, 6, 11, 12, 22, 24

EXCEL OM Data File **ModBExB1.xls** can be found at **www.pearsonhighered.com/heizer.**

OM in Action LP at UPS

On an *average* day, the $50 billion shipping giant UPS delivers 15 million packages to 6 million customers in 220 countries. On a *really* busy day, say a few days before Christmas, it handles almost twice that number, or 300 packages per second. It does all this with a fleet of 500+ planes, making it the 11th largest commercial airline in the world.

When UPS decided it should use linear programming to map its entire operation—every pickup and delivery center and every sorting facility (more than 1,500 locations)—to find the best routes to move the millions of packages, it invested close to a decade in developing VOLCANO. This LP-based optimization system (which stands for *Volume, Location,* and *Aircraft Network Optimization*) is used to determine the least-cost set of routes, fleet assignments, and package flows.

Constraints include the number of planes, airport restrictions, and plane aircraft speed, capacity, and range.

The VOLCANO system is credited with saving UPS hundreds of millions of dollars. But that's just the start. UPS is investing $600 million more to optimize the whole supply chain to include drivers—the employees closest to the customer—so they will be able to update schedules, priorities, and time conflicts on the fly.

The UPS "airline" is not alone. Southwest runs its massive LP model (called *ILOG Optimizer)* every day to schedule its thousands of flight legs. The program has 90,000 constraints and 2 million variables. Continental's LP program is called *OptSolver,* and Delta's is called *Coldstart.* Airlines, like many other firms, manage their millions of daily decisions with LP.

Sources: Aviation Daily (February 9, 2004); **Compass.ups.com** (May 2008); and *Interfaces* (January–February 2004).

Linear Programming Applications

The foregoing examples each contained just two variables (X_1 and X_2). Most real-world problems (as we see in the UPS *OM in Action* box above) contain many more variables, however. Let's use the principles already developed to formulate a few more-complex problems. The practice you will get by "paraphrasing" the following LP situations should help develop your skills for applying linear programming to other common operations situations.

STUDENT TIP
Now we look at three larger problems—ones that have more than two decision variables each and therefore are not graphed.

Production-Mix Example

LO6 *Formulate* production-mix, diet, and labor scheduling problems

Example 2 involves another *production-mix* decision. Limited resources must be allocated among various products that a firm produces. The firm's overall objective is to manufacture the selected products in such quantities as to maximize total profits.

Example 2

A PRODUCTION-MIX PROBLEM

Failsafe Electronics Corporation primarily manufactures four highly technical products, which it supplies to aerospace firms that hold NASA contracts. Each of the products must pass through the following departments before they are shipped: wiring, drilling, assembly, and inspection. The time requirements in each department (in hours) for each unit produced and its corresponding profit value are summarized in this table:

	DEPARTMENT				
PRODUCT	WIRING	DRILLING	ASSEMBLY	INSPECTION	UNIT PROFIT
XJ201	.5	3	2	.5	$ 9
XM897	1.5	1	4	1.0	$12
TR29	1.5	2	1	.5	$15
BR788	1.0	3	2	.5	$11

The production time available in each department each month and the minimum monthly production requirement to fulfill contracts are as follows:

DEPARTMENT	CAPACITY (HOURS)	PRODUCT	MINIMUM PRODUCTION LEVEL
Wiring	1,500	XJ201	150
Drilling	2,350	XM897	100
Assembly	2,600	TR29	200
Inspection	1,200	BR788	400

APPROACH ▶ Formulate this production-mix situation as an LP problem. The production manager first specifies production levels for each product for the coming month. He lets:

$$X_1 = \text{number of units of XJ201 produced}$$
$$X_2 = \text{number of units of XM897 produced}$$
$$X_3 = \text{number of units of TR29 produced}$$
$$X_4 = \text{number of units of BR788 produced}$$

SOLUTION ▶ The LP formulation is:

Objective: Maximize profit $= 9X_1 + 12X_2 + 15X_3 + 11X_4$

subject to:

$$.5X_1 + 1.5X_2 + 1.5X_3 + 1X_4 \leq 1{,}500 \text{ hours of wiring available}$$
$$3X_1 + 1X_2 + 2X_3 + 3X_4 \leq 2{,}350 \text{ hours of drilling available}$$
$$2X_1 + 4X_2 + 1X_3 + 2X_4 \leq 2{,}600 \text{ hours of assembly available}$$
$$.5X_1 + 1X_2 + .5X_3 + .5X_4 \leq 1{,}200 \text{ hours of inspection}$$
$$X_1 \geq 150 \text{ units of XJ201}$$
$$X_2 \geq 100 \text{ units of XM897}$$
$$X_3 \geq 200 \text{ units of TR29}$$
$$X_4 \geq 400 \text{ units of BR788}$$
$$X_1, X_2, X_3, X_4 \geq 0$$

INSIGHT ▶ There can be numerous constraints in an LP problem. The constraint right-hand sides may be in different units, but the objective function uses one common unit—dollars of profit, in this case. Because there are more than two decision variables, this problem is not solved graphically.

LEARNING EXERCISE ▶ Solve this LP problem as formulated. What is the solution? [Answer: $X_1 = 150, X_2 = 300, X_3 = 200, X_4 = 400$.]

RELATED PROBLEMS ▶ 7, 8, 10, 19, 20, 21, 23, 28

Diet Problem Example

Example 3 illustrates the *diet problem*, which was originally used by hospitals to determine the most economical diet for patients. Known in agricultural applications as the *feed-mix problem*, the diet problem involves specifying a food or feed ingredient combination that will satisfy stated nutritional requirements at a minimum cost level.

Example 3

A DIET PROBLEM

The Feed 'N Ship feedlot fattens cattle for local farmers and ships them to meat markets in Kansas City and Omaha. The owners of the feedlot seek to determine the amounts of cattle feed to buy to satisfy minimum nutritional standards and, at the same time, minimize total feed costs.

Each grain stock contains different amounts of four nutritional ingredients: A, B, C, and D. Here are the ingredient contents of each grain, in *ounces per pound of grain*:

	FEED		
INGREDIENT	STOCK X	STOCK Y	STOCK Z
A	3 oz	2 oz	4 oz
B	2 oz	3 oz	1 oz
C	1 oz	0 oz	2 oz
D	6 oz	8 oz	4 oz

The cost per pound of grains X, Y, and Z is \$0.02, \$0.04, and \$0.025, respectively. The minimum requirement per cow per month is 64 ounces of ingredient A, 80 ounces of ingredient B, 16 ounces of ingredient C, and 128 ounces of ingredient D.

The feedlot faces one additional restriction—it can obtain only 500 pounds of stock Z per month from the feed supplier, regardless of its need. Because there are usually 100 cows at the Feed 'N Ship feedlot at any given time, this constraint limits the amount of stock Z for use in the feed of each cow to no more than 5 pounds, or 80 ounces, per month.

APPROACH ▶ Formulate this as a minimization LP problem.

Let: X_1 = number of pounds of stock X purchased per cow each month
X_2 = number of pounds of stock Y purchased per cow each month
X_3 = number of pounds of stock Z purchased per cow each month

SOLUTION ▶

$$\begin{aligned} &\text{Objective: Minimize cost} = .02X_1 + .04X_2 + .025X_3 \\ &\text{subject to: Ingredient A requirement:} \quad 3X_1 + 2X_2 + 4X_3 \geq 64 \\ &\text{Ingredient B requirement:} \quad 2X_1 + 3X_2 + 1X_3 \geq 80 \\ &\text{Ingredient C requirement:} \quad 1X_1 + 0X_2 + 2X_3 \geq 16 \\ &\text{Ingredient D requirement:} \quad 6X_1 + 8X_2 + 4X_3 \geq 128 \\ &\text{Stock Z limitation:} \quad X_3 \leq 5 \\ &X_1, X_2, X_3 \geq 0 \end{aligned}$$

The cheapest solution is to purchase 40 pounds of grain X_1, at a cost of \$0.80 per cow.

INSIGHT ▶ Because the cost per pound of stock X is so low, the optimal solution excludes grains Y and Z.

LEARNING EXERCISE ▶ The cost of a pound of stock X just increased by 50%. Does this affect the solution? [Answer: Yes, when the cost per pound of grain X is \$0.03, X_1 = 16 pounds, X_2 = 16 pounds, X_3 = 0, and cost = \$1.12 per cow.]

RELATED PROBLEMS ▶ 6, 30

Labor Scheduling Example

Labor scheduling problems address staffing needs over a specific time period. They are especially useful when managers have some flexibility in assigning workers to jobs that require overlapping or interchangeable talents. Large banks and hospitals frequently use LP to tackle their labor scheduling. Example 4 describes how one bank uses LP to schedule tellers.

Example 4

SCHEDULING BANK TELLERS

Mexico City Bank of Commerce and Industry is a busy bank that has requirements for between 10 and 18 tellers depending on the time of day. Lunchtime, from noon to 2 P.M., is usually heaviest. The table below indicates the workers needed at various hours that the bank is open.

TIME PERIOD	NUMBER OF TELLERS REQUIRED	TIME PERIOD	NUMBER OF TELLERS REQUIRED
9 A.M.–10 A.M.	10	1 P.M.–2 P.M.	18
10 A.M.–11 A.M.	12	2 P.M.–3 P.M.	17
11 A.M.–Noon	14	3 P.M.–4 P.M.	15
Noon–1 P.M.	16	4 P.M.–5 P.M.	10

The bank now employs 12 full-time tellers, but many people are on its roster of available part-time employees. A part-time employee must put in exactly 4 hours per day but can start anytime between 9 A.M. and 1 P.M. Part-timers are a fairly inexpensive labor pool because no retirement or lunch benefits are provided them. Full-timers, on the other hand, work from 9 A.M. to 5 P.M. but are allowed 1 hour for lunch. (Half the full-timers eat at 11 A.M., the other half at noon.) Full-timers thus provide 35 hours per week of productive labor time.

By corporate policy, the bank limits part-time hours to a maximum of 50% of the day's total requirement.

Part-timers earn \$6 per hour (or \$24 per day) on average, whereas full-timers earn \$75 per day in salary and benefits on average.

APPROACH ▶ The bank would like to set a schedule, using LP, that would minimize its total manpower costs. It will release 1 or more of its full-time tellers if it is profitable to do so.

We can let:

F = full-time tellers
P_1 = part-timers starting at 9 A.M. (leaving at 1 P.M.)

P_2 = part-timers starting at 10 A.M. (leaving at 2 P.M.)
P_3 = part-timers starting at 11 A.M. (leaving at 3 P.M.)
P_4 = part-timers starting at noon (leaving at 4 P.M.)
P_5 = part-timers starting at 1 P.M. (leaving at 5 P.M.)

SOLUTION ▶ Objective function:

$$\text{Minimize total daily manpower cost} = \$75F + \$24(P_1 + P_2 + P_3 + P_4 + P_5)$$

Constraints: For each hour, the available labor-hours must be at least equal to the required labor-hours:

$$\begin{array}{lll}
F + P_1 & \geq 10 & \textit{(9 A.M. to 10 A.M. needs)} \\
F + P_1 + P_2 & \geq 12 & \textit{(10 A.M. to 11 A.M. needs)} \\
\frac{1}{2}F + P_1 + P_2 + P_3 & \geq 14 & \textit{(11 A.M. to noon needs)} \\
\frac{1}{2}F + P_1 + P_2 + P_3 + P_4 & \geq 16 & \textit{(noon to 1 P.M. needs)} \\
F \quad + P_2 + P_3 + P_4 + P_5 & \geq 18 & \textit{(1 P.M. to 2 P.M. needs)} \\
F \quad + P_3 + P_4 + P_5 & \geq 17 & \textit{(2 P.M. to 3 P.M. needs)} \\
F \quad + P_4 + P_5 & \geq 15 & \textit{(3 P.M. to 4 P.M. needs)} \\
F \quad + P_5 & \geq 10 & \textit{(4 P.M. to 5 P.M. needs)}
\end{array}$$

Only 12 full-time tellers are available, so:

$$F \leq 12$$

Part-time worker-hours cannot exceed 50% of total hours required each day, which is the sum of the tellers needed each hour:

$$4(P_1 + P_2 + P_3 + P_4 + P_5) \leq .50(10 + 12 + 14 + 16 + 18 + 17 + 15 + 10)$$

or:

$$4P_1 + 4P_2 + 4P_3 + 4P_4 + 4P_5 \leq 0.50(112)$$
$$F, P_1, P_2, P_3, P_4, P_5 \geq 0$$

There are two alternative optimal schedules that Mexico City Bank can follow. The first is to employ only 10 full-time tellers ($F = 10$) and to start 7 part-timers at 10 A.M. ($P_2 = 7$), 2 part-timers at 11 A.M. and noon ($P_3 = 2$ and $P_4 = 2$), and 3 part-timers at 1 P.M. ($P_5 = 3$). No part-timers would begin at 9 A.M.

The second solution also employs 10 full-time tellers, but starts 6 part-timers at 9 A.M. ($P_1 = 6$), 1 part-timer at 10 A.M. ($P_2 = 1$), 2 part-timers at 11 A.M. and noon ($P_3 = 2$ and $P_4 = 2$), and 3 part-timers at 1 P.M. ($P_5 = 3$). The cost of either of these two policies is \$1,086 per day.

INSIGHT ▶ It is not unusual for multiple optimal solutions to exist in large LP problems. In this case, it gives management the option of selecting, at the same cost, between schedules. To find an alternate optimal solution, you may have to enter the constraints in a different sequence.

LEARNING EXERCISE ▶ The bank decides to give part-time employees a raise to \$7 per hour. Does the solution change? [Answer: Yes, cost = \$1,142, $F = 10$, $P_1 = 6$, $P_2 = 1$, $P_3 = 2$, $P_4 = 5$, $P_5 = 0$.]

RELATED PROBLEM ▶ 18

The Simplex Method of LP

Simplex method
An algorithm for solving linear programming problems of all sizes.

Most real-world linear programming problems have more than two variables and thus are too complex for graphical solution. A procedure called the simplex method may be used to find the optimal solution to such problems. The simplex method is actually an algorithm (or a set of instructions) with which we examine corner points in a methodical fashion until we arrive at the best solution—highest profit or lowest cost. Computer programs (such as Excel OM and POM for Windows) and Excel spreadsheets are available to solve linear programming problems via the simplex method.

For details regarding the algebraic steps of the simplex algorithm, see Tutorial 3 at our text Web site or refer to a management science textbook.[2]

[2]See, for example, Barry Render, Ralph M. Stair, and Michael Hanna, *Quantitative Analysis for Management*, 11th ed. (Pearson Education, Inc., Upper Saddle River, NJ, 2013): Chapters 7–9; or Raju Balakrishnan, Barry Render, and Ralph M. Stair, *Managerial Decision Modeling with Spreadsheets*, 3rd ed. (Pearson Education, Inc., Upper Saddle River, NJ, 2012): Chapters 2–4.

Summary

This text introduces a special kind of model, linear programming. LP has proven to be especially useful when trying to make the most effective use of an organization's resources.

The first step in dealing with LP models is problem formulation, which involves identifying and creating an objective function and constraints. The second step is to solve the problem. If there are only two decision variables, the problem can be solved graphically, using the corner-point method or the iso-profit/iso-cost line method. With either approach, we first identify the feasible region, then find the corner point yielding the greatest profit or least cost. LP is used in a wide variety of business applications, as the examples and homework problems in this text reveal.

Key Terms

Linear programming (LP)
Objective function
Constraints
Graphical solution approach
Decision variables
Feasible region
Iso-profit line method
Corner-point method
Parameter
Sensitivity analysis
Shadow price (or dual value)
Iso-cost
Simplex method

Discussion Questions

1. List at least four applications of linear programming problems.
2. What is a "corner point"? Explain why solutions to linear programming problems focus on corner points.
3. Define the feasible region of a graphical LP problem. What is a feasible solution?
4. Each linear programming problem that has a feasible region has an infinite number of solutions. Explain.
5. Under what circumstances is the objective function more important than the constraints in a linear programming model?
6. Under what circumstances are the constraints more important than the objective function in a linear programming model?
7. Why is the diet problem, in practice, applicable for animals but not particularly for people?
8. How many feasible solutions are there in a linear program? Which ones do we need to examine to find the optimal solution?
9. Define shadow price (or dual value).
10. Explain how to use the iso-cost line in a graphical minimization problem.
11. Compare how the corner-point and iso-profit line methods work for solving graphical problems.
12. Where a constraint crosses the vertical or horizontal axis, the quantity is fairly obvious. How does one go about finding the quantity coordinates where two constraints cross, not at an axis?
13. Suppose a linear programming (maximation) problem has been solved and that the optimal value of the objective function is \$300. Suppose an additional constraint is added to this problem. Explain how this might affect each of the following:
    a) The feasible region.
    b) The optimal value of the objective function.

Using Software to Solve LP Problems

All LP problems can be solved with the simplex method, using software such as Excel OM and POM for Windows or Excel. This approach produces valuable economic information such as the shadow price, or dual value, and provides complete sensitivity analysis on other inputs to the problems. Excel uses Solver, which requires that you enter your own constraints. Excel OM and POM for Windows require only that problem data be entered. In the following section we illustrate how to create an Excel spreadsheet for LP problems.

USING EXCEL SPREADSHEETS

Excel offers the ability to analyze linear programming problems using built-in problem-solving tools. Excel's tool is named Solver. Solver is limited to 200 changing cells (variables), each with 2 boundary constraints and up to 100 additional constraints. These capabilities make Solver suitable for the solution of complex, real-world problems.

We use Excel to set up the Glickman Electronics problem in Program 2. The objective and constraints are repeated here:

Objective function: Maximize profit = \$7(No. of x-pods) + \$5(No. of BlueBerrys)

Subject to: 4(x-pods) + 3(BlueBerrys) $\le$ 240

2(x-pods) + 1(BlueBerry) $\le$ 100

Program **2**

Using Excel to Formulate the Glickman Electronics Problem

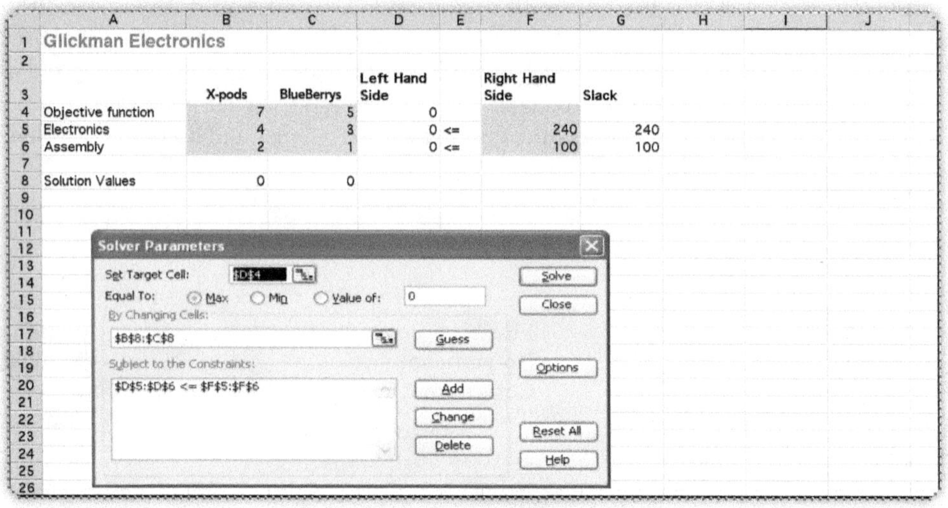

		COMPUTATIONS	
VALUE	CELL	EXCEL FORMULA	ACTION
Left Hand Side	D4	=SUMPRODUCT($B$8:$C$8, B4:C4)	Copy to D5:D6
Slack	G5	=F5–D5	Copy to G6
			Select *Data Tab, Solver* (in the *Data Analysis* section) for Excel 2007, 2010. *Select Tools, Solver* for Excel 2011 for Mac or Excel 2003.
			Set Solver parameters as displayed
			Press Solve

The Excel screen in Program 3 shows Solver's solution to the Glickman Electronics Company problem. Note that the optimal solution is now shown in the *changing cells* (cells B8 and C8, which served as the variables). The Reports selection performs more extensive analysis of the solution and its environment. Excel's sensitivity analysis capability was illustrated earlier in Program 1.

Program **3**

Excel Solution to Glickman Electronics LP Problem

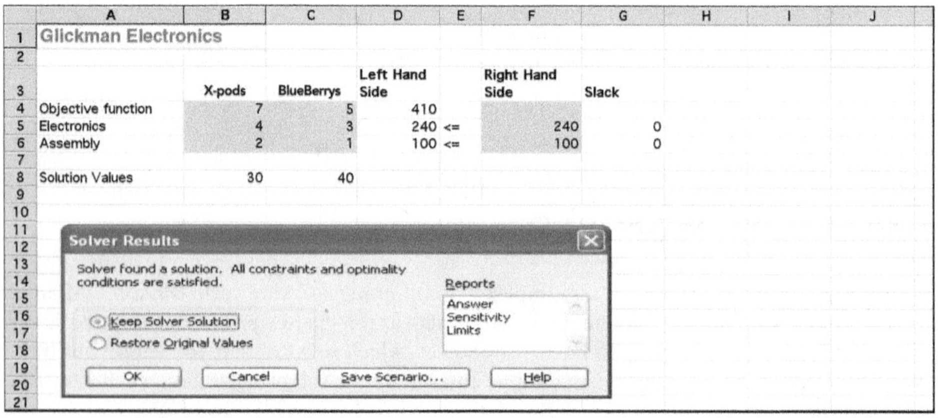

USING EXCEL OM AND POM FOR WINDOWS

Excel OM and POM for Windows can handle relatively large LP problems. As output, the software provides optimal values for the variables, optimal profit or cost, and sensitivity analysis. In addition, POM for Windows provides graphical output for problems with only two variables.

Solved Problems

Virtual Office Hours help is available at www.myomlab.com.

SOLVED PROBLEM 1

Smith's, a Niagara, New York, clothing manufacturer that produces men's shirts and pajamas, has two primary resources available: sewing-machine time (in the sewing department) and cutting-machine time (in the cutting department). Over the next month, owner Barbara Smith can schedule up to 280 hours of work on sewing machines and up to 450 hours of work on cutting machines. Each shirt produced requires 1.00 hour of sewing time and 1.50 hours of cutting time. Producing each pair of pajamas requires .75 hours of sewing time and 2 hours of cutting time.

To express the LP constraints for this problem mathematically, we let:

X_1 = number of shirts produced

X_2 = number of pajamas produced

SOLUTION

First constraint: $1X_1 + .75X_2 \leq 280$ hours of sewing-machine time available—our first scarce resource

Second constraint: $1.5X_1 + ②X_2 \leq 450$ hours of cutting-machine time available—our second scarce resource

Note: This means that each pair of pajamas takes 2 hours of the cutting resource.

Smith's accounting department analyzes cost and sales figures and states that each shirt produced will yield a $4 contribution to profit and that each pair of pajamas will yield a $3 contribution to profit.

This information can be used to create the LP *objective function* for this problem:

Objective function: Maximize total contribution to profit $= \$4X_1 + \$3X_2$

SOLVED PROBLEM 2

We want to solve the following LP problem for Kevin Caskey Wholesale Inc. using the corner-point method:

Objective: Maximize profit $= \$9X_1 + \$7X_2$

Constraints:

$$2X_1 + 1X_2 \leq 40$$
$$X_1 + 3X_2 \leq 30$$
$$X_1, X_2 \geq 0$$

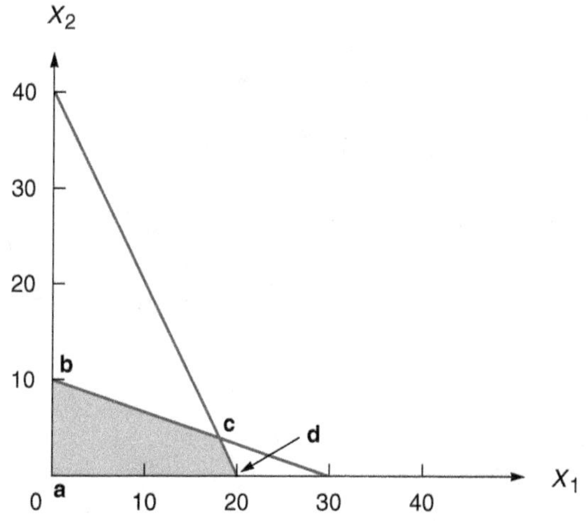

Figure 10

K. Caskey Wholesale Inc.'s Feasible Region

SOLUTION

Figure 10 illustrates these constraints:

Corner-point **a**: ($X_1 = 0, X_2 = 0$) Profit = 0

Corner-point **b**: ($X_1 = 0, X_2 = 10$) Profit $= 9(0) + 7(10) = \$70$

Corner-point **d**: ($X_1 = 20, X_2 = 0$) Profit $= 9(20) + 7(0) = \$180$

Corner-point **c** is obtained by solving equations $2X_1 + 1X_2 = 40$ and $X_1 + 3X_2 = 30$ simultaneously. Multiply the second equation by −2 and add it to the first.

$$\begin{aligned} 2X_1 + 1X_2 &= 40 \\ -2X_1 - 6X_2 &= -60 \\ \hline -5X_2 &= -20 \\ \text{Thus } X_2 &= 4 \end{aligned}$$

And $X_1 + 3(4) = 30$ or $X_1 + 12 = 30$ or $X_1 = 18$

Corner-point **c**: ($X_1 = 18, X_2 = 4$) Profit $= 9(18) + 7(4) = \$190$

Hence the optimal solution is:

$(x_1 = 18, x_2 = 4)$ Profit = $190

SOLVED PROBLEM 3

Holiday Meal Turkey Ranch is considering buying two different types of turkey feed. Each feed contains, in varying proportions, some or all of the three nutritional ingredients essential for fattening turkeys. Brand Y feed costs the ranch $.02 per pound. Brand Z costs $.03 per pound. The rancher would like to determine the lowest-cost diet that meets the minimum monthly intake requirement for each nutritional ingredient.

The following table contains relevant information about the composition of brand Y and brand Z feeds, as well as the minimum monthly requirement for each nutritional ingredient per turkey.

COMPOSITION OF EACH POUND OF FEED			
INGREDIENT	BRAND Y FEED	BRAND Z FEED	MINIMUM MONTHLY REQUIREMENT
A	5 oz	10 oz	90 oz
B	4 oz	3 oz	48 oz
C	.5 oz	0	1.5 oz
Cost/lb	$.02	$.03	

SOLUTION

If we let:

X_1 = number of pounds of brand Y feed purchased

X_2 = number of pounds of brand Z feed purchased

then we may proceed to formulate this linear programming problem as follows:

Objective: Minimize cost (in cents) $= 2X_1 + 3X_2$

subject to these constraints:

$5X_1 + 10X_2 \geq 90$ oz (*ingredient A constraint*)

$4X_1 + 3X_2 \geq 48$ oz (*ingredient B constraint*)

$\frac{1}{2}X_1 \geq 1\frac{1}{2}$ oz (*ingredient C constraint*)

Figure 11 illustrates these constraints.

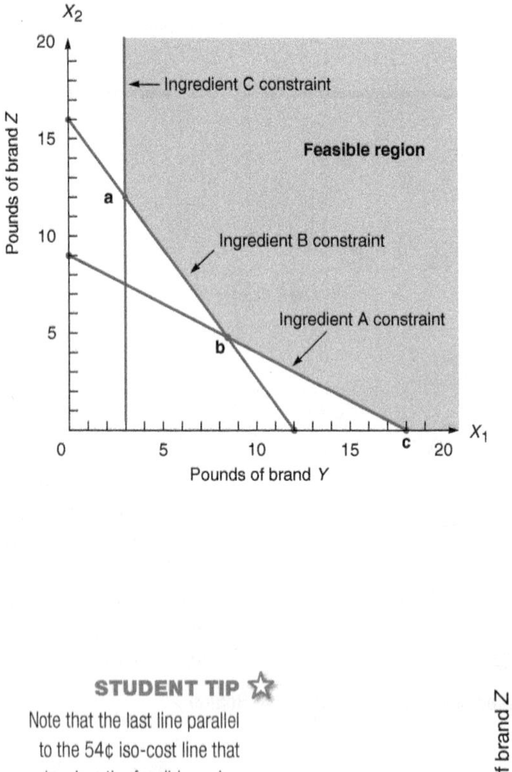

Figure 11

Feasible Region for the Holiday Meal Turkey Ranch Problem

The iso-cost line approach may be used to solve LP minimization problems such as that of the Holiday Meal Turkey Ranch. As with iso-profit lines, we need not compute the cost at each corner point, but instead draw a series of parallel cost lines. The last cost point to touch the feasible region provides us with the optimal solution corner.

For example, we start in Figure 12 by drawing a 54¢ cost line, namely, $54 = 2X_1 + 3X_2$. Obviously, there are many points in the feasible region that would yield a lower total cost. We proceed to move our iso-cost line toward the lower left, in a plane parallel to the 54¢ solution line. The last point we touch while still in contact with the feasible region is the same as corner point **b** of Figure 11. It has the coordinates ($X_1 = 8.4$, $X_2 = 4.8$) and an associated cost of 31.2 cents.

STUDENT TIP ☆

Note that the last line parallel to the 54¢ iso-cost line that touches the feasible region indicates the optimal corner point.

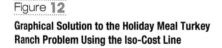

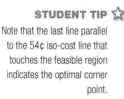

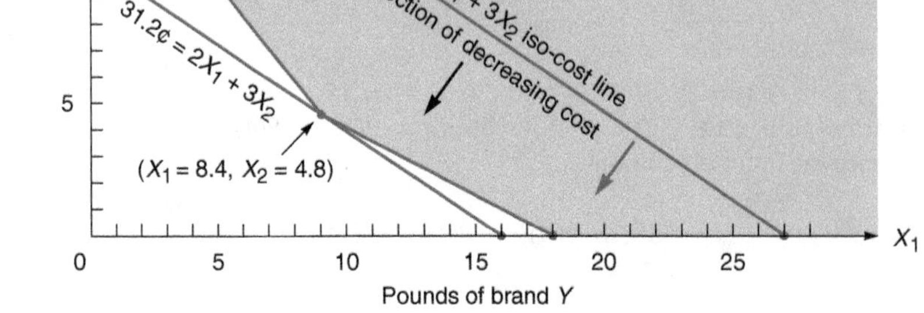

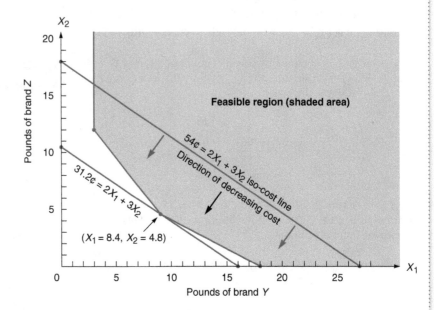

Figure 12

Graphical Solution to the Holiday Meal Turkey Ranch Problem Using the Iso-Cost Line

18, 16, 23 ...

Problems

Note: PX means the problem may be solved with POM for Windows and/or Excel OM.

• **1** Solve the following linear programming problem graphically:

Maximize profit $= 4X + 6Y$
Subject to:
$X + 2Y \leq 8$
$5X + 4Y \leq 20$
$X, Y \geq 0$ PX

• **2** Solve the following linear programming problem graphically:

Maximize profit $= X + 10Y$
Subject to:
$4X + 3Y \leq 36$
$2X + 4Y \leq 40$
$Y \geq 3$
$X, Y \geq 0$ PX

• **3** Solve the following linear program graphically:

Minimize cost $= X_1 + X_2$
$8X_1 + 16X_2 \geq 64$
$X_1 \geq 0$
$X_2 \geq -2$ PX

(*Note:* X_2 values can be negative in this problem.)

•• **4** Consider the following linear programming problem:

Maximize profit $= 30X_1 + 10X_2$
Subject to:
$3X_1 + X_2 \leq 300$
$X_1 + X_2 \leq 200$
$X_1 \leq 100$
$X_2 \geq 50$
$X_1 - X_2 \leq 0$
$X_1, X_2 \geq 0$

a) Solve the problem graphically.
b) Is there more than one optimal solution? Explain. PX

• **5** Solve the following LP problem graphically:

Minimize cost $= 24X + 15Y$
Subject to:
$7X + 11Y \geq 77$
$16X + 4Y \geq 80$
$X, Y \geq 0$

•• **6** Doug Turner Food Processors wishes to introduce a new brand of dog biscuits composed of chicken- and liver-flavored biscuits that meet certain nutritional requirements. The liver-flavored biscuits contain 1 unit of nutrient A and 2 units of nutrient B; the chicken-flavored biscuits contain 1 unit of nutrient A and 4 units of nutrient B. According to federal requirements, there must be at least 40 units of nutrient A and 60 units of nutrient B in a package of the new mix. In addition, the company has decided that there can be no more than 15 liver-flavored biscuits in a package. If it costs 1¢ to make 1 liver-flavored biscuit and 2¢ to make 1 chicken-flavored, what is the optimal product mix for a package of the biscuits to minimize the firm's cost?

a) Formulate this as a linear programming problem.
b) Solve this problem graphically, giving the optimal values of all variables.
c) What is the total cost of a package of dog biscuits using the optimal mix? PX

• **7** The Attaran Corporation manufactures two electrical products: portable air conditioners and portable heaters. The assembly process for each is similar in that both require a certain amount of wiring and drilling. Each air conditioner takes 3 hours of wiring and 2 hours of drilling. Each heater must go through 2 hours of wiring and 1 hour of drilling. During the next production period, 240 hours of wiring time are available and up to 140 hours of drilling time may be used. Each air conditioner sold yields a profit of $25. Each heater assembled may be sold for a $15 profit.

Formulate and solve this LP production-mix situation, and find the best combination of air conditioners and heaters that yields the highest profit. PX

• **8** The Jean-Pierre Amor Company manufactures two lines of designer yard gates, called model A and model B. Every gate requires blending a certain amount of steel and zinc; the company has available a total of 25,000 lb of steel and 6,000 lb of zinc. Each model A gate requires a mixture of 125 lb of steel and 20 lb of zinc, and each yields a profit of $90. Each model B gate requires 100 lb of steel and 30 lb of zinc and can be sold for a profit of $70.

Find by graphical linear programming the best production mix of yard gates. PX

•• **9** Green Vehicle Inc. manufactures electric cars and small delivery trucks. It has just opened a new factory where the C1 car and the T1 truck can both be manufactured. To make either vehicle, processing in the assembly shop and in the paint shop are required. It takes 1/40 of a day and 1/60 of a day to paint a truck of type T1 and a car of type C1 in the paint shop, respectively. It takes 1/50 of a day to assemble either type of vehicle in the assembly shop.

A T1 truck and a C1 car yield profits of $300 and $220, respectively, per vehicle sold.

a) Define the objective function and constraint equations.
b) Graph the feasible region.
c) What is a maximum-profit daily production plan at the new factory?
d) How much profit will such a plan yield, assuming whatever is produced is sold? PX

• **10** The Lifang Wu Corporation manufactures two models of industrial robots, the Alpha 1 and the Beta 2. The firm employs 5 technicians, working 160 hours each per month, on its assembly line. Management insists that full employment (that is, *all* 160 hours of time) be maintained for each worker during next month's operations. It requires 20 labor-hours to assemble each Alpha 1 robot and 25 labor-hours to assemble each Beta 2 model. Wu wants to see at least 10 Alpha 1s and at least 15 Beta 2s produced during the production period. Alpha 1s generate a $1,200 profit per unit, and Beta 2s yield $1,800 each.

Determine the most profitable number of each model of robot to produce during the coming month. PX

• **11** The Sweet Smell Fertilizer Company markets bags of manure labeled "not less than 60 lb dry weight." The packaged manure is a combination of compost and sewage wastes. To provide good-quality fertilizer, each bag should contain at least 30 lb of compost but no more than 40 lb of sewage. Each pound of compost costs Sweet Smell 5¢ and each pound of sewage costs 4¢. Use a graphical LP method to determine the least-cost blend of compost and sewage in each bag. PX

• **12** Consider Paul Jordan's following linear programming formulation:

$$\begin{aligned} \text{Minimize cost} &= \$1X_1 + \$2X_2 \\ \text{Subject to:} \quad X_1 + 3X_2 &\geq 90 \\ 8X_1 + 2X_2 &\geq 160 \\ 3X_1 + 2X_2 &\geq 120 \\ X_2 &\leq 70 \end{aligned}$$

a) Graphically illustrate the feasible region to indicate to Jordan which corner point produces the optimal solution.
b) What is the cost of this solution?

• **13** The LP relationships that follow were formulated by Richard Martin at the Long Beach Chemical Company. Which ones are invalid for use in a linear programming problem, and why?

$$\begin{aligned} \text{Maximize} &= 6X_1 + \tfrac{1}{2}X_1X_2 + 5X_3 \\ \text{Subject to:} \quad 4X_1X_2 + 2X_3 &\leq 70 \\ 7.9X_1 - 4X_2 &\geq 15.6 \\ 3X_1 + 3X_2 + 3X_3 &\geq 21 \\ 19X_2 - \tfrac{1}{3}X_3 &= 17 \\ -X_1 - X_2 + 4X_3 &= 5 \\ 4X_1 + 2X_2 + 3\sqrt{X_3} &\leq 80 \end{aligned}$$

•• **14** Kalyan Singhal Corp. makes three products, and it has three machines available as resources as given in the following LP problem:

$$\begin{aligned} \text{Maximize contribution} &= 4X_1 + 4X_2 + 7X_3 \\ \text{Subject to:} \quad 1X_1 + 7X_2 + 4X_3 &\leq 100 \text{ (hours on machine 1)} \\ 2X_1 + 1X_2 + 7X_3 &\leq 110 \text{ (hours on machine 2)} \\ 8X_1 + 4X_2 + 1X_3 &\leq 100 \text{ (hours on machine 3)} \end{aligned}$$

a) Determine the optimal solution using LP software.
b) Is there unused time available on any of the machines with the optimal solution?
c) What would it be worth to the firm to make an additional hour of time available on the third machine?
d) How much would the firm's profit increase if an extra 10 hours of time were made available on the second machine at no extra cost?

•• **15** Consider the following LP problem developed at Zafar Malik's Carbondale, Illinois, optical scanning firm:

$$\begin{aligned} \text{Maximize profit} &= \$1X_1 + \$1X_2 \\ \text{Subject to:} \quad 2X_1 + 1X_2 &\leq 100 \\ 1X_1 + 2X_2 &\leq 100 \end{aligned}$$

a) What is the optimal solution to this problem? Solve it graphically.
b) If a technical breakthrough occurred that raised the profit per unit of X_1 to \$3, would this affect the optimal solution?
c) Instead of an increase in the profit coefficient X_1 to \$3, suppose that profit was overestimated and should only have been \$1.25. Does this change the optimal solution?

••• **16** The Hills County, Michigan, superintendent of education is responsible for assigning students to the three high schools in his county. He recognizes the need to bus a certain number of students, because several sectors, A–E, of the county are beyond walking distance to a school. The superintendent partitions the county into five geographic sectors as he attempts to establish a plan that will minimize the total number of student miles traveled by bus. He also recognizes that if a student happens to live in a certain sector and is assigned to the high school in that sector, there is no need to bus him because he can walk to school. The three schools are located in sectors B, C, and E.

Hans Magelssen/Shutterstock

The accompanying table reflects the number of high-school-age students living in each sector and the distance in miles from each sector to each school:

	DISTANCE TO SCHOOL			
SECTOR	SCHOOL IN SECTOR B	SCHOOL IN SECTOR C	SCHOOL IN SECTOR E	NUMBER OF STUDENTS
A	5	8	6	700
B	0	4	12	500
C	4	0	7	100
D	7	2	5	800
E	12	7	0	400
				2,500

Each high school has a capacity of 900 students.
a) Set up the objective function and constraints of this problem using linear programming so that the total number of student miles traveled by bus is minimized.
b) Solve the problem.

•• **17** The Rio Credit Union has \$250,000 available to invest in a 12-month commitment. The money can be placed in Brazilian treasury notes yielding an 8% return or in riskier high-yield bonds at an average rate of return of 9%. Credit union regulations require diversification to the extent that at least 50% of the investment be placed in Treasury notes. It is also decided that no more than 40% of the investment be placed in bonds. How much should the Rio Credit Union invest in each security so as to maximize its return on investment?

•• **18** Wichita's famous Sethi Restaurant is open 24 hours a day. Servers report for duty at 3 A.M., 7 A.M., 11 A.M., 3 P.M., 7 P.M., or 11 P.M., and each works an 8-hour shift. The following table shows the minimum number of workers needed during the 6 periods into which the day is divided:

PERIOD	TIME	NUMBER OF SERVERS REQUIRED
1	3 A.M.–7 A.M.	3
2	7 A.M.–11 A.M.	12
3	11 A.M.–3 P.M.	16
4	3 P.M.–7 P.M.	9
5	7 P.M.–11 P.M.	11
6	11 P.M.–3 A.M.	4

Owner Avanti Sethi's scheduling problem is to determine how many servers should report for work at the start of each time period in order to minimize the total staff required for one day's operation. (*Hint:* Let X_i equal the number of servers beginning work in time period i, where $i = 1, 2, 3, 4, 5, 6$.) PX

• **19.** A craftsman named William Barnes builds two kinds of birdhouses, one for wrens and a second for bluebirds. Each wren birdhouse takes 4 hours of labor and 4 units of lumber. Each bluebird house requires 2 hours of labor and 12 units of lumber. The craftsman has available 60 hours of labor and 120 units of lumber. Wren houses yield a profit of $6 each, and bluebird houses yield a profit of $15 each.

a) Write out the objective and constraints.
b) Solve graphically. PX

•• **20.** Each coffee table produced by Kevin Watson Designers nets the firm a profit of $9. Each bookcase yields a $12 profit. Watson's firm is small and its resources limited. During any given production period (of 1 week), 10 gallons of varnish and 12 lengths of high-quality redwood are available. Each coffee table requires approximately 1 gallon of varnish and 1 length of redwood. Each bookcase takes 1 gallon of varnish and 2 lengths of wood.

Formulate Watson's production-mix decision as a linear programming problem, and solve. How many tables and bookcases should be produced each week? What will the maximum profit be? PX

•• **21.** Par, Inc., produces a standard golf bag and a deluxe golf bag on a weekly basis. Each golf bag requires time for cutting and dyeing and time for sewing and finishing, as shown in the following table:

	HOURS REQUIRED PER BAG	
PRODUCT	CUTTING AND DYEING	SEWING AND FINISHING
Standard bag	1/2	1
Deluxe bag	1	2/3

The profits per bag and weekly hours available for cutting and dyeing and for sewing and finishing are as follows:

PRODUCT	PROFIT PER UNIT ($)
Standard bag	10
Deluxe bag	8

ACTIVITY	WEEKLY HOURS AVAILABLE
Cutting and dyeing	300
Sewing and finishing	360

Par, Inc., will sell whatever quantities it produces of these two products.

a) Find the mix of standard and deluxe golf bags to produce per week that maximizes weekly profit from these activities.
b) What is the value of the profit? PX

• **22.** Solve the following linear programming problem graphically:

$$\begin{aligned} \text{Minimize cost} &= 4X_1 + 5X_2 \\ \text{Subject to:} \quad X_1 + 2X_2 &\geq 80 \\ 3X_1 + X_2 &\geq 75 \\ X_1, X_2 &\geq 0 \end{aligned}$$

PX

•• **23.** Leach Distributors packages and distributes industrial supplies. A standard shipment can be packaged in a class A container, a class K container, or a class T container. A single class A container yields a profit of $9; a class K container, a profit of $7; and a class T container, a profit of $15. Each shipment prepared requires a certain amount of packing material and a certain amount of time.

RESOURCES NEEDED PER STANDARD SHIPMENT		
CLASS OF CONTAINER	PACKING MATERIAL (POUNDS)	PACKING TIME (HOURS)
A	2	2
K	1	6
T	3	4
Total resource available each week:	130 pounds	240 hours

Hugh Leach, head of the firm, must decide the optimal number of each class of container to pack each week. He is bound by the previously mentioned resource restrictions but also decides that he must keep his 6 full-time packers employed all 240 hours (6 workers × 40 hours) each week.

Formulate and solve this problem using LP software. PX

•• **24.** How many corner points are there in the feasible region of the following problem?

$$\begin{aligned} \text{Minimize cost} &= X - Y \\ \text{Subject to:} \quad X &\leq 4 \\ -X &\leq 2 \\ X + 2Y &\leq 6 \\ -X + 2Y &\leq 8 \\ Y &\geq 0 \end{aligned}$$

(*Note:* X values can be negative in this problem.)

•• **25.** The Denver advertising agency promoting the new Breem dishwashing detergent wants to get the best exposure possible for the product within the $100,000 advertising budget ceiling placed on it. To do so, the agency needs to decide how much of the budget to spend on each of its two most effective media: (1) television spots during the afternoon hours and (2) large ads in the city's Sunday newspaper. Each television spot costs $3,000; each Sunday newspaper ad costs $1,250. The expected exposure, based on industry ratings, is 35,000 viewers for each TV commercial and 20,000 readers for each newspaper advertisement. The agency director, Deborah Kellogg, knows from experience that it is important to use both media in order to reach the broadest spectrum of potential Breem customers. She decides that at least 5 but no more than 25 television spots should be ordered, and that at least 10 newspaper ads should be contracted. How many times should each of the two media be used to obtain maximum exposure while staying within the budget? Use the graphical method to solve. PX

••• **26.** Tri-State Manufacturing has three factories (1, 2, and 3) and three warehouses (A, B, and C). The following table shows the shipping costs between each factory and warehouse, the factory manufacturing capabilities (in thousands), and the warehouse capacities (in thousands). Management would like to keep the warehouses filled to capacity in order to generate demand.

(*contd.*)

TO / FROM	WAREHOUSE A	WAREHOUSE B	WAREHOUSE C	PRODUCTION CAPABILITY
Factory 1	\$ 6	\$ 5	\$ 3	6
Factory 2	\$ 8	\$10	\$ 8	8
Factory 3	\$11	\$14	\$18	10
Capacity	7	12	5	

a) Write the objective function and the constraint equations. Let X_{1A} = 1,000s of units shipped from factory 1 to warehouse A, and so on.
b) Solve by computer. Px

•••• **27.** A fertilizer manufacturer has to fulfill supply contracts to its two main customers (650 tons to Customer A and 800 tons to Customer B). It can meet this demand by shipping existing inventory from any of its three warehouses. Warehouse 1 (W1) has 400 tons of inventory on hand, Warehouse 2 (W2) has 500 tons, and Warehouse 3 (W3) has 600 tons. The company would like to arrange the shipping for the lowest cost possible, where the per-ton transit costs are as follows:

	W1	W2	W3
Customer A	\$7.50	\$6.25	\$6.50
Customer B	\$6.75	\$7.00	\$8.00

a) Explain what each of the six decision variables (V) is: (*Hint:* Look at the Solver report below.)
V A1: ____________
V A2: ____________
V A3: ____________
V B1: ____________
V B2: ____________
V B3: ____________

b) Write out the objective function in terms of the variables (V A1, V A2, etc.) and the objective coefficients.
c) Aside from nonnegativity of the variables, what are the five constraints? Write a short description for each constraint, and write out the formula (and circle the type of equality/inequality).

	Description	Variables and Coefficients	What Type?	RHS
C1:	____________	Formula: ____________	(= > | = | = <)	____________
C2:	____________	Formula: ____________	(= > | = | = <)	____________
C3:	____________	Formula: ____________	(= > | = | = <)	____________
C4:	____________	Formula: ____________	(= > | = | = <)	____________
C5:	____________	Formula: ____________	(= > | = | = <)	____________

After you formulate and enter the linear program for Problem 27 in Excel, the Solver gives you the following sensitivity report:

Adjustable Cells

CELL	NAME	FINAL VALUE	REDUCED COST	OBJECTIVE COEFFICIENT	ALLOWABLE INCREASE	ALLOWABLE DECREASE
\$B\$6	V A1	0	1.5	7.5	1E+30	1.5
\$C\$6	V A2	100	0	6.25	0.25	0.75
\$D\$6	V A3	550	0	6.5	0.75	0.25
\$E\$6	V B1	400	0	6.75	0.5	1E+30
\$F\$6	V B2	400	0	7	0.75	0.5
\$G\$6	V B3	0	0.75	8	1E+30	0.75

Constraints

CELL	NAME	FINAL VALUE	SHADOW PRICE	CONSTRAINT R.H. SIDE	ALLOWABLE INCREASE	ALLOWABLE DECREASE
\$H\$7	C1	650	6.5	650	50	550
\$H\$8	C2	800	7.25	800	50	400
\$H\$9	C3	400	−0.5	400	400	50
\$H\$10	C4	500	−0.25	500	550	50
\$H\$11	C5	550	0	600	1E+30	50

d) How many of the constraints are binding?
e) What is the range of optimality on variable V A3?
f) If we could ship 10 tons less to Customer A, how much money *might* we be able to save? If we could choose to short *either* Customer A or Customer B by 10 tons, which would we prefer to short? Why? Px

•••• **28.** Baton Rouge's Mt. Cedar Hospital is a large, private, 600-bed facility complete with laboratories, operating rooms, and X-ray equipment. In seeking to increase revenues, Mt. Cedar's administration has decided to make a 90-bed addition on a portion of adjacent land currently used for staff parking. The administrators feel that the labs, operating rooms, and X-ray department are not being fully utilized at present and do not need to be expanded to handle additional patients. The addition of 90 beds, however, involves deciding how many beds should be allocated to the medical staff (for medical patients) and how many to the surgical staff (for surgical patients).

The hospital's accounting and medical records departments have provided the following pertinent information: The average hospital stay for a medical patient is 8 days, and the average medical patient generates $2,280 in revenues. The average surgical patient is in the hospital 5 days and generates $1,515 in revenues. The laboratory is capable of handling 15,000 tests per year more than it *was* handling. The average medical patient requires 3.1 lab tests, the average surgical patient 2.6 lab tests. Furthermore, the average medical patient uses 1 X-ray, the average surgical patient 2 X-rays. If the hospital were expanded by 90 beds, the X-ray department could handle up to 7,000 X-rays without significant additional cost. Finally, the administration estimates that up to 2,800 additional operations could be performed in existing operating-room facilities. Medical patients, of course, require no surgery, whereas each surgical patient generally has one surgery performed.

Formulate this problem so as to determine how many medical beds and how many surgical beds should be added to maximize revenues. Assume that the hospital is open 365 days per year. PX

•••• **29.** Bowman Builders manufactures steel storage sheds for commercial use. Joe Bowman, president of Bowman Builders, is contemplating producing sheds for home use. The activities necessary to build an experimental model and related data are given in Table 2.

a) What is the project normal time completion date?
b) Formulate an LP problem to crash this project to 10 weeks.

TABLE 2 Data for Problem 29

ACTIVITY	NORMAL TIME	CRASH TIME	NORMAL COST ($)	CRASH COST ($)	IMMEDIATE PREDECESSORS
A	3	2	1,000	1,600	—
B	2	1	2,000	2,700	—
C	1	1	300	300	—
D	7	3	1,300	1,600	*A*
E	6	3	850	1,000	*B*
F	2	1	4,000	5,000	*C*
G	4	2	1,500	2,000	*D, E*

•••• **30.** You have just been hired as a planner for the municipal school system, and your first assignment is to redesign the subsidized lunch program. In particular, you are to formulate the least expensive lunch menu that will still meet all state and federal nutritional guidelines.

The guidelines are as follows: A meal must be between 500 and 800 calories. It must contain at least 200 calories of protein, at least 200 calories of carbohydrates, and no more than 400 calories of fat. It also needs to have at least 200 calories of a food classified as a fruit or vegetable.

Table 3 provides a list of the foods you can consider as possible menu items, with contract-determined prices and nutritional information. Note that all percentages sum to 100% per food—as all calories are protein, carbohydrate, or fat calories. For example, a serving of applesauce has 100 calories, all of which are carbohydrates, and it counts as a fruit/veg food. You are allowed to use fractional servings, such as 2.25 servings of turkey breast and a 0.33 portion of salad. Costs and nutritional attributes scale likewise: e.g., a 0.33 portion of salad costs $.30 and has 33 calories.

TABLE 3 Data for Problem 30

FOOD	COST/SERVING	CALORIES/SERVING	% PROTEIN	% CARBS	% FAT	FRUIT/VEG
Applesauce	$0.30	100	0%	100%	0%	Y
Canned corn	$0.40	150	20%	80%	0%	Y
Fried chicken	$0.90	250	55%	5%	40%	N
French fries	$0.20	400	5%	35%	60%	N
Mac and cheese	$0.50	430	20%	30%	50%	N
Turkey breast	$1.50	300	67%	0%	33%	N
Garden salad	$0.90	100	15%	40%	45%	Y

Formulate and solve as a linear problem. Print out your formulation in Excel showing the objective function coefficients and constraint matrix in standard form.

- Display, on a separate page, the full *Answer Report* as generated by Excel Solver.
- Highlight *and label as Z* the objective value for the optimal solution on the Answer Report.
- Highlight the nonzero decision variables for the optimal solution on the Answer Report.
- Display, on a separate page, the full *Sensitivity Report* as generated by Excel Solver. PX

Refer to MyOMLab for these additional homework problems: 31–40

CASE STUDY

Quain Lawn and Garden, Inc.

Bill and Jeanne Quain spent a career as a husband-and-wife real estate investment partnership in Atlantic City, New Jersey. When they finally retired to a 25-acre farm in nearby Cape May County, they became ardent amateur gardeners. Bill planted shrubs and fruit trees, and Jeanne spent her hours potting all sizes of plants. When the volume of shrubs and plants reached the point that the Quains began to think of their hobby in a serious vein, they built a greenhouse adjacent to their home and installed heating and watering systems.

By 2012, the Quains realized their retirement from real estate had really only led to a second career—in the plant and shrub business—and they filed for a New Jersey business license. Within a matter of months, they asked their attorney to file incorporation documents and formed the firm Quain Lawn and Garden, Inc.

Early in the new business's existence, Bill Quain recognized the need for a high-quality commercial fertilizer that he could blend himself, both for sale and for his own nursery. His goal was to keep his costs to a minimum while producing a top-notch product that was especially suited to the New Jersey climate.

Working with chemists at Rutgers University, Quain blended "Quain-Grow." It consists of four chemical compounds, C-30, C-92, D-21, and E-11. The cost per pound for each compound is indicated in the following table:

CHEMICAL COMPOUND	COST PER POUND
C-30	$.12
C-92	.09
D-21	.11
E-11	.04

The specifications for Quain-Grow are established as:

a) Chemical E-11 must constitute at least 15% of the blend.
b) C-92 and C-30 must together constitute at least 45% of the blend.
c) D-21 and C-92 can together constitute no more than 30% of the blend.
d) Quain-Grow is packaged and sold in 50-lb bags.

Discussion Questions

1. Formulate an LP problem to determine what blend of the four chemicals will allow Quain to minimize the cost of a 50-lb bag of the fertilizer.
2. Solve to find the best solution.

- **Additional Case Studies:** Visit **www.myomlab.com** or **www.pearsonhighered.com/heizer** for these free case studies:
Chase Manhattan Bank: This scheduling case involves finding the optimal number of full-time versus part-time employees at a bank.
Coastal States Chemical: The company must prepare for a shortage of natural gas.

Bibliography

Balakrishman, R., B. Render, and R. M. Stair. *Managerial Decision Modeling with Spreadsheets*, 3rd ed. Upper Saddle River, NJ: Prentice Hall, 2012.

Denton, Brian T. "AusWest Timbers Uses an Optimization Model to Improve Its Manufacturing Process." *Interfaces* 38, no. 4 (July–August 2008): 341–344.

Duran, G., et al. "Scheduling the Chilean Soccer League by Integer Programming." *Interfaces* 37, no. 6 (November–December 2007): 539–555.

Harrod, Steven. "A Spreadsheet-Based, Matrix Formulation Linear Programming Lesson." *Decision Sciences Journal of Innovative Education* 7, no. 1 (January 2009): 249.

Martin, C. H. "Ohio University's College of Business Uses Integer Programming to Schedule Classes." *Interfaces* 34 (November–December 2004): 460–465.

Matthews, C. H. "Using Linear Programming to Minimize the Cost of Nurse Personnel." *Journal of Health Care Finance* (September 2005).

Pasupathy, K., and A. Medina-Borja. "Integrating Excel, Access, and Visual Basic to Deploy Performance Measurement and Evaluation at the American Red Cross." *Interfaces* 38, no. 4 (July–August 2008): 324–340.

Render, B., R. M. Stair, and Michael Hanna. *Quantitative Analysis for Management*, 11th ed. Upper Saddle River, NJ: Prentice Hall, 2012.

Sodhi, M. S., and S. Norri. "A Fast and Optimal Modeling Approach Applied to Crew Rostering at London Underground." *Annals of OR* 127 (March 2004): 259.

Taylor, Bernard. *Introduction to Management Science*, 10th ed. Upper Saddle River, NJ: Prentice Hall, 2011.

APPENDIX

SOLUTIONS TO EVEN-NUMBERED PROBLEMS

2 Profit = \$100 at $X = 0, Y = 10$

4 **(b)** Yes; $P = \$3{,}000$ at (75, 75) and (50, 150)

6 **(a)** Min $X_1 + 2X_2$
Subject to: $X_1 + X_2 \geq 40$
$2X_1 + 4X_2 \geq 60$
$x_1 \leq 15$
(b) Cost = \$.65 at (15, 25)
(c) 65¢

8 $x_1 = 200, x_2 = 0$, profit = \$18,000

10 10 Alpha 1s, 24 Beta 2s, profit = \$55,200

12 **(a)** $x_1 = 25.71, x_2 = 21.43$
(b) Cost = \$68.57

14 **(a)** $x_1 = 7.95, x_2 = 5.95, x_3 = 12.6, P = \$143.76$
(b) No unused time
(c) 26¢
(d) \$7.86

16 **(a)** Let X_{ij} = number of students bused from sector i to school j.
Objective: minimize total travel miles =
$5X_{AB} + 8X_{AC} + 6X_{AE}$
$+ 0X_{BB} + 4X_{BC} + 12X_{BE}$
$+ 4x_{CB} + 0X_{CC} + 7X_{CE}$
$+ 7X_{DB} + 2X_{DC} + 5x_{DE}$
$+ 12X_{EB} + 7X_{EC} + 0X_{EE}$
Subject to:
$X_{AB} + X_{AC} + X_{AE} = 700$ (number of students in sector A)
$X_{BB} + X_{BC} + X_{BE} = 500$ (number students in sector B)
$X_{CB} + X_{CC} + X_{CE} = 100$ (number students in sector C)
$X_{DB} + X_{DC} + X_{DE} = 800$ (number students in sector D)
$X_{EB} + X_{EC} + X_{EE} = 400$ (number of students in sector E)
$X_{AB} + X_{BB} + X_{CB} + X_{DB} + X_{EB} \leq 900$ (school B capacity)
$X_{AC} + X_{BC} + X_{CC} + X_{DC} + X_{EC} \leq 900$ (school C capacity)
$X_{AE} + X_{BE} + X_{CE} + X_{DE} + X_{EE} \leq 900$ (school E capacity)
(b) Solution: $X_{AB} = 400$
$X_{AE} = 300$
$X_{BB} = 500$
$X_{CC} = 100$
$X_{DC} = 800$
$X_{EE} = 400$
Distance = 5,400 "student miles"

18 Hire 30 workers; three solutions are feasible; two of these are:
16 begin at 7 A.M.
9 begin at 3 P.M.
2 begin at 7 P.M.
3 begin at 11 P.M.
An alternate optimum is:
3 begin at 3 A.M.
9 begin at 7 A.M.
7 begin at 11 A.M.
2 begin at 3 P.M.
9 begin at 7 P.M.
0 begin at 11 P.M.

20 Max $P = 9x_1 + 12x_2$
Subject to:
$x_1 + x_2 \leq 10$
$x_1 + 2x_2 \leq 12$
$x_1 = 8, x_2 = 2$; profit = \$96

22 $x_1 = 14, x_2 = 33$, cost = 221

24 5 corner points

26 **(a)** Minimize $= 6X_{1A} + 5X_{1B} + 3X_{1C} + 8X_{2A} + 10X_{2B} + 8X_{2C} + 11X_{3A} + 14X_{3B} + 18X_{3C}$
Subject to:
$X_{1A} + X_{2A} + X_{3A} = 7$
$X_{1B} + X_{2B} + X_{3B} = 12$
$X_{1C} + X_{2C} + X_{3C} = 5$
$X_{1A} + X_{1B} + X_{1C} \leq 6$
$X_{2A} + X_{2B} + X_{2C} \leq 8$
$X_{3A} + X_{3B} + X_{3C} \leq 10$
(b) Minimum cost = \$219,000

28 One approach results in 2,790 medical patients and 2,104 surgical patients, with a revenue of \$9,551,659 per year (which can change slightly to \$9,548,760 with rounding). This yields 61 integer medical beds and 29 integer surgical beds.

30 Apple sauce = 0, Canned corn = 1.33, Fried chicken = 0.46, French fries = 0, Mac & Cheese = 1.13, Turkey = 0, Garden salad = 0, Cost = \$1.51.

Rapid Review

Main Heading	Review Material	MyOMLab
WHY USE LINEAR PROGRAMMING?	■ **Linear programming (LP)**—A mathematical technique designed to help operations managers plan and make decisions relative to allocation of resources.	
REQUIREMENTS OF A LINEAR PROGRAMMING PROBLEM	■ **Objective function**—A mathematical expression in linear programming that maximizes or minimizes some quantity (often profit or cost, but any goal may be used). ■ **Constraints**—Restrictions that limit the degree to which a manager can pursue an objective. All LP problems have four properties in common: 1. LP problems seek to *maximize* or *minimize* some quantity. We refer to this property as the *objective function* of an LP problem. 2. The presence of restrictions, or *constraints*, limits the degree to which we can pursue our objective. We want, therefore, to maximize or minimize a quantity (the objective function) subject to limited resources (the constraints). 3. There must be *alternative courses of action* to choose from. 4. The objective and constraints in linear programming problems must be expressed in terms of *linear equations* or inequalities.	
FORMULATING LINEAR PROGRAMMING PROBLEMS	One of the most common linear programming applications is the *product-mix problem*. Two or more products are usually produced using limited resources. For example, a company might like to determine how many units of each product it should produce to maximize overall profit, given its limited resources. An important aspect of linear programming is that certain interactions will exist between variables. The more units of one product that a firm produces, the fewer it can make of other products.	Virtual Office Hours for Solved Problem: 1 **ACTIVE MODEL 1**
GRAPHICAL SOLUTION TO A LINEAR PROGRAMMING PROBLEM	■ **Graphical solution approach**—A means of plotting a solution to a two-variable problem on a graph. ■ **Decision variables**—Choices available to a decision maker. Constraints of the form $X \geq 0$ are called *nonnegativity constraints*. ■ **Feasible region**—The set of all feasible combinations of decision variables. Any point inside the feasible region represents a *feasible solution*, while any point outside the feasible region represents an *infeasible solution*. ■ **Iso-profit line method**—An approach to identifying the optimum point in a graphic linear programming problem. The line that touches a particular point of the feasible region will pinpoint the optimal solution. ■ **Corner-point method**—Another method for solving graphical linear programming problems. The mathematical theory behind linear programming states that an optimal solution to any problem will lie at a *corner point*, or an *extreme point*, of the feasible region. Hence, it is necessary to find only the values of the variables at each corner; the optimal solution will lie at one (or more) of them. This is the corner-point method. 	Problems: 1, 2, 4, 7–10, 15, 19–21 Virtual Office Hours for Solved Problem: 2
SENSITIVITY ANALYSIS	■ **Parameter**—A numerical value that is given in a model. ■ **Sensitivity analysis**—An analysis that projects how much a solution may change if there are changes in the variables or input data. Sensitivity analysis is also called *postoptimality analysis*. There are two approaches to determining just how sensitive an optimal solution is to changes: (1) a trial-and-error approach and (2) the analytic postoptimality method.	Problems: 14, 15, 27, 30

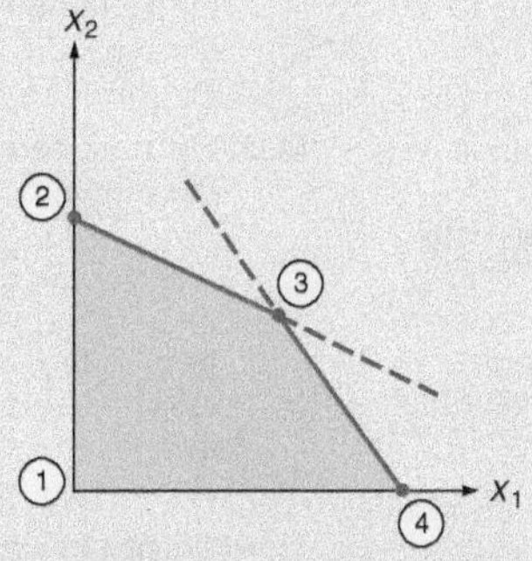

Main Heading	Review Material	MyOMLab
	To use the analytic postoptimality method, after an LP problem has been solved, we determine a range of changes in problem parameters that will not affect the optimal solution or change the variables in the solution. LP software has this capability. While using the information in a sensitivity report to answer what-if questions, we assume that we are considering a change to only a *single* input data value at a time. That is, the sensitivity information does not generally apply to simultaneous changes in several input data values. ■ **Shadow price** (or **dual value**)—The value of one additional unit of a scarce resource in LP. The shadow price is valid as long as the right-hand side of the constraint stays in a range within which all current corner points continue to exist. The information to compute the upper and lower limits of this range is given by the entries labeled Allowable Increase and Allowable Decrease in the sensitivity report.	
SOLVING MINIMIZATION PROBLEMS	■ **Iso-cost**—An approach to solving a linear programming minimization problem graphically. The iso-cost line approach to solving minimization problems is analogous to the iso-profit approach for maximization problems, but successive iso-cost lines are drawn *inward* instead of outward.	Virtual Office Hours for Solved Problem: 3 Problems: 3, 5, 6, 11, 12, 22, 24
LINEAR PROGRAMMING APPLICATIONS	The *diet problem*, known in agricultural applications as the *feed-mix problem*, involves specifying a food or feed ingredient combination that will satisfy stated nutritional requirements at a minimum cost level. *Labor scheduling problems* address staffing needs over a specific time period. They are especially useful when managers have some flexibility in assigning workers to jobs that require overlapping or interchangeable talents.	Problems: 16–18, 23, 25–29
THE SIMPLEX METHOD OF LP	■ **Simplex method**—An algorithm for solving linear programming problems of all sizes. The simplex method is actually a set of instructions with which we examine corner points in a methodical fashion until we arrive at the best solution—highest profit or lowest cost. Computer programs (such as Excel OM and POM for Windows) and Excel's Solver add-in are available to solve linear programming problems via the simplex method.	

Self Test

■ **Before taking the self-test,** refer to the learning objectives listed at the beginning of the text and the key terms listed at the end of the text.

LO1. Which of the following is *not* a valid LP constraint formulation?
- **a)** $3X + 4Y \leq 12$
- **b)** $2X \times 2Y \leq 12$
- **c)** $3Y + 2Z = 18$
- **d)** $100 \geq X + Y$
- **e)** $2.5X + 1.5Z = 30.6$

LO2. Using a *graphical solution procedure* to solve a maximization problem requires that we:
- **a)** move the iso-profit line up until it no longer intersects with any constraint equation.
- **b)** move the iso-profit line down until it no longer intersects with any constraint equation.
- **c)** apply the method of simultaneous equations to solve for the intersections of constraints.
- **d)** find the value of the objective function at the origin.

LO3. Consider the following linear programming problem:

$$\begin{aligned} \text{Maximize } & 4X + 10Y \\ \text{Subject to: } & 3X + 4Y \leq 480 \\ & 4X + 2Y \leq 360 \\ & X, Y \geq 0 \end{aligned}$$

The feasible corner points are (48,84), (0,120), (0,0), and (90,0). What is the maximum possible value for the objective function?
a) 1,032 **b)** 1,200 **c)** 360 **d)** 1,600 **e)** 840

LO4. A zero shadow price for a resource ordinarily means that:
- **a)** the resource is scarce.
- **b)** the resource constraint was redundant.
- **c)** the resource has not been used up.
- **d)** something is wrong with the problem formulation.
- **e)** none of the above.

LO5. For these two constraints, which point is in the feasible region of this minimization problem?

$$14x + 6y \geq 42 \quad \text{and} \quad x + y \geq 3$$

- **a)** $x = -1, y = 1$
- **b)** $x = 0, y = 4$
- **c)** $x = 2, y = 1$
- **d)** $x = 5, y = 1$
- **e)** $x = 2, y = 0$

LO6. When applying LP to diet problems, the objective function is usually designed to:
- **a)** maximize profits from blends of nutrients.
- **b)** maximize ingredient blends.
- **c)** minimize production losses.
- **d)** maximize the number of products to be produced.
- **e)** minimize the costs of nutrient blends.

Answers: LO1. b; LO2. a; LO3. b; LO4. c; LO5. d; LO6. e.

Design of Goods and Services

OUTLINE

GLOBAL COMPANY PROFILE: *Regal Marine*

10 OM STRATEGY DECISIONS

- *Design of Goods and Services*
- Managing Quality
- Process Strategy
- Location Strategies
- Layout Strategies
- Human Resources
- Supply-Chain Management
- Inventory Management
- Scheduling
- Maintenance

Product Strategy Provides Competitive Advantage at Regal Marine

Forty years after its founding by potato farmer Paul Kuck, Regal Marine has become a powerful force on the waters of the world. The world's third-largest boat manufacturer (by global sales), Regal exports to 30 countries, including Russia and China. Almost one-third of its sales are overseas.

Product design is critical in the highly competitive pleasure boat business: "We keep in touch with our customers and we respond to the marketplace," says Kuck. "We're introducing six new models this year alone. I'd say we're definitely on the aggressive end of the spectrum."

With changing consumer tastes, compounded by material changes and ever-improving marine engineering, the design function is under constant pressure. Added to these pressures is the

CAD/CAM is used to design the rain cover of a new product. This process results in faster and more efficient design and production.

Here the deck, suspended from ceiling cranes, is being finished prior to being moved to join the hull. Regal is one of the first boat builders in the world to earn the ISO 9001 quality certification.

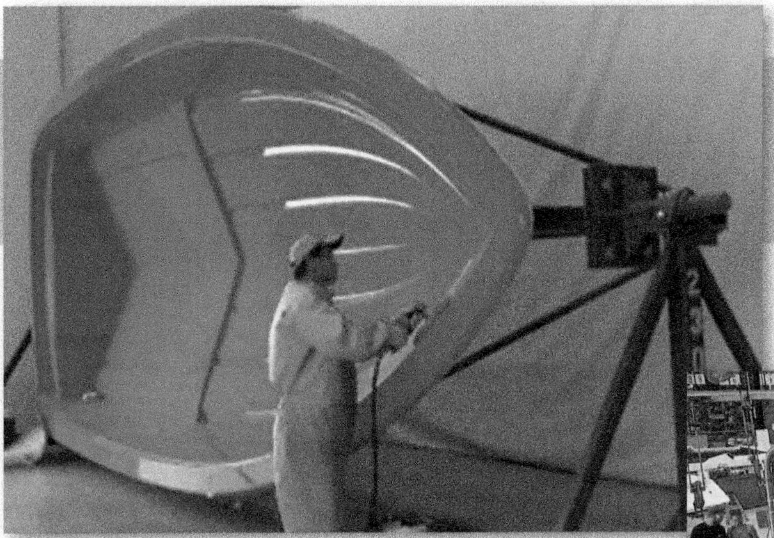

Here the finishing touches are being put on a mold used for forming the hull.

Once a hull has been pulled from the mold, it travels down a monorail assembly path. JIT inventory delivers engines, wiring, seats, flooring, and interiors when needed.

constant issue of cost competitiveness combined with the need to provide good value for customers.

Consequently, Regal Marine is a frequent user of computer-aided design (CAD). New designs come to life via Regal's three-dimensional CAD system, borrowed from automotive technology. Regal's naval architect's goal is to continue to reduce the time from concept to prototype to production. The sophisticated CAD system not only has reduced product development time and cost, but also has reduced problems with tooling and production, resulting in a superior product.

All of Regal's products, from its $14,000 19-foot boat to the $500,000 52-foot Sports yacht, follow a similar production process. Hulls and decks are separately hand-produced by spraying preformed molds with three to five layers of a fiberglass laminate. The hulls and decks harden and are removed to become the lower and upper structure of the boat. As they move to the assembly line, they are joined and components added at each workstation.

Wooden components, precut in-house by computer-driven routers, are delivered on a just-in-time basis for installation at one station. Engines—one of the few purchased components—are installed at another. Racks of electrical wiring harnesses, engineered and rigged in-house, are then installed. An in-house upholstery department delivers customized seats, beds, dashboards, or other cushioned components. Finally, chrome fixtures are put in place, and the boat is sent to Regal's test tank for watertight, gauge, and system inspection.

At the final stage, smaller boats, such as this one, are placed in this test tank, where a rain machine ensures watertight fits.

LEARNING OBJECTIVES

- LO1 ***Define*** product life cycle
- LO2 ***Describe*** a product development system
- LO3 ***Build*** a house of quality
- LO4 ***Explain*** how time-based competition is implemented by OM
- LO5 ***Describe*** how goods and services are defined by OM
- LO6 ***Describe*** the documents needed for production
- LO7 ***Explain*** how the customer participates in the design and delivery of services
- LO8 ***Apply*** decision trees to product issues

Goods and Services Selection

STUDENT TIP Product strategy is critical to achieving competitive advantage.

Global firms like Regal Marine know that the basis for an organization's existence is the good or service it provides society. Great products are the keys to success. Anything less than an excellent product strategy can be devastating to a firm. To maximize the potential for success, many companies focus on only a few products and then concentrate on those products. For instance, Honda's focus, its core competency, is engines. Virtually all of Honda's sales (autos, motorcycles, generators, lawn mowers) are based on its outstanding engine technology. Likewise, Intel's focus is on microprocessors, and Michelin's is on tires.

However, because most products have a limited and even predictable life cycle, companies must constantly be looking for new products to design, develop, and take to market. Operations managers insist on strong communication among customer, product, processes, and suppliers that results in a high success rate for their new products. 3M's goal is to produce 30% of its profit from products introduced in the past 4 years. DuPont generates almost 40% of its revenue from products launched in the past 5 years. Benchmarks, of course, vary by industry; Regal introduces six new boats a year, and Rubbermaid introduces a new product each day!

VIDEO 1 Product Strategy at Regal Marine

The importance of new products cannot be overestimated. As Figure 1 shows, leading companies generate a substantial portion of their sales from products less than 5 years old. The need for new products is why Gillette developed its multiblade razors, in spite of continuing high sales of its phenomenally successful Sensor razor, and why Disney continues to innovate with new rides and new parks even though it is already the world's leading family entertainment company.

Despite constant efforts to introduce viable new products, many new products do not succeed. Product selection, definition, and design occur frequently—perhaps hundreds of times for each financially successful product. DuPont estimates that it takes 250 ideas to yield one *marketable* product. Operations managers and their organizations build cultures that accept

Figure 1
Innovation and New Products

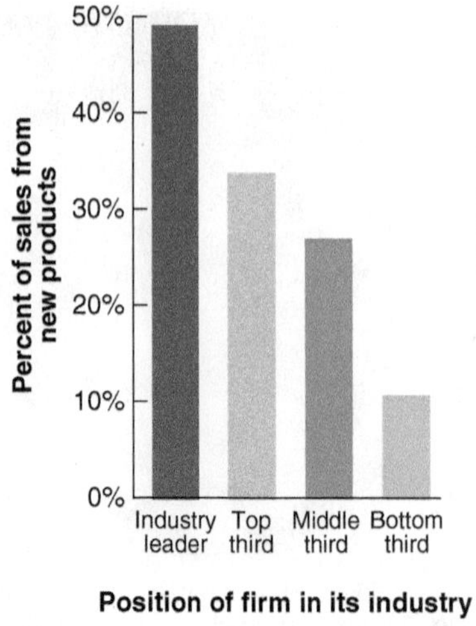

The higher the percentage of sales from the last 5 years, the more likely the firm is to be a leader.

this risk and tolerate failure. They learn to accommodate a high volume of new product ideas while maintaining the production activities to which they are already committed.

STUDENT TIP
Motorola went through 3,000 working models before it developed its first pocket cell phone.

Note that many *service firms* also refer to their offerings as products. For instance, when Allstate Insurance offers a new homeowner's policy, it is referred to as a new "product." Similarly, when Citicorp opens a mortgage department, it offers a number of new mortgage "products." Although the term *products* may often refer to tangible goods, it also refers to offerings by service organizations.

An effective product strategy links product decisions with investment, market share, and product life cycle, and defines the breadth of the product line. The *objective of the* **product decision** *is to develop and implement a product strategy that meets the demands of the marketplace with a competitive advantage.* As one of the 10 decisions of OM, product strategy may focus on developing a competitive advantage via differentiation, low cost, rapid response, or a combination of these.

Product decision
The selection, definition, and design of products.

Product Strategy Options Support Competitive Advantage

A world of options exists in the selection, definition, and design of products. Product selection is choosing the good or service to provide customers or clients. For instance, hospitals specialize in various types of patients and medical procedures. A hospital's management may decide to operate a general-purpose hospital or a maternity hospital or, as in the case of the Canadian hospital Shouldice, to specialize in hernias. Hospitals select their products when they decide what kind of hospital to be. Numerous other options exist for hospitals, just as they exist for Taco Bell and Toyota.

Service organizations like Shouldice Hospital *differentiate* themselves through their product. Shouldice differentiates itself by offering a distinctly unique and high-quality product. Its world-renowned specialization in hernia-repair service is so effective it allows patients to return

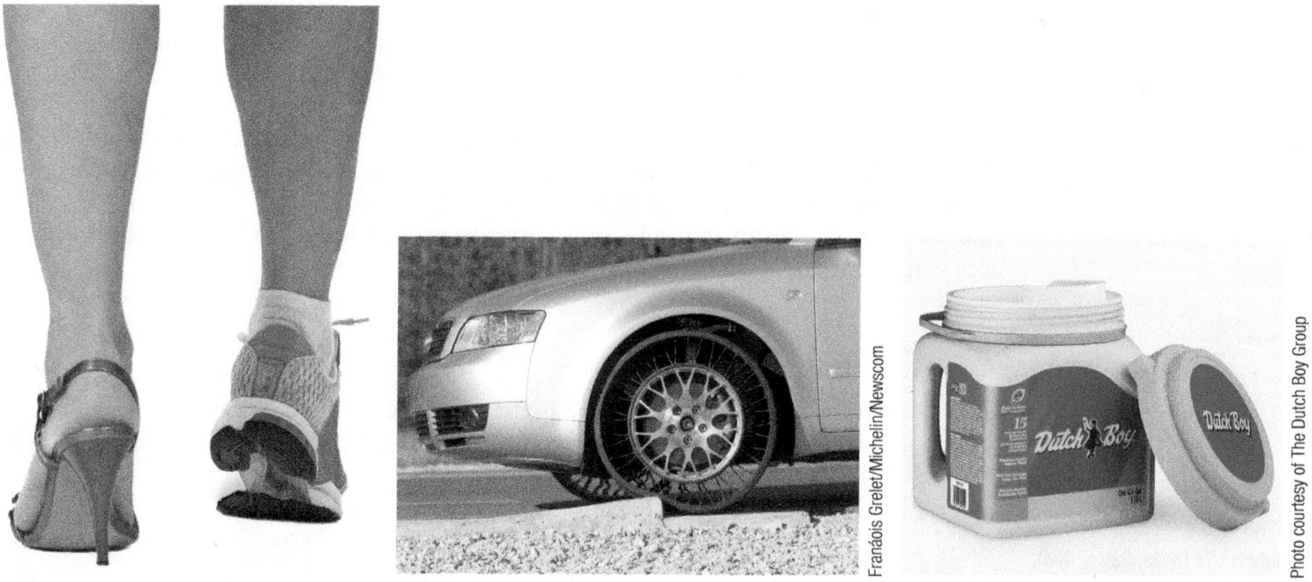

Frandois Grelet/Michelin/Newscom

Photo courtesy of The Dutch Boy Group

(a) Markets: In its creative way, the market has moved athletic shoes from utilitarian footwear into fashionable accessories.

(b) Technology: Michelin's latest technology: radical new tires that don't go flat.

(c) Packaging: Sherwin Williams's Dutch Boy has revolutionized the paint industry with its square Twist & Pour paint container.

Product Innovation Can Be Driven By Markets, Technology, and Packaging. Whether it is design focused on changes in the market (a), the application of technology at Michelin (b), or a new container at Sherwin-Williams (c), operations managers need to remind themselves that the creative process is ongoing with major production implications.

to normal living in 8 days as opposed to the average 2 weeks—and with very few complications. The entire production system is designed for this one product. Local anesthetics are used; patients enter and leave the operating room on their own; meals are served in a common dining room, encouraging patients to get out of bed for meals and join fellow patients in the lounge. As Shouldice demonstrates, product selection affects the entire production system.

Taco Bell has developed and executed a *low-cost* strategy through product design. By designing a product (its menu) that can be produced with a minimum of labor in small kitchens, Taco Bell has developed a product line that is both low cost and high value. Successful product design has allowed Taco Bell to increase the food content of its products from 27¢ to 45¢ of each sales dollar.

Toyota's strategy is *rapid response* to changing consumer demand. By executing the fastest automobile design in the industry, Toyota has driven the speed of product development down to well under 2 years in an industry whose standard is still over 2 years. The shorter design time allows Toyota to get a car to market before consumer tastes change and to do so with the latest technology and innovations.

Product decisions are fundamental to an organization's strategy and have major implications throughout the operations function. For instance, GM's steering columns are a good example of the strong role product design plays in both quality and efficiency. The redesigned steering column is simpler, with about 30% fewer parts than its predecessor. The result: Assembly time is one-third that of the older column, and the new column's quality is about seven times higher. As an added bonus, machinery on the new line costs a third less than that on the old line.

Product Life Cycles

Products are born. They live and they die. They are cast aside by a changing society. It may be helpful to think of a product's life as divided into four phases. Those phases are introduction, growth, maturity, and decline.

Product life cycles may be a matter of a few days (a concert t-shirt), months (seasonal fashions), years (Madden NFL football video game), or decades (Boeing 737). Regardless of the length of the cycle, the task for the operations manager is the same: to design a system that helps introduce new products successfully. If the operations function cannot perform effectively at this stage, the firm may be saddled with losers—products that cannot be produced efficiently and perhaps not at all.

LO1 *Define* product life cycle

Figure 2 shows the four life cycle stages and the relationship of product sales, cash flow, and profit over the life cycle of a product. Note that typically a firm has a negative cash flow while it develops a product. When the product is successful, those losses may be recovered. Eventually, the successful product may yield a profit prior to its decline. However, the profit is fleeting—hence, the constant demand for new products.

Life Cycle and Strategy

Just as operations managers must be prepared to develop new products, they must also be prepared to develop *strategies* for new and *existing* products. Periodic examination of

Figure 2
Product Life Cycle, Sales, Cost, and Profit

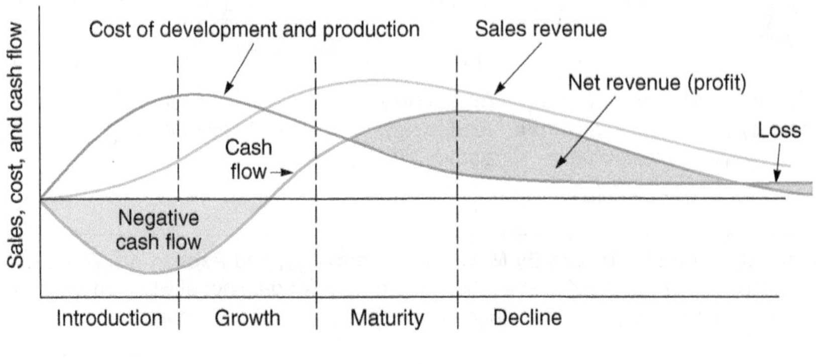

products is appropriate because *strategies change as products move through their life cycle*. Successful product strategies require determining the best strategy for each product based on its position in its life cycle. A firm, therefore, identifies products or families of products and their position in the life cycle. Let us review some strategy options as products move through their life cycles.

Introductory Phase Because products in the introductory phase are still being "fine-tuned" for the market, as are their production techniques, they may warrant unusual expenditures for (1) research, (2) product development, (3) process modification and enhancement, and (4) supplier development. For example, when the iPhone was first introduced, the features desired by the public were still being determined. At the same time, operations managers were still groping for the best manufacturing techniques.

Growth Phase In the growth phase, product design has begun to stabilize, and effective forecasting of capacity requirements is necessary. Adding capacity or enhancing existing capacity to accommodate the increase in product demand may be necessary.

Maturity Phase By the time a product is mature, competitors are established. So high-volume, innovative production may be appropriate. Improved cost control, reduction in options, and a paring down of the product line may be effective or necessary for profitability and market share.

Decline Phase Management may need to be ruthless with those products whose life cycle is at an end. Dying products are typically poor products in which to invest resources and managerial talent. Unless dying products make some unique contribution to the firm's reputation or its product line or can be sold with an unusually high contribution, their production should be terminated.[1]

Product-by-Value Analysis

The effective operations manager selects items that show the greatest promise. This is the Pareto principle applied to product mix: Resources are to be invested in the critical few and not the trivial many. **Product-by-value analysis** lists products in descending order of their *individual dollar contribution* to the firm. It also lists the *total annual dollar contribution* of the product. Low contribution on a per-unit basis by a particular product may look substantially different if it represents a large portion of the company's sales.

Product-by-value analysis
A list of products, in descending order of their individual dollar contribution to the firm, as well as the *total annual dollar contribution* of the product.

A product-by-value report allows management to evaluate possible strategies for each product. These may include increasing cash flow (e.g., increasing contribution by raising selling price or lowering cost), increasing market penetration (improving quality and/or reducing cost or price), or reducing costs (improving the production process). The report may also tell management which product offerings should be eliminated and which fail to justify further investment in research and development or capital equipment. Product-by-value analysis focuses attention on the strategic direction for each product.

Generating New Products

STUDENT TIP
Societies reward those who supply new products that reflect their needs.

Because products die; because products must be weeded out and replaced; because firms generate most of their revenue and profit from new products—product selection, definition, and design take place on a continuing basis. Consider recent product changes: TV to HDTV, radio to satellite radio, coffee shops to Starbucks lifestyle coffee, traveling circuses to Cirque du Soleil, landlines to cell phones, cell phone to iPhone, Walkman to iPod, mops to Swiffers—and the list goes on. Knowing how to successfully find and develop new products is a requirement.

[1]*Contribution* is defined as the difference between direct cost and selling price. Direct costs are labor and material that go into the product.

Aggressive new product development requires that organizations build structures internally that have open communication with customers, innovative product development cultures, aggressive R&D, strong leadership, formal incentives, and training. Only then can a firm profitably and energetically focus on specific opportunities such as the following:

1. *Understanding the customer* is the premier issue in new-product development. Many commercially important products are initially thought of and even prototyped by users rather than producers. Such products tend to be developed by "lead users"—companies, organizations, or individuals that are well ahead of market trends and have needs that go far beyond those of average users. The operations manager must be "tuned in" to the market and particularly these innovative lead users.
2. *Economic change* brings increasing levels of affluence in the long run but economic cycles and price changes in the short run. In the long run, for instance, more and more people can afford automobiles, but in the short run, a recession may weaken the demand for automobiles.
3. *Sociological and demographic change* may appear in such factors as decreasing family size. This trend alters the size preference for homes, apartments, and automobiles.
4. *Technological change* makes possible everything from cell phones to iPads to artificial hearts.
5. *Political and legal change* brings about new trade agreements, tariffs, and government requirements.
6. Other changes may be brought about through *market practice, professional standards, suppliers*, and *distributors*.

Operations managers must be aware of these dynamics and be able to anticipate changes in product opportunities, the products themselves, product volume, and product mix.

Product Development

Product Development System

LO2 *Describe* a product development system

An effective product strategy links product decisions with other business functions, such as R&D, engineering, marketing, and finance. A firm requires cash for product development, an understanding of the marketplace, and the necessary human talents. The product development system may well determine not only product success but also the firm's future. Figure 3 shows the stages of product development. In this system, product options go through a series of steps, each having its own screening and evaluation criteria, but providing a continuing flow of information to prior steps.

Optimum product development depends not only on support from other parts of the firm but also on the successful integration of all 10 of the OM decisions, from product design to maintenance. Identifying products that appear likely to capture market share, be cost-effective, and be profitable but are, in fact, very difficult to produce may lead to failure rather than success.

Quality Function Deployment (QFD)

Quality function deployment (QFD)

A process for determining customer requirements (customer "wants") and translating them into the attributes (the "hows") that each functional area can understand and act on.

House of quality

A part of the quality function deployment process that utilizes a planning matrix to relate customer "wants" to "how" the firm is going to meet those "wants."

Quality function deployment (QFD) refers to both (1) determining what will satisfy the customer and (2) translating those customer desires into the target design. The idea is to capture a rich understanding of customer wants and to identify alternative process solutions. This information is then integrated into the evolving product design. QFD is used early in the design process to help determine *what will satisfy the customer* and *where to deploy quality efforts*.

One of the tools of QFD is the **house of quality**, a graphic technique for defining the relationship between customer desires and product (or service). Only by defining this relationship in a rigorous way can managers design products and processes with features desired by customers.

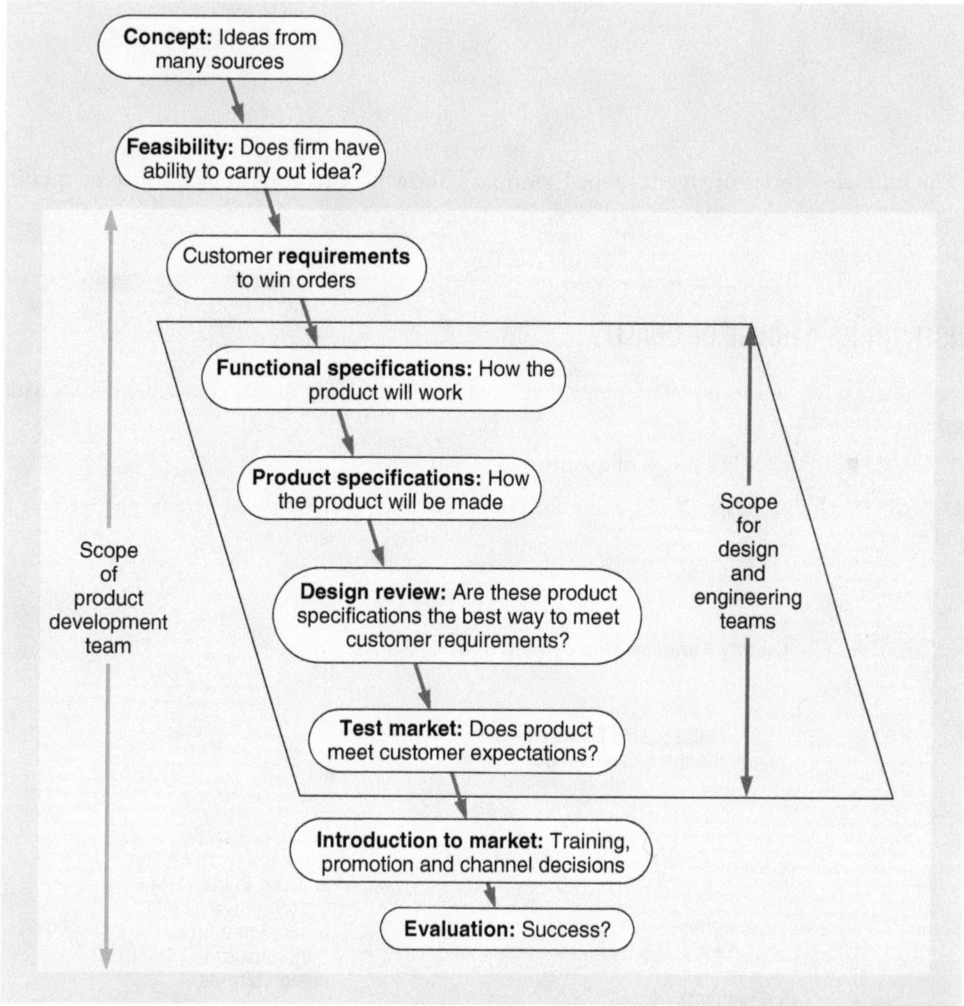

Figure 3

Product Development Stages

Product concepts are developed from a variety of sources, both external and internal to the firm. Concepts that survive the product idea stage progress through various stages, with nearly constant review, feedback, and evaluation in a highly participative environment to minimize failure.

Defining this relationship is the first step in building a world-class production system. To build the house of quality, we perform seven basic steps:

LO3 *Build* a house of quality

1. Identify customer *wants*. (What do customers want in this product?)
2. Identify *how* the good/service will satisfy customer wants. (Identify specific product characteristics, features, or attributes and show how they will satisfy customer *wants*.)
3. Relate customer *wants* to product *hows*. (Build a matrix, as in Example 1, that shows this relationship.)
4. Identify relationships between the firm's *hows*. (How do our *hows* tie together? For instance, in the following example, there is a high relationship between low electricity requirements and auto focus, auto exposure, and number of pixels because they all require electricity. This relationship is shown in the "roof" of the house in Example 1.)
5. Develop importance ratings. (Using the *customer's* importance ratings and weights for the relationships shown in the matrix, compute *our* importance ratings, as in Example 1.)
6. Evaluate competing products. (How well do competing products meet customer wants? Such an evaluation, as shown in the two columns on the right of the figure in Example 1, would be based on market research.)
7. Determine the desirable technical attributes, your performance, and the competitor's performance against these attributes. (This is done at the bottom of the figure in Example 1.)

The following series of overlays for Example 1 show how to construct a house of quality.

Example 1

CONSTRUCTING A HOUSE OF QUALITY

Great Cameras, Inc., wants a methodology that strengthens its ability to meet customer desires with its new digital camera.

APPROACH ▶ Use QFD's house of quality.

SOLUTION ▶ Build the house of quality for Great Cameras, Inc. We do so here using Overlays 1, 2, 3, and 4.

To view the building of the house of quality, please visit www.pearsonhighered.com/heizer and download the House of Quality PowerPoint file.

Quality Function Deployment's (QFD) House of Quality

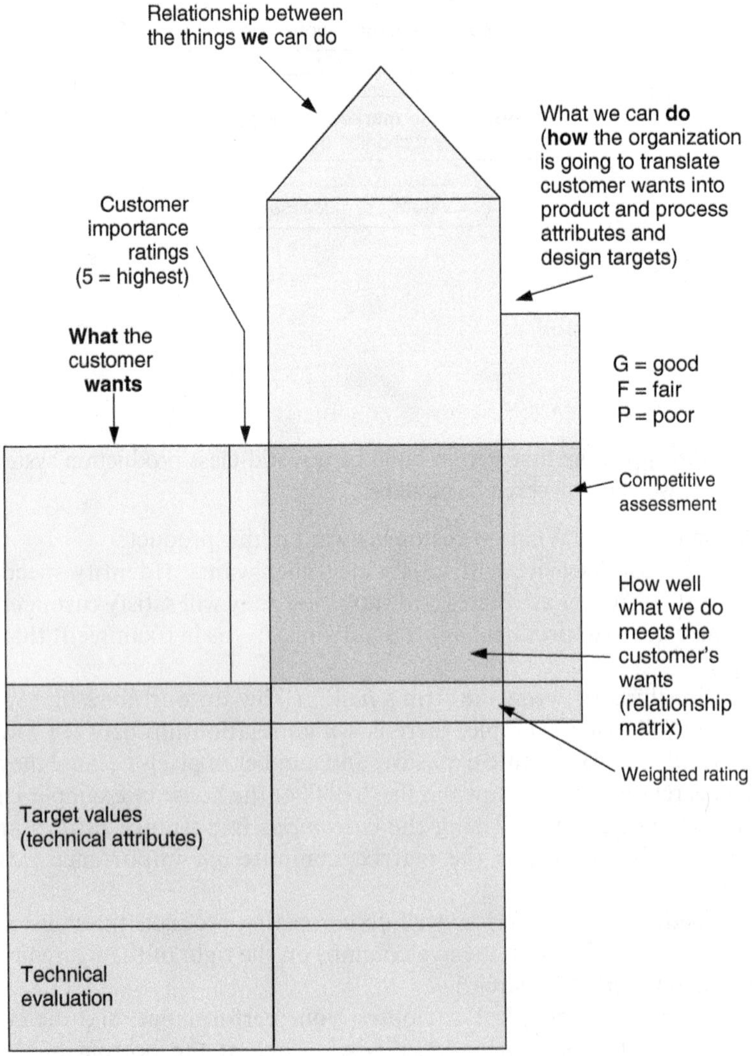

INSIGHT ▶ QFD provides an analytical tool that structures design features and technical issues, as well as providing importance rankings and competitor comparison.

LEARNING EXERCISE ▶ If the market research for another country indicates that "lightweight" has the most important customer ranking (5), and reliability a 3, what is the new total importance ranking for low electricity requirements, aluminum components, and ergonomic design? [Answer: 18, 15, 27, respectively.]

RELATED PROBLEMS ▶ 1, 2, 3, 4

Another use of quality function deployment (QFD) is to show how the quality effort will be *deployed*. As Figure 4 shows, *design characteristics* of House 1 become the inputs to House 2, which are satisfied by *specific components* of the product. Similarly, the concept is carried to House 3, where the specific components are to be satisfied through particular *production processes*. Once those production processes are defined, they become requirements of House 4 to be satisfied by a *quality plan* that will ensure conformance of those processes. The quality plan is a set of specific tolerances, procedures, methods, and sampling techniques that will ensure that the production process meets the customer requirements.

The QFD effort is devoted to meeting customer requirements. The *sequence* of houses is a very effective way of identifying, communicating, and deploying production resources. In this way we produce quality products, meet customer requirements, and win orders.

Organizing for Product Development

Let's look at four approaches to organizing for product development. *First*, the traditional U.S. approach to product development is an organization with distinct departments: a research and development department to do the necessary research; an engineering department to design the product; a manufacturing engineering department to design a product that can be produced; and a production department that produces the product. The distinct advantage of this approach is that fixed duties and responsibilities exist. The distinct disadvantage is lack of forward thinking: How will downstream departments in the process deal with the concepts, ideas, and designs presented to them, and ultimately what will the customer think of the product?

A *second* and popular approach is to assign a product manager to "champion" the product through the product development system and related organizations. However, a *third*, and perhaps the best, product development approach used in the U.S. seems to be the use of teams.

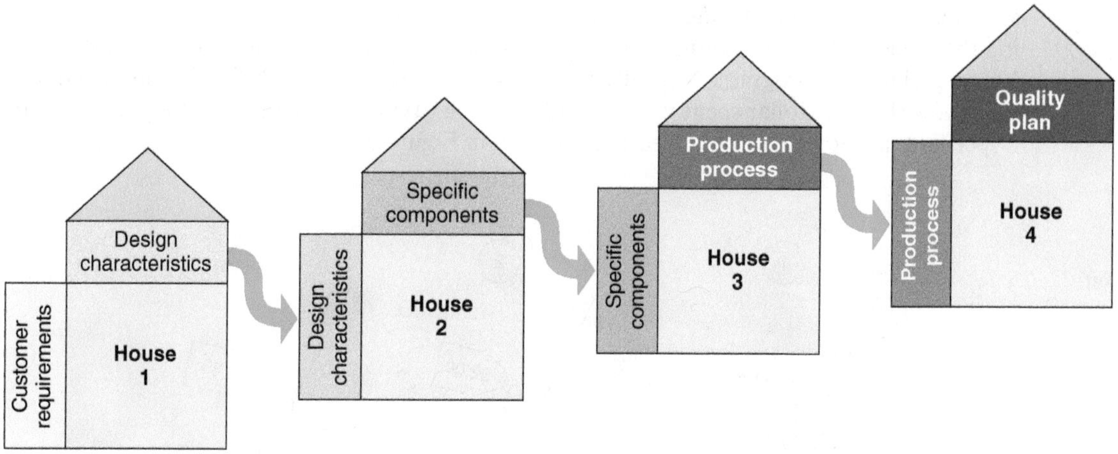

Figure 4

House of Quality Sequence Indicates How to Deploy Resources to Achieve Customer Requirements

Such teams are known variously as *product development teams, design for manufacturability teams*, and *value engineering teams*.

The Japanese use a *fourth* approach. They bypass the team issue by not subdividing organizations into research and development, engineering, production, and so forth. Consistent with the Japanese style of group effort and teamwork, these activities are all in one organization. Japanese culture and management style are more collegial and the organization less structured than in most Western countries. Therefore, the Japanese find it unnecessary to have "teams" provide the necessary communication and coordination. However, the typical Western style, and the conventional wisdom, is to use teams.

Product development teams
Teams charged with moving from market requirements for a product to achieving product success.

Product development teams are charged with the responsibility of moving from market requirements for a product to achieving a product success (refer to Figure 3). Such teams often include representatives from marketing, manufacturing, purchasing, quality assurance, and field service personnel. Many teams also include representatives from vendors. Regardless of the formal nature of the product development effort, research suggests that success is more likely in an open, highly participative environment where those with potential contributions are allowed to make them. The objective of a product development team is to make the good or service a success. This includes marketability, manufacturability, and serviceability.

Concurrent engineering
Use of cross-functional teams in product design and preproduction manufacturing.

Use of such teams is also called **concurrent engineering** and implies a team representing all affected areas (known as a *cross-functional* team). Concurrent engineering also implies speedier product development through simultaneous performance of various aspects of product development. The team approach is the dominant structure for product development by leading organizations in the U.S.

Manufacturability and Value Engineering

Manufacturability and value engineering
Activities that help improve a product's design, production, maintainability, and use.

Manufacturability and value engineering activities are concerned with improvement of design and specifications at the research, development, design, and preproduction stages of product development. In addition to immediate, obvious cost reduction, design for manufacturability and value engineering may produce other benefits. These include:

1. Reduced complexity of the product.
2. Reduction of environmental impact.
3. Additional standardization of components.
4. Improvement of functional aspects of the product.
5. Improved job design and job safety.
6. Improved maintainability (serviceability) of the product.
7. Robust design.

Manufacturability and value engineering activities may be the best cost-avoidance technique available to operations management. They yield value improvement by focusing on achieving the functional specifications necessary to meet customer requirements in an optimal way. Value engineering programs typically reduce costs between 15% and 70% without reducing quality, with every dollar spent yielding \$10 to \$25 in savings. The cost reduction achieved for a specific bracket via value engineering is shown in Figure 5.

Figure 5
Cost Reduction of a Bracket via Value Engineering

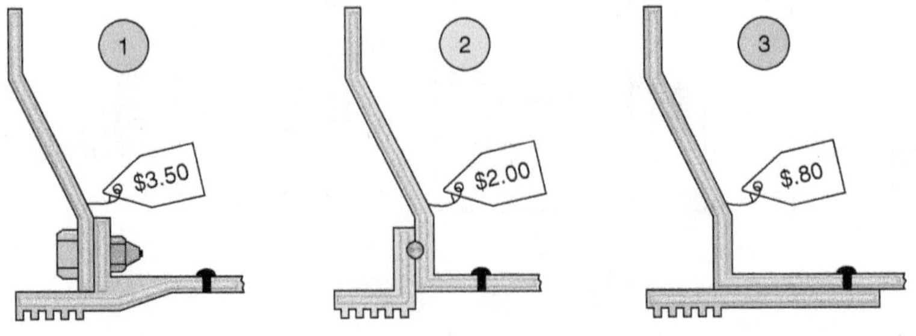

STUDENT TIP
Each time the bracket is redesigned and simplified, we are able to produce it for less.

Issues for Product Design

In addition to developing an effective system and organization structure for product development, several considerations are important to the design of a product. We will now review six of these: (1) robust design, (2) modular design, (3) computer-aided design/computer-aided manufacturing (CAD/CAM), (4) virtual reality technology, (5) value analysis, and (6) sustainability/life cycle assessment (LCA).

Robust Design

Robust design means that the product is designed so that small variations in production or assembly do not adversely affect the product. For instance, Lucent developed an integrated circuit that could be used in many products to amplify voice signals. As originally designed, the circuit had to be manufactured very expensively to avoid variations in the strength of the signal. But after testing and analyzing the design, Lucent engineers realized that if the resistance of the circuit was reduced—a minor change with no associated costs—the circuit would be far less sensitive to manufacturing variations. The result was a 40% improvement in quality.

Robust design
A design that can be produced to requirements even with unfavorable conditions in the production process.

Modular Design

Products designed in easily segmented components are known as **modular designs**. Modular designs offer flexibility to both production and marketing. Operations managers find modularity helpful because it makes product development, production, and subsequent changes easier. Marketing may like modularity because it adds flexibility to the ways customers can be satisfied. For instance, virtually all premium high-fidelity sound systems are produced and sold this way. The customization provided by modularity allows customers to mix and match to their own taste. This is also the approach taken by Harley-Davidson, where relatively few different engines, chassis, gas tanks, and suspension systems are mixed to produce a huge variety of motorcycles. It has been estimated that many automobile manufacturers can, by mixing the available modules, never make two cars alike. This same concept of modularity is carried over to many industries, from airframe manufacturers to fast-food restaurants. Airbus uses the same wing modules on several planes, just as McDonald's and Burger King use relatively few modules (cheese, lettuce, buns, sauces, pickles, meat patties, french fries, etc.) to make a variety of meals.

Modular design
A design in which parts or components of a product are subdivided into modules that are easily interchanged or replaced.

Computer-Aided Design (CAD) and Computer-Aided Manufacturing (CAM)

Computer-aided design (CAD) is the use of computers to interactively design products and prepare engineering documentation. CAD uses three-dimensional drawing to save time and money by shortening development cycles for virtually all products (see the 3-D design photo in the Regal Marine Global Company Profile that opens this text). The speed and ease with which sophisticated designs can be manipulated, analyzed, and modified with CAD makes review of numerous options possible before final commitments are made. Faster development, better products, and accurate flow of information to other departments all contribute to a tremendous payoff for CAD. The payoff is particularly significant because most product costs are determined at the design stage.

Computer-aided design (CAD)
Interactive use of a computer to develop and document a product.

One extension of CAD is **design for manufacture and assembly (DFMA)** software, which focuses on the effect of design on assembly. For instance, DFMA allows Ford to build new vehicles in a virtual factory where designers examine how to put a transmission in a car on the production line, even while both the transmission and the car are still in the design stage.

Design for manufacture and assembly (DFMA)
Software that allows designers to look at the effect of design on manufacturing of the product.

CAD systems have moved to the Internet through e-commerce, where they link computerized design with purchasing, outsourcing, manufacturing, and long-term maintenance. This move also speeds up design efforts as staff around the world can work on their unique work schedules. Rapid product change also supports the trend toward "mass customization," and, when carried

This prototype wheel for a tire (at the left of the photo) is being built using 3-D System's 3-D printing technology. This technology uses data from CAD and builds structures layer by layer in .001-inch increments. The technique reduces the time it takes to create a sample from weeks to hours while also reducing costs. The technique is also known as rapid prototyping.

to an extreme, allows customers to enter a supplier's design libraries and make changes. The result is faster and less expensive customized products. As product life cycles shorten, designs become more complex, and global collaboration has grown, the European Community (EU) has developed a standard for the exchange of product data (STEP; ISO 10303). STEP permits 3-D product information to be expressed in a standard format so it can be exchanged internationally.

Standard for the exchange of product data (STEP)
A standard that provides a format allowing the electronic transmission of three-dimensional data.

Computer-aided manufacturing (CAM)
The use of information technology to control machinery.

3-D printing
An extension of CAD that builds prototypes and small lots.

Computer-aided manufacturing (CAM) refers to the use of specialized computer programs to direct and control manufacturing equipment. When CAD information is translated into instructions for CAM, the result of these two technologies is CAD/CAM. The combination is a powerful tool for manufacturing efficiency. Fewer defective units are produced, translating into less rework and lower inventory. More precise scheduling also contributes to less inventory and more efficient use of personnel.

A related extension of CAD is 3-D printing. This technology is particularly useful for prototype development and small lot production (as shown in the photo above). 3-D printing speeds development by avoiding a more lengthy and formal manufacturing process, as we see in the *OM in Action* box "3-D Printers Hit the Mainstream."

Virtual Reality Technology

Virtual reality
A visual form of communication in which images substitute for reality and typically allow the user to respond interactively.

Virtual reality is a visual form of communication in which images substitute for the real thing but still allow the user to respond interactively. The roots of virtual reality technology in operations are in CAD. Once design information is in a CAD system, it is also in electronic digital form for other uses, such as developing 3-D layouts of everything from retail stores and restaurant layouts to amusement parks. Procter & Gamble, for instance, builds walk-in virtual

OM in Action 3-D Printers Hit the Mainstream

3-D printers are revolutionizing the product design process. With instructions from 3-D CAD models, these printers "build" products by laying down successive thin layers of plastic, metal, glass, or ceramics. Indeed, for many firms, 3-D printers have become indispensable.

The medical field uses the machines to make custom hearing aids. Invisalign Corp. produces individualized braces for teeth. Architects use the technology to produce models of buildings, and consumer electronics companies build prototypes of their latest gadgets. Microsoft uses 3-D printers to help design computer mouse devices and keyboards, while Mercedes, Honda, Boeing, and Lockheed Martin use them to fashion prototypes and to make parts that go into final products. Eventually, "a person who buys a BMW will want a part of the car with their name on it or to customize the seats to the contours of their bodies," says 3-D Systems's CEO. "We're printing with chocolate in our research labs today, so Godiva might print a candy bar with your face on it."

Large industrial 3-D systems cost from $5,000 to $1 million. The total current market is about $1.7 billion, and it is expected to reach $3.7 billion by 2015. However, the cost of 3-D printing continues to drop. Now anyone can buy a 3-D printer, hook it up to a Wi-Fi network, and begin downloading files that will turn into real objects. Another beauty and value of 3-D printing is that it has the power to unleash a world of creative energy: People who previously only thought about an invention or improved product can now quickly make it real.

Sources: BusinessWeek (April 30, 2012); and *The Wall Street Journal* (July 16, 2011).

stores to rapidly generate and test ideas. Changes to mechanical design, layouts, and even amusement park rides are much less expensive at the design stage than they are later.

Value Analysis

Although value engineering focuses on *preproduction* design and manufacturing issues, value analysis, a related technique, takes place *during* the production process, when it is clear that a new product is a success. **Value analysis** seeks improvements that lead to either a better product, or a product made more economically, or a product with less environmental impact. The techniques and advantages for value analysis are the same as for value engineering, although minor changes in implementation may be necessary because value analysis is taking place while the product is being produced.

Value analysis
A review of successful products that takes place during the production process.

Sustainability and Life Cycle Assessment (LCA)

Product design requires that managers evaluate product options. Addressing sustainability and life cycle assessment (LCA) are two ways of doing this. *Sustainability* means meeting the needs of the present without compromising the ability of future generations to meet their needs. An LCA is a formal evaluation of the environmental impact of a product.

Product Development Continuum

STUDENT TIP
Fast communication, rapid technological change, and short product life cycles push product development.

As product life cycles shorten, the need for faster product development increases. And as technological sophistication of new products increases, so do the expense and risk. For instance, drug firms invest an average of 12 to 15 years and $1 billion before receiving regulatory approval for a new drug. And even then, only 1 of 5 will actually be a success. Those operations managers who master this art of product development continually gain on slower product developers. To the swift goes the competitive advantage. This concept is called **time-based competition**.

Time-based competition
Competition based on time; rapidly developing products and moving them to market.

Often, the first company into production may have its product adopted for use in a variety of applications that will generate sales for years. It may become the "standard." Consequently, there is often more concern with getting the product to market than with optimum product design or process efficiency. Even so, rapid introduction to the market may be good management because until competition begins to introduce copies or improved versions, the product can sometimes be priced high enough to justify somewhat inefficient production design and methods.

Because time-based competition is so important, instead of developing new products from scratch (which has been the focus thus far in this text), a number of other strategies can be used. Figure 6 shows a continuum that goes from new, internally developed products (on the lower left) to "alliances." *Enhancements* and *migrations* use the organization's existing product strengths for innovation and therefore are typically faster while at the same time being less risky than developing entirely new products.

LO4 *Explain* how time-based competition is implemented by OM

Enhancements may be changes in color, size, weight, or features, such as are taking place in cellular phones (see the *OM in Action* box "The Frenzied Pace of Cell Phone Innovation"), or even changes in commercial aircraft. Boeing's enhancements of the 737 since its introduction in 1967 has made the 737 the largest-selling commercial aircraft in history.

Boeing also uses its engineering prowess in air frames to *migrate* from one model to the next. This allows Boeing to speed development while reducing both cost and risk for new designs. This approach is also referred to as building on *product platforms*. Similarly, Volkswagen is using a versatile automobile platform (the MQB chassis) for small to midsize front-wheel-drive cars. This includes VW's Polo, Golf, Passat, Tiguan, and Skoda Octavia, and may eventually include 44 different vehicles. The advantages are downward pressure on cost as well as faster development. Hewlett-Packard has done the same in the printer business. Enhancements and platform migrations are a way of building on existing expertise, speeding product development, and extending a product's life cycle.

Figure 6

Product Development
Continuum

Product Development Continuum

External development strategies

Alliances

Joint ventures

Purchase technology or expertise
by acquiring the developer

Internal development strategies

Migrations of existing products

Enhancements to existing products

New internally developed products

Internal	Cost of product development	Shared
Lengthy	Speed of product development	Rapid and/or Existing
High	Risk of product development	Shared

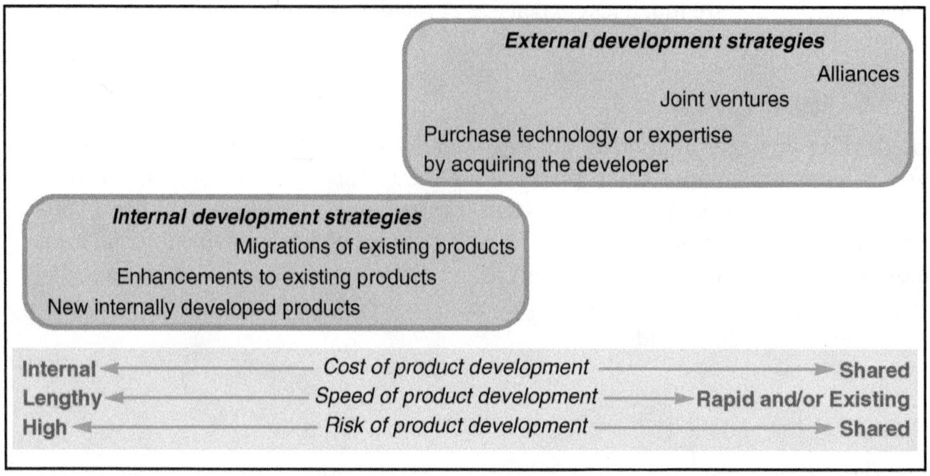

STUDENT TIP ☆

Managers seek a variety of
approaches to obtain speed to
market. The president of one
U.S. firm says: "If I miss one
product cycle, I'm dead."

The product development strategies on the lower left of Figure 6 are *internal* development strategies, while the three approaches we now introduce can be thought of as *external* development strategies. Firms use both. The external strategies are (1) purchase the technology, (2) establish joint ventures, and (3) develop alliances.

Purchasing Technology by Acquiring a Firm

Microsoft and Cisco Systems are examples of companies on the cutting edge of technology that often speed development by *acquiring entrepreneurial firms* that have already developed the technology that fits their mission. The issue then becomes fitting the purchased organization, its technology, its product lines, and its culture into the buying firm, rather than a product development issue.

Joint ventures

Firms establishing joint ownership to pursue new products or
markets.

Joint Ventures

In an effort to reduce the weight of new cars, GM is in a joint venture with Tokyo-based Teijin Ltd. to bring lightweight carbon fiber to GM's customers. Joint ventures such as this are

OM in Action **The Frenzied Pace of Cell Phone Innovation**

In the shrinking world marketplace, innovations rapidly become global trends. The process shakes up the structure of one industry after another, from clothing fashions, to computers, to video games. But nowhere has this impact been more evident in recent years than in the cell phone industry. The industry sells 1 billion phones each year, but product life cycle is short—very short. And the competition is intense. Higher market share and higher margins go to the innovator, perpetuating the race.

Contemporary cell phones may be a curvy, boxy, or a clamshell fashion item; have a keyboard for quick and easy typing; have a built-in radio or a digital music player; have a camera; have Internet access; function as a computer on cellular or wireless (Wi-Fi) networks; and have games or personal organizers. Mattel and Nokia even have Barbie phones for preteen girls, complete with prepaid minutes and customized ringtones and faceplates. The rapid changes in features and market preference force manufacturers into a frenzied race to keep up. The

swiftest innovators replace models in a matter of months—not years. Companies that can't keep up with the rapid product cycle times drop out of the race.

Apple's iPhone complicated the market even more with added sophistication, including over half a million apps from games to education and attachments for ultrasound and blood pressure. Technological advances now blur the distinction between cell phones, smart phones, tablets, and computers. Developing new products is always a challenge, but in the dynamic global marketplace of cell phones, product development has taken on a new dimension, with new technology and new markets occurring at breakneck speed. Wired consumers seek the latest innovation, local retailers rush to offer it, and telecommunication providers build it.

Sources: The Wall Street Journal (March 17–18, 2012); *Supply Chain Management Review* (October, 2007); and *International Business Times* (March 3, 2009).

combined ownership, usually between just two firms, to form a new entity. Ownership can be 50–50, or one owner can assume a larger portion to ensure tighter control. Joint ventures are often appropriate for exploiting specific product opportunities that may not be central to the firm's mission. Such ventures are more likely to work when the risks are known and can be equitably shared.

Alliances

When new products are central to the mission, but substantial resources are required and sizable risk is present, then alliances may be a good strategy for product development. **Alliances** are cooperative agreements that allow firms to remain independent but use complementing strengths to pursue strategies consistent with their individual missions. Alliances are particularly beneficial when the products to be developed also have technologies that are in ferment. For example, Microsoft is pursuing alliances with a variety of companies to deal with the convergence of computing, the Internet, and television broadcasting. Alliances in this case are appropriate because the technological unknowns, capital demands, and risks are significant. Similarly, three firms, Mercedes-Benz, Ford Motor, and Ballard Power Systems, have formed an alliance to develop "green" cars powered by fuel cells. Alliances are much more difficult to achieve and maintain than joint ventures because of the ambiguities associated with them. It may be helpful to think of an alliance as an incomplete contract between the firms. The firms remain separate.

Alliances
Cooperative agreements that allow firms to remain independent, but pursue strategies consistent with their individual missions.

Enhancements, migration, acquisitions, joint ventures, and alliances are all strategies for speeding product development. Moreover, they typically reduce the risk associated with product development while enhancing the human and capital resources available.

Defining a Product

STUDENT TIP
Before anything can be produced, a product's functions and attributes must be defined.

Once new goods or services are selected for introduction, they must be defined. First, a good or service is defined in terms of its *functions*—that is, what it is to *do*. The product is then designed, and the firm determines how the functions are to be achieved. Management typically has a variety of options as to how a product should achieve its functional purpose. For instance, when an alarm clock is produced, aspects of design such as the color, size, or location of buttons may make substantial differences in ease of manufacture, quality, and market acceptance.

LO5 *Describe* how products and services are defined by OM

Rigorous specifications of a product are necessary to assure efficient production. Equipment, layout, and human resources cannot be determined until the product is defined, designed, and documented. Therefore, every organization needs documents to define its products. This is true of everything from meat patties, to cheese, to computers, to a medical procedure. In the case of cheese, a written specification is typical. Indeed, written specifications or standard grades exist and provide the definition for many products. For instance, Monterey Jack cheese has a written description that specifies the characteristics necessary for each Department of Agriculture grade. A portion of the Department of Agriculture grade for Monterey Jack Grade AA is shown in Figure 7. Similarly, McDonald's Corp. has 60 specifications for potatoes that are to be made into french fries.

Most manufactured items, as well as their components, are defined by a drawing, usually referred to as an engineering drawing. An **engineering drawing** shows the dimensions, tolerances, materials, and finishes of a component. The engineering drawing will be an item on a bill of material. An engineering drawing is shown in Figure 8. The **bill of material (BOM)** lists the hierarchy of components, their description, and the quantity of each required to make one unit of a product. A bill of material for a manufactured item is shown in Figure 9(a). Note that subassemblies and components (lower-level items) are indented at each level to indicate their subordinate position. An engineering drawing shows how to make one item on the bill of material.

Engineering drawing
A drawing that shows the dimensions, tolerances, materials, and finishes of a component.

Bill of material (BOM)
A list of the hierarchy of components, their description, and the quantity of each required to make one unit of a product.

Figure 7

Monterey Jack

A portion of the general requirements for the U.S. grades of Monterey Jack cheese is shown here.

Source: Based on 58.2469 Specifications for U.S. grades of Monterey (Monterey Jack) cheese, (May 10, 1996).

§ 58.2469 Specifications for U.S. grades of Monterey (Monterey Jack) cheese

(a) *U.S. grade AA.* Monterey Cheese shall conform to the following requirements:

(1) *Flavor.* Is fine and highly pleasing, free from undesirable flavors and odors. May possess a very slight acid or feed flavor.

(2) *Body and texture.* A plug drawn from the cheese shall be reasonably firm. It shall have numerous small mechanical openings evenly distributed throughout the plug. It shall not possess sweet holes, yeast holes, or other gas holes.

(3) *Color.* Shall have a natural, uniform, bright, attractive appearance.

(4) *Finish and appearance—bandaged and paraffin-dipped.* The rind shall be sound, firm, and smooth, providing a good protection to the cheese.

Code of Federal Regulation, Parts 53 to 109, General Service Administration.

David Murray/Dorling Kindersley Media Library

In the food-service industry, bills of material manifest themselves in *portion-control standards*. The portion-control standard for Hard Rock Cafe's hickory BBQ bacon cheeseburger is shown in Figure 9(b). In a more complex product, a bill of material is referenced on other bills of material of which they are a part. In this manner, subunits (subassemblies) are part of the next higher unit (their parent bill of material) that ultimately makes a final product. In addition to being defined by written specifications, portion-control documents, or bills of material, products can be defined in other ways. For example, products such as chemicals, paints, and petroleums may be defined by formulas or proportions that describe how they are to be made. Movies are defined by scripts, and insurance coverage by legal documents known as policies.

Make-or-Buy Decisions

Make-or-buy decision
The choice between producing a component or a service and purchasing it from an outside source.

For many components of products, firms have the option of producing the components themselves or purchasing them from outside sources. Choosing between these options is known as the make-or-buy decision. The **make-or-buy decision** distinguishes between what the firm wants to *produce* and what it wants to *purchase*. Because of variations in quality, cost, and delivery schedules, the make-or-buy decision is critical to product definition. Many items can be purchased as a "standard item" produced by someone else. Examples are the standard bolts listed twice on the bill of material shown in Figure 9(a), for which there will be SAE (Society

Figure 8

Engineering Drawings Such as This One Show Dimensions, Tolerances, Materials, and Finishes

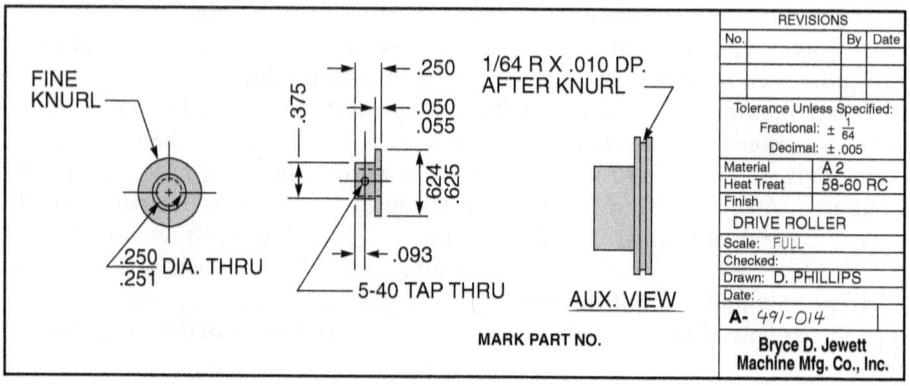

(a) **Bill of Material for a Panel Weldment**

NUMBER	DESCRIPTION	QTY
A 60-71	PANEL WELDM'T	1
A 60-7	LOWER ROLLER ASSM.	1
R 60-17	ROLLER	1
R 60-428	PIN	1
P 60-2	LOCKNUT	1
A 60-72	GUIDE ASSM. REAR	1
R 60-57-1	SUPPORT ANGLE	1
A 60-4	ROLLER ASSEM.	1
02-50-1150	BOLT	1
A 60-73	GUIDE ASSM. FRONT	1
A 60-74	SUPPORT WELDM'T	1
R 60-99	WEAR PLATE	1
02-50-1150	BOLT	1

(b) **Hard Rock Cafe's Hickory BBQ Bacon Cheeseburger**

DESCRIPTION	QTY
Bun	1
Hamburger patty	8 oz.
Cheddar cheese	2 slices
Bacon	2 strips
BBQ onions	1/2 cup
Hickory BBQ sauce	1 oz.
Burger set	
Lettuce	1 leaf
Tomato	1 slice
Red onion	4 rings
Pickle	1 slice
French fries	5 oz.
Seasoned salt	1 tsp.
11-inch plate	1
HRC flag	1

Figure 9

Bills of Material Take Different Forms in a (a) Manufacturing Plant and (b) Restaurant, but in Both Cases, the Product Must Be Defined

STUDENT TIP

Hard Rock's recipe here serves the same purpose as a bill of material in a factory: It defines the product for production.

of Automotive Engineers) specifications. Therefore, there typically is no need for the firm to duplicate this specification in another document.

Group Technology

Engineering drawings may also include codes to facilitate group technology. **Group technology** identifies components by a coding scheme that specifies size, shape, and the type of processing (such as drilling). This facilitates standardization of materials, components, and processes as well as the identification of families of parts. As families of parts are identified, activities and machines can be grouped to minimize setups, routings, and material handling. An example of how families of parts may be grouped is shown in Figure 10. Group technology provides a systematic way to review a family of components to see if an existing component might suffice on a new project. Using existing or standard components eliminates all the costs connected with the design and development of the new part, which is a major cost reduction.

Group technology

A product and component coding system that specifies the size, shape, and type of processing; it allows similar products to be grouped.

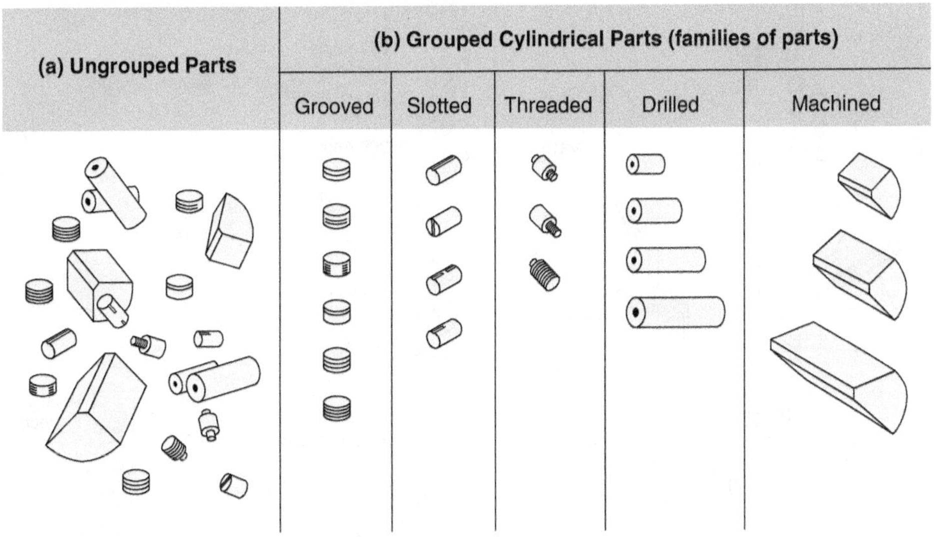

Figure 10

A Variety of Group Technology Coding Schemes Move Manufactured Components from (a) Ungrouped to (b) Grouped (families of parts)

STUDENT TIP ☆ Production personnel need clear, specific documents to help them make the product.

Documents for Production

Once a product is selected, designed, and ready for production, production is assisted by a variety of documents. We will briefly review some of these.

Assembly drawing An exploded view of the product.

An assembly drawing simply shows an exploded view of the product. An assembly drawing is usually a three-dimensional drawing, known as an *isometric drawing*; the relative locations of components are drawn in relation to each other to show how to assemble the unit [see Figure 11(a)].

Assembly chart A graphic means of identifying how components flow into subassemblies and final products.

The assembly chart shows in schematic form how a product is assembled. Manufactured components, purchased components, or a combination of both may be shown on an assembly chart. The assembly chart identifies the point of production at which components flow into subassemblies and ultimately into a final product. An example of an assembly chart is shown in Figure 11(b).

Route sheet A listing of the operations necessary to produce a component with the material specified in the bill of material.

The route sheet lists the operations necessary to produce the component with the material specified in the bill of material. The route sheet for an item will have one entry for each operation to be performed on the item. When route sheets include specific methods of operation and labor standards, they are often known as *process sheets*.

Work order An instruction to make a given quantity of a particular item.

The work order is an instruction to make a given quantity of a particular item, usually to a given schedule. The ticket that a waiter writes in your favorite restaurant is a work order. In a hospital or factory, the work order is a more formal document that provides authorization to draw items from inventory, to perform various functions, and to assign personnel to perform those functions.

Engineering change notice (ECN) A correction or modification of an engineering drawing or bill of material.

Configuration management A system by which a product's planned and changing components are accurately identified.

Engineering change notices (ECNs) change some aspect of the product's definition or documentation, such as an engineering drawing or a bill of material. For a complex product that has a long manufacturing cycle, such as a Boeing 777, the changes may be so numerous that no two 777s are built exactly alike—which is indeed the case. Such dynamic design change has fostered the development of a discipline known as configuration management, which is concerned with product identification, control, and documentation. Configuration management is the system by which a product's planned and changing configurations are accurately identified and for which control and accountability of change are maintained.

Product life-cycle management (PLM) Software programs that tie together many phases of product design and manufacture.

Product Life-Cycle Management (PLM)

Product life-cycle management (PLM) is an umbrella of software programs that attempts to bring together phases of product design and manufacture—including tying together many of

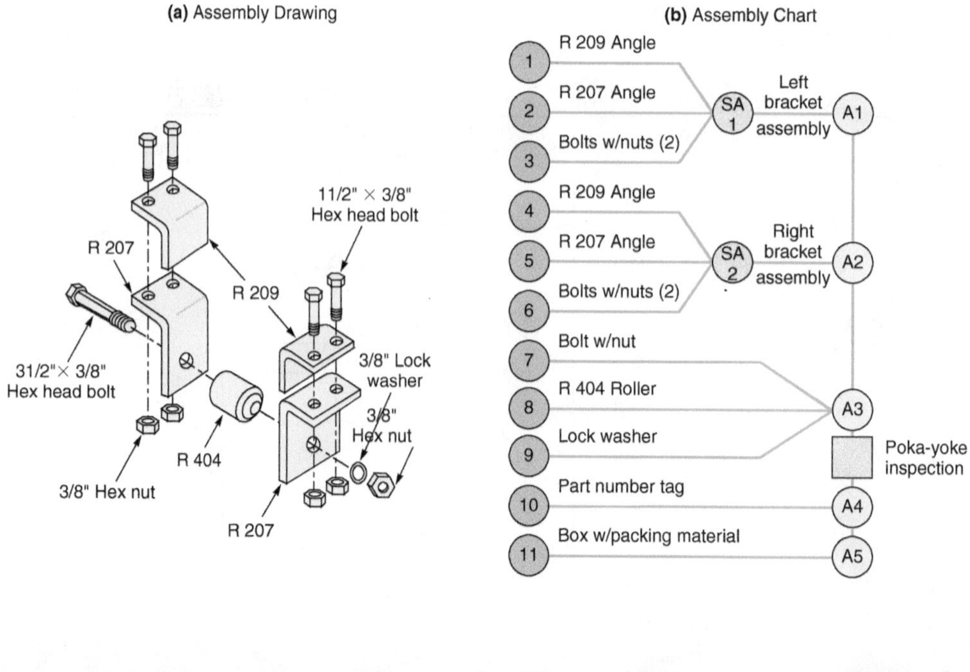

Figure 11 **Assembly Drawing and Assembly Chart**

Source: Assembly drawing and assembly chart produced by author.

J.R. Simplot Company

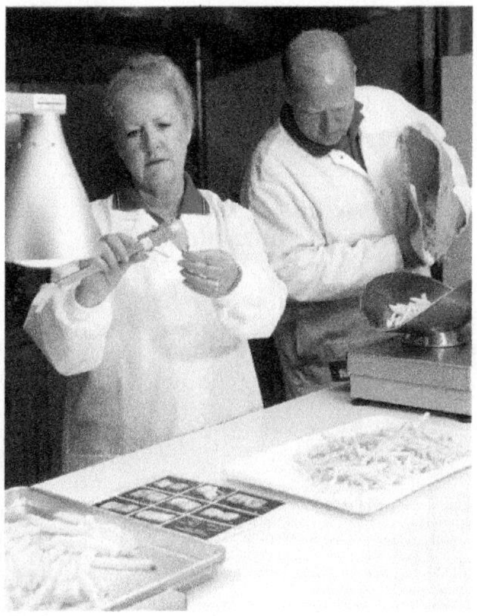

J.R. Simplot

Each year the JR Simplot potato-processing facility in Caldwell, Idaho, produces billions of french fries for quick-service restaurant chains and many other customers, both domestically and overseas (left photo). Sixty specifications (including a special blend of frying oil, a unique steaming process, and exact time and temperature for prefrying and drying) define how these potatoes become french fries. Further, 40% of all french fries must be 2 to 3 inches long, 40% must be over 3 inches long, and a few stubby ones constitute the final 20%. Quality control personnel use a micrometer to measure the fries (right photo).

the techniques discussed in the prior two sections, *Defining a Product* and *Documents for Production*. The idea behind PLM software is that product design and manufacture decisions can be performed more creatively, faster, and more economically when the data are integrated and consistent.

LO6 *Describe* the documents needed for production

Although there is not one standard, PLM products often start with product design (CAD/CAM); move on to design for manufacture and assembly (DFMA); and then into product routing, materials, layout, assembly, maintenance, and even environmental issues. Integration of these tasks makes sense because many of these decision areas require overlapping pieces of data. PLM software is now a tool of many large organizations, including Lockheed Martin, GE, Procter & Gamble, Toyota, and Boeing. Boeing estimates that PLM will cut final assembly of its 787 jet from 2 weeks to 3 days. PLM is now finding its way into medium and small manufacture as well.

Shorter life cycles, more technologically challenging products, more regulations regarding materials and manufacturing processes, and more environmental issues all make PLM an appealing tool for operations managers. Major vendors of PLM software include SAP PLM (www.mySAP.com), Parametric Technology Corp. (www.ptc.com), UGS Corp. (www.ugs.com), and Proplanner (www.proplanner.com).

Service Design

STUDENT TIP
Services also need to be defined and documented.

Much of our discussion so far has focused on what we can call tangible products—that is, goods. On the other side of the product coin are, of course, services. Service industries include banking, finance, insurance, transportation, and communications. The products offered by service firms range from a medical procedure that leaves only the tiniest scar after an appendectomy, to a shampoo and cut at a hair salon, to a great sandwich. Designing services is challenging because they have a unique characteristic—customer interaction.

Process–chain–network (PCN) analysis
Analysis that focuses on the ways in which processes can be designed to optimize interaction between firms and their customers.

Process–Chain–Network (PCN) Analysis

Process–chain–network (PCN) analysis, developed by Professor Scott Sampson, focuses on the ways in which processes can be designed to optimize interaction between firms and their customers.[2]

[2]See Scott Sampson, "Visualizing Service Operations," *Journal of Service Research* (May 2012). More details about PCN analysis are available at **services.byu.edu.**

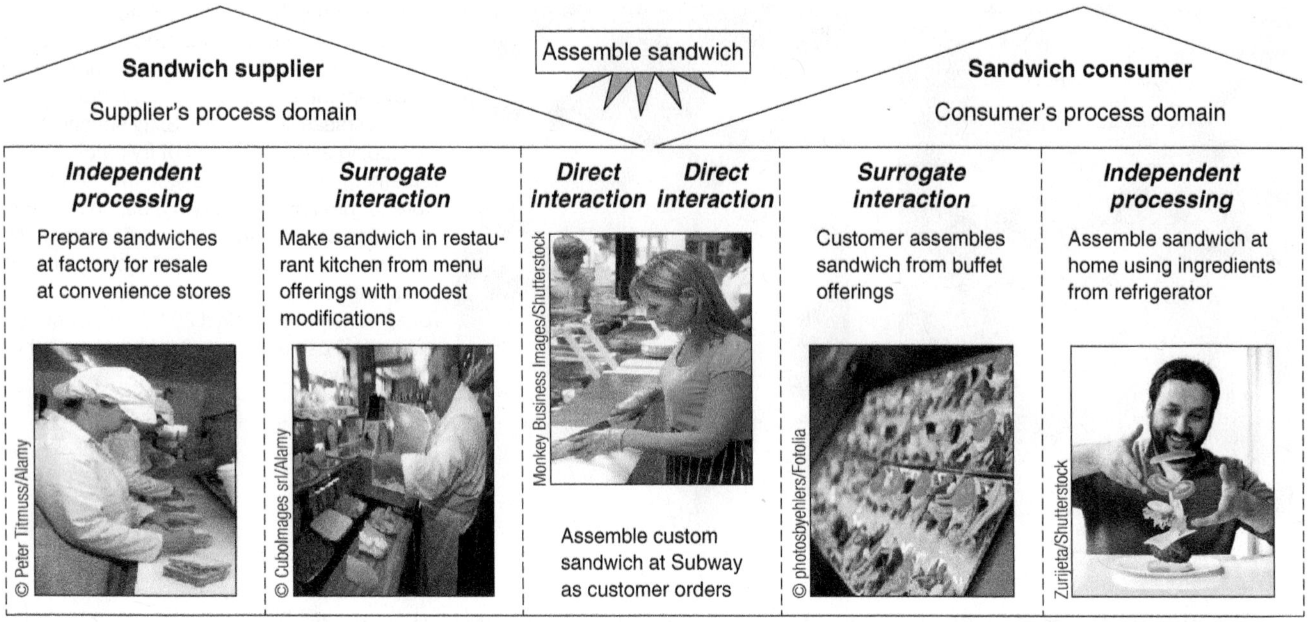

Figure 12
Customer Interaction Is a Strategic Choice

Process chain
A sequence of steps that accomplishes an identifiable purpose (of providing value to process participants).

A process chain is a sequence of steps that accomplishes an activity, such as building a home, completing a tax return, or preparing a sandwich. A process participant can be a manufacturer, a service provider, or a customer. A network is a set of participants.

Each participant has a *process domain* that includes the set of activities over which it has control. The domain and interactions between two participants for sandwich preparation are shown in the PCN diagram (Figure 12). The activities are organized into three *process regions* for each participant:

1. The *direct interaction* region includes process steps that involve interaction between participants. For example, a sandwich buyer directly interacts with employees of a sandwich store (e.g., Subway, in the middle of Figure 12).
2. The *surrogate (substitute) interaction* region includes process steps in which one participant is acting on another participant's resources, such as their information, materials, or technologies. This occurs when the sandwich *supplier* is making sandwiches in the restaurant kitchen (left side of Figure 12) or, alternately, when the *customer* has access to buffet ingredients and assembles the sandwich himself (right side of the figure). Under surrogate interaction, *direct* interaction is limited.
3. The *independent processing* region includes steps in which the sandwich supplier and/or the sandwich customer is acting on resources where each has maximum control. Most make-to-stock production fits in this region (left side of Figure 12; think of the firm that assembles all those prepackaged sandwiches available in vending machines and convenience stores). Similarly, those sandwiches built at home occur to the right, in the customer's independent processing domain.

LO7 *Explain* how the customer participates in the design and delivery of services

All three process regions have similar operating issues—quality control, facility location and layout, job design, inventory, and so on—but the appropriate way of handling the issues differs across regions. Service operations exist only within the area of *direct* and *surrogate interaction.*

From the operations manager's perspective, the valuable aspect of PCN analysis is insight to aid in positioning and designing processes that can achieve strategic objectives. A firm's operations are strategic in that they can define what type of business the firm is in and what value proposition it desires to provide to customers. For example, a firm may assume a low-cost strategy, operating on the left of Figure 12 as a manufacturer of premade sandwiches. Other firms (e.g., Subway) adopt a differentiation strategy with high customer interaction. Each of the process regions depicts a unique operational strategy.

Firms wanting to achieve high economies of scale or more control in their operations should probably position toward the independent processing region of their process domain. Firms intending to provide a value offering that focuses on customization should be positioned more toward the consumer's process domain. PCN analysis can be applied in a wide variety of business settings.

Adding Service Efficiency

Service productivity is notoriously low, in part because of customer involvement in the *design* or *delivery* of the service, or both. This complicates the product design challenge. We will now discuss a number of ways to increase service efficiency and, among these, several ways to limit this interaction.

Limit the Options Because customers may participate in the *design* of the service (e.g., for a funeral or a hairstyle), design specifications may take the form of everything from a menu (in a restaurant), to a list of options (for a funeral), to a verbal description (a hairstyle). However, by providing a list of options (in the case of the funeral) or a series of photographs (in the case of the hairstyle), ambiguity may be reduced. An early resolution of the product's definition can aid efficiency as well as aid in meeting customer expectations.

Delay Customization Design the product so that *customization is delayed* as late in the process as possible. This is the way a hair salon operates. Although shampoo and condition are done in a standard way with lower-cost labor, the color and styling (customizing) are done last. It is also the way most restaurants operate: How would you like that cooked? Which dressing would you prefer with your salad?

Modularization *Modularize* the service so that customization takes the form of changing modules. This strategy allows for "custom" services to be designed as standard modular entities. Just as modular design allows you to buy a high-fidelity sound system with just the features you want, modular flexibility also lets you buy meals, clothes, and insurance on a mix-and-match (modular) basis. Investments (portfolios of stocks and bonds) and education (college curricula) are examples of how the modular approach can be used to customize a service.

Automation Divide the service into small parts and identify those parts that lend themselves to automation. For instance, by isolating check-cashing activity via ATM, banks have been very effective at designing a product that both increases customer service and reduces costs. Similarly, airlines have moved to ticketless service via kiosks. A technique such as kiosks reduces both costs and lines at airports—thereby increasing customer satisfaction—and providing a win–win "product" design.

Moment of Truth High customer interaction means that in the service industry there is a *moment of truth* when the relationship between the provider and the customer is crucial. At that moment, the customer's satisfaction with the service is defined. The moment of truth is the moment that exemplifies, enhances, or detracts from the customer's expectations. That moment may be as simple as a smile from a Starbucks barista or having the checkout clerk focus on you rather than talking over his shoulder to the clerk at the next counter. Moments of truth can occur when you order at McDonald's, get a haircut, or register for college courses. The operations manager's task is to identify moments of truth and design operations that meet or exceed the customer's expectations.

Documents for Services

Because of the high customer interaction of most services, the documents for moving the product to production often take the form of explicit *job instructions* or *script*. For instance, regardless of how good a bank's products may be in terms of checking, savings, trusts, loans, mortgages, and so forth, if the interaction between participants is not done well, the product may be poorly received. Example 2 shows the kind of documentation a bank may use to move a product (drive-up window banking) to "production." Similarly, a telemarketing service has the product design communicated to production personnel in the form of a *telephone script*, while a *manuscript* is used for books, and a *storyboard* is used for movie and TV production.

Example 2

SERVICE DOCUMENTATION FOR PRODUCTION

First Bank Corp. wants to ensure effective delivery of service to its drive-up customers.

APPROACH ▶ Develop a "production" document for the tellers at the drive-up window that provides the information necessary to do an effective job.

SOLUTION ▶

Documentation for Tellers at Drive-up Windows

Customers who use the drive-up teller windows rather than walk-in lobbies require a different customer relations technique. The distance and machinery between the teller and the customer raises communication barriers. Guidelines to ensure good customer relations at the drive-up window are:

- Be especially discreet when talking to the customer through the microphone.
- Provide written instructions for customers who must fill out forms you provide.
- Mark lines to be completed or attach a note with instructions.
- Always say "please" and "thank you" when speaking through the microphone.
- Establish eye contact with the customer if the distance allows it.
- If a transaction requires that the customer park the car and come into the lobby, apologize for the inconvenience.

Source: Adapted with permission from *Teller Operations* (Chicago, IL: The Institute of Financial Education, 1999): 32.

INSIGHT ▶ By providing documentation in the form of a script/guideline for tellers, the likelihood of effective communication and a good product/service is improved.

LEARNING EXERCISE ▶ Modify the guidelines above to show how they would be different for a drive-through restaurant. [Answer: Written instructions, marking lines to be completed, or coming into the store are seldom necessary, but techniques for making change and proper transfer of the order should be included.]

RELATED PROBLEM ▶ 7

Application of Decision Trees to Product Design

STUDENT TIP A decision tree is a great tool for thinking through a problem.

LO8 *Apply* decision trees to product issues

Decision trees can be used for new-product decisions as well as for a wide variety of other management problems when uncertainty is present. They are particularly helpful when there are a series of decisions and various outcomes that lead to *subsequent* decisions followed by other outcomes. To form a decision tree, we use the following procedure:

1. Be sure that all possible alternatives and states of nature (beginning on the left and moving right) are included in the tree. This includes an alternative of "doing nothing."
2. Payoffs are entered at the end of the appropriate branch. This is the place to develop the payoff of achieving this branch.
3. The objective is to determine the expected value of each course of action. We accomplish this by starting at the end of the tree (the right-hand side) and working toward the beginning of the tree (the left), calculating values at each step and "pruning" alternatives that are not as good as others from the same node.

Example 3 shows the use of a decision tree applied to product design.

Example 3

DECISION TREE APPLIED TO PRODUCT DESIGN

Silicon, Inc., a semiconductor manufacturer, is investigating the possibility of producing and marketing a microprocessor. Undertaking this project will require either purchasing a sophisticated CAD system or hiring and training several additional engineers. The market for the product could be either favorable or unfavorable. Silicon, Inc., of course, has the option of not developing the new product at all.

With favorable acceptance by the market, sales would be 25,000 processors selling for \$100 each. With unfavorable acceptance, sales would be only 8,000 processors selling for \$100 each. The cost of CAD equipment is \$500,000, but that of hiring and training three new engineers is only \$375,000. However, manufacturing costs should drop from \$50 each when manufacturing without CAD to \$40 each when manufacturing with CAD.

The probability of favorable acceptance of the new microprocessor is .40; the probability of unfavorable acceptance is .60.

APPROACH ▶ Use of a decision tree seems appropriate as Silicon, Inc., has the basic ingredients: a choice of decisions, probabilities, and payoffs.

SOLUTION ▶ In Figure 13 we draw a decision tree with a branch for each of the three decisions, assign the respective probabilities and payoff for each branch, and then compute the respective EMVs. The expected monetary values (EMVs) have been circled at each step of the decision tree. For the top branch:

$$\text{EMV (Purchase CAD system)} = (.4)(\$1{,}000{,}000) + (.6)(-\$20{,}000) = \$388{,}000$$

This figure represents the results that will occur if Silicon, Inc., purchases CAD.

The expected value of hiring and training engineers is the second series of branches:

$$\text{EMV (Hire/train engineers)} = (.4)(\$875{,}000) + (.6)(\$25{,}000) = \$365{,}000$$

Figure 13
Decision Tree for Development of a New Product

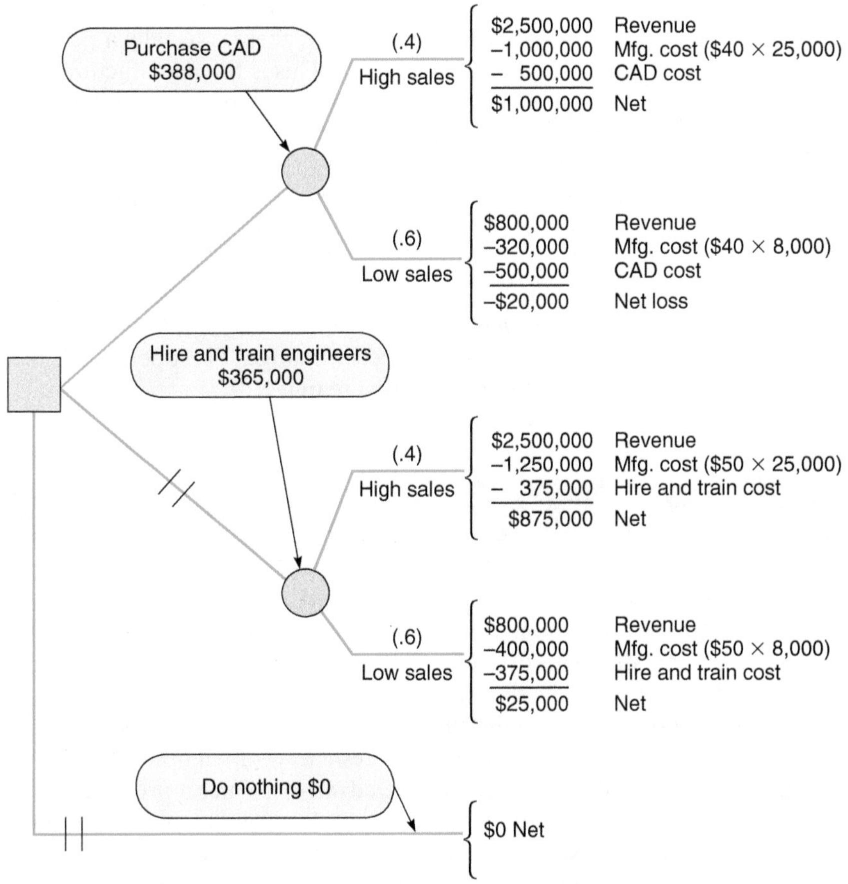

STUDENT TIP ☆
The manager's options are to purchase CAD, hire/train engineers, or do nothing. Purchasing CAD has the highest EMV.

The EMV of doing nothing is $0.

Because the top branch has the highest expected monetary value (an EMV of $388,000 vs. $365,000 vs. $0), it represents the best decision. Management should purchase the CAD system.

INSIGHT ▶ Use of the decision tree provides both objectivity and structure to our analysis of the Silicon, Inc., decision.

LEARNING EXERCISE ▶ If Silicon, Inc., thinks the probabilities of high sales and low sales may be equal, at .5 each, what is the best decision? [Answer: Purchase CAD remains the best decision, but with an EMV of $490,000.]

RELATED PROBLEMS ▶ 10, 11, 12, 13, 14, 15, 16, 18

ACTIVE **MODEL** 1 This example is further illustrated in Active Model 5.1 at **www.pearsonhighered.com/heizer**.

STUDENT TIP ☆
One of the arts of management is knowing when a product should move from development to production.

Transition to Production

Eventually, a product, whether a good or service, has been selected, designed, and defined. It has progressed from an idea to a functional definition, and then perhaps to a design. Now, management must make a decision as to further development and production or termination of the product idea. One of the arts of management is knowing when to move a product from development to production; this move is known as *transition to production*. The product development staff is always interested in making improvements in a product. Because this staff tends to see product development as evolutionary, they may never have a completed product, but as we noted earlier, the cost of late product introduction is high. Although these conflicting pressures exist, management must make a decision—more development or production.

Once this decision is made, there is usually a period of trial production to ensure that the design is indeed producible. This is the manufacturability test. This trial also gives the operations staff the opportunity to develop proper tooling, quality control procedures, and training of personnel to ensure that production can be initiated successfully. Finally, when the product is deemed both marketable and producible, line management will assume responsibility.

To ensure that the transition from development to production is successful some companies appoint a *project manager*; others use *product development teams*. Both approaches allow a wide range of resources and talents to be brought to bear to ensure satisfactory production of a product that is still in flux. A third approach is *integration of the product development and manufacturing organizations*. This approach allows for easy shifting of resources between the two organizations as needs change. The operations manager's job is to make the transition from R&D to production seamless.

Summary

Effective product strategy requires selecting, designing, and defining a product and then transitioning that product to production. Only when this strategy is carried out effectively can the production function contribute its maximum to the organization. The operations manager must build a product development system that has the ability to conceive, design, and produce products that will yield a competitive advantage for the firm. As products move through their life cycle (introduction, growth, maturity, and decline), the options that the operations manager should pursue change. Both manufactured and service products have a variety of techniques available to aid in performing this activity efficiently.

Written specifications, bills of material, and engineering drawings aid in defining products. Similarly, assembly drawings, assembly charts, route sheets, and work orders are often used to assist in the actual production of the product. Once a product is in production, value analysis is appropriate to ensure maximum product value. Engineering change notices and configuration management provide product documentation.

Key Terms

Product decision
Product-by-value analysis
Quality function deployment (QFD)
House of quality
Product development teams
Concurrent engineering
Manufacturability and value engineering
Robust design
Modular design
Computer-aided design (CAD)
Design for manufacture and assembly (DFMA)
Standard for the exchange of product data (STEP)
Computer-aided manufacturing (CAM)
3-D printing
Virtual reality
Value analysis
Time-based competition
Joint ventures
Alliances
Engineering drawing
Bill of material (BOM)
Make-or-buy decision
Group technology
Assembly drawing
Assembly chart
Route sheet
Work order
Engineering change notice (ECN)
Configuration management
Product life-cycle management (PLM)
Process–Chain–Network (PCN) analysis
Process chain

Ethical Dilemma

John Sloan, president of Sloan Toy Company, Inc., in Oregon, has just reviewed the design of a new pull-toy locomotive for 1- to 3-year-olds. John's design and marketing staff are very enthusiastic about the market for the product and the potential of follow-on circus train cars. The sales manager is looking forward to a very good reception at the annual toy show in Dallas next month. John, too, is delighted, as he is faced with a layoff if orders do not improve.

John's production people have worked out the manufacturing issues and produced a successful pilot run. However, the quality testing staff suggests that under certain conditions, a hook to attach cars to the locomotive and the crank for the bell can be broken off. This is an issue because children can choke on small parts such as these. In the quality test, 1- to 3-year-olds were unable to break off these parts; there were *no* failures. But when the test simulated the force of an adult tossing the locomotive into a toy box or a 5-year-old throwing it on the floor, there were failures. The estimate is that one of the two parts can be broken off 4 times out of 100,000 throws. Neither the design nor the material people know how to make the toy safer and still perform as designed. The failure rate is low and certainly normal for this type of toy, but not at the Six Sigma level that John's firm strives for. And, of course, someone, someday may sue. A child choking on the broken part is a serious matter. Also, John was recently reminded in a discussion with legal counsel that U.S. case law suggests that new products may not be produced if there is "actual or foreseeable knowledge of a problem" with the product.

The design of successful, ethically produced new products, as suggested in this text, is a complex task. What should John do?

Nikolay Stefanvo Dimitrov/Shutterstock

Discussion Questions

1. Why is it necessary to document a product explicitly?
2. What techniques do we use to define a product?
3. In what ways is product strategy linked to product decisions?
4. Once a product is defined, what documents are used to assist production personnel in its manufacture?
5. What is time-based competition?
6. Describe the differences between joint ventures and alliances.
7. Describe four organizational approaches to product development. Which of these is generally thought to be best?
8. Explain what is meant by robust design.
9. What are three specific ways in which computer-aided design (CAD) benefits the design engineer?
10. What information is contained in a bill of material?
11. What information is contained in an engineering drawing?
12. What information is contained in an assembly chart? In a process sheet?
13. Explain what is meant in service design by the "moment of truth."
14. Explain how the house of quality translates customer desires into product/service attributes.
15. What strategic advantages does computer-aided design provide?
16. What is a process chain?
17. Why are the direct interaction and surrogate interaction regions in a PCN diagram important in service design?
18. Why are documents for service useful? Provide examples of four types.

Solved Problem

Virtual Office Hours help is available at www.myomlab.com.

SOLVED PROBLEM 1

Sarah King, president of King Electronics, Inc., has two design options for her new line of high-resolution cathode-ray tubes (CRTs) for CAD workstations. The life cycle sales forecast for the CRT is 100,000 units.

Design option A has a .90 probability of yielding 59 good CRTs per 100 and a .10 probability of yielding 64 good CRTs per 100. This design will cost $1,000,000.

Design option B has a .80 probability of yielding 64 good units per 100 and a .20 probability of yielding 59 good units per 100. This design will cost $1,350,000.

Good or bad, each CRT will cost $75. Each good CRT will sell for $150. Bad CRTs are destroyed and have no salvage value. We ignore any disposal costs in this problem.

SOLUTION

We draw the decision tree to reflect the two decisions and the probabilities associated with each decision. We then determine the payoff associated with each branch. The resulting tree is shown in Figure 14.

For design A:

$$\text{EMV(design A)} = (.9)(\$350{,}000) + (.1)(\$1{,}100{,}000) = \$425{,}000$$

For design B:

$$\text{EMV(design B)} = (.8)(\$750{,}000) + (.2)(\$0) = \$600{,}000$$

The highest payoff is design option B, at $600,000.

Figure 14
Decision Tree for Solved Problem 1

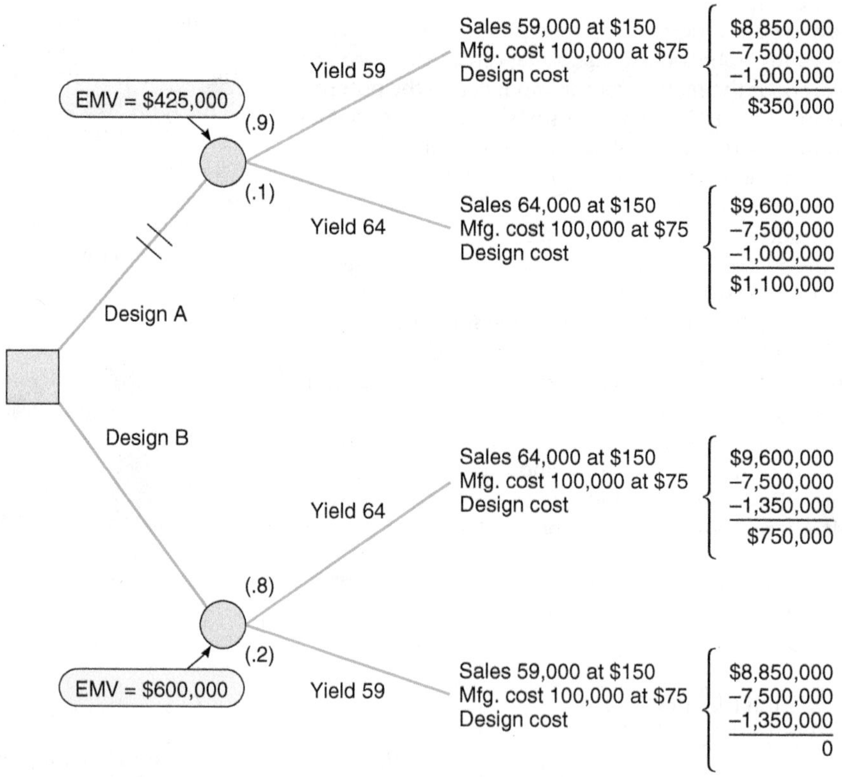

Problems

Note: Px means the problem may be solved with POM for Windows and/or Excel OM.

•• **1** Construct a house of quality matrix for a wristwatch. Be sure to indicate specific customer wants that you think the general public desires. Then complete the matrix to show how an operations manager might identify specific attributes that can be measured and controlled to meet those customer desires.

•• **2** Using the house of quality, pick a real product (a good or service) and analyze how an existing organization satisfies customer requirements.

•• **3** Prepare a house of quality for a mousetrap.

•• **4** Conduct an interview with a prospective purchaser of a new bicycle and translate the customer's *wants* into the specific *hows* of the firm.

•• **5** Prepare a bill of material for (a) a pair of eyeglasses and its case or (b) a fast-food sandwich (visit a local sandwich shop like Subway, McDonald's, Blimpie, Quizno's; perhaps a clerk or the manager will provide you with details on the quantity or weight of various ingredients—otherwise, estimate the quantities).

•• **6** Draw an assembly chart for a pair of eyeglasses and its case.

•• **7** Prepare a script for telephone callers at the university's annual "phone-a-thon" fund raiser.

•• **8** Prepare an assembly chart for a table lamp.

••• **9** Prepare a product-by-value analysis for the following products, and given the position in its life cycle, identify the issues likely to confront the operations manager and his or her possible actions. Product Alpha has annual sales of 1,000 units and a contribution of $2,500; it is in the introductory stage. Product Bravo has annual sales of 1,500 units and a contribution of $3,000; it is in the growth stage. Product Charlie has annual sales of 3,500 units and a contribution of $1,750; it is in the decline stage.

•• **10** Given the contribution made on each of the three products in the following table and their position in the life cycle, identify a reasonable operations strategy for each:

PRODUCT	PRODUCT CONTRIBUTION (% OF SELLING PRICE)	COMPANY CONTRIBUTION (%: TOTAL ANNUAL CONTRIBUTION DIVIDED BY TOTAL ANNUAL SALES)	POSITION IN LIFE CYCLE
Kindle Fire	30	40	Growth
Netbook computer	30	50	Introduction
Hand calculator	50	10	Decline

•• **11** Draw a two-participant PCN diagram (similar to Figure 12) for one of the following processes:

a) The process of having your computer repaired.
b) The process of pizza preparation.
c) The process of procuring tickets for a concert.

•• **12** Review strategic process positioning options for the regions in Figure 12, discussing the operational impact (in terms of the 10 strategic OM decisions) for:

a) Manufacturing the sandwiches.
b) Direct interaction.
c) Establishing a sandwich buffet.

••• **13** Select a service business that involves interaction between customers and service providers, and create a PCN diagram similar to Figure 12. Pick a key step that could be performed either by the service provider or by the customers. Show process positioning options for the step. Describe how the options compare in terms of efficiency, economies of scale, and opportunity for customization.

•• **14** The product design group of Iyengar Electric Supplies, Inc., has determined that it needs to design a new series of switches. It must decide on one of three design strategies. The market forecast is for 200,000 units. The better and more sophisticated the design strategy and the more time spent on value engineering, the less will be the variable cost. The chief of engineering design, Dr. W. L. Berry, has decided that the following costs are a good estimate of the initial and variable costs connected with each of the three strategies:

a) *Low-tech:* A low-technology, low-cost process consisting of hiring several new junior engineers. This option has a fixed cost of $45,000 and variable-cost probabilities of .3 for $.55 each, .4 for $.50, and .3 for $.45.
b) *Subcontract:* A medium-cost approach using a good outside design staff. This approach would have a fixed cost of $65,000 and variable-cost probabilities of .7 of $.45, .2 of $.40, and .1 of $.35.
c) *High-tech:* A high-technology approach using the very best of the inside staff and the latest computer-aided design technology. This approach has a fixed cost of $75,000 and variable-cost probabilities of .9 of $.40 and .1 of $.35.

What is the best decision based on an expected monetary value (EMV) criterion? (*Note:* We want the lowest EMV, as we are dealing with costs in this problem.)

•• **15** MacDonald Products, Inc., of Clarkson, New York, has the option of (a) proceeding immediately with production of a new top-of-the-line stereo TV that has just completed prototype testing or (b) having the value analysis team complete a study. If Ed Lusk, VP for operations, proceeds with the existing prototype (option a), the firm can expect sales to be 100,000 units at $550 each, with a probability of .6, and a .4 probability of 75,000 at $550. If, however, he uses the value analysis team (option b), the firm expects sales of 75,000 units at $750, with a probability of .7, and a .3 probability of 70,000 units at $750. Value analysis, at a cost of $100,000, is only used in option b. Which option has the highest expected monetary value (EMV)?

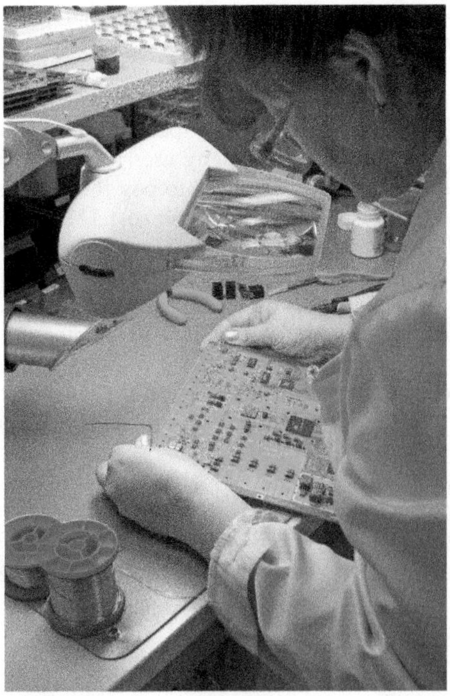

Romanchuck Dimitry/Shutterstock

•• **16** Residents of Mill River have fond memories of ice skating at a local park. An artist has captured the experience in a drawing and is hoping to reproduce it and sell framed copies to current and former residents. He thinks that if the market is good he can sell 400 copies of the elegant version at $125 each. If the market is not good, he will sell only 300 at $90 each. He can make a deluxe version of the same drawing instead. He feels that if the market is good he can sell 500 copies of the deluxe version at $100 each. If the market is not good, he will sell only

400 copies at $70 each. In either case, production costs will be approximately $35,000. He can also choose to do nothing. If he believes there is a 50% probability of a good market, what should he do? Why? PX

•• **17** Ritz Products's materials manager, Tej Dhakar, must determine whether to make or buy a new semiconductor for the wrist TV that the firm is about to produce. One million units are expected to be produced over the life cycle. If the product is made, start-up and production costs of the *make* decision total $1 million, with a probability of .4 that the product will be satisfactory and a .6 probability that it will not. If the product is not satisfactory, the firm will have to reevaluate the decision. If the decision is reevaluated, the choice will be whether to spend another $1 million to redesign the semiconductor or to purchase. Likelihood of success the second time that the make decision is made is .9. If the second *make* decision also fails, the firm must purchase. Regardless of when the purchase takes place, Dhakar's best judgment of cost is that Ritz will pay $.50 for each purchased semiconductor plus $1 million in vendor development cost.

a) Assuming that Ritz must have the semiconductor (stopping or doing without is not a viable option), what is the best decision?
b) What criteria did you use to make this decision?
c) What is the worst that can happen to Ritz as a result of this particular decision? What is the best that can happen? PX

•• **18** Sox Engineering designs and constructs air conditioning and heating systems for hospitals and clinics. Currently, the company's staff is overloaded with design work. There is a major design project due in 8 weeks. The penalty for completing the design late is $14,000 per week, since any delay will cause the facility to open later than anticipated and cost the client significant revenue. If the company uses its inside engineers to complete the design, it will have to pay them overtime for all work. Sox has estimated that it will cost $12,000 per week (wages and overhead), including late weeks, to have company engineers complete the design. Sox is also considering having an outside engineering firm do the design. A bid of $92,000 has been received for the completed design. Yet another option for completing the design is to conduct a joint design by having a third engineering company complete all electromechanical components of the design at a cost of $56,000. Sox would then complete the rest of the design and control systems at an estimated cost of $30,000.

Sox has estimated the following probabilities of completing the project within various time frames when using each of the three options. Those estimates are shown in the following table:

	PROBABILITY OF COMPLETING THE DESIGN			
OPTION	ON TIME	1 WEEK LATE	2 WEEKS LATE	3 WEEKS LATE
Internal Engineers	.4	.5	.1	—
External Engineers	.2	.4	.3	.1
Joint Design	.1	.3	.4	.2

What is the best decision based on an expected monetary value criterion? (*Note:* You want the lowest EMV because we are dealing with costs in this problem.) PX

••• **19** Use the data in Solved Problem 1 to examine what happens to the decision if Sarah King can increase yields from 59,000 to 64,000 by applying an expensive phosphorus to the screen at an added manufacturing cost of $250,000. Prepare the modified decision tree. What are the payoffs, and which branch has the greatest EMV?

•••• **20** Using the house of quality sequence, as described in Figure 4, determine how you might deploy resources to achieve the desired quality for a product or service whose production process you understand.

•••• **21** McBurger, Inc., wants to redesign its kitchens to improve productivity and quality. Three designs, called designs K1, K2, and K3, are under consideration. No matter which design is used, daily production of sandwiches at a typical McBurger restaurant is for 500 sandwiches. A sandwich costs $1.30 to produce. Non-defective sandwiches sell, on the average, for $2.50 per sandwich. Defective sandwiches cannot be sold and are scrapped. The goal is to choose a design that maximizes the expected profit at a typical restaurant over a 300-day period. Designs K1, K2, and K3 cost $100,000, $130,000, and $180,000, respectively. Under design K1, there is a .80 chance that 90 out of each 100 sandwiches are non-defective and a .20 chance that 70 out of each 100 sandwiches are non-defective. Under design K2, there is a .85 chance that 90 out of each 100 sandwiches are non-defective and a .15 chance that 75 out of each 100 sandwiches are non-defective. Under design K3, there is a .90 chance that 95 out of each 100 sandwiches are non-defective and a .10 chance that 80 out of each 100 sandwiches are non-defective. What is the expected profit level of the design that achieves the maximum expected 300-day profit level?

Refer to MyOMLab **for these additional homework problems: 22–28**

CASE STUDIES

De Mar's Product Strategy

De Mar, a plumbing, heating, and air-conditioning company located in Fresno, California, has a simple but powerful product strategy: *Solve the customer's problem no matter what, solve the problem when the customer needs it solved, and make sure the customer feels good when you leave.* De Mar offers guaranteed, same-day service for customers requiring it. The company provides 24-hour-a-day, 7-day-a-week service at no extra charge for customers whose air conditioning dies on a hot summer Sunday or whose toilet overflows at 2:30 A.M. As assistant service coordinator Janie Walter puts it: "We will be there to fix your A/C on the fourth of July, and it's not a penny extra. When our competitors won't get out of bed, we'll be there!"

De Mar guarantees the price of a job to the penny before the work begins. Whereas most competitors guarantee their work for 30 days, De Mar guarantees all parts and labor for one year. The company assesses no travel charge because "it's not fair to charge customers for driving out." Owner Larry Harmon says: "We are in an industry that doesn't have the best reputation. If we start making money our main goal, we are in trouble. So I stress customer satisfaction; money is the by-product."

De Mar uses selective hiring, ongoing training and education, performance measures, and compensation that incorporate customer satisfaction, strong teamwork, peer pressure, empowerment, and aggressive promotion to implement its strategy. Says credit manager Anne Semrick: "The person who wants a nine-to-five job needs to go somewhere else."

De Mar is a premium pricer. Yet customers respond because De Mar delivers value—that is, benefits for costs. In 8 years, annual sales increased from about $200,000 to more than $3.3 million.

Discussion Questions

1. What is De Mar's product? Identify the tangible parts of this product and its service components.
2. How should other areas of De Mar (marketing, finance, personnel) support its product strategy?
3. Even though De Mar's product is primarily a service product, how should each of the 10 strategic OM decisions in the text be managed to ensure that the product is successful?

Source: Reprinted with the permission of The Free Press, from *On Great Service: A Framework for Action* by Leonard L. Berry. Copyright © 1995 by Leonard L. Berry.

Product Design at Regal Marine

Video Case

With hundreds of competitors in the boat business, Regal Marine must work to differentiate itself from the flock. As we saw in the *Global Company Profile* that opened this text, Regal continuously introduces innovative, high-quality new boats. Its differentiation strategy is reflected in a product line consisting of 22 models.

To maintain this stream of innovation, and with so many boats at varying stages of their life cycles, Regal constantly seeks design input from customers, dealers, and consultants. Design ideas rapidly find themselves in the styling studio, where they are placed onto CAD machines in order to speed the development process. Existing boat designs are always evolving as the company tries to stay stylish and competitive. Moreover, with life cycles as short as 3 years, a steady stream of new products is required. A few years ago, the new product was the three-passenger $11,000 Rush, a small but powerful boat capable of pulling a water-skier. This was followed with a 20-foot inboard–outboard performance boat with so many innovations that it won prize after prize in the industry. Another new boat is a redesigned 52-foot sports yacht that sleeps six in luxury staterooms. With all these models and innovations, Regal designers and production personnel are under pressure to respond quickly.

By getting key suppliers on board early and urging them to participate at the design stage, Regal improves both innovations and quality while speeding product development. Regal finds that the sooner it brings suppliers on board, the faster it can bring new boats to the market. After a development stage that constitutes concept and styling, CAD designs yield product specifications. The first stage in actual production is the creation of the "plug," a foam-based carving used to make the molds for fiberglass hulls and decks. Specifications from the CAD system drive the carving process. Once the plug is carved, the permanent molds for each new hull and deck design are formed. Molds take about 4 to 8 weeks to make and are all hand-

made. Similar molds are made for many of the other features in Regal boats—from galley and stateroom components to lavatories and steps. Finished molds can be joined and used to make thousands of boats.

Discussion Questions*

1. How does the concept of product life cycle apply to Regal Marine products?
2. What strategy does Regal use to stay competitive?
3. What kind of engineering savings is Regal achieving by using CAD technology rather than traditional drafting techniques?
4. What are the likely benefits of the CAD design technology?

*You may wish to view the video that accompanies this case before addressing these questions.

Bibliography

Alexy Oliver, P. Criscuelo, and A. Salter. "Managing Unsolicited Ideas for R&D." *California Management Review* 54, no. 3 (Spring 2012): 116–139.

Brown, Bruce, and S.D. Anthony; "How P&G Tripled Its Innovation Success Rate." *Harvard Business Review* 89, no. 6 (June 2011): 64–72.

Camevalli, J. A., and P. A. C. Miguel. "Review, Analysis, and Classification of the Literature on QFD." *International Journal of Production Economics* 114, no. 2 (August 2008): 737.

Ernst, David, and James Bamford. "Your Alliances Are too Stable." *Harvard Business Review* 83, no. 5 (June 2005): 133–141.

Gerwin, Donald. "Coordinating New Product Development in Strategic Alliances." *The Academy of Management Review* 29, no. 2 (April 2004): 241–257.

Haines, Steven. *Managing Product Management*, New York; McGraw-Hill, 2012.

Krishnan, V., and Karl T. Ulrich. "Product Development Decisions: A Review of the Literature." *Management Science* 47, no. 1 (January 2001): 1–21.

Loch, C. H., and C. Terwiesch. "Rush and Be Wrong or Wait and Be Late?" *Production and Operations Management* 14, no. 3 (Fall 2005): 331–343.

Miguel, P. A. C., and J. A. Camevalli. "Benchmarking Practices of Quality Function Deployment." *Benchmarking* 15, no. 6 (2008): 657.

Phyper, J. D., and D. MacLean. *Good to Green: Managers' Business Risks and Opportunities in an Age of Environmental Awareness.* New York: Wiley, 2009.

Pisano, Gary P., and Roberto Verganti. "Which Kind of Collaboration Is Right for You?" *Harvard Business Review* 86, no. 12 (December 2008):78–86.

Reeves, Martin, and Mike Deimler. "Adaptability: The New Competitive Advantage." *Harvard Business Review* 90, no. 7 (July–August 2011): 135–141.

Saaksvuori, A., and A. Immonen. *Product Lifecycle Management.* Berlin: Springer-Verlag, 2004.

Seider, Warren D., et al. *Product and Process Design Principles.* 3rd. ed. New York: Wiley, 2008.

Ulrich, K., and S. Eppinger. *Product Design and Development*, 4th ed. New York: McGraw-Hill, 2008.

APPENDIX
SOLUTIONS TO EVEN-NUMBERED PROBLEMS

2 House of quality for a lunch:

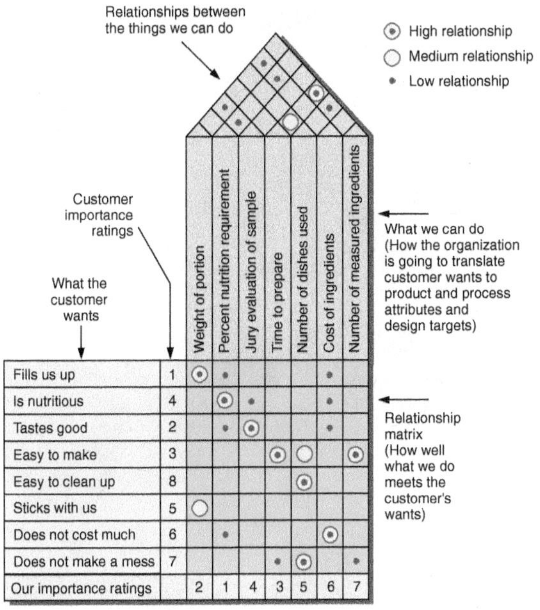

4 Individual answer. Build a house of quality similar to the one shown in Problem 2, entering the *wants* on the left and entering the *hows* at the top.

6 An assembly chart for the eyeglasses is shown below:

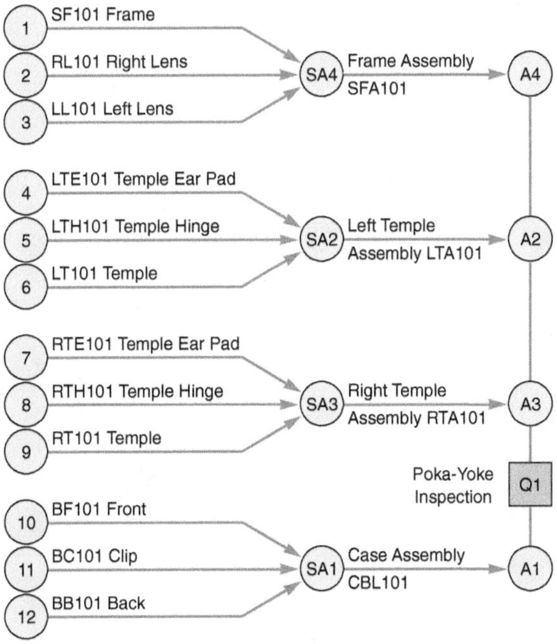

8 Assembly chart for a table lamp:

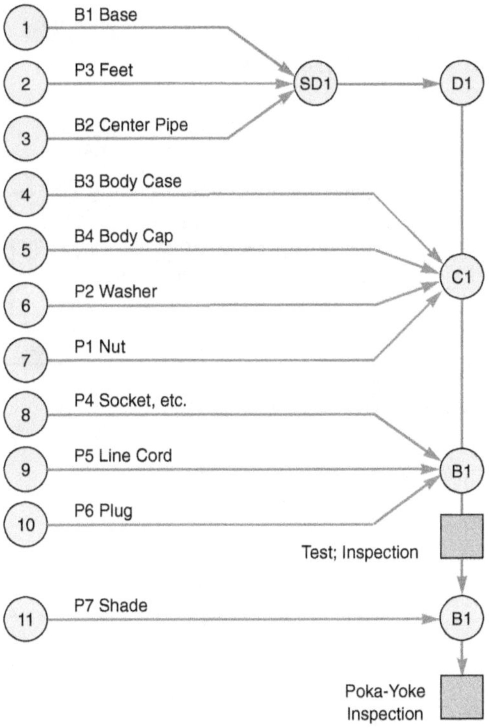

10 *Possible strategies:*
Kindle Fire (growth phase):
Increase capacity and improve balance of production system.
Attempt to make production facilities more efficient.
Netbook (introductory phase):
Increase R&D to better define required product characteristics.
Modify and improve production process.
Develop supplier and distribution systems.
Hand calculator (decline phase):
Concentrate on production and distribution cost reduction.

12 All 10 strategic OM decisions are impacted by their position in the PCN diagram. Comparing just one of these 10 decisions, *product design*:

(a) *Manufacturing*: Must commit to product decisions based on historical data of user preferences (e.g., more risk, no direct interaction)

(b) *Direct interaction*: The sandwich maker must build a system and hire personnel capable of making sandwiches for an end user who may literally be coaching the sandwich maker (e.g., "more mustard, no onions") as the sandwiches are made

(c) *Sandwich buffet*: Commit to purchase, prepare, and sanitarily display the sandwich components which may (or may not) be selected by the end user

14 Low technology, cost = $145,000
16 Deluxe version, EMV = $4,000
18 Joint design, EMV is lowest at $109,8000
20 House of Quality Sequence for Ice Cream

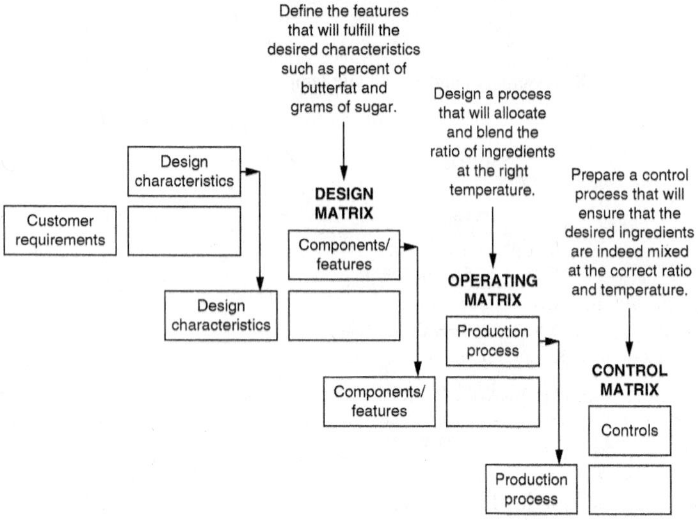

Rapid Review

Main Heading	Review Material	MyOMLab
GOODS AND SERVICES SELECTION	Although the term *products* may often refer to tangible goods, it also refers to offerings by service organizations. *The objective of the product decision is to develop and implement a product strategy that meets the demands of the marketplace with a competitive advantage.* ■ **Product decision**—The selection, definition, and design of products. The four phases of the product life cycle are introduction, growth, maturity, and decline. ■ **Product-by-value analysis**—A list of products, in descending order of their individual dollar contribution to the firm, as well as the *total annual dollar* contribution of the product.	Problem: 9 **VIDEO 1** Product Strategy at Regal Marine
GENERATING NEW PRODUCTS	Product selection, definition, and design take place on a continuing basis. Changes in product opportunities, the products themselves, product volume, and product mix may arise due to understanding the customer, economic change, sociological and demographic change, technological change, political/legal change, market practice, professional standards, suppliers, or distributors.	
PRODUCT DEVELOPMENT	■ **Quality function deployment (QFD)**—A process for determining customer requirements (customer "wants") and translating them into attributes (the "hows") that each functional area can understand and act on. ■ **House of quality**—A part of the quality function deployment process that utilizes a planning matrix to relate customer wants to how the firm is going to meet those wants. ■ **Product development teams**—Teams charged with moving from market requirements for a product to achieving product success. ■ **Concurrent engineering**—Use of participating teams in design and engineering activities. ■ **Manufacturability and value engineering**—Activities that help improve a product's design, production, maintainability, and use.	
ISSUES FOR PRODUCT DESIGN	■ **Robust design**—A design that can be produced to requirements even with unfavorable conditions in the production process. ■ **Modular design**—A design in which parts or components of a product are subdivided into modules that are easily interchanged or replaced. ■ **Computer-aided design (CAD)**—Interactive use of a computer to develop and document a product. ■ **Design for manufacture and assembly (DFMA)**—Software that allows designers to look at the effect of design on manufacturing of a product. ■ **Standard for the exchange of product data (STEP)**—A standard that provides a format allowing the electronic transmission of three-dimensional data. ■ **Computer-aided manufacturing (CAM)**—The use of information technology to control machinery. ■ **3-D printing**—An extension of CAD that builds prototypes and small lots. ■ **Virtual reality**—A visual form of communication in which images substitute for reality and typically allow the user to respond interactively. ■ **Value analysis**—A review of successful products that takes place during the production process. Sustainability is meeting the needs of the present without compromising the ability of future generations to meet their needs. Life cycle assessment (LCA) is part of ISO 14000; it assesses the environmental impact of a product from material and energy inputs to disposal and environmental releases.	
PRODUCT DEVELOPMENT CONTINUUM	■ **Time-based competition**—Competition based on time; rapidly developing products and moving them to market. *Internal development strategies* include (1) new internally developed products, (2) enhancements to existing products, and (3) migrations of existing products. *External development strategies* include (1) purchase the technology or expertise by acquiring the developer, (2) establish joint ventures, and (3) develop alliances. ■ **Joint ventures**—Firms establishing joint ownership to pursue new products or markets. ■ **Alliances**—Cooperative agreements that allow firms to remain independent but pursue strategies consistent with their individual missions.	

Rapid Review continued

Main Heading	Review Material	MyOMLab
DEFINING A PRODUCT	■ **Engineering drawing**—A drawing that shows the dimensions, tolerances, materials, and finishes of a component. ■ **Bill of material (BOM)**—A list of the components, their description, and the quantity of each required to make one unit of a product. ■ **Make-or-buy decision**—The choice between producing a component or a service and purchasing it from an outside source. ■ **Group technology**—A product and component coding system that specifies the size, shape, and type of processing; it allows similar products to be grouped.	
DOCUMENTS FOR PRODUCTION	■ **Assembly drawing**—An exploded view of a product. ■ **Assembly chart**—A graphic means of identifying how components flow into subassemblies and final products ■ **Route sheet**—A list of the operations necessary to produce a component with the material specified in the bill of material. ■ **Work order**—An instruction to make a given quantity of a particular item. ■ **Engineering change notice (ECN)**—A correction or modification of an engineering drawing or bill of material. ■ **Configuration management**—A system by which a product's planned and changing components are accurately identified. ■ **Product life cycle management (PLM)**—Software programs that tie together many phases of product design and manufacture.	
SERVICE DESIGN	■ **Process–chain–network (PCN) analysis**—A way to design processes to optimize interaction between firms and their customers. ■ **Process chain**—A sequence of steps that provide value to process participants. To enhance service efficiency, companies: (1) limit options, (2) delay customization, (3) modularize, (4) automate, and (5) design for the "moment of truth."	
APPLICATION OF DECISION TREES TO PRODUCT DESIGN	To form a decision tree, (1) include all possible alternatives (including "do nothing") and states of nature; (2) enter payoffs at the end of the appropriate branch; and (3) determine the expected value of each course of action by starting at the end of the tree and working toward the beginning, calculating values at each step and "pruning" inferior alternatives.	Problems: 10, 14–21 Virtual Office Hours for Solved Problem: 1 ACTIVE MODEL 1
TRANSITION TO PRODUCTION	One of the arts of management is knowing when to move a product from development to production; this move is known as *transition to production*.	

Self Test

■ **Before taking the self-test,** refer to the learning objectives listed at the beginning of the text and the key terms listed at the end of the text.

LO1. A product's life cycle is divided into four stages, including:
- **a)** introduction.
- **b)** growth.
- **c)** maturity.
- **d)** all of the above.

LO2. Product development systems include:
- **a)** bills of material.
- **b)** routing charts.
- **c)** functional specifications.
- **d)** product-by-values analysis.
- **e)** configuration management.

LO3. A house of quality is:
- **a)** a matrix relating customer "wants" to the firm's "hows."
- **b)** a schematic showing how a product is put together.
- **c)** a list of the operations necessary to produce a component.
- **d)** an instruction to make a given quantity of a particular item.
- **e)** a set of detailed instructions about how to perform a task.

LO4. Time-based competition focuses on:
- **a)** moving new products to market more quickly.
- **b)** reducing the life cycle of a product.
- **c)** linking QFD to PLM.
- **d)** design database availability.
- **e)** value engineering.

LO5. Products are defined by:
- **a)** value analysis.
- **b)** value engineering.
- **c)** routing sheets.
- **d)** assembly charts.
- **e)** engineering drawings.

LO6. A route sheet:
- **a)** lists the operations necessary to produce a component.
- **b)** is an instruction to make a given quantity of a particular item.
- **c)** is a schematic showing how a product is assembled.
- **d)** is a document showing the flow of product components.
- **e)** all of the above.

LO7. The three process regions in a process–chain–network diagram are:
- **a)** manufacture, supplier, customer
- **b)** direct and surrogate, customer, provider
- **c)** independent, dependent, customer interaction
- **d)** direct interaction, surrogate interaction, independent processing

LO8. Decision trees use:
- **a)** probabilities.
- **b)** payoffs.
- **c)** logic.
- **d)** options.
- **e)** all of the above.

Answers: LO1. d; LO2. c; LO3. a; LO4. a; LO5. e; LO6. a; LO7. d; LO8. e.

Managing Quality

OUTLINE

GLOBAL COMPANY PROFILE: *Arnold Palmer Hospital*

- Quality and Strategy
- Defining Quality
- Total Quality Management
- Tools of TQM
- The Role of Inspection
- TQM In Services

10 OM STRATEGY DECISIONS

- Design of Goods and Services
- *Managing Quality*
- Process Strategy
- Location Strategies
- Layout Strategies
- Human Resources
- Supply-Chain Management
- Inventory Management
- Scheduling
- Maintenance

From Chapter 6 of *Operations Management, Sustainability and Supply Chain Management*, Eleventh Edition.

GLOBAL COMPANY PROFILE
Arnold Palmer Hospital

Managing Quality Provides a Competitive Advantage at Arnold Palmer Hospital

Since 1989, Arnold Palmer Hospital, named after its famous golfing benefactor, has touched the lives of over 7 million children and women and their families. Its patients come not only from its Orlando location but from all 50 states and around the world. More than 12,000 babies are delivered every year at Arnold Palmer, and its huge neonatal intensive care unit boasts one of the highest survival rates in the U.S.

Every hospital professes quality health care, but at Arnold Palmer quality is the mantra—practiced in a fashion like the Ritz-Carlton practices it in the hotel industry. The hospital typically scores in the top 10% of national benchmark studies in terms of patient satisfaction. And its managers follow patient questionnaire results daily. If anything is amiss, corrective action takes place immediately.

Virtually every quality management technique we present in this text is employed at Arnold Palmer Hospital:

- *Continuous improvement:* The hospital constantly seeks new ways to lower infection rates, readmission rates, deaths, costs, and hospital stay times.

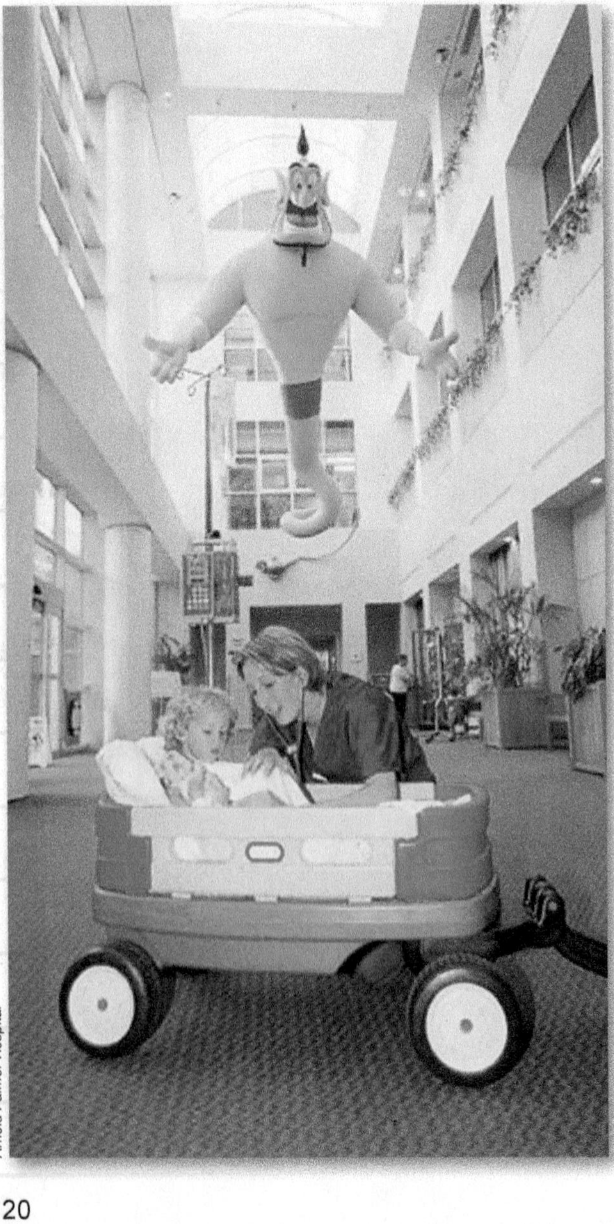

Arnold Palmer Hospital

The lobby of Arnold Palmer Hospital, with its 20-foot-high Genie, is clearly intended as a warm and friendly place for children.

Arnold Palmer Hospital

The Storkboard is a visible chart of the status of each baby about to be delivered, so all nurses and doctors are kept up to date at a glance.

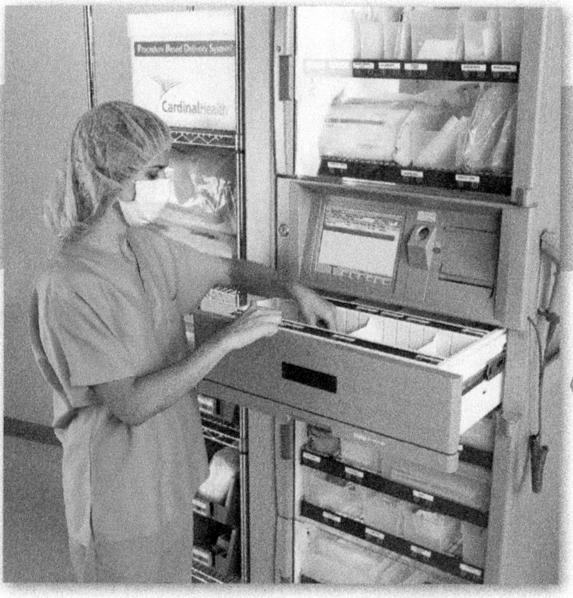

CareFusion Pyxis

This PYXIS inventory station gives nurses quick access to medicines and supplies needed in their departments. When the nurse removes an item for patient use, the item is automatically billed to that account, and usage is noted at the main supply area.

The hospital has redesigned its neonatal rooms. In the old system, there were 16 neonatal beds in an often noisy and large room. The new rooms are semiprivate, with a quiet simulated-night atmosphere. These rooms have proven to help babies develop and improve more quickly.

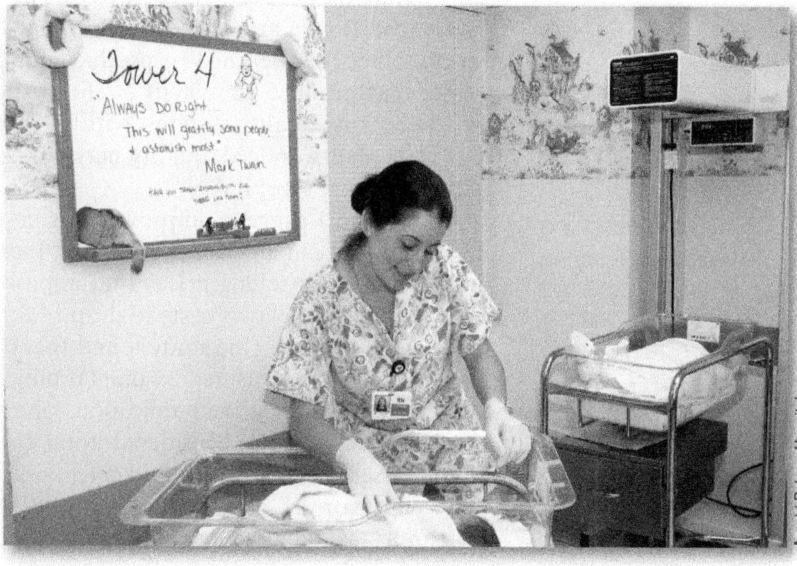

Arnold Palmer Hospital

- *Employee empowerment:* When employees see a problem, they are trained to take care of it; staff are empowered to give gifts to patients displeased with some aspect of service.
- *Benchmarking:* The hospital belongs to a 2,000-member organization that monitors standards in many areas and provides monthly feedback to the hospital.

Arnold Palmer Hospital

When Arnold Palmer Hospital began planning for a new 11-story hospital across the street from its existing building, it decided on a circular pod design, creating a patient-centered environment. Rooms use warm colors, have pull-down Murphy beds for family members, 14-foot ceilings, and natural lighting with oversized windows. The pod concept also means there is a nursing station within a few feet of each 10-bed pod, saving much wasted walking time by nurses to reach the patient.

- *Just-in-time:* Supplies are delivered to Arnold Palmer on a JIT basis. This keeps inventory costs low and keeps quality problems from hiding.
- *Tools such as Pareto charts and flowcharts:* These tools monitor processes and help the staff graphically spot problem areas and suggest ways they can be improved.

From their first day of orientation, employees from janitors to nurses learn that the patient comes first. Staff standing in hallways will never be heard discussing their personal lives or commenting on confidential issues of health care. This culture of quality at Arnold Palmer Hospital makes a hospital visit, often traumatic to children and their parents, a warmer and more comforting experience.

EARNING OBJECTIVES

LO1 *Define* quality and TQM

LO2 *Describe* the ISO international quality standards

LO3 *Explain* what Six Sigma is

LO4 *Explain* how benchmarking is used in TQM

LO5 *Explain* quality robust products and Taguchi concepts

LO6 *Use* the seven tools of TQM

Quality and Strategy

As Arnold Palmer Hospital and many other organizations have found, quality is a wonderful tonic for improving operations. Managing quality helps build successful strategies of *differentiation*, *low cost*, and *response*. For instance, defining customer quality expectations has helped Bose Corp. successfully *differentiate* its stereo speakers as among the best in the world. Nucor has learned to produce quality steel at *low cost* by developing efficient processes that produce consistent quality. And Dell Computers rapidly *responds* to customer orders because quality systems, with little rework, have allowed it to achieve rapid throughput in its plants. Indeed, quality may be the key success factor for these firms, just as it is at Arnold Palmer Hospital.

VIDEO 1
The Culture of Quality at Arnold Palmer Hospital

STUDENT TIP
High-quality products and services are the most profitable.

As Figure 1 suggests, improvements in quality help firms increase sales and reduce costs, both of which can increase profitability. Increases in sales often occur as firms speed response, increase or lower selling prices, and improve their reputation for quality products. Similarly, improved quality allows costs to drop as firms increase productivity and lower rework, scrap, and warranty costs. One study found that companies with the highest quality were five times as productive (as measured by units produced per labor-hour) as companies with the poorest quality. Indeed, when the implications of an organization's long-term costs and the potential for increased sales are considered, total costs may well be at a minimum when 100% of the goods or services are perfect and defect free.

Quality, or the lack of quality, affects the entire organization from supplier to customer and from product design to maintenance. Perhaps more importantly, *building* an organization that can achieve quality is a demanding task. Figure 2 lays out the flow of activities for an organization to use to achieve total quality management (TQM). A successful quality strategy begins with an organizational culture that fosters quality, followed by an understanding of the principles of quality, and then engaging employees in the necessary activities to implement quality. When these things are done well, the organization typically satisfies its customers and obtains a competitive advantage. The ultimate goal is to win customers. Because quality causes so many other good things to happen, it is a great place to start.

Figure 1
Ways Quality Improves Profitability

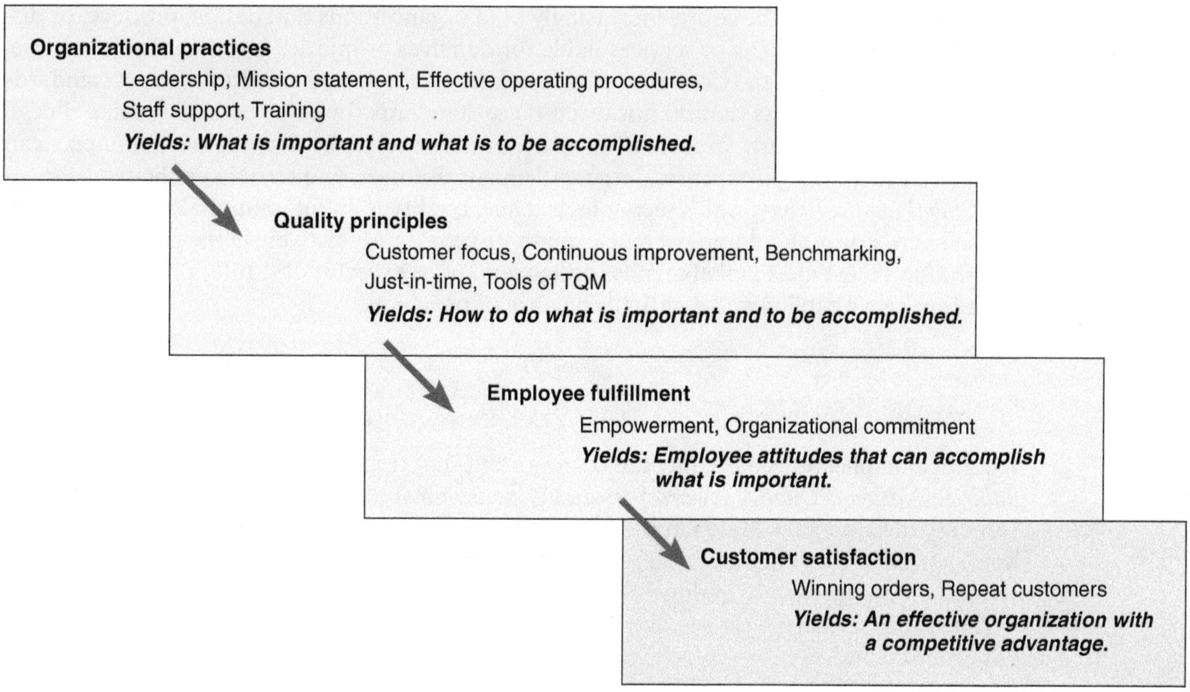

Figure 2

The Flow of Activities Necessary to Achieve Total Quality Management

Defining Quality

An operations manager's objective is to build a total quality management system that identifies and satisfies customer needs. Total quality management takes care of the customer. Consequently, we accept the definition of quality as adopted by the American Society for Quality (ASQ; **www.asq.org**): "The totality of features and characteristics of a product or service that bears on its ability to satisfy stated or implied needs."

Quality
The ability of a product or service to meet customer needs.

Others, however, believe that definitions of quality fall into several categories. Some definitions are *user based*. They propose that quality "lies in the eyes of the beholder." Marketing people like this approach and so do customers. To them, higher quality means better performance, nicer features, and other (sometimes costly) improvements. To production managers, quality is *manufacturing based*. They believe that quality means conforming to standards and "making it right the first time." Yet a third approach is *product based*, which views quality as a precise and measurable variable. In this view, for example, really good ice cream has high butterfat levels.

LO1 *Define* quality and TQM

This text develops approaches and techniques to address all three categories of quality. The characteristics that connote quality must first be identified through research (a user-based approach to quality). These characteristics are then translated into specific product attributes (a product-based approach to quality). Then, the manufacturing process is organized to ensure that products are made precisely to specifications (a manufacturing-based approach to quality). A process that ignores any one of these steps will not result in a quality product.

STUDENT TIP
To create a quality good or service, operations managers need to know what the customer expects.

Implications of Quality

In addition to being a critical element in operations, quality has other implications. Here are three other reasons why quality is important:

1. *Company reputation:* An organization can expect its reputation for quality—be it good or bad—to follow it. Quality will show up in perceptions about the firm's new products, employment practices, and supplier relations. Self-promotion is not a substitute for quality products.

2. *Product liability:* The courts increasingly hold organizations that design, produce, or distribute faulty products or services liable for damages or injuries resulting from their use. Legislation such as the Consumer Product Safety Act sets and enforces product standards by banning products that do not reach those standards. Impure foods that cause illness, nightgowns that burn, tires that fall apart, or auto fuel tanks that explode on impact can all lead to huge legal expenses, large settlements or losses, and terrible publicity.
3. *Global implications:* In this technological age, quality is an international, as well as OM, concern. For both a company and a country to compete effectively in the global economy, products must meet global quality, design, and price expectations. Inferior products harm a firm's profitability and a nation's balance of payments.

Malcolm Baldrige National Quality Award

The global implications of quality are so important that the U.S. has established the *Malcolm Baldrige National Quality Award* for quality achievement. The award is named for former Secretary of Commerce Malcolm Baldrige. Winners include such firms as Motorola, Milliken, Xerox, FedEx, Ritz-Carlton Hotels, AT&T, Cadillac, and Texas Instruments. (For details about the Baldrige Award and its 1,000-point scoring system, visit **www.quality.nist.gov**.)

The Japanese have a similar award, the Deming Prize, named after an American, Dr. W. Edwards Deming.

ISO 9000 International Quality Standards

ISO 9000
A set of quality standards developed by the International Organization for Standardization (ISO).

The move toward global supply chains has placed so much emphasis on quality that the world has united around a single quality standard, ISO 9000. ISO 9000 is *the* quality standard with international recognition. Its focus is to enhance success through eight quality management principles: (1) top management leadership, (2) customer satisfaction, (3) continual improvement, (4) involvement of people, (5) process analysis, (6) use of data-driven decision making, (7) a systems approach to management, and (8) mutually beneficial supplier relationships.

LO2 *Describe* the ISO international quality standards

The ISO standard encourages establishment of quality management procedures, detailed documentation, work instructions, and recordkeeping. Like the Baldrige Awards, the assessment includes self-appraisal and problem identification. Unlike the Baldrige, ISO certified organizations must be reaudited every three years.

In 2009, the latest modification of the standard, ISO 9004: 2009, emphasized how an organization can use a quality management approach to achieve *sustained* success. This version encourages organizations to plan for their economic survival through continuing and systematic improvement in performance, efficiency, and effectiveness.

STUDENT TIP ☆
International quality standards grow in prominence every year. See **www.iso.ch.**

Over one million certifications have been awarded to firms in 178 countries, including over 30,000 in the U.S. To do business globally, it is critical for a firm to be certified and listed in the ISO directory.

Cost of Quality (COQ)

Cost of quality (COQ)
The cost of doing things wrong—that is, the price of nonconformance.

Four major categories of costs are associated with quality. Called the cost of quality (COQ), they are:

- *Prevention costs:* costs associated with reducing the potential for defective parts or services (e.g., training, quality improvement programs).
- *Appraisal costs:* costs related to evaluating products, processes, parts, and services (e.g., testing, labs, inspectors).
- *Internal failure costs:* costs that result from production of defective parts or services before delivery to customers (e.g., rework, scrap, downtime).
- *External failure costs:* costs that occur after delivery of defective parts or services (e.g., rework, returned goods, liabilities, lost goodwill, costs to society).

TABLE 1 Leaders in the Field of Quality Management

LEADER	PHILOSOPHY/CONTRIBUTION
W. Edwards Deming	Deming insisted management accept responsibility for building good systems. The employee cannot produce products that on average exceed the quality of what the process is capable of producing. His 14 points for implementing quality improvement are presented in this text.
Joseph M. Juran	A pioneer in teaching the Japanese how to improve quality, Juran believed strongly in top-management commitment, support, and involvement in the quality effort. He was also a believer in teams that continually seek to raise quality standards. Juran varies from Deming somewhat in focusing on the customer and defining quality as fitness for use, not necessarily the written specifications.
Armand Feigenbaum	His 1961 book *Total Quality Control* laid out 40 steps to quality improvement processes. He viewed quality not as a set of tools but as a total field that integrated the processes of a company. His work in how people learn from each other's successes led to the field of cross-functional teamwork.
Philip B. Crosby	*Quality Is Free* was Crosby's attention-getting book published in 1979. Crosby believed that in the traditional trade-off between the cost of improving quality and the cost of poor quality, the cost of poor quality is understated. The cost of poor quality should include all of the things that are involved in not doing the job right the first time. Crosby coined the term *zero defects* and stated, "There is absolutely no reason for having errors or defects in any product or service."

Source: Based on *Quality Is Free* by Philip B. Crosby, (New York, McGraw-Hill, 1979) p. 58.

The first three costs can be reasonably estimated, but external costs are very hard to quantify. When GE had to recall 3.1 million dishwashers (because of a defective switch alleged to have started seven fires), the cost of repairs exceeded the value of all the machines. This leads to the belief by many experts that the cost of poor quality is consistently underestimated.

Observers of quality management believe that, on balance, the cost of quality products is only a fraction of the benefits. They think the real losers are organizations that fail to work aggressively at quality. For instance, Philip Crosby stated that quality is free. "What costs money are the unquality things—all the actions that involve not doing it right the first time."[1]

Takumi is a Japanese character that symbolizes a broader dimension than quality, a deeper process than education, and a more perfect method than persistence.

Leaders in Quality Besides Crosby there are several other giants in the field of quality management, including Deming, Feigenbaum, and Juran. Table 1 summarizes their philosophies and contributions.

Ethics and Quality Management

For operations managers, one of the most important jobs is to deliver healthy, safe, and quality products and services to customers. The development of poor-quality products, because of inadequate design and production processes, results not only in higher production costs but also leads to injuries, lawsuits, and increased government regulation.

If a firm believes that it has introduced a questionable product, ethical conduct must dictate the responsible action. This may be a worldwide recall, as conducted by both Johnson & Johnson (for Tylenol) and Perrier (for sparkling water), when each of these products was found to be contaminated. A manufacturer must accept responsibility for any poor-quality product released to the public.

There are many stakeholders involved in the production and marketing of poor-quality products, including stockholders, employees, customers, suppliers, distributors, and creditors. As a matter of ethics, management must ask if any of these stakeholders are being wronged. Every company needs to develop core values that become day-to-day guidelines for everyone from the CEO to production-line employees.

[1]Philip B. Crosby, *Quality Is Free* (New York: McGraw-Hill, 1979). Further, J. M. Juran states, in his book *Juran on Quality by Design* (The Free Press 1992, p. 119), that costs of poor quality "are huge, but the amounts are not known with precision. In most companies the accounting system provides only a minority of the information needed to quantify this cost of poor quality. It takes a great deal of time and effort to extend the accounting system so as to provide full coverage."

TABLE 2 Deming's 14 Points for Implementing Quality Improvement

1.	Create consistency of purpose.
2.	Lead to promote change.
3.	Build quality into the product; stop depending on inspections to catch problems.
4.	Build long-term relationships based on performance instead of awarding business on the basis of price.
5.	Continuously improve product, quality, and service.
6.	Start training.
7.	Emphasize leadership.
8.	Drive out fear.
9.	Break down barriers between departments.
10.	Stop haranguing workers.
11.	Support, help, and improve.
12.	Remove barriers to pride in work.
13.	Institute a vigorous program of education and self-improvement.
14.	Put everybody in the company to work on the transformation.

Source: Deming, W. Edwards. *Out of the Crisis*, pp. 23–24, © 2000 W. Edwards Deming Institute, published by The MIT Press. Reprinted by permission.

Total Quality Management

Total quality management (TQM)
Management of an entire organization so that it excels in all aspects of products and services that are important to the customer.

Total quality management (TQM) refers to a quality emphasis that encompasses the entire organization, from supplier to customer. TQM stresses a commitment by management to have a continuing companywide drive toward excellence in all aspects of products and services that are important to the customer. Each of the 10 decisions made by operations managers deals with some aspect of identifying and meeting customer expectations. Meeting those expectations requires an emphasis on TQM if a firm is to compete as a leader in world markets.

STUDENT TIP Here are 7 concepts that make up the heart of an effective TQM program.

Quality expert W. Edwards Deming used 14 points (see Table 2) to indicate how he implemented TQM. We develop these into seven concepts for an effective TQM program: (1) continuous improvement, (2) Six Sigma, (3) employee empowerment, (4) benchmarking, (5) just-in-time (JIT), (6) Taguchi concepts, and (7) knowledge of TQM tools.

Continuous Improvement

Total quality management requires a never-ending process of continuous improvement that covers people, equipment, suppliers, materials, and procedures. The basis of the philosophy is that every aspect of an operation can be improved. The end goal is perfection, which is never achieved but always sought.

PDCA
A continuous improvement model of plan, do, check. act.

Plan-Do-Check-Act Walter Shewhart, another pioneer in quality management, developed a circular model known as **PDCA** (plan, do, check, act) as his version of continuous improvement. Deming later took this concept to Japan during his work there after World War II. The PDCA cycle (also called a Deming circle or a Shewhart circle) is shown in Figure 3 as a circle to stress the continuous nature of the improvement process.

Figure 3
PDCA Cycle

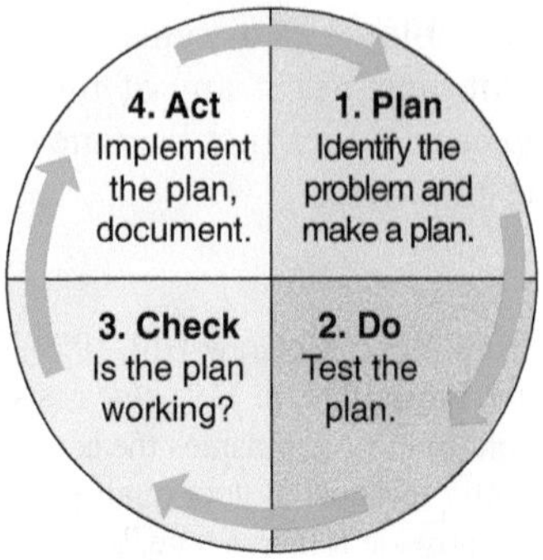

The Japanese use the word *kaizen* to describe this ongoing process of unending improvement—the setting and achieving of ever-higher goals. In the U.S., *TQM* and *zero defects* are also used to describe continuous improvement efforts. But whether it's PDCA, kaizen, TQM, or zero defects, the operations manager is a key player in building a work culture that endorses continuous improvement.

Six Sigma

The term **Six Sigma**, popularized by Motorola, Honeywell, and General Electric, has two meanings in TQM. In a *statistical* sense, it describes a process, product, or service with an extremely high capability (99.9997% accuracy). For example, if 1 million passengers pass through the St. Louis Airport with checked baggage each month, a Six Sigma program for baggage handling will result in only 3.4 passengers with misplaced luggage. The more common *three-sigma* program would result in 2,700 passengers with misplaced bags every month. See Figure 4.

Six Sigma
A program to save time, improve quality, and lower costs.

The second TQM definition of Six Sigma is a *program* designed to reduce defects to help lower costs, save time, and improve customer satisfaction. Six Sigma is a comprehensive system—a strategy, a discipline, and a set of tools—for achieving and sustaining business success:

LO3 *Explain* what Six Sigma is

- It is a *strategy* because it focuses on total customer satisfaction.
- It is a *discipline* because it follows the formal Six Sigma Improvement Model known as DMAIC. This five-step process improvement model (1) *Defines* the project's purpose, scope, and outputs and then identifies the required process information, keeping in mind the customer's definition of quality; (2) *Measures* the process and collects data; (3) *Analyzes* the data, ensuring repeatability (the results can be duplicated) and reproducibility (others get the same result); (4) *Improves*, by modifying or redesigning, existing processes and procedures; and (5) *Controls* the new process to make sure performance levels are maintained.
- It is a *set of seven tools* that we introduce shortly in this text: check sheets, scatter diagrams, cause-and-effect diagrams, Pareto charts, flowcharts, histograms, and statistical process control.

Motorola developed Six Sigma in the 1980s, in response to customer complaints about its products and in response to stiff competition. The company first set a goal of reducing defects by 90%. Within one year, it had achieved such impressive results—through benchmarking competitors, soliciting new ideas from employees, changing reward plans, adding training, and revamping critical processes—that it documented the procedures into what it called Six Sigma. Although the concept was rooted in manufacturing, GE later expanded Six Sigma into services, including human resources, sales, customer services, and financial/credit services. The concept of wiping out defects turns out to be the same in both manufacturing and services.

Implementing Six Sigma Implementing Six Sigma is a big commitment. Indeed, successful Six Sigma programs in every firm, from GE to Motorola to DuPont to Texas Instruments, require a major time commitment, especially from top management. These leaders have to formulate the plan, communicate their buy-in and the firm's objectives, and take a visible role in setting the example for others.

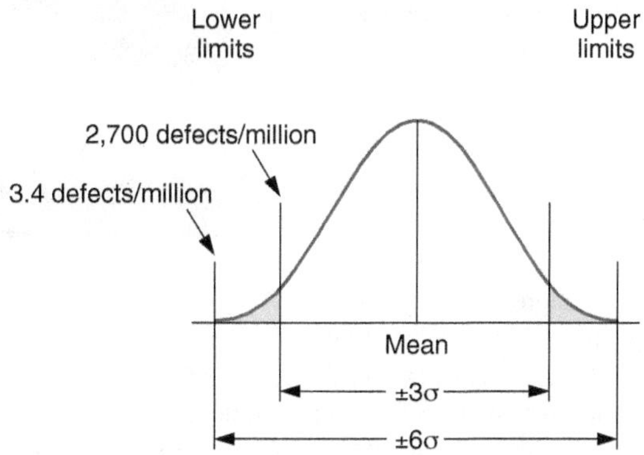

Figure 4
Defects per Million for $\pm 3\sigma$ vs. $\pm 6\sigma$

STUDENT TIP
Recall that $\pm 3\sigma$ provides 99.73% accuracy, while $\pm 6\sigma$ is 99.9997%.

Successful Six Sigma projects are clearly related to the strategic direction of a company. It is a management-directed, team-based, and expert-led approach.[2]

Employee Empowerment

Employee empowerment
Enlarging employee jobs so that the added responsibility and authority is moved to the lowest level possible in the organization.

Employee empowerment means involving employees in every step of the production process. Consistently, research suggests that some 85% of quality problems have to do with materials and processes, not with employee performance. Therefore, the task is to design equipment and processes that produce the desired quality. This is best done with a high degree of involvement by those who understand the shortcomings of the system. Those dealing with the system on a daily basis understand it better than anyone else. One study indicated that TQM programs that delegate responsibility for quality to shop-floor employees tend to be twice as likely to succeed as those implemented with "top-down" directives.[3]

When nonconformance occurs, the worker is seldom wrong. Either the product was designed wrong, the system that makes the product was designed wrong, or the employee was improperly trained. Although the employee may be able to help solve the problem, the employee rarely causes it.

Techniques for building employee empowerment include (1) building communication networks that include employees; (2) developing open, supportive supervisors; (3) moving responsibility from both managers and staff to production employees; (4) building high-morale organizations; and (5) creating such formal organization structures as teams and quality circles.

Quality circle
A group of employees meeting regularly with a facilitator to solve work-related problems in their work area.

Teams can be built to address a variety of issues. One popular focus of teams is quality. Such teams are often known as quality circles. A **quality circle** is a group of employees who meet regularly to solve work-related problems. The members receive training in group planning, problem solving, and statistical quality control. They generally meet once a week (usually after work but sometimes on company time). Although the members are not rewarded financially, they do receive recognition from the firm. A specially trained team member, called the *facilitator*, usually helps train the members and keeps the meetings running smoothly. Teams with a quality focus have proven to be a cost-effective way to increase productivity as well as quality.

Benchmarking

Benchmarking
Selecting a demonstrated standard of performance that represents the very best performance for a process or an activity.

Benchmarking is another ingredient in an organization's TQM program. **Benchmarking** involves selecting a demonstrated standard of products, services, costs, or practices that represent the very best performance for processes or activities very similar to your own. The idea is to

Workers at this TRW airbag manufacturing plant in Marshall, Illinois, are their own inspectors. Empowerment is an essential part of TQM. This man is checking the quality of a crash sensor he built.

[2]To train employees in how to improve quality and its relationship to customers, there are three other key players in the Six Sigma program: Master Black Belts, Black Belts, and Green Belts.

[3]"The Straining of Quality," *The Economist* (January 14, 1995): 55. We also see that this is one of the strengths of Southwest Airlines, which offers bare-bones domestic service but whose friendly and humorous employees help it obtain number-one ranking for quality. (See *Fortune* [March 6, 2006]: 65–69.)

TABLE 3 Best Practices for Resolving Customer Complaints

BEST PRACTICE	JUSTIFICATION
Make it easy for clients to complain.	It is free market research.
Respond quickly to complaints.	It adds customers and loyalty.
Resolve complaints on the first contact.	It reduces cost.
Use computers to manage complaints.	Discover trends, share them, and align your services.
Recruit the best for customer service jobs.	It should be part of formal training and career advancement.

Source: Based on Canadian Government Guide on Complaint Mechanism.

develop a target at which to shoot and then to develop a standard or benchmark against which to compare your performance. The steps for developing benchmarks are:

1. Determine what to benchmark.
2. Form a benchmark team.
3. Identify benchmarking partners.
4. Collect and analyze benchmarking information.
5. Take action to match or exceed the benchmark.

LO4 *Explain* how benchmarking is used in TQM

Typical performance measures used in benchmarking include percentage of defects, cost per unit or per order, processing time per unit, service response time, return on investment, customer satisfaction rates, and customer retention rates.

In the ideal situation, you find one or more similar organizations that are leaders in the particular areas you want to study. Then you compare yourself (benchmark yourself) against them. The company need not be in your industry. Indeed, to establish world-class standards, it may be best to look outside your industry. If one industry has learned how to compete via rapid product development while yours has not, it does no good to study your industry.

This is exactly what Xerox and Mercedes-Benz did when they went to L.L. Bean for order-filling and warehousing benchmarks. Xerox noticed that L.L. Bean was able to "pick" orders three times as fast as it could. After benchmarking, Xerox was immediately able to pare warehouse costs by 10%. Mercedes-Benz observed that L.L. Bean warehouse employees used flowcharts to spot wasted motions. The auto giant followed suit and now relies more on problem solving at the worker level.

Benchmarks often take the form of "best practices" found in other firms or in other divisions. Table 3 illustrates best practices for resolving customer complaints.

Likewise, Britain's Great Ormond Street Hospital benchmarked the Ferrari Racing Team's pit stops to improve one aspect of medical care. (See the *OM in Action* box "A Hospital Benchmarks Against the Ferrari Racing Team?")

Internal Benchmarking When an organization is large enough to have many divisions or business units, a natural approach is the internal benchmark. Data are usually much more accessible than from outside firms. Typically, one internal unit has superior performance worth learning from.

Xerox's almost religious belief in benchmarking has paid off not only by looking outward to L.L. Bean but by examining the operations of its various country divisions. For example, Xerox Europe, a $6 billion subsidiary of Xerox Corp., formed teams to see how better sales could result through internal benchmarking. Somehow, France sold five times as many color copiers as did other divisions in Europe. By copying France's approach, namely, better sales training and use of dealer channels to supplement direct sales, Norway increased sales by 152%, Holland by 300%, and Switzerland by 328%!

Benchmarks can and should be established in a variety of areas. Total quality management requires no less.[4]

[4]Note that benchmarking is good for evaluating how well you are doing the thing you are doing compared with the industry, but the more imaginative approach to process improvement is to ask, Should we be doing this at all? Comparing your warehousing operations to the marvelous job that L.L. Bean does is fine, but maybe you should be outsourcing the warehousing function.

OM in Action — A Hospital Benchmarks Against the Ferrari Racing Team?

After surgeons successfully completed a 6-hour operation to fix a hole in a 3-year-old boy's heart, Dr. Angus McEwan supervised one of the most dangerous phases of the procedure: the boy's transfer from surgery to the intensive care unit.

Thousands of such "handoffs" occur in hospitals every day, and devastating mistakes can happen during them. In fact, at least 35% of preventable hospital mishaps take place because of handoff problems. Risks come from many sources: using temporary nursing staff, frequent shift changes for interns, surgeons working in larger teams, and an ever-growing tangle of wires and tubes connected to patients.

Using an unlikely benchmark, Britain's largest children's hospital turned to Italy's Formula One Ferrari racing team for help in revamping patient handoff techniques. Armed with videos and slides, the racing team described how they analyze pit crew performance. It also explained how its system for recording errors stressed the small ones that go unnoticed in pit-stop handoffs.

To move forward, Ferrari invited a team of doctors to attend practice sessions at the British Grand Prix in order to get closer looks at pit stops. Ferrari's technical director, Nigel Stepney, then watched a video of a hospital handoff. Stepney was not impressed. "In fact, he was amazed at how clumsy, chaotic, and informal the process appeared," said one hospital official. At that meeting, Stepney described how each Ferrari crew member is required to do a specific job, in a specific sequence, and in silence. The hospital handoff, in contrast, had several conversations going on at once, while different members of its team disconnected or reconnected patient equipment, but in no particular order.

Associated Press

Results of the benchmarking process: handoff errors fell over 40%, with a bonus of faster handoff time.

Sources: The Wall Street Journal (December 3, 2007) and (November 14, 2006).

Just-in-Time (JIT)

The philosophy behind just-in-time (JIT) is one of continuing improvement and enforced problem solving. JIT systems are designed to produce or deliver goods just as they are needed. JIT is related to quality in three ways:

- *JIT cuts the cost of quality:* This occurs because scrap, rework, inventory investment, and damage costs are directly related to inventory on hand. Because there is less inventory on hand with JIT, costs are lower. In addition, inventory hides bad quality, whereas JIT immediately *exposes* bad quality.
- *JIT improves quality:* As JIT shrinks lead time, it keeps evidence of errors fresh and limits the number of potential sources of error. JIT creates, in effect, an early warning system for quality problems, both within the firm and with vendors.
- *Better quality means less inventory and a better, easier-to-employ JIT system:* Often the purpose of keeping inventory is to protect against poor production performance resulting from unreliable quality. If consistent quality exists, JIT allows firms to reduce all the costs associated with inventory.

Taguchi Concepts

Most quality problems are the result of poor product and process design. Genichi Taguchi has provided us with three concepts aimed at improving both product and process quality: *quality robustness*, *quality loss function*, and *target-oriented quality*.

Quality robust
Products that are consistently built to meet customer needs in spite of adverse conditions in the production process.

Quality robust products are products that can be produced uniformly and consistently in adverse manufacturing and environmental conditions. Taguchi's idea is to remove the *effects* of adverse conditions instead of removing the causes. Taguchi suggests that removing

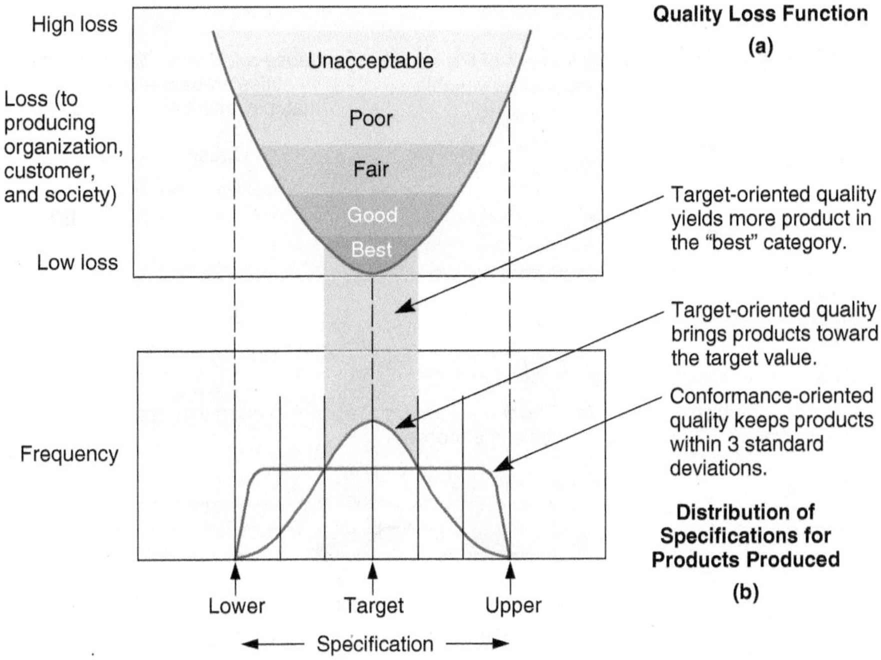

Figure 5

(a) Quality Loss Function and (b) Distribution of Products Produced

Taguchi aims for the target because products produced near the upper and lower acceptable specifications result in higher quality loss function.

the effects is often cheaper than removing the causes and more effective in producing a robust product. In this way, small variations in materials and process do not destroy product quality.

A quality loss function (QLF) identifies all costs connected with poor quality and shows how these costs increase as the product moves away from being exactly what the customer wants. These costs include not only customer dissatisfaction but also warranty and service costs; internal inspection, repair, and scrap costs; and costs that can best be described as costs to society. Notice that Figure 5(a) shows the quality loss function as a curve that increases at an increasing rate. It takes the general form of a simple quadratic formula:

Quality loss function (QLF)
A mathematical function that identifies all costs connected with poor quality and shows how these costs increase as product quality moves from what the customer wants.

$$L = D^2C$$

where L = loss to society

D^2 = square of the distance from the target value

C = cost of the deviation at the specification limit

LO5 *Explain* quality robust products and Taguchi concepts

All the losses to society due to poor performance are included in the loss function. The smaller the loss, the more desirable the product. The farther the product is from the target value, the more severe the loss.

Taguchi observed that traditional conformance-oriented specifications (i.e., the product is good as long as it falls within the tolerance limits) are too simplistic. As shown in Figure 5(b), conformance-oriented quality accepts all products that fall within the tolerance limits, producing more units farther from the target. Therefore, the loss (cost) is higher in terms of customer satisfaction and benefits to society. Target-oriented quality, on the other hand, strives to keep the product at the desired specification, producing more (and better) units near the target. Target-oriented quality is a philosophy of continuous improvement to bring the product exactly on target.

Target-oriented quality
A philosophy of continuous improvement to bring a product exactly on target.

Knowledge of TQM Tools

To empower employees and implement TQM as a continuing effort, everyone in the organization must be trained in the techniques of TQM. In the following section, we focus on some of the diverse and expanding tools that are used in the TQM crusade.

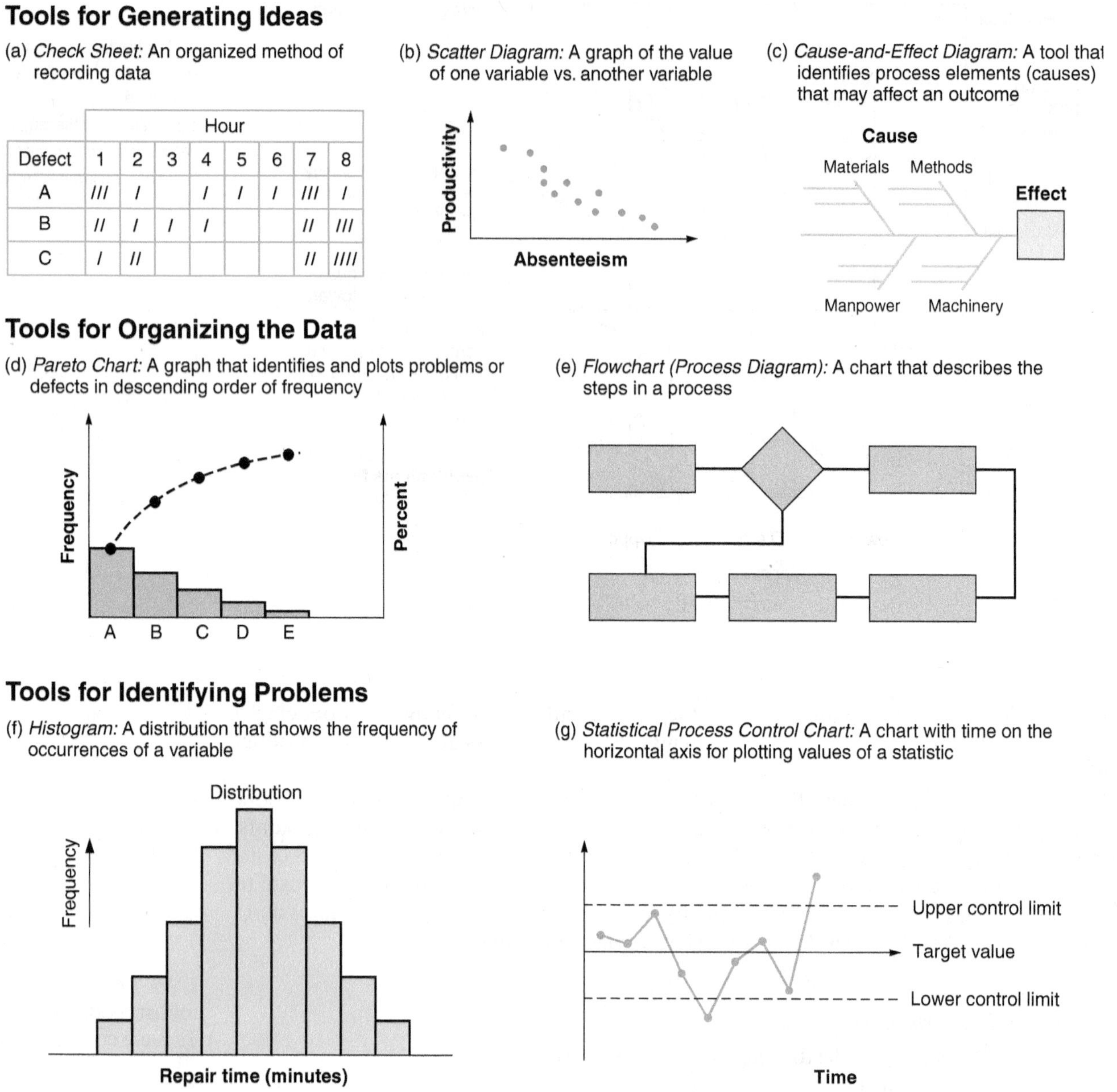
Tools for Generating Ideas
(a) Check Sheet: An organized method of recording data
Hour
Defect
(b) Scatter Diagram: A graph of the value of one variable vs. another variable
Productivity
Absenteeism
(c) Cause-and-Effect Diagram: A tool that identifies process elements (causes) that may affect an outcome
Cause
Materials
Methods
Effect
Manpower
Machinery
Tools for Organizing the Data
(d) Pareto Chart: A graph that identifies and plots problems or defects in descending order of frequency
Frequency
Percent
A B C D E
(e) Flowchart (Process Diagram): A chart that describes the steps in a process
Tools for Identifying Problems
(f) Histogram: A distribution that shows the frequency of occurrences of a variable
Distribution
Frequency
Repair time (minutes)
(g) Statistical Process Control Chart: A chart with time on the horizontal axis for plotting values of a statistic
Upper control limit
Target value
Lower control limit
Time

Defect	1	2	3	4	5	6	7	8
A	///	/		/	/	/	///	/
B	//	/	/	/			//	///
C	/	//					//	////

Figure 6
Seven Tools of TQM

STUDENT TIP ☆ These tools will prove useful in many of your courses and throughout your career.

Tools of TQM

Seven tools that are particularly helpful in the TQM effort are shown in Figure 6. We will now introduce these tools.

Check Sheets

LO6 *Use the seven tools of TQM*

A check sheet is any kind of a form that is designed for recording data. In many cases, the recording is done so the patterns are easily seen while the data are being taken [see Figure 6(a)]. Check sheets help analysts find the facts or patterns that may aid subsequent analysis. An example might be a drawing that shows a tally of the areas where defects are occurring or a check sheet showing the type of customer complaints.

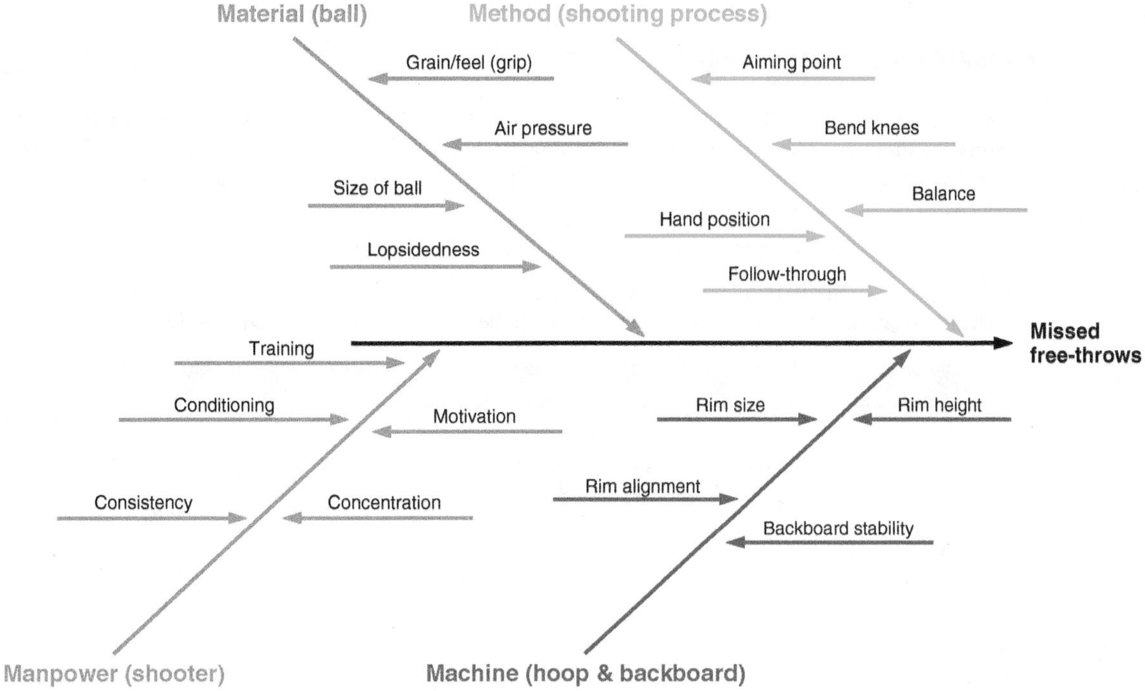

Figure 7

Fish-Bone Chart (or Cause-and-Effect Diagram) for Problems with Missed Free-Throws

Source: Adapted from MoreSteam.com, 2007.

Scatter Diagrams

Scatter diagrams show the relationship between two measurements. An example is the positive relationship between length of a service call and the number of trips a repair person makes back to the truck for parts. Another example might be a plot of productivity and absenteeism, as shown in Figure 6(b). If the two items are closely related, the data points will form a tight band. If a random pattern results, the items are unrelated.

Cause-and-Effect Diagrams

Another tool for identifying quality issues and inspection points is the cause-and-effect diagram, also known as an Ishikawa diagram or a fish-bone chart. Figure 7 illustrates a chart (note the shape resembling the bones of a fish) for a basketball quality control problem—missed free-throws. Each "bone" represents a possible source of error.

Cause-and-effect diagram
A schematic technique used to discover possible locations of quality problems.

The operations manager starts with four categories: material, machinery/equipment, manpower, and methods. These four *M*s are the "causes." They provide a good checklist for initial analysis. Individual causes associated with each category are tied in as separate bones along that branch, often through a brainstorming process. For example, the method branch in Figure 7 has problems caused by hand position, follow-through, aiming point, bent knees, and balance. When a fish-bone chart is systematically developed, possible quality problems and inspection points are highlighted.

Pareto Charts

Pareto charts are a method of organizing errors, problems, or defects to help focus on problem-solving efforts. They are based on the work of Vilfredo Pareto, a 19th-century economist. Joseph M. Juran popularized Pareto's work when he suggested that 80% of a firm's problems are a result of only 20% of the causes.

Pareto charts
A graphic way of classifying problems by their level of importance, often referred to as the 80–20 rule.

Example 1 indicates that of the five types of complaints identified, the vast majority were of one type—poor room service.

Example 1

A PARETO CHART AT THE HARD ROCK HOTEL

The Hard Rock Hotel in Bali has just collected the data from 75 complaint calls to the general manager during the month of October. The manager wants to prepare an analysis of the complaints. The data provided are room service, 54; check-in delays, 12; hours the pool is open, 4; minibar prices, 3; and miscellaneous, 2.

APPROACH ▶ A Pareto chart is an excellent choice for this analysis.

SOLUTION ▶ The Pareto chart shown below indicates that 72% of the calls were the result of one cause: room service. The majority of complaints will be eliminated when this one cause is corrected.

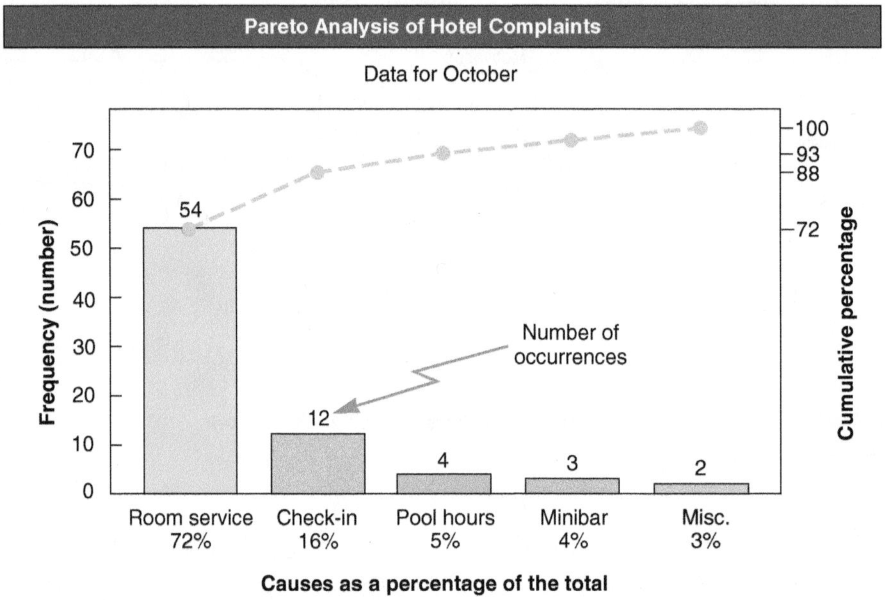

INSIGHT ▶ This visual means of summarizing data is very helpful—particularly with large amounts of data, as in the Southwestern University case study at the end of this text. We can immediately spot the top problems and prepare a plan to address them.

LEARNING EXERCISE ▶ Hard Rock's bar manager decides to do a similar analysis on complaints she has collected over the past year: too expensive, 22; weak drinks, 15; slow service, 65; short hours, 8; unfriendly bartender, 12. Prepare a Pareto chart. [Answer: slow service, 53%; expensive, 18%; drinks, 12%; bartender, 10%; hours, 7%.]

RELATED PROBLEMS ▶ 1, 3, 7b, 12, 13, 16c

ACTIVE MODEL 1 This example is further illustrated in Active Model 6.1 at **www.pearsonhighered.com/heizer**.

Pareto analysis indicates which problems may yield the greatest payoff. Pacific Bell discovered this when it tried to find a way to reduce damage to buried phone cable, the number-one cause of phone outages. Pareto analysis showed that 41% of cable damage was caused by construction work. Armed with this information, Pacific Bell was able to devise a plan to reduce cable cuts by 24% in one year, saving $6 million.

Likewise, Japan's Ricoh Corp., a copier maker, used the Pareto principle to tackle the "callback" problem. Callbacks meant the job was not done right the first time and that a second visit, at Ricoh's expense, was needed. Identifying and retraining only the 11% of the customer engineers with the most callbacks resulted in a 19% drop in return visits.

Flowcharts

Flowcharts
Block diagrams that graphically describe a process or system.

Flowcharts graphically present a process or system using annotated boxes and interconnected lines [see Figure 6(e)]. They are a simple but great tool for trying to make sense of a process or explain a process. Example 2 uses a flowchart to show the process of completing an MRI at a hospital.

Example 2

A FLOWCHART FOR HOSPITAL MRI SERVICE

Arnold Palmer Hospital has undertaken a series of process improvement initiatives. One of these is to make the MRI service efficient for patient, doctor, and hospital. The first step, the administrator believes, is to develop a flowchart for this process.

APPROACH ▶ A process improvement staffer observed a number of patients and followed them (and information flow) from start to end. Here are the 11 steps:

1. Physician schedules MRI after examining patient (START).
2. Patient taken to the MRI lab with test order and copy of medical records.
3. Patient signs in, completes required paperwork.
4. Patient is prepped by technician for scan.
5. Technician carries out the MRI scan.
6. Technician inspects film for clarity.
7. If MRI not satisfactory (20% of time), Steps 5 and 6 are repeated.
8. Patient taken back to hospital room.
9. MRI is read by radiologist and report is prepared.
10. MRI and report are transferred electronically to physician.
11. Patient and physician discuss report (END).

SOLUTION ▶ Here is the flowchart:

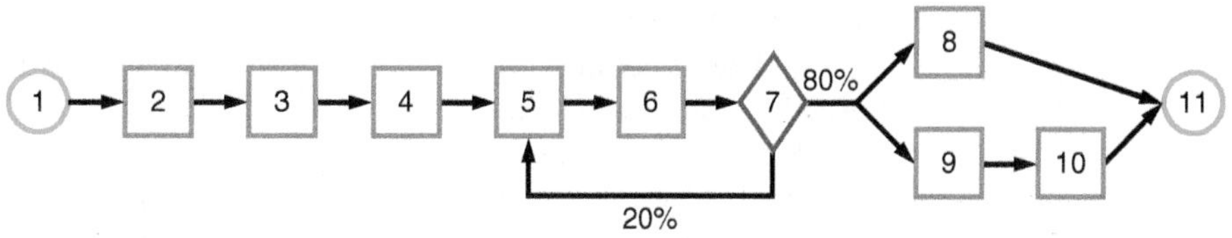

STUDENT TIP Flowcharting any process is an excellent way to understand and then try to improve that process.

INSIGHT ▶ With the flowchart in hand, the hospital can analyze each step and identify value-added activities and activities that can be improved or eliminated.

LEARNING EXERCISE ▶ If the patient's blood pressure is over 200/120 when being prepped for the MRI, she is taken back to her room for 2 hours and the process returns to Step 2. How does the flowchart change? Answer:

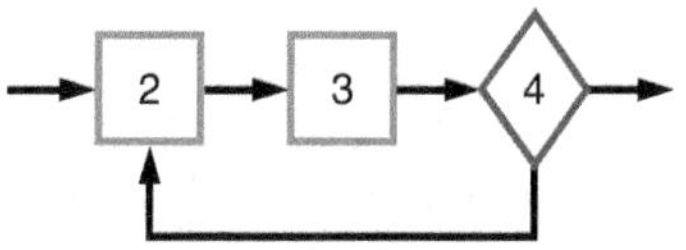

RELATED PROBLEMS ▶ 6, 15

Histograms

Histograms show the range of values of a measurement and the frequency with which each value occurs [see Figure 6(f)]. They show the most frequently occurring readings as well as the variations in the measurements. Descriptive statistics, such as the average and standard deviation, may be calculated to describe the distribution. However, the data should always be plotted so the shape of the distribution can be "seen." A visual presentation of the distribution may also provide insight into the cause of the variation.

Statistical Process Control (SPC)

Statistical process control (SPC) monitors standards, makes measurements, and takes corrective action as a product or service is being produced. Samples of process outputs are examined; if they are within acceptable limits, the process is permitted to continue. If they fall outside certain specific ranges, the process is stopped and, typically, the assignable cause located and removed.

Statistical process control (SPC)
A process used to monitor standards, make measurements, and take corrective action as a product or service is being produced.

Figure 8

Control Chart for Percentage of Free-throws Missed by the Orlando Magic in Their First Nine Games of the New Season

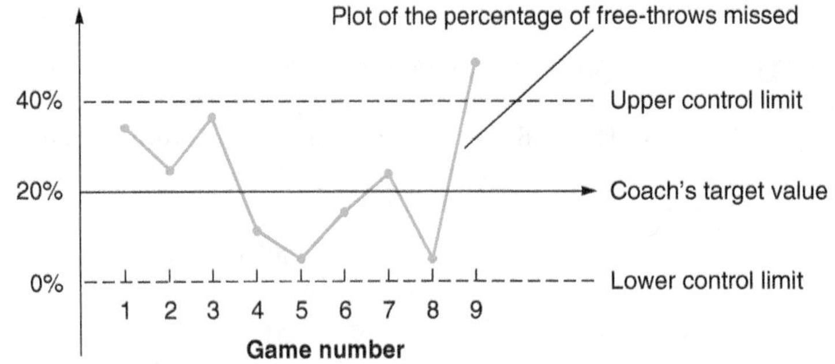

Fernando Medina

Control charts
Graphic presentations of process data over time, with predetermined control limits.

Control charts are graphic presentations of data over time that show upper and lower limits for the process we want to control [see Figure 6(g)]. Control charts are constructed in such a way that new data can be quickly compared with past performance data. We take samples of the process output and plot the average of each of these samples on a chart that has the limits on it. The upper and lower limits in a control chart can be in units of temperature, pressure, weight, length, and so on.

Figure 8 shows the plot of sample averages in a control chart. When the samples fall within the upper and lower control limits and no discernible pattern is present, the process is said to be in control with only natural variation present. Otherwise, the process is out of control or out of adjustment.

The Role of Inspection

To make sure a system is producing at the expected quality level, control of the process is needed. The best processes have little variation from the standard expected. The operations manager's task is to build such systems and to verify, often by inspection, that they are performing to standard. This **inspection** can involve measurement, tasting, touching, weighing, or testing of the product (sometimes even destroying it when doing so). Its goal is to detect a bad process immediately. Inspection does not correct deficiencies in the system or defects in the products; nor does it change a product or increase its value. Inspection only finds deficiencies and defects. Moreover, inspections are expensive and do not add value to the product.

Inspection
A means of ensuring that an operation is producing at the quality level expected.

Inspection should be thought of as a vehicle for improving the system. Operations managers need to know critical points in the system: (1) *when to inspect* and (2) *where to inspect.*

When and Where to Inspect

Deciding when and where to inspect depends on the type of process and the value added at each stage. Inspections can take place at any of the following points:

1. At your supplier's plant while the supplier is producing.
2. At your facility upon receipt of goods from your supplier.
3. Before costly or irreversible processes.
4. During the step-by-step production process.
5. When production or service is complete.
6. Before delivery to your customer.
7. At the point of customer contact.

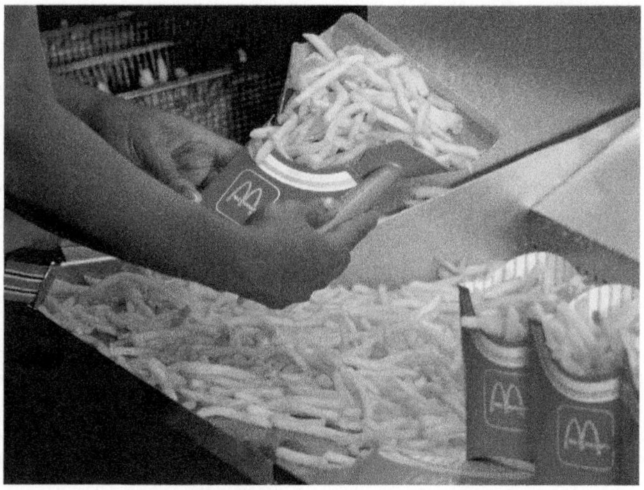

Ralf-Finn Hestoft/Corbis-NY

Good methods analysis and the proper tools can result in poka-yokes that improve both quality and speed. Here, two poka-yokes are demonstrated. First, the aluminum scoop automatically positions the french fries vertically, and second, the properly sized container ensures that the portion served is correct. McDonald's thrives by bringing rigor and consistency to the restaurant business.

The seven tools of TQM discussed in the previous section aid in this "when and where to inspect" decision. However, inspection is not a substitute for a robust product produced by well-trained employees in a good process. In one well-known experiment conducted by an independent research firm, 100 defective pieces were added to a "perfect" lot of items and then subjected to 100% inspection. The inspectors found only 68 of the defective pieces in their first inspection. It took another three passes by the inspectors to find the next 30 defects. The last two defects were never found. So the bottom line is that there is variability in the inspection process. Additionally, inspectors are only human: They become bored, they become tired, and the inspection equipment itself has variability. Even with 100% inspection, inspectors cannot guarantee perfection. Therefore, good processes, employee empowerment, and source control are a better solution than trying to find defects by inspection. You cannot inspect quality into the product.

STUDENT TIP
One of our themes of quality is that "quality cannot be inspected into a product."

For example, at Velcro Industries, as in many other organizations, quality was viewed by machine operators as the job of "those quality people." Inspections were based on random sampling, and if a part showed up bad, it was thrown out. The company decided to pay more attention to the system (operators, machine repair and design, measurement methods, communications, and responsibilities) and to invest more money in training. Over time as defects declined, Velcro was able to pull half its quality control people out of the process.

Source Inspection

The best inspection can be thought of as no inspection at all; this "inspection" is always done at the source—it is just doing the job properly with the operator ensuring that this is so. This may be called source inspection (or source control) and is consistent with the concept of employee empowerment, where individual employees self-check their own work. The idea is that each supplier, process, and employee *treats the next step in the process as the customer*, ensuring perfect product to the next "customer." This inspection may be assisted by the use of checklists and controls such as a fail-safe device called a *poka-yoke*, a name borrowed from the Japanese.

Source inspection
Controlling or monitoring at the point of production or purchase—at the source.

A poka-yoke is a foolproof device or technique that ensures production of good units every time. These special devices avoid errors and provide quick feedback of problems. A simple example of a poka-yoke device is the diesel gas pump nozzle that will not fit into the "unleaded" gas tank opening on your car. In McDonald's, the french fry scoop and standard-size bag used to measure the correct quantity are poka-yokes. Similarly, in a hospital, the prepackaged surgical coverings that contain exactly the items needed for a medical procedure are poka-yokes.

Poka-yoke
Literally translated, "foolproof"; it has come to mean a device or technique that ensures the production of a good unit every time.

Checklists are a type of poka-yoke to help ensure consistency and completeness in carrying out a task. A basic example is a to-do list. This tool may take the form of preflight checklists used by airplane pilots, surgical safety checklists used by doctors, or software quality assurance lists used by programmers. The *OM in Action* box "Safe Patients, Smart Hospitals" illustrates the important role checklists have in hospital quality.

Checklist
A type of poka-yoke that lists the steps needed to ensure consistency and completeness in a task.

The idea of source inspection, poka-yokes, and checklists is to guarantee 100% good product or service at each step of a process.

OM in Action Safe Patients, Smart Hospitals

Simple and avoidable errors are made in hospitals each day, causing patients to die. Inspired by two tragic medical mistakes—his father's misdiagnosed cancer and sloppiness that killed an 18-month-old child at Johns Hopkins—Dr. Peter Pronovost has made it his mission, often swimming upstream against the medical culture, to improve patient safety and prevent deaths.

He began by developing a basic 5-step checklist to reduce catheter infections. Inserted into veins in the groin, neck, or chest to administer fluids and medicines, catheters can save lives. But every year, 80,000 Americans get infections from *central venous catheters* (or lines) and over 30,000 of these patients die. Pronovost's checklist has dropped infection rates at hospitals that use it down to zero, saving thousands of lives and tens of millions of dollars.

His steps for doctors and nurses are simple: (1) wash your hands; (2) use sterile gloves, masks, and drapes; (3) use antiseptic on the area being opened for the catheter; (4) avoid veins in the arms and legs; and (5) take the catheter out as soon as possible. He also created a special cart, where all supplies needed are stored.

Dr. Provonost believes that many hospital errors are due to lack of standardization, poor communications, and a noncollaborative culture that is "antiquated and toxic." He points out that checklists in the airline industry are a science, and *every* crew member works as part of the safety team. Provonost's book has shown that one person, with small changes, can make a huge difference.

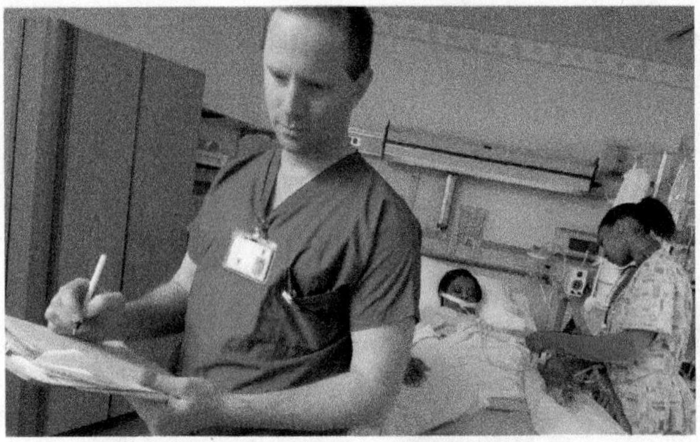
David Joel/Getty Images Inc.-Photographer's Choice Royalty Free

Sources: Safe Patients, Smart Hospitals (Penguin Publishers, 2011); and *The Wall Street Journal* (March 2, 2011).

Service Industry Inspection

In *service*-oriented organizations, inspection points can be assigned at a wide range of locations, as illustrated in Table 4. Again, the operations manager must decide where inspections are justified and may find the seven tools of TQM useful when making these judgments.

Inspection of Attributes versus Variables

Attribute inspection
An inspection that classifies items as being either good or defective.

Variable inspection
Classifications of inspected items as falling on a continuum scale, such as dimension or strength.

When inspections take place, quality characteristics may be measured as either *attributes* or *variables*. **Attribute inspection** classifies items as being either good or defective. It does not address the *degree* of failure. For example, the lightbulb burns or it does not. **Variable inspection** measures such dimensions as weight, speed, size, or strength to see if an item falls within an acceptable

TABLE 4 Examples of Inspection in Services

ORGANIZATION	WHAT IS INSPECTED	STANDARD
Jones Law Offices	Receptionist performance	Phone answered by the second ring
	Billing	Accurate, timely, and correct format
	Attorney	Promptness in returning calls
Hard Rock Hotel	Reception desk	Use customer's name
	Doorman	Greet guest in less than 30 seconds
	Room	All lights working, spotless bathroom
	Minibar	Restocked and charges accurately posted to bill
Arnold Palmer Hospital	Billing	Accurate, timely, and correct format
	Pharmacy	Prescription accuracy, inventory accuracy
	Lab	Audit for lab-test accuracy
	Nurses	Charts immediately updated
	Admissions	Data entered correctly and completely
Olive Garden Restaurant	Busboy	Serves water and bread within one minute
	Busboy	Clears all entrée items and crumbs prior to dessert
	Waiter	Knows and suggests specials, desserts
Nordstrom Department Store	Display areas	Attractive, well organized, stocked, good lighting
	Stockrooms	Rotation of goods, organized, clean
	Salesclerks	Neat, courteous, very knowledgeable

range. If a piece of electrical wire is supposed to be 0.01 inch in diameter, a micrometer can be used to see if the product is close enough to pass inspection.

Knowing whether attributes or variables are being inspected helps us decide which statistical quality control approach to take.

TQM in Services

The personal component of services is more difficult to measure than the quality of the tangible component. Generally, the user of a service, like the user of a good, has features in mind that form a basis for comparison among alternatives. Lack of any one feature may eliminate the service from further consideration. Quality also may be perceived as a bundle of attributes in which many lesser characteristics are superior to those of competitors. This approach to product comparison differs little between goods and services. However, what is very different about the selection of services is the poor definition of the (1) *intangible differences between products* and (2) *the intangible expectations customers have of those products*. Indeed, the intangible attributes may not be defined at all. They are often unspoken images in the purchaser's mind. This is why all of those marketing issues such as advertising, image, and promotion can make a difference.

The operations manager plays a significant role in addressing several major aspects of service quality. First, the *tangible component of many services is important*. How well the service is designed and produced does make a difference. This might be how accurate, clear, and complete your checkout bill at the hotel is, how warm the food is at Taco Bell, or how well your car runs after you pick it up at the repair shop.

Second, another aspect of service and service quality is the process. Notice in Table 5 that 9 out of 10 of the determinants of service quality are related to *the service process*. Such things as reliability and courtesy are part of the process. An operations manager can *design processes (service products) that have these attributes* and can ensure their quality through the TQM techniques discussed in this text. (See the Alaska Airlines photo).

Third, the operations manager should realize that the customer's expectations are the standard against which the service is judged. Customers' perceptions of service quality result from a comparison of their "before-service expectations" with their "actual-service experience." In

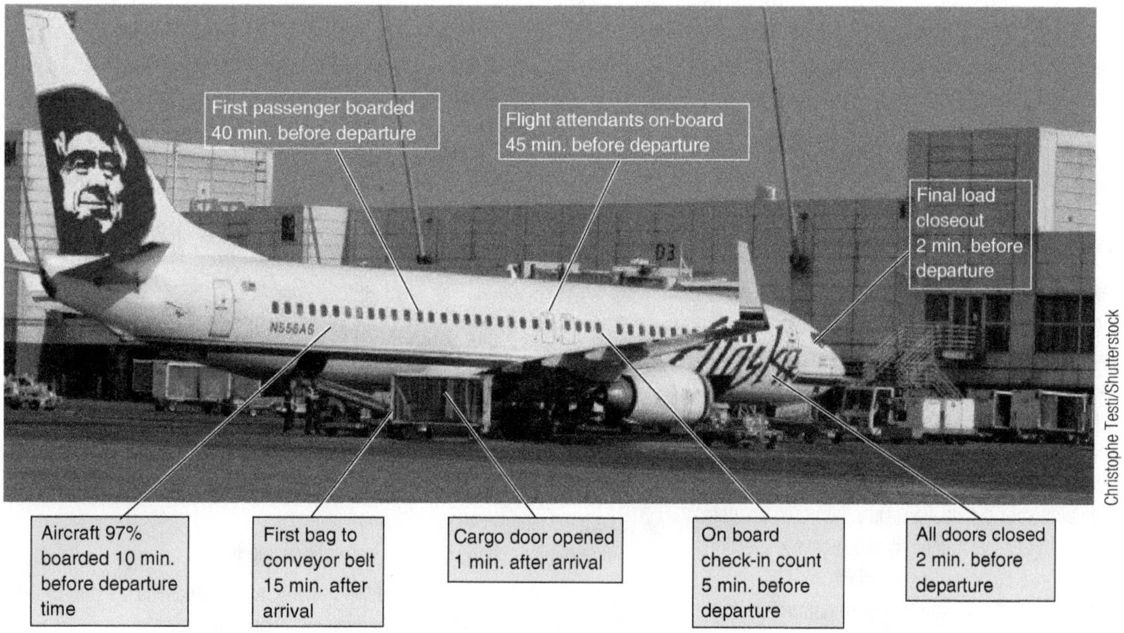

Like many service organizations, Alaska Airlines sets quality standards in areas such as courtesy, appearance, and time. Shown here are some of Alaska Airlines's 50 quality checkpoints, based on a timeline for each departure.

TABLE 5 Determinants of Service Quality

Reliability involves consistency of performance and dependability. It means that the firm performs the service right the first time and that the firm honors its promises.
Responsiveness concerns the willingness or readiness of employees to provide service. It involves timeliness of service.
Competence means possession of the required skills and knowledge to perform the service.
Access involves approachability and ease of contact.
Courtesy involves politeness, respect, consideration, and friendliness of contact personnel (including receptionists, telephone operators, etc.).
Communication means keeping customers informed in language they can understand and listening to them. It may mean that the company has to adjust its language for different consumers—increasing the level of sophistication with a well-educated customer and speaking simply and plainly with a novice.
Credibility involves trustworthiness, believability, and honesty. It involves having the customer's best interests at heart.
Security is the freedom from danger, risk, or doubt.
Understanding/knowing the customer involves making the effort to understand the customer's needs.
Tangibles include the physical evidence of the service.

Sources: Adapted from A. Parasuranam, Valarie A. Zeithaml, and Leonard L. Berry, "A Conceptual Model of Service Quality and Its Implications for Future Research," *Journal of Marketing* (1985): 49. Copyright © 1985 by the American Marketing Association. Reprinted with permission.

other words, service quality is judged on the basis of whether it meets expectations. The *manager may be able to influence both the quality of the service and the expectation.* Don't promise more than you can deliver.

Fourth, the manager must expect exceptions. There is a standard quality level at which the regular service is delivered, such as the bank teller's handling of a transaction. However, there are "exceptions" or "problems" initiated by the customer or by less-than-optimal operating conditions (e.g., the computer "crashed"). This implies that the quality control system must recognize and *have a set of alternative plans for less-than-optimal operating conditions.*

Service recovery
Training and empowering frontline workers to solve a problem immediately.

Well-run companies have service recovery strategies. This means they train and empower frontline employees to immediately solve a problem. For instance, staff at Marriott Hotels are drilled in the LEARN routine—*L*isten, *E*mpathize, *A*pologize, *R*eact, *N*otify—with the final step ensuring that the complaint is fed back into the system. And at the Ritz-Carlton, staff members are trained not to say merely "sorry" but "please accept my apology." The Ritz gives them a budget for reimbursing upset guests.

Designing the product, managing the service process, matching customer expectations to the product, and preparing for the exceptions are keys to quality services. The *OM in Action* box "Richey International's Spies" provides another glimpse of how OM managers improve quality in services.

VIDEO 2
TQM at Ritz-Carlton Hotels

OM in Action Richey International's Spies

How do luxury hotels maintain quality? They inspect. But when the product is one-on-one service, largely dependent on personal behavior, how do you inspect? You hire spies!

Richey International is the spy. Preferred Hotels and Resorts Worldwide and Intercontinental Hotels have both hired Richey to do quality evaluations via spying. Richey employees posing as customers perform the inspections. However, even then management must have established what the customer expects and specific services that yield customer satisfaction. Only then do managers know where and how to inspect. Aggressive training and objective inspections reinforce behavior that will meet those customer expectations.

The hotels use Richey's undercover inspectors to ensure performance to exacting standards. The hotels do not know when the evaluators will arrive. Nor what aliases they will use. Over 50 different standards are evaluated before the inspectors even check in at a luxury hotel. Over the next 24 hours, using checklists, tape recordings, and photos, written reports are prepared. The reports include evaluation of standards such as:

- Does the doorman greet each guest in less than 30 seconds?
- Does the front-desk clerk use the guest's name during check-in?
- Are the bathroom tub and shower spotlessly clean?
- How many minutes does it take to get coffee after the guest sits down for breakfast?
- Did the waiter make eye contact?
- Were minibar charges posted correctly on the bill?

Established standards, aggressive training, and inspections are part of the TQM effort at these hotels. Quality does not happen by accident.

Sources: Hotel and Motel Management (August 2002); *The Wall Street Journal* (May 12, 1999); and *Forbes* (October 5, 1998).

Summary

Quality is a term that means different things to different people. We define quality as "the totality of features and characteristics of a product or service that bears on its ability to satisfy stated or implied needs." Defining quality expectations is critical to effective and efficient operations.

Quality requires building a total quality management (TQM) environment because quality cannot be inspected into a product. The text also addresses seven TQM *concepts*: continuous improvement, Six Sigma, employee empowerment, benchmarking, just-in-time, Taguchi concepts, and knowledge of TQM tools. The seven TQM *tools* introduced in this text are check sheets, scatter diagrams, cause-and-effect diagrams, Pareto charts, flowcharts, histograms, and statistical process control (SPC).

Key Terms

Quality
ISO 9000
Cost of quality (COQ)
Total quality management (TQM)
PDCA
Six Sigma
Employee empowerment
Quality circle
Benchmarking
Quality robust
Quality loss function (QLF)
Target-oriented quality
Cause-and-effect diagram, Ishikawa diagram, or fish-bone chart
Pareto charts
Flowcharts
Statistical process control (SPC)
Control charts
Inspection
Source inspection
Poka-yoke
Checklists
Attribute inspection
Variable inspection
Service recovery

Ethical Dilemma

A lawsuit a few years ago made headlines worldwide when a McDonald's drive-through customer spilled a cup of scalding hot coffee on herself. Claiming the coffee was too hot to be safely consumed in a car, the badly burned 80-year-old woman won $2.9 million in court. (The judge later reduced the award to $640,000.) McDonald's claimed the product was served to the correct specifications and was of proper quality. Further, the cup read "Caution—Contents May Be Hot." McDonald's coffee, at 180°, is substantially hotter (by corporate rule) than typical restaurant coffee, despite hundreds of coffee-scalding complaints in the past 10 years. Similar court cases, incidentally, resulted in smaller verdicts, but again in favor of the plaintiffs. For example, Motor City Bagel Shop was sued for a spilled cup of coffee by a drive-through patron, and Starbucks by a customer who spilled coffee on her own ankle.

Are McDonald's, Motor City, and Starbucks at fault in situations such as these? How do quality and ethics enter into these cases?

Discussion Questions

1. Explain how improving quality can lead to reduced costs.
2. As an Internet exercise, determine the Baldrige Award criteria. See the Web site **www.quality.nist.gov.**
3. Which 3 of Deming's 14 points do you think are most critical to the success of a TQM program? Why?
4. List the seven concepts that are necessary for an effective TQM program. How are these related to Deming's 14 points?
5. Name three of the important people associated with the quality concepts of this text. In each case, write a sentence about each one summarizing his primary contribution to the field of quality management.
6. What are seven tools of TQM?
7. How does fear in the workplace (and in the classroom) inhibit learning?
8. How can a university control the quality of its output (that is, its graduates)?
9. Philip Crosby said that quality is free. Why?
10. List the three concepts central to Taguchi's approach.
11. What is the purpose of using a Pareto chart for a given problem?
12. What are the four broad categories of "causes" to help initially structure an Ishikawa diagram or cause-and-effect diagram?
13. Of the several points where inspection may be necessary, which apply especially well to manufacturing?
14. What roles do operations managers play in addressing the major aspects of service quality?
15. Explain, in your own words, what is meant by *source inspection*.
16. What are 10 determinants of service quality?
17. Name several products that do not require high quality.
18. What does the formula $L = D^2C$ mean?
19. In this text, we have suggested that building quality into a process and its people is difficult. Inspections are also difficult. To indicate just how difficult inspections are, count the number of *E*s (both capital *E* and lowercase *e*) in the *OM in Action* box "Richey International's Spies" (include the title but not the source note). How many did you find? If each student does this individually, you are very likely to find a distribution rather than a single number!

Solved Problem

Virtual Office Hours help is available at www.myomlab.com.

SOLVED PROBLEM 1

Northern Airlines's frequent flyer complaints about redeeming miles for free, discounted, and upgraded travel are summarized below, in five categories, from 600 letters received this year.

COMPLAINT	FREQUENCY
Could not get through to customer service to make requests	125
Seats not available on date requested	270
Had to pay fees to get "free" seats	62
Seats were available but only on flights at odd hours	110
Rules kept changing whenever customer called	33

Develop a Pareto chart for the data.

SOLUTION

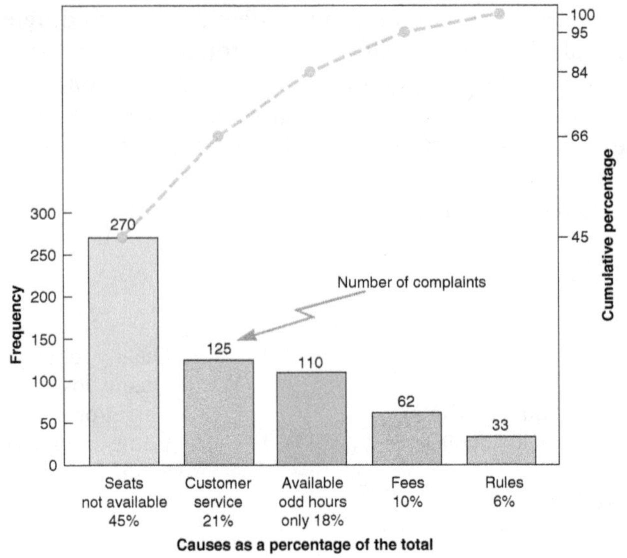

Problems

• **1** An avant-garde clothing manufacturer runs a series of high-profile, risqué ads on a billboard on Highway 101 and regularly collects protest calls from people who are offended by them. The company has no idea how many people in total see the ads, but it has been collecting statistics on the number of phone calls from irate viewers:

TYPE	DESCRIPTION	NUMBER OF COMPLAINTS
R	Offensive racially/ethnically	10
M	Demeaning to men	4
W	Demeaning to women	14
I	Ad is incomprehensible	6
O	Other	2

a) Depict this data with a Pareto chart. Also depict the cumulative complaint line.
b) What percent of the total complaints can be attributed to the most prevalent complaint?

• **2** Develop a scatter diagram for two variables of interest [say pages in the newspaper by day of the week; see the example in Figure 6(b)].

• **3** Develop a Pareto chart of the following causes of poor grades on an exam:

REASON FOR POOR GRADE	FREQUENCY
Insufficient time to complete	15
Late arrival to exam	7
Difficulty understanding material	25
Insufficient preparation time	2
Studied wrong material	2
Distractions in exam room	9
Calculator batteries died during exam	1
Forgot exam was scheduled	3
Felt ill during exam	4

• **4** Develop a histogram of the time it took for you or your friends to receive six recent orders at a fast-food restaurant.

• • **5** Kathleen McFadden's restaurant in Boston has recorded the following data for eight recent customers:

CUSTOMER NUMBER, i	MINUTES FROM TIME FOOD ORDERED UNTIL FOOD ARRIVED (y)	NO. OF TRIPS TO KITCHEN BY WAITRESS (x)
1	10.50	4
2	12.75	5
3	9.25	3
4	8.00	2
5	9.75	3
6	11.00	4
7	14.00	6
8	10.75	5

a) McFadden wants you to graph the eight points (x_i, y_i), $i = 1, 2, \ldots 8$. She has been concerned because customers have been waiting too long for their food, and this graph is intended to help her find possible causes of the problem.
b) This is an example of what type of graph?

• • **6** Develop a flowchart [as in Figure 6(e) and Example 2] showing all the steps involved in planning a party.

• • **7** Consider the types of poor driving habits that might occur at a traffic light. Make a list of the 10 you consider most likely to happen. Add the category of "other" to that list.
a) Compose a check sheet [like that in Figure 6(a)] to collect the frequency of occurrence of these habits. Using your check sheet, visit a busy traffic light intersection at four different times of the day, with two of these times being during high-traffic periods (rush hour, lunch hour). For 15 to 20 minutes each visit, observe the frequency with which the habits you listed occurred.
b) Construct a Pareto chart showing the relative frequency of occurrence of each habit.

•• **8** Draw a fish-bone chart detailing reasons why an airline customer might be dissatisfied.

•• **9** Consider the everyday task of getting to work on time or arriving at your first class on time in the morning. Draw a fish-bone chart showing reasons why you might arrive late in the morning.

•• **10** Construct a cause-and-effect diagram to reflect "student dissatisfied with university registration process." Use the "four *Ms*" or create your own organizing scheme. Include at least 12 causes.

•• **11** Draw a fish-bone chart depicting the reasons that might give rise to an incorrect fee statement at the time you go to pay for your registration at school.

••• **12** Mary Beth Marrs, the manager of an apartment complex, feels overwhelmed by the number of complaints she is receiving. Below is the check sheet she has kept for the past 12 weeks. Develop a Pareto chart using this information. What recommendations would you make?

WEEK	GROUNDS	PARKING/ DRIVES	POOL	TENANT ISSUES	ELECTRICAL/ PLUMBING
1	✓✓✓	✓✓	✓	✓✓✓	
2	✓	✓✓✓	✓✓	✓✓	✓
3	✓✓✓	✓✓✓	✓✓	✓	
4	✓	✓✓✓✓	✓	✓	✓✓
5	✓✓	✓✓✓	✓✓✓✓	✓✓	
6	✓	✓✓✓✓	✓✓		
7		✓✓✓	✓✓	✓✓	
8	✓	✓✓✓✓	✓✓	✓✓✓	✓
9	✓	✓✓	✓		
10	✓	✓✓✓✓	✓✓	✓✓	
11		✓✓✓	✓✓	✓	
12	✓✓	✓✓✓	✓✓✓	✓	

• **13** Use Pareto analysis to investigate the following data collected on a printed-circuit-board assembly line:

DEFECT	NUMBER OF DEFECT OCCURRENCES
Components not adhering	143
Excess adhesive	71
Misplaced transistors	601
Defective board dimension	146
Mounting holes improperly positioned	12
Circuitry problems on final test	90
Wrong component	212

a) Prepare a graph of the data.
b) What conclusions do you reach?

•• **14** A list of 16 issues that led to incorrect formulations in Tuncey Bayrak's jam manufacturing unit in NewEngland is provided below:

List of Issues

1. Incorrect measurement	9. Variability in scale accuracy
2. Antiquated scales	10. Equipment in disrepair
3. Lack of clear instructions	11. Technician calculation off
4. Damaged raw material	12. Jars mislabeled
5. Operator misreads display	13. Temperature controls off
6. Inadequate cleanup	14. Incorrect weights
7. Incorrect maintenance	15. Priority miscommunication
8. Inadequate flow controls	16. Inadequate instructions

Create a fish-bone diagram and categorize each of these issues correctly, using the "four *Ms*" method.

•• **15** Develop a flowchart for one of the following:

a) Filling up with gasoline at a self-serve station.
b) Determining your account balance and making a withdrawal at an ATM.
c) Getting a cone of yogurt or ice cream from an ice cream store.

•••• **16** Boston Electric Generators has been getting many complaints from its major customer, Home Station, about the quality of its shipments of home generators. Daniel Shimshak, the plant manager, is alarmed that a customer is providing him with the only information the company has on shipment quality. He decides to collect information on defective shipments through a form he has asked his drivers to complete on arrival at customers' stores. The forms for the first 279 shipments have been turned in. They show the following over the past 8 weeks:

WEEK	NO. OF SHIPMENTS	NO. OF SHIPMENTS WITH DEFECTS	*REASON FOR DEFECTIVE SHIPMENT*			
			INCORRECT BILL OF LADING	INCORRECT TRUCKLOAD	DAMAGED PRODUCT	TRUCKS LATE
1	23	5	2	2	1	
2	31	8	1	4	1	2
3	28	6	2	3	1	
4	37	11	4	4	1	2
5	35	10	3	4	2	1
6	40	14	5	6	3	
7	41	12	3	5	3	1
8	44	15	4	7	2	2

Even though Daniel increased his capacity by adding more workers to his normal contingent of 30, he knew that for many weeks he exceeded his regular output of 30 shipments per week. A review of his turnover over the past 8 weeks shows the following:

WEEK	NO. OF NEW HIRES	NO. OF TERMINATIONS	TOTAL NO. OF WORKERS
1	1	0	30
2	2	1	31
3	3	2	32
4	2	0	34
5	2	2	34
6	2	4	32
7	4	1	35
8	3	2	36

a) Develop a scatter diagram using total number of shipments and number of defective shipments. Does there appear to be any relationship?
b) Develop a scatter diagram using the variable "turnover" (number of new hires plus number of terminations) and the number of defective shipments. Does the diagram depict a relationship between the two variables?
c) Develop a Pareto chart for the type of defects that have occurred.
d) Draw a fish-bone chart showing the possible causes of the defective shipments.

••• **17** A recent Gallup poll of 519 adults who flew in the past year found the following number of complaints about flying: cramped seats (45), cost (16), dislike or fear of flying (57), security measures (119), poor service (12), connecting flight problems (8), overcrowded planes (42), late planes/waits (57), food (7), lost luggage (7), and other (51).

a) What percentage of those surveyed found nothing they disliked?
b) Draw a Pareto chart summarizing these responses. Include the "no complaints" group.
c) Use the "four *Ms*" method to create a fish-bone diagram for the 10 specific categories of dislikes (exclude "other" and "no complaints").
d) If you were managing an airline, what two or three specific issues would you tackle to improve customer service? Why?

▶ **Refer to MyOMLab for these additional homework problems: 6.18–6.21**

CASE STUDIES

Southwestern University: (C)

The popularity of Southwestern University's football program under its new coach Phil Flamm surged in each of the 5 years since his arrival at the Stephenville, Texas, college. With a football stadium close to maxing out at 54,000 seats and a vocal coach pushing for a new stadium, SWU president Joel Wisner faced some difficult decisions. After a phenomenal upset victory over its archrival, the University of Texas, at the homecoming game in the fall, Dr. Wisner was not as happy as one would think. Instead of ecstatic alumni, students, and faculty, all Wisner heard were complaints. "The lines at the concession stands were too long"; "Parking was harder to find and farther away than in the old days" (that is, before the team won regularly); "Seats weren't comfortable"; "Traffic was backed up halfway to Dallas"; and on and on. "A college president just can't win," muttered Wisner to himself.

At his staff meeting the following Monday, Wisner turned to his VP of administration, Leslie Gardner. "I wish you would take care of these football complaints, Leslie," he said. "See what the *real* problems are and let me know how you've resolved them." Gardner wasn't surprised at the request. "I've already got a handle on it, Joel," she replied. "We've been randomly surveying 50 fans per game for the past year to see what's on their minds. It's all part of my campuswide TQM effort. Let me tally things up and I'll get back to you in a week."

When she returned to her office, Gardner pulled out the file her assistant had compiled (see Table 6). "There's a lot of information here," she thought.

TABLE 6 **Fan Satisfaction Survey Results ($N = 250$)**

		OVERALL GRADE				
		A	B	C	D	F
Game Day	A. Parking	90	105	45	5	5
	B. Traffic	50	85	48	52	15
	C. Seating	45	30	115	35	25
	D. Entertainment	160	35	26	10	19
	E. Printed Program	66	34	98	22	30
Tickets	A. Pricing	105	104	16	15	10
	B. Season Ticket Plans	75	80	54	41	0
Concessions	A. Prices	16	116	58	58	2
	B. Selection of Foods	155	60	24	11	0
	C. Speed of Service	35	45	46	48	76
Respondents						
Alumnus	113					
Student	83					
Faculty/Staff	16					
None of the above	38					

(table cont'd)

Open-Ended Comments on Survey Cards:

Parking a mess	More hot dog stands	Put in bigger seats	My company will buy a skybox—build it!
Add a skybox	Seats are all metal	Friendly ushers	Programs overpriced
Get better cheerleaders	Need skyboxes	Need better seats	Want softer seats
Double the parking attendants	Seats stink	Expand parking lots	Beat those Longhorns!
Everything is okay	Go SWU!	Hate the bleacher seats	I'll pay for a skybox
Too crowded	Lines are awful	Hot dogs cold	Seats too small
Seats too narrow	Seats are uncomfortable	$3 for a coffee? No way!	Band was terrific
Great food	I will pay more for better view	Get some skyboxes	Love Phil Flamm
Phil F. for President!	Get a new stadium	Love the new uniforms	Everything is great
I smelled drugs being smoked	Student dress code needed	Took an hour to park	Build new stadium
Stadium is ancient	I want cushioned seats	Coach is terrific	Move games to Dallas
Seats are like rocks	Not enough police	More water fountains	No complaints
Not enough cops for traffic	Students too rowdy	Better seats	Dirty bathroom
Game starts too late	Parking terrible	Seats not comfy	
Hire more traffic cops	Toilets weren't clean	Bigger parking lot	
Need new band	Not enough handicap spots in lot	I'm too old for bench seats	
Great!	Well done, SWU	Cold coffee served at game	

Discussion Questions

1. Using at least two different quality tools, analyze the data and present your conclusions.
2. How could the survey have been more useful?
3. What is the next step?

The Culture of Quality at Arnold Palmer Hospital

Video Case

Founded in 1989, Arnold Palmer Hospital is one of the largest hospitals for women and children in the U.S., with 431 beds in two facilities totaling 676,000 square feet. Located in downtown Orlando, Florida, and named after its famed golf benefactor, the hospital, with more than 2,000 employees, serves an 18-county area in central Florida and is the only Level 1 trauma center for children in that region. Arnold Palmer Hospital provides a broad range of medical services including neonatal and pediatric intensive care, pediatric oncology and cardiology, care for high-risk pregnancies, and maternal intensive care.

The Issue of Assessing Quality Health Care

Quality health care is a goal all hospitals profess, but Arnold Palmer Hospital has actually developed comprehensive and scientific means of asking customers to judge the quality of care they receive. Participating in a national benchmark comparison against other hospitals, Arnold Palmer Hospital consistently scores in the top 10% in overall patient satisfaction. Executive Director Kathy Swanson states, "Hospitals in this area will be distinguished largely on the basis of their customer satisfaction. We must have accurate information about how our patients and their families judge the quality of our care, so I follow the questionnaire results daily. The in-depth survey helps me and others on my team to gain quick knowledge from patient feedback." Arnold Palmer Hospital employees are empowered to provide gifts in value up to $200 to patients who find reason to complain about any hospital service such as food, courtesy, responsiveness, or cleanliness.

Swanson doesn't focus just on the customer surveys, which are mailed to patients one week after discharge, but also on a variety of internal measures. These measures usually start at the grassroots level, where the staff sees a problem and develops ways to track performance. The hospital's longstanding philosophy supports the concept that each patient is important and respected as a person. That patient has the right to comprehensive, compassionate family-centered health care provided by a knowledgeable physician-directed team.

Some of the measures Swanson carefully monitors for continuous improvement are morbidity, infection rates, readmission rates, costs per case, and length of stays. The tools she uses daily include Pareto charts, flowcharts, and process charts, in addition to benchmarking against hospitals both nationally and in the southeast region.

The result of all of these efforts has been a quality culture as manifested in Arnold Palmer's high ranking in patient satisfaction and one of the highest survival rates of critically ill babies.

Discussion Questions*

1. Why is it important for Arnold Palmer Hospital to get a patient's assessment of health care quality? Does the patient have the expertise to judge the health care she receives?
2. How would you build a culture of quality in an organization such as Arnold Palmer Hospital?
3. What techniques does Arnold Palmer Hospital practice in its drive for quality and continuous improvement?
4. Develop a fish-bone diagram illustrating the quality variables for a patient who just gave birth at Arnold Palmer Hospital (or any other hospital).

*You may wish to view the video that accompanies this case before answering these questions.

Source: From Executive Director Kathy Swanson of Arnold Palmer Hospital.

Quality at the Ritz-Carlton Hotel Company — Video Case

Ritz-Carlton. The name alone evokes images of luxury and quality. As the first hotel company to win the Malcolm Baldrige National Quality Award, the Ritz treats quality as if it is the heartbeat of the company. This means a daily commitment to meeting customer expectations and making sure that each hotel is free of any deficiency.

In the hotel industry, quality can be hard to quantify. Guests do not purchase a product when they stay at the Ritz: They buy an experience. Thus, creating the right combination of elements to make the experience stand out is the challenge and goal of every employee, from maintenance to management.

Before applying for the Baldrige Award, company management undertook a rigorous self-examination of its operations in an attempt to measure and quantify quality. Nineteen processes were studied, including room service delivery, guest reservation and registration, message delivery, and breakfast service. This period of self-study included statistical measurement of process work flows and cycle times for areas ranging from room service delivery times and reservations to valet parking and housekeeping efficiency. The results were used to develop performance benchmarks against which future activity could be measured.

With specific, quantifiable targets in place, Ritz-Carlton managers and employees now focus on continuous improvement. The goal is 100% customer satisfaction: If a guest's experience does not meet expectations, the Ritz-Carlton risks losing that guest to competition.

One way the company has put more meaning behind its quality efforts is to organize its employees into "self-directed" work teams. Employee teams determine work scheduling, what work needs to be done, and what to do about quality problems in their own areas. In order to see the relationship of their specific area to the overall goals, employees are also given the opportunity to take additional training in hotel operations. Ritz-Carlton believes that a more educated and informed employee is in a better position to make decisions in the best interest of the organization.

Discussion Questions*

1. In what ways could the Ritz-Carlton monitor its success in achieving quality?
2. Many companies say that their goal is to provide quality products or services. What actions might you expect from a company that intends quality to be more than a slogan or buzzword?
3. Why might it cost the Ritz-Carlton less to "do things right" the first time?
4. How could control charts, Pareto diagrams, and cause-and-effect diagrams be used to identify quality problems at a hotel?
5. What are some nonfinancial measures of customer satisfaction that might be used by the Ritz-Carlton?

*You may wish to view the video that accompanies this case before addressing these questions.

Source: Adapted from C. T. Horngren, S. M. Datar, and G. Foster, *Cost Accounting*, 14th ed. (Upper Saddle River, NJ: Prentice Hall, 2012).

- **Additional Case Study:** Visit **www.myomlab.com** or **www.pearsonhighered.com/heizer** for this free case study:
  Westover Electrical, Inc.: This electric motor manufacturer has a large log of defects in its wiring process.

Bibliography

Besterfield, Dale H. *Quality Control*, 8th ed. Upper Saddle River, NJ: Prentice Hall, 2009.

Brown, Mark G. *Baldrige Award Winning Quality*, 19th ed. University Park, IL: Productivity Press, 2010.

Crosby, P. B. *Quality Is Still Free*. New York: McGraw-Hill, 1996.

Evans, J. R., and W. M. Lindsay. *Managing for Quality and Performance Excellence*. 8th ed. Mason, OH: Thompson-Southwestern, 2012.

Feigenbaum, A. V. "Raising the Bar." *Quality Progress* 41, no. 7 (July 2008): 22–28.

Foster, Thomas. *Managing Quality*, 4th ed. Upper Saddle River, NJ: Pearson/Prentice Hall, 2010.

Gitlow, Howard S. *A Guide to Lean Six Sigma Management Skills*. University Park, IL: Productivity Press, 2009.

Gonzalez-Benito, J., and O. Gonzalez-Benito. "Operations Management Practices Linked to the Adoption of ISO 14001." *International Journal of Production Economics* 113, no. 1 (May 2008): 60.

Gryna, F. M., R. C. H. Chua, and J. A. DeFeo. *Juran's Quality Planning and Analysis for Enterprise Quality*, 5th ed. New York: McGraw-Hill, 2007.

Mitra, Amit. *Fundamentals of Quality Control and Improvement*. New York: Wiley, 2009.

Pande, P. S., R. P. Neuman, R. R. Cavanagh. *What Is Design for Six Sigma?* New York: McGraw-Hill, 2005.

Petroski, Henry. *To Forgive Design: Understanding Failure*. Cambridge, MA: Belknap, 2012.

Schroeder, Roger G., et al. "Six Sigma: Definition and Underlying Theory." *Journal of Operations Management* 26, no. 4 (2008): 536–554.

Stewart, D. M. "Piecing Together Service Quality: A Framework for Robust Service." *Production and Operations Management* (Summer 2003): 246–265.

Summers, Donna. *Quality Management*, 2nd ed. Upper Saddle River, NJ: Prentice Hall, 2009.

APPENDIX

SOLUTIONS TO EVEN-NUMBERED PROBLEMS

2 Individual answer, in the style of Figure 6(b).

4 Individual answer, in the style of Figure 6(f).

6 Partial flowchart for planning a party:

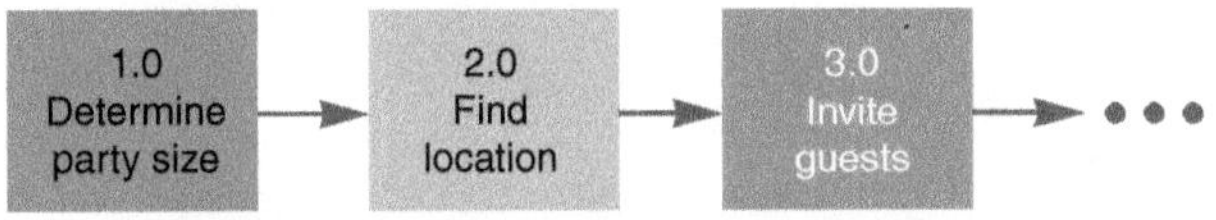

8 See figure on next page for a partial fish-bone. Individual answer in the style of Figure 7.

10 Individual answer, in the style of Figure 7 in the chapter.

12 Pareto chart, in the style of Example 1 with parking/drives most frequent, pool second, etc.

14 See figure below.
Issues: Materials: 4, 12, 14; Methods: 3, 7, 15, 16; Manpower: 1, 5, 6, 11; Machines: 2, 8, 9, 10, 13.

16 **(a)** A scatter diagram in the style of Figure 6(b) that shows a strong positive relationship between shipments and defects

(b) A scatter diagram in the style of Figure 6(b) that shows a mild relationship between shipments and turnover

(c) A Pareto chart in the style of Figure 6(d) that shows frequency of each type of defect

(d) A fishbone chart in the style of Figure 6(c) with the 4 *Ms* showing possible causes of increasing defects in shipments

▼ *Figure for Problem 8.*

Partial Fish-Bone Chart for Dissatisfied Airline Customer

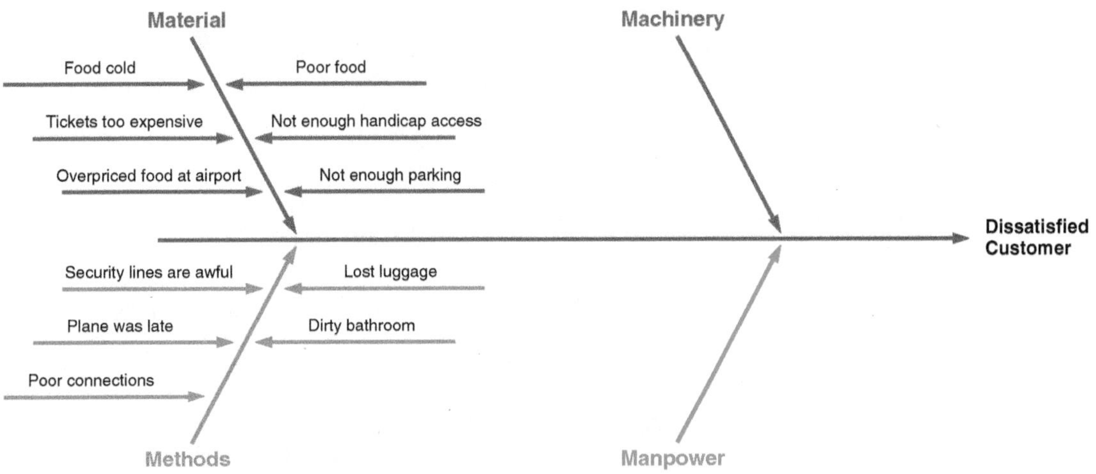

▼ *Figure for Problem 14.*

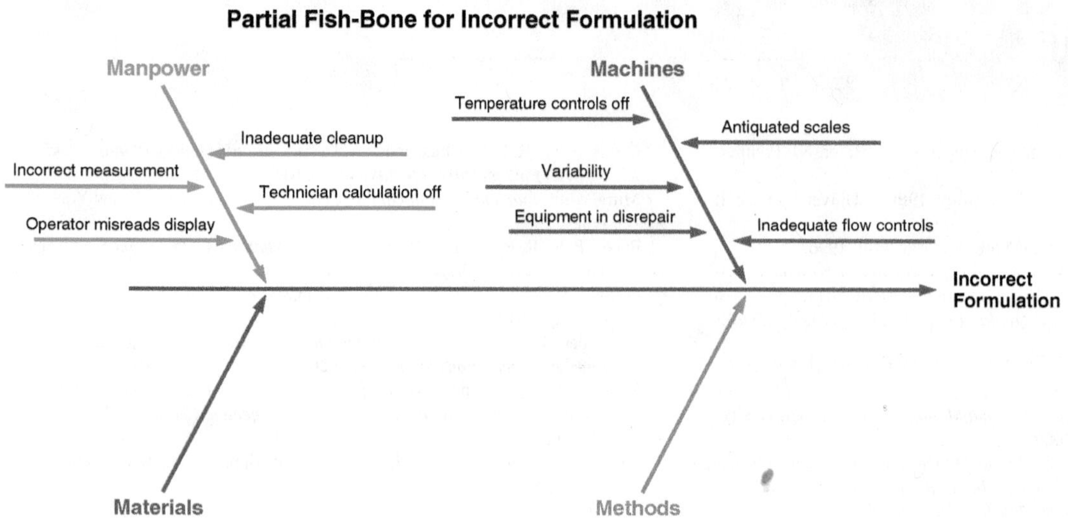

Rapid Review

Main Heading	Review Material	MyOMLab
QUALITY AND STRATEGY	Managing quality helps build successful strategies of differentiation, low cost, and *response.* Two ways that quality improves profitability are: ▪ *Sales gains* via improved response, price flexibility, increased market share, and/or improved reputation ▪ *Reduced costs* via increased productivity, lower rework and scrap costs, and/or lower warranty costs	**VIDEO 1** The Culture and Quality at Arnold Palmer Hospital
DEFINING QUALITY	An operations manager's objective is to build a total quality management system that identifies and satisfies customer needs. ▪ **Quality**—The ability of a product or service to meet customer needs. The American Society for Quality (ASQ) defines quality as "the totality of features and characteristics of a product or service that bears on its ability to satisfy stated or implied needs." The two most well-known quality awards are: ▪ *U.S.*: Malcolm Baldrige National Quality Award, named after a former secretary of commerce ▪ *Japan*: Deming Prize, named after an American, Dr. W. Edwards Deming ▪ **ISO 9000**—A set of quality standards developed by the International Organization for Standardization (ISO). ISO 9000 is the only quality standard with international recognition. To do business globally, being listed in the ISO directory is critical. ▪ **Cost of quality (COQ)**—The cost of doing things wrong; that is, the price of nonconformance. The four major categories of costs associated with quality are *prevention costs, appraisal costs, internal failure costs,* and *external failure costs.* Four leaders in the field of quality management are W. Edwards Deming, Joseph M. Juran, Armand Feigenbaum, and Philip B. Crosby.	
TOTAL QUALITY MANAGEMENT	▪ **Total quality management (TQM)**—Management of an entire organization so that it excels in all aspects of products and services that are important to the customer. Seven concepts for an effective TQM program are (1) continuous improvement, (2) Six Sigma, (3) employee empowerment, (4) benchmarking, (5) just-in-time (JIT), (6) Taguchi concepts, and (7) knowledge of TQM tools. ▪ **PDCA**—A continuous improvement model that involves four stages: plan, do, check, and act. The Japanese use the word *kaizen* to describe the ongoing process of unending improvement—the setting and achieving of ever-higher goals. ▪ **Six Sigma**—A program to save time, improve quality, and lower costs. In a statistical sense, Six Sigma describes a process, product, or service with an extremely high capability—99.9997% accuracy, or 3.4 defects per million. ▪ **Employee empowerment**—Enlarging employee jobs so that the added responsibility and authority are moved to the lowest level possible in the organization. Business literature suggests that some 85% of quality problems have to do with materials and processes, not with employee performance. ▪ **Quality circle**—A group of employees meeting regularly with a facilitator to solve work-related problems in their work area. ▪ **Benchmarking**—Selecting a demonstrated standard of performance that represents the very best performance for a process or an activity. The philosophy behind just-in-time (JIT) involves continuing improvement and enforced problem solving. JIT systems are designed to produce or deliver goods just as they are needed. ▪ **Quality robust**—Products that are consistently built to meet customer needs, in spite of adverse conditions in the production process. ▪ **Quality loss function (QLF)**—A mathematical function that identifies all costs connected with poor quality and shows how these costs increase as product quality moves from what the customer wants: $L = D^2C$. ▪ **Target-oriented quality**—A philosophy of continuous improvement to bring the product exactly on target.	Problems: 1, 3, 5, 13, 14, 16, and 17

Rapid Review continued

Main Heading	Review Material	MyOMLab
TOOLS OF TQM	TQM tools that generate ideas include the *check sheet* (organized method of recording data), *scatter diagram* (graph of the value of one variable vs. another variable), and *cause-and-effect diagram*. Tools for organizing the data are the *Pareto chart* and *flowchart*. Tools for identifying problems are the *histogram* (distribution showing the frequency of occurrences of a variable) and *statistical process control chart*. ■ **Cause-and-effect diagram**—A schematic technique used to discover possible locations of quality problems. (Also called an Ishikawa diagram or a fish-bone chart.) The 4 *M*s (material, machinery/equipment, manpower, and methods) may be broad "causes." ■ **Pareto chart**—A graphic that identifies the few critical items as opposed to many less important ones. ■ **Flowchart**—A block diagram that graphically describes a process or system. ■ **Statistical process control (SPC)**—A process used to monitor standards, make measurements, and take corrective action as a product or service is being produced. ■ **Control chart**—A graphic presentation of process data over time, with predetermined control limits.	ACTIVE MODEL 1 Virtual Office Hours for Solved Problem: 1
THE ROLE OF INSPECTION	■ **Inspection**—A means of ensuring that an operation is producing at the quality level expected. ■ **Source inspection**—Controlling or monitoring at the point of production or purchase: at the source. ■ **Poka-yoke**—Literally translated, "foolproof"; it has come to mean a device or technique that ensures the production of a good unit every time. ■ **Checklist**—A type of poka-yoke that lists the steps needed to ensure consistency and completeness in a task. ■ **Attribute inspection**—An inspection that classifies items as being either good or defective. ■ **Variable inspection**—Classifications of inspected items as falling on a continuum scale, such as dimension, size, or strength.	
TQM IN SERVICES	Determinants of service quality: reliability, responsiveness, competence, access, courtesy, communication, credibility, security, understanding/knowing the customer, and tangibles. ■ **Service recovery**—Training and empowering frontline workers to solve a problem immediately.	**VIDEO 2** TQM at Ritz-Carlton Hotels

Self Test

■ **Before taking the self-test,** refer to the learning objectives listed at the beginning of the text and the key terms listed at the end of the text.

LO1. In this chapter, *quality* is defined as:
- **a)** the degree of excellence at an acceptable price and the control of variability at an acceptable cost.
- **b)** how well a product fits patterns of consumer preferences.
- **c)** the totality of features and characteristics of a product or service that bears on its ability to satisfy stated or implied needs.
- **d)** being impossible to define, but you know what it is.

LO2. ISO 9000 is an international standard that addresses ______.

LO3. If 1 million passengers pass through the Jacksonville Airport with checked baggage each year, a successful Six Sigma program for baggage handling would result in how many passengers with misplaced luggage?
- **a)** 3.4
- **b)** 6.0
- **c)** 34
- **d)** 2,700
- **e)** 6 times the monthly standard deviation of passengers

LO4. The process of identifying other organizations that are best at some facet of your operations and then modeling your organization after them is known as:
- **a)** continuous improvement.
- **b)** employee empowerment.
- **c)** benchmarking.
- **d)** copycatting.
- **e)** patent infringement.

LO5. The Taguchi method includes all except which of the following major concepts?
- **a)** Employee involvement
- **b)** Remove the effects of adverse conditions
- **c)** Quality loss function
- **d)** Target specifications

LO6. The seven tools of total quality management are ______, ______, ______, ______, ______, ______, and ______.

Answers: LO1. c; LO2. quality management systems; LO3. a; LO4. c; LO5. a; LO6. check sheets, scatter diagrams, cause-and-effect diagrams, Pareto charts, flowcharts, histograms, SPC charts.

Statistical Process Control

OUTLINE

- Statistical Process Control (SPC)
- Process Capability
- Acceptance Sampling

LEARNING OBJECTIVES

LO1 ***Explain*** the purpose of a control chart

LO2 ***Explain*** the role of the central limit theorem in SPC

LO3 ***Build*** $\bar{x}$-charts and *R*-charts

LO4 ***List*** the five steps involved in building control charts

LO5 ***Build*** *p*-charts and *c*-charts

LO6 ***Explain*** process capability and compute C_p and C_{pk}

LO7 ***Explain*** acceptance sampling

As part of its statistical process control system, Flowers Bakery, in Georgia, uses a digital camera to inspect just-baked sandwich buns as they move along the production line. Items that don't measure up in terms of color, shape, seed distribution, or size are identified and removed automatically from the conveyor.

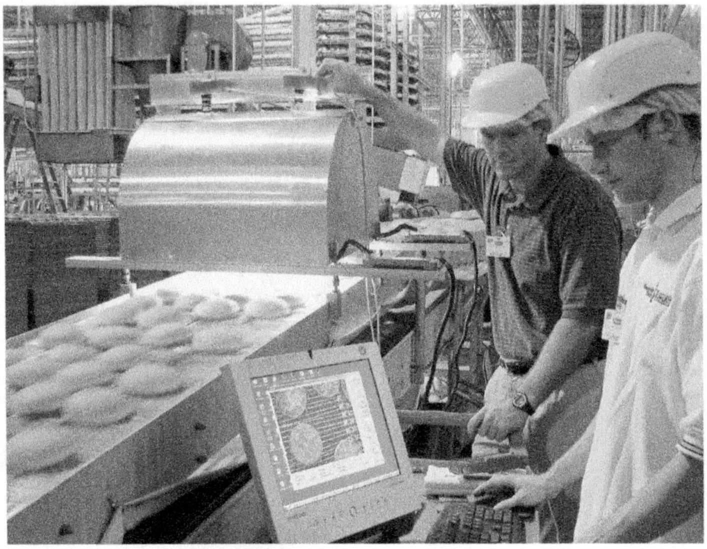

Georgia Institute of Technology

Statistical Process Control (SPC)

In this supplement, we address statistical process control—the same techniques used at BetzDearborn, at Arnold Palmer Hospital, at GE, and at Southwest Airlines to achieve quality standards. Statistical process control (SPC) is the application of statistical techniques to ensure that processes meet standards. All processes are subject to a certain degree of variability. While studying process data in the 1920s, Walter Shewhart of Bell Laboratories made the distinction between the common (natural) and special (assignable) causes of variation. He developed a simple but powerful tool to separate the two—the control chart.

Statistical process control (SPC)
A process used to monitor standards by taking measurements and corrective action as a product or service is being produced.

Control chart
A graphical presentation of process data over time.

A process is said to be operating *in statistical control* when the only source of variation is common (natural) causes. The process must first be brought into statistical control by detecting and eliminating special (assignable) causes of variation.[1] Then its performance is predictable, and its ability to meet customer expectations can be assessed. The *objective* of a process control system is to *provide a statistical signal when assignable causes of variation are present.* Such a signal can quicken appropriate action to eliminate assignable causes.

Natural Variations Natural variations affect almost every process and are to be expected. Natural variations are the many sources of variation that occur within a process, even one that is in statistical control. Natural variations form a pattern that can be described as a *distribution*.

Natural variations
Variability that affects every production process to some degree and is to be expected; also known as common cause.

As long as the distribution (output measurements) remains within specified limits, the process is said to be "in control," and natural variations are tolerated.

[1]Removing assignable causes is work. Quality expert W. Edwards Deming observed that a state of statistical control is not a natural state for a manufacturing process. Deming instead viewed it as an achievement, arrived at by elimination, one by one, by determined effort, of special causes of excessive variation.

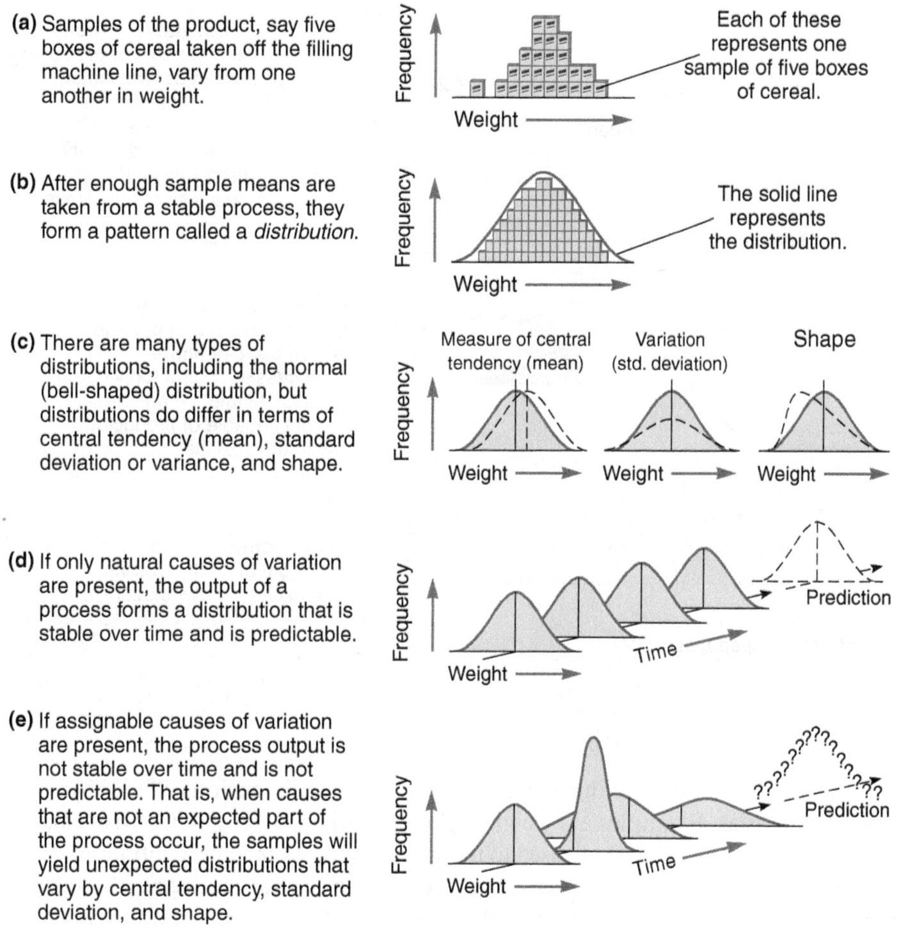
(a) Samples of the product, say five boxes of cereal taken off the filling machine line, vary from one another in weight.
Each of these represents one sample of five boxes of cereal.
Frequency
Weight
(b) After enough sample means are taken from a stable process, they form a pattern called a *distribution*.
The solid line represents the distribution.
Frequency
Weight
(c) There are many types of distributions, including the normal (bell-shaped) distribution, but distributions do differ in terms of central tendency (mean), standard deviation or variance, and shape.
Measure of central tendency (mean)
Variation (std. deviation)
Shape
Frequency
Weight
Weight
Weight
(d) If only natural causes of variation are present, the output of a process forms a distribution that is stable over time and is predictable.
Prediction
Frequency
Weight
Time
(e) If assignable causes of variation are present, the process output is not stable over time and is not predictable. That is, when causes that are not an expected part of the process occur, the samples will yield unexpected distributions that vary by central tendency, standard deviation, and shape.
Prediction
Frequency
Weight
Time

Figure S1
Natural and Assignable Variation

Assignable Variations Assignable variation in a process can be traced to a specific reason. Factors such as machine wear, misadjusted equipment, fatigued or untrained workers, or new batches of raw material are all potential sources of assignable variations.

Assignable variation
Variation in a production process that can be traced to specific causes.

Natural and assignable variations distinguish two tasks for the operations manager. The first is to *ensure that the process is capable* of operating under control with only natural variation. The second is, of course, to *identify and eliminate assignable variations* so that the processes will remain under control.

Samples Because of natural and assignable variation, statistical process control uses averages of small samples (often of four to eight items) as opposed to data on individual parts. Individual pieces tend to be too erratic to make trends quickly visible.

Figure S1 provides a detailed look at the important steps in determining process variation. The horizontal scale can be weight (as in the number of ounces in boxes of cereal) or length (as in fence posts) or any physical measure. The vertical scale is frequency. The samples of five boxes of cereal in Figure S1 **(a)** are weighed; **(b)** form a distribution, and **(c)** can vary. The distributions formed in **(b)** and **(c)** will fall in a predictable pattern **(d)** if only natural variation is present. If assignable causes of variation are present, then we can expect either the mean to vary or the dispersion to vary, as is the case in **(e)**.

Control Charts The process of building control charts is based on the concepts presented in Figure S2. This figure shows three distributions that are the result of outputs from three types of processes. We plot small samples and then examine characteristics of the resulting data to see if the process is within "control limits." The purpose of control charts is to help distinguish between natural variations and variations due to assignable causes. As seen in Figure S2, a process is **(a)** in control *and the process is capable of producing within established control limits*, **(b)** in control *but the process is not capable of producing within established limits*, or **(c)** out of control. We now look at ways to build control charts that help the operations manager keep a process under control.

LO1 *Explain* the purpose of a control chart

Figure S2

Process Control: Three Types of Process Outputs

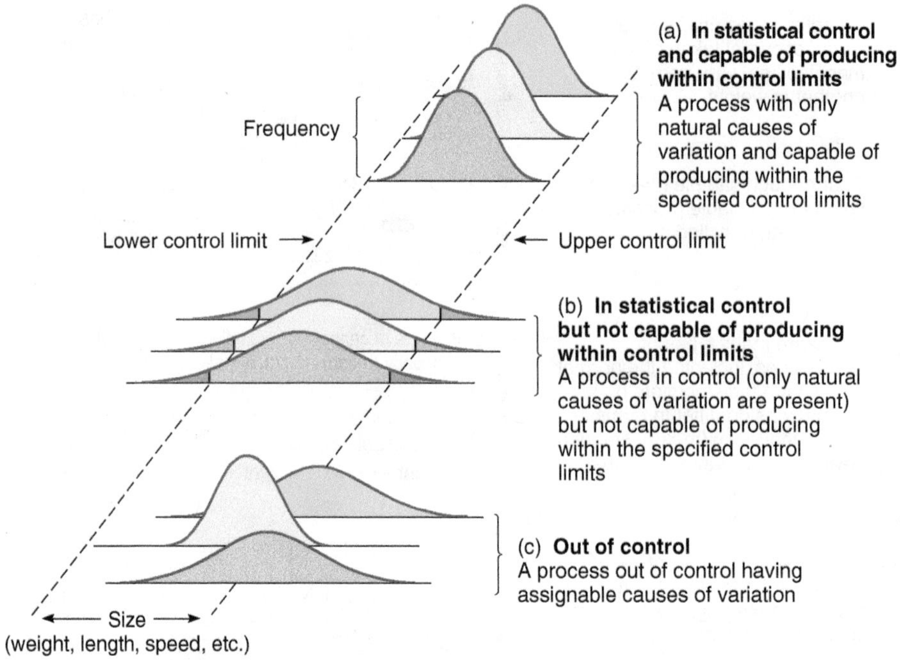
Frequency
Lower control limit
Upper control limit
(a) In statistical control and capable of producing within control limits
A process with only natural causes of variation and capable of producing within the specified control limits
(b) In statistical control but not capable of producing within control limits
A process in control (only natural causes of variation are present) but not capable of producing within the specified control limits
(c) Out of control
A process out of control having assignable causes of variation
Size
(weight, length, speed, etc.)

Control Charts for Variables

The variables of interest here are those that have continuous dimensions. They have an infinite number of possibilities. Examples are weight, speed, length, or strength. Control charts for the mean, $\bar{x}$ or *x*-bar, and the range, *R*, are used to monitor processes that have continuous dimensions. The $\bar{x}$-chart tells us whether changes have occurred in the central tendency (the mean, in this case) of a process. These changes might be due to such factors as tool wear, a gradual increase in temperature, a different method used on the second shift, or new and stronger materials. The *R*-chart values indicate that a gain or loss in dispersion has occurred. Such a change may be due to worn bearings, a loose tool, an erratic flow of lubricants to a machine, or to sloppiness on the part of a machine operator. The two types of charts go hand in hand when monitoring variables because they measure the two critical parameters: central tendency and dispersion.

$\bar{x}$-chart

A quality control chart for variables that indicates when changes occur in the central tendency of a production process.

R-chart

A control chart that tracks the "range" within a sample; it indicates that a gain or loss in uniformity has occurred in dispersion of a production process.

The Central Limit Theorem

The theoretical foundation for $\bar{x}$-charts is the central limit theorem. This theorem states that regardless of the distribution of the population, the distribution of $\bar{x}$s (each of which is a mean of a sample drawn from the population) will tend to follow a normal curve as the number of samples increases. Fortunately, even if each sample (*n*) is fairly small (say, 4 or 5), the distributions of the averages will still roughly follow a normal curve. The theorem also states that: (1) the mean of the distribution of the $\bar{x}$s (called $\bar{\bar{x}}$) will equal the mean of the overall population (called μ); and (2) the standard deviation of the *sampling distribution*, $\sigma_{\bar{x}}$, will be the *population (process) standard deviation*, divided by the square root of the sample size, *n*. In other words:[2]

Central limit theorem

The theoretical foundation for $\bar{x}$-charts, which states that regardless of the distribution of the population of all parts or services, the distribution of $\bar{x}$s tends to follow a normal curve as the number of samples increases.

$$\bar{\bar{x}} = \mu \qquad \text{(S1)}$$

and

$$\sigma_{\bar{x}} = \frac{\sigma}{\sqrt{n}} \qquad \text{(S2)}$$

LO2 *Explain* the role of the central limit theorem in SPC

[2]The standard deviation is easily calculated as $\sigma = \sqrt{\frac{\sum_{i=1}^{n}(x_i - \bar{x})^2}{n-1}}$. For a good review of this and other statistical terms, refer to Tutorial 1, "Statistical Review for Managers," at our free Web site, **www.pearsonhighered.com/heizer**.

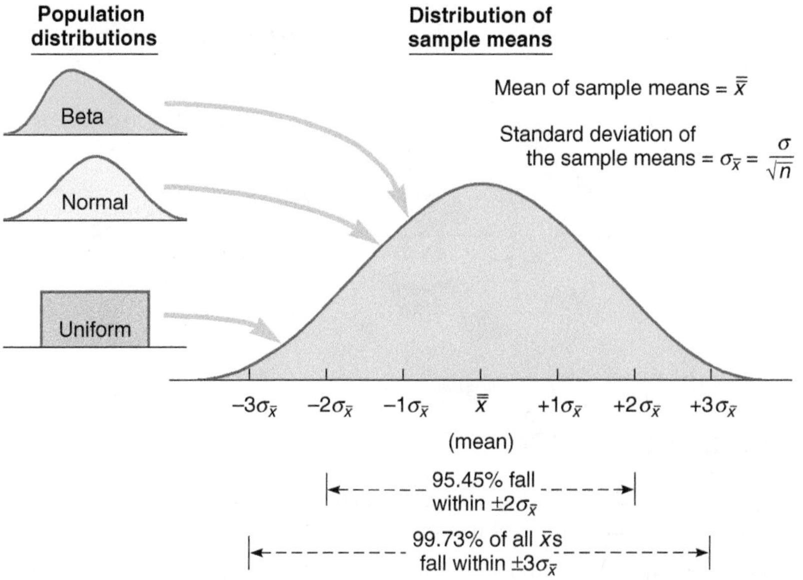

Figure **S3**

The Relationship Between Population and Sampling Distributions

Even though the population distributions will differ (e.g., normal, beta, uniform), each with its own mean (μ) and standard deviation (σ), the distribution of sample means always approaches a normal distribution.

Figure S3 shows three possible population distributions, each with its own mean, μ, and standard deviation, σ. If a series of random samples ($\bar{x}_1$, $\bar{x}_2$, $\bar{x}_3$, $\bar{x}_4$, and so on), each of size n, is drawn from any population distribution (which could be normal, beta, uniform, and so on), the resulting distribution of $\bar{x}_i$s will approximate a normal distribution (see Figure S3).

Moreover, the sampling distribution, as is shown in Figure S4, will have less variability than the process distribution. Because the sampling distribution is normal, we can state that:

- 95.45% of the time, the sample averages will fall within $\pm 2\sigma_{\bar{x}}$ if the process has only natural variations.
- 99.73% of the time, the sample averages will fall within $\pm 3\sigma_{\bar{x}}$ if the process has only natural variations.

If a point on the control chart falls outside of the $\pm 3\sigma_{\bar{x}}$ control limits, then we are 99.73% sure the process has changed. This is the theory behind control charts.

Setting Mean Chart Limits ($\bar{x}$-Charts)

If we know, through past data, the standard deviation of the population (process), σ, we can set upper and lower control limits[3] by using these formulas:

$$\text{Upper control limit (UCL)} = \bar{\bar{x}} + z\sigma_{\bar{x}} \quad \text{(S3)}$$

$$\text{Lower control limit (LCL)} = \bar{\bar{x}} - z\sigma_{\bar{x}} \quad \text{(S4)}$$

LO3 *Build* $\bar{x}$-charts and *R*-charts

where

$\bar{\bar{x}}$ = mean of the sample means or a target value set for the process
z = number of normal standard deviations (2 for 95.45% confidence, 3 for 99.73%)
$\sigma_{\bar{x}}$ = standard deviation of the sample means = $\sigma/\sqrt{n}$
σ = population (process) standard deviation
n = sample size

Example S1 shows how to set control limits for sample means using standard deviations.

[3]Lower control limits cannot take negative values in control charts. So the LCL = max $(0, \bar{\bar{x}} - z\sigma_{\bar{x}})$.

Figure S4

The Sampling Distribution of Means Is Normal and Has Less Variability Than the Process Distribution

In this figure, the process distribution from which the sample was drawn was also normal, but it could have been any distribution.

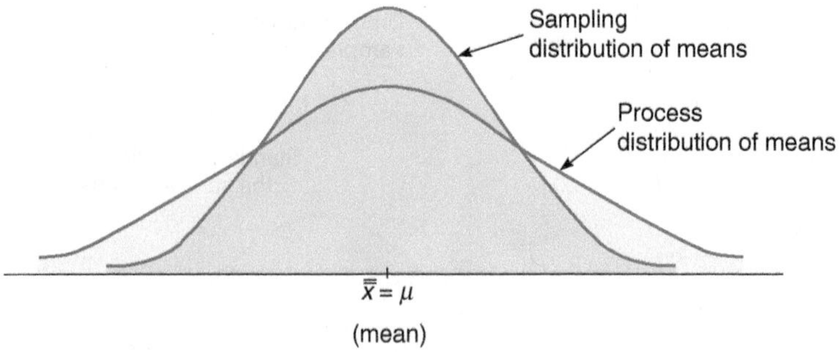

Example S1

SETTING CONTROL LIMITS USING SAMPLES

The weights of boxes of Oat Flakes within a large production lot are sampled each hour. Managers want to set control limits that include 99.73% of the sample means.

APPROACH ▶ Randomly select and weigh nine ($n = 9$) boxes each hour. Then find the overall mean and use Equations (S3) and (S4) to compute the control limits. Here are the nine boxes chosen for Hour 1:

STUDENT TIP ☆
If you want to see an example of such variability in your supermarket, go to the soft drink section and line up a few 2-liter bottles of Coke or Pepsi.

SOLUTION ▶

$$\text{The average weight in the first sample} = \frac{17 + 13 + 16 + 18 + 17 + 16 + 15 + 17 + 16}{9}$$
$$= 16.1 \text{ ounces.}$$

Also, the *population (process)* standard deviation (σ) is known to be 1 ounce. We do not show each of the boxes randomly selected in hours 2 through 12, but here are all 12 hourly samples:

WEIGHT OF SAMPLE		WEIGHT OF SAMPLE		WEIGHT OF SAMPLE	
HOUR	(AVG. OF 9 BOXES)	HOUR	(AVG. OF 9 BOXES)	HOUR	(AVG. OF 9 BOXES)
1	16.1	5	16.5	9	16.3
2	16.8	6	16.4	10	14.8
3	15.5	7	15.2	11	14.2
4	16.5	8	16.4	12	17.3

The average mean $\bar{\bar{x}}$ of the 12 samples is calculated to be exactly 16 ounces $\left[\bar{\bar{x}} = \frac{\sum_{i=1}^{12}(\text{Avg of 9 Boxes})}{12}\right]$.

We therefore have $\bar{\bar{x}} = 16$ ounces, $\sigma = 1$ ounce, $n = 9$, and $z = 3$. The control limits are:

$$UCL_{\bar{x}} = \bar{\bar{x}} + z\sigma_{\bar{x}} = 16 + 3\left(\frac{1}{\sqrt{9}}\right) = 16 + 3\left(\frac{1}{3}\right) = 17 \text{ ounces}$$

$$LCL_{\bar{x}} = \bar{\bar{x}} - z\sigma_{\bar{x}} = 16 - 3\left(\frac{1}{\sqrt{9}}\right) = 16 - 3\left(\frac{1}{3}\right) = 15 \text{ ounces}$$

The 12 samples are then plotted on the following control chart:

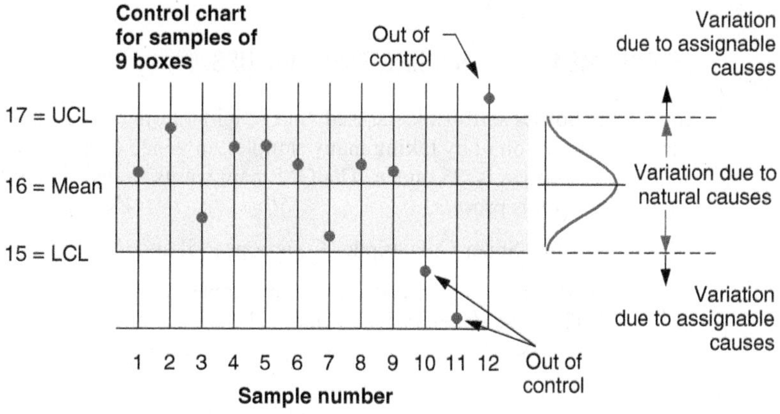

INSIGHT ▶ Because the means of recent sample averages fall outside the upper and lower control limits of 17 and 15, we can conclude that the process is becoming erratic and is *not* in control.

LEARNING EXERCISE ▶ If Oat Flakes's population standard deviation (σ) is 2 (instead of 1), what is your conclusion? [Answer: LCL = 14, UCL = 18; the process would be in control.]

RELATED PROBLEMS ▶ S1, S2, S4, S8, S10a,b

EXCEL OM Data File **CH06SExS1.XLS** can be found at **www.pearsonhighered.com/heizer**.

Because process standard deviations are often not available, we usually calculate control limits based on the average *range* values rather than on standard deviations. Table S1 provides the necessary conversion for us to do so. The *range* (R_i) is defined as the difference between the largest and smallest items in one sample. For example, the heaviest box of Oat Flakes in Hour 1 of Example S1 was 18 ounces and the lightest was 13 ounces, so the range for that hour is 5 ounces. We use Table S1 and the equations:

$$UCL_{\bar{x}} = \bar{\bar{x}} + A_2\bar{R} \tag{S5}$$

and:

$$LCL_{\bar{x}} = \bar{\bar{x}} - A_2\bar{R} \tag{S6}$$

where $\bar{R} = \frac{\sum_{i=1}^{n} R_i}{n}$ = average range of the samples; R_i = range for one sample

A_2 = value found in Table S1

$\bar{\bar{x}}$ = mean of the sample means

Example S2 shows how to set control limits for sample means by using Table S1 and the average range.

TABLE S1 **Factors for Computing Control Chart Limits (3 sigma)**

SAMPLE SIZE, n	MEAN FACTOR, A_2	UPPER RANGE, D_4	LOWER RANGE, D_3
2	1.880	3.268	0
3	1.023	2.574	0
4	.729	2.282	0
5	.577	2.115	0
6	.483	2.004	0
7	.419	1.924	0.076
8	.373	1.864	0.136
9	.337	1.816	0.184
10	.308	1.777	0.223
12	.266	1.716	0.284

Source: Reprinted by permission of American Society for Testing Materials. Copyright 1951. Taken from Special Technical Publication 15–C, "Quality Control of Materials," pp. 63 and 72. Copyright ASTM INTERNATIONAL. Reprinted with permission.

Example S2

SETTING MEAN LIMITS USING TABLE VALUES

Super Cola bottles soft drinks labeled "net weight 12 ounces." Indeed, an overall process average of 12 ounces has been found by taking many samples, in which each sample contained 5 bottles. The average range of the process is .25 ounce. The OM team wants to determine the upper and lower control limits for averages in this process.

APPROACH ▶ Super Cola applies Equations (S5) and (S6) and uses the A_2 column of Table S1.

SOLUTION ▶ Looking in Table S1 for a sample size of 5 in the mean factor A_2 column, we find the value .577. Thus, the upper and lower control chart limits are:

$$\begin{aligned} UCL_{\bar{x}} &= \bar{\bar{x}} + A_2\bar{R} \\ &= 12 + (.577)(.25) \\ &= 12 + .144 \\ &= 12.144 \text{ ounces} \\ LCL_{\bar{x}} &= \bar{\bar{x}} - A_2\bar{R} \\ &= 12 - .144 \\ &= 11.856 \text{ ounces} \end{aligned}$$

INSIGHT ▶ The advantage of using this range approach, instead of the standard deviation, is that it is easy to apply and may be less confusing.

LEARNING EXERCISE ▶ If the sample size was $n = 4$ and the average range = .20 ounces, what are the revised $UCL_{\bar{x}}$ and $LCL_{\bar{x}}$? [Answer: 12.146, 11.854.]

RELATED PROBLEMS ▶ S3a, S5, S6, S7, S9, S10b,c,d S11, S34

EXCEL OM Data File **CH06SExS2.xls** can be found at **www.pearsonhighered.com/heizer**.

Setting Range Chart Limits (*R*-Charts)

In Examples S1 and S2, we determined the upper and lower control limits for the process *average*. In addition to being concerned with the process average, operations managers are interested in the process *dispersion*, or *range*. Even though the process average is under control, the dispersion of the process may not be. For example, something may have worked itself loose in

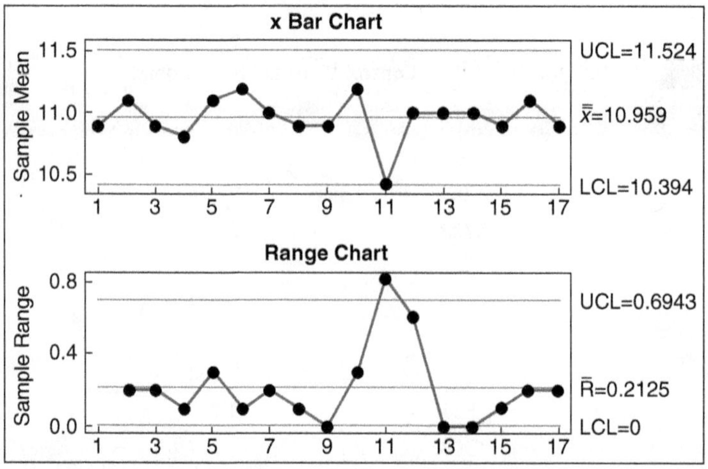

VIDEO S1
Farm to Fork: Quality of Darden Restaurants

Salmon filets are monitored by Darden Restaurant's SPC software, which includes $\bar{x}$- and *R*-charts. Darden uses average weight as a measure of central tendency for salmon filets. The range is the difference between the heaviest and the lightest filets in each sample. The video case study "Farm to Fork," at the end of this supplement, asks you to interpret these figures.

a piece of equipment that fills boxes of Oat Flakes. As a result, the average of the samples may remain the same, but the variation within the samples could be entirely too large. For this reason, operations managers use control charts for ranges to monitor the process variability, as well as control charts for averages, which monitor the process central tendency. The theory behind the control charts for ranges is the same as that for process average control charts. Limits are established that contain ± 3 standard deviations of the distribution for the average range $\overline{R}$. We can use the following equations to set the upper and lower control limits for ranges:

$$\text{UCL}_R = D_4\overline{R} \tag{S7}$$

$$\text{LCL}_R = D_3\overline{R} \tag{S8}$$

where

UCL_R = upper control chart limit for the range
LCL_R = lower control chart limit for the range
D_4 and D_3 = values from Table S1

Example S3 shows how to set control limits for sample ranges using Table S1 and the average range.

Example S3

SETTING RANGE LIMITS USING TABLE VALUES

The average *range* of a product at Clinton Manufacturing is 5.3 pounds. With a sample size of 5, owner Roy Clinton wants to determine the upper and lower control chart limits.

APPROACH ▶ Looking in Table S1 for a sample size of 5, he finds that $D_4 = 2.115$ and $D_3 = 0$.

SOLUTION ▶ The range control limits are:

$$\text{UCL}_R = D_4\overline{R} = (2.115)(5.3 \text{ pounds}) = 11.2 \text{ pounds}$$

$$\text{LCL}_R = D_3\overline{R} = (0)(5.3 \text{ pounds}) = 0$$

INSIGHT ▶ Computing ranges with Table S1 is straightforward and an easy way to evaluate dispersion.

LEARNING EXERCISE ▶ Clinton decides to increase the sample size to $n = 7$ (with no change in average range, $\overline{R}$). What are the new UCL_R and LCL_R values? [Answer: 10.197, 0.403.]

RELATED PROBLEMS ▶ S3b, S5, S6, S7, S9, S10c, S11, S12, S34

Using Mean and Range Charts

The normal distribution is defined by two parameters, the *mean* and *standard deviation*. The $\overline{x}$ (mean)-chart and the R-chart mimic these two parameters. The $\overline{x}$-chart is sensitive to shifts in the process mean, whereas the R-chart is sensitive to shifts in the process standard deviation. Consequently, by using both charts we can track changes in the process distribution.

For instance, the samples and the resulting $\overline{x}$-chart in Figure S5(a) show the shift in the process mean, but because the dispersion is constant, no change is detected by the R-chart. Conversely, the samples and the $\overline{x}$-chart in Figure S5(b) detect no shift (because none is present), but the R-chart does detect the shift in the dispersion. Both charts are required to track the process accurately.

LO4 *List* the five steps involved in building control charts

Steps to Follow When Using Control Charts There are five steps that are generally followed in using $\overline{x}$- and R-charts:

1. Collect 20 to 25 samples, often of $n = 4$ or $n = 5$ observations each, from a stable process and compute the mean and range of each.
2. Compute the overall means ($\overline{\overline{x}}$ and $\overline{R}$), set appropriate control limits, usually at the 99.73% level, and calculate the preliminary upper and lower control limits. Refer to

Figure S5

Mean and Range Charts Complement Each Other by Showing the Mean and Dispersion of the Normal Distribution

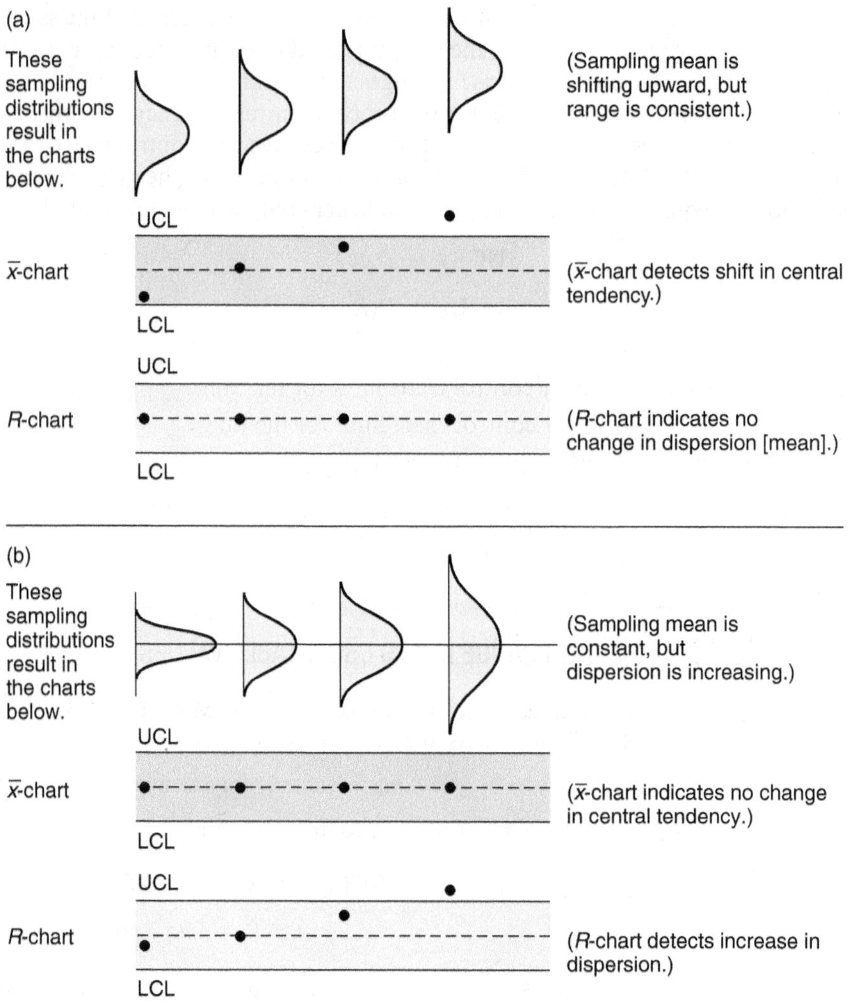

STUDENT TIP ☆

Mean ($\bar{x}$) charts are a measure of *central tendency*, while range (*R*) charts are a measure of *dispersion*. SPC requires both charts for a complete assessment because a sample mean could be out of control while the range is in control and vice versa.

TABLE S2

Common *z* Values

DESIRED CONTROL LIMIT (%)	Z-VALUE (STANDARD DEVIATION REQUIRED FOR DESIRED LEVEL OF CONFIDENCE)
90.0	1.65
95.0	1.96
95.45	2.00
99.0	2.58
99.73	3.00

Table S2 for other control limits. *If the process is not currently stable and in control*, use the desired mean, μ, instead of $\bar{\bar{x}}$ to calculate limits.

3. Graph the sample means and ranges on their respective control charts and determine whether they fall outside the acceptable limits.
4. Investigate points or patterns that indicate the process is out of control. Try to assign causes for the variation, address the causes, and then resume the process.
5. Collect additional samples and, if necessary, revalidate the control limits using the new data.

Control Charts for Attributes

LO5 *Build p*-charts and *c*-charts

Control charts for $\bar{x}$ and *R* do not apply when we are sampling *attributes*, which are typically classified as *defective* or *nondefective*. Measuring defectives involves counting them (for example, number of bad lightbulbs in a given lot, or number of letters or data entry records typed with errors), whereas *variables* are usually measured for length or weight. There are two kinds of attribute control charts: (1) those that measure the *percent* defective in a sample—called *p*-charts—and (2) those that count the *number* of defects—called *c*-charts.

p-chart
A quality control chart that is used to control attributes.

p-Charts Using *p*-charts is the chief way to control attributes. Although attributes that are either good or bad follow the binomial distribution, the normal distribution can be used to calculate *p*-chart limits when sample sizes are large. The procedure resembles the $\bar{x}$-chart approach, which is also based on the central limit theorem.

Donna McWilliam/AP Wide World Photos

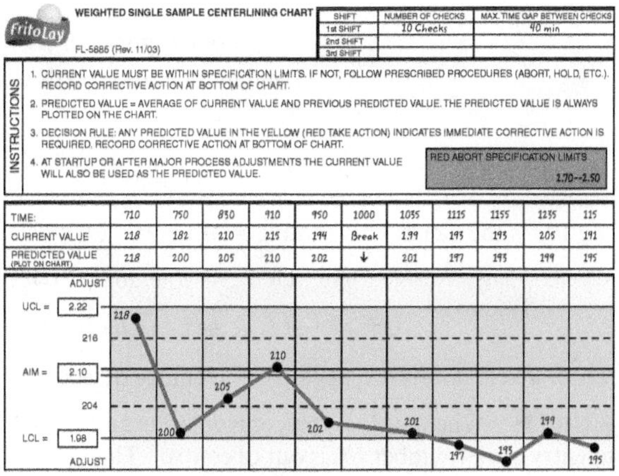

Frito-Lay uses $\bar{x}$ charts to control production quality at critical points in the process. About every 40 minutes, three batches of chips are taken from the conveyor (on the left) and analyzed electronically to get an average salt content, which is plotted on an $\bar{x}$-chart (on the right). Points plotted in the green zone are "in control," while those in the yellow zone are "out of control." The SPC chart is displayed where all production employees can monitor process stability.

The formulas for p-chart upper and lower control limits follow:

$$\text{UCL}_p = \bar{p} + z\sigma_{\hat{p}} \tag{S9}$$

$$\text{LCL}_p = \bar{p} - z\sigma_{\hat{p}} \tag{S10}$$

VIDEO S2
Frito-Lay's Quality-Controlled Potato Chips

where $\bar{p}$ = mean fraction (percent) defective in the samples
z = number of standard deviations ($z = 2$ for 95.45% limits; $z = 3$ for 99.73% limits)
$\sigma_{\hat{p}}$ = standard deviation of the sampling distribution

$\sigma_{\hat{p}}$ is estimated by the formula:

$$\sigma_{\hat{p}} = \sqrt{\frac{\bar{p}(1 - \bar{p})}{n}} \tag{S11}$$

where n = number of observations in *each* sample[4]

Example S4 shows how to set control limits for p-charts for these standard deviations.

Example S4

SETTING CONTROL LIMITS FOR PERCENT DEFECTIVE

Clerks at Mosier Data Systems key in thousands of insurance records each day for a variety of client firms. CEO Donna Mosier wants to set control limits to include 99.73% of the random variation in the data entry process when it is in control.

APPROACH ▶ Samples of the work of 20 clerks are gathered (and shown in the table). Mosier carefully examines 100 records entered by each clerk and counts the number of errors. She also computes the fraction defective in each sample. Equations (S9), (S10), and (S11) are then used to set the control limits.

SAMPLE NUMBER	NUMBER OF ERRORS	FRACTION DEFECTIVE	SAMPLE NUMBER	NUMBER OF ERRORS	FRACTION DEFECTIVE
1	6	.06	11	6	.06
2	5	.05	12	1	.01
3	0	.00	13	8	.08
4	1	.01	14	7	.07
5	4	.04	15	5	.05
6	2	.02	16	4	.04
7	5	.05	17	11	.11
8	3	.03	18	3	.03
9	3	.03	19	0	.00
10	2	.02	20	4	.04
				80	

[4]If the sample sizes are not the same, other techniques must be used.

SOLUTION ▶

$$\bar{p} = \frac{\text{Total number of errors}}{\text{Total number of records examined}} = \frac{80}{(100)(20)} = .04$$

$$\sigma_{\hat{p}} = \sqrt{\frac{(.04)(1 - .04)}{100}} = .02 \text{ (rounded up from .0196)}$$

(*Note:* 100 is the size of *each* sample $= n$.)

$$UCL_p = \bar{p} + z\sigma_{\hat{p}} = .04 + 3(.02) = .10$$

$$LCL_p = \bar{p} - z\sigma_{\hat{p}} = .04 - 3(.02) = 0$$

(because we cannot have a negative percentage defective)

INSIGHT ▶ When we plot the control limits and the sample fraction defectives, we find that only one data-entry clerk (number 17) is out of control. The firm may wish to examine that individual's work a bit more closely to see if a serious problem exists (see Figure S6).

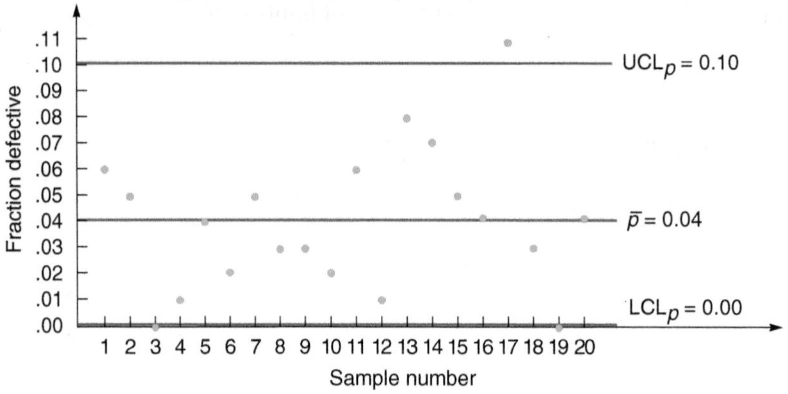

Figure **S6**

***p*-Chart for Data Entry for Example S4**

STUDENT TIP ☆
We are always pleased to be at zero or below the center line in a *p*-chart.

LEARNING EXERCISE ▶ Mosier decides to set control limits at 95.45% instead. What are the new UCL_p and LCL_p? [Answer: 0.08, 0]

RELATED PROBLEMS ▶ S13, S14, S15, S16, S17, S18, S19, S20, S25, S35

EXCEL OM Data File **Ch06SExS4.xls** can be found at **www.pearsonhighered.com/heizer**.

ACTIVE **MODEL** S1 This example is further illustrated in Active Model S6.1 at **www.pearsonhighered. com/heizer**.

The *OM in Action* box "Trying to Land a Seat with Frequent Flyer Miles" provides a real-world follow-up to Example S4.

c-chart
A quality control chart used to control the number of defects per unit of output.

***c*-Charts** In Example S4, we counted the number of defective records entered. A defective record was one that was not exactly correct because it contained at least one defect. However, a bad record may contain more than one defect. We use *c*-charts to control the *number* of defects per unit of output (or per insurance record, in the preceding case).

OM in Action Trying to Land a Seat with Frequent Flyer Miles

How hard is it to redeem your 25,000 frequent flyer points for airline tickets? That depends on the airline. (It also depends on the city. Don't try to get into or out of San Francisco!) When the consulting firm Idea Works made 280 requests for a standard mileage award to each of 24 airlines' Web sites (a total of 6,720 requests), the success rates ranged from a low of 25.7% and 27.1% (at US Airways and Delta, respectively) to a high of 100% at GOL-Brazil and 99.3% at Southwest.

The overall average of 68.6% for the two dozen carriers provides the center line in a *p*-chart. With 3-sigma upper and lower control limits of 82.5% and 54.7%, the other top and bottom performers are easily spotted. "Out of control" (but in a positive *outperforming* way) are GOL and Southwest, Lufthansa (85.0%), Singapore (90.7%), Virgin Australia (91.4%), and Air Berlin (96.4%).

Out of control *on the negative side* are US Airways and Delta, plus Emirates (35.7%), AirTran (47.1%), Turkish (49.3%), and SAS (52.9%).

Control charts can help airlines see where they stand relative to competitors in such customer service activities as lost bags, on-time rates, and ease of redeeming mileage points. "I think airlines are getting the message that availability is important. Are airlines where they need to be? I don't think so," says the president of Idea Works.

Sources: Wall Street Journal (May 26, 2011); and *St. Louis Business Journal* (May 26, 2011).

Charles O'Rear/Corbis-NY

Sampling wine from these wooden barrels, to make sure it is aging properly, uses both SPC (for alcohol content and acidity) and subjective measures (for taste).

Control charts for defects are helpful for monitoring processes in which a large number of potential errors can occur, but the actual number that do occur is relatively small. Defects may be errors in newspaper words, bad circuits in a microchip, blemishes on a table, or missing pickles on a fast-food hamburger.

The Poisson probability distribution,[5] which has a variance equal to its mean, is the basis for *c*-charts. Because $\bar{c}$ is the mean number of defects per unit, the standard deviation is equal to $\sqrt{\bar{c}}$. To compute 99.73% control limits for $\bar{c}$, we use the formula:

$$\text{Control limits} = \bar{c} \pm 3\sqrt{\bar{c}} \qquad \text{(S12)}$$

Example S5 shows how to set control limits for a $\bar{c}$-chart.

Example S5

SETTING CONTROL LIMITS FOR NUMBER OF DEFECTS

Red Top Cab Company receives several complaints per day about the behavior of its drivers. Over a 9-day period (where days are the units of measure), the owner, Gordon Hoft, received the following numbers of calls from irate passengers: 3, 0, 8, 9, 6, 7, 4, 9, 8, for a total of 54 complaints. Hoft wants to compute 99.73% control limits.

APPROACH ▶ He applies Equation (S6–12).

SOLUTION ▶ $\bar{c} = \frac{54}{9} = 6$ complaints per day

Thus:

$$UCL_c = \bar{c} + 3\sqrt{\bar{c}} = 6 + 3\sqrt{6} = 6 + 3(2.45) = 13.35, \text{ or } 13$$

$$LCL_c = \bar{c} - 3\sqrt{\bar{c}} = 6 - 3\sqrt{6} = 6 - 3(2.45) = 0 \leftarrow \text{(since it cannot be negative)}$$

INSIGHT ▶ After Hoft plotted a control chart summarizing these data and posted it prominently in the drivers' locker room, the number of calls received dropped to an average of three per day. Can you explain why this occurred?

LEARNING EXERCISE ▶ Hoft collects 3 more days' worth of complaints (10, 12, and 8 complaints) and wants to combine them with the original 9 days to compute updated control limits. What are the revised UCL_c and LCL_c? [Answer: 14.94, 0.]

RELATED PROBLEMS ▶ S21, S22, S23, S24

EXCEL OM Data File **Ch06SExS5.xls** can be found at **www.pearsonhighered.com/heizer**.

[5]A Poisson probability distribution is a discrete distribution commonly used when the items of interest (in this case, defects) are infrequent or occur in time or space.

STUDENT TIP ☆
This is a really useful table. When you are not sure which control chart to use, turn here for clarification.

TABLE S3 Helping You Decide Which Control Chart to Use

VARIABLE DATA USING AN $\bar{X}$-CHART AND AN *R*-CHART
1. Observations are *variables*, which are usually products measured for size or weight. Examples are the width or length of a wire and the weight of a can of Campbell's soup. **2.** Collect 20 to 25 samples, usually of $n = 4$, $n = 5$, or more, each from a stable process, and compute the means for an $\bar{x}$-chart and the ranges for an *R*-chart. **3.** We track samples of *n* observations each, as in Example S1.
ATTRIBUTE DATA USING A P-CHART
1. Observations are *attributes* that can be categorized as good or bad (or pass–fail, or functional–broken); that is, in two states. **2.** We deal with fraction, proportion, or percent defectives. **3.** There are several samples, with many observations in each. For example, 20 samples of $n = 100$ observations in each, as in Example S4.
ATTRIBUTE DATA USING A *C*-CHART
1. Observations are *attributes* whose defects per unit of output can be counted. **2.** We deal with the number counted, which is a small part of the possible occurrences. **3.** Defects may be: number of blemishes on a desk; crimes in a year; broken seats in a stadium; typos in a chapter of this text; flaws in a bolt of cloth; or complaints in a day, as is shown in Example S5.

Managerial Issues and Control Charts

In an ideal world, there is no need for control charts. Quality is uniform and so high that employees need not waste time and money sampling and monitoring variables and attributes. But because most processes have not reached perfection, managers must make three major decisions regarding control charts.

First, managers must select the points in their process that need SPC. They may ask "Which parts of the job are critical to success?" or "Which parts of the job have a tendency to become out of control?"

Second, managers need to decide if variable charts (i.e., $\bar{x}$ and *R*) or attribute charts (i.e., *p* and *c*) are appropriate. Variable charts monitor weights or dimensions. Attribute charts are more of a "yes–no" or "go–no go" gauge and tend to be less costly to implement. Table S3 can help you understand when to use each of these types of control charts.

Third, the company must set clear and specific SPC policies for employees to follow. For example, should the data-entry process be halted if a trend is appearing in percent defective records being keyed? Should an assembly line be stopped if the average length of five successive samples is above the centerline? Figure S7 illustrates some of the patterns to look for over time in a process.

Figure **S7**

Patterns to Look for on Control Charts

Source: Adapted from Bertrand L. Hansen, *Quality Control: Theory and Applications* (1991): 65. Reprinted by permission of Prentice Hall, Upper Saddle River, NJ.

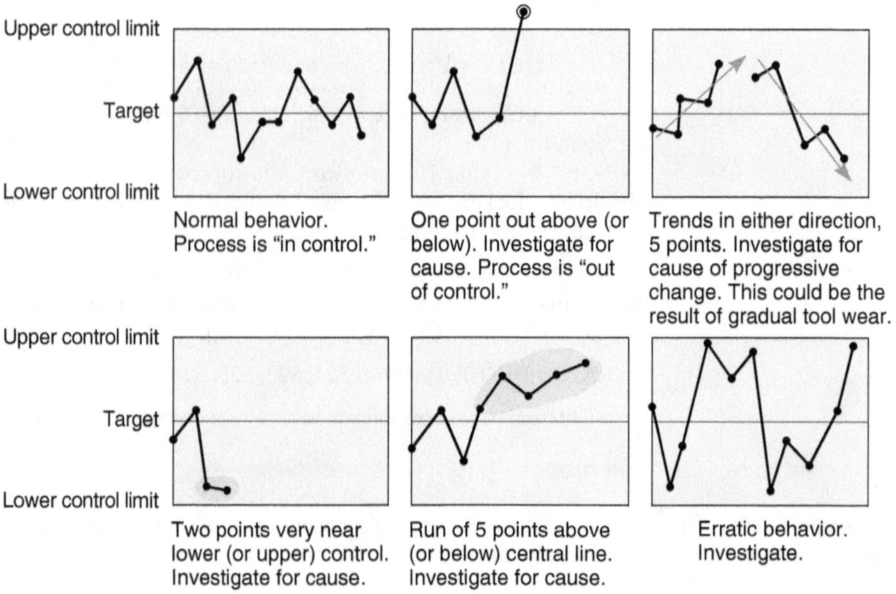

Upper control limit
Target
Lower control limit
Normal behavior. Process is "in control."
One point out above (or below). Investigate for cause. Process is "out of control."
Trends in either direction, 5 points. Investigate for cause of progressive change. This could be the result of gradual tool wear.
Upper control limit
Target
Lower control limit
Two points very near lower (or upper) control. Investigate for cause.
Run of 5 points above (or below) central line. Investigate for cause.
Erratic behavior. Investigate.

STUDENT TIP ☆
Workers in companies such as Frito-Lay are trained to follow rules like these.

A tool called a run test is available to help identify the kind of abnormalities in a process that we see in Figure S7. In general, a run of 5 points above or below the target or centerline may suggest that an assignable, or nonrandom, variation is present. When this occurs, even though all the points may fall inside the control limits, a flag has been raised. This means the process may not be statistically in control. A variety of run tests are described in books on the subject of quality methods.

Run test
A test used to examine the points in a control chart to see if nonrandom variation is present.

Process Capability

STUDENT TIP
Here we deal with whether a process meets the specification it was *designed* to yield.

Statistical process control means keeping a process in control. This means that the natural variation of the process must be stable. But a process that is in statistical control may not yield goods or services that meet their *design specifications* (tolerances). The ability of a process to meet design specifications, which are set by engineering design or customer requirements, is called process capability. Even though that process may be statistically in control (stable), the output of that process may not conform to specifications.

Process capability
The ability to meet design specifications.

For example, let's say the time a customer expects to wait for the completion of a lube job at Quik Lube is 12 minutes, with an acceptable tolerance of ± 2 minutes. This tolerance gives an upper specification of 14 minutes and a lower specification of 10 minutes. The lube process has to be capable of operating within these design specifications—if not, some customers will not have their requirements met. As a manufacturing example, the tolerances for Harley-Davidson cam gears are extremely low, only 0.0005 inch—and a process must be designed that is capable of achieving this tolerance.

There are two popular measures for quantitatively determining if a process is capable: process capability ratio (C_p) and process capability index (C_{pk}).

LO6 *Explain* process capability and compute C_p and C_{pk}

Process Capability Ratio (C_p)

For a process to be capable, its values must fall within upper and lower specifications. This typically means the process capability is within ± 3 standard deviations from the process mean. Since this range of values is 6 standard deviations, a capable process tolerance, which is the difference between the upper and lower specifications, must be greater than or equal to 6.

The process capability ratio, C_p, is computed as:

C_p
A ratio for determining whether a process meets design specifications; a ratio of the specification to the process variation.

$$C_p = \frac{\text{Upper specification} - \text{Lower specification}}{6\sigma} \tag{S13}$$

Example S6 shows the computation of C_p.

Example S6

PROCESS CAPABILITY RATIO (C_p)

In a GE insurance claims process, $\bar{x} = 210.0$ minutes, and $\sigma = .516$ minutes.

The design specification to meet customer expectations is 210 ± 3 minutes. So the Upper Specification is 213 minutes and the lower specification is 207 minutes. The OM manager wants to compute the process capability ratio.

APPROACH ▶ GE applies Equation (S13).

SOLUTION ▶ $C_p = \dfrac{\text{Upper specification} - \text{Lower specification}}{6\sigma} = \dfrac{213 - 207}{6(.516)} = 1.938$

INSIGHT ▶ Since a ratio of 1.00 means that 99.73% of a process's outputs are within specifications, this ratio suggests a very capable process, with nonconformance of less than 4 claims per million.

LEARNING EXERCISE ▶ If $\sigma = .60$ (instead of .516), what is the new C_p? [Answer: 1.667, a very capable process still.]

RELATED PROBLEMS ▶ S26, S27

ACTIVE MODEL S2 This example is further illustrated in Active Model S6.2 at **www.pearsonhighered.com/heizer**.

EXCEL OM Data File **Ch06SExS6.xls** can be found at **www.pearsonhighered.com/heizer**.

A capable process has a C_p of at least 1.0. If the C_p is less than 1.0, the process yields products or services that are outside their allowable tolerance. With a C_p of 1.0, 2.7 parts in 1,000 can be expected to be "out of spec."[6] The higher the process capability ratio, the greater the likelihood the process will be within design specifications. Many firms have chosen a C_p of 1.33 (a 4-sigma standard) as a target for reducing process variability. This means that only 64 parts per million can be expected to be out of specification.

We mentioned the concept of *Six Sigma* quality, championed by GE and Motorola. This standard equates to a C_p of 2.0, with only 3.4 defective parts per million (very close to zero defects) instead of the 2.7 parts per 1,000 with 3-sigma limits.

Although C_p relates to the spread (dispersion) of the process output relative to its tolerance, it does not look at how well the process average is centered on the target value.

Process Capability Index (C_{pk})

C_{pk}
A proportion of variation (3σ) between the center of the process and the nearest specification limit.

The process capability index, C_{pk}, measures the difference between the desired and actual dimensions of goods or services produced.

The formula for C_{pk} is:

$$C_{pk} = \text{Minimum of}\left[\frac{\text{Upper specification limit} - \bar{X}}{3\sigma}, \frac{\bar{X} - \text{Lower specification limit}}{3\sigma}\right] \quad \text{(S14)}$$

where $\bar{X}$ = process mean
σ = standard deviation of the process population

When the C_{pk} index for both the upper and lower specification limits equals 1.0, the process variation is centered and the process is capable of producing within ± 3 standard deviations (fewer than 2,700 defects per million). A C_{pk} of 2.0 means the process is capable of producing fewer than 3.4 defects per million. For C_{pk} to exceed 1, σ must be less than $\frac{1}{3}$ of the difference between the specification and the process mean ($\bar{X}$). Figure S8 shows the meaning of various measures of C_{pk}, and Example S7 shows an application of C_{pk}.

Example S7

PROCESS CAPABILITY INDEX (C_{pk})

You are the process improvement manager and have developed a new machine to cut insoles for the company's top-of-the-line running shoes. You are excited because the company's goal is no more than 3.4 defects per million and this machine may be the innovation you need. The insoles cannot be more than $\pm$.001 of an inch from the required thickness of .250 . You want to know if you should replace the existing machine, which has a C_{pk} of 1.0.

APPROACH ▶ You decide to determine the C_{pk}, using Equation (S14), for the new machine and make a decision on that basis.

SOLUTION ▶ Upper specification limit = .251 inch

Lower specification limit = .249 inch

Mean of the new process $\bar{X}$ = .250 inch.

Estimated standard deviation of the new process = σ = .0005 inch.

$$C_{pk} = \text{Minimum of}\left[\frac{\text{Upper specification limit} - \bar{X}}{3\sigma}, \frac{\bar{X} - \text{Lower specification limit}}{3\sigma}\right]$$

$$C_{pk} = \text{Minimum of}\left[\frac{(.251) - .250}{(3).0005}, \frac{.250 - (.249)}{(3).0005}\right]$$

[6]This is because a C_p of 1.0 has 99.73% of outputs within specifications. So 1.00 − .9973 = .0027; with 1,000 parts, there are .0027 × 1,000 = 2.7 defects.

For a C_p of 2.0, 99.99966% of outputs are "within spec." So 1.00 − .9999966 = .0000034; with 1 million parts, there are 3.4 defects.

Both calculations result in: $\frac{.001}{.0015} = .67.$

INSIGHT ▶ Because the new machine has a C_{pk} of only 0.67, the new machine should *not* replace the existing machine.

LEARNING EXERCISE ▶ If the insoles can be ±.002 (instead of .001) from the required .250 , what is the new C_{pk}? [Answer: 1.33 and the new machine *should* replace the existing one.]

RELATED PROBLEMS ▶ S27, S28, S29, S30, S31

EXCEL OM Data File **Ch06SExS7.xls** can be found at **www.pearsonhighered.com/heizer**.

ACTIVE MODEL S2 This example is further illustrated in Active Model S6.2 at **www.pearsonhighered.com/heizer**.

Note that C_p and C_{pk} will be the same when the process is centered. However, if the mean of the process is not centered on the desired (specified) mean, then the smaller numerator in Equation (S14) is used (the minimum of the difference between the upper specification limit and the mean or the lower specification limit and the mean). This application of C_{pk} is shown in Solved Problem S4. C_{pk} is the standard criterion used to express process performance.

Acceptance Sampling[7]

Acceptance sampling is a form of testing that involves taking random samples of "lots," or batches, of finished products and measuring them against predetermined standards. Sampling is more economical than 100% inspection. The quality of the sample is used to judge the quality of all items in the lot. Although both attributes and variables can be inspected by acceptance sampling, attribute inspection is more commonly used, as illustrated in this section.

Acceptance sampling
A method of measuring random samples of lots or batches of products against predetermined standards.

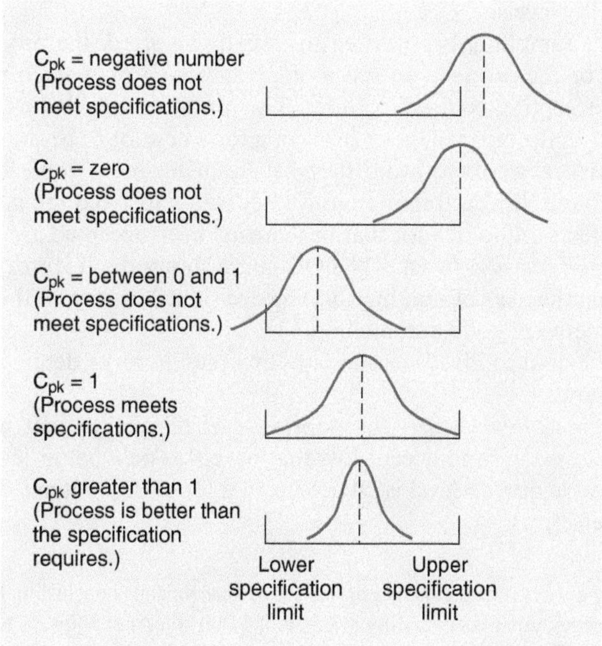

Figure S8

Meanings of C_{pk} Measures

A C_{pk} index of 1.0 for both the upper and lower specification limits indicates that the process variation is within the upper and lower specification limits. As the C_{pk} index goes above 1.0, the process becomes increasingly target oriented, with fewer defects. If the C_{pk} is less than 1.0, the process will not produce within the specified tolerance. Because a process may not be centered, or may "drift," a C_{pk} above 1 is desired.

[7]Refer to Tutorial 2 on our free Web site **www.pearsonhighered.com/heizer** for an extended discussion of acceptance sampling.

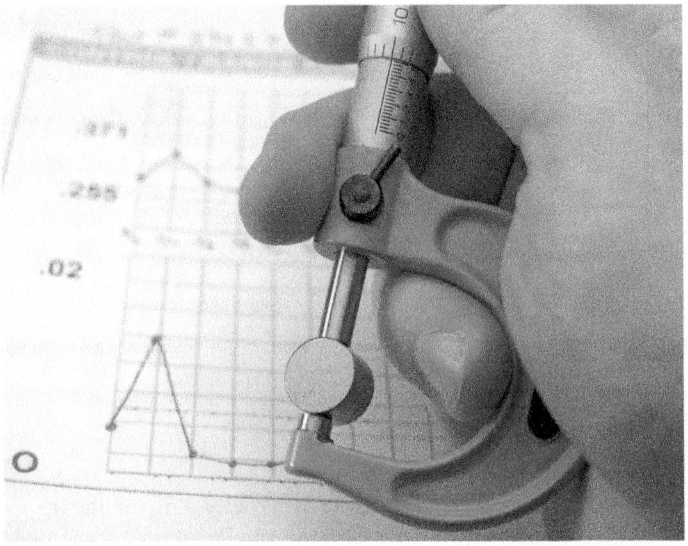

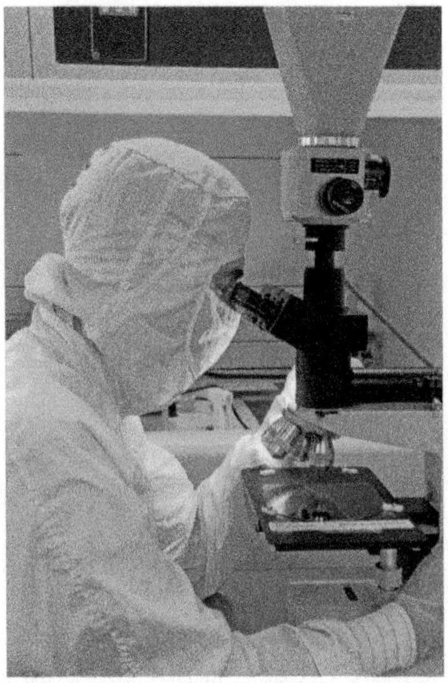

Raw data for Statistical Process Control is collected in a wide variety of ways. Here physical measures using a micrometer (on the left) and a microscope (on the right) are being made.

LO7 *Explain* acceptance sampling

Acceptance sampling can be applied either when materials arrive at a plant or at final inspection, but it is usually used to control incoming lots of purchased products. A lot of items rejected, based on an unacceptable level of defects found in the sample, can (1) be returned to the supplier or (2) be 100% inspected to cull out all defects, with the cost of this screening usually billed to the supplier. However, acceptance sampling is not a substitute for adequate process controls. In fact, the current approach is to build statistical quality controls at suppliers so that acceptance sampling can be eliminated.

Operating Characteristic Curve

Operating characteristic (OC) curve
A graph that describes how well an acceptance plan discriminates between good and bad lots.

The operating characteristic (OC) curve describes how well an acceptance plan discriminates between good and bad lots. A curve pertains to a specific plan—that is, to a combination of n (sample size) and c (acceptance level). It is intended to show the probability that the plan will accept lots of various quality levels.

With acceptance sampling, two parties are usually involved: the producer of the product and the consumer of the product. In specifying a sampling plan, each party wants to avoid costly mistakes in accepting or rejecting a lot. The producer usually has the responsibility of replacing all defects in the rejected lot or of paying for a new lot to be shipped to the customer. The producer, therefore, wants to avoid the mistake of having a good lot rejected (producer's risk). On the other hand, the customer or consumer wants to avoid the mistake of accepting a bad lot because defects found in a lot that has already been accepted are usually the responsibility of the customer (consumer's risk). The OC curve shows the features of a particular sampling plan, including the risks of making a wrong decision. The steeper the curve, the better the plan distinguishes between good and bad lots.[8]

Producer's risk
The mistake of having a producer's good lot rejected through sampling.

Consumer's risk
The mistake of a customer's acceptance of a bad lot overlooked through sampling.

Figure S9 can be used to illustrate one sampling plan in more detail. Four concepts are illustrated in this figure.

Acceptable quality level (AQL)
The quality level of a lot considered good.

The acceptable quality level (AQL) is the poorest level of quality that we are willing to accept. In other words, we wish to accept lots that have this or a better level of quality, but no worse. If an acceptable quality level is 20 defects in a lot of 1,000 items or parts, then AQL is $20/1{,}000 = 2\%$ defectives.

[8]Note that sampling always runs the danger of leading to an erroneous conclusion. Let us say that in one company the total population under scrutiny is a load of 1,000 computer chips, of which in reality only 30 (or 3%) are defective. This means that we would want to accept the shipment of chips, because for this particular firm 4% is the allowable defect rate. However, if a random sample of $n = 50$ chips was drawn, we could conceivably end up with 0 defects and accept that shipment (that is, it is okay), or we could find all 30 defects in the sample. If the latter happened, we could wrongly conclude that the whole population was 60% defective and reject them all.

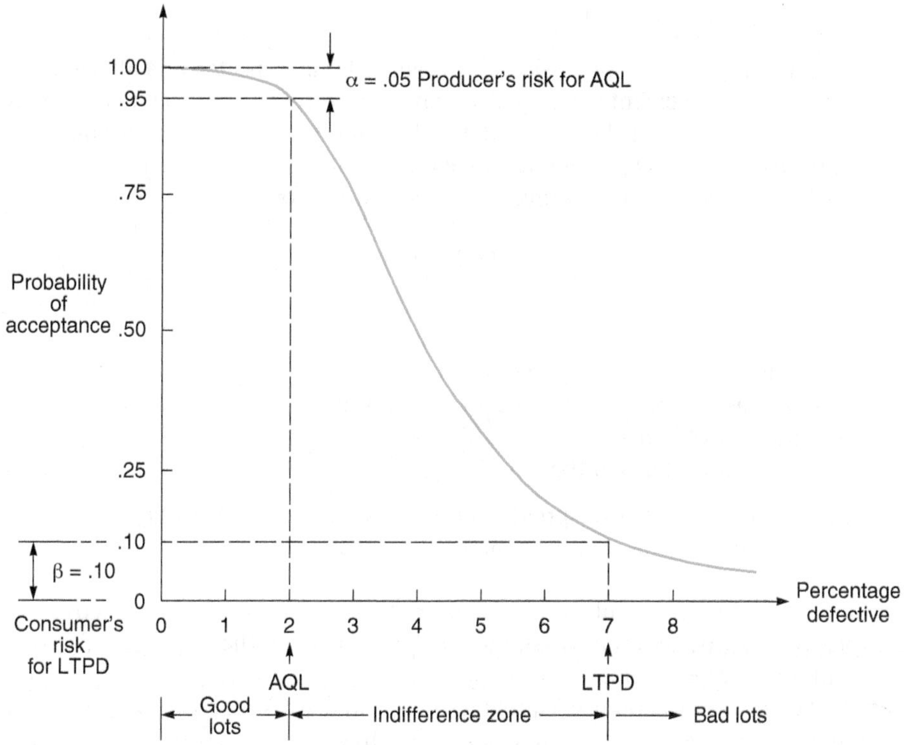

Figure **S9**

An Operating Characteristic (OC) Curve Showing Producer's and Consumer's Risks

A good lot for this particular acceptance plan has less than or equal to 2% defectives. A bad lot has 7% or more defectives.

STUDENT TIP
Figure S9 is further illustrated in Active Model S3 on our Web site, **www.pearsonhighered.com/heizer.**

The lot tolerance percentage defective (LTPD) is the quality level of a lot that we consider bad. We wish to reject lots that have this or a poorer level of quality. If it is agreed that an unacceptable quality level is 70 defects in a lot of 1,000, then the LTPD is $70/1{,}000 = 7\%$ defective.

Lot tolerance percentage defective (LTPD)
The quality level of a lot considered bad.

To derive a sampling plan, producer and consumer must define not only "good lots" and "bad lots" through the AQL and LTPD, but they must also specify risk levels.

Producer's risk (α) is the probability that a "good" lot will be rejected. This is the risk that a random sample might result in a much higher proportion of defects than the population of all items. A lot with an acceptable quality level of AQL still has an α chance of being rejected. Sampling plans are often designed to have the producer's risk set at $\alpha = .05$, or 5%.

Consumer's risk (β) is the probability that a "bad" lot will be accepted. This is the risk that a random sample may result in a lower proportion of defects than the overall population of items. A common value for consumer's risk in sampling plans is $\beta = .10$, or 10%.

The probability of rejecting a good lot is called a type I error. The probability of accepting a bad lot is a type II error.

Type I error
Statistically, the probability of rejecting a good lot.

Type II error
Statistically, the probability of accepting a bad lot.

Sampling plans and OC curves may be developed by computer (as seen in the software available with this text), by published tables, or by calculation, using binomial or Poisson distributions.

Faro Technologies

This laser tracking device, by Faro Technologies, enables quality control personnel to measure and inspect parts and tools during production. The portable tracker can measure objects from 262 feet away and takes to up 1,000 accurate readings per second.

Average Outgoing Quality

In most sampling plans, when a lot is rejected, the entire lot is inspected and all defective items replaced. Use of this replacement technique improves the average outgoing quality in terms of percent defective. In fact, given (1) any sampling plan that replaces all defective items encountered and (2) the true incoming percent defective for the lot, it is possible to determine the **average outgoing quality (AOQ)** in percentage defective. The equation for AOQ is:

Average outgoing quality (AOQ)
The percentage defective in an average lot of goods inspected through acceptance sampling.

$$AOQ = \frac{(P_d)(P_a)(N - n)}{N} \quad (S15)$$

where

P_d = true percentage defective of the lot
P_a = probability of accepting the lot for a given sample size and quantity defective
N = number of items in the lot
n = number of items in the sample

The maximum value of AOQ corresponds to the highest average percentage defective or the lowest average quality for the sampling plan. It is called the *average outgoing quality limit (AOQL)*.

Acceptance sampling is useful for screening incoming lots. When the defective parts are replaced with good parts, acceptance sampling helps to increase the quality of the lots by reducing the outgoing percent defective.

Figure S10 compares acceptance sampling, SPC, and C_{pk}. As the figure shows, (a) acceptance sampling by definition accepts some bad units, (b) control charts try to keep the process in control, but (c) the C_{pk} index places the focus on improving the process. As operations managers, that is what we want to do—improve the process.

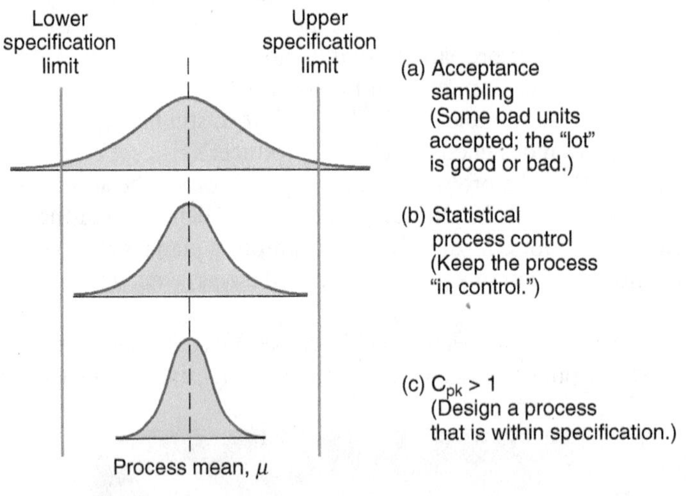

Figure **S10**

The Application of Statistical Process Control Techniques Contributes to the Identification and Systematic Reduction of Process Variability

Summary

Statistical process control is a major statistical tool of quality control. Control charts for SPC help operations managers distinguish between natural and assignable variations. The $\bar{x}$-chart and the R-chart are used for variable sampling, and the p-chart and the c-chart for attribute sampling. The C_{pk} index is a way to express process capability. Operating characteristic (OC) curves facilitate acceptance sampling and provide the manager with tools to evaluate the quality of a production run or shipment.

Key Terms

Statistical process control (SPC)
Control chart
Natural variations
Assignable variation
$\bar{x}$-chart
R-chart
Central limit theorem
p-chart
c-chart
Run test
Process capability
C_p
C_{pk}
Acceptance sampling
Operating characteristic (OC) curve
Producer's risk
Consumer's risk
Acceptable quality level (AQL)
Lot tolerance percentage defective (LTPD)
Type I error
Type II error
Average outgoing quality (AOQ)

Discussion Questions

1. List Shewhart's two types of variation. What are they also called?
2. Define "in statistical control."
3. Explain briefly what an $\bar{x}$-chart and an R-chart do.
4. What might cause a process to be out of control?
5. List five steps in developing and using $\bar{x}$-charts and R-charts.
6. List some possible causes of assignable variation.
7. Explain how a person using 2-sigma control charts will more easily find samples "out of bounds" than 3-sigma control charts. What are some possible consequences of this fact?
8. When is the desired mean, μ, used in establishing the centerline of a control chart instead of $\bar{\bar{x}}$?
9. Can a production process be labeled as "out of control" because it is too good? Explain.
10. In a control chart, what would be the effect on the control limits if the sample size varied from one sample to the next?
11. Define C_{pk} and explain what a C_{pk} of 1.0 means. What is C_p?
12. What does a run of 5 points above or below the centerline in a control chart imply?
13. What are the acceptable quality level (AQL) and the lot tolerance percentage defective (LTPD)? How are they used?
14. What is a run test and when is it used?
15. Discuss the managerial issues regarding the use of control charts.
16. What is an OC curve?
17. What is the purpose of acceptance sampling?
18. What two risks are present when acceptance sampling is used?
19. Is a *capable* process a *perfect* process? That is, does a capable process generate only output that meets specifications? Explain.

Using Software for SPC

Excel, Excel OM, and POM for Windows may be used to develop control charts for most of the problems in this text.

CREATING EXCEL SPREADSHEETS TO DETERMINE CONTROL LIMITS FOR A C-CHART

Excel and other spreadsheets are extensively used in industry to maintain control charts. Program S1 is an example of how to use Excel to determine the control limits for a *c*-chart. *c*-charts are used when the number of defects per unit of output is known. The data from Example S5 are used. In this example, 54 complaints occurred over 9 days. Excel also contains a built-in graphing ability with Chart Wizard.

Program **S1**

An Excel Spreadsheet for Creating a *c*-Chart for Example S5

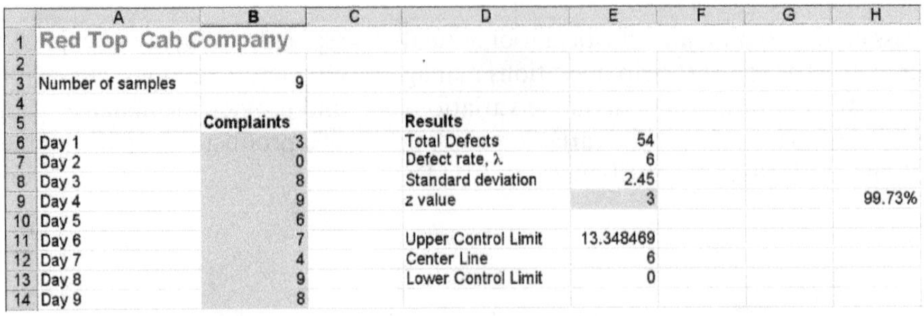

	A	B	C	D	E	F	G	H
1	Red Top Cab Company							
2								
3	Number of samples	9						
4								
5		Complaints		Results				
6	Day 1	3		Total Defects	54			
7	Day 2	0		Defect rate, λ	6			
8	Day 3	8		Standard deviation	2.45			
9	Day 4	9		z value	3			99.73%
10	Day 5	6						
11	Day 6	7		Upper Control Limit	13.348469			
12	Day 7	4		Center Line	6			
13	Day 8	9		Lower Control Limit	0			
14	Day 9	8						

VALUE	CELL	EXCEL FORMULA
Total Defects	E6	=SUM(B6:B14)
Defect rate, λ	E7	=E6/B3
Standard deviation	E8	=SQRT(E7)
Upper Control Limit	E11	=E7+E9*E8
Center Line	E12	=E7
Lower Control Limit	E13	=IF(E7-E9*E8>0,E7-E9*E8,0)

USING EXCEL OM

Excel OM's Quality Control module has the ability to develop $\bar{x}$-charts, *p*-charts, and *c*-charts. It also handles OC curves, acceptance sampling, and process capability. Program S2 illustrates Excel OM's spreadsheet approach to computing the $\bar{x}$ control limits for the Oat Flakes company in Example S1.

Program **S2**

Excel OM Input and Selected Formulas for the Oat Flakes Company in Example S1

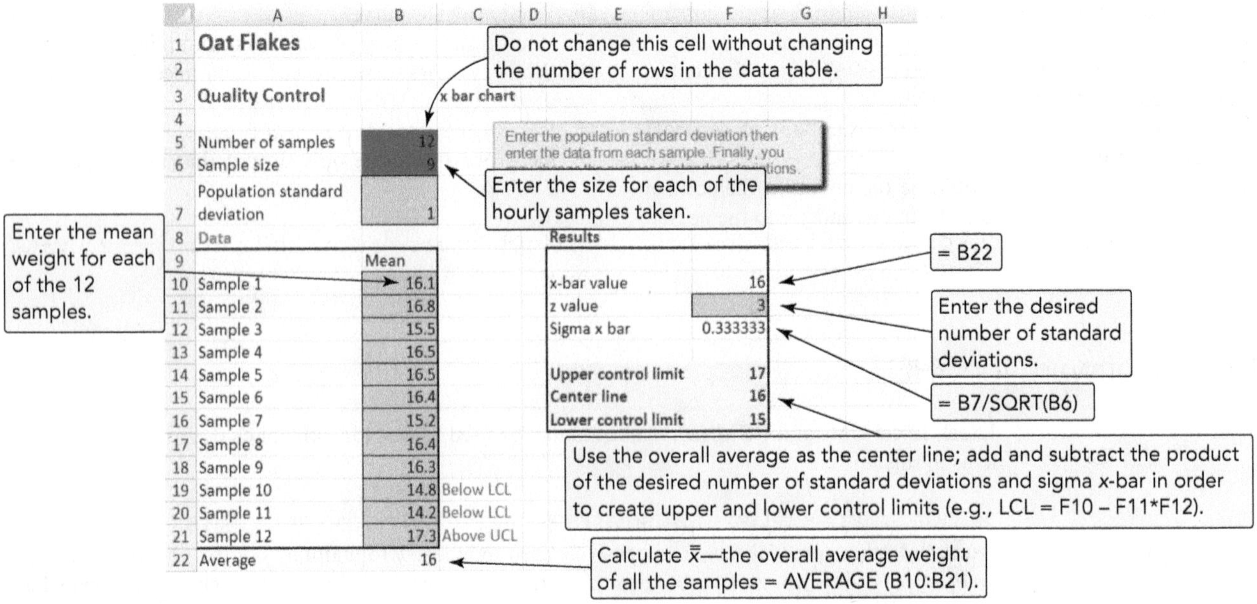

P USING POM FOR WINDOWS

The POM for Windows Quality Control module has the ability to compute all the SPC control charts we introduced in this supplement, as well as OC curves, acceptance sampling, and process capability.

Solved Problems

Virtual Office Hours help is available at www.myomlab.com.

SOLVED PROBLEM S1

A manufacturer of precision machine parts produces round shafts for use in the construction of drill presses. The average diameter of a shaft is .56 inch. Inspection samples contain 6 shafts each. The average range of these samples is .006 inch. Determine the upper and lower $\overline{x}$ control chart limits.

SOLUTION

The mean factor A_2 from Table S1, where the sample size is 6, is seen to be .483. With this factor, you can obtain the upper and lower control limits:

$$\begin{aligned} UCL_{\overline{x}} &= .56 + (.483)(.006) \\ &= .56 + .0029 \\ &= .5629 \text{ inch} \\ LCL_{\overline{x}} &= .56 - .0029 \\ &= .5571 \text{ inch} \end{aligned}$$

SOLVED PROBLEM S2

Nocaf Drinks, Inc., a producer of decaffeinated coffee, bottles Nocaf. Each bottle should have a net weight of 4 ounces. The machine that fills the bottles with coffee is new, and the operations manager wants to make sure that it is properly adjusted. Bonnie Crutcher, the operations manager, randomly selects and weighs $n = 8$ bottles and records the average and range in ounces for each sample. The data for several samples is given in the following table. Note that every sample consists of 8 bottles.

SAMPLE	SAMPLE RANGE	SAMPLE AVERAGE	SAMPLE	SAMPLE RANGE	SAMPLE AVERAGE
A	.41	4.00	E	.56	4.17
B	.55	4.16	F	.62	3.93
C	.44	3.99	G	.54	3.98
D	.48	4.00	H	.44	4.01

Is the machine properly adjusted and in control?

SOLUTION

We first find that $\overline{\overline{x}} = 4.03$ and $\overline{R} = .505$. Then, using Table S1, we find:

$$\begin{aligned} UCL_{\overline{x}} &= \overline{\overline{x}} + A_2\overline{R} = 4.03 + (.373)(.505) = 4.22 \\ LCL_{\overline{x}} &= \overline{\overline{x}} - A_2\overline{R} = 4.03 - (.373)(.505) = 3.84 \\ UCL_R &= D_4\overline{R} = (1.864)(.505) = .94 \\ LCL_R &= D_3\overline{R} = (.136)(.505) = .07 \end{aligned}$$

It appears that the process average and range are both in statistical control.

The operations manager needs to determine if a process with a mean (4.03) slightly above the desired mean of 4.00 is satisfactory; if it is not, the process will need to be changed.

SOLVED PROBLEM S3

Altman Distributors, Inc., fills catalog orders. Samples of size $n = 100$ orders have been taken each day over the past 6 weeks. The average defect rate was .05. Determine the upper and lower limits for this process for 99.73% confidence.

SOLUTION

$z = 3, \overline{p} = .05$. Using Equations (S9), (S10), and (S11):

$$\begin{aligned} UCL_p &= \overline{p} + 3\sqrt{\frac{\overline{p}(1-\overline{p})}{n}} = .05 + 3\sqrt{\frac{(.05)(1-.05)}{100}} \\ &= .05 + 3(0.0218) = .1154 \\ LCL_p &= \overline{p} - 3\sqrt{\frac{\overline{p}(1-\overline{p})}{n}} = .05 - 3(0.0218) \\ &= .05 - .0654 = 0 \quad \text{(because percentage defective cannot be negative)} \end{aligned}$$

SOLVED PROBLEM S4

Ettlie Engineering has a new catalyst injection system for your countertop production line. Your process engineering department has conducted experiments and determined that the mean is 8.01 grams with a standard deviation of .03. Your specifications are: $\mu = 8.0$ and $\sigma = .04$, which means an upper specification limit of $8.12 [= 8.0 + 3(.04)]$ and a lower specification limit of $7.88 [= 8.0 - 3(.04)]$.

What is the C_{pk} performance of the injection system?

SOLUTION

Using Equation (S14):

$$C_{pk} = \text{Minimum of}\left[\frac{\text{Upper specification limit} - \overline{X}}{3\sigma}, \frac{\overline{X} - \text{Lower specification limit}}{3\sigma}\right]$$

where

$\overline{X} =$ process mean

$\sigma =$ standard deviation of the process population

$$C_{pk} = \text{Minimum of}\left[\frac{8.12 - 8.01}{(3)(.03)}, \frac{8.01 - 7.88}{(3)(.03)}\right]$$

$$\left[\frac{.11}{.09} = 1.22, \frac{.13}{.09} = 1.44\right]$$

The minimum is 1.22, so the C_{pk} is within specifications and has an implied error rate of less than 2,700 defects per million.

SOLVED PROBLEM S5

Airlines lose thousands of checked bags every day, and America South Airlines is no exception to the industry rule. Over the past 6 weeks, the number of bags "misplaced" on America South flights has been 18, 10, 4, 6, 12, and 10. The head of customer service wants to develop a *c*-chart at 99.73% levels.

SOLUTION

She first computes $\bar{c} = \dfrac{18 + 10 + 4 + 6 + 12 + 10}{6} = \dfrac{60}{6} = 10$ bags/week

Then, using Equation (S12):

$$UCL_c = \bar{c} + 3\sqrt{\bar{c}} = 10 + 3\sqrt{10} = 10 + 3(3.16) = 19.48 \text{ bags}$$

$$LCL_c = \bar{c} - 3\sqrt{\bar{c}} = 10 - 3\sqrt{10} = 10 - 3(3.16) = .52 \text{ bag}$$

Problems

Note: Px means the problem may be solved with POM for Windows and/or Excel OM/Excel.

• **S1** Boxes of Honey-Nut Oatmeal are produced to contain 14 ounces, with a standard deviation of .1 ounce. Set up the 3-sigma $\bar{x}$-chart for a sample size of 36 boxes.

• **S2** The overall average on a process you are attempting to monitor is 50 units. The process population standard deviation is 1.72. Determine the upper and lower control limits for a mean chart, if you choose to use a sample size of 5.

a) Set $z = 3$.
b) Now set $z = 2$. How do the control limits change?

• **S3** Thirty-five samples of size 7 each were taken from a fertilizer-bag-filling machine. The results were overall mean = 57.75 lb; average range = 1.78 lb.

a) Determine the upper and lower control limits of the $\bar{x}$-chart, where $\sigma = 3$.
b) Determine the upper and lower control limits of the R-chart, where $\sigma = 3$.

• **S4** Pioneer Chicken advertises "lite" chicken with 30% fewer calories than standard chicken. When the process for "lite" chicken breast production is in control, the average chicken breast contains 420 calories, and the standard deviation in caloric content of the chicken breast population is 25 calories.

Pioneer wants to design an $\bar{x}$-chart to monitor the caloric content of chicken breasts, where 25 chicken breasts would be chosen at random to form each sample.

a) What are the lower and upper control limits for this chart if these limits are chosen to be *four* standard deviations from the target?
b) What are the limits with three standard deviations from the target?

• **S5** Greg Stock is attempting to monitor a filling process that has an overall average of 705 cc. The average range is 6 cc. If you use a sample size of 10, what are the upper and lower control limits for the mean and range?

• • **S6** Sampling four pieces of precision-cut wire (to be used in computer assembly) every hour for the past 24 hours has produced the following results:

HOUR	$\bar{x}$	R	HOUR	$\bar{x}$	R
1	3.25"	.71"	13	3.11"	.85"
2	3.10	1.18	14	2.83	1.31
3	3.22	1.43	15	3.12	1.06
4	3.39	1.26	16	2.84	.50
5	3.07	1.17	17	2.86	1.43
6	2.86	.32	18	2.74	1.29
7	3.05	.53	19	3.41	1.61
8	2.65	1.13	20	2.89	1.09
9	3.02	.71	21	2.65	1.08
10	2.85	1.33	22	3.28	.46
11	2.83	1.17	23	2.94	1.58
12	2.97	.40	24	2.64	.97

Develop appropriate control charts and determine whether there is any cause for concern in the cutting process. Plot the information and look for patterns.

• • **S7** Auto pistons at Wemming Chung's plant in Shanghai are produced in a forging process, and the diameter is a critical factor that must be controlled. From sample sizes of 10 pistons produced each day, the mean and the range of this diameter have been as follows:

DAY	MEAN (mm)	RANGE (mm)
1	156.9	4.2
2	153.2	4.6
3	153.6	4.1
4	155.5	5.0
5	156.6	4.5

a) What is the value of $\bar{\bar{x}}$?
b) What is the value of $\bar{R}$?
c) What are the $UCL_{\bar{x}}$ and $LCL_{\bar{x}}$, using 3σ? Plot the data.
d) What are the UCL_R and LCL_R, using 3σ? Plot the data.
e) If the true diameter mean should be 155 mm and you want this as your center (nominal) line, what are the new $UCL_{\bar{x}}$ and $LCL_{\bar{x}}$?

• • **S8** Benjamin Neve's bowling ball factory in Pennsyvania makes bowling balls of adult size and weight only. The standard deviation in the weight of a bowling ball produced at the factory is known to be 0.12 pounds. Each day for 24 days, the average weight, in pounds, of nine of the bowling balls produced that day has been assessed as follows:

DAY	AVERAGE (lb)	DAY	AVERAGE (lb)
1	16.3	13	16.3
2	15.9	14	15.9
3	15.8	15	16.3
4	15.5	16	16.2
5	16.3	17	16.1
6	16.2	18	15.9
7	16.0	19	16.2
8	16.1	20	15.9
9	15.9	21	15.9
10	16.2	22	16.0
11	15.9	23	15.5
12	15.9	24	15.8

a) Establish a control chart for monitoring the average weights of the bowling balls in which the upper and lower control limits are each two standard deviations from the mean. What are the values of the control limits?

b) If three standard deviations are used in the chart, how do these values change? Why?

• • **S9** Organic Grains LLC uses statistical process control to ensure that its health-conscious, low-fat, multigrain sandwich loaves have the proper weight. Based on a previously stable and in-control process, the control limits of the $\bar{x}$- and R-charts are $UCL_{\bar{x}} = 6.56$, $LCL_{\bar{x}} = 5.84$, $UCL_R = 1.141$, $LCL_R = 0$. Over the past few days, they have taken five random samples of four loaves each and have found the following:

	NET WEIGHT			
SAMPLE	LOAF #1	LOAF #2	LOAF #3	LOAF #4
1	6.3	6.0	5.9	5.9
2	6.0	6.0	6.3	5.9
3	6.3	4.8	5.6	5.2
4	6.2	6.0	6.2	5.9
5	6.5	6.6	6.5	6.9

Is the process still in control? Explain why or why not.

• • • **S10** A process that is considered to be in control measures an ingredient in ounces. Below are the last 10 samples (each of size $n = 5$) taken. The population process standard deviation, σ, is 1.36.

SAMPLES									
1	2	3	4	5	6	7	8	9	10
10	9	13	10	12	10	10	13	8	10
9	9	9	10	10	10	11	10	8	12
10	11	10	11	9	8	10	8	12	9
9	11	10	10	11	12	8	10	12	8
12	10	9	10	10	9	9	8	9	12

a) What is $\sigma_{\bar{x}}$?
b) If $z = 3$, what are the control limits for the mean chart?
c) What are the control limits for the range chart?
d) Is the process in control?

• • • **S11** Twelve samples, each containing five parts, were taken from a process that produces steel rods. The length of each rod in the samples was determined. The results were tabulated and sample means and ranges were computed. The results were:

SAMPLE	SAMPLE MEAN (in.)	RANGE (in.)
1	10.002	0.011
2	10.002	0.014
3	9.991	0.007
4	10.006	0.022
5	9.997	0.013
6	9.999	0.012
7	10.001	0.008
8	10.005	0.013
9	9.995	0.004
10	10.001	0.011
11	10.001	0.014
12	10.006	0.009

a) Determine the upper and lower control limits and the overall means for $\bar{x}$-charts and R-charts.
b) Draw the charts and plot the values of the sample means and ranges.
c) Do the data indicate a process that is in control?
d) Why or why not?

• • **S12** Eagletrons are all-electric automobiles produced by Mogul Motors, Inc. One of the concerns of Mogul Motors is that the Eagletrons be capable of achieving appropriate maximum speeds. To monitor this, Mogul executives take samples of eight Eagletrons at a time. For each sample, they determine the average maximum speed and the range of the maximum speeds within the sample. They repeat this with 35 samples to obtain 35 sample means and 35 ranges. They find that the average sample mean is 88.50 miles per hour, and the average range is 3.25 miles per hour. Using these results, the executives decide to establish an R chart. They would like this chart to be established so that when it shows that the range of a sample is not within the control limits, there is only approximately a 0.0027 probability that this is due to natural variation. What will be the upper control limit (UCL) and the lower control limit (LCL) in this chart?

• • **S13** The defect rate for data entry of insurance claims has historically been about 1.5%.
a) What are the upper and lower control chart limits if you wish to use a sample size of 100 and 3-sigma limits?
b) What if the sample size used were 50, with 3σ?
c) What if the sample size used were 100, with 2σ?
d) What if the sample size used were 50, with 2σ?
e) What happens to $\sigma_{\hat{p}}$ when the sample size is larger?
f) Explain why the lower control limit cannot be less than 0.

• • **S14** You are attempting to develop a quality monitoring system for some parts purchased from Charles Sox Manufacturing Co. These parts are either good or defective. You have decided to take a sample of 100 units. Develop a table of the appropriate upper and lower control chart limits for various values of the average fraction defective in the samples taken. The values for $\bar{p}$ in this table should range from 0.02 to 0.10 in increments of 0.02. Develop the upper and lower limits for a 99.73% confidence level.

$N = 100$		
$\bar{P}$	UCL	LCL
0.02		
0.04		
0.06		
0.08		
0.10		

• • **S15** The results of an inspection of DNA samples taken over the past 10 days are given below. Sample size is 100.

DAY	1	2	3	4	5	6	7	8	9	10
DEFECTIVES	7	6	6	9	5	6	0	8	9	1

a) Construct a 3-sigma p-chart using this information.
b) Using the control chart in part (a), and finding that the number of defectives on the next three days are 12, 5, and 13, is the process in control?

• **S16** In the past, the defective rate for your product has been 1.5%. What are the upper and lower control chart limits if you wish to use a sample size of 500 and $z = 3$?

• **S17** Refer to Problem S16. If the defective rate was 3.5% instead of 1.5%, what would be the control limits ($z = 3$)?

• • **S18** Five data entry operators work at the data processing department of the Birmingham Bank. Each day for 30 days, the number of defective records in a sample of 250 records typed by these operators has been noted, as follows:

SAMPLE NO.	NO. DEFECTIVE	SAMPLE NO.	NO. DEFECTIVE	SAMPLE NO.	NO. DEFECTIVE
1	7	11	18	21	17
2	5	12	5	22	12
3	19	13	16	23	6
4	10	14	4	24	7
5	11	15	11	25	13
6	8	16	8	26	10
7	12	17	12	27	14
8	9	18	4	28	6
9	6	19	6	29	12
10	13	20	16	30	3

a) Establish 3σ upper and lower control limits.
b) Why can the lower control limit not be a negative number?
c) The industry standards for the upper and lower control limits are 0.10 and 0.01, respectively. What does this imply about Birmingham Bank's own standards?

• • **S19** Houston North Hospital is trying to improve its image by providing a positive experience for its patients and their relatives. Part of the "image" program involves providing tasty, inviting patient meals that are also healthful. A questionnaire accompanies each meal served, asking the patient, among other things, whether he or she is satisfied or unsatisfied with the meal. A 100-patient sample of the survey results over the past 7 days yielded the following data:

DAY	NO. OF UNSATISFIED PATIENTS	SAMPLE SIZE
1	24	100
2	22	100
3	8	100
4	15	100
5	10	100
6	26	100
7	17	100

Construct a p-chart that plots the percentage of patients unsatisfied with their meals. Set the control limits to include 99.73% of the random variation in meal satisfaction. Comment on your results.

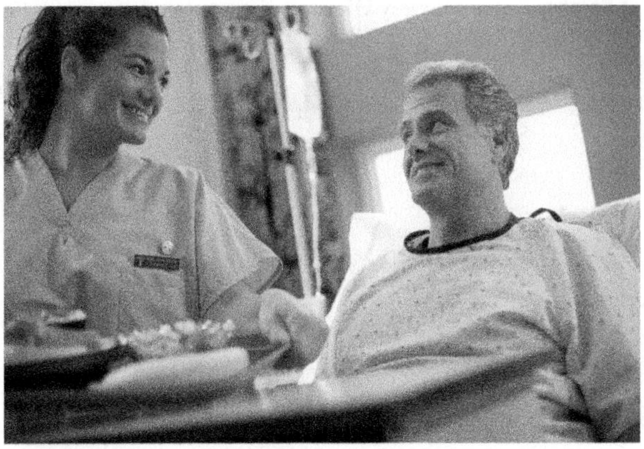

© Corbis Super RF/Alamy

• • **S20** Jamison Kovach Supply Company manufactures paper clips and other office products. Although inexpensive, paper clips have provided the firm with a high margin of profitability. Sample size is 200. Results are given for the last 10 samples:

SAMPLE	1	2	3	4	5	6	7	8	9	10
DEFECTIVES	5	7	4	4	6	3	5	6	2	8

a) Establish upper and lower control limits for the control chart and graph the data.
b) Is the process in control?
c) If the sample size were 100 instead, how would your limits and conclusions change?

• **S21** Peter Ittig's department store, Ittig Brothers, is Amherst's largest independent clothier. The store receives an average of six returns per day. Using $z = 3$, would nine returns in a day warrant action?

• • **S22** An ad agency tracks the complaints, by week received, about the billboards in its city:

WEEK	NO. OF COMPLAINTS
1	4
2	5
3	4
4	11
5	3
6	9

a) What type of control chart would you use to monitor this process? Why?
b) What are the 3-sigma control limits for this process? Assume that the historical complaint rate is unknown.
c) Is the process mean in control, according to the control limits? Why or why not?
d) Assume now that the historical complaint rate has been four calls a week. What would the 3-sigma control limits for this process be now? Is the process in control according to the control limits?

• • **S23** The school board is trying to evaluate a new math program introduced to second-graders in five elementary schools across the county this year. A sample of the student scores on standardized math tests in each elementary school yielded the following data:

SCHOOL	NO. OF TEST ERRORS
A	52
B	27
C	35
D	44
E	55

Construct a c-chart for test errors, and set the control limits to contain 99.73% of the random variation in test scores. What does the chart tell you? Has the new math program been effective?

• • **S24** Telephone inquiries of 100 IRS "customers" are monitored daily at random. Incidents of incorrect information or other nonconformities (such as impoliteness to customers) are recorded. The data for last week follow:

DAY	NO. OF NONCONFORMITIES
1	5
2	10
3	23
4	20
5	15

a) Construct a 3-standard deviation *c*-chart of nonconformities.
b) What does the control chart tell you about the IRS telephone operators? PX

• • • **S25** The accounts receivable department at Rick Wing Manufacturing has been having difficulty getting customers to pay the full amount of their bills. Many customers complain that the bills are not correct and do not reflect the materials that arrived at their receiving docks. The department has decided to implement SPC in its billing process. To set up control charts, 10 samples of 50 bills each were taken over a month's time and the items on the bills checked against the bill of lading sent by the company's shipping department to determine the number of bills that were not correct. The results were:

SAMPLE NO.	NO. OF INCORRECT BILLS	SAMPLE NO.	NO. OF INCORRECT BILLS
1	6	6	5
2	5	7	3
3	11	8	4
4	4	9	7
5	0	10	2

a) Determine the value of *p*-bar, the mean fraction defective. Then determine the control limits for the *p*-chart using a 99.73% confidence level (3 standard deviations). Is this process in control? If not, which samples were out of control?
b) How might you use the quality tools to determine the source of the billing defects and where you might start your improvement efforts to eliminate the causes? PX

• **S26** The difference between the upper specification and the lower specification for a process is 0.6″. The standard deviation is 0.1″. What is the process capability ratio, C_p? Interpret this number. PX

• • **S27** Meena Chavan Corp.'s computer chip production process yields DRAM chips with an average life of 1,800 hours and $\sigma = 100$ hours. The tolerance upper and lower specification limits are 2,400 hours and 1,600 hours, respectively. Is this process capable of producing DRAM chips to specification? PX

• • **S28** Linda Boardman, Inc., an equipment manufacturer in Boston, has submitted a sample cutoff valve to improve your manufacturing process. Your process engineering department has conducted experiments and found that the valve has a mean (μ) of 8.00 and a standard deviation (σ) of .04. Your desired performance is $\mu = 8.0 \pm 3\sigma$, where $\sigma = .045$. What is the C_{pk} of the Boardman valve? PX

• • **S29** The specifications for a plastic liner for concrete highway projects calls for a thickness of 3.0 mm $\pm .1$ mm. The standard deviation of the process is estimated to be .02 mm. What are the upper and lower specification limits for this product? The process is known to operate at a mean thickness of 3.0 mm. What is the C_{pk} for this process? About what percentage of all units of this liner will meet specifications? PX

• • **S30** The manager of an organic yogurt processing plant desires a quality specification with a mean of 16 ounces, an upper specification limit of 16.5, and a lower specification limit of 15.5. The process has a mean of 16 ounces and a standard deviation of 1 ounce. Determine the C_{pk} of the process. PX

• • **S31** A process filling small bottles with baby formula has a target of 3 ounces ± 0.150 ounce. Two hundred bottles from the process were sampled. The results showed the average amount of formula placed in the bottles to be 3.042 ounces. The standard deviation of the amounts was 0.034 ounce. Determine the value of C_{pk}. Roughly what proportion of bottles meet the specifications? PX

• • • **S32** As the supervisor in charge of shipping and receiving, you need to determine *the average outgoing quality* in a plant where the known incoming lots from your assembly line have an average defective rate of 3%. Your plan is to sample 80 units of every 1,000 in a lot. The number of defects in the sample is not to exceed 3. Such a plan provides you with a probability of acceptance of each lot of .79 (79%). What is your average outgoing quality? PX

• • • **S33** An acceptance sampling plan has lots of 500 pieces and a sample size of 60. The number of defects in the sample may not exceed 2. This plan, based on an OC curve, has a probability of .57 of accepting lots when the incoming lots have a defective rate of 4%, which is the historical average for this process. What do you tell your customer the average outgoing quality is? PX

• • • **S34** West Battery Corp. has recently been receiving complaints from retailers that its 9-volt batteries are not lasting as long as other name brands. James West, head of the TQM program at West's Austin plant, believes there is no problem because his batteries have had an average life of 50 hours, about 10% longer than competitors' models. To raise the lifetime above this level would require a new level of technology not available to West. Nevertheless, he is concerned enough to set up hourly assembly line checks. Previously, after ensuring that the process was running properly, West took size $n = 5$ samples of 9-volt batteries for each of 25 hours to establish the standards for control chart limits. Those samples are shown in the following table:

West Battery Data—Battery Lifetimes (in hours)

HOUR SAMPLE TAKEN	SAMPLE 1	2	3	4	5	$\bar{X}$	R
1	51	50	49	50	50	50.0	2
2	45	47	70	46	36	48.8	34
3	50	35	48	39	47	43.8	15
4	55	70	50	30	51	51.2	40
5	49	38	64	36	47	46.8	28
6	59	62	40	54	64	55.8	24
7	36	33	49	48	56	44.4	23
8	50	67	53	43	40	50.6	27

(cont'd)

HOUR SAMPLE TAKEN	SAMPLE 1	2	3	4	5	$\bar{x}$	R
9	44	52	46	47	44	46.6	8
10	70	45	50	47	41	50.6	29
11	57	54	62	45	36	50.8	26
12	56	54	47	42	62	52.2	20
13	40	70	58	45	44	51.4	30
14	52	58	40	52	46	49.6	18
15	57	42	52	58	59	53.6	17
16	62	49	42	33	55	48.2	29
17	40	39	49	59	48	47.0	20
18	64	50	42	57	50	52.6	22
19	58	53	52	48	50	52.2	10
20	60	50	41	41	50	48.4	19
21	52	47	48	58	40	49.0	18
22	55	40	56	49	45	49.0	16
23	47	48	50	50	48	48.6	3
24	50	50	49	51	51	50.2	2
25	51	50	51	51	62	53.0	12

With these limits established, West now takes 5 more hours of data, which are shown in the following table:

HOUR	SAMPLE 1	2	3	4	5
26	48	52	39	57	61
27	45	53	48	46	66
28	63	49	50	45	53
29	57	70	45	52	61
30	45	38	46	54	52

a) Determine means and the upper and lower control limits for $\bar{x}$ and R (using the first 25 hours only).
b) Is the manufacturing process in control?
c) Comment on the lifetimes observed. Px

• • • • **S35** One of New England Air's top competitive priorities is on-time arrivals. Quality VP Clair Bond decided to personally monitor New England Air's performance. Each week for the past 30 weeks, Bond checked a random sample of 100 flight arrivals for on-time performance. The table that follows contains the number of flights that did not meet New England Air's definition of "on time":

SAMPLE (WEEK)	LATE FLIGHTS	SAMPLE (WEEK)	LATE FLIGHTS
1	2	16	2
2	4	17	3
3	10	18	7
4	4	19	3
5	1	20	2
6	1	21	3
7	13	22	7
8	9	23	4
9	11	24	3
10	0	25	2
11	3	26	2
12	4	27	0
13	2	28	1
14	2	29	3
15	8	30	4

a) Using a 95% confidence level, plot the overall percentage of late flights ($\bar{p}$) and the upper and lower control limits on a control chart.
b) Assume that the airline industry's upper and lower control limits for flights that are not on time are .1000 and .0400, respectively. Draw them on your control chart.
c) Plot the percentage of late flights in each sample. Do all samples fall within New England Air's control limits? When one falls outside the control limits, what should be done?
d) What can Clair Bond report about the quality of service? Px

▶ **Refer to MyOMLab for these additional homework problems: S6.36–S6.52**

CASE STUDIES

Bayfield Mud Company

In November 2012, John Wells, a customer service representative of Bayfield Mud Company, was summoned to the Houston warehouse of Wet-Land Drilling, Inc., to inspect three boxcars of mudtreating agents that Bayfield had shipped to the Houston firm. (Bayfield's corporate offices and its largest plant are located in Orange, Texas, which is just west of the Louisiana–Texas border.) Wet-Land had filed a complaint that the 50-pound bags of treating agents just received from Bayfield were short-weight by approximately 5%.

The short-weight bags were initially detected by one of Wet-Land's receiving clerks, who noticed that the railroad scale tickets indicated that net weights were significantly less on all three boxcars than those of identical shipments received on October 25, 2012. Bayfield's traffic department was called to determine if lighter-weight pallets were used on the shipments. (This might explain the lighter net weights.) Bayfield indicated, however, that no changes had been made in loading or palletizing procedures. Thus, Wet-Land engineers randomly checked 50 bags and discovered that the average net weight was 47.51 pounds. They noted from past shipments that the process yielded bag net weights averaging exactly 50.0 pounds, with an acceptable standard deviation σ of 1.2 pounds. Consequently, they concluded that the sample indicated a significant short-weight. (The reader may wish to verify this conclusion.) Bayfield was then contacted, and Wells was sent to investigate the complaint. Upon arrival, Wells verified the complaint and issued a 5% credit to Wet-Land.

Wet-Land management, however, was not completely satisfied with the issuance of credit. The charts followed by their mud engineers on the drilling platforms were based on 50-pound bags of treating agents. Lighter-weight bags might result in poor chemical control during the drilling operation and thus adversely affect drilling efficiency. (Mud-treating agents are used to control the pH and other chemical properties of the core during drilling operation.) This defect could cause severe economic consequences because of the extremely high cost of oil and natural gas well-drilling operations. Consequently, special-use instructions had to accompany the delivery of these shipments to the drilling platforms. Moreover, the short-weight shipments had to be isolated in Wet-Land's warehouse, causing extra handling and poor space utilization. Thus, Wells was informed that Wet-Land might seek a new supplier of mud-treating agents if, in the future, it received bags that deviated significantly from 50 pounds.

The quality control department at Bayfield suspected that the lightweight bags might have resulted from "growing pains" at the Orange plant. Because of the earlier energy crisis, oil and natural gas exploration activity had greatly increased. In turn, this increased activity created increased demand for products produced by related industries, including drilling muds. Consequently, Bayfield had

		RANGE				*RANGE*	
TIME	AVERAGE WEIGHT (POUNDS)	SMALLEST	LARGEST	TIME	AVERAGE WEIGHT (POUNDS)	SMALLEST	LARGEST
6:00 A.M.	49.6	48.7	50.7	6:00 P.M.	46.8	41.0	51.2
7:00	50.2	49.1	51.2	7:00	50.0	46.2	51.7
8:00	50.6	49.6	51.4	8:00	47.4	44.0	48.7
9:00	50.8	50.2	51.8	9:00	47.0	44.2	48.9
10:00	49.9	49.2	52.3	10:00	47.2	46.6	50.2
11:00	50.3	48.6	51.7	11:00	48.6	47.0	50.0
12 noon	48.6	46.2	50.4	12 midnight	49.8	48.2	50.4
1:00 P.M.	49.0	46.4	50.0	1:00 A.M.	49.6	48.4	51.7
2:00	49.0	46.0	50.6	2:00	50.0	49.0	52.2
3:00	49.8	48.2	50.8	3:00	50.0	49.2	50.0
4:00	50.3	49.2	52.7	4:00	47.2	46.3	50.5
5:00	51.4	50.0	55.3	5:00	47.0	44.1	49.7
6:00	51.6	49.2	54.7	6:00	48.4	45.0	49.0
7:00	51.8	50.0	55.6	7:00	48.8	44.8	49.7
8:00	51.0	48.6	53.2	8:00	49.6	48.0	51.8
9:00	50.5	49.4	52.4	9:00	50.0	48.1	52.7
10:00	49.2	46.1	50.7	10:00	51.0	48.1	55.2
11:00	49.0	46.3	50.8	11:00	50.4	49.5	54.1
12 midnight	48.4	45.4	50.2	12 noon	50.0	48.7	50.9
1:00 A.M.	47.6	44.3	49.7	1:00 P.M.	48.9	47.6	51.2
2:00	47.4	44.1	49.6	2:00	49.8	48.4	51.0
3:00	48.2	45.2	49.0	3:00	49.8	48.8	50.8
4:00	48.0	45.5	49.1	4:00	50.0	49.1	50.6
5:00	48.4	47.1	49.6	5:00	47.8	45.2	51.2
6:00	48.6	47.4	52.0	6:00	46.4	44.0	49.7
7:00	50.0	49.2	52.2	7:00	46.4	44.4	50.0
8:00	49.8	49.0	52.4	8:00	47.2	46.6	48.9
9:00	50.3	49.4	51.7	9:00	48.4	47.2	49.5
10:00	50.2	49.6	51.8	10:00	49.2	48.1	50.7
11:00	50.0	49.0	52.3	11:00	48.4	47.0	50.8
12 noon	50.0	48.8	52.4	12 midnight	47.2	46.4	49.2
1:00 P.M.	50.1	49.4	53.6	1:00 A.M.	47.4	46.8	49.0
2:00	49.7	48.6	51.0	2:00	48.8	47.2	51.4
3:00	48.4	47.2	51.7	3:00	49.6	49.0	50.6
4:00	47.2	45.3	50.9	4:00	51.0	50.5	51.5
5:00	46.8	44.1	49.0	5:00	50.5	50.0	51.9

to expand from a one-shift (6:00 A.M. to 2:00 P.M.) to a two-shift (2:00 P.M. to 10:00 P.M.) operation in mid-2010, and finally to a three-shift operation (24 hours per day) in the fall of 2012.

The additional night-shift bagging crew was staffed entirely by new employees. The most experienced foremen were temporarily assigned to supervise the night-shift employees. Most emphasis was placed on increasing the output of bags to meet ever-increasing demand. It was suspected that only occasional reminders were made to double-check the bag weight-feeder. (A double-check is performed by systematically weighing a bag on a scale to determine if the proper weight is being loaded by the weight-feeder. If there is significant deviation from 50 pounds, corrective adjustments are made to the weight-release mechanism.)

To verify this expectation, the quality control staff randomly sampled the bag output and prepared the chart on the previous page. Six bags were sampled and weighed each hour.

Discussion Questions

1. What is your analysis of the bag-weight problem?
2. What procedures would you recommend to maintain proper quality control?

Source: Professor Jerry Kinard, Western Carolina University. Reprinted with permission.

Frito-Lay's Quality-Controlled Potato Chips

Video Case

Frito-Lay, the multi-billion-dollar snack food giant, produces billions of pounds of product every year at its dozens of U.S. and Canadian plants. From the farming of potatoes—in Florida, North Carolina, and Michigan—to factory and to retail stores, the ingredients and final product of Lay's chips, for example, are inspected at least 11 times: in the field, before unloading at the plant, after washing and peeling, at the sizing station, at the fryer, after seasoning, when bagged (for weight), at carton filling, in the warehouse, and as they are placed on the store shelf by Frito-Lay personnel. Similar inspections take place for its other famous products, including Cheetos, Fritos, Ruffles, and Tostitos.

In addition to these employee inspections, the firm uses proprietary vision systems to look for defective potato chips. Chips are pulled off the high-speed line and checked twice if the vision system senses them to be too brown.

The company follows the very strict standards of the American Institute of Baking (AIB), standards that are much tougher than those of the U.S. Food and Drug Administration. Two unannounced AIB site visits per year keep Frito-Lay's plants on their toes. Scores, consistently in the "excellent" range, are posted, and every employee knows exactly how the plant is doing.

There are two key metrics in Frito-Lay's continuous improvement quality program: (1) total customer complaints (measured on a complaints per million bag basis) and (2) hourly or daily statistical process control scores (for oil, moisture, seasoning, and salt content, for chip thickness, for fryer temperature, and for weight).

In the Florida plant, Angela McCormack, who holds engineering and MBA degrees, oversees a 15-member quality assurance staff. They watch all aspects of quality, including training employees on the factory floor, monitoring automated processing equipment, and developing and updating statistical process control (SPC) charts. The upper and lower control limits for one check point, salt content in Lay's chips, are 2.22% and 1.98%, respectively. To see exactly how these limits are created using SPC, watch the video that accompanies this case.

Discussion Questions*

1. Angela is now going to evaluate a new salt process delivery system and wants to know if the upper and lower control limits at 3 standard deviations for the new system will meet the upper and lower control specifications noted above.

   The data (in percents) from the initial trial samples are:

   Sample 1: 1.98, 2.11, 2.15, 2.06
   Sample 2: 1.99, 2.0, 2.08, 1.99
   Sample 3: 2.20, 2.10. 2.20, 2.05
   Sample 4: 2.18, 2.01, 2.23, 1.98
   Sample 5: 2.01, 2.08, 2.14, 2.16

   Provide the report to Angela.
2. What are the advantages and disadvantages of Frito-Lay drivers stocking their customers' shelves?
3. Why is quality a critical function at Frito-Lay?

*You may wish to view the video that accompanies this case before answering these questions.

Farm to Fork: Quality at Darden Restaurants

Video Case

Darden Restaurants, the $5.2 billion owner of such popular brands as Olive Garden, Red Lobster, Seasons 52, and Bahama Breeze, serves more than 300 million meals annually in its 1,700 restaurants across the U.S. and Canada. Before any one of these meals is placed before a guest, the ingredients for each recipe must pass quality control inspections at the source, ranging from measurement and weighing to tasting, touching, or lab testing. Darden has differentiated itself from its restaurant peers by developing the gold standard in continuous improvement.

To assure both customers and the company that quality expectations are met, Darden uses a rigorous inspection process, employing statistical process control (SPC) as part of its "Farm to Fork" program. More than 50 food scientists, microbiologists, and public health professionals report to Ana Hooper, vice president of quality assurance.

As part of Darden's Point Source program, Hooper's team, based in Southeast Asia (in China, Thailand, and Singapore) and Latin America (in Equador, Honduras, and Chile), approves and inspects—and works with Darden buyers to purchase—more than 50 million pounds of seafood each year for restaurant use. Darden used to build quality in at the end by inspecting shipments as they reached U.S. distribution centers. Now, thanks to coaching and partnering with vendors abroad, Darden needs but a few domestic inspection labs to verify compliance to its exacting standards. Food vendors in source countries know that when supplying Darden, they are subject to regular audits that are stricter than U.S. Food and Drug Administration (FDA) standards.

Two Quality Success Stories

Quality specialists' jobs include raising the bar and improving quality and safety at all plants in their geographic area. The Thai quality representative, for example, worked closely with several of Darden's largest shrimp vendors to convert them to a production-line-integrated quality assurance program. The vendors were able to improve the quality of shrimp supplied and reduce the percentage of defects by 19%.

Likewise, when the Darden quality teams visited fields of growers/shippers in Mexico recently, it identified challenges such as low employee hygiene standards, field food safety problems, lack of portable toilets, child labor, and poor working conditions. Darden addressed these concerns and hired third-party independent food safety verification firms to ensure continued compliance to standards.

SPC Charts

SPC charts, are particularly important. These charts document pre-cooked food weights; meat, seafood and poultry temperatures; blemishes on produce; and bacteria counts on shrimp—just to name a few. Quality assurance is part of a much bigger process that is key to Darden's success—its supply chain. That's because quality comes from the source and flows through distribution to the restaurant and guests.

Discussion Questions*

1. How does Darden build quality into the supply chain?
2. Select two potential problems—one in the Darden supply chain and one in a restaurant—that can be analyzed with a fish-bone chart. Draw a complete chart to deal with each problem.
3. Darden applies SPC in many product attributes. Identify where these are probably used.
4. The SPC chart on illustrates Darden's use of control charts to monitor the weight of salmon filets. Given these data, what conclusion do you, as a Darden quality control inspector, draw? What report do you issue to your supervisor? How do you respond to the salmon vendor?

*You might want to view the video that accompanies this case before answering these questions.

- **Additional Case Study:** Visit **www.myomlab.com** or **www.pearsonhighered.com/heizer** for this free case study:
  Green River Chemical Company: Involves a company that needs to set up a control chart to monitor sulfate content because of customer complaints.

Bibliography

Bakir, S. T. "A Quality Control Chart for Work Performance Appraisal." *Quality Engineering* 17, no. 3 (2005): 429.

Besterfield, Dale H. *Quality Control*, 8th ed. Upper Saddle River, NJ: Prentice Hall, 2009.

Elg, M., J. Olsson, and J. J. Dahlgaard. "Implementing Statistical Process Control." *The International Journal of Quality and Reliability Management* 25, no. 6 (2008): 545.

Goetsch, David L., and Stanley B. Davis. *Quality Management*, 6th ed. Upper Saddle River, NJ: Prentice Hall, 2009.

Gryna, F. M., R. C. H. Chua, and J. A. DeFeo. *Juran's Quality Planning and Analysis*, 5th ed. New York: McGraw-Hill, 2007.

Lin, H., and G. Sheen. "Practical Implementation of the Capability Index C_{pk} Based on Control Chart Data." *Quality Engineering* 17, no. 3 (2005): 371.

Matthes, N., et al. "Statistical Process Control for Hospitals." *Quality Management in Health Care* 16, no. 3 (July–September 2007): 205.

Mitra, Amit. *Fundamentals of Quality Control and Improvement*, 3rd ed. New York: Wiley, 2008.

Montgomery, D. C., C. L. Jennings, and M. E. Pfund. *Managing, Controlling, and Improving Quality*. New York: Wiley, 2011.

Roth, H. P. "How SPC Can Help Cut Costs." *Journal of Corporate Accounting and Finance* 16, no. 3 (March–April 2005): 21–30.

Sower, V. E. *Essentials of Quality*. New York: Wiley, 2011.

Summers, Donna. *Quality Management*, 2nd ed. Upper Saddle River, NJ: Prentice Hall, 2009.

APPENDIX

SOLUTIONS TO EVEN-NUMBERED PROBLEMS

S2 **(a)** $UCL_{\bar{x}} = 52.31$
$LCL_{\bar{x}} = 47.69$
(b) $UCL_{\bar{x}} = 51.54$
$LCL_{\bar{x}} = 48.46$

S4 **(a)** $UCL_{\bar{x}} = 440$ calories
$LCL_{\bar{x}} = 400$ calories
(b) $UCL_{\bar{x}} = 435$ calories
$LCL_{\bar{x}} = 405$ calories

S6 $UCL_{\bar{x}} = 3.728$
$LCL_{\bar{x}} = 2.236$
$UCL_R = 2.336$
$LCL_R = 0.0$
The process is in control.

S8 **(a)** $UCL_{\bar{x}} = 16.08$
$LCL_{\bar{x}} = 15.92$
(b) $UCL_{\bar{x}} = 16.12$
$LCL_{\bar{x}} = 15.88$

S10 **(a)** $\sigma_{\bar{x}} = 0.61$
(b) Using $\sigma_{\bar{x}}$, $UCL_{\bar{x}} = 11.83$, and $LCL_{\bar{x}} = 8.17$.
(c) Using A_2, $UCL_{\bar{x}} = 11.90$, and $LCL_{\bar{x}} = 8.10$.
(c) $UCL_R = 6.98$; $LCL_R = 0$
(d) Yes

S12 $UCL_R = 6.058$; $LCL_R = 0.442$
Averages are increasing.

S14

UCL	LCL
.062	0
.099	0
.132	0
.161	0
.190	.01

S16 $UCL_p = .0313$; $LCL_p = 0$

S18 **(a)** $UCL_p = 0.076$; $LCL_p = 0.002$

S20 **(a)** $UCL_p = .0581$
$LCL_p = 0$
(b) in control
(c) $UCL_p = .1154$
$LCL_p = 0$

S22 **(a)** *c*-chart
(b) $UCL_c = 13.35$
$LCL_c = 0$
(c) in control
(d) not in control

S24 **(a)** $UCL_c = 26.063$
$LCL_c = 3.137$
(b) No point out of control.

S26 $C_p = 1.0$. The process is barely capable.

S28 $C_{pk} = 1.125$. Process *is* centered and will produce within tolerance.

S30 $C_{pk} = .1667$

S32 $AOQ = 2.2\%$

S34 **(a)** $UCL_{\bar{x}} = 61.131$, $LCL_{\bar{x}} = 38.421$, $UCL_R = 41.62$, $LCL_R = 0$
(b) Yes, the process is in control for both $\bar{x}$- and *R*-charts.
(c) They support West's claim. But variance from the mean needs to be reduced and controlled.

Rapid Review

Main Heading	Review Material	MyOMLab

STATISTICAL PROCESS CONTROL (SPC)

- **Statistical process control (SPC)**—A process used to monitor standards by taking measurements and corrective action as a product or service is being produced.
- **Control chart**—A graphical presentation of process data over time.

A process is said to be operating *in statistical control* when the only source of variation is common (natural) causes. The process must first be brought into statistical control by detecting and eliminating special (assignable) causes of variation.

The objective of a process control system is to provide a statistical signal when assignable causes of variation are present.

- **Natural variations**—The variability that affects every production process to some degree and is to be expected; also known as common cause.

When natural variations form a *normal distribution,* they are characterized by two parameters:

- Mean, μ (the measure of central tendency—in this case, the average value)
- Standard deviation, σ (the measure of dispersion)

As long as the distribution (output measurements) remains within specified limits, the process is said to be "in control," and natural variations are tolerated.

- **Assignable variation**—Variation in a production process that can be traced to specific causes.

Control charts for the mean, $\bar{x}$, and the range, R, are used to monitor *variables* (outputs with continuous dimensions), such as weight, speed, length, or strength.

- **$\bar{x}$-chart**—A quality control chart for variables that indicates when changes occur in the central tendency of a production process.
- ***R*-chart**—A control chart that tracks the range within a sample; it indicates that a gain or loss in uniformity has occurred in dispersion of a production process.
- **Central limit theorem**—The theoretical foundation for $\bar{x}$-charts, which states that regardless of the distribution of the population of all parts or services, the $\bar{x}$ distribution will tend to follow a normal curve as the number of samples increases:

$$\bar{\bar{x}} = \mu \quad \text{(S1)}$$

$$\sigma_{\bar{x}} = \frac{\sigma}{\sqrt{n}} \quad \text{(S2)}$$

The $\bar{x}$-chart limits, if we know the true standard deviation σ of the process population, are:

$$\text{Upper control limit (UCL)} = \bar{\bar{x}} + z\sigma_{\bar{x}} \quad \text{(S3)}$$

$$\text{Lower control limit (LCL)} = \bar{\bar{x}} - z\sigma_{\bar{x}} \quad \text{(S4)}$$

where z = confidence level selected (e.g., $z = 3$ is 99.73% confidence).

The *range, R*, of a sample is defined as the difference between the largest and smallest items. If we do not know the true standard deviation, σ, of the population, the $\bar{x}$-chart limits are:

$$\text{UCL}_{\bar{x}} = \bar{\bar{x}} + A_2\bar{R} \quad \text{(S5)}$$

$$\text{LCL}_{\bar{x}} = \bar{\bar{x}} - A_2\bar{R} \quad \text{(S6)}$$

In addition to being concerned with the process average, operations managers are interested in the process dispersion, or range. The *R*-chart control limits for the range of a process are:

$$\text{UCL}_R = D_4\bar{R} \quad \text{(S7)}$$

$$\text{LCL}_R = D_3\bar{R} \quad \text{(S8)}$$

Attributes are typically classified as *defective* or *nondefective*. The two attribute charts are (1) *p*-charts (which measure the *percent* defective in a sample), and (2) *c*-charts (which *count* the number of defects in a sample).

- ***p*-chart**—A quality control chart that is used to control attributes:

$$\text{UCL}_p = \bar{p} + z\sigma_{\hat{p}} \quad \text{(S9)}$$

$$\text{LCL}_p = \bar{p} - z\sigma_{\hat{p}} \quad \text{(S10)}$$

$$\sigma_{\hat{p}} = \sqrt{\frac{\bar{p}(1-\bar{p})}{n}} \quad \text{(S11)}$$

MyOMLab:

Problems: S1–S25, S34

VIDEO S1
Farm to Fork: Quality at Darden Restaurants

Virtual Office Hours for Solved Problems: S1–S3

ACTIVE MODEL S1

VIDEO S2

Frito-Lay's Quality-Controlled Potato Chips

Main Heading	Review Material	MyOMLab
	■ ***c*-chart**—A quality control chart used to control the number of defects per unit of output. The Poisson distribution is the basis for *c*-charts, whose 99.73% limits are computed as: $$\text{Control limits} = \bar{c} \pm 3\sqrt{\bar{c}} \quad (S12)$$ ■ **Run test**—A test used to examine the points in a control chart to determine whether nonrandom variation is present.	Virtual Office Hours for Solved Problem: S5
PROCESS CAPABILITY	■ **Process capability**—The ability to meet design specifications. ■ $\mathbf{C_p}$—A ratio for determining whether a process meets design specifications. $$C_p = \frac{(\text{Upper specification} - \text{Lower specification})}{6\sigma} \quad (S13)$$ ■ $\mathbf{C_{pk}}$—A proportion of variation (3σ) between the center of the process and the nearest specification limit: $$C_{pk} = \text{Minimum of}\left[\frac{\text{Upper spec limit} - \overline{X}}{3\sigma}, \frac{\overline{X} - \text{Lower spec limit}}{3\sigma}\right] \quad (S14)$$	Problems: S25–S31 Virtual Office Hours for Solved Problems: S4 ACTIVE MODEL S2
ACCEPTANCE SAMPLING	■ **Acceptance sampling—**A method of measuring random samples of lots or batches of products against predetermined standards. ■ **Operating characteristic (OC) curve—**A graph that describes how well an acceptance plan discriminates between good and bad lots. ■ **Producer's risk—**The mistake of having a producer's good lot rejected through sampling. ■ **Consumer's risk—**The mistake of a customer's acceptance of a bad lot overlooked through sampling. ■ **Acceptable quality level (AQL)—**The quality level of a lot considered good. ■ **Lot tolerance percent defective (LTPD)—**The quality level of a lot considered bad. ■ **Type I error—**Statistically, the probability of rejecting a good lot. ■ **Type II error—**Statistically, the probability of accepting a bad lot. ■ **Average outgoing quality (AOQ)—**The percent defective in an average lot of goods inspected through acceptance sampling: $$AOQ = \frac{(P_d)(P_a)(N - n)}{N} \quad (S15)$$	Problems:S32, S33 ACTIVE MODEL S3

Self Test

■ **Before taking the self-test,** refer to the learning objectives listed at the beginning of the text and the key terms listed at the end of the text.

LO1. If the mean of a particular sample is within control limits and the range of that sample is not within control limits:
- **a)** the process is in control, with only assignable causes of variation.
- **b)** the process is not producing within the established control limits.
- **c)** the process is producing within the established control limits, with only natural causes of variation.
- **d)** the process has both natural and assignable causes of variation.

LO2. The central limit theorem:
- **a)** is the theoretical foundation of the *c*-chart.
- **b)** states that the average of assignable variations is zero.
- **c)** allows managers to use the normal distribution as the basis for building some control charts.
- **d)** states that the average range can be used as a proxy for the standard deviation.
- **e)** controls the steepness of an operating characteristic curve.

LO3. The type of chart used to control the central tendency of variables with continuous dimensions is:
- **a)** $\bar{x}$-chart.
- **b)** *R*-chart.
- **c)** *p*-chart.
- **d)** *c*-chart.
- **e)** none of the above.

LO4. If parts in a sample are measured and the mean of the sample measurement is outside the control limits:
- **a)** the process is out of control, and the cause should be established.
- **b)** the process is in control but not capable of producing within the established control limits.
- **c)** the process is within the established control limits, with only natural causes of variation.
- **d)** all of the above are true.

LO5. Control charts for attributes are:
- **a)** *p*-charts.
- **b)** *c*-charts.
- **c)** *R*-charts.
- **d)** $\bar{x}$-charts.
- **e)** both a and b.

LO6. The ability of a process to meet design specifications is called:
- **a)** Taguchi.
- **b)** process capability.
- **c)** capability index.
- **d)** acceptance sampling.
- **e)** average outgoing quality.

LO7. The _______ risk is the probability that a lot will be rejected despite the quality level exceeding or meeting the _______.

Answers: LO1. b; LO2. c; LO3. a; LO4. a; LO5. e; LO6. b; LO7. producer's, AQL

Process Strategy

OUTLINE

GLOBAL COMPANY PROFILE: *Harley-Davidson*

- Four Process Strategies
- Selection of Equipment
- Process Analysis and Design
- Special Considerations for Service Process Design
- Production Technology
- Technology in Services
- Process Redesign

10 OM STRATEGY DECISIONS

- Design of Goods and Services
- Managing Quality
- *Process Strategy*
- Location Strategies
- Layout Strategies
- Human Resources
- Supply-Chain Management
- Inventory Management
- Scheduling
- Maintenance

GLOBAL COMPANY PROFILE
Harley-Davidson

Repetitive Manufacturing Works at Harley-Davidson

Since Harley-Davidson's founding in Milwaukee in 1903, it has competed with hundreds of manufacturers, foreign and domestic. The competition has been tough. Recent competitive battles have been with the Japanese, and earlier battles were with the German, English, and Italian manufacturers. But after over 100 years, Harley is the only major U.S. motorcycle company. The company now has five U.S. facilities and an assembly plant in Brazil. The Sportster powertrain is manufactured in Wauwatosa, Wisconsin, and the sidecars, saddlebags, windshields, and other specialty items are produced in Tomahawk, Wisconsin. The Touring and Softail bikes are assembled in York, Pennsylvania, while the Sportster models, Dyna models, and VRSC models of motorcycles are produced in Kansas City, Missouri.

As a part of management's lean manufacturing effort, Harley groups production of parts that require similar processes together. The result is work cells. Using the latest technology, work cells perform in one location all the operations necessary for production of a specific module. Raw materials are moved to the work cells and then the modules proceed to the assembly line. As a double check on quality, Harley has also installed "light curtain" technology which uses an infrared

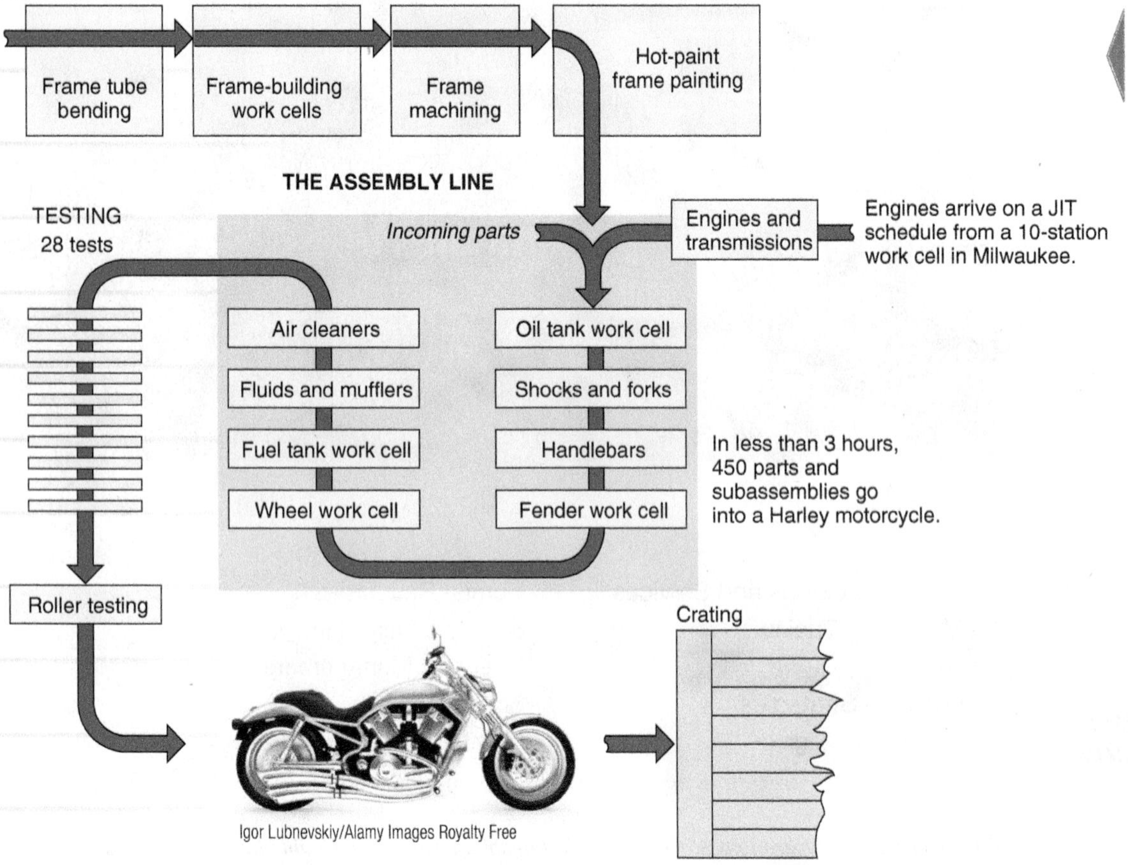

Igor Lubnevskiy/Alamy Images Royalty Free

Flowchart Showing the Production Process at Harley-Davidson's York Assembly Plant

Associated Press

Wheel assembly modules are prepared in a work cell for JIT delivery to the assembly line.

Steven Rubin/The Image Works

For manufacturers like Harley-Davidson, which produces a large number of end products from a relatively small number of options, modular bills of material provide an effective solution.

sensor to verify the bin from which an operator is taking parts. Materials go to the assembly line on a just-in-time basis, or as Harley calls it, using a Materials as Needed (MAN) system.

The 12.5-million-square-foot York facility includes manufacturing cells that perform tube bending, frame-building, machining, painting, and polishing. Innovative manufacturing techniques use robots to load machines and highly automated production to reduce machining time. Automation and precision sensors play a key role in maintaining tolerances and producing a quality product. Each day the York facility produces up to 600 heavy-duty factory-custom motorcycles. Bikes are assembled with different engine displacements, multiple wheel options, colors, and accessories. The result is a huge number of variations in the motorcycles available, which allows customers to individualize their purchase. (See **www.Harley-Davidson.com** for an example of modular customization.) The Harley-Davidson production system works because high-quality modules are brought together on a tightly scheduled repetitive production line.

Harley-Davidson Motor Company

Engines, having arrived just-in-time from the Milwaukee engine plant in their own protective shipping containers, are placed on an overhead conveyor for movement to the assembly line.

Catherine Karnow/Woodfin Camp & Associates, Inc.

It all comes together on the line. Any employee who spots a problem has the authority to stop the line until the problem in corrected. The multicolored "andon" light above the motorcycle on the frame of the carrier signals the severity of the problem.

LEARNING OBJECTIVES

LO1 ***Describe*** four process strategies

LO2 ***Compute*** crossover points for different processes

LO3 ***Use*** the tools of process analysis

LO4 ***Describe*** customer interaction in service processes

LO5 ***Identify*** recent advances in production technology

Four Process Strategies

A major decision for an operations manager is finding the best way to produce so as not to waste our planet's resources. Let's look at ways to help managers design a process for achieving this goal.

Process strategy
An organization's approach to transforming resources into goods and services.

A process strategy is an organization's approach to transforming resources into goods and services. *The objective is to create a process that can produce products that meets customer requirements within cost and other managerial constraints.* The process selected will have a long-term effect on efficiency and flexibility of production, as well as on cost and quality of the goods produced.

Virtually every good or service is made by using some variation of one of four process strategies: (1) process focus, (2) repetitive focus, (3) product focus, and (4) mass customization. The relationship of these four strategies to volume and variety is shown in Figure 1. We examine *Arnold Palmer Hospital* as an example of a process-focused firm, *Harley-Davidson* as a repetitive producer, *Frito-Lay* as a product-focused operation, and *Dell* as a mass customizer.

LO1 *Describe* four process strategies

Process Focus

The vast majority of global production is devoted to making *low-volume, high-variety* products in places called "job shops." Such facilities are organized around specific activities or processes. In a factory, these processes might be departments devoted to welding, grinding, and painting. In an office, the processes might be accounts payable, sales, and payroll. In a restaurant, they might be bar, grill, and bakery. Such facilities are process focused in terms of equipment, layout,

Figure 1
Process Selected Must Fit with Volume and Variety

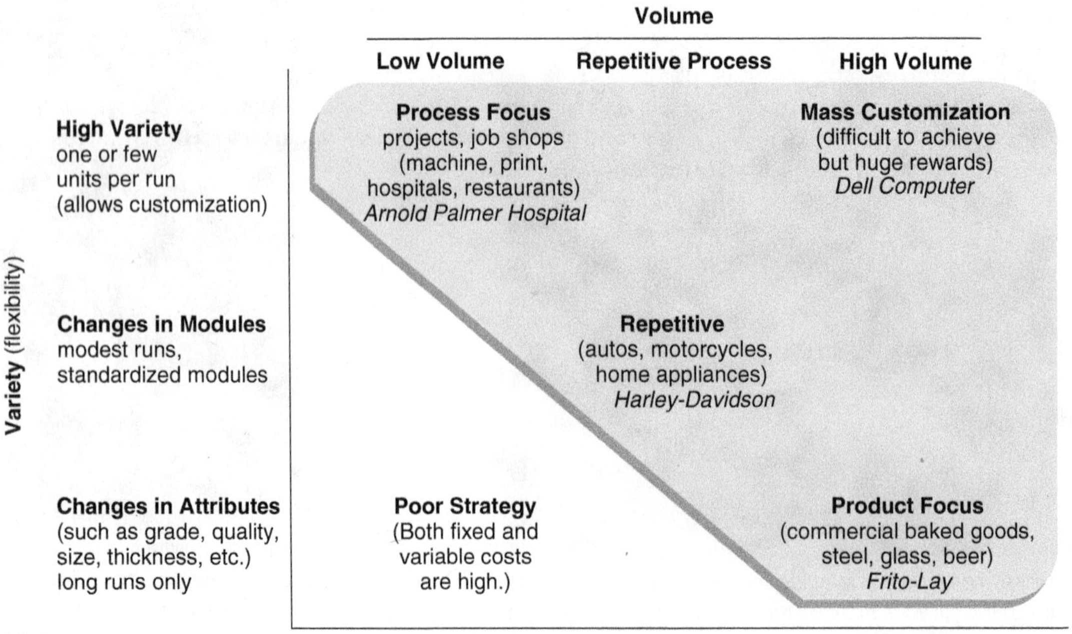

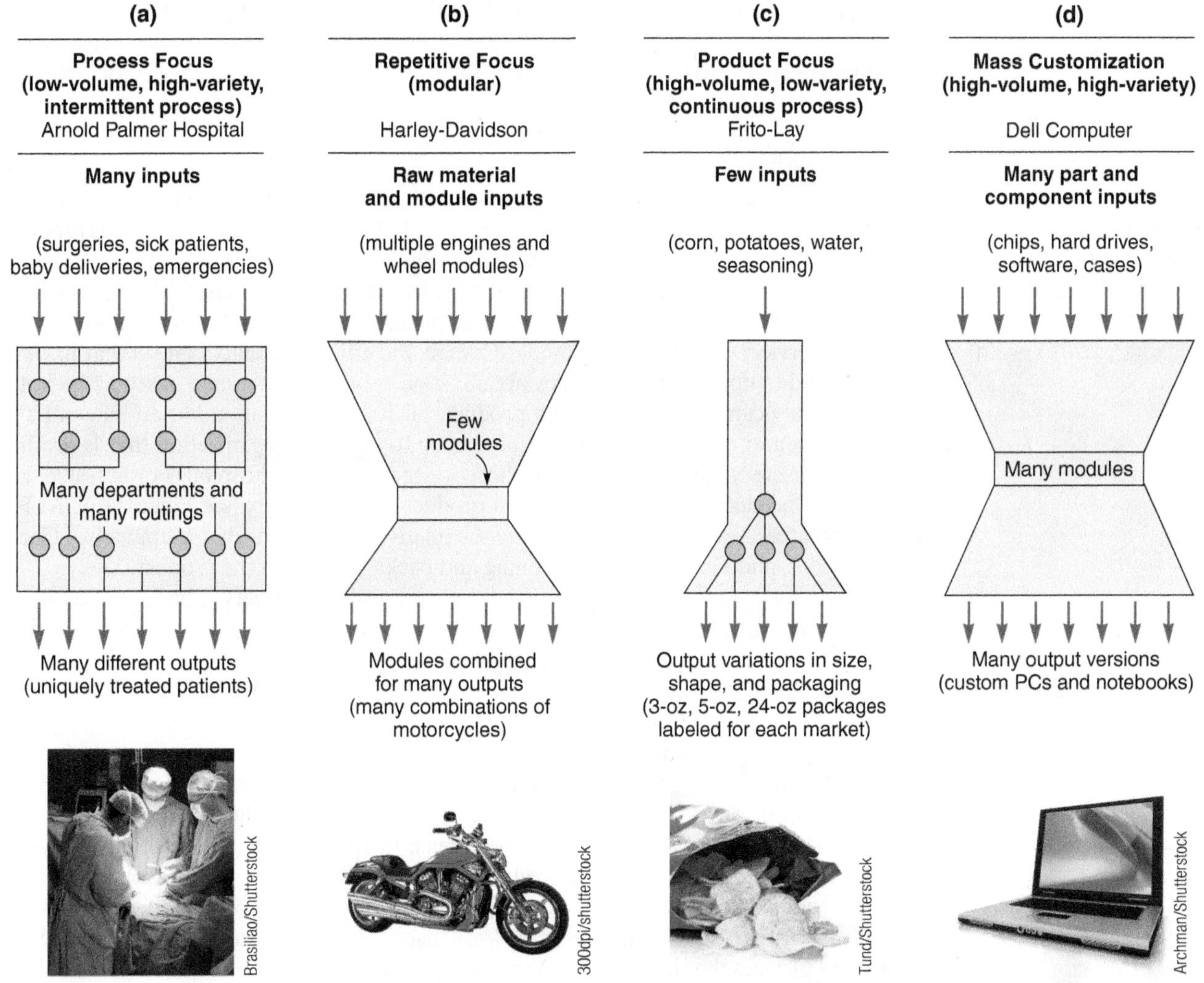

Figure 2

Four Process Options with an Example of Each

and supervision. They provide a high degree of product flexibility as products move between the specialized processes. Each process is designed to perform a variety of activities and handle frequent changes. Consequently, they are also called *intermittent processes.*

Process focus
A production facility organized around processes to facilitate low-volume, high-variety production.

Referring to Figure 2(a), imagine a diverse group of patients entering Arnold Palmer Hospital, a process-focused facility, to be routed to specialized departments, treated in a distinct way, and then exiting as uniquely cared-for individuals.

Process-focused facilities have high variable costs with extremely low utilization of facilities, as low as 5%. This is the case for many restaurants, hospitals, and machine shops. However, some facilities that lend themselves to electronic controls do somewhat better.

Repetitive Focus

Repetitive processes, as we saw in the Global Company Profile on Harley-Davidson, use modules (see Figure 2b). Modules are parts or components previously prepared, often in a product-focused (continuous) process.

Modules
Parts or components of a product previously prepared, often in a continuous process.

The repetitive process is the classic assembly line. Widely used in the assembly of virtually all automobiles and household appliances, it has more structure and consequently less flexibility than a process-focused facility.

Repetitive process
A product-oriented production process that uses modules.

Fast-food firms are another example of a repetitive process using modules. This type of production allows more customizing than a product-focused facility; modules (for example, meat, cheese, sauce, tomatoes, onions) are assembled to get a quasi-custom product, a cheeseburger. In this manner, the firm obtains both the economic advantages of the product-focused model (where many of the modules are prepared) and the custom advantage of the low-volume, high-variety model.

Product Focus

Product focus

A facility organized around products; a product-oriented, high-volume, low-variety process.

High-volume, low-variety processes are **product focused**. The facilities are organized around *products*. They are also called *continuous processes* because they have very long, continuous production runs. Products such as glass, paper, tin sheets, lightbulbs, beer, and potato chips are made via a continuous process. Some products, such as lightbulbs, are discrete; others, such as rolls of paper, are made in a continuous flow. Still others, such as repaired hernias at Canada's famous Shouldice Hospital, are services. It is only with standardization and effective quality control that firms have established product-focused facilities. An organization producing the same lightbulb or hot dog bun day after day can organize around a product. Such an organization has an inherent ability to set standards and maintain a given quality, as opposed to an organization that is producing unique products every day, such as a print shop or general-purpose hospital. For example, Frito-Lay's family of products is also produced in a product-focused facility [see Figure 2(c)]. At Frito-Lay, corn, potatoes, water, and seasoning are the relatively few inputs, but outputs (like Cheetos, Ruffles, Tostitos, and Fritos) vary in seasoning and packaging within the product family.

A product-focused facility produces high volume and low variety. The specialized nature of the facility requires high fixed cost, but low variable costs reward high facility utilization.

Mass Customization Focus

Our increasingly wealthy and sophisticated world demands individualized goods and services. A peek at the rich variety of goods and services that operations managers are called on to supply is shown in Table 1. The explosion of variety has taken place in automobiles, movies, breakfast cereals, and thousands of other areas. In spite of this proliferation of products, operations managers have improved product quality while reducing costs. Consequently, the variety of products continues to grow. Operations managers use *mass customization* to produce this vast array of goods and services. **Mass customization** is the rapid, low-cost production of goods and services that fulfill increasingly unique customer desires. But mass customization (see the upper-right section of Figure 1) is not just about variety; it is about making precisely *what* the customer wants *when* the customer wants it economically.

Mass customization

Rapid, low-cost production that caters to constantly changing unique customer desires.

Mass customization brings us the variety of products traditionally provided by low-volume manufacture (a process focus) at the cost of standardized high-volume (product-focused) production. However, achieving mass customization is a challenge that requires sophisticated operational capabilities. Building agile processes that rapidly and inexpensively produce custom products

TABLE 1 Mass Customization Provides More Choices Than Ever

	NUMBER OF CHOICES[a]	
ITEM	1970S	21ST CENTURY
Vehicle styles	18	1,212
Bicycle types	8	211,000[c]
Software titles	0	400,000
Web sites	0	255,000,000[d]
Movie releases per year	267	774[e]
New book titles	40,530	300,000+
Houston TV channels	5	185
Breakfast cereals	160	340
Items (SKUs) in supermarkets	14,000[b]	150,000[f]
LCD TVs	0	102

Source: Various; however, many of the data are from the Federal Reserve Bank of Dallas.
[a]Variety available in America; worldwide the variety increases even more. [b]1989.
[c]Possible combinations for one manufacturer. [d]Royal Pingdom Estimate (2010).
[e]www.movieweb.com (2011). [f]SKUs managed by H. E. Butts grocery chain.

requires a limited product line and modular design. The link between sales, design, production, supply chain, and logistics must be tight.

Dell Computer [see Figure 2(d)] has demonstrated that the payoff for mass customization can be substantial. More traditional manufacturers include Toyota, which recently announced delivery of custom-ordered cars in 5 days. Similarly, electronic controls allow designers in the textile industry to rapidly revamp their lines and respond to changes.

The service industry is also moving toward mass customization. For instance, not very many years ago, most people had the same telephone service. Now, not only is the phone service full of options, from caller ID to voice mail, but contemporary phones are hardly phones. They may also be part camera, computer, game player, GPS, and Web browser. Insurance companies are adding and tailoring new products with shortened development times to meet the unique needs of their customers. And firms like iTunes, Spotify, Rhapsody, Amazon, and eMusic maintain a music inventory on the Internet that allows customers to select a dozen songs of their choosing and have them made into a custom playlist. Similarly, the number of new books and movies increases each year. Mass customization places new demands on operations managers who must create and align the processes that provide this expanding variety of goods and services.

Making Mass Customization Work Mass customization suggests a high-volume system in which products are built-to-order. Build-to-order (BTO) means producing to customer orders, not forecasts. But high-volume build-to-order is difficult. Some major challenges are:

Build-to-order (BTO)
Produce to customer order rather than to a forecast.

- *Product design* must be imaginative. Successful build-to-order designs include a limited product line and modules. Ping Inc., a premier golf club manufacturer, uses different combinations of club heads, grips, shafts, and angles to make 20,000 variations of its golf clubs.
- *Process design* must be flexible and able to accommodate changes in both design and technology. For instance, postponement allows for customization late in the production process. Toyota installs unique interior modules very late in production for its popular Scion, a process also typical with customized vans.
- *Inventory management* requires tight control. To be successful with build-to-order, a firm must avoid being stuck with unpopular or obsolete components. With virtually no raw material, Dell puts custom computers together in less than a day.
- *Tight schedules* that track orders and material from design through delivery are another requirement of mass customization. Align Technology, a well-known name in orthodontics, figured out how to achieve competitive advantage by delivering custom-made clear plastic aligners within 3 weeks of the first visit to the dentist's office (see the *OM in Action* box "Mass Customization for Straight Teeth").
- *Responsive partners* in the supply chain can yield effective collaboration. Forecasting, inventory management, and ordering for JCPenney shirts are all handled for the retailer by its supplier in Hong Kong.

Postponement
The delay of any modifications or customization to a product as long as possible in the production process.

Mass customization/build-to-order is the new imperative for operations. There are advantages to mass customization and building to order: first, by meeting the demands of the market

OM in Action Mass Customization for Straight Teeth

Align Technology of Santa Clara, California, wants to straighten your teeth with a clear plastic removable aligner. The company is a mass customizer for orthodontic treatments. Each patient is *very* custom, requiring a truly unique product; no two patients are alike. Based on dental impressions, X-rays, and photos taken at the dentist's office and sent to Align headquarters, the firm builds a precise 3-D computer model and file of the patient's mouth. This digitized file is then sent to Costa Rica, where technicians develop a comprehensive treatment plan, which is then returned to the dentist for approval. After approval, data from the virtual models and treatment plan are used to program 3-D printers to form molds. The molds are then shipped to Juarez, Mexico, where a series of customized teeth aligners—usually about 19 pairs—are made. The time required for this process: about 3 weeks from start to finish.

The clear aligners take the place of the traditional "wire and brackets." Align calls the product "complex to make, easy to use." With good OM, mass customization works, even for a very complex, very individualized product, such as teeth aligners.

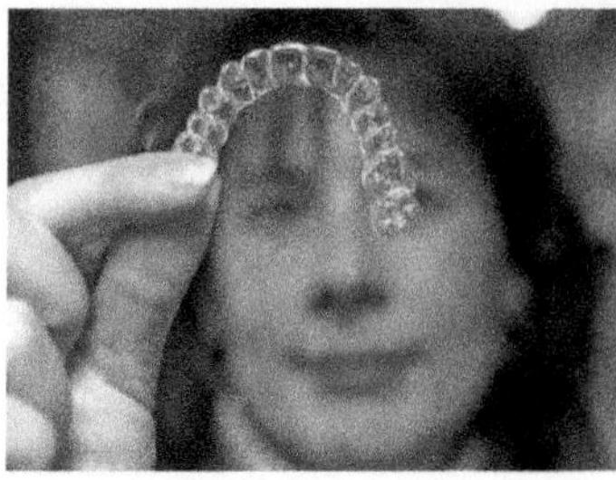

HUGH GRANNUM KRT/Newscom

Sources: BusinessWeek (April 30, 2012); Laura Rock Kopezak and M. Eric Johnson, "Aligning the Supply Chain," Case #6-0024, Dartmouth College, 2006; and www.invisalign.com.

TABLE 2 Comparison of the Characteristics of Four Types of Processes

PROCESS FOCUS (LOW VOLUME, HIGH VARIETY) (E.G., ARNOLD PALMER HOSPITAL)	REPETITIVE FOCUS (MODULAR) (E.G., HARLEY-DAVIDSON)	PRODUCT FOCUS (HIGH VOLUME, LOW VARIETY) (E.G., FRITO-LAY)	MASS CUSTOMIZATION (HIGH VOLUME, HIGH VARIETY) (E.G., DELL COMPUTER)
1. Small quantity and large variety of products	1. Long runs, a standardized product from modules	1. Large quantity and small variety of products	1. Large quantity and large variety of products
2. Broadly skilled operators	2. Moderately trained employees	2. Less broadly skilled operators	2. Flexible operators
3. Instructions for each job	3. Few changes in job instructions	3. Standardized job instructions	3. Custom orders requiring many job instructions
4. High inventory	4. Low inventory	4. Low inventory	4. Low inventory relative to the value of the product
5. Finished goods are made to order and not stored	5. Finished goods are made to frequent forecasts	5. Finished goods are made to a forecast and stored	5. Finished goods are build-to-order (BTO)
6. Scheduling is complex	6. Scheduling is routine	6. Scheduling is routine	6. Sophisticated scheduling accommodates custom orders
7. Fixed costs are low and variable costs high	7. Fixed costs are dependent on flexibility of the facility	7. Fixed costs are high and variable costs low	7. Fixed costs tend to be high and variable costs low

place, firms win orders and stay in business; in addition, they trim costs (from personnel to inventory to facilities) that exist because of inaccurate sales forecasting.

Process Comparison

The characteristics of the four processes are shown in Table 2 and Figure 2, and each may provide a strategic advantage. For instance, unit costs will be less in the product (continuous) or repetitive case when high volume (and high utilization) exists. However, a low-volume differentiated product is likely to be produced more economically under process focus. And mass customization requires exceptional competence in product and process design, scheduling, supply chain, and inventory management. Proper evaluation and selection of process strategies are critical.

Crossover chart
A chart of costs at the possible volumes for more than one process.

Crossover Charts The comparison of processes can be further enhanced by looking at the point where the total cost of the processes changes. For instance, Figure 3 shows three alternative processes compared on a single chart. Such a chart is sometimes called a crossover chart. Process A has the lowest cost for volumes below V_1, process B has the lowest cost between V_1 and V_2, and process C has the lowest cost at volumes above V_2.

Example 1 illustrates how to determine the exact volume where one process becomes more expensive than another.

Example 1

CROSSOVER CHART

Kleber Enterprises would like to evaluate three accounting software products (A, B, and C) to support changes in its internal accounting processes. The resulting processes will have cost structures similar to those shown in Figure 3. The costs of the software for these processes are:

	TOTAL FIXED COST	DOLLARS REQUIRED PER ACCOUNTING REPORT
Software A	$200,000	$60
Software B	$300,000	$25
Software C	$400,000	$10

LO2 *Compute* crossover points for different processes

APPROACH ▶ Solve for the crossover point for software A and B and then the crossover point for software B and C.

SOLUTION ▶ Software A yields a process that is most economical up to V_1, but to exactly what number of reports (volume)? To determine the volume at V_1, we set the cost of software A equal to the cost of software B. V_1 is the unknown volume:

$$200{,}000 + (60)V_1 = 300{,}000 + (25)V_1$$
$$35V_1 = 100{,}000$$
$$V_1 = 2{,}857$$

This means that software A is most economical from 0 reports to 2,857 reports (V_1).

Similarly, to determine the crossover point for V_2, we set the cost of software B equal to the cost of software C:

$$300{,}000 + (25)V_2 = 400{,}000 + (10)V_2$$
$$15V_2 = 100{,}000$$
$$V_2 = 6{,}666$$

This means that software B is most economical if the number of reports is between 2,857 (V_1) and 6,666 (V_2) and that software C is most economical if reports exceed 6,666 (V_2).

INSIGHT ▶ As you can see, the software and related process chosen is highly dependent on the forecasted volume.

LEARNING EXERCISE ▶ If the vendor of software A reduces the fixed cost to $150,000, what is the new crossover point between A and B? [Answer: 4,286.]

RELATED PROBLEMS ▶ 5, 6, 7, 8, 9, 10, 11, 12, 14

ACTIVE **MODEL** 1 This example is further illustrated in Active Model 7.1 at **www.pearsonhighered.com/heizer**.

EXCEL **OM** Data File **Ch07Ex1.xls** can be found at **www.pearsonhighered.com/heizer**.

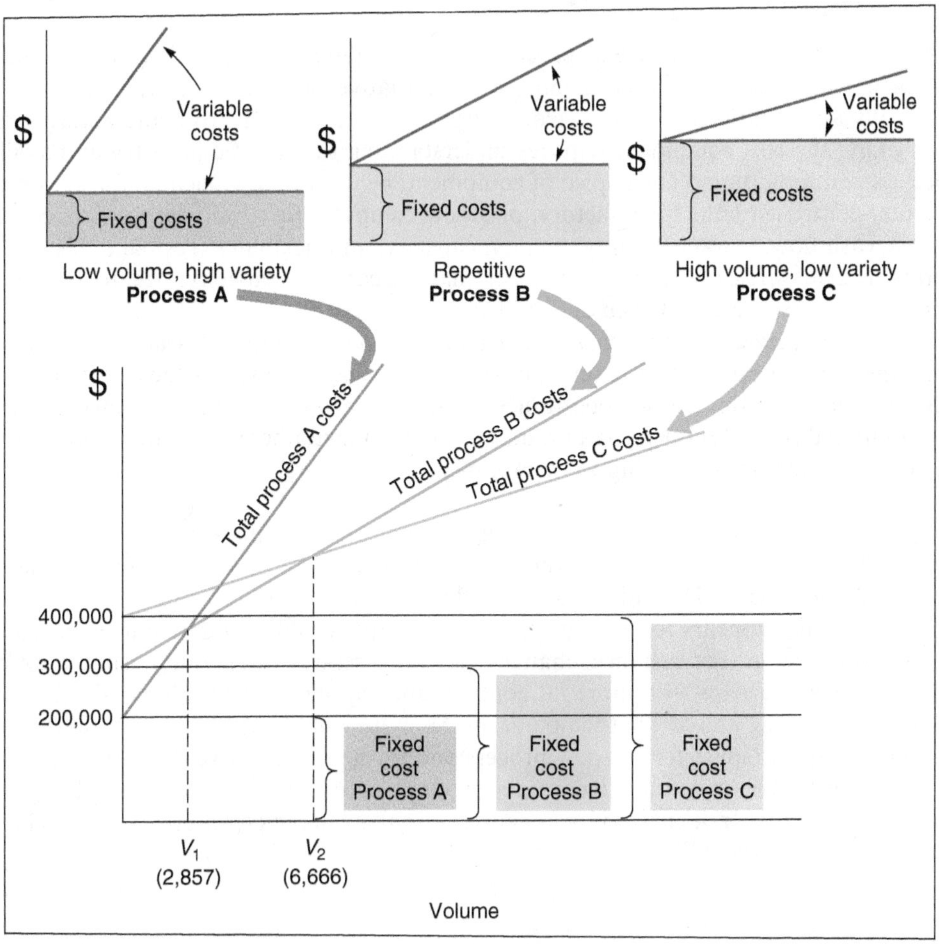

Figure 3
Crossover Charts

☆ **STUDENT TIP**
Different processes can be expected to have different costs. However, at any given volume, only one will have the lowest cost.

VIDEO 1
Process Strategy at Wheeled Coach Ambulance

Focused Processes In an ongoing quest for efficiency, industrialized societies continue to move toward specialization. The focus that comes with specialization contributes to efficiency. Managers who focus on a limited number of activities, products, and technologies do better. As the variety of products in a facility increase, overhead costs increase even faster. Similarly, as the variety of products, customers, and technology increases, so does complexity. The resources necessary to cope with the complexity expand disproportionately. A focus on depth of product line as opposed to breadth is typical of outstanding firms, of which Intel, L.M. Ericsson, and Bosch are world-class examples. *Focus*, defined here as specialization, simplification, and concentration, yields efficiency. Focus also contributes to building a core competence that fosters market and financial success. The focus can be:

- *Customers* (such as Winterhalter Gastronom, a German company that focuses on dishwashers for hotels and restaurants, for whom spotless glasses and dishes are critical)
- *Products* with similar attributes (such as Nucor Steel's Crawford, Ohio, plant, which processes only high-quality sheet steels, and Gallagher, a New Zealand company, which has 45% of the world market in electric fences)
- *Service* (such as Orlando's Arnold Palmer Hospital, with a focus on children and women; or Shouldice Hospital, in Canada, with a focus on hernia repair)
- *Technology* (such as Texas Instruments, with a focus on only certain specialized kinds of semiconductors; and SAP, which in spite of a world of opportunities, remains focused on software)

VIDEO 2
Process Analysis at Arnold Palmer Hospital

The key for the operations manager is to move continuously toward specialization, focusing on the core competence necessary to excel at that speciality.

Selection of Equipment

STUDENT TIP
A process that is going to win orders often depends on the selection of the proper equipment.

Ultimately, selection of a particular process strategy requires decisions about equipment and technology. These decisions can be complex, as alternative methods of production are present in virtually all operations functions, from hospitals, to restaurants, to manufacturing facilities. Picking the best equipment requires understanding the specific industry and available processes and technology. The choice of equipment, be it an X-ray machine for a hospital, a computer-controlled lathe for a factory, or a new computer for an office, requires considering cost, cash flow, market stability, quality, capacity, and flexibility. To make this decision, operations managers develop documentation that indicates the capacity, size, tolerances, and maintenance requirements of each option.

Flexibility
The ability to respond with little penalty in time, cost, or customer value.

In this age of rapid technological change and short product life cycles, adding flexibility to the production process can be a major competitive advantage. **Flexibility** is the ability to respond with little penalty in time, cost, or customer value. This may mean modular, movable, or digitally controlled equipment. Honda's process flexibility, for example, has allowed it to become the industry leader at responding to market dynamics by modifying production volume and product mix.

Building flexibility into a production process can be difficult and expensive, but if it is not present, change may mean starting over. Consider what would be required for a rather simple change—such as McDonald's adding the flexibility necessary to serve you a charbroiled hamburger. What appears to be rather straightforward would require changes in many of the 10 OM decisions. For instance, changes may be necessary in (1) purchasing (a different quality of meat, perhaps with more fat content, and supplies such as charcoal), (2) quality standards (how long and at what temperature the patty will cook), (3) equipment (the charbroiler), (4) layout (space for the new process and for new exhaust vents), (5) training, and (6) maintenance. You may want to consider the implications of another simple change, such as a change from paper menus to iPad menus as discussed in the *OM in Action* box "The iPad Menu . . . A New Process."

OM in Action **The iPad Menu . . . a New Process**

Mass customization begins with the order. And at restaurants from California to Boston, the order now starts with an iPad. *Stacked Restaurants* lets customers choose ingredients for their sandwiches using an iPad on the table. Diners also get a great photo of the menu item (which stimulates sales), a list of ingredients and nutritional information (a plus for those with allergies or watching their diet), and an opportunity to build their own meal (mass customization).

Some restaurants, in addition to having the enticing photo of the meal, find that they can add a description and photo of just what a medium-rare steak looks like. They can further enrich the dining experience by adding a "recipe" tab or "history" tab with descriptions of the item's origins and tradition. *Steakhouses,* a chain in San Francisco, Atlanta, and Chicago, find the tabs great for its lengthy wine lists. Other restaurants find that the customer's ability to order immediately and the instantaneous placement of the order to the kitchen is a significant advantage as it reinforces their *response strategy.*

Stacked Restaurants

Using iPads means developing a new process. iPads are not cheap, but they are accurate and fast, with lots of options; you can even pay at the table via the iPad. And they are fun to use.

Sources: USA Today (February 16, 2011) and (July 25, 2012); and *Commercial Integrator* (March 28, 2011).

Changing processes or equipment can be difficult and expensive. It is best to get this critical decision right the first time.

Process Analysis and Design

STUDENT TIP
Here we look at five tools that help understand processes.

When analyzing and designing processes, we ask questions such as the following:

- Is the process designed to achieve competitive advantage in terms of differentiation, response, or low cost?
- Does the process eliminate steps that do not add value?
- Does the process maximize customer value as perceived by the customer?
- Will the process win orders?

LO3 *Use* the tools of process analysis

A number of tools help us understand the complexities of process design and redesign. They are simply ways of making sense of what happens or must happen in a process. Let's look at five of them: flowcharts, time-function mapping, value-stream mapping, process charts, and service blueprinting.

Flowchart

The first tool is the **flowchart**, which is a schematic or drawing of the movement of material, product, or people. For instance, the flowchart in the *Global Company Profile* for this text shows the assembly processes for Harley-Davidson. Such charts can help understanding, analysis, and communication of a process.

Flowchart
A drawing used to analyze movement of people or material.

Time-Function Mapping

A second tool for process analysis and design is a flowchart, but with time added on the horizontal axis. Such charts are sometimes called **time-function mapping**, or **process mapping**. With time-function mapping, nodes indicate the activities and the arrows indicate the flow direction, with time on the horizontal axis. This type of analysis allows users to identify and eliminate waste such as extra steps, duplication, and delay. Figure 4 shows the use of process mapping before and after process improvement at American National Can Company. In this example, substantial reduction in waiting time and process improvement in order processing contributed to a savings of 46 days.

Time-function mapping (or process mapping)
A flowchart with time added on the horizontal axis.

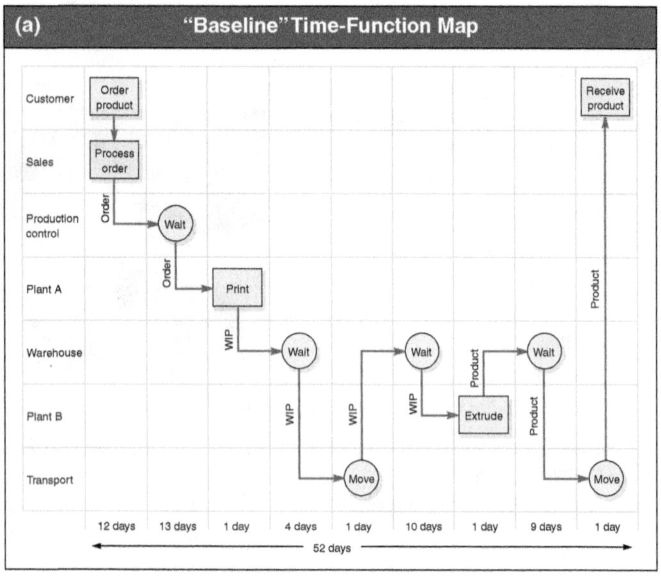

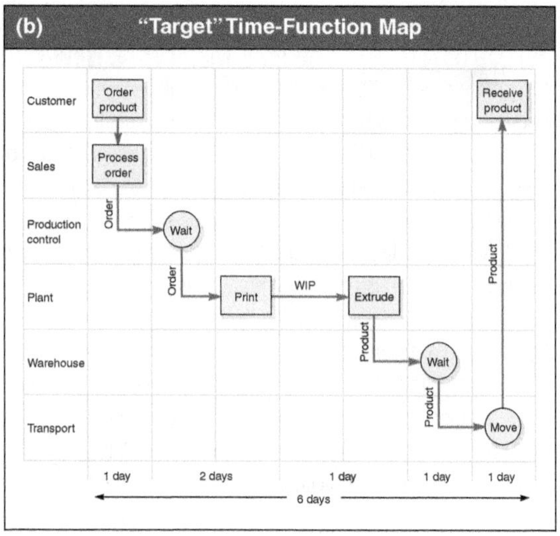

Figure 4

Time-Function Mapping (Process Mapping) for a Product Requiring Printing and Extruding Operations at American National Can Company

This technique clearly shows that waiting and order processing contributed substantially to the 46 days that can be eliminated in this operation.

Source: Excerpted from Elaine J. Labach, "Faster, Better, and Cheaper," *Target* no. 5:43 with permission of the Association for Manufacturing Excellence, 380 West Palatine Road, Wheeling, IL 60090-5863, 847/520-3282. **www.ame.org**. Reprinted with permission of Target Magazine.

Value-Stream Mapping

Value-stream mapping (VSM)
A process that helps managers understand how to add value in the flow of material and information through the entire production process.

A variation of time-function mapping is value-stream mapping (VSM); however, value-stream mapping takes an expanded look at where value is added (and not added) in the entire production process, including the supply chain. As with time-function mapping, the idea is to start with the customer and understand the production process, but value-stream mapping extends the analysis back to suppliers.

Value-stream mapping takes into account not only the process but, as shown in Example 2, also the management decisions and information systems that support the process.

Example 2

VALUE-STREAM MAPPING

Motorola has received an order for 11,000 cell phones per month and wants to understand how the order will be processed through manufacturing.

APPROACH ▶ To fully understand the process from customer to supplier, Motorola prepares a value-stream map.

SOLUTION ▶ Although value-stream maps appear complex, their construction is easy. Here are the steps needed to complete the value-stream map shown in Figure 5.

1. Begin with symbols for customer, supplier, and production to ensure the big picture.
2. Enter customer order requirements.
3. Calculate the daily production requirements.
4. Enter the outbound shipping requirements and delivery frequency.
5. Determine inbound shipping method and delivery frequency.
6. Add the process steps (i.e., machine, assemble) in sequence, left to right.
7. Add communication methods, add their frequency, and show the direction with arrows.
8. Add inventory quantities (shown with △) between every step of the entire flow.
9. Determine total working time (value-added time) and delay (non-value-added time).

Figure 5
Value-Stream Mapping (VSM)

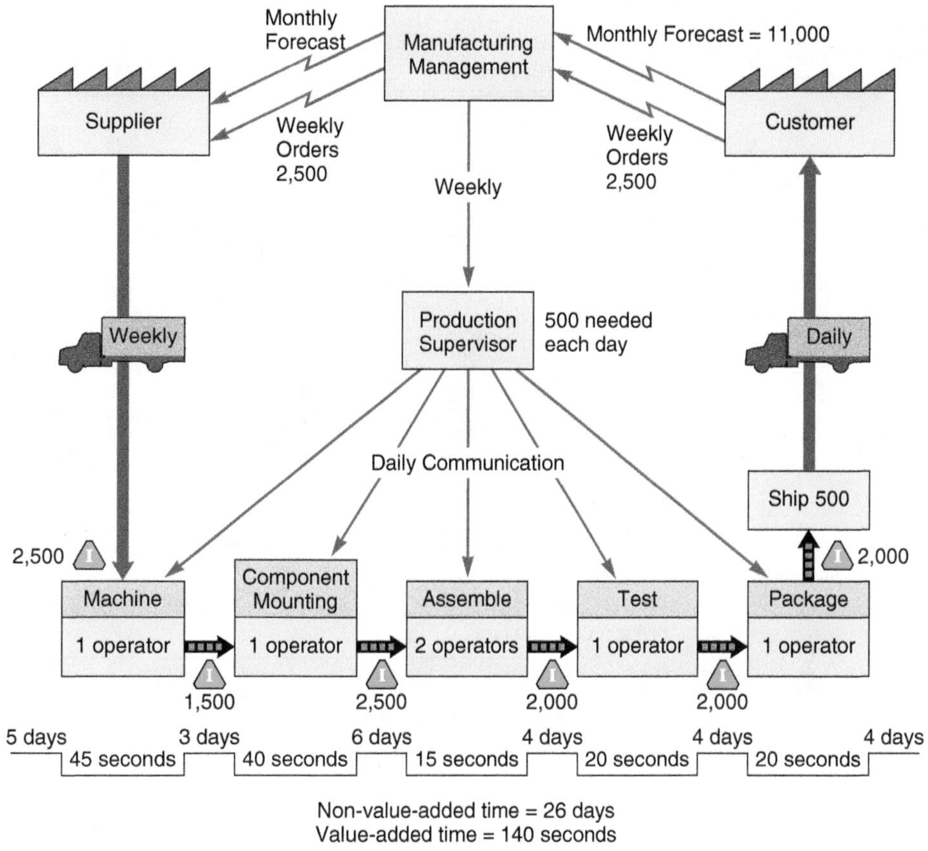

INSIGHT ▶ From Figure 5 we note that large inventories exist in incoming raw material and between processing steps, and that the value-added time is low as a proportion of the entire process.

LEARNING EXERCISE ▶ How might raw material inventory be reduced? [Answer: Have deliveries twice per week rather than once per week.]

RELATED PROBLEMS ▶ 13

Process Charts

The fourth tool is the *process chart*. Process charts use symbols, time, and distance to provide an objective and structured way to analyze and record the activities that make up a process. They allow us to focus on value-added activities. For instance, the process chart shown in Figure 6, which includes the present method of hamburger assembly at a fast-food restaurant, includes a value-added line to help us distinguish between value-added activities and waste. Identifying all value-added operations (as opposed to inspection, storage, delay, and transportation, which add no value) allows us to determine the percent of value added to total activities.[1] We can see from the computation at the bottom of Figure 6 that the percentage of value added in this case is 85.7%. The operations manager's job is to reduce waste and increase the percent of value added. The non-value-added items are a waste; they are resources lost to the firm and to society forever.

Process charts
Charts that use symbols to analyze the movement of people or material.

[1]Waste includes *inspection* (if the task is done properly, then inspection is unnecessary); *transportation* (movement of material within a process may be a necessary evil, but it adds no value); *delay* (an asset sitting idle and taking up space is waste); *storage* (unless part of a "curing" process, storage is waste).

Figure 6

Process Chart Showing a Hamburger Assembly Process at a Fast-Food Restaurant

Present Method [X]	PROCESS CHART	Proposed Method [ ]
SUBJECT CHARTED *Hamburger Assembly Process*		DATE *12/1/12*
DEPARTMENT	CHART BY *KH*	SHEET NO. *1* OF *1*

DIST. IN FEET	TIME IN MINS.	CHART SYMBOLS	PROCESS DESCRIPTION
	—	○ ⇨ □ D ▽	*Meat Patty in Storage*
1.5	*.05*	○ ⇨ □ D ▽	*Transfer to Broiler*
	2.50	○ ⇨ □ D ▽	*Broiler*
	.05	○ ⇨ □ D ▽	*Visual Inspection*
1.0	*.05*	○ ⇨ □ D ▽	*Transfer to Rack*
	.15	○ ⇨ □ D ▽	*Temporary Storage*
.5	*.10*	○ ⇨ □ D ▽	*Obtain Buns, Lettuce, etc.*
	.20	○ ⇨ □ D ▽	*Assemble Order*
.5	*.05*	○ ⇨ □ D ▽	*Place in Finish Rack*
		○ ⇨ □ D ▽	
3.5	*3.15*	*2 4 1 – 2*	TOTALS

Value-added time = Operation time/Total time = (2.50+.20)/3.15 = 85.7%

○ = operation; ⇨ = transport; □ = inspect; D = delay; ▽ = storage.

Service Blueprinting

Service blueprinting

A process analysis technique that lends itself to a focus on the customer and the provider's interaction with the customer.

Products with a high service content may warrant use of yet a fifth process technique. Service blueprinting is a process analysis technique that focuses on the customer and the provider's interaction with the customer. For instance, the activities at level one of Figure 7 are under the control of the customer. In the second level are activities of the service provider interacting with the customer. The third level includes those activities that are performed away from, and not immediately visible to, the customer. Each level suggests different management issues. For instance, the top level may suggest educating the customer or modifying expectations, whereas the second level may require a focus on personnel selection and training. Finally, the third level lends itself to more typical process innovations. The service blueprint shown in Figure 7 also notes potential failure points and shows how poka-yoke techniques can be added to improve quality. The consequences of these failure points can be greatly reduced if identified at the design stage when modifications or appropriate poka-yokes can be included. A time dimension is included in Figure 7 to aid understanding, extend insight, and provide a focus on customer service.

STUDENT TIP ☆

Service blueprinting helps evaluate the impact of customer interaction with the process.

Each of these five process analysis tools has strengths and variations. Flowcharts provide a quick way to view the big picture and try to make sense of the entire system. Time-function mapping adds some rigor and a time element to the macro analysis. Value-stream mapping extends beyond the immediate organization to customers and suppliers. Process charts are designed to provide a much more detailed view of the process, adding items such as value-added time, delay, distance, storage, and so forth. Service blueprinting, on the other hand, is designed to help us focus on the customer interaction part of the process. Because customer interaction is often an important variable in process design, we now examine some additional aspects of service process design.

Special Considerations for Service Process Design

STUDENT TIP ☆

Customer interaction with service processes increases the design challenge.

Interaction with the customer often affects process performance adversely. But a service, by its very nature, implies that some interaction and customization is needed. Recognizing that the customer's unique desires tend to play havoc with a process, the more the manager designs the process to accommodate these special requirements, the more effective and efficient the process will be. The trick is to find the right combination.

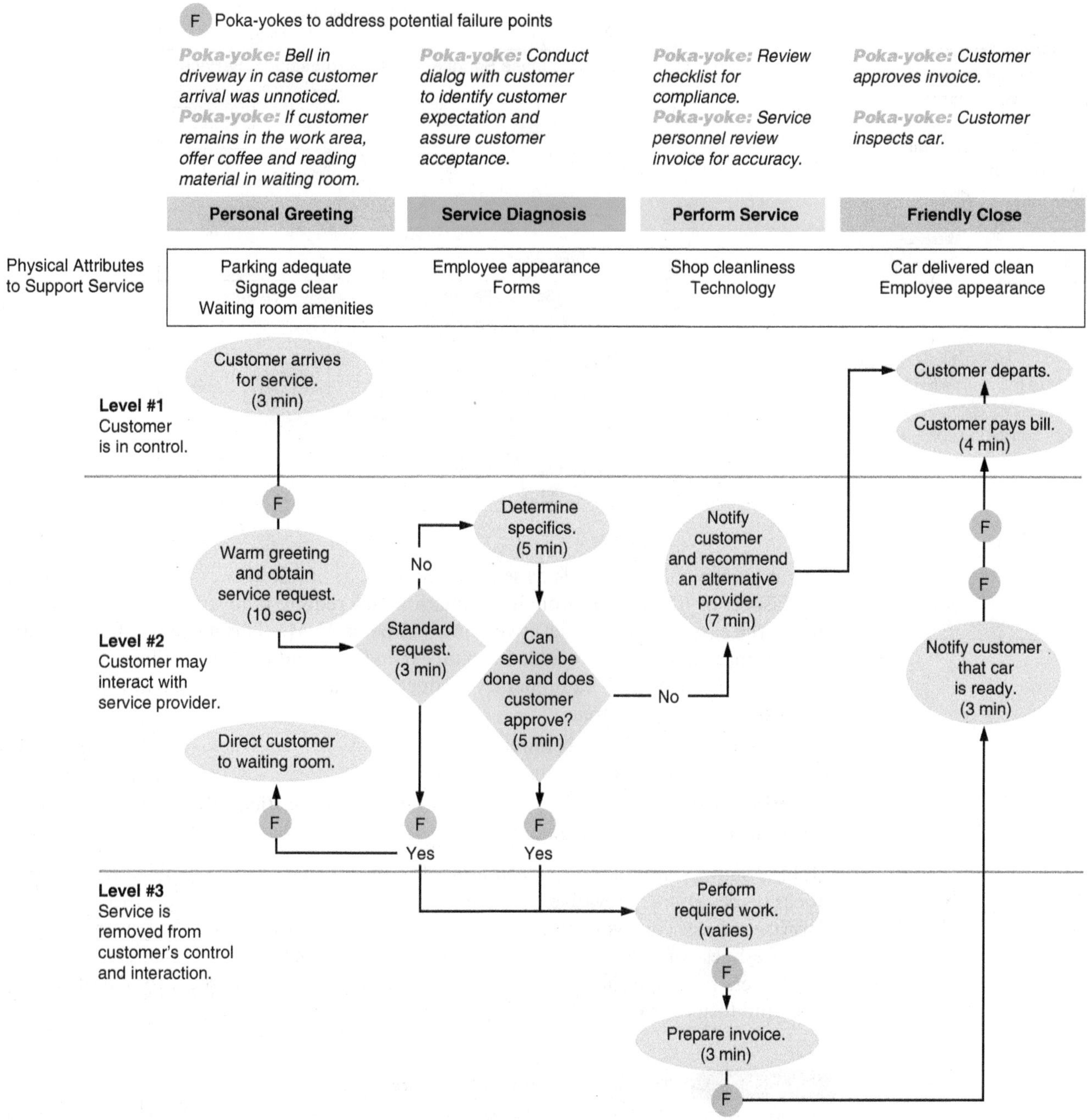

Figure 7

Service Blueprint for Service at Speedy Lube, Inc.

The four quadrants of Figure 8 provide additional insight on how operations managers modify service processes to find the best level of specialization and focus while maintaining the necessary customer interaction and customization. For instance:

LO4 *Describe* customer interaction in service processes

- In the upper sections (quadrants) of *mass service* and *professional service*, where *labor content is high*, we expect the manager to focus extensively on human resources. This is often done with personalized services, requiring high labor involvement and therefore significant personnel selection and training issues. This is particularly true in the professional service quadrant.
- The quadrants with *low customization* tend to (1) standardize or restrict some offerings, as do fast-food restaurants, (2) automate, as have airlines with ticket-vending machines, or

Figure 8

Services Moving Toward Specialization and Focus Within the Service Process Matrix

Source: From "Services Moving toward Specialization and Focus with the Service Process Matrix" by Roger Schmenner, from *MIT Sloan Management Review*, 1986. Copyright © 1986 by Massachusetts Institute of Technology. Reprinted by permission of Tribune Media Services.

STUDENT TIP

Notice how services find a competitive opportunity by moving from the rectangles to the ovals.

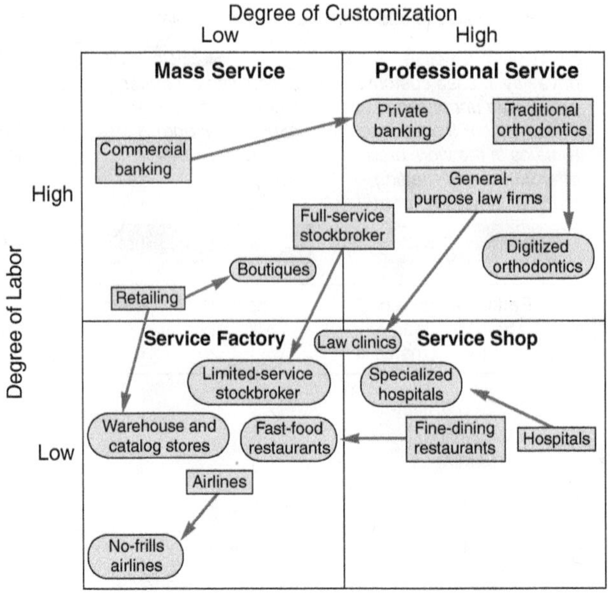

(3) remove some services, such as seat assignments, as has Southwest Airlines. Offloading some aspect of the service through automation may require innovations in process design. Such is the case with airline ticket vending and bank ATMs. This move to standardization and automation may require added capital expenditure and new OM skills for the purchase and maintenance of such equipment. A reduction in a customization capability will require added strength in other areas.

- Because customer feedback is lower in the quadrants with *low customization*, tight control may be required to maintain quality standards.
- Operations with *low labor intensity* may lend themselves particularly well to innovations in process technology and scheduling.

Table 3 shows some additional techniques for innovative process design in services. Managers focus on designing innovative processes that enhance the service. For instance, supermarket *self-service* reduces cost while it allows customers to check for the specific features they want, such as freshness or color. Dell Computer provides another version of self-service by allowing customers to design their own product on the Web. Customers seem to like this, and it is cheaper and faster for Dell.

TABLE 3 Techniques for Improving Service Productivity

STRATEGY	TECHNIQUE	EXAMPLE
Separation	*Structuring service* so customers must go where the service is offered	Bank customers go to a manager to open a new account, to loan officers for loans, and to tellers for deposits
Self-service	*Self-service* so customers examine, compare, and check out at their own pace	Supermarkets and department stores Internet ordering
Postponement	*Customizing at delivery*	Customizing vans at delivery rather than at production
Focus	*Restricting* the offerings	Limited-menu restaurant
Modules	*Modular* selection of service *Modular* production	Investment and insurance selection Prepackaged food modules in restaurants
Automation	*Separating services* that may lend themselves to some type of automation	Automatic teller machines
Scheduling	Precise personnel *scheduling*	Scheduling airline ticket counter personnel at 15-minute intervals
Training	*Clarifying the service* options *Explaining how to avoid problems*	Investment counselor, funeral directors After-sale maintenance personnel

Production Technology

STUDENT TIP
Here are nine technologies that can improve employee safety, product quality, and productivity.

Advances in technology that enhance production and productivity have a wide range of applications in both manufacturing and services. In this section, we introduce nine areas of technology: (1) machine technology, (2) automatic identification systems (AIS), (3) process control, (4) vision systems, (5) robots, (6) automated storage and retrieval systems (ASRSs), (7) automated guided vehicles (AGVs), (8) flexible manufacturing systems (FMSs), and (9) computer-integrated manufacturing (CIM).

LO5 *Identify* recent advances in production technology

Machine Technology

Most of the world's machinery that performs operations such as cutting, drilling, boring, and milling is undergoing tremendous progress in both precision and control. New machinery turns out metal components that vary less than a micron—1/76 the width of a human hair. They can accelerate water to three times the speed of sound to cut titanium for surgical tools. Machinery of the 21st century is often five times more productive than that of previous generations while being smaller and using less power. And continuing advances in lubricants now allow the use of water-based lubricants rather than oil-based. Water-based lubricants enhance sustainability by eliminating hazardous waste and allowing shavings to be easily recovered and recycled.

The intelligence now available for the control of new machinery via computers allows more complex and precise items to be made faster. Electronic controls increase speed by reducing changeover time, reducing waste (because of fewer mistakes), and enhancing flexibility. Machinery with its own computer and memory is called computer numerical control (CNC) machinery.

Computer numerical control (CNC)
Machinery with its own computer and memory.

Advanced versions of such technology are used on Pratt & Whitney's turbine blade plant in Connecticut. The machinery has improved the loading and alignment task so much that Pratt has cut the total time for the grinding process of a turbine blade from 10 days to 2 hours. The new machinery has also contributed to process improvements that mean the blades now travel just 1,800 feet in the plant, down from 8,100 feet, cutting throughput time from 22 days to 7 days.

With RFID, a cashier could scan the entire contents of a shopping cart in seconds.

Automatic Identification Systems (AISs) and RFID

New equipment, from numerically controlled manufacturing machinery to ATM machines, is controlled by digital electronic signals. Electrons are a great vehicle for transmitting information, but they have a major limitation—most OM data does not start out in bits and bytes. Therefore, operations managers must get the data into an electronic form. Making data digital is done via computer keyboards, bar codes, radio frequencies, optical characters, and so forth. These automatic identification systems (AISs) help us move data into electronic form, where it is easily manipulated.

Automatic identification system (AIS)
A system for transforming data into electronic form, for example, bar codes.

Because of its decreasing cost and increasing pervasiveness, radio frequency identification (RFID) warrants special note. RFID is integrated circuitry with its own tiny antennas that use radio waves to send signals a limited range—usually a matter of yards. These RFID tags provide unique identification that enables the tracking and monitoring of parts, pallets, people, and pets—virtually everything that moves. RFID requires no line of sight between tag and reader.

Radio frequency identification (RFID)
A wireless system in which integrated circuits with antennas send radio waves.

Process Control

Process control is the use of information technology to monitor and control a physical process. For instance, process control is used to measure the moisture content and thickness of paper as it travels over a paper machine at thousands of feet per minute. Process control is also used to determine and control temperatures, pressures, and quantities in petroleum refineries, petrochemical processes, cement plants, steel mills, nuclear reactors, and other product-focused facilities.

Process control
The use of information technology to control a physical process.

Process control systems operate in a number of ways, but the following are typical:

- Sensors collect data, which is read on some periodic basis, perhaps once a minute or second.
- Measurements are translated into digital signals, which are transmitted to a computer.
- Computer programs read the file and analyze the data.
- The resulting output may take numerous forms. These include messages on computer consoles or printers, signals to motors to change valve settings, warning lights or horns, or statistical process control charts.

Vision Systems

Vision systems
Systems that use video cameras and computer technology in inspection roles.

Vision systems combine video cameras and computer technology and are often used in inspection roles. Visual inspection is an important task in most food-processing and manufacturing organizations. Moreover, in many applications, visual inspection performed by humans is tedious, mind-numbing, and error prone. Thus vision systems are widely used when the items being inspected are very similar. For instance, vision systems are used to inspect Frito-Lay's potato chips so that imperfections can be identified as the chips proceed down the production line. The systems are also used to ensure that sealant is present and in the proper amount on Whirlpool's washing-machine transmissions. Vision systems are consistently accurate, do not become bored, and are of modest cost. These systems are vastly superior to individuals trying to perform these tasks.

Robots

Robot
A flexible machine with the ability to hold, move, or grab items. It functions through electronic impulses that activate motors and switches.

When a machine is flexible and has the ability to hold, move, and perhaps "grab" items, we tend to use the word *robot*. **Robots** are mechanical devices that use electronic impulses to activate motors and switches. Robots may be used effectively to perform tasks that are especially monotonous or dangerous or those that can be improved by the substitution of mechanical for human effort. Such is the case when consistency, accuracy, speed, strength, or power can be enhanced by the substitution of machines for people. Ford, for example, uses robots to do 98% of the welding and most of the painting on some automobiles.

Automated Storage and Retrieval Systems (ASRSs)

Automated storage and retrieval system (ASRS)
Computer-controlled warehouses that provide for the automatic placement of parts into and from designated places in a warehouse.

Because of the tremendous labor involved in error-prone warehousing, computer-controlled warehouses have been developed. These systems, known as **automated storage and retrieval systems (ASRSs)**, provide for the automatic placement and withdrawal of parts and products into and from designated places in a warehouse. Such systems are commonly used in distribution facilities of retailers such as Walmart, Tupperware, and Benetton. These systems are also found in inventory and test areas of manufacturing firms.

Sophisticated process control is required to monitor complex processes that vary from beer at Anheuser-Busch, to steel at Nucor, to nuclear reactors at Dominion Resources (shown here).

Automated Guided Vehicles (AGVs)

Automated material handling can take the form of monorails, conveyors, robots, or automated guided vehicles. **Automated guided vehicles (AGVs)** are electronically guided and controlled carts used in manufacturing and warehousing to move parts and equipment. They are also used in offices to move mail and in hospitals and in jails to deliver supplies and meals.

Automated guided vehicle (AGV)
Electronically guided and controlled cart used to move materials.

Flexible Manufacturing Systems (FMSs)

When a central computer provides instructions to each workstation *and* to the material-handling equipment such as robots, ASRSs and AGVs (as just noted above), the system is known as an automated work cell or, more commonly, a **flexible manufacturing system (FMS)**. An FMS is flexible because both the material-handling devices and the machines themselves are controlled by easily changed electronic signals (computer programs). Operators simply load new programs, as necessary, to produce different products. The result is a system that can economically produce low volume but high variety. For example, the Lockheed Martin facility, near Dallas, efficiently builds one-of-a-kind spare parts for military aircraft. The costs associated with changeover and low utilization have been reduced substantially. FMSs bridge the gap between product-focused and process-focused facilities.

Flexible manufacturing system (FMS)
A system that uses electronic signals from a centralized computer to automate production and material flow.

Computer-Integrated Manufacturing (CIM)

Flexible manufacturing systems can be extended backward electronically into the engineering and inventory control departments and forward to the warehousing and shipping departments. In this way, computer-aided design (CAD) generates the necessary electronic instructions to run a numerically controlled machine. In a computer-integrated manufacturing environment, a design change initiated at a CAD terminal can result in that change being made in the part produced on the shop floor in a matter of minutes. When this capability is integrated with inventory control, warehousing, and shipping as a part of a flexible manufacturing system, the entire system is called **computer-integrated manufacturing (CIM)** (Figure 9).

Computer-integrated manufacturing (CIM)
A manufacturing system in which CAD, FMS, inventory control, warehousing, and shipping are integrated.

Flexible manufacturing systems and computer-integrated manufacturing are reducing the distinction between low-volume/high-variety and high-volume/low-variety production. Information technology is allowing FMS and CIM to handle increasing variety while expanding to include a growing range of volumes.

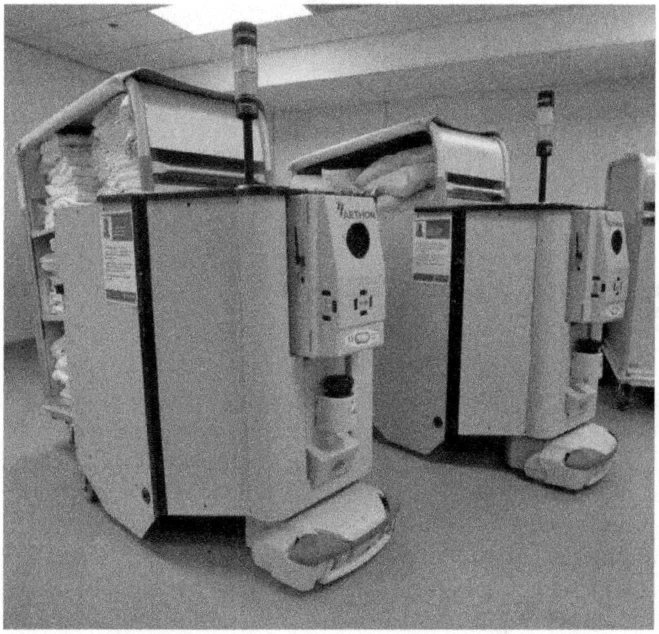

Automated guided vehicles (AGVs) such as these *TUGs* from Aethon are used extensively for routine delivery tasks. Here they are transporting clean linens in a hospital.

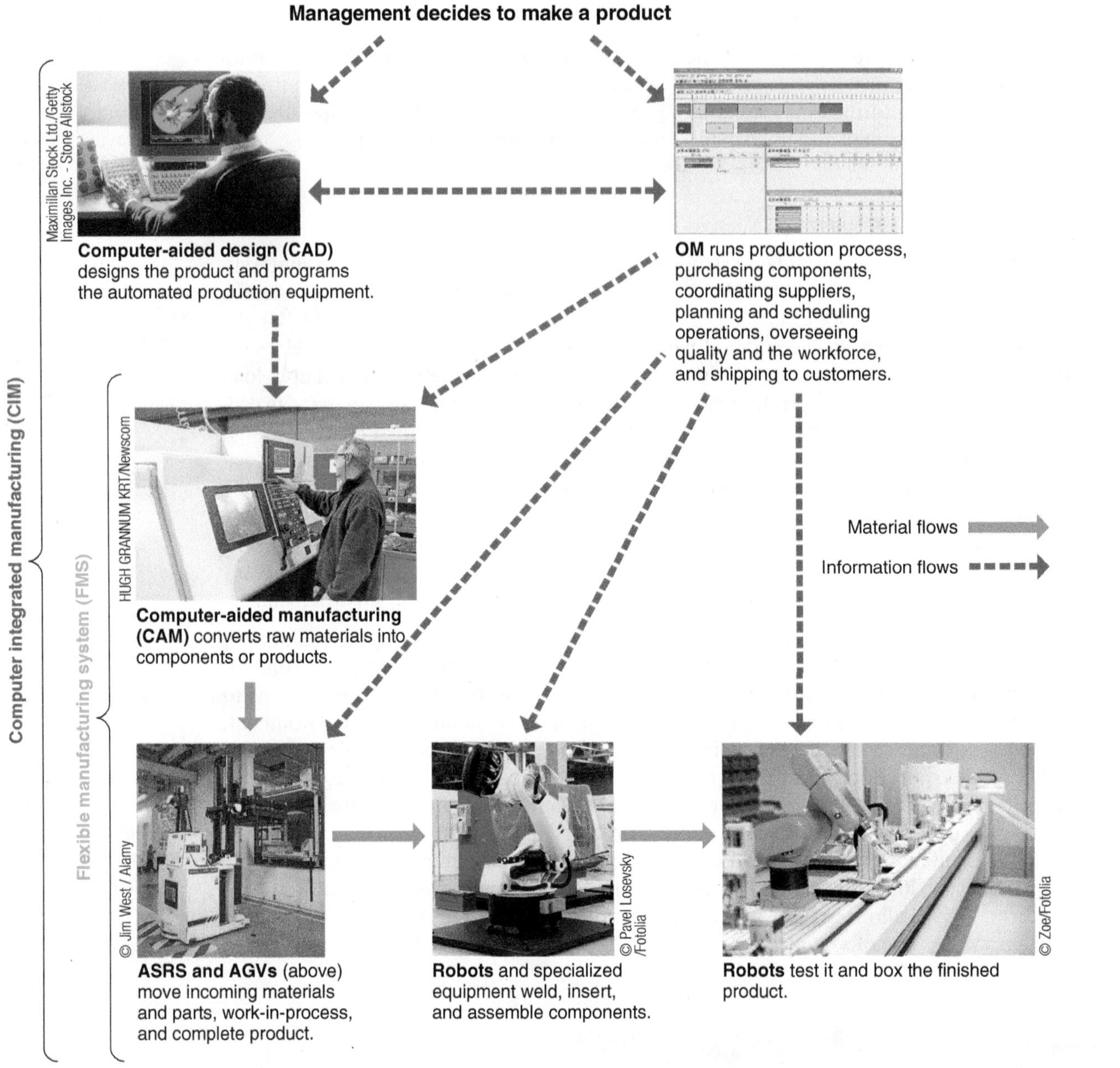
Management decides to make a product
Maximillan Stock Ltd./Getty Images Inc. - Stone Allstock
Computer-aided design (CAD) designs the product and programs the automated production equipment.
OM runs production process, purchasing components, coordinating suppliers, planning and scheduling operations, overseeing quality and the workforce, and shipping to customers.
HUGH GRANNUM KRT/Newscom
Computer-aided manufacturing (CAM) converts raw materials into components or products.
Material flows
Information flows
Computer integrated manufacturing (CIM)
Flexible manufacturing system (FMS)
© Jim West / Alamy
ASRS and AGVs (above) move incoming materials and parts, work-in-process, and complete product.
© Pavel Losevsky /Fotolia
Robots and specialized equipment weld, insert, and assemble components.
© Zoe/Fotolia
Robots test it and box the finished product.

Figure 9

Computer-Integrated Manufacturing (CIM)

CIM includes computer-aided design (CAD), computer-aided manufacturing (CAM), flexible manufacturing systems (FMSs), automated storage and retrieval systems (ASRSs), automated guided vehicles (AGVs), and robots to provide an integrated and flexible manufacturing process.

Technology in Services

Just as we have seen rapid advances in technology in the manufacturing sector, so we also find dramatic changes in the service sector. These range from electronic diagnostic equipment at auto repair shops, to blood- and urine-testing equipment in hospitals, to retinal security scanners at airports. The hospitality industry provides other examples, as discussed in the *OM in Action* box "Technology Changes the Hotel Industry." The McDonald's approach is to use self-serve kiosks. The labor savings when ordering and speedier checkout service provide valuable productivity increases for both the restaurant and the customer.

In retail stores, POS terminals download prices quickly to reflect changing costs or market conditions, and sales are tracked in 15-minute segments to aid scheduling. Drug companies, such

OM in Action Technology Changes the Hotel Industry

Technology is introducing "intelligent rooms" to the hotel industry. Hotel management can now precisely track a maid's time through the use of a security system. When a maid enters a room, a card is inserted that notifies the front-desk computer of the maid's location. "We can show her a printout of how long she takes to do a room," says one manager.

Security systems also enable guests to use their own credit cards as keys to unlock their doors. There are also other uses for the system. The computer can bar a guest's access to the room after checkout time and automatically control the air conditioning or heat, turning it on at check-in and off at checkout.

Minibars are now equipped with sensors that alert the central computer system at the hotel when an item is removed. Such items are immediately billed to the room. And now, with a handheld infrared unit, housekeeping staff can check, from the hallway, to see if a room is physically occupied. This both eliminates the embarrassment of having a hotel staffer walk in on a guest and improves security for housekeepers.

At Loew's Portofino Bay Hotel at Universal Studios, Orlando, guest smart cards act as credit cards in both the theme park and the hotel, and staff smart cards (programmed for different levels of security access) create an audit trail of employee movement. At the Mandarin Oriental Hotel in Las Vegas, guests arriving in their rooms after check-in are greeted by the drapes opening, lights turning on, and the TV displaying a customized message with the guest's name.

Sources: New York Times (November 10, 2008); *Hotel and Motel Management* (November 5, 2007); and **Hotel Marketing.com** (March 28, 2011).

as Purdue Pharma LP, track critical medications with radio frequency identification (RFID) tags to reduce counterfeiting and theft.

Table 4 provides a glimpse of the impact of technology on services. Operations managers in services, as in manufacturing, must be able to evaluate the impact of technology on their firm. This ability requires particular skill when evaluating reliability, investment analysis, human resource requirements, and maintenance/service.

TABLE 4 Examples of Technology's Impact on Services

SERVICE INDUSTRY	EXAMPLE
Financial Services	Debit cards, electronic funds transfer, automatic teller machines, Internet stock trading, online banking via cell phone
Education	Online newspapers and journals, interactive assignments via WebCT, Blackboard, and smartphones
Utilities and government	Automated one-person garbage trucks, optical mail scanners, flood-warning systems, meters that allow homeowners to control energy usage and costs
Restaurants and foods	Wireless orders from waiters to the kitchen, robot butchering, transponders on cars that track sales at drive-throughs
Communications	Interactive TV, e-books via Kindle
Hotels	Electronic check-in/check-out, electronic key/lock systems, mobile Web bookings
Wholesale/retail trade	Point-of-sale (POS) terminals, e-commerce, electronic communication between store and supplier, bar-coded data, RFID
Transportation	Automatic toll booths, satellite-directed navigation systems, Wi-Fi in automobiles
Health care	Online patient-monitoring systems, online medical information systems, robotic surgery
Airlines	Ticketless travel, scheduling, Internet purchases, boarding passes downloaded as two-dimensional bar codes on smartphones

Pharmaceutical companies are counting on RFID to aid the tracking and tracing of drugs in the distribution system to reduce losses that total over $30 billion a year.

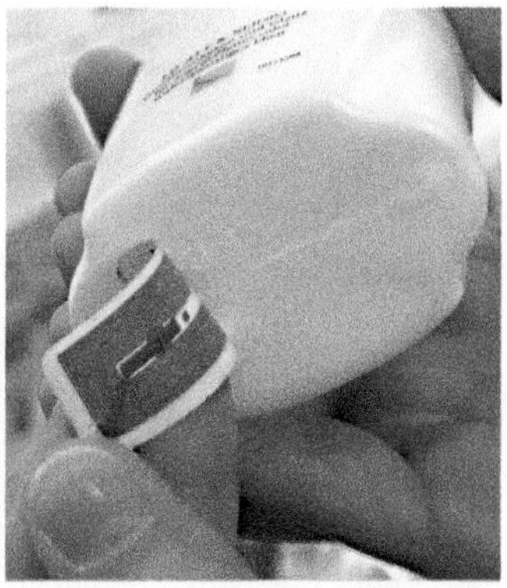

Kruell/laif/Redux Photos

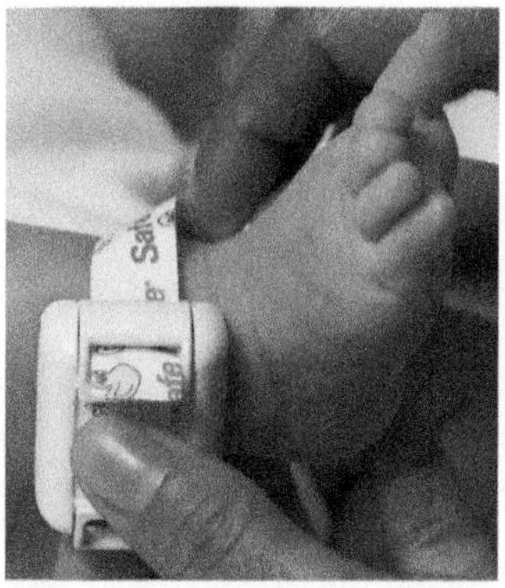

Safe Place Infant Security Solution tracks infants with small, lightweight RFID transmitters and soft, comfortable banding. For instance, when a protected infant approaches a monitored exit, the transmitter triggers the exit's lock and notifies staff to ensure a fast response.

Process Redesign

Process redesign
The fundamental rethinking of business processes to bring about dramatic improvements in performance.

Often a firm finds that the initial assumptions of its process are no longer valid. The world is a dynamic place, and customer desires, product technology, and product mix change. Consequently, processes are redesigned. Process redesign (sometimes called process reengineering) is the fundamental rethinking of business processes to bring about dramatic improvements in performance. Effective process redesign relies on reevaluating the purpose of the process and questioning both purpose and underlying assumptions. It works only if the basic process and its objectives are reexamined.

Process redesign also focuses on those activities that cross functional lines. Because managers are often in charge of specific "functions" or specialized areas of responsibility, those activities (processes) that cross from one function or specialty to another may be neglected. Redesign casts aside all notions of how the process is currently being done and focuses on dramatic improvements in cost, time, and customer value. Any process is a candidate for radical redesign. The process can be a factory layout, a purchasing procedure, a new way of processing credit applications, or a new order-fulfillment process.

Shell Lubricants, for example, reinvented its order-fulfillment process by replacing a group of people who handled different parts of an order with one individual who does it all. As a result, Shell has cut the cycle time of turning an order into cash by 75%, reduced operating expenses by 45%, and boosted customer satisfaction 105%—all by introducing a new way of handling orders. Time, cost, and customer satisfaction—the dimension of performance shaped by operations—get major boosts from operational innovation.

Summary

Effective operations managers understand how to use process strategy as a competitive weapon. They select a production process with the necessary quality, flexibility, and cost structure to meet product and volume requirements. They also seek creative ways to combine the low unit cost of high-volume, low-variety manufacturing with the customization available through low-volume, high-variety facilities. Managers use the techniques of lean production and employee participation to encourage the development of efficient equipment and processes. They design their equipment and processes to have capabilities beyond the tolerance required by their customers, while ensuring the flexibility needed for adjustments in technology, features, and volumes.

Key Terms

Process strategy
Process focus
Modules
Repetitive process
Product focus
Mass customization
Build-to-order (BTO)
Postponement
Crossover chart
Flexibility
Flowchart
Time-function mapping (or process mapping)
Value-stream mapping (VSM)
Process charts
Service blueprinting
Computer numerical control (CNC)
Automatic identification system (AIS)
Radio frequency identification (RFID)
Process control
Vision systems
Robot
Automated storage and retrieval system (ASRS)
Automated guided vehicle (AGV)
Flexible manufacturing system (FMS)
Computer-integrated manufacturing (CIM)
Process redesign

Ethical Dilemma

For the sake of efficiency and lower costs, Premium Standard Farms of Princeton, Missouri, has turned pig production into a standardized product-focused process. Slaughterhouses have done this for a hundred years—but after the animal was dead. Doing it while the animal is alive is a relatively recent innovation. Here is how it works.

Impregnated female sows wait for 40 days in metal stalls so small that they cannot turn around. After an ultrasound test, they wait 67 days in a similar stall until they give birth. Two weeks after delivering 10 or 11 piglets, the sows are moved back to breeding rooms for another cycle. After 3 years, the sow is slaughtered. Animal-welfare advocates say such confinement drives pigs crazy. Premium Standard replies that its hogs are in fact comfortable, arguing that only 1% die before Premium Standard wants them to and that their system helps reduce the cost of pork products.

Discuss the productivity and ethical implications of this industry and these two divergent opinions.

Glenda M. Powers/Shutterstock

Discussion Questions

1. What is process strategy?
2. What type of process is used for making each of the following products?
   - **(a)** beer
   - **(b)** wedding invitations
   - **(c)** automobiles
   - **(d)** paper
   - **(e)** Big Macs
   - **(f)** custom homes
   - **(g)** motorcycles
3. What is service blueprinting?
4. What is process redesign?
5. What are the techniques for improving service productivity?
6. Name the four quadrants of the service process matrix. Discuss how the matrix is used to classify services into categories.
7. What is CIM?
8. What do we mean by a process-control system, and what are the typical elements in such systems?
9. Identify *manufacturing* firms that compete on each of the four processes shown in Figure 1.
10. Identify the competitive advantage of each of the four firms identified in Discussion Question 9.
11. Identify *service* firms that compete on each of the four processes shown in Figure 1.
12. Identify the competitive advantage of each of the four firms identified in Discussion Question 11.
13. What are numerically controlled machines?
14. Describe briefly what an automatic identification system (AIS) is and how service organizations could use AIS to increase productivity and at the same time increase the variety of services offered.
15. Name some of the advances being made in technology that enhance production and productivity.
16. Explain what a flexible manufacturing system (FMS) is.
17. In what ways do CAD and FMS connect?

Solved Problem

Virtual Office Hours help is available at www.myomlab.com.

SOLVED PROBLEM 1

Bagot Copy Shop has a volume of 125,000 black-and-white copies per month. Two salespeople have made presentations to Gordon Bagot for machines of equal quality and reliability. The *Print Shop 5* has a cost of \$2,000 per month and a variable cost of \$.03. The other machine (a *Speed Copy 100*) will cost only \$1,500 per month but the toner is more expensive, driving the cost per copy up to \$.035. If cost and volume are the only considerations, which machine should Bagot purchase?

SOLUTION

$$2{,}000 + .03X = 1{,}500 + .035X$$
$$2{,}000 - 1{,}500 = .035X - .03X$$
$$500 = .005X$$
$$100{,}000 = X$$

Because Bagot expects his volume to exceed 100,000 units, he should choose the *Print Shop 5*.

Problems

Note: Px means the problem may be solved with POM for Windows and/or Excel OM.

• **1** Prepare a flowchart for one of the following:
a) the registration process at a school
b) the process at the local car wash
c) a shoe shine
d) some other process with the approval of the instructor

• **2** Prepare a process chart for one of the activities in Problem 1.

•• **3** Prepare a time-function map for one of the activities in Problem 1.

•• **4** Prepare a service blueprint for one of the activities in Problem 1.

• **5** Borges Machine Shop, Inc., has a 1-year contract for the production of 200,000 gear housings for a new off-road vehicle. Owner Luis Borges hopes the contract will be extended and the volume increased next year. Borges has developed costs for three alternatives. They are general-purpose equipment (GPE), flexible manufacturing system (FMS), and expensive, but efficient, dedicated machine (DM). The cost data follow:

	GENERAL-PURPOSE EQUIPMENT (GPE)	FLEXIBLE MANUFACTURING SYSTEM (FMS)	DEDICATED MACHINE (DM)
Annual contracted units	200,000	200,000	200,000
Annual fixed cost	$100,000	$200,000	$500,000
Per unit variable cost	$ 15.00	$ 14.00	$ 13.00

Which process is best for this contract? Px

• **6** Using the data in Problem 5, determine the economical volume for each process. Px

• **7** Using the data in Problem 5, determine the best process for each of the following volumes: (1) 75,000, (2) 275,000, and (3) 375,000.

• **8** Refer to Problem 5. If a contract for the second and third years is pending, what are the implications for process selection?

•• **9** Stan Fawcett's company is considering producing a gear assembly that it now purchases from Salt Lake Supply, Inc. Salt Lake Supply charges $4 per unit, with a minimum order of 3,000 units. Stan estimates that it will cost $15,000 to set up the process and then $1.82 per unit for labor and materials.
a) Draw a graph illustrating the crossover (or indifference) point.
b) Determine the number of units where either choice has the same cost. Px

•• **10** Ski Boards, Inc., wants to enter the market quickly with a new finish on its ski boards. It has three choices: (a) Refurbish the old equipment at a cost of $800, (b) make major modifications at a cost of $1,100, or (c) purchase new equipment at a net cost of $1,800. If the firm chooses to refurbish the equipment, materials and labor will be $1.10 per board. If it chooses to make modifications, materials and labor will be $0.70 per board. If it buys new equipment, variable costs are estimated to be $.40 per board.
a) Graph the three total cost lines on the same chart.
b) Which alternative should Ski Boards, Inc., choose if it thinks it can sell more than 3,000 boards?
c) Which alternative should the firm use if it thinks the market for boards will be between 1,000 and 2,000? Px

Eric Limon/Shutterstock

•• **11** Tim Urban, owner/manager of Urban's Motor Court in Key West, is considering outsourcing the daily room cleanup for his motel to Duffy's Maid Service. Tim rents an average of 50 rooms for each of 365 nights (365 × 50 equals the total rooms rented for the year). Tim's cost to clean a room is $12.50. The Duffy's Maid Service quote is $18.50 per room plus a fixed cost of $25,000 for sundry items such as uniforms with the motel's name. Tim's annual fixed cost for space, equipment, and supplies is $61,000. Which is the preferred process for Tim, and why? Px

•• **12** Matthew Bailey, as manager of Designs by Bailey, is upgrading his CAD software. The high-performance (HP) software rents for $3,000 per month per workstation. The standard-performance (SP) software rents for $2,000 per month per workstation. The productivity figures that he has available suggest that the HP software is faster for his kind of design. Therefore, with the HP software he will need five engineers and with the SP software he will need six. This translates into a variable cost of $200 per drawing for the HP system and $240 per drawing for the SP system. At his projected volume of 80 drawings per month, which system should he rent? Px

•• **13** Using Figure 5 in the discussion of value-stream mapping as a starting point, analyze an opportunity for improvement in a process with which you are familiar and develop an improved process.

••• **14** Metters Cabinets, Inc., needs to choose a production method for its new office shelf, the Maxistand. To help accomplish this, the firm has gathered the following production cost data:

PROCESS TYPE	ANNUALIZED FIXED COST OF PLANT & EQUIP.	*VARIABLE COSTS (PER UNIT) ($)* LABOR	MATERIAL	ENERGY
Mass Customization	$1,260,000	30	18	12
Intermittent	$1,000,000	24	26	20
Repetitive	$1,625,000	28	15	12
Continuous	$1,960,000	25	15	10

Metters Cabinets projects an annual demand of 24,000 units for the Maxistand. The Maxistand will sell for $120 per unit.
a) Which process type will maximize the annual profit from producing the Maxistand?
b) What is the value of this annual profit? Px

CASE STUDIES

Rochester Manufacturing's Process Decision

Rochester Manufacturing Corporation (RMC) is considering moving some of its production from traditional numerically controlled machines to a flexible manufacturing system (FMS). Its computer numerical control machines have been operating in a high-variety, low-volume manner. Machine utilization, as near as it can determine, is hovering around 10%. The machine tool salespeople and a consulting firm want to put the machines together in an FMS. They believe that a $3 million expenditure on machinery and the transfer machines will handle about 30% of RMC's work. There will, of course, be transition and startup costs in addition to this.

The firm has not yet entered all its parts into a comprehensive group technology system, but believes that the 30% is a good estimate of products suitable for the FMS. This 30% should fit very nicely into a "family." A reduction, because of higher utilization, should take place in the number of pieces of machinery. The firm should be able to go from 15 to about 4 machines, and personnel should go from 15 to perhaps as low as 3. Similarly, floor space reduction will go from 20,000 square feet to about 6,000. Throughput of orders should also improve with processing of this family of parts in 1 to 2 days rather than 7 to 10. Inventory reduction is estimated to yield a one-time $750,000 savings, and annual labor savings should be in the neighborhood of $300,000.

Although the projections all look very positive, an analysis of the project's return on investment showed it to be between 10% and 15% per year. The company has traditionally had an expectation that projects should yield well over 15% and have payback periods of substantially less than 5 years.

Discussion Questions

1. As a production manager for RMC, what do you recommend? Why?
2. Prepare a case by a conservative plant manager for maintaining the status quo until the returns are more obvious.
3. Prepare the case for an optimistic sales manager that you should move ahead with the FMS now.

Process Analysis at Arnold Palmer Hospital

Video Case

The Arnold Palmer Hospital (APH) in Orlando, Florida, is one of the busiest and most respected hospitals for the medical treatment of children and women in the U.S. Since its opening on golfing legend Arnold Palmer's birthday September 10, 1989, more than 1.6 million children and women have passed through its doors. It is the fourth busiest labor and delivery hospital in the U.S. and one of the largest neonatal intensive care units in the Southeast. APH ranks in the top 10% of hospitals nationwide in patient satisfaction.

"Part of the reason for APH's success," says Executive Director Kathy Swanson, "is our continuous improvement process. Our goal is 100% patient satisfaction. But getting there means constantly examining and reexamining everything we do, from patient flow, to cleanliness, to layout space, to a work-friendly environment, to speed of medication delivery from the pharmacy to a patient. Continuous improvement is a huge and never-ending task."

One of the tools the hospital uses consistently is process charts [like those in Figures 4 to 7 in this text. Staffer Diane Bowles, who carries the title "clinical practice improvement consultant," charts scores of processes. Bowles's flowcharts help study ways to improve the turnaround of a vacated room (especially important in a hospital that has pushed capacity for years), speed up the admission process, and deliver warm meals warm.

Lately, APH has been examining the flow of maternity patients (and their paperwork) from the moment they enter the hospital until they are discharged, hopefully with their healthy baby, a day or two later. The flow of maternity patients follows these steps:

1. Enter APH's Labor & Delivery (L&D) check-in desk entrance.
2. If the baby is born en route or if birth is imminent, the mother and baby are taken directly to Labor & Delivery on the second floor and registered and admitted directly at the bedside. If there are no complications, the mother and baby go to Step 6.
3. If the baby is *not* yet born, the front desk asks if the mother is preregistered. (Most do preregister at the 28- to 30-week pregnancy mark.) If she is not, she goes to the registration office on the first floor.
4. The pregnant woman is then taken to L&D Triage on the 8th floor for assessment. If she is in active labor, she is taken to an L&D room on the 2nd floor until the baby is born. If she is not ready, she goes to Step 5.
5. Pregnant women not ready to deliver (i.e., no contractions or false alarms) are either sent home to return on a later date and reenter the system at that time, or if contractions are not yet close enough, they are sent to walk around the hospital grounds (to encourage progress) and then return to L&D Triage at a prescribed time.
6. When the baby is born, if there are no complications, after 2 hours the mother and baby are transferred to a "mother–baby care unit" room on floors 3, 4, or 5 for an average of 40–44 hours.
7. If there *are* complications with the mother, she goes to an operating room and/or intensive care unit. From there, she goes back to a mother–baby care room upon stabilization—or is discharged at another time if not stabilized. Complications for the baby may result in a stay in the neonatal intensive care unit (NICU) before transfer to the baby nursery near the mother's room. If the baby is not stable enough for discharge with the mother, the baby is discharged later.
8. Mother and/or baby, when ready, are discharged and taken by wheelchair to the discharge exit for pickup to travel home.

Discussion Questions*

1. As Diane's new assistant, you need to flowchart this process. Explain how the process might be improved once you have completed the chart.
2. If a mother is scheduled for a Caesarean-section birth (i.e., the baby is removed from the womb surgically), how would this flowchart change?
3. If *all* mothers were electronically (or manually) preregistered, how would the flowchart change? Redraw the chart to show your changes.
4. Describe in detail a process that the hospital could analyze, besides the ones mentioned in this case.

*You may wish to view the video that accompanies this case before addressing these questions.

Process Strategy at Wheeled Coach

Video Case

Wheeled Coach, based in Winter Park, Florida, is the world's largest manufacturer of ambulances. Working four 10-hour days each week, 350 employees make only custom-made ambulances; virtually every vehicle is unique. Wheeled Coach accommodates the marketplace by providing a wide variety of options and an engineering staff accustomed to innovation and custom design. Continuing growth, which now requires that more than 20 ambulances roll off the assembly line each week, makes process design a continuing challenge. Wheeled Coach's response has been to build a focused factory: Wheeled Coach builds nothing but ambulances. Within the focused factory, Wheeled Coach established work cells for every major module feeding an assembly line, including aluminum bodies, electrical wiring harnesses, interior cabinets, windows, painting, and upholstery.

Labor standards drive the schedule so that every work cell feeds the assembly line on schedule, just-in-time for installations. The chassis, usually that of a Ford truck, moves to a station at which the aluminum body is mounted. Then the vehicle is moved to painting. Following a custom paint job, it moves to the assembly line, where it will spend 7 days. During each of these 7 workdays, each work cell delivers its respective module to the appropriate position on the assembly line. During the first day, electrical wiring is installed; on the second day, the unit moves forward to the station at which cabinetry is delivered and installed, then to a window and lighting station, on to upholstery, to fit and finish, to further customizing, and finally to inspection and road testing.

Discussion Questions*

1. Why do you think major auto manufacturers do not build ambulances?
2. What is an alternative process strategy to the assembly line that Wheeled Coach currently uses?
3. Why is it more efficient for the work cells to prepare "modules" and deliver them to the assembly line than it would be to produce the component (e.g., interior upholstery) on the line?
4. How does Wheeled Coach manage the tasks to be performed at each work station?

*You may wish to view the video that accompanies this case before addressing these questions.

- **Additional Case Study:** Visit **www.myomlab.com** or **www.pearsonhighered.com/heizer** for this free case study:
Matthew Yachts, Inc.: Examines a possible process change as the market for yachts changes.

Bibliography

Davenport, T. H. "The Coming Commoditization of Processes." *Harvard Business Review* 83, no. 6 (June 2005): 101–108.

Debo, L. G., L. B. Toktay, and L. N. Van Wassenhove. "Market Segmentation and Product Technology Selection for Remanufacturable Products." *Management Science* 51, no. 8 (August 2005): 1193–1205.

Duray, R., P. T. Ward, G. W. Milligan, and W. L. Berry. "Approaches to Mass Customization: Configurations and Empirical Validation." *Journal of Operations Management* 18, no. 6 (November 2000): 605–625.

Duray, R. "Mass Customization Origins: Mass or Custom Manufacturing." *International Journal of Operations and Production Management* 22, no. 3 (2002): 314–328.

Hall, Joseph M., and M. Eric Johnson. "When Should a Process Be Art, Not Science?" *Harvard Business Review* 87, no. 3 (March 2009): 58–65.

Hegde, V. G., et al. "Customization: Impact on Product and Process Performance." *Production and Operations Management* 14, no. 4 (Winter 2005): 388–399.

Inderfurth, Karl, I. M. Langella. "An Approach for Solving Disassembly-to-order Problems under Stochastic Yields." In *Logistik Management.* Heidelberg: Physica, 2004: 309–331.

Rugtusanatham, M. Johnny, and Fabrizio Salvador. "From Mass Production to Mass Customization." *Production and Operations Management* 17, no. 3 (May–June 2008): 385–396.

Swamidass, Paul M. *Innovations in Competitive Manufacturing*. Dordrecht, NL: Kluwer, 2000.

Welborn, Cliff. "Mass Customization." *OR/MS Today* (December 2007): 38–42.

Zhang, M., Y. Qi, and X. Zhao. "The Impact of Mass Customization Practices on Performance." *International Journal of Mass Customization* 4, no. 1–2 (2011): 44–66.

Zipkin, Paul. "The Limits of Mass Customization." *MIT Sloan Management Review* 40, no. 1 (Spring 2001): 81–88.

APPENDIX

SOLUTIONS TO EVEN-NUMBERED PROBLEMS

2

PROCESS CHART

Present Method [X] Proposed Method [ ]
SUBJECT CHARTED Shoe Shine DATE 1/15/13
CHART BY J.C.
DEPARTMENT SHEET NO. 1 OF 1

DIST. IN FEET	TIME IN MINS.	CHART SYMBOLS	PROCESS DESCRIPTION
	.67	○⇨□D▽	Clean/Brush Shoes
1.	.05	○⇨□D▽	Obtain Polish
	.5	○⇨□D▽	Open and Apply Polish
	.75	○⇨□D▽	Buff
	.05	○⇨□D▽	Inspect
	.25	○⇨□D▽	Collect Payment
1.	2.27	4 1 1	Totals

4

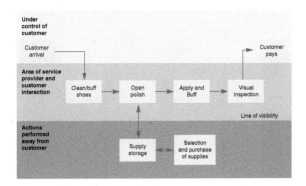

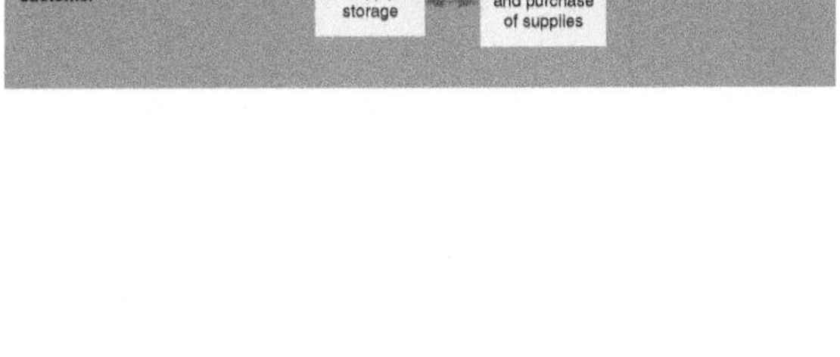

6 GPE is best below 100,000.
FMS is best between 100,000 and 300,000.
DM is best over 300,000.

8 Optimal process will change at 100,000 and 300,000.

10 **(a)**

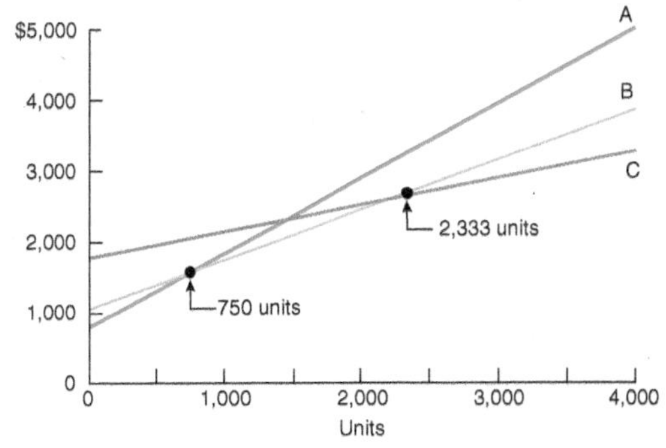

(b) Plan c
(c) Plan b

12 Rent HP software since projected volume of 80 is above the crossover point of 75.

14 **(a)** Intermittent
(b) $200,000

Rapid Review

Main Heading	Review Material	MyOMLab
FOUR PROCESS STRATEGIES	■ **Process strategy**—An organization's approach to transforming resources into goods and services. *The objective of a process strategy is to build a production process that meets customer requirements and product specifications within cost and other managerial constraints.* Virtually every good or service is made by using some variation of one of four process strategies. ■ **Process focus**—A facility organized around processes to facilitate low-volume, high-variety production. The vast majority of global production is devoted to making low-volume, high-variety products in process-focused facilities, also known as job shops or *intermittent process* facilities. Process-focused facilities have high variable costs with extremely low utilization (5% to 25%) of facilities. ■ **Modules**—Parts or components of a product previously prepared, often in a continuous process. ■ **Repetitive process**—A product-oriented production process that uses modules. The repetitive process is the classic assembly line. It allows the firm to use modules and combine the economic advantages of the product-focused model with the customization advantages of the process-focus model. ■ **Product focus**—A facility organized around products; a product-oriented, high-volume, low-variety process. Product-focused facilities are also called *continuous processes* because they have very long, continuous production runs. The specialized nature of a product-focused facility requires high fixed cost; however, low variable costs reward high facility utilization. ■ **Mass customization**—Rapid, low-cost production that caters to constantly changing unique customer desires. ■ **Build-to-order (BTO)**—Produce to customer order rather than to a forecast. Major challenges of a build-to-order system include: *Product design, Process design, Inventory management, Tight schedules* and *Responsive partners.* ■ **Postponement**—The delay of any modifications or customization to a product as long as possible in the production process. ■ **Crossover chart**—A chart of costs at the possible volumes for more than one process.	Problems: 5–12, 14 **VIDEO 1** Process Strategy at Wheeled Coach Ambulance **ACTIVE MODEL 1** **VIDEO 2** Process Analysis at Arnold Palmer Hospital Virtual Office Hours for Solved Problem: 1
SELECTION OF EQUIPMENT	Picking the best equipment involves understanding the specific industry and available processes and technology. The choice requires considering cost, quality, capacity, and flexibility. ■ **Flexibility**—The ability to respond with little penalty in time, cost, or customer value.	
PROCESS ANALYSIS AND DESIGN	Five tools of process analysis are (1) flowcharts, (2) time-function mapping, (3) value-stream mapping, (4) process charts, and (5) service blueprinting. ■ **Flowchart**—A drawing used to analyze movement of people or materials. ■ **Time-function mapping** (or **process mapping**)—A flowchart with time added on the horizontal axis. ■ **Value-stream mapping (VSM)**—A tool that helps managers understand how to add value in the flow of material and information through the entire production process. ■ **Process charts**—Charts that use symbols to analyze the movement of people or material. Process charts allow managers to focus on value-added activities and to compute the percentage of value-added time (= operation time/total time). ■ **Service blueprinting**—A process analysis technique that lends itself to a focus on the customer and the provider's interaction with the customer.	Problems: 2–3

Rapid Review continued

MyOMLab

Main Heading	Review Material
SPECIAL CONSIDERATIONS FOR SERVICE PROCESS DESIGN	Services can be classified into one of four quadrants, based on relative degrees of labor and customization: 1. *Service factory* 2. *Service shop* 3. *Mass service* 4. *Professional service* Techniques for improving service productivity include: ■ *Separation*—Structuring service so customers must go where the service is offered ■ *Self-service*—Customers examining, comparing, and evaluating at their own pace ■ *Postponement*—Customizing at delivery ■ *Focus*—Restricting the offerings ■ *Modules*—Modular selection of service; modular production ■ *Automation*—Separating services that may lend themselves to a type of automation ■ *Scheduling*—Precise personnel scheduling ■ *Training*—Clarifying the service options; explaining how to avoid problems
PRODUCTION TECHNOLOGY	■ **Computer numerical control (CNC)**—Machinery with its own computer and memory. ■ **Automatic identification system (AIS)**—A system for transforming data into electronic form (e.g., bar codes). ■ **Radio frequency identification (RFID)**—A wireless system in which integrated circuits with antennas send radio waves. ■ **Process control**—The use of information technology to control a physical process. ■ **Vision systems**—Systems that use video cameras and computer technology in inspection roles. ■ **Robot**—A flexible machine with the ability to hold, move, or grab items. ■ **Automated storage and retrieval systems (ASRS)**—Computer-controlled warehouses that provide for the automatic placement of parts into and from designated places within a warehouse. ■ **Automated guided vehicle (AGV)**—Electronically guided and controlled cart used to move materials. ■ **Flexible manufacturing system (FMS)**—Automated work cell controlled by electronic signals from a common centralized computer facility. ■ **Computer-integrated manufacturing (CIM)**—A manufacturing system in which CAD, FMS, inventory control, warehousing, and shipping are integrated.
TECHNOLOGY IN SERVICES	Many rapid technological developments have occurred in the service sector. These range from POS terminals and RFID to online newspapers and e-books.
PROCESS REDESIGN	■ **Process redesign**—The fundamental rethinking of business processes to bring about dramatic improvements in performance. Process redesign often focuses on activities that cross functional lines.

Self Test

■ **Before taking the self-test,** refer to the learning objectives listed at the beginning of the text and the key terms listed at the end of the text.

LO1. Low-volume, high-variety processes are also known as:
- **a)** continuous processes.
- **b)** process focused.
- **c)** repetitive processes.
- **d)** product focused.

LO2. A crossover chart for process selection focuses on:
- **a)** labor costs.
- **b)** material cost.
- **c)** both labor and material costs.
- **d)** fixed and variable costs.
- **e)** fixed costs.

LO3. Tools for process analysis include all of the following except:
- **a)** flowchart.
- **b)** vision systems.
- **c)** service blueprinting.
- **d)** time-function mapping.
- **e)** value-stream mapping.

LO4. Customer feedback in process design is lower as:
- **a)** the degree of customization is increased.
- **b)** the degree of labor is increased.
- **c)** the degree of customization is lowered.
- **d)** both a and b.
- **e)** both b and c.

LO5. Computer-integrated manufacturing (CIM) includes manufacturing systems that have:
- **a)** computer-aided design, direct numerical control machines, and material-handling equipment controlled by automation.
- **b)** transaction processing, a management information system, and decision support systems.
- **c)** automated guided vehicles, robots, and process control.
- **d)** robots, automated guided vehicles, and transfer equipment.

Answers: LO1. b; LO2. d; LO3. b; LO4. c; LO5. a.

Capacity and Constraint Management

OUTLINE

From Supplement 7 of *Operations Management, Sustainability and Supply Chain Management*, Eleventh Edition. Jay Heizer, Barry Render.

LEARNING OBJECTIVES

- **LO1** ***Define*** capacity
- **LO2** ***Determine*** design capacity, effective capacity, and utilization
- **LO3** ***Perform*** bottleneck analysis
- **LO4** ***Compute*** break-even
- **LO5** ***Determine*** expected monetary value of a capacity decision
- **LO6** ***Compute*** net present value

John Garrett/Getty Images Inc. - Stone Allstock

When designing a concert hall, management hopes that the forecasted capacity (the product mix—opera, symphony, and special events—and the technology needed for these events) is accurate and adequate for operation above the break-even point. However, in many concert halls, even when operating at full capacity, break-even is not achieved, and supplemental funding must be obtained.

Capacity

LO1 *Define* capacity

What should be the seating capacity of a concert hall? How many customers per day should an Olive Garden or a Hard Rock Cafe be able to serve? How large should a Frito-Lay plant be to produce 75,000 bags of Ruffles in an 8-hour shift? In this supplement we look at tools that help a manager make these decisions.

After selection of a production process, managers need to determine capacity. Capacity is the "throughput," or the number of units a facility can hold, receive, store, or produce in a given time. Capacity decisions often determine capital requirements and therefore a large portion of fixed cost. Capacity also determines whether demand will be satisfied or whether facilities will be idle. If a facility is too large, portions of it will sit unused and add cost to existing production. If a facility is too small, customers—and perhaps entire markets—will be lost. Determining facility size, with an objective of achieving high levels of utilization and a high return on investment, is critical.

Capacity
The "throughput," or number of units a facility can hold, receive, store, or produce in a period of time.

Capacity planning can be viewed in three time horizons. In Figure S1 we note that long-range capacity (generally greater than 3 years) is a function of adding facilities and equipment that have a long lead time. In the intermediate range (usually 3 to 36 months), we can add equipment, personnel, and shifts; we can subcontract; and we can build or use inventory. This is the "aggregate planning" task. In the short run (usually up to 3 months), we are primarily concerned with scheduling jobs and people, as well as allocating machinery. Modifying capacity in the short run is difficult, as we are usually constrained by existing capacity.

STUDENT TIP
Too little capacity loses customers and too much capacity is expensive. Like Goldilocks's porridge, capacity needs to be *just* right.

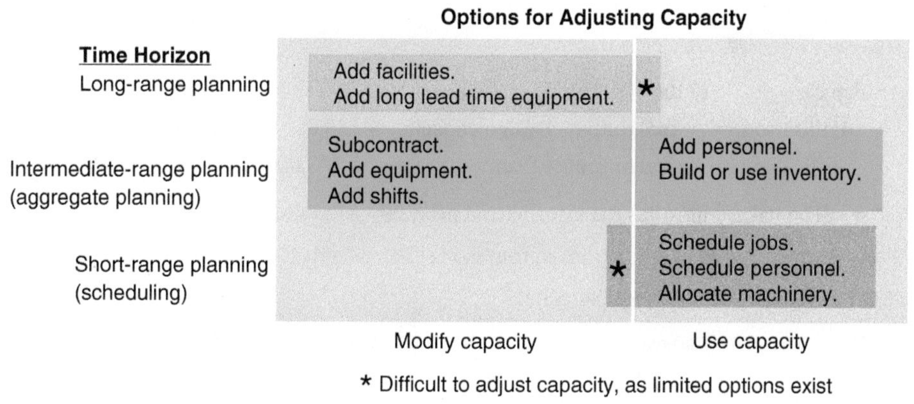

Figure **S1**

Time Horizons and Capacity Options

Design and Effective Capacity

Design capacity is the maximum theoretical output of a system in a given period under ideal conditions. It is normally expressed as a rate, such as the number of tons of steel that can be produced per week, per month, or per year. For many companies, measuring capacity can be straightforward: it is the maximum number of units the company is capable of producing in a specific time. However, for some organizations, determining capacity can be more difficult. Capacity can be measured in terms of beds (a hospital), active members (a church), or billable hours (a CPA firm). Other organizations use total work time available as a measure of overall capacity.

Design capacity
The theoretical maximum output of a system in a given period under ideal conditions.

Most organizations operate their facilities at a rate less than the design capacity. They do so because they have found that they can operate more efficiently when their resources are not stretched to the limit. For example, Ian's Bistro has tables set with 2 or 4 chairs seating a total of 270 guests. But the tables are never filled that way. Some tables will have 1 or 3 guests; tables can be pulled together for parties of 6 or 8. There are always unused chairs. *Design capacity* is 270, but *effective capacity* is often closer to 220, which is 81% of design capacity.

Effective capacity is the capacity a firm *expects* to achieve given the current operating constraints. Effective capacity is often lower than design capacity because the facility may have been designed for an earlier version of the product or a different product mix than is currently being produced.

Effective capacity
The capacity a firm can expect to achieve, given its product mix, methods of scheduling, maintenance, and standards of quality.

Two measures of system performance are particularly useful: utilization and efficiency. **Utilization** is simply the percent of *design capacity* actually achieved. **Efficiency** is the percent of *effective capacity* actually achieved. Depending on how facilities are used and managed, it may be difficult or impossible to reach 100% efficiency. Operations managers tend to be evaluated on efficiency. The key to improving efficiency is often found in correcting quality problems and in effective scheduling, training, and maintenance. Utilization and efficiency are computed below:

Utilization
Actual output as a percent of design capacity.

Efficiency
Actual output as a percent of effective capacity.

$$\text{Utilization} = \text{Actual output/Design capacity} \quad \text{(S1)}$$

$$\text{Efficiency} = \text{Actual output/Effective capacity} \quad \text{(S2)}$$

In Example S1 we determine these values.

Example S1

DETERMINING CAPACITY UTILIZATION AND EFFICIENCY

Sara James Bakery has a plant for processing *Deluxe* breakfast rolls and wants to better understand its capability. Determine the design capacity, utilization, and efficiency for this plant when producing this *Deluxe* roll.

APPROACH ▶ Last week the facility produced 148,000 rolls. The effective capacity is 175,000 rolls. The production line operates 7 days per week, with three 8-hour shifts per day. The line was designed to process the nut-filled, cinnamon-flavored *Deluxe* roll at a rate of 1,200 per hour. The firm first computes the design capacity and then uses Equation (S1) to determine utilization and Equation (S2) to determine efficiency.

SOLUTION ▶

$$\text{Design capacity} = (7 \text{ days} \times 3 \text{ shifts} \times 8 \text{ hours}) \times (1{,}200 \text{ rolls per hour}) = 201{,}600 \text{ rolls}$$
$$\text{Utilization} = \text{Actual output}/\text{Design capacity} = 148{,}000/201{,}600 = 73.4\%$$
$$\text{Efficiency} = \text{Actual output}/\text{Effective capacity} = 148{,}000/175{,}000 = 84.6\%$$

INSIGHT ▶ The bakery now has the information necessary to evaluate efficiency.

LEARNING EXERCISE ▶ If the actual output is 150,000, what is the efficiency? [Answer: 85.7%.]

RELATED PROBLEMS ▶ S1, S2, S4, S5, S7

ACTIVE **MODEL** S1 This example is further illustrated in Active Model S7.1 at **www.pearsonhighered.com/heizer.**

LO2 *Determine* design capacity, effective capacity, and utilization

Design capacity, utilization, and efficiency are all important measures for an operations manager. But managers often need to know the expected output of a facility or process. To do this, we solve for actual (or in this case, future or expected) output as shown in Equation (S3):

$$\text{Actual (or Expected) output} = (\text{Effective capacity})(\text{Efficiency}) \qquad \text{(S3)}$$

Expected output is sometimes referred to as *rated capacity*. With a knowledge of effective capacity and efficiency, a manager can find the expected output of a facility. We do so in Example S2.

Example S2

DETERMINING EXPECTED OUTPUT

The manager of Sara James Bakery (see Example S1) now needs to increase production of the increasingly popular *Deluxe* roll. To meet this demand, she will be adding a second production line.

APPROACH ▶ The manager must determine the expected output of this second line for the sales department. Effective capacity on the second line is the same as on the first line, which is 175,000 *Deluxe* rolls. The first line is operating at an efficiency of 84.6%, as computed in Example S1. But output on the second line will be less than the first line because the crew will be primarily new hires; so the efficiency can be expected to be no more than 75%. What is the expected output?

SOLUTION ▶ Use Equation (S3) to determine the expected output:

$$\text{Expected output} = (\text{Effective capacity})\,(\text{Efficiency}) = (175{,}000)\,(.75) = 131{,}250 \text{ rolls}$$

INSIGHT ▶ The sales department can now be told the expected output is 131,250 *Deluxe* rolls.

LEARNING EXERCISE ▶ After 1 month of training, the crew on the second production line is expected to perform at 80% efficiency. What is the revised expected output of *Deluxe* rolls? [Answer: 140,000.]

RELATED PROBLEMS ▶ S3, S6, S8

If the expected output is inadequate, additional capacity may be needed. Much of the remainder of this supplement addresses how to effectively and efficiently add that capacity.

Capacity and Strategy

Sustained profits come from building competitive advantage, not just from a good financial return on a specific process. Capacity decisions must be integrated into the organization's mission and strategy. Investments are not to be made as isolated expenditures, but as part of a coordinated plan that will place the firm in an advantageous position. The questions to be asked are, "Will these investments eventually win profitable customers?" and "What competitive advantage (such as process flexibility, speed of delivery, improved quality, and so on) do we obtain?"

All 10 OM decisions we discuss in this text, as well as other organizational elements such as marketing and finance, are affected by changes in capacity. Change in capacity will have sales and cash flow implications, just as capacity changes have quality, supply chain, human resource, and maintenance implications. All must be considered.

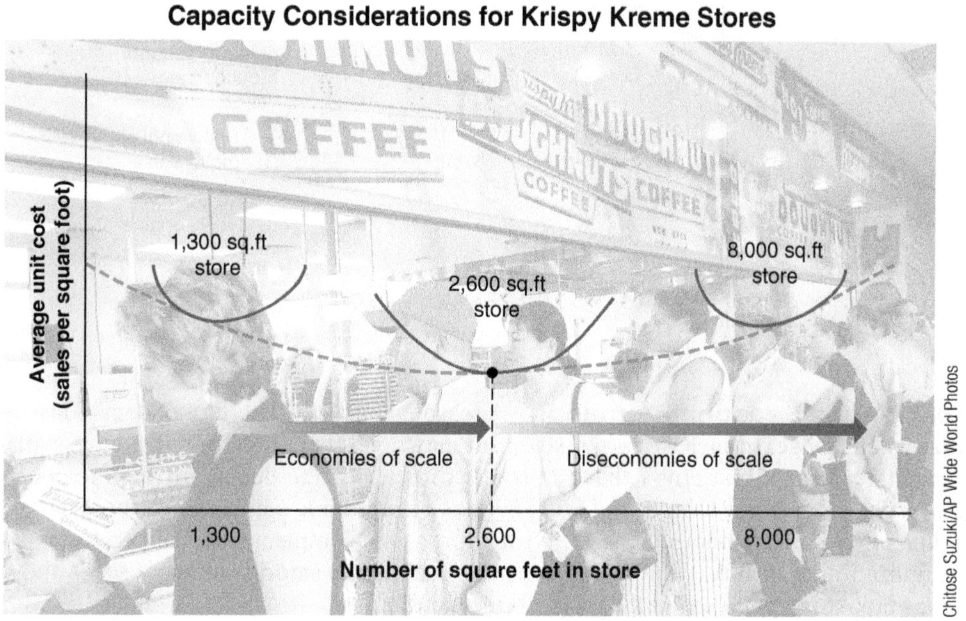

Figure S2

Economies and Diseconomies of Scale

Krispy Kreme originally had 8,000-square-foot stores but found them too large and too expensive for many markets. Then they tried tiny 1,300-square-foot stores, which required less investment, but such stores were too small to provide the mystique of seeing and smelling Krispy Kreme doughnuts being made. Krispy Kreme finally got it right with a 2,600-foot-store.

Capacity Considerations

In addition to tight integration of strategy and investments, there are four special considerations for a good capacity decision:

1. *Forecast demand accurately:* Product additions and deletions, competition actions, product life cycle, and unknown sales volumes all add challenge to accurate forecasting.
2. *Match technology increments and sales volume:* Capacity options are often constrained by technology. Some capacity increments may be large (e.g., steel mills or power plants), while others may be small (hand-crafted Louis Vuitton handbags). This complicates the difficult but necessary job of matching capacity to sales.
3. *Find the optimum operating size (volume):* Economies and diseconomies of scale often dictate an optimal size for a facility. As Figure S2 suggests, most businesses have an optimal size—at least until someone comes along with a new business model. For decades, very large integrated steel mills were considered optimal. Then along came Nucor, CMC, and other minimills, with a new process and a new business model that radically reduced the optimum size of a steel mill.
4. *Build for change:* Managers build flexibility into facilities and equipment; changes will occur in processes, as well as products, product volume, and product mix.

STUDENT TIP
Each industry and technology has an optimum size.

Next, we note that rather than strategically manage capacity, managers may tactically manage demand.

Managing Demand

Even with good forecasting and facilities built to accomodate that forecast, there may be a poor match between the actual demand that occurs and available capacity. A poor match may mean demand exceeds capacity or capacity exceeds demand. However, in both cases, firms have options.

Demand Exceeds Capacity When *demand exceeds capacity*, the firm may be able to curtail demand simply by raising prices, scheduling long lead times (which may be inevitable), and discouraging marginally profitable business. However, because inadequate facilities reduce revenue below what is possible, the long-term solution is usually to increase capacity.

Capacity Exceeds Demand When *capacity exceeds demand*, the firm may want to stimulate demand through price reductions or aggressive marketing, or it may accommodate the market through product changes. When decreasing customer demand is combined with old and inflexible processes, layoffs and plant closings may be necessary to bring capacity in line with demand.

Figure S3
By Combining Products That Have Complementary Seasonal Patterns, Capacity Can Be Better Utilized

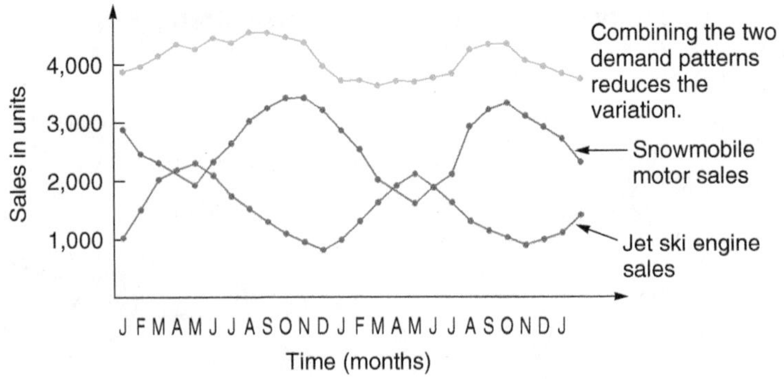

Adjusting to Seasonal Demands A seasonal or cyclical pattern of demand is another capacity challenge. In such cases, management may find it helpful to offer products with complementary demand patterns—that is, products for which the demand is high for one when low for the other. For example, in Figure S3 the firm is adding a line of snowmobile motors to its line of jet skis to smooth demand. With appropriate complementing of products, perhaps the utilization of facility, equipment, and personnel can be smoothed (as we see in the *OM in Action* box "Matching Airline Capacity to Demand").

Tactics for Matching Capacity to Demand Various tactics for adjusting capacity to demand include:

1. Making staffing changes (increasing or decreasing the number of employees or shifts)
2. Adjusting equipment (purchasing additional machinery or selling or leasing out existing equipment)
3. Improving processes to increase throughput (e.g., reducing setup times at M2 Global Technology added the equivalent of 17 shifts of capacity)
4. Redesigning products to facilitate more throughput
5. Adding process flexibility to better meet changing product preferences
6. Closing facilities

The foregoing tactics can be used to adjust demand to existing facilities. The strategic issue is, of course, how to have a facility of the correct size.

Service-Sector Demand and Capacity Management

In the service sector, scheduling customers is *demand management*, and scheduling the workforce is *capacity management*.

Joe McNally/Getty Images

Recessions (e.g., 2008–2010) and terrorist attacks (e.g., September 11, 2001) can make even the best capacity decision for an airline look bad. And excess capacity for an airline can be very expensive, with storage costs running as high as $60,000 per month per aircraft. Here, as a testimonial to excess capacity, aircraft sit idle in the Mojave Desert.

OM in Action Matching Airline Capacity to Demand

Airlines constantly struggle to control their capital expenditures and to adapt to unstable demand patterns.

Southwest and Lufthansa have each taken their own approach to increasing capacity while holding down capital investment. To manage capacity constraints on the cheap, Southwest squeezes seven flight segments out of its typical plane schedule per day—one more than most competitors. Its operations personnel find that quick ground turnaround, long a Southwest strength, is a key to this capital-saving technique.

Lufthansa has cut hundreds of millions of dollars in new jet purchases by squashing rows of seats 2 inches closer together. On the A320, for example, Lufthansa added two rows of seats, giving the plane 174 seats instead of 162. For its European fleet, this is the equivalent of having 12 more Airbus A320 jets. But Lufthansa will tell you that squeezing in more seats is not quite as bad as it sounds, as the new generation of ultra-thin seats provides passengers with more leg room. Using a strong mesh, similar to that in fancy office chairs (instead of inches of foam padding), and moving magazine pockets to the top of seat backs, there is actually more knee room than with the old chairs.

Unstable demands in the airline industry provide another capacity challenge. Seasonal patterns (e.g., fewer people fly in the winter), compounded by spikes in demand during major holidays and summer vacations, play havoc with efficient use of capacity. Airlines attack costly seasonality in several ways. First, they schedule more planes for maintenance and renovations during slow winter months, curtailing winter capacity; second, they seek out contra-seasonal routes. And when capacity is substantially above demand, placing planes in storage (as shown in the photo) may be the most economical answer.

Airlines also use revenue management to maximize per-seat pricing of available capacity, regardless of current demand patterns.

Sources: The Wall Street Journal (February 29, 2012) and (October 6, 2011).

Demand Management When demand and capacity are fairly well matched, demand management can often be handled with appointments, reservations, or a first-come, first-served rule. In some businesses, such as doctors' and lawyers' offices, an *appointment system* is the schedule and is adequate. *Reservations systems* work well in rental car agencies, hotels, and some restaurants as a means of minimizing customer waiting time and avoiding disappointment over unfilled service. In retail shops, a post office, or a fast-food restaurant, a *first-come, first-served* rule for serving customers may suffice. Each industry develops its own approaches to matching demand and capacity. Other more aggressive approaches to demand management include many variations of discounts: "early bird" specials in restaurants, discounts for matinee performances or for seats at odd hours on an airline, and cheap weekend hotel rooms.

Capacity Management When managing demand is not feasible, then managing capacity through changes in full-time, temporary, or part-time staff may be an option. This is the approach in many services. For instance, hospitals may find capacity limited by a shortage of board-certified radiologists willing to cover the graveyard shifts. Getting fast and reliable radiology readings can be the difference between life and death for an emergency room patient. As the photo below illustrates, when an overnight reading is required (and 40% of CT scans are done between 8 P.M. and 8 A.M.), the image can be sent by e-mail to a doctor in Europe or Australia for immediate analysis.

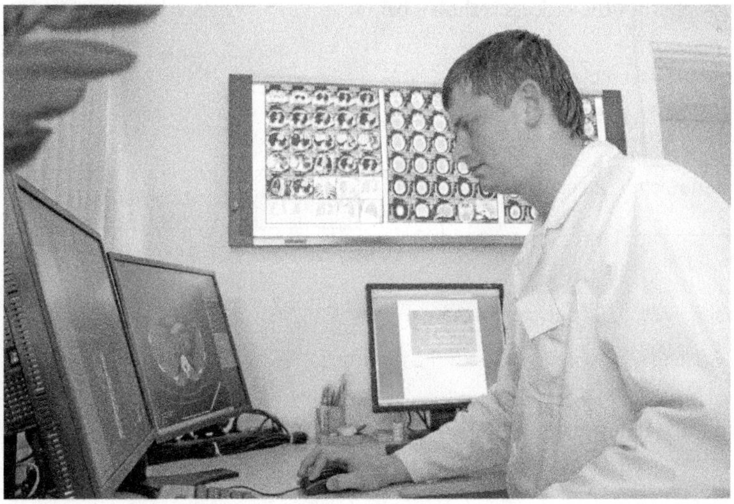

Many U.S. hospitals use services abroad to manage capacity for radiologists during night shifts. Night Hawk, an Idaho-based service with 50 radiologists in Zurich and Sydney, contracts with 900 facilities (20% of all U.S. hospitals). These trained experts, wide awake and alert in their daylight hours, usually return a diagnosis in 10 to 20 minutes, with a guarantee of 30 minutes.

Bottleneck Analysis and the Theory of Constraints

Capacity analysis
A means of determining throughput capacity of workstations or an entire production system.

Bottleneck
The limiting factor or constraint in a system.

As managers seek to match capacity to demand, decisions must be made about the size of specific operations or work areas in the larger system. Each of the interdependent work areas can be expected to have its own unique capacity. **Capacity analysis** involves determining the throughput capacity of workstations in a system and ultimately the capacity of the entire system.

A key concept in capacity analysis is the role of a constraint or bottleneck. A **bottleneck** is an operation that is the limiting factor or constraint. The term *bottleneck* refers to the literal neck of a bottle that constrains flow or, in the case of a production system, constrains throughput. A bottleneck has the lowest effective capacity of any operation in the system and thus limits the system's output. Bottlenecks occur in all facets of life—from job shops where a machine is constraining the work flow to highway traffic where two lanes converge into one inadequate lane, resulting in traffic congestion.

Bottleneck time
The time of the longest (slowest) process; the bottleneck.

The **bottleneck time** is the time of the slowest workstation (the one that takes the longest) in a production system. For example, the flowchart in Figure S4 shows a simple assembly line. Individual station times are 2, 4, and 3 minutes, respectively. The bottleneck time is 4 minutes. This is because station B is the slowest station. Even if we were to speed up station A, the entire production process would not be faster. Inventory would simply pile up in front of station B even more than now. Likewise, if station C could work faster, we could not tap its excess capacity because station B will not be able to feed products to it any faster than 1 every 4 minutes.

Figure **S4**
Three-Station Assembly Line
A box represents an operation, a triangle represents inventory, and arrows represent precedence relationships

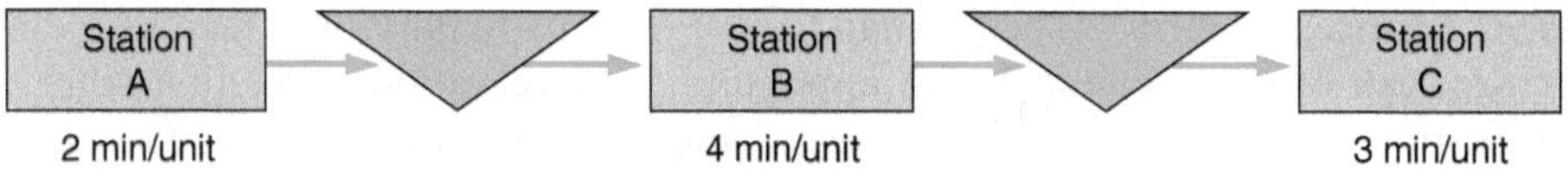

Throughput time
The time it takes for a product to go through the production process with no waiting.

The **throughput time**, on the other hand, is the time it takes a unit to go through production from start to end. The time to produce a new completed unit in Figure S4 is 9 minutes (= 2 minutes + 4 minutes + 3 minutes).

The following two examples illustrate capacity analysis for slightly more complex systems. Example S3 introduces the concept of parallel processes.

Example S3

CAPACITY ANALYSIS WITH PARALLEL PROCESSES

Howard Kraye's sandwich shop provides healthy sandwiches for customers. Howard has two identical sandwich assembly lines. A customer first places an order. The order is then sent to one of two assembly lines. Each assembly line has two workers and two operations: (1) worker 1 retrieves and cuts the bread (15 seconds/sandwich) and (2) worker 2 adds ingredients (20 seconds/sandwich) and places the sandwich onto the toaster conveyor belt. The toaster then heats the sandwich (20 seconds/sandwich). Finally, another employee wraps and packages the heated sandwich coming out of the toaster, and delivers it to the customers (37.5 seconds/sandwich). A flowchart of the process is shown below.

LO3 *Perform* bottleneck analysis

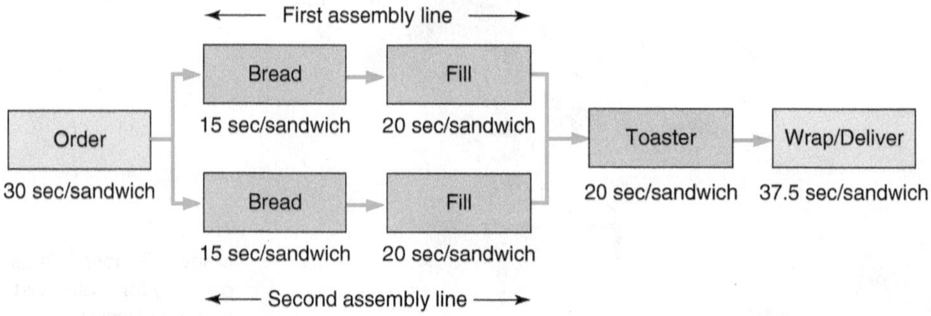

APPROACH ▶ Howard should first determine the bottleneck of the process and the throughput time of the entire operation.

SOLUTION ▶ The wrapping and delivering operation, with a time of 37.5 seconds, appears to be the bottleneck for the entire operation. The capacity per hour equals 3,600 seconds per hour/37.5 seconds per sandwich = 96 sandwiches per hour. The throughput time equals 30 + 15 + 20 + 20 + 37.5 = 122.5 seconds (or 2 minutes and 2.5 seconds), assuming no wait time in line to begin with.

INSIGHT ▶ Doubling the resources at a workstation effectively cuts the time at that station in half (If n parallel [redundant] operations are added, the time of the combined workstation operation will equal $1/n$ times the original time).

LEARNING EXERCISE ▶ If Howard hires an additional wrapper, what will be the new hourly capacity? [Answer: The new bottleneck is now the order-taking station: Capacity = 3,600 seconds per hour/30 seconds per sandwich = 120 sandwiches per hour]

RELATED PROBLEMS ▶ S9, S10, S11, S12, S13

Example 4 introduces the concept of simultaneous processing.

Example S4

CAPACITY ANALYSIS WITH SIMULTANEOUS PROCESSES

Dr. Cynthia Knott's dentistry practice has been cleaning customers' teeth for decades. The process for a basic dental cleaning is relatively straightforward: (1) the customer checks in (2 minutes); (2) a lab technician takes and develops four X-rays (2 and 4 minutes, respectively); (3) the dentist processes and examines the X-rays (5 minutes) *while* the hygienist cleans the teeth (24 minutes); (4) the dentist meets with the patient to poke at a few teeth, explain the X-ray results, and tell the patient to floss more often (8 minutes); and (5) the customer pays and books her next appointment (6 minutes). A flowchart of the customer visit is shown below.

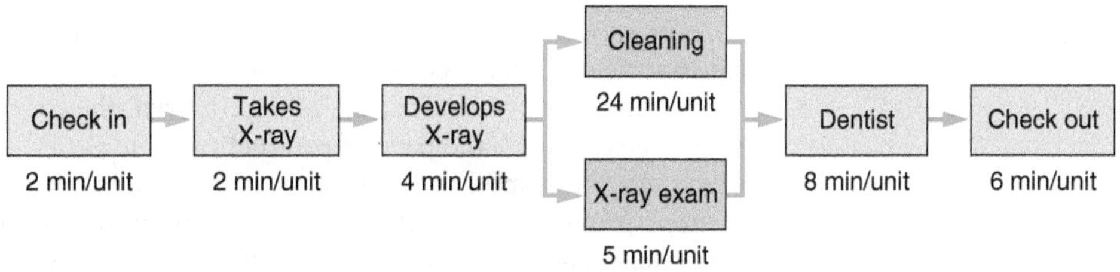

APPROACH ▶ With simultaneous processes, an order or a product is essentially *split* into different paths to be rejoined later on. To find the bottleneck time, each operation is treated separately, just as though all operations were on a sequential path. To find the throughput time, the time over *all* paths must be computed, and it is the *longest* path.

SOLUTION ▶ The bottleneck in this system is cleaning (the hygienist) at 24 minutes per patient, resulting in an hourly system capacity of 60 minutes/24 minutes per patient = 2.5 patients. The throughput time is the maximum of the two paths through the system. The path through the X-ray exam is 2 + 2 + 4 + 5 + 8 + 6 = 27 minutes, while the path through the hygienist is 2 + 2 + 4 + 24 + 8 + 6 = 46 minutes. Thus a patient should be out the door after 46 minutes (i.e., the maximum of 27 and 46).

INSIGHT ▶ With simultaneous processing, all operation times in the entire system are not simply added together to compute throughput time because some operations are occurring simultaneously. Instead, the longest path through the system is deemed the throughput time.

LEARNING EXERCISE ▶ Suppose that the same technician now has the hygienist start immediately after the X-rays are taken (allowing the hygienist to start 4 minutes sooner). The technician then develops the X-rays while the hygienist is cleaning teeth. The dentist still examines the X-rays while the teeth cleaning is occurring. What would be the new system capacity and throughput time? [Answer: The X-ray development operation is now on the parallel path with cleaning and X-ray exam, reducing the total patient visit duration by 4 minutes, for a throughput time of 42 minutes (the maximum of 27 and 42). However, the hygienist is still the bottleneck, so the capacity remains 2.5 patients per hour.]

RELATED PROBLEMS ▶ S14, S15

To summarize: (1) the *bottleneck* is the operation with the longest (slowest) process time, after dividing by the number of parallel (redundant) operations, (2) the *system capacity* is the inverse of the *bottleneck time*, and (3) the *throughput time* is the total time through the longest path in the system, assuming no waiting.

Theory of Constraints

Theory of constraints (TOC)
A body of knowledge that deals with anything that limits an organization's ability to achieve its goals.

The **theory of constraints (TOC)** has been popularized by the book *The Goal: A Process of Ongoing Improvement,* by Goldratt and Cox.[1] TOC is a body of knowledge that deals with anything that limits or constrains an organization's ability to achieve its goals. Constraints can be physical (e.g., process or personnel availability, raw materials, or supplies) or non-physical (e.g., procedures, morale, and training). Recognizing and managing these limitations through a five-step process is the basis of TOC.

Step 1: Identify the constraints.
Step 2: Develop a plan for overcoming the identified constraints.
Step 3: Focus resources on accomplishing Step 2.
Step 4: Reduce the effects of the constraints by offloading work or by expanding capability. Make sure that the constraints are recognized by all those who can have an impact on them.
Step 5: When one set of constraints is overcome, go back to Step 1 and identify new constraints.

Bottleneck Management

STUDENT TIP ☆
There are always bottlenecks; a manager must identify and manage them.

A crucial constraint in any system is the bottleneck, and managers must focus significant attention on it. We present four principles of bottleneck management:

1. *Release work orders to the system at the pace set by the bottleneck's capacity:* The theory of constraints utilizes the concept of ***drum, buffer, rope*** to aid in the implementation of bottleneck and non-bottleneck scheduling. In brief, the *drum* is the beat of the system. It provides the schedule—the pace of production. The *buffer* is the resource, usually inventory, which may be helpful to keep the bottleneck operating at the pace of the drum. Finally, the *rope* provides the synchronization or communication necessary to pull units through the system. The rope can be thought of as signals between workstations.
2. *Lost time at the bottleneck represents lost capacity for the whole system:* This principle implies that the bottleneck should always be kept busy with work. Well-trained and cross-trained employees and inspections prior to the bottleneck can reduce lost capacity at a bottleneck.
3. *Increasing the capacity of a non-bottleneck station is a mirage:* Increasing the capacity of *non-bottleneck* stations has no impact on the system's overall capacity. Working faster on a non-bottleneck station may just create extra inventory, with all of its adverse effects. This implies that non-bottlenecks should have planned idle time. Extra work or setups at non-bottleneck stations will not cause delay, which allows for smaller batch sizes and more frequent product changeovers at non-bottleneck stations.
4. *Increasing the capacity of the bottleneck increases capacity for the whole system:* Managers should focus improvement efforts on the bottleneck. Bottleneck capacity may be improved by various means, including offloading some of the bottleneck operations to another workstation (e.g., let the beer foam settle next to the tap at the bar, not under it, so the next beer can be poured), increasing capacity of the bottleneck (adding resources, working longer or working faster), subcontracting, developing alternative routings, and reducing setup times.

Even when managers have process and quality variability under control, changing technology, personnel, products, product mixes, and volumes can create multiple and shifting bottlenecks. Identifying and managing bottlenecks is a required operations task, but by definition, bottlenecks cannot be "eliminated." A system will always have at least one.

[1]See E. M. Goldratt and J. Cox, *The Goal: A Process of Ongoing Improvement*, 3rd rev. ed., Great Barrington, MA: North River Press, 2004.

Break-Even Analysis

Break-even analysis is the critical tool for determining the capacity a facility must have to achieve profitability. The objective of **break-even analysis** is to find the point, in dollars and units, at which costs equal revenue. This point is the break-even point. Firms must operate above this level to achieve profitability. As shown in Figure S5, break-even analysis requires an estimation of fixed costs, variable costs, and revenue.

Break-even analysis
A means of finding the point, in dollars and units, at which costs equal revenues.

Fixed costs are costs that continue even if no units are produced. Examples include depreciation, taxes, debt, and mortgage payments. *Variable costs* are those that vary with the volume of units produced. The major components of variable costs are labor and materials. However, other costs, such as the portion of the utilities that varies with volume, are also variable costs. The difference between selling price and variable cost is *contribution*. Only when total contribution exceeds total fixed cost will there be profit.

Another element in break-even analysis is the *revenue function*. In Figure S5, revenue begins at the origin and proceeds upward to the right, increasing by the selling price of each unit. Where the revenue function crosses the total cost line (the sum of fixed and variable costs) is the break-even point, with a profit corridor to the right and a loss corridor to the left.

Assumptions A number of assumptions underlie the basic break-even model. Notably, costs and revenue are shown as straight lines. They are shown to increase linearly—that is, in direct proportion to the volume of units being produced. However, neither fixed costs nor variable costs (nor, for that matter, the revenue function) need be a straight line. For example, fixed costs change as more capital equipment or warehouse space is used; labor costs change with overtime or as marginally skilled workers are employed; the revenue function may change with such factors as volume discounts.

Single-Product Case

LO4 *Compute* break-even

The formulas for the break-even point in units and dollars for a single product are shown below. Let:

BEP_x = break-even point in units	TR = total revenue = Px
$BEP_\$$ = break-even point in dollars	F = fixed costs
P = price per unit (after all discounts)	V = variable costs per unit
x = number of units produced	TC = total costs = $F + Vx$

The break-even point occurs where total revenue equals total costs. Therefore:

$$TR = TC \quad \text{or} \quad Px = F + Vx$$

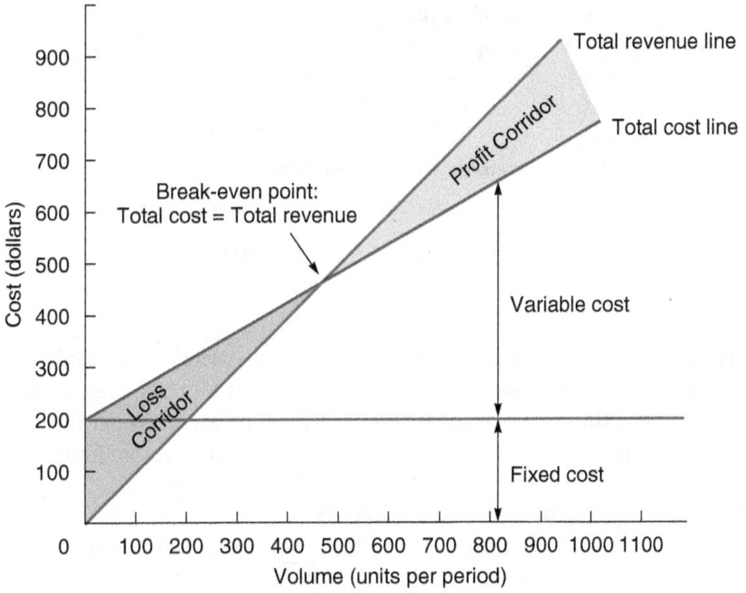

Figure S5
Basic Break-Even Point

Solving for x, we get:

$$\text{Break-even point in units } (BEP_x) = \frac{F}{P - V}$$

and:

$$\text{Break-even point in dollars } (BEP_\$) = BEP_x P = \frac{F}{P - V} P = \frac{F}{(P - V)/P} = \frac{F}{1 - V/P}$$

$$\text{Profit} = TR - TC = Px - (F + Vx) = Px - F - Vx = (P - V)x - F$$

Using these equations, we can solve directly for break-even point and profitability. The two break-even formulas of particular interest are:

$$\text{Break-even in units } (BEP_x) = \frac{\text{Total fixed cost}}{\text{Price} - \text{Variable cost}} = \frac{F}{P - V} \tag{S4}$$

$$\text{Break-even in dollars } (BEP_\$) = \frac{\text{Total fixed cost}}{1 - \dfrac{\text{Variable cost}}{\text{Price}}} = \frac{F}{1 - \dfrac{V}{P}} \tag{S5}$$

In Example S5, we determine the break-even point in dollars and units for one product.

Example S5

SINGLE PRODUCT BREAK-EVEN ANALYSIS

Stephens, Inc., wants to determine the minimum dollar volume and unit volume needed at its new facility to break even.

APPROACH ▶ The firm first determines that it has fixed costs of $10,000 this period. Direct labor is $1.50 per unit, and material is $.75 per unit. The selling price is $4.00 per unit.

SOLUTION ▶ The break-even point in dollars is computed as follows:

$$BEP_\$ = \frac{F}{1 - (V/P)} = \frac{\$10{,}000}{1 - [(1.50 + .75)/(4.00)]} = \frac{\$10{,}000}{.4375} = \$22{,}857.14$$

The break-even point in units is:

$$BEP_x = \frac{F}{P - V} = \frac{\$10{,}000}{4.00 - (1.50 + .75)} = 5{,}714$$

Note that we use total variable costs (that is, both labor and material).

INSIGHT ▶ The management of Stevens, Inc., now has an estimate in both units and dollars of the volume necessary for the new facility.

LEARNING EXERCISE ▶ If Stevens finds that fixed cost will increase to $12,000, what happens to the break-even in units and dollars? [Answer: The break-even in units increases to 6,857, and break-even in dollars increases to $27,428.57.]

RELATED PROBLEMS ▶ S16, S17, S18, S19, S20, S21, S22, S23, S24, S25

EXCEL **OM** Data File **Ch07SExS3.xls** can be found at **www.pearsonhighered.com/heizer**.

ACTIVE **MODEL** S2 This example is further illustrated in Active Model S7.2 at **www.pearsonhighered.com/heizer**.

Multiproduct Case

Most firms, from manufacturers to restaurants, have a variety of offerings. Each offering may have a different selling price and variable cost. Utilizing break-even analysis, we modify Equation (S5) to reflect the proportion of sales for each product. We do this by "weighting" each product's contribution by its proportion of sales. The formula is then:

$$\text{Break-even point in dollars } (BEP_\$) = \frac{F}{\sum\left[\left(1 - \dfrac{V_i}{P_i}\right) \times (W_i)\right]} \tag{S6}$$

Jupiter Images Royalty Free

Paper machines such as the one shown here require a high capital investment. This investment results in a high fixed cost but allows production of paper at a very low variable cost. The production manager's job is to maintain utilization above the break-even point to achieve profitability.

where V = variable cost per unit
P = price per unit
F = fixed cost
W = percent each product is of total dollar sales
i = each product

Example S6 shows how to determine the break-even point for the multiproduct case at the Le Bistro restaurant.

Example S6

MULTIPRODUCT BREAK-EVEN ANALYSIS

Le Bistro, like most other resturants, makes more than one product and would like to know its break-even point in dollars.

APPROACH ▶ Information for Le Bistro follows. Fixed costs are \$3,000 per month.

ITEM	PRICE	COST	ANNUAL FORECASTED SALES UNITS
Sandwich	\$5.00	\$3.00	9,000
Drinks	1.50	.50	9,000
Baked potato	2.00	1.00	7,000

With a variety of offerings, we proceed with break-even analysis just as in a single-product case, except that we weight each of the products by its proportion of total sales using Equation (S6).

SOLUTION ▶ Multiproduct Break-Even: Determining Contribution

1	2	3	4	5	6	7	8
ITEM (i)	SELLING PRICE (P)	VARIABLE COST (V)	(V/P)	1 − (V/P)	ANNUAL FORECASTED SALES \$	% OF SALES	WEIGHTED CONTRIBUTION (COL. 5 × COL. 7)
Sandwich	\$5.00	\$3.00	.60	.40	\$45,000	.621	.248
Drinks	1.50	0.50	.33	.67	13,500	.186	.125
Baked potato	2.00	1.00	.50	.50	14,000	.193	.097
					\$72,500	1.000	.470

Note: Revenue for sandwiches is \$45,000 (=5.00 × 9,000), which is 62.1% of the total revenue of \$72,500. Therefore, the contribution for sandwiches is "weighted" by .621. The weighted contribution is .621 × .40 = .248. In this manner, its *relative* contribution is properly reflected.

Using this approach for each product, we find that the total weighted contribution is .47 for each dollar of sales, and the break-even point in dollars is \$76,596:

$$BEP_\$ = \frac{F}{\Sigma\left[\left(1 - \frac{V_i}{P_i}\right) \times (W_i)\right]} = \frac{\$3{,}000 \times 12}{.47} = \frac{\$36{,}000}{.47} = \$76{,}596$$

The information given in this example implies total daily sales (52 weeks at 6 days each) of:

$$\frac{\$76{,}596}{312 \text{ days}} = \$245.50$$

INSIGHT ▶ The management of Le Bistro now knows that it must generate average sales of $245.50 each day to break even. Management also knows that if the forecasted sales of $72,500 are correct, Le Bistro will lose money, as break-even is $76,596.

LEARNING EXERCISE ▶ If the manager of Le Bistro wants to make an additional $1,000 per month in salary, and considers this a fixed cost, what is the new break-even point in average sales per day? [Answer: $327.33.]

RELATED PROBLEMS ▶ S26, S27

Break-even figures by product provide the manager with added insight as to the realism of his or her sales forecast. They indicate exactly what must be sold each day, as we illustrate in Example S7.

Example S7

UNIT SALES AT BREAK-EVEN

Le Bistro also wants to know the break-even for the number of sandwiches that must be sold every day.

APPROACH ▶ Using the data in Example S6, we take the forecast sandwich sales of 62.1% times the daily break-even of $245.50 divided by the selling price of each sandwich ($5.00).

SOLUTION ▶ At break-even, sandwich sales must then be:

$$\frac{.621 \times \$245.50}{5.00} = \text{Number of sandwiches} = 30.5 \approx 31 \text{ sandwiches each day}$$

INSIGHT ▶ With knowledge of individual product sales, the manager has a basis for determining material and labor requirements.

LEARNING EXERCISE ▶ At a dollar break-even of $327.33 per day, how many sandwiches must Le Bistro sell each day? [Answer: ≈ 41.]

RELATED PROBLEMS ▶ S26b, S27b

Once break-even analysis has been prepared, analyzed, and judged to be reasonable, decisions can be made about the type and capacity of equipment needed. Indeed, a better judgment of the likelihood of success of the enterprise can now be made.

Reducing Risk with Incremental Changes

When demand for goods and services can be forecast with a reasonable degree of precision, determining a break-even point and capacity requirements can be rather straightforward. But, more likely, determining the capacity and how to achieve it will be complicated, as many factors are difficult to measure and quantify. Factors such as technology, competitors, building restrictions, cost of capital, human resource options, and regulations make the decision interesting. To complicate matters further, demand growth is usually in small units, while capacity additions are likely to be both instantaneous and in large units. This contradiction adds to the capacity decision risk. To reduce risk, incremental changes that hedge demand forecasts may be a good option. Figure S6 illustrates four approaches to new capacity.

STUDENT TIP ☆ Capacity decisions require matching capacity to forecasts, which is always difficult.

Alternative Figure S6(a) *leads* capacity—that is, acquires capacity to stay ahead of demand, with new capacity being acquired at the beginning of period 1. This capacity handles increased demand until the beginning of period 2. At the beginning of period 2, new capacity is again acquired, allowing the organization to stay ahead of demand until the beginning of period 3. This process can be continued indefinitely into the future. Here capacity is acquired *incrementally*—at the beginning of period 1 *and* at the beginning of period 2.

VIDEO S1 Capacity Planning at Arnold Palmer Hospital

But managers can also elect to make a larger increase at the beginning of period 1 [Figure S6(b)]—an increase that may satisfy expected demand until the beginning of period 3. Excess capacity gives operations managers flexibility. For instance, in the hotel industry, added (extra)

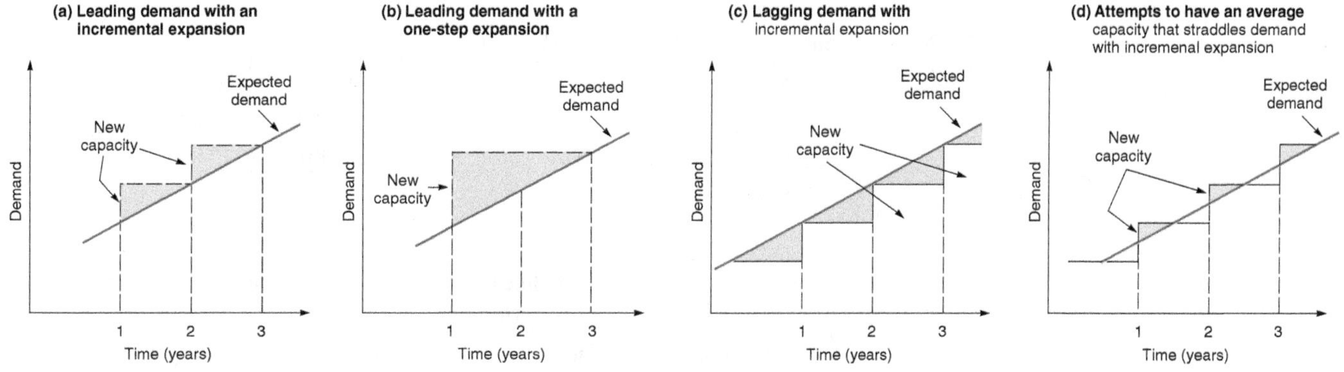

Figure S6
Four Approaches to Capacity Expansion

capacity in the form of rooms can allow a wider variety of room options and perhaps flexibility in room cleanup schedules. In manufacturing, excess capacity can be used to do more setups, shorten production runs, and drive down inventory costs.

Figure S6(c) shows an option that *lags* capacity, perhaps using overtime or subcontracting to accommodate excess demand. Finally, Figure S6(d) *straddles* demand by building capacity that is "average," sometimes lagging demand and sometimes leading it. Both the lag and straddle option have the advantage of delaying capital expenditure.

In cases where the business climate is stable, deciding between alternatives can be relatively easy. The total cost of each alternative can be computed, and the alternative with the least total cost can be selected. However, when capacity requirements are subject to significant unknowns, "probabilistic" models may be appropriate. One technique for making successful capacity planning decisions with an uncertain demand is decision theory, including the use of expected monetary value.

STUDENT TIP
Uncertainty in capacity decisions makes EMV a helpful tool.

Applying Expected Monetary Value (EMV) to Capacity Decisions

Determining expected monetary value (EMV) requires specifying alternatives and various states of nature. For capacity-planning situations, the state of nature usually is future demand or market favorability. By assigning probability values to the various states of nature, we can make decisions that maximize the expected value of the alternatives. Example S8 shows how to apply EMV to a capacity decision.

LO5 *Determine* expected monetary value of a capacity decision

Example S8

EMV APPLIED TO CAPACITY DECISION

Southern Hospital Supplies, a company that makes hospital gowns, is considering capacity expansion.

APPROACH: ▶ Southern's major alternatives are to do nothing, build a small plant, build a medium plant, or build a large plant. The new facility would produce a new type of gown, and currently the potential or marketability for this product is unknown. If a large plant is built and a favorable market exists, a profit of $100,000 could be realized. An unfavorable market would yield a $90,000 loss. However, a medium plant would earn a $60,000 profit with a favorable market. A $10,000 loss would result from an unfavorable market. A small plant, on the other hand, would return $40,000 with favorable market conditions and lose only $5,000 in an unfavorable market. Of course, there is always the option of doing nothing.

Recent market research indicates that there is a .4 probability of a favorable market, which means that there is also a .6 probability of an unfavorable market. With this information, the alternative that will result in the highest expected monetary value (EMV) can be selected.

SOLUTION ▶ Compute the EMV for each alternative:

$$\text{EMV (large plant)} = (.4)(\$100{,}000) + (.6)(-\$90{,}000) = -\$14{,}000$$
$$\text{EMV (medium plant)} = (.4)(\$60{,}000) + (.6)(-\$10{,}000) = +\$18{,}000$$
$$\text{EMV (small plant)} = (.4)(\$40{,}000) + (.6)(-\$5{,}000) = +\$13{,}000$$
$$\text{EMV (do nothing)} = \$0$$

Based on EMV criteria, Southern should build a medium plant.

INSIGHT ▶ If Southern makes many decisions like this, then determining the EMV for each alternative and selecting the highest EMV is a good decision criterion.

LEARNING EXERCISE ▶ If a new estimate of the loss from a medium plant in an unfavorable market increases to –\$20,000, what is the new EMV for this alternative? [Answer: \$12,000, which changes the decision because the small plant EMV is now higher.]

RELATED PROBLEMS ▶ S28, S29

Applying Investment Analysis to Strategy-Driven Investments

STUDENT TIP ☆ An operations manager may be held responsible for return on investment (ROI).

Once the strategy implications of potential investments have been considered, traditional investment analysis is appropriate. We introduce the investment aspects of capacity next.

Investment, Variable Cost, and Cash Flow

Because capacity and process alternatives exist, so do options regarding capital investment and variable cost. Managers must choose from among different financial options as well as capacity and process alternatives. Analysis should show the capital investment, variable cost, and cash flows as well as net present value for each alternative.

Net Present Value

Net present value
A means of determining the discounted value of a series of future cash receipts.

Determining the discount value of a series of future cash receipts is known as the net present value technique. By way of introduction, let us consider the time value of money. Say you invest \$100.00 in a bank at 5% for 1 year. Your investment will be worth \$100.00 + (\$100.00)(.05) = \$105.00. If you invest the \$105.00 for a second year, it will be worth \$105.00 + (\$105.00)(.05) = \$110.25 at the end of the second year. Of course, we could calculate the future value of \$100.00 at 5% for as many years as we wanted by simply extending this analysis. However, there is an easier way to express this relationship mathematically. For the first year:

$$\$105 = \$100(1 + .05)$$

For the second year:

$$\$110.25 = \$105(1 + .05) = \$100(1 + .05)^2$$

In general:

$$F = P(1 + i)^N \tag{S7}$$

where F = future value (such as \$110.25 or \$105)
P = present value (such as \$100.00)
i = interest rate (such as .05)
N = number of years (such as 1 year or 2 years)

LO6 *Compute* net present value

In most investment decisions, however, we are interested in calculating the present value of a series of future cash receipts. Solving for P, we get:

$$P = \frac{F}{(1 + i)^N} \tag{S8}$$

TABLE S1 Present Value of $1

YEAR	5%	6%	7%	8%	9%	10%	12%	14%
1	.952	.943	.935	.926	.917	.909	.893	.877
2	.907	.890	.873	.857	.842	.826	.797	.769
3	.864	.840	.816	.794	.772	.751	.712	.675
4	.823	.792	.763	.735	.708	.683	.636	.592
5	.784	.747	.713	.681	.650	.621	.567	.519
6	.746	.705	.666	.630	.596	.564	.507	.456
7	.711	.665	.623	.583	.547	.513	.452	.400
8	.677	.627	.582	.540	.502	.467	.404	.351
9	.645	.592	.544	.500	.460	.424	.361	.308
10	.614	.558	.508	.463	.422	.386	.322	.270
15	.481	.417	.362	.315	.275	.239	.183	.140
20	.377	.312	.258	.215	.178	.149	.104	.073

When the number of years is not too large, the preceding equation is effective. However, when the number of years, N, is large, the formula is cumbersome. For 20 years, you would have to compute $(1 + i)^{20}$. Interest-rate tables, such as Table S1, can help. We restate the present value equation:

$$P = \frac{F}{(1 + i)^N} = FX \qquad \text{(S9)}$$

where X = a factor from Table S1 defined as $= 1/(1 + i)^N$ and F = future value

Thus, all we have to do is find the factor X and multiply it by F to calculate the present value, P. The factors, of course, are a function of the interest rate, i, and the number of years, N. Table S1 lists some of these factors.

Equations (S8) and (S9) are used to determine the present value of one future cash amount, but there are situations in which an investment generates a series of uniform and equal cash amounts. This type of investment is called an *annuity*. For example, an investment might yield $300 per year for 3 years. Easy-to-use factors have been developed for the present value of annuities. These factors are shown in Table S2. The basic relationship is:

$$S = RX$$

where X = factor from Table S2
S = present value of a series of uniform annual receipts
R = receipts that are received every year for the life of the investment (the annuity)

TABLE S2 Present Value of an Annuity of $1

YEAR	5%	6%	7%	8%	9%	10%	12%	14%
1	.952	.943	.935	.926	.917	.909	.893	.877
2	1.859	1.833	1.808	1.783	1.759	1.736	1.690	1.647
3	2.723	2.673	2.624	2.577	2.531	2.487	2.402	2.322
4	3.546	3.465	3.387	3.312	3.240	3.170	3.037	2.914
5	4.329	4.212	4.100	3.993	3.890	3.791	3.605	3.433
6	5.076	4.917	4.766	4.623	4.486	4.355	4.111	3.889
7	5.786	5.582	5.389	5.206	5.033	4.868	4.564	4.288
8	6.463	6.210	5.971	5.747	5.535	5.335	4.968	4.639
9	7.108	6.802	6.515	6.247	5.985	5.759	5.328	4.946
10	7.722	7.360	7.024	6.710	6.418	6.145	5.650	5.216
15	10.380	9.712	9.108	8.559	8.060	7.606	6.811	6.142
20	12.462	11.470	10.594	9.818	9.128	8.514	7.469	6.623

The present value of a uniform annual series of amounts is an extension of the present value of a single amount, and thus Table S2 can be directly developed from Table S1. The factors for any given interest rate in Table S2 are the cumulative sum of the values in Table S1. In Table S1, for example, .943, .890, and .840 are the factors for years 1, 2, and 3 when the interest rate is 6%. The cumulative sum of these factors is 2.673. Now look at the point in Table S2 where the interest rate is 6% and the number of years is 3. The factor for the present value of an annuity is 2.673, as you would expect.

Example S9 shows how to determine the present value of an annuity.

Example S9

DETERMINING NET PRESENT VALUE OF FUTURE RECEIPTS OF EQUAL VALUE

River Road Medical Clinic is thinking of investing in a sophisticated new piece of medical equipment. It will generate $7,000 per year in receipts for 5 years.

APPROACH ▶ Determine the present value of this cash flow; assume an interest rate of 6%.

SOLUTION ▶ The factor from Table S2 (4.212) is obtained by finding that value when the interest rate is 6% and the number of years is 5:

$$S = RX = \$7{,}000(4.212) = \$29{,}484$$

INSIGHT ▶ There is another way of looking at this example. If you went to a bank and took a loan for $29,484 today, your payments would be $7,000 per year for 5 years if the bank used an interest rate of 6% compounded yearly. Thus, $29,484 is the present value.

LEARNING EXERCISE ▶ If the interest rate is 8%, what is the present value? [Answer: $27,951.]

RELATED PROBLEMS ▶ S30, S31, S32, S33, S34, S35

EXCEL OM Data File **Ch07SExS9.xls** can be found at **www.pearsonhighered.com/heizer**.

The net present value method is straightforward: You simply compute the present value of all cash flows for each investment alternative. When deciding among investment alternatives, you pick the investment with the highest net present value. Similarly, when making several investments, those with higher net present values are preferable to investments with lower net present values.

Solved Problem S4 shows how to use the net present value to choose between investment alternatives.

Although net present value is one of the best approaches to evaluating investment alternatives, it does have its faults. Limitations of the net present value approach include the following:

1. Investments with the same net present value may have significantly different projected lives and different salvage values.
2. Investments with the same net present value may have different cash flows. Different cash flows may make substantial differences in the company's ability to pay its bills.
3. The assumption is that we know future interest rates, which we do not.
4. Payments are always made at the end of the period (week, month, or year), which is not always the case.

Summary

Managers tie equipment selection and capacity decisions to the organization's missions and strategy. Four additional considerations are critical: (1) accurately forecasting demand; (2) understanding the equipment, processes, and capacity increments; (3) finding the optimum operating size; and (4) ensuring the flexibility needed for adjustments in technology, product features and mix, and volumes.

Techniques that are particularly useful to operations managers when making capacity decisions include good forecasting, bottleneck analysis, break-even analysis, expected monetary value, cash flow, and net present value.

The single most important criterion for investment decisions is the contribution to the overall strategic plan and the winning of profitable orders. Successful firms select the correct process and capacity.

Key Terms

Capacity
Design capacity
Effective capacity
Utilization
Efficiency
Capacity analysis
Bottleneck
Bottleneck time
Throughput time
Theory of constraints (TOC)
Break-even analysis
Net present value

Discussion Questions

1. Distinguish between design capacity and effective capacity.
2. What is effective capacity?
3. What is efficiency?
4. How is actual, or expected, output computed?
5. Explain why doubling the capacity of a bottleneck may not double the system capacity.
6. Distinguish between bottleneck time and throughput time.
7. What is the theory of constraints?
8. What are the assumptions of break-even analysis?
9. What keeps plotted revenue data from falling on a straight line in a break-even analysis?
10. Under what conditions would a firm want its capacity to lag demand? to lead demand?
11. Explain how net present value is an appropriate tool for comparing investments.
12. Describe the five-step process that serves as the basis of the theory of constraints.
13. What are the techniques available to operations managers to deal with a bottleneck operation? Which of these does not decrease throughput time?

Using Software for Break-Even Analysis

Excel, Excel OM, and POM for Windows all handle break-even and cost–volume analysis problems.

USING EXCEL

It is a straightforward task to develop the formulas to do a break-even analysis in Excel. Although we do not demonstrate the basics here, Active Model S2 provides a working example. You can see similar spreadsheet analysis in the Excel OM preprogrammed software that accompanies this text.

X USING EXCEL OM

Excel OM's Break-Even Analysis module provides the Excel formulas needed to compute the break-even points, and the solution and graphical output.

P USING POM FOR WINDOWS

Similar to Excel OM, POM for Windows also contains a break-even/cost–volume analysis module.

Solved Problems

Virtual Office Hours help is available at www.myomlab.com.

SOLVED PROBLEM S1

Sara James Bakery, described in Examples S1 and S2, has decided to increase its facilities by adding one additional process line. The firm will have two process lines, each working 7 days a week, 3 shifts per day, 8 hours per shift, with effective capacity of 300,000 rolls. This addition, however, will reduce overall system efficiency to 85%. Compute the expected production with this new effective capacity.

SOLUTION

$$\begin{aligned}\text{Expected production} &= (\text{Effective capacity})(\text{Efficiency})\\ &= 300{,}000(.85)\\ &= 255{,}000 \text{ rolls per week}\end{aligned}$$

SOLVED PROBLEM S2

Marty McDonald has a business packaging software in Wisconsin. His annual fixed cost is \$10,000, direct labor is \$3.50 per package, and material is \$4.50 per package. The selling price will be \$12.50 per package. What is the break-even point in dollars? What is break-even in units?

SOLUTION

$$BEP_{\$} = \frac{F}{1-(V/P)} = \frac{\$10{,}000}{1-(\$8.00/\$12.50)} = \frac{\$10{,}000}{.36} = \$27{,}777$$

$$BEP_x = \frac{F}{P-V} = \frac{\$10{,}000}{\$12.50-\$8.00} = \frac{\$10{,}000}{\$4.50} = 2{,}222 \text{ units}$$

SOLVED PROBLEM S3

John has been asked to determine whether the \$22.50 cost of tickets for the community dinner theater will allow the group to achieve break-even and whether the 175 seating capacity is adequate. The cost for each performance of a 10-performance run is \$2,500. The facility rental cost for the entire 10 performances is \$10,000. Drinks and parking are extra charges and have their own price and variable costs, as shown below:

1	2	3	4	5	6	7	8	9
	SELLING PRICE (P)	VARIABLE COST (V)	PERCENT VARIABLE COST (V/P)	CONTRIBUTION 1 − (V/P)	ESTIMATED QUANTITY OF SALES UNITS (SALES)	DOLLAR SALES (SALES × P)	PERCENT OF SALES	CONTRIBUTION WEIGHTED BY PERCENT SALES (COL.5 × COL. 8)
Tickets with dinner	\$22.50	\$10.50	0.467	0.533	175	\$3,938	0.741	0.395
Drinks	\$ 5.00	\$ 1.75	0.350	0.650	175	\$ 875	0.165	0.107
Parking	\$ 5.00	\$ 2.00	0.400	0.600	100	\$ 500	0.094	0.056
					450	\$5,313	1.000	0.558

SOLUTION

$$BEP_{\$} = \frac{F}{\sum\left[\left(1 - \frac{V_i}{P_i}\right) \times (W_i)\right]} = \frac{\$(10 \times 2{,}500) + \$10{,}000}{0.558} = \frac{\$35{,}000}{0.558} = \$62{,}724$$

Revenue for each performance (from column 7) = \$5,313
Total forecasted revenue for the 10 performances = (10 × \$5,313) = \$53,130
Forecasted revenue with this mix of sales shows a break-even of \$62,724

Thus, given this mix of costs, sales, and capacity John determines that the theater will not break even.

SOLVED PROBLEM S4

Your boss has told you to evaluate the cost of two machines. After some questioning, you are assured that they have the costs shown at the right. Assume:

a) The life of each machine is 3 years.
b) The company thinks it knows how to make 14% on investments no riskier than this one.

Determine via the present value method which machine to purchase.

	MACHINE A	MACHINE B
Original cost	\$13,000	\$20,000
Labor cost per year	2,000	3,000
Floor space per year	500	600
Energy (electricity) per year	1,000	900
Maintenance per year	2,500	500
Total annual cost	\$ 6,000	\$ 5,000
Salvage value	\$ 2,000	\$ 7,000

SOLUTION

		MACHINE A			*MACHINE B*		
		COLUMN 1	COLUMN 2	COLUMN 3	COLUMN 4	COLUMN 5	COLUMN 6
Now	Expense	1.000	\$13,000	\$13,000	1.000	\$20,000	\$20,000
1 yr.	Expense	.877	6,000	5,262	.877	5,000	4,385
2 yr.	Expense	.769	6,000	4,614	.769	5,000	3,845
3 yr.	Expense	.675	6,000	4,050	.675	5,000	3,375
				\$26,926			\$31,605
3 yr.	Salvage revenue	.675	\$ 2,000	−1,350	.675	\$ 7,000	−4,725
				\$25,576			\$26,880

We use 1.0 for payments with no discount applied against them (that is, when payments are made now, there is no need for a discount). The other values in columns 1 and 4 are from the 14% column and the respective year in Table S1 (for example, the intersection of 14% and 1 year is .877, etc.). Columns 3 and 6 are the products of the present value figures times the combined costs. This computation is made for each year and for the salvage value.

The calculation for machine A for the first year is:

$$.877 \times (\$2{,}000 + \$500 + \$1{,}000 + \$2{,}500) = \$5{,}262$$

The salvage value of the product is *subtracted* from the summed costs, because it is a receipt of cash. Since the sum of the net costs for machine B is larger than the sum of the net costs for machine A, machine A is the low-cost purchase, and your boss should be so informed.

SOLVED PROBLEM S5

T. Smunt Manufacturing Corp. has the process displayed below. The drilling operation occurs separately from and simultaneously with the sawing and sanding operations. The product only needs to go through one of the three assembly operations (the assembly operations are "parallel").

a) Which operation is the bottleneck?
b) What is the throughput time for the overall system?
c) If the firm operates 8 hours per day, 22 days per month, what is the monthly capacity of the manufacturing process?
d) Suppose that a second drilling machine is added, and it takes the same time as the original drilling machine. What is the new bottleneck time of the system?
e) Suppose that a second drilling machine is added, and it takes the same time as the original drilling machine. What is the new throughput time?

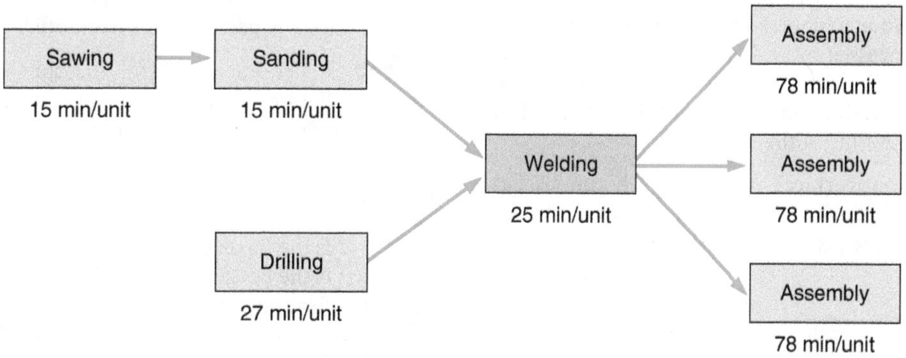

SOLUTION

a) The time for *assembly* is 78 minutes/3 operators = 26 minutes per unit, so the station that takes the longest time, hence the bottleneck, is *drilling*, at 27 minutes.
b) System throughput time is the maximum of (15 + 15 + 25 + 78), (27 + 25 + 78) = maximum of (133, 130) = 133 minutes
c) Monthly capacity = (60 minutes)(8 hours)(22 days)/27 minutes per unit = 10,560 minutes per month/27 minutes per unit = 391.11 units/month.
d) The bottleneck shifts to *Assembly*, with a time of 26 minutes per unit.
e) Redundancy does not affect throughput time. It is still 133 minutes.

Problems

Note: Px means the problem may be solved with POM for Windows and/or Excel OM.

• **S1** Amy Xia's plant was designed to produce 7,000 hammers per day but is limited to making 6,000 hammers per day because of the time needed to change equipment between styles of hammers. What is the utilization?

• **S2** For the past month, the plant in Problem S1, which has an effective capacity of 6,500, has made only 4,500 hammers per day because of material delay, employee absences, and other problems. What is its efficiency?

• **S3** If a plant has an effective capacity of 6,500 and an efficiency of 88%, what is the actual (planned) output?

• **S4** A plant has an effective capacity of 900 units per day and produces 800 units per day with its product mix; what is its efficiency?

• **S5** Material delays have routinely limited production of household sinks to 400 units per day. If the plant efficiency is 80%, what is the effective capacity?

• **S6** The effective capacity and efficiency for the next quarter at MMU Mfg. in Waco, Texas, for each of three departments are shown:

DEPARTMENT	EFFECTIVE CAPACITY	RECENT EFFICIENCY
Design	93,600	.95
Fabrication	156,000	1.03
Finishing	62,400	1.05

Compute the expected production for next quarter for each department.

•• **S7** Southeastern Oklahoma State University's business program has the facilities and faculty to handle an enrollment of 2,000 new students per semester. However, in an effort to limit class sizes to a "reasonable" level (under 200, generally), Southeastern's dean, Holly Lutze, placed a ceiling on enrollment of 1,500 new students. Although there was ample demand for business courses last semester, conflicting schedules allowed only 1,450 new students to take business courses. What are the utilization and efficiency of this system?

•• **S8** Underidealconditions,aservicebayataFastLubecan serve 6 cars per hour. The effective capacity and efficiency of a Fast Lube service bay are known to be 5.5 and 0.880, respectively. What is the minimum number of service bays Fast Lube needs to achieve an anticipated servicing of 200 cars per 8-hour day?

• **S9** A production line at V. J. Sugumaran's machine shop has three stations. The first station can process a unit in 10 minutes. The second station has two identical machines, each of which can process a unit in 12 minutes. (Each unit only needs to be processed on one of the two machines.) The third station can process a unit in 8 minutes. Which station is the bottleneck station?

• • **S10** A work cell at Chris Ellis Commercial Laundry has a workstation with two machines, and each unit produced at the station needs to be processed by both of the machines. (The same unit cannot be worked on by both machines simultaneously.) Each machine has a production capacity of 4 units per hour. What is the throughput time of the work cell?

• • **S11** The three-station work cell illustrated in Figure S7 has a product that must go through one of the two machines at station 1 (they are parallel) before proceeding to station 2.

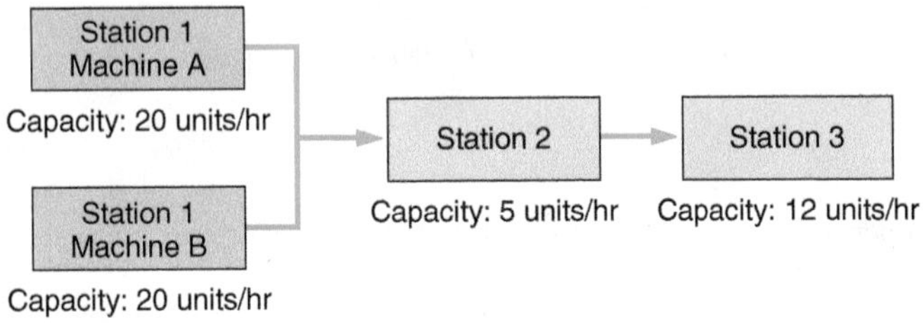

Figure **S7**

a) What is the bottleneck time of the system?
b) What is the bottleneck station of this work cell?
c) What is the throughput time?
d) If the firm operates 10 hours per day, 5 days per week, what is the weekly capacity of this work cell?

• • **S12** The three-station work cell at Pullman Mfg., Inc. is illustrated in Figure S8. It has two machines at station 1 in parallel (i.e., the product needs to go through only one of the two machines before proceeding to station 2).
a) What is the throughput time of this work cell?
b) What is the bottleneck time of this work cell?
c) What is the bottleneck station?

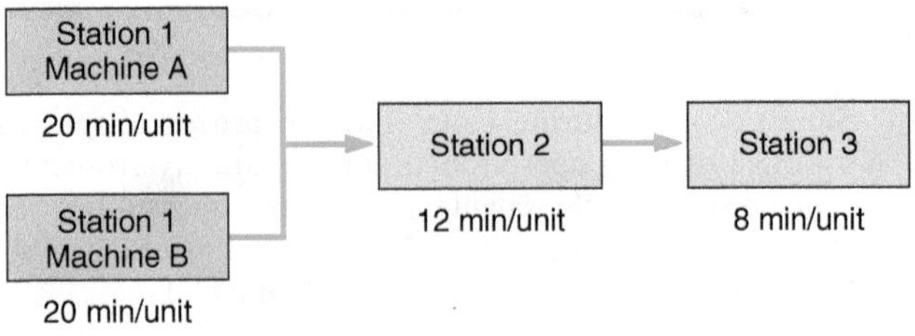

Figure **S8**

d) If the firm operates 8 hours per day, 6 days per week, what is the weekly capacity of this work cell?

• • **S13** The Pullman Mfg., Inc, three-station work cell illustrated in Figure S8 has two machines at station 1 in parallel. (The product needs to go through only one of the two machines before proceeding to station 2.) The manager, Ms. Hartley, has asked you to evaluate the system if she adds a parallel machine at station 2.
a) What is the throughput time of the new work cell?
b) What is the bottleneck time of the new work cell?
c) If the firm operates 8 hours per day, 6 days per week, what is the weekly capacity of this work cell?
d) How did the addition of the second machine at workstation 2 affect the performance of the work cell from Problem S12?

• **S14** Klassen Toy Company, Inc., assembles two parts (parts 1 and 2): Part 1 is first processed at workstation A for 15 minutes per unit and then processed at workstation B for 10 minutes per unit. Part 2 is simultaneously processed at workstation C for 20 minutes per unit. Work stations B and C feed the parts to an assembler at workstation D, where the two parts are assembled. The time at workstation D is 15 minutes.
a) What is the bottleneck of this process?
b) What is the hourly capacity of the process?

• • **S15** A production process at Kenneth Day Manufacturing is shown in Figure S9. The drilling operation occurs separately from, and simultaneously with, the sawing and sanding operations. A product needs to go through only one of the three assembly operations (the operations are in parallel).
a) Which operation is the bottleneck?
b) What is the bottleneck time?
c) What is the throughput time of the overall system?
d) If the firm operates 8 hours per day, 20 days per month, what is the monthly capacity of the manufacturing process?

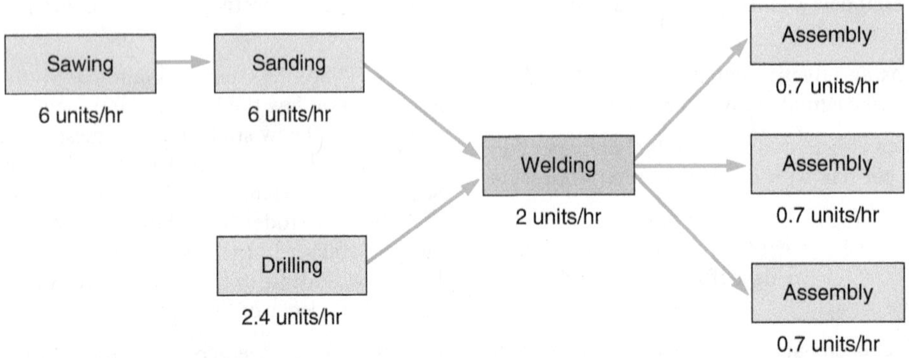

Figure **S9**

• **S16** Smithson Cutting is opening a new line of scissors for supermarket distribution. It estimates its fixed cost to be $500.00 and its variable cost to be $0.50 per unit. Selling price is expected to average $0.75 per unit.
a) What is Smithson's break-even point in units?
b) What is the break-even point in dollars? PX

• **S17** Markland Manufacturing intends to increase capacity by overcoming a bottleneck operation by adding new equipment. Two vendors have presented proposals. The fixed costs for proposal A are $50,000, and for proposal B, $70,000. The variable cost for A is $12.00, and for B, $10.00. The revenue generated by each unit is $20.00.
a) What is the break-even point in units for proposal A?
b) What is the break-even point in units for proposal B? PX

• **S18** Using the data in Problem S17:
a) What is the break-even point in dollars for proposal A if you add $10,000 installation to the fixed cost?
b) What is the break-even point in dollars for proposal B if you add $10,000 installation to the fixed cost? PX

• **S19** Given the data in Problem S17, at what volume (units) of output would the two alternatives yield the same profit? PX

•• **S20** Janelle Heinke, the owner of Ha'Peppas!, is considering a new oven in which to bake the firm's signature dish, vegetarian pizza. Oven type A can handle 20 pizzas an hour. The fixed costs associated with oven A are $20,000 and the variable costs are $2.00 per pizza. Oven B is larger and can handle 40 pizzas an hour. The fixed costs associated with oven B are $30,000 and the variable costs are $1.25 per pizza. The pizzas sell for $14 each.
a) What is the break-even point for each oven?
b) If the owner expects to sell 9,000 pizzas, which oven should she purchase?
c) If the owner expects to sell 12,000 pizzas, which oven should she purchase?
d) At what volume should Janelle switch ovens? PX

Corbis RF

•• **S21** Given the following data, calculate a) BEP_x; b) $BEP_\$$; and c) the profit at 100,000 units:

$$P = \$8/\text{unit} \quad V = \$4/\text{unit} \quad F = \$50{,}000$$ PX

•• **S22** You are considering opening a copy service in the student union. You estimate your fixed cost at $15,000 and the variable cost of each copy sold at $.01. You expect the selling price to average $.05.
a) What is the break-even point in dollars?
b) What is the break-even point in units? PX

•• **S23** An electronics firm is currently manufacturing an item that has a variable cost of $.50 per unit and a selling price of $1.00 per unit. Fixed costs are $14,000. Current volume is 30,000 units. The firm can substantially improve the product quality by adding a new piece of equipment at an additional fixed cost of $6,000. Variable cost would increase to $.60, but volume should jump to 50,000 units due to a higher-quality product. Should the company buy the new equipment? PX

•• **S24** The electronics firm in Problem S23 is now considering the new equipment and increasing the selling price to $1.10 per unit. With the higher-quality product, the new volume is expected to be 45,000 units. Under these circumstances, should the company purchase the new equipment and increase the selling price? PX

•••• **S25** Zan Azlett and Angela Zesiger have joined forces to start A&Z Lettuce Products, a processor of packaged shredded lettuce for institutional use. Zan has years of food processing experience, and Angela has extensive commercial food preparation experience. The process will consist of opening crates of lettuce and then sorting, washing, slicing, preserving, and finally packaging the prepared lettuce. Together, with help from vendors, they think they can adequately estimate demand, fixed costs, revenues, and variable cost per 5-pound bag of lettuce. They think a largely manual process will have monthly fixed costs of $37,500 and variable costs of $1.75 per bag. A more mechanized process will have fixed costs of $75,000 per month with variable costs of $1.25 per 5-pound bag. They expect to sell the shredded lettuce for $2.50 per 5-pound bag.
a) What is the break-even quantity for the manual process?
b) What is the revenue at the break-even quantity for the manual process?
c) What is the break-even quantity for the mechanized process?
d) What is the revenue at the break-even quantity for the mechanized process?
e) What is the monthly profit or loss of the *manual* process if they expect to sell 60,000 bags of lettuce per month?
f) What is the monthly profit or loss of the *mechanized* process if they expect to sell 60,000 bags of lettuce per month?
g) At what quantity would Zan and Angela be indifferent to the process selected?
h) Over what range of demand would the *manual* process be preferred over the mechanized process? Over what range of demand would the *mechanized* process be preferred over the manual process? PX

•••• **S26** As a prospective owner of a club known as the Red Rose, you are interested in determining the volume of sales dollars necessary for the coming year to reach the break-even point. You have decided to break down the sales for the club into four categories, the first category being beer. Your estimate of the beer sales is that 30,000 drinks will be served. The selling price for each unit will average $1.50; the cost is $.75. The second major category is meals, which you expect to be 10,000 units with an average price of $10.00 and a cost of $5.00. The third major category is desserts and wine, of which you also expect to sell 10,000 units, but with an average price of $2.50 per unit sold and a cost of $1.00 per unit. The final category is lunches and inexpensive sandwiches, which you expect to total 20,000 units at an average price of $6.25 with a food cost of $3.25. Your fixed cost (i.e. rent, utilities, and so on) is $1,800 per month plus $2,000 per month for entertainment.

a) What is your break-even point in dollars per month?
b) What is the expected number of meals each day if you are open 30 days a month?

••• **S27** As manager of the St. Cloud Theatre Company, you have decided that concession sales will support themselves. The following table provides the information you have been able to put together thus far:

ITEM	SELLING PRICE	VARIABLE COST	% OF REVENUE
Soft drink	$1.00	$.65	25
Wine	1.75	.95	25
Coffee	1.00	.30	30
Candy	1.00	.30	20

Last year's manager, Jim Freeland, has advised you to be sure to add 10% of variable cost as a waste allowance for all categories.

You estimate labor cost to be $250.00 (5 booths with 2 people each). Even if nothing is sold, your labor cost will be $250.00, so you decide to consider this a fixed cost. Booth rental, which is a contractual cost at $50.00 for *each* booth per night, is also a fixed cost.

a) What is the break-even volume per evening performance?
b) How much wine would you expect to sell each evening at the break-even point?

•• **S28** James Lawson's Bed and Breakfast, in a small historic Mississippi town, must decide how to subdivide (remodel) the large old home that will become its inn. There are three alternatives: Option A would modernize all baths and combine rooms, leaving the inn with four suites, each suitable for two to four adults. Option B would modernize only the second floor; the results would be six suites, four for two to four adults, two for two adults only. Option C (the status quo option) leaves all walls intact. In this case, there are eight rooms available, but only two are suitable for four adults, and four rooms will not have private baths. Below are the details of profit and demand patterns that will accompany each option:

	ANNUAL PROFIT UNDER VARIOUS DEMAND PATTERNS			
ALTERNATIVES	HIGH	P	AVERAGE	P
A (modernize all)	$90,000	.5	$25,000	.5
B (modernize 2nd)	$80,000	.4	$70,000	.6
C (status quo)	$60,000	.3	$55,000	.7

Which option has the highest expected monetary value? Px

•••• **S29** As operations manager of Holz Furniture, you must make a decision about adding a line of rustic furniture. In discussing the possibilities with your sales manager, Steve Gilbert, you decide that there will definitely be a market and that your firm should enter that market. However, because rustic furniture has a different finish than your standard offering, you decide you need another process line. There is no doubt in your mind about the decision, and you are sure that you should have a second process. But you do question how large to make it. A large process line is going to cost $400,000; a small process line will cost $300,000. The question, therefore, is the demand for rustic furniture. After extensive discussion with Mr. Gilbert and Tim Ireland of Ireland Market Research, Inc., you determine that the best estimate you can make is that there is a two-out-of-three chance of profit from sales as large as $600,000 and a one-out-of-three chance as low as $300,000.

With a large process line, you could handle the high figure of $600,000. However, with a small process line you could not and would be forced to expand (at a cost of $150,000), after which time your profit from sales would be $500,000 rather than the $600,000 because of the lost time in expanding the process. If you do not expand the small process, your profit from sales would be held to $400,000. If you build a small process and the demand is low, you can handle all of the demand.

Should you open a large or small process line?

•• **S30** What is the net present value of an investment that costs $75,000 and has a salvage value of $45,000? The annual profit from the investment is $15,000 each year for 5 years. The cost of capital at this risk level is 12%. Px

• **S31** The initial cost of an investment is $65,000 and the cost of capital is 10%. The return is $16,000 per year for 8 years. What is the net present value? Px

• **S32** What is the present value of $5,600 when the interest rate is 8% and the return of $5,600 will not be received for 15 years? Px

•• **S33** Tim Smunt has been asked to evaluate two machines. After some investigation, he determines that they have the costs shown in the following table. He is told to assume that:

1. The life of each machine is 3 years.
2. The company thinks it knows how to make 12% on investments no more risky than this one.
3. Labor and maintenance are paid at the end of the year.

	MACHINE A	MACHINE B
Original cost	$10,000	$20,000
Labor per year	2,000	4,000
Maintenance per year	4,000	1,000
Salvage value	2,000	7,000

Determine, via the present value method, which machine Tim should recommend.

•••• **S34** Your boss has told you to evaluate two ovens for Tink-the-Tinkers, a gourmet sandwich shop. After some questioning of vendors and receipt of specifications, you are assured that the ovens have the attributes and costs shown in the following table. The following two assumptions are appropriate:

1. The life of each machine is 5 years.
2. The company thinks it knows how to make 14% on investments no more risky than this one.

a) Determine via the present value method which machine to tell your boss to purchase.
b) What assumption are you making about the ovens?
c) What assumptions are you making in your methodology?

	THREE SMALL OVENS AT $1,250 EACH	TWO LARGE OVENS AT $2,500 EACH
Original cost	$3,750	$5,000
Labor per year in excess of larger models	$ 750 (total)	
Cleaning/ maintenance	$ 750 ($250 each)	$ 400 ($200 each)
Salvage value	$ 750 ($250 each)	$1,000 ($500 each)

•••• **S35** Bold's Gym, a health club chain, is considering expanding into a new location: the initial investment would be $1 million in equipment, renovation, and a 6-year lease, and its annual upkeep and expenses would be $75,000 (paid at the beginning of the year). Its planning horizon is 6 years out, and at the end, it can sell the equipment for $50,000. Club capacity is 500 members who would pay an annual fee of $600. Bold's expects to have no problems filling membership slots. Assume that the interest rate is 10%. (See Table S1.)

a) What is the present value profit/loss of the deal?
b) The club is considering offering a special deal to the members in the first year. For $3,000 upfront they get a full 6-year membership (i.e., 1 year free). Would it make financial sense to offer this deal?

Refer to MyOMLab for these additional homework problems: S7.36–S7.45

CASE STUDY

Capacity Planning at Arnold Palmer Hospital

Video Case

Since opening day, Arnold Palmer Hospital has experienced an explosive growth in demand for its services. One of only six hospitals in the U.S. to specialize in health care for women and children, Arnold Palmer Hospital has cared for over 1,500,000 patients who came to the Orlando facility from all 50 states and more than 100 other countries. With patient satisfaction scores in the top 10% of U.S. hospitals surveyed (over 95% of patients would recommend the hospital to others), one of Arnold Palmer Hospital's main focuses is delivery of babies. Originally built with 281 beds and a capacity for 6,500 births per year, the hospital steadily approached and then passed 10,000 births. Looking at Table S3, Executive Director Kathy Swanson knew an expansion was necessary.

With continuing population growth in its market area serving 18 central Florida counties, Arnold Palmer Hospital was delivering the equivalent of a kindergarten class of babies every day and still not meeting demand. Supported with substantial additional demographic analysis, the hospital was ready to move ahead with a capacity expansion plan and a new 11-story hospital building across the street from the existing facility.

Thirty-five planning teams were established to study such issues as (1) specific forecasts, (2) services that would transfer to the new facility, (3) services that would remain in the existing facility, (4) staffing needs, (5) capital equipment, (6) pro forma accounting data, and (7) regulatory requirements. Ultimately, Arnold Palmer Hospital was ready to move ahead with a budget of $100 million and a commitment to an additional 150 beds. But given the growth of the central Florida region, Swanson decided to expand the hospital in stages: the top two floors would be empty interiors ("shell") to be completed at a later date, and the fourth-floor operating room could be doubled in size when needed. "With the new facility in place, we are now able to handle up to 16,000 births per year," says Swanson.

TABLE S3 Births at Arnold Palmer Hospital

YEAR	BIRTHS
1995	6,144
1996	6,230
1997	6,432
1998	6,950
1999	7,377
2000	8,655
2001	9,536
2002	9,825
2003	10,253
2004	10,555
2005	12,316
2006	13,070
2007	14,028
2008	14,241
2009	13,050
2010	12,571
2011	12,978

Discussion Questions*

1. Given the capacity planning discussion in the text (see Figure S6), what approach is being taken by Arnold Palmer Hospital toward matching capacity to demand?
2. What kind of major changes could take place in Arnold Palmer Hospital's demand forecast that would leave the hospital with an underutilized facility (namely, what are the risks connected with this capacity decision)?
3. Use regression analysis to forecast the point at which Swanson needs to "build out" the top two floors of the new building, namely, when demand will exceed 16,000 births.

*You may wish to view the video that accompanies the case before addressing these questions.

- **Additional Case Study:** Visit **www.myomlab.com** or **www.pearsonhighered.com/heizer** for this free case study:
  Southwestern University (D): Requires the development of a multiproduct break-even solution.

Bibliography

Anupindi, Ravi, S. Deshmukh, and S. Chopra. *Managing Business Process Flows*, 2nd ed. Upper Saddle River, NJ: Prentice Hall (2007).

Bowers, John, et al. "Modeling Outpatient Capacity for a Diagnosis and Treatment Center." *Health Care Management Science* 8, no. 3 (August 2005): 205.

Chambers, Chester, Eli M. Snir, and Asad Ata. "The Use of Flexible Manufacturing Capacity in Pharmaceutical Product Introductions." *Decision Sciences* 40, no. 2 (May 2009): 243–268.

Chen, Wen-Chih, and C. Chien. "Evaluating Capacity Pooling Strategy in Semiconductor Manufacturing: A Productivity Perspective Study." *International Journal of Production Research* 49, no 12 (June 2011): 3635–3652.

Goldratt, Eliyaha. *The Choice*. Great Barrington, MA: North River Press (2009).

Goodale, John C., Rohit Verma, and Madeleine E. Pullman. "A Market Utility-Based Model for Capacity Scheduling in Mass Services." *Production and Operations Management* 12, no. 2 (Summer 2003): 165–185.

Gupta, M. C., and L. H. Boyd. "Theory of Constraints: A Theory for Operations Management." *International Journal of Operations Management* 28, no. 10 (2008): 991.

Jonsson, Patrik, and Stig-Arne Mattsson. "Use and Applicability of Capacity Planning Methods." *Production and Inventory Management Journal* (3rd/4th Quarter 2002): 89–95.

Li, Shanling, and L. Wang. "Outsourcing and Capacity Planning in an Uncertain Global Environment." *European Journal of Operational Research* 207, no. 1 (November 2010): 131–141.

May, Jerrold H., W. E. Spangler, D. P. Strum, and L. G. Vargas. "The Surgical Scheduling Problem: Current Research and Future Opportunities." *Production & Operations Management* 20, no. 3 (May–June 2011): 392–405.

Mincsovics, G. Z., and N. P. Dellaert. "Workload-Dependent Capacity Control in Production-to-Order Systems." *IIE Transactions,* 41, no. 10 (October 2009): 853–865.

Roy, Anjan. "Strategic Positioning and Capacity Utilization: Factors in Planning for Profitable Growth in Banking." *Journal of Performance Management* 23, no. 3 (November 2010): 23.

Tanrisever, Fehmi, D. Morrice, and D. Morton. "Managing Capacity Flexibility in Make-to-Order Production Environments." *European Journal of Operational Research* 216, no. 2 (January 2012): 334–345.

Tibben-Lembke, Ronald S. "Theory of Constraints at UniCo." *International Journal of Production Research* 47, no. 7 (January 2009): 1815.

Watson, Kevin J., John H. Blackstone, and Stanley C. Gardiner. "The Evolution of a Management Philosophy: The Theory of Constraints." *Journal of Operations Management* 25, no. 2 (March 2007): 387–402.

APPENDIX
SOLUTIONS TO EVEN-NUMBERED PROBLEMS

S2 69.2%

S4 88.9%

S6 Design = 88,920
Fabrication = 160,680
Finishing = 65,520

S8 5.17 (or 6) bays

S10 15 min/unit

S12 **(a)** Throughput time = 40 min
(b) Bottleneck time = 12 min.
(c) Station 2
(d) Weekly capacity = 240 units

S14 **(a)** Work station C at 20 min/unit
(b) 3 units/hr

S16 **(a)** 2,000 units
(b) $1,500

S18 **(a)** $150,000
(b) $160,000

S20 **(a)** $BEP_A = 1{,}667$;
$BEP_B = 2{,}353$
(b, c) Oven A slightly more profitable
(d) 13,333 pizzas

S22 **(a)** $18,750
(b) 375,000

S24 Yes, purchase new equipment and raise price. Profit = $2,500

S26 $BEP_{\$} = \$7{,}584.83$ per mo
Daily meals = 9

S28 Option B; $74,000

S30 $4,590

S32 NPV = $1,764

S34 **(a)** Purchase two large ovens.
(b) Equal quality, equal capacity.
(c) Payments are made at end of each time period. And future interest rates are known.

Rapid Review

Main Heading	Review Material	MyOMLab

CAPACITY

- **Capacity**—The "throughput," or number of units a facility can hold, receive, store, or produce in a period of time.

Capacity decisions often determine capital requirements and therefore a large portion of fixed cost. Capacity also determines whether demand will be satisfied or whether facilities will be idle.

Determining facility size, with an objective of achieving high levels of utilization and a high return on investment, is critical.

Capacity planning can be viewed in three time horizons:

1. *Long-range* (> 1 year)—Adding facilities and long lead-time equipment
2. *Intermediate-range* (3–18 months)—"Aggregate planning" tasks, including adding equipment, personnel, and shifts; subcontracting; and building or using inventory
3. *Short-range* (< 3 months)—Scheduling jobs and people, and allocating machinery

- **Design capacity**—The theoretical maximum output of a system in a given period, under ideal conditions.

Most organizations operate their facilities at a rate less than the design capacity.

- **Effective capacity**—The capacity a firm can expect to achieve, given its product mix, methods of scheduling, maintenance, and standards of quality.
- **Utilization**—Actual output as a percent of design capacity.
- **Efficiency**—Actual output as a percent of effective capacity.

$$\text{Utilization} = \text{Actual output}/\text{Design capacity} \qquad \text{(S1)}$$

$$\text{Efficiency} = \text{Actual output}/\text{Effective capacity} \qquad \text{(S2)}$$

$$\text{Actual (or Expected) output} = \text{(Effective capacity) (Efficiency)} \qquad \text{(S3)}$$

Expected output is sometimes referred to as *rated capacity.*

When demand exceeds capacity, a firm may be able to curtail demand simply by raising prices, increasing lead times (which may be inevitable), and discouraging marginally profitable business.

When capacity exceeds demand, a firm may want to stimulate demand through price reductions or aggressive marketing, or it may accommodate the market via product changes.

In the service sector, scheduling customers is *demand management,* and scheduling the workforce is *capacity management.*

When demand and capacity are fairly well matched, demand management in services can often be handled with appointments, reservations, or a first-come, first-served rule. Otherwise, discounts based on time of day may be used (e.g., "early bird" specials, matinee pricing).

When managing demand in services is not feasible, managing capacity through changes in full-time, temporary, or part-time staff may be an option.

MyOMLab: Problems: S1–S8

Virtual Office Hours for Solved Problem: S1

ACTIVE MODEL S1

BOTTLENECK ANALYSIS AND THE THEORY OF CONSTRAINTS

- **Capacity analysis**—Determining throughput capacity of workstations or an entire production system.
- **Bottleneck**—The limiting factor or constraint in a system.
- **Bottleneck time**—The time of the longest (slowest) process, the bottleneck.
- **Throughput time**—The time it takes for a product to go through the production process with no waiting: the longest path through the system.

If n parallel (redundant) operations are added, the process time of the combined operations will equal $1/n$ times the process time of the original.

With simultaneous processing, an order or product is essentially *split* into different paths to be rejoined later on. The longest path through the system is deemed the throughput time.

- **Theory of constraints (TOC)**—A body of knowledge that deals with anything limiting an organization's ability to achieve its goals.

MyOMLab: Problems: S9–S15

Virtual Office Hours for Solved Problem S5

Main Heading	Review Material	MyOMLab
BREAK-EVEN ANALYSIS	■ **Break-even analysis**—A means of finding the point, in dollars and units, at which costs equal revenues. *Fixed costs* are costs that exist even if no units are produced. Variable costs are those that vary with the volume of units produced. In the break-even model, costs and revenue are assumed to increase linearly. $$\text{Break-even in units} = \frac{\text{Total Fixed cost}}{\text{Price} - \text{Variable cost}} = \frac{F}{P - V} \quad \text{(S4)}$$ $$\text{Break-even in dollars} = \frac{\text{Total Fixed cost}}{1 - \dfrac{\text{Variable cost}}{\text{Price}}} = \frac{F}{1 - \left(\dfrac{V}{P}\right)} \quad \text{(S5)}$$ $$\text{Multiproduct break-even point in dollars} = BEP_{\$} = \frac{F}{\sum\left[\left(1 - \dfrac{V_i}{P_i}\right) \times (W_i)\right]} \quad \text{(S6)}$$	Problems: S16–S27 Virtual Office Hours for Solved Problem: S3 ACTIVE MODEL S2
REDUCING RISK WITH INCREMENTAL CHANGES	Demand growth is usually in small units, while capacity additions are likely to be both instantaneous and in large units. To reduce risk, incremental changes that hedge demand forecasts may be a good option. Four approaches to capacity expansion are (1) *leading* strategy, with incremental expansion, (2) *leading* strategy with one step expansion, (3) *lag* strategy, and (4) *straddle* strategy. Both lag strategy and straddle strategy delay capital expenditure.	**VIDEO S1** Capacity Planning at Arnold Palmer Hospital
APPLYING EXPECTED MONETARY VALUE	Determining expected monetary value requires specifying alternatives and various states of nature (e.g., demand or market favorability). By assigning probability values to the various states of nature, we can make decisions that maximize the expected value of the alternatives.	Problems: S28–S29
APPLYING INVESTMENT ANALYSIS TO STRATEGY-DRIVEN INVESTMENTS	■ **Net present value**—A means of determining the discounted value of a series of future cash receipts. $$F = P(1 + i)^N \quad \text{(S7)}$$ $$P = \frac{F}{(1 + i)^N} \quad \text{(S8)}$$ $$P = \frac{F}{(1 + i)^N} = FX \quad \text{(S9)}$$ When making several investments, those with higher net present values are preferable to investments with lower net present values.	Problems: S30–S35 Virtual Office Hours for Solved Problem: S4

Self Test

■ **Before taking the self-test,** refer to the learning objectives listed at the beginning of the text and the key terms listed at the end of the text.

LO1. Capacity decisions should be made on the basis of:
a) building sustained competitive advantage.
b) good financial returns.
c) a coordinated plan.
d) integration into the company's strategy.
e) all of the above.

LO2. Effective capacity is:
a) the capacity a firm expects to achieve, given the current operating constraints.
b) the percentage of design capacity actually achieved.
c) the percentage of capacity actually achieved.
d) actual output.
e) efficiency.

LO3. System capacity is based on:
a) the bottleneck.
b) throughput time.
c) time of the fastest station.
d) throughput time plus waiting time.
e) none of the above.

LO4. The break-even point is:
a) adding processes to meet the point of changing product demands.
b) improving processes to increase throughput.
c) the point in dollars or units at which cost equals revenue.
d) adding or removing capacity to meet demand.
e) the total cost of a process alternative.

LO5. Expected monetary value is most appropriate:
a) when the payoffs are equal.
b) when the probability of each decision alternative is known.
c) when probabilities are the same.
d) when both revenue and cost are known.
e) when probabilities of each state of nature are known.

LO6. Net present value:
a) is greater if cash receipts occur later rather than earlier.
b) is greater if cash receipts occur earlier rather than later.
c) is revenue minus fixed cost.
d) is preferred over break-even analysis.
e) is greater if $100 monthly payments are received in a lump sum ($1,200) at the end of the year.

Answers: LO1. e; LO2. a; LO3. a; LO4. c; LO5. b; LO6. b.

Location Strategies

OUTLINE

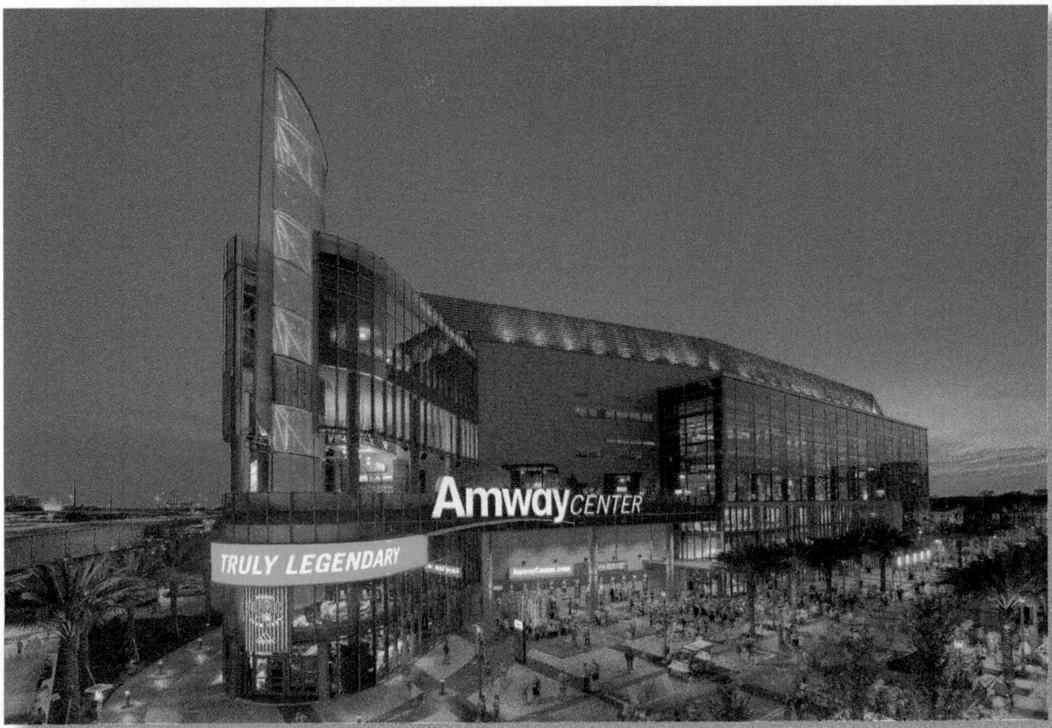

10 OM STRATEGY DECISIONS

- Design of Goods and Services
- Managing Quality
- Process Strategy
- *Location Strategies*
- Layout Strategies
- Human Resources
- Supply-Chain Management
- Inventory Management
- Scheduling
- Maintenance

GLOBAL COMPANY PROFILE
FedEx

Location Provides Competitive Advantage for FedEx

Overnight-delivery powerhouse FedEx has believed in the hub concept for its 43-year existence. Even though Fred Smith, founder and CEO, got a C on his college paper proposing a hub for small-package delivery, the idea has proven extremely successful. Starting with one central location in Memphis, Tennessee (now called its *superhub*), the $39 billion firm has added a European hub in Paris, an Asian hub in Guangzhou, China, a Latin American hub in Miami, and a Canadian hub in Toronto. FedEx's fleet of 687 planes flies into 375 airports worldwide, then delivers to the door with more than 80,000 vans and trucks.

Oliver Berg/EPA/Newscom

At the FedEx hub in Memphis, Tennessee, approximately 100 FedEx aircraft converge each night around midnight with more than 5 million documents and packages.

AP Wide World Photos

At the preliminary sorting area, packages and documents are sorted and sent to a secondary sorting area. The Memphis facility covers 1.5 million square feet; it is big enough to hold 33 football fields. Packages are sorted and exchanged until 4 A.M.

FedEx Corporation

Packages and documents that have already gone through the primary and secondary sorts are checked by city, state, and zip code. They are then placed in containers that are loaded onto aircraft for delivery to their final destinations in 215 countries.

Matt York/AP Wide World Photos

FedEx's fleet of 687 planes makes it the largest airline in the world. More than 80,000 trucks complete the delivery process.

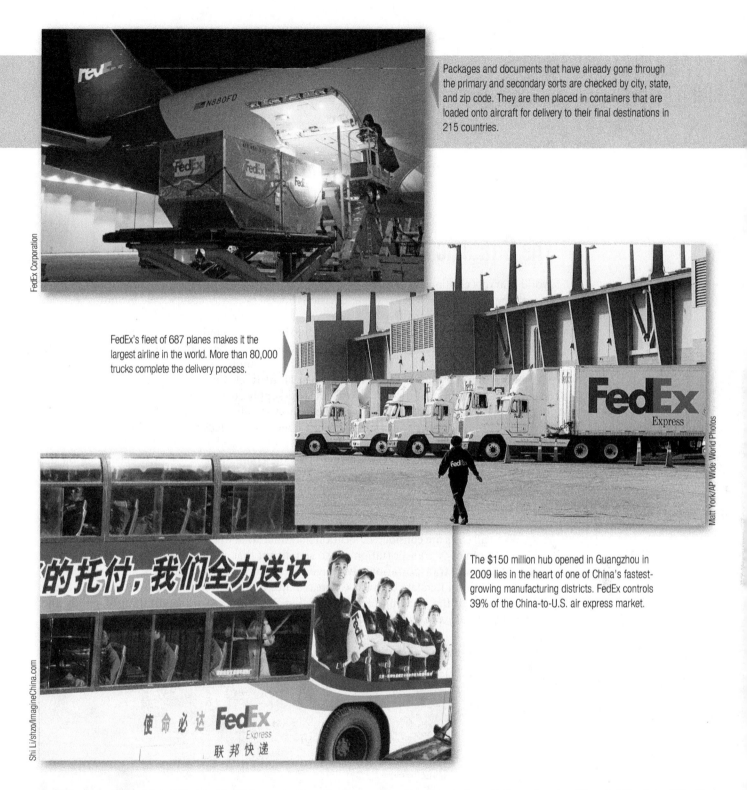

Shi Li/shzo/ImagineChina.com

The $150 million hub opened in Guangzhou in 2009 lies in the heart of one of China's fastest-growing manufacturing districts. FedEx controls 39% of the China-to-U.S. air express market.

Why was Memphis picked as FedEx's central location? (1) It is located in the middle of the U.S. (2) It has very few hours of bad weather closures, perhaps contributing to the firm's excellent flight-safety record.

Each night, except Sunday, FedEx brings to Memphis packages from throughout the world that are going to cities for which FedEx does not have direct flights. The central hub permits service to a far greater number of points with fewer aircraft than the traditional City-A-to-City-B system. It also allows FedEx to match aircraft flights with package loads each night and to reroute flights when load volume requires it, a major cost savings. Moreover, FedEx also believes that the central hub system helps reduce mishandling and delay in transit because there is total control over the packages from pickup point through delivery.

LEARNING OBJECTIVES

LO1 ***Identify*** and explain seven major factors that affect location decisions

LO2 ***Compute*** labor productivity

LO3 ***Apply*** the factor-rating method

LO4 ***Complete*** a locational cost–volume analysis graphically and mathematically

LO5 ***Use*** the center-of-gravity method

LO6 ***Understand*** the differences between service- and industrial-sector location analysis

The Strategic Importance of Location

VIDEO 1
Hard Rock's Location Selection

World markets continue to expand, and the global nature of business is accelerating. Indeed, one of the most important strategic decisions made by many companies, including FedEx, Mercedes-Benz, and Hard Rock, is where to locate their operations. When FedEx opened its Asian hub in Guangzhou, China, it set the stage for "round-the-world" flights linking its Paris and Memphis package hubs to Asia. When Mercedes-Benz announced its plans to build its first major overseas plant in Vance, Alabama, it completed a year of competition among 170 sites in 30 states and two countries. When Hard Rock Cafe opened in Moscow, it ended 3 years of advance preparation of a Russian food-supply chain. The strategic impact, cost, and international aspect of these decisions indicate how significant location decisions are.

Firms throughout the world are using the concepts and techniques of this text to address the location decision because location greatly affects both fixed and variable costs. Location has a major impact on the overall risk and profit of the company. For instance, depending on the product and type of production or service taking place, transportation costs alone can total as much as 25% of the product's selling price. That is, one-fourth of a firm's total revenue may be needed just to cover freight expenses of the raw materials coming in and finished products going out. Other costs that may be influenced by location include taxes, wages, raw material costs, and rents. When all costs are considered, location may alter total operating expenses as much as 50%.

The economics of transportation are so significant that companies—and even cities—have coalesced around a transportation advantage. For centuries, rivers and ports, and more recently rail hubs and then interstate highways, were a major ingredient in the location decision. Today airports are often the deciding factor, providing fast, low-cost transportation of goods and people. The book *Aerotropolis* defines an "airport–integration region, extending as far as

From Dubai to Chongqing to Honduras, location decisions are often taking shape in urban developments based on airport hubs. The ideal "aerotropolis" is an amalgam of office parks, cargo complexes, convention hotels, and even factories that sometimes line the runway. Welcome to the new global city.

© Kathy deWitt/Alamy

[1]John D. Kasarda and Greg Lindsay. *Aerotropolis*. New York: Farrar, Straus, and Giroux, 2011.

60 miles from the inner cluster of hotel, office, distribution, and logistics facilities."[1] The airport is not just a piece of the city but becomes an "airport city."

Companies make location decisions relatively infrequently, usually because demand has outgrown the current plant's capacity or because of changes in labor productivity, exchange rates, costs, or local attitudes. Companies may also relocate their manufacturing or service facilities because of shifts in demographics and customer demand.

Location options include (1) expanding an existing facility instead of moving, (2) maintaining current sites while adding another facility elsewhere, or (3) closing the existing facility and moving to another location.

The location decision often depends on the type of business. For industrial location decisions, the strategy is usually minimizing costs, although innovation and creativity may also be critical. For retail and professional service organizations, the strategy focuses on maximizing revenue. Warehouse location strategy, however, may be driven by a combination of cost and speed of delivery. *The objective of location strategy is to maximize the benefit of location to the firm.*

Location and Costs Because location is such a significant cost and revenue driver, location often has the power to make (or break) a company's business strategy. Key multinationals in every major industry, from automobiles to cellular phones, now have or are planning a presence in each of their major markets. Location decisions to support a low-cost strategy require particularly careful consideration.

Once management is committed to a specific location, many costs are firmly in place and difficult to reduce. For instance, if a new factory location is in a region with high energy costs, even good management with an outstanding energy strategy is starting at a disadvantage. Management is in a similar bind with its human resource strategy if labor in the selected location is expensive, ill-trained, or has a poor work ethic. Consequently, hard work to determine an optimal facility location is a good investment.

TABLE 1

Competitiveness of 142 Selected Countries, Based on Annual Surveys of 13,000 Business Executives

COUNTRY	2011–2012 RANKING
Switzerland	1
Singapore	2
Sweden	3
Finland	4
U.S.	5
⋮	
Japan	9
U.K.	10
⋮	
Canada	12
⋮	
Israel	22
⋮	
China	26
⋮	
Mexico	58
⋮	
Vietnam	65
Russia	66
⋮	
Haiti	141
Chad	142

Source: www.weforum.org, 2012. Used with permission of World Economic Forum.

Factors That Affect Location Decisions

Selecting a facility location is becoming much more complex with globalization. Globalization has taken place because of the development of (1) market economics; (2) better international communications; (3) more rapid, reliable travel and shipping; (4) ease of capital flow between countries; and (5) high differences in labor costs. Many firms now consider opening new offices, factories, retail stores, or banks outside their home country. Location decisions transcend national borders. In fact, as Figure 1 shows, the sequence of location decisions often begins with choosing a country in which to operate.

One approach to selecting a country is to identify what the parent organization believes are key success factors (KSFs) needed to achieve competitive advantage. Six possible country KSFs are listed at the top of Figure 1. Using such factors (including some negative ones, such as crime) the World Economic Forum biannually ranks the global competitiveness of 142 countries (see Table 1). Switzerland placed first because of its high rates of saving and investment, openness to trade, quality education, and efficient government.

Once a firm decides which country is best for its location, it focuses on a region of the chosen country and a community. The final step in the location decision process is choosing a specific site within a community. The company must pick the one location that is best suited for shipping and receiving, zoning, utilities, size, and cost. Again, Figure 1 summarizes this series of decisions and the factors that affect them.

Besides globalization, a number of other factors affect the location decision. Among these are labor productivity, foreign exchange, culture, changing attitudes toward the industry, and proximity to markets, suppliers, and competitors.

LO1 *Identify* and explain seven major factors that affect location decisions

Labor Productivity

When deciding on a location, management may be tempted by an area's low wage rates. However, wage rates cannot be considered by themselves, as Otis Elevator discovered when

Figure 1
Some Considerations and Factors That Affect Location Decisions

Country Decision

Key Success Factors

1. Political risks, government rules, attitudes, incentives
2. Cultural and economic issues
3. Location of markets
4. Labor talent, attitudes, productivity, costs
5. Availability of supplies, communications, energy
6. Exchange rates and currency risk

Region/Community Decision

1. Corporate desires
2. Attractiveness of region (culture, taxes, climate, etc.)
3. Labor availability, costs, attitudes toward unions
4. Cost and availability of utilities
5. Environmental regulations of state and town
6. Government incentives and fiscal policies
7. Proximity to raw materials and customers
8. Land/construction costs

Site Decision

1. Site size and cost
2. Air, rail, highway, and waterway systems
3. Zoning restrictions
4. Proximity of services/supplies needed
5. Environmental impact issues

LO2 *Compute* labor productivity

it opened its plant in Mexico (see the *OM in Action* box "Otis Elevator Pulls the Plug on Mexico"). Management must also consider productivity.

Differences exist in productivity in various countries. What management is really interested in is the combination of production and the wage rate. For example, if Otis Elevator pays \$70 per day with 60 units produced per day in South Carolina, it will spend less on labor than at a Mexican plant that pays \$25 per day with production of 20 units per day:

$$\frac{\text{Labor cost per day}}{\text{Production (units per day)}} = \text{Labor cost per unit}$$

1. Case 1: South Carolina plant:

$$\frac{\$70 \text{ Wages per day}}{60 \text{ Units produced per day}} = \frac{\$70}{60} = \$1.17 \text{ per unit}$$

OM in Action Otis Elevator Pulls the Plug on Mexico

Globalization has come full circle at Otis Elevator Co. The U.S. manufacturer, whose elevators zip up and down structures from the Empire State Building to the Eiffel Tower, is pulling the plug on the Mexican factory it opened in 1998. The new plant's location: South Carolina. More startling: Otis says the move will save it money.

As the cost of producing in Mexican *macquiladoras* (there are some 3,000 such assembly plants employing almost 1 million workers) has risen, international companies such as Otis, GE, and Ford have started returning jobs to the U.S. When Otis moved to Mexico, "It was clearly for cost-related reasons," says the firm's CEO.

Times have changed, and Otis's new automated facility in South Carolina will undercut Mexican production costs by using advanced automation and fewer workers. But it will also be closer to its customers—about 70% of whom are on the U.S. East Coast—which should save 17% on freight and logistics. The new layout will place designers and engineers in the same building as final assembly for the first time. "We really needed to rationalize our supply chain, and the way to do it was to do everything in one place," adds the CEO.

Sources: The Wall Street Journal (October 6, 2011); *BusinessWeek* (September 16, 2011); and *South Carolina Now* (July 7, 2011).

2. Case 2: Juarez, Mexico, plant:

$$\frac{\$25 \text{ Wages per day}}{20 \text{ Units produced per day}} = \frac{\$25}{20} = \$1.25 \text{ per unit}$$

Employees with poor training, poor education, or poor work habits may not be a good buy even at low wages. By the same token, employees who cannot or will not always reach their places of work are not much good to the organization, even at low wages. (Labor cost per unit is sometimes called the *labor content* of the product.)

STUDENT TIP
Final cost is the critical factor, and low productivity can negate low wages.

Exchange Rates and Currency Risk

Although wage rates and productivity may make a country seem economical, unfavorable exchange rates may negate any savings. Sometimes, though, firms can take advantage of a particularly favorable exchange rate by relocating or exporting to a foreign country. However, the values of foreign currencies continually rise and fall in most countries. Such changes could well make what was a good location in 2013 a disastrous one in 2017.

Costs

We can divide location costs into two categories, tangible and intangible. **Tangible costs** are those costs that are readily identifiable and precisely measured. They include utilities, labor, material, taxes, depreciation, and other costs that the accounting department and management can identify. In addition, such costs as transportation of raw materials, transportation of finished goods, and site construction are all factored into the overall cost of a location. Government incentives, as we see in the *OM in Action* box "How Alabama Won the Auto Industry," certainly affect a location's cost.[2]

Tangible costs
Readily identifiable costs that can be measured with some precision.

Intangible costs are less easily quantified. They include quality of education, public transportation facilities, community attitudes toward the industry and the company, and quality and attitude of prospective employees. They also include quality-of-life variables, such as climate and sports teams, that may influence personnel recruiting.

Intangible costs
A category of location costs that cannot be easily quantified, such as quality of life and government.

OM in Action How Alabama Won the Auto Industry

Almost 20 years ago, Alabama persuaded Mercedes-Benz to build its first U.S. auto plant in the town of Vance by offering the luxury carmaker $253 million worth of incentives—$169,000 for every job Mercedes promised the state.

Taxpayers considered the deal such a boondoggle that they voted Governor Jim Folsom out of office long before the first Mercedes SUV rolled off the new assembly line in 1997. Today, with 50,000 car-related jobs in Alabama, the deal looks a little more like a bargain—suggesting that the practice of paying millions of taxpayer dollars to lure big employers can *sometimes* have a big payoff.

Mercedes surpassed its pledge to create 1,500 jobs at the Vance plant and currently has a workforce of about 4,000.

In 2001, Honda opened a factory 70 miles east of the Mercedes plant to build its Odyssey minivan. Toyota Motor Corp.'s plant near Huntsville started producing engines in 2002. Those two automakers also received incentives.

To cement Alabama's reputation as the South's busiest auto-making center, Hyundai Motor Co. of South Korea picked a site near Montgomery for its first U.S. assembly plant. The factory began production in 2005, employing 2,650 workers to make 300,000 sedans and SUVs a year.

Is the state giving away more than it gets in return? That's what many economists argue. Other former foes of incentives now argue that manufacturers' arrivals herald "Alabama's new day."

Sources: New York Times (February 18, 2011); and *The Wall Street Journal* (May 25, 2011) and (August 14, 2007).

[2]So what's a city, county, or state to do? According to *Forbes* (June 19, 2006): 42, "Keep taxes low. Don't grant favors. Pursue non-discriminatory reforms like reining in debt and public spending. Remove barriers rather than trying to steer economic growth to this favored corporation or that one."

TABLE 2

Ranking Corruption in Selected Countries (score of 10 represents a corruption-free country)

RANK	SCORE
1 New Zealand	9.4
2 Denmark Finland	9.3 (tie)
⋮	
10 Canada	8.7
⋮	
24 U.S.	7.1
⋮	
36 Israel	5.8
⋮	
73 Brazil, Tunisia	3.8 (tie)
⋮	
143 Russia	2.4
⋮	
175 Haiti	1.8
⋮	
182 Somalia, North Korea	1.0 (tie)

Source: Transparency International's 2011 survey, at **www.transparency.org.** Used with permission of Transparency International.

Political Risk, Values, and Culture

The political risk associated with national, state, and local governments' attitudes toward private and intellectual property, zoning, pollution, and employment stability may be in flux. Governmental positions at the time a location decision is made may not be lasting ones. However, management may find that these attitudes can be influenced by their own leadership.

Worker values may also differ from country to country, region to region, and small town to city. Worker views regarding turnover, unions, and absenteeism are all relevant factors. In turn, these values can affect a company's decision whether to make offers to current workers if the firm relocates to a new location. The case study at the end of this text, "Southern Recreational Vehicle Company," describes a St. Louis firm that actively chose *not to relocate* any of its workers when it moved to Mississippi.

One of the greatest challenges in a global operations decision is dealing with another country's culture. Cultural variations in punctuality by employees and suppliers make a marked difference in production and delivery schedules. Bribery and other forms of corruption also create substantial economic inefficiency, as well as ethical and legal problems in the global arena. As a result, operations managers face significant challenges when building effective supply chains across cultures. Table 2 provides one ranking of corruption in countries around the world.

Proximity to Markets

For many firms, locating near customers is extremely important. Particularly, service organizations, like drugstores, restaurants, post offices, or barbers, find that proximity to market is *the* primary location factor. Manufacturing firms find it useful to be close to customers when transporting finished goods is expensive or difficult (perhaps because they are bulky, heavy, or fragile). To be near U.S. markets foreign-owned auto giants such as Mercedes, Honda, Toyota, and Hyundai are building millions of cars each year in the U.S.

In addition, with just-in-time production, suppliers want to locate near users. For a firm like Coca-Cola, whose product's primary ingredient is water, it makes sense to have bottling plants in many cities rather than shipping heavy (and sometimes fragile glass) containers cross country.

Proximity to Suppliers

Firms locate near their raw materials and suppliers because of (1) perishability, (2) transportation costs, or (3) bulk. Bakeries, dairy plants, and frozen seafood processors deal with *perishable* raw materials, so they often locate close to suppliers. Companies dependent on inputs of heavy or bulky raw materials (such as steel producers using coal and iron ore) face expensive inbound *transportation costs*, so transportation costs become a major factor. And goods for which there is a *reduction in bulk* during production (e.g., trees to lumber) typically need facilities near the raw material.

Proximity to Competitors (Clustering)

Clustering
The location of competing companies near each other, often because of a critical mass of information, talent, venture capital, or natural resources.

Both manufacturing and service organizations also like to locate, somewhat surprisingly, near competitors. This tendency, called **clustering**, often occurs when a major resource is found in that region. Such resources include natural resources, information resources, venture capital resources, and talent resources. Table 3 presents nine examples of industries that exhibit clustering, and the reasons why.

Italy may be the true leader when it comes to clustering, however, with northern zones of that country holding world leadership in such specialties as ceramic tile (Modena), gold jewelry (Vicenza), machine tools (Busto Arsizio), cashmere and wool (Biella), designer eyeglasses (Belluma), and pasta machines (Parma).

TABLE 3 Clustering of Companies

INDUSTRY	LOCATIONS	REASON FOR CLUSTERING
Wine making	Napa Valley (U.S.), Bordeaux region (France)	Natural resources of land and climate
Software firms	Silicon Valley, Boston, Bangalore, Israel	Talent resources of bright graduates in scientific/technical areas, venture capitalists nearby
Clean energy	Colorado	Critical mass of talent and information, with 1,000 companies
Theme parks (e.g., Disney World, Universal Studios, and Sea World)	Orlando, Florida	A hot spot for entertainment, warm weather, tourists, and inexpensive labor
Electronics firms (e.g., Sony, IBM, HP, Motorola, and Panasonic)	Northern Mexico	NAFTA, duty-free export to U.S. (24% of all TVs are built here)
Computer hardware manufacturing	Singapore, Taiwan	High technological penetration rates and per capita GDP, skilled/educated workforce with large pool of engineers
Fast-food chains (e.g., Wendy's, McDonald's, Burger King, Pizza Hut)	Sites within 1 mile of one another	Stimulate food sales, high traffic flows
General aviation aircraft (e.g., Cessna, Learjet, Boeing, Raytheon)	Wichita, Kansas	Mass of aviation skills (60–70% of world's small planes/jets built here)
Athletic footwear, outdoor wear	Portland, Oregon	300 companies, many spawned by Nike, deep talent pool and outdoor culture

Methods of Evaluating Location Alternatives

Four major methods are used for solving location problems: the factor-rating method, locational cost–volume analysis, the center-of-gravity method, and the transportation model. This section describes these approaches.

The Factor-Rating Method

There are many factors, both qualitative and quantitative, to consider in choosing a location. Some of these factors are more important than others, so managers can use weightings to make the decision process more objective. The **factor-rating method** is popular because a wide variety of factors, from education to recreation to labor skills, can be objectively included. Figure 1 listed a few of the many factors that affect location decisions.

Factor-rating method
A location method that instills objectivity into the process of identifying hard-to-evaluate costs.

The factor-rating method has six steps:

1. Develop a list of relevant factors called *key success factors* (such as those in Figure 1).
2. Assign a weight to each factor to reflect its relative importance in the company's objectives.
3. Develop a scale for each factor (for example, 1 to 10 or 1 to 100 points).
4. Have management score each location for each factor, using the scale in Step 3.
5. Multiply the score by the weights for each factor and total the score for each location.
6. Make a recommendation based on the maximum point score, considering the results of other quantitative approaches as well.

Example 1

LO3 *Apply* the factor-rating method

FACTOR-RATING METHOD FOR AN EXPANDING THEME PARK

Five Flags over Florida, a U.S. chain of 10 family-oriented theme parks, has decided to expand overseas by opening its first park in Europe. It wishes to select between France and Denmark.

APPROACH ▶ The ratings sheet in Table 4 lists key success factors that management has decided are important; their weightings and their rating for two possible sites—Dijon, France, and Copenhagen, Denmark—are shown.

STUDENT TIP ☆
These weights do not need to be on a 0–1 scale or total to 1. We can use a 1–10 scale, 1–100 scale, or any other scale we prefer.

TABLE 4 Weights, Scores, and Solution

		SCORES (OUT OF 100)		WEIGHTED SCORES	
KEY SUCCESS FACTOR	WEIGHT	FRANCE	DENMARK	FRANCE	DENMARK
Labor availability and attitude	.25	70	60	(.25)(70) = 17.5	(.25)(60) = 15.0
People-to-car ratio	.05	50	60	(.05)(50) = 2.5	(.05)(60) = 3.0
Per capita income	.10	85	80	(.10)(85) = 8.5	(.10)(80) = 8.0
Tax structure	.39	75	70	(.39)(75) = 29.3	(.39)(70) = 27.3
Education and health	.21	60	70	(.21)(60) = 12.6	(.21)(70) = 14.7
Totals	1.00			70.4	68.0

SOLUTION ▶ Table 4 uses weights and scores to evaluate alternative site locations. Given the option of 100 points assigned to each factor, the French location is preferable.

INSIGHT ▶ By changing the points or weights slightly for those factors about which there is some doubt, we can analyze the sensitivity of the decision. For instance, we can see that changing the scores for "labor availability and attitude" by 10 points can change the decision. The numbers used in factor weighting can be subjective and the model's results are not "exact" even though this is a quantitative approach.

LEARNING EXERCISE ▶ If the weight for "tax structure" drops to .20 and the weight for "education and health" increases to .40, what is the new result? [Answer: Denmark is now chosen, with a 68.0 vs. a 67.5 score for France.]

RELATED PROBLEMS ▶ 5, 6, 7, 8, 9, 10, 11, 12, 13, 14, 15, 24, 25

EXCEL OM Data File **Ch08Ex1.xls** can be found at **www.pearsonhighered.com/heizer**.

When a decision is sensitive to minor changes, further analysis of the weighting and the points assigned may be appropriate. Alternatively, management may conclude that these intangible factors are not the proper criteria on which to base a location decision. Managers therefore place primary weight on the more quantitative aspects of the decision.

Locational Cost–Volume Analysis

Locational cost–volume analysis
A method of making an economic comparison of location alternatives.

Locational cost–volume analysis is a technique for making an economic comparison of location alternatives. By identifying fixed and variable costs and graphing them for each location, we can determine which one provides the lowest cost. Locational cost–volume analysis can be done mathematically or graphically. The graphic approach has the advantage of providing the range of volume over which each location is preferable.

The three steps to locational cost–volume analysis are as follows:

1. Determine the fixed and variable cost for each location.
2. Plot the costs for each location, with costs on the vertical axis of the graph and annual volume on the horizontal axis.
3. Select the location that has the lowest total cost for the expected production volume.

Example 2

LOCATIONAL COST–VOLUME ANALYSIS FOR A PARTS MANUFACTURER

Esmail Mohebbi, owner of European Ignitions Manufacturing, needs to expand his capacity. He is considering three locations—Athens, Brussels, and Lisbon—for a new plant. The company wishes to find the most economical location for an expected volume of 2,000 units per year.

APPROACH ▶ Mohebbi conducts locational cost–volume analysis. To do so, he determines that fixed costs per year at the sites are $30,000, $60,000, and $110,000, respectively; and variable costs are $75 per unit, $45 per unit, and $25 per unit, respectively. The expected selling price of each ignition system produced is $120.

SOLUTION ▶ For each of the three locations, Mohebbi can plot the fixed costs (those at a volume of zero units) and the total cost (fixed costs + variable costs) at the expected volume of output. These lines have been plotted in Figure 2.

Figure 2

Crossover Chart for Locational Cost–Volume Analysis

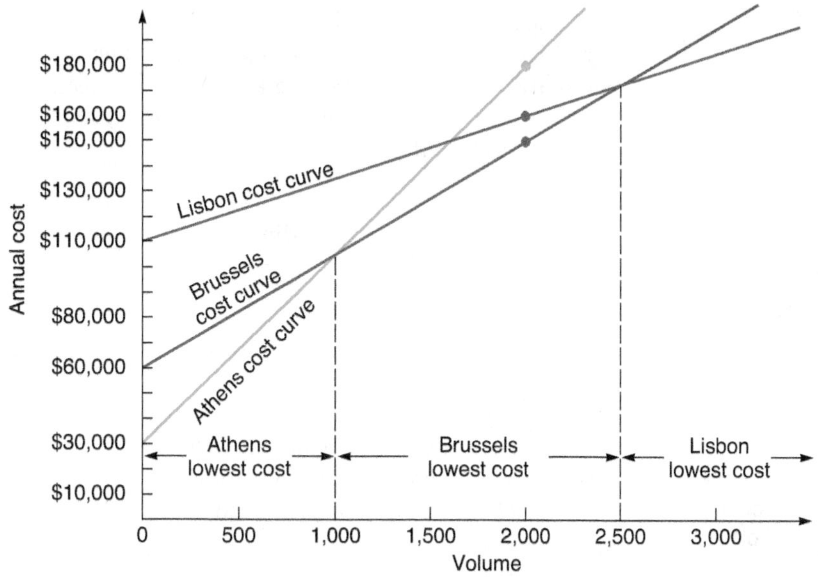

For Athens:

$$\text{Total cost} = \$30{,}000 + \$75(2{,}000) = \$180{,}000$$

For Brussels:

$$\text{Total cost} = \$60{,}000 + \$45(2{,}000) = \$150{,}000$$

For Lisbon:

$$\text{Total cost} = \$110{,}000 + \$25(2{,}000) = \$160{,}000$$

LO4 *Complete* a locational cost–volume analysis graphically and mathematically

With an expected volume of 2,000 units per year, Brussels provides the lowest cost location. The expected profit is:

$$\text{Total revenue} - \text{Total cost} = \$120(2{,}000) - \$150{,}000 = \$90{,}000 \text{ per year}$$

The crossover point for Athens and Brussels is:

$$30{,}000 + 75(x) = 60{,}000 + 45(x)$$
$$30(x) = 30{,}000$$
$$x = 1{,}000$$

and the crossover point for Brussels and Lisbon is:

$$60{,}000 + 45(x) = 110{,}000 + 25(x)$$
$$20(x) = 50{,}000$$
$$x = 2{,}500$$

INSIGHT ▶ As with every other OM model, locational cost–volume results can be sensitive to input data. For example, for a volume of less than 1,000, Athens would be preferred. For a volume greater than 2,500, Lisbon would yield the greatest profit.

LEARNING EXERCISE ▶ The variable cost for Lisbon is now expected to be $22 per unit. What is the new crossover point between Brussels and Lisbon? [Answer: 2,174 units.]

RELATED PROBLEMS ▶ 16, 17, 18, 19

EXCEL OM Data File **Ch08Ex2.xls** can be found at **www.pearsonhighered.com/heizer**.

Center-of-Gravity Method

Center-of-gravity method
A mathematical technique used for finding the best location for a single distribution point that services several stores or areas.

The **center-of-gravity method** is a mathematical technique used for finding the location of a distribution center that will minimize distribution costs. The method takes into account the location of markets, the volume of goods shipped to those markets, and shipping costs in finding the best location for a distribution center.

The first step in the center-of-gravity method is to place the locations on a coordinate system. This will be illustrated in Example 3. The origin of the coordinate system and the scale used are arbitrary, just as long as the relative distances are correctly represented. This can be done easily by placing a grid over an ordinary map. The center of gravity is determined using Equations (1) and (2):

$$x\text{-coordinate of the center of gravity} = \frac{\sum_i d_{ix} Q_i}{\sum_i Q_i} \quad (1)$$

$$y\text{-coordinate of the center of gravity} = \frac{\sum_i d_{iy} Q_i}{\sum_i Q_i} \quad (2)$$

where $d_{ix} = x$-coordinate of location i
$d_{iy} = y$-coordinate of location i
$Q_i =$ Quantity of goods moved to or from location i

LO5 *Use* the center-of-gravity method

Note that Equations (1) and (2) include the term Q_i, the quantity of supplies transferred to or from location *i*.

Since the number of containers shipped each month affects cost, distance alone should not be the principal criterion. The center-of-gravity method assumes that cost is directly proportional to both distance and volume shipped. The ideal location is that which minimizes the weighted distance between the warehouse and its retail outlets, where the distance is weighted by the number of containers shipped.[3]

Example 3

CENTER OF GRAVITY

Quain's Discount Department Stores, a chain of four large Target-type outlets, has store locations in Chicago, Pittsburgh, New York, and Atlanta; they are currently being supplied out of an old and inadequate warehouse in Pittsburgh, the site of the chain's first store. The firm wants to find some "central" location in which to build a new warehouse.

APPROACH ▶ Quain's will apply the center-of-gravity method. It gathers data on demand rates at each outlet (see Table 5).

TABLE 5 Demand for Quain's Discount Department Stores

STORE LOCATION	NUMBER OF CONTAINERS SHIPPED PER MONTH
Chicago	2,000
Pittsburgh	1,000
New York	1,000
Atlanta	2,000

[3]Equations (1) and (2) compute a center of gravity (COG) under "squared Euclidean" distances and may actually result in transportation costs slightly (less than 2%) higher than an *optimal* COG computed using "Euclidean" (straight-line) distances. The latter, however, is a more complex and involved procedure mathematically, so the formulas we present are generally used as an attractive substitute. See C. Kuo and R. E. White, "A Note on the Treatment of the Center-of-Gravity Method in Operations Management Textbooks," *Decision Sciences Journal of Innovative Education* 2: 219–227.

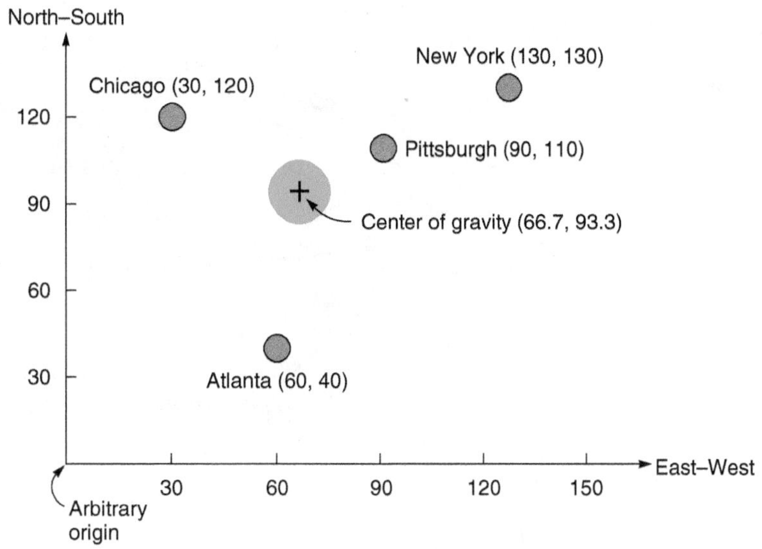

Figure 3

Coordinate Locations of Four Quain's Department Stores and Center of Gravity

Its current store locations are shown in Figure 3. For example, location 1 is Chicago, and from Table 5 and Figure 3, we have:

$$d_{1x} = 30$$
$$d_{1y} = 120$$
$$Q_1 = 2{,}000$$

SOLUTION ▶ Using the data in Table 5 and Figure 3 for each of the other cities, and Equations (1) and (2), we find:

x-coordinate of the center of gravity:

$$= \frac{(30)(2000) + (90)(1000) + (130)(1000) + (60)(2000)}{2000 + 1000 + 1000 + 2000} = \frac{400{,}000}{6{,}000}$$
$$= 66.7$$

y-coordinate of the center of gravity:

$$= \frac{(120)(2000) + (110)(1000) + (130)(1000) + (40)(2000)}{2000 + 1000 + 1000 + 2000} = \frac{560{,}000}{6{,}000}$$
$$= 93.3$$

This location (66.7, 93.3) is shown by the crosshairs in Figure 3.

INSIGHT ▶ By overlaying a U.S. map on this figure, we find this location is near central Ohio. The firm may well wish to consider Columbus, Ohio, or a nearby city as an appropriate location. But it is important to have both north–south and east–west interstate highways near the city selected to make delivery times quicker.

LEARNING EXERCISE ▶ The number of containers shipped per month to Atlanta is expected to grow quickly to 3,000. How does this change the center of gravity, and where should the new warehouse be located? [Answer: (65.7, 85.7), which is closer to Cincinnati, Ohio.]

RELATED PROBLEMS ▶ 20, 21, 22, 23

EXCEL OM Data File **Ch08Ex3.xls** can be found at **www.pearsonhighered.com/heizer.**

ACTIVE **MODEL** 1 This example is further illustrated in Active Model 8.1 at **www.pearsonhighered.com/heizer**.

Figure 4

Worldwide Distribution of Volkswagens and Parts

Source: The Economist, 2012. Copyright © 2012 by The Economist Newspaper Limted. Reprinted with permission.

VW's supply network

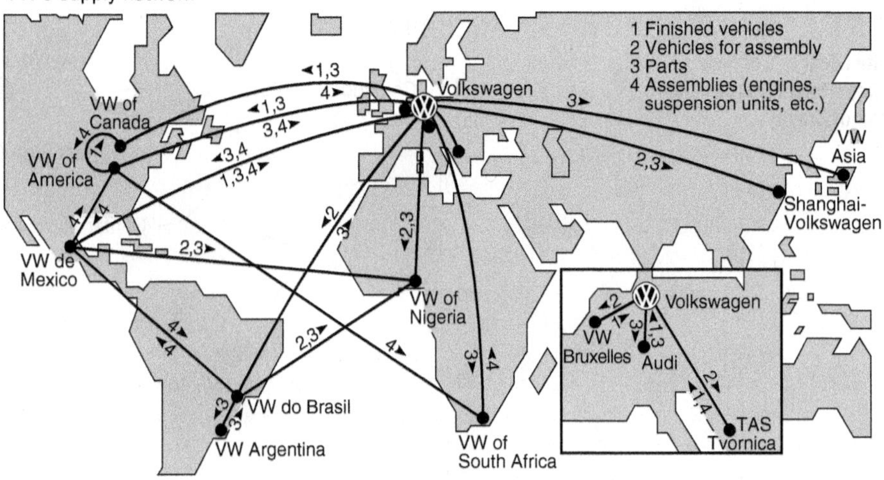

Transportation Model

Transportation model
A technique for solving a class of linear programming problems.

The objective of the **transportation model** is to determine the best pattern of shipments from several points of supply (sources) to several points of demand (destinations) so as to minimize total production and transportation costs. Every firm with a network of supply-and-demand points faces such a problem. The complex Volkswagen supply network (shown in Figure 4) provides one such illustration. We note in Figure 4, for example, that VW of Mexico ships vehicles for assembly and parts to VW of Nigeria, sends assemblies to VW of Brasil, and receives parts and assemblies from headquarters in Germany.

Although the linear programming (LP) technique can be used to solve this type of problem, more efficient, special-purpose algorithms have been developed for the transportation application. The transportation model finds an initial feasible solution and then makes step-by-step improvement until an optimal solution is reached.

Service Location Strategy

STUDENT TIP
Retail stores often attract more shoppers when competitors are close.

While the focus in industrial-sector location analysis is on *minimizing cost,* the focus in the service sector is on *maximizing revenue.* This is because manufacturing firms find that costs tend to vary substantially among locations, while service firms find that location often has more impact on revenue than cost. Therefore, for the service firm, a specific location often influences revenue more than it does cost. This means that the location focus for service firms should be on determining the volume of customers and revenue.

There are eight major determinants of volume and revenue for the service firm:

1. Purchasing power of the customer-drawing area
2. Service and image compatibility with demographics of the customer-drawing area
3. Competition in the area
4. Quality of the competition
5. Uniqueness of the firm's and competitors' locations
6. Physical qualities of facilities and neighboring businesses
7. Operating policies of the firm
8. Quality of management

Realistic analysis of these factors can provide a reasonable picture of the revenue expected. The techniques used in the service sector include regression analysis (see the *OM in Action* box, "How La Quinta Selects Profitable Hotel Sites"), traffic counts, demographic analysis, purchasing power analysis, the factor-rating method, the center-of-gravity method, and geographic information systems. Table 6 provides a summary of location strategies for both service and goods-producing organizations.

OM in Action How La Quinta Selects Profitable Hotel Sites

One of the most important decisions a lodging chain makes is location. Those that pick good sites more accurately and quickly than competitors have a distinct advantage. La Quinta Inns, headquartered in San Antonio, Texas, is a moderately priced chain of 800 inns. To model motel selection behavior and predict success of a site, La Quinta turned to regression analysis.

The hotel started by testing 35 independent variables, trying to find which of them would have the highest correlation with predicted profitability, the dependent variable. Variables included: the number of hotel rooms in the vicinity and their average room rates; local attractions such as office buildings and hospitals that drew potential customers to a 4-mile-radius trade area; local population and unemployment rate: the number of inns in a region; and physical characteristics of the site, such as ease of access or sign visibility.

In the end, the regression model chosen, with an R^2 of 51%, included four predictive variables: (1) the price of the inn, (2) median income levels, (3) the state population per inn, and (4) the location of nearby colleges (which serves as a proxy for other demand generators). La Quinta then used the regression model to predict profitability and developed a cutoff that gave the best results for predicting success or failure of a site. A spreadsheet is now used to implement the model, which applies the decision rule and suggests "build" or "don't build." The CEO likes the model so much that he no longer feels obliged to personally select new sites.

© Mike Booth/Alamy

Source: S. Kimes and J. Fitzsimmons, *Interfaces* 20, no. 2: 12–20; and G. Keller, *Statistics for Management and Economics*, 8th ed. Cincinnati-Cengage, 2008: 679.

TABLE 6 Location Strategies—Service vs. Goods-Producing Organizations

SERVICE/RETAIL/PROFESSIONAL	*GOODS-PRODUCING*
REVENUE FOCUS	COST FOCUS
Volume/revenue Drawing area; purchasing power Competition; advertising/pricing **Physical quality** Parking/access; security/lighting; appearance/image **Cost determinants** Rent Management caliber Operation policies (hours, wage rates)	**Tangible costs** Transportation cost of raw material Shipment cost of finished goods Energy and utility cost; labor; raw material; taxes, and so on **Intangible and future costs** Attitude toward union Quality of life Education expenditures by state Quality of state and local government
TECHNIQUES	TECHNIQUES
Regression models to determine importance of various factors Factor-rating method Traffic counts Demographic analysis of drawing area Purchasing power analysis of area Center-of-gravity method Geographic information systems	Transportation method Factor-rating method Locational cost–volume analysis Crossover charts
ASSUMPTIONS	ASSUMPTIONS
Location is a major determinant of revenue High customer-contact issues are critical Costs are relatively constant for a given area; therefore, the revenue function is critical	Location is a major determinant of cost Most major costs can be identified explicitly for each site Low customer contact allows focus on the identifiable costs Intangible costs can be evaluated

☆ **STUDENT TIP**
This table helps differentiate between service- and manufacturing-sector decisions.

LO6 *Understand* the differences between service- and industrial-sector location analysis

Geographic Information Systems

Geographic information systems are an important tool to help firms make successful, analytical decisions with regard to location. A geographic information system (GIS) stores and displays information that can be linked to a geographical location. For instance, retailers, banks, food chains, gas stations, and print shop franchises can all use geographically coded files from a GIS to conduct demographic analyses. By combining population, age, income, traffic flow,

Geographic information system (GIS)
A system that stores and displays information that can be linked to a geographic location.

and density figures with geography, a retailer can pinpoint the best location for a new store or restaurant.

Here are some of the geographic databases available in many GISs:

- Census data by block, tract, city, county, congressional district, metropolitan area, state, and zip code
- Maps of every street, highway, bridge, and tunnel in the U.S.
- Utilities such as electrical, water, and gas lines
- All rivers, mountains, lakes, and forests
- All major airports, colleges, and hospitals

For example, airlines use GISs to identify airports where ground services are the most effective. This information is then used to help schedule and to decide where to purchase fuel, meals, and other services.

Commercial office building developers use GISs in the selection of cities for future construction. Building new office space takes several years, so developers value the database approach that a GIS can offer. GIS is used to analyze factors that influence the location decisions by addressing five elements for each city: (1) residential areas, (2) retail shops, (3) cultural and entertainment centers, (4) crime incidence, and (5) transportation options. For example, one study of Tampa, Florida, showed that the city's central business district lacks the characteristics to sustain a viable high-demand office market, suggesting that builders should look elsewhere.

Here are five more examples of how location-scouting GIS software is turning commercial real estate into a science.

- *Carvel Ice Cream:* This 76-year-old chain of ice cream shops uses GIS to create a demographic profile of what a typically successful neighborhood for a Carvel looks like—mostly in terms of income and ages.
- *Saber Roofing:* Rather than send workers out to estimate the costs for reroofing jobs, this Redwood City, California, firm pulls up aerial shots of the building via Google Earth. The

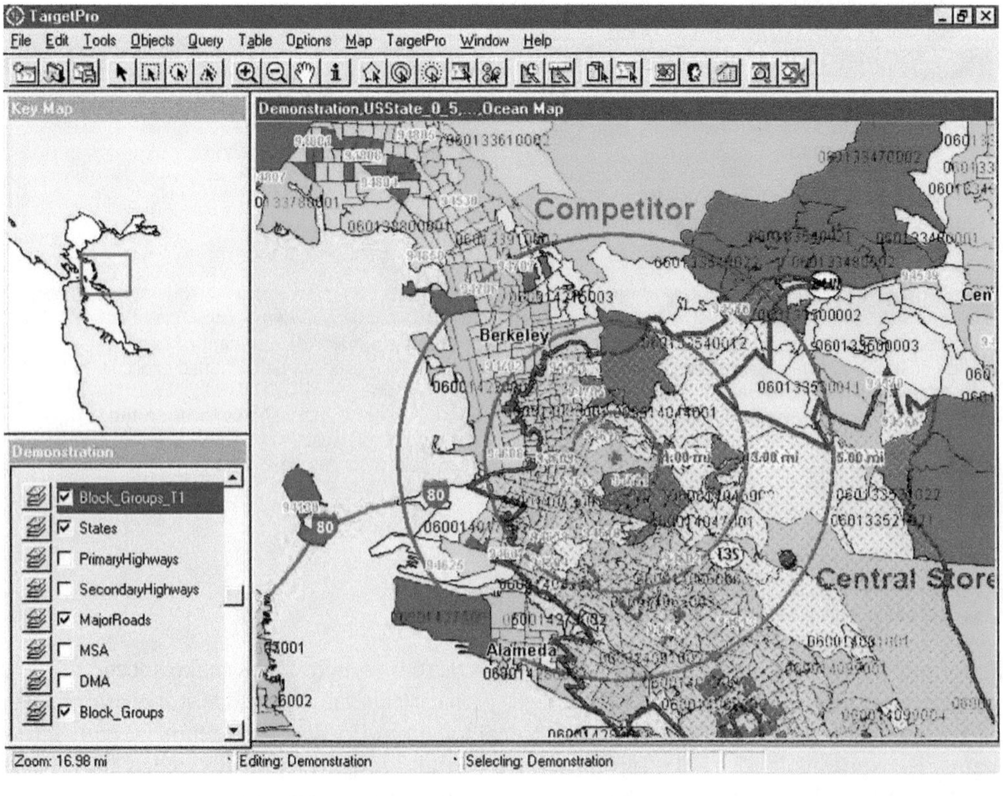

Geographic information systems (GISs) are used by a variety of firms, including Darden Restaurants, to identify target markets by income, ethnicity, product use, age, etc. Here, data from MapInfo helps with competitive analysis. Three concentric blue rings, each representing various mile radii, were drawn around the competitor's store. The heavy red line indicates the "drive" time to the firm's own central store (the red dot).

owner can measure roofs, eyeball the conditions, and e-mail the client an estimate, saving hundreds of miles of driving daily. In one case, while on the phone, a potential client was told her roof was too steep for the company to tackle after the Saber employee quickly looked up the home on Google Earth.

- *Arby's:* As this fast-food chain learned, specific products can affect behavior. Using MapInfo, Arby's discovered that diners drove up to 20% farther for their roast beef sandwich (which they consider a "destination" product) than for its chicken sandwich.
- *Home Depot:* Wanting a store in New York City, even though Home Depot demographics are usually for customers who own big homes, the company opened in Queens when GIS software predicted it would do well. Although most people there live in apartments and very small homes, the store has become one of the chain's highest-volume outlets. Similarly, Home Depot thought it had saturated Atlanta two decades ago, but GIS analysis suggested expansion. There are now over 40 Home Depots in that area.
- *Jo-Ann Stores:* This fabric and craft retailer's 70 superstores were doing well a few years ago, but managers were afraid more big-box stores could not justify building expenses. So Jo-Ann used its GIS to create an ideal customer profile—female homeowners with families—and mapped it against demographics. The firm found it could build 700 superstores, which in turn increased the sales from $105 to $150 per square foot.

Other packages similar to MapInfo are Hemisphere Solutions (by Unisys Corp.), Atlas GIS (from Strategic Mapping, Inc.), Arc/Info (by ESRI), SAS/GIS (by SAS Institute, Inc.), Market Base (by National Decision Systems, Inc.), and MapPoint 2011 (by Microsoft).

To illustrate how extensive some of these GISs can be, consider Microsoft's MapPoint 2011, which includes a comprehensive set of map and demographic data. Its North American maps have more than 7 million miles of streets and 2 million points of interest to allow users to locate restaurants, airports, hotels, gas stations, ATMs, museums, campgrounds, and freeway exits. Demographic data includes statistics for population, age, income, education, and housing for 1980, 1990, 2000, and 2010. These data can be mapped by state, county, city, zip code, or census tract. MapPoint 2011 produces maps that identify business trends; pinpoint market graphics; locate clients, customers, and competitors; and visualize sales performance and product distribution. The European version of MapPoint includes 8 million kilometers of roads as well as 400,000 points of interest (see www.mapapps.net).

The *Video Case Study* "Locating the Next Red Lobster Restaurant" that appears at the end of this text describes how that chain uses its GIS to define trade areas based on market size and population density.

VIDEO 2
Locating the Next Red Lobster Restaurant

Summary

Location may determine up to 50% of operating expense. Location is also a critical element in determining revenue for the service, retail, or professional firm. Industrial firms need to consider both tangible and intangible costs. Industrial location problems are typically addressed via a factor-rating method, locational cost–volume analysis, the center-of-gravity method, and the transportation method of linear programming.

For service, retail, and professional organizations, analysis is typically made of a variety of variables including purchasing power of a drawing area, competition, advertising and promotion, physical qualities of the location, and operating policies of the organization.

Key Terms

Tangible costs
Intangible costs
Clustering
Factor-rating method
Locational cost–volume analysis
Center-of-gravity method
Transportation model
Geographic information system (GIS)

Ethical Dilemma

In this text, we have discussed a number of location decisions. Consider another: United Airlines announced its competition to select a town for a new billion-dollar aircraft-repair base. The bidding for the prize of 7,500 jobs paying at least $25 per hour was fast and furious, with Orlando offering $154 million in incentives and Denver more than twice that amount. Kentucky's governor angrily rescinded Louisville's offer of $300 million, likening the bidding to "squeezing every drop of blood out of a turnip."

When United finally selected from among the 93 cities bidding on the base, the winner was Indianapolis and its $320 million offer of taxpayers' money.

But a few years later, with United near bankruptcy, and having fulfilled its legal obligation, the company walked away from the massive center. This left the city and state governments out all that money, with no new tenant in sight. The city now even owns the tools, neatly arranged in each of the 12 elaborately equipped hangar bays. United outsourced its maintenance to mechanics at a southern firm (which pays one-third of what United paid in salary and benefits in Indianapolis).

What are the ethical, legal, and economic implications of such location bidding wars? Who pays for such giveaways? Are local citizens allowed to vote on offers made by their cities, counties, or states? Should there be limits on these incentives?

Discussion Questions

1. How is FedEx's location a competitive advantage? Discuss.
2. Why do so many U.S. firms build facilities in other countries?
3. Why do so many foreign companies build facilities in the U.S.?
4. What is clustering?
5. How does factor weighting incorporate personal preference in location choices?
6. What are the advantages and disadvantages of a qualitative (as opposed to a quantitative) approach to location decision making?
7. Provide two examples of clustering in the service sector.
8. What are the major factors that firms consider when choosing a country in which to locate?
9. What factors affect region/community location decisions?
10. Although most organizations may make the location decision infrequently, there are some organizations that make the decision quite regularly and often. Provide one or two examples. How might their approach to the location decision differ from the norm?
11. List factors, other than globalization, that affect the location decision.
12. Explain the assumptions behind the center-of-gravity method. How can the model be used in a service facility location?
13. What are the three steps to locational cost–volume analysis?
14. "Manufacturers locate near their resources, retailers locate near their customers." Discuss this statement, with reference to the proximity-to-markets arguments covered in the text. Can you think of a counter-example in each case? Support your choices.
15. Why shouldn't low wage rates alone be sufficient to select a location?
16. List the techniques used by service organizations to select locations.
17. Contrast the location of a food distributor and a supermarket. (The distributor sends truckloads of food, meat, produce, etc., to the supermarket.) Show the relevant considerations (factors) they share; show those where they differ.
18. Elmer's Fudge Factory is planning to open 10 retail outlets in Oregon over the next 2 years. Identify (and weight) those factors relevant to the decision. Provide this list of factors and weights.
19. What is meant by "aerotropolis"?

Using Software to Solve Location Problems

This section presents three ways to solve location problems with computer software. First, you can create your own spreadsheets to compute factor ratings, the center of gravity, and locational cost–volume analysis. Second, Excel OM (free with your text and found at our Web site) is programmed to solve all three models. Third, POM for Windows is also found at **www.pearsonhighered.com/heizer** and can solve all problems labeled with a P.

CREATING YOUR OWN EXCEL SPREADSHEETS

Excel spreadsheets are easily developed to solve most of the problems in this text. Consider the Quain's Department Store center-of-gravity analysis in Example 3. You can see from Program 1 how the formulas are created.

X USING EXCEL OM

Excel OM may be used to solve Example 1 (with the Factor Rating module), Example 2 (with the Cost–Volume Analysis module), and Example 3 (with the Center-of-Gravity module), as well as other location problems.

P USING POM FOR WINDOWS

POM for Windows also includes three different facility location models: the factor-rating method, the center-of-gravity model, and locational cost–volume analysis.

Program 1

An Excel Spreadsheet for Creating a Center-of-Gravity Analysis for Example 3, Quain's Discount Department Stores

	A	B	C	D	E
1	**Quain's Discount Department Stores**				
2					
3	Store Locations	Number of Containers Shipped per Month	x	y	
4	Chicago	2000	30	120	
5	Pittsburgh	1000	90	110	
6	New York	1000	130	130	
7	Atlanta	2000	60	40	
8					
9	**Results**				
10	**Sum**	**6000**			
11	**Weighted Ave (COG)**		**66.667**	**93.333**	
12					
13					
14					

COMPUTATIONS

VALUE	CELL	EXCEL FORMULA	EXCEL FORMULA
Total containers shipped	B10	=SUM(B4:B7)	
Weighted average*	C11	=IF($B$10>0,SUMPRODUCT($B$4:$B$7,C4:C7)/$B$10,0)	Copy to D11

*Note that the formula in cell C11 includes an If test in case weights do not sum to 1.

Solved Problems

Virtual Office Hours help is available at www.myomlab.com.

SOLVED PROBLEM 1

Just as cities and communities can be compared for location selection by the weighted approach model, as we saw earlier in this text, so can actual site decisions within those cities. Table 7 illustrates four factors of importance to Washington, DC, and the health officials charged with opening that city's first public drug treatment clinic. Of primary concern (and given a weight of 5) was location of the clinic so it would be as accessible as possible to the largest number of patients. Due to a tight budget, the annual lease cost was also of some concern. A suite in the city hall, at 14th and U Streets, was highly rated because its rent would be free. An old office building near the downtown bus station received a much lower rating because of its cost. Equally important as lease cost was the need for confidentiality of patients and, therefore, for a relatively inconspicuous clinic. Finally, because so many of the staff at the clinic would be donating their time, the safety, parking, and accessibility of each site were of concern as well.

Using the factor-rating method, which site is preferred?

SOLUTION

From the three rightmost columns in Table 7, the weighted scores are summed. The bus terminal area has a low score and can be excluded from further consideration. The other two sites are virtually identical in total score. The city may now want to consider other factors, including political ones, in selecting between the two remaining sites.

TABLE 7 Potential Clinic Sites in Washington, DC

		*POTENTIAL LOCATIONS**			*WEIGHTED SCORES*		
FACTOR	IMPORTANCE WEIGHT	HOMELESS SHELTER (2ND AND D, SE)	CITY HALL (14TH AND U, NW)	BUS TERMINAL AREA (7TH AND H, NW)	HOMELESS SHELTER	CITY HALL	BUS TERMINAL AREA
Accessibility for addicts	5	9	7	7	45	35	35
Annual lease cost	3	6	10	3	18	30	9
Inconspicuous	3	5	2	7	15	6	21
Accessibility for health staff	2	3	6	2	6	12	4
					Total scores: 84	83	69

* All sites are rated on a 1 to 10 basis, with 10 as the highest score and 1 as the lowest.

Source: From *Service Management and Operations*, 2nd ed., by Haksever/Render/Russell/Murdick, p. 266. Copyright © 2000. Reprinted by permission of Prentice Hall, Inc., Upper Saddle River, NJ.

SOLVED PROBLEM 2

Ching-Chang Kuo is considering opening a new foundry in Denton, Texas; Edwardsville, Illinois; or Fayetteville, Arkansas, to produce high-quality rifle sights. He has assembled the following fixed-cost and variable-cost data:

		PER-UNIT COSTS		
LOCATION	FIXED COST PER YEAR	MATERIAL	VARIABLE LABOR	OVERHEAD
Denton	$200,000	$ .20	$ .40	$ .40
Edwardsville	$180,000	$ .25	$ .75	$ .75
Fayetteville	$170,000	$1.00	$1.00	$1.00

a) Graph the total cost lines.
b) Over what range of annual volume is each facility going to have a competitive advantage?
c) What is the volume at the intersection of the Edwardsville and Fayetteville cost lines?

SOLUTION

a) A graph of the total cost lines is shown in Figure 5.
b) Below 8,000 units, the Fayetteville facility will have a competitive advantage (lowest cost); between 8,000 units and 26,666 units, Edwardsville has an advantage; and above 26,666, Denton has the advantage. (We have made the assumption in this problem that other costs—that is, delivery and intangible factors—are constant regardless of the decision.)
c) From Figure 5, we see that the cost line for Fayetteville and the cost line for Edwardsville cross at about 8,000. We can also determine this point with a little algebra:

$$\$180{,}000 + 1.75Q = \$170{,}000 + 3.00Q$$
$$\$10{,}000 = 1.25Q$$
$$8{,}000 = Q$$

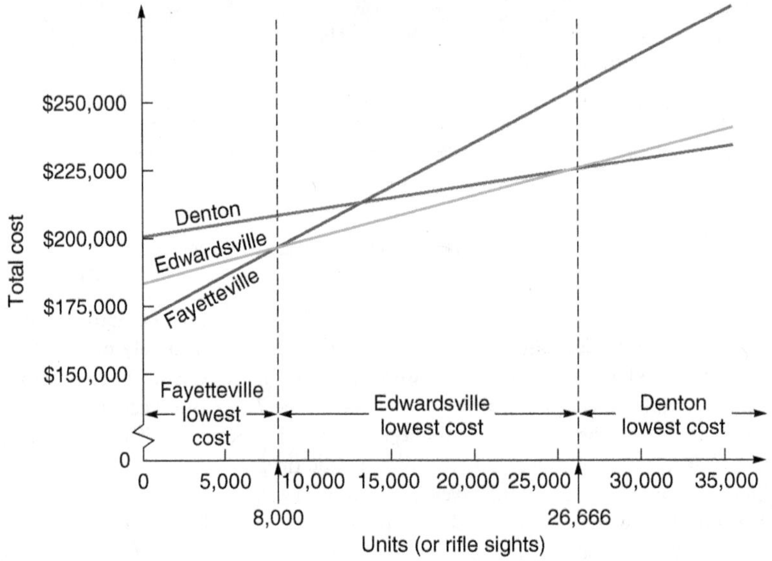

Figure 5
Graph of Total Cost Lines for Ching-Chang Kuo

SOLVED PROBLEM 3

The Metropolis Public Library plans to expand with its first major branch library in the city's growing north side. The branch will serve six census tracts. Here are the coordinates of each tract and the population within it:

CENSUS TRACT	CENTER OF TRACT	POPULATION IN TRACT
503—Logan Square	(3, 4)	45,000
519—Albany Park	(4, 5)	25,000
522—Rogers Park	(3, 6)	62,000
538—Kentwood	(4, 7)	51,000
540—Roosevelt	(2, 3)	32,000
561—Western	(5, 2)	29,000

Using the center-of-gravity method, what should be the coordinate location of the branch library?

SOLUTION

$$x\text{-coordinate} = \frac{\sum_i d_{ix}Q_i}{\sum_i Q_i} = \frac{3(45{,}000) + 4(25{,}000) + 3(62{,}000) + 4(51{,}000) + 2(32{,}000) + 5(29{,}000)}{244{,}000} = 3.42$$

$$y\text{-coordinate} = \frac{\sum_i d_{iy}Q_i}{\sum_i Q_i} = \frac{4(45{,}000) + 5(25{,}000) + 6(62{,}000) + 7(51{,}000) + 3(32{,}000) + 2(29{,}000)}{244{,}000} = 4.87$$

The new branch library will sit just west of Logan Square and Rogers Park, at the (3.42, 4.87) tract location.

Problems

Note: Px means the problem may be solved with POM for Windows and/or Excel OM.

• **1** In Myanmar (formerly Burma), 6 laborers, each making the equivalent of \$3 per day, can produce 40 units per day. In rural China, 10 laborers, each making the equivalent of \$2 per day, can produce 45 units. In Billings, Montana, 2 laborers, each making \$60 per day, can make 100 units. Based on labor costs only, which location would be most economical to produce the item?

• **2** Refer to Problem 1. Shipping cost from Myanmar to Denver, Colorado, the final destination, is \$1.50 per unit. Shipping cost from China to Denver is \$1 per unit, while the shipping cost from Billings to Denver is \$.25 per unit. Considering both labor and transportation costs, which is the most favorable production location?

•• **3** You have been asked to analyze the bids for 200 polished disks used in solar panels. These bids have been submitted by three suppliers: Thailand Polishing, India Shine, and Sacramento Glow. Thailand Polishing has submitted a bid of 2,000 baht. India Shine has submitted a bid of 2,000 rupees. Sacramento Glow has submitted a bid of \$200. You check with your local bank and find that \$1 = 10 baht and \$1 = 8 rupees. Which company should you choose?

• **4** Refer to Problem 3. If the final destination is New Delhi, India, and there is a 30% import tax, which firm should you choose?

•• **5** Subway, with more than 20,000 outlets in the U.S., is planning for a new restaurant in Buffalo, New York. Three locations are being considered. The following table gives the factors for each site.

FACTOR	WEIGHT	MAITLAND	BAPTIST CHURCH	NORTHSIDE MALL
Space	.30	60	70	80
Costs	.25	40	80	30
Traffic density	.20	50	80	60
Neighborhood income	.15	50	70	40
Zoning laws	.10	80	20	90

a) At which site should Subway open the new restaurant?
b) If the weights for Space and Traffic density are reversed, how would this affect the decision? Px

• **6** Ken Gilbert owns the Knoxville Warriors, a minor league baseball team in Tennessee. He wishes to move the Warriors south, to either Mobile (Alabama) or Jackson (Mississippi). The table below gives the factors that Gilbert thinks are important, their weights, and the scores for Mobile and Jackson.

FACTOR	WEIGHT	MOBILE	JACKSON
Incentive	.4	80	60
Player satisfaction	.3	20	50
Sports interest	.2	40	90
Size of city	.1	70	30

a) Which site should he select?
b) Jackson just raised its incentive package, and the new score is 75. Why doesn't this impact your decision in part (a)? Px

Andrea Catenaro Doherty/Shutterstock

•• **7** Northeastern Insurance Company is considering opening an office in the U.S. The two cities under consideration are Philadelphia and New York. The factor ratings (higher scores are better) for the two cities are given in the following table. In which city should Northeastern locate?

FACTOR	WEIGHT	PHILADELPHIA	NEW YORK
Customer convenience	.25	70	80
Bank accessibility	.20	40	90
Computer support	.20	85	75
Rental costs	.15	90	55
Labor costs	.10	80	50
Taxes	.10	90	50

•• **8** Marilyn Helm Retailers is attempting to decide on a location for a new retail outlet. At the moment, the firm has three alternatives—stay where it is but enlarge the facility; locate along the main street in nearby Newbury; or locate in a new shopping mall in Hyde Park. The company has selected the four factors listed in the following table as the basis for evaluation and has assigned weights as shown:

FACTOR	FACTOR DESCRIPTION	WEIGHT
1	Average community income	.30
2	Community growth potential	.15
3	Availability of public transportation	.20
4	Labor availability, attitude, and cost	.35

Helm has rated each location for each factor, on a 100-point basis. These ratings are given below:

	LOCATION		
FACTOR	PRESENT LOCATION	NEWBURY	HYDE PARK
1	40	60	50
2	20	20	80
3	30	60	50
4	80	50	50

a) What should Helm do?
b) A new subway station is scheduled to open across the street from the present location in about a month, so its third factor score should be raised to 40. How does this change your answer? Px

•• **9** A location analysis for Cook Controls, a small manufacturer of parts for high-technology cable systems, has been narrowed down to four locations. Cook will need to train assemblers, testers, and robotics maintainers in local training centers. Lori Cook, the president, has asked each potential site to offer training programs, tax breaks, and other industrial incentives. The critical factors, their weights, and the ratings for each location are shown in the following table. High scores represent favorable values.

		LOCATION			
FACTOR	WEIGHT	AKRON, OH	BILOXI, MS	CARTHAGE, TX	DENVER, CO
Labor availability	.15	90	80	90	80
Technical school quality	.10	95	75	65	85
Operating cost	.30	80	85	95	85
Land and construction cost	.15	60	80	90	70
Industrial incentives	.20	90	75	85	60
Labor cost	.10	75	80	85	75

a) Compute the composite (weighted average) rating for each location.
b) Which site would you choose?
c) Would you reach the same conclusion if the weights for operating cost and labor cost were reversed? Recompute as necessary and explain. Px

••• **10** Pan American Refineries, headquartered in Houston, must decide among three sites for the construction of a new oil-processing center. The firm has selected the six factors listed below as a basis for evaluation and has assigned rating weights from 1 to 5 on each factor:

FACTOR	FACTOR NAME	RATING WEIGHT
1	Proximity to port facilities	5
2	Power-source availability and cost	3
3	Workforce attitude and cost	4
4	Distance from Houston	2
5	Community desirability	2
6	Equipment suppliers in area	3

Subhajit Chakraborty, the CEO, has rated each location for each factor on a 1- to 100-point basis.

FACTOR	LOCATION A	LOCATION B	LOCATION C
1	100	80	80
2	80	70	100
3	30	60	70
4	10	80	60
5	90	60	80
6	50	60	90

a) Which site will be recommended based on *total* weighted scores?
b) If location B's score for Proximity to port facilities was reset at 90, how would the result change?
c) What score would location B need on Proximity to port facilities to change its ranking? Px

•• **11** A company is planning on expanding and building a new plant in one of three Southeast Asian countries. Chris Ellis, the manager charged with making the decision, has determined that five key success factors can be used to evaluate the prospective countries. Ellis used a rating system of 1 (least desirable country) to 5 (most desirable) to evaluate each factor.

KEY SUCCESS FACTOR	WEIGHT	*CANDIDATE COUNTRY RATINGS*		
		TAIWAN	THAILAND	SINGAPORE
Technology	0.2	4	5	1
Level of education	0.1	4	1	5
Political and legal aspects	0.4	1	3	3
Social and cultural aspects	0.1	4	2	3
Economic factors	0.2	3	3	2

a) Which country should be selected for the new plant?
b) Political unrest in Thailand results in a lower score, 2, for Political and legal aspects. Does your conclusion change?
c) What if Thailand's score drops even further, to a 1, for Political and legal aspects? Px

• **12** Rollins College is contemplating opening a European campus where students from the main campus could go to take courses for 1 of the 4 college years. At the moment, it is considering five countries: Holland, Great Britain, Italy, Belgium, and Greece. The college wishes to consider eight factors in its decision. The first two factors are given weights of 0.2, while the rest are assigned weights of 0.1. The following table illustrates its assessment of each factor for each country (5 is best).

FACTOR	FACTOR DESCRIPTION	HOLLAND	GREAT BRITAIN	ITALY	BELGIUM	GREECE
1	Stability of government	5	5	3	5	4
2	Degree to which the population can converse in English	4	5	3	4	3
3	Stability of the monetary system	5	4	3	4	3
4	Communications infrastructure	4	5	3	4	3
5	Transportation infrastructure	5	5	3	5	3
6	Availability of historic/ cultural sites	3	4	5	3	5
7	Import restrictions	4	4	3	4	4
8	Availability of suitable quarters	4	4	3	4	3

a) In which country should Rollins College choose to set up its European campus?
b) How would the decision change if the "degree to which the population can converse in English" was not an issue? Px

•• **13** Daniel Tracy, owner of Martin Manufacturing, must expand by building a new factory. The search for a location for this factory has been narrowed to four sites: A, B, C, or D. The following table shows the results thus far obtained by Tracy by using the factor-rating method to analyze the problem. The scale used for each factor scoring is 1 through 5.

FACTOR	WEIGHT	SITE SCORES A	B	C	D
Quality of labor	10	5	4	4	5
Construction cost	8	2	3	4	1
Transportation costs	8	3	4	3	2
Proximity to markets	7	5	3	4	4
Taxes	6	2	3	3	4
Weather	6	2	5	5	4
Energy costs	5	5	4	3	3

a) Which site should Tracy choose?
b) If site D's score for Energy costs increases from a 3 to a 5, do results change?
c) If site A's Weather score is adjusted to a 4, what is the impact? What should Tracy do at this point? Px

••• **14** An American consulting firm is planning to expand globally by opening a new office in one of four countries: Germany, Italy, Spain, or Greece. The chief partner entrusted with the decision, L. Wayne Shell, has identified eight key success factors that he views as essential for the success of any consultancy. He used a rating system of 1 (least desirable country) to 5 (most desirable) to evaluate each factor.

KEY SUCCESS FACTOR	WEIGHT	CANDIDATE COUNTRY RATINGS GERMANY	ITALY	SPAIN	GREECE
Level of education					
Number of consultants	.05	5	5	5	2
National literacy rate	.05	4	2	1	1
Political aspects					
Stability of government	0.2	5	5	5	2
Product liability laws	0.2	5	2	3	5
Environmental regulations	0.2	1	4	1	3
Social and cultural aspects					
Similarity in language	0.1	4	2	1	1
Acceptability of consultants	0.1	1	4	4	3
Economic factors					
Incentives	0.1	2	3	1	5

a) Which country should be selected for the new office?
b) If Spain's score were lowered in the Stability of government factor, to a 4, how would its overall score change? On this factor, at what score for Spain *would* the rankings change? Px

•• **15** A British hospital chain wishes to make its first entry into the U.S. market by building a medical facility in the Midwest, a region with which its director, Doug Moodie, is comfortable because he got his medical degree at Northwestern University. After a preliminary analysis, four cities are chosen for further consideration. They are rated and weighted according to the factors shown below:

FACTOR	WEIGHT	CITY CHICAGO	MILWAUKEE	MADISON	DETROIT
Costs	2.0	8	5	6	7
Need for a facility	1.5	4	9	8	4
Staff availability	1.0	7	6	4	7
Local incentives	0.5	8	6	5	9

a) Which city should Moodie select?
b) Assume a minimum score of 5 is now required for all factors. Which city should be chosen? Px

•• **16** The fixed and variable costs for three potential manufacturing plant sites for a rattan chair weaver are shown:

SITE	FIXED COST PER YEAR	VARIABLE COST PER UNIT
1	$ 500	$11
2	1,000	7
3	1,700	4

a) Over what range of production is each location optimal?
b) For a production of 200 units, which site is best? Px

• **17** Peter Billington Stereo, Inc., supplies car radios to auto manufacturers and is going to open a new plant. The company is undecided between Detroit and Dallas as the site. The fixed costs in Dallas are lower due to cheaper land costs, but the variable costs in Dallas are higher because shipping distances would increase. Given the following costs:

COST	DALLAS	DETROIT
Fixed costs	$600,000	$800,000
Variable costs	$28/radio	$22/radio

a) Perform an analysis of the volume over which each location is preferable.
b) How does your answer change if Dallas's fixed costs increase by 10%?

••• **18** Hyundai Motors is considering three sites—A, B, and C—at which to locate a factory to build its new-model automobile, the Hyundai Sport C150. The goal is to locate at a minimum-cost site, where cost is measured by the annual fixed plus variable costs of production. Hyundai Motors has gathered the following data:

SITE	ANNUALIZED FIXED COST	VARIABLE COST PER AUTO PRODUCED
A	$10,000,000	$2,500
B	$20,000,000	$2,000
C	$25,000,000	$1,000

The firm knows it will produce between 0 and 60,000 Sport C150s at the new plant each year, but, thus far, that is the extent of its knowledge about production plans.

a) For what values of volume, V, of production, if any, is site C a recommended site?
b) What volume indicates site A is optimal?
c) Over what range of volume is site B optimal? Why?

•• **19** Peggy Lane Corp., a producer of machine tools, wants to move to a larger site. Two alternative locations have been identified: Bonham and McKinney. Bonham would have fixed costs of $800,000 per year and variable costs of $14,000 per standard unit produced. McKinney would have annual fixed costs of $920,000 and variable costs of $13,000 per standard unit. The finished items sell for $29,000 each.

a) At what volume of output would the two locations have the same profit?
b) For what range of output would Bonham be superior (have higher profits)?
c) For what range would McKinney be superior?
d) What is the relevance of break-even points for these cities?

•• **20** The following table gives the map coordinates and the shipping loads for a set of cities that we wish to connect through a central hub.

CITY	MAP COORDINATE (*x*, *y*)	SHIPPING LOAD
A	(5, 10)	5
B	(6, 8)	10
C	(4, 9)	15
D	(9, 5)	5
E	(7, 9)	15
F	(3, 2)	10
G	(2, 6)	5

a) Near which map coordinates should the hub be located?
b) If the shipments from city A triple, how does this change the coordinates?

•• **21** A chain of home health care firms in Louisiana needs to locate a central office from which to conduct internal audits and other periodic reviews of its facilities. These facilities are scattered throughout the state, as detailed in the following table. Each site, except for Houma, will be visited three times each year by a team of workers, who will drive from the central office to the site. Houma will be visited five times a year. Which coordinates represent a good central location for this office? What other factors might influence the office location decision? Where would you place this office? Explain.

	MAP COORDINATES	
CITY	*x*	*y*
Covington	9.2	3.5
Donaldsonville	7.3	2.5
Houma	7.8	1.4
Monroe	5.0	8.4
Natchitoches	2.8	6.5
New Iberia	5.5	2.4
Opelousas	5.0	3.6
Ruston	3.8	8.5

•• **22** A small rural county has experienced unprecedented growth over the past 6 years, and as a result, the local school district built the new 500-student North Park Elementary School. The district has three older and smaller elementary schools: Washington, Jefferson, and Lincoln. Now the growth pressure is being felt at the secondary level. The school district would like to build a centrally located middle school to accommodate students and reduce busing costs. The older middle school is adjacent to the high school and will become part of the high school campus.

a) What are the coordinates of the central location?
b) What other factors should be considered before building a school?

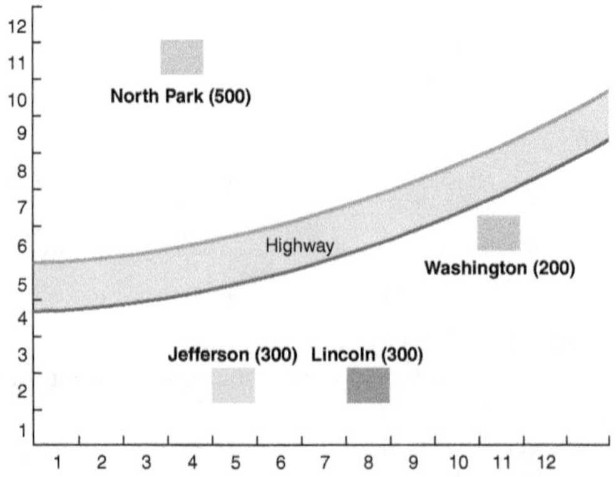

•• **23** Todd's Video, a major video rental and TV sales chain headquartered in New Orleans, is about to open its first outlet in Mobile, Alabama, and wants to select a site that will place the new outlet in the center of Mobile's population base. Todd examines the seven census tracts in Mobile, plots the coordinates of the center of each from a map, and looks up the population base in each to use as a weighting. The information gathered appears in the following table.

CENSUS TRACT	POPULATION IN CENSUS TRACT	*x*, *y* MAP COORDINATES
101	2,000	(25, 45)
102	5,000	(25, 25)
103	10,000	(55, 45)
104	7,000	(50, 20)
105	10,000	(80, 50)
106	20,000	(70, 20)
107	14,000	(90, 25)

a) At what center-of-gravity coordinates should the new store be located?

b) Census tracts 103 and 105 are each projected to grow by 20% in the next year. How will this influence the new store's coordinates?

•••• **24** Eagle Electronics must expand by building a second facility. The search has been narrowed down to locating the new facility in one of four cities: Atlanta (A), Baltimore (B), Chicago (C), or Dallas (D). The factors, scores, and weights follow:

			SCORES BY SITE			
I	FACTOR	WEIGHT (W_i)	A	B	C	D
1	Labor quality	20	5	4	4	5
2	Quality of life	16	2	3	4	1
3	Transportation	16	3	4	3	2
4	Proximity to markets	14	5	3	4	4
5	Proximity to suppliers	12	2	3	3	4
6	Taxes	12	2	5	5	4
7	Energy supplies	10	5	4	3	3

a) Using the factor-rating method, what is the recommended site for Eagle Electronics's new facility?

b) For what range of values for the weight (currently $w_7 = 10$) does the site given as the answer to part (a) remain a recommended site?

•••• **25** The EU has made changes in airline regulation that dramatically affect major European carriers such as British International Air (BIA), KLM, Air France, Alitalia, and Swiss International Air. With ambitious expansion plans, BIA has decided it needs a second service hub on the continent, to complement its large Heathrow (London) repair facility. The location selection is critical, and with the potential for 4,000 new skilled blue-collar jobs on the line, virtually every city in western Europe is actively bidding for BIA's business.

After initial investigations by Holmes Miller, head of the Operations Department, BIA has narrowed the list to 9 cities. Each is then rated on 12 factors, as shown in the table below.

a) Help Miller rank the top three cities that BIA should consider as its new site for servicing aircraft.

b) After further investigation, Miller decides that an existing set of hangar facilities for repairs is not nearly as important as earlier thought. If he lowers the weight of that factor to 30, does the ranking change?

c) After Miller makes the change in part (b), Germany announces it has reconsidered its offer of financial incentives, with an additional 200-million-euro package to entice BIA. Accordingly, BIA has raised Germany's rating to 10 on that factor. Is there any change in top rankings in part (b)?

Refer to MyOMLab for these additional homework problems: 8.26–8.34

DATA FOR PROBLEM 25

		LOCATION								
			ITALY			*FRANCE*			*GERMANY*	
FACTOR	IMPORTANCE WEIGHT	MILAN	ROME	GENOA	PARIS	LYON	NICE	MUNICH	BONN	BERLIN
Financial incentives	85	8	8	8	7	7	7	7	7	7
Skilled labor pool	80	4	6	5	9	9	7	10	8	9
Existing facility	70	5	3	2	9	6	5	9	9	2
Wage rates	70	9	8	9	4	6	6	4	5	5
Competition for jobs	70	7	3	8	2	8	7	4	8	9
Ease of air traffic access	65	5	4	6	2	8	8	4	8	9
Real estate cost	40	6	4	7	4	6	6	3	4	5
Communication links	25	6	7	6	9	9	9	10	9	8
Attractiveness to relocating executives	15	4	8	3	9	6	6	2	3	3
Political considerations	10	6	6	6	8	8	8	8	8	8
Expansion possibilities	10	10	2	8	1	5	4	4	5	6
Union strength	10	1	1	1	5	5	5	6	6	6

CASE STUDIES

Southern Recreational Vehicle Company

In October 2012, the top management of Southern Recreational Vehicle Company of St. Louis, Missouri, announced its plans to relocate its manufacturing and assembly operations to a new plant in Ridgecrest, Mississippi. The firm, a major producer of pickup campers and camper trailers, had experienced 5 consecutive years of declining profits as a result of spiraling production costs. The costs of labor and raw materials had increased alarmingly, utility costs had gone up sharply, and taxes and transportation expenses had steadily climbed upward. In spite of increased sales, the company suffered its first net loss since operations were begun in 1982.

When management initially considered relocation, it closely scrutinized several geographic areas. Of primary importance to the relocation decision were the availability of adequate transportation facilities, state and municipal tax structures, an adequate labor supply, positive community attitudes, reasonable site costs, and financial inducements. Although several communities offered essentially the same incentives, the management of Southern Recreational Vehicle Company was favorably impressed by the efforts of the Mississippi Power and Light Company to attract "clean, labor-intensive" industry and the enthusiasm exhibited by state and local officials, who actively sought to bolster the state's economy by enticing manufacturing firms to locate within its boundaries.

Two weeks prior to the announcement, management of Southern Recreational Vehicle Company finalized its relocation plans. An existing building in Ridgecrest's industrial park was selected (the physical facility had previously housed a mobile home manufacturer that had gone bankrupt due to inadequate financing and poor management); initial recruiting was begun through the state employment office; and efforts to lease or sell the St. Louis property were initiated. Among the inducements offered Southern Recreational Vehicle Company to locate in Ridgecrest were:

1. Exemption from county and municipal taxes for 5 years
2. Free water and sewage services
3. Construction of a second loading dock—free of cost—at the industrial site
4. An agreement to issue $500,000 in industrial bonds for future expansion
5. Public-financed training of workers in a local industrial trade school

In addition to these inducements, other factors weighed heavily in the decision to locate in the small Mississippi town. Labor costs would be significantly less than those incurred in St. Louis; organized labor was not expected to be as powerful (Mississippi is a right-to-work state); and utility costs and taxes would be moderate. All in all, the management of Southern Recreational Vehicle Company felt that its decision was sound.

On October 15, the following announcement was attached to each employee's paycheck:

> To: Employees of Southern Recreational Vehicle Company
>
> From: Gerald O'Brian, President
>
> The Management of Southern Recreational Vehicle Company regretfully announces its plans to cease all manufacturing operations in St. Louis on December 31. Because of increased operating costs and the unreasonable demands forced upon the company by the union, it has become impossible to operate profitably. I sincerely appreciate the fine service that each of you has rendered to the company during the past years. If I can be of assistance in helping you find suitable employment with another firm, please let me know. Thank you again for your cooperation and past service.

Discussion Questions

1. Evaluate the inducements offered Southern Recreational Vehicle Company by community leaders in Ridgecrest, Mississippi.
2. What problems would a company experience in relocating its executives from a heavily populated industrialized area to a small rural town?
3. Evaluate the reasons cited by O'Brian for relocation. Are they justifiable?
4. What legal and ethical responsibilities does a firm have to its employees when a decision to cease operations is made?

Source: Reprinted by permission of Professor Jerry Kinard, Western Carolina University.

Locating the Next Red Lobster Restaurant — Video Case

From its first Red Lobster in 1968, Darden Restaurants has grown the chain to 690 locations, with over $2.6 billion in U.S. sales annually. The casual dining market may be crowded, with competitors such as Chili's, Ruby Tuesday, Applebee's, TGI Friday's, and Outback, but Darden's continuing success means the chain thinks there is still plenty of room to grow. Robert Reiner, director of market development, is charged with identifying the sites that will maximize new store sales without cannibalizing sales at the existing Red Lobster locations.

Characteristics for identifying a good site have not changed in 40 years; they still include real estate prices, customer age, competition, ethnicity, income, family size, population density, nearby hotels, and buying behavior, to name just a few. What *has* changed is the powerful software that allows Reiner to analyze a new site in 5 minutes, as opposed to the 8 hours he spent just a few years ago.

Darden has partnered with MapInfo Corp., whose geographic information system (GIS) contains a powerful module for analyzing a trade area (see the discussion of GIS in the text). With the U.S. geocoded down to the individual block, MapInfo allows Reiner to create a psychographic profile of existing and potential Red Lobster trade areas. "We can now target areas with greatest sales potential," says Reiner.

The U.S. is segmented into 72 "clusters" of customer profiles by MapInfo. If, for example, cluster #7, Equestrian Heights (see MapInfo description below), represents 1.7% of a household base within a Red Lobster trade area, but this segment also accounts for

2.4% of sales, Reiner computes that this segment is effectively spending 1.39 times more than average (Index = 2.4/1.7) and adjusts his analysis of a new site to reflect this added weight.

CLUSTER	PSYTE 2003	SNAP SHOT DESCRIPTION
7	Equestrian Heights	They may not have a stallion in the barn, but they likely pass a corral on the way home. These families with teens live in older, larger homes adjacent to, or between, suburbs but not usually tract housing. Most are married with teenagers, but 40% are empty nesters. They use their graduate and professional school education—56% are dual earners. Over 90% are white, non-Hispanic. Their mean family income is $99,000, and they live within commuting distance of central cities. They have white-collar jobs during the week but require a riding lawn mower to keep the place up on weekends.

When Reiner maps the U.S., a state, or a region for a new site, he wants one that is at least 3 miles from the nearest Red Lobster and won't negatively impact its sales by more than 8%; MapInfo pinpoints the best spot. The software also recognizes the nearness of non-Darden competition and assigns a probability of success (as measured by reaching sales potential).

The specific spot selected depends on Darden's seven real estate brokers, whose list of considerations include proximity to a vibrant retail area, proximity to a freeway, road visibility, nearby hotels, and a corner location at a primary intersection.

"Picking a new Red Lobster location is one of the most critical functions we can do at Darden," says Reiner. "And the software we use serves as an independent voice in assessing the quality of an existing or proposed location."

Discussion Questions*

1. Visit the Web site for MapInfo (**www.mapinfo.com**). Describe the psychological profiling (PSYTE) clustering system. Select an industry, other than restaurants, and explain how the software can be used for that industry.
2. What are the major differences in site location for a restaurant versus a retail store versus a manufacturing plant?
3. Red Lobster also defines its trade areas based on market size and population density. Here are its seven density classes:

DENSITY CLASS	DESCRIPTION	HOUSEHOLDS per sq. MILE
1	Super Urban	8,000+
2	Urban	4,000–7,999
3	Light Urban	2,000–3,999
4	First Tier Suburban	1,000–1,999
5	Second Tier Suburban	600–999
6	Exurban/Small	100–599
7	Rural	0–99

Note: Density classes are based on the households and land area within 3 miles of the geography (e.g., census tract) using population-weighted centroids.

The majority (92%) of the Red Lobster restaurants fall into three of these classes. Which three classes do you think the chain has the most restaurants in? Why?

*You may wish to view the video that accompanies this case before answering the questions.

Where to Place the Hard Rock Cafe

Video Case

Some people would say that Oliver Munday, Hard Rock's vice president for cafe development, has the best job in the world. Travel the world to pick a country for Hard Rock's next cafe, select a city, and find the ideal site. It's true that selecting a site involves lots of incognito walking around, visiting nice restaurants, and drinking in bars. But that is not where Mr. Munday's work begins, nor where it ends. At the front end, selecting the country and city first involves a great deal of research. At the back end, Munday not only picks the final site and negotiates the deal but then works with architects and planners and stays with the project through the opening and first year's sales.

Munday is currently looking heavily into global expansion in Europe, Latin America, and Asia. "We've got to look at political risk, currency, and social norms—how does our brand fit into the country," he says. Once the country is selected, Munday focuses on the region and city. His research checklist is extensive, as seen in the accompanying table.

Site location now tends to focus on the tremendous resurgence of "city centers," where nightlife tends to concentrate. That's what Munday selected in Moscow and Bogota, although in both locations he chose to find a local partner and franchise the operation. In these two political environments, "Hard Rock wouldn't dream of operating by ourselves," says Munday. The location decision also is at least a 10- to 15-year commitment by Hard Rock, which employs tools such

Hard Rock's Standard Market Report (for offshore sites)

A. Demographics (local, city, region, SMSA), with trend analysis
   1. Population of area
   2. Economic indicators
B. Visitor market, with trend analysis
   1. Tourists/business visitors
   2. Hotels
   3. Convention center
   4. Entertainment
   5. Sports
   6. Retail
C. Transportation
   1. Airport ← subcategories include: (a) age of airport, (b) no. of passengers, (c) airlines, (d) direct flights, (e) hubs
   2. Rail
   3. Road
   4. Sea/river
D. Restaurants and nightclubs (a selection in key target market areas)
E. Political risk
F. Real estate market
G. Hard Rock Cafe comparable market analysis

as locational cost-volume analysis to help decide whether to purchase land and build, or to remodel an existing facility.

Currently, Munday is considering four European cities for Hard Rock's next expansion. Although he could not provide the names, for competitive reasons, the following is known:

FACTOR	*EUROPEAN CITY UNDER CONSIDERATION* A	B	C	D	IMPORTANCE OF THIS FACTOR AT THIS TIME
A. Demographics	70	70	60	90	20
B. Visitor market	80	60	90	75	20
C. Transportation	100	50	75	90	20
D. Restaurants/ nightclubs	80	90	65	65	10
E. Low political risk	90	60	50	70	10
F. Real estate market	65	75	85	70	10
G. Comparable market analysis	70	60	65	80	10

Discussion Questions*

1. From Munday's Standard Market Report checklist, select any other four categories, such as population (A1), hotels (B2), or restaurants/nightclubs (D), and provide three subcategories that should be evaluated. (See item C1 [airport] for a guide.)
2. Which is the highest rated of the four European cities under consideration, using the table above?
3. Why does Hard Rock put such serious effort into its location analysis?
4. Under what conditions do you think Hard Rock prefers to franchise a cafe?

*You may wish to view the video case before answering the questions.

- **Additional Case Study:** Visit **www.myomlab.com** or **www.pearsonhighered.com/heizer** for this free case study: **Southwestern University (E):** The university faces three choices as to where to locate its football stadium.

Bibliography

Ballou, Ronald H. *Business Logistics Management*, 5th ed. Upper Saddle River, NJ: Prentice Hall, 2004.

Bartness, A. D. "The Plant Location Puzzle." *Harvard Business Review* 72, no. 2 (March–April 1994).

Denton, B. "Decision Analysis, Location Models, and Scheduling Problems." *Interfaces* 30, no. 3 (May–June 2005): 262–263.

Drezner, Z. *Facility Location: Applications and Theory*. Berlin: Springer-Verlag, 2002.

Florida, R. *The Flight of the Creative Class: The New Global Competition for Talent*. New York: HarperCollins, 2005.

Klamroth, K. *Single Facility Location Problems*. Berlin: Springer-Verlag, 2002.

Kennedy, M. *Introducing Geographic Information Systems with ArcGIS*. New York: Wiley, 2006.

Mentzer, John T. "Seven Keys to Facility Location." *Supply Chain Management Review* 12, no. 5 (May 2008): 25.

Partovi, F. Y. "An Analytic Model for Locating Facilities Strategically." *Omega* 34, no. 1 (January 2006): 41.

Porter, Michael E., and Scott Stern. "Innovation: Location Matters." *MIT Sloan Management Review* (Summer 2001): 28–36.

Render, B., R. M. Stair, and M. Hanna. *Quantitative Analysis for Management*, 11th ed. Upper Saddle River, NJ: Prentice Hall, 2012.

Snyder, L. V. "Facility Location Under Uncertainty." *IIE Transactions* 38, no. 7 (July 2006): 547.

Tallman, Stephen, et al. "Knowledge, Clusters, and Competitive Advantage." *The Academy of Management Review* 29, no. 2 (April 2004): 258–271.

White, G. "Location, Location, Location." *Nation's Restaurant News* 42, no. 27 (July 14, 2008): S10–S11.

APPENDIX

SOLUTIONS TO EVEN-NUMBERED PROBLEMS

2 China, $1.44

4 India is $.05 less than elsewhere.

6 **(a)** Mobile = 53; Jackson = 60; select Jackson.
(b) Jackson now = 66.

8 **(a)** Hyde Park, with 54.5 points.
(b) Present location = 51 points.

10 **(a)** Location C, with a total *weighted* score of 1,530.
(b) Location B = 1,360
(c) B can never be in first place.

12 **(a)** Great Britain, at 36;
(b) Great Britain is now 31; Holland is 30.

14 **(a)** Italy is highest.
(b) Spain always lowest.

16 **(a)** Site 1 up to 125, site 2 from 125 to 233, site 3 above 233
(b) Site 2

18 **(a)** Above 10,000 cars, site C is lowest cost
(b) Site A optimal from 0–10,000 cars.
(c) Site B is never optimal.

20 **(a)** (5.15, 7.31)
(b) (5.13, 7.67)

22 **(a)** (6.23, 6.08);
(b) safety, etc.

24 **(a)** Site C is best, with a score of 374
(b) For all positive values of w_7 such that $w_7 \leq 14$

Rapid Review

Main Heading	Review Material	MyOMLab
THE STRATEGIC IMPORTANCE OF LOCATION	Location has a major impact on the overall risk and profit of the company. Transportation costs alone can total as much as 25% of the product's selling price. When all costs are considered, location may alter total operating expenses as much as 50%. Companies make location decisions relatively infrequently, usually because demand has outgrown the current plant's capacity or because of changes in labor productivity, exchange rates, costs, or local attitudes. Companies may also relocate their manufacturing or service facilities because of shifts in demographics and customer demand. Location options include (1) expanding an existing facility instead of moving, (2) maintaining current sites while adding another facility elsewhere, and (3) closing the existing facility and moving to another location. For industrial location decisions, the location strategy is usually minimizing costs. For retail and professional service organizations, the strategy focuses on maximizing revenue. Warehouse location strategy may be driven by a combination of cost and speed of delivery. *The objective of location strategy is to maximize the benefit of location to the firm.* When innovation is the focus, overall competitiveness and innovation are affected by (1) the presence of high-quality and specialized inputs such as scientific and technical talent, (2) an environment that encourages investment and intense local rivalry, (3) pressure and insight gained from a sophisticated local market, and (4) local presence of related and supporting industries.	**VIDEO 1** Hard Rock's Location Selection
FACTORS THAT AFFECT LOCATION DECISIONS	Globalization has taken place because of the development of (1) market economics; (2) better international communications; (3) more rapid, reliable travel and shipping; (4) ease of capital flow between countries; and (5) large differences in labor costs. Labor cost per unit is sometimes called the *labor content* of the product: Labor cost per unit = Labor cost per day ÷ Production (that is, units per day) Sometimes firms can take advantage of a particularly favorable exchange rate by relocating or exporting to (or importing from) a foreign country. ■ **Tangible costs**—Readily identifiable costs that can be measured with some precision. ■ **Intangible costs**—A category of location costs that cannot be easily quantified, such as quality of life and government. Many service organizations find that proximity to market is *the* primary location factor. Firms locate near their raw materials and suppliers because of (1) perishability, (2) transportation costs, or (3) bulk. ■ **Clustering**—Location of competing companies near each other, often because of a critical mass of information, talent, venture capital, or natural resources.	Problems: 1–4
METHODS OF EVALUATING LOCATION ALTERNATIVES	■ **Factor-rating method**—A location method that instills objectivity into the process of identifying hard-to-evaluate costs. The six steps of the factor-rating method are: 1. Develop a list of relevant factors called *key success factors*. 2. Assign a weight to each factor to reflect its relative importance in the company's objectives. 3. Develop a scale for each factor (for example, 1 to 10 or 1 to 100 points). 4. Have management score each location for each factor, using the scale in step 3. 5. Multiply the score by the weight for each factor and total the score for each location. 6. Make a recommendation based on the maximum point score, considering the results of other quantitative approaches as well. ■ **Locational cost–volume analysis**—A method used to make an economic comparison of location alternatives. The three steps to locational cost–volume analysis are: 1. Determine the fixed and variable cost for each location. 2. Plot the costs for each location, with costs on the vertical axis of the graph and annual volume on the horizontal axis. 3. Select the location that has the lowest total cost for the expected production volume.	Problems: 5–25 Virtual Office Hours for Solved Problems: 1, 2 **ACTIVE MODEL 1**

Main Heading	Review Material	MyOMLab
	■ **Center-of-gravity method**—A mathematical technique used for finding the best location for a single distribution point that services several stores or areas. The center-of-gravity method chooses the ideal location that minimizes the *weighted* distance between itself and the locations it serves, where the distance is weighted by the number of containers shipped, Q_i: $x\text{-coordinate of the center of gravity} = \sum_i d_{ix}Q_i \div \sum_i Q_i \quad (1)$ $y\text{-coordinate of the center of gravity} = \sum_i d_{iy}Q_i \div \sum_i Q_i \quad (2)$ ■ **Transportation model**—A technique for solving a class of linear programming problems. The transportation model determines the best pattern of shipments from several points of supply to several points of demand in order to minimize total production and transportation costs.	Virtual Office Hours for Solved Problem: 3
SERVICE LOCATION STRATEGY	The eight major determinants of volume and revenue for the service firm are: 1. Purchasing power of the customer-drawing area 2. Service and image compatibility with demographics of the customer-drawing area 3. Competition in the area 4. Quality of the competition 5. Uniqueness of the firm's and competitors' locations 6. Physical qualities of facilities and neighboring businesses 7. Operating policies of the firm 8. Quality of management	
GEOGRAPHIC INFORMATION SYSTEMS	■ **Geographic information system (GIS)**—A system that stores and displays information that can be linked to a geographic location. Some of the geographic databases available in many GISs include (1) census data by block, tract, city, county, congressional district, metropolitan area, state, and zip code; (2) maps of every street, highway, bridge, and tunnel in the United States; (3) utilities such as electrical, water, and gas lines; (4) all rivers, mountains, lakes, and forests; and (5) all major airports, colleges, and hospitals.	**VIDEO 2** Locating the Next Red Lobster Restaurant

Self Test

■ **Before taking the self-test**, refer to the learning objectives listed at the beginning of the text and the key terms listed at the end of the text.

LO1. The factors involved in location decisions include
- **a)** foreign exchange.
- **b)** attitudes.
- **c)** labor productivity.
- **d)** all of the above.

LO2. If Fender Guitar pays $30 per day to a worker in its Ensenada, Mexico, plant, and the employee completes four instruments per 8-hour day, the labor cost/unit is
- **a)** $30.00.
- **b)** $3.75.
- **c)** $7.50.
- **d)** $4.00.
- **e)** $8.00.

LO3. Evaluating location alternatives by comparing their composite (weighted-average) scores involves
- **a)** factor-rating analysis.
- **b)** cost–volume analysis.
- **c)** transportation model analysis.
- **d)** linear regression analysis.
- **e)** crossover analysis.

LO4. On the cost–volume analysis chart where the costs of two or more location alternatives have been plotted, the quantity at which two cost curves cross is the quantity at which:
- **a)** fixed costs are equal for two alternative locations.
- **b)** variable costs are equal for two alternative locations.
- **c)** total costs are equal for all alternative locations.
- **d)** fixed costs equal variable costs for one location.
- **e)** total costs are equal for two alternative locations.

LO5. A regional bookstore chain is about to build a distribution center that is centrally located for its eight retail outlets. It will most likely employ which of the following tools of analysis?
- **a)** Assembly-line balancing
- **b)** Load–distance analysis
- **c)** Center-of-gravity model
- **d)** Linear programming
- **e)** All of the above

LO6. What is the major difference in focus between location decisions in the service sector and in the manufacturing sector?
- **a)** There is no difference in focus.
- **b)** The focus in manufacturing is revenue maximization, while the focus in service is cost minimization.
- **c)** The focus in service is revenue maximization, while the focus in manufacturing is cost minimization.
- **d)** The focus in manufacturing is on raw materials, while the focus in service is on labor.

Answers: LO1. d; LO2. c; LO3. a; LO4. e; LO5. c; LO6. c.

Layout Strategies

OUTLINE

GLOBAL COMPANY PROFILE: ***McDonald's***

- The Strategic Importance of Layout Decisions
- Types of Layout
- Office Layout
- Retail Layout
- Warehouse and Storage Layouts
- Fixed-Position Layout
- Process-Oriented Layout
- Work Cells
- Repetitive and Product-Oriented Layout

10 OM STRATEGY DECISIONS

- Design of Goods and Services
- Managing Quality
- Process Strategy
- Location Strategies
- *Layout Strategies*
- Human Resources
- Supply-Chain Management
- Inventory Management
- Scheduling
- Maintenance

McDonald's Looks for Competitive Advantage Through Layout

In its over half-century of existence, McDonald's has revolutionized the restaurant industry by inventing the limited-menu fast-food restaurant. It has also made seven major innovations. The first, the introduction of *indoor seating* (1950s), was a layout issue, as was the second, *drive-through windows* (1970s). The third, adding *breakfasts* to the menu (1980s), was a product strategy. The fourth, *adding play areas* (late 1980s), was again a layout decision.

In the 1990s, McDonald's completed its fifth innovation, a radically new *redesign of the kitchens* in its 14,000 North American outlets to facilitate a mass customization process. Dubbed the "Made by You" kitchen system, sandwiches were assembled to order with the revamped layout.

In 2004, the chain began the rollout of its sixth innovation, a new food ordering layout: the *self-service kiosk*. Self-service kiosks have been infiltrating the service sector since the introduction of ATMs in 1985 (there are over 1.5 million ATMs in banking). Alaska Airlines was the first airline to provide self-service airport check-in, in 1996. Most passengers of the major airlines now check themselves in for flights. Kiosks take up less space than an employee and reduce waiting line time.

Now, McDonald's is working on its seventh innovation, and not surprisingly, it also deals with restaurant layout. The company, on an unprecedented scale, is redesigning all 30,000 eateries around the globe to take on a *21st century look*. The dining area will be separated into three sections with distinct personalities: (1) the "linger" zone focuses on young adults and offers

Rick Wilking/Corbis

McDonald's finds that kiosks reduce both space requirements and waiting; order taking is faster. An added benefit is that customers like them. Also, kiosks are reliable—they don't call in sick. And, most importantly, sales are up 10%–15% (an average of $1) when a customer orders from a kiosk, which consistently recommends the larger size and other extras.

Nancy Siesel/Redux

The redesigned kitchen of a McDonald's in Manhattan. The more efficient layout requires less labor, reduces waste, and provides faster service. A graphic of this "assembly line" is shown in Figure 11.

comfortable furniture and Wi-Fi connections; (2) the "grab and go" zone features tall counters, bar stools, and flat-screen TVs; and (3) the "flexible" zone has colorful family booths, flexible seating, and kid-oriented music. The cost per outlet: a whopping \$300,000–\$400,000 renovation fee.

As McDonald's has discovered, facility layout is indeed a source of competitive advantage.

© ZUMA Press, Inc./Alamy

Flexible Zone
This area is geared for family and larger groups, with movable tables and chairs.

Callie Lipkin Photography, Inc.

Grab & Go Zone
This section has tall counters with bar stools for customers who eat alone. Flat-screen TVs keep them company.

Callie Lipkin Photography, Inc.

Linger Zone
Cozy booths, plus Wi-Fi connections, make these areas attractive to those who want to hang out and socialize.

LEARNING OBJECTIVES

- **LO1** ***Discuss*** important issues in office layout
- **LO2** ***Define*** the objectives of retail layout
- **LO3** ***Discuss*** modern warehouse management and terms such as ASRS, cross-docking, and random stocking
- **LO4** ***Identify*** when fixed-position layouts are appropriate
- **LO5** ***Explain*** how to achieve a good process-oriented facility layout
- **LO6** ***Define*** work cell and the requirements of a work cell
- **LO7** ***Define*** product-oriented layout
- **LO8** ***Explain*** how to balance production flow in a repetitive or product-oriented facility

The Strategic Importance of Layout Decisions

Layout is one of the key decisions that determines the long-run efficiency of operations. Layout has strategic implication because it establishes an organization's competitive priorities in regard to capacity, processes, flexibility, and cost, as well as quality of work life, customer contact, and image. An effective layout can help an organization achieve a strategy that supports differentiation, low cost, or response. Benetton, for example, supports a *differentiation* strategy by heavy investment in warehouse layouts that contribute to fast, accurate sorting and shipping to its 5,000 outlets. Walmart store layouts support a strategy of *low cost*, as do its warehouse layouts. Hallmark's office layouts, where many professionals operate with open communication in work cells, support *rapid development* of greeting cards. *The objective of layout strategy is to develop an effective and efficient layout that will meet the firm's competitive requirements.* These firms have done so.

In all cases, layout design must consider how to achieve the following:

- Higher utilization of space, equipment, and people
- Improved flow of information, materials, and people
- Improved employee morale and safer working conditions
- Improved customer/client interaction
- Flexibility (whatever the layout is now, it will need to change)

In our increasingly short-life-cycle, mass-customized world, layout designs need to be viewed as dynamic.This means considering small, movable, and flexible equipment. Store displays need to be movable, office desks and partitions modular, and warehouse racks prefabricated. To make quick and easy changes in product models and in production rates, operations managers must design flexibility into layouts. To obtain flexibility in layout, managers cross-train their workers, maintain equipment, keep investments low, place workstations close together, and use small, movable equipment. In some cases, equipment on wheels is appropriate, in anticipation of the next change in product, process, or volume.

Types of Layout

Layout decisions include the best placement of machines (in production settings), offices and desks (in office settings), or service centers (in settings such as hospitals or department stores). An effective layout facilitates the flow of materials, people, and information within and between areas. To achieve these objectives, a variety of approaches has been developed. We will discuss seven of them in this text:

1. *Office layout:* Positions workers, their equipment, and spaces/offices to provide for movement of information.
2. *Retail layout:* Allocates display space and responds to customer behavior.
3. *Warehouse layout:* Addresses trade-offs between space and material handling.
4. *Fixed-position layout:* Addresses the layout requirements of large, bulky projects such as ships and buildings.
5. *Process-oriented layout:* Deals with low-volume, high-variety production (also called "job shop," or intermittent production).

TABLE 1 Layout Strategies

	OBJECTIVES	EXAMPLES
Office	Locate workers requiring frequent contact close to one another	Allstate Insurance Microsoft Corp.
Retail	Expose customer to high-margin items	Kroger's Supermarket Walgreens Bloomingdale's
Warehouse (storage)	Balance low-cost storage with low cost material handling	Federal-Mogul's warehouse The Gap's distribution center
Project (fixed position)	Move material to the limited storage areas around the site	Ingall Ship Building Corp. Trump Plaza Pittsburgh Airport
Job shop (process oriented)	Manage varied material flow for each product	Arnold Palmer Hospital Hard Rock Cafe Olive Garden
Work cell (product families)	Identify a product family, build teams, cross-train team members	Hallmark Cards Wheeled Coach Ambulances
Repetitive/continuous (product oriented)	Equalize the task time at each workstation	Sony's TV assembly line Toyota Scion

6. *Work-cell layout:* Arranges machinery and equipment to focus on production of a single product or group of related products.
7. *Product-oriented layout:* Seeks the best personnel and machine utilization in repetitive or continuous production.

Examples for each of these classes of layouts are noted in Table 1.

Because only a few of these seven classes can be modeled mathematically, layout and design of physical facilities are still something of an art. However, we do know that a good layout requires determining the following:

- *Material handling equipment:* Managers must decide about equipment to be used, including conveyors, cranes, automated storage and retrieval systems, and automatic carts to deliver and store material.
- *Capacity and space requirements:* Only when personnel, machines, and equipment requirements are known can managers proceed with layout and provide space for each component. In the case of office work, operations managers must make judgments about the space requirements for each employee. They must also consider allowances for requirements that address safety, noise, dust, fumes, temperature, and space around equipment and machines.
- *Environment and aesthetics:* Layout concerns often require decisions about windows, planters, and height of partitions to facilitate air flow, reduce noise and provide privacy.
- *Flows of information:* Communication is important to any organization and must be facilitated by the layout. This issue may require decisions about proximity, as well as decisions about open spaces versus half-height dividers versus private offices.
- *Cost of moving between various work areas:* There may be unique considerations related to moving materials or to the importance of having certain areas next to each other. For example, moving molten steel is more difficult than moving cold steel.

Office Layout

Office layouts require the grouping of workers, their equipment, and spaces to provide for comfort, safety, and movement of information. The main distinction of office layouts is the importance placed on the flow of information. Office layouts are in constant flux as the technological changes sweeping society alter the way offices function.

Office layout
The grouping of workers, their equipment, and spaces/offices to provide for comfort, safety, and movement of information.

Even though the movement of information is increasingly electronic, analysis of office layouts still requires a task-based approach. Managers therefore examine both electronic and conventional communication patterns, separation needs, and other conditions affecting employee effectiveness. A useful tool for such an analysis is the *relationship chart* shown in Figure 1. This

Figure 1

Office Relationship Chart

Source: Adapted from Richard Muther, *Simplified Systematic Layout Planning*, 3rd ed. (Kansas City, Mgt. & Ind'l Research Publications). Used by permission of the publisher.

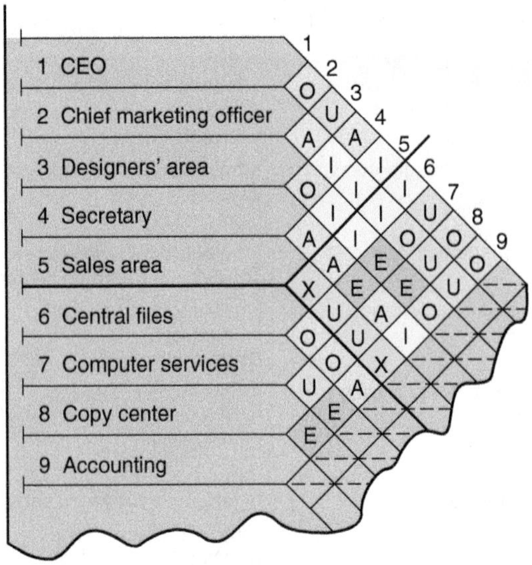

Value	CLOSENESS
A	Absolutely necessary
E	Especially important
I	Important
O	Ordinary OK
U	Unimportant
X	Not desirable

LO1 *Discuss* important issues in office layout

chart, prepared for an office of product designers, indicates that the chief marketing officer must be (1) near the designers' area, (2) less near the secretary and central files, and (3) not at all near the copy center or accounting department.

On the other hand, some layout considerations are universal (many of which apply to factories as well as to offices). They have to do with working conditions, teamwork, authority, and status. Should offices be private or open cubicles, have low file cabinets to foster informal communication or high cabinets to reduce noise and contribute to privacy? (See the *OM in Action* box "Layout and the Shrinking Office").

Workspace can inspire informal and productive encounters if it balances three physical and social aspects[1]:

- *Proximity*: Spaces should naturally bring people together.
- *Privacy*: People must be able to control access to their conversations.
- *Permission*: The culture should signal that non-work interactions are encouraged.

As a final comment on office layout, we note two major trends. First, technology, such as cell phones, iPods, faxes, the Internet, laptop computers, and tablets, allows increasing layout

OM in Action Layout and the Shrinking Office

Your future office may be a lot smaller than you had planned. But that's not all bad. As employees become more mobile and less tied to their desks, the workspace per employee nationwide (across all industries) has dropped from 400 square feet in 1985 to 250 square feet today. And it's heading towards 150 square feet within 10 years.

"A lot of thinking about the office has changed," says the president of Steelcase, the leading office furniture maker. "The work setting was a reflection of your status. A job focuses more on collaboration than on the individual now."

Intel, for example, was known for decades for its endless rows of gray cubicles, low ceilings, and fluorescent lighting. Never one of those tech companies to offer beanbag chairs, designer desks, or pinball machines, Intel has just completed a major re-layout of over 1 million square feet of office space. Gray walls are now yellow, purple, and white; cubicle walls are low enough to see other employees; and lounges have been equipped with flat-screen TVs, comfy chairs, and sleek kitchens. The whole idea was to get people to work more in groups rather than be isolated at their desks.

© nyul

This also saves money. With less space needed per person, one newly laid-out floor at Intel holds 1,000 employees, up from 600. In some departments where employees are on the road a lot, two people may be assigned to one desk. Even tradition-bound firms in accounting and banking are embracing open-floor layouts. The thinking is that downsizing makes people interact more and become more productive.

Sources: The New York Times (January 19, 2011); and *The Wall Street Journal* (January 4, 2012).

[1]Fayurd, A. L., and J. Weeks. "Who Moved My Cube?" *Harvard Business Review* (July-August, 2011): 102.

flexibility by moving information electronically and allowing employees to work offsite. Second, modern firms create dynamic needs for space and services.

Here are two examples:[2]

- When Deloitte & Touche found that 30% to 40% of desks were empty at any given time, the firm developed its "hoteling programs." Consultants lost their permanent offices; anyone who plans to be in the building (rather than out with clients) books an office through a "concierge," who hangs that consultant's name on the door for the day and stocks the space with requested supplies.
- Cisco Systems cut rent and workplace service costs by 37% and saw productivity benefits of $2.4 billion per year by reducing square footage, reconfiguring space, creating movable, everything-on-wheels offices, and designing "get away from it all" innovation areas.

Retail Layout

Retail layouts are based on the idea that sales and profitability vary directly with customer exposure to products. Thus, most retail operations managers try to expose customers to as many products as possible. Studies do show that the greater the rate of exposure, the greater the sales and the higher the return on investment. The operations manager can change exposure with store arrangement and the allocation of space to various products within that arrangement.

Retail layout
An approach that addresses flow, allocates space, and responds to customer behavior

Five ideas are helpful for determining the overall arrangement of many stores:

1. Locate the high-draw items around the periphery of the store. Thus, we tend to find dairy products on one side of a supermarket and bread and bakery products on another. An example of this tactic is shown in Figure 2.
2. Use prominent locations for high-impulse and high-margin items. Best Buy puts fast-growing, high-margin digital goods—such as cameras and printers—in the front and center of its stores.
3. Distribute what are known in the trade as "power items"—items that may dominate a purchasing trip—to both sides of an aisle, and disperse them to increase the viewing of other items.
4. Use end-aisle locations because they have a very high exposure rate.
5. Convey the mission of the store by carefully selecting the position of the lead-off department. For instance, if prepared foods are part of a supermarket's mission, position the bakery and deli up front to appeal to convenience-oriented customers. Walmart's push to increase sales of clothes means those departments are in broad view upon entering a store.

STUDENT TIP
The goal in a retail layout is to maximize profit per square foot of store space.

LO2 *Define* the objectives of retail layout

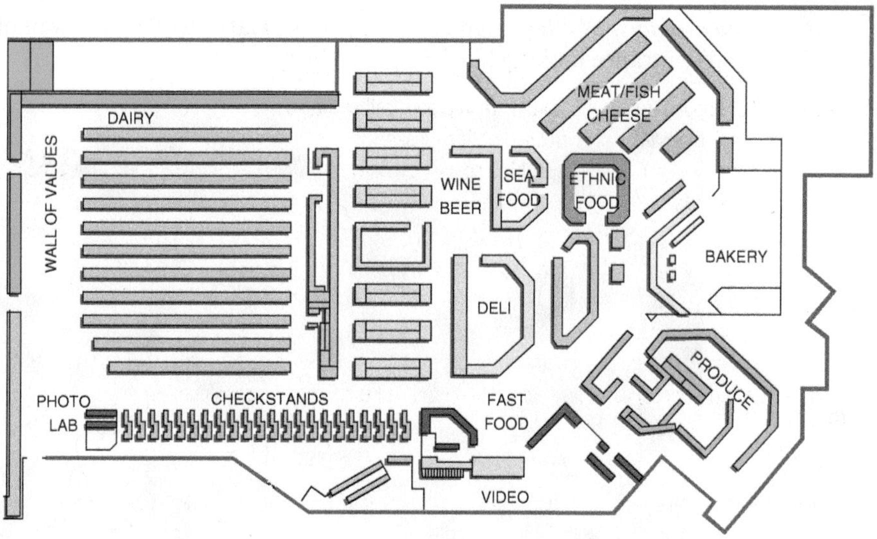

Figure 2
Store Layout with Dairy and Bakery, High-Draw Items, in Different Areas of the Store

[2]"Square Feet. Oh, How Square!" *BusinessWeek* (July 3, 2006): 100–101.

Once the overall layout of a retail store has been decided, products need to be arranged for sale. Many considerations go into this arrangement. However, the main *objective of retail layout is to maximize profitability per square foot of floor space* (or, in some stores, on linear foot of shelf space). Big-ticket, or expensive, items may yield greater dollar sales, but the profit per square foot may be lower. Computerized programs are available to assist managers in evaluating the profitability of various merchandising plans for hundreds of categories: this technique is known as category management.

Slotting fees
Fees manufacturers pay to get shelf space for their products.

An additional, and somewhat controversial, issue in retail layout is called slotting. **Slotting fees** are fees manufacturers pay to get their goods on the shelf in a retail store or supermarket chain. The result of massive new-product introductions, retailers can now demand up to $25,000 to place an item in their chain. During the last decade, marketplace economics, consolidations, and technology have provided retailers with this leverage. The competition for shelf space is advanced by POS systems and scanner technology, which improve supply-chain management and inventory control. Many small firms question the legality and ethics of slotting fees, claiming the fees stifle new products, limit their ability to expand, and cost consumers money. Walmart is one of the few major retailers that does not demand slotting fees, removing a barrier to entry. (See the *Ethical Dilemma* at the end of this text.)

Servicescapes

Servicescape
The physical surroundings in which a service takes place, and how they affect customers and employees.

Although a major goal of retail layout is to maximize profit through product exposure, there are other aspects of the service that managers consider. The term **servicescape** describes the physical surroundings in which the service is delivered and how the surroundings have a humanistic effect on customers and employees. To provide a good service layout, a firm considers three elements:

1. *Ambient conditions*, which are background characteristics such as lighting, sound, smell, and temperature. All these affect workers *and* customers and can affect how much is spent and how long a person stays in the building.
2. *Spatial layout and functionality*, which involve customer circulation path planning, aisle characteristics (such as width, direction, angle, and shelf spacing), and product grouping.
3. *Signs, symbols, and artifacts*, which are characteristics of building design that carry social significance (such as carpeted areas of a department store that encourage shoppers to slow down and browse).

Examples of each of these three elements of servicescape are:

- *Ambient conditions:* Fine-dining restaurants with linen tablecloths and candlelit atmosphere; Mrs. Field's Cookie bakery smells permeating the shopping mall; leather chairs at Starbucks.
- *Layout/functionality:* Kroger's long aisles and high shelves; Best Buy's wide center aisle.
- *Signs, symbols, and artifacts:* Walmart's greeter at the door; Hard Rock Cafe's wall of guitars; Disneyland's entrance looking like hometown heaven.

© imagebroker/Alamy

A critical element contributing to the bottom line at Hard Rock Cafe is the layout of each cafe's retail shop space. The retail space, from 600 to 1,300 square feet in size, is laid out in conjunction with the restaurant area to create the maximum traffic flow before and after eating. The payoffs for cafes like this one in London are huge. Almost half of a cafe's annual sales are generated from these small shops, which have very high retail sales per square foot.

Warehouse and Storage Layouts

The objective of warehouse layout *is to find the optimum trade-off between handling cost and costs associated with warehouse space*. Consequently, management's task is to maximize the utilization of the total "cube" of the warehouse—that is, utilize its full volume while maintaining low material handling costs. We define *material handling costs* as all the costs related to the transaction. This consists of incoming transport, storage, and outgoing transport of the materials to be warehoused. These costs include equipment, people, material, supervision, insurance, and depreciation. Effective warehouse layouts do, of course, also minimize the damage and spoilage of material within the warehouse.

Warehouse layout
A design that attempts to minimize total cost by addressing trade-offs between space and material handling.

Management minimizes the sum of the resources spent on finding and moving material plus the deterioration and damage to the material itself. The variety of items stored and the number of items "picked" has direct bearing on the optimum layout. A warehouse storing a few unique items lends itself to higher density than a warehouse storing a variety of items. Modern warehouse management is, in many instances, an automated procedure using *automated storage and retrieval systems* (ASRSs).

STUDENT TIP
In warehouse layout, we want to maximize use of the whole building—from floor to ceiling.

The Stop & Shop grocery chain, with 350 supermarkets in New England, has recently completed the largest ASRS in the world. The 1.3-million-square-foot distribution center in Freetown, Massachusetts, employs 77 rotating-fork automated storage and retrieval machines. These 77 cranes each access 11,500 pick slots on 90 aisles—a total of 64,000 pallets of food. The Wolfsburg, Germany, parking garage photo (below) indicates that an ASRS can take many forms.

An important component of warehouse layout is the relationship between the receiving/unloading area and the shipping/loading area. Facility design depends on the type of supplies unloaded, what they are unloaded from (trucks, rail cars, barges, and so on), and where they are unloaded. In some companies, the receiving and shipping facilities, or *docks*, as they are called, are even in the same area; sometimes they are receiving docks in the morning and shipping docks in the afternoon.

LO3 *Discuss* modern warehouse management and terms such as ASRS, cross-docking, and random stocking

Cross-Docking

Cross-docking means to avoid placing materials or supplies in storage by processing them as they are received. In a manufacturing facility, product is received directly by the assembly line. In a distribution center, labeled and presorted loads arrive at the shipping dock for immediate rerouting, thereby avoiding formal receiving, stocking/storing, and order-selection activities. Because these activities add no value to the product, their elimination is 100% cost savings. Walmart, an early advocate of cross-docking, uses the technique as a major component of

Cross-docking
Avoiding the placement of materials or supplies in storage by processing them as they are received for shipment.

Automated storage and retrieval systems are not found only in traditional warehouses. This parking garage in Wolfsburg, Germany, occupies only 20% of the space of a traditionally designed garage. The ASRS "retrieves" autos in less time, without the potential of the cars being damaged by an attendant.

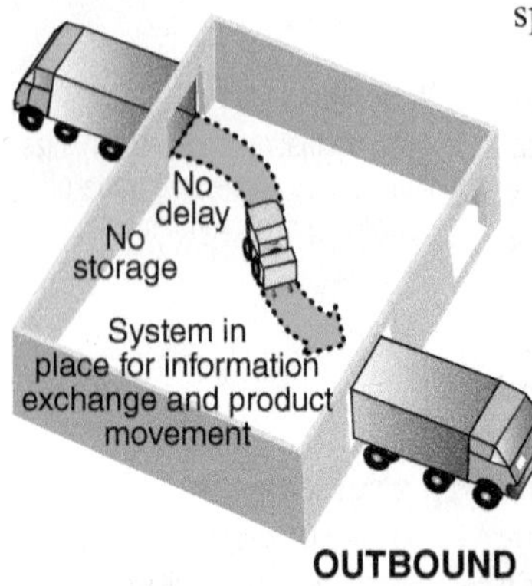

its continuing low-cost strategy. With cross-docking, Walmart reduces distribution costs and speeds restocking of stores, thereby improving customer service. Although cross-docking reduces product handling, inventory, and facility costs, it requires both (1) tight scheduling and (2) accurate inbound product identification.

Random Stocking

Random stocking
Used in warehousing to locate stock wherever there is an open location.

Automatic identification systems (AISs), usually in the form of bar codes, allow accurate and rapid item identification. When automatic identification systems are combined with effective management information systems, operations managers know the quantity and location of every unit. This information can be used with human operators or with automatic storage and retrieval systems to load units anywhere in the warehouse—randomly. Accurate inventory quantities and locations mean the potential utilization of the whole facility because space does not need to be reserved for certain stock-keeping units (SKUs) or part families. Computerized random stocking systems often include the following tasks:

1. Maintaining a list of "open" locations
2. Maintaining accurate records of existing inventory and its locations
3. Sequencing items to minimize the travel time required to "pick" orders
4. Combining orders to reduce picking time
5. Assigning certain items or classes of items, such as high-usage items, to particular warehouse areas so that the total distance traveled within the warehouse is minimized

Random stocking systems can increase facility utilization and decrease labor cost, but they require accurate records.

Customizing

Customizing
Using warehousing to add value to a product through component modification, repair, labeling, and packaging.

Although we expect warehouses to store as little product as possible and hold it for as short a time as possible, we are now asking warehouses to customize products. Warehouses can be places where value is added through customizing. Warehouse customization is a particularly useful way to generate competitive advantage in markets where products have multiple configurations. For instance, a warehouse can be a place where computer components are put together, software loaded, and repairs made. Warehouses may also provide customized labeling and packaging for retailers so items arrive ready for display.

Increasingly, this type of work goes on adjacent to major airports, in facilities such as the FedEx terminal in Memphis. Adding value at warehouses adjacent to major airports also facilitates overnight delivery. For example, if your computer has failed, the replacement may be sent to you from such a warehouse for delivery the next morning. When your old machine arrives back at the warehouse, it is repaired and sent to someone else. These value-added activities at "quasi-warehouses" contribute to strategies of differentiation, low cost, and rapid response.

Fixed-Position Layout

Fixed-position layout
A system that addresses the layout requirements of stationary projects.

In a fixed-position layout, the project remains in one place and workers and equipment come to that one work area. Examples of this type of project are a ship, a highway, a bridge, a house, and an operating table in a hospital operating room.

The techniques for addressing the fixed-position layout are complicated by three factors. First, there is limited space at virtually all sites. Second, at different stages of a project, different materials are needed; therefore, different items become critical as the project develops. Third, the volume of materials needed is dynamic. For example, the rate of use of steel panels for the hull of a ship changes as the project progresses.

LO4 *Identify* when fixed-position layouts are appropriate

Because problems with fixed-position layouts are so difficult to solve well onsite, an alternative strategy is to complete as much of the project as possible offsite. This approach is used in the shipbuilding industry when standard units—say, pipe-holding brackets—are assembled on a nearby assembly line (a product-oriented facility). In an attempt to add efficiency to shipbuilding,

Here are three versions of the fixed-position layout.

Craig Ruttle/AP World Wide Photos

A house built via traditional fixed-position layout would be constructed onsite, with equipment, materials, and workers brought to the site. Then a "meeting of the trades" would assign space for various time periods. However, the home pictured here can be built at a much lower cost. The house is built in two movable modules in a factory. Scaffolding and hoists make the job easier, quicker, and cheaper, and the indoor work environment aids labor productivity.

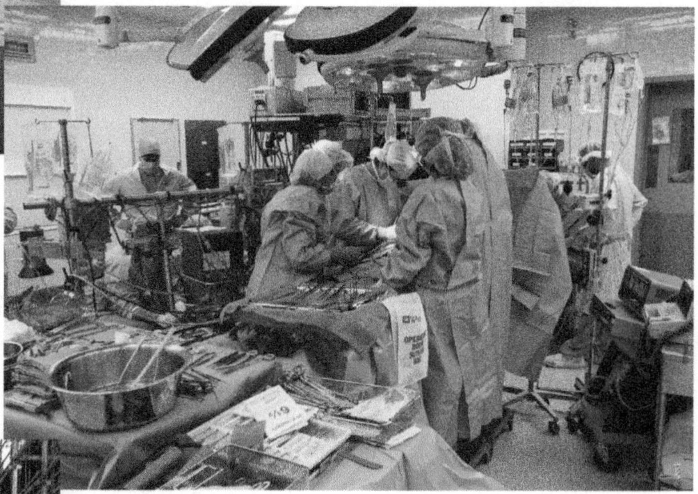

Dick Blume/The Image Works

A service example of a fixed-position layout is an operating room; the patient remains stationary on the table, and medical personnel and equipment are brought to the site.

Corbis Images

In shipbuilding, there is limited space next to the fixed-position layout. Shipyards call these loading areas platens, and they are assigned for various time periods to each contractor.

Ingall Ship Building Corporation has moved toward product-oriented production when sections of a ship (modules) are similar or when it has a contract to build the same section of several similar ships. Also, as the top photo on the page shows, many home builders are moving from a fixed-position layout strategy to one that is more product oriented. About one-third of all new homes in the U.S. are built this way. In addition, many houses that are built onsite (fixed position) have the majority of components such as doors, windows, fixtures, trusses, stairs, and wallboard built as modules in more efficient offsite processes.

Process-Oriented Layout

Process-oriented layout
A layout that deals with low-volume, high-variety production in which like machines and equipment are grouped together.

A process-oriented layout can simultaneously handle a wide variety of products or services. This is the traditional way to support a product differentiation strategy. It is most efficient when making products with different requirements or when handling customers, patients, or clients

Figure 3

An Emergency Room Process Layout Showing the Routing of Two Patients

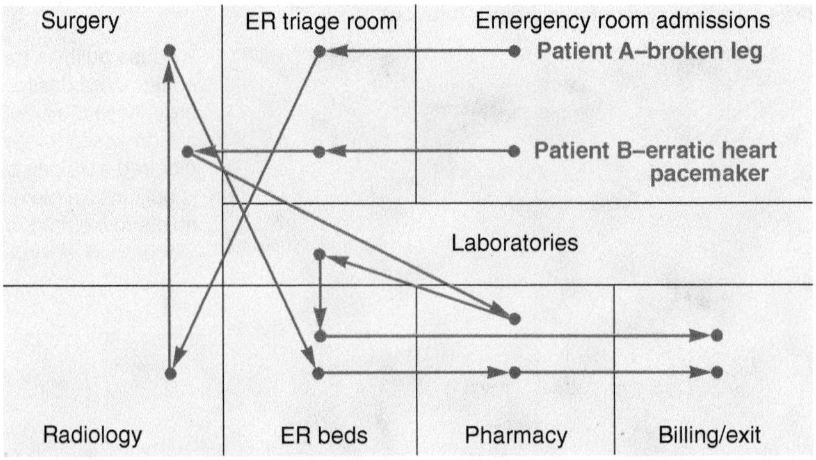

STUDENT TIP

Patient A (broken leg) proceeds (blue arrow) to ER triage, to radiology, to surgery, to a bed, to pharmacy, to billing. Patient B (pacemaker problem) moves (red arrow) to ER triage, to surgery, to pharmacy, to lab, to a bed, to billing.

with different needs. A process-oriented layout is typically the low-volume, high-variety strategy. In this job-shop environment, each product or each small group of products undergoes a different sequence of operations. A product or small order is produced by moving it from one department to another in the sequence required for that product. A good example of the process-oriented layout is a hospital or clinic. Figure 3 illustrates the process for two patients, A and B, at an emergency clinic in Chicago. An inflow of patients, each with his or her own needs, requires routing through admissions, laboratories, operating rooms, radiology, pharmacies, nursing beds, and so on. Equipment, skills, and supervision are organized around these processes.

VIDEO 1
Laying Out Arnold Palmer Hospital's New Facility

A big advantage of process-oriented layout is its flexibility in equipment and labor assignments. The breakdown of one machine, for example, need not halt an entire process; work can be transferred to other machines in the department. Process-oriented layout is also especially good for handling the manufacture of parts in small batches, or job lots, and for the production of a wide variety of parts in different sizes or forms.

Job lots
Groups or batches of parts processed together.

The disadvantages of process-oriented layout come from the general-purpose use of the equipment. Orders take more time to move through the system because of difficult scheduling, changing setups, and unique material handling. In addition, general-purpose equipment requires high labor skills, and work-in-process inventories are higher because of imbalances in the production process. High labor-skill needs also increase the required level of training and experience, and high work-in-process levels increase capital investment.

LO5 *Explain* how to achieve a good process-oriented facility layout

When designing a process layout, the most common tactic is to arrange departments or work centers so as to minimize the costs of material handling. In other words, departments with large flows of parts or people between them should be placed next to one another. Material handling costs in this approach depend on (1) the number of loads (or people) to be moved between two departments during some period of time and (2) the distance-related costs of moving loads (or people) between departments. Cost is assumed to be a function of distance between departments. The objective can be expressed as follows:

$$\text{Minimize cost} = \sum_{i=1}^{n} \sum_{j=1}^{n} X_{ij}C_{ij} \quad (1)$$

where n = total number of work centers or departments
i,j = individual departments
X_{ij} = number of loads moved from department i to department j
C_{ij} = cost to move a load between department i and department j

Process-oriented facilities (and fixed-position layouts as well) try to minimize loads, or trips, multiplied by distance-related costs. The term C_{ij} combines distance and other costs into one factor. We thereby assume not only that the difficulty of movement is equal but also that the pickup and setdown costs are constant. Although they are not always constant, for simplicity's sake we summarize these data (that is, distance, difficulty, and pickup and setdown costs) in this one variable, cost. The best way to understand the steps involved in designing a process layout is to look at an example.

Example 1

DESIGNING A PROCESS LAYOUT

Walters Company management wants to arrange the six departments of its factory in a way that will minimize interdepartmental material-handling costs. They make an initial assumption (to simplify the problem) that each department is 20×20 feet and that the building is 60 feet long and 40 feet wide.

APPROACH AND SOLUTION ▶ The process layout procedure that they follow involves six steps:

Step 1: *Construct a "from–to matrix"* showing the flow of parts or materials from department to department (see Figure 4).

Figure 4

Interdepartmental Flow of Parts

STUDENT TIP ☆ The high flows between 1 and 3 and between 3 and 6 are immediately apparent. Departments 1, 3, and 6, therefore, should be close together.

Number of loads per week

Department	Assembly (1)	Painting (2)	Machine Shop (3)	Receiving (4)	Shipping (5)	Testing (6)
Assembly (1)		50	100	0	0	20
Painting (2)			30	50	10	0
Machine Shop (3)				20	0	100
Receiving (4)					50	0
Shipping (5)						0
Testing (6)						

Step 2: *Determine the space requirements* for each department. (Figure 5 shows available plant space.)

Figure 5

Building Dimensions and One Possible Department Layout

STUDENT TIP ☆ Think of this as a starting, initial, layout. Our goal is to improve it, if possible.

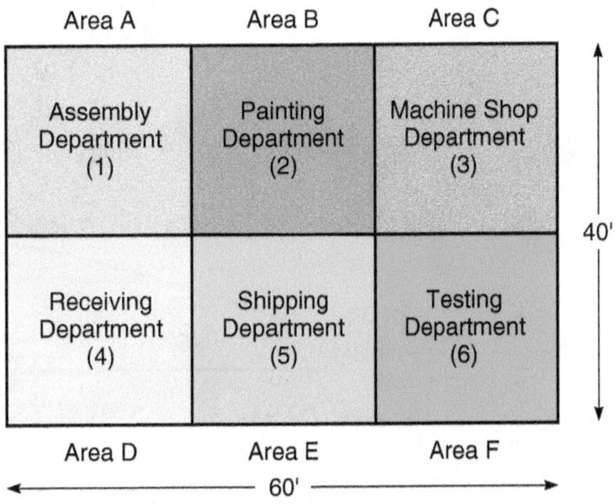

Step 3: *Develop an initial schematic diagram* showing the sequence of departments through which parts must move. Try to place departments with a heavy flow of materials or parts next to one another. (See Figure 6.)

Figure 6

Interdepartmental Flow Graph Showing Number of Weekly Loads

STUDENT TIP ☆ This shows that 100 loads also move weekly between Assembly and the Machine Shop. We will probably want to move these two departments closer to one another to minimize the flow of parts through the factory.

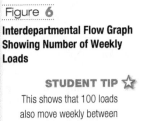

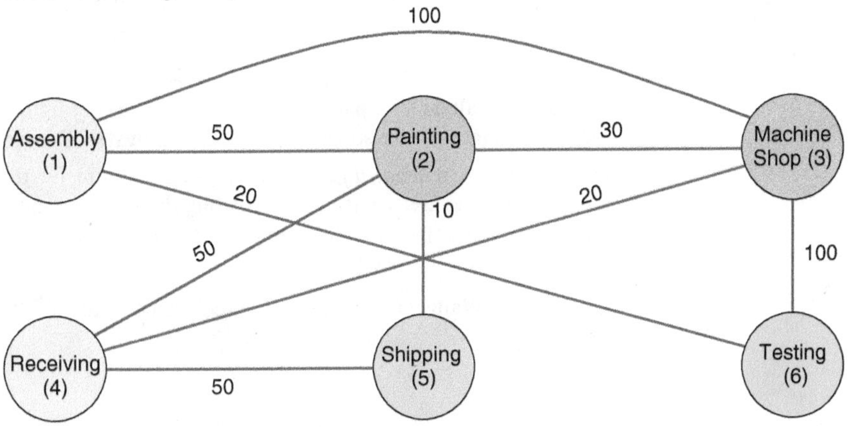

Step 4: *Determine the cost of this layout* by using the material-handling cost equation:

$$\text{Cost} = \sum_{i=1}^{n} \sum_{j=1}^{n} X_{ij}C_{ij}$$

For this problem, Walters Company assumes that a forklift carries all interdepartmental loads. The cost of moving one load between adjacent departments is estimated to be \$1. Moving a load between nonadjacent departments costs \$2. Looking at Figures 4 and 5, we thus see that the handling cost between departments 1 and 2 is \$50 (\$1 × 50 loads), \$200 between departments 1 and 3 (\$2 × 100 loads), \$40 between departments 1 and 6 (\$2 × 20 loads), and so on. Work areas that are diagonal to one another, such as 2 and 4, are treated as adjacent. The total cost for the layout shown in Figure 6 is:

$$\begin{aligned}\text{Cost} = &\underset{(1\text{ and }2)}{\$50} + \underset{(1\text{ and }3)}{\$200} + \underset{(1\text{ and }6)}{\$40} + \underset{(2\text{ and }3)}{\$30} + \underset{(2\text{ and }4)}{\$50}\\ &+ \underset{(2\text{ and }5)}{\$10} + \underset{(3\text{ and }4)}{\$40} + \underset{(3\text{ and }6)}{\$100} + \underset{(4\text{ and }5)}{\$50}\\ = &\ \$570\end{aligned}$$

Step 5: By trial and error (or by a more sophisticated computer program approach that we discuss shortly), *try to improve the layout* pictured in Figure 5 to establish a better arrangement of departments.

By looking at both the flow graph (Figure 6) and the cost calculations, we see that placing departments 1 and 3 closer together appears desirable. They currently are nonadjacent, and the high volume of flow between them causes a large handling expense. Looking the situation over, we need to check the effect of shifting departments and possibly raising, instead of lowering, overall costs.

One possibility is to switch departments 1 and 2. This exchange produces a second departmental flow graph (Figure 7), which shows a reduction in cost to \$480, a savings in material handling of \$90:

$$\begin{aligned}\text{Cost} = &\underset{(1\text{ and }2)}{\$50} + \underset{(1\text{ and }3)}{\$100} + \underset{(1\text{ and }6)}{\$20} + \underset{(2\text{ and }3)}{\$60} + \underset{(2\text{ and }4)}{\$50}\\ &+ \underset{(2\text{ and }5)}{\$10} + \underset{(3\text{ and }4)}{\$40} + \underset{(3\text{ and }6)}{\$100} + \underset{(4\text{ and }5)}{\$50}\\ = &\ \$480\end{aligned}$$

Figure 7
Second Interdepartmental Flow Graph

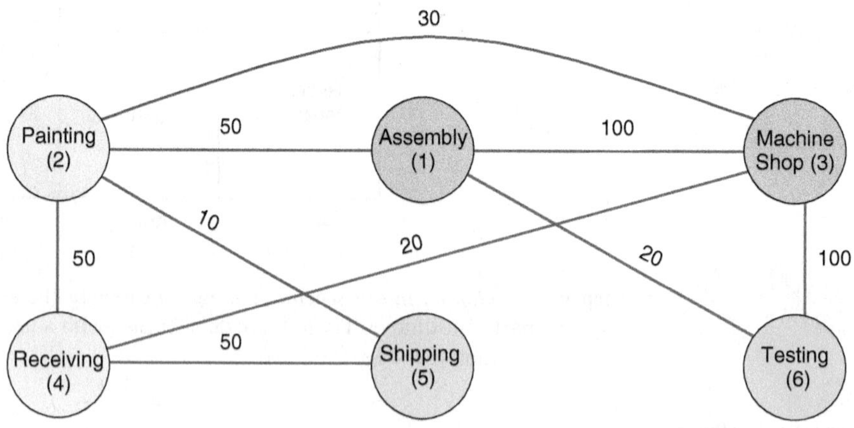

STUDENT TIP
Notice how Assembly and Machine Shop are now adjacent. Testing stayed close to the Machine Shop also.

Suppose Walters Company is satisfied with the cost figure of \$480 and the flow graph of Figure 7. The problem may not be solved yet. Often, a sixth step is necessary:

Step 6: *Prepare a detailed plan* arranging the departments to fit the shape of the building and its nonmovable areas (such as the loading dock, washrooms, and stairways). Often this step involves ensuring that the final plan can be accommodated by the electrical system, floor loads, aesthetics, and other factors.

In the case of Walters Company, space requirements are a simple matter (see Figure 8).

Figure 8
A Feasible Layout for Walters Company

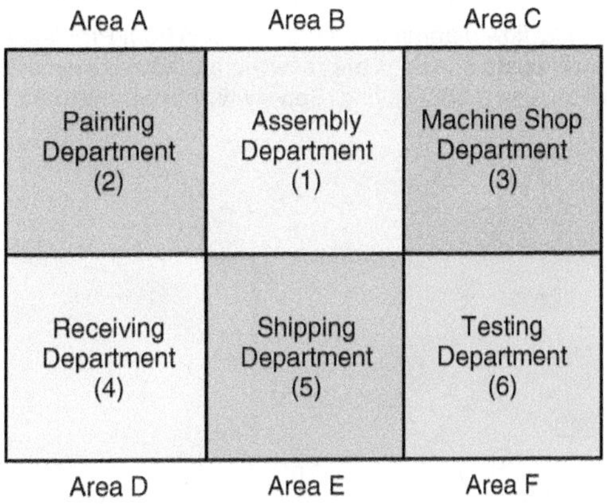

STUDENT TIP ☆
Here we see the departments moved to areas A–F to try to improve the flow.

INSIGHT ▶ This switch of departments is only one of a large number of possible changes. For a six-department problem, there are actually 720 (or $6! = 6 \times 5 \times 4 \times 3 \times 2 \times 1$) potential arrangements! In layout problems, we may not find the optimal solution and may have to be satisfied with a "reasonable" one.

LEARNING EXERCISE ▶ Can you improve on the layout in Figures 7 and 8? [Answer: Yes, it can be lowered to $430 by placing Shipping in area A, Painting in area B, Assembly in area C, Receiving in area D (no change), Machine Shop in area E, and Testing in area F (no change).]

RELATED PROBLEMS ▶ 1, 2, 3, 4, 5, 6, 7, 8, 9

EXCEL OM Data File **Ch09Ex1.xls** can be found at **www.pearsonhighered.com/heizer**.

ACTIVE MODEL 1 Example 1 is further illustrated in Active Model 9.1 at **www.pearsonhighered.com/heizer**.

Computer Software for Process-Oriented Layouts

The graphic approach in Example 1 is fine for small problems. It does not, however, suffice for larger problems. When 20 departments are involved in a layout problem, more than 600 *trillion* different department configurations are possible. Fortunately, computer programs have been written to handle large layouts. These programs (see the Proplanner graphic on the next page) often add sophistication with flowcharts, multiple-story capability, storage and container placement, material volumes, time analysis, and cost comparisons. These programs tend to be interactive—that is, require participation by the user. And most only claim to provide "good," not "optimal," solutions.

UGS/Siemens

Siemens Corp. software such as this allows operations managers to quickly place and connect symbols for factory equipment for a full three-dimensional view of the layout. Such presentations provide added insight into the issues of facility layout in terms of process, material handling, efficiency, and safety. (Images created with Tecnomatix Plant Simulation software, courtesy of Siemens PLM Software)

Proplanner Software for Process-Oriented Layouts

With the click of a mouse, material flow diagrams, such as this one from Proplanner, can manipulate layouts to show the cost savings from an improved layout. In this example, pump housings are received and stored nearer to the point of use, reducing total in-plant travel distance from over 3.5 million feet to 2.2 million feet, a 38% saving. See **www.proplanner.com** for video demonstrations of this and other related tools.

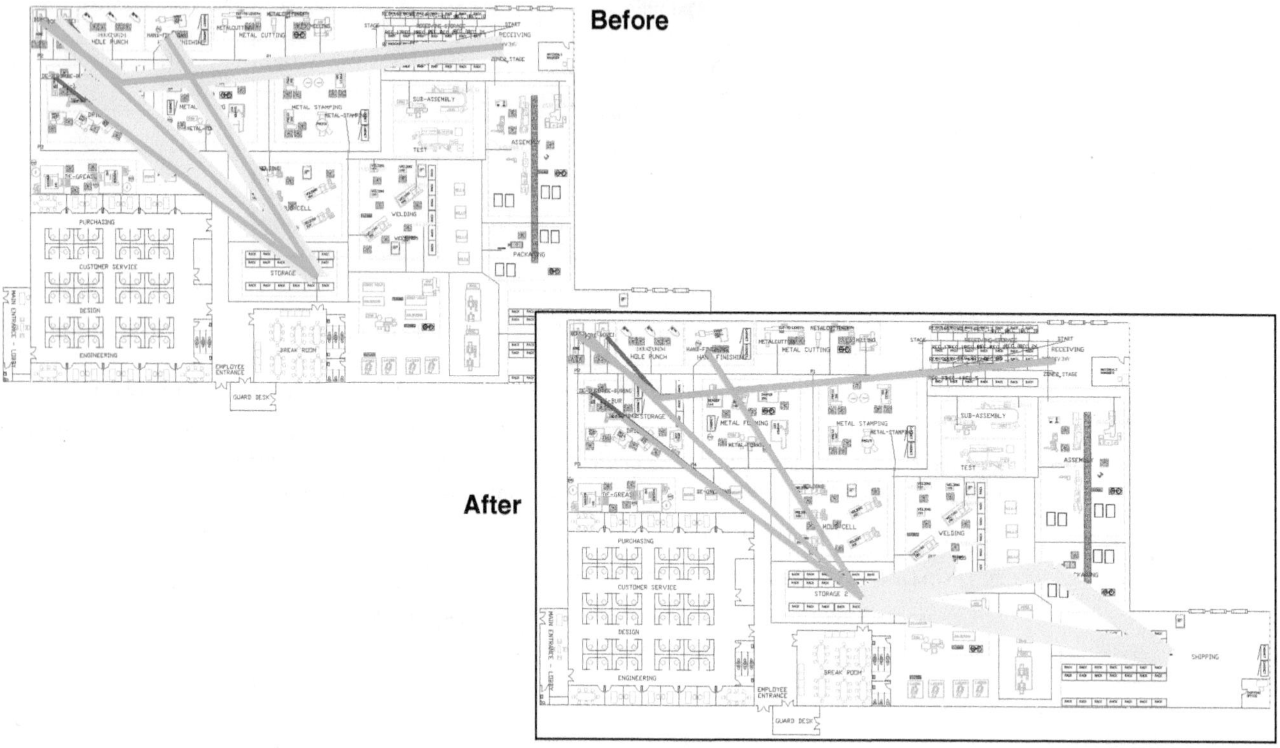

Work Cells

Work cell
An arrangement of machines and personnel that focuses on making a single product or family of related products.

A **work cell** reorganizes people and machines that would ordinarily be dispersed in various departments into a group so that they can focus on making a single product or a group of related products (Figure 9). Cellular work arrangements are used when volume warrants a special arrangement of machinery and equipment. These work cells are reconfigured as product designs change or volume fluctuates. The advantages of work cells are:

1. *Reduced work-in-process inventory* because the work cell is set up to provide one-piece flow from machine to machine.
2. *Less floor space* required because less space is needed between machines to accommodate work-in-process inventory.
3. *Reduced raw material and finished goods inventories* because less work-in-process allows more rapid movement of materials through the work cell.
4. *Reduced direct labor cost* because of improved communication among employees, better material flow, and improved scheduling.
5. *Heightened sense of employee participation* in the organization and the product: employees accept the added responsibility of product quality because it is directly associated with them and their work cell.
6. *Increased equipment and machinery utilization* because of better scheduling and faster material flow.
7. *Reduced investment in machinery and equipment* because good utilization reduces the number of machines and the amount of equipment and tooling.

LO6 *Define* work cell and the requirements of a work cell

Requirements of Work Cells

The requirements of cellular production include:

- Identification of families of products, often through the use of group technology codes or equivalents

Figure 9

Improving Layouts by Moving to the Work Cell Concept

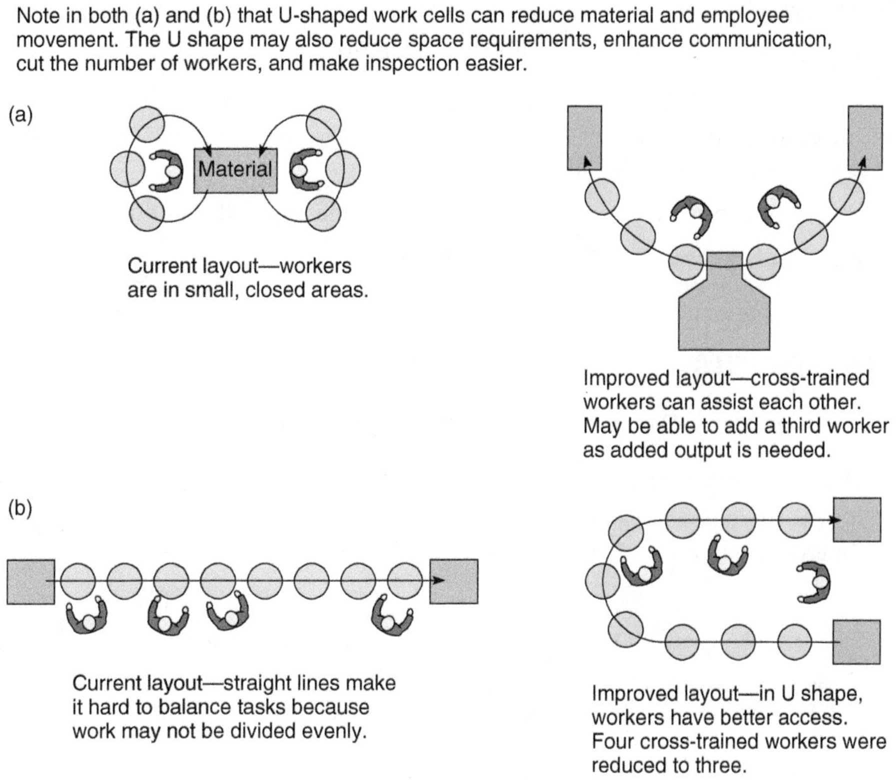

Note in both (a) and (b) that U-shaped work cells can reduce material and employee movement. The U shape may also reduce space requirements, enhance communication, cut the number of workers, and make inspection easier.
(a)
Material
Current layout—workers are in small, closed areas.
Improved layout—cross-trained workers can assist each other. May be able to add a third worker as added output is needed.
(b)
Current layout—straight lines make it hard to balance tasks because work may not be divided evenly.
Improved layout—in U shape, workers have better access. Four cross-trained workers were reduced to three.

- A high level of training, flexibility, and empowerment of employees
- Being self-contained, with its own equipment and resources
- Testing (poka-yoke) at each station in the cell

Work cells have at least five advantages over assembly lines and process facilities: (1) because tasks are grouped, inspection is often immediate; (2) fewer workers are needed; (3) workers can reach more of the work area; (4) the work area can be more efficiently balanced; and (5) communication is enhanced. Work cells are sometimes organized in a U shape, as shown on the right side of Figure 9.

As noted in the following *OM in Action* box, Canon is one of many organizations that have had success with work cells.

STUDENT TIP

Using work cells is a big step toward manufacturing efficiency. They can make jobs more interesting, save space, and cut inventory.

Staffing and Balancing Work Cells

Once the work cell has the appropriate equipment located in the proper sequence, the next task is to staff and balance the cell. Efficient production in a work cell requires appropriate staffing.

OM in Action — Work Cells Increase Productivity at Canon

Look quickly at Canon's factory near Tokyo, and you might think you stepped back a few decades. Instead of the swiftly moving assembly lines you might expect to see in a high-cost, sophisticated digital camera and photo copier giant, you see workers gathered in small work cell groups. Each cell is responsible for one product or a small family of products. The product focus encourages employees to exchange ideas about how to improve the assembly process. They also accept more responsibility for their work.

Canon's work cells have increased productivity by 30%. But how?

First, conveyor belts and their spare parts take up space, an expensive commodity in Japan. The shift to the cell system has freed 12 miles of conveyor-belt space at 54 plants and allowed Canon to close 29 parts warehouses, saving $280 million in real estate costs.

Employees are encouraged to work in ever-tighter cells, with prizes given to those who free up the most space.

Second, the cells enable Canon to change the product mix more quickly to meet market demands for innovative products—a big advantage as product life cycles become shorter and shorter.

Third, staff morale has increased because instead of performing a single task over and over, employees are trained to put together whole machines. Some of Canon's fastest workers are so admired that they have become TV celebrities.

Work cells improve both morale and productivity—a win–win for Canon.

Sources: Super Factory (July 2008); and *Financial Times* (September 23, 2003): 14.

Takt time
Pace of production to meet customer demands.

This involves two steps. First, determine the takt time,[3] which is the pace (frequency) of production units necessary (time per unit) to meet customer orders:

$$\text{Takt time} = \text{Total work time available}/\text{Units required} \qquad (2)$$

Second, determine the number of operators required. This requires dividing the total operation time in the work cell by the takt time:

$$\text{Workers required} = \text{Total operation time required}/\text{Takt time} \qquad (3)$$

Example 2 considers these two steps when staffing work cells.

Example 2

STAFFING WORK CELLS

Stephen Hall's company in Dayton makes auto mirrors. The major customer is the Honda plant nearby. Honda expects 600 mirrors delivered daily, and the work cell producing the mirrors is scheduled for 8 hours. Hall wants to determine the takt time and the number of workers required.

APPROACH ▶ Hall uses Equations (2) and (3) and develops a work balance chart to help determine the time for each operation in the work cell, as well as total time.

SOLUTION ▶

$$\text{Takt time} = (8 \text{ hours} \times 60 \text{ minutes})/600 \text{ units} = 480/600 = .8 \text{ minute} = 48 \text{ seconds}$$

Therefore, the customer requirement is one mirror every 48 seconds.

The *work balance chart* in Figure 10 shows that 5 operations are necessary, for a total operation time of 140 seconds:

$$\begin{aligned}\text{Workers required} &= \text{Total operation time required}/\text{Takt time}\\ &= (50 + 45 + 10 + 20 + 15)/48\\ &= 140/48 = 2.92\end{aligned}$$

Figure 10
Work Balance Chart for Mirror Production

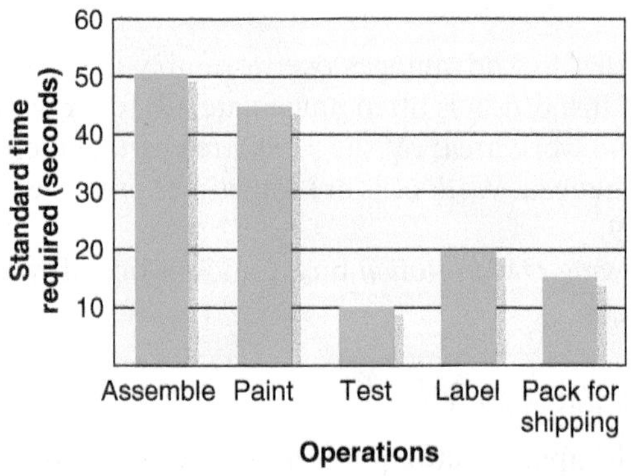

INSIGHT ▶ To produce one unit every 48 seconds will require 2.92 people. With three operators this work cell will be producing one unit each 46.67 seconds (140 seconds/3 employees = 46.67) and 617 units per day (480 minutes available × 60 seconds/46.67 seconds for each unit = 617).

LEARNING EXERCISE ▶ If testing time is expanded to 20 seconds, what is the staffing requirement? [Answer: 3.125 employees.]

RELATED PROBLEMS ▶ 10

A *work balance chart* (like the one in Example 2) is also valuable for evaluating the operation times in work cells. Some consideration must be given to determining the bottleneck operation. Bottleneck operations can constrain the flow through the cell. Imbalance in a work cell is seldom an issue if the operation is manual, as cell members by definition are part of a cross-trained team. Consequently, the inherent flexibility of work cells typically overcomes modest imbalance issues within a cell. However, if the imbalance is a machine constraint, then an adjustment in

[3]*Takt* is German for "time," "measure," or "beat" and is used in this context as the rate at which completed units must be produced to satisfy customer demand.

machinery, process, or operations may be necessary. In such situations the use of traditional assembly-line-balancing analysis, the topic of our next section, may be helpful.

The success of work cells is not limited to manufacturing. Kansas City's Hallmark, which has over half the U.S. greeting card market and produces some 40,000 different cards, has modified the offices into a cellular design. In the past, its 700 creative professionals would take up to 2 years to develop a new card. Hallmark's decision to create work cells consisting of artists, writers, lithographers, merchandisers, and accountants, all located in the same area, has resulted in card preparation in a fraction of the time that the old layout required. Work cells have also yielded higher performance and better service for the American Red Cross blood donation process.[4]

The Focused Work Center and the Focused Factory

When a firm has *identified a family of similar products that have a large and stable demand*, it may organize a focused work center. A focused work center (also called a "plant within a plant") moves production to a large work cell that remains part of the present facility. For example, bumpers and dashboards in Toyota's Texas plant are produced in a focused work center, and the Levi's departments in JCPenney are managed and run in a stand-alone boutique setting.

Focused work center
A permanent or semi-permanent product-oriented arrangement of machines and personnel.

If the focused work center is in a separate facility, it is often called a focused factory. For example, separate plants that produce seat belts, fuel tanks, and exhaust systems for Toyota are focused factories. A fast-food restaurant is also a focused factory—most are easily reconfigured for adjustments to product mix and volume. Burger King changes the number of personnel and task assignments rather than moving machines and equipment. In this manner, Burger King balances the assembly line to meet changing production demands. In effect, the "layout" changes numerous times each day.

Focused factory
A facility designed to produce similar products or components.

The term *focused factories* may also refer to facilities that are focused in ways other than by product line or layout. For instance, facilities may focus on their core competence, such as low cost, quality, new product introduction, or flexibility.

Focused facilities in both manufacturing and services appear to be better able to stay in tune with their customers, to produce quality products, and to operate at higher margins. This is true whether they are auto manufacturers like Toyota; restaurants like McDonald's and Burger King; or a hospital like Arnold Palmer.

Repetitive and Product-Oriented Layout

Product-oriented layouts are organized around products or families of similar high-volume, low-variety products. Repetitive production and continuous production, use product layouts. The assumptions are that:

1. Volume is adequate for high equipment utilization
2. Product demand is stable enough to justify high investment in specialized equipment
3. Product is standardized or approaching a phase of its life cycle that justifies investment in specialized equipment
4. Supplies of raw materials and components are adequate and of uniform quality (adequately standardized) to ensure that they will work with the specialized equipment

LO7 *Define* product-oriented layout

Two types of a product-oriented layout are fabrication and assembly lines. The fabrication line builds components, such as automobile tires or metal parts for a refrigerator, on a series of machines, while an assembly line puts the fabricated parts together at a series of workstations. However, both are repetitive processes, and in both cases, the line must be "balanced"; that is, the time spent to perform work on one machine must equal or "balance" the time spent to perform work on the next machine in the fabrication line, just as the time spent at one workstation by one assembly-line employee must "balance" the time spent at the next workstation by the next employee. The same issues arise when designing the "disassembly lines" of slaughterhouses and automobile recyclers.

Fabrication line
A machine-paced, product-oriented facility for building components.

Assembly line
An approach that puts fabricated parts together at a series of workstations; used in repetitive processes.

[4]Mark Pagell and Steven A. Melnyk, "Assessing the Impact of Alternative Manufacturing Layouts in a Service Setting," *Journal of Operations Management* 22 (2004): 413–429.

A well-balanced assembly line has the advantage of high personnel and facility utilization and equity among employees' workloads. Some union contracts require that workloads be nearly equal among those on the same assembly line. The term most often used to describe this process is assembly-line balancing. Indeed, the *objective of the product-oriented layout is to minimize imbalance in the fabrication or assembly line.*

Assembly-line balancing
Obtaining output at each workstation on a production line so delay is minimized.

The main advantages of product-oriented layout are:

1. The low variable cost per unit usually associated with high-volume, standardized products
2. Low material-handling costs
3. Reduced work-in-process inventories
4. Easier training and supervision
5. Rapid throughput

The disadvantages of product layout are:

1. The high volume required because of the large investment needed to establish the process
2. Work stoppage at any one point can tie up the whole operation
3. The process flexibility necessary for a variety of products and production rates can be a challenge

VIDEO 2
Facility Layout at Wheeled Coach Ambulances

Because the problems of fabrication lines and assembly lines are similar, we focus our discussion on assembly lines. On an assembly line, the product typically moves via automated means, such as a conveyor, through a series of workstations until completed. This is the way fast-food hamburgers are made (see Figure 11), automobiles and some planes (see the photo of the Boeing 737 on the next page) are assembled, and television sets and ovens are produced. Product-oriented layouts use more automated and specially designed equipment than do process layouts.

Assembly-Line Balancing

LO8 *Explain* how to balance production flow in a repetitive or product-oriented facility

Line balancing is usually undertaken to minimize imbalance between machines or personnel while meeting a required output from the line. To produce at a specified rate, management must know the tools, equipment, and work methods used. Then the time requirements for each assembly task (e.g., drilling a hole, tightening a nut, or spray-painting a part) must be determined. Management also needs to know the *precedence relationship* among the activities—that is, the sequence in which various tasks must be performed. Example 3 shows how to turn these task data into a precedence diagram.

Elapsed time	0:00	0:11	0:31	0:45		1:30
Task time (seconds)		11	20	14	0	45
Task	1. Order	2. Bun toasting	3. Assembly with condiments	4. Wrapping of patty with bun	5. Order picked up immediately to keep it fresh	6. Customer service (order and payment)

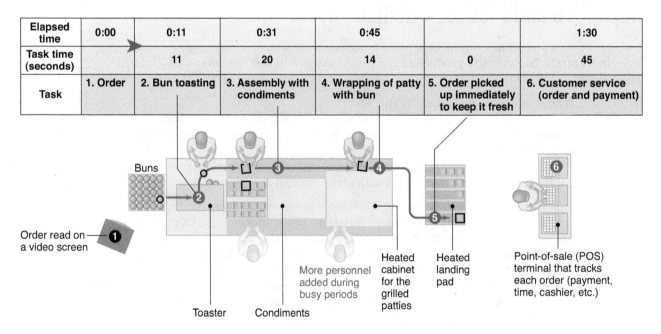

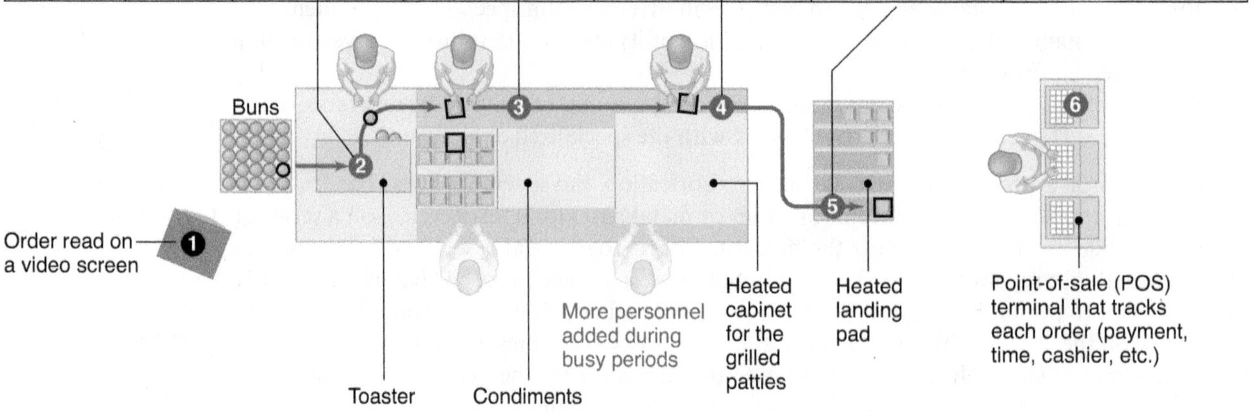

Figure 11
McDonald's Hamburger Assembly Line

The Boeing 737, the world's most popular commercial airplane, is produced on a moving production line, traveling at 2 inches a minute through the final assembly process. The moving line, one of several lean manufacturing innovations at the Renton, Washington, facility, has enhanced quality, reduced flow time, slashed inventory levels, and cut space requirements. Final assembly is only 11 days—a time savings of 50%—and inventory is down more than 55%.

Example 3

DEVELOPING A PRECEDENCE DIAGRAM FOR AN ASSEMBLY LINE

Boeing wants to develop a precedence diagram for an electrostatic wing component that requires a total assembly time of 65 minutes.

APPROACH ▶ Staff gather tasks, assembly times, and sequence requirements for the component in Table 2.

TABLE 2 Precedence Data for Wing Component

TASK	ASSEMBLY TIME (MINUTES)	TASK MUST FOLLOW TASK LISTED BELOW	
A	10	—	This means that tasks B and E cannot be done until task A has been completed.
B	11	A	
C	5	B	
D	4	B	
E	11	A	
F	3	C, D	
G	7	F	
H	11	E	
I	3	G, H	
	Total time 65		

SOLUTION ▶ Figure 12 shows the precedence diagram.

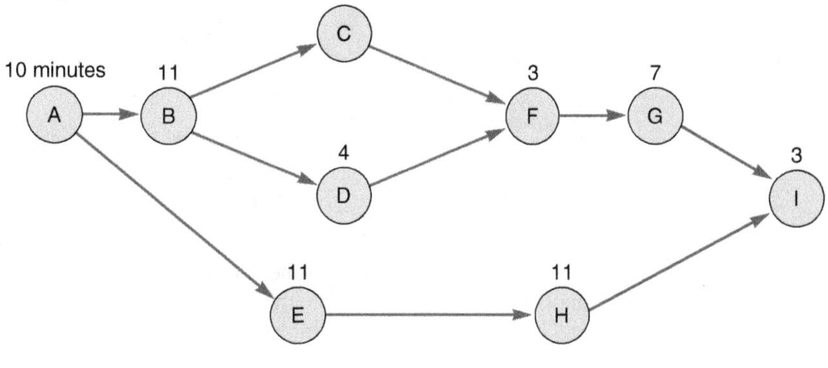

Figure 12
Precedence Diagram

INSIGHT ▶ The diagram helps structure an assembly line and workstations, and it makes it easier to visualize the sequence of tasks.

LEARNING EXERCISE ▶ If task D had a second preceding task (C), how would Figure 12 change? [Answer: There would also be an arrow pointing from C to D.]

RELATED PROBLEMS ▶ 12a, 14a, 15a, 16a, 19a

Once we have constructed a precedence chart summarizing the sequences and performance times, we turn to the job of grouping tasks into job stations so that we can meet the specified production rate. This process involves three steps:

Cycle time
The maximum time that a product is allowed at each workstation.

1. Take the units required (demand or production rate) per day and divide them into the productive time available per day (in minutes or seconds). This operation gives us what is called the cycle time[5]—namely, the maximum time allowed at each workstation if the production rate is to be achieved:

$$\text{Cycle time} = \frac{\text{Production time available per day}}{\text{Units required per day}} \tag{4}$$

2. Calculate the theoretical minimum number of workstations. This is the total task-duration time (the time it takes to make the product) divided by the cycle time. Fractions are rounded to the next higher whole number:

$$\text{Minimum number of workstations} = \frac{\sum_{i=1}^{n} \text{Time for task } i}{\text{Cycle time}} \tag{5}$$

where n is the number of assembly tasks.

3. Balance the line by assigning specific assembly tasks to each workstation. An efficient balance is one that will complete the required assembly, follow the specified sequence, and keep the idle time at each workstation to a minimum. A formal procedure for doing this is the following:
   - **a.** Identify a master list of tasks.
   - **b.** Eliminate those tasks that have been assigned.
   - **c.** Eliminate those tasks whose precedence relationship has not been satisfied.
   - **d.** Eliminate those tasks for which inadequate time is available at the workstation.
   - **e.** Use one of the line-balancing "heuristics" described in Table 3. The five choices are (1) longest task time, (2) most following tasks, (3) ranked positional weight, (4) short-

TABLE 3 Layout Heuristics That May Be Used to Assign Tasks to Workstations in Assembly-Line Balancing

1. *Longest task (operation) time*	From the available tasks, choose the task with the largest (longest) time.
2. *Most following tasks*	From the available tasks, choose the task with the largest number of following tasks.
3. *Ranked positional weight*	From the available tasks, choose the task for which the sum of the times for each following task is longest. (In Example 4 we see that the ranked positional weight of task C = 5(C) + 3(F) + 7(G) + 3(I) = 18, whereas the ranked positional weight of task D = 4(D) + 3(F) + 7(G) + 3(I) = 17; therefore, C would be chosen first, using this heuristic.)
4. *Shortest task (operations) time*	From the available tasks, choose the task with the shortest task time.
5. *Least number of following tasks*	From the available tasks, choose the task with the least number of subsequent tasks.

[5]*Cycle time* is the maximum time allowed to accomplish a task or process step. Several process steps may be necessary to complete the product. *Takt time*, discussed earlier, is determined by the customer and is the speed at which completed units must be produced to satisfy customer demand.

est task time, and (5) least number of following tasks. You may wish to test several of these heuristics to see which generates the "best" solution—that is, the smallest number of workstations and highest efficiency. Remember, however, that although heuristics provide solutions, they do not guarantee an optimal solution.

Heuristic
Problem solving using procedures and rules rather than mathematical optimization.

Example 4 illustrates a simple line-balancing procedure.

Example 4

BALANCING THE ASSEMBLY LINE

On the basis of the precedence diagram and activity times given in Example 3, Boeing determines that there are 480 productive minutes of work available per day. Furthermore, the production schedule requires that 40 units of the wing component be completed as output from the assembly line each day. It now wants to group the tasks into workstations.

APPROACH ▶ Following the three steps above, we compute the cycle time using Equation (4) and minimum number of workstations using Equation (5), and we assign tasks to workstations—in this case using the *most following tasks* heuristic.

SOLUTION ▶

$$\text{Cycle time (in minutes)} = \frac{480 \text{ minutes}}{40 \text{ units}} = 12 \text{ minutes/unit}$$

$$\text{Minimum number of workstations} = \frac{\text{Total task time}}{\text{Cycle time}} = \frac{65}{12} = 5.42, \text{ or } 6 \text{ stations}$$

Figure 13 shows one solution that does not violate the sequence requirements and that groups tasks into six one-person stations. To obtain this solution, activities with the most following tasks were moved into workstations to use as much of the available cycle time of 12 minutes as possible. The first workstation consumes 10 minutes and has an idle time of 2 minutes.

Figure 13
A Six-Station Solution to the Line-Balancing Problem

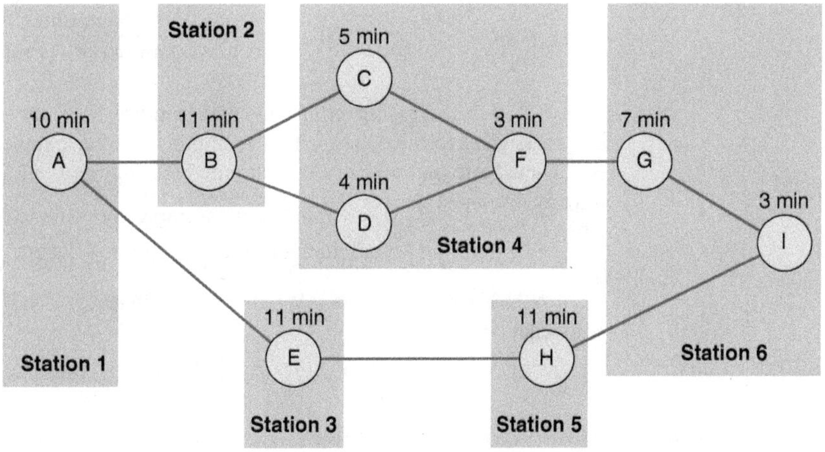

STUDENT TIP ☆
Tasks C, D, and F can be grouped together in one workstation, provided that the physical facilities and skill levels meet the work requirements.

INSIGHT ▶ This is a reasonably well-balanced assembly line. The second and third workstations use 11 minutes. The fourth workstation groups three small tasks and balances perfectly at 12 minutes. The fifth has 1 minute of idle time, and the sixth (consisting of tasks G and I) has 2 minutes of idle time per cycle. Total idle time for this solution is 7 minutes per cycle.

LEARNING EXERCISE ▶ If task I required 6 minutes (instead of 3 minutes), how would this change the solution? [Answer: The cycle time would not change, and the *theoretical* minimum number of workstations would still be 6 (rounded up from 5.67), but it would take 7 stations to balance the line.]

RELATED PROBLEMS ▶ 11, 12, 13, 14, 15, 16, 17, 18, 19, 20, 21, 22, 23

EXCEL OM Data File **Ch09Ex4.xls** can be found at **www.pearsonhighered.com/heizer**.

We can compute the efficiency of a line balance by dividing the total task times by the product of the number of workstations required times the assigned (actual) cycle time of the *longest* workstation:

$$\text{Efficiency} = \frac{\sum \text{Task times}}{(\textit{Actual}\text{ number of workstations}) \times (\text{Largest assigned cycle time})} \quad (6)$$

Operations managers compare different levels of efficiency for various numbers of workstations. In this way, a firm can determine the sensitivity of the line to changes in the production rate and workstation assignments.

Example 5

DETERMINING LINE EFFICIENCY

Boeing needs to calculate the efficiency for Example 4.

APPROACH ▶ Equation (6) is applied.

SOLUTION ▶ $\text{Efficiency} = \frac{65\text{ minutes}}{(6\text{ stations}) \times (12\text{ minutes})} = \frac{65}{72} = 90.3\%$

Note that opening a seventh workstation, for whatever reason, would decrease the efficiency of the balance to 77.4% (assuming that at least one of the workstations still required 12 minutes):

$$\text{Efficiency} = \frac{65\text{ minutes}}{(7\text{ stations}) \times (12\text{ minutes})} = 77.4\%$$

INSIGHT ▶ Increasing efficiency may require that some tasks be divided into smaller elements and reassigned to other tasks. This facilitates a better balance between workstations and means higher efficiency. Note that we can also compute efficiency as 1 − (% Idle time) i.e., [1 − (Idle time)/(Total time in workstations)], where:

$$\text{Idle time} = (\text{Actual number of workstations} \times \text{largest assigned cycle time}) - \sum \text{Task times}$$

LEARNING EXERCISE ▶ What is the efficiency if an eighth workstation is opened? [Answer: Efficiency = 67.7%.]

RELATED PROBLEMS ▶ 12f, 13c, 14f, 16c, 17b, 18b, 19e, g

Large-scale line-balancing problems, like large process-layout problems, are often solved by computers. Computer programs such as Assembly Line Pro, Proplanner, Timer Pro, Flexible Line Balancing, and Promodel are available to handle the assignment of workstations on assembly lines with numerous work activities. Such software evaluates the thousands, or even millions, of possible workstation combinations much more efficiently than could ever be done by hand.

Summary

Layouts make a substantial difference in operating efficiency. The seven layout situations discussed in this text are (1) office, (2) retail, (3) warehouse, (4) fixed position, (5) process oriented, (6) work cells, and (7) product oriented. A variety of techniques have been developed to solve these layout problems. Office layouts often seek to maximize information flows, retail firms focus on product exposure, and warehouses attempt to optimize the trade-off between storage space and material handling cost.

The fixed-position layout problem attempts to minimize material handling costs within the constraint of limited space at the site. Process layouts minimize travel distances times the number of trips. Product layouts focus on reducing waste and the imbalance in an assembly line. Work cells are the result of identifying a family of products that justify a special configuration of machinery and equipment that reduces material travel and adjusts imbalances with cross-trained personnel.

Often, the issues in a layout problem are so wide-ranging that finding an optimal solution is not possible. For this reason, layout decisions, although the subject of substantial research effort, remain something of an art.

Key Terms

Office layout
Retail layout
Slotting fees
Servicescape
Warehouse layout
Cross-docking
Random stocking
Customizing
Fixed-position layout
Process-oriented layout
Job lots
Work cell
Takt time
Focused work center
Focused factory
Fabrication line
Assembly line
Assembly-line balancing
Cycle time
Heuristic

Ethical Dilemma

Although buried by mass customization and a proliferation of new products of numerous sizes and variations, grocery chains continue to seek to maximize payoff from their layout. Their layout includes a marketable commodity—shelf space—and they charge for it. This charge is known as a *slotting fee*. Recent estimates are that food manufacturers now spend some 13% of sales on trade promotions, which is paid to grocers to get them to promote and discount the manufacturer's products. A portion of these fees is for slotting, but slotting fees drive up the manufacturer's cost. They also put the small company with a new product at a disadvantage, because small companies with limited resources may be squeezed out of the marketplace. Slotting fees may also mean that customers may no longer be able to find the special local brand. How ethical are slotting fees?

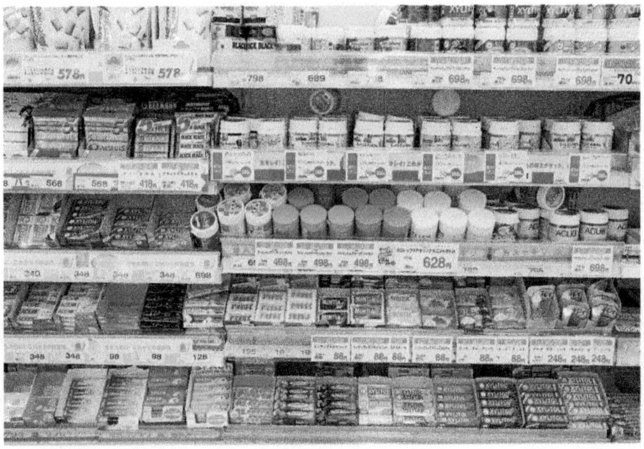

© Image Source/Alamy

Discussion Questions

1. What are the seven layout strategies presented in this text?
2. What are the three factors that complicate a fixed-position layout?
3. What are the advantages and disadvantages of process layout?
4. How would an analyst obtain data and determine the number of trips in:
   (a) a hospital?
   (b) a machine shop?
   (c) an auto-repair shop?
5. What are the advantages and disadvantages of product layout?
6. What are the four assumptions (or preconditions) of establishing layout for high-volume, low-variety products?
7. What are the alternative forms of work cells discussed in this textbook?
8. What are the advantages and disadvantages of work cells?
9. What are the requirements for a focused work center or focused factory to be appropriate?
10. What are the two major trends influencing office layout?
11. What layout variables would you consider particularly important in an office layout where computer programs are written?

12. What layout innovations have you noticed recently in retail establishments?
13. What are the variables that a manager can manipulate in a retail layout?
14. Visit a local supermarket and sketch its layout. What are your observations regarding departments and their locations?
15. What is random stocking?
16. What information is necessary for random stocking to work?
17. Explain the concept of cross-docking.
18. What is a heuristic? Name several that can be used in assembly-line balancing.

Using Software to Solve Layout Problems

In addition to the many commercial software packages available for addressing layout problems, Excel OM and POM for Windows, both of which accompany this text, contain modules for the process problem and the assembly-line-balancing problem.

USING EXCEL OM

Excel OM can assist in evaluating a series of department work assignments like the one we saw for the Walters Company in Example 1. The layout module can generate an optimal solution by enumeration or by computing the "total movement" cost for each layout you wish to examine. As such, it provides a speedy calculator for each flow–distance pairing.

Program 1 illustrates our inputs in the top two tables. We first enter department flows, then provide distances between work areas. Entering area assignments on a trial-and-error basis in the upper left of the top table generates movement computations at the bottom of the screen. Total movement is recalculated each time we try a new area assignment. It turns out that the assignment shown is optimal at 430 feet of movement.

USING POM FOR WINDOWS

The POM for Windows facility layout module can be used to place up to 10 departments in 10 rooms to minimize the total distance traveled as a function of the distances between the rooms and the flow between departments. The program exchanges departments until no exchange will reduce the total amount of movement, meaning an optimal solution has been reached.

The POM for Windows and Excel OM modules for line balancing can handle a line with up to 99 tasks, each with up to six immediate predecessors. In this program, cycle time can be entered as either (1) *given*, if known, or (2) the *demand* rate can be entered with time available as shown. All five "heuristic rules" are used: (1) longest operation (task) time, (2) most following tasks, (3) ranked positional weight, (4) shortest operation (task) time, and (5) least number of following tasks. No one rule can guarantee an optimal solution, but POM for Windows displays the number of stations needed for each rule.

Program 1

Using Excel OM's Process Layout Module to Solve the Walters Company Problem in Example 1

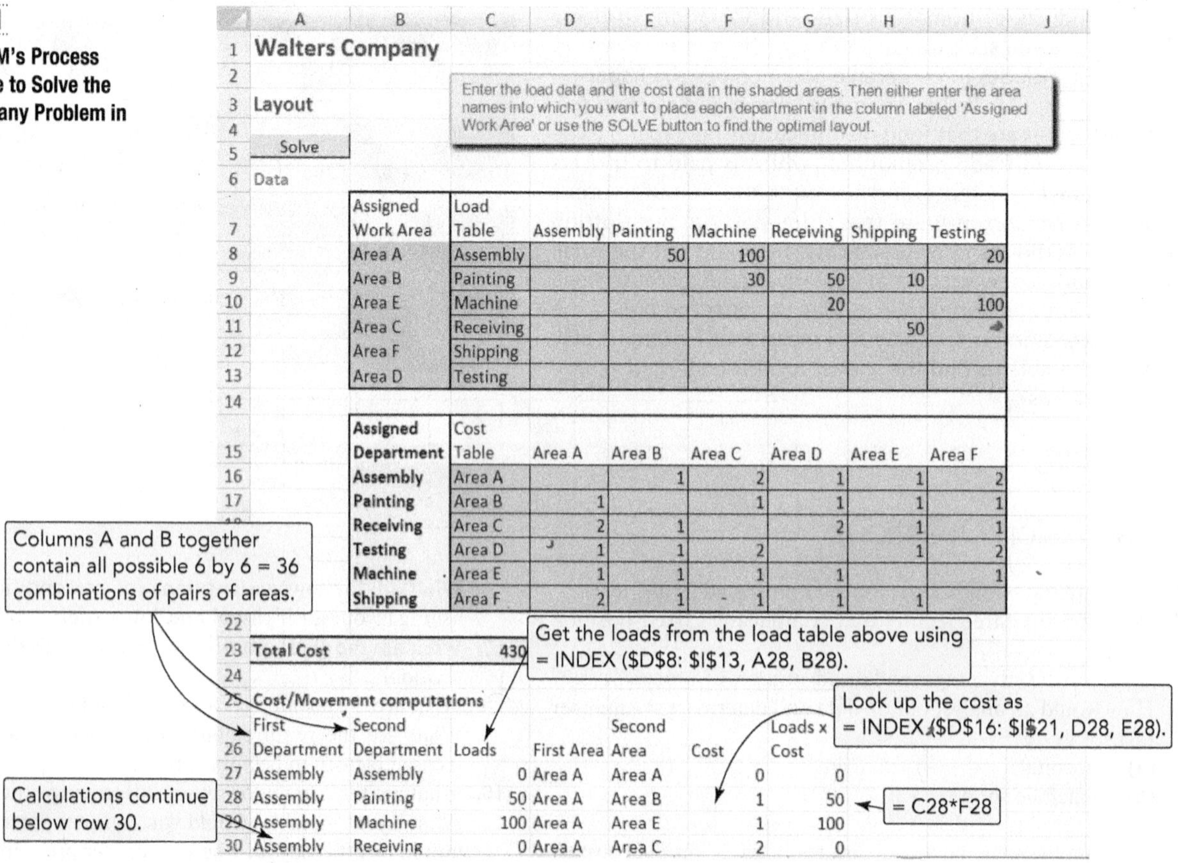

Solved Problems

Virtual Office Hours help is available at www.myomlab.com.

SOLVED PROBLEM 1

Aero Maintenance is a small aircraft engine maintenance facility located in Wichita, Kansas. Its new administrator, Ann Daniel, decides to improve material flow in the facility, using the process-layout method she studied at Wichita State University. The current layout of Aero Maintenance's eight departments is shown in Figure 14.

The only physical restriction perceived by Daniel is the need to keep the entrance in its current location. All other departments can be moved to a different work area (each 10 feet square) if layout analysis indicates a move would be beneficial.

First, Daniel analyzes records to determine the number of material movements among departments in an average month. These data are shown in Figure 15. Her objective, Daniel decides, is to lay out the departments so as to minimize the total movement (distance traveled) of material in the facility. She writes her objective as:

$$\text{Minimize material movement} = \sum_{i=1}^{8} \sum_{j=1}^{8} X_{ij}C_{ij}$$

where X_{ij} = number of material movements per month (loads or trips) moving from department i to department j

C_{ij} = distance in feet between departments i and j (which, in this case, is the equivalent of cost per load to move between departments)

Note that this is only a slight modification of the cost-objective equation shown earlier in the text.

Daniel assumes that adjacent departments, such as entrance (now in work area A) and receiving (now in work area B), have a walking distance of 10 feet. Diagonal departments are also considered adjacent and assigned a distance of 10 feet. Nonadjacent departments, such as the entrance and parts (now in area C) or the entrance and inspection (area G) are 20 feet apart, and nonadjacent rooms, such as entrance and metallurgy (area D), are 30 feet apart. (Hence, 10 feet is considered 10 units of cost, 20 feet is 20 units of cost, and 30 feet is 30 units of cost.)

Given the above information, redesign Aero Maintenance's layout to improve its material flow efficiency.

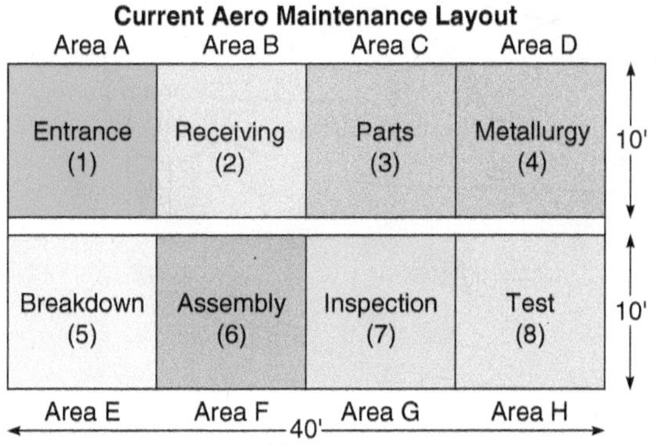

Figure 14

Aero Maintenance Layout

Figure 15

Number of Material Movements (Loads) Between Departments in 1 Month

Department	Entrance (1)	Receiving (2)	Parts (3)	Metallurgy (4)	Breakdown (5)	Assembly (6)	Inspection (7)	Test (8)
Entrance (1)		100	100	0	0	0	0	0
Receiving (2)			0	50	20	0	0	0
Parts (3)				30	30	0	0	0
Metallurgy (4)					20	0	0	20
Breakdown (5)						20	0	10
Assembly (6)							30	0
Inspection (7)								0
Test (8)								

(continued)

SOLUTION

First, establish Aero Maintenance's current layout, as shown in Figure 16. Then, by analyzing the current layout, compute material movement:

$$
\begin{aligned}
\text{Total movement} &= \underbrace{(100 \times 10)}_{\text{1 to 2}} + \underbrace{(100 \times 20)}_{\text{1 to 3}} + \underbrace{(50 \times 20)}_{\text{2 to 4}} + \underbrace{(20 \times 10)}_{\text{2 to 5}} \\
&\quad + \underbrace{(30 \times 10)}_{\text{3 to 4}} + \underbrace{(30 \times 20)}_{\text{3 to 5}} + \underbrace{(20 \times 30)}_{\text{4 to 5}} + \underbrace{(20 \times 10)}_{\text{4 to 8}} \\
&\quad + \underbrace{(20 \times 10)}_{\text{5 to 6}} + \underbrace{(10 \times 30)}_{\text{5 to 8}} + \underbrace{(30 \times 10)}_{\text{5 to 7}} \\
&= 1{,}000 + 2{,}000 + 1{,}000 + 200 + 300 + 600 + 600 \\
&\quad + 200 + 200 + 300 + 300 \\
&= 6{,}700 \text{ feet}
\end{aligned}
$$

Figure 16

Current Material Flow

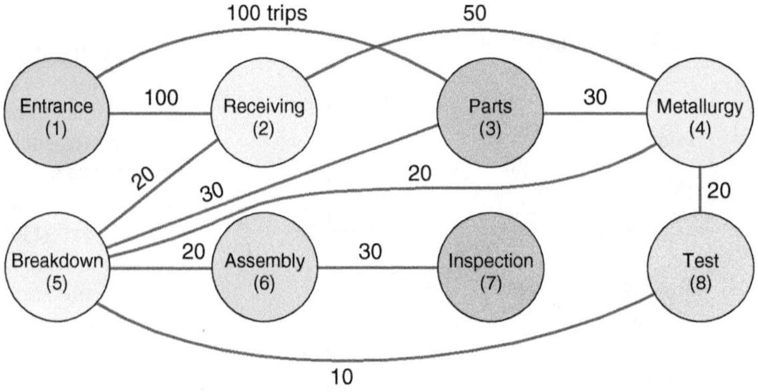

Propose a new layout that will reduce the current figure of 6,700 feet. Two useful changes, for example, are to switch departments 3 and 5 and to interchange departments 4 and 6. This change would result in the schematic shown in Figure 17:

$$
\begin{aligned}
\text{Total movement} &= \underbrace{(100 \times 10)}_{\text{1 to 2}} + \underbrace{(100 \times 10)}_{\text{1 to 3}} + \underbrace{(50 \times 10)}_{\text{2 to 4}} + \underbrace{(20 \times 10)}_{\text{2 to 5}} \\
&\quad + \underbrace{(30 \times 10)}_{\text{3 to 4}} + \underbrace{(30 \times 20)}_{\text{3 to 5}} + \underbrace{(20 \times 10)}_{\text{4 to 5}} + \underbrace{(20 \times 20)}_{\text{4 to 8}} \\
&\quad + \underbrace{(20 \times 10)}_{\text{5 to 6}} + \underbrace{(10 \times 10)}_{\text{5 to 8}} + \underbrace{(30 \times 10)}_{\text{6 to 7}} \\
&= 1{,}000 + 1{,}000 + 500 + 200 + 300 + 600 + 200 \\
&\quad + 400 + 200 + 100 + 300 \\
&= 4{,}800 \text{ feet}
\end{aligned}
$$

Do you see any room for further improvement?

Figure 17

Improved Layout

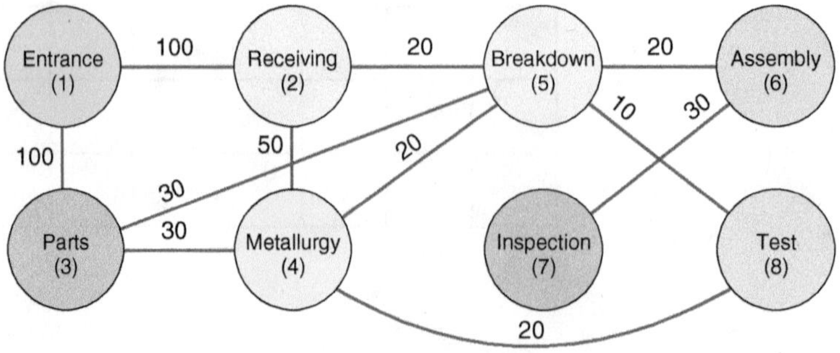

SOLVED PROBLEM 2

The assembly line whose activities are shown in Figure 18 has an 8-minute cycle time. Draw the precedence graph and find the minimum possible number of one-person workstations. Then arrange the work activities into workstations so as to balance the line. What is the efficiency of your line balance?

TASK	PERFORMANCE TIME (MINUTES)	TASK MUST FOLLOW THIS TASK
A	5	—
B	3	A
C	4	B
D	3	B
E	6	C
F	1	C
G	4	D, E, F
H	2	G
	28	

Figure 18

Four-Station Solution to the Line-Balancing Problem

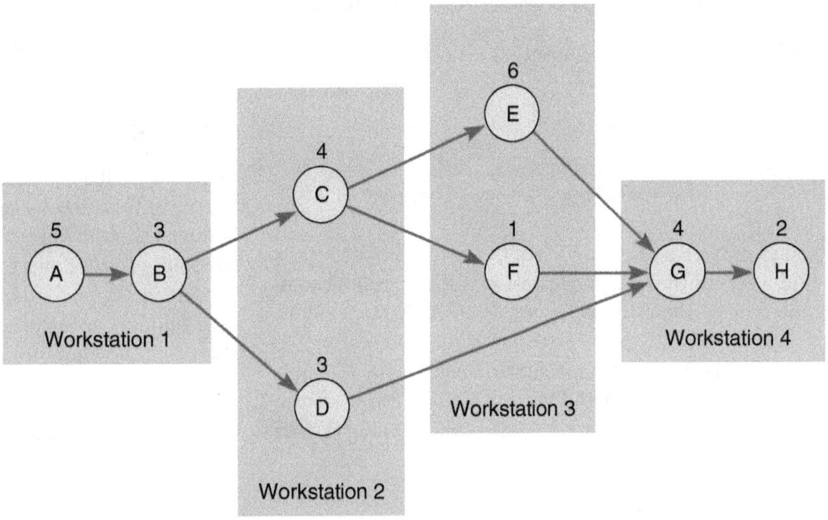

SOLUTION

The theoretical minimum number of workstations is:

$$\frac{\Sigma t_i}{\text{Cycle time}} = \frac{28 \text{ minutes}}{8 \text{ minutes}} = 3.5, \text{ or } 4 \text{ stations}$$

The precedence graph and one good layout are shown in Figure 18:

$$\text{Efficiency} = \frac{\text{Total task time}}{(\text{Actual number of workstations}) \times (\text{Largest assigned cycle time})} = \frac{28}{(4)(8)} = 87.5\%$$

Problems

Note: PX means the problem may be solved with POM for Windows and/or Excel OM.

•• **1** Gordon Miller's job shop has four work areas, A, B, C, and D. Distances in feet between centers of the work areas are:

	A	B	C	D
A	—	4	9	7
B	—	—	6	8
C	—	—	—	10
D	—	—	—	—

Workpieces moved, in hundreds of workpieces per week, between pairs of work areas, are:

	A	B	C	D
A	—	8	7	4
B	—	—	3	2
C	—	—	—	6
D	—	—	—	—

It costs Gordon $1 to move 1 work piece 1 foot. What is the weekly total material handling cost of the layout? PX

•• **2** A Missouri job shop has four departments—machining (M), dipping in a chemical bath (D), finishing (F), and plating (P)—assigned to four work areas. The operations manager, Mary Marrs, has gathered the following data for this job shop as it is currently laid out (Plan A).

100s of Workpieces Moved Between Work Areas Each Year Plan A

	M	D	F	P
M	—	6	18	2
D	—	—	4	2
F	—	—	—	18
P	—	—	—	—

Distances Between Work Areas (Departments) in Feet

	M	D	F	P
M	—	20	12	8
D	—	—	6	10
F	—	—	—	4
P	—	—	—	—

It costs $0.50 to move 1 workpiece 1 foot in the job shop. Marrs's goal is to find a layout that has the lowest material handling cost.

a) Determine cost of the current layout, Plan A, from the data above.
b) One alternative is to switch those departments with the high loads, namely, finishing (F) and plating (P), which alters the distance between them and machining (M) and dipping (D), as follows:

Distances Between Work Areas (Departments) in Feet Plan B

	M	D	F	P
M	—	20	8	12
D	—	—	10	6
F	—	—	—	4
P	—	—	—	—

What is the cost of *this* layout?

c) Marrs now wants you to evaluate Plan C, which also switches milling (M) and drilling (D), below.

Distance Between Work Areas (Departments) in Feet Plan C

	M	D	F	P
M	—	20	10	6
D	—	—	8	12
F	—	—	—	4
P	—	—	—	—

What is the cost of *this* layout?

d) Which layout is best from a cost perspective?

• **3** Three departments—milling (M), drilling (D), and sawing (S)—are assigned to three work areas in Victor Berardis's machine shop in Vent, Ohio. The number of work pieces moved per day and the distances between the centers of the work areas, in feet, follow.

Pieces Moved Between Work Areas Each Day

	M	D	S
M	—	23	32
D	—	—	20
S	—	—	—

Distances Between Centers of Work Areas (Departments) in Feet

	M	D	S
M	—	10	5
D	—	—	8
S	—	—	—

It costs $2 to move 1 workpiece 1 foot.
What is the cost?

•• **4** Roy Creasey Enterprises, a machine shop, is planning to move to a new, larger location. The new building will be 60 feet long by 40 feet wide. Creasey envisions the building as having six distinct production areas, roughly equal in size. He feels strongly about safety and intends to have marked pathways throughout the building to facilitate the movement of people and materials. See the following building schematic.

Building Schematic (with work areas 1–6)

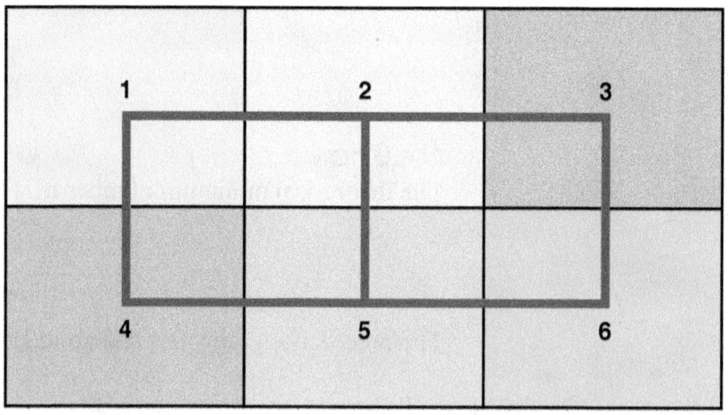

His foreman has completed a month-long study of the number of loads of material that have moved from one process to another in the current building. This information is contained in the following flow matrix.

Flow Matrix Between Production Processes

FROM \ TO	MATERIALS	WELDING	DRILLS	LATHES	GRINDERS	BENDERS
Materials	0	100	50	0	0	50
Welding	25	0	0	50	0	0
Drills	25	0	0	0	50	0
Lathes	0	25	0	0	20	0
Grinders	50	0	100	0	0	0
Benders	10	0	20	0	0	0

Finally, Creasey has developed the following matrix to indicate distances between the work areas shown in the building schematic.

Distance Between Work Areas						
	1	2	3	4	5	6
1		20	40	20	40	60
2			20	40	20	40
3				60	40	20
4					20	40
5						20
6						

What is the appropriate layout of the new building? Px

•• **5** Munson Manufacturing, in Gainesville, Florida, wants to arrange its four work centers so as to minimize interdepartmental parts handling costs. The flows and existing facility layout are shown in Figure 19.

Parts Moved Between Work Centers

	A	B	C	D
A	—	450	550	50
B	350	—	200	0
C	0	0	—	750
D	0	0	0	—

Existing Layout

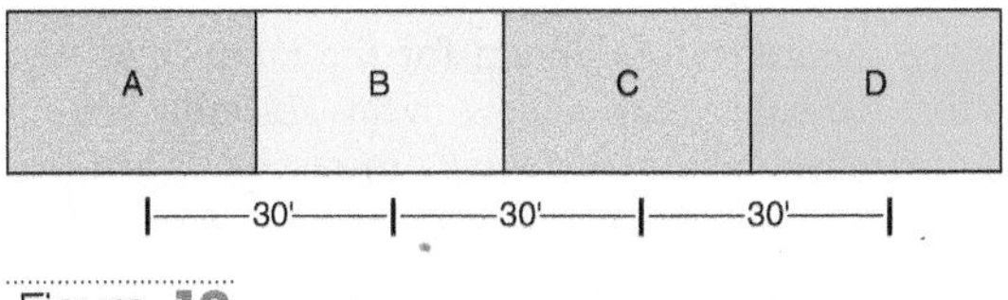

Figure 19
Munson Manufacturing

a) What is the "load × distance," or "movement cost," of the layout shown?
b) Provide an improved layout and compute its movement cost. Px

••• **6** You have just been hired as the director of operations for Reid Chocolates, a purveyor of exceptionally fine candies. Reid Chocolates has two kitchen layouts under consideration for its recipe making and testing department. The strategy is to provide the best kitchen layout possible so that food scientists can devote their time and energy to product improvement, not wasted effort in the kitchen. You have been asked to evaluate these two kitchen layouts and to prepare a recommendation for your boss, Mr. Reid, so that he can proceed to place the contract for building the kitchens. [See Figure 20(a), and Figure 20(b).] Px

Number of trips between work centers:

From: \ To:		Refrigerator 1	Counter 2	Sink 3	Storage 4	Stove 5
Refrig.	1	0	8	13	0	0
Counter	2	5	0	3	3	8
Sink	3	3	12	0	4	0
Storage	4	3	0	0	0	5
Stove	5	0	8	4	10	0

Figure 20(a)
Layout Options

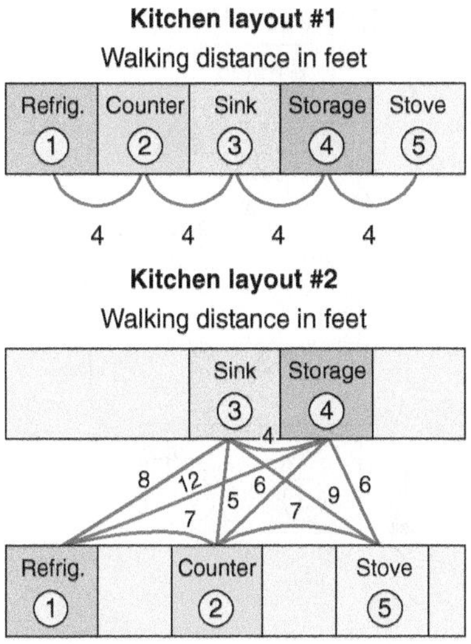

Figure 20(b)

••• **7** Reid Chocolates (see Problem 6) is considering a third layout, as shown below. Evaluate its effectiveness in trip-distance feet. Px

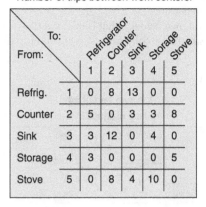

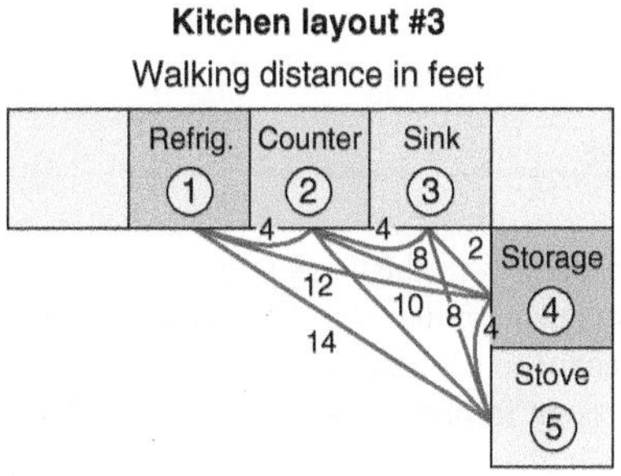

••• **8** Reid Chocolates (see Problems 6 and 7) has yet two more layouts to consider.

a) Layout 4 is shown below. What is the total trip distance?
b) Layout 5, which also follows, has what total trip distance?

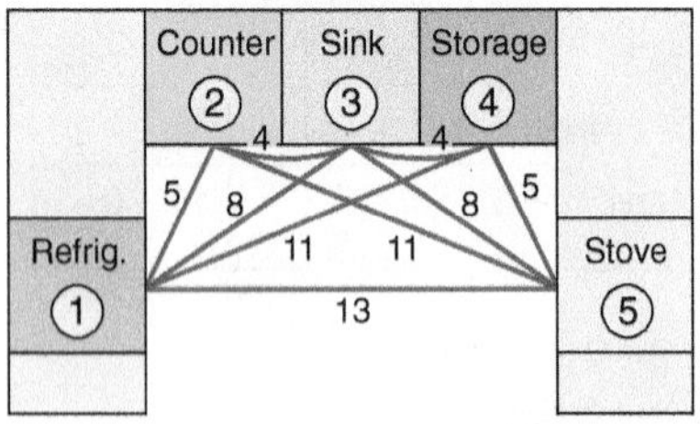

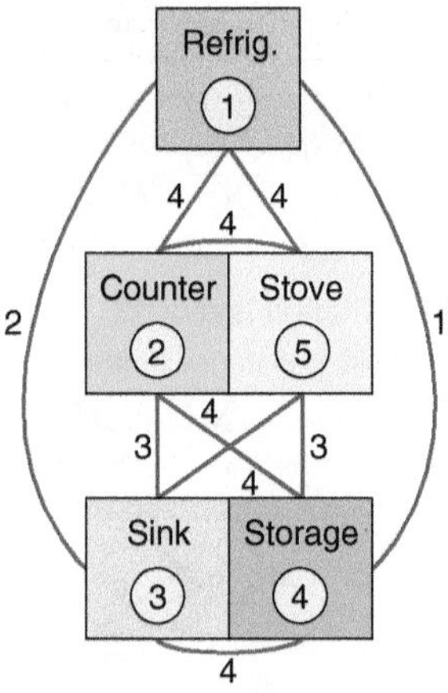

•• **9** Six processes are to be laid out in six areas along a long corridor at Rita Gibson Accounting Services in Daytona Beach. The distance between adjacent work centers is 40 feet. The number of trips between work centers is given in the following table:

	TRIPS BETWEEN PROCESSES					
	TO					
FROM	A	B	C	D	E	F
A		18	25	73	12	54
B			96	23	31	45
C				41	22	20
D					19	57
E						48
F						

a) Assign the processes to the work areas in a way that minimizes the total flow, using a method that places processes with highest flow adjacent to each other.
b) What assignment minimizes the total traffic flow? PX

•• **10** After an extensive product analysis using group technology, Leon Bazil has identified a product he believes should be pulled out of his process facility and handled in a work cell. Leon has identified the following operations as necessary for the work cell. The customer expects delivery of 250 units per day, and the work day is 420 minutes.

a) What is the takt time?
b) How many employees should be cross-trained for the cell?
c) Which operations may warrant special consideration?

OPERATION	STANDARD TIME (min)
Shear	1.1
Bend	1.1
Weld	1.7
Clean	3.1
Paint	1.0

•• **11** Stanford Rosenberg Computing wants to establish an assembly line for producing a new product, the Personal Digital Assistant (PDA). The tasks, task times, and immediate predecessors for the tasks are as follows:

TASK	TIME (sec)	IMMEDIATE PREDECESSORS
A	12	—
B	15	A
C	8	A
D	5	B, C
E	20	D

Rosenberg's goal is to produce 180 PDAs per hour.

a) What is the cycle time?
b) What is the theoretical minimum for the number of workstations that Rosenberg can achieve in this assembly line?
c) Can the theoretical minimum actually be reached when workstations are assigned? PX

••• **12** Illinois Furniture, Inc., produces all types of office furniture. The "Executive Secretary" is a chair that has been designed using ergonomics to provide comfort during long work hours. The chair sells for $130. There are 480 minutes available during the day, and the average daily demand has been 50 chairs. There are eight tasks:

TASK	PERFORMANCE TIME (min)	TASK MUST FOLLOW TASK LISTED BELOW
A	4	—
B	7	—
C	6	A, B
D	5	C
E	6	D
F	7	E
G	8	E
H	6	F, G

a) Draw a precedence diagram of this operation.
b) What is the cycle time for this operation?
c) What is the *theoretical* minimum number of workstations?
d) Assign tasks to workstations.
e) What is the idle time per cycle?
f) How much total idle time is present in an 8-hour shift?
g) What is the efficiency of the assembly line, given your answer in (d)? PX

•• **13** Sue Helms Appliances wants to establish an assembly line to manufacture its new product, the Micro Popcorn Popper. The goal is to produce five poppers per hour. The tasks, task times, and immediate predecessors for producing one Micro Popcorn Popper are as follows:

TASK	TIME (min)	IMMEDIATE PREDECESSORS
A	10	—
B	12	A
C	8	A, B
D	6	B, C
E	6	C
F	6	D, E

a) What is the *theoretical* minimum for the smallest number of workstations that Helms can achieve in this assembly line?
b) Graph the assembly line and assign workers to workstations. Can you assign them with the theoretical minimum?
c) What is the efficiency of *your* assignment? PX

•• **14** The Action Toy Company has decided to manufacture a new train set, the production of which is broken into six steps. The demand for the train is 4,800 units per 40-hour workweek:

TASK	PERFORMANCE TIME (sec)	PREDECESSORS
A	20	None
B	30	A
C	15	A
D	15	A
E	10	B, C
F	30	D, E

a) Draw a precedence diagram of this operation.
b) Given the demand, what is the cycle time for this operation?
c) What is the *theoretical* minimum number of workstations?
d) Assign tasks to workstations.
e) How much total idle time is present each cycle?
f) What is the efficiency of the assembly line with five stations? With six stations? PX

•• **15** The following table details the tasks required for Indiana-based Frank Pianki Industries to manufacture a fully portable industrial vacuum cleaner. The times in the table are in minutes. Demand forecasts indicate a need to operate with a cycle time of 10 minutes.

ACTIVITY	ACTIVITY DESCRIPTION	IMMEDIATE PREDECESSORS	TIME
A	Attach wheels to tub	—	5
B	Attach motor to lid	—	1.5
C	Attach battery pack	B	3
D	Attach safety cutoff	C	4
E	Attach filters	B	3
F	Attach lid to tub	A, E	2
G	Assemble attachments	—	3
H	Function test	D, F, G	3.5
I	Final inspection	H	2
J	Packing	I	2

a) Draw the appropriate precedence diagram for this production line.
b) Assign tasks to workstations and determine how much idle time is present each cycle.
c) Discuss how this balance could be improved to 100%.
d) What is the *theoretical* minimum number of workstations? PX

•• **16** Tailwind, Inc., produces high-quality but expensive training shoes for runners. The Tailwind shoe, which sells for $210, contains both gas- and liquid-filled compartments to provide more stability and better protection against knee, foot, and back injuries. Manufacturing the shoes requires 10 separate tasks. There are 400 minutes available for manufacturing the shoes in the plant each day. Daily demand is 60. The information for the tasks is as follows:

TASK	PERFORMANCE TIME (min)	TASK MUST FOLLOW TASK LISTED BELOW
A	1	—
B	3	A
C	2	B
D	4	B
E	1	C, D
F	3	A
G	2	F
H	5	G
I	1	E, H
J	3	I

a) Draw the precedence diagram.
b) Assign tasks to the minimum feasible number of workstations according to the "ranked positioned weight" decision rule.
c) What is the efficiency of the process you completed in (b)?
d) What is the idle time per cycle? PX

•• **17** The Mach 10 is a one-person sailboat manufactured by Creative Leisure. The final assembly plant is in Cupertino, California. The assembly area is available for production of the Mach 10 for 200 minutes per day. (The rest of the time it is busy making other products.) The daily demand is 60 boats. Given the information in the table on the next page,

a) Draw the precedence diagram and assign tasks using five workstations.

b) What is the efficiency of the assembly line, using your answer to (a)?
c) What is the *theoretical* minimum number of workstations?
d) What is the idle time per boat produced? Px

TASK	PERFORMANCE TIME (min)	TASK MUST FOLLOW TASK LISTED BELOW
A	1	—
B	1	A
C	2	A
D	1	C
E	3	C
F	1	C
G	1	D, E, F
H	2	B
I	1	G, H

© Alex Segre/Alamy

•• **18** Because of the expected high demand for Mach 10, Creative Leisure has decided to increase manufacturing time available to produce the Mach 10 (see Problem 17).
a) If demand remained the same but 300 minutes were available each day on the assembly line, how many workstations would be needed?
b) What would be the efficiency of the new system, using the actual number of workstations from (a)?
c) What would be the impact on the system if 400 minutes were available? Px

••• **19** Dr. Lori Baker, operations manager at Nesa Electronics, prides herself on excellent assembly-line balancing. She has been told that the firm needs to complete 96 instruments per 24-hour day. The assembly-line activities are:

TASK	TIME (min)	PREDECESSORS
A	3	—
B	6	—
C	7	A
D	5	A, B
E	2	B
F	4	C
G	5	F
H	7	D, E
I	1	H
J	6	E
K	4	G, I, J
	50	

a) Draw the precedence diagram.
b) If the daily (24-hour) production rate is 96 units, what is the highest allowable cycle time?
c) If the cycle time after allowances is given as 10 minutes, what is the daily (24-hour) production rate?
d) With a 10-minute cycle time, what is the theoretical minimum number of stations with which the line can be balanced?
e) With a 10-minute cycle time and six workstations, what is the efficiency?
f) What is the total idle time per cycle with a 10-minute cycle time and six workstations?
g) What is the best work station assignment you can make without exceeding a 10-minute cycle time and what is its efficiency? Px

•• **20** Suppose production requirements in Solved Problem 2 increase and require a reduction in cycle time from 8 minutes to 7 minutes. Balance the line once again, using the new cycle time. Note that it is not possible to combine task times so as to group tasks into the minimum number of workstations. This condition occurs in actual balancing problems fairly often. Px

•• **21** The preinduction physical examination given by the U.S. Army involves the following seven activities:

ACTIVITY	AVERAGE TIME (min)
Medical history	10
Blood tests	8
Eye examination	5
Measurements (e.g., weight, height, blood pressure)	7
Medical examination	16
Psychological interview	12
Exit medical evaluation	10

These activities can be performed in any order, with two exceptions: Medical history must be taken first, and Exit medical evaluation is last. At present, there are three paramedics and two physicians on duty during each shift. Only physicians can perform exit evaluations and conduct psychological interviews. Other activities can be carried out by either physicians or paramedics.
a) Develop a layout and balance the line.
b) How many people can be processed per hour?

c) Which activity accounts for the current bottleneck?
d) What is the total idle time per cycle?
e) If one more physician and one more paramedic can be placed on duty, how would you redraw the layout? What is the new throughput?

••• **22** Samuel Smith's company wants to establish an assembly line to manufacture its new product, the iStar phone. Samuel's goal is to produce 60 iStars per hour. Tasks, task times, and immediate predecessors are as follows:

TASK	TIME (sec)	IMMEDIATE PREDECESSORS	TASK	TIME (sec)	IMMEDIATE PREDECESSORS
A	40	—	F	25	C
B	30	A	G	15	C
C	50	A	H	20	D, E
D	40	B	I	18	F, G
E	6	B	J	30	H, I

a) What is the theoretical minimum for the number of workstations that Samuel can achieve in this assembly line?
b) Use the *most following tasks* heuristic to balance an assembly line for the iStar phone.
c) How many workstations are in your answer to (b)?
d) What is the efficiency of your answer to (b)? Px

•••• **23** As the Cottrell Bicycle Co. of St. Louis completes plans for its new assembly line, it identifies 25 different tasks in the production process. VP of Operations Jonathan Cottrell now faces the job of balancing the line. He lists precedences and provides time estimates for each step based on work-sampling techniques. His goal is to produce 1,000 bicycles per standard 40-hour workweek.

TASK	TIME (sec)	PRECEDENCE TASKS	TASK	TIME (sec)	PRECEDENCE TASKS
K3	60	—	E3	109	F3
K4	24	K3	D6	53	F4
K9	27	K3	D7	72	F9, E2, E3
J1	66	K3	D8	78	E3, D6
J2	22	K3	D9	37	D6
J3	3	—	C1	78	F7
G4	79	K4, K9	B3	72	D7, D8, D9, C1
G5	29	K9, J1	B5	108	C1
F3	32	J2	B7	18	B3
F4	92	J2	A1	52	B5
F7	21	J3	A2	72	B5
F9	126	G4	A3	114	B7, A1, A2
E2	18	G5, F3			

a) Balance this operation, using various heuristics. Which is best and why?
b) What happens if the firm can change to a 41-hour workweek? Px

Refer to MyOMLab for these additional homework problems: 9.24–9.27

CASE STUDIES

State Automobile License Renewals

Henry Coupe, the manager of a metropolitan branch office of the state department of motor vehicles, attempted to analyze the driver's license-renewal operations. He had to perform several steps. After examining the license-renewal process, he identified those steps and associated times required to perform each step, as shown in the following table:

State Automobile License Renewal Process Times

STEP	AVERAGE TIME TO PERFORM (sec)
1. Review renewal application for correctness	15
2. Process and record payment	30
3. Check file for violations and restrictions	60
4. Conduct eye test	40
5. Photograph applicant	20
6. Issue temporary license	30

Coupe found that each step was assigned to a different person. Each application was a separate process in the sequence shown. He determined that his office should be prepared to accommodate a maximum demand of processing 120 renewal applicants per hour.

He observed that work was unevenly divided among clerks and that the clerk responsible for checking violations tended to shortcut her task to keep up with the others. Long lines built up during the maximum-demand periods.

Coupe also found that Steps 1 to 4 were handled by general clerks who were each paid $12 per hour. Step 5 was performed by a photographer paid $16 per hour. (Branch offices were charged $10 per hour for each camera to perform photography.) Step 6, issuing temporary licenses, was required by state policy to be handled by uniformed motor vehicle officers. Officers were paid $18 per hour but could be assigned to any job except photography.

A review of the jobs indicated that Step 1, reviewing applications for correctness, had to be performed before any other step could be taken. Similarly, Step 6, issuing temporary licenses, could not be performed until all the other steps were completed.

Henry Coupe was under severe pressure to increase productivity and reduce costs, but he was also told by the regional director that he must accommodate the demand for renewals. Otherwise, "heads would roll."

Discussion Questions

1. What is the maximum number of applications per hour that can be handled by the present configuration of the process?
2. How many applications can be processed per hour if a second clerk is added to check for violations?
3. If the second clerk could be added *anywhere* you choose (and not necessarily to check for violations, as in Question 2), what is the maximum number of applications the process can handle? What is the new configuration?
4. How would you suggest modifying the process to accommodate 120 applications per hour? What is the cost per application of this new configuration?

Source: Modified from a case by W. Earl Sasser, Paul R. Olson, and D. Daryl Wyckoff, *Management of Services Operations: Text, Cases, and Readings* (Boston: Allyn & Bacon).

Laying Out Arnold Palmer Hospital's New Facility — Video Case

When Orlando's Arnold Palmer Hospital began plans to create a new 273-bed, 11-story hospital across the street from its existing facility, which was bursting at the seams in terms of capacity, a massive planning process began. The $100 million building, opened in 2006, was long overdue, according to Executive Director Kathy Swanson: "We started Arnold Palmer Hospital in 1989, with a mission to provide quality services for children and women in a comforting, family-friendly environment. Since then we have served well over 1.5 million women and children and now deliver more than 12,000 babies a year. By 2001, we simply ran out of room, and it was time for us to grow."

The new hospital's unique, circular pod design provides a maximally efficient layout in all areas of the hospital, creating a patient-centered environment. *Servicescape* design features include a serene environment created through the use of warm colors, private rooms with pull-down Murphy beds for family members, 14-foot ceilings, and natural lighting with oversized windows in patient rooms. But these radical new features did not come easily. "This pod concept with a central nursing area and pie-shaped rooms resulted from over 1,000 planning meetings of 35 user groups, extensive motion and time studies, and computer simulations of the daily movements of nurses," says Swanson.

In a traditional linear hospital layout, called the *racetrack* design, patient rooms line long hallways, and a nurse might walk 2.7 miles per day serving patient needs at Arnold Palmer. "Some nurses spent 30% of their time simply walking. With the nursing shortage and the high cost of health care professionals, efficiency is a major concern," added Swanson. With the nursing station in the center of 10- or 12-bed circular pods, no patient room is more than 14 feet from a station. The time savings are in the 20% range. Swanson pointed to Figures 21 and 22 as examples of the old and new walking and trip distances.*

"We have also totally redesigned our neonatal rooms," says Swanson. "In the old system, there were 16 neonatal beds in a large and often noisy rectangular room. The new building features semiprivate rooms for these tiny babies. The rooms are much improved, with added privacy and a quiet, simulated night atmosphere, in addition to pull-down beds for parents to use. Our research shows that babies improve and develop much more quickly with this layout design. Layout and environment indeed impact patient care!"

*Layout and walking distances, including some of the numbers in Figures 21 and 22, have been simplified for purposes of this case.

Figure 21

Traditional Hospital Layout

Patient rooms are on two linear hallways with exterior windows. Supply rooms are on interior corridors. This layout is called a "racetrack" design.

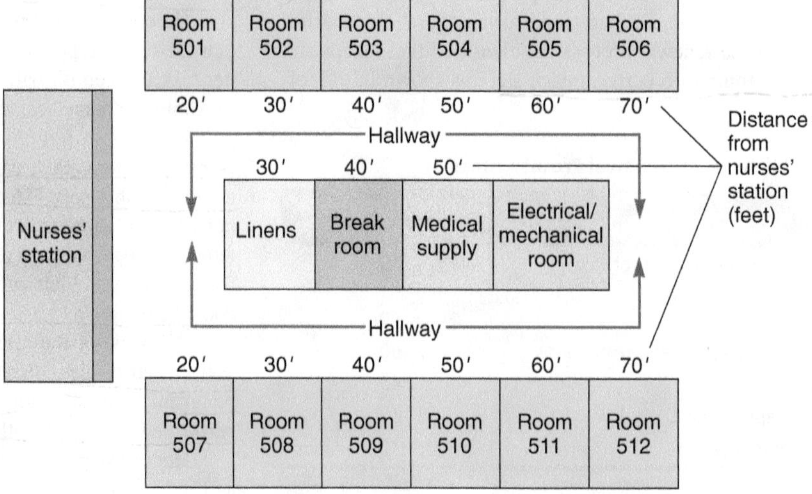

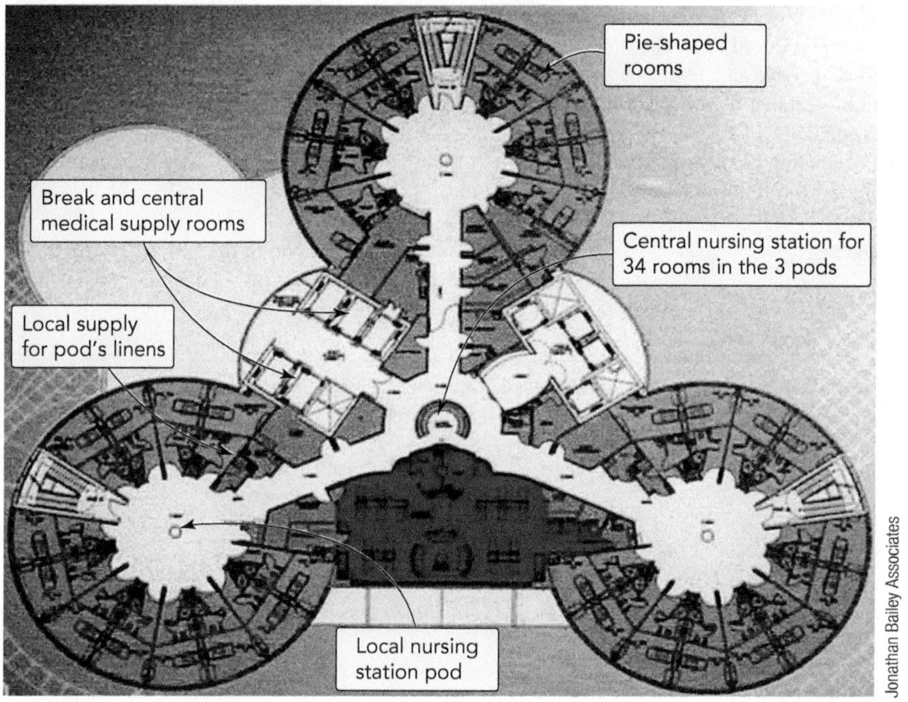

Figure 22
New Pod Design for Hospital Layout

Note that each room is 14 feet from the pod's *local* nursing station. The *break rooms* and the *central medical station* are each about 60 feet from the local nursing pod. Pod *linen supply* rooms are also 14 feet from the local nursing station.

Discussion Questions*

1. Identify the many variables that a hospital needs to consider in layout design.
2. What are the advantages of the circular pod design over the traditional linear hallway layout found in most hospitals?
3. Figure 21 illustrates a sample linear hallway layout. During a period of random observation, nurse Thomas Smith's day includes 6 trips from the nursing station to each of the 12 patient rooms (back and forth), 20 trips to the medical supply room, 5 trips to the break room, and 12 trips to the linen supply room. What is his total distance traveled in miles?
4. Figure 22 illustrates an architect's drawing of Arnold Palmer Hospital's new circular pod system. If nurse Susan Jones's day includes 7 trips from the nursing pod to each of the 12 rooms (back and forth), 20 trips to central medical supply, 6 trips to the break room, and 12 trips to the pod linen supply, how many miles does she walk during her shift? What are the differences in the travel times between the two nurses for this random day?
5. The concept of *servicescapes* is discussed in this text. Describe why this is so important at Arnold Palmer Hospital and give examples of its use in layout design.

*You may wish to view the video that accompanies this case before addressing these questions.

Facility Layout at Wheeled Coach

Video Case

When President Bob Collins began his career at Wheeled Coach, the world's largest manufacturer of ambulances, there were only a handful of employees. Now the firm's Florida plant has a workforce of 350. The physical plant has also expanded, with offices, R&D, final assembly, and wiring, cabinetry, and upholstery work cells in one large building. Growth has forced the painting work cell into a separate building, aluminum fabrication and body installation into another, inspection and shipping into a fourth, and warehousing into yet another.

Like many other growing companies, Wheeled Coach was not able to design its facility from scratch. And although management realizes that material handling costs are a little higher than an ideal layout would provide, Collins is pleased with the way the facility has evolved and employees have adapted. The aluminum cutting work cell lies adjacent to body fabrication, which, in turn, is located next to the body-installation work cell. And while the vehicle must be driven across a street to one building for painting and then to another for final assembly, at least the ambulance is on wheels. Collins is also satisfied with the flexibility shown in the design of the work cells. Cell construction is flexible and can accommodate changes in product mix and volume. In addition, work cells are typically small and movable, with many work benches and staging racks borne on wheels so that they can be easily rearranged and products transported to the assembly line.

Assembly-line balancing is one key problem facing Wheeled Coach and every other repetitive manufacturer. Produced on a schedule calling for four 10-hour work days per week, once an ambulance is on one of the six final assembly lines, it *must* move forward each day to the next workstation. Balancing just enough workers and tasks at each of the seven workstations is a never-ending challenge. Too many workers end up running into each other; too few can't finish an ambulance in seven days. Constant shifting of design and mix and improved analysis has led to frequent changes.

Discussion Questions*

1. What analytical techniques are available to help a company like Wheeled Coach deal with layout problems?
2. What suggestions would you make to Bob Collins about his layout?
3. How would you measure the "efficiency" of this layout?

*You may wish to view the video that accompanies this case before addressing these questions.

- **Additional Case Study:** Visit **www.myomlab.com** or **www.pearsonhighered.com/heizer** *for this free case study:*
  Microfix, Inc.: This company needs to balance its PC manufacturing assembly line and deal with sensitivity analysis of time estimates.

Bibliography

Aghazadeh, S. M., S. Hafeznezami, L. Najjar, and Z. Hug. "The Influence of Work-Cells and Facility Layout on Manufacturing Efficiency." *Journal of Facilities Management* 9, no. 3 (2011): 213–224.

Birchfield, J. C., and J. Birchfield. *Design and Layout of Foodservice Facilities*, 3rd ed. New York, Wiley & Sons, 2007.

Francis, R. L., L. F. McGinnis, and J. A. White. *Facility Layout and Location*, 3rd ed. Upper Saddle River, NJ: Prentice Hall, 1998.

Heragu, S. S. *Facilities Design*, 3rd ed. New York: CRC Press, 2008.

Heyer, N., and U. Wemmerlöv. *Reorganizing the Factory: Competing through Cellular Manufacturing*. Portland, OR: Productivity Press, 2002.

Johnson, Alan. "Getting the Right Factory Layout." *Manufacturer's Monthly* (July 2008): 16.

Kator, C. "Crossdocking on the Rise." *Modern Materials Handling* 63, no. 6 (June 2008): 15.

Larson, S. "Extreme Makover—OR Edition." *Nursing Management* (November 2005): 26.

Roodbergen, K. J., and I. F. A. Vis. "A Model for Warehouse Layout." *IIE Transactions* 38, no. 10 (October 2006): 799–811.

Stanowy, A. "Evolutionary Strategy for Manufacturing Cell Design." *Omega* 34, no. 1 (January 2006): 1.

Taghavi, A., and A. Murat. "A Heuristic Procedure for the Integrated Facility Layout Design and Flow Assignment Problem." *Computers & Industrial Engineering* 61, no. 1 (August 2011): 55–63.

Tompkins, James A. *Facility Planning*, 4th ed. New York: Wiley, 2009.

Upton, David. "What Really Makes Factories Flexible?" *Harvard Business Review* 73, no. 4 (July–August 1995): 74–84.

Zhao, T., and C. L. Tseng. "Flexible Facility Interior Layout." *The Journal of the Operational Research Society* 58, no. 6 (June 2007): 729–740.

APPENDIX
SOLUTIONS TO EVEN-NUMBERED PROBLEMS

2 (**a**) $23,400
(**b**) $20,600
(**c**) $22,000
(**d**) Plan B

4 Benders to area 1; Materials to 2; Welders to 3; Drills to 4; Grinder to 5; and Lathes to 6; Trips × Distance = 13,000 ft.

6 Layout #1, distance = 600 with areas fixed
Layout #2, distance = 602 with areas fixed

8 Layout #4, distance = 609
Layout #5, distance = 478

10 (**a**) 1.68 minutes
(**b**) 4.76 5
(**c**) cleaning

12 (**b**) Cycle time = 9.6 min.;
(**e**) Idle time/cycle = 15 min.
(**f**) 15 hours/day idle.
(**g**) 8 workstations with 76.6% efficiency is possible.

14 (**a**)

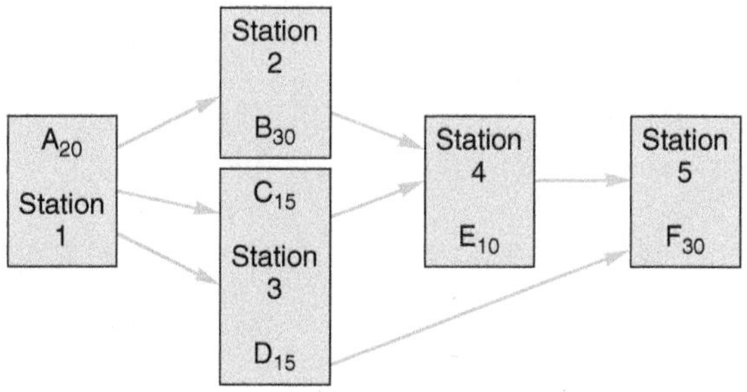

(**b**) cycle time = 30 sec./unit
(**c**) 4 stations = *theoretical* minimum, but 5 are needed
(**d**) Station 1–Task A; 2–B; 3–C, D; 4–E; 5–F
(**e**) Total idle = 30 sec.
(**f**) E = 80% with 5 stations; E = 66.6% with 6 stations

16 (**a, b**) Cycle time = 6.67 min/unit. Multiple solutions with 5 stations. Here is a sample: A, F, G to station 1; B, C to station 2; D, E to station 3; H to station 4; and I, J to station 5. (**c**) Actual efficiency with 5 stations = 83% (**d**) Idle time = 5 min/cycle.

18 (**a**) Minimum no. of workstations = 2.6 (or 3).
(**b**) Efficiency = 86.7%.
(**c**) Cycle time = 6.67 min/unit with 400 min/day; minimum no. of workstations = 1.95 (or 2).

20 Minimum (theoretical) = 4 stations. Efficiency = 93.3% with 5 stations and 6 min. cycle time. Several assignments with 5 are possible.

22 (**a**) Theoretical min. no. workstations = 5
(**b**) There are several possibilities. For example, Station 1–Task A; 2–C; 3–B and F; 4–D and G; 5–E, H, and I; 6–J. Or 1–A; 2–C; 3–B and F; 4–D and G; 5–E, H and I; 6–J.
(**c**) $n = 6$
(**d**) Efficiency = .7611

Rapid Review

Main Heading	Review Material	MyOMLab
THE STRATEGIC IMPORTANCE OF LAYOUT DECISIONS	Layout has numerous strategic implications because it establishes an organization's competitive priorities in regard to capacity, processes, flexibility, and cost, as well as quality of work life, customer contact, and image. *The objective of layout strategy is to develop an effective and efficient layout that will meet the firm's competitive requirements.*	
TYPES OF LAYOUT	Types of layout and examples of their typical objectives include: 1. *Office layout*: Locate workers requiring frequent contact close to one another. 2. *Retail layout*: Expose customers to high-margin items. 3. *Warehouse layout*: Balance low-cost storage with low-cost material handling. 4. *Fixed-position layout*: Move material to the limited storage areas around the site. 5. *Process-oriented layout*: Manage varied material flow for each product. 6. *Work-cell layout*: Identify a product family, build teams, and cross-train team members. 7. *Product-oriented layout*: Equalize the task time at each workstation.	
OFFICE LAYOUT	■ **Office layout**—The grouping of workers, their equipment, and spaces/offices to provide for comfort, safety, and movement of information. A *relationship chart* displays a "closeness value" between each pair of people and/or departments that need to be placed in the office layout.	
RETAIL LAYOUT	■ **Retail layout**—An approach that addresses flow, allocates space, and responds to customer behavior. Retail layouts are based on the idea that sales and profitability vary directly with customer exposure to products. The main *objective of retail layout is to maximize profitability per square foot of floor space* (or, in some stores, per linear foot of shelf space). ■ **Slotting fees**—Fees manufacturers pay to get shelf space for their products. ■ **Servicescape**—The physical surroundings in which a service takes place and how they affect customers and employees.	
WAREHOUSE AND STORAGE LAYOUTS)	■ **Warehouse layout**—A design that attempts to minimize total cost by addressing trade-offs between space and material handling. The variety of items stored and the number of items "picked" has direct bearing on the optimal layout. Modern warehouse management is often an automated procedure using *automated storage and retrieval systems* (ASRSs). ■ **Cross-docking**—Avoiding the placement of materials or supplies in storage by processing them as they are received for shipment. Cross-docking requires both tight scheduling and accurate inbound product identification. ■ **Random stocking**—Used in warehousing to locate stock wherever there is an open location. ■ **Customizing**—Using warehousing to add value to a product through component modification, repair, labeling, and packaging.	
FIXED-POSITION LAYOUT	■ **Fixed-position layout**—A system that addresses the layout requirements of stationary projects. Fixed-position layouts involve three complications: (1) there is limited space at virtually all sites, (2) different materials are needed at different stages of a project, and (3) the volume of materials needed is dynamic.	
PROCESS-ORIENTED LAYOUT	■ **Process-oriented layout**—A layout that deals with low-volume, high-variety production in which like machines and equipment are grouped together. ■ **Job lots**—Groups or batches of parts processed together. $$\text{Minimize cost} = \sum_{i=1}^{n} \sum_{j=1}^{n} X_{ij}C_{ij} \quad (1)$$	Problems: 1–9 Virtual Office Hours for Solved Problem: 1 **VIDEO 1** Laying Out Arnold Palmer Hospital's New Facility **ACTIVE MODEL 1**

Rapid Review *continued*

Main Heading	Review Material	MyOMLab
WORK CELLS	▪ **Work cell**—An arrangement of machines and personnel that focuses on making a single product or family of related products. ▪ **Takt time**—Pace of production to meet customer demands. Takt time = Total work time available/Units required (2) Workers required = Total operation time required/Takt time (3) ▪ **Focused work center**—A permanent or semi-permanent product-oriented arrangement of machines and personnel. ▪ **Focused factory**—A facility designed to produce similar products or components.	Problem: 10
REPETITIVE AND PRODUCT-ORIENTED LAYOUT	▪ **Fabrication line**—A machine-paced, product-oriented facility for building components. ▪ **Assembly line**—An approach that puts fabricated parts together at a series of workstations; a repetitive process. ▪ **Assembly-line balancing**—Obtaining output at each workstation on a production line in order to minimize delay. ▪ **Cycle time**—The maximum time that a product is allowed at each workstation. Cycle time = Production time available per day ÷ Units required per day (4) $\text{Minimum number of workstations} = \sum_{i=1}^{n} \text{Time for task } i/(\text{Cycle time})$ (5) ▪ **Heuristic**—Problem solving using procedures and rules rather than mathematical optimization. Line-balancing heuristics include *longest task (operation) time, most following tasks, ranked positional weight, shortest task (operation) time,* and *least number of following tasks.* $\text{Efficiency} = \dfrac{\Sigma\text{Task times}}{(\textit{Actual}\text{ number of workstations}) \times (\text{Largest assigned cycle time})}$ (6)	Problems: 11–22 **VIDEO 2** Facility Layout at Wheeled Coach Ambulances Virtual Office Hours for Solved Problem: 2

Self Test

▪ **Before taking the self-test,** refer to the learning objectives listed at the beginning of the text and the key terms listed at the end of the text.

LO1. Which of the statements below best describes *office layout*?
- **a)** Groups workers, their equipment, and spaces/offices to provide for movement of information.
- **b)** Addresses the layout requirements of large, bulky projects such as ships and buildings.
- **c)** Seeks the best personnel and machine utilization in repetitive or continuous production.
- **d)** Allocates shelf space and responds to customer behavior.
- **e)** Deals with low-volume, high-variety production.

LO2. Which of the following does *not* support the retail layout objective of maximizing customer exposure to products?
- **a)** Locate high-draw items around the periphery of the store.
- **b)** Use prominent locations for high-impulse and high-margin items.
- **c)** Maximize exposure to expensive items.
- **d)** Use end-aisle locations.
- **e)** Convey the store's mission with the careful positioning of the lead-off department.

LO3. The major problem addressed by the warehouse layout strategy is:
- **a)** minimizing difficulties caused by material flow varying with each product.
- **b)** requiring frequent contact close to one another.
- **c)** addressing trade-offs between space and material handling.
- **d)** balancing product flow from one workstation to the next.
- **e)** none of the above.

LO4. A fixed-position layout:
- **a)** groups workers to provide for movement of information.
- **b)** addresses the layout requirements of large, bulky projects such as ships and buildings.
- **c)** seeks the best machine utilization in continuous production.
- **d)** allocates shelf space based on customer behavior.
- **e)** deals with low-volume, high-variety production.

LO5. A process-oriented layout:
- **a)** groups workers to provide for movement of information.
- **b)** addresses the layout requirements of large, bulky projects such as ships and buildings.
- **c)** seeks the best machine utilization in continuous production.
- **d)** allocates shelf space based on customer behavior.
- **e)** deals with low-volume, high-variety production.

LO6. For a focused work center or focused factory to be appropriate, the following three factors are required:
- **a)** ______________________
- **b)** ______________________
- **c)** ______________________

LO7. Before considering a product-oriented layout, it is important to be certain that:
- **a)** ______________________
- **b)** ______________________
- **c)** ______________________
- **d)** ______________________

LO8. An assembly line is to be designed for a product whose completion requires 21 minutes of work. The factory works 400 minutes per day. Can a production line with five workstations make 100 units per day?
- **a)** Yes, with exactly 100 minutes to spare.
- **b)** No, but four workstations would be sufficient.
- **c)** No, it will fall short even with a perfectly balanced line.
- **d)** Yes, but the line's efficiency is very low.
- **e)** Cannot be determined from the information given.

Answers: LO1. a; LO2. c; LO3. c; LO4. b; LO5. e; LO6. family of products, stable forecast (demand), volume; LO7. adequate volume, stable demand, standardized product, adequate/quality supplies; LO8. c.

Waiting-Line Models

OUTLINE

- Queuing Theory
- Characteristics of a Waiting-Line System
- Queuing Costs
- The Variety of Queuing Models
- Other Queuing Approaches

LEARNING OBJECTIVES

- **LO1** ***Describe*** the characteristics of arrivals, waiting lines, and service systems
- **LO2** ***Apply*** the single-server queuing model equations
- **LO3** ***Conduct*** a cost analysis for a waiting line
- **LO4** ***Apply*** the multiple-server queuing model formulas
- **LO5** ***Apply*** the constant-service-time model equations
- **LO6** ***Perform*** a limited-population model analysis

Paris's EuroDisney, Tokyo's Disney Japan, and the U.S.'s Disney World and Disneyland all have one feature in common—long lines and seemingly endless waits. However, Disney is one of the world's leading companies in the scientific analysis of queuing theory. It analyzes queuing behaviors and can predict which rides will draw what length crowds. To keep visitors happy, Disney makes lines appear to be constantly moving forward, entertains people while they wait, and posts signs telling visitors how many minutes until they reach each ride.

Jeff Greenberg/PhotoEdit Inc.

Queuing Theory

Queuing theory
A body of knowledge about waiting lines.

Waiting line (queue)
Items or people in a line awaiting service.

The body of knowledge about waiting lines, often called queuing theory, is an important part of operations and a valuable tool for the operations manager. Waiting lines are a common situation—they may, for example, take the form of cars waiting for repair at a Midas Muffler Shop, copying jobs waiting to be completed at a Kinko's print shop, or vacationers waiting to enter the Space Mountain ride at Disney. Table 1 lists just a few OM uses of waiting-line models.

Waiting-line models are useful in both manufacturing and service areas. Analysis of queues in terms of waiting-line length, average waiting time, and other factors helps us to understand service systems (such as bank teller stations), maintenance activities (that might repair broken machinery), and shop-floor control activities. Indeed, patients waiting in a doctor's office and broken drill presses

TABLE 1 Common Queuing Situations

SITUATION	ARRIVALS IN QUEUE	SERVICE PROCESS
Supermarket	Grocery shoppers	Checkout clerks at cash register
Highway toll booth	Automobiles	Collection of tolls at booth
Doctor's office	Patients	Treatment by doctors and nurses
Computer system	Programs to be run	Computer processes jobs
Telephone company	Callers	Switching equipment forwards calls
Bank	Customers	Transactions handled by teller
Machine maintenance	Broken machines	Repair people fix machines
Harbor	Ships and barges	Dock workers load and unload

waiting in a repair facility have a lot in common from an OM perspective. Both use human and equipment resources to restore valuable production assets (people and machines) to good condition.

Characteristics of a Waiting-Line System

In this section, we take a look at the three parts of a waiting-line, or queuing, system (as shown in Figure 1):

1. *Arrivals or inputs to the system:* These have characteristics such as population size, behavior, and a statistical distribution.
2. *Queue discipline, or the waiting line itself:* Characteristics of the queue include whether it is limited or unlimited in length and the discipline of people or items in it.
3. *The service facility:* Its characteristics include its design and the statistical distribution of service times.

We now examine each of these three parts.

LO1 *Describe* the characteristics of arrivals, waiting lines, and service systems.

Arrival Characteristics

The input source that generates arrivals or customers for a service system has three major characteristics:

1. *Size* of the arrival population
2. *Behavior* of arrivals
3. *Pattern* of arrivals (statistical distribution)

Size of the Arrival (Source) Population Population sizes are considered either unlimited (essentially infinite) or limited (finite). When the number of customers or arrivals on hand at any given moment is just a small portion of all potential arrivals, the arrival population is considered unlimited, or infinite. Examples of unlimited populations include cars arriving at a big-city car wash, shoppers arriving at a supermarket, and students arriving to register for classes at a large university. Most queuing models assume such an infinite arrival population. An example of a limited, or finite, population is found in a copying shop that has, say, eight copying machines. Each of the copiers is a potential "customer" that may break down and require service.

Unlimited, or infinite, population
A queue in which a virtually unlimited number of people or items could request the services, or in which the number of customers or arrivals on hand at any given moment is a very small portion of potential arrivals.

Limited, or finite, population
A queue in which there are only a limited number of potential users of the service.

Pattern of Arrivals at the System Customers arrive at a service facility either according to some known schedule (for example, one patient every 15 minutes or one student every half hour) or else they arrive *randomly*. Arrivals are considered random when they are independent of one another and their occurrence cannot be predicted exactly. Frequently in queuing

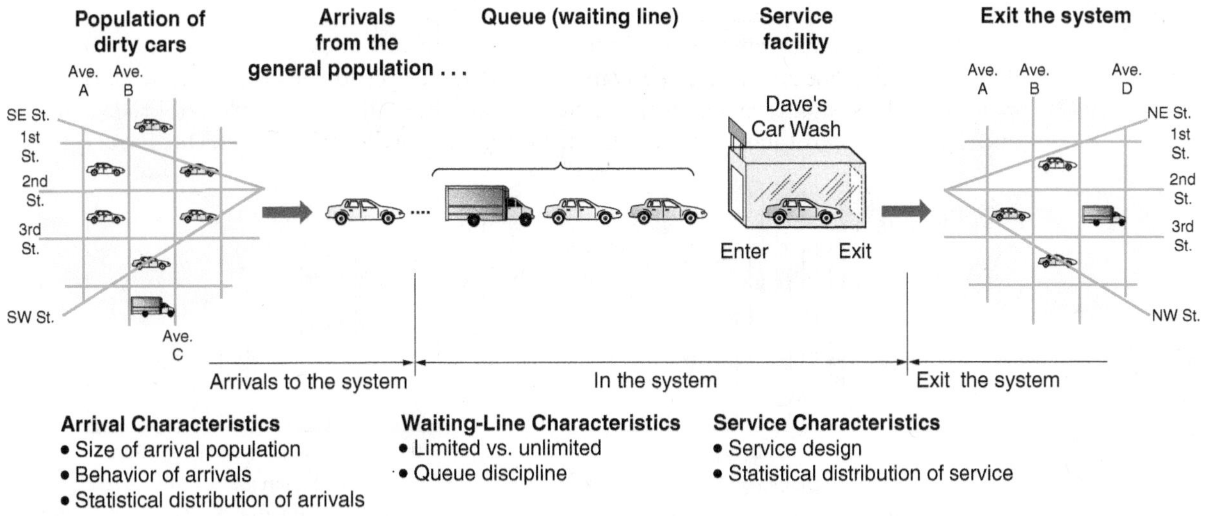

Figure 1
Three Parts of a Waiting Line, or Queuing System, at Dave's Car Wash

problems, the number of arrivals per unit of time can be estimated by a probability distribution known as the Poisson distribution.[1] For any given arrival time (such as 2 customers per hour or 4 trucks per minute), a discrete Poisson distribution can be established by using the formula:

Poisson distribution
A discrete probability distribution that often describes the arrival rate in queuing theory.

$$P(x) = \frac{e^{-\lambda}\lambda^x}{x!} \quad \text{for } x = 0, 1, 2, 3, 4, \ldots \qquad (1)$$

where $P(x)$ = probability of x arrivals
x = number of arrivals per unit of time
λ = average arrival rate
e = 2.7183 (which is the base of the natural logarithms)

With the help of the table in the Appendix: "Values of e-l for Use in the Poisson Distribution", which gives the value of $e^{-\lambda}$ for use in the Poisson distribution, these values are easy to compute. Figure 2 illustrates the Poisson distribution for $\lambda = 2$ and $\lambda = 4$. This means that if the average arrival rate is $\lambda = 2$ customers per hour, the probability of 0 customers arriving in any random hour is about 13%, probability of 1 customer is about 27%, 2 customers about 27%, 3 customers about 18%, 4 customers about 9%, and so on. The chances that 9 or more will arrive are virtually nil. Arrivals, of course, are not always Poisson distributed (they may follow some other distribution). Patterns, therefore, should be examined to make certain that they are well approximated by Poisson before that distribution is applied.

Behavior of Arrivals Most queuing models assume that an arriving customer is a patient customer. Patient customers are people or machines that wait in the queue until they are served and do not switch between lines. Unfortunately, life is complicated by the fact that people have been known to balk or to renege. Customers who *balk* refuse to join the waiting line because it is too long to suit their needs or interests. *Reneging* customers are those who enter the queue but then become impatient and leave without completing their transaction. Actually, both of these situations just serve to highlight the need for queuing theory and waiting-line analysis.

Waiting-Line Characteristics

The waiting line itself is the second component of a queuing system. The length of a line can be either limited or unlimited. A queue is *limited* when it cannot, either by law or because of physical restrictions, increase to an infinite length. A small barbershop, for example, will have only a limited number of waiting chairs. Queuing models are treated in this text under an assumption of *unlimited* queue length. A queue is *unlimited* when its size is unrestricted, as in the case of the toll booth serving arriving automobiles.

A second waiting-line characteristic deals with *queue discipline*. This refers to the rule by which customers in the line are to receive service. Most systems use a queue discipline known

Figure 2
Two Examples of the Poisson Distribution for Arrival Times

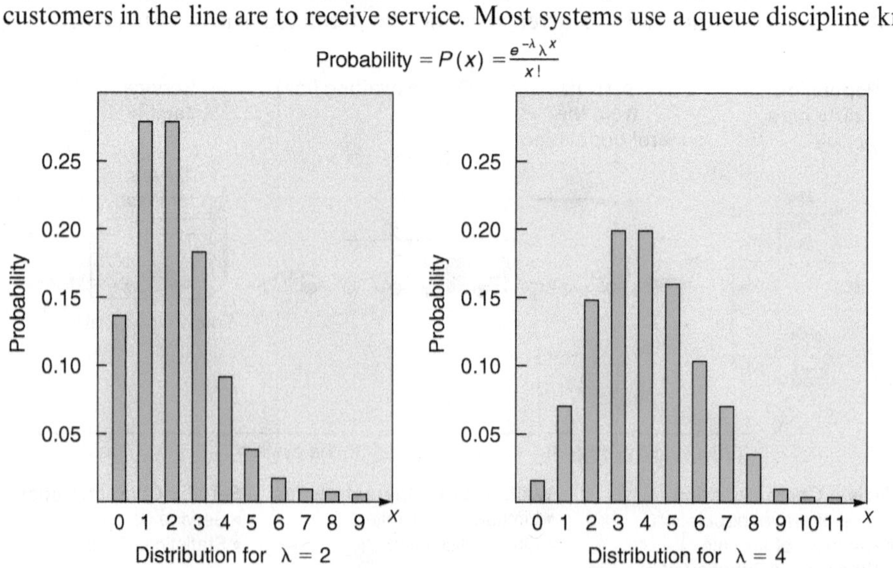

STUDENT TIP
Notice that even though the mean arrival rate might be $\lambda = 2$ per hour, there is still a small chance that as many as 9 customers arrive in an hour.

[1]When the arrival rates follow a Poisson process with mean arrival rate, λ, the time between arrivals follows a negative exponential distribution with mean time between arrivals of $1/\lambda$. The negative exponential distribution, then, is also representative of a Poisson process but describes the time between arrivals and specifies that these time intervals are completely random.

OM in Action Zero Wait Time Guarantee at This Michigan Hospital's ER

Other hospitals smirked a few years ago when Michigan's Oakwood Healthcare chain rolled out an emergency room (ER) guarantee that promised a written apology and movie tickets to patients not seen by a doctor within 30 minutes. Even employees cringed at what sounded like a cheap marketing ploy.

But if you have visited an ER lately and watched some patients wait for hours on end—the *official* average wait is 47 minutes—you can understand why Oakwood's patient satisfaction levels have soared. The 30-minute guarantee was such a huge success that fewer than 1% of the 191,000 ER patients asked for free tickets. The following year, Oakwood upped the stakes again, offering a 15-minute guarantee. Then Oakwood started its Zero Wait Program in the ERs. Patients who enter any Oakwood emergency department are *immediately* cared for by a healthcare professional.

Oakwood's CEO even extended the ER guarantee to on-time surgery, 45-minute meal service orders, and other custom room services. "Medicine is a service business," says Larry Alexander, the head of an ER in Sanford, Florida. "And people are in the mindset of the fast-food industry."

How did Oakwood make good on its promise to eliminate the ER queue? It first studied queuing theory, then reengineered its billing, records, and lab operations to drive down service time. Then, to improve service capability, Oakwood upgraded its technical staff. Finally, it replaced its ER physicians with a crew willing to work longer hours.

Sources: Wall Street Journal (October 19, 2010); *Time* (January 26, 2011); and *Crain's Detroit Business* (March 4, 2002).

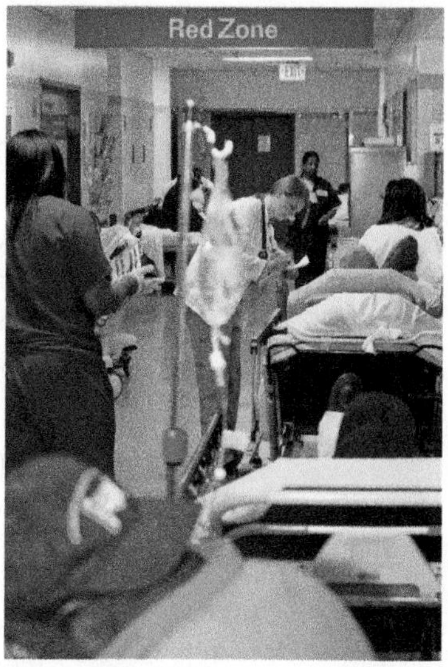

Associated Press

Queuing Costs

☆ **STUDENT TIP**

The two costs we consider here are cost of servers and cost of lost time waiting.

As described in the *OM in Action* box "Zero Wait Time Guarantee at This Michigan Hospital's ER," operations managers must recognize the trade-off that takes place between two costs: the cost of providing good service and the cost of customer or machine waiting time. Managers want queues that are short enough so that customers do not become unhappy and either leave without buying, or buy, but never return. However, managers may be willing to allow some waiting if it is balanced by a significant savings in service costs.

One means of evaluating a service facility is to look at total expected cost. Total cost is the sum of expected service costs plus expected waiting costs.

As you can see in Figure 5, service costs increase as a firm attempts to raise its level of service. Managers in *some* service centers can vary capacity by having standby personnel and machines that they can assign to specific service stations to prevent or shorten excessively long lines. In grocery stores, for example, managers and stock clerks can open extra checkout counters. In banks and airport check-in points, part-time workers may be called in to help. As the level of service improves (that is, speeds up), however, the cost of time spent waiting in lines decreases. (Refer to Figure 5.) Waiting cost may reflect lost produc-

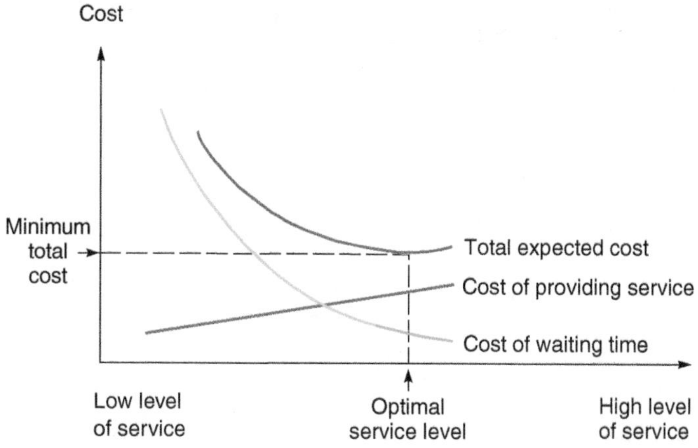

Figure 5
The Trade-off Between Waiting Costs and Service Costs

tivity of workers while tools or machines await repairs or may simply be an estimate of the cost of customers lost because of poor service and long queues. In some service systems (for example, an emergency ambulance service), the cost of long waiting lines may be intolerably high.

The Variety of Queuing Models

A wide variety of queuing models may be applied in operations management. We will introduce you to four of the most widely used models. These are outlined in Table 2, and examples of each follow in the next few sections. More complex models are described in queuing theory textbooks[3] or can be developed through the use of simulation. Note that all four queuing models listed in Table 2 have three characteristics in common. They all assume:

STUDENT TIP ☆ This is the main section of text. We illustrate four important queuing models.

1. Poisson distribution arrivals
2. FIFO discipline
3. A single-service phase

In addition, they all describe service systems that operate under steady, ongoing conditions. This means that arrival and service rates remain stable during the analysis.

Model A (M/M/1): Single-Server Queuing Model with Poisson Arrivals and Exponential Service Times

LO2 *Apply* the single-server queuing model equations

The most common case of queuing problems involves the *single-server*, or single-channel, waiting line. In this situation, arrivals form a single line to be serviced by a single station (see Figure 3). We assume that the following conditions exist in this type of system:

1. Arrivals are served on a first-in, first-out (FIFO) basis, and every arrival waits to be served, regardless of the length of the line or queue.
2. Arrivals are independent of preceding arrivals, but the average number of arrivals (*arrival rate*) does not change over time.
3. Arrivals are described by a Poisson probability distribution and come from an infinite (or very, very large) population.
4. Service times vary from one customer to the next and are independent of one another, but their average rate is known.

TABLE 2 Queuing Models Described in This Text

MODEL	NAME (TECHNICAL NAME IN PARENTHESES)	EXAMPLE	NUMBER OF SERVERS (CHANNELS)	NUMBER OF PHASES	ARRIVAL RATE PATTERN	SERVICE TIME PATTERN	POPULATION SIZE	QUEUE DISCIPLINE
A	Single-server system (M/M/1)	Information counter at department store	Single	Single	Poisson	Exponential	Unlimited	FIFO
B	Multiple-server (M/M/S)	Airline ticket counter	Multi-server	Single	Poisson	Exponential	Unlimited	FIFO
C	Constant service (M/D/1)	Automated car wash	Single	Single	Poisson	Constant	Unlimited	FIFO
D	Limited population (finite population)	Shop with only a dozen machines that might break	Single	Single	Poisson	Exponential	Limited	FIFO

[3]See, for example, Donald Gross, et al. *Fundamentals of Queuing Theory*, 4th ed. New York: Wiley, 2008.

Roy/EXPLORER/Photo Researchers

The giant Moscow McDonald's boasts 900 seats, 800 workers, and $80 million in annual sales (vs. less than $2 million in a U.S. outlet). Americans would balk at the average waiting time of 45 minutes, but Russians are used to such long lines. McDonald's represents good service in Moscow.

5. Service times occur according to the negative exponential probability distribution.
6. The service rate is faster than the arrival rate.

When these conditions are met, the series of equations shown in Table 3 can be developed. Examples 1 and 2 illustrate how Model A (which in technical journals is known as the M/M/1 model) may be used.[4]

TABLE 3 Queuing Formulas for Model A: Single-Server System, also Called M/M/1

λ = mean number of arrivals per time period
μ = mean number of people or items served per time period (average service rate)
L_s = average number of units (customers) in the system (waiting and being served) $= \dfrac{\lambda}{\mu - \lambda}$
W_s = average time a unit spends in the system (waiting time plus service time) $= \dfrac{1}{\mu - \lambda}$
L_q = average number of units waiting in the queue $= \dfrac{\lambda^2}{\mu(\mu - \lambda)}$
W_q = average time a unit spends waiting in the queue $= \dfrac{\lambda}{\mu(\mu - \lambda)} = \dfrac{L_q}{\lambda}$
ρ = utilization factor for the system $= \dfrac{\lambda}{\mu}$
P_0 = probability of 0 units in the system (that is, the service unit is idle) $= 1 - \dfrac{\lambda}{\mu}$
$P_{n>k}$ = probability of more than k units in the system, where n is the number of units in the system $= \left(\dfrac{\lambda}{\mu}\right)^{k+1}$

[4]In queuing notation, the first letter refers to the arrivals (where M stands for Poisson distribution); the second letter refers to service (where M is again a Poisson distribution, which is the same as an exponential rate for service—and a D is a constant service rate); the third symbol refers to the number of servers. So an M/D/1 system (our Model C) has Poisson arrivals, constant service, and one server.

Example 1

A SINGLE-SERVER QUEUE

Tom Jones, the mechanic at Golden Muffler Shop, is able to install new mufflers at an average rate of 3 per hour (or about 1 every 20 minutes), according to a negative exponential distribution. Customers seeking this service arrive at the shop on the average of 2 per hour, following a Poisson distribution. They are served on a first-in, first-out basis and come from a very large (almost infinite) population of possible buyers.

We would like to obtain the operating characteristics of Golden Muffler's queuing system.

APPROACH ▶ This is a single-server (M/M/1) system, and we apply the formulas in Table 3.

SOLUTION ▶

$$\lambda = 2 \text{ cars arriving per hour}$$
$$\mu = 3 \text{ cars serviced per hour}$$
$$L_s = \frac{\lambda}{\mu - \lambda} = \frac{2}{3 - 2} = \frac{2}{1}$$
$$= 2 \text{ cars in the system, on average}$$
$$W_s = \frac{1}{\mu - \lambda} = \frac{1}{3 - 2} = 1$$
$$= 1\text{-hour average time in the system}$$
$$L_q = \frac{\lambda^2}{\mu(\mu - \lambda)} = \frac{2^2}{3(3 - 2)} = \frac{4}{3(1)} = \frac{4}{3}$$
$$= 1.33 \text{ cars waiting in line, on average}$$
$$W_q = \frac{\lambda}{\mu(\mu - \lambda)} = \frac{2}{3(3 - 2)} = \frac{2}{3}\text{ hour}$$
$$= 40\text{-minute average waiting time per car}$$
$$\rho = \frac{\lambda}{\mu} = \frac{2}{3}$$
$$= 66.6\% \text{ of time mechanic is busy}$$
$$P_0 = 1 - \frac{\lambda}{\mu} = 1 - \frac{2}{3}$$
$$= .33 \text{ probability there are 0 cars in the system}$$

Probability of More Than *k* Cars in the System

K	$P_{n>k} = (2/3)^{k+1}$
0	.667 ← Note that this is equal to $1 - P_0 = 1 - .33 = .667$.
1	.444
2	.296
3	.198 ← Implies that there is a 19.8% chance that more than 3 cars are in the system.
4	.132
5	.088
6	.058
7	.039

INSIGHT ▶ Recognize that arrival and service times are converted to the same rate. For example, a service time of 20 minutes is stated as an average *rate* of 3 mufflers *per hour*. It's also important to differentiate between time in the *queue* and time in the *system*.

LEARNING EXERCISE ▶ If $\mu = 4$ cars/hour instead of the current 3 arrivals, what are the new values of L_s, W_s, L_q, W_q, and P_0? [Answer: 1 car, 30 min., .5 cars, 15 min., 50%, .50.]

RELATED PROBLEMS ▶ 1, 2, 3, 4, 6, 7, 8, 9a–e, 10, 11a–c, 12a–d

EXCEL OM Data File **ModDExD1.xls** can be found at **www.pearsonhighered.com/heizer.**

ACTIVE MODEL 1 This example is further illustrated in Active Model D.1 at **www.pearsonhighered.com/heizer.**

Once we have computed the operating characteristics of a queuing system, it is often important to do an economic analysis of their impact. Although the waiting-line model described above is valuable in predicting potential waiting times, queue lengths, idle times, and so on, it does not identify optimal decisions or consider cost factors. As we saw earlier, the solution to a queuing problem may require management to make a trade-off between the increased cost of providing better service and the decreased waiting costs derived from providing that service.

Example 2 examines the costs involved in Example 1.

Example 2

ECONOMIC ANALYSIS OF EXAMPLE 1

Golden Muffler Shop's owner is interested in cost factors as well as the queuing parameters computed in Example 1. He estimates that the cost of customer waiting time, in terms of customer dissatisfaction and lost goodwill, is $15 per hour spent *waiting* in line. Jones, the mechanic, is paid $11 per hour.

APPROACH ▶ First compute the average daily customer waiting time, then the daily salary for Jones, and finally the total expected cost.

LO3 *Conduct* a cost analysis for a waiting line

SOLUTION ▶ Because the average car has a $\frac{2}{3}$-hour wait (W_q) and because there are approximately 16 cars serviced per day (2 arrivals per hour times 8 working hours per day), the total number of hours that customers spend waiting each day for mufflers to be installed is:

$$\frac{2}{3}(16) = \frac{32}{3} = 10\frac{2}{3} \text{ hour}$$

Hence, in this case:

$$\text{Customer waiting-time cost} = \$15\left(10\frac{2}{3}\right) = \$160 \text{ per day}$$

The only other major cost that Golden's owner can identify in the queuing situation is the salary of Jones, the mechanic, who earns $11 per hour, or $88 per day. Thus:

$$\begin{aligned}\text{Total expected costs} &= \$160 + \$88 \\ &= \$248 \text{ per day}\end{aligned}$$

This approach will be useful in Solved Problem 2.

INSIGHT ▶ L_q and W_q are the two most important queuing parameters when it comes to cost analysis. Calculating customer wait times, we note, is based on average time waiting in the queue (W_q) times the number of arrivals per hour (λ) times the number of hours per day. This is because this example is set on a daily basis. This is the same as using L_q, since $L_q = W_q\lambda$.

LEARNING EXERCISE ▶ If the customer waiting time is actually $20 per hour and Jones gets a salary increase to $15 per hour, what are the total daily expected costs? [Answer: $333.33.]

RELATED PROBLEMS ▶ 12e–f, 13, 22, 23, 24

Model B (M/M/S): Multiple-Server Queuing Model

LO4 *Apply* the multiple-server queuing model formulas

Now let's turn to a multiple-server (multiple-channel) queuing system in which two or more servers are available to handle arriving customers. We still assume that customers awaiting service form one single line and then proceed to the first available server. Multiple-server, single-phase waiting lines are found in many banks today: a common line is formed, and the customer at the head of the line proceeds to the first free teller. (Refer to Figure 3 for a typical multiple-server configuration.)

The multiple-server system presented in Example 3 again assumes that arrivals follow a Poisson probability distribution and that service times are exponentially distributed. Service is first-come, first-served, and all servers are assumed to perform at the same rate. Other assumptions listed earlier for the single-server model also apply.

The queuing equations for Model B (which also has the technical name M/M/S) are shown in Table 4. These equations are obviously more complex than those used in the single-server model, yet they are used in exactly the same fashion and provide the same type of information as the simpler model. (*Note:* The POM for Windows and Excel OM software described later in this text can prove very useful in solving multiple-server and other queuing problems.)

To shorten lines (or wait times), each Costco register is staffed with two employees. This approach has improved efficiency by 20–30%.

Photo courtesy of Costco Wholesale, 2012

TABLE 4 Queuing Formulas for Model B: Multiple-Server System, also Called M/M/S

M = number of servers (channels) open

λ = average arrival rate

μ = average service rate at each server (channel)

The probability that there are zero people or units in the system is:

$$P_0 = \frac{1}{\left[\sum_{n=0}^{M-1} \frac{1}{n!}\left(\frac{\lambda}{\mu}\right)^n\right] + \frac{1}{M!}\left(\frac{\lambda}{\mu}\right)^M \frac{M\mu}{M\mu - \lambda}} \quad \text{for } M\mu > \lambda$$

The average number of people or units in the system is:

$$L_s = \frac{\lambda\mu(\lambda/\mu)^M}{(M-1)!(M\mu-\lambda)^2}P_0 + \frac{\lambda}{\mu}$$

The average time a unit spends in the waiting line and being serviced (namely, in the system) is:

$$W_s = \frac{\mu(\lambda/\mu)^M}{(M-1)!(M\mu-\lambda)^2}P_0 + \frac{1}{\mu} = \frac{L_s}{\lambda}$$

The average number of people or units in line waiting for service is:

$$L_q = L_s - \frac{\lambda}{\mu}$$

The average time a person or unit spends in the queue waiting for service is:

$$W_q = W_s - \frac{1}{\mu} = \frac{L_q}{\lambda}$$

Example 3

A MULTIPLE-SERVER QUEUE

The Golden Muffler Shop has decided to open a second garage bay and hire a second mechanic to handle installations. Customers, who arrive at the rate of about $\lambda = 2$ per hour, will wait in a single line until 1 of the 2 mechanics is free. Each mechanic installs mufflers at the rate of about $\mu = 3$ per hour.

The company wants to find out how this system compares with the old single-server waiting-line system.

APPROACH ▶ Compute several operating characteristics for the $M = 2$ server system, using the equations in Table 4, and compare the results with those found in Example 1.

SOLUTION ▶

$$P_0 = \frac{1}{\left[\sum_{n=0}^{1} \frac{1}{n!}\left(\frac{2}{3}\right)^n\right] + \frac{1}{2!}\left(\frac{2}{3}\right)^2 \frac{2(3)}{2(3) - 2}}$$

$$= \frac{1}{1 + \frac{2}{3} + \frac{1}{2}\left(\frac{4}{9}\right)\left(\frac{6}{6-2}\right)} = \frac{1}{1 + \frac{2}{3} + \frac{1}{3}} = \frac{1}{2}$$

$= .5$ probability of zero cars in the system

Then:

$$L_s = \frac{(2)(3)(2/3)^2}{1![2(3) - 2]^2}\left(\frac{1}{2}\right) + \frac{2}{3} = \frac{8/3}{16}\left(\frac{1}{2}\right) + \frac{2}{3} = \frac{3}{4}$$

$= .75$ average number of cars in the system

$$W_s = \frac{L_s}{\lambda} = \frac{3/4}{2} = \frac{3}{8} \text{ hour}$$

$= 22.5$ minutes average time a car spends in the system

$$L_q = L_s - \frac{\lambda}{\mu} = \frac{3}{4} - \frac{2}{3} = \frac{9}{12} - \frac{8}{12} = \frac{1}{12}$$

$= .083$ average number of cars in the queue (waiting)

$$W_q = \frac{L_q}{\lambda} = \frac{.083}{2} = .0415 \text{ hour}$$

$= 2.5$ minutes average time a car spends in the queue (waiting)

INSIGHT ▶ It is very interesting to see the big differences in service performance when an additional server is added.

LEARNING EXERCISE ▶ If $\mu = 4$ per hour, instead of $\mu = 3$, what are the new values for P_0, L_s, W_s, L_q, and W_q? [Answers: 0.6, .53 cars, 16 min, .033 cars, 1 min.]

RELATED PROBLEMS ▶ 7h, 9f, 11d, 15, 20

EXCEL OM Data File **ModDExD3.xls** can be found at **www.pearsonhighered.com/heizer**.

ACTIVE MODEL 2 This example is further illustrated in Active Model D.2 at **www.pearsonhighered.com/heizer**.

We can summarize the characteristics of the two-server model in Example 3 and compare them to those of the single-server model in Example 1 as follows:

	SINGLE SERVER	TWO SERVERS (CHANNELS)
P_0	.33	.5
L_s	2 cars	.75 car
W_s	60 minutes	22.5 minutes
L_q	1.33 cars	.083 car
W_q	40 minutes	2.5 minutes

The increased service has a dramatic effect on almost all characteristics. For instance, note that the time spent waiting in line drops from 40 minutes to only 2.5 minutes.

Use of Waiting-Line Tables Imagine the work a manager would face in dealing with $M = 3$, 4, or 5 server waiting-line models if a computer was not readily available. The arithmetic becomes increasingly troublesome. Fortunately, much of the burden of manually examining multiple-server queues can be avoided by using Table 5. This table, the result of hundreds of computations, represents the relationship between three things: (1) a ratio, λ/μ, (2) number of servers open, and (3) the average number of customers in the queue, L_q (which is what we'd like to find). For any combination of the ratio λ/μ and $M = 1, 2, 3, 4$, or 5 servers, you can quickly look in the body of the table to read off the appropriate value for L_q.

TABLE 5 Values of L_q for M = 1–5 Servers (channels) and Selected Values of λ/μ

POISSON ARRIVALS, EXPONENTIAL SERVICE TIMES					
	NUMBER OF SERVERS (CHANNELS), M				
λ/μ	1	2	3	4	5
.10	.0111				
.15	.0264	.0008			
.20	.0500	.0020			
.25	.0833	.0039			
.30	.1285	.0069			
.35	.1884	.0110			
.40	.2666	.0166			
.45	.3681	.0239	.0019		
.50	.5000	.0333	.0030		
.55	.6722	.0449	.0043		
.60	.9000	.0593	.0061		
.65	1.2071	.0767	.0084		
.70	1.6333	.0976	.0112		
.75	2.2500	.1227	.0147		
.80	3.2000	.1523	.0189		
.85	4.8166	.1873	.0239	.0031	
.90	8.1000	.2285	.0300	.0041	
.95	18.0500	.2767	.0371	.0053	
1.0		.3333	.0454	.0067	
1.2		.6748	.0904	.0158	
1.4		1.3449	.1778	.0324	.0059
1.6		2.8444	.3128	.0604	.0121
1.8		7.6734	.5320	.1051	.0227
2.0			.8888	.1739	.0398
2.2			1.4907	.2770	.0659
2.4			2.1261	.4305	.1047
2.6			4.9322	.6581	.1609
2.8			12.2724	1.0000	.2411
3.0				1.5282	.3541
3.2				2.3856	.5128
3.4				3.9060	.7365
3.6				7.0893	1.0550
3.8				16.9366	1.5184
4.0					2.2164
4.2					3.3269
4.4					5.2675
4.6					9.2885
4.8					21.6384

Example 4 illustrates the use of Table 5.

Example 4

USE OF WAITING-LINE TABLES

Alaska National Bank is trying to decide how many drive-in teller windows to open on a busy Saturday. CEO Ted Eschenbach estimates that customers arrive at a rate of about $\lambda = 18$ per hour, and that each teller can service about $\mu = 20$ customers per hour.

APPROACH ▶ Ted decides to use Table 5 to compute L_q and W_q.

SOLUTION ▶ The ratio is $\lambda/\mu = \frac{18}{20} = .90$. Turning to the table, under $\lambda/\mu = .90$, Ted sees that if only $M = 1$ service window is open, the average number of customers in line will be 8.1. If two windows are open, L_q drops to .2285 customers, to .03 for $M = 3$ tellers, and to .0041 for $M = 4$ tellers. Adding more open windows at this point will result in an average queue length of 0.

It is also a simple matter to compute the average waiting time in the queue, W_q, since $W_q = L_q/\lambda$. When one service window is open, W_q = 8.1 customers/(18 customers per hour) = .45 hours = 27 minutes waiting time; when two tellers are open, W_q = .2285 customers/(18 customers per hour) = .0127 hours $\cong \frac{3}{4}$ minute; and so on.

INSIGHT ▶ If a computer is not readily available, Table 5 makes it easy to find L_q and to then compute W_q. Table 5 is especially handy to compare L_q for different numbers of servers (M).

LEARNING EXERCISE ▶ The number of customers arriving on a Thursday afternoon at Alaska National is 15/hour. The service rate is still 20 customers/hour. How many people are in the queue if there are 1, 2, or 3 servers? [Answer: 2.25, .1227, .0147.]

RELATED PROBLEM ▶ 5

You might also wish to check the calculations in Example 3 against tabled values just to practice the use of Table 5. You may need to interpolate if your exact value is not found in the first column. Other common operating characteristics besides L_q are published in tabular form in queuing theory textbooks.

David Young-Wolff/PhotoEdit, Inc.

Stephen Brashear/AP Wide World Photos

Long check-in lines (left photo) such as at Los Angeles International (LAX) are a common airport sight. This is an M/M/S model—passengers wait in a single queue for one of several agents. But at Anchorage International Airport (right photo), Alaska Air has jettisoned the traditional wall of ticket counters. Instead, 1.2 million passengers per year use self-service check-in machines and staffed "bag drop" stations. Looking nothing like a typical airport, the new system doubled the airline's check-in capacity and cut staff needs in half, all while speeding travelers through in less than 15 minutes, even during peak hours.

Model C (M/D/1): Constant-Service-Time Model

LO5 *Apply* the constant-service-time model equations

Some service systems have constant, instead of exponentially distributed, service times. When customers or equipment are processed according to a fixed cycle, as in the case of an automatic car wash or an amusement park ride, constant service times are appropriate. Because constant rates are certain, the values for L_q, W_q, L_s, and W_s are always less than they would be in Model A, which has variable service rates. As a matter of fact, both the average queue length and the average waiting time in the queue are halved with Model C. Constant-service-model formulas are given in Table 6. Model C also has the technical name M/D/1 in the literature of queuing theory.

TABLE 6 Queuing Formulas for Model C: Constant Service, also Called M/D/1

Average length of queue: $L_q = \dfrac{\lambda^2}{2\mu(\mu - \lambda)}$
Average waiting time in queue: $W_q = \dfrac{\lambda}{2\mu(\mu - \lambda)}$
Average number of customers in system: $L_s = L_q + \dfrac{\lambda}{\mu}$
Average time in system: $W_s = W_q + \dfrac{1}{\mu}$

Example 5 gives a constant-service-time analysis.

Example 5

A CONSTANT-SERVICE-TIME MODEL

Inman Recycling, Inc., collects and compacts aluminum cans and glass bottles in Reston, Louisiana. Its truck drivers currently wait an average of 15 minutes before emptying their loads for recycling. The cost of driver and truck time while they are in queues is valued at $60 per hour. A new automated compactor can be purchased to process truckloads at a *constant* rate of 12 trucks per hour (that is, 5 minutes per truck). Trucks arrive according to a Poisson distribution at an average rate of 8 per hour. If the new compactor is put in use, the cost will be amortized at a rate of $3 per truck unloaded.

APPROACH ▶ CEO Tony Inman hires a summer college intern to conduct an analysis to evaluate the costs versus benefits of the purchase. The intern uses the equation for W_q in Table 6.

SOLUTION ▶

Current waiting cost/trip = (1/4 hr waiting now)($60/hr cost) = $15/trip

New system: λ = 8 trucks/hr arriving μ = 12 trucks/hr served

$$\text{Average waiting time in queue} = W_q = \frac{\lambda}{2\mu(\mu - \lambda)} = \frac{8}{2(12)(12 - 8)} = \frac{1}{12}\text{ hr}$$

Waiting cost/trip with new compactor = (1/12 hr wait)($60/hr cost) = $5/trip

Savings with new equipment = $15(current system) − $5(new system) = $10/trip
Cost of new equipment amortized: = $ 3/trip
Net savings = $ 7/trip

INSIGHT ▶ Constant service times, usually attained through automation, help control the variability inherent in service systems. This can lower average queue length and average waiting time. Note the 2 in the denominator of the equations for L_q and W_q in Table 6.

LEARNING EXERCISE ▶ With the new constant-service-time system, what are the average waiting time in the queue, average number of trucks in the system, and average waiting time in the system? [Answer: 0.0833 hours, 1.33, 0.1667 hours.]

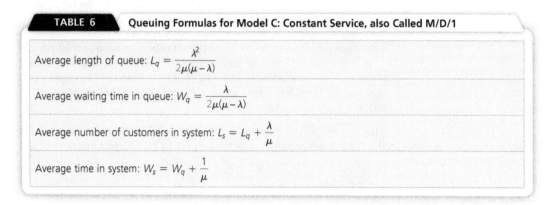

RELATED PROBLEMS ▶ 14, 16, 21

EXCEL OM Data File **ModDExD5.xls** can be found at **www.pearsonhighered.com/heizer**.

ACTIVE MODEL 3 This example is further illustrated in Active Model D.3 at **www.pearsonhighered.com/heizer**.

Little's Law

A practical and useful relationship in queuing for any system in a *steady state* is called Little's Law. A steady state exists when a queuing system is in its normal operating condition (e.g., after customers waiting at the door when a business opens in the morning are taken care of). Little's Law can be written as either:

$$L = \lambda W \text{ (which is the same as } W = L/\lambda) \quad (2)$$

or:

$$L_q = \lambda W_q \text{ (which is the same as } W_q = L_q/\lambda) \quad (3)$$

The advantage of these formulas is that once two of the parameters are known, the other one can easily be found. This is important because in certain waiting-line situations, one of these might be easier to determine than the other.

Little's Law is also important because it makes no assumptions about the probability distributions for arrivals and service times, the number of servers, or service priority rules. The law applies to all the queuing systems discussed in this text, except the limited-population model, which we discuss next.

Model D: Limited-Population Model

LO6 *Perform* a limited-population model analysis

When there is a limited population of potential customers for a service facility, we must consider a different queuing model. This model would be used, for example, if we were considering equipment repairs in a factory that has 5 machines, if we were in charge of maintenance for a fleet of 10 commuter airplanes, or if we ran a hospital ward that has 20 beds. The limited-population model allows any number of repair people (servers) to be considered.

This model differs from the three earlier queuing models because there is now a *dependent* relationship between the length of the queue and the arrival rate. Let's illustrate the extreme situation: If your factory had five machines and all were broken and awaiting repair, the arrival rate would drop to zero. In general, then, as the *waiting line* becomes longer in the limited population model, the *arrival rate* of customers or machines drops.

Table 7 displays the queuing formulas for the limited-population model. Note that they employ a different notation than Models A, B, and C. To simplify what can become

TABLE 7 Queuing Formulas and Notation for Model D: Limited-Population Formulas

Service factor: $X = \frac{T}{T + U}$	Average number of units running: $J = NF(1 - X)$
Average number waiting: $L_q = N(1 - F)$	Average number being serviced: $H = FNX$
Average waiting time: $W_q = \frac{L_q(T + U)}{N - L_q} = \frac{T(1 - F)}{XF}$	Number in population: $N = J + L_q + H$
Notation	
D = probability that a unit will have to wait in queue	N = number of potential customers
F = efficiency factor	T = average service time
H = average number of units being served	U = average time between unit service requirements
J = average number of units in working order	W_q = average time a unit waits in line
L_q = average number of units waiting for service	X = service factor
M = number of servers (channels)	

time-consuming calculations, finite queuing tables have been developed that determine D and F. D represents the probability that a machine needing repair will have to wait in line. F is a waiting-time efficiency factor. D and F are needed to compute most of the other finite model formulas.

A small part of the published finite queuing tables is illustrated in this section. Table 8 provides data for a population of $N = 5$.[5]

To use Table 8, we follow four steps:

1. Compute X (the service factor), where $X = T/(T + U)$.
2. Find the value of X in the table and then find the line for M (where M is the number of servers).
3. Note the corresponding values for D and F.
4. Compute L_q, W_q, J, H, or whichever are needed to measure the service system's performance.

Example 6 illustrates these steps.

Example 6

A LIMITED-POPULATION MODEL

Past records indicate that each of the 5 massive laser computer printers at the U.S. Department of Energy (DOE), in Washington, DC, needs repair after about 20 hours of use. Breakdowns have been determined to be Poisson distributed. The one technician on duty can service a printer in an average of 2 hours, following an exponential distribution. Printer downtime costs $120 per hour. Technicians are paid $25 per hour. Should the DOE hire a second technician?

APPROACH ▶ Assuming the second technician can also repair a printer in an average of 2 hours, we can use Table 8 (because there are $N = 5$ machines in this limited population) to compare the costs of 1 vs. 2 technicians.

SOLUTION ▶

1. First, we note that $T = 2$ hours and $U = 20$ hours.
2. Then, $X = \frac{T}{T+U} = \frac{2}{2+20} = \frac{2}{22} = .091$ (close to .090 [to use for determining D and F]).
3. For $M = 1$ server, $D = .350$ and $F = .960$.
4. For $M = 2$ servers, $D = .044$ and $F = .998$.
5. The average number of printers working is $J = NF(1 - X)$.
   For $M = 1$, this is $J = (5)(.960)(1 - .091) = 4.36$.
   For $M = 2$, it is $J = (5)(.998)(1 - .091) = 4.54$.
6. The cost analysis follows:

NUMBER OF TECHNICIANS	AVERAGE NUMBER PRINTERS DOWN $(N - J)$	AVERAGE COST/HR FOR DOWNTIME $(N - J)$($120/HR)	COST/HR. FOR TECHNICIANS (AT $25/HR)	TOTAL COST/HR
1	.64	$76.80	$25.00	$101.80
2	.46	$55.20	$50.00	$105.20

INSIGHT ▶ This analysis suggests that having only one technician on duty will save a few dollars per hour ($105.20 − $101.80 = $3.40). This may seem like a small amount, but it adds up to over $7,000 per year.

LEARNING EXERCISE ▶ DOE has just replaced its printers with a new model that seems to break down after about 18 hours of use. Recompute the costs. [Answer: For $M = 1$, $F = .95$, $J = 4.275$, and total cost/hr = $112.00. For $M = 2$, $F = .997$, $J = 4.487$, and total cost/hr = $111.56.]

RELATED PROBLEMS ▶ 17, 18, 19

EXCEL OM Data File **ModDExD6.xls** can be found at **www.pearsonhighered.com/heizer**.

[5]Limited, or finite, queuing tables are available to handle arrival populations of up to 250. Although there is no definite number that we can use as a dividing point between limited and unlimited populations, the general rule of thumb is this: If the number in the queue is a significant proportion of the arrival population, use a limited population queuing model. For a complete set of N-values, see L. G. Peck and R. N. Hazelwood, *Finite Queuing Tables.* New York: Wiley, 1958.

TABLE 8 Finite Queuing Tables for a Population of $N = 5$*

X	M	D	F	X	M	D	F	X	M	D	F	X	M	D	F	X	M	D	F
.012	1	.048	.999		1	.404	.945		1	.689	.801	.330	4	.012	.999		3	.359	.927
.019	1	.076	.998	.110	2	.065	.996	.210	3	.032	.998		3	.112	.986		2	.779	.728
.025	1	.100	.997		1	.421	.939		2	.211	.973		2	.442	.904		1	.988	.384
.030	1	.120	.996	.115	2	.071	.995		1	.713	.783		1	.902	.583	.540	4	.085	.989
.034	1	.135	.995		1	.439	.933	.220	3	.036	.997	.340	4	.013	.999		3	.392	.917
.036	1	.143	.994	.120	2	.076	.995		2	.229	.969		3	.121	.985		2	.806	.708
.040	1	.159	.993		1	.456	.927		1	.735	.765		2	.462	.896		1	.991	.370
.042	1	.167	.992	.125	2	.082	.994	.230	3	.041	.997		1	.911	.569	.560	4	.098	.986
.044	1	.175	.991		1	.473	.920		2	.247	.965	.360	4	.017	.998		3	.426	.906
.046	1	.183	.990	.130	2	.089	.933		1	.756	.747		3	.141	.981		2	.831	.689
.050	1	.198	.989		1	.489	.914	.240	3	.046	.996		2	.501	.880		1	.993	.357
.052	1	.206	.988	.135	2	.095	.993		2	.265	.960		1	.927	.542	.580	4	.113	.984
.054	1	.214	.987		1	.505	.907		1	.775	.730	.380	4	.021	.998		3	.461	.895
.056	2	.018	.999	.140	2	.102	.992	.250	3	.052	.995		3	.163	.976		2	.854	.670
	1	.222	.985		1	.521	.900		2	.284	.955		2	.540	.863		1	.994	.345
.058	2	.019	.999	.145	3	.011	.999		1	.794	.712		1	.941	.516	.600	4	.130	.981
	1	.229	.984		2	.109	.991	.260	3	.058	.994	.400	4	.026	.977		3	.497	.883
.060	2	.020	.999		1	.537	.892		2	.303	.950		3	.186	.972		2	.875	.652
	1	.237	.983	.150	3	.012	.999		1	.811	.695		2	.579	.845		1	.996	.333
.062	2	.022	.999		2	.115	.990	.270	3	.064	.994		1	.952	.493	.650	4	.179	.972
	1	.245	.982		1	.553	.885		2	.323	.944	.420	4	.031	.997		3	.588	.850
.064	2	.023	.999	.155	3	.013	.999		1	.827	.677		3	.211	.966		2	.918	.608
	1	.253	.981		2	.123	.989	.280	3	.071	.993		2	.616	.826		1	.998	.308
.066	2	.024	.999		1	.568	.877		2	.342	.938		1	.961	.471	.700	4	.240	.960
	1	.260	.979	.160	3	.015	.999		1	.842	.661	.440	4	.037	.996		3	.678	.815
.068	2	.026	.999		2	.130	.988	.290	4	.007	.999		3	.238	.960		2	.950	.568
	1	.268	.978		1	.582	.869		3	.079	.992		2	.652	.807		1	.999	.286
.070	2	.027	.999	.165	3	.016	.999		2	.362	.932		1	.969	.451	.750	4	.316	.944
	1	.275	.977		2	.137	.987		1	.856	.644	.460	4	.045	.995		3	.763	.777
.075	2	.031	.999		1	.597	.861	.300	4	.008	.999		3	.266	.953		2	.972	.532
	1	.294	.973	.170	3	.017	.999		3	.086	.990		2	.686	.787	.800	4	.410	.924
.080	2	.035	.998		2	.145	.985		2	.382	.926		1	.975	.432		3	.841	.739
	1	.313	.969		1	.611	.853		1	.869	.628	.480	4	.053	.994		2	.987	.500
.085	2	.040	.998	.180	3	.021	.999	.310	4	.009	.999		3	.296	.945	.850	4	.522	.900
	1	.332	.965		2	.161	.983		3	.094	.989		2	.719	.767		3	.907	.702
.090	2	.044	.998		1	.638	.836		2	.402	.919		1	.980	.415		2	.995	.470
	1	.350	.960	.190	3	.024	.998		1	.881	.613	.500	4	.063	.992	.900	4	.656	.871
.095	2	.049	.997		2	.117	.980	.320	4	.010	.999		3	.327	.936		3	.957	.666
	1	.368	.955		1	.665	.819		3	.103	.988		2	.750	.748		2	.998	.444
.100	2	.054	.997	.200	3	.028	.998		2	.422	.912		1	.985	.399	.950	4	.815	.838
	1	.386	.950		2	.194	.976		1	.892	.597	.520	4	.073	.991		3	.989	.631
.105	2	.059	.997																

*See notation in Table 7.

Other Queuing Approaches

STUDENT TIP ☆
When the assumptions of the 4 models we just introduced do not hold true, there are other approaches still available to us.

Many practical waiting-line problems that occur in service systems have characteristics like those of the four mathematical models already described. Often, however, *variations* of these specific cases are present in an analysis. Service times in an automobile repair shop, for example, tend to follow the normal probability distribution instead of the exponential. A college registration system in which seniors have first choice of courses and hours over other students is an example of a first-come, first-served model with a preemptive priority queue discipline. A physical examination for military recruits is an example of a multiphase system, one that differs from the single-phase models discussed earlier in this text. A recruit first lines up to have blood drawn at one station, then waits for an eye exam at the next station, talks to a psychiatrist at the third, and is examined by a doctor for medical problems at the fourth. At each phase, the recruit must enter another queue and wait his or her turn. Many models, some very complex, have been developed to deal with situations such as these.

Summary

Queues are an important part of the world of operations management. In this text, we describe several common queuing systems and present mathematical models for analyzing them.

The most widely used queuing models include Model A, the basic single-server, single-phase system with Poisson arrivals and exponential service times; Model B, the multiple-server equivalent of Model A; Model C, a constant-service-rate model; and Model D, a limited-population system. All four models allow for Poisson arrivals; first-in, first-out service; and a single-service phase. Typical operating characteristics we examine include average time spent waiting in the queue and system, average number of customers in the queue and system, idle time, and utilization rate.

A variety of queuing models exists for which all the assumptions of the traditional models need not be met. In these cases, we use more complex mathematical models or turn to a technique called *simulation*.

Key Terms

Queuing theory
Waiting line (queue)
Unlimited, or infinite, population
Limited, or finite, population
Poisson distribution
First-in, first-out (FIFO) rule
Single-server queuing system
Multiple-server queuing system
Single-phase system
Multiphase system
Negative exponential probability distribution

Discussion Questions

1. Name the three parts of a typical queuing system.
2. When designing a waiting line system, what "qualitative" concerns need to be considered?
3. Name the three factors that govern the structure of "arrivals" in a queuing system.
4. State the seven common measures of queuing system performance.
5. State the assumptions of the "basic" single-server queuing model (Model A, or M/M/1).
6. Is it good or bad to operate a supermarket bakery system on a strict first-come, first-served basis? Why?
7. Describe what is meant by the waiting-line terms *balk* and *renege*. Provide an example of each.
8. Which is larger, W_s or W_q? Explain.
9. Briefly describe three situations in which the first-in, first-out (FIFO) discipline rule is not applicable in queuing analysis.
10. Describe the behavior of a waiting line where $\lambda > \mu$. Use both analysis and intuition.
11. Discuss the likely outcome of a waiting line system where $\mu > \lambda$ but only by a tiny amount (e.g., $\mu = 4.1$, $\lambda = 4$).
12. Provide examples of four situations in which there is a limited, or finite, waiting line.
13. What are the components of the following queuing systems? Draw and explain the configuration of each.
    a) Barbershop
    b) Car wash
    c) Laundromat
    d) Small grocery store

14. Do doctors' offices generally have random arrival rates for patients? Are service times random? Under what circumstances might service times be constant?
15. What happens if two single-server systems have the same mean arrival and service rates, but the service time is constant in one and exponential in the other?
16. What dollar value do you place on yourself per hour that you spend waiting in lines? What value do your classmates place on themselves? Why do the values differ?
17. Why is Little's Law a useful queuing concept?

Using Software to Solve Queuing Problems

Both Excel OM and POM for Windows may be used to analyze all but the last two homework problems in this text.

USING EXCEL OM

Excel OM's Waiting-Line program handles all four of the models developed in this text. Program 1 illustrates our first model, the M/M/1 system, using the data from Example 1.

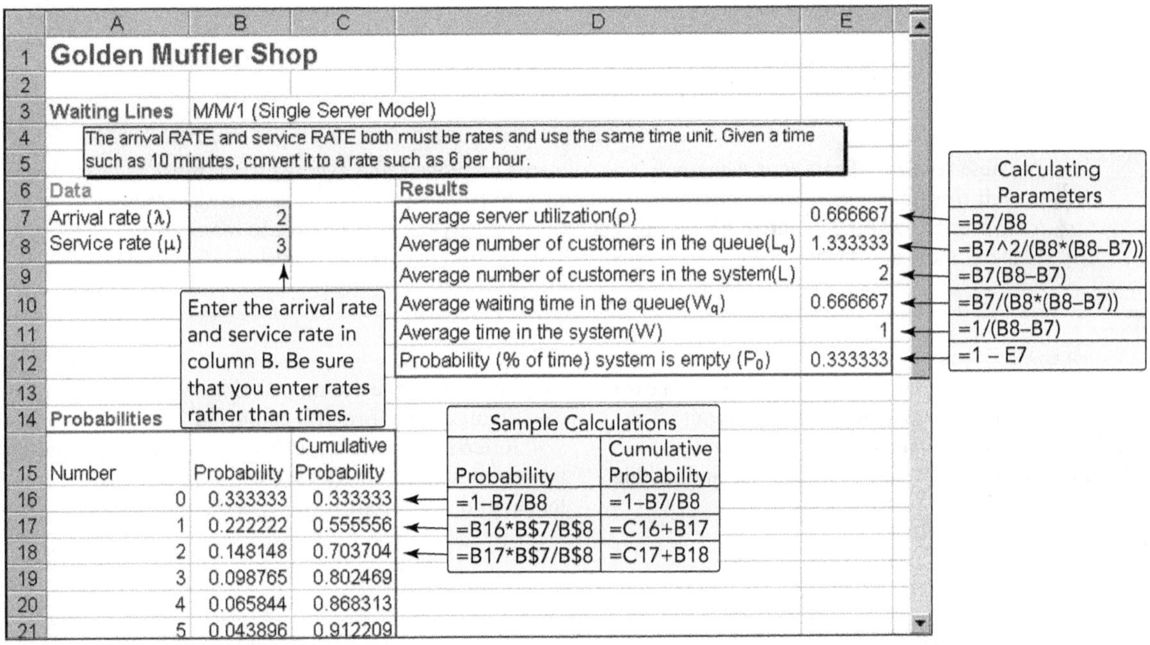

Program 1

Using Excel OM for Queuing

Example 1's (Golden Muffler Shop) data are illustrated in the M/M/1 model.

USING POM FOR WINDOWS

There are several POM for Windows queuing models from which to select in that program's Waiting-Line module. The program can include an economic analysis of cost data, and, as an option, you may display probabilities of various numbers of people/items in the system.

Solved Problems

Virtual Office Hours help is available www.myomlab.com.

SOLVED PROBLEM 1

Sid Das Brick Distributors in Jamaica currently employs 1 worker whose job is to load bricks on outgoing company trucks. An average of 24 trucks per day, or 3 per hour, arrive at the loading platform, according to a Poisson distribution. The worker loads them at a rate of 4 trucks per hour, following approximately the exponential distribution in his service times.

Das believes that adding an additional brick loader will substantially improve the firm's productivity. He estimates that a 2-person crew loading each truck will double the loading rate (μ) from 4 trucks per hour to 8 trucks per hour. Analyze the effect on the queue of such a change and compare the results to those achieved with one worker. What is the probability that there will be more than 3 trucks either being loaded or waiting?

SOLUTION

	NUMBER OF BRICK LOADERS	
	1	2
Truck arrival rate (λ)	3/hr	3/hr
Loading rate (μ)	4/hr	8/hr
Average number in system (L_s)	3 trucks	.6 truck
Average time in system (W_s)	1 hr	.2 hr
Average number in queue (L_q)	2.25 trucks	.225 truck
Average time in queue (W_q)	.75 hr	.075 hr
Utilization rate (ρ)	.75	.375
Probability system empty (P_0)	.25	.625

Probability of More than *k* Trucks in System

	PROBABILITY $n > K$	
K	1 LOADER	2 LOADERS
0	.75	.375
1	.56	.141
2	.42	.053
3	.32	.020

These results indicate that when only one loader is employed, the average truck must wait three-quarters of an hour before it is loaded. Furthermore, there is an average of 2.25 trucks waiting in line to be loaded. This situation may be unacceptable to management. Note also the decline in queue size after the addition of a second loader.

SOLVED PROBLEM 2

Truck drivers working for Sid Das (see Solved Problem 1) earn an average of $10 per hour. Brick loaders receive about $6 per hour. Truck drivers waiting *in the queue or at the loading platform* are drawing a salary but are productively idle and unable to generate revenue during that time. What would be the *hourly* cost savings to the firm if it employed 2 loaders instead of 1?

Referring to the data in Solved Problem 1, we note that the average number of trucks *in the system* is 3 when there is only 1 loader and .6 when there are 2 loaders.

SOLUTION

	NUMBER OF LOADERS	
	1	2
Truck driver idle time costs [(Average number of trucks) × (Hourly rate)] = (3)($10) =	$30	$ 6 = (.6)($10)
Loading costs	6	12 = (2)($6)
Total expected cost per hour	$36	$18

The firm will save $18 per hour by adding another loader.

SOLVED PROBLEM 3

Sid Das is considering building a second platform or gate to speed the process of loading trucks. This system, he thinks, will be even more efficient than simply hiring another loader to help out on the first platform (as in Solved Problem 1).

Assume that the worker at each platform will be able to load 4 trucks per hour each and that trucks will continue to arrive at the rate of 3 per hour. Then apply the appropriate equations to find the waiting line's new operating conditions. Is this new approach indeed speedier than the other two that Das has considered in the Solved Problems above?

SOLUTION

$$P_0 = \frac{1}{\left[\sum_{n=0}^{1} \frac{1}{n!}\left(\frac{3}{4}\right)^n\right] + \frac{1}{2!}\left(\frac{3}{4}\right)^2 \frac{2(4)}{2(4) - 3}}$$

$$= \frac{1}{1 + \frac{3}{4} + \frac{1}{2}\left(\frac{3}{4}\right)^2\left(\frac{8}{8 - 3}\right)} = .4545$$

$$L_s = \frac{3(4)(3/4)^2}{(1)!(8 - 3)^2}(.4545) + \frac{3}{4} = .873$$

$$W_s = \frac{.873}{3} = .291 \text{ hr}$$

$$L_q = .873 - 3/4 = .123$$

$$W_q = \frac{.123}{3} = .041 \text{ hr}$$

Looking back at Solved Problem 1, we see that although length of the *queue* and average time in the queue are lowest when a second platform is open, the average number of trucks in the *system* and average time spent waiting in the system are smallest when two workers are employed at a *single* platform. Thus, we would probably recommend not building a second platform.

SOLVED PROBLEM 4

St. Elsewhere Hospital's cardiac care unit (CCU) has 5 beds, which are virtually always occupied by patients who have just undergone major heart surgery. Two registered nurses are on duty in the CCU in each of the three 8-hour shifts. About every 2 hours (following a Poisson distribution), one of the patients requires a nurse's attention. The nurse will then spend an average of 30 minutes (exponentially distributed) assisting the patient and updating medical records regarding the problem and care provided.

Because immediate service is critical to the 5 patients, two important questions are: What is the average number of patients being attended by the nurses? What is the average time that a patient spends waiting for one of the nurses to arrive?

SOLUTION

$N = 5$ patients

$M = 2$ nurses

$T = 30$ minutes

$U = 120$ minutes

$$X = \frac{T}{T + U} = \frac{30}{30 + 120} = .20$$

From Table 8, with $X = .20$ and $M = 2$, we see that:

$F = .976$

$H =$ average number being attended to $= FNX$

$= (.976)(5)(.20) = .98 \approx 1$ patient at any given time

$W_q =$ average waiting time for a nurse $= \dfrac{T(1 - F)}{XF}$

$$= \frac{30(1 - .976)}{(.20)(.976)} = 3.69 \text{ minutes}$$

Problems

Note: PX means the problem may be solved with POM for Windows and/or Excel OM.

• **1** Customers arrive at Rich Dunn's Styling Shop at a rate of 3 per hour, distributed in a Poisson fashion. Rich can perform haircuts at a rate of 5 per hour, distributed exponentially.

a) Find the average number of customers waiting for haircuts.
b) Find the average number of customers in the shop.
c) Find the average time a customer waits until it is his or her turn.
d) Find the average time a customer spends in the shop.
e) Find the percentage of time that Rich is busy. PX

• **2** There is only one copying machine in the student lounge of the business school. Students arrive at the rate of $\lambda = 40$ per hour (according to a Poisson distribution). Copying takes an average of 40 seconds, or $\mu = 90$ per hour (according to an exponential distribution). Compute the following:

a) The percentage of time that the machine is used.
b) The average length of the queue.
c) The average number of students in the system.
d) The average time spent waiting in the queue.
e) The average time in the system. PX

• **3** Paul Fenster owns and manages a chili-dog and soft-drink stand near the Kean U. campus. While Paul can service 30 customers per hour on the average (μ), he gets only 20 customers per hour (λ). Because Paul could wait on 50% more customers than actually visit his stand, it doesn't make sense to him that he should have any waiting lines.

Paul hires you to examine the situation and to determine some characteristics of his queue. After looking into the problem, you find it follows the six conditions for a single-server waiting line (as seen in Model A). What are your findings? PX

• **4** Dr. Tarun Gupta, a Michigan vet, is running a rabies vaccination clinic for dogs at the local grade school. Tarun can "shoot" a dog every 3 minutes. It is estimated that the dogs will arrive independently and randomly throughout the day at a rate of one dog every 6 minutes according to a Poisson distribution. Also assume that Tarun's shooting times are exponentially distributed. Compute the following:

a) The probability that Tarun is idle.
b) The proportion of the time that Tarun is busy.
c) The average number of dogs being vaccinated and waiting to be vaccinated.
d) The average number of dogs waiting to be vaccinated.
e) The average time a dog waits before getting vaccinated.
f) The average amount of time a dog spends waiting in line and being vaccinated. PX

•• **5** The pharmacist at Arnold Palmer Hospital, Wende Huehn-Brown, receives 12 requests for prescriptions each hour, Poisson distributed. It takes her a mean time of 4 minutes to fill each, following a negative exponential distribution. Use the waiting-line table, Table 5, and $W_q = L_q/\lambda$, to answer these questions.

a) What is the average number of prescriptions in the queue?
b) How long will the average prescription spend in the queue?
c) Wende decides to hire a second pharmacist, Ajay Aggerwal, with whom she went to school and who operates at the same speed in filling prescriptions. How will the answers to parts (a) and (b) change? PX

• **6** Calls arrive at Lynn Ann Fish's hotel switchboard at a rate of 2 per minute. The average time to handle each is 20 seconds. There is only one switchboard operator at the current time. The Poisson and exponential distributions appear to be relevant in this situation.

a) What is the probability that the operator is busy?
b) What is the average time that a customer must wait before reaching the operator?
c) What is the average number of calls waiting to be answered? PX

•• **7** Automobiles arrive at the drive-through window at the downtown Baton Rouge, Louisiana, post office at the rate of 4 every 10 minutes. The average service time is 2 minutes. The Poisson distribution is appropriate for the arrival rate and service times are exponentially distributed.

a) What is the average time a car is in the system?
b) What is the average number of cars in the system?
c) What is the average number of cars waiting to receive service?
d) What is the average time a car is in the queue?
e) What is the probability that there are no cars at the window?
f) What percentage of the time is the postal clerk busy?
g) What is the probability that there are exactly 2 cars in the system?
h) By how much would your answer to part (a) be reduced if a second drive-through window, with its own server, were added? PX

• **8** Virginia's Ron McPherson Electronics Corporation retains a service crew to repair machine breakdowns that occur on average $\lambda = 3$ per 8-hour workday (approximately Poisson in nature). The crew can service an average of $\mu = 8$ machines per workday, with a repair time distribution that resembles the exponential distribution.

a) What is the utilization rate of this service system?
b) What is the average downtime for a broken machine?
c) How many machines are waiting to be serviced at any given time?
d) What is the probability that more than 1 machine is in the system? The probability that more than 2 are broken and waiting to be repaired or being serviced? More than 3? More than 4? PX

•• **9** Neve Commercial Bank is the only bank in the town of York, Pennsylvania. On a typical Friday, an average of 10 customers per hour arrive at the bank to transact business. There is currently one teller at the bank, and the average time required to transact business is 4 minutes. It is assumed that service times may be described by the exponential distribution. If a single teller is used, find:

a) The average time in the line.
b) The average number in the line.
c) The average time in the system.
d) The average number in the system.
e) The probability that the bank is empty.
f) CEO Benjamin Neve is considering adding a second teller (who would work at the same rate as the first) to reduce the waiting time for customers. A single line would be used, and the customer at the front of the line would go to the first available bank teller. He assumes that this will cut the waiting time in half. If a second teller is added, find the new answers to parts (a) to (e). PX

•• **10** Beate Klingenberg manages a Poughkeepsie, New York, movie theater complex called Cinema 8. Each of the eight auditoriums plays a different film; the schedule staggers starting times to avoid the large crowds that would occur if all four movies started at the same time. The theater has a single ticket booth and a cashier who can maintain an average service rate of 280 patrons per hour. Service times are assumed to follow an exponential distribution. Arrivals on a normally active day are Poisson distributed and average 210 per hour.

To determine the efficiency of the current ticket operation, Beate wishes to examine several queue-operating characteristics.

a) Find the average number of moviegoers waiting in line to purchase a ticket.
b) What percentage of the time is the cashier busy?
c) What is the average time that a customer spends in the system?
d) What is the average time spent waiting in line to get to the ticket window?
e) What is the probability that there are more than two people in the system? More than three people? More than four? PX

•• **11** Bill Youngdahl has been collecting data at the TU student grill. He has found that, between 5:00 P.M. and 7:00 P.M., students arrive at the grill at a rate of 25 per hour (Poisson distributed) and service time takes an average of 2 minutes (exponential distribution). There is only 1 server, who can work on only 1 order at a time.

a) What is the average number of students in line?
b) What is the average time a student is in the grill area?
c) Suppose that a second server can be added to team up with the first (and, in effect, act as 1 faster server). This would reduce the average service time to 90 seconds. How would this affect the average time a student is in the grill area?
d) Suppose a second server is added and the 2 servers act independently, with *each* taking an average of 2 minutes. What would be the average time a student is in the system? Px

••• **12** The wheat harvesting season in the American Midwest is short, and farmers deliver their truckloads of wheat to a giant central storage bin within a 2-week span. Because of this, wheat-filled trucks waiting to unload and return to the fields have been known to back up for a block at the receiving bin. The central bin is owned cooperatively, and it is to every farmer's benefit to make the unloading/storage process as efficient as possible. The cost of grain deterioration caused by unloading delays and the cost of truck rental and idle driver time are significant concerns to the cooperative members. Although farmers have difficulty quantifying crop damage, it is easy to assign a waiting and unloading cost for truck and driver of $18 per hour. During the 2-week harvest season, the storage bin is open and operated 16 hours per day, 7 days per week, and can unload 35 trucks per hour according to an exponential distribution. Full trucks arrive all day long (during the hours the bin is open) at a rate of about 30 per hour, following a Poisson pattern.

To help the cooperative get a handle on the problem of lost time while trucks are waiting in line or unloading at the bin, find the following:
a) The average number of trucks in the unloading system
b) The average time per truck in the system
c) The utilization rate for the bin area
d) The probability that there are more than three trucks in the system at any given time
e) The total daily cost to the farmers of having their trucks tied up in the unloading process
f) As mentioned, the cooperative uses the storage bin heavily only 2 weeks per year. Farmers estimate that enlarging the bin would cut unloading costs by 50% next year. It will cost $9,000 to do so during the off-season. Would it be worth the expense to enlarge the storage area? Px

••• **13** Janson's Department Store in Stark, Ohio, maintains a successful catalog sales department in which a clerk takes orders by telephone. If the clerk is occupied on one line, incoming phone calls to the catalog department are answered automatically by a recording machine and asked to wait. As soon as the clerk is free, the party who has waited the longest is transferred and serviced first. Calls come in at a rate of about 12 per hour. The clerk can take an order in an average of 4 minutes. Calls tend to follow a Poisson distribution, and service times tend to be exponential.

The cost of the clerk is $10 per hour, but because of lost goodwill and sales, Janson's loses about $25 per hour of customer time spent waiting for the clerk to take an order.
a) What is the average time that catalog customers must wait before their calls are transferred to the order clerk?
b) What is the average number of customers waiting to place an order?
c) Pamela Janson is considering adding a second clerk to take calls. The store's cost would be the same $10 per hour. Should she hire another clerk? Explain your decision. Px

• **14** Altug's Coffee Shop decides to install an automatic coffee vending machine outside one of its stores to reduce the number of people standing in line inside. Mehmet Altug charges $3.50 per cup. However, it takes too long for people to make change. The service time is a constant 3 minutes, and the arrival rate is 15 per hour (Poisson distributed).
a) What is the average wait in line?
b) What is the average number of people in line?
c) Mehmet raises the price to $5 per cup and takes 60 seconds off the service time. However, because the coffee is now so expensive, the arrival rate drops to 10 per hour. Now what are the average wait time and the average number of people in the queue (waiting)? Px

••• **15** The typical subway station in Washington, DC, has six turnstiles, each of which can be controlled by the station manager to be used for either entrance or exit control—but never for both. The manager must decide at different times of the day how many turnstiles to use for entering passengers and how many to use for exiting passengers.

At the George Washington University (GWU) Station, passengers enter the station at a rate of about 84 per minute between the hours of 7 A.M. and 9 A.M. Passengers exiting trains at the stop reach the exit turnstile area at a rate of about 48 per minute during the same morning rush hours. Each turnstile can allow an average of 30 passengers per minute to enter or exit. Arrival and service times have been thought to follow Poisson and exponential distributions, respectively. Assume riders form a common queue at both entry and exit turnstile areas and proceed to the first empty turnstile.

The GWU station manager, Ernie Forman, does not want the average passenger at his station to have to wait in a turnstile line for more than 6 seconds, nor does he want more than 8 people in any queue at any average time.
a) How many turnstiles should be opened in each direction every morning?
b) Discuss the assumptions underlying the solution of this problem using queuing theory. Px

•• **16** Renuka Jain's Car Wash takes a constant time of 4.5 minutes in its automated car wash cycle. Autos arrive following a

Poisson distribution at the rate of 10 per hour. Renuka wants to know:

a) The average waiting time in line.
b) The average length of the line.

••• **17** Debra Bishop's cabinet-making shop, in Des Moines, has five tools that automate the drilling of holes for the installation of hinges. These machines need setting up for each order of cabinets. The orders appear to follow the Poisson distribution, averaging 3 per 8-hour day. There is a single technician for setting these machines. Her service times are exponential, averaging 2 hours each.

a) What is the service factor for this system?
b) What is the average number of machines in service and available for drilling?
c) What impact on machines in service would there be if a second technician were available?

••• **18** Two technicians, working separately, monitor a group of 5 computers that run an automated manufacturing facility. It takes an average of 15 minutes (exponentially distributed) to adjust a computer that develops a problem. Computers run for an average of 85 minutes (Poisson distributed) without requiring adjustments. Determine the following:

a) The average number of computers waiting for adjustment
b) The average number being adjusted
c) The average number of computers not in working order

••• **19** One mechanic services 5 drilling machines for a steel plate manufacturer. Machines break down on an average of once every 6 working days, and breakdowns tend to follow a Poisson distribution. The mechanic can handle an average of one repair job per day. Repairs follow an exponential distribution.

a) On the average, how many machines are waiting for service?
b) On the average, how many drills are in running order?
c) How much would waiting time be reduced if a second mechanic were hired?

••• **20** Ted Glickman, the administrator at D.C. General Hospital emergency room, faces the problem of providing treatment for patients who arrive at different rates during the day. There are four doctors available to treat patients when needed. If not needed, they can be assigned other responsibilities (such as doing lab tests, reports, X-ray diagnoses) or else rescheduled to work at other hours.

It is important to provide quick and responsive treatment, and Ted thinks that, on the average, patients should not have to sit in the waiting area for more than 5 minutes before being seen by a doctor. Patients are treated on a first-come, first-served basis and see the first available doctor after waiting in the queue. The arrival pattern for a typical day is as follows:

TIME	ARRIVAL RATE
9 A.M.–3 P.M.	6 patients/hour
3 P.M.–8 P.M.	4 patients/hour
8 P.M.–midnight	12 patients/hour

Arrivals follow a Poisson distribution, and treatment times, 12 minutes on the average, follow the exponential pattern.

a) How many doctors should be on duty during each period to maintain the level of patient care expected?
b) What condition would exist if only one doctor were on duty between 9 A.M. and 3 P.M.?

••• **21** The Pontchartrain Bridge is a 16-mile toll bridge that crosses Lake Pontchartrain in New Orleans. Currently, there are 7 toll booths, each staffed by an employee. Since Hurricane Katrina, the Port Authority has been considering replacing the employees with machines. Many factors must be considered because the employees are unionized. However, one of the Port Authority's concerns is the effect that replacing the employees with machines will have on the times that drivers spend in the system. Customers arrive to any one toll booth at a rate of 10 per minute. In the exact change lanes with employees, the service time is essentially constant at 5 seconds for each driver. With machines, the average service time would still be 5 seconds, but it would be exponential rather than constant, because it takes time for the coins to rattle around in the machine. Contrast the two systems for a single lane.

••• **22** The registration area has just opened at a large convention of dentists in Orlando. There are 200 people arriving per hour (Poisson distributed), and the cost of their waiting time in the queue is valued at \$100 per person per hour. The Orlando Convention Center provides servers to register guests at a fee of \$15 per person per hour. It takes about one minute to register an attendee (exponentially distributed). A single waiting line, with multiple servers, is set up.

a) What is the minimum number of servers for this system?
b) What is the optimal number of servers for this system?
c) What is the cost for the system, per hour, at the optimum number of servers?
d) What is the server utilization rate with the minimum number of servers?

•• **23** Refer to Problem 22. A new registration manager, Dwayne Cole, is hired who initiates a program to entertain the people in line with a juggler whom he pays \$15/hour. This reduces the waiting costs to \$50 per hour.

a) What is the optimal number of servers?
b) What is the cost for the system, per hour, at the optimal service level?

•••• **24** The Chattanooga Furniture store gets an average of 50 customers per shift. Marilyn Helms, the manager, wants to calculate whether she should hire 1, 2, 3, or 4 salespeople. She has determined that average waiting times will be 7 minutes with one salesperson, 4 minutes with two salespeople, 3 minutes with three salespeople, and 2 minutes with four salespeople. She has estimated the cost per minute that customers wait at \$1. The cost per salesperson per shift (including fringe benefits) is \$70.

How many salespeople should be hired?

Refer to MyOMLab for these additional homework problems: 25–33

CASE STUDIES

New England Foundry

For more than 75 years, New England Foundry, Inc. (NEFI), has manufactured wood stoves for home use. In recent years, with increasing energy prices, president George Mathison has seen sales triple. This dramatic increase has made it difficult for George to maintain quality in all his wood stoves and related products.

Unlike other companies manufacturing wood stoves, NEFI is in the business of making *only* stoves and stove-related products. Its major products are the Warmglo I, the Warmglo II, the Warmglo III, and the Warmglo IV. The Warmglo I is the smallest wood stove, with a heat output of 30,000 BTUs, and the Warmglo IV is the largest, with a heat output of 60,000 BTUs.

The Warmglo III outsold all other models by a wide margin. Its heat output and available accessories were ideal for the typical home. The Warmglo III also had a number of other outstanding features that made it one of the most attractive and heat-efficient stoves on the market. These features, along with the accessories, resulted in expanding sales and prompted George to build a new factory to manufacture the Warmglo III model. An overview diagram of the factory is shown in Figure 6.

The new foundry used the latest equipment, including a new Disamatic that helped in manufacturing stove parts. Regardless of new equipment or procedures, casting operations have remained basically unchanged for hundreds of years. To begin with, a wooden pattern is made for every cast-iron piece in the stove. The wooden pattern is an exact duplicate of the cast-iron piece that is to be manufactured. All NEFI patterns are made by Precision Patterns, Inc. and are stored in the pattern shop and maintenance room. Next, a specially formulated sand is molded around the wooden pattern. There can be two or more sand molds for each pattern. The sand is mixed and the molds are made in the molding room. When the wooden pattern is removed, the resulting sand molds form a negative image of the desired casting. Next, molds are transported to the casting room, where molten iron is poured into them and allowed to cool. When the iron has solidified, molds are moved into the cleaning, grinding, and preparation room, where they are dumped into large vibrators that shake most of the sand from the casting. The rough castings are then subjected to both sandblasting to remove the rest of the sand and grinding to finish some of their surfaces. Castings are then painted with a special heat-resistant paint, assembled into workable stoves, and inspected for manufacturing defects that may have gone undetected. Finally, finished stoves are moved to storage and shipping, where they are packaged and transported to the appropriate locations.

At present, the pattern shop and the maintenance department are located in the same room. One large counter is used by both maintenance personnel, who store tools and parts (which are mainly used by the casting department), and sand molders, who need various patterns for the molding operation. Pete Nawler and Bob Dillman, who work behind the counter, can service a total of 10 people per hour (about 5 per hour each). On average, 4 people from casting and 3 from molding arrive at the counter each hour. People from molding and casting departments arrive randomly, and to be served, they form a single line.

Pete and Bob have always had a policy of first come, first served. Because of the location of the pattern shop and maintenance department, it takes an average of 3 minutes for an individual from the casting department to walk to the pattern and maintenance room, and it takes about 1 minute for an individual to walk from the molding department to the pattern and maintenance room.

After observing the operation of the pattern shop and maintenance room for several weeks, George decided to make some changes to the factory layout. An overview of these changes appears in Figure 7.

Separating the maintenance shop from the pattern shop would have a number of advantages. It would take people from the casting department only 1 minute instead of 3 to get to the new maintenance room. The time from molding to the pattern shop would be unchanged. Using motion and time studies, George was also able to determine that improving the layout of the maintenance room would allow Bob to serve 6 people from the casting department per hour; improving the layout of the pattern department would allow Pete to serve 7 people from the molding shop per hour.

Discussion Questions

1. How much time would the new layout save?
2. If casting personnel were paid \$9.50 per hour and molding personnel were paid \$11.75 per hour, how much could be saved per hour with the new factory layout?
3. Should George have made the change in layout?

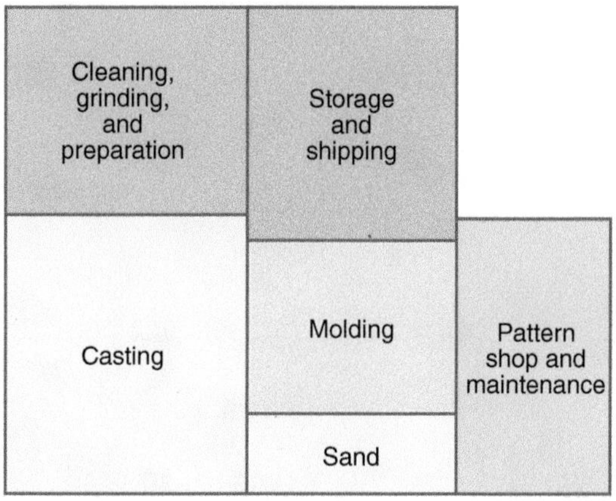

Figure 6
Overview of Factory

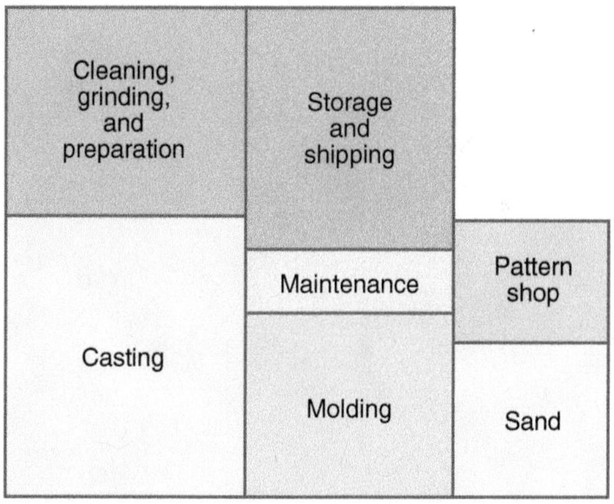

Figure 7
Overview of Factory after Changes

☆ The Winter Park Hotel

Lori Cook, manager of the Winter Park Hotel, is considering how to restructure the front desk to reach an optimum level of staff efficiency and guest service. At present, the hotel has five clerks on duty, each with a separate waiting line, during peak check-in time of 3:00 P.M. to 5:00 P.M. Observation of arrivals during this period shows that an average of 90 guests arrive each hour (although there is no upward limit on the number that could arrive at any given time). It takes an average of 3 minutes for the front-desk clerk to register each guest.

Ms. Cook is considering three plans for improving guest service by reducing the length of time that guests spend waiting in line. The first proposal would designate one employee as a quick-service clerk for guests registering under corporate accounts, a market segment that fills about 30% of all occupied rooms. Because corporate guests are preregistered, their registration takes just 2 minutes. With these guests separated from the rest of the clientele, the average time for registering a typical guest would climb to 3.4 minutes. Under this plan, noncorporate guests would choose any of the remaining four lines.

The second plan is to implement a single-line system. All guests could form a single waiting line to be served by whichever of five clerks became available. This option would require sufficient lobby space for what could be a substantial queue.

The use of an automatic teller machine (ATM) for check-ins is the basis of the third proposal. This ATM would provide about the same service rate as would a clerk. Because initial use of this technology might be minimal, Cook estimates that 20% of customers, primarily frequent guests, would be willing to use the machines. (This might be a conservative estimate if guests perceive direct benefits from using the ATM, as bank customers do. Citibank reports that some 95% of its Manhattan customers use its ATMs.) Ms. Cook would set up a single queue for customers who prefer human check-in clerks. This line would be served by the five clerks, although Cook is hopeful that the ATM will allow a reduction to four.

Discussion Questions

1. Determine the average amount of time that a guest spends checking in. How would this change under each of the stated options?
2. Which option do you recommend?

• **Additional Case Study:** Visit **www.myomlab.com** or **www.pearsonhighered.com/heizer** for this additional free case study:
Pantry Shopper: The case requires the redesign of a checkout system for a supermarket.

Bibliography

Balakrishnan, R., B. Render, and R. M. Stair. *Managerial Decision Modeling with Spreadsheets*, 3rd ed. Upper Saddle River, NJ: Prentice Hall, 2012.

Canonaco, P., et al. "A Queuing Network Model for the Management of Berth Crane Operations." *Computers & Operations Research* 35, no. 8 (August 2008): 2432.

Cochran, J. K., and K. Roche. "A Queueing-Based Decision Support Methodology to Estimate Hospital Inpatient Bed Demand." *Journal of the Operational Research Society* 59, no. 11 (November 2008): 1471–1483.

Gross, Donald, John F. Shortle, James M. Thompson, and Carl M. Harris. *Fundamentals of Queuing Theory*, 4th ed. New York: Wiley, 2008.

Parlar, M., and M. Sharafali. "Dynamic Allocation of Airline Check-In Counters: A Queueing Optimization Problem." *Management Science* 54, no. 8 (August 2008): 1410–1425.

Prabhu, N. U. *Foundations of Queuing Theory.* Dordecht, Netherlands: Kluwer Academic Publishers, 1997.

Render, B., R. M. Stair, and M. Hanna. *Quantitative Analysis for Management*, 11th ed. Upper Saddle River, NJ: Prentice Hall, 2012.

Stanford, D. A., E. Renouf, and V. C. McAlister. "Waiting for Liver Transplantation in Canada." *Health Care Management Science* 11, no. 2 (June 2008): 196–208.

Yan Kovic, N., and L. V. Green. "Identifying Good Nursing Levels: A Queuing Approach." *Operations Research* 59, no. 4 (July/August 2011): 942–955.

APPENDIX

SOLUTIONS TO EVEN-NUMBERED PROBLEMS

2 **(a)** 44%
(b) .36 people
(c) .8 people
(d) .53 min
(e) 1.2 min

4 **(a)** .5
(b) .5
(c) 1
(d) .5
(e) .05 hr
(f) .1 hr

6 **(a)** .667
(b) .667 min
(c) 1.33

8 **(a)** .375
(b) 1.6 hr (or .2 days)
(c) .225
(d) 0.141, 0.053, 0.020, 0.007

10 **(a)** 2.25
(b) .75
(c) .857 min. (.014 hr)
(d) .64 min. (.011 hr)
(e) 42%, 32%, 24%

12 **(a)** 6 trucks
(b) 12 min
(c) .857
(d) .54
(e) $1,728/day
(f) Yes, save $3,096 in the first year.

14 **(a)** .075 hrs (4.5 min)
(b) 1.125 people
(c) .0083 hrs (0.5 min), 0.083 people

16 **(a)** .113 hr. = 6.8 min
(b) 1.13 cars

18 **(a)** .05
(b) .743
(c) .793

20 **(a)** 3, 2, 4 MDs, respectively
(b) Because $\lambda > \mu$, an indefinite queue buildup can occur.

22 **(a)** 4 servers
(b) 6 servers
(c) $109
(d) 83.33%

24 2 salespeople ($340)

Rapid Review

Main Heading	Review Material	MyOMLab
QUEUING THEORY	■ **Queuing theory**—A body of knowledge about waiting lines. ■ **Waiting line (queue)**—Items or people in a line awaiting service.	
CHARACTERISTICS OF A WAITING-LINE SYSTEM	The three parts of a waiting-line, or queuing, system are: *Arrivals or inputs to the system; queue discipline, or the waiting line itself;* and *the service facility*. ■ **Unlimited, or infinite, population**—A queue in which a virtually unlimited number of people or items could request the services, or in which the number of customers or arrivals on hand at any given moment is a very small portion of potential arrivals. ■ **Limited**, or **finite, population**—A queue in which there are only a limited number of potential users of the service. ■ **Poisson distribution**—A discrete probability distribution that often describes the arrival rate in queuing theory: $$P(x) = \frac{e^{-\lambda}\lambda^x}{x!} \textit{ for } x = 0, 1, 2, 3, 4, \ldots \qquad (1)$$ A queue is *limited* when it cannot, either by law or because of physical restrictions, increase to an infinite length. A queue is *unlimited* when its size is unrestricted. *Queue discipline* refers to the rule by which customers in the line are to receive service: ■ **First-in, first-out (FIFO) rule**—A queue discipline in which the first customers in line receive the first service. ■ **Single-server (single-channel) queuing system**—A service system with one line and one server. ■ **Multiple-server (multiple-channel) queuing system**—A service system with one waiting line but with more than one server (channel). ■ **Single-phase system**—A system in which the customer receives service from only one station and then exits the system. ■ **Multiphase system**—A system in which the customer receives services from several stations before exiting the system. ■ **Negative exponential probability distribution**—A continuous probability distribution often used to describe the service time in a queuing system.	
QUEUING COSTS	Operations managers must recognize the trade-off that takes place between two costs: the cost of providing good service and the cost of customer or machine waiting time. 	
THE VARIETY OF QUEUING MODELS	***Model A:*** *Single-Server System (M/M/1):* *Queuing Formulas:* λ = mean number of arrivals per time period μ = mean number of people or items served per time period L_s = average number of units in the system = $\lambda/(\mu - \lambda)$ W_s = average time a unit spends in the system = $1/(\mu - \lambda)$ L_q = average number of units waiting in the queue = $\lambda^2/[\mu(\mu - \lambda)]$	Problems: 1–24 Virtual Office Hours for Solved Problems: 1–2 **ACTIVE MODELS 1, 2, 3**

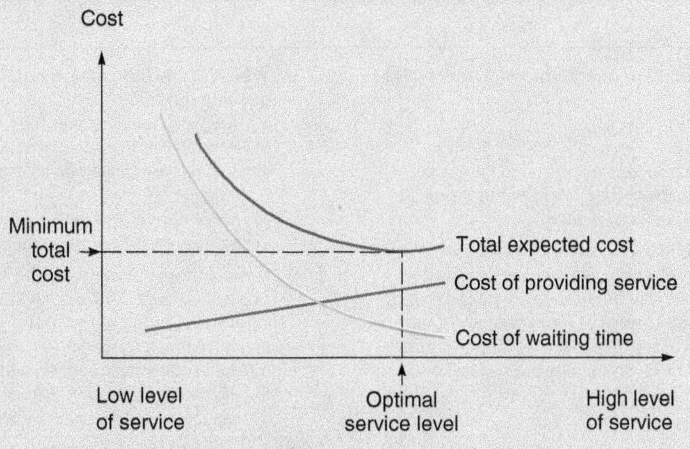

Main Heading	Review Material	MyOMLab
	W_q = average time a unit spends waiting in the queue = $\lambda/[\mu(\mu-\lambda)] = L_q/\lambda$ ρ = utilization factor for the system = λ/μ P_0 = probability of 0 units in the system (i.e., the service unit is idle) = $1-(\lambda/\mu)$ $P_{n>k}$ = probability of > k units in the system = $(\lambda/\mu)^{k+1}$ ***Model B:*** *Multiple-Server System (M/M/S):* $$P_0 = \frac{1}{\left[\sum_{n=0}^{M-1}\frac{1}{n!}\left(\frac{\lambda}{\mu}\right)^n\right]+\frac{1}{M!}\left(\frac{\lambda}{\mu}\right)^M\frac{M\mu}{M\mu-\lambda}} \quad \text{for } M\mu > \lambda$$ $$L_s = \frac{\lambda\mu(\lambda/\mu)^M}{(M-1)!(M\mu-\lambda)^2}P_0 + \frac{\lambda}{\mu}$$ $$W_s = L_s/\lambda \qquad L_q = L_s - (\lambda/\mu) \qquad W_q = L_q/\lambda$$ ***Model C:*** *Constant Service (M/D/1):* $$L_q = \lambda^2/[2\mu(\mu-\lambda)] \qquad W_q = \lambda/[2\mu(\mu-\lambda)]$$ $$L_s = L_q + (\lambda/\mu) \qquad W_s = W_q + (1/\mu)$$ *Little's Law* A useful relationship in queuing for any system in a steady state is called Little's Law: $$L = \lambda W \text{ (which is the same as } W = L/\lambda) \quad (2)$$ $$L_q = \lambda W_q \text{ (which is the same as } W_q = L_q/\lambda) \quad (3)$$ ***Model D:*** *Limited Population* With a limited population, there is a *dependent* relationship between the length of the queue and the arrival rate. As the *waiting* line becomes longer, the *arrival rate* drops.	Virtual Office Hours for Solved Problems: 3–4
OTHER QUEUING APPROACHES	Often, *variations* of the four basic queuing models are present in an analysis. Many models, some very complex, have been developed to deal with such variations.	

Self Test

■ **Before taking the self-test,** refer to the learning objectives listed at the beginning of the text and the key terms listed at the end of the text.

LO1. Which of the following is *not* a key operating characteristic for a queuing system?
a) Utilization rate
b) Percent idle time
c) Average time spent waiting in the system and in the queue
d) Average number of customers in the system and in the queue
e) Average number of customers who renege

LO2. Customers enter the waiting line at a cafeteria's only cash register on a first-come, first-served basis. The arrival rate follows a Poisson distribution, while service times follow an exponential distribution. If the average number of arrivals is 6 per minute and the average service rate of a single server is 10 per minute, what is the average number of customers in the system?
a) 0.6 **b)** 0.9
c) 1.5 **d)** 0.25
e) 1.0

LO3. In performing a cost analysis of a queuing system, the waiting time cost is sometimes based on the time in the queue and sometimes based on the time in the system. The waiting cost should be based on time in the system for which of the following situations?
a) Waiting in line to ride an amusement park ride
b) Waiting to discuss a medical problem with a doctor
c) Waiting for a picture and an autograph from a rock star
d) Waiting for a computer to be fixed so it can be placed back in service

LO4. Which of the following is *not* an assumption in a multiple-server queuing model?
a) Arrivals come from an infinite, or very large, population.
b) Arrivals are Poisson distributed.
c) Arrivals are treated on a first-in, first-out basis and do not balk or renege.
d) Service times follow the exponential distribution.
e) Servers each perform at their own individual speeds.

LO5. If everything else remains the same, including the mean arrival rate and service rate, except that the service time becomes constant instead of exponential:
a) the average queue length will be halved.
b) the average waiting time will be doubled.
c) the average queue length will increase.
d) we cannot tell from the information provided.

LO6. A company has one computer technician who is responsible for repairs on the company's 20 computers. As a computer breaks, the technician is called to make the repair. If the repairperson is busy, the machine must wait to be repaired. This is an example of:
a) a multiple-server system.
b) a finite population system.
c) a constant service rate system.
d) a multiphase system.
e) all of the above.

Answers: LO1. e; LO2. c; LO3. d; LO4. e; LO5. a; LO6. b.

Project Management

OUTLINE

From Chapter 3 of *Operations Management, Sustainability and Supply Chain Management*, Eleventh Edition. Jay Heizer, Barry Render.

GLOBAL COMPANY PROFILE
Bechtel Group

Project Management Provides a Competitive Advantage for Bechtel

Now in its 115th year, the San Francisco–based Bechtel Group (www.bechtel.com) is the world's premier manager of massive construction and engineering projects. Known for billion-dollar projects, Bechtel is famous for its construction feats on the Hoover Dam, the Boston Central Artery/Tunnel project, and rebuilding of Kuwait's oil and gas infrastructure after the invasion by Iraq in 1990. With 53,000 employees and revenues over $25 billion, Bechtel is the largest project manager in the U.S.

© philipus/Alamy

A massive dredge hired by Bechtel removes silt from Iraq's port at Umm Qasr. This paved the way for large-scale deliveries of U.S. food and the return of commercial shipping.

Associated Press

In addition to major construction projects, Bechtel used its project management skills to provide emergency response to major catastrophes as it did here in the wake of Hurricane Katrina.

Conditions weren't what Bechtel expected when it won a series of billion-dollar contracts from the U.S. government to help reconstruct Iraq in 2003–2006. Saddam Hussein's defeat by Allied forces hadn't caused much war damage. Instead, what Bechtel found was a country that had been crumbling for years. None of the sewage plants in Baghdad worked. Power flicked on and off. Towns and cities in the anti-Hussein south had been left to decay as punishment. And to complicate matters even more, scavengers were stealing everything from museum artifacts to electric power lines. Bechtel's job was to oversee electric power, sewage, transportation, and airport repairs.

Bechtel's crews travelled under armed escort and slept in trailers surrounded by razor wire. But the company's efforts have paid off. Iraq's main seaport, Umm Qasr, was reopened when Bechtel dredged the water and repaired the grain elevators. Electrical generation was back to prewar levels in 10 months. Bechtel refurbished more than 1,200 schools.

With a global procurement program, Bechtel easily tapped the company's network of suppliers and buyers worldwide to help rebuild Iraq's

Bill Pogue/Getty Images Inc. - Stone Allstock

Managing massive construction projects such as this is the strength of Bechtel. With large penalties for late completion and incentives for early completion, a good project manager is worth his or her weight in gold.

infrastructure. Other interesting recent Bechtel projects include:

- Constructing 30 high-security data centers worldwide for Equinix, Inc. ($1.2 billion).
- Building and running a rail line between London and the Channel Tunnel ($4.6 billion).
- Developing an oil pipeline from the Caspian Sea region to Russia ($850 million).
- Expanding the Dubai Airport in the United Arab Emirates ($600 million) and the Miami International Airport ($2 billion).
- Building liquefied natural gas plants in Trinidad, West Indies ($1 billion).
- Building a new subway for Athens, Greece ($2.6 billion).
- Constructing a natural gas pipeline in Thailand ($700 million).
- Building 30 plants for iMotors.com, a company that sells refurbished autos online ($300 million).
- Building a highway to link the north and south of Croatia ($303 million).

When companies or countries seek out firms to manage massive projects, they go to Bechtel, which, again and again, through outstanding project management, has demonstrated its competitive advantage.

Thomas Hartwell/U.S. Agency for International Development (USAID)

Reconstructed terminal at Baghdad International Airport.

Joe Cavaretta/Associated Press

Bechtel was the construction contractor for the Hoover Dam. This dam, on the Colorado River, is the highest in the Western Hemisphere.

LEARNING OBJECTIVES

LO1 ***Use*** a Gantt chart for scheduling

LO2 ***Draw*** AOA and AON networks

LO3 ***Complete*** forward and backward passes for a project

LO4 ***Determine*** a critical path

LO5 ***Calculate*** the variance of activity times

LO6 ***Crash*** a project

STUDENT TIP ☆ Wherever your career takes you, one of the most useful tools you can have, as a manager, is the ability to manage a project.

The Importance of Project Management

When Bechtel, the subject of the opening Global Company Profile, begins a project, it quickly has to mobilize substantial resources, often consisting of manual workers, construction professionals, cooks, medical personnel, and even security forces. Its project management team develops a supply chain to access materials to build everything from ports to bridges, dams, and monorails. Bechtel is just one example of a firm that faces modern phenomena: growing project complexity and collapsing product/service life cycles. This change stems from awareness of the strategic value of time-based competition and a quality mandate for continuous improvement. Each new product/service introduction is a unique event—a project. In addition, projects are a common part of our everyday life. We may be planning a wedding or a surprise birthday party, remodeling a house, or preparing a semester-long class project.

VIDEO 1 Project Management at Hard Rock's Rockfest

Scheduling projects can be a difficult challenge for operations managers. The stakes in project management are high. Cost overruns and unnecessary delays occur due to poor scheduling and poor controls.

Projects that take months or years to complete are usually developed outside the normal production system. Project organizations within the firm may be set up to handle such jobs and are often disbanded when the project is complete. On other occasions, managers find projects just a part of their job. The management of projects involves three phases (see Figure 1):

1. *Planning:* This phase includes goal setting, defining the project, and team organization.
2. *Scheduling:* This phase relates people, money, and supplies to specific activities and relates activities to each other.
3. *Controlling:* Here the firm monitors resources, costs, quality, and budgets. It also revises or changes plans and shifts resources to meet time and cost demands.

We begin this text with a brief overview of these functions. Three popular techniques to allow managers to plan, schedule, and control—Gantt charts, PERT, and CPM—are also described.

Project Planning

Projects can be defined as a series of related tasks directed toward a major output. In some firms a project organization is developed to make sure existing programs continue to run smoothly on a day-to-day basis while new projects are successfully completed.

Project organization An organization formed to ensure that programs (projects) receive the proper management and attention.

For companies with multiple large projects, such as a construction firm, a project organization is an effective way of assigning the people and physical resources needed. It is a temporary organization structure designed to achieve results by using specialists from throughout the firm.

The project organization may be most helpful when:

1. Work tasks can be defined with a specific goal and deadline.
2. The job is unique or somewhat unfamiliar to the existing organization.
3. The work contains complex interrelated tasks requiring specialized skills.

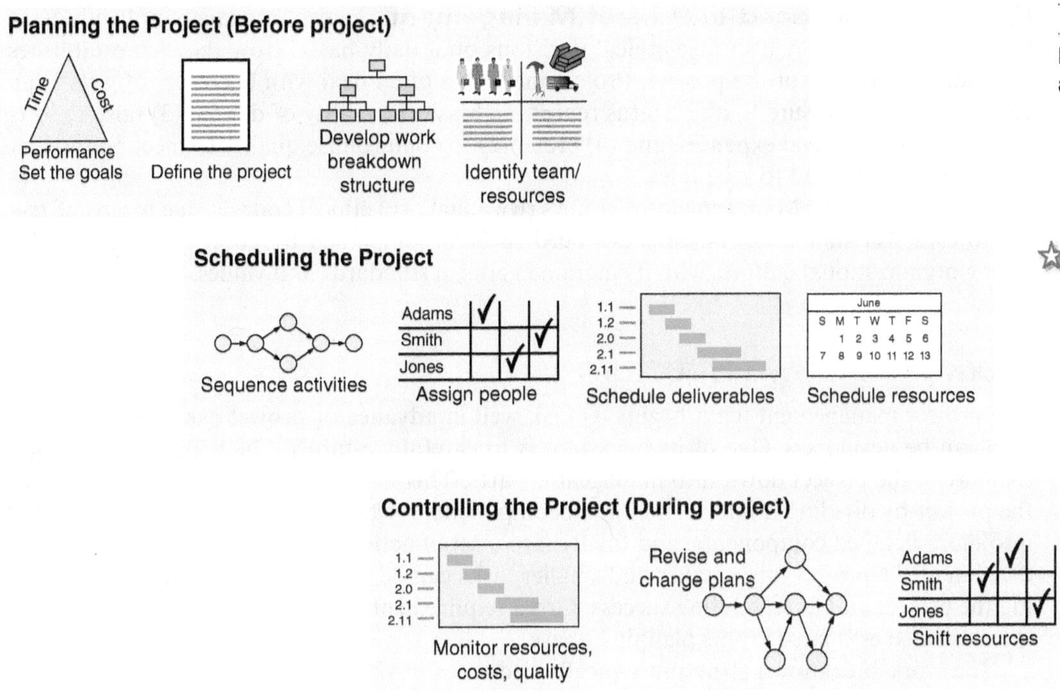

Figure 1
Project Planning, Scheduling, and Controlling

STUDENT TIP
Managers must "make the plan and then work the plan."

4. The project is temporary but critical to the organization.
5. The project cuts across organizational lines.

The Project Manager

An example of a project organization is shown in Figure 2. Project team members are temporarily assigned to a project and report to the project manager. The manager heading the project coordinates activities with other departments and reports directly to top management. Project managers receive high visibility in a firm and are responsible for making sure that (1) all necessary activities are finished in proper sequence and on time; (2) the project comes in within budget; (3) the project meets its quality goals; and (4) the people assigned to the project receive the motivation, direction, and information needed to do their jobs. This means that project managers should be good coaches and communicators, and be able to organize activities from a variety of disciplines.

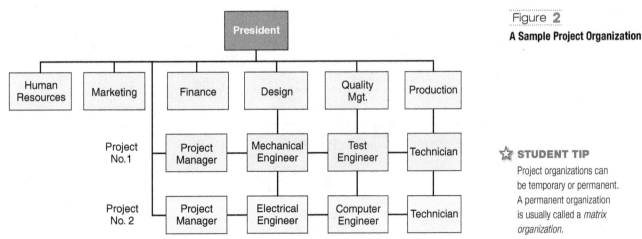

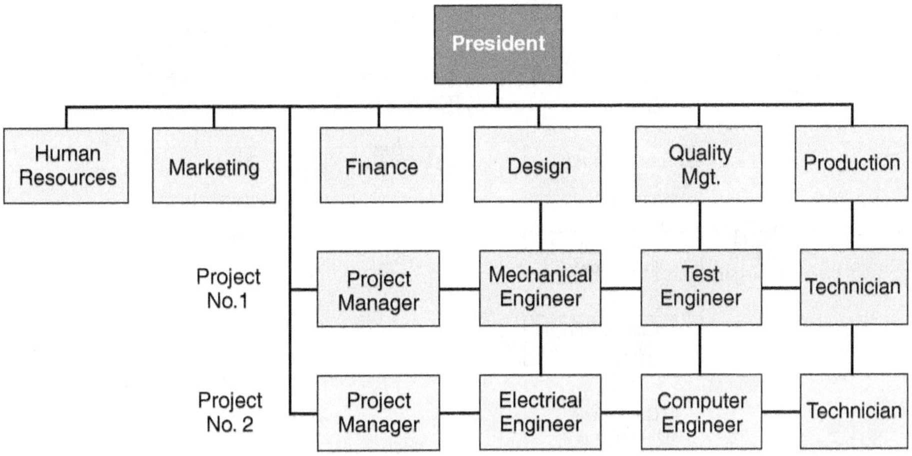

Figure 2
A Sample Project Organization

STUDENT TIP
Project organizations can be temporary or permanent. A permanent organization is usually called a *matrix organization*.

Ethical Issues Faced in Project Management Project managers not only have high visibility but they also face ethical decisions on a daily basis. How they act establishes the code of conduct for the project. Project managers often deal with (1) offers of gifts from contractors, (2) pressure to alter status reports to mask the reality of delays, (3) false reports for charges of time and expenses, and (4) pressures to compromise quality to meet bonuses or avoid penalties related to schedules.

Using the Project Management Institute's **(www.pmi.org)** ethical codes is one means of trying to establish standards. These codes need to be accompanied by good leadership and a strong organizational culture, with its ingrained ethical standards and values.

Work Breakdown Structure

Work breakdown structure (WBS)
A hierarchical description of a project into more and more detailed components.

The project management team begins its task well in advance of project execution so that a plan can be developed. One of its first steps is to carefully establish the project's objectives, then break the project down into manageable parts. This work breakdown structure (WBS) defines the project by dividing it into its major subcomponents (or tasks), which are then subdivided into more detailed components, and finally into a set of activities and their related costs. The division of the project into smaller and smaller tasks can be difficult, but is critical to managing the project and to scheduling success. Gross requirements for people, supplies, and equipment are also estimated in this planning phase.

The work breakdown structure typically decreases in size from top to bottom and is indented like this:

Level
1 Project
2 Major tasks in the project
3 Subtasks in major tasks
4 Activities (or "work packages") to be completed

This hierarchical framework can be illustrated with the development of Microsoft's operating system Windows 8. As we see in Figure 3, the project, creating a new operating system, is labeled 1.0. The first step is to identify the major tasks in the project (level 2). Three examples would be software design (1.1), cost management plan (1.2), and system testing (1.3). Two major subtasks for 1.1 are development of graphical user interfaces (GUIs) (1.1.1) and creating compatibility with previous versions of Windows (1.1.2). The major subtasks for 1.1.2 are level-4 activities, such as creating a team to handle compatibility with Windows 7 (1.1.2.1),

Figure 3
Work Breakdown Structure

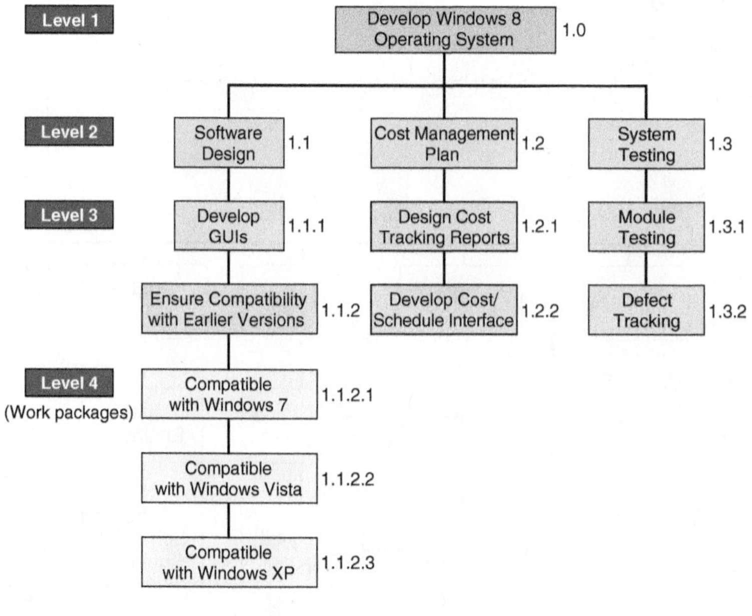

creating a team for Windows Vista (1.1.2.2), and creating a team for Windows XP (1.1.2.3). There are usually many level-4 activities.

Project Scheduling

Project scheduling involves sequencing and allotting time to all project activities. At this stage, managers decide how long each activity will take and compute the resources needed at each stage of production. Managers may also chart separate schedules for personnel needs by type of skill (management, engineering, or pouring concrete, for example) and material needs.

One popular project scheduling approach is the Gantt chart. **Gantt charts** are low-cost means of helping managers make sure that (1) activities are planned, (2) order of performance is documented, (3) activity time estimates are recorded, and (4) overall project time is developed. As Figure 4 shows, Gantt charts are easy to understand. Horizontal bars are drawn for each project activity along a time line. This illustration of a routine servicing of a Delta jetliner during a 40-minute layover shows that Gantt charts also can be used for scheduling repetitive operations. In this case, the chart helps point out potential delays. The *OM in Action* box on Delta provides additional insights.

Gantt charts
Planning charts used to schedule resources and allocate time.

On simple projects, scheduling charts such as these permit managers to observe the progress of each activity and to spot and tackle problem areas. Gantt charts, though, do not adequately illustrate the interrelationships between the activities and the resources.

STUDENT TIP
Gantt charts are simple and visual, making them widely used.

PERT and CPM, the two widely used network techniques that we shall discuss shortly, *do* have the ability to consider precedence relationships and interdependency of activities. On complex projects, the scheduling of which is almost always computerized, PERT and CPM thus have an edge over the simpler Gantt charts. Even on huge projects, though, Gantt charts can be used as summaries of project status and may complement the other network approaches.

LO1 *Use* a Gantt chart for scheduling

To summarize, whatever the approach taken by a project manager, project scheduling serves several purposes:

1. It shows the relationship of each activity to others and to the whole project.
2. It identifies the precedence relationships among activities.
3. It encourages the setting of realistic time and cost estimates for each activity.
4. It helps make better use of people, money, and material resources by identifying critical bottlenecks in the project.

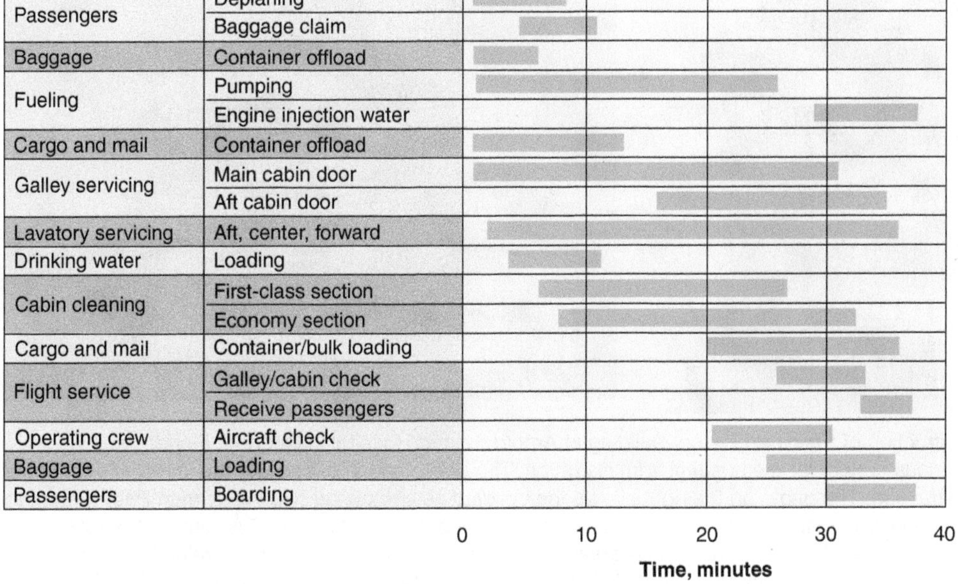

Figure 4
Gantt Chart of Service Activities for a Delta Jet during a 40-Minute Layover
Delta saves $50 million a year with this turnaround time, which is a reduction from its traditional 60-minute routine.

OM in Action Delta's Ground Crew Orchestrates a Smooth Takeoff

Flight 574's engines screech its arrival as the jet lumbers down Richmond's taxiway with 140 passengers arriving from Atlanta. In 40 minutes, the plane is to be airborne again.

However, before this jet can depart, there is business to attend to: passengers, luggage, and cargo to unload and load; thousands of gallons of jet fuel and countless drinks to restock; cabin and restrooms to clean; toilet holding tanks to drain; and engines, wings, and landing gear to inspect.

The 10-person ground crew knows that a miscue anywhere—a broken cargo loader, lost baggage, misdirected passengers—can mean a late departure and trigger a chain reaction of headaches from Richmond to Atlanta to every destination of a connecting flight.

Carla Sutera, the operations manager for Delta's Richmond International Airport, views the turnaround operation like a pit boss awaiting a race car. Trained crews are in place for Flight 574 with baggage carts and tractors, hydraulic cargo loaders, a truck to load food and drinks, another to lift the cleanup crew, another to put fuel on, and a fourth to take water off. The "pit crew" usually performs so smoothly that most passengers never suspect the proportions of the effort. Gantt charts, such as the one in Figure 4, aid Delta and other airlines with the staffing and scheduling that are needed for this task.

Sources: Knight Ridder Tribune Business News (July 16, 2005) and (November 21, 2002).

Jeff Topping/Getty Images

Project Controlling

VIDEO 2
Project Management at Arnold Palmer Hospital

The control of projects, like the control of any management system, involves close monitoring of resources, costs, quality, and budgets. Control also means using a feedback loop to revise the project plan and having the ability to shift resources to where they are needed most. Computerized PERT/CPM reports and charts are widely available today from scores of competing software firms. Some of the more popular of these programs are Primavera (by Primavera Systems, Inc.), MacProject (by Apple Computer Corp.), MindView (by Match Ware), HP Project (by Hewlett-Packard), Fast Track (by AEC Software), and Microsoft Project (by Microsoft Corp.), which we illustrate in this text.

STUDENT TIP To use project management software, you first need to understand the next two sections in this text.

These programs produce a broad variety of reports, including (1) detailed cost breakdowns for each task, (2) total program labor curves, (3) cost distribution tables, (4) functional cost and hour summaries, (5) raw material and expenditure forecasts, (6) variance reports, (7) time analysis reports, and (8) work status reports.

Jonathan Bailey Associates

Pia Gandolfo/Jonathan Bailey Associates

Construction of the new 11-story building at Arnold Palmer Hospital in Orlando, Florida, was an enormous project for the hospital administration. The photo on the left shows the first six floors under construction. The photo on the right shows the building as completed two years later. Prior to beginning actual construction, regulatory and funding issues added, as they do with most projects, substantial time to the overall project. Cities have zoning and parking issues; the EPA has drainage and waste issues; and regulatory authorities have their own requirements, as do issuers of bonds. The $100 million, 4-year project at Arnold Palmer Hospital is discussed in the Video Case Study at the end of this text.

Project Management Techniques: PERT and CPM

Program evaluation and review technique (PERT) and the critical path method (CPM) were both developed in the 1950s to help managers schedule, monitor, and control large and complex projects. CPM arrived first, as a tool developed to assist in the building and maintenance of chemical plants at duPont. Independently, PERT was developed in 1958 for the U.S. Navy.

Program evaluation and review technique (PERT)
A project management technique that employs three time estimates for each activity.

Critical path method (CPM)
A project management technique that uses only one time factor per activity.

The Framework of PERT and CPM

PERT and CPM both follow six basic steps:

1. Define the project and prepare the work breakdown structure.
2. Develop the relationships among the activities. Decide which activities must precede and which must follow others.
3. Draw the network connecting all the activities.
4. Assign time and/or cost estimates to each activity.
5. Compute the *longest* time path through the network. This is called the critical path.
6. Use the network to help plan, schedule, monitor, and control the project.

Critical path
The computed *longest* time path(s) through a network.

Step 5, finding the critical path, is a major part of controlling a project. The activities on the critical path represent tasks that will delay the entire project if they are not completed on time. Managers can gain the flexibility needed to complete critical tasks by identifying noncritical activities and replanning, rescheduling, and reallocating labor and financial resources.

Although PERT and CPM differ to some extent in terminology and in the construction of the network, their objectives are the same. Furthermore, the analysis used in both techniques is very similar. The major difference is that PERT employs three time estimates for each activity. These time estimates are used to compute expected values and standard deviations for the activity. CPM makes the assumption that activity times are known with certainty and hence requires only one time factor for each activity.

For purposes of illustration, the rest of this section concentrates on a discussion of PERT. Most of the comments and procedures described, however, apply just as well to CPM.

PERT and CPM are important because they can help answer questions such as the following about projects with thousands of activities:

1. When will the entire project be completed?
2. What are the critical activities or tasks in the project—that is, which activities will delay the entire project if they are late?
3. Which are the noncritical activities—the ones that can run late without delaying the whole project's completion?
4. What is the probability that the project will be completed by a specific date?
5. At any particular date, is the project on schedule, behind schedule, or ahead of schedule?
6. On any given date, is the money spent equal to, less than, or greater than the budgeted amount?
7. Are there enough resources available to finish the project on time?
8. If the project is to be finished in a shorter amount of time, what is the best way to accomplish this goal at the least cost?

Network Diagrams and Approaches

The first step in a PERT or CPM network is to divide the entire project into significant activities in accordance with the work breakdown structure. There are two approaches for drawing a project network: activity on node (AON) and activity on arrow (AOA). Under the AON convention, *nodes* designate activities. Under AOA, *arrows* represent activities. Activities consume time and resources. The basic difference between AON and AOA is that the nodes in an AON diagram represent activities. In an AOA network, the nodes represent the starting and finishing times of an activity and are also called *events*. So nodes in AOA consume neither time nor resources.

Activity-on-node (AON)
A network diagram in which nodes designate activities.

Activity-on-arrow (AOA)
A network diagram in which arrows designate activities.

Although both AON and AOA are popular in practice, many of the project management software packages, including Microsoft Project, use AON networks. For this reason, although we illustrate both types of networks in the next examples, we focus on AON networks in subsequent discussions in this text.

Example 1

PREDECESSOR RELATIONSHIPS FOR POLLUTION CONTROL AT MILWAUKEE PAPER

Milwaukee Paper Manufacturing had long delayed the expense of installing advanced computerized air pollution control equipment in its facility. But when the board of directors adopted a new proactive policy on sustainability, it did not just *authorize* the budget for the state-of-the-art equipment. It directed the plant manager, Julie Ann Williams, to complete the installation in time for a major announcement of the policy, on Earth Day, exactly 16 weeks away! Under strict deadline from her bosses, Williams needs to be sure that installation of the filtering system progresses smoothly and on time.

Given the following information, develop a table showing activity precedence relationships.

APPROACH ▶ Milwaukee Paper has identified the eight activities that need to be performed in order for the project to be completed. When the project begins, two activities can be simultaneously started: building the internal components for the device (activity A) and the modifications necessary for the floor and roof (activity B). The construction of the collection stack (activity C) can begin when the internal components are completed. Pouring the concrete floor and installation of the frame (activity D) can be started as soon as the internal components are completed and the roof and floor have been modified.

After the collection stack has been constructed, two activities can begin: building the high-temperature burner (activity E) and installing the pollution control system (activity F). The air pollution device can be installed (activity G) after the concrete floor has been poured, the frame has been installed, and the high-temperature burner has been built. Finally, after the control system and pollution device have been installed, the system can be inspected and tested (activity H).

SOLUTION ▶ Activities and precedence relationships may seem rather confusing when they are presented in this descriptive form. It is therefore convenient to list all the activity information in a table, as shown in Table 1. We see in the table that activity A is listed as an *immediate predecessor* of activity C. Likewise, both activities D and E must be performed prior to starting activity G.

TABLE 1 Milwaukee Paper Manufacturing's Activities and Predecessors

ACTIVITY	DESCRIPTION	IMMEDIATE PREDECESSORS
A	Build internal components	—
B	Modify roof and floor	—
C	Construct collection stack	A
D	Pour concrete and install frame	A, B
E	Build high-temperature burner	C
F	Install pollution control system	C
G	Install air pollution device	D, E
H	Inspect and test	F, G

INSIGHT ▶ To complete a network, all predecessors must be clearly defined.

LEARNING EXERCISE ▶ What is the impact on this sequence of activities if Environmental Protection Agency (EPA) approval is required after *Inspect and Test?* [Answer: The immediate predecessor for the new activity would be H, *Inspect and Test*, with *EPA approval* as the last activity.]

Activity-on-Node Example

Note that in Example 1, we only list the *immediate* predecessors for each activity. For instance, in Table 1, since activity A precedes activity C, and activity C precedes activity E, the fact that activity A precedes activity E is *implicit*. This relationship need not be explicitly shown in the activity precedence relationships.

LO2 *Draw* AOA and AON networks

When there are many activities in a project with fairly complicated precedence relationships, it is difficult for an individual to comprehend the complexity of the project from just the tabular information. In such cases, a visual representation of the project, using a *project network*, is convenient and useful. A project network is a diagram of all the activities and the precedence relationships that exist between these activities in a project. Example 2 illustrates how to construct an AON project network for Milwaukee Paper Manufacturing.

Example 2

AON GRAPH FOR MILWAUKEE PAPER

Draw the AON network for Milwaukee Paper, using the data in Example 1.

APPROACH ▶ In the AON approach, we denote each activity by a node. The lines, or arrows, represent the precedence relationships between the activities.

SOLUTION ▶ In this example, there are two activities (A and B) that do not have any predecessors. We draw separate nodes for each of these activities, as shown in Figure 5. Although not required, it is usually convenient to have a unique starting activity for a project. We have therefore included a *dummy activity* called *Start* in Figure 5. This dummy activity does not really exist and takes up zero time and resources. Activity *Start* is an immediate predecessor for both activities A and B, and serves as the unique starting activity for the entire project.

Dummy activity
An activity having no time that is inserted into a network to maintain the logic of the network.

Figure 5
Beginning AON Network for Milwaukee Paper

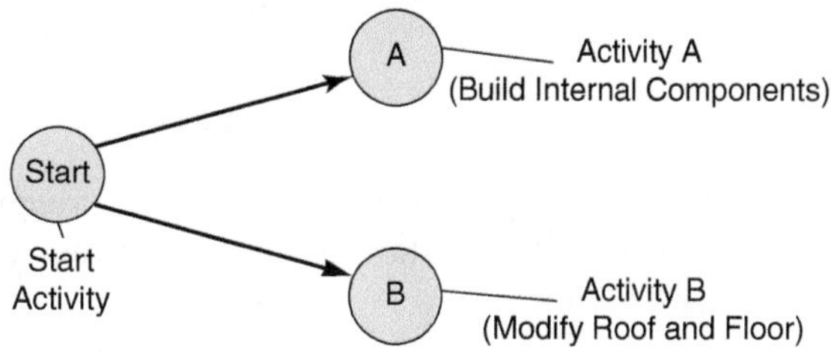

We now show the precedence relationships using lines with arrow symbols. For example, an arrow from activity Start to activity A indicates that Start is a predecessor for activity A. In a similar fashion, we draw an arrow from Start to B.

Next, we add a new node for activity C. Since activity A precedes activity C, we draw an arrow from node A to node C (see Figure 6). Likewise, we first draw a node to represent activity D. Then, since activities A and B both precede activity D, we draw arrows from A to D and from B to D (see Figure 6).

Figure 6
Intermediate AON Network for Milwaukee Paper

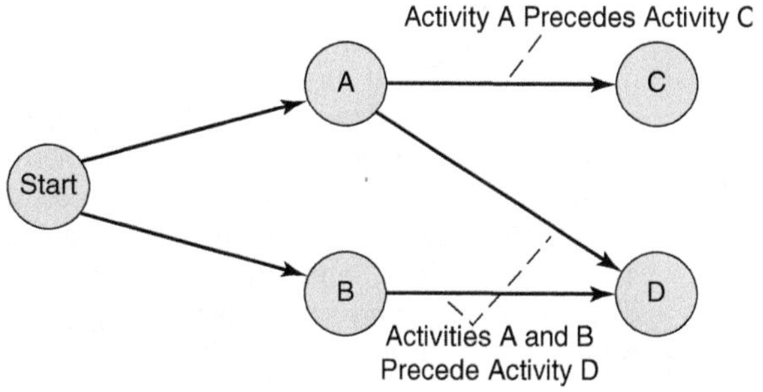

We proceed in this fashion, adding a separate node for each activity and a separate line for each precedence relationship that exists. The complete AON project network for the Milwaukee Paper Manufacturing project is shown in Figure 7.

Figure 7
Complete AON Network for Milwaukee Paper

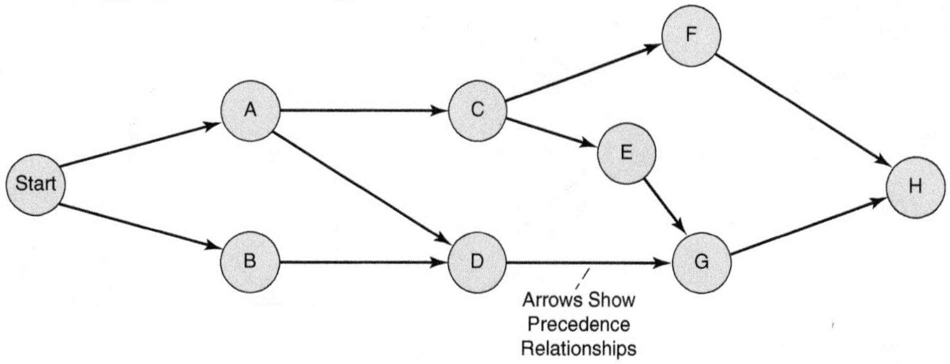

INSIGHT ▶ Drawing a project network properly takes some time and experience. We would like the lines to be straight and arrows to move to the right when possible.

LEARNING EXERCISE ▶ If *EPA Approval* occurs after *Inspect and Test*, what is the impact on the graph? [Answer: A straight line is extended to the right beyond H (with a node I added) to reflect the additional activity.]

RELATED PROBLEMS ▶ 3, 6, 7, 9a, 10, 12, 15a

When we first draw a project network, it is not unusual to place our nodes (activities) in the network in such a fashion that the arrows (precedence relationships) are not straight lines. That is, the lines could be intersecting each other, and even facing in opposite directions. For example, if we had switched the location of the nodes for activities E and F in Figure 7, the lines from F to H and E to G would have intersected. Although such a project network is perfectly valid, it is good practice to place the nodes in such a fashion that all arrows point in the same direction.

As with the unique starting node, it is convenient to have the project network finish with a unique ending node. In the Milwaukee Paper example, it turns out that a unique activity, H, is the last activity in the project. We therefore automatically have a unique ending node.

In situations in which a project has multiple ending activities, we include a "dummy" ending activity. We illustrate this type of situation in Solved Problem 1 at the end of this text.

Activity-on-Arrow Example

In an AOA project network we can represent activities by arrows. A node represents an *event*, which marks the start or completion time of an activity. We usually identify an event (node) by a number.

Example 3

ACTIVITY-ON-ARROW FOR MILWAUKEE PAPER

Draw the complete AOA project network for Milwaukee Paper's problem.

APPROACH ▶ Using the data from Table 1 in Example 1, draw one activity at a time, starting with A.

SOLUTION ▶ We see that activity A starts at event 1 and ends at event 2. Likewise, activity B starts at event 1 and ends at event 3. Activity C, whose only immediate predecessor is activity A, starts at node 2 and ends at node 4. Activity D, however, has two predecessors (i.e., A and B). Hence, we need both activities A and B to end at event 3, so that activity D can start at that event. However, we cannot have multiple activities with common starting and ending nodes in an AOA network. To overcome this difficulty, in such cases, we may need to add a dummy line (activity) to enforce the precedence relationship. The dummy activity, shown in Figure 8 as a dashed line, is inserted between events 2 and 3 to make the diagram reflect the precedence between A and D. The remainder of the AOA project network for Milwaukee Paper's example is also shown.

Figure 8
Complete AOA Network (with Dummy Activity) for Milwaukee Paper

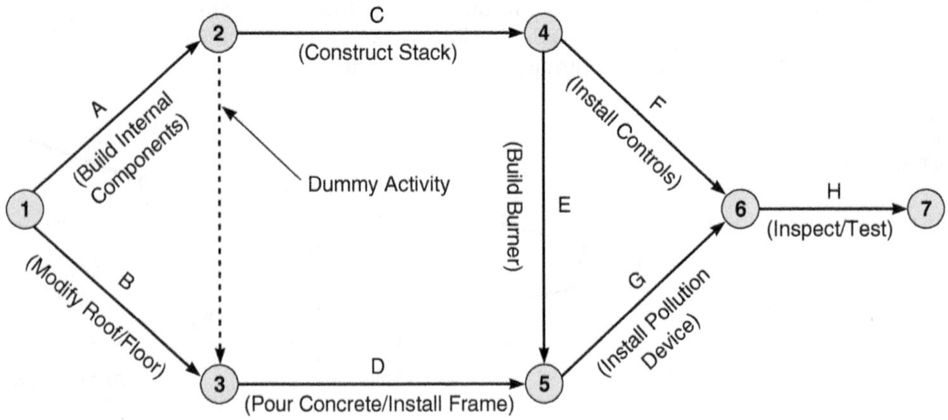

STUDENT TIP ☆
The dummy activity consumes no time, but note how it changes precedence. Now activity D cannot begin until *both* B and the dummy are complete.

INSIGHT ▶ Dummy activities are common in AOA networks. They do not really exist in the project and take zero time.

LEARNING EXERCISE ▶ A new activity, *EPA Approval*, follows activity H. Add it to Figure 8. [Answer: Insert an arrowed line from node 7, which ends at a new node 8, and is labeled I (EPA Approval).]

RELATED PROBLEMS ▶ 4, 5, 9b

TABLE 2 **Time Estimates for Milwaukee Paper Manufacturing**

ACTIVITY	DESCRIPTION	TIME (WEEKS)
A	Build internal components	2
B	Modify roof and floor	3
C	Construct collection stack	2
D	Pour concrete and install frame	4
E	Build high-temperature burner	4
F	Install pollution control system	3
G	Install air pollution device	5
H	Inspect and test	2
	Total time (weeks)	25

STUDENT TIP
Does this mean the project will take 25 weeks to complete? No. Don't forget that several of the activities are being performed at the same time. It would take 25 weeks if they were done sequentially.

Determining the Project Schedule

Look back at Figure 7 (in Example 2) for a moment to see Milwaukee Paper's completed AON project network. Once this project network has been drawn to show all the activities and their precedence relationships, the next step is to determine the project schedule. That is, we need to identify the planned starting and ending time for each activity.

Let us assume Milwaukee Paper estimates the time required for each activity, in weeks, as shown in Table 2. The table indicates that the total time for all eight of the company's activities is 25 weeks. However, since several activities can take place simultaneously, it is clear that the total project completion time may be less than 25 weeks. To find out just how long the project will take, we perform the critical path analysis for the network.

Critical path analysis
A process that helps determine a project schedule.

As mentioned earlier, the critical path is the *longest* time path through the network. To find the critical path, we calculate two distinct starting and ending times for each activity. These are defined as follows:

Earliest start (ES) = earliest time at which an activity can start, assuming all predecessors have been completed
Earliest finish (EF) = earliest time at which an activity can be finished
Latest start (LS) = latest time at which an activity can start so as to not delay the completion time of the entire project
Latest finish (LF) = latest time by which an activity has to finish so as to not delay the completion time of the entire project

We use a two-pass process, consisting of a forward pass and a backward pass, to determine these time schedules for each activity. The early start and finish times (ES and EF) are determined during the forward pass. The late start and finish times (LS and LF) are determined during the backward pass.

Forward pass
A process that identifies all the early times.

LO3 *Complete* forward and backward passes for a project

Forward Pass

To clearly show the activity schedules on the project network, we use the notation shown in Figure 9. The ES of an activity is shown in the top left corner of the node denoting that activ-

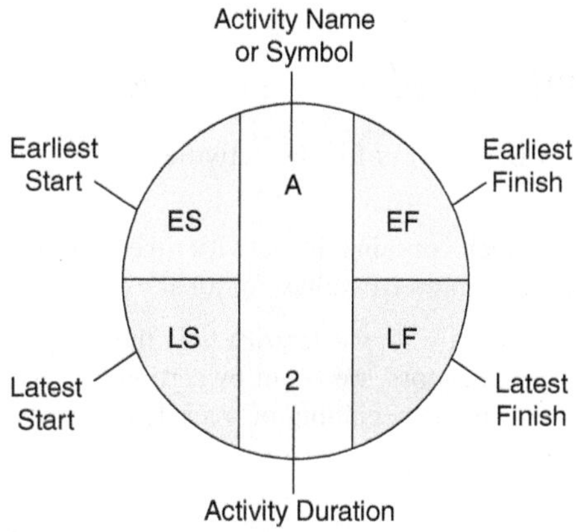

Figure 9
Notation Used in Nodes for Forward and Backward Pass

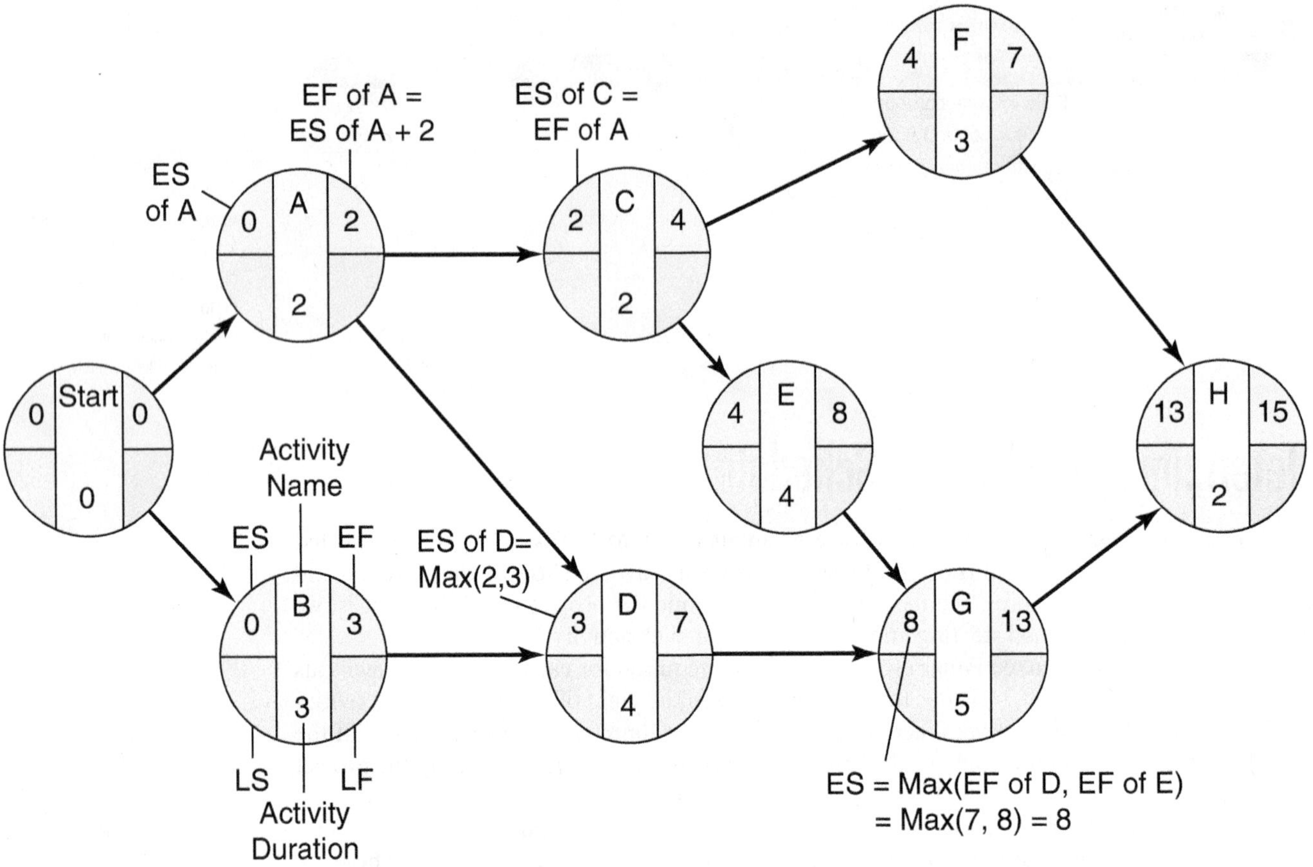

Figure 10 **Earliest Start and Earliest Finish Times for Milwaukee Paper**

To view all the layers of this figure, please visit www.pearsonhighered.com/heizer and download the Earliest Start and Finish Times PowerPoint file.

ity. The EF is shown in the top right corner. The latest times, LS and LF, are shown in the bottom-left and bottom-right corners, respectively.

Earliest Start Time Rule Before an activity can start, *all* its immediate predecessors must be finished:

- If an activity has only a single immediate predecessor, its ES equals the EF of the predecessor.
- If an activity has multiple immediate predecessors, its ES is the maximum of all EF values of its predecessors. That is:

STUDENT TIP *All* predecessor activities must be completed before an acitivity can begin.

$$ES = \text{Max}\ \{\text{EF of all immediate predecessors}\} \tag{1}$$

Earliest Finish Time Rule The earliest finish time (EF) of an activity is the sum of its earliest start time (ES) and its activity time. That is:

$$EF = ES + \text{Activity time} \tag{2}$$

Example 4

COMPUTING EARLIEST START AND FINISH TIMES FOR MILWAUKEE PAPER

Calculate the earliest start and finish times for the activities in the Milwaukee Paper Manufacturing project.

APPROACH ▶ Use Table 2, which contains the activity times. Complete the project network for the company's project, along with the ES and EF values for all activities.

SOLUTION ▶ With the help of Figure 10, we describe how these values are calculated.

Since activity Start has no predecessors, we begin by setting its ES to 0. That is, activity Start can begin at time 0, which is the same as the beginning of week 1. If activity Start has an ES of 0, its EF is also 0, since its activity time is 0.

Next, we consider activities A and B, both of which have only Start as an immediate predecessor. Using the earliest start time rule, the ES for both activities A and B equals zero, which is the EF of activity Start. Now, using the earliest finish time rule, the EF for A is 2 (= 0 + 2), and the EF for B is 3 (= 0 + 3).

Since activity A precedes activity C, the ES of C equals the EF of A (= 2). The EF of C is therefore 4 (= 2 + 2).

We now come to activity D. Both activities A and B are immediate predecessors for D. Whereas A has an EF of 2, activity B has an EF of 3. Using the earliest start time rule, we compute the ES of activity D as follows:

$$\text{ES of D} = \text{Max(EF of A, EF of B)} = \text{Max}(2, 3) = 3$$

The EF of D equals 7 (= 3 + 4). Next, both activities E and F have activity C as their only immediate predecessor. Therefore, the ES for both E and F equals 4 (= EF of C). The EF of E is 8 (= 4 + 4), and the EF of F is 7 (= 4 + 3).

Activity G has both activities D and E as predecessors. Using the earliest start time rule, its ES is therefore the maximum of the EF of D and the EF of E. Hence, the ES of activity G equals 8 (= maximum of 7 and 8), and its EF equals 13 (= 8 + 5).

Finally, we come to activity H. Since it also has two predecessors, F and G, the ES of H is the maximum EF of these two activities. That is, the ES of H equals 13 (= maximum of 13 and 7). This implies that the EF of H is 15 (= 13 + 2). Since H is the last activity in the project, this also implies that the earliest time in which the entire project can be completed is 15 weeks.

INSIGHT ▶ The ES of an activity that has only one predecessor is simply the EF of that predecessor. For an activity with more than one predecessor, we must carefully examine the EFs of all immediate predecessors and choose the largest one.

LEARNING EXERCISE ▶ A new activity I, *EPA Approval*, takes 1 week. Its predecessor is activity H. What are I's ES and EF? [Answer: 15, 16]

RELATED PROBLEMS ▶ 11, 14c

EXCEL OM Data File **Ch03Ex4.xls** can be found at **www.pearsonhighered.com/heizer**.

Although the forward pass allows us to determine the earliest project completion time, it does not identify the critical path. To identify this path, we need to now conduct the backward pass to determine the LS and LF values for all activities.

Backward Pass

Just as the forward pass began with the first activity in the project, the **backward pass** begins with the last activity in the project. For each activity, we first determine its LF value, followed by its LS value. The following two rules are used in this process.

Backward pass
An activity that finds all the late start and late finish times.

Latest Finish Time Rule This rule is again based on the fact that before an activity can start, all its immediate predecessors must be finished:

- If an activity is an immediate predecessor for just a single activity, its LF equals the LS of the activity that immediately follows it.
- If an activity is an immediate predecessor to more than one activity, its LF is the minimum of all LS values of all activities that immediately follow it. That is:

$$\text{LF} = \text{Min}\{\text{LS of all immediate following activities}\} \quad (3)$$

Latest Start Time Rule The latest start time (LS) of an activity is the difference of its latest finish time (LF) and its activity time. That is:

$$\text{LS} = \text{LF} - \text{Activity time} \quad (4)$$

Example 5

COMPUTING LATEST START AND FINISH TIMES FOR MILWAUKEE PAPER

Calculate the latest start and finish times for each activity in Milwaukee Paper's pollution project.

APPROACH ▶ Use Figure 10 as a beginning point. Overlay 1 of Figure 10 shows the complete project network for Milwaukee Paper, along with added LS and LF values for all activities. In what follows, we see how these values were calculated.

SOLUTION ▶ We begin by assigning an LF value of 15 weeks for activity H. That is, we specify that the latest finish time for the entire project is the same as its earliest finish time. Using the latest start time rule, the LS of activity H is equal to 13 (= 15 − 2).

Since activity H is the lone succeeding activity for both activities F and G, the LF for both F and G equals 13. This implies that the LS of G is 8 (= 13 − 5), and the LS of F is 10 (= 13 − 3).

Proceeding in this fashion, we see that the LF of E is 8 (= LS of G), and its LS is 4 (= 8 − 4). Likewise, the LF of D is 8 (= LS of G), and its LS is 4 (= 8 − 4).

We now consider activity C, which is an immediate predecessor to two activities: E and F. Using the latest finish time rule, we compute the LF of activity C as follows:

$$\text{LF of C} = \text{Min(LS of E, LS of F)} = \text{Min}(4, 10) = 4$$

The LS of C is computed as 2 (= 4 − 2). Next, we compute the LF of B as 4 (= LS of D) and its LS as 1 (= 4 − 3).

We now consider activity A. We compute its LF as 2 (= minimum of LS of C and LS of D). Hence, the LS of activity A is 0 (= 2 − 2). Finally, both the LF and LS of activity Start are equal to 0.

INSIGHT ▶ The LF of an activity that is the predecessor of only one activity is just the LS of that following activity. If the activity is the predecessor to more than one activity, its LF is the smallest LS value of all activities that follow immediately.

LEARNING EXERCISE ▶ A new activity I, *EPA Approval*, takes 1 week. Its predecessor is activity H. What are I's LS and LF? [Answer: 15, 16]

RELATED PROBLEMS ▶ 11, 14c.

Calculating Slack Time and Identifying the Critical Path(s)

Slack time
Free time for an activity. Also referred to as free float or free slack.

After we have computed the earliest and latest times for all activities, it is a simple matter to find the amount of slack time that each activity has. Slack is the length of time an activity can be delayed without delaying the entire project. Mathematically:

$$\text{Slack} = \text{LS} - \text{ES} \quad \text{or} \quad \text{Slack} = \text{LF} - \text{EF} \tag{5}$$

Example 6

CALCULATING SLACK TIMES FOR MILWAUKEE PAPER

Calculate the slack for the activities in the Milwaukee Paper project.

APPROACH ▶ Start with the data in Overlay 1 of Figure 10 in Example 5 and develop Table 3 one line at a time.

SOLUTION ▶ Table 3 summarizes the ES, EF, LS, LF, and slack time for all of the firm's activities. Activity B, for example, has 1 week of slack time since its LS is 1 and its ES is 0 (alternatively, its LF is 4 and its EF is 3). This means that activity B can be delayed by up to 1 week, and the whole project can still be finished in 15 weeks.

On the other hand, activities A, C, E, G, and H have *no* slack time. This means that none of them can be delayed without delaying the entire project. Conversely, if plant manager Julie Ann Williams wants to reduce the total project times, she will have to reduce the length of one of these activities.

Overlay 2 of Figure 10 shows the slack computed for each activity.

INSIGHT ▶ Slack may be computed from either early/late starts or early/late finishes. The key is to find which activities have zero slack.

TABLE 3 Milwaukee Paper's Schedule and Slack Times

ACTIVITY	EARLIEST START ES	EARLIEST FINISH EF	LATEST START LS	LATEST FINISH LF	SLACK LS – ES	ON CRITICAL PATH
A	0	2	0	2	0	Yes
B	0	3	1	4	1	No
C	2	4	2	4	0	Yes
D	3	7	4	8	1	No
E	4	8	4	8	0	Yes
F	4	7	10	13	6	No
G	8	13	8	13	0	Yes
H	13	15	13	15	0	Yes

LEARNING EXERCISE ▶ A new activity I, *EPA Approval*, follows activity H and takes 1 week. Is it on the critical path? [Answer: Yes, it's LS – ES = 0]

RELATED PROBLEMS ▶ 6, 11, 27

ACTIVE **MODEL** 1 This example is further illustrated in Active Model 1 at **www.pearsonhighered.com/heizer**.

The activities with zero slack are called *critical activities* and are said to be on the critical path. The critical path is a continuous path through the project network that:

LO4 *Determine* a critical path

- Starts at the first activity in the project (Start in our example).
- Terminates at the last activity in the project (H in our example).
- Includes only critical activities (i.e., activities with no slack time).

Example 7

SHOWING CRITICAL PATH WITH BLUE ARROWS

Show Milwaukee Paper's critical path and find the project completion time.

APPROACH ▶ We use Table 3 and Overlay 3 of Figure 10. Overlay 3 of Figure 10 indicates that the total project completion time of 15 weeks corresponds to the longest path in the network. That path is Start-A-C-E-G-H in network form. It is shown with thick blue arrows.

INSIGHT ▶ The critical path follows the activities with slack = 0. This is considered the longest path through the network.

LEARNING EXERCISE ▶ Why are activities B, D, and F not on the path with the thick blue line? [Answer: They are not critical and have slack values of 1, 1, and 6 weeks, respectively.]

RELATED PROBLEMS ▶ 3, 4, 5, 6, 7, 12, 14b, 15, 17, 20a, 22a, 23, 26

Total Slack Time Look again at the project network in Overlay 3 of Figure 10. Consider activities B and D, which have slack of 1 week each. Does it mean that we can delay *each* activity by 1 week, and still complete the project in 15 weeks? The answer is no.

Let's assume that activity B is delayed by 1 week. It has used up its slack of 1 week and now has an EF of 4. This implies that activity D now has an ES of 4 and an EF of 8. Note that these are also its LS and LF values, respectively. That is, activity D also has no slack time now. Essentially, the slack of 1 week that activities B and D had is, for that path, *shared* between them. Delaying either activity by 1 week causes not only that activity, but also the other activity, to lose its slack. This type of a slack time is referred to as *total slack*. Typically, when two or more noncritical activities appear successively in a path, they share total slack.

To plan, monitor, and control the huge number of details involved in sponsoring a rock festival attended by more than 100,000 fans, managers use Microsoft Project and the tools discussed in this text. The *Video Case Study* "Managing Hard Rock's Rockfest," at the end of the text, provides more details of the management task.

Variability in Activity Times

In identifying all earliest and latest times so far, and the associated critical path(s), we have adopted the CPM approach of assuming that all activity times are known and fixed constants. That is, there is no variability in activity times. However, in practice, it is likely that activity completion times vary depending on various factors.

For example, building internal components (activity A) for Milwaukee Paper Manufacturing is estimated to finish in 2 weeks. Clearly, supply-chain issues such as late arrival of materials, absence of key personnel, and so on could delay this activity. Suppose activity A actually ends up taking 3 weeks. Since A is on the critical path, the entire project will now be delayed by 1 week to 16 weeks. If we had anticipated completion of this project in 15 weeks, we would obviously miss our Earth Day deadline.

Although some activities may be relatively less prone to delays, others could be extremely susceptible to delays. For example, activity B (modify roof and floor) could be heavily dependent on weather conditions. A spell of bad weather could significantly affect its completion time.

STUDENT TIP ☆
PERT's ability to handle three time estimates for each activity enables us to compute the probability that we can complete the project by a target date.

This means that we cannot ignore the impact of variability in activity times when deciding the schedule for a project. PERT addresses this issue.

Three Time Estimates in PERT

In PERT, we employ a probability distribution based on three time estimates for each activity, as follows:

Optimistic time
The "best" activity completion time that could be obtained in a PERT network.

Pessimistic time
The "worst" activity time that could be expected in a PERT network.

Most likely time
The most probable time to complete an activity in a PERT network.

Optimistic time (a) = time an activity will take if everything goes as planned. In estimating this value, there should be only a small probability (say, 1/100) that the activity time will be $< a$.

Pessimistic time (b) = time an activity will take assuming very unfavorable conditions. In estimating this value, there should also be only a small probability (also 1/100) that the activity time will be $> b$.

Most likely time (m) = most realistic estimate of the time required to complete an activity.

When using PERT, we often assume that activity time estimates follow the beta probability distribution (see Figure 11). This continuous distribution is often appropriate for determining the expected value and variance for activity completion times.

To find the *expected activity time*, t, the beta distribution weights the three time estimates as follows:

$$t = (a + 4m + b)/6 \tag{6}$$

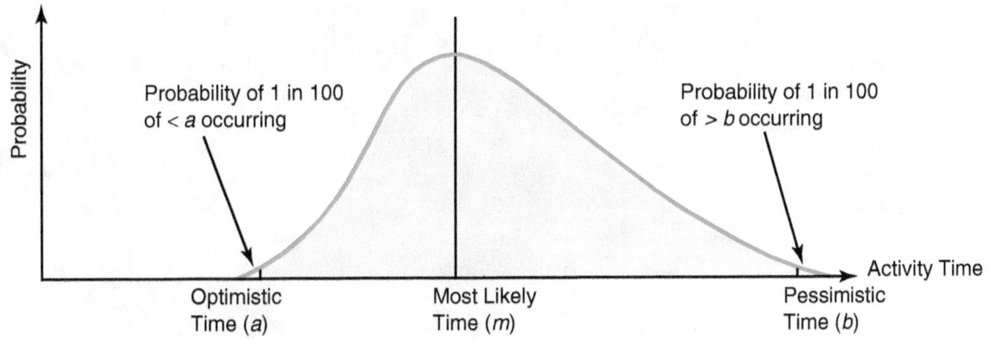

Figure 11
Beta Probability Distribution with Three Time Estimates

That is, the most likely time (m) is given four times the weight as the optimistic time (a) and pessimistic time (b). The time estimate t computed using Equation (6) for each activity is used in the project network to compute all earliest and latest times.

To compute the *dispersion* or *variance of activity completion time*, we use the formula:[1]

$$\text{Variance} = [(b - a)/6]^2 \qquad (7)$$

Example 8

EXPECTED TIMES AND VARIANCES FOR MILWAUKEE PAPER

LO5 *Calculate* the variance of activity times

Julie Ann Williams and the project management team at Milwaukee Paper want an expected time and variance for Activity F (Installing the Pollution Control System) where:

$$a = 1 \text{ week}, m = 2 \text{ weeks}, b = 9 \text{ weeks}$$

APPROACH ▶ Use Equations (6) and (7) to compute the expected time and variance for F.

SOLUTION ▶ The expected time for Activity F is:

$$t = \frac{a + 4m + b}{6} = \frac{1 + 4(2) + 9}{6} = \frac{18}{6} = 3 \text{ weeks}$$

The variance for Activity F is:

$$\text{Variance} = \left[\frac{(b - a)}{6}\right]^2 = \left[\frac{(9 - 1)}{6}\right]^2 = \left(\frac{8}{6}\right)^2 = \frac{64}{36} = 1.78$$

INSIGHT ▶ Williams now has information that allows her to understand and manage Activity F. The expected time is, in fact, the activity time used in our earlier computation and identification of the critical path.

LEARNING EXERCISE ▶ Review the expected times and variances for all of the other activities in the project. These are shown in Table 4.

TABLE 4 Time Estimates (in weeks) for Milwaukee Paper's Project

ACTIVITY	OPTIMISTIC a	MOST LIKELY m	PESSIMISTIC b	EXPECTED TIME $t = (a + 4m + b)/6$	VARIANCE $[(b - a)/6]^2$
A	1	2	3	2	$[(3 - 1)/6]^2 = 4/36 = .11$
B	2	3	4	3	$[(4 - 2)/6]^2 = 4/36 = .11$
C	1	2	3	2	$[(3 - 1)/6]^2 = 4/36 = .11$
D	2	4	6	4	$[(6 - 2)/6]^2 = 16/36 = .44$
E	1	4	7	4	$[(7 - 1)/6]^2 = 36/36 = 1.00$
F	1	2	9	3	$[(9 - 1)/6]^2 = 64/36 = 1.78$
G	3	4	11	5	$[(11 - 3)/6]^2 = 64/36 = 1.78$
H	1	2	3	2	$[(3 - 1)/6]^2 = 4/36 = .11$

STUDENT TIP Can you see why the variance is higher in some activities than in others? Note the spread between the optimistic and pessimistic times.

RELATED PROBLEMS ▶ 13, 14a, 17a,b, 21a

EXCEL OM Data File **Ch03Ex8.xls** can be found at **www.pearsonhighered.com/heizer**.

[1]This formula is based on the statistical concept that from one end of the beta distribution to the other is 6 standard deviations (±3 standard deviations from the mean). Since $(b - a)$ is 6 standard deviations, the variance is $[(b - a)/6]^2$.

We see here a ship being built at the Hyundai shipyard, Asia's largest shipbuilder, in Korea. Managing this project uses the same techniques as managing the remodeling of a store, installing a new production line, or implementing a new computer system.

Paul Chesley/Getty Images

Probability of Project Completion

The critical path analysis helped us determine that Milwaukee Paper's expected project completion time is 15 weeks. Julie Ann Williams knows, however, that there is significant variation in the time estimates for several activities. Variation in activities that are on the critical path can affect the overall project completion time—possibly delaying it. This is one occurrence that worries the plant manager considerably.

PERT uses the variance of critical path activities to help determine the variance of the overall project. Project variance is computed by summing variances of *critical* activities:

$$\sigma_p^2 = \text{Project variance} = \quad (\text{variances of activities on critical path}) \qquad (8)$$

Example 9

COMPUTING PROJECT VARIANCE AND STANDARD DEVIATION FOR MILWAUKEE PAPER

Milwaukee Paper's managers now wish to know the project's variance and standard deviation.

APPROACH ▶ Because the activities are independent, we can add the variances of the activities on the critical path and then take the square root to determine the project's standard deviation.

SOLUTION ▶ From Example 8 (Table 4), we have the variances of all of the activities on the critical path. Specifically, we know that the variance of activity A is 0.11, variance of activity C is 0.11, variance of activity E is 1.00, variance of activity G is 1.78, and variance of activity H is 0.11.

Compute the total project variance and project standard deviation:

$$\text{Project variance}(\sigma_p^2) = 0.11 + 0.11 + 1.00 + 1.78 + 0.11 = 3.11$$

which implies:

$$\text{Project standard deviation}(\sigma_p) = \sqrt{\text{Project variance}} = \sqrt{3.11} = 1.76 \text{ weeks}$$

INSIGHT ▶ Management now has an estimate not only of expected completion time for the project but also of the standard deviation of that estimate.

LEARNING EXERCISE ▶ If the variance for activity A is actually 0.30 (instead of 0.11), what is the new project standard deviation? [Answer: 1.817.]

RELATED PROBLEM ▶ 17e

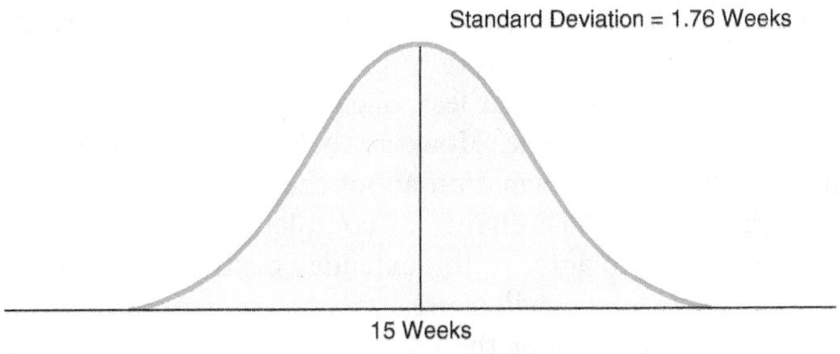

Figure 12
Probability Distribution for Project Completion Times at Milwaukee Paper

How can this information be used to help answer questions regarding the probability of finishing the project on time? PERT makes two more assumptions: (1) total project completion times follow a normal probability distribution, and (2) activity times are statistically independent. With these assumptions, the bell-shaped normal curve shown in Figure 12 can be used to represent project completion dates. This normal curve implies that there is a 50% chance that the manufacturer's project completion time will be less than 15 weeks and a 50% chance that it will exceed 15 weeks.

Example 10

PROBABILITY OF COMPLETING A PROJECT ON TIME

Julie Ann Williams would like to find the probability that her project will be finished on or before the 16-week Earth Day deadline.

APPROACH ▶ To do so, she needs to determine the appropriate area under the normal curve. This is the area to the left of the 16th week.

SOLUTION ▶ The standard normal equation can be applied as follows:

$$Z = (\text{Due date} - \text{Expected date of completion})/\sigma_p \quad (9)$$
$$= (16 \text{ weeks} - 15 \text{ weeks})/1.76 \text{ weeks} = 0.57$$

where Z is the number of standard deviations the due date or target date lies from the mean or expected date.

Referring to the Normal Table in the Appendix: "Normal Curve Areas", we find a Z value of 0.57 to the right of the mean indicates a probability of 0.7157. Thus, there is a 71.57% chance that the pollution control equipment can be put in place in 16 weeks or less. This is shown in Figure 13.

STUDENT TIP ☆ Here is a chance to review your statistical skills and use of a normal distribution table Appendix: "Normal Curve Areas".

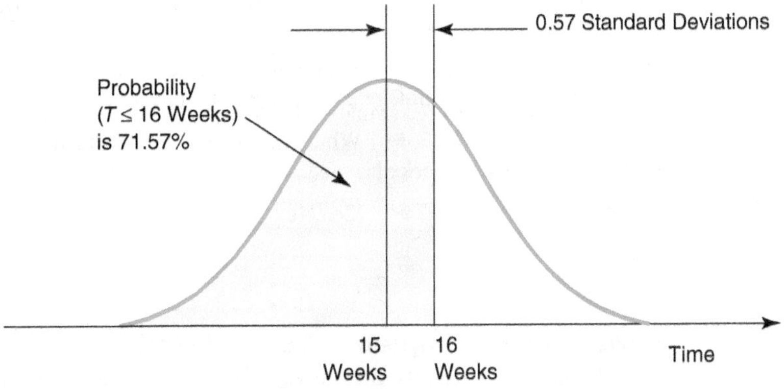

Figure 13
Probability That Milwaukee Paper Will Meet the 16-Week Deadline

INSIGHT ▶ The shaded area to the left of the 16th week (71.57%) represents the probability that the project will be completed in less than 16 weeks.

LEARNING EXERCISE ▶ What is the probability that the project will be completed on or before the 17th week? [Answer: About 87.2%.]

RELATED PROBLEMS ▶ 14d, 17f, 21d, e, 22b, 24

Determining Project Completion Time for a Given Confidence Level Let's say Julie Ann Williams is worried that there is only a 71.57% chance that the pollution control equipment can be put in place in 16 weeks or less. She thinks that it may be possible to plead with the board of directors for more time. However, before she approaches the board, she wants to arm herself with sufficient information about the project. Specifically, she wants to find the deadline by which she has a 99% chance of completing the project. She hopes to use her analysis to convince the board to agree to this extended deadline, even though she is aware of the public relations damage the delay will cause.

Clearly, this due date would be greater than 16 weeks. However, what is the exact value of this new due date? To answer this question, we again use the assumption that Milwaukee Paper's project completion time follows a normal probability distribution with a mean of 15 weeks and a standard deviation of 1.76 weeks.

Example 11

COMPUTING PROBABILITY FOR ANY COMPLETION DATE

Julie Ann Williams wants to find the due date that gives her company's project a 99% chance of *on-time* completion.

APPROACH ▶ She first needs to compute the Z-value corresponding to 99%, as shown in Figure 14. Mathematically, this is similar to Example 10, except the unknown is now the due date rather than Z.

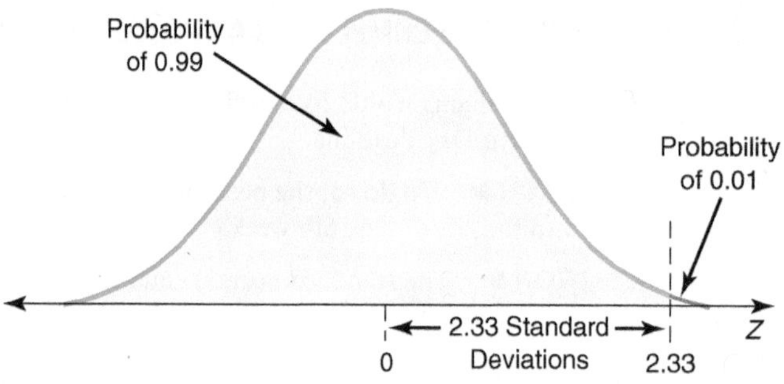

Figure 14
Z-Value for 99% Probability of Project Completion at Milwaukee Paper

SOLUTION ▶ Referring again to the Normal Table in the Appendix: "Normal Curve Areas", we identify a Z-value of 2.33 as being closest to the probability of 0.99. That is, Julie Ann Williams's due date should be 2.33 standard deviations above the mean project completion time. Starting with the standard normal equation [see Equation (9)], we can solve for the due date and rewrite the equation as:

$$\text{Due date} = \text{Expected completion time} + (Z \times \sigma_p) \quad (10)$$
$$= 15 + (2.33 \times 1.76) = 19.1 \text{ weeks}$$

INSIGHT ▶ If Williams can get the board to agree to give her a new deadline of 19.1 weeks (or more), she can be 99% sure of finishing the project by that new target date.

LEARNING EXERCISE ▶ What due date gives the project a 95% chance of on-time completion? [Answer: About 17.9 weeks.]

RELATED PROBLEMS ▶ 22c, 24e

Variability in Completion Time of Noncritical Paths In our discussion so far, we have focused exclusively on the variability in the completion times of activities on the critical path. This seems logical since these activities are, by definition, the more important activities in a project network. However, when there is variability in activity times, it is important that we also investigate the variability in the completion times of activities on *noncritical* paths.

Consider, for example, activity D in Milwaukee Paper's project. Recall from Overlay 3 in Figure 10 (in Example 7) that this is a noncritical activity, with a slack time of 1 week. We have therefore not considered the variability in D's time in computing the probabilities of project completion times. We observe, however, that D has a variance of 0.44 (see Table 4 in

Example 8). In fact, the pessimistic completion time for D is 6 weeks. This means that if D ends up taking its pessimistic time to finish, the project will not finish in 15 weeks, even though D is not a critical activity.

For this reason, when we find probabilities of project completion times, it may be necessary for us to not focus only on the critical path(s). Indeed, some research has suggested that expending project resources to reduce the variability of activities not on the critical path can be an effective element in project management. We may need also to compute these probabilities for noncritical paths, especially those that have relatively large variances. It is possible for a noncritical path to have a smaller probability of completion within a due date, when compared with the critical path. Determining the variance and probability of completion for a noncritical path is done in the same manner as Examples 9 and 10.

What Project Management Has Provided So Far Project management techniques have thus far been able to provide Julie Ann Williams with several valuable pieces of management information:

1. The project's expected completion date is 15 weeks.
2. There is a 71.57% chance that the equipment will be in place within the 16-week deadline. PERT analysis can easily find the probability of finishing by any date Williams is interested in.
3. Five activities (A, C, E, G, and H) are on the critical path. If any one of these is delayed for any reason, the entire project will be delayed.
4. Three activities (B, D, F) are not critical and have some slack time built in. This means that Williams can borrow from their resources, and, if necessary, she may be able to speed up the whole project.
5. A detailed schedule of activity starting and ending dates, slack, and critical path activities has been made available (see Table 3 in Example 6).

Cost-Time Trade-Offs and Project Crashing

While managing a project, it is not uncommon for a project manager to be faced with either (or both) of the following situations: (1) the project is behind schedule, and (2) the scheduled project completion time has been moved forward. In either situation, some or all of the remaining activities need to be speeded up (usually by adding resources) to finish the project by the desired due date. The process by which we shorten the duration of a project in the cheapest manner possible is called project crashing.

Crashing
Shortening activity time in a network to reduce time on the critical path so total completion time is reduced.

CPM is a technique in which each activity has a *normal* or *standard* time that we use in our computations. Associated with this normal time is the *normal* cost of the activity. However, another time in project management is the *crash time*, which is defined as the shortest duration required to complete an activity. Associated with this crash time is the *crash cost* of the activity. Usually, we can shorten an activity by adding extra resources (e.g., equipment, people) to it. Hence, it is logical for the crash cost of an activity to be higher than its normal cost.

The amount by which an activity can be shortened (i.e., the difference between its normal time and crash time) depends on the activity in question. We may not be able to shorten some activities at all. For example, if a casting needs to be heat-treated in the furnace for 48 hours, adding more resources does not help shorten the time. In contrast, we may be able to shorten some activities significantly (e.g., frame a house in 3 days instead of 10 days by using three times as many workers).

Likewise, the cost of crashing (or shortening) an activity depends on the nature of the activity. Managers are usually interested in speeding up a project at the least additional cost. Hence, when choosing which activities to crash, and by how much, we need to ensure the following:

- The amount by which an activity is crashed is, in fact, permissible
- Taken together, the shortened activity durations will enable us to finish the project by the due date
- The total cost of crashing is as small as possible

LO6 *Crash* a project

Crashing a project involves four steps:

STEP 1: Compute the crash cost per week (or other time period) for each activity in the network. If crash costs are linear over time, the following formula can be used:

$$\text{Crash cost per period} = \frac{(\text{Crash cost} - \text{Normal cost})}{(\text{Normal time} - \text{Crash time})} \qquad (11)$$

STEP 2: Using the current activity times, find the critical path(s) in the project network. Identify the critical activities.

STEP 3: If there is only one critical path, then select the activity on this critical path that (a) can still be crashed and (b) has the smallest crash cost per period. Crash this activity by one period.

If there is more than one critical path, then select one activity from each critical path such that (a) each selected activity can still be crashed and (b) the total crash cost per period of *all* selected activities is the smallest. Crash each activity by one period. Note that the same activity may be common to more than one critical path.

STEP 4: Update all activity times. If the desired due date has been reached, stop. If not, return to Step 2.

We illustrate project crashing in Example 12.

Example 12

PROJECT CRASHING TO MEET A DEADLINE AT MILWAUKEE PAPER

Suppose the plant manager at Milwaukee Paper Manufacturing has been given only 13 weeks (instead of 16 weeks) to install the new pollution control equipment. As you recall, the length of Julie Ann Williams's critical path was 15 weeks, but she must now complete the project in 13 weeks.

APPROACH ▶ Williams needs to determine which activities to crash, and by how much, to meet this 13-week due date. Naturally, Williams is interested in speeding up the project by 2 weeks, at the least additional cost.

SOLUTION ▶ The company's normal and crash times, and normal and crash costs, are shown in Table 5. Note, for example, that activity B's normal time is 3 weeks (the estimate used in computing the critical path), and its crash time is 1 week. This means that activity B can be shortened by up to 2 weeks if extra resources are provided. The cost of these additional resources is $4,000 (= difference between the crash cost of $34,000 and the normal cost of $30,000). If we assume that the crashing cost is linear over time (i.e., the cost is the same each week), activity B's crash cost per week is $2,000 (= $4,000/2).

TABLE 5 **Normal and Crash Data for Milwaukee Paper Manufacturing**

	TIME (WEEKS)		*COST ($)*			
ACTIVITY	NORMAL	CRASH	NORMAL	CRASH	CRASH COST PER WEEK ($)	CRITICAL PATH?
A	2	1	22,000	22,750	750	Yes
B	3	1	30,000	34,000	2,000	No
C	2	1	26,000	27,000	1,000	Yes
D	4	3	48,000	49,000	1,000	No
E	4	2	56,000	58,000	1,000	Yes
F	3	2	30,000	30,500	500	No
G	5	2	80,000	84,500	1,500	Yes
H	2	1	16,000	19,000	3,000	Yes

This calculation for Activity B is shown in Figure 15. Crash costs for all other activities can be computed in a similar fashion.

Figure 15

Crash and Normal Times and Costs for Activity B

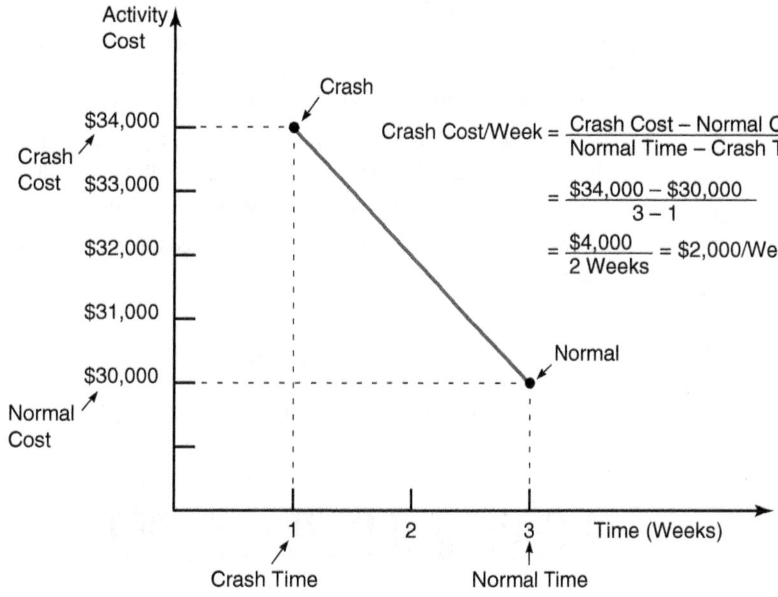

Steps 2, 3, and 4 can now be applied to reduce Milwaukee Paper's project completion time at a minimum cost. We show the project network for Milwaukee Paper again in Figure 16.

Figure 16

Critical Path and Slack Times for Milwaukee Paper

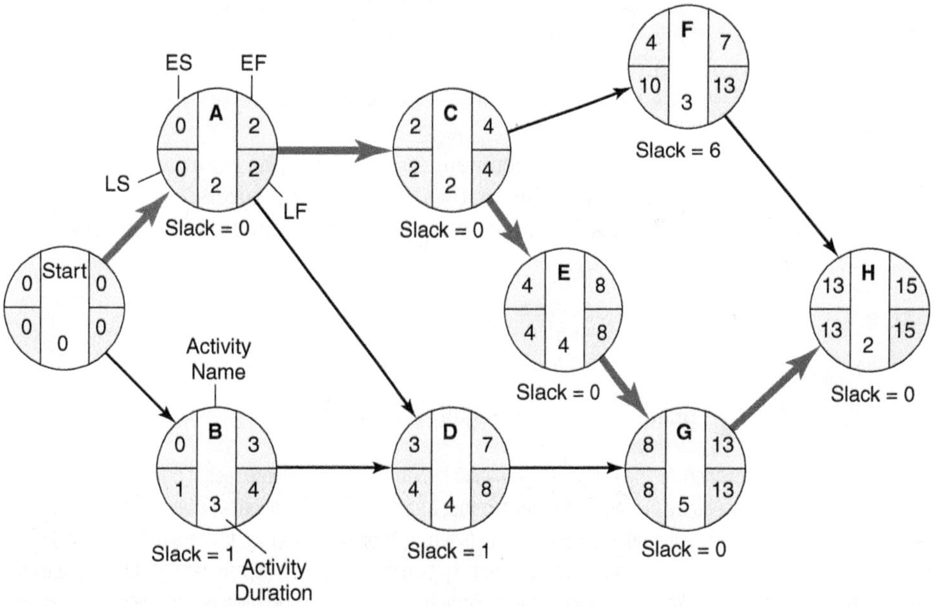

The current critical path (using normal times) is Start–A–C–E–G–H, in which Start is just a dummy starting activity. Of these critical activities, activity A has the lowest crash cost per week of $750. Julie Ann Williams should therefore crash activity A by 1 week to reduce the project completion time to 14 weeks. The cost is an additional $750. Note that activity A cannot be crashed any further, since it has reached its crash limit of 1 week.

At this stage, the original path Start–A–C–E–G–H remains critical with a completion time of 14 weeks. However, a new path Start–B–D–G–H is also critical now, with a completion time of 14 weeks. Hence, any further crashing must be done to both critical paths.

On each of these critical paths, we need to identify one activity that can still be crashed. We also want the total cost of crashing an activity on each path to be the smallest. We might be tempted to simply pick the activities with the smallest crash cost per period in each path. If we did this, we would select activity C from the first path and activity D from the second path. The total crash cost would then be $2,000 (= $1,000 + $1,000).

But we spot that activity G is common to both paths. That is, by crashing activity G, we will simultaneously reduce the completion time of both paths. Even though the $1,500 crash cost for activity G is higher than that for activities C and D, we would still prefer crashing G, since the total crashing cost will now be only $1,500 (compared with the $2,000 if we crash C and D).

INSIGHT ▶ To crash the project down to 13 weeks, Williams should crash activity A by 1 week and activity G by 1 week. The total additional cost will be $2,250 (= $750 + $1,500). This is important because many contracts for projects include bonuses or penalties for early or late finishes.

LEARNING EXERCISE ▶ Say the crash cost for activity B is $31,000 instead of $34,000. How does this change the answer? [Answer: no change.]

RELATED PROBLEMS ▶ 16, 18, 19, 20, 25

EXCEL OM Data File **Ch3Ex12.xls** can be found at **www.pearsonhighered.com/heizer**.

A Critique of PERT and CPM

As a critique of our discussions of PERT, here are some of its features about which operations managers need to be aware:

Advantages

1. Especially useful when scheduling and controlling large projects.
2. Straightforward concept and not mathematically complex.
3. Graphical networks help highlight relationships among project activities.
4. Critical path and slack time analyses help pinpoint activities that need to be closely watched.
5. Project documentation and graphs point out who is responsible for various activities.
6. Applicable to a wide variety of projects.
7. Useful in monitoring not only schedules but costs as well.

OM in Action — Rebuilding the Pentagon After 9/11

On September 11, 2001, American Airlines Flight 77 slammed into the Pentagon. The world was shocked by this and the other terrorist attacks on the Twin Towers in New York City. One hundred and twenty-five people died when a large portion of the Pentagon was severely damaged. Among the first to react were construction workers renovating another portion of the Pentagon. Their heroism saved lives and eased suffering. Within hours of the disaster, heavy equipment began arriving on the site, accompanied by hundreds of volunteer construction workers driven by patriotism and pride.

Just four days after the attack, Walker Evey, named program manager for "Project Phoenix," promised to rebuild the damaged portions of the Pentagon "faster than anyone has a right to expect . . . and to have people back in the damaged portion of the building, right where the plane hit, by September 11, 2002."

Preliminary construction reports estimated it would take 3 to 4 years and $750 million to rebuild. By directing the project with teamwork, handshake contracts, creativity, and ingenuity—not to mention emotional 20-hour days 6 to 7 days a week—Evey's Project Phoenix met its psychological and physical goal. In less than 11 months, and for only $501 million, workers demolished and rebuilt the damaged sections—400,000 square feet of structure, 2 million square feet of offices, 50,000 tons of debris—using 1,000 construction workers from 80 companies. By September 9, 2002, more than 600 military and civilian personnel were sitting at their desks in rebuilt Pentagon offices.

Mai/Mai/Getty Images/Time Life Pictures

Outside, the blackened gash is long gone. Instead, some 4,000 pieces of limestone—mined from the same Indiana vein that the Pentagon's original stone came from 65 years ago—have been placed on the building's façade. For this impressive accomplishment, the Pentagon and Walker Evey were nominated for the Project Management Institute's Project of the Year Award.

Sources: MIT Sloan Management Review (March 23, 2011); *Knight-Ridder Tribune Business News* (February 1, 2004); *U.S. News & World Report* (September 16, 2002).

Limitations

1. Project activities have to be clearly defined, independent, and stable in their relationships.
2. Precedence relationships must be specified and networked together.
3. Time estimates tend to be subjective and are subject to fudging by managers who fear the dangers of being overly optimistic or not pessimistic enough.
4. There is the inherent danger of placing too much emphasis on the longest, or critical, path. Near-critical paths need to be monitored closely as well.

Using Microsoft Project to Manage Projects

The approaches discussed so far are effective for managing small projects. However, for large or complex projects, specialized project management software is much preferred. In this section, we provide a brief introduction to the most popular example of such specialized software, Microsoft Project. A time-limited version of Microsoft Project may be requested with this text.

Microsoft Project is extremely useful in drawing project networks, identifying the project schedule, and managing project costs and other resources.

Milwaukee Paper Co. Activities

ACTIVITY	TIME (WKS)	PREDECESSORS
A	2	—
B	3	—
C	2	A
D	4	A, B
E	4	C
F	3	C
G	5	D, E
H	2	F, G

Entering Data Let us again consider the Milwaukee Paper Manufacturing project. Recall that this project has eight activities (repeated in the margin). The first step is to define the activities and their precedence relationships. To do so, we select **File|New** to open a blank project. We type the project start date (as July 1), then enter all activity information (see Program 1). For each activity (or task, as Microsoft Project calls it), we fill in the name and duration. The description of the activity is also placed in the ***Task Name*** column in Program 1. As we enter activities and durations, the software automatically inserts start and finish dates.

The next step is to define precedence relationships between these activities. To do so, we enter the relevant activity numbers (e.g., 1, 2) in the ***Predecessors*** column.

Viewing the Project Schedule When all links have been defined, the complete project schedule can be viewed as a Gantt chart. We can also select **View|Network Diagram** to view the schedule as a project network (shown in Program 2). The critical path is shown in red on the

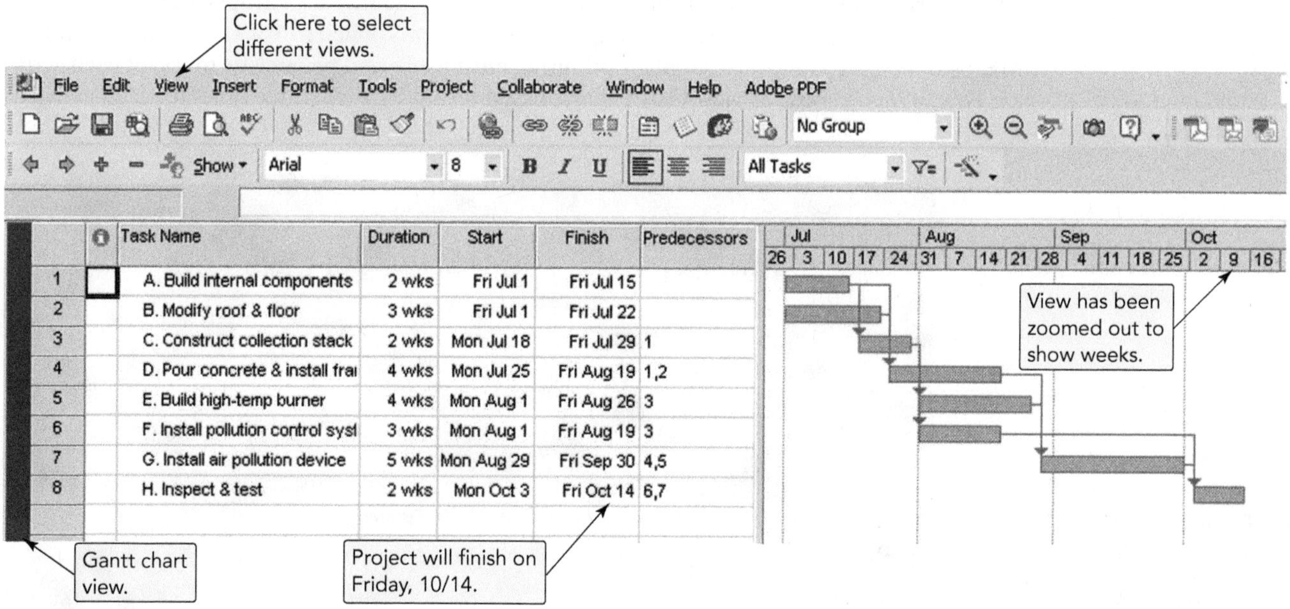

Program 1

Gantt Chart in Microsoft Project for Milwaukee Paper Manufacturing

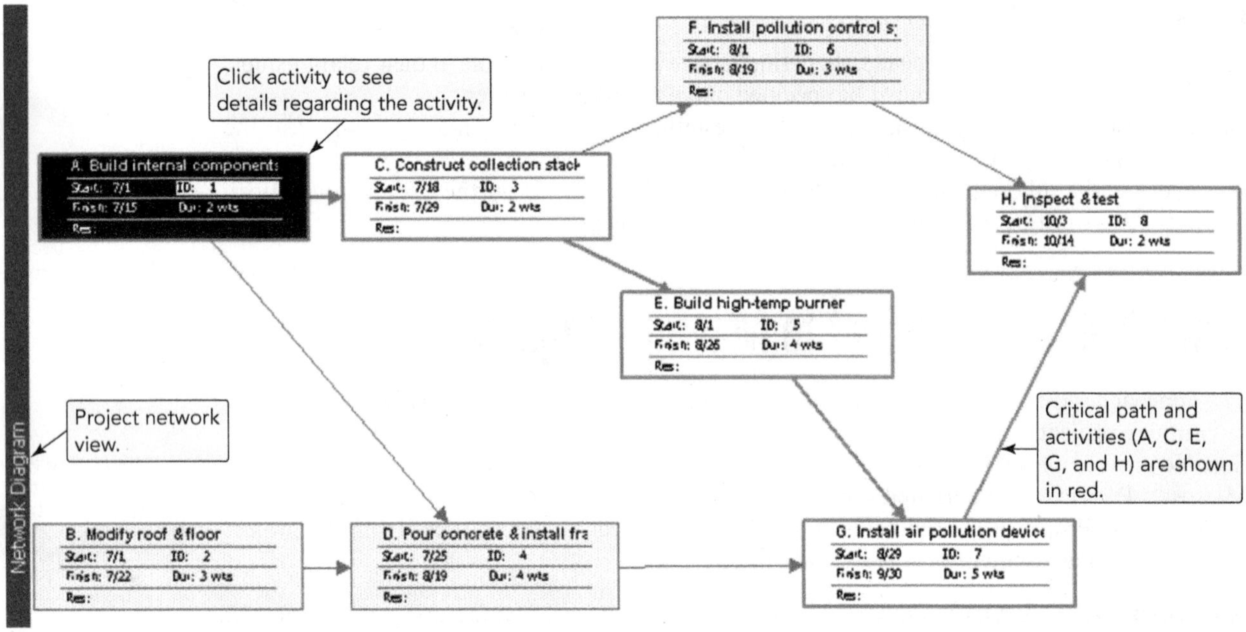

Program 2

Project Network in Microsoft Project for Milwaukee Paper Manufacturing

screen in the network diagram. We can click on any of the activities in the project network to view details of the activities. Likewise, we can easily add or remove activities from the project network. Each time we do so, Microsoft Project automatically updates all start dates, finish dates, and the critical path(s). If desired, we can manually change the layout of the network (e.g., reposition activities) by changing the options in Format|Layout.

STUDENT TIP ☆
Now that you understand the workings of PERT and CPM, you are ready to master this useful program. Knowing such software gives you an edge over others in the job market.

Programs 1 and 2 show that if Milwaukee Paper's project starts July 1, it can be finished on October 14. The start and finish dates for all activities are also clearly identified. Project management software, we see, can greatly simplify the scheduling procedures discussed earlier in this text.

PERT Analysis Microsoft Project does not perform the PERT probability calculations discussed in Examples 10 and 11. However, by clicking View|Toolbars|PERT Analysis, we can get Microsoft Project to allow us to enter optimistic, most likely, and pessimistic times for each activity. We can then choose to view Gantt charts based on any of these three times for each activity.

Using PERT/CPM, Taco Bell built and opened this fast-food restaurant in Compton, California, in just 2 days! Typically, 2 months are needed to accomplish such a task. Good project management means a faster revenue stream instead of money tied up in construction.

David Young-Wolff/PhotoEdit Inc.

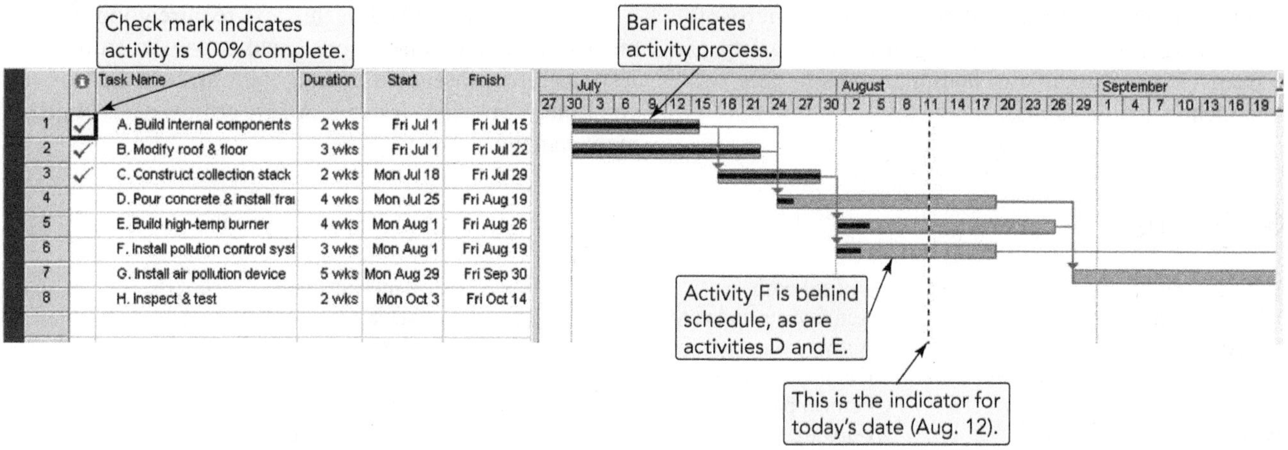

Program 3

Tracking Project Progress in Microsoft Project

Tracking the Time Status of a Project Perhaps the biggest advantage of using software to manage projects is that it can track the progress of the project. In this regard, Microsoft Project has many features available to track individual activities in terms of time, cost, resource usage, and so on.

An easy way to track the time progress of tasks is to enter the percent of work completed for each task. One way to do so is to double-click on any activity in the *Task Name* column in Program 1. A window is displayed that allows us to enter the percent of work completed for each task.

The table in the margin provides data regarding the percent of each of Milwaukee Paper's activities that are completed as of today. (Assume that today is Friday, August 12, i.e., the end of the sixth week of the project schedule.)

Pollution Project Percentage Completed on Aug. 12

ACTIVITY	COMPLETED
A	100
B	100
C	100
D	10
E	20
F	20
G	0
H	0

As shown in Program 3, the Gantt chart immediately reflects this updated information by drawing a thick line within each activity's bar. The length of this line is proportional to the percent of that activity's work that has been completed.

How do we know if we are on schedule? Notice that there is a vertical line shown on the Gantt chart corresponding to today's date. Microsoft Project will automatically move this line to correspond with the current date. If the project is on schedule, we should see all bars to the *left* of today's line indicate that they have been completed. For example, Program 3 shows that activities A, B, and C are on schedule. In contrast, activities D, E, and F appear to be behind schedule. These activities need to be investigated further to determine the reason for the delay. This type of easy *visual* information is what makes such software so useful in practice for project management.

We encourage you to load the copy of Microsoft Project that may be ordered with your text and to create a project network for work you are currently doing.

Summary

PERT, CPM, and other scheduling techniques have proven to be valuable tools in controlling large and complex projects. Managers use such techniques to segment projects into discrete activities (work breakdown structures), indentifying specific resources and time requirements for each. With PERT and CPM, managers can understand the status of each activity, including its earliest start, latest start, earliest finish, and latest finish (ES, LS, EF, and LF) times. By controlling the trade-off between ES and LS, managers can identify the activities that have slack and can address resource allocation, perhaps by smoothing resources. Effective project management also allows managers to focus on the activities that are critical to timely project completion. By understanding the project's critical path, they know where crashing makes the most economic sense.

Good project management also allows firms to efficiently create products and services for global markets and to respond effectively to global competition. Microsoft Project, illustrated in this text, is one of a wide variety of software packages available to help managers handle network modeling problems.

The models described in this text require good management practices, detailed work breakdown structures, clear responsibilities assigned to activities, and straightforward and timely reporting systems. All are critical parts of project management.

Key Terms

Project organization
Work breakdown structure (WBS)
Gantt charts
Program evaluation and review technique (PERT)
Critical path method (CPM)
Critical path
Activity-on-node (AON)
Activity-on-arrow (AOA)
Dummy activity
Critical path analysis
Forward pass
Backward pass
Slack time
Optimistic time
Pessimistic time
Most likely time
Crashing

Ethical Dilemma

Two examples of massively mismanaged projects are TAURUS and the "Big Dig." The first, formally called the London Stock Exchange Automation Project, cost $575 million before it was finally abandoned. Although most IT projects have a reputation for cost overruns, delays, and underperformance, TAURUS set a new standard.

But even TAURUS paled next to the biggest, most expensive public works project in U.S. history—Boston's 15-year-long Central Artery/Tunnel Project. Called the Big Dig, this was perhaps the poorest and most felonious case of project mismanagement in decades. From a starting $2 billion budget to a final price tag of $15 billion, the Big Dig cost more than the Panama Canal, Hoover Dam, or Interstate 95, the 1,919-mile highway between Maine and Florida.

Read about one of these two projects (or another of your choice) and explain why it faced such problems. How and why do project managers allow such massive endeavors to fall into such a state? What do you think are the causes?

Discussion Questions

1. Give an example of a situation in which project management is needed.
2. Explain the purpose of project organization.
3. What are the three phases involved in the management of a large project?
4. What are some of the questions that can be answered with PERT and CPM?
5. Define *work breakdown structure*. How is it used?
6. What is the use of Gantt charts in project management?
7. What is the difference between an activity-on-arrow (AOA) network and an activity-on-node (AON) network? Which is primarily used in this text?
8. What is the significance of the critical path?
9. What would a project manager have to do to crash an activity?
10. Describe how expected activity times and variances can be computed in a PERT network.
11. Define *earliest start, earliest finish, latest finish*, and *latest start* times.
12. Students are sometimes confused by the concept of critical path, and want to believe that it is the *shortest* path through a network. Convincingly explain why this is not so.
13. What are dummy activities? Why are they used in activity-on-arrow (AOA) project networks?
14. What are the three time estimates used with PERT?
15. Would a project manager ever consider crashing a noncritical activity in a project network? Explain convincingly.
16. How is the variance of the total project computed in PERT?
17. Describe the meaning of slack, and discuss how it can be determined.
18. How can we determine the probability that a project will be completed by a certain date? What assumptions are made in this computation?
19. Name some of the widely used project management software programs.

Using Software to Solve Project Management Problems

In addition to the Microsoft Project software illustrated earlier, both Excel OM and POM for Windows are available to readers of this text as project management tools.

USING EXCEL OM

Excel OM has a Project Scheduling module. Program 4 uses the data from the Milwaukee Paper Manufacturing example in this text (see Examples 4 and 5). The PERT/CPM analysis also handles activities with three time estimates.

Program 4

Excel OM's Use of Milwaukee Paper Manufacturing's Data from Examples 4 and 5

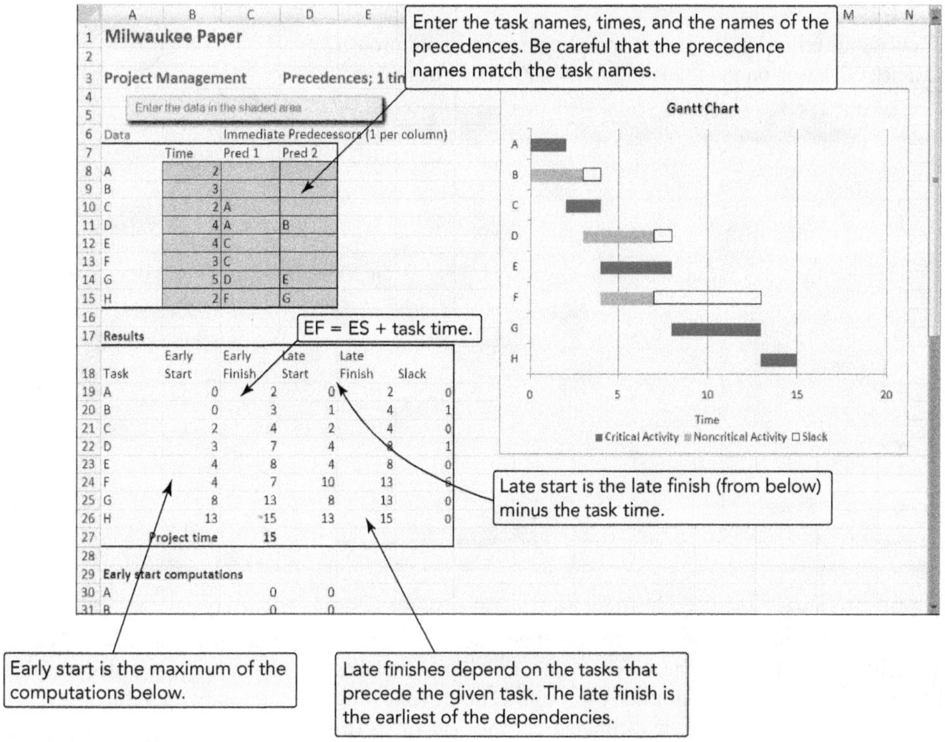
Enter the task names, times, and the names of the precedences. Be careful that the precedence names match the task names.
EF = ES + task time.
Late start is the late finish (from below) minus the task time.
Early start is the maximum of the computations below.
Late finishes depend on the tasks that precede the given task. The late finish is the earliest of the dependencies.
Milwaukee Paper
Project Management
Gantt Chart
Time
Critical Activity
Noncritical Activity
Slack

P USING POM FOR WINDOWS

POM for Window's Project Scheduling module can also find the expected project completion time for a CPM and PERT network with either one or three time estimates. POM for Windows also performs project crashing. For further details refer to Appendix: Using Excel OM and POM for Windows.

Solved Problems

Virtual Office Hours help is available at www.myomlab.com.

SOLVED PROBLEM 1

Construct an AON network based on the following:

ACTIVITY	IMMEDIATE PREDECESSOR(S)
A	—
B	—
C	—
D	A, B
E	C

SOLUTION

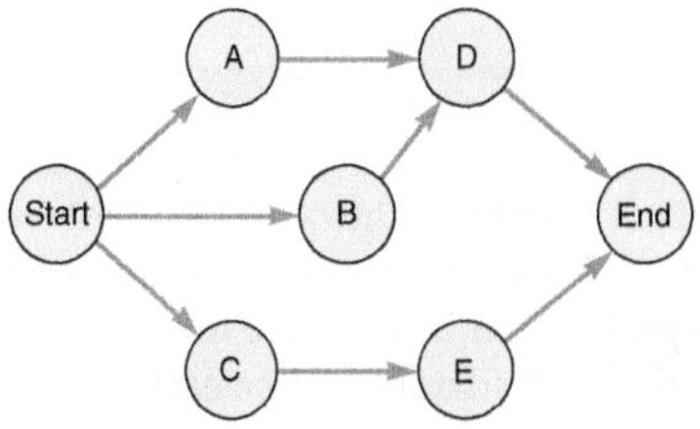
Start
A
B
C
D
E
End

SOLVED PROBLEM 2

Insert a dummy activity and event to correct the following AOA network:

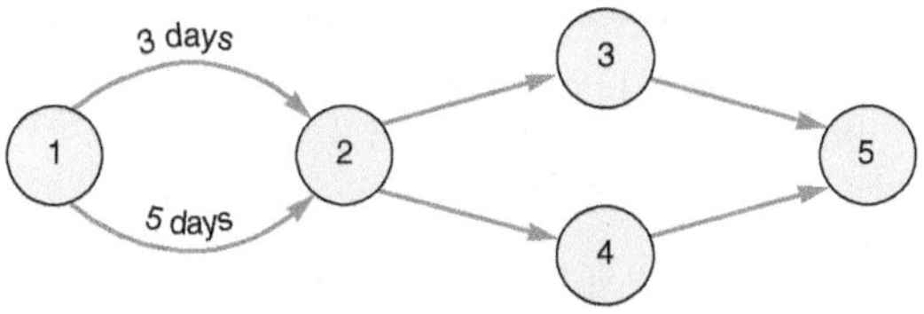
3 days
5 days
1
2
3
4
5

SOLUTION

Since we cannot have two activities starting and ending at the same node, we add the following dummy activity and dummy event to obtain the correct AOA network:

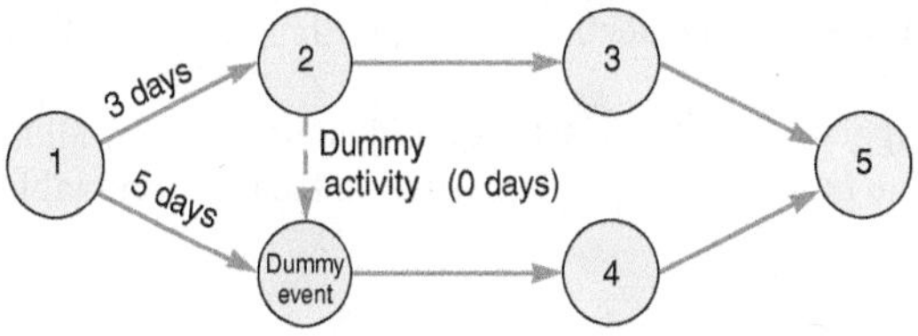
3 days
5 days
1
2
3
4
5
Dummy activity (0 days)
Dummy event

SOLVED PROBLEM 3

Calculate the critical path, project completion time T, and project variance σ_p^2, based on the following AON network information:

ACTIVITY	TIME	VARIANCE	ES	EF	LS	LF	SLACK
A	2	$\frac{2}{6}$	0	2	0	2	0
B	3	$\frac{2}{6}$	0	3	1	4	1
C	2	$\frac{4}{6}$	2	4	2	4	0
D	4	$\frac{4}{6}$	3	7	4	8	1
E	4	$\frac{2}{6}$	4	8	4	8	0
F	3	$\frac{1}{6}$	4	7	10	13	6
G	5	$\frac{1}{6}$	8	13	8	13	0

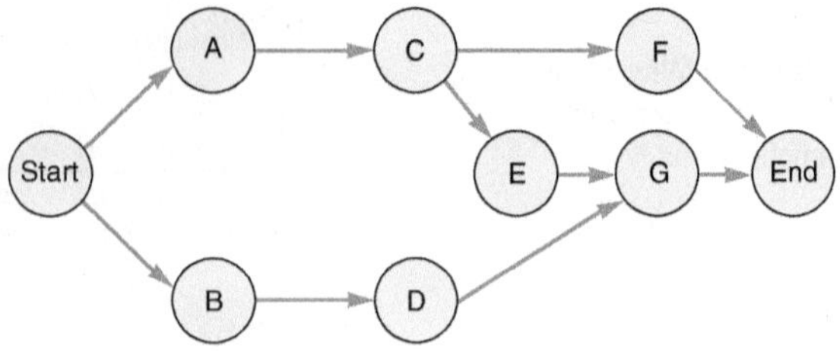

SOLUTION

We conclude that the critical path is Start–A–C–E–G–End:

$$\text{Total project time} = T = 2 + 2 + 4 + 5 = 13$$

and

$$\sigma_p^2 = \Sigma \text{ Variances on the critical path}$$
$$= \frac{2}{6} + \frac{4}{6} + \frac{2}{6} + \frac{1}{6} = \frac{9}{6} = 1.5$$

SOLVED PROBLEM 4

To complete the wing assembly for an experimental aircraft, Jim Gilbert has laid out the seven major activities involved. These activities have been labeled A through G in the following table, which also shows their estimated completion times (in weeks) and immediate predecessors. Determine the expected time and variance for each activity.

ACTIVITY	a	m	b	IMMEDIATE PREDECESSORS
A	1	2	3	—
B	2	3	4	—
C	4	5	6	A
D	8	9	10	B
E	2	5	8	C, D
F	4	5	6	D
G	1	2	3	E

SOLUTION

Expected times and variances can be computed using Equations (6) and (7) presented in this text. The results are summarized in the following table:

ACTIVITY	EXPECTED TIME (IN WEEKS)	VARIANCE
A	2	$\frac{1}{9}$
B	3	$\frac{1}{9}$
C	5	$\frac{1}{9}$
D	9	$\frac{1}{9}$
E	5	1
F	5	$\frac{1}{9}$
G	2	$\frac{1}{9}$

SOLVED PROBLEM 5

Referring to Solved Problem 4, now Jim Gilbert would like to determine the critical path for the entire wing assembly project as well as the expected completion time for the total project. In addition, he would like to determine the earliest and latest start and finish times for all activities.

SOLUTION

The AON network for Gilbert's project is shown in Figure 17. Note that this project has multiple activities (A and B) with no immediate predecessors, and multiple activities (F and G) with no successors. Hence, in addition to a unique starting activity (Start), we have included a unique finishing activity (End) for the project.

Figure 17 shows the earliest and latest times for all activities. The results are also summarized in the following table:

	ACTIVITY TIME				
ACTIVITY	ES	EF	LS	LF	SLACK
A	0	2	5	7	5
B	0	3	0	3	0
C	2	7	7	12	5
D	3	12	3	12	0
E	12	17	12	17	0
F	12	17	14	19	2
G	17	19	17	19	0

Expected project length = 19 weeks
Variance of the critical path = 1.333
Standard deviation of the critical path = 1.155 weeks

The activities along the critical path are B, D, E, and G. These activities have zero slack as shown in the table.

Figure 17

Critical Path for Solved Problem 5

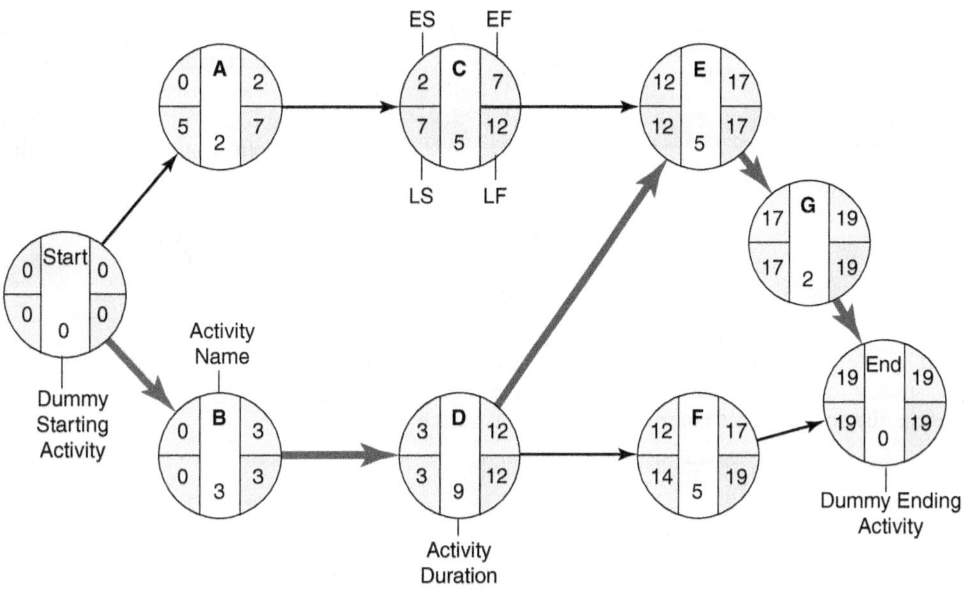

SOLVED PROBLEM 6

The following information has been computed from a project:

$$\text{Expected total project time} = T = 62 \text{ weeks}$$

$$\text{Project variance } (\sigma_p^2) = 81$$

What is the probability that the project will be completed 18 weeks *before* its expected completion date?

SOLUTION

The desired completion date is 18 weeks before the expected completion date, 62 weeks. The desired completion date is 44 (or 62–18) weeks:

$$\sigma_p = \sqrt{\text{Project variance}}$$

$$Z = \frac{\text{Due date} - \text{Expected completion date}}{\sigma_p}$$

$$= \frac{44 - 62}{9} = \frac{-18}{9} = -2.0$$

The normal curve appears as follows:

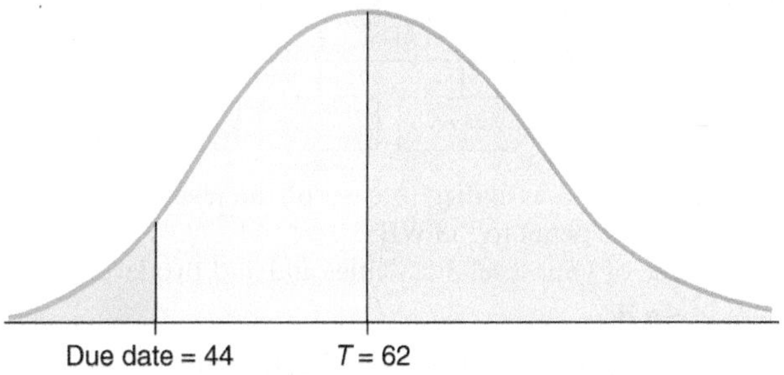

Because the normal curve is symmetrical and table values are calculated for positive values of Z, the area desired is equal to 1– (table value). For $Z = +2.0$ the area from the table is .97725. Thus, the area corresponding to a Z value of –2.0 is .02275 (or 1 – .97725). Hence, the probability of completing the project 18 weeks before the expected completion date is approximately .023, or 2.3%.

SOLVED PROBLEM 7

Determine the least cost of reducing the project completion date by 3 months based on the following information:

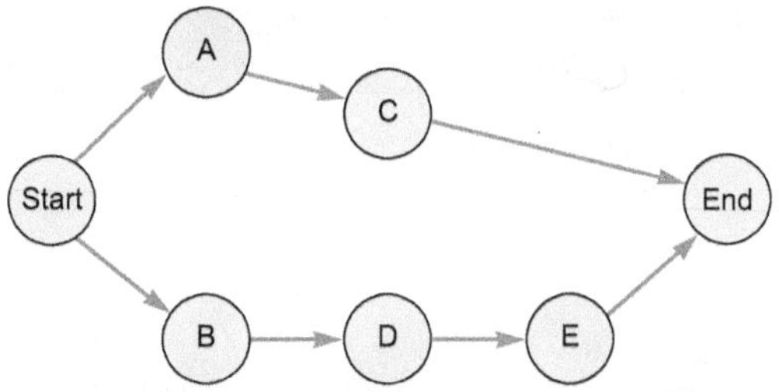

ACTIVITY	NORMAL TIME (MONTHS)	CRASH TIME (MONTHS)	NORMAL COST	CRASH COST
A	6	4	$2,000	$2,400
B	7	5	3,000	3,500
C	7	6	1,000	1,300
D	6	4	2,000	2,600
E	9	8	8,800	9,000

SOLUTION

The first step in this problem is to compute ES, EF, LS, LF, and slack for each activity.

ACTIVITY	ES	EF	LS	LF	SLACK
A	0	6	9	15	9
B	0	7	0	7	0
C	6	13	15	22	9
D	7	13	7	13	0
E	13	22	13	22	0

The critical path consists of activities B, D, and E.

(cont'd)

Next, crash cost/month must be computed for each activity:

ACTIVITY	NORMAL TIME–CRASH TIME	CRASH COST–NORMAL COST	CRASH COST/ MONTH	CRITICAL PATH?
A	2	$400	$200/month	No
B	2	500	250/month	Yes
C	1	300	300/month	No
D	2	600	300/month	Yes
E	1	200	200/month	Yes

Finally, we will select that activity on the critical path with the smallest crash cost/month. This is activity E. Thus, we can reduce the total project completion date by 1 month for an additional cost of $200. We still need to reduce the project completion date by 2 more months. This reduction can be achieved at least cost along the critical path by reducing activity B by 2 months for an additional cost of $500. Neither reduction has an effect on noncritical activities. This solution is summarized in the following table:

ACTIVITY	MONTHS REDUCED	COST
E	1	$200
B	2	500
		Total: $700

Problems

Note: Px means the problem may be solved with POM for Windows and/or Excel OM.

• **1** The work breakdown structure (WBS) for building a house (levels 1 and 2) is shown below:

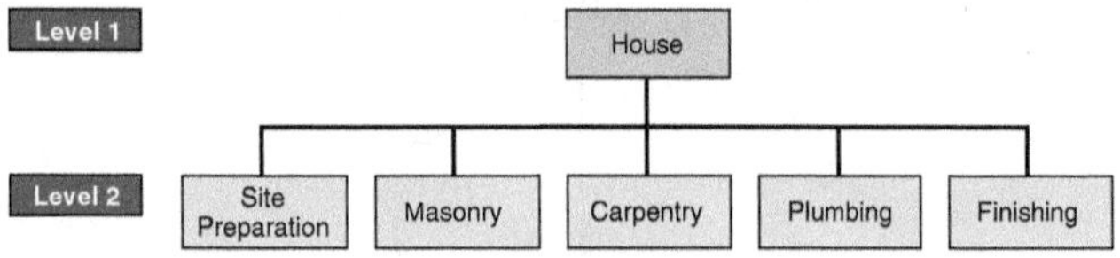

a) Add two level-3 activities to each of the level-2 activities to provide more detail to the WBS.
b) Select one of your level-3 activities and add two level-4 activities below it.

•• **2** Robert Day has decided to run for a seat as Congressman from the House of Representatives, District 34, in Connecticut. He views his 8-month campaign for office as a major project and wishes to create a work breakdown structure (WBS) to help control the detailed scheduling. So far, he has developed the following pieces of the WBS:

LEVEL	LEVEL ID NO.	ACTIVITY
1	1.0	Develop political campaign
2	1.1	Fund-raising plan
3	1.11	________
3	1.12	________
3	1.13	________
2	1.2	Develop a position on major issues
3	1.21	________
3	1.22	________
3	1.23	________
2	1.3	Staffing for campaign
3	1.31	________
3	1.32	________
3	1.33	________
3	1.34	________
2	1.4	Paperwork compliance for candidacy
3	1.41	________
3	1.42	________
2	1.5	Ethical plan/issues
3	1.51	________

Help Mr. Day by providing details where the blank lines appear. Are there any other major (level-2) activities to create? If so, add an ID no. 1.6 and insert them.

© Blend Images/Alamy

• **3** Draw the activity-on-node (AON) project network associated with the following activities for Carl Betterton's construction project. How long should it take Carl and his team to complete this project? What are the critical path activities?

ACTIVITY	IMMEDIATE PREDECESSOR(S)	TIME (DAYS)
A	—	3
B	A	4
C	A	6
D	B	6
E	B	4
F	C	4
G	D	6
H	E, F	8

• **4** Given the activities whose sequence is described by the following table, draw the appropriate activity-on-arrow (AOA) network diagram.

a) Which activities are on the critical path?
b) What is the length of the critical path?

ACTIVITY	IMMEDIATE PREDECESSOR(S)	TIME (DAYS)
A	—	5
B	A	2
C	A	4
D	B	5
E	B	5
F	C	5
G	E, F	2
H	D	3
I	G, H	5

• **5** Using AOA, diagram the network described below for Lillian Fok's construction project. Calculate its critical path. How long is the minimum duration of this network?

ACTIVITY	NODES	TIME (WEEKS)	ACTIVITY	NODES	TIME (WEEKS)
J	1–2	10	N	3–4	2
K	1–3	8	O	4–5	7
L	2–4	6	P	3–5	5
M	2–3	3			

•• **6** Stephen Hall is developing a program in supply chain management certification for managers. Hall has listed a number of activities that must be completed before a training program of this nature could be conducted. The activities, immediate predecessors, and times appear in the accompanying table:

ACTIVITY	IMMEDIATE PREDECESSOR(S)	TIME (DAYS)
A	—	2
B	—	5
C	—	1
D	B	10
E	A, D	3
F	C	6
G	E, F	8

a) Develop an AON network for this problem.
b) What is the critical path?
c) What is the total project completion time?
d) What is the slack time for each individual activity? Px

•• **7** Task time estimates for the modification of an assembly line at Jim Goodale's Carbondale, Illinois, factory are as follows:

ACTIVITY	TIME (IN HOURS)	IMMEDIATE PREDECESSORS
A	6.0	—
B	7.2	—
C	5.0	A
D	6.0	B, C
E	4.5	B, C
F	7.7	D
G	4.0	E, F

a) Draw the project network using AON.
b) Identify the critical path.
c) What is the expected project length?
d) Draw a Gantt chart for the project. Px

•• **8** The City Commission of Nashville has decided to build a botanical garden and picnic area in the heart of the city for the recreation of its citizens. The precedence table for all the activities required to construct this area successfully is given. Draw the Gantt chart for the whole construction activity.

CODE	ACTIVITY	DESCRIPTION	TIME (IN HOURS)	IMMEDIATE PREDECESSOR(S)
A	Planning	Find location; determine resource requirements	20	None
B	Purchasing	Requisition of lumber and sand	60	Planning
C	Excavation	Dig and grade	100	Planning
D	Sawing	Saw lumber into appropriate sizes	30	Purchasing
E	Placement	Position lumber in correct locations	20	Sawing, excavation
F	Assembly	Nail lumber together	10	Placement
G	Infill	Put sand in and under the equipment	20	Assembly
H	Outfill	Put dirt around the equipment	10	Assembly
I	Decoration	Put grass all over the garden, landscape, paint	30	Infill, outfill

•• **9** Refer to the table in Problem 8.
a) Draw the AON network for the construction activity.
b) Draw the AOA network for the construction activity.

• **10** The activities needed to build a prototype laser scanning machine at Dave Fletcher Corp. are listed in the following table. Construct an AON network for these activities.

ACTIVITY	IMMEDIATE PREDECESSOR(S)	ACTIVITY	IMMEDIATE PREDECESSOR(S)
A	—	E	B
B	—	F	B
C	A	G	C, E
D	A	H	D, F

• **11** Dave Fletcher (see Problem 10) was able to determine the activity times for constructing his laser scanning machine. Fletcher would like to determine ES, EF, LS, LF, and slack for each activity. The total project completion time and the critical path should also be determined. Here are the activity times:

ACTIVITY	TIME (WEEKS)	ACTIVITY	TIME (WEEKS)
A	6	E	4
B	7	F	6
C	3	G	10
D	2	H	7

• **12** The activities described by the following table are given for the Howard Corporation in Kansas:

ACTIVITY	IMMEDIATE PREDECESSOR(S)	TIME
A	—	9
B	A	7
C	A	3
D	B	6
E	B	9
F	C	4
G	E, F	6
H	D	5
I	G, H	3

a) Draw the appropriate AON PERT diagram for J.C. Howard's management team.
b) Find the critical path.
c) What is the project completion time? PX

• **13** A renovation of the gift shop at Orlando Amway Center has six activities (in hours). For the following estimates of a, m, and b, calculate the expected time and the standard deviation for each activity:

ACTIVITY	a	m	b
A	11	15	19
B	27	31	41
C	18	18	18
D	8	13	19
E	17	18	20
F	16	19	22

PX

•• **14** Kelle Carpet and Trim installs carpet in commercial offices. Peter Kelle has been very concerned with the amount of time it took to complete several recent jobs. Some of his workers are very unreliable. A list of activities and their optimistic completion time, the most likely completion time, and the pessimistic completion time (all in days) for a new contract are given in the following table:

ACTIVITY	TIME (DAYS) a	m	b	IMMEDIATE PREDECESSOR(S)
A	3	6	8	—
B	2	4	4	—
C	1	2	3	—
D	6	7	8	C
E	2	4	6	B, D
F	6	10	14	A, E
G	1	2	4	A, E
H	3	6	9	F
I	10	11	12	G
J	14	16	20	C
K	2	8	10	H, I

a) Determine the expected completion time and variance for each activity.
b) Determine the total project completion time and the critical path for the project.
c) Determine ES, EF, LS, LF, and slack for each activity.
d) What is the probability that Kelle Carpet and Trim will finish the project in 40 days or less? PX

•• **15** The following is a table of activities associated with a project at Rafay Ishfaq's software firm in Chicago, their durations, and what activities each must precede:

ACTIVITY	DURATION (WEEKS)	PRECEDES
A (start)	1	B, C
B	1	E
C	4	F
E	2	F
F (end)	2	—

a) Draw an AON diagram of the project, including activity durations.
b) Define the critical path, listing all critical activities in chronological order.
c) What is the project duration (in weeks)?
d) What is the slack (in weeks) associated with any and all noncritical paths through the project?

•• **16** Assume that the activities in Problem 15 have the following costs to shorten: A, \$300/week; B, \$100/week; C, \$200/week; E, \$100/week; and F, \$400/week. Assume also that you can crash an activity down to 0 weeks in duration and that every week you can shorten the project is worth \$250 to you. What activities would you crash? What is the total crashing cost?

••• **17** Bill Fennema, president of Fennema Hospitality, has developed the tasks, durations, and predecessor relationships in the following table for building new motels. Draw the AON network and answer the questions that follow.

ACTIVITY	IMMEDIATE PREDECESSOR(S)	TIME ESTIMATES (IN WEEKS) OPTIMISTIC	MOST LIKELY	PESSIMISTIC
A	—	4	8	10
B	A	2	8	24
C	A	8	12	16
D	A	4	6	10
E	B	1	2	3
F	E, C	6	8	20
G	E, C	2	3	4
H	F	2	2	2
I	F	6	6	6
J	D, G, H	4	6	12
K	I, J	2	2	3

a) What is the expected (estimated) time for activity C?
b) What is the variance for activity C?
c) Based on the calculation of estimated times, what is the critical path?
d) What is the estimated time of the critical path?
e) What is the activity variance along the critical path?
f) What is the probability of completion of the project before week 36? PX

••• **18** What is the minimum cost of crashing the following project that Roger Solano manages at Slippery Rock University by 4 days?

ACTIVITY	NORMAL TIME (DAYS)	CRASH TIME (DAYS)	NORMAL COST	CRASH COST	IMMEDIATE PREDECESSOR(S)
A	6	5	$ 900	$1,000	—
B	8	6	300	400	—
C	4	3	500	600	—
D	5	3	900	1,200	A
E	8	5	1,000	1,600	C

PX

•• **19** Three activities are candidates for crashing on a project network for a large computer installation (all are, of course, critical). Activity details are in the following table:

ACTIVITY	PREDECESSOR	NORMAL TIME	NORMAL COST	CRASH TIME	CRASH COST
A	—	7 days	$6,000	6 days	$6,600
B	A	4 days	1,200	2 days	3,000
C	B	11 days	4,000	9 days	6,000

a) What action would you take to reduce the critical path by 1 day?
b) Assuming no other paths become critical, what action would you take to reduce the critical path one additional day?
c) What is the total cost of the 2-day reduction? PX

••• **20** Development of Version 2.0 of a particular accounting software product is being considered by Jose Noguera's technology firm in Baton Rouge. The activities necessary for the completion of this project are listed in the following table:

ACTIVITY	NORMAL TIME (WEEKS)	CRASH TIME (WEEKS)	NORMAL COST	CRASH COST	IMMEDIATE PREDECESSOR(S)
A	4	3	$2,000	$2,600	—
B	2	1	2,200	2,800	—
C	3	3	500	500	—
D	8	4	2,300	2,600	A
E	6	3	900	1,200	B
F	3	2	3,000	4,200	C
G	4	2	1,400	2,000	D, E

a) What is the project completion date?
b) What is the total cost required for completing this project on normal time?
c) If you wish to reduce the time required to complete this project by 1 week, which activity should be crashed, and how much will this increase the total cost?
d) What is the maximum time that can be crashed? How much would costs increase? PX

••• **21** The estimated times and immediate predecessors for the activities in a project at Howard Umrah's retinal scanning company are given in the following table. Assume that the activity times are independent.

ACTIVITY	IMMEDIATE PREDECESSOR	TIME (WEEKS) *a*	*m*	*b*
A	—	9	10	11
B	—	4	10	16
C	A	9	10	11
D	B	5	8	11

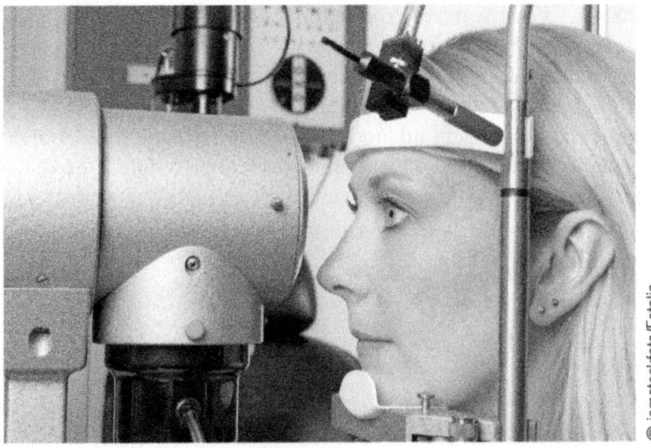
© jamstockfoto/Fotolia

a) Calculate the expected time and variance for each activity.
b) What is the expected completion time of the critical path? What is the expected completion time of the other path in the network?
c) What is the variance of the critical path? What is the variance of the other path in the network?
d) If the time to complete path A–C is normally distributed, what is the probability that this path will be finished in 22 weeks or less?
e) If the time to complete path B–D is normally distributed, what is the probability that this path will be finished in 22 weeks or less?
f) Explain why the probability that the *critical path* will be finished in 22 weeks or less is not necessarily the probability that the *project* will be finished in 22 weeks or less. PX

••• **22** Rich Cole Control Devices, Inc., produces custom-built relay devices for auto makers. The most recent project undertaken by Cole requires 14 different activities. Cole's managers would like to determine the total project completion time (in days) and those activities that lie along the critical path. The appropriate data are shown in the following table.
a) What is the probability of being done in 53 days?
b) What date results in a 99% probability of completion?

ACTIVITY	IMMEDIATE PREDECESSOR(S)	OPTIMISTIC TIME	MOST LIKELY TIME	PESSIMISTIC TIME
A	—	4	6	7
B	—	1	2	3
C	A	6	6	6
D	A	5	8	11
E	B, C	1	9	18
F	D	2	3	6
G	D	1	7	8
H	E, F	4	4	6
I	G, H	1	6	8
J	I	2	5	7
K	I	8	9	11
L	J	2	4	6
M	K	1	2	3
N	L, M	6	8	10

PX

••• **23** Four Squares Productions, a firm hired to coordinate the release of the movie *Pirates of the Caribbean: On Stranger Tides* (starring Johnny Depp), identified 16 activities to be completed before the release of the film.

a) How many weeks in advance of the film release should Four Squares have started its marketing campaign? What is the critical path? The tasks (in time units of weeks) are as follows:

ACTIVITY	IMMEDIATE PREDECESSORS	OPTIMISTIC TIME	MOST LIKELY TIME	PESSIMISTIC TIME
A	—	1	2	4
B	—	3	3.5	4
C	—	10	12	13
D	—	4	5	7
E	—	2	4	5
F	A	6	7	8
G	B	2	4	5.5
H	C	5	7.7	9
I	C	9.9	10	12
J	C	2	4	5
K	D	2	4	6
L	E	2	4	6
M	F, G, H	5	6	6.5
N	J, K, L	1	1.1	2
O	I, M	5	7	8
P	N	5	7	9

b) If activities I and J were not necessary, what impact would this have on the critical path and the number of weeks needed to complete the marketing campaign?

Tracy Whiteside/Shutterstock

•• **24** Using PERT, Adam Munson was able to determine that the expected project completion time for the construction of a pleasure yacht is 21 months, and the project variance is 4.

a) What is the probability that the project will be completed in 17 months?
b) What is the probability that the project will be completed in 20 months?
c) What is the probability that the project will be completed in 23 months?
d) What is the probability that the project will be completed in 25 months?
e) What is the due date that yields a 95% chance of completion?

••• **25** Clark Products makes pizza ovens for commercial use. Michael Clark, CEO, is contemplating producing smaller ovens for use in high school and college kitchens. The activities necessary to build an experimental model and related data are given in the following table:

ACTIVITY	NORMAL TIME (WEEKS)	CRASH TIME (WEEKS)	NORMAL COST ($)	CRASH COST ($)	IMMEDIATE PREDECESSOR(S)
A	3	2	1,000	1,600	—
B	2	1	2,000	2,700	—
C	1	1	300	300	—
D	7	3	1,300	1,600	A
E	6	3	850	1,000	B
F	2	1	4,000	5,000	C
G	4	2	1,500	2,000	D, E

a) What is the project completion date?
b) Crash this project to 10 weeks at the least cost.
c) Crash this project to 7 weeks (which is the maximum it can be crashed) at the least cost.

••• **26** The Tesla 6 is a new custom-designed sports car. An analysis of the task of building the Tesla 6 reveals the following list of relevant activities, their immediate predecessors, and their duration:[2]

JOB LETTER	DESCRIPTION	IMMEDIATE PREDECESSOR(S)	NORMAL TIME (DAYS)
A	Start	—	0
B	Design	A	8
C	Order special accessories	B	0.1
D	Build frame	B	1
E	Build doors	B	1
F	Attach axles, wheels, gas tank	D	1
G	Build body shell	B	2
H	Build transmission and drivetrain	B	3
I	Fit doors to body shell	G, E	1
J	Build engine	B	4
K	Bench-test engine	J	2
L	Assemble chassis	F, H, K	1
M	Road-test chassis	L	0.5
N	Paint body	I	2
O	Install wiring	N	1
P	Install interior	N	1.5
Q	Accept delivery of special accessories	C	5
R	Mount body and accessories on chassis	M, O, P, Q	1
S	Road test car	R	0.5
T	Attach exterior trim	S	1
U	Finish	T	0

[2]*Source:* Adapted from James A. D. Stoner, *Management*, 6th ed. (Upper Saddle River, NJ: Pearson 1995).

a) Draw a network diagram for the project.
b) Mark the critical path and state its length.
c) If the Tesla 6 had to be completed 2 days earlier, would it help to:
   i) Buy preassembled transmissions and drivetrains?
   ii) Install robots to halve engine-building time?
   iii) Speed delivery of special accessories by 3 days?
d) How might resources be borrowed from activities on the non-critical path to speed activities on the critical path? Px

Refer to MyOMLab for these additional homework problems: 27–33

CASE STUDIES

Southwestern University: (A)

Southwestern University (SWU), a large state college in Stephenville, Texas, 30 miles southwest of the Dallas/Fort Worth metroplex, enrolls close to 20,000 students. In a typical town–gown relationship, the school is a dominant force in the small city, with more students during fall and spring than permanent residents.

A longtime football powerhouse, SWU is a member of the Big Eleven conference and is usually in the top 20 in college football rankings. To bolster its chances of reaching the elusive and long-desired number-one ranking, in 2006, SWU hired the legendary Phil Flamm as its head coach.

One of Flamm's demands on joining SWU had been a new stadium. With attendance increasing, SWU administrators began to face the issue head-on. After 6 months of study, much political arm wrestling, and some serious financial analysis, Dr. Joel Wisner, president of Southwestern University, had reached a decision to expand the capacity at its on-campus stadium.

Adding thousands of seats, including dozens of luxury skyboxes, would not please everyone. The influential Flamm had argued the need for a first-class stadium, one with built-in dormitory rooms for his players and a palatial office appropriate for the coach of a future NCAA champion team. But the decision was made, and *everyone*, including the coach, would learn to live with it.

The job now was to get construction going immediately after the 2012 season ended. This would allow exactly 270 days until the 2013 season opening game. The contractor, Hill Construction (Bob Hill being an alumnus, of course), signed his contract. Bob Hill looked at the tasks his engineers had outlined and looked President Wisner in the eye. "I guarantee the team will be able to take the field on schedule next year," he said with a sense of confidence. "I sure hope so," replied Wisner. "The contract penalty of $10,000 per day for running late is nothing compared to what Coach Flamm will do to you if our opening game with Penn State is delayed or canceled." Hill, sweating slightly, did not need to respond. In football-crazy Texas, Hill Construction would be *mud* if the 270-day target was missed.

Back in his office, Hill again reviewed the data (see Table 6) and noted that optimistic time estimates can be used as crash times. He then gathered his foremen. "Folks, if we're not 75% sure we'll finish this stadium in less than 270 days, I want this project crashed! Give me the cost figures for a target date of 250 days—also for 240 days. I want to be *early*, not just on time!"

Discussion Questions

1. Develop a network drawing for Hill Construction and determine the critical path. How long is the project expected to take?
2. What is the probability of finishing in 270 days?
3. If it is necessary to crash to 250 or 240 days, how would Hill do so, and at what costs? As noted in the case, assume that optimistic time estimates can be used as crash times.

TABLE 6 Southwestern University Project

			TIME ESTIMATES (DAYS)			
ACTIVITY	DESCRIPTION	PREDECESSOR(S)	OPTIMISTIC	MOST LIKELY	PESSIMISTIC	CRASH COST/DAY
A	Bonding, insurance, tax structuring	—	20	30	40	$1,500
B	Foundation, concrete footings for boxes	A	20	65	80	3,500
C	Upgrading skybox stadium seating	A	50	60	100	4,000
D	Upgrading walkways, stairwells, elevators	C	30	50	100	1,900
E	Interior wiring, lathes	B	25	30	35	9,500
F	Inspection approvals	E	0.1	0.1	0.1	0
G	Plumbing	D, F	25	30	35	2,500
H	Painting	G	10	20	30	2,000
I	Hardware/AC/metal workings	H	20	25	60	2,000
J	Tile/carpet/windows	H	8	10	12	6,000
K	Inspection	J	0.1	0.1	0.1	0
L	Final detail work/cleanup	I, K	20	25	60	4,500

Project Management at Arnold Palmer Hospital

Video Case

The equivalent of a new kindergarten class is born every day at Orlando's Arnold Palmer Hospital. With more than 13,000 births in the mid-2000s in a hospital that was designed 15 years earlier for a capacity of 6,500 births a year, the newborn intensive care unit was stretched to the limit. Moreover, with continuing strong population growth in central Florida, the hospital was often full. It was clear that new facilities were needed. After much analysis, forecasting, and discussion, the management team decided to build a new 273-bed building across the street from the existing hospital. But the facility had to be built in accordance with the hospital's Guiding Principles and its uniqueness as a health center dedicated to the specialized needs of women and infants. Those Guiding Principles are: *Family-centered focus, a healing environment where privacy and dignity are respected, sanctuary of caring that includes warm, serene surroundings with natural lighting, sincere and dedicated staff providing the highest quality care, and patient-centered flow and function.*

The vice president of business development, Karl Hodges, wanted a hospital that was designed from the inside out by the people who understood the Guiding Principles, who knew most about the current system, and who were going to use the new system, namely, the doctors and nurses. Hodges and his staff spent 13 months discussing expansion needs with this group, as well as with patients and the community, before developing a proposal for the new facility. An administrative team created 35 user groups, which held over 1,000 planning meetings (lasting from 45 minutes to a whole day). They even created a "Supreme Court" to deal with conflicting views on the multifaceted issues facing the new hospital.

Funding and regulatory issues added substantial complexity to this major expansion, and Hodges was very concerned that the project stay on time and within budget. Tom Hyatt, director of facility development, was given the task of onsite manager of the $100 million project, in addition to overseeing ongoing renovations, expansions, and other projects. The activities in the multiyear project for the new building at Arnold Palmer are shown in Table 7.

Discussion Questions*

1. Develop the network for planning and construction of the new hospital at Arnold Palmer.
2. What is the critical path and how long is the project expected to take?
3. Why is the construction of this 11-story building any more complex than construction of an equivalent office building?
4. What percent of the whole project duration was spent in planning that occurred prior to the proposal and reviews? Prior to the actual building construction? Why?

*You may wish to view the video accompanying this case before addressing these questions.

TABLE 7 Expansion Planning and Arnold Palmer Hospital Construction Activities and Times[a]

ACTIVITY	SCHEDULED TIME	PRECEDENCE ACTIVITY(IES)
1. Proposal and review	1 month	—
2. Establish master schedule	2 weeks	1
3. Architect selection process	5 weeks	1
4. Survey whole campus and its needs	1 month	1
5. Conceptual architect's plans	6 weeks	3
6. Cost estimating	2 months	2, 4, 5
7. Deliver plans to board for consideration/decision	1 month	6
8. Surveys/regulatory review	6 weeks	6
9. Construction manager selection	9 weeks	6
10. State review of need for more hospital beds ("Certificate of Need")	3.5 months	7, 8
11. Design drawings	4 months	10
12. Construction documents	5 months	9, 11
13. Site preparation/demolish existing building	9 weeks	11
14. Construction start/building pad	2 months	12, 13
15. Relocate utilities	6 weeks	12
16. Deep foundations	2 months	14
17. Building structure in place	9 months	16
18. Exterior skin/roofing	4 months	17
19. Interior buildout	12 months	17
20. Building inspections	5 weeks	15, 19
21. Occupancy	1 month	20

[a]This list of activities is abbreviated for purposes of this case study. For simplification, assume each week = .25 months (i.e., 2 weeks = .5 month, 6 weeks = 1.5 months, etc.).

Managing Hard Rock's Rockfest

Video Case

At the Hard Rock Cafe, like many organizations, project management is a key planning tool. With Hard Rock's constant growth in hotels and cafes, remodeling of existing cafes, scheduling for Hard Rock Live concert and event venues, and planning the annual Rockfest, managers rely on project management techniques and software to maintain schedule and budget performance.

"Without Microsoft Project," says Hard Rock Vice-President Chris Tomasso, "there is no way to keep so many people on the same page." Tomasso is in charge of the Rockfest event, which is attended by well over 100,000 enthusiastic fans. The challenge is pulling it off within a tight 9-month planning horizon. As the event approaches, Tomasso devotes greater energy to its activities. For the first 3 months, Tomasso updates his Microsoft Project charts monthly. Then at the 6-month mark, he updates his progress weekly. At the 9-month mark, he checks and corrects his schedule twice a week.

Early in the project management process, Tomasso identifies 10 major tasks (called level-2 activities in a work breakdown structure, or WBS):[†] talent booking, ticketing, marketing/PR, online promotion, television, show production, travel, sponsorships, operations, and merchandising. Using a WBS, each of these is further divided into a series of subtasks. Table 8 identifies 26 of the major activities and subactivities, their immediate predecessors, and time estimates. Tomasso enters all these into the Microsoft Project software.[‡] Tomasso alters the Microsoft Project document and the time line as the project progresses. "It's okay to change it as long as you keep on track," he states.

The day of the rock concert itself is not the end of the project planning. "It's nothing but surprises. A band not being able to get to the venue because of traffic jams is a surprise, but an 'anticipated' surprise. We had a helicopter on stand-by ready to fly the band in," says Tomasso.

On completion of Rockfest in July, Tomasso and his team have a 3-month reprieve before starting the project planning process again.

[†]The level-1 activity is the Rockfest concert itself.

[‡]There are actually 127 activities used by Tomasso; the list is abbreviated for this case study.

TABLE 8 Some of the Major Activities and Subactivities in the Rockfest Plan

ACTIVITY	DESCRIPTION	PREDECESSOR(S)	TIME (WEEKS)
A	Finalize site and building contracts	—	7
B	Select local promoter	A	3
C	Hire production manager	A	3
D	Design promotional Web site	B	5
E	Set TV deal	D	6
F	Hire director	E	4
G	Plan for TV camera placement	F	2
H	Target headline entertainers	B	4
I	Target support entertainers	H	4
J	Travel accommodations for talent	I	10
K	Set venue capacity	C	2
L	Ticketmaster contract	D, K	3
M	On-site ticketing	L	8
N	Sound and staging	C	6
O	Passes and stage credentials	G, R	7
P	Travel accommodations for staff	B	20
Q	Hire sponsor coordinator	B	4
R	Finalize sponsors	Q	4
S	Define/place signage for sponsors	R, X	3
T	Hire operations manager	A	4
U	Develop site plan	T	6
V	Hire security director	T	7
W	Set police/fire security plan	V	4
X	Power, plumbing, AC, toilet services	U	8
Y	Secure merchandise deals	B	6
Z	Online merchandise sales	Y	6

Discussion Questions§

1. Identify the critical path and its activities for Rockfest. How long does the project take?
2. Which activities have a slack time of 8 weeks or more?
3. Identify five major challenges a project manager faces in events such as this one.
4. Why is a work breakdown structure useful in a project such as this? Take the 26 activities and break them into what you think should be level-2, level-3, and level-4 tasks.

§You may wish to view the video accompanying this case before addressing these questions.

- **Additional Case Study:** Visit **www.myomlab.com** or **www.pearsonhighered.com/heizer** for this free case study:
Shale Oil Company: This oil refinery must shut down for maintenance of a major piece of equipment.

Bibliography

Balakrishnan, R., B. Render, and R. M. Stair. *Managerial Decision Modeling with Spreadsheets*, 3rd ed. Upper Saddle River, NJ: Prentice Hall, 2012.

Cleland, D. L., and L. R. Ireland. *Project Management*, 6th ed. New York: McGraw-Hill/Irwin, 2010.

Gray, C. L., and E. W. Larson. *Project Management with MS Project.* New York: McGraw-Hill/Irwin, 2008.

Helgadottir, Hilder. "The Ethical Dimension of Project Management." *International Journal of Project Management* 26, no. 7 (October 2008): 743.

Karlos, A., et al. "Foundations of Project Management." *International Journal of Project Management* 27, no. 1 (January 2009): 1.

Kerzner, H. *Project Management Case Studies*, 3rd ed. New York: Wiley, 2009.

Matta, N. F., and R. N. Ashkenas. "Why Good Projects Fail Anyway." *Harvard Business Review* 85, no. 5 (September 2003): 109–114.

Maylor, Harvey. *Project Management*, 5th ed. Upper Saddle River, NJ: Prentice Hall, 2011.

Meredith, J. R., and S. Mantel. *Project Management*, 8th ed. New York: Wiley, 2011.

Oates, David. "Understanding and Solving the Causes of Project Failure." *Knowledge Management Review* 9, no. 5 (May–June 2006): 5.

Render, B., R. M. Stair, and M. Hanna. *Quantitative Analysis for Management*, 11th ed. Upper Saddle River, NJ: Prentice Hall, 2012.

Verzuh, Eric. *The Fast Forward MBA in Project Management.* New York: Wiley, 2008.

Wysocki, R. K. *Effective Project Management*, 6th ed. New York: Wiley, 2012.

APPENDIX

SOLUTIONS TO EVEN-NUMBERED PROBLEMS

2 Here are some detailed activities for the first two activities for Day's WBS:

1.11 Set initial goals for fundraising.
1.12 Set strategy, including identifying sources and solicitation.
1.13 Raise the funds.
1.21 Identify voters' concerns.
1.22 Analyze competitor's voting record.
1.23 Establish position on issues.

4

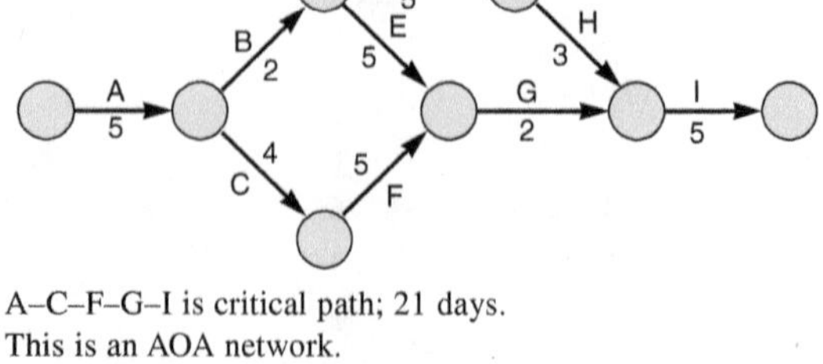

A–C–F–G–I is critical path; 21 days.
This is an AOA network.

6 **(a)**

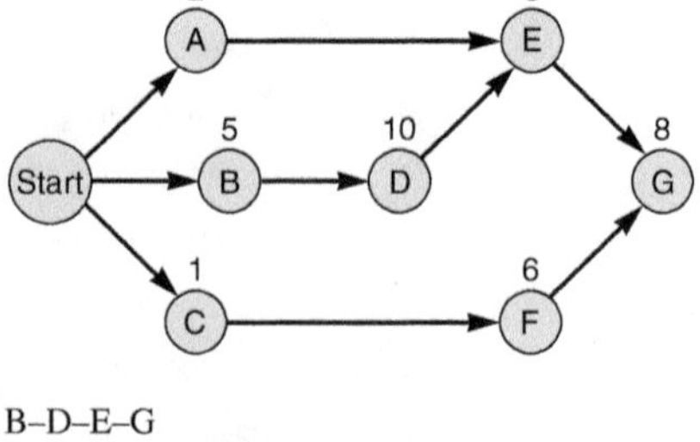

(b) B–D–E–G
(c) 26 days
(d)

Activity	Slack
A	13
B	0
C	11
D	0
E	0
F	11
G	0

8

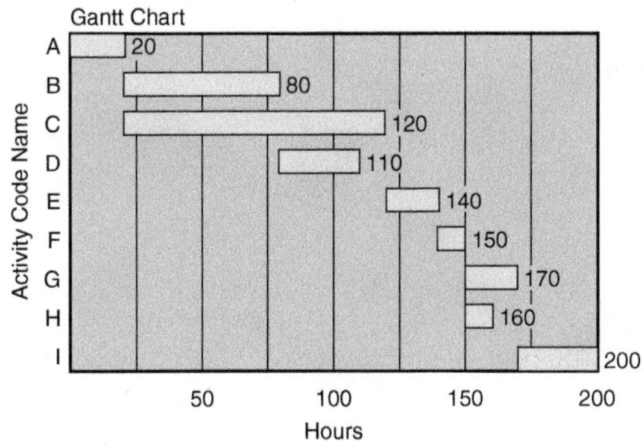

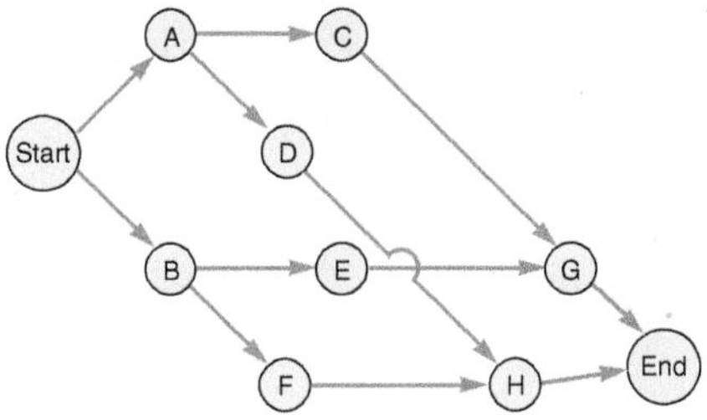

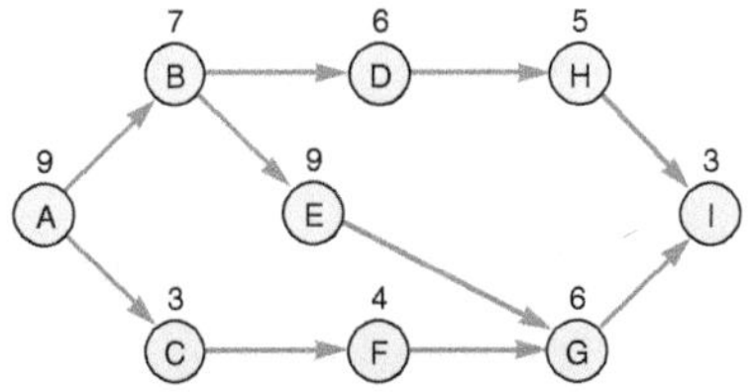

(b) A–B–E–G–I is critical path.
(c) 34

14 **(a)**

A, 5.83, 0.69	G, 2.17, 0.25
B, 3.67, 0.11	H, 6.00, 1.00
C, 2.00, 0.11	I, 11.00, 0.11
D, 7.00, 0.11	J, 16.33, 1.00
E, 4.00, 0.44	K, 7.33, 1.78
F, 10.00, 1.78	

(b) Critical path is C–D–E–F–H–K. Time = 36.33 days.
(c) Slacks are 7.17, 5.33, 0, 0, 0, 0, 2.83, 0, 2.83, 18, and 0, respectively, for A through K.
(d) $P = .946$

16 Crash C to 3 weeks at $200 total for one week. Now both paths are critical. Not worth it to crash further.

18 Critical path currently is C–E for 12 days. $1,100 to crash by 4 days. Watch for parallel critical paths as you crash.

20 **(a)** 16 (A–D–G)
(b) $12,300
(c) D; 1 wk. for $75
(d) 7 wk.; $1,600

22 **(a)** A–C–E–H–I–K–M–N; 50 days
(b) 82.1%
(c) 58 days

24 **(a)** .0228
(b) .3085
(c) .8413
(d) .97725
(e) 24 mo.

26 **(a)**

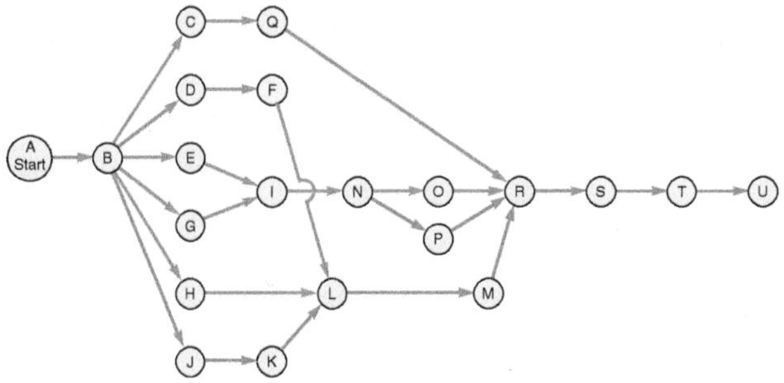

(b) Critical path is A–B–J–K–L–M–R–S–T–U for 18 days.
(c) **i.** No, transmissions and drivetrains are not on the critical path.
ii. No, halving engine-building time will reduce the critical path by only 1 day.
iii. No, it is not on the critical path.
(d) Reallocating workers not involved with critical-path activities to activities along the critical path will reduce the critical path length.

Rapid Review

Main Heading	Review Material	MyOMLab
THE IMPORTANCE OF PROJECT MANAGEMENT	The management of projects involves three phases: 1. *Planning*—This phase includes goal setting, defining the project, and team organization. 2. *Scheduling*—This phase relates people, money, and supplies to specific activities and relates activities to each other. 3. *Controlling*—Here the firm monitors resources, costs, quality, and budgets. It also revises or changes plans and shifts resources to meet time and cost demands.	**VIDEO 1** Project Management at Hard Rock's Rockfest
PROJECT PLANNING	Projects can be defined as a series of related tasks directed toward a major output. ■ **Project organization**—An organization formed to ensure that programs (projects) receive the proper management and attention. ■ **Work breakdown structure (WBS)**—Defines a project by dividing it into more and more detailed components.	Problem 1
PROJECT SCHEDULING	■ **Gantt charts**—Planning charts used to schedule resources and allocate time. Project scheduling serves several purposes: 1. It shows the relationship of each activity to others and to the whole project. 2. It identifies the precedence relationships among activities. 3. It encourages the setting of realistic time and cost estimates for each activity. 4. It helps make better use of people, money, and material resources by identifying critical bottlenecks in the project.	Problem 8
PROJECT CONTROLLING	Computerized programs produce a broad variety of PERT/CPM reports, including (1) detailed cost breakdowns for each task, (2) total program labor curves, (3) cost distribution tables, (4) functional cost and hour summaries, (5) raw material and expenditure forecasts, (6) variance reports, (7) time analysis reports, and (8) work status reports.	**VIDEO 2** Project Management at Arnold Palmer Hospital
PROJECT MANAGEMENT TECHNIQUES: PERT AND CPM	■ **Program evaluation and review technique (PERT)**—A project management technique that employs three time estimates for each activity. ■ **Critical path method (CPM)**—A project management technique that uses only one estimate per activity. ■ **Critical path**—The computed *longest* time path(s) through a network. PERT and CPM both follow six basic steps. The activities on the critical path will delay the entire project if they are not completed on time. ■ **Activity-on-node (AON)**—A network diagram in which nodes designate activities. ■ **Activity-on-arrow (AOA)**—A network diagram in which arrows designate activities. In an AOA network, the nodes represent the starting and finishing times of an activity and are also called *events*. ■ **Dummy activity**—An activity having no time that is inserted into a network to maintain the logic of the network. A dummy ending activity can be added to the end of an AON diagram for a project that has multiple ending activities.	Problems: 3–7, 9, 10, 12, 15 Virtual Office Hours for Solved Problems: 1, 2
DETERMINING THE PROJECT SCHEDULE	■ **Critical path analysis**—A process that helps determine a project schedule. To find the critical path, we calculate two distinct starting and ending times for each activity: ■ *Earliest start (ES)* = Earliest time at which an activity can start, assuming that all predecessors have been completed ■ *Earliest finish (EF)* = Earliest time at which an activity can be finished ■ *Latest start (LS)* = Latest time at which an activity can start, without delaying the completion time of the entire project ■ *Latest finish (LF)* = Latest time by which an activity has to finish so as to not delay the completion time of the entire project ■ **Forward pass**—A process that identifies all the early start and early finish times. $\text{ES} = \text{Max}\{\text{EF of all immediate predecessors}\}$ (1) $\text{EF} = \text{ES} + \text{Activity time}$ (2) ■ **Backward pass**—A process that identifies all the late start and late finish times. $\text{LF} = \text{Min}\{\text{LS of all immediate following activities}\}$ (3) $\text{LS} = \text{LF} - \text{Activity time}$ (4)	Problems: 11, 14, 15, 17, 20, 22, 23, 26

Rapid Review continued

Main Heading	Review Material	MyOMLab
	▪ **Slack time**—Free time for an activity. Slack = LS − ES or Slack = LF − EF (5) The activities with zero slack are called *critical activities* and are said to be on the critical path. The critical path is a continuous path through the project network that starts at the first activity in the project, terminates at the last activity in the project, and includes only critical activities.	Virtual Office Hours for Solved Problem: 3 **ACTIVE MODEL 1**
VARIABILITY IN ACTIVITY TIMES	▪ **Optimistic time** (a)—The "best" activity completion time that could be obtained in a PERT network. ▪ **Pessimistic time** (b)—The "worst" activity time that could be expected in a PERT network. ▪ **Most likely time** (m)—The most probable time to complete an activity in a PERT network. When using PERT, we often assume that activity time estimates follow the beta distribution. Expected activity time $t = (a + 4m + b)/6$ (6) Variance of activity completion time = $[(b - a)/6]^2$ (7) σ_p^2 = Project variance = Σ (variances of activities on critical path) (8) Z = (Due date − Expected date of completion)/ σ_p (9) Due date = Expected completion time + $(Z - \sigma_p)$ (10)	Problems: 13, 14. 21, 24 Virtual Office Hours for Solved Problems: 4, 5, 6
COST–TIME TRADE-OFFS AND PROJECT CRASHING	▪ **Crashing**—Shortening activity time in a network to reduce time on the critical path so total completion time is reduced. $\text{Crash cost per period} = \dfrac{\text{(Crash cost – Normal cost)}}{\text{(Normal time – Crash time)}}$ (11)	Problems: 16, 18, 19, 25 Virtual Office Hours for Solved Problem: 7
A CRITIQUE OF PERT AND CPM	As with every technique for problem solving, PERT and CPM have a number of advantages as well as several limitations.	
USING MICROSOFT PROJECT TO MANAGE PROJECTS	Microsoft Project, the most popular example of specialized project management software, is extremely useful in drawing project networks, identifying the project schedule, and managing project costs and other resources.	

Self Test

▪ **Before taking the self-test,** refer to the learning objectives listed at the beginning of the text and the key terms listed at the end of the text.

LO1. Which of the following statements regarding Gantt charts is true?
- **a)** Gantt charts give a timeline and precedence relationships for each activity of a project.
- **b)** Gantt charts use the four standard spines: Methods, Materials, Manpower, and Machinery.
- **c)** Gantt charts are visual devices that show the duration of activities in a project.
- **d)** Gantt charts are expensive.
- **e)** All of the above are true.

LO2. Which of the following is true about AOA and AON networks?
- **a)** In AOA, arrows represent activities.
- **b)** In AON, nodes represent activities.
- **c)** Activities consume time and resources.
- **d)** Nodes are also called *events* in AOA.
- **e)** All of the above.

LO3. Slack time equals:
- **a)** ES + t.
- **b)** LS − ES.
- **c)** zero.
- **d)** EF − ES.

LO4. The critical path of a network is the:
- **a)** shortest-time path through the network.
- **b)** path with the fewest activities.
- **c)** path with the most activities.
- **d)** longest-time path through the network.

LO5. PERT analysis computes the variance of the total project completion time as:
- **a)** the sum of the variances of all activities in the project.
- **b)** the sum of the variances of all activities on the critical path.
- **c)** the sum of the variances of all activities not on the critical path.
- **d)** the variance of the final activity of the project.

LO6. The crash cost per period:
- **a)** is the difference in costs divided by the difference in times (crash and normal).
- **b)** is considered to be linear in the range between normal and crash.
- **c)** needs to be determined so that the smallest cost values on the critical path can be considered for time reduction first.
- **d)** all of the above.

Answers: LO1. c; LO2. e; LO3. b; LO4. d; LO5. b; LO6. d.

Supply Chain Management

OUTLINE

10 OM STRATEGY DECISIONS

- Design of Goods and Services
- Managing Quality
- Process Strategy
- Location Strategies
- Layout Strategies
- Human Resources
- *Supply Chain Management*
- Inventory Management
- Scheduling
- Maintenance

GLOBAL COMPANY PROFILE
Darden Restaurants

Darden's Supply Chain Yields a Competitive Edge

Darden Restaurants, Inc., is the largest publicly traded casual dining restaurant company in the world. It serves over 400 million meals annually from more than 1,900 restaurants in North America. Its well-known flagship brands—Olive Garden and Red Lobster—annually generate $3.5 and $2.5 billion, respectively. Darden's other brands include Bahama Breeze, Seasons 52, The Capital Grille, and LongHorn Steakhouse. The firm employs more than 180,000 people and is the 32nd largest employer in the U.S.

"Operations is typically thought of as an execution of strategy. For us it is the strategy," Darden's former chairman, Joe R. Lee, stated.

In the restaurant business, a winning strategy requires a winning supply chain. Nothing is more important than sourcing and delivering healthy, high-quality food; and there are very few

Darden Restaurants

Qualifying Worldwide Sources: Part of Darden's supply chain begins with a crab harvest in the frigid waters off the coast of Alaska. But long before a supplier is qualified to sell to Darden, a total quality team is appointed. The team provides guidance, assistance, support, and training to the suppliers to ensure that overall objectives are understood and desired results accomplished.

Darden Restaurants

Aquaculture Certification: Shrimp in this Asian plant are certified to ensure traceability. The focus is on quality control certified by the Aquaculture Certification Council, of which Darden is a member. Farming and inspection practices yield safe and wholesome shrimp.

Darden Restaurants

Product tracking: Darden's seafood inspection team developed an integral system that uses a *Lot ID* to track seafood from its origin through shipping and receipt. Darden uses a modified atmosphere packaging (MAP) process to extend the shelf life and preserve the quality of its fresh fish. The tracking includes time temperature monitoring.

other industries where supplier performance is so closely tied to the customer.

Darden sources its food from five continents and thousands of suppliers. To meet Darden's needs for fresh ingredients, the company has developed four distinct supply chains: one for seafood; one for dairy/produce/other refrigerated foods; a third for other food items, like baked goods; and a fourth for restaurant supplies (everything from dishes to ovens to uniforms). Over $2 billion is spent in these supply chains annually. (See the *Video Case Study* at the end of this text for details.)

Darden's four supply channels have some common characteristics. They all require *supplier qualification*, have *product tracking*, are subject to *independent audits*, and employ *just-in-time delivery*. With best-in-class techniques and processes, Darden creates worldwide supply chain partnerships and alliances that are rapid, transparent, and efficient. Darden achieves competitive advantage through its superior supply chain.

Darden Restaurants

Darden Restaurants

JIT Delivery: For many products, temperature monitoring begins immediately and is tracked through the entire supply chain, to the kitchen at each of Darden's 1,900 restaurants, and ultimately to the guest.

LEARNING OBJECTIVES	
LO1	***Explain*** the strategic importance of the supply chain
LO2	***Identify*** six sourcing strategies
LO3	***Explain*** issues and opportunities in the supply chain
LO4	***Describe*** the steps in supplier selection
LO5	***Explain*** major issues in logistics management
LO6	***Compute*** the percentage of assets committed to inventory and inventory turnover

STUDENT TIP Competition today is not between companies; it is between supply chains.

The Supply Chain's Strategic Importance

Like Darden, most firms spend a huge portion of their sales dollars on purchases. Because an increasing percentage of an organization's costs are determined by purchasing, relationships with suppliers are increasingly integrated and long term. Combined efforts that improve innovation, speed design, and reduce costs are common. Such efforts, when part of a corporate-wide strategy, can dramatically improve all partners' competitiveness. This integrated focus places added emphasis on managing supplier relationships.

Supply chain management The coordination of all supply chain activities involved in enhancing customer value.

Supply chain management describes the coordination of all supply chain activities, starting with raw materials and ending with a satisfied customer. Thus, a supply chain includes suppliers; manufacturers and/or service providers; and distributors, wholesalers, and/or retailers who deliver the product and/or service to the final customer. Figure 1 provides an example of the breadth of links and activities that a supply chain may cover.

The objective of supply chain management is to coordinate activities within the supply chain to maximize the supply chain's competitive advantage and benefits to the ultimate consumer. Just as with championship teams, a central feature of successful supply chains is members acting in ways that benefit the team (the supply chain).

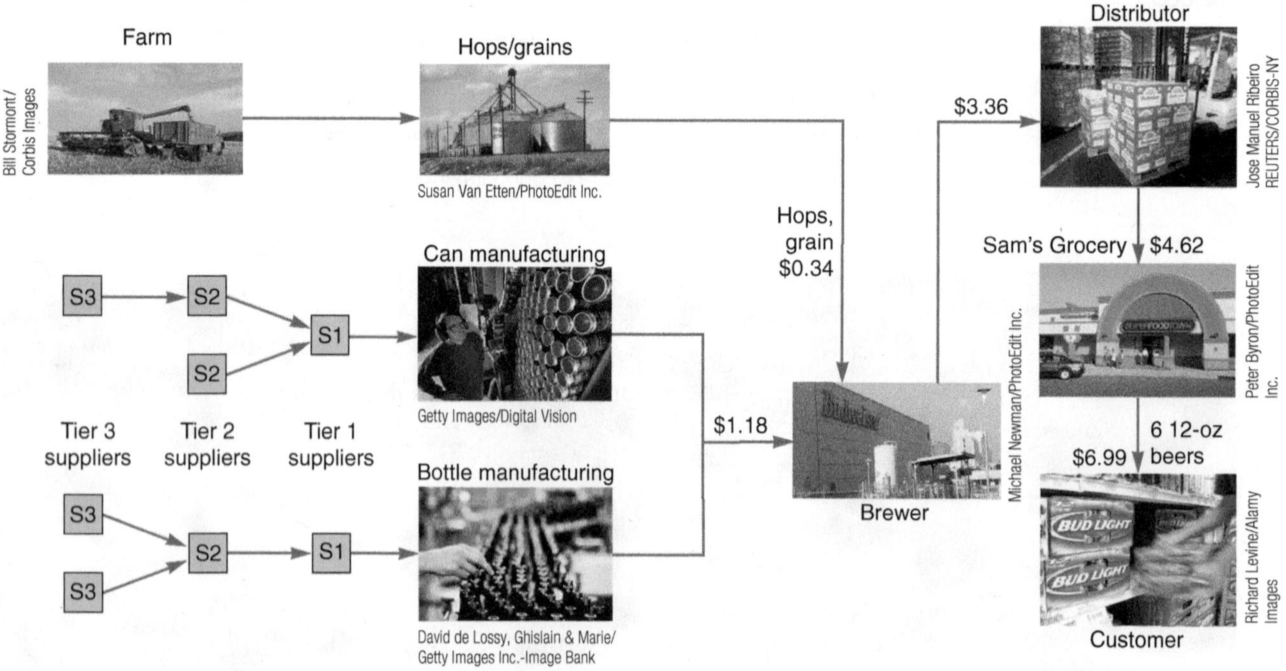

Figure 1
A Supply Chain for Beer
The supply chain includes all the interactions among suppliers, manufacturers, distributors, and customers. A well-functioning supply chain has information flowing between all partners. The chain includes transportation, scheduling information, cash and credit transfers, as well as ideas, designs, and material transfers. Even can and bottle manufacturers have their own tiers of suppliers providing components such as lids, labels, packing containers, etc. (Costs are approximate and include substantial taxes.)

With collaboration, costs for both buyers and suppliers can drop. For example, when both parties are willing to share sales and cost information, profit can increase for both. Examples of supply chain coordination include:

- Walmart cooperates with its top 200 supplier factories in China to reach the goal of 20% energy efficiency improvement.
- Mercury Marine, the large boat-engine producer, uses the Internet to enhance design with boat builders and engine dealers as it fights off competition from Honda, Yamaha, and Volvo.
- Unifi, the leading U.S. maker of synthetic yarn, shares daily production-scheduling and quality-control information with raw materials supplier DuPont.

As Table 1 indicates, a huge part of a firm's revenue is typically spent on purchases, so supply chains are a good place to look for savings. Example 1 further illustrates the amount of leverage available to the operations manager through the supply chain. These percentages indicate the strong role that supply chains play in potential profitability. Effective cost cutting may help a firm reach its profit goals more easily than would an increased sales effort.

TABLE 1

Supply Chain Costs as a Percentage of Sales

INDUSTRY	% PURCHASED
Automobile	67
Beverages	52
Chemical	62
Food	60
Lumber	61
Metals	65
Paper	55
Petroleum	79
Restaurants	35
Transportation	62

Example 1

SUPPLY CHAIN STRATEGY VS. SALES STRATEGY TO ACHIEVE A TARGET PROFIT

Hau Lee Furniture, Inc., spends 60% of its sales dollars in the supply chain and has a current gross profit of $10,000. Hau wishes to increase gross profit by $5,000 (50%). He would like to compare two strategies: reducing material costs vs. increasing sales.

APPROACH ▶ Use the table below to make the analysis.

SOLUTION ▶ The current material costs and production costs are 60% and 20%, respectively, of sales dollars, with fixed cost at a constant $10,000. Analysis indicates that an improvement in the supply chain that would *reduce material costs by 8.3%* ($5,000/$60,000) would produce a 50% net profit gain for Hau; whereas a *much larger 25% increase in sales* ($25,000/$100,000) would be required to produce the same result.

	CURRENT SITUATION	SUPPLY CHAIN STRATEGY	SALES STRATEGY
Sales	$100,000	$100,000	$125,000
Cost of materials	$60,000 (60%)	$55,000 (55%)	$75,000 (60%)
Production costs	$20,000 (20%)	$20,000 (20%)	$25,000 (20%)
Fixed costs	$10,000 (10%)	$10,000 (10%)	$10,000 (8%)
Profit	$10,000 (10%)	$15,000 (15%)	$15,000 (12%)

INSIGHT ▶ Supply chain savings flow directly to the bottom line. In general, supply chain costs need to shrink by a much lower percentage than sales revenue needs to increase to attain a profit goal. Effective management of the supply chain can generate substantial benefits.

LEARNING EXERCISE ▶ If Hau wants to double the original gross profits (from $10,000 to $20,000), what would be required of the supply chain and sales strategies? [Answer: Supply chain strategy = 16.7% *reduction* in material costs; sales strategy = 50% *increase* in sales.]

RELATED PROBLEMS ▶ 3, 4

LO1 *Explain* the strategic importance of the supply chain

As firms strive to increase their competitiveness via product customization, high quality, cost reductions, and speed to market, added emphasis is placed on the supply chain. Through long-term strategic relationships, suppliers become "partners" as they contribute to competitive advantage.

To ensure that the supply chain supports a firm's strategy, managers need to consider the supply chain issues shown in Table 2. Activities of supply chain managers cut across accounting, finance, marketing, and the operations discipline. Just as the OM function supports the firm's overall strategy, the supply chain must support the OM strategy. Strategies of low cost or rapid response demand different things from a supply chain than a strategy of differentiation. For instance, a low-cost strategy, as Table 2 indicates, requires suppliers be selected based primarily on cost. Such suppliers

OM in Action — A Rose Is a Rose, but Only If It Is Fresh

Supply chains for food and flowers must be fast, and they must be good. When the food supply chain has a problem, the best that can happen is the customer does not get fed on time; the worst that happens is the customer gets food poisoning and dies. In the floral industry, the timing and temperature are also critical. Indeed, flowers are the most perishable agricultural item—even more so than fish. Flowers not only need to move fast, but they must also be kept cool, at a constant temperature of 33 to 37 degrees. And they must be provided preservative-treated water while in transit. Roses are especially delicate, fragile, and perishable.

Seventy percent of the roses sold in the U.S. market arrive by air from rural Colombia and Ecuador. Roses move through this supply chain via an intricate but fast transportation network. This network stretches from growers who cut, grade, bundle, pack and ship, to importers who make the deal, to the U.S. Department of Agriculture personnel who quarantine and inspect for insects, diseases, and parasites, to U.S. Customs agents who inspect and approve, to facilitators who provide clearance and labeling, to wholesalers who distribute, to retailers who arrange and sell, and finally to the customer. Each and every minute the product is deteriorating. The time and temperature sensitivity of perishables like roses requires sophistication and refined standards in the supply chain. Success yields quality and low losses. After all, when it's Valentine's Day, what good is a shipment of roses that arrives wilted or late? This is a difficult supply chain; only an excellent one will get the job done.

© Africa Studio

Sources: IIE Solutions (February 2002): 26–32; *Analytics* (Feb. 13, 2007); and *RFID Journal* (June 4, 2007).

should have the ability to design low-cost products that meet the functional requirements, minimize inventory, and drive down lead times. However, if you want roses that are fresh, build a supply chain that focuses on response (see the *OM in Action* box "A Rose Is a Rose, but Only if It Is Fresh").

Firms must achieve integration of strategy up and down the supply chain, and must expect that strategy to be different for different products and to change as products move through their life cycle. Darden Restaurants, as noted in the opening *Global Company Profile*, has mastered worldwide product and service complexity by segmenting its supply chain and at the same time integrating four unique supply chains into its overall strategy.

VIDEO 1
Darden's Global Supply Chain

Sourcing Issues: Make-or-Buy vs. Outsourcing

As suggested in Table 2, a firm needs to determine strategically how to design the supply chain. However, prior to embarking on supply chain design, operations managers must first consider the "make-or-buy" and outsourcing decisions.

TABLE 2 How Corporate Strategy Impacts Supply Chain Decisions*

	LOW-COST STRATEGY	RESPONSE STRATEGY	DIFFERENTIATION STRATEGY
Primary supplier selection criteria	• Cost	• Capacity • Speed • Flexibility	• Product development skills • Willing to share information • Jointly and rapidly develop products
Supply chain inventory	• Minimize inventory to hold down costs	• Use buffer stocks to ensure speedy supply	• Minimize inventory to avoid product obsolescence
Distribution network	• Inexpensive transportation • Sell through discount distributors/retailers	• Fast transportation • Provide premium customer service	• Gather and communicate market research data • Knowledgeable sales staff
Product design characteristics	• Maximize performance • Minimize cost	• Low setup time • Rapid production ramp-up	• Modular design to aid product differentiation

*See related table and discussion in Marshall L. Fisher, "What Is the Right Supply Chain for Your Product?" *Harvard Business Review* (March–April 1997): 105.

Make-or-Buy Decisions

A wholesaler or retailer buys everything that it sells; a manufacturing operation hardly ever does. Manufacturers, restaurants, and assemblers of products buy components and subassemblies that go into final products. Choosing products and services that can be advantageously obtained *externally* as opposed to produced *internally* is known as the **make-or-buy decision**. Supply chain personnel evaluate alternative suppliers and provide current, accurate, and complete data relevant to the buy alternative.

Make-or-buy decision
A choice between producing a component or service in-house or purchasing it from an outside source.

Outsourcing

Outsourcing transfers some of what are traditional internal activities and resources of a firm to outside vendors, making it slightly different from the traditional make-or-buy decision. Outsourcing, is part of the continuing trend toward using the efficiency that comes with specialization. The vendor performing the outsourced service is an expert in that particular specialty. This leaves the outsourcing firm to focus on its key success factors and its core competencies.

Outsourcing
Transferring a firm's activities that have traditionally been internal to external suppliers.

Six Sourcing Strategies

LO2 *Identify* six sourcing strategies

Having decided *what* to outsource, managers have six strategies to consider.

Many Suppliers

With the many-suppliers strategy, a supplier responds to the demands and specifications of a "request for quotation," with the order usually going to the low bidder. This is a common strategy when products are commodities. This strategy plays one supplier against another and places the burden of meeting the buyer's demands on the supplier. Suppliers aggressively compete with one another. This approach holds the supplier responsible for maintaining the necessary technology, expertise, and forecasting abilities, as well as cost, quality, and delivery competencies. Long-term "partnering" relationships are not the goal.

STUDENT TIP
Supply chain strategies come in many varieties; choosing the correct one is the trick.

Few Suppliers

A strategy of few suppliers implies that rather than looking for short-term attributes, such as low cost, a buyer is better off forming a long-term relationship with a few dedicated suppliers. Long-term suppliers are more likely to understand the broad objectives of the procuring firm and the end customer. Using few suppliers can create value by allowing suppliers to have economies of scale and a learning curve that yields both lower transaction costs and lower production costs. This strategy also encourages those suppliers to provide design innovations and technological expertise.

Ford chooses suppliers even before parts are designed. Motorola evaluates suppliers on rigorous criteria, but in many instances has eliminated traditional supplier bidding, placing added emphasis on quality and reliability. On occasion these relationships yield contracts that extend through the product's life cycle. The British retailer Marks & Spencer finds that cooperation with its suppliers yields new products that win customers for the supplier and themselves. The move toward tight integration of the suppliers and purchasers is occurring in both manufacturing and services.

VIDEO 2
Supply Chain Management at Regal Marine

As with all other strategies, a downside exists. With few suppliers, the cost of changing partners is huge, so both buyer and supplier run the risk of becoming captives of the other. Poor supplier performance is only one risk the purchaser faces. The purchaser must also be concerned about trade secrets and suppliers that make other alliances or venture out on their own. This happened when the U.S. Schwinn Bicycle Co., needing additional capacity, taught Taiwan's Giant Manufacturing Company to make and sell bicycles. Giant Manufacturing is now the largest bicycle manufacturer in the world, and Schwinn was acquired out of bankruptcy by Pacific Cycle LLC.

Figure 2
Vertical Integration Can Be Forward or Backward

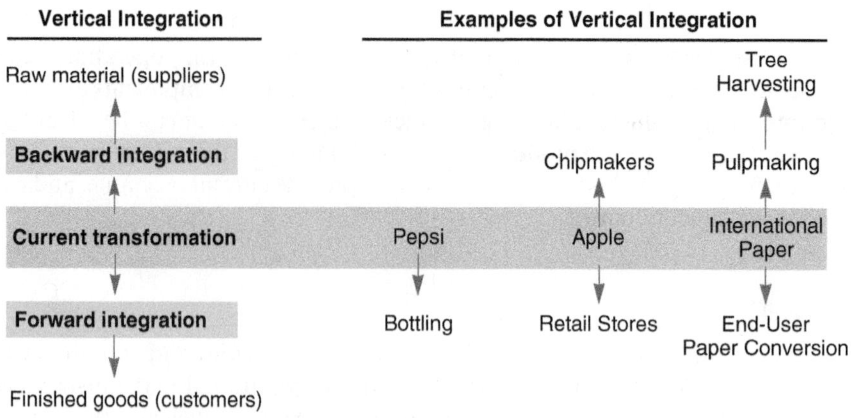

Vertical Integration

Vertical integration
Developing the ability to produce goods or services previously purchased or actually buying a supplier or a distributor.

Purchasing can be extended to take the form of vertical integration. By **vertical integration**, we mean developing the ability to produce goods or services previously purchased or to actually buy a supplier or a distributor. As shown in Figure 2, vertical integration can take the form of *forward* or *backward integration*.

Backward integration suggests a firm purchase its suppliers, as in the case of Apple deciding to manufacture its own semiconductors. Apple also uses forward integration by establishing its own revolutionary retail stores.

Vertical integration can offer a strategic opportunity for the operations manager. For firms with the capital, managerial talent, and required demand, vertical integration may provide substantial opportunities for cost reduction, higher quality, timely delivery, and inventory reduction. Vertical integration appears to work best when the organization has a large market share and the management talent to operate an acquired vendor successfully.

The relentless march of specialization continues, meaning that a model of "doing everything" or "vertical integration" is increasingly difficult. Backward integration may be particularly dangerous for firms in industries undergoing technological change if management cannot keep abreast of those changes or invest the financial resources necessary for the next wave of technology. Research and development costs are too high and technology changes too rapid for one company to sustain leadership in every component. Most organizations are better served concentrating on their own specialty and leveraging suppliers' contributions.

Joint Ventures

Because vertical integration is so dangerous, firms may opt for some form of formal collaboration. Firms may engage in collaboration to enhance their new product prowess or technological skills. But firms also engage in collaboration to secure supply or reduce costs. One version of a joint venture is the current Daimler–BMW effort to develop and produce standard automobile components. Given the global consolidation of the auto industry, these two rivals in the luxury segment of the automobile market are at a disadvantage in volume. Their relatively low volume means fewer units over which to spread fixed costs, hence the interest in consolidating to cut development and production costs. As in all other such collaborations, the trick is to cooperate without diluting the brand or conceding a competitive advantage.

Keiretsu Networks

Keiretsu
A Japanese term that describes suppliers who become part of a company coalition.

Many large Japanese manufacturers have found another strategy: it is part collaboration, part purchasing from few suppliers, and part vertical integration. These manufacturers are often financial supporters of suppliers through ownership or loans. The supplier becomes part of a company coalition known as a ***keiretsu***. Members of the *keiretsu* are assured long-term relationships and are therefore expected to collaborate as partners, providing technical expertise and stable quality production to the manufacturer. Members of the *keiretsu* can also have second- and even third-tier suppliers as part of the coalition.

Virtual Companies

Virtual companies rely on a variety of good, stable supplier relationships to provide services on demand. Suppliers may provide a variety of services that include doing the payroll, hiring personnel, designing products, providing consulting services, manufacturing components, conducting tests, or distributing products. The relationships may be short- or long-term and may include true partners, collaborators, or simply able suppliers and subcontractors. Whatever the formal relationship, the result can be exceptionally lean performance. The advantages of virtual companies include specialized management expertise, low capital investment, flexibility, and speed. The result is efficiency.

Virtual companies
Companies that rely on a variety of supplier relationships to provide services on demand. Also known as hollow corporations or network companies.

The apparel business provides a *traditional* example of virtual organizations. The designers of clothes seldom manufacture their designs; rather, they license the manufacture. The manufacturer may then rent space, lease sewing machines, and contract for labor. The result is an organization that has low overhead, remains flexible, and can respond rapidly to the market.

A *contemporary* example is exemplified by Vizio, Inc., a California-based producer of flat-screen TVs that has fewer than 100 employees but huge sales. Vizio uses modules to assemble its own brand of TVs. Because the key components of TVs are now readily available and sold almost as commodities, innovative firms such as Vizio can specify the components, hire a contract manufacturer, and market the TVs with very little startup cost. In a virtual company, the supply chain is the company. Managing it is dynamic and demanding.

Supply Chain Risk

In this age of increasing specialization, low communication cost, and fast transportation, companies are making less and buying more. This means more reliance on supply chains and more risk. Managing integrated supply chains is a strategic challenge. Having fewer suppliers makes the supplier and customer more dependent on each other, increasing risk for both. This risk is

© Joe Gough/Fotolia

Supply chain risks arise in many ways. As this mishap illustrates, expected shipments can literally sink into the ocean.

STUDENT TIP ☆
The environment, controls, and process performance all affect supply-chain risk.

compounded by globalization and logistical complexity. In any supply chain, vendor reliability and quality may be challenging. But the new model of a tight, fast, low-inventory supply chain, operating across political and cultural boundaries, adds a new dimension to risk. As organizations go global, shipping time may increase, logistics may be less reliable, and tariffs and quotas may block companies from doing business. In addition, international supply chains complicate information flows and increase political/currency risks.

Risks and Mitigation Tactics

Supply chain risks arise in numerous ways. Table 3 identifies major categories of risks and tactics to help manage them. The development of a successful strategic plan for supply chain management requires careful research, a thorough assessment of the risks involved, and innovative planning. Companies need to focus not only on reducing potential disruptions but also on how to prepare for responses to inevitable negative events. Flexible, secure supply chains and sufficient insurance against a variety of disruptions are a start. They may also choose to diversify their supplier base by using multiple sources for critical components. **Cross-sourcing** represents a hybrid technique where two suppliers each provide a different component, but they have the capability of producing each other's component—that is, acting as a backup source. Another option is to create excess capacity that can be used in response to problems in the supply chain. Such contingency plans can reduce risk.

Cross-sourcing
Using one supplier for a component and a second supplier for another component, where each supplier acts as a backup for the other.

TABLE 3 Supply Chain Risks and Tactics

RISK	RISK REDUCTION TACTICS	EXAMPLE
Supplier failure to deliver	Use multiple suppliers; effective contracts with penalties; subcontractors on retainer; pre-planning	**McDonald's** planned its supply chain 6 years before its opening in Russia. Every plant—bakery, meat, chicken, fish, and lettuce—is closely monitored to ensure strong links.
Supplier quality failures	Careful supplier selection, training, certification, and monitoring	**Darden Restaurants** has placed extensive controls, including third-party audits, on supplier processes and logistics to ensure constant monitoring and reduction of risk.
Logistics delays or damage	Multiple/redundant transportation modes and warehouses; secure packaging; effective contracts with penalties	**Walmart,** with its own trucking fleet and numerous distribution centers located throughout the U.S., finds alternative origins and delivery routes bypassing problem areas.
Distribution	Careful selection, monitoring, and effective contracts with penalties	**Toyota** trains its dealers around the world, invoking principles of the Toyota Production System to help dealers improve customer service, used-car logistics, and body and paint operations.
Information loss or distortion	Redundant databases; secure IT systems; training of supply chain partners on the proper interpretations and uses of information	**Boeing** utilizes a state-of-the-art international communication system that transmits engineering, scheduling, and logistics data to Boeing facilities and suppliers worldwide.
Political	Political risk insurance; cross-country diversification; franchising and licensing	**Hard Rock Café** reduces political risk by franchising and licensing, rather than owning, when the political and cultural barriers seem significant.
Economic	Hedging to combat exchange rate risk; purchasing contracts that address price fluctuations	**Honda and Nissan** are moving more manufacturing out of Japan as the exchange rate for the yen makes Japanese-made autos more expensive.
Natural catastrophes	Insurance; alternate sourcing; cross-country diversification	**Toyota,** after its experience with fires, earthquakes, and tsunamis, now attempts to have at least two suppliers, each in a different geographical region, for each component.
Theft, vandalism, and terrorism	Insurance; patent protection; security measures including RFID and GPS; diversification	**Domestic Port Radiation Initiative:** The U.S. government has set up radiation portal monitors that scan nearly all imported containers for radiation.

Provided by South Carolina State Ports Authority

As this photo of the port of Charleston suggests, with over 16 million containers entering the U.S. annually, tracking location, content, and condition of trucks and containers is a challenge. But new technology may improve both security and JIT shipments.

Security and JIT

There is probably no society more open than the U.S. This includes its borders and ports—but they are swamped. Millions of containers enter U.S. ports each year, along with thousands of planes, cars, and trucks each day. Even under the best of conditions, some 5% of the container movements are misrouted, stolen, damaged, or excessively delayed.

Since the September 11, 2001, terrorist attacks, supply chains have become more complex. However, technological innovations in the supply chain are improving both security and inventory management, making logistics more reliable. Technology is now capable of knowing truck and container location, content, and condition. New devices can even detect broken container seals. Motion detectors can also be installed inside containers. Other sensors record interior data including temperature, shock, radioactivity, and whether a container is moving. Tracking lost containers, identifying delays, or just reminding individuals in the supply chain that a shipment is on its way will help expedite shipments.

Managing the Integrated Supply Chain

As managers move toward integration of the supply chain, substantial efficiencies are possible. The cycle of materials—as they flow from suppliers, to production, to warehousing, to distribution, to the customer—takes place among separate and often very independent organizations. It can lead to actions that may not optimize the entire chain. On the other hand, the supply chain is full of opportunities to reduce waste and enhance value. We now look at some of the significant *issues* and *opportunities*.

VIDEO 3
Arnold Palmer Hospital's Supply Chain

Issues in Managing the Integrated Supply Chain

LO3 *Explain* issues and opportunities in the supply chain

Three issues complicate development of an efficient, integrated supply chain: local optimization, incentives, and large lots.

Local Optimization Members of the chain are inclined to focus on maximizing local profit or minimizing immediate cost based on their limited knowledge. Slight upturns in demand are overcompensated for because no one wants to be caught short. Similarly, slight downturns are overcompensated for because no one wants to be caught holding excess inventory. So fluctuations are magnified. For instance, a pasta distributor does not want to run out of pasta for its retail customers; the natural response to an extra large order from the retailer is to compensate with an even larger order to the manufacturer on the assumption that retail sales are picking up. Neither the distributor nor the manufacturer knows that the retailer had a major one-time promotion that moved a lot of pasta. This is exactly the issue that complicated the implementation of efficient distribution at the Italian pasta maker Barilla.

Incentives (Sales Incentives, Quantity Discounts, Quotas, and Promotions) Incentives push merchandise into the chain for sales that have not occurred. This generates fluctuations that are ultimately expensive to all members of the chain.

Large Lots There is often a bias toward large lots because large lots tend to reduce unit costs. A logistics manager wants to ship large lots, preferably in full trucks, and a production manager wants long production runs. Both actions drive down unit shipping and production costs, but they increase holding costs and fail to reflect actual sales.

These three common occurrences—local optimization, incentives, and large lots—contribute to distortions of information about what is really occurring in the supply chain. A well-running supply system needs to be based on accurate information about how many products are truly being pulled through the chain. The inaccurate information is unintentional, but it results in distortions and fluctuations, causing what is known as the bullwhip effect.

Bullwhip effect

The increasing fluctuation in orders that often occurs as orders move through the supply chain.

The bullwhip effect occurs as orders are relayed from retailers, to distributors, to wholesalers, to manufacturers, with fluctuations increasing at each step in the sequence. The "bullwhip" fluctuations in the supply chain increase the costs associated with inventory, transportation, shipping, and receiving, while decreasing customer service and profitability. A number of specific opportunities exist for reducing the bullwhip effect and improving supply chain performance.

Opportunities in Managing the Integrated Supply Chain

Opportunities for effective management in the supply chain include the following 10 items.

Pull data

Accurate sales data that initiate transactions to "pull" product through the supply chain.

Accurate "Pull" Data Accurate pull data are generated by sharing (1) point-of-sales (POS) information so that each member of the chain can schedule effectively and (2) computer-assisted ordering (CAO). This implies using POS systems that collect sales data and then adjusting that data for market factors, inventory on hand, and outstanding orders. Then a net order is sent directly to the supplier who is responsible for maintaining the finished-goods inventory.

Lot Size Reduction Lot sizes are reduced through aggressive management. This may include (1) developing economical shipments of less than truckload lots; (2) providing discounts based on total annual volume rather than size of individual shipments; and (3) reducing the cost of ordering through techniques such as standing orders and various forms of electronic purchasing.

Single-stage control of replenishment

Fixing responsibility for monitoring and managing inventory for the retailer.

Single-Stage Control of Replenishment Single-stage control of replenishment means designating a member in the chain as responsible for monitoring and managing inventory in the supply chain based on the "pull" from the end user. This approach removes distorted information and multiple forecasts that create the bullwhip effect. Control may be in the hands of:

- A sophisticated retailer who understands demand patterns. Walmart does this for some of its inventory with radio frequency ID (RFID) tags.
- A distributor who manages the inventory for a particular distribution area. Distributors who handle grocery items, beer, and soft drinks may do this. Anheuser-Busch manages beer inventory and delivery for many of its customers.
- A manufacturer who has a well-managed forecasting, manufacturing, and distribution system. TAL Apparel Ltd., discussed in the *OM in Action* box, "The JCPenney Supply Chain for Dress Shirts," does this for JCPenney.

Vendor-managed inventory (VMI)

A system in which a supplier maintains material for the buyer, often delivering directly to the buyer's using department.

Vendor-Managed Inventory Vendor-managed inventory (VMI) means the use of a local supplier (usually a distributor) to maintain inventory for the manufacturer or retailer. The supplier delivers directly to the purchaser's using department rather than to a receiving dock or stockroom. If the supplier can maintain the stock of inventory for a variety of customers who use the same

OM in Action — The JCPenney Supply Chain for Dress Shirts

Purchase a white Stafford wrinkle-free dress shirt, size 17 neck, 34/35 sleeve at JCPenney at Atlanta's Northlake Mall on a Tuesday, and the supply chain responds. Within a day, TAL Apparel Ltd. in Hong Kong downloads a record of the sale. After a run through its forecasting model, TAL decides how many shirts to make and in what styles, colors, and sizes. By Wednesday afternoon, the replacement shirt is packed to be shipped directly to the JCPenney Northlake Mall store. The system bypasses the JCPenney warehouse—indeed all warehouses—as well as the JCPenney corporate decision makers.

In a second instance, two shirts are sold, leaving none in stock. TAL, after downloading the data, runs its forecasting model but comes to the decision that this store needs to have two in stock. Without consulting JCPenney, a TAL factory in Taiwan makes two new shirts. It sends one by ship, but because of the outage, the other goes by air.

As retailers deal with mass customization, fads, and seasonal swings, they also strive to cut costs—making a responsive supply chain critical. Before globalization of the supply chain, JCPenney would have had thousands of shirts warehoused across the country. Now JCPenney stores, like those of many retailers, hold a very limited inventory of shirts.

Losevsky Photo and Video/Shutterstock

JCPenney's supplier, TAL, is providing both sales forecasting and inventory management, a situation not acceptable to many retailers. But what is most startling is that TAL also places its own orders! A supply chain like this works only when there is trust between partners. The rapid changes in supply chain management not only place increasing technical demands on suppliers but also increase demands for trust between the parties.

Sources: Apparel (April 2006); *The Wall Street Journal* (September 11, 2003); and *International Trade Forum* (Issue 3, 2005)

product or whose differences are very minor (say, at the packaging stage), then there should be a net savings. These systems work without the immediate direction of the purchaser.

Collaborative Planning, Forecasting, and Replenishment (CPFR) As with single-stage control and vendor-managed inventory, collaborative planning, forecasting, and replenishment (CPFR) is another effort to manage inventory in the supply chain. With CPFR, members of the supply chain share planning, demand, forecasting, and inventory information. Partners in a CPFR effort begin with collaboration on product definition and a joint marketing plan. Promotion, advertising, forecasts, joint order commitments, and timing of shipments are all included in the plan in a concerted effort to drive down inventory and related costs. CPFR can help to significantly reduce the bullwhip effect.

Collaborative planning, forecasting, and replenishment (CPFR)
A system in which members of a supply chain share information in a joint effort to reduce supply chain costs.

Blanket Orders Blanket orders are unfilled orders with a vendor and are also called "open orders" or "incomplete orders." A blanket order is a contract to purchase certain items from a vendor. It is not an authorization to ship anything. Shipment is made only on receipt of an agreed-on document, perhaps a shipping requisition or shipment release.

Blanket order
A long-term purchase commitment to a supplier for items that are to be delivered against short-term releases to ship.

Standardization The purchasing department should make special efforts to increase levels of standardization. That is, rather than obtaining a variety of similar components with labeling, coloring, packaging, or perhaps even slightly different engineering specifications, the purchasing agent should try to have those components standardized.

Postponement Postponement withholds any modification or customization to the product (keeping it generic) as long as possible. The concept is to minimize internal variety while maximizing external variety. For instance, after analyzing the supply chain for its printers, Hewlett-Packard (HP) determined that if the printer's power supply was moved out of the printer itself and into a power cord, HP could ship the basic printer anywhere in the world. HP modified the printer, its power cord, its packaging, and its documentation so that only the power cord and documentation needed to be added at the final distribution point. This modification allowed the firm to manufacture and hold centralized inventories of the generic printer for shipment as demand changed. Only the unique power system and documentation had to be held in each country. This understanding of the entire supply chain reduced both risk and investment in inventory.

Postponement
Delaying any modifications or customization to a product as long as possible in the production process.

Electronic Ordering and Funds Transfer Electronic ordering and bank transfers are traditional approaches to speeding transactions and reducing paperwork. Transactions between firms often use electronic data interchange (EDI), which is a standardized data-transmittal format for computerized communications between organizations. EDI also provides for the use of advanced shipping notice (ASN), which notifies the purchaser that the vendor is ready to ship. Although some firms are still moving to EDI and ASN, the Internet's ease of use and lower cost is proving more popular.

Drop shipping
Shipping directly from the supplier to the end consumer rather than from the seller, saving both time and reshipping costs.

Drop Shipping and Special Packaging Drop shipping means the supplier will ship directly to the end consumer, rather than to the seller, saving both time and reshipping costs. Other cost-saving measures include the use of special packaging, labels, and optimal placement of labels and bar codes on containers. The final location down to the department and number of units in each shipping container can also be indicated. Substantial savings can be obtained through management techniques such as these. Some of these techniques can be of particular benefit to wholesalers and retailers by reducing shrinkage (lost, damaged, or stolen merchandise) and handling cost.

For instance, Dell Computer has decided that its core competence does not include stocking peripherals. So if you order a PC from Dell, with a printer and perhaps other components, the computer comes from Dell, but the printer and many of the other components will be drop shipped from the manufacturer.

Building the Supply Base

LO4 *Describe* the steps in supplier selection

For those goods and services a firm buys, suppliers, also known as *vendors,* must be selected and actively managed. Supplier selection considers numerous factors, such as strategic fit, supplier competence, delivery, and quality performance. Because a firm may have some competence in all areas and may have exceptional competence in only a few, selection can be challenging. Procurement policies also need to be established. Those might address issues such as percent of business done with any one supplier or with minority businesses. We now examine supplier selection as a four-stage process: (1) supplier evaluation, (2) supplier development, (3) negotiations, and (4) contracting.

Supplier Evaluation

The first stage of supplier selection, *supplier evaluation,* involves finding potential suppliers and determining the likelihood of their becoming *good* suppliers. If good suppliers are not selected, then all other supply chain efforts are wasted. As firms move toward long-term suppliers, the issues of financial strength, quality, management, research, technical ability, and potential for a close, long-term relationship play an increasingly important role. Evaluation criteria critical to the firm might include these categories as well as production process capability, location, and information systems.

Supplier Certification International quality certifications such as ISO 9000 and ISO 14000 are designed to provide an external verification that a firm follows sound quality management and environmental management standards. Buying firms can use such certifications to pre-qualify potential suppliers. Despite the existence of the ISO standards, firms often create their own supplier certification programs. Buyers audit potential suppliers and award a certified status to those that meet the specified qualification. A certification process often involves three steps: (1) qualification, (2) education, and (3) the certification performance process. Once certified, the supplier may be awarded special treatment and priority, allowing the buying firm to reduce or eliminate incoming inspection of materials. Such an arrangement may facilitate JIT production for the buying firm. Most large companies use some sort of supplier certification program.

Supplier Development

The second stage of supplier selection is *supplier development.* Assuming that a firm wants to proceed with a particular supplier, how does it integrate this supplier into its system? The buyer makes sure the supplier has an appreciation of quality requirements, product specifications, schedules and delivery, and procurement policies. Supplier development may include everything from training, to engineering and production help, to procedures for information transfer.

Negotiations

While the prices that consumers pay are often inflexible (printed on the price tag, listed in the catalog, etc.), a significant number of final prices paid in business-to-business transactions are negotiated. In addition to the price itself, several other aspects of the full product "package" must be determined. These may include credit and delivery terms, quality standards, and cooperative advertising agreements. In fact, negotiation represents a significant element in a purchasing manager's job, and well-honed negotiation skills are highly valued.

Here are three classic types of negotiation strategies: the cost-based model, the market-based price model, and competitive bidding.

Cost-Based Price Model The cost-based price model requires that the supplier open its books to the purchaser. The contract price is then based on time and materials or on a fixed cost with an escalation clause to accommodate changes in the vendor's labor and materials cost.

Market-Based Price Model In the market-based price model, price is based on a published, auction, or index price. Many commodities (agricultural products, paper, metal, etc.) are priced this way. Paperboard prices, for instance, are available via the *Official Board Markets* weekly publication (**www.advanstar.com**).

Competitive Bidding When suppliers are not willing to discuss costs or where near-perfect markets do not exist, competitive bidding is often appropriate. Competitive bidding is the typical policy in many firms for the majority of their purchases. Bidding policies usually require that the purchasing agent have several potential suppliers and quotations from each. The major disadvantage of this method, as mentioned earlier, is that the development of long-term relations between buyer and seller is hindered. It may also make difficult the communication and performance that are vital for engineering changes, quality, and delivery.

Yet a fourth approach is *to combine one or more* of the preceding negotiation techniques. The supplier and purchaser may agree to review cost data, accept some form of market-based cost, or agree that the supplier will "remain competitive."

Contracting

Supply chain partners often develop contracts to spell out terms of the relationship. Contracts are designed to share risks, share benefits, and create incentive structures to encourage supply chain members to adopt policies that are optimal for the entire chain. The idea is to make the total pie (of supply chain profits) bigger and then divide the bigger pie among all participants. The goal is collaboration. Some common features of contracts include *quantity discounts* (lower prices for larger orders), *buybacks* (common in the magazine and book business where there is a buyback of unsold units), and *revenue sharing* (where both partners share the risk of uncertainty by sharing revenue).

Centralized Purchasing

Companies with multiple facilities (e.g., multiple manufacturing plants or multiple retail outlets) must determine which items to purchase centrally and which to allow local sites to purchase for themselves. Unmonitored decentralized purchasing can create havoc. For example, different plants for Nestle USA's brands used to pay 29 different prices for its vanilla ingredient *to the same supplier*! Important cost, efficiency, and "single-voice" benefits often accrue from a centralized purchasing function. Typical benefits include:

- Leverage purchase volume for better pricing
- Develop specialized staff expertise
- Develop stronger supplier relationships
- Maintain professional control over the purchasing process

- Devote more resources to the supplier selection and negotiation process
- Reduce the duplication of tasks
- Promote standardization

However, local managers enjoy having their own purchasing control, and decentralized purchasing can offer certain inventory control, transportation cost, or lead-time benefits. Often firms use a hybrid approach—using centralized purchasing for some items and/or sites while allowing local purchasing for others.

E-Procurement

E-procurement
Purchasing facilitated through the Internet.

E-procurement speeds purchasing, reduces costs, and integrates the supply chain. It reduces the traditional barrage of paperwork, and at the same time provides purchasing personnel with an extensive database of supplier, delivery, and quality data.

Online Catalogs and Exchanges Purchase of standard items is often accomplished via online catalogs. Such catalogs support cost comparisons and incorporate voice and video clips, making the process efficient for both buyers and sellers.

Online exchanges are typically industry-specific Internet sites that bring buyers and sellers together. Marriott and Hyatt created one of the first, Avendra (**www.avendra.com**), which facilitates economic purchasing of the huge range of goods needed by the 5,000 hospitality industry customers now in the exchange. Online catalogs and exchanges can help move companies from a multitude of individual phone calls, faxes, and emails to a centralized system and drive billions of dollars of waste out of the supply chain.

Online Auctions In addition to catalogs, some suppliers and buyers have established online auction sites. Operations managers find online auctions a fertile area for disposing of excess raw material and discontinued or excess inventory. Online auctions lower entry barriers, encourage sellers to join, and simultaneously increase the potential number of buyers. The key for intermediaries is to find and build a huge base of potential bidders, improve client buying procedures, and qualify new suppliers.

In a traditional auction, a seller offers a product or service and generates competition between bidders—bidding the price up. In contrast, buyers often utilize online *reverse auctions* (or *Dutch auctions*). In reverse auctions, a buyer initiates the process by submitting a description of the desired product or service. Potential suppliers then submit bids, which may include price and other delivery information. Thus, price competition occurs on the selling side of the transaction—bidding the price down. Note that, as with traditional supplier selection decisions, price is important but may not be the only factor in winning the bid.

Logistics Management

Logistics management
An approach that seeks efficiency of operations through the integration of all material acquisition, movement, and storage activities.

Procurement activities may be combined with various shipping, warehousing, and inventory activities to form a logistics system. The purpose of logistics management is to obtain efficiency of operations through the integration of all material acquisition, movement, and storage activities. When transportation and inventory costs are substantial on both the input and output sides of the production process, an emphasis on logistics may be appropriate. Many firms opt for outsourcing the logistics function, as logistics specialists can often bring expertise not available in-house. For instance, logistics companies often have tracking technology that reduces transportation losses and supports delivery schedules that adhere to precise delivery windows. The potential for competitive advantage is found via both reduced costs and improved customer service.

Shipping Systems

STUDENT TIP ☆
Time, cost, and reliability variables make logistics decisions demanding.

Firms recognize that the transportation of goods to and from their facilities can represent as much as 25% of the cost of products. Because of this high cost, firms constantly evaluate their means of shipping. Six major means of shipping are trucking, railroads, airfreight, waterways, pipelines, and multimodal.

Trucking The vast majority of manufactured goods moves by truck. The flexibility of shipping by truck is only one of its many advantages. Companies that have adopted JIT programs in recent years have put increased pressure on truckers to pick up and deliver on time, with no damage, with paperwork in order, and at low cost. Trucking firms are using computers to monitor weather, find the most effective route, reduce fuel cost, and analyze the most efficient way to unload. To improve logistics efficiency, the industry is establishing Web sites such as Schneider National's connection (**www.schneider.com**), which lets shippers and truckers find each other to use some of this idle capacity.

LO5 *Explain* major issues in logistics management

Railroads Railroads in the U.S. employ 215,000 people and ship 40% of the ton-miles of all commodities, including 93% of coal, 57% of cereal grains, and 52% of basic chemicals. Containerization has made shipping of truck trailers on railroad flat cars a popular means of distribution. More than 40 million trailer loads are moved in the U.S. each year by rail.

Airfreight Airfreight represents less than 1% of tonnage shipped in the U.S. However, the proliferation of airfreight carriers such as FedEx, UPS, and DHL makes it a fast-growing mode of shipping. Clearly, for national and international movement of lightweight items, such as medical and emergency supplies, flowers, fruits, and electronic components, airfreight offers speed and reliability.

Waterways Waterways are one of the nation's oldest means of freight transportation, dating back to construction of the Erie Canal in 1817. Included in U.S. waterways are the nation's rivers, canals, the Great Lakes, coastlines, and oceans connecting to other countries. The usual cargo on internal waterways is bulky, low-value cargo such as iron ore, grains, cement, coal, chemicals, limestone, and petroleum products. Internationally, millions of containers holding all sorts of industrial and consumer goods are shipped at very low cost via huge oceangoing ships each year. Water transportation is often preferred when cost is more important than speed.

Pipelines Pipelines are an important form of transporting crude oil, natural gas, and other petroleum and chemical products.

Multimodal Multimodal shipping combines shipping methods, and is a common means of getting a product to its final destination, particularly for international shipments. The use of standardized containers facilitates easy transport from truck to rail to ship and back again, without having to unload products from the containers until the very end.

While freight rates are often based on very complicated pricing systems, in general, clients pay for speed. Faster methods such as airfreight tend to be much more expensive, while slower methods, such as waterways, provide a much cheaper shipping rate per unit. The size of shipments follows a similar pattern. The faster methods tend to involve smaller shipment sizes, while the slower methods involve very large shipment sizes.

Warehousing

Warehouses come in all shapes and sizes, from tiny rooms in the back of a store to enormous facilities that could fit multiple football fields. Warehouses may be extremely expensive to operate, but the alternatives (e.g., either no storage at all or storage at local operating facilities, along with the related logistics issues) may be much more costly. The fundamental purpose of a warehouse is to store goods. However, some warehouses also provide other crucial functions. For example, a warehouse can serve as a *consolidation point,* gathering shipments from multiple sources to send outbound in one cheaper, fully loaded truck. Alternatively, a warehouse can provide a *break-bulk* function by accepting a cheaper full truckload inbound shipment and then dividing it for distribution to individual sites. Further, similar to a major airport hub, a warehouse can serve simply as a *cross-docking* facility—accepting shipments from a variety of sources and recombining them for distribution to a variety of destinations, often without actually storing any goods during the transition. Finally, a warehouse can serve as a point of *postponement* in the process, providing final customer-specific value-added processing to the product before final shipment.

Channel assembly
Postpones final assembly of a product so the distribution channel can assemble it.

Channel assembly represents one way to implement postponement. **Channel assembly** sends individual components and modules, rather than finished products, to the distributor. The distributor then assembles, tests, and ships. Channel assembly treats distributors more as

OM in Action DHL's Role in the Supply Chain

It's the dead of night at DHL International's air express hub in Brussels, yet the massive building is alive with busy forklifts and sorting workers. The boxes going on and off the DHL plane range from Dell computers and Cisco routers to Caterpillar mufflers and Komatsu hydraulic pumps. Sun Microsystems computers from California are earmarked for Finland; DVDs from Teac's plant in Malaysia are destined for Bulgaria.

The door-to-door movement of time-sensitive packages is key to the global supply chain. JIT, short product life cycles, mass customization, and reduced inventories depend on logistics firms such as DHL, FedEx, and UPS. These powerhouses are in continuous motion.

With a decentralized network covering 225 countries and territories (more than are in the UN), DHL is a true multinational. The Brussels headquarters has only 450 of the company's 124,000 employees but includes 26 nationalities.

DHL has assembled an extensive global network of express logistics centers for strategic goods. In its Brussels logistics center, for instance, DHL upgrades, repairs, and configures Fijitsu computers, InFocus projectors, and Johnson & Johnson medical equipment. It stores and provides parts for EMC and Hewlett-Packard and replaces Nokia and Philips phones. "If something breaks down on a Thursday at 4 o'clock, the relevant warehouse knows at 4:05, and the part is on a DHL plane at 7 or 8 that evening," says Robert Kuijpers, DHL International's CEO.

Sources: Materials Handling World (December 14, 2011); **www.dhlsupplychainmatters.com**; and *Forbes* (October 8, 1999)

manufacturing partners than as distributors. This technique has proven successful in industries where products are undergoing rapid change, such as PCs. With this strategy, finished-goods inventory is reduced because units are built to a shorter, more accurate forecast. Consequently, market response is better, with lower investment—a nice combination.

Third-Party Logistics (3PL)

Supply chain managers outsource logistics to meet three goals: drive down inventory investment, lower delivery costs, and improve delivery reliability and speed. Specialized logistics firms support these goals by coordinating the supplier's inventory system with the service capabilities of the delivery firm. FedEx, for example, has a successful history of using the Internet for online tracking. At **fedex.com**, a customer can compute shipping costs, print labels, adjust invoices, and track package status. FedEx, UPS, and DHL play a core role in other firms' logistics processes. For instance, UPS works with Nike at a shipping hub in Louisville, Kentucky, to store and immediately expedite shipments. The *OM in Action* box "DHL's Role in the Supply

FedEx Corporation

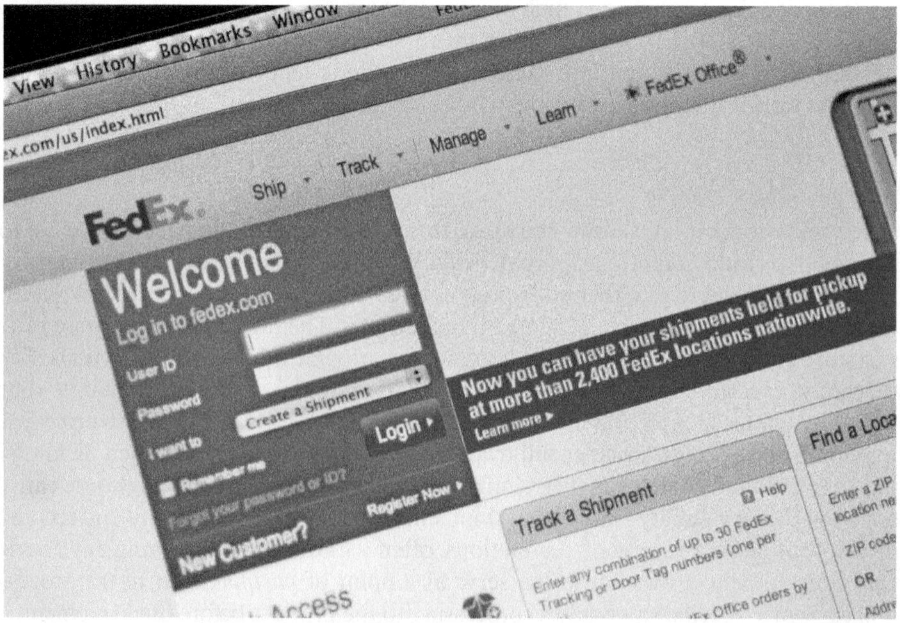

© NetPhotos/Alamy

Speed and accuracy in the supply chain are supported by bar-code tracking of shipments. At each step of a journey, from initial pickup (left) to final destination, bar codes are read and stored. Within seconds, this tracking information is available online to customers worldwide (right).

Chain" provides another example of how outsourcing logistics can reduce costs while shrinking inventory and delivery times.

Distribution Management

Management of the supply chain focuses on incoming materials, but just as importantly, *distribution management* focuses on the outbound flow of products. Designing distribution networks to meet customer expectations suggests three criteria: (1) *rapid response,* (2) *product choice,* and (3) *service.*

Office Depot, for example, addresses these customer concerns by having several stores in a town for convenience and quick response time. But it also offers an online shopping presence to accommodate customers requiring a much larger selection of products (**www.officedepot.com**). It may even offer delivery directly to large customers. These varying expectations suggest both different distribution channels and multiple outlets.

So how many stores should Office Depot open in your town? As Figure 3(a) indicates, an increase in the number of facilities generally implies a quicker response and increased customer satisfaction. On the cost side, three logistics-related costs [see Figure 3(b)] are shown: *inventory costs*, *transportation costs*, and *facility costs.* Taken together, *total logistics costs* tend to follow the top curve, first declining, and then rising. For this particular example, it appears that total logistics costs are minimized with three facilities. However, when revenue is considered [see Figure 3(c)], we note that profit is maximized with four facilities.

Whether creating a network of warehouses or retail outlets, finding the optimal number of facilities represents a critical and often dynamic decision. Barely a year after adding 3 million square feet of warehouse capacity, market dynamics caused Amazon.com to close three of its U.S. distribution centers.

Just as firms need an effective *supplier management* program, an effective *distribution management* program may make the difference between supply chain success and failure. For example, in addition to facilities, packaging and logistics are necessary for the network to perform well. Packaging and logistics are also important distribution decisions, because the manufacturer is usually held responsible for breakages and serviceability. Further, selection and development of dealers or retailers are necessary to ensure ethical and enthusiastic representation of the firm's products. Top-notch supply chain performance requires good *downstream* (distributors and retailers) management, just as it does good *upstream* (suppliers) management.

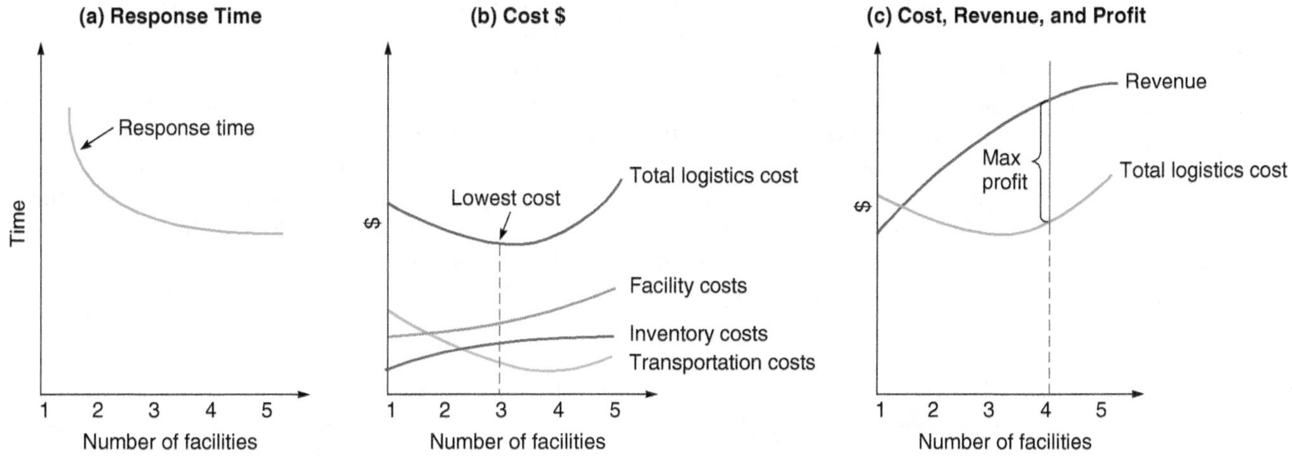

Figure 3
Number of Facilities in a Distribution Network

The focus should be on profit maximization (c) rather than cost minimization (b).

Ethics and Sustainable Supply Chain Management

Let's look at two issues that OM managers must address every day when dealing with supply chains: ethics and sustainability.

STUDENT TIP ☆ Because so much money passes through the supply chain, the opportunity for ethical lapses is significant.

Supply Chain Management Ethics

We consider three aspects of ethics: personal ethics, ethics within the supply chain, and ethical behavior regarding the environment. As the supply chain becomes increasingly international, each of these becomes even more significant.

Personal Ethics Ethical decisions are critical to the long-term success of any organization. However, the supply chain is particularly susceptible to ethical lapses. With sales personnel anxious to sell and purchasing agents spending huge sums, temptations abound. Salespeople become friends with customers, do favors for them, take them to lunch, or present small (or large) gifts. Determining when tokens of friendship become bribes can be challenging. Many companies have strict rules and codes of conduct that limit what is acceptable.

Recognizing these issues, the Institute for Supply Management has developed the following principles and standards to be used as guidelines for ethical behavior:

- *Promote and uphold* responsibilities to one's employer; positive supplier and customer relationships; sustainability and social responsibility; protection of confidential and proprietary information; applicable laws, regulations, and trade agreements; and development of professional competence.
- *Avoid* perceived impropriety; conflicts of interest; behaviors that negatively influence supply chain decisions; and improper reciprocal agreements.

Ethics Within the Supply Chain In this age of hyper-specialization, much of any organization's resources are purchased, putting great stress on ethics in the supply chain. Managers may be tempted to ignore ethical lapses by suppliers or offload pollution to suppliers. But firms must establish standards for their suppliers, just as they have established standards for themselves. Society expects ethical performance throughout the supply chain. For instance, Gap, Inc., reported that of its 3,000-plus factories worldwide, about 90% failed their initial evaluation. Gap found that 10% to 25% of its Chinese factories engaged in psychological or verbal abuse, and more than 50% of the factories in sub-Saharan Africa operated without proper safety devices. The challenge of enforcing ethical standards is significant, but responsible firms such as Gap are finding ways to deal with this difficult issue.

Ethical Behavior Regarding the Environment While ethics on both a personal basis and in the supply chain are important, so is ethical behavior in regard to the environment. Good ethics extends to doing business in a way that supports conservation and renewal of resources. This requires evaluation of the entire environmental impact, from raw material, to manufacture, through use and final disposal. For instance, Darden Restaurants and Walmart both require their shrimp and fish suppliers in Southeast Asia to abide by the standards of the Global Aquaculture Alliance. These standards must be met if suppliers want to maintain the business relationship. Operations managers also ensure that sustainability is reflected in the performance of second- and third-tier suppliers. Enforcement can be done by in-house inspectors, third-party auditors, governmental agencies, or nongovernmental watchdog organizations. All four approaches are used.

Establishing Sustainability in Supply Chains

Reverse logistics
The process of sending returned products back up the supply chain for value recovery or disposal.

The incoming supply chain garners most of the attention, but it is only part of the challenge of sustainability. The "return" supply chain is also significant. **Reverse logistics** involves the processes for sending returned products back up the supply chain for resale, repair, reuse, remanufacture, recycling, or disposal. The operations manager's goal should be to limit burning

TABLE 4 Management Challenges of Reverse Logistics

ISSUE	FORWARD LOGISTICS	REVERSE LOGISTICS
Forecasting	Relatively straightforward	More uncertain
Product quality	Uniform	Not uniform
Product packaging	Uniform	Often damaged
Pricing	Relatively uniform	Dependent on many factors
Speed	Often very important	Often not a priority
Distribution costs	Easily visible	Less directly visible
Inventory management	Consistent	Not consistent

Adapted from the Reverse Logistics Executive Council (**www.rlec.org**).

or burying of returned products and instead strive for reuse. Reverse logistics initiates a new set of challenges, as shown in Table 4.

Although sometimes used as a synonym for reverse logistics, a closed-loop supply chain refers more to the proactive design of a supply chain that tries to optimize all forward and reverse flows. A closed-loop supply chain prepares for returns prior to product introduction. For instance, Kodak introduced an excellent closed-loop supply chain for single-use cameras in the early 1990s, which is still used. Customers return the entire camera to the photo developer. In addition to printing the pictures, the developer returns the cameras to a subcontractor to refurbish the cameras for reloading with film and future use for Kodak. Customers are unable to distinguish refurbished cameras from original ones.

Closed-loop supply chain
A supply chain designed to optimize both forward and reverse flows.

Measuring Supply Chain Performance

STUDENT TIP
If you can't measure it, you can't control it.

Like all other managers, supply chain managers require standards (or *metrics*, as they are often called) to evaluate performance. We now introduce several inventory-based metrics.

Assets Committed to Inventory

LO6 *Compute* the percentage of assets committed to inventory and inventory turnover

Supply chain managers make scheduling and quantity decisions that determine the assets committed to inventory. Three specific measures can be helpful here. The first is the amount of money invested in inventory, usually expressed as a percentage of assets, as shown in Equation (1) and Example 2:

$$\text{Percentage invested in inventory} = (\text{Total inventory investment}/\text{Total assets}) \times 100 \qquad (1)$$

Example 2

TRACKING HOME DEPOT'S INVENTORY INVESTMENT

Home Depot's management wishes to track its investment in inventory as one of its performance measures. Recently, Home Depot had \$11.4 billion invested in inventory and total assets of \$44.4 billion.

APPROACH ▶ Determine the investment in inventory and total assets and then use Equation (1).

SOLUTION ▶ Percent invested in inventory = $(11.4/44.4) \times 100 = 25.7\%$

INSIGHT ▶ Over one-fourth of Home Depot assets are committed to inventory.

LEARNING EXERCISE ▶ If Home Depot can drive its investment down to 20% of assets, how much money will it free up for other uses? [Answer: $11.4 - (44.4 \times 2) = \$2.52$ billion.]

RELATED PROBLEMS ▶ 5b, 6b

Inventory turnover
Cost of goods sold divided by average inventory.

TABLE 5

Inventory as Percentage of Total Assets (with examples of exceptional performance)

Manufacturer (Toyota 5%)	15%
Wholesale (Coca-Cola 2.9%)	34%
Restaurants (McDonald's .05%)	2.9%
Retail (Home Depot 25.7%)	27%

Specific comparisons with competitors may assist evaluation. Total assets committed to inventory in manufacturing approach 15%, in wholesale 34%, and retail 27%—with wide variations, depending on the specific business model, the business cycle, and management (see Table 5).

The second common measure of supply chain performance is *inventory turnover* (see Table 6). Its reciprocal, *weeks of supply*, is the third. **Inventory turnover** is computed on an annual basis, using Equation (2):

$$\text{Inventory turnover} = \text{Cost of goods sold/Inventory investment} \quad (2)$$

Cost of goods sold is the cost to produce the goods or services sold for a given period. Inventory investment is the average inventory value for the same period. This may be the average of several periods of inventory or beginning and ending inventory added together and divided by 2. Often, average inventory investment is based on nothing more than the inventory investment at the end of the period—typically at year-end.[1]

In Example 3, we look at inventory turnover applied to PepsiCo.

Example 3

INVENTORY TURNOVER AT PEPSICO, INC.

PepsiCo, Inc., manufacturer and distributor of drinks, Frito-Lay, and Quaker Foods, provides the following in a recent annual report (shown here in $ billions). Determine PepsiCo's turnover.

Net revenue		$32.5
Cost of goods sold		$14.2
Inventory:		
Raw material inventory	$.74	
Work-in-process inventory	$.11	
Finished goods inventory	$.84	
Total inventory investment		$1.69

APPROACH ▶ Use the inventory turnover computation in Equation (2) to measure inventory performance. Cost of goods sold is $14.2 billion. Total inventory is the sum of raw material at $.74 billion, work-in-process at $.11 billion, and finished goods at $.84 billion, for total inventory investment of $1.69 billion.

SOLUTION ▶
$$\begin{aligned}\text{Inventory turnover} &= \text{Cost of goods sold/Inventory investment}\\ &= 14.2/1.69\\ &= 8.4\end{aligned}$$

INSIGHT ▶ We now have a standard, popular measure by which to evaluate performance.

LEARNING EXERCISE ▶ If Coca-Cola's cost of goods sold is $10.8 billion and inventory investment is $.76 billion, what is its inventory turnover? [Answer: 14.2.]

RELATED PROBLEMS ▶ 5a, 6c, 7

Weeks of supply, as shown in Example 4, may have more meaning in the wholesale and retail portions of the service sector than in manufacturing. It is computed below as the reciprocal of inventory turnover:

$$\text{Weeks of supply} = \text{Inventory investment/(Annual cost of goods sold/52 weeks)} \quad (3)$$

[1]Inventory quantities often fluctuate wildly, and various types of inventory exist (e.g., raw material; work-in-process; finished goods; and maintenance, repair, and operating supplies [MRO]). Therefore, care must be taken when using inventory values; they may reflect more than just supply chain performance.

Example 4

DETERMINING WEEKS OF SUPPLY AT PEPSICO

Using the PepsiCo data in Example 3, management wants to know the weeks of supply.

APPROACH ▶ We know that inventory investment is \$1.69 billion and that weekly sales equal annual cost of goods sold (\$14.2 billion) divided by 52 = \$14.2/52 = \$.273 billion.

SOLUTION ▶ Using Equation (3), we compute weeks of supply as:

$$\text{Weeks of supply} = (\text{Inventory investment}/\text{Average weekly cost of goods sold})$$
$$= 1.69/.273 = 6.19 \text{ weeks}$$

INSIGHT ▶ We now have a standard measurement by which to evaluate a company's continuing performance or by which to compare companies.

LEARNING EXERCISE ▶ If Coca-Cola's average inventory investment is \$.76 billion and its average weekly cost of goods sold is \$.207 billion, what is the firm's weeks of supply? [Answer: 3.67 weeks.]

RELATED PROBLEMS ▶ 6a, 8

Supply chain management is critical in driving down inventory investment. The rapid movement of goods is key. Walmart, for example, has set the pace in the retailing sector with its world-renowned supply chain management. By doing so, it has established a competitive advantage. With its own truck fleet, distribution centers, and a state-of-the-art communication system, Walmart (with the help of its suppliers) replenishes store shelves an average of twice per week. Competitors resupply every other week. Economical and speedy resupply means both rapid response to product changes and customer preferences, as well as lower inventory investment. Similarly, while many manufacturers struggle to move inventory turnover up to 10 times per year, Dell Computer has inventory turns exceeding 90 and supply measured in *days*—not weeks. Supply chain management provides a competitive advantage when firms effectively respond to the demands of global markets and global sources.

TABLE 6

Examples of Annual Inventory Turnover

FOOD, BEVERAGE, RETAIL	
Anheuser Busch	15
Coca-Cola	14
Home Depot	5
McDonald's	112
MANUFACTURING	
Dell Computer	90
Johnson Controls	22
Toyota (overall)	13
Nissan (assembly)	150

Benchmarking the Supply Chain

While metric values convey their own meaning and are useful when compared to past data, another important use compares these values to those of benchmark firms. Several organizations and websites allow companies to submit their own data and receive reports on how they stack up against other firms in their own industry or against world-class firms from any industry. Table 7 provides a few examples of metric values for typical firms and for benchmark firms in the consumer packaged goods industry. World-class benchmarks are the result of well-managed supply chains that drive down costs, lead times, late deliveries, and shortages while improving service levels.

TABLE 7 **Supply Chain Metrics in the Consumer Packaged Goods Industry**

	TYPICAL FIRMS	BENCHMARK FIRMS
Order fill rate	71%	98%
Order fulfillment lead time (days)	7	3
Cash-to-cash cycle time (days)	100	30
Inventory days of supply	50	20

Source: Institute for Industrial Engineers

The SCOR Model

Perhaps the best-known benchmarking system is the five-part **Supply Chain Operations Reference (SCOR) model**. As shown in Figure 4, the five parts are Plan (planning activities for supply and demand), Source (purchasing activities), Make (production activities), Deliver (distribution activities), and Return (closed-loop supply chain activities). The system is maintained by the

Supply Chain Operations Reference (SCOR) model
A set of processes, metrics, and best practices developed by the Supply Chain Council.

Figure 4
The Supply Chain Operations Reference (SCOR) Model

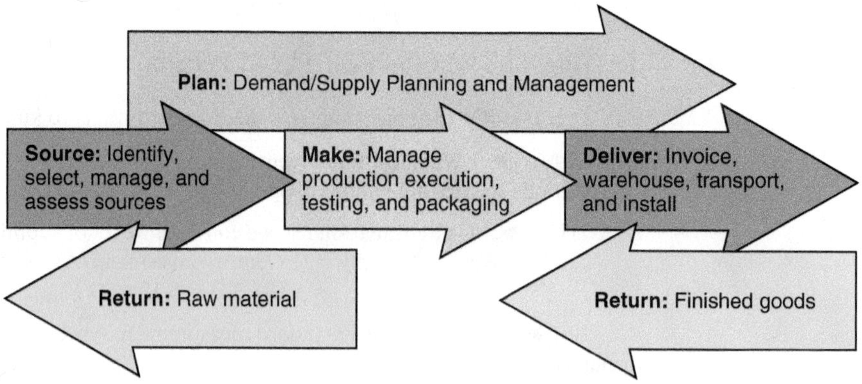

non-profit Supply Chain Council (SCC) (**www.supplychain.org**). Firms use SCOR to identify, measure, reorganize, and improve supply chain processes.

The SCOR model defines over 200 process elements, 550 measurable metrics, and 500 best practices. The best practices describe the techniques used by benchmark firms that have scored very well on the metrics. SCOR combines these metrics with "Performance Attributes" (see Table 8) to facilitate comparisons of companies that compete by using different strategies (for example, low cost vs. responsiveness).

Benchmarking can be very useful, but it is not always adequate for excellence in the supply chain. Audits based on continuing communication, understanding, trust, performance, and corporate strategy are necessary. The relationships should manifest themselves in the mutual belief that "we are in this together" and go well beyond written agreements.

TABLE 8 **SCOR Model Metrics to Help Firms Benchmark Performance Against the Industry**

PERFORMANCE ATTRIBUTE	SAMPLE METRIC	CALCULATION
Supply chain reliability	Perfect order fulfillment	(Total perfect orders)/(Total number of orders)
Supply chain responsiveness	Average order fulfillment cycle time	(Sum of actual cycle times for all orders delivered)/(Total number of orders delivered)
Supply chain agility	Upside supply chain flexibility	Time required to achieve an unplanned 20% increase in delivered quantities
Supply chain costs	Supply chain management cost	Cost to plan + Cost to source + Cost to deliver + Cost to return
Supply chain asset management	Cash-to-cash cycle time	Inventory days of supply + Days of receivables outstanding − Days of payables outstanding

Summary

Competition is no longer between companies but between supply chains. The key to success is to collaborate with members on both the supply side and the distribution side of the supply chain to make decisions that will benefit the whole channel. For many firms, the supply chain determines a substantial portion of product cost and quality, as well as opportunities for responsiveness and differentiation. The challenge of building a great supply chain is significant, but with good sourcing tactics, a thoughtful logistics plan, and active management of the distribution network, each link in the chain can be firmly forged. A number of metrics are available to help managers evaluate their supply chain performance and benchmark against the industry. Skillful supply chain management provides a great strategic opportunity for competitive advantage.

Key Terms

Supply chain management
Make-or-buy decision
Outsourcing
Vertical integration
Keiretsu
Virtual companies
Cross-sourcing
Bullwhip effect
Pull data
Single-stage control of replenishment
Vendor-managed inventory (VMI)
Collaborative planning, forecasting, and replenishment (CPFR)
Blanket order
Postponement
Drop shipping
E-procurement
Logistics management
Channel assembly
Reverse logistics
Closed-loop supply chain
Inventory turnover
Supply Chain Operations Reference (SCOR) model

Ethical Dilemma

As a buyer for a discount retail chain, you find yourself caught in a maelstrom. Just last month, your chain began selling an economy-priced line of clothing endorsed by a famous movie star. To be price competitive, you have followed the rest of the industry and sourced the clothing from a low-wage region of Asia. Initial sales have been brisk; however, the movie star has recently called you screaming and crying because an investigative news outlet has reported that the clothes with her name on them are being made by children.

Outraged, you fly to the outsourcing manufacturing facility only to find that conditions are not quite as clear-cut as you had originally imagined. You feel uncomfortable riding through the streets. Poverty is everywhere. Children are chasing foreigners and begging for money. When you enter the plant, you observe a very clean facility. The completely female workforce appears to be very industrious, but many of them do appear to be young. You confront the plant manager and explain your firm's strict international sourcing policies. You demand to know why these girls aren't in school. The manager provides the following response: "The truth is that some of these workers may be underage. We check IDs, but the use of falsified records is commonplace in this country. Plus, you don't understand the alternatives. If you shut this plant down, you will literally take food off the table for these families. There are no other opportunities in this town at this time, and there's no comprehensive welfare system in our country. As for the young women, school is not an option. In this town, only boys receive an education past the sixth grade. If you shut us down, these girls will be out on the street, begging, stealing, or prostituting themselves. Your business offers them a better existence. Please don't take that away!"

What do you say to your company, the movie star, the media, and the protestors picketing your stores? Is the best option to shut down and try someplace else?

Discussion Questions

1. Define *supply chain management.*
2. What are the objectives of supply chain management?
3. What is the objective of logistics management?
4. How do we distinguish between the types of risk in the supply chain?
5. What is vertical integration? Give examples of backward and forward integration.
6. What are three basic approaches to negotiations?
7. How does a traditional adversarial relationship with suppliers change when a firm makes a decision to move to a few suppliers?
8. What is the difference between postponement and channel assembly?
9. What is CPFR?
10. What is the value of online auctions in e-commerce?
11. Explain how FedEx uses the Internet to meet requirements for quick and accurate delivery.
12. How does Walmart use drop shipping?
13. What are blanket orders? How do they differ from invoiceless purchasing?
14. What can purchasing do to implement just-in-time deliveries?
15. What is e-procurement?
16. How does Darden Restaurants, described in the *Global Company Profile*, find competitive advantage in its supply chain?
17. What is SCOR, and what purpose does it serve?

Solved Problem

Virtual Office Hours help is available at www.myomlab.com.

SOLVED PROBLEM 1

Jack's Pottery Outlet has total end-of-year assets of \$5 million. The first-of-the-year inventory was \$375,000, with a year-end inventory of \$325,000. The annual cost of goods sold was \$7 million. The owner, Eric Jack, wants to evaluate his supply chain performance by measuring his percent of assets in inventory, his inventory turnover, and his weeks of supply. We use Equations (1), (2), and (3) to provide these measures.

SOLUTION

First, determine *average inventory*:

$$(\$375{,}000 + \$325{,}000)/2 = \$350{,}000$$

Then, use Equation (1) to determine percent invested in inventory:

$$\text{Percent invested in inventory} = (\text{Total inventory investment}/\text{Total assets}) \times 100$$
$$= (350{,}000/5{,}000{,}000) \times 100$$
$$= 7\%$$

Third, determine inventory turnover, using Equation (2):

$$\text{Inventory turnover} = \text{Cost of goods sold}/\text{Inventory investment}$$
$$= 7{,}000{,}000/350{,}000$$
$$= 20$$

Finally, to determine weeks of inventory, use Equation (3), adjusted to weeks:

$$\text{Weeks of inventory} = \text{Inventory investment}/\text{Weekly cost of goods sold}$$
$$= 350{,}000/(7{,}000{,}000/52)$$
$$= 350{,}000/134{,}615$$
$$= 2.6$$

We conclude that Jack's Pottery Outlet has 7% of its assets invested in inventory, that the inventory turnover is 20, and that weeks of supply is 2.6.

Problems

•• **1** Choose a local establishment that is a member of a relatively large chain. From interviews with workers and information from the Internet, identify the elements of the supply chain. Determine whether the supply chain supports a low-cost, rapid response, or differentiation strategy. Are the supply chain characteristics significantly different from one product to another?

•• **2** Using sources from the Internet, identify some of the problems faced by a company of your choosing as it moves toward, or operates as, a virtual organization. Does its operating as a virtual organization simply exacerbate old problems, or does it create new ones?

••• **3** Hau Lee Furniture, Inc., described in Example 1 of this text, finds its current profit of $10,000 inadequate. The bank is insisting on an improved profit picture prior to approval of a loan for some new equipment. Hau would like to improve the profit line to $25,000 so he can obtain the bank's approval for the loan.

a) What percentage improvement is needed in the *supply chain strategy* for profit to improve to $25,000? What is the cost of material with a $25,000 profit?
b) What percentage improvement is needed in the *sales strategy* for profit to improve to $25,000? What must sales be for profit to improve to $25,000?

•••• **4** Kamal Fatehl, production manager of Kennesaw Manufacturing, finds his profit at $15,000 (as shown in the statement below)—inadequate for expanding his business. The bank is insisting on an improved profit picture prior to approval of a loan for some new equipment. Kamal would like to improve the profit line to $25,000 so he can obtain the bank's approval for the loan.

		% OF SALES
Sales	$250,000	100%
Cost of supply chain purchases	175,000	70%
Other production costs	30,000	12%
Fixed costs	30,000	12%
Profit	15,000	6%

a) What percentage improvement is needed in a *supply chain strategy* for profit to improve to $25,000? What is the cost of material with a $25,000 profit?
b) What percentage improvement is needed in a *sales strategy* for profit to improve to $25,000? What must sales be for profit to improve to $25,000? (*Hint:* See Example 1.)

•• **5** Baker Mfg. Inc. (see Table 9) wishes to compare its inventory turnover to those of industry leaders, who have turnover of about 13 times per year and 8% of their assets invested in inventory.

a) What is Baker's inventory turnover?
b) What is Baker's percent of assets committed to inventory?
c) How does Baker's performance compare to the industry leaders?

TABLE 9 **For Problems 5 and 6**

ARROW DISTRIBUTING CORP.	
Net revenue	$16,500
Cost of sales	$13,500
Inventory	$ 1,000
Total assets	$ 8,600
BAKER MFG. INC.	
Net revenue	$27,500
Cost of sales	$21,500
Inventory	$ 1,250
Total assets	$16,600

•• **6** Arrow Distributing Corp. (see Table 9) likes to track inventory by using weeks of supply as well as by inventory turnover.

a) What is its weeks of supply?
b) What percent of Arrow's assets are committed to inventory?
c) What is Arrow's inventory turnover?
d) Is Arrow's supply chain performance, as measured by these inventory metrics, better than that of Baker in Problem 5?

• **7** The grocery industry has an annual inventory turnover of about 14 times. Organic Grocers, Inc. had a cost of goods sold last year of $10.5 million; its average inventory was $1.0 million. What was Organic Grocers's inventory turnover, and how does that performance compare with that of the industry?

•• **8** Mattress Wholesalers, Inc., is constantly trying to reduce inventory in its supply chain. Last year, cost of goods sold was $7.5 million and inventory was $1.5 million. This year, cost of goods sold is $8.6 million and inventory investment is $1.6 million.

a) What were the weeks of supply last year?
b) What are the weeks of supply this year?
c) Is Mattress Wholesalers making progress in its inventory-reduction effort?

© Tyler Olson/Fotolia

CASE STUDIES

Darden's Global Supply Chains

Video Case

Darden Restaurants (subject of the *Global Company Profile* at the beginning of this text), owner of popular brands such as Olive Garden and Red Lobster, requires unique supply chains to serve more than 300 million meals annually. Darden's strategy is operations excellence, and Senior VP Jim Lawrence's task is to ensure competitive advantage via Darden's supply chains. For a firm with purchases exceeding $1.5 billion, managing the supply chains is a complex and challenging task.

Darden, like other casual dining restaurants, has unique supply chains that reflect its menu options. Darden's supply chains are rather shallow, often having just one tier of suppliers. But it has four distinct supply chains.

First, "smallware" is a restaurant industry term for items such as linens, dishes, tableware and kitchenware, and silverware. These are purchased, with Darden taking title as they are received at the Darden Direct Distribution (DDD) warehouse in Orlando, Florida. From this single warehouse, smallware items are shipped via common carrier (trucking companies) to Olive Garden, Red Lobster, Bahama Breeze, and Seasons 52 restaurants.

Second, frozen, dry, and canned food products are handled economically by Darden's 11 distribution centers in North America, which are managed by major U.S. food distributors, such as MBM, Maines, and Sygma. This is Darden's second supply line.

Third, the fresh food supply chain (not frozen and not canned), where product life is measured in days, includes dairy products, produce, and meat. This supply chain is B2B, where restaurant managers directly place orders with a preselected group of independent suppliers.

Fourth, Darden's worldwide seafood supply chain is the final link. Here Darden has developed independent suppliers of salmon, shrimp, tilapia, scallops, and other fresh fish that are source inspected by Darden's overseas representatives to ensure quality. These fresh products are flown to the U.S. and shipped to 16 distributors, with 22 locations, for quick delivery to the restaurants. With suppliers in 35 countries, Darden must be on the cutting edge when it comes to collaboration, partnering, communication, and food safety. It does this with heavy travel schedules for purchasing and quality control personnel, native-speaking employees onsite, and aggressive communication. Communication is a critical element; Darden tries to develop as much forecasting transparency as possible. "Point of sale (POS) terminals," says Lawrence, "feed actual sales every night to suppliers."

Discussion Questions*

1. What are the advantages of each of Darden's four supply chains?
2. What are the complications of having four supply chains?
3. Where would you expect ownership/title to change in each of Darden's four supply chains?
4. How do Darden's four supply chains compare with those of other firms, such as Dell or an automobile manufacturer? Why do the differences exist, and how are they addressed?

*You may wish to view the video that accompanies this case before answering these questions.

Supply Chain Management at Regal Marine

Video Case

Like most other manufacturers, Regal Marine finds that it must spend a huge portion of its revenue on purchases. Regal has also found that the better its suppliers understand its end users, the better are both the supplier's product and Regal's final product. As one of the 10 largest U.S. power boat manufacturers, Regal is trying to differentiate its products from the vast number of boats supplied by 300 other companies. Thus, the firm works closely with suppliers to ensure innovation, quality, and timely delivery.

Regal has done a number of things to drive down costs while driving up quality, responsiveness, and innovation. First, working on partnering relationships with suppliers ranging from providers of windshields to providers of instrument panel controls, Regal has brought timely innovation at reasonable cost to its product. Key vendors are so tightly linked with the company that they meet with designers to discuss material changes to be incorporated into new product designs.

Second, the company has joined about 15 other boat manufacturers in a purchasing group, known as American Boat Builders Association, to work with suppliers on reducing the costs of large purchases. Third, Regal is working with a number of local vendors to supply hardware and fasteners directly to the assembly line on a just-in-time basis. In some of these cases, Regal has worked out an arrangement with the vendor so that title does not transfer until parts are used by Regal. In other cases, title transfers when items are delivered to the property. This practice drives down total inventory and the costs associated with large-lot delivery.

Finally, Regal works with a personnel agency to outsource part of the recruiting and screening process for employees. In all these cases, Regal is demonstrating innovative approaches to supply chain management that help the firm and, ultimately, the end user.

Discussion Questions*

1. What other techniques might Regal use to improve supply chain management?
2. What kind of response might members of the supply chain expect from Regal because of their "partnering" in the supply chain?
3. Why is supply chain management important to Regal?

*You may wish to view the video that accompanies this case before answering the questions.

Arnold Palmer Hospital's Supply Chain

Video Case

Arnold Palmer Hospital, one of the nation's top hospitals dedicated to serving women and children, is a large business with over 2,000 employees working in a 431-bed facility totaling 676,000 square feet in Orlando, Florida. Like many other hospitals, and other companies, Arnold Palmer Hospital had been a long-time member of a large buying group, one servicing 900 members. But the group did have a few limitations. For example, it might change suppliers for a particular product every year (based on a new lower-cost bidder) or stock only a product that was not familiar to the physicians at Arnold Palmer Hospital. The buying group was also not able to negotiate contracts with local manufacturers to secure the best pricing.

So in 2003, Arnold Palmer Hospital, together with seven other partner hospitals in central Florida, formed its own much smaller, but still powerful (with $200 million in annual purchases) Healthcare Purchasing Alliance (HPA) corporation. The new alliance saved the HPA members $7 million in its first year with two main changes. First, it was structured and staffed to assure that the bulk of the savings associated with its contracting efforts went to its eight members. Second, it struck even better deals with vendors by guaranteeing a *committed* volume and signing not 1-year deals but 3- to 5-year contracts. "Even with a new internal cost of $400,000 to run HPA, the savings and ability to contract for what our member hospitals really want makes the deal a winner," says George DeLong, head of HPA.

Effective supply chain management in manufacturing often focuses on development of new product innovations and efficiency through buyer–vendor collaboration. However, the approach in a service industry has a slightly different emphasis. At Arnold Palmer Hospital, supply chain opportunities often manifest themselves through the Medical Economic Outcomes Committee. This committee (and its subcommittees) consists of users (including the medical and nursing staff) who evaluate purchase options with a goal of better medicine while achieving economic targets. For instance, the heart pacemaker negotiation by the cardiology subcommittee allowed for the standardization to two manufacturers, with annual savings of $2 million for just this one product.

Arnold Palmer Hospital is also able to develop custom products that require collaboration down to the third tier of the supply chain. This is the case with custom packs that are used in the operating room. The custom packs are delivered by a distributor, McKesson General Medical, but assembled by a pack company that uses materials the hospital wanted purchased from specific manufacturers. The HPA allows Arnold Palmer Hospital to be creative in this way. With major cost savings, standardization, blanket purchase orders, long-term contracts, and more control of product development, the benefits to the hospital are substantial.

Discussion Questions*

1. How does this supply chain differ from that in a manufacturing firm?
2. What are the constraints on making decisions based on economics alone at Arnold Palmer Hospital?
3. What role do doctors and nurses play in supply chain decisions in a hospital? How is this participation handled at Arnold Palmer Hospital?
4. Doctor Smith just returned from the Annual Physician's Orthopedic Conference, where she saw a new hip joint replacement demonstrated. She decides she wants to start using the replacement joint at Arnold Palmer Hospital. What process will Dr. Smith have to go through at the hospital to introduce this new product into the supply chain for future surgical use?

*You may wish to view the video that accompanies this case before answering the questions.

- **Additional Case Studies:** Visit **www.myomlab.com** or **www.pearsonhighered.com/heizer** for these free case studies:
Amazon.com: Discusses opportunities and issues in an innovative business model for the Internet.
Dell's Value Chain: Discusses Dell's very successful collaborative supply chain.

Bibliography

Blackburn, Joseph, and Gary Scudder. "Supply Chain Strategies for Perishable Products." *Production and Operations Management* 18, no. 2 (March–April 2009): 129–137.
Boyer, Kenneth K., and G. Tomas M. Hult. "Extending the Supply Chain: Integrating Operations and Marketing in the Online Grocery Industry." *Journal of Operations Management* 23, no. 6 (September 2005): 642–661.
Chopra, Sunil, and Peter Meindl. *Supply Chain Management*, 4th ed. Upper Saddle River, NJ: Prentice Hall (2010).
Crook, T. Russell, and James G. Combs. "Sources and Consequences of Bargaining Power in Supply Chains." *Journal of Operations Management* 25, no. 2 (March 2007): 546–555.
Hu, J., and C. L. Munson. "Speed versus Reliability Trade-offs in Supplier Selection." *International Journal Procurement Management* 1, no. 1/2 (2007): 238–259.
Kersten, Wolfgang, and Thorsten Blecker (eds.). *Managing Risk in Supply Chains*. Berlin: Erich Schmidt Verlag GmbH & Co. (2006).
Kreipl, Stephan, and Michael Pinedo. "Planning and Scheduling in Supply Chains." *Production and Operations Management* 13, no. 1 (Spring 2004): 77–92.
Linton, J. D., R. Klassen, and V. Jayaraman. "Sustainable Supply Chains: An Introduction." *Journal of Operations Management* 25, no. 6 (November, 2007): 1075–1082.
Monczka, R. M., R. B. Handfield, L. C. Gianipero, and J. L. Patterson. *Purchasing and Supply Chain Management*, 5th ed. Mason, OH: Cengage (2012).
Narayanan, Sriram, Ann S. Marucheck, and Robert B. Handfield. "Electronic Data Interchange: Research Review and Future Directions." *Decisions Sciences* 40, no. 1 (February 2009): 121–163.
Pisano, Gary P., and Roberto Verganti. "Which Kind of Collaboration Is Right for You?" *Harvard Business Review* 86, no. 12 (December, 2008): 78–86.
Sinha, K. K., and E. J. Kohnke. "Health Care Supply Chain Design." *Decision Sciences* 40, no. 2 (May 2009): 197–212.
Stanley, L. L., and V. R. Singhal. "Service Quality Along the Supply Chain." *Journal of Operations Management* 19, no. 3 (May 2001): 287–306.
Wisner, Joel, K. Tan, and G. Keong Leong. *Principles of Supply Chain Management,* 4th ed., Mason, OH: Cengage (2012).

APPENDIX
SOLUTIONS TO EVEN-NUMBERED PROBLEMS

2 Problems include communication, product valuation, selecting virtual partners

4 (a) Only a 5.7% decrease in material (supply chain) costs are required to yield a profit of $25,000, but (b) a 22.2% increase in sales is necessary for a $25,000 profit.

6 **(a)** Weeks of supply = 3.85
(b) % of assets in inventory = 11.63%
(c) Turnover = 13.5
(d) No, but note they are in different industries

8 **(a)** Last year = 10.4
(b) This year = 9.67
(c) Yes

Rapid Review

Main Heading	Review Material	MyOMLab
THE SUPPLY CHAIN'S STRATEGIC IMPORTANCE	Most firms spend a huge portion of their sales dollars on purchases. ■ **Supply chain management**—Management of activities related to procuring materials and services, transforming them into intermediate goods and final products, and delivering them through a distribution system. *The objective is to build a chain of suppliers that focuses on maximizing value to the ultimate customer.* Competition is no longer between companies; it is between supply chains.	**VIDEO 1** Darden's Global Supply Chain Problems: 3, 4
SOURCING ISSUES: MAKE-OR-BUY VS. OUTSOURCING	■ **Make-or-buy decision**—A choice between producing a component or service within the firm or purchasing it from an outside source. ■ **Outsourcing**—Transferring to external suppliers a firm's activities that have traditionally been internal.	
SIX SOURCING STRATEGIES	Six supply chain strategies for goods and services to be obtained from outside sources are: 1. Negotiating with many suppliers and playing one supplier against another 2. Developing long-term partnering relationships with a few suppliers 3. Vertical integration 4. Joint ventures 5. Developing *keiretsu* networks 6. Developing virtual companies that use suppliers on an as-needed basis. ■ **Vertical integration**—Developing the ability to produce goods or services previously purchased or actually buying a supplier or a distributor. ■ ***Keiretsu***—A Japanese term that describes suppliers who become part of a company coalition. ■ **Virtual companies**—Companies that rely on a variety of supplier relationships to provide services on demand. Also known as hollow corporations or network companies.	**VIDEO 2** Supply Chain Management at Regal Marine
SUPPLY CHAIN RISK	The development of a supply chain plan requires a thorough assessment of the risks involved. ■ **Cross-sourcing**—Using one supplier for a component and a second supplier for another component, where each supplier acts as a backup for the other.	
MANAGING THE INTEGRATED SUPPLY CHAIN	Supply chain integration success begins with mutual agreement on goals, followed by mutual trust, and continues with compatible organizational cultures. Three issues complicate the development of an efficient, integrated supply chain: local optimization, incentives, and large lots. ■ **Bullwhip effect**—Increasing fluctuation in orders or cancellations that often occurs as orders move through the supply chain. ■ **Pull data**—Accurate sales data that initiate transactions to "pull" product through the supply chain. ■ **Single-stage control of replenishment**—Fixing responsibility for monitoring and managing inventory for the retailer. ■ **Vendor-managed inventory (VMI)**—A system in which a supplier maintains material for the buyer, often delivering directly to the buyer's using department. ■ **Collaborative planning, forecasting, and replenishment (CPFR)**—A system in which members of a supply chain share information in a joint effort to reduce supply chain costs. ■ **Blanket order**—A long-term purchase commitment to a supplier for items that are to be delivered against short-term releases to ship. The purchasing department should make special efforts to increase levels of standardization. ■ **Postponement**—Delaying any modifications or customization to a product as long as possible in the production process. Postponement strives to minimize internal variety while maximizing external variety. ■ **Drop shipping**—Shipping directly from the supplier to the end consumer rather than from the seller, saving both time and reshipping costs. Online catalogs move companies from a multitude of individual phone calls, faxes, and e-mails to a centralized online system and drive billions of dollars of waste out of the supply chain.	**VIDEO 3** Arnold Palmer Hospital's Supply Chain
BUILDING THE SUPPLY BASE	Supplier selection is a four-stage process: (1) supplier evaluation, (2) supplier development, (3) negotiations, and (4) contracting. *Supplier evaluation* involves finding potential vendors and determining the likelihood of their becoming good suppliers. *Supplier development* may include everything from training, to engineering and production help, to procedures for information transfer.	

Main Heading	Review Material	MyOMLab
	Negotiations involve approaches taken by supply chain personnel to set prices. Three classic types of negotiation strategies are (1) the cost-based price model, (2) the market-based price model, and (3) competitive bidding. *Contracting* involves a design to share risks, share benefits, and create incentives so as to optimize the whole supply chain. ■ **E-procurement**—Purchasing facilitated through the Internet.	
LOGISTICS MANAGEMENT	■ **Logistics management**—An approach that seeks efficiency of operations through the integration of all material acquisition, movement, and storage activities. Six major means of distribution are trucking, railroads, airfreight, waterways, pipelines, and multimodal. The vast majority of manufactured goods move by truck. Third-party logistics involves the outsourcing of the logistics function. ■ **Channel assembly**—A system that postpones final assembly of a product so the distribution channel can assemble it.	
DISTRIBUTION MANAGEMENT	Distribution management focused on the outbound flow of final products. Total logistics costs are the sum of facility costs, inventory costs, and transportation costs (Figure 3). The optimal number of distribution facilities focuses on maximizing profit.	
ETHICS AND SUSTAINABLE SUPPLY CHAIN MANAGEMENT	Ethics includes personal ethics, ethics within the supply chain, and ethical behavior regarding the environment. The Institute for Supply Management has developed a set of Principles and Standards for ethical conduct. ■ **Reverse logistics**—The process of sending returned products back up the supply chain for value recovery or disposal. ■ **Closed-loop supply chain**—A supply chain designed to optimize all forward and reverse flows.	
MEASURING SUPPLY CHAIN PERFORMANCE	Typical supply chain benchmark metrics include lead time, time spent placing an order, percent of late deliveries, percent of rejected material, and number of shortages per year: Percent invested in inventory = (Total inventory investment/Total assets) × 100 (1) ■ **Inventory turnover**—Cost of goods sold divided by average inventory: Inventory turnover = Cost of goods sold ÷ Inventory investment (2) Weeks of supply = Inventory investment ÷ (Annual cost of goods sold/52 weeks) (3) ■ **Supply Chain Operations Reference (SCOR) model**—A set of processes, metrics, and best practices developed by the Supply Chain Council. The five parts of the SCOR model are Plan, Source, Make, Deliver, and Return.	Problems: 5–8 Virtual Office Hours for Solved Problem: 1

Self Test

■ **Before taking the self-test,** refer to the learning objectives listed at the beginning of the text and the key terms listed at the end of the text.

LO1. The objective of supply chain management is to _______.

LO2. The term *vertical integration* means to:
- **a)** develop the ability to produce products that complement or supplement the original product.
- **b)** produce goods or services previously purchased.
- **c)** develop the ability to produce the specified good more efficiently.
- **d)** all of the above.

LO3. The bullwhip effect can be aggravated by:
- **a)** local optimization.
- **b)** sales incentives.
- **c)** quantity discounts.
- **d)** promotions.
- **e)** all of the above.

LO4. Supplier selection requires:
- **a)** supplier evaluation and effective third-party logistics.
- **b)** supplier development and logistics.
- **c)** negotiations, supplier evaluation, supplier development, and contracts.
- **d)** an integrated supply chain.
- **e)** inventory and supply chain management.

LO5. A major issue in logistics is:
- **a)** cost of purchases.
- **b)** supplier evaluation.
- **c)** product customization.
- **d)** cost of shipping alternatives.
- **e)** excellent e-procurement.

LO6. Inventory turnover =
- **a)** Cost of goods sold ÷ Weeks of supply
- **b)** Weeks of supply ÷ Annual cost of goods sold
- **c)** Annual cost of goods sold ÷ 52 weeks
- **d)** Inventory investment ÷ Cost of goods sold
- **e)** Cost of goods sold ÷ Inventory investment

Answers: LO1. build a chain of suppliers that focuses on maximizing value to the ultimate customer; LO2. b; LO3. e; LO4. c; LO5. d; LO6. e.

Simulation

OUTLINE

- What Is Simulation
- Advantages and Disadvantages of Simulation
- Monte Carlo Simulation
- Simulation and Inventory Analysis

LEARNING OBJECTIVES

LO1 ***List*** the advantages and disadvantages of modeling with simulation

LO2 ***Perform*** the five steps in a Monte Carlo simulation

LO3 ***Simulate*** an inventory problem

LO4 ***Use*** Excel spreadsheets to create a simulation

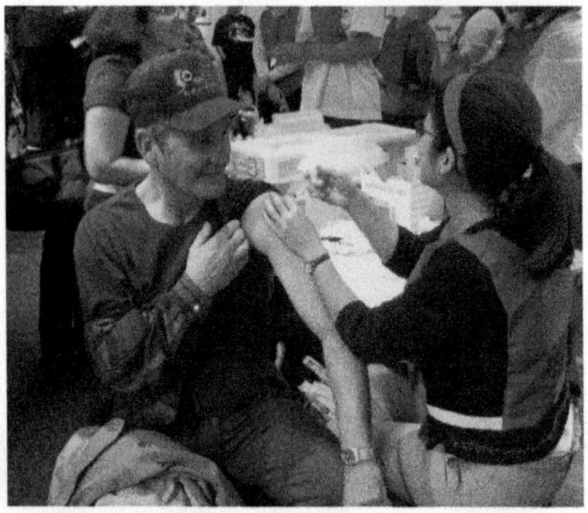

Department of Health & Social Services, Christine Lynch/AP Wide World Photos

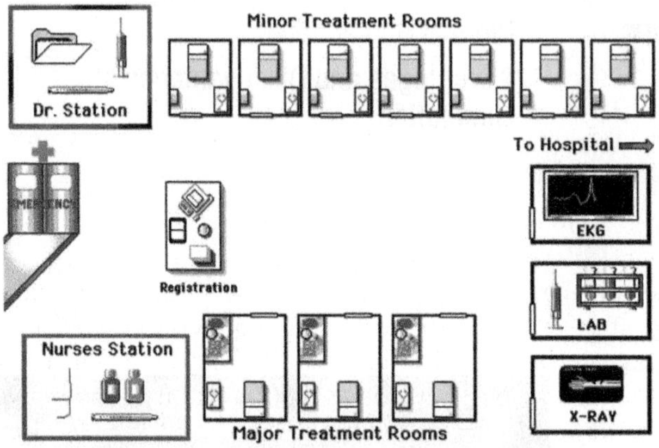

Micro Saint® Sharp image used with permission of Alion Science and Technolgy Corp.

When Bay Medical Center faced severe overcrowding at its outpatient clinic, it turned to computer simulation to try to reduce bottlenecks and improve patient flow. A simulation language called Micro Saint analyzed current data relating to patient service times between clinic rooms. By simulating different numbers of doctors and staff, simulating the use of another clinic for overflow, and simulating a redesign of the existing clinic, Bay Medical Center was able to make decisions based on an understanding of both costs and benefits. This resulted in better patient service at lower cost.

Source: Micro Analysis and Design Simulation Software, Inc., Boulder, CO.

What Is Simulation?

Simulation models abound in our world. The city of Atlanta, for example, uses them to control traffic. Europe's Airbus Industries uses them to test the aerodynamics of proposed jets. The U.S. Army simulates war games on computers. Business students use management gaming to simulate realistic business competition. And thousands of organizations like Bay Medical Center develop simulation models to help make operations decisions.

Most of the large companies in the world use simulation models. Table 1 lists just a few areas in which simulation is now being applied.

Simulation
The attempt to duplicate the features, appearance, and characteristics of a real system, usually via a computerized model.

Simulation is the attempt to duplicate the features, appearance, and characteristics of a real system. In this text, we will show how to simulate part of an operations management system by building a mathematical model that comes as close as possible to representing the reality

TABLE 1 Some Applications of Simulation

Ambulance location and dispatching	Bus scheduling
Assembly-line balancing	Design of library operations
Parking lot and harbor design	Taxi, truck, and railroad dispatching
Distribution system design	Production facility scheduling
Scheduling aircraft	Plant layout
Labor-hiring decisions	Capital investments
Personnel scheduling	Production scheduling
Traffic-light timing	Sales forecasting
Voting pattern prediction	Inventory planning and control

of the system. The model will then be used to estimate the effects of various actions. The idea behind simulation is threefold:

1. To imitate a real-world situation mathematically
2. Then to study its properties and operating characteristics
3. Finally, to draw conclusions and make action decisions based on the results of the simulation

In this way, a real-life system need not be touched until the advantages and disadvantages of a major policy decision are first measured on the model.

To use simulation, an OM manager should:

1. Define the problem.
2. Introduce the important variables associated with the problem.
3. Construct a numerical model.
4. Set up possible courses of action for testing by specifying values of variables.
5. Run the experiment.
6. Consider the results (possibly modifying the model or changing data inputs).
7. Decide what course of action to take.

These steps are illustrated in Figure 1.

The problems tackled by simulation may range from very simple to extremely complex, from bank-teller lines to an analysis of the U.S. economy. Although small simulations can be conducted by hand, effective use of the technique requires a computer. Large-scale models, simulating perhaps years of business decisions, are virtually all handled by computer.

In this text, we examine the basic principles of simulation and then tackle some problems in the areas of waiting-line analysis and inventory control. Why do we use simulation in these areas when mathematical models described in other chapters can solve similar problems? The answer is that simulation provides an alternative approach for problems that are very complex mathematically. It can handle, for example, inventory problems in which demand or lead time is not constant.

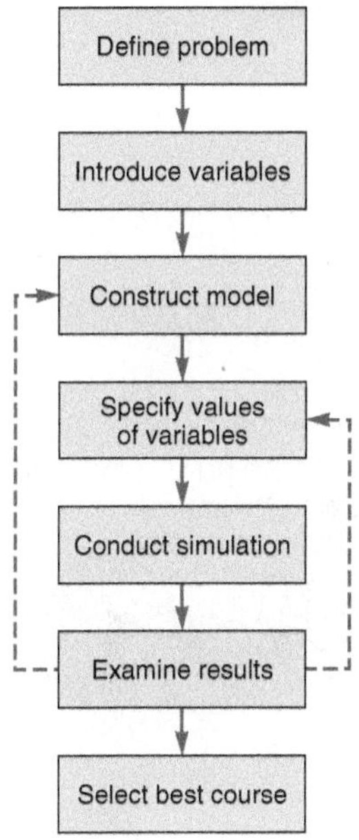

Figure 1

The Process of Simulation

Advantages and Disadvantages of Simulation

Simulation is a tool that has become widely accepted by managers for several reasons. The main *advantages* of simulation are as follows:

1. It can be used to analyze large and complex real-world situations that cannot be solved by conventional operations management models.
2. Real-world complications can be included that most OM models cannot permit. For example, simulation can use *any* probability distribution the user defines; it does not require standard distributions.
3. "Time compression" is possible. The effects of OM policies over many months or years can be obtained by computer simulation in a short time.
4. Simulation allows "what-if?" types of questions. Managers like to know in advance what options will be most attractive. With a computerized model, a manager can try out several policy decisions within a matter of minutes.
5. Simulations do not interfere with real-world systems. It may be too disruptive, for example, to experiment physically with new policies or ideas in a hospital or manufacturing plant.

STUDENT TIP
There are many reasons it's better to simulate a real-world system than to experiment with it.

LO1 *List* the advantages and disadvantages of modeling with simulation

The main *disadvantages* of simulation are as follows:

1. Good simulation models can take a long time to develop.
2. It is a repetitive approach that may produce different solutions in repeated runs. It does not generate optimal solutions to problems (as does linear programming).
3. Managers must generate all of the conditions and constraints for solutions that they want to examine. The simulation model does not produce answers without adequate, realistic input.
4. Each simulation model is unique. Its solutions and inferences are not usually transferable to other problems.

Computer simulation models have been developed to address a variety of productivity issues at fast-food restaurants such as Burger King. In one, the ideal distance between the drive-through order station and the pickup window was simulated. For example, because a longer distance reduced waiting time, 12 to 13 additional customers could be served per hour—a benefit of about $20,000 in extra sales per restaurant per year. In another simulation, a second drive-through window was considered. This model predicted a sales increase of 15%.

Donna Shader

Monte Carlo Simulation

Monte Carlo method
A simulation technique that uses random elements when chance exists in their behavior.

When a system contains elements that exhibit *chance* in their behavior, the **Monte Carlo method** of simulation may be applied. The basis of Monte Carlo simulation is experimentation on chance (or *probabilistic*) elements by means of random sampling.

The technique breaks down into five simple steps:

1. Setting up a probability distribution for important variables.
2. Building a cumulative probability distribution for each variable.
3. Establishing an interval of random numbers for each variable.
4. Generating random numbers.
5. Actually simulating a series of trials.

Let's examine these steps in turn.

LO2 *Perform* the five steps in a Monte Carlo simulation

Step 1. Establishing Probability Distributions. The basic idea in the Monte Carlo simulation is to generate values for the variables making up the model under study. In real-world systems, a lot of variables are probabilistic in nature. To name just a few: inventory demand; lead time for orders to arrive; times between machine breakdowns; times between customer arrivals at a service facility; service times; times required to complete project activities; and number of employees absent from work each day.

One common way to establish a *probability distribution* for a given variable is to examine historical outcomes. We can find the probability, or relative frequency, for each possible outcome of a variable by dividing the frequency of observation by the total number of observations. Here's an example.

The daily demand for radial tires at Barry's Auto Tire over the past 200 days is shown in columns 1 and 2 of Table 2. Assuming that past arrival rates will hold in the future, we can convert this demand to a probability distribution by dividing each demand frequency by the total demand, 200. The results are shown in column 3.

Cumulative probability distribution
The accumulation of individual probabilities of a distribution.

Step 2. Building a Cumulative Probability Distribution for Each Variable. The conversion from a regular probability distribution, such as in column 3 of Table 2, to a **cumulative probability distribution** is an easy job. In column 4, we see that the cumulative probability for each level of demand is the sum of the number in the probability column (column 3) added to the previous cumulative probability.

STUDENT TIP ☆
To establish a probability distribution for tires, we assume that historical demand is a good indicator of future demand.

TABLE 2 Demand for Barry's Auto Tire

(1) DEMAND FOR TIRES	(2) FREQUENCY	(3) PROBABILITY OF OCCURRENCE	(4) CUMULATIVE PROBABILITY
0	10	10/200 = .05	.05
1	20	20/200 = .10	.15
2	40	40/200 = .20	.35
3	60	60/200 = .30	.65
4	40	40/200 = .20	.85
5	30	30/200 = .15	1.00
	200 days	200/200 = 1.00	

TABLE 3 The Assignment of Random-Number Intervals for Barry's Auto Tire

DAILY DEMAND	PROBABILITY	CUMULATIVE PROBABILITY	INTERVAL OF RANDOM NUMBERS
0	.05	.05	01 through 05
1	.10	.15	06 through 15
2	.20	.35	16 through 35
3	.30	.65	36 through 65
4	.20	.85	66 through 85
5	.15	1.00	86 through 00

STUDENT TIP
You may start random-number intervals at either 01 or 00, but the text starts at 01 so that the top of each range is the cumulative probability.

Step 3. Setting Random-Number Intervals. Once we have established a cumulative probability distribution for each variable in the simulation, we must assign a set of numbers to represent each possible value or outcome. These are referred to as random-number intervals. Basically, a random number is a series of digits (say, two digits from 01, 02, . . . , 98, 99, 00) that have been selected by a totally random process—a process in which each random number has an equal chance of being selected.

Random-number intervals
A set of numbers to represent each possible value or outcome in a computer simulation.

Random number
A series of digits that have been selected by a totally random process.

If, for example, there is a 5% chance that demand for Barry's radial tires will be 0 units per day, then we will want 5% of the random numbers available to correspond to a demand of 0 units. If a total of 100 two-digit numbers is used in the simulation, we could assign a demand of 0 units to the first 5 random numbers: 01, 02, 03, 04, and 05.[1] Then a simulated demand for 0 units would be created every time one of the numbers 01 to 05 was drawn. If there is also a 10% chance that demand for the same product will be 1 unit per day, we could let the next 10 random numbers (06, 07, 08, 09, 10, 11, 12, 13, 14, and 15) represent that demand—and so on for other demand levels.

Similarly, we can see in Table 3 that the length of each interval on the right corresponds to the probability of 1 of each of the possible daily demands. Thus, in assigning random numbers

TABLE 4 Table of 2-Digit Random Numbers

52	06	50	88	53	30	10	47	99	37	66	91	35	32	00	84	57	07
37	63	28	02	74	35	24	03	29	60	74	85	90	73	59	55	17	60
82	57	68	28	05	94	03	11	27	79	90	87	92	41	09	25	36	77
69	02	36	49	71	99	32	10	75	21	95	90	94	38	97	71	72	49
98	94	90	36	06	78	23	67	89	85	29	21	25	73	69	34	85	76
96	52	62	87	49	56	59	23	78	71	72	90	57	01	98	57	31	95
33	69	27	21	11	60	95	89	68	48	17	89	34	09	93	50	44	51
50	33	50	95	13	44	34	62	64	39	55	29	30	64	49	44	30	16
88	32	18	50	62	57	34	56	62	31	15	40	90	34	51	95	26	14
90	30	36	24	69	82	51	74	30	35	36	85	01	55	92	64	09	85
50	48	61	18	85	23	08	54	17	12	80	69	24	84	92	16	49	59
27	88	21	62	69	64	48	31	12	73	02	68	00	16	16	46	13	85
45	14	46	32	13	49	66	62	74	41	86	98	92	98	84	54	33	40
81	02	01	78	82	74	97	37	45	31	94	99	42	49	27	64	89	42
66	83	14	74	27	76	03	33	11	97	59	81	72	00	64	61	13	52
74	05	81	82	93	09	96	33	52	78	13	06	28	30	94	23	37	39
30	34	87	01	74	11	46	82	59	94	25	34	32	23	17	01	58	73
59	55	72	33	62	13	74	68	22	44	42	09	32	46	71	79	45	89
67	09	80	98	99	25	77	50	03	32	36	63	65	75	94	19	95	88
60	77	46	63	71	69	44	22	03	85	14	48	69	13	30	50	33	24
60	08	19	29	36	72	30	27	50	64	85	72	75	29	87	05	75	01
80	45	86	99	02	34	87	08	86	84	49	76	24	08	01	86	29	11
53	84	49	63	26	65	72	84	85	63	26	02	75	26	92	62	40	67
69	84	12	94	51	36	17	02	15	29	16	52	56	43	26	22	08	62
37	77	13	10	02	18	31	19	32	85	31	94	81	43	31	58	33	51

Source: Reprinted from A *Million Random Digits with 100,000 Normal Deviates*. New York: The Free Press, 1995. Used by permission.

[1]Alternatively, we could have assigned the random numbers 00, 01, 02, 03, and 04 to represent a demand of 0 units. The 2 digits 00 can be thought of as either 0 or 100. As long as 5 numbers out of 100 are assigned to the 0 demand, it does not make any difference which 5 they are.

to the daily demand for 3 radial tires, the range of the random-number interval (36 through 65) corresponds *exactly* to the probability (or proportion) of that outcome. A daily demand for 3 radial tires occurs 30% of the time. All of the 30 random numbers greater than 35 up to and including 65 are assigned to that event.

Step 4. Generating Random Numbers. Random numbers may be generated for simulation problems in two ways. If the problem is large and the process under study involves many simulation trials, computer programs are available to generate the needed random numbers. If the simulation is being done by hand, the numbers may be selected from a table of random digits.

Step 5. Simulating the Experiment. We may simulate outcomes of an experiment by simply selecting random numbers from Table 4. Beginning anywhere in the table, we note the interval in Table 3 into which each number falls. For example, if the random number chosen is 81 and the interval 66 through 85 represents a daily demand for 4 tires, then we select a demand of 4 tires. Example 1 carries the simulation further.

Example 1

SIMULATING DEMAND

Barry's Auto Tire wants to simulate 10 days of demand for radial tires.

APPROACH ▶ Earlier, we went through Steps 1 and 2 in the Monte Carlo method (in Table 2) and Step 3 (in Table 3). Now we need to generate random numbers (Step 4) and simulate demand (Step 5).

SOLUTION ▶ We select the random numbers needed from Table 4, starting in the upper-left-hand corner and continuing down the first column, and record the corresponding daily demand:

DAY NUMBER	RANDOM NUMBER	SIMULATED DAILY DEMAND
1	52	3
2	37	3
3	82	4
4	69	4
5	98	5
6	96	5
7	33	2
8	50	3
9	88	5
10	90	5
		39 Total 10-day demand
		39/10 = 3.9 = tires average daily demand

INSIGHT ▶ It is interesting to note that the average demand of 3.9 tires in this 10-day simulation differs substantially from the *expected* daily demand, which we may calculate from the data in Table 3:

$$\begin{aligned}\text{Expected demand} &= \sum_{i=1}^{5}(\text{probability of } i \text{ units}) \times (\text{demand of } i \text{ units})\\ &= (.05)(0) + (.10)(1) + (.20)(2) + (.30)(3) + (.20)(4) + (.15)(5)\\ &= 0 + .1 + .4 + .9 + .8 + .75\\ &= 2.95 \text{ tires}\end{aligned}$$

However, if this simulation was repeated hundreds or thousands of times, the average *simulated* demand would be nearly the same as the *expected* demand.

LEARNING EXERCISE ▶ Resimulate the 10 days, this time with random numbers from column 2 of Table 4. What is the average daily demand? [Answer: 2.5.]

RELATED PROBLEMS ▶ 1, 18

OM in Action — Simulation Software Takes the Kinks out of Starbucks's Lines

The animation on the computer screen is not encouraging. Starbucks is running a digital simulation of customers ordering new warm sandwiches and pastries at a "virtual" store.

At first, things seem to go well, as animated workers rush around, preparing orders. But then they can't keep up. Soon the customers are stacking up in line, and the goal of serving each person in less than 3 minutes is blown. The line quickly reaches the point at which customers decide the snack or drink isn't worth the wait—called the "balking point" in queuing theory.

Fortunately for Starbucks, the customers departing without their Frappuccinos and decaf slim lattes are digital. The simulation software is helping operations managers find out what caused the backup before the scene repeats itself in the real world.

© Jeff Greenberg/Alamy

Simulation software is also used to find the point where capital expenditures will pay off. In large chains such as Starbucks, adding even a minor piece of equipment can add up. A $200 blender in each of Starbucks's more than 10,000 stores globally can cost the firm $2 million.

Sources: The Wall Street Journal (August 4, 2009); and *Business Wire* (February 13, 2006) and (June 15, 2005).

Naturally, it would be risky to draw any hard and fast conclusions about the operation of a firm from only a short simulation like Example 1. Seldom would anyone actually want to go to the effort of simulating such a simple model containing only one variable. Simulating by hand does, however, demonstrate the important principles involved and may be useful in small-scale studies.

Simulation and Inventory Analysis

Commonly used EOQ models are based on the assumption that both product demand and reorder lead time are known, constant values. In most real-world inventory situations, though, demand and lead time are variables, so accurate analysis becomes extremely difficult to handle by any means other than simulation.

STUDENT TIP Most real-world inventory systems have probabilistic events and benefit from a simulation approach.

In this section, we present an inventory problem with two decision variables and two probabilistic components. The owner of the hardware store in Example 2 would like to establish *order quantity* and *reorder point* decisions for a particular product that has probabilistic (uncertain) daily demand and reorder lead time. He wants to make a series of simulation runs, trying out various order quantities and reorder points, to minimize his total inventory cost for the item. Inventory costs in this case will include ordering, holding, and stockout costs.

Example 2 — AN INVENTORY SIMULATION WITH TWO VARIABLES

Simkin's Hardware Store, in Reno, sells the Ace model electric drill. Daily demand for this particular product is relatively low but subject to some variability. Lead times tend to be variable as well. Mark Simkin wants to develop a simulation to test an inventory policy of ordering 10 drills, with a reorder point of 5. In other words, every time the on-hand inventory level at the end of the day is 5 or less, Simkin will call his supplier that evening and place an order for 10 more drills. Simkin notes that if the lead time is 1 day, the order will not arrive the next morning but rather at the beginning of the following workday. Stockouts become lost sales, not backorders.

APPROACH ▶ Simkin wants to follow the 5 steps in the Monte Carlo simulation process.

SOLUTION ▶ Over the past 300 days, Simkin has observed the sales shown in column 2 of Table 5. He converts this historical frequency into a probability distribution for the variable daily demand (column 3). A cumulative probability distribution is formed in column 4 of Table 5. Finally, Simkin establishes an interval of random numbers to represent each possible daily demand (column 5).

When Simkin places an order to replenish his inventory of drills, there is a delivery lag of from 1 to 3 days. This means that lead time may also be considered a probabilistic variable. The number of days

LO3 *Simulate* an inventory problem

TABLE 5 Probabilities and Random-Number Intervals for Daily Ace Drill Demand

(1) DEMAND FOR ACE DRILL	(2) FREQUENCY	(3) PROBABILITY	(4) CUMULATIVE PROBABILITY	(5) INTERVAL OF RANDOM NUMBERS
0	15	.05	.05	01 through 05
1	30	.10	.15	06 through 15
2	60	.20	.35	16 through 35
3	120	.40	.75	36 through 75
4	45	.15	.90	76 through 90
5	30	.10	1.00	91 through 00
	300 days	1.00		

that it took to receive the past 50 orders is presented in Table 6. In a fashion similar to the creation of the demand variable, Simkin establishes a probability distribution for the lead time variable (column 3 of Table 6), computes the cumulative distribution (column 4), and assigns random-number intervals for each possible time (column 5).

TABLE 6 Probabilities and Random-Number Intervals for Reorder Lead Time

(1) LEAD TIME (DAYS)	(2) FREQUENCY	(3) PROBABILITY	(4) CUMULATIVE PROBABILITY	(5) RANDOM-NUMBER INTERVAL
1	10	.20	.20	01 through 20
2	25	.50	.70	21 through 70
3	15	.30	1.00	71 through 00
	50 orders	1.00		

The entire process is simulated in Table 7 for a 10-day period. We assume that beginning inventory (column 3) is 10 units on day 1. We took the random numbers (column 4) from column 2 of Table 4.

TABLE 7 Simkin Hardware's First Inventory Simulation. Order Quantity = 10 Units; Reorder Point = 5 Units

(1) DAY	(2) UNITS RECEIVED	(3) BEGINNING INVENTORY	(4) RANDOM NUMBER	(5) DEMAND	(6) ENDING INVENTORY	(7) LOST SALES	(8) ORDER?	(9) RANDOM NUMBER	(10) LEAD TIME
1		10	06	1	9	0	No		
2	0	9	63	3	6	0	No		
3	0	6	57	3	3[a]	0	Yes	02[b]	1
4	0	3	94[c]	5	0	2	No[d]		
5	10[e]	10	52	3	7	0	No		
6	0	7	69	3	4	0	Yes	33	2
7	0	4	32	2	2	0	No		
8	0	2	30	2	0	0	No		
9	10[f]	10	48	3	7	0	No		
10	0	7	88	4	3	0	Yes	14	1
					Totals: 41	2			

[a]This is the first time inventory dropped to the reorder point of five drills. Because no prior order was outstanding, an order is placed.
[b]The random number 02 is generated to represent the first lead time. It was drawn from column 2 of Table 4 as the next number in the list being used. A separate column could have been used from which to draw lead-time random numbers if we had wanted to do so, but in this example, we did not do so.
[c]Again, notice that the random digits 02 were used for lead time (see footnote b). So the next number in the column is 94.
[d]No order is placed on day 4 because there is an order outstanding from the previous day that has not yet arrived.
[e]The lead time for the first order placed is 1 day, but as noted in the text, an order does not arrive the next morning but rather the beginning of the following day. Thus, the first order arrives at the start of day 5.
[f]This is the arrival of the order placed at the close of business on day 6. Fortunately for Simkin, no lost sales occurred during the 2-day lead time before the order arrived.

Table 7 was filled in by proceeding 1 day (or line) at a time, working from left to right. It is a four-step process:

1. Begin each simulated day by checking to see whether any ordered inventory has just arrived. If it has, increase current inventory by the quantity ordered (10 units, in this case).
2. Generate a daily demand from the demand probability distribution for the selected random number.
3. Compute: Ending inventory = Beginning inventory minus Demand. If on-hand inventory is insufficient to meet the day's demand, satisfy as much demand as possible and note the number of lost sales.
4. Determine whether the day's ending inventory has reached the reorder point (5 units). If it has, and if there are no outstanding orders, place an order. Lead time for a new order is simulated for the selected random number corresponding to the distribution in Table 6.

INSIGHTS ▶ Simkin's inventory simulation yields some interesting results. The average daily ending inventory is:

$$\text{Average ending inventory} = \frac{41 \text{ total units}}{10 \text{ days}} = 4.1 \text{ units/day}$$

We also note the average lost sales and number of orders placed per day:

$$\text{Average lost sales} = \frac{2 \text{ sales lost}}{10 \text{ days}} = .2 \text{ units/day}$$

$$\text{Average number of orders placed} = \frac{3 \text{ orders}}{10 \text{ days}} = .3 \text{ orders/day}$$

LEARNING EXERCISE ▶ How would these 3 averages change if the random numbers for day 10 were 04 and 93 instead of 88 and 14? [Answer: 4.4, .2 (no change), and .2.]

RELATED PROBLEMS ▶ 11, 13, 16, 17, 18

Now that we have worked through Example 2 we want to emphasize something very important: This simulation should be extended many more days before we draw any conclusions as to the cost of the order policy being tested. If a hand simulation is being conducted, 100 days would provide a better representation. If a computer is doing the calculations, 1,000 days would be helpful in reaching accurate cost estimates. (Moreover, remember that even with a 1,000-day simulation, the generated distribution should be compared with the desired distribution to ensure valid results.)

Summary

Simulation involves building mathematical models that attempt to act like real operating systems. In this way, a real-world situation can be studied without imposing on the actual system. Although simulation models can be developed manually, simulation by computer is generally more desirable. The Monte Carlo approach uses random numbers to represent variables, such as inventory demand or people waiting in line, which are then simulated in a series of trials. Simulation is widely used as an operations tool because its advantages usually outweigh its disadvantages.

Key Terms

Simulation
Monte Carlo method
Cumulative probability distribution
Random-number intervals
Random number

Discussion Questions

1. State the seven steps, beginning with "Defining the Problem," that an operations manager should perform when using simulation to analyze a problem.
2. List the advantages of simulation.
3. List the disadvantages of simulation.
4. Explain the difference between *simulated* average demand and *expected* average demand.

5. What is the role of random numbers in a Monte Carlo simulation?
6. Why might the results of a simulation differ each time you make a run?
7. What is Monte Carlo simulation? What principles underlie its use, and what steps are followed in applying it?
8. List six ways that simulation can be used in business.
9. Why is simulation such a widely used technique?
10. What are the advantages of special-purpose simulation languages (see below)?
11. In the simulation of an order policy for drills at Simkin's hardware (Example 2, would the results (of Table 7) change significantly if a longer period were simulated? Why is the 10-day simulation valid or invalid?
12. Why is a computer necessary in conducting a real-world simulation?
13. Why might a manager be forced to use simulation instead of an analytical model in dealing with a problem of:
    a) inventory order policy?
    b) ships docking in a port to unload?
    c) bank-teller service windows?
    d) the U.S. economy?

Using Software in Simulation

Computers are critical in simulating complex tasks. They can generate random numbers, simulate thousands of time periods in a matter of seconds or minutes, and provide management with reports that improve decision making. A computer approach is almost a necessity in order to draw valid conclusions from a simulation.

Computer programming languages can help the simulation process. *General-purpose languages*, such as BASIC or C++, constitute one approach. *Special-purpose simulation languages*, such as GPSS and SIMSCRIPT, have a few advantages: (1) they require less programming time for large simulations, (2) they are usually more efficient and easier to check for errors, and (3) random-number generators are already built in as subroutines.

Commercial, easy-to-use prewritten simulation programs are also available. Some are generalized to handle a wide variety of situations ranging from queuing to inventory. These include programs such as Extend, Modsim, Witness, MAP/1, Enterprise Dynamics, Simfactory, ProModel, Micro Saint, and ARENA.

Spreadsheet software such as Excel can also be used to develop simulations quickly and easily. Such packages have built-in random-number generators and develop outputs through "data-fill" table commands.

USING EXCEL SPREADSHEETS

The ability to generate random numbers and then "look up" these numbers in a table to associate them with a specific event makes spreadsheets excellent tools for conducting simulations. Program 1 illustrates an Excel simulation for Example 1.

Notice that the cumulative probabilities are calculated in column E of Program 1. This procedure reduces the chance of error and is useful in larger simulations involving more levels of demand.

LO4 *Use* Excel spreadsheets to create a simulation

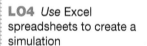

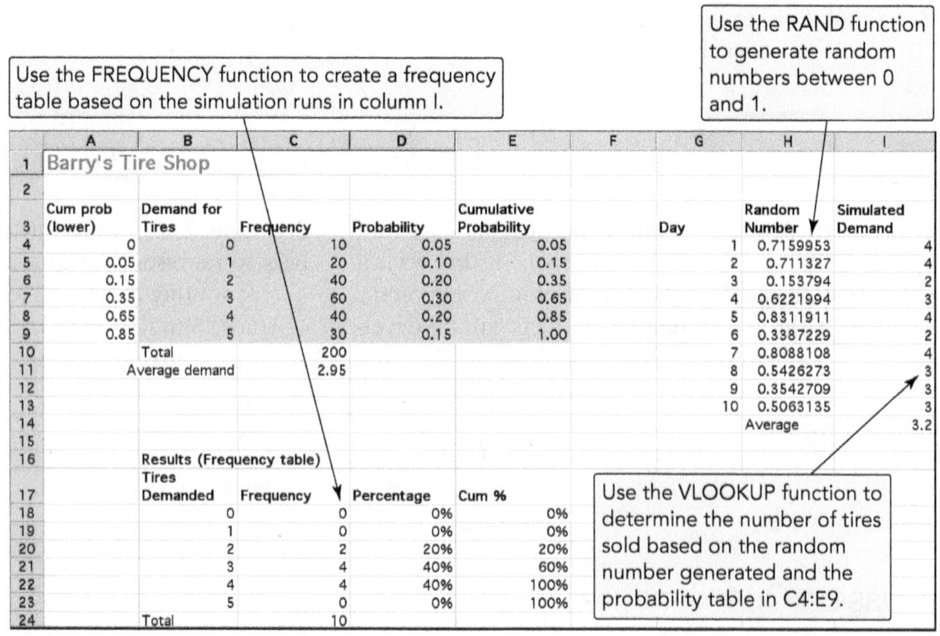

	A	B	C	D	E	F	G	H	I
1	Barry's Tire Shop								
2									
3	Cum prob (lower)	Demand for Tires	Frequency	Probability	Cumulative Probability		Day	Random Number	Simulated Demand
4	0	0	10	0.05	0.05		1	0.7159953	4
5	0.05	1	20	0.10	0.15		2	0.711327	4
6	0.15	2	40	0.20	0.35		3	0.153794	2
7	0.35	3	60	0.30	0.65		4	0.6221994	3
8	0.65	4	40	0.20	0.85		5	0.8311911	4
9	0.85	5	30	0.15	1.00		6	0.3387229	2
10		Total	200				7	0.8088108	4
11		Average demand	2.95				8	0.5426273	3
12							9	0.3542709	3
13							10	0.5063135	3
14								Average	3.2
15									
16		Results (Frequency table)							
17		Tires Demanded	Frequency	Percentage	Cum %				
18		0	0	0%	0%				
19		1	0	0%	0%				
20		2	2	20%	20%				
21		3	4	40%	60%				
22		4	4	40%	100%				
23		5	0	0%	100%				
24		Total	10						

Program 1

Using Excel to Simulate Tire Demand for Barry's Auto Tire Shop

The output shows a simulated average of 3.2 tires per day (in cell I14).

The = VLOOKUP function in column I looks up the random number (generated in column H) in the leftmost column of the defined lookup table ($A$4:$B$9). The = VLOOKUP function moves downward through this column until it finds a cell that is bigger than the random number. It then goes to the previous row and gets the value from column B of the table. In column H, for example, the first random number shown is .716. Excel looked down the left-hand column of the lookup table ($A$4:$B$9) of Program 1 until it found .85. From the previous row it retrieved the value in column B which is 4. Pressing the F9 function key recalculates the random numbers and the simulation.

VALUE	CELL	EXCEL FORMULA	ACTION
Cumulative probability	A4	=0	
Cumulative probability	A5	=A4+D4	Copy to A6:A9
Random Number	H4	=RAND()	Copy to H5:H13
Demand	I4	=VLOOKUP(H4,$A$4:$B$9,2,TRUE)	Copy to I5:I13
Average	I14	=AVERAGE(I4:I13)	
Frequency	C18	=FREQUENCY($I$4:$I$13,$B$18:$B$23)	Array copy to C19:C23
Total	C24	=SUM(C18:C23)	
Percentage	D18	=C18/$C$24	Copy to D19:D23
Average simulated demand	D25	=SUMPRODUCT(B18:B23,D18:D23)	
Cumulative Percentage	E18	=D18	
Cumulative Percentage	E19	=E18 + D19	Copy to E20:E23
			Press the F9 Key to simulate

PX USING POM FOR WINDOWS AND EXCEL OM

POM for Windows and Excel OM are capable of handling any simulation that contains only one random variable, such as Example 1.

Solved Problems

Virtual Office Hours help is available at www.myomlab.com.

SOLVED PROBLEM 1

Higgins Plumbing and Heating maintains a stock of 30-gallon water heaters that it sells to homeowners and installs for them. Owner Jim Higgins likes the idea of having a large supply on hand to meet any customer demand. However, he also recognizes that it is expensive to do so. He examines water heater sales over the past 50 weeks and notes the following:

WATER HEATER SALES PER WEEK	NUMBER OF WEEKS THIS NUMBER WAS SOLD
4	6
5	5
6	9
7	12
8	8
9	7
10	3
	50 weeks total data

a) If Higgins maintains a constant supply of 8 water heaters in any given week, how many times will he stockout during a 20-week simulation? We use random numbers from the 7th column of Table 4, beginning with the random digit 10.
b) What is the average number of sales per week over the 20-week period?
c) Using an analytic nonsimulation technique, determine the expected number of sales per week. How does this compare with the answer in part (b)?

SOLUTION

HEATER SALES	PROBABILITY	CUMULATIVE PROBABILITY	RANDOM-NUMBER INTERVALS
4	.12	.12	01 through 12
5	.10	.22	13 through 22
6	.18	.40	23 through 40
7	.24	.64	41 through 64
8	.16	.80	65 through 80
9	.14	.94	81 through 94
10	.06	1.00	95 through 00
	1.00		

a)

WEEK	RANDOM NUMBER	SIMULATED SALES	WEEK	RANDOM NUMBER	SIMULATED SALES
1	10	4	11	08	4
2	24	6	12	48	7
3	03	4	13	66	8
4	32	6	14	97	10
5	23	6	15	03	4
6	59	7	16	96	10
7	95	10	17	46	7
8	34	6	18	74	8
9	34	6	19	77	8
10	51	7	20	44	7

With a supply of 8 heaters, Higgins will stock out three times during the 20-week period (in weeks 7, 14, and 16).

b) Average sales by simulation = total sales/20 weeks = 135/20 = 6.75 per week

c) Using expected values, we obtain:

$$E\text{(sales)} = .12(4 \text{ heaters}) + .10(5) + .18(6) + .24(7) + .16(8) + .14(9) + .06(10) = 6.88 \text{ heaters}$$

With a longer simulation, these two approaches will lead to even closer values.

SOLVED PROBLEM 2

Random numbers may be used to simulate continuous distributions. As a simple example, assume that fixed cost equals \$300, profit contribution equals \$10 per item sold, and you expect an equally likely chance of 0 to 99 units to be sold. That is, profit equals $-\$300 + \$10X$, where X is the number sold. The mean amount you expect to sell is 49.5 units.

a) Calculate the expected value.
b) Simulate the sale of 5 items, using the following double-digit randomly-selected numbers of items sold:
   37 77 13 10 85
c) Calculate the expected value of (b) and compare with the results of (a).

SOLUTION

a) Expected value $= -300 + 10(49.5) = \$195$

b) $-300 + \$10(37) = \$70$
   $-300 + \$10(77) = \$470$
   $-300 + \$10(13) = -\$170$
   $-300 + \$10(10) = -\$200$
   $-300 + \$10(85) = \$550$

c) The mean of these simulated sales is \$144. If the sample size were larger, we would expect the two values to be closer.

Problems

Note Px means the problem may be solved with POM for Windows and/or Excel OM or Excel.

The problems that follow involve simulations that can be done by hand. However, to obtain accurate and meaningful results, long periods must be simulated. This task is usually handled by a computer. If you are able to program some of the problems in Excel or a computer language with which you are familiar, we suggest you try to do so. If not, the hand simulations will still help you understand the simulation process.

• **1** The daily demand for tuna sandwiches at an Ohio University cafeteria vending machine is 8, 9, 10, or 11, with probabilities 0.4, 0.3, 0.2, or 0.1, respectively. Assume the following random numbers have been generated: 09, 55, 73, 67, 53, 59, 04, 23, 88, and 84. Using these numbers, generate daily sandwich sales for 10 days Px

• **2** The number of machine breakdowns per day at Yuwen Chen's factory is 0, 1, or 2, with probabilities 0.5, 0.3, or 0.2, respectively. The following random numbers have been generated: 13, 14, 02, 18, 31, 19, 32, 85, 31, and 94. Use these numbers to generate the number of breakdowns for 10 consecutive days. What proportion of these days had at least one breakdown? Px

• **3** The table below shows the partial results of a Monte Carlo simulation. Assume that the simulation began at 8:00 A.M., and there is only one server.

CUSTOMER NUMBER	ARRIVAL TIME	SERVICE TIME
1	8:01	6
2	8:06	7
3	8:09	8
4	8:15	6
5	8:20	6

a) When does service begin for customer number 3?
b) When will customer number 5 leave?
c) What is the average waiting time in line?
d) What is the average time in the system?

• **4** Barbara Flynn sells papers at a newspaper stand for \$.35. The papers cost her \$.25, giving her a \$.10 profit on each one she sells. From past experience Barbara knows that:
a) 20% of the time she sells 100 papers.
b) 20% of the time she sells 150 papers.
c) 30% of the time she sells 200 papers.
d) 30% of the time she sells 250 papers.

Assuming that Barbara believes the cost of a lost sale to be \$.05 and any unsold papers cost her \$.25, simulate her profit outlook over 5 days if she orders 200 papers for each of the 5 days. Use the following random numbers: 52, 06, 50, 88, and 53. Px

•• **5** Arnold Palmer Hospital is studying the number of emergency surgery kits that it uses on weekends. Over the past 40 weekends, the number of kits used was as follows:

NUMBER OF KITS	FREQUENCY
4	4
5	6
6	10
7	12
8	8

The following random numbers have been generated: 11, 52, 59, 22, 03, 03, 50, 86, 85, 15, 32, 47. Simulate 12 weekends of emergency kit usage. What is the average number of kits used during these 12 weekends? Px

• **6** Susan Sherer's grocery store has noted the following figures with regard to the number of people who arrive at the store's three checkout stands and the time it takes to check them out:

ARRIVALS/MINUTE	FREQUENCY
0	.3
1	.5
2	.2

SERVICE TIME/MINUTE	FREQUENCY
1	.1
2	.3
3	.4
4	.2

Simulate the utilization of the three checkout stands over 5 minutes, using the following random numbers: 07, 60, 77, 49, 76, 95, 51, 16, and 14. Record the results at the end of the 5-minute period. Start at time = 0. Px

• **7** A warehouse manager at Mary Beth Marrs Corp. needs to simulate the demand placed on a product that does not fit standard models. The concept being measured is "demand during lead time," where both lead time and daily demand are variable. The historical record for this product, along with the cumulative distribution, appear in the table. Random numbers have been generated to simulate the next 5 order cycles; they are 91, 45, 37, 65, and 51. What are the five demand values? What is their average?

DEMAND DURING LEAD TIME	PROBABILITY	CUMULATIVE PROBABILITY
100	.01	.01
120	.15	.16
140	.30	.46
160	.15	.61
180	.04	.65
200	.10	.75
220	.25	1.00

Px

•• **8** The time between arrivals at the drive-through window of Barry Harmon's fast-food restaurant follows the distribution given in the table. The service-time distribution is also given. Use the random numbers provided to simulate the activity of the first 4 arrivals. Assume that the window opens at 11:00 A.M. and that the first arrival occurs afterward, based on the first interarrival time generated.

TIME BETWEEN ARRIVALS	PROBABILITY	SERVICE TIME	PROBABILITY
1	.2	1	.3
2	.3	2	.5
3	.3	3	.2
4	.2		

Random numbers for arrivals: 14, 74, 27, 03
Random numbers for service times: 88, 32, 36, 24
At what time does the fourth customer leave the system? Px

• **9** Phantom Controls monitors and repairs control circuit boxes on elevators installed in multistory buildings in downtown Chicago. The company has the contract for 108 buildings. When a box malfunctions, Phantom installs a new one and rebuilds the failed unit in its repair facility in Gary, Indiana. The data for failed boxes over the last 2 years is shown in the following table:

NUMBER OF FAILED BOXES PER MONTH	PROBABILITY
0	.10
1	.14
2	.26
3	.20
4	.18
5	.12

Simulate 2 years (24 months) of operation for Phantom and determine the average number of failed boxes per month from the simulation. Was it common to have fewer than 7 failures over 3 months of operation? (Start your simulation at the top of the 10th column of Table 4 of this text, $RN = 37$, and go down in the table.) Px

• **10** The number of cars arriving at Patti Miles's Car Wash, in Orono, Maine, during the last 200 hours of operation is observed to be the following:

NUMBER OF CARS ARRIVING	FREQUENCY
3 or fewer	0
4	20
5	30
6	50
7	60
8	40
9 or more	0
	200

a) Set up a probability and cumulative-probability distribution for the variable of car arrivals.
b) Establish random-number intervals for the variable.
c) Simulate 15 hours of car arrivals and compute the average number of arrivals per hour. Select the random numbers needed from column 1, Table 4, beginning with the digits 52. Px

•• **11** Leonard Presby's newsstand uses naive forecasting to order tomorrow's papers. The number of newspapers ordered corresponds to the previous day's demands. Today's demand for papers was 22. Presby buys the newspapers for $.20 and sells them for $.50. Whenever there is unsatisfied demand, Presby estimates the lost goodwill cost at $.10. Complete the accompanying table, and answer the questions that follow.

DEMAND	PROBABILITY
21	.25
22	.15
23	.10
24	.20
25	.30

DAY	PAPERS ORDERED	RANDOM NUMBER	DEMAND	REVENUE	COST	GOODWILL COST	NET PROFIT
1	22	37					
2		19					
3		52					
4		8					
5		22					
6		61					

a) What is the demand on day 3?
b) What is the total net profit at the end of the 6 days?
c) What is the lost goodwill on day 6?
d) What is the net profit on day 2?
e) How many papers has Presby ordered for day 5? Px

••• **12** Central Hospital in York, Pennsylvania, has an emergency room that is divided into six departments: (1) an initial exam station to treat minor problems or to make a diagnosis; (2) an X-ray department; (3) an operating room; (4) a cast-fitting room; (5) an observation room (for recovery and general observation before final diagnosis or release); and (6) an outprocessing department (where clerks check out patients and arrange for payment or insurance forms).

The probabilities that a patient will go from one department to another are presented in the following table:

FROM	TO	PROBABILITY
Initial exam at emergency room entrance	X-ray department	.45
	Operating room	.15
	Observation room	.10
	Outprocessing clerk	.30
X-ray department	Operating room	.10
	Cast-fitting room	.25
	Observation room	.35
	Outprocessing clerk	.30
Operating room	Cast-fitting room	.25
	Observation room	.70
	Outprocessing clerk	.05
Cast-fitting room	Observation room	.55
	X-ray department	.05
	Outprocessing clerk	.40
Observation room	Operating room	.15
	X-ray department	.15
	Outprocessing clerk	.70

a) Simulate the trail followed by 10 emergency room patients. Proceed, one patient at a time, from each one's entry at the initial exam station until he or she leaves through outprocessing. You should be aware that a patient can enter the same department more than once.
b) Using your simulation data, determine the chances that a patient enters the X-ray department twice.

•• **13** Every home football game for the past 8 years at Southwestern University has been sold out. The revenues from ticket sales are significant, but the sale of food, beverages, and souvenirs has contributed greatly to the overall profitability of the football program. One particular souvenir is the football program for each game. The number of programs sold at each game is described by the probability distribution given in the following table.

NUMBERS OF PROGRAMS SOLD	PROBABILITY
2,300	0.15
2,400	0.22
2,500	0.24
2,600	0.21
2,700	0.18

Each program costs \$.80 to produce and sells for \$2.00. Any programs that are not sold are donated to a recycling center and do not produce any revenue.

a) Simulate the sales of programs at 10 football games. Use the last column in the random-number table (Table 4) and begin at the top of the column.
b) If the university decided to print 2,500 programs for each game, what would the average profits be for the 10 games that were simulated?
c) If the university decided to print 2,600 programs for each game, what would the average profits be for the 10 games that were simulated? PX

• **14** Refer to the data in Solved Problem 1, which deals with Higgins Plumbing and Heating. Higgins has now collected 100 weeks of data and finds the following distribution for sales:

WATER HEATER SALES PER WEEK	NUMBER OF WEEKS THIS NUMBER WAS SOLD	WATER HEATER SALES PER WEEK	NUMBER OF WEEKS THIS NUMBER WAS SOLD
3	2	8	12
4	9	9	12
5	10	10	10
6	15	11	5
7	25		100

a) Assuming that Higgins maintains a constant supply of 8 heaters, simulate the number of stockouts incurred over a 20-week period (using the seventh column of Table 4).
b) Conduct this 20-week simulation two more times and compare your answers with those in (a). Did they change significantly? Why or why not?
c) What is the new expected number of sales per week? PX

••• **15** Connecticut Tanning has two tanning beds. One bed serves the company's regular members exclusively. The second bed serves strictly walk-in customers (those without appointments) on a first-come, first-served basis. Orv Karan, the store manager, has noticed on several occasions during the busy 5 hours of the day (2:00 P.M. until 7:00 P.M.) that potential walk-in customers will most often walk away from the store if they see one person already waiting for the second bed. He wonders if capturing this lost demand would justify adding a third bed. Leasing and maintaining a tanning bed costs Connecticut Tanning \$600 per month. The price paid per customer varies according to the time in the bed, but Orv has calculated the average net income for every 10 minutes of tanning time to be \$2. A study of the pattern of arrivals during the busy hours and the time spent tanning has revealed the following:

TIME BETWEEN ARRIVALS (MINUTES)	PROBABILITY	TIME IN TANNING BED (MINUTES)	PROBABILITY
5	0.30	10	0.20
10	0.25	15	0.30
15	0.20	20	0.40
20	0.15	25	0.10
25	0.10		

a) Simulate 4 hours of operation (arrivals over 4 hours). Use the 14th column of Table 4 for arrival times and the 8th column for tanning times. Assume there is one person who has just entered the bed at 2:00 P.M. for a 20-minute tan. Indicate which customers balk at waiting for the bed to become available. How many customers were lost over the 4 hours?
b) If the store is open an average of 24 days a month, will capturing all lost sales justify adding a new tanning bed?

••• **16** Kathryn Marley owns and operates the largest Mercedes-Benz auto dealership in Pittsburgh. In the past 36 months, her sales have ranged from a low of 6 new cars to a high of 12 new cars, as reflected in the following table:

SALES OF NEW CARS/MONTH	FREQUENCY
6	3
7	4
8	6
9	12
10	9
11	1
12	1
	36 months

Marley believes that sales will continue during the next 24 months at about the same historical rates, and that delivery times will also continue to follow the following pace (stated in probability form):

DELIVERY TIME (MONTHS)	PROBABILITY
1	.44
2	.33
3	.16
4	.07
	1.00

Marley's current policy is to order 14 cars at a time (two full truckloads, with 7 autos on each truck), and to place a new order whenever the stock on hand reaches 12 autos.

a) What are the results of this policy when simulated over the next 2 years?
b) Marley establishes the following relevant costs: (1) carrying cost per Mercedes per month is \$600; (2) cost of a lost sale averages \$4,350; and (3) cost of placing an order is \$570. What is the total inventory cost of this policy?

•• **17** Dumoor Appliance Center sells and services several brands of major appliances. Past sales for a particular model of refrigerator have resulted in the following probability distribution for demand:

Demand per week	0	1	2	3	4
Probability	0.20	0.40	0.20	0.15	0.05

The lead-time in weeks is described by the following distribution:

Lead time (weeks)	1	2	3
Probability	0.15	0.35	0.50

Based on cost considerations as well as storage space, the company has decided to order 10 of these each time an order is placed. The holding cost is $1 per week for each unit that is left in inventory at the end of the week. The stockout cost has been set at $40 per stockout. The company has decided to place an order whenever there are only two refrigerators left at the end of the week. Simulate 10 weeks of operation for Dumoor Appliance, assuming that there are currently 5 units in inventory. Determine what the weekly stockout cost and weekly holding cost would be for the problem. Use the random numbers in the first column of Table 4 for demand and the second column for lead time.

•• **18** Repeat the simulation in Problem 17, assuming that the reorder point is 4 units rather than 2. Compare the costs for these two situations. Use the same random numbers as in Problem 17.

Refer to MyOMLab for these additional homework problems: 19–25

CASE STUDY

Alabama Airlines's Call Center

Alabama Airlines opened its doors in December 2001 as a commuter service with its headquarters and hub located in Birmingham. The airline was started and managed by two former pilots, David Douglas and George Devenney. It acquired a fleet of 12 used prop-jet planes and the airport gates vacated by Delta Air Lines's 2001 downsizing due to the September 11 terrorist attacks.

TABLE 8 Incoming Call Distribution

TIME BETWEEN CALLS (MINUTES)	PROBABILITY
1	.11
2	.21
3	.22
4	.20
5	.16
6	.10

With business growing quickly, Douglas turned his attention to Alabama Air's "800" reservations system. Between midnight and 6:00 A.M., only one telephone reservations agent had been on duty. The time between incoming calls during this period is distributed as shown in Table 8. Carefully observing and timing the agent, Douglas estimated that the time required to process passenger inquiries is distributed as shown in Table 9.

TABLE 9 Service-Time Distribution

TIME TO PROCESS CUSTOMER INQUIRIES (MINUTES)	PROBABILITY
1	.20
2	.19
3	.18
4	.17
5	.13
6	.10
7	.03

All customers calling Alabama Air go "on hold" and are served in the order of the calls received unless the reservations agent is available for immediate service. Douglas is deciding whether a second agent should be on duty to cope with customer demand. To maintain customer satisfaction, Alabama Air wants a customer to be "on hold" for no more than 3 to 4 minutes; it also wants to maintain a "high" operator utilization.

Furthermore, the airline is planning a new TV advertising campaign. As a result, it expects an increase in "800" line phone inquiries. Based on similar campaigns in the past, the incoming call distribution from midnight to 6:00 A.M. is expected to be as shown in Table 10. (The same service-time distribution will apply.)

TABLE 10 Incoming Call Distribution

TIME BETWEEN CALLS (MINUTES)	PROBABILITY
1	.22
2	.25
3	.19
4	.15
5	.12
6	.07

Discussion Questions

1. Given the original call distribution, what would you advise Alabama Air to do for the current reservation system? Create a simulation model to investigate the scenario. Describe the model carefully and justify the duration of the simulation, assumptions, and measures of performance.
2 What are your recommendations regarding operator utilization and customer satisfaction if the airline proceeds with the advertising campaign?

Source: Professor Zbigniew H. Przasnyski, Loyola Marymount University. Reprinted by permission.

• **Additional Case Study:** Visit **www.myomlab.com** or **www.pearsonhighered.com/heizer** for this free case study:
Saigon Transport: This Vietnamese shipping company is trying to determine the ideal truck fleet size.

Bibliography

Boh,W. F., S. A. Slaughter, and J. A. Espinosa. "Learning from Experience in Software Development." *Management Science* 53, no. 8 (August 2007): 1315–1332.

Couto, J. P., and J. C. Teixeira. "Using a Linear Model for Learning Curve Effect on Highrise Floor Construction." *Construction Management & Economics* 23 (May 2005): 355.

McDonald, A., and L. Schrattenholzer. "Learning Curves and Technology Assessment." *International Journal of Technology Management* 23 (2002): 718.

Morrison, J. Bradley. "Putting the Learning Curve into Context." *Journal of Business Research* 61, no. 1 (November 2008): 1182.

Ngwenyama, O., A. Guergachi, and T. McLaren. "Using the Learning Curve to Maximize IT Productivity." *International Journal of Production Economics* 105, no. 2 (February 2007): 524.

Smunt, T. L., and C. A. Watts. "Improving Operations Planning with Learning Curves." *Journal of Operations Management* 21 (January 2003): 93.

Weston, M. *Learning Curves*. New York: Crown Publishing, 2000.

APPENDIX

SOLUTIONS TO EVEN-NUMBERED PROBLEMS

2 0, 0, 0, 0, 0, 0, 0, 2, 0, 2

4 Profits = 20, −15, 20, 17.50, 20; average equals $12.50.

6 At the end of 5 min, two checkouts are still busy and one is available.

8

Arrivals	*Arrival Time*	*Service Time*	*Departure Time*
1	11:01	3	11:04
2	11:04	2	11:06
3	11:06	2	11:08
4	11:07	1	11:09

10 **(a, b)**

No. Cars	Prob.	Cum. Prob.	R.N. Interval
3 or fewer	0	0	—
4	.10	.10	01 through 10
5	.15	.25	11 through 25
6	.25	.50	26 through 50
7	.30	.80	51 through 80
8	.20	1.00	81 through 00
9 or more	0	—	—

(c) Average no arrivals/hr = 105/15 = 7 cars

12 Here are the random-number intervals for the first two departments. Random number intervals correspond to probability of occurrence.

From	To	R.N. Interval
Initial exam	X-ray	01 through 45
	OR	46 through 60
	Observ.	61 through 70
	Out	71 through 00

From	To	R.N. Interval
X-ray	OR	01 through 10
	Cast	11 through 35
	Observ.	36 through 70
	Out	71 through 00

Each simulation could produce different results. Some will indeed show a person entering X-ray twice.

14 **(a)** 5 times
(b) 6.95 times; yes
(c) 7.16 heaters

16 **(a)** Expected average demand is about 8.75, average lead time is 1.86, average end inventory = 6.50, average lost sales = 4.04. Values and costs will vary with different sets of random numbers. Random numbers were selected from right-hand column of Appendix: Table of Random Numbers (07, 60, 77, 49, etc).
(b) $520,110, or $21,671 per month

18 Total stockout cost = $80; total holding cost = $40; so total cost = $120 with ROP = 4 vs. total cost = $223 with ROP = 2 in Problem 17. Weekly costs are found by dividing by 10.

Rapid Review

Main Heading | **Review Material**

WHAT IS SIMULATION?

Most of the large companies in the world use simulation models.

- **Simulation**—The attempt to duplicate the features, appearance, and characteristics of a real system, usually via a computerized model.

The idea behind simulation is threefold:

1. To imitate a real-world situation mathematically
2. Then to study its properties and operating characteristics
3. Finally, to draw conclusions and make action decisions based on the results of the simulation

In this way, a real-life system need not be touched until the advantages and disadvantages of a major policy decision are first measured on the model.

To use simulation, an OM manager should:

1. Define the problem.
2. Introduce the important variables associated with the problem.
3. Construct a numerical model.
4. Set up possible courses of action for testing by specifying values of variables.
5. Run the experiment.
6. Consider the results (possibly modifying the model or changing data inputs).
7. Decide what course of action to take.

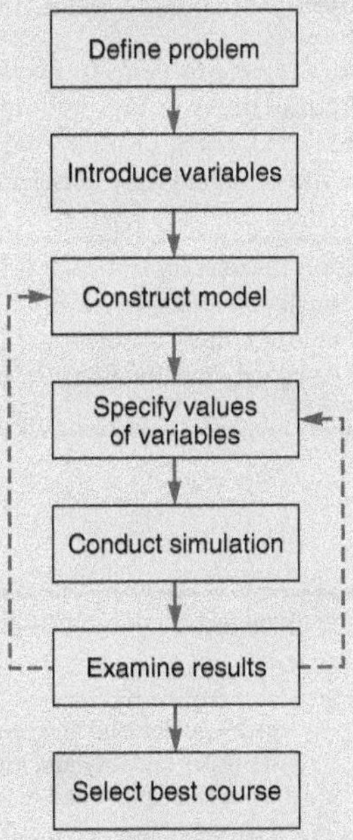

Figure 1
The Process of Simulation

ADVANTAGES AND DISADVANTAGES OF SIMULATION

The main *advantages* of simulation are:

1. It can be used to analyze large and complex real-world situations that cannot be solved using conventional operations management models.
2. Real-world complications can be included that most OM models cannot permit. For example, simulation can use any probability distribution the user defines; it does not require standard distributions.
3. "Time compression" is possible. The effects of OM policies over many months or years can be obtained by computer simulation in a short time.
4. Simulation allows "what-if?" types of questions. Managers like to know in advance what options will be most attractive. With a computerized model, a manager can try out several policy decisions within a matter of minutes.
5. Simulations do not interfere with real-world systems. It may be too disruptive, for example, to experiment physically with new policies or ideas.

The main *disadvantages* of simulation are:

1. Good simulation models can be very expensive; they may take many months to develop.
2. It is a repetitive approach that may produce different solutions in repeated runs. It does not generate optimal solutions to problems.

Main Heading	Review Material	MyOMLab
	3. Managers must generate all of the conditions and constraints for solutions that they want to examine. The simulation model does not produce answers without adequate, realistic input. 4. Each simulation model is unique. Its solutions and inferences are not usually transferable to other problems.	
MONTE CARLO SIMULATION	■ **Monte Carlo method**—A simulation technique that selects random numbers assigned to a distribution. The Monte Carlo method breaks down into five simple steps: 1. Setting up a probability distribution for important variables 2. Building a cumulative probability distribution for each variable 3. Establishing an interval of random numbers for each variable 4. Generating random numbers 5. Actually simulating a series of trials One common way to establish a *probability distribution* for a given variable is to examine historical outcomes. We can find the probability, or relative frequency, for each possible outcome of a variable by dividing the frequency of observation by the total number of observations. ■ **Cumulative probability distribution**—The accumulation (summary) of probabilities of a distribution. ■ **Random-number intervals**—A set of numbers to represent each possible value or outcome in a computer simulation. ■ **Random number**—A series of digits that have been selected using a totally random process. Random numbers may be generated for simulation problems in two ways: (1) If the problem is large and the process under study involves many simulation trials, computer programs are available to generate the needed random numbers; or (2) if the simulation is being done by hand, the numbers may be selected from a table of random digits.	Problems: 1–10, 14 Virtual Office Hours for Solved Problems: 1, 2
SIMULATION AND INVENTORY ANALYSIS	The commonly used EOQ models are based on the assumption that both product demand and reorder lead time are known, constant values. In most real-world inventory situations, though, demand and lead time are variables, so accurate analysis becomes extremely difficult to handle by any means other than simulation.	Problems: 11, 12, 13, 15, 16, 17, 18

Self Test

■ **Before taking the self-test,** refer to the learning objectives listed at the beginning of the text and the key terms listed at the end of the text.

LO1. Which of the following is *not* an advantage of simulation?
- **a)** Simulation is relatively straightforward and flexible.
- **b)** Good simulation models are usually inexpensive to develop.
- **c)** "Time compression" is possible.
- **d)** Simulation can study the interactive effects of individual variables.
- **e)** Simulations do not interfere with real-world systems.

LO2. The five steps required to implement the Monte Carlo simulation technique are ______, ______, ______, ______, and ______.

LO3. Two particularly good candidates to be probabilistic components in the simulation of an inventory problem are:
- **a)** order quantity and reorder point.
- **b)** setup cost and holding cost.
- **c)** daily demand and reorder lead time.
- **d)** order quantity and reorder lead time.
- **e)** reorder point and reorder lead time.

LO4. One important reason that spreadsheets are excellent tools for conducting simulations is that they can:
- **a)** generate random numbers.
- **b)** easily provide animation of the simulation.
- **c)** provide more security than manual simulations.
- **d)** prohibit "time compression" from corrupting the results.
- **e)** be easily programmed.

Answers: LO1. b; LO2. set up a probability distribution for each of the important variables, build a cumulative probability distribution for each of the important variables, establish an interval of random numbers for each variable, generate sets of random numbers, actually simulate a set of trials; LO3, c; LO4, a.

Operations Strategy in a Global Environment

OUTLINE

GLOBAL COMPANY PROFILE: *Boeing*

GLOBAL COMPANY PROFILE
Boeing

Boeing's Global Supply-Chain Strategy Yields Competitive Advantage

Boeing's strategy for its 787 Dreamliner is unique for its technologically advanced product design and vast global supply chain.

The Dreamliner incorporates the latest in a wide range of aerospace technologies, from airframe and engine design to super-lightweight titanium-graphite laminate and carbon-fiber composites. The electronic monitoring system that allows the airplane to report maintenance requirements in real time to ground-based computer systems is another product innovation. Boeing's collaboration with General Electric and Rolls-Royce has resulted in the development of more efficient engines and an emissions reduction of 20%. The advances in engine technology contribute as much as 8% of the increased fuel/payload efficiency of the new airplane, representing a nearly two-generation jump in technology.

With the 787's state-of-the-art design, more spacious interior, and global suppliers, Boeing has garnered record sales worldwide.

Some of the International Suppliers of Boeing 787 Components

SUPPLIER	HQ COUNTRY	COMPONENT
Latecoere	France	Passenger doors
Labinel	France	Wiring
Dassault	France	Design and product life cycle management software
Messier-Bugatti	France	Electric brakes
Thales	France	Electrical power conversion system
Messier-Dowty	France	Landing gear structure
Diehl	Germany	Interior lighting
Cobham	UK	Fuel pumps and valves
Rolls-Royce	UK	Engines
Smiths Aerospace	UK	Central computer system
BAE Systems	UK	Electronics
Alenia Aeronautica	Italy	Upper center fuselage
Toray Industries	Japan	Carbon fiber for wing and tail units
Fuji Heavy Industries	Japan	Center wing box
Kawasaki Heavy Ind.	Japan	Forward fuselage, fixed sections of wing
Teijin Seiki	Japan	Hydraulic actuators
Mitsubishi Heavy Ind.	Japan	Wing box
Chengdu Aircraft	China	Rudder
Hafei Aviation	China	Parts
Korean Airlines	South Korea	Wingtips
Saab	Sweden	Cargo and access doors

Boeing's design group at its Everett, Washington, facility led an international team of aerospace companies in development of this state-of-the-art plane. Technologically advanced design, new manufacturing processes, and a committed international supply chain have helped Boeing and its partners achieve unprecedented levels of performance in design and manufacture.

State-of-the-art composite sections of the 787 are built around the world and shipped to Boeing for final assembly.

Components from Boeing's worldwide supply chain come together on assembly lines in Everett, Washington, and Charleston, South Carolina. Although components come from throughout the world, about 35% of the 787 structure comes from Japanese companies.

The 787 is global not only because it has a range of 8,300 miles, but also because it is built all over the world. With a huge financial commitment of over $5 billion, Boeing needed partners. The global nature of both the technology and the aircraft market meant finding exceptional engineering talent and suppliers, wherever they might be. It also meant developing a culture of collaboration and integration with firms willing to step up to the risk associated with this revolutionary and very expensive new product.

State-of-the-art technology, multinational aircraft certifications, the cross-culture nature of the communications, and logistical challenges all added to the supply chain risk. In the end, Boeing accepted the challenge of teaming with more than 300 suppliers in over a dozen countries. Twenty of these suppliers are developing technologies, design concepts, and major systems for the 787. Some of them are shown in the table. The partners brought commitment to the table. The expectation is that countries that have a stake in the Dreamliner are more likely to buy from Boeing than from its European competitor, Airbus.

Japanese companies are producing over 35% of the project, and Italy's Alenia Aeronautica is building an additional 10% of the plane.

The innovative Dreamliner, with its global range and worldwide supply chain, is setting new levels of operational efficiency. As a result, it is the fastest-selling commercial jet in history. Boeing's Dreamliner reflects the global nature of business in the 21st century.

Boeing's collaborative technology enables a "virtual workspace" that allows engineers on the 787, including partners in Australia, Japan, Italy, Canada and across the United States, to make concurrent design changes to the airplane in real time. Designing, building, and testing the 787 digitally before production reduced design errors and improved production efficiencies.

LEARNING OBJECTIVES

LO1 ***Define*** mission and strategy

LO2 ***Identify*** and explain three strategic approaches to competitive advantage

LO3 ***Understand*** the significance of key success factors and core competencies

LO4 ***Use*** factor rating to evaluate both country and outsource providers

LO5 ***Identify*** and explain four global operations strategy options

A Global View of Operations and Supply Chains

Today's successful operations manager has a global view of operations strategy. Since the early 1990s, nearly 3 billion people in developing countries have overcome the cultural, religious, ethnic, and political barriers that constrain productivity. And now they are all players on the global economic stage. As these barriers disappear, simultaneous advances are being made in technology, reliable shipping, and inexpensive communication. These changes mean that, increasingly, firms find their customers and suppliers located around the world. The unsurprising result is the growth of world trade (see Figure 1), global capital markets, and the international movement of people. This means increasing economic integration and interdependence of countries—in a word, globalization. In response, organizations are hastily extending their distribution channels and supply chains globally. The result is innovative strategies where firms compete not just with their own expertise but with the talent in their entire global supply chain. For instance:

- Boeing is competitive because both its sales and supply chain are worldwide.
- Italy's Benetton moves inventory to stores around the world faster than its competition with rapid communication and by building exceptional flexibility into design, production, and distribution.
- Sony purchases components from a supply chain that extends to Thailand, Malaysia, and elsewhere around the world for assembly of its electronic products, which in turn are distributed around the world.
- Volvo, considered a Swedish company, was recently purchased by a Chinese company, Geely. But the current Volvo S40 is assembled in Belgium, South Africa, Malaysia, and China, on a platform shared with the Mazda 3 (built in Japan) and the Ford Focus (built in Europe.)

Figure 1

Growth of World Trade as a Percent of World GDP

Sources: World Bank; and World Trade Organization.

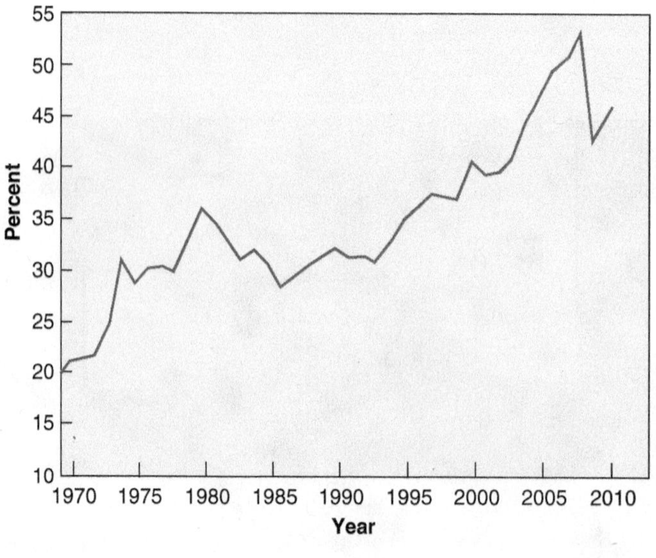

- China's Haier (pronounced "higher") is now producing compact refrigerators (it has one-third of the U.S. market) and refrigerated wine cabinets (it has half of the U.S. market) in South Carolina.

Globalization means customers, talent, and suppliers are worldwide. The new standards of global competitiveness impact quality, variety, customization, convenience, timeliness, and cost. Globalization strategies contribute efficiency, adding value to products and services, but they also complicate the operations manager's job. Complexity, risk, and competition are intensified, forcing companies to adjust for a shrinking world.

We have identified six reasons domestic business operations decide to change to some form of international operation. They are:

1. Improve the supply chain.
2. Reduce costs (labor, taxes, tariffs, etc.).
3. Improve operations.
4. Understand markets.
5. Improve products.
6. Attract and retain global talent.

Let us examine, in turn, each of the six reasons.

Improve the Supply Chain The supply chain can often be improved by locating facilities in countries where unique resources are available. These resources may be human resource expertise, low-cost labor, or raw material. For example, auto-styling studios from throughout the world have migrated to the auto mecca of southern California to ensure the necessary expertise in contemporary auto design. Similarly, world athletic shoe production has migrated from South Korea to Guangzhou, China; this location takes advantage of the low-cost labor and production competence in a city where 40,000 people work making athletic shoes for the world. And a perfume manufacturer wants a presence in Grasse, France, where much of the world's perfume essences are prepared from the flowers of the Mediterranean.

Reduce Costs Many international operations seek to take advantage of the tangible opportunities to reduce their costs. Foreign locations can help lower both direct and indirect costs. (See the *OM in Action* box "U.S. Cartoon Production at Home in Manila.") Less stringent government regulations on a wide variety of operation practices (e.g., environmental control, health and safety, etc.) reduce costs. Opportunities to cut the cost of taxes and tariffs also encourage foreign operations. In Mexico, the creation of maquiladoras (free trade zones) allows manufacturers to cut their costs of taxation by paying only on the value added by Mexican workers. If a U.S. manufacturer, such as Caterpillar, brings a $1,000 engine to a maquiladora operation for assembly work costing $200, tariff duties will be charged only on the $200 of work performed in Mexico.

Maquiladoras
Mexican factories located along the U.S.–Mexico border that receive preferential tariff treatment.

OM in Action U.S. Cartoon Production at Home in Manila

Fred Flintstone is not from Bedrock. He is actually from Manila, capital of the Philippines. So are Tom and Jerry, Aladdin, and Donald Duck. More than 90% of American television cartoons are produced in Asia and India, with the Philippines leading the way. With their natural advantage of English as an official language and a strong familiarity with U.S. culture, animation companies in Manila now employ more than 1,700 people. Filipinos understand Western culture, and "you need to have a group of artists that can understand the humor that goes with it," says Bill Dennis, a Hanna-Barbera executive.

Major studios like Disney, Marvel, Warner Brothers, and Hanna-Barbera send *storyboards*—cartoon action outlines—and voice tracks to the Philippines. Artists there draw, paint, and film about 20,000 sketches for a 30-minute episode. The cost of $130,000 to produce an episode in the Philippines compares with $160,000 in Korea and $500,000 in the United States.

Sources: Animation Insider (March 30, 2011); *The New York Times* (February 26, 2004): and *The Wall Street Journal* (August 9, 2005).

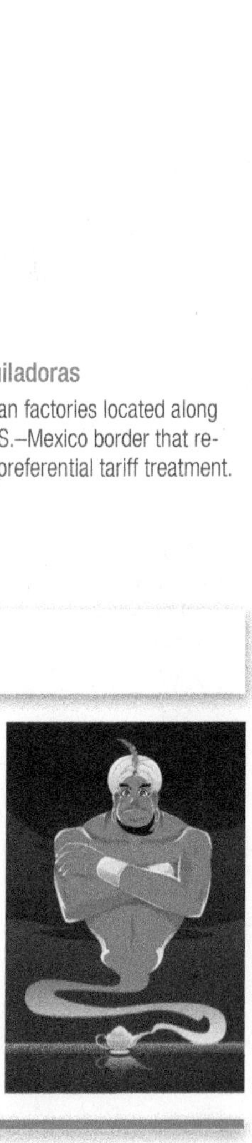

© artisticco/Fotolia

Shifting low-skilled jobs to another country has several potential advantages. First, and most obviously, the firm may reduce costs. Second, moving the lower-skilled jobs to a lower-cost location frees higher cost workers for more valuable tasks. Third, reducing wage costs allows the savings to be invested in improved products and facilities (and the retraining of existing workers, if necessary) at the home location.

Trade agreements have also helped reduce tariffs and thereby reduce the cost of operating facilities in foreign countries. The World Trade Organization (WTO) has helped reduce tariffs from 40% in 1940 to less than 3% today. Another important trade agreement is the North American Free Trade Agreement (NAFTA). NAFTA seeks to phase out all trade and tariff barriers among Canada, Mexico, and the U.S. Other trade agreements that are accelerating global trade include APEC (the Pacific Rim countries), SEATO (Australia, New Zealand, Japan, Hong Kong, South Korea, New Guinea, and Chile), MERCOSUR (Argentina, Brazil, Paraguay, and Uruguay), and CAFTA (Central America, Dominican Republic, and United States).

World Trade Organization (WTO)
An international organization that promotes world trade by lowering barriers to the free flow of goods across borders.

North American Free Trade Agreement (NAFTA)
A free trade agreement between Canada, Mexico, and the United States.

European Union (EU)
A European trade group that has 27 member states.

Another trading group is the European Union (EU).[1] The European Union has reduced trade barriers among the participating European nations through standardization and a common currency, the euro. However, this major U.S. trading partner, with almost 500 million people, is also placing some of the world's most restrictive conditions on products sold in the EU. Everything from recycling standards to automobile bumpers to hormone-free farm products must meet EU standards, complicating international trade.

Improve Operations Operations learn from better understanding of differences in the way business is handled in different countries. Japanese manufacturing has improved inventory management, just as the Scandinavians have contributed to improved ergonomics throughout the world.

Another reason to have international operations is to reduce response time to meet customers' changing product and service requirements. Customers who purchase goods and services from U.S. firms are increasingly located in foreign countries. Providing them with quick and adequate service is often improved by locating facilities in their home countries.

Understand Markets Because international operations require interaction with foreign customers, suppliers, and other competitive businesses, international firms inevitably learn about opportunities for new products and services. Europe led the way with cell phone innovations, and now the Japanese lead with the latest cell phone fads. Knowledge of these markets not only helps firms understand where the market is going but also helps firms diversify their customer base, add production flexibility, and smooth the business cycle.

Another reason to go into foreign markets is the opportunity to expand the *life cycle* (i.e., stages a product goes through) of an existing product. While some products in the U.S. are in a "mature" stage of their product life cycle, they may represent state-of-the-art products in less developed countries.

Improve Products Learning does not take place in isolation. Firms serve themselves and their customers well when they remain open to the free flow of ideas. For example, Toyota and BMW will manage joint research and share development costs on battery research for the next generation of green cars. Their relationship also provides Toyota with BMW's highly regarded diesel engines for its European market, where diesel-powered vehicles make up more than half of the market. The payoff is reduced risk in battery development for both, a state-of-the-art diesel engine for Toyota in Europe, and lower per-unit

[1]The 27 members of the European Union (EU) as of 2013 were Austria, Belgium, Bulgaria, Cyprus, Czech Republic, Denmark, Estonia, Finland, France, Germany, Greece, Hungary, Ireland, Italy, Latvia, Lithuania, Luxembourg, Malta, the Netherlands, Poland, Portugal, Romania, Slovakia, Slovenia, Spain, Sweden, and United Kingdom. Not all have adopted the euro. In addition, Croatia, Iceland, Macedonia, Montenegro, and Turkey are candidates for entry into the European Union.

Kraipit Phanvut/SIPA Press

A worldwide strategy places added burdens on operations management. Because of economic and lifestyle differences, designers must target products to each market. For instance, clothes washers sold in northern countries must spin-dry clothes much better than those in warmer climates, where consumers are likely to line-dry them. Similarly, as shown here, Whirlpool refrigerators sold in Bangkok are manufactured in bright colors because they are often put in living rooms.

diesel engine cost for BMW. Similarly, international learning in operations is taking place as South Korea's Samsung and Germany's Robert Bosch join together to produce lithium-ion batteries to the benefit of both.

Attract and Retain Global Talent Global organizations can attract and retain better employees by offering more employment opportunities. They need people in all functional areas and areas of expertise worldwide. Global firms can recruit and retain good employees because they provide both greater growth opportunities and insulation against unemployment during times of economic downturn. During economic downturns in one country or continent, a global firm has the means to relocate unneeded personnel to more prosperous locations.

So, to recap, successfully achieving a competitive advantage in our shrinking world means maximizing all of the possible opportunities, from tangible to intangible, that international operations can offer.

Cultural and Ethical Issues

While there are great forces driving firms toward globalization, many challenges remain. One of these challenges is reconciling differences in social and cultural behavior. With issues ranging from bribery, to child labor, to the environment, managers sometimes do not know how to respond when operating in a different culture. What one country's culture deems acceptable may be considered unacceptable or illegal in another. It is not by chance that there are fewer female managers in the Middle East than in India.

In the last decade, changes in international laws, agreements, and codes of conduct have been applied to define ethical behavior among managers around the world. The WTO, for example, helps to make uniform the protection of both governments and industries from foreign firms that engage in unethical conduct. Even on issues where significant differences between cultures exist, as in the area of bribery or the protection of intellectual property, global uniformity is slowly being accepted by most nations.

In spite of cultural and ethical differences, we live in a period of extraordinary mobility of capital, information, goods, and even people. We can expect this to continue. The financial sector, the telecommunications sector, and the logistics infrastructure of the world are healthy institutions that foster efficient and effective use of capital, information, and goods. Globalization, with all its opportunities and risks, is here. It must be embraced as managers develop their missions and strategies.

STUDENT TIP Getting an education and managing an organization both require a mission and strategy.

Developing Missions and Strategies

An effective operations management effort must have a *mission* so it knows where it is going and a *strategy* so it knows how to get there. This is the case for a small domestic organization as well as a large international organization.

Mission

Mission The purpose or rationale for an organization's existence.

LO1 *Define* mission and strategy

Economic success, indeed survival, is the result of identifying missions to satisfy a customer's needs and wants. We define the organization's **mission** as its purpose—what it will contribute to society. Mission statements provide boundaries and focus for organizations and the concept around which the firm can rally. The mission states the rationale for the organization's existence. Developing a good strategy is difficult, but it is much easier if the mission has been well defined. Figure 2 provides examples of mission statements.

Once an organization's mission has been decided, each functional area within the firm determines its supporting mission. By *functional area* we mean the major disciplines required by the firm, such as marketing, finance/accounting, and production/operations. Missions for each function are developed to support the firm's overall mission. Then within that function lower-level supporting missions are established for the OM functions. Figure 3 provides such a hierarchy of sample missions.

Strategy

Strategy How an organization expects to achieve its missions and goals.

LO2 *Identify* and explain three strategic approaches to competitive advantage

With the mission established, strategy and its implementation can begin. **Strategy** is an organization's action plan to achieve the mission. Each functional area has a strategy for achieving its mission and for helping the organization reach the overall mission. These strategies exploit opportunities and strengths, neutralize threats, and avoid weaknesses. In the following sections, we will describe how strategies are developed and implemented.

Firms achieve missions in three conceptual ways: (1) differentiation, (2) cost leadership, and (3) response. This means operations managers are called on to deliver goods and services that are (1) *better*, or at least different, (2) *cheaper*, and (3) more *responsive*. Operations managers translate these *strategic concepts* into tangible tasks to be accomplished. Any one or combination of these three strategic concepts can generate a system that has a unique advantage over competitors.

VIDEO 1 Operations Strategy at Regal Marine

Figure 2
Mission Statements for Three Organizations
Sources: Mission statement from Merck. Copyright © by Merck & Co., Inc. Reprinted with permission.

Merck
The mission of Merck is to provide society with superior products and services—innovations and solutions that improve the quality of life and satisfy customer needs—to provide employees with meaningful work and advancement opportunities and investors with a superior rate of return.
PepsiCo
Our mission is to be the world's premier consumer products company focused on convenient foods and beverages. We seek to produce financial rewards to investors as we provide opportunities for growth and enrichment to our employees, our business partners and the communities in which we operate. And in everything we do, we strive for honesty, fairness and integrity.
Arnold Palmer Hospital
Arnold Palmer Hospital for Children provides state of the art, family-centered healthcare focused on restoring the joy of childhood in an environment of compassion, healing, and hope.

Sample Company Mission	
To manufacture and service an innovative, growing, and profitable worldwide microwave communications business that exceeds our customers' expectations.	
Sample Operations Management Mission	
To produce products consistent with the company's mission as the worldwide low-cost manufacturer.	
Sample OM Department Missions	
Product design	To design and produce products and services with outstanding quality and inherent customer value.
Quality management	To attain the exceptional value that is consistent with our company mission and marketing objectives by close attention to design, supply chain, production, and field service opportunities.
Process design	To determine, design, and develop the production process and equipment that will be compatible with low-cost product, high quality, and a good quality of work life.
Location	To locate, design, and build efficient and economical facilities that will yield high value to the company, its employees, and the community.
Layout design	To achieve, through skill, imagination, and resourcefulness in layout and work methods, production effectiveness and efficiency while supporting a high quality of work life.
Human resources	To provide a good quality of work life, with well-designed, safe, rewarding jobs, stable employment, and equitable pay, in exchange for outstanding individual contribution from employees at all levels.
Supply-chain management	To collaborate with suppliers to develop innovative products from stable, effective, and efficient sources of supply.
Inventory	To achieve low investment in inventory consistent with high customer service levels and high facility utilization.
Scheduling	To achieve high levels of throughput and timely customer delivery through effective scheduling.
Maintenance	To achieve high utilization of facilities and equipment by effective preventive maintenance and prompt repair of facilities and equipment.

Figure 3

Sample Missions for a Company, the Operations Function, and Major OM Departments

Achieving Competitive Advantage Through Operations

Each of the three strategies provides an opportunity for operations managers to achieve competitive advantage. **Competitive advantage** implies the creation of a system that has a unique advantage over competitors. The idea is to create customer value in an efficient and sustainable way. Pure forms of these strategies may exist, but operations managers will more likely be called on to implement some combination of them. Let us briefly look at how managers achieve competitive advantage via *differentiation*, *low cost*, and *response*.

Competitive advantage
The creation of a unique advantage over competitors.

Competing on Differentiation

STUDENT TIP
For many organizations, the operations function provides *the* competitive advantage.

Safeskin Corporation is number one in latex exam gloves because it has differentiated itself and its products. It did so by producing gloves that were designed to prevent allergic reactions about which doctors were complaining. When other glove makers caught up, Safeskin developed hypoallergenic gloves. Then it added texture to its gloves. Then it developed a synthetic disposable glove for those allergic to latex—always staying ahead of the competition. Safeskin's strategy is to develop a reputation for designing and producing reliable state-of-the-art gloves, thereby differentiating itself.

Differentiation is concerned with providing *uniqueness*. A firm's opportunities for creating uniqueness are not located within a particular function or activity but can arise in virtually everything the firm does. Moreover, because most products include some service, and most services include some product, the opportunities for creating this uniqueness are limited only by imagination. Indeed, differentiation should be thought of as going beyond both physical characteristics and service attributes to encompass everything about the product or service that influences the value that the customers derive from it. Therefore, effective operations managers assist in defining everything about a product or service that will influence the potential value to the customer. This may be the convenience of a broad product line, product features, or a service related to the product. Such services can manifest themselves through convenience (location of distribution centers, stores, or branches), training, product delivery and installation, or repair and maintenance services.

Differentiation
Distinguishing the offerings of an organization in a way that the customer perceives as adding value.

In the service sector, one option for extending product differentiation is through an *experience*. Differentiation by experience in services is a manifestation of the growing "experience economy." The idea of experience differentiation is to engage the customer—to use people's five senses so they become immersed, or even an active participant, in the product. Disney does this with the Magic Kingdom. People no longer just go on a ride; they are immersed in the Magic Kingdom—surrounded by dynamic visual and sound experiences that complement the physical ride. Some rides further engage the customer with changes in air flow and smells, as well as having them steer the ride or shoot at targets or villains.

Experience differentiation
Engaging a customer with a product through imaginative use of the five senses, so the customer "experiences" the product.

VIDEO 2
Hard Rock's Global Strategy

Theme restaurants, such as Hard Rock Cafe, likewise differentiate themselves by providing an "experience." Hard Rock engages the customer with classic rock music, big-screen rock videos, memorabilia, and staff who can tell stories. In many instances, a full-time guide is available to explain the displays, and there is always a convenient retail store so the guest can take home a tangible part of the experience. The result is a "dining experience" rather than just a meal. In a less dramatic way, both Starbucks and your local supermarket deliver an experience when they provide music and the aroma of fresh coffee or freshly baked bread.

Competing on Cost

Southwest Airlines has been a consistent moneymaker while other U.S. airlines have lost billions. Southwest has done this by fulfilling a need for low-cost and short-hop flights. Its operations strategy has included use of secondary airports and terminals, first-come, first-served seating, few fare options, smaller crews flying more hours, snacks-only or no-meal flights, and no downtown ticket offices.

Additionally, and less obviously, Southwest has very effectively matched capacity to demand and effectively utilized this capacity. It has done this by designing a route structure that matches the capacity of its Boeing 737, the only plane in its fleet. Second, it achieves more air miles than other airlines through faster turnarounds—its planes are on the ground less.

One driver of a low-cost strategy is a facility that is effectively utilized. Southwest and others with low-cost strategies understand this and use financial resources effectively. Identifying the optimum size (and investment) allows firms to spread overhead costs, providing a cost advantage. For instance, Walmart continues to pursue its low-cost strategy with superstores, open 24 hours a day. For 20 years, it has successfully grabbed market share. Walmart has driven down store overhead costs, shrinkage, and distribution costs. Its rapid transportation of goods, reduced warehousing costs, and direct shipment from manufacturers have resulted in high inventory turnover and made it a low-cost leader.

Likewise, Franz Colruyt, a Belgian discount food retailer, is also an aggressive cost cutter. Colruyt cuts overhead by using converted factory warehouses, movie theaters, and garages as outlets. Customers find no background music, shopping bags, or bright lights: all have been eliminated to cut costs. Walmart and Colruyt are winning with a low-cost strategy.

Low-cost leadership entails achieving maximum *value* as defined by your customer. It requires examining each of the 10 OM decisions in a relentless effort to drive down costs while meeting customer expectations of value. A low-cost strategy does *not* imply low value or low quality.

Low-cost leadership
Achieving maximum value, as perceived by the customer.

Competing on Response

The third strategy option is response. Response is often thought of as *flexible* response, but it also refers to *reliable* and *quick* response. Indeed, we define response as including the entire range of values related to timely product development and delivery, as well as reliable scheduling and flexible performance.

Response
A set of values related to rapid, flexible, and reliable performance.

Flexible response may be thought of as the ability to match changes in a marketplace where design innovations and volumes fluctuate substantially.

Hewlett-Packard is an exceptional example of a firm that has demonstrated flexibility in both design and volume changes in the volatile world of personal computers. HP's products often have a life cycle of months, and volume and cost changes during that brief life cycle are dramatic. However, HP has been successful at institutionalizing the ability to change products and volume to respond to dramatic changes in product design and costs—thus building a *sustainable competitive advantage*.

The second aspect of response is the *reliability* of scheduling. One way the German machine industry has maintained its competitiveness despite having the world's highest labor costs is through reliable response. This response manifests itself in reliable scheduling. German machine firms have meaningful schedules—and they perform to these schedules. Moreover, the results of these schedules are communicated to the customer and the customer can, in turn, rely on them. Consequently, the competitive advantage generated through reliable response has value to the end customer.

The third aspect of response is *quickness*. Johnson Electric Holdings, Ltd., with headquarters in Hong Kong, makes 13 million tiny motors each month. The motors go in cordless tools, household appliances, and personal care items such as hair dryers; dozens are found in each automobile. Johnson's major competitive advantage is speed: speed in product development, speed in production, and speed in delivery.

Whether it is a production system at Johnson Electric or a pizza delivered in 5 minutes by Pizza Hut, the operations manager who develops systems that respond quickly can have a competitive advantage.

In practice, differentiation, low cost, and response can increase productivity and generate a sustainable competitive advantage. Proper implementation of the ten decisions by operations managers (see Figure 4) will allow these advantages to be achieved.

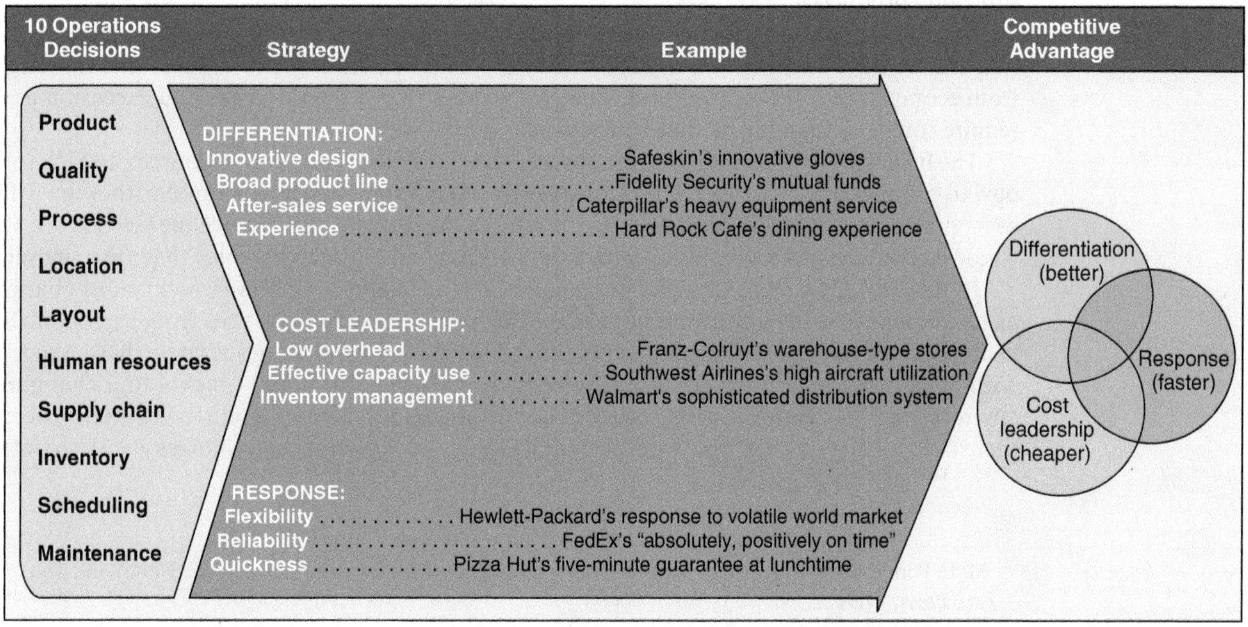

Figure 4
Achieving Competitive Advantage Through Operations

Response strategy wins orders at Super Fast Pizza. Using a wireless connection, orders are transmitted to $20,000 kitchens in vans. The driver, who works solo, receives a printed order, goes to the kitchen area, pulls premade pizzas from the cooler, and places them in the oven—it takes about 1 minute. The driver then delivers the pizza—sometimes even arriving before the pizza is ready.

Darren Hauck/AP Photo

Issues in Operations Strategy

Resources view

A method managers use to evaluate the resources at their disposal and manage or alter them to achieve competitive advantage.

Value-chain analysis

A way to identify those elements in the product/service chain that uniquely add value.

Five forces model

A method of analyzing the five forces in the competitive environment.

Whether the OM strategy is differentiation, cost, or response (as shown in Figure 4), OM is a critical player. Therefore, prior to establishing and attempting to implement a strategy, some alternate perspectives may be helpful. One perspective is to take a resources view. This means thinking in terms of the financial, physical, human, and technological resources available and ensuring that the potential strategy is compatible with those resources. Another perspective is Porter's value-chain analysis.[2] Value-chain analysis is used to identify activities that represent strengths, or potential strengths, and may be opportunities for developing competitive advantage. These are areas where the firm adds its unique *value* through product research, design, human resources, supply-chain management, process innovation, or quality management. Porter also suggests analysis of competitors via what he calls his five forces model.[3] These potential competing forces are immediate rivals, potential entrants, customers, suppliers, and substitute products.

In addition to the competitive environment, the operations manager needs to understand that the firm is operating in a system with many other external factors. These factors range from economic, to legal, to cultural. They influence strategy development and execution and require constant scanning of the environment.

The firm itself is also undergoing constant change. Everything from resources, to technology, to product life cycles is in flux. Consider the significant changes required within the firm as its products move from introduction, to growth, to maturity, and to decline (see Figure 5). These internal changes, combined with external changes, require strategies that are dynamic.

In the *Global Company Profile*, Boeing provides an example of how strategy must change as technology and the environment change. Boeing can now build planes from carbon fiber, using a global supply chain. Like many other OM strategies, Boeing's strategy has changed with technology and globalization. Microsoft has also had to adapt quickly to a changing environment. Faster processors, new computer languages, changing customer preferences, increased security issues, the Internet, and Google have all driven changes at Microsoft.

[2]M. E. Porter, *Competitive Advantage: Creating and Sustaining Superior Performance.* New York: The Free Press, 1985.

[3]Michael E. Porter, *Competitive Strategy: Techniques for Analyzing Industries and Competitors.* New York: The Free Press, 1980, 1998.

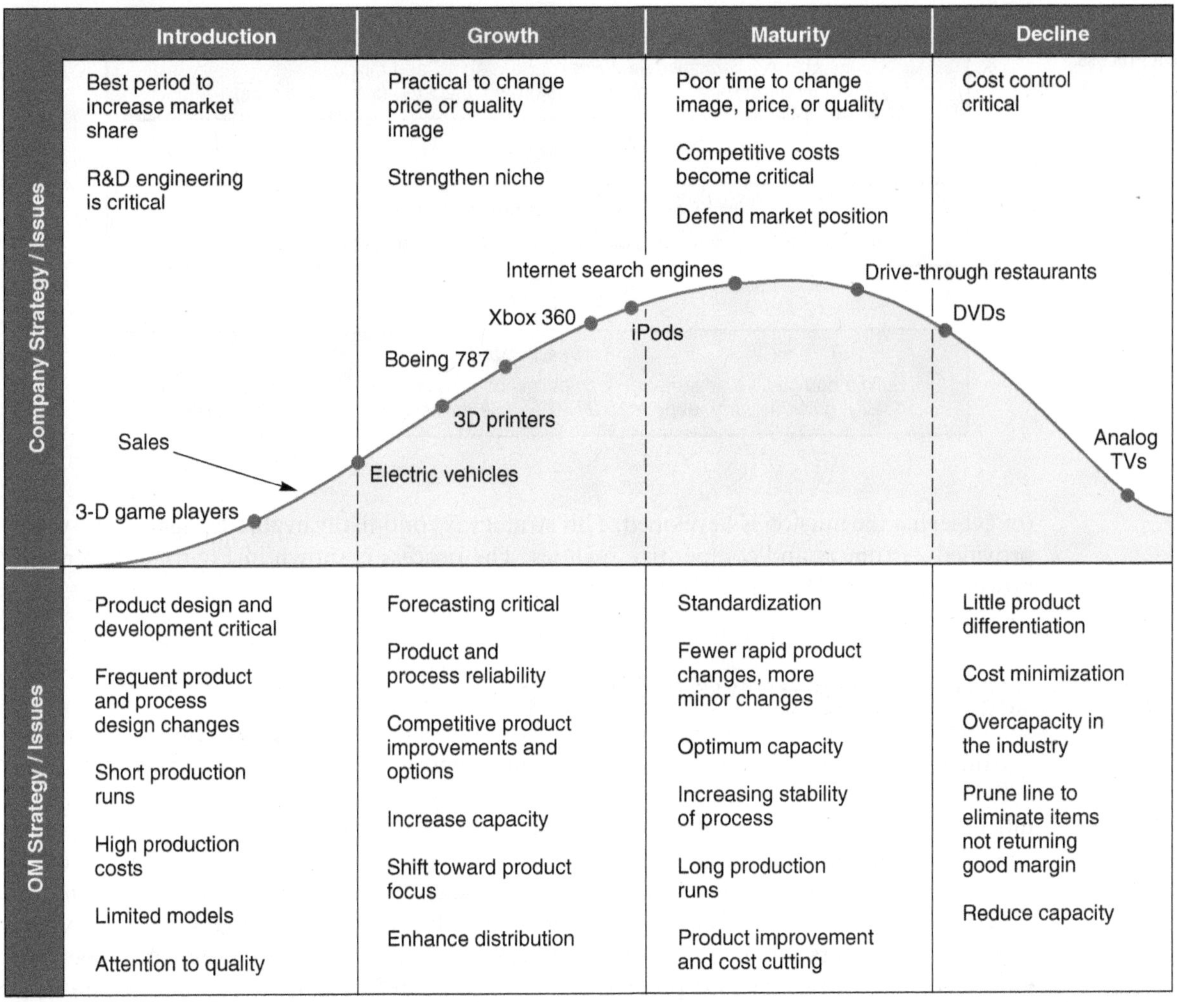
Introduction
Growth
Maturity
Decline
Company Strategy / Issues
Best period to increase market share
R&D engineering is critical
Practical to change price or quality image
Strengthen niche
Poor time to change image, price, or quality
Competitive costs become critical
Defend market position
Cost control critical
Internet search engines
Drive-through restaurants
Xbox 360
iPods
DVDs
Boeing 787
3D printers
Sales
Analog TVs
Electric vehicles
3-D game players
OM Strategy / Issues
Product design and development critical
Frequent product and process design changes
Short production runs
High production costs
Limited models
Attention to quality
Forecasting critical
Product and process reliability
Competitive product improvements and options
Increase capacity
Shift toward product focus
Enhance distribution
Standardization
Fewer rapid product changes, more minor changes
Optimum capacity
Increasing stability of process
Long production runs
Product improvement and cost cutting
Little product differentiation
Cost minimization
Overcapacity in the industry
Prune line to eliminate items not returning good margin
Reduce capacity

Figure 5
Strategy and Issues During a Product's Life

These forces have moved Microsoft's product strategy from operating systems to office products, to Internet service provider, and now to integrator of computers, cell phones, games, and television.

The more thorough the analysis and understanding of both the external and internal factors, the more likely that a firm can find the optimum use of its resources. Once a firm understands itself and the environment, a SWOT analysis, which we discuss next, is in order.

Strategy Development and Implementation

A SWOT analysis is a formal review of internal strengths and weaknesses and external opportunities and threats. Beginning with SWOT analyses, organizations position themselves, through their strategy, to have a competitive advantage. A firm may have excellent design skills or great talent at identifying outstanding locations. However, it may recognize limitations of its manufacturing process or in finding good suppliers. The idea is to maximize opportunities and minimize threats in the environment while maximizing the advantages of the organization's strengths and minimizing the weaknesses. Any preconceived ideas about mission are then reevaluated to ensure they are consistent with the SWOT analysis. Subsequently, a strategy

STUDENT TIP
A SWOT analysis provides an excellent model for evaluating a strategy.

SWOT analysis
A method of determining internal strengths and weaknesses and external opportunities and threats.

Figure 6
Strategy Development Process

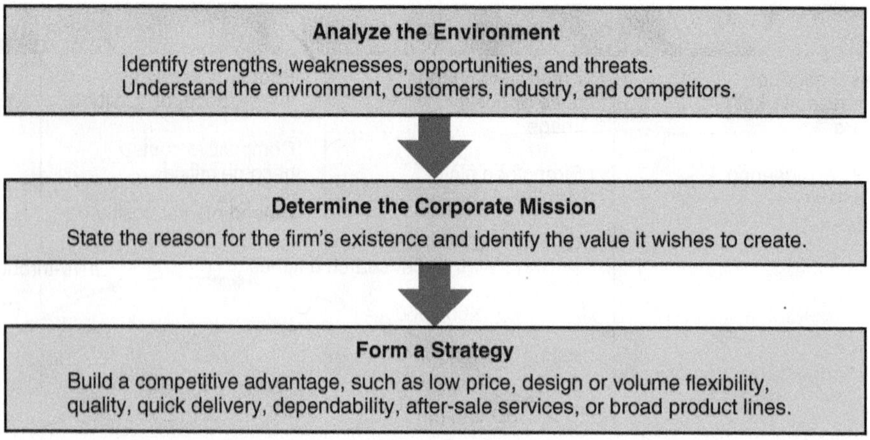

for achieving the mission is developed. This strategy is continually evaluated against the value provided customers and competitive realities. The process is shown in Figure 6. From this process, key success factors are identified.

Analyze the Environment
Identify strengths, weaknesses, opportunities, and threats.
Understand the environment, customers, industry, and competitors.
Determine the Corporate Mission
State the reason for the firm's existence and identify the value it wishes to create.
Form a Strategy
Build a competitive advantage, such as low price, design or volume flexibility, quality, quick delivery, dependability, after-sale services, or broad product lines.

Key Success Factors and Core Competencies

Key success factors (KSFs)
Activities or factors that are *key* to achieving competitive advantage.

Core competencies
A set of skills, talents, and capabilities in which a firm is particularly strong.

Because no firm does everything exceptionally well, a successful strategy requires determining the firm's key success factors and core competencies. **Key success factors (KSFs)** are those activities that are necessary for a firm to achieve its goals. Key success factors can be so significant that a firm must get them right to survive. A KSF for McDonald's, for example, is layout. Without an effective drive-through and an efficient kitchen, McDonald's cannot be successful. KSFs are often necessary, but not sufficient for competitive advantage. On the other hand, **core competencies** are the set of unique skills, talents, and capabilities that a firm does at a world-class standard. They allow a firm to set itself apart and develop a competitive advantage. Organizations that prosper identify their core competencies and nurture them. While McDonald's KSFs may include layout, its core competency may be consistency and quality. Honda Motors's core competence is gas-powered engines—engines for automobiles, motorcycles, lawn mowers, generators, snow blowers, and more. The idea is to build KSFs and core competencies that provide a competitive advantage and support a successful strategy and mission. A core competency may be the ability to perform the KSFs or a combination of KSFs. The operations manager begins this inquiry by asking:

LO3 *Understand* the significance of key success factors and core competencies

- "What tasks must be done particularly well for a given strategy to succeed?"
- "Which activities provide a competitive advantage?"
- "Which elements contain the highest likelihood of failure, and which require additional commitment of managerial, monetary, technological, and human resources?"

Automobiles

Julie Lucht/ Shutterstock

Generators

American Honda Motor Co., Inc.

Motorcycles

Courtesy of www .HondaNews.com

Water Pumps

American Honda Motor Co., Inc.

Marine Motors

American Honda Motor Co., Inc.

Race Cars

American Honda Motor Co., Inc.

4-Wheel Scooters

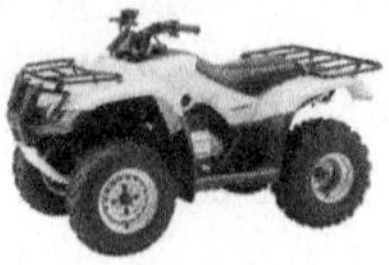

American Honda Motor Co., Inc.

Snow Blowers

American Honda Motor Co., Inc.

Honda's core competence is the design and manufacture of gas-powered engines. This competence has allowed Honda to become a leader in the design and manufacture of a wide range of gas-powered products. Tens of millions of these products are produced and shipped around the world.

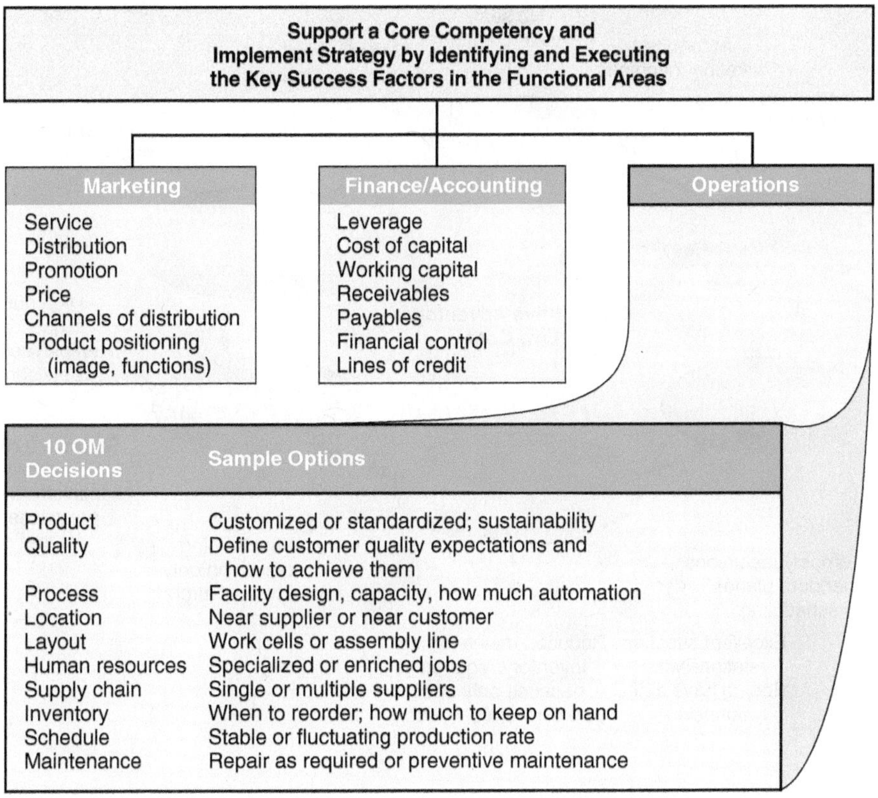

Figure 7
Implement Strategy by Identifying and Executing Key Success Factors That Support Core Competencies

Only by identifying and strengthening key success factors and core competencies can an organization achieve sustainable competitive advantage. In this text we focus on the 10 strategic OM decisions that typically include the KSFs. These decisions, plus major decision areas for marketing and finance, are shown in Figure 7.

STUDENT TIP
These 10 decisions are used to implement a specific strategy and yield a competitive advantage.

Integrating OM with Other Activities

Whatever the KSFs and core competencies, they must be supported by the related activities. One approach to identifying the activities is an **activity map**, which links competitive advantage, KSFs, and supporting activities. For example, Figure 8 shows how Southwest Airlines, whose core competency is operations, built a set of integrated activities to support its low-cost competitive advantage. Notice how the KSFs support operations and in turn are supported by other activities. The activities fit together and reinforce each other. In this way, all of the areas support the company's objectives. For example, short-term scheduling in the airline industry is dominated by volatile customer travel patterns. Day-of-week preference, holidays, seasonality, college schedules, and so on all play roles in changing flight schedules. Consequently, airline scheduling, although an OM activity, is tied to marketing. Effective scheduling in the trucking industry is reflected in the amount of time trucks travel loaded. But maximizing the time trucks travel loaded requires the integration of information from deliveries completed, pickups pending, driver availability, truck maintenance, and customer priority. Success requires integration of all of these activities.

Activity map
A graphical link of competitive advantage, KSFs, and supporting activities.

The better the activities are integrated and reinforce each other, the more sustainable the competitive advantage. By focusing on enhancing its core competence and KSFs with a supporting set of activities, firms such as Southwest Airlines have built successful strategies.

Building and Staffing the Organization

Once a strategy, KSFs, and the necessary integration have been identified, the second step is to group the necessary activities into an organizational structure. Then, managers must staff the

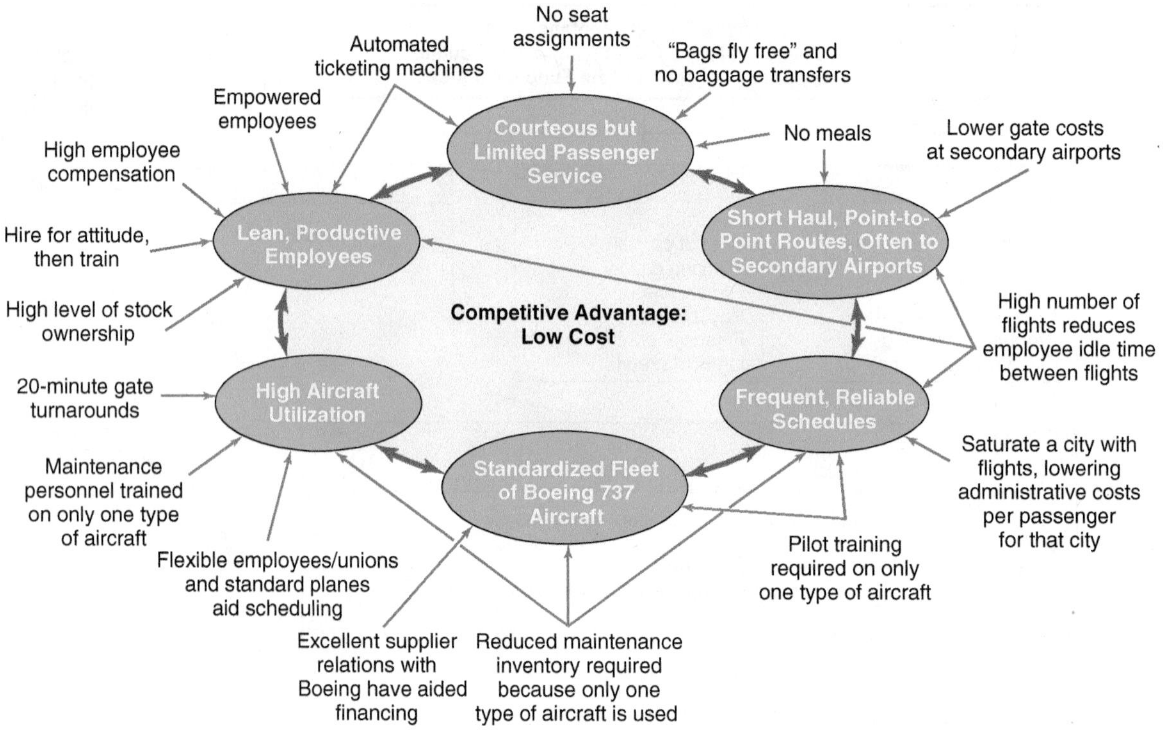

Figure 8

Activity Mapping of Southwest Airlines's Low-Cost Competitive Advantage

To achieve a low-cost competitive advantage, Southwest has identified a number of key success factors (connected by red arrows) and support activities (shown by blue arrows). As this figure indicates, Southwest's low-cost strategy is highly dependent on a very well-run operations function.

organization with personnel who will get the job done. The manager works with subordinate managers to build plans, budgets, and programs that will successfully implement strategies that achieve missions. Firms tackle this organization of the operations function in a variety of ways. Organization charts indicate the way some firms have organized to perform the required activities. *The operations manager's job is to implement an OM strategy, provide competitive advantage, and increase productivity.*

Implementing the 10 Strategic OM Decisions

As mentioned earlier, the implementation of the 10 strategic OM decisions is influenced by a variety of issues—from missions and strategy to key success factors and core competencies—while addressing such issues as product mix, product life cycle, and competitive environment. Because each product brings its own mix of attributes, the importance and method of implementation of the 10 strategic OM decisions will vary. Throughout this text, we discuss how these decisions are implemented in ways that provide competitive advantage. How this might be done for two drug companies, one seeking competitive advantage via differentiation and the other via low cost, is shown in Table 1.

Strategic Planning, Core Competencies, and Outsourcing

Outsourcing
Transferring a firm's activities that have traditionally been internal to external suppliers.

As organizations develop missions, goals, and strategies, they identify their strengths—what they do as well as or better than their competitors—as their *core competencies*. By contrast, *non-core activities*, which can be a sizable portion of an organization's total business, are good candidates for outsourcing. **Outsourcing** is transferring activities that have traditionally been internal to external suppliers.

TABLE 1 Operations Strategies of Two Drug Companies*

COMPETITIVE ADVANTAGE	BRAND NAME DRUGS, INC. PRODUCT DIFFERENTIATION STRATEGY	GENERIC DRUG CORP. LOW-COST STRATEGY
Product selection and design	Heavy R&D investment; extensive labs; focus on development in a broad range of drug categories	Low R&D investment; focus on development of generic drugs
Quality	Quality is major priority, standards exceed regulatory requirements	Meets regulatory requirements on a country-by-country basis, as necessary
Process	Product and modular production process; tries to have long product runs in specialized facilities; builds capacity ahead of demand	Process focused; general production processes; "job shop" approach, short-run production; focus on high utilization
Location	Still located in city where it was founded	Recently moved to low-tax, low-labor-cost environment
Layout	Layout supports automated product-focused production	Layout supports process-focused "job shop" practices
Human resources	Hire the best; nationwide searches	Very experienced top executives provide direction; other personnel paid below industry average
Supply chain	Long-term supplier relationships	Tends to purchase competitively to find bargains
Inventory	Maintains high finished goods inventory primarily to ensure all demands are met	Process focus drives up work-in-process inventory; finished goods inventory tends to be low
Scheduling	Centralized production planning	Many short-run products complicate scheduling
Maintenance	Highly trained staff; extensive parts inventory	Highly trained staff to meet changing demands

*Notice how the 10 decisions are altered to build two distinct strategies in the same industry.

Outsourcing is not a new concept, but it does add complexity and risk to the supply chain. Because of its potential, outsourcing continues to expand. The expansion is accelerating due to three global trends: (1) increased technological expertise, (2) more reliable and cheaper transportation, and (3) the rapid development and deployment of advancements in telecommunications and computers. This rich combination of economic advances is contributing to both lower cost and more specialization. As a result more firms are candidates for outsourcing of non-core activities.

VIDEO 3
Outsourcing Offshore at Darden

Outsourcing implies an agreement (typically a legally binding contract) with an external organization. The classic make-or-buy decision, concerning which products to make and which to buy, is the basis of outsourcing. When firms such as Apple find that their core competency is in creativity, innovation, and product design, they may want to outsource manufacturing.

Keith Dannemiller/Alamy

Contract manufacturers such as Flextronics provide outsourcing service to IBM, Cisco Systems, HP, Microsoft, Sony, Nortel, Ericsson, and Sun, among many others. Flextronics is a high-quality producer that has won over 450 awards, including the Malcolm Baldrige Award. One of the side benefits of outsourcing is that client firms such as IBM can actually improve their performance by using the competencies of an outstanding firm like Flextronics. But there are risks involved in outsourcing.

Outsourcing manufacturing is an extension of the long-standing practice of *subcontracting* production activities, which when done on a continuing basis is known as *contract manufacturing*. Contract manufacturing is becoming standard practice in many industries, from computers to automobiles. For instance, Johnson & Johnson, like many other big drug companies whose core competency is research and development, often farms out manufacturing to contractors. On the other hand, Sony's core competency is electromechanical design of chips. This is its core competency, but Sony is also one of the best in the world when it comes to rapid response and specialized production of these chips. Therefore, Sony finds that it wants to be its own *manufacturer*, while specialized providers come up with major innovations in such areas as software, human resources, and distribution. These areas are the providers' business, not Sony's, and the provider may very well be better at it than Sony.

Other examples of outsourcing non-core activities include:

- DuPont's legal services routed to the Philippines
- IBM's handing of travel services and payroll and Hewlett-Packard's provision of IT services to P&G
- Production of the Audi A4 convertible and Mercedes CLK convertible by Wilheim Karmann in Osnabruck, Germany
- Blue Cross sending hip resurfacing surgery patients to India

Managers evaluate their strategies and core competencies and ask themselves how to use the assets entrusted to them. Do they want to be the company that does low-margin work at 3%–4% or the innovative firm that makes a 30%–40% margin? PC and iPod contract manufacturers in China and Taiwan earn 3%–4%, but Apple, which innovates, designs, and sells, has a margin 10 times as large.

The Theory of Comparative Advantage

Theory of comparative advantage
A theory which states that countries benefit from specializing in (and exporting) goods and services in which they have relative advantage, and they benefit from importing goods and services in which they have a relative disadvantage.

The motivation for international outsourcing comes from the **theory of comparative advantage**. This theory focuses on the economic concept of relative advantage. According to the theory, if an external provider, regardless of its geographic location, can perform activities more productively than the purchasing firm, then the external provider should do the work. This allows the purchasing firm to focus on what it does best—its core competencies. Consistent with the theory of comparative advantage, outsourcing continues to grow. But outsourcing the wrong activities can be a disaster. And even outsourcing non-core activities has risks.

Risks of Outsourcing

STUDENT TIP ☆ The substantial risk of outsourcing requires managers to invest in the effort to make sure they do it right.

Risk management starts with a realistic analysis of uncertainty and results in a strategy that minimizes the impact of these uncertainties. Indeed, outsourcing *is* risky, with roughly half of all outsourcing agreements failing because of inadequate planning and analysis. Timely delivery and quality standards can be major problems, as can underestimating increases in inventory and logistics costs. Some potential advantages and disadvantages of outsourcing are shown in Table 2. A survey of North American companies found that, as a group, those that outsourced customer service saw a drop in their score on the American Consumer Satisfaction Index. The declines were roughly the same whether companies outsourced domestically or overseas.[4]

However, when outsourcing is overseas, additional issues must be considered. These issues include financial attractiveness, people skills and availability, and the general business

[4]J. Whitaker, M. S. Krishnan, and C. Fornell. "How Offshore Outsourcing Affects Customer Satisfaction." *The Wall Street Journal* (July 7, 2008): R4.

TABLE 2 Potential Advantages and Disadvantages of Outsourcing

ADVANTAGES	DISADVANTAGES
Cost savings	Increased logistics and inventory costs
Gaining outside expertise	Loss of control (quality, delivery, etc.)
Improving operations and service	Potential creation of future competition
Maintaining a focus on core competencies	Negative impact on employees
Accessing outside technology	Risks may not manifest themselves for years

environment. Another risk of outsourcing overseas is the political backlash that results from moving jobs to foreign countries. The perceived loss of jobs has fueled anti-outsourcing rhetoric. This rhetoric is contributing to a process known as *reshoring* (also called homeshoring and backsourcing), the return of business activity to the originating country. (See the *OM in Action* box "Reshoring to Small-Town U.S.A.")

In addition to the external risks, operations managers must deal with other issues that outsourcing brings. These include: (1) changes in employment levels, (2) changes in facilities, (3) adjustments to quality control systems, (4) changes in manufacturing processes needed to receive components in a different state of assembly, and (5) vastly expanded logistics issues, including insurance, tariffs, customs, and timing.

To summarize, managers can find substantial efficiencies in outsourcing non-core activities, but they must be cautious in outsourcing those elements of the product or service that provide a competitive advantage. The next section provides a methodology that helps analyze the outsourcing decision process.

Rating Outsource Providers

Research indicates that the most common reason for the failure of outsourcing agreements is that the decisions are made without sufficient analysis. The *factor-rating method* provides an objective way to evaluate outsource providers. We assign points for each factor to each provider and then importance weights to each of the factors. We now apply the technique in Example 1 to compare outsourcing providers being considered by a firm.

LO4 *Use* factor rating to evaluate both country and outsource providers

OM in Action Reshoring to Small-Town U.S.A.

U.S. companies continue their global search for efficiency by outsourcing call centers and back-office operations, but many find they need to look no farther than a place like Dubuque, Iowa.

To U.S. firms facing quality problems with their outsourcing operations overseas and bad publicity at home, small-town America is emerging as a pleasant alternative. Dubuque (population 57,313), Nacogdoches, Texas (population 29,914), or Twin Falls, Idaho (population 34,469), may be the perfect call center location. Even though the pay is low, the jobs are some of the best available to small-town residents.

By moving out of big cities to the cheaper labor and real estate of small towns, companies can save millions and still increase productivity. A call center in a town that just lost its major manufacturing plant finds the jobs easy to fill.

IBM, which has been criticized in the past for moving jobs to India and other offshore locations, picked Dubuque for its new remote computer-services center with 1,300 jobs.

Taking advantage of even cheaper wages in other countries will not stop soon, though. Is India the unstoppable overseas call center capital that people think it is? Not at all. Despite its population of 1.3 billion, only a small percentage of its workers have the language skills and technical education to work in Western-style industries. Already, India has been warned that if call centers can't recruit at reasonable wages, its jobs will move to the Philippines, South Africa, and Ghana. And indeed, Dell, Apple, and Britain's Powergen are reshoring from Indian call centers, claiming their costs had become too high.

Sherwin Crasto/Reuters/CORBIS-NY

Sources: Business Week (December 2, 2010); *The Wall Street Journal* (January 15, 2009), (April 18–19, 2009), and (May 30–31, 2009).

Example 1

RATING PROVIDER SELECTION CRITERIA

National Architects, Inc., a San Francisco–based designer of high-rise office buildings, has decided to outsource its information technology (IT) function. Three outsourcing providers are being actively considered: one in the U.S., one in India, and one in Israel.

APPROACH ▶ National's VP–Operations, Susan Cholette, has made a list of seven criteria she considers critical. After putting together a committee of four other VPs, she has rated each firm (on a 1–5 scale, with 5 being highest) and has also placed an importance weight on each of the factors, as shown in Table 3.

TABLE 3 Factor Ratings Applied to National Architects's Potential IT Outsourcing Providers

FACTOR (CRITERION)*	IMPORTANCE WEIGHT	OUTSOURCE PROVIDERS		
		BIM (U.S.)	S.P.C. (INDIA)	TELCO (ISRAEL)
1. Can reduce operating costs	.2	3	3	5
2. Can reduce capital investment	.2	4	3	3
3. Skilled personnel	.2	5	4	3
4. Can improve quality	.1	4	5	2
5. Can gain access to technology not in company	.1	5	3	5
6. Can create additional capacity	.1	4	2	4
7. Aligns with policy/philosophy/culture	.1	2	3	5
Total Weighted Score		3.9	3.3	3.8

*These seven major criteria are based on a survey of 165 procurement executives, as reported in J. Schildhouse, *Inside Supply Management* (December 2005): 22–29.

SOLUTION ▶ Susan multiplies each rating by the weight and sums the products in each column to generate a total score for each outsourcing provider. She selects BIM, which has the highest overall rating.

INSIGHT ▶ When the total scores are as close (3.9 vs 3.8) as they are in this case, it is important to examine the sensitivity of the results to inputs. For example, if one of the importance weights or factor scores changes even marginally, the final selection may change. Management preference may also play a role here.

LEARNING EXERCISE ▶ Susan decides that "Skilled personnel" should instead get a weight of 0.1 and "Aligns with policy/philosophy/culture" should increase to 0.2. How do the total scores change? [Answer: BIM = 3.6, S.P.C. = 3.2, and Telco = 4.0, so Telco would be selected.]

RELATED PROBLEMS ▶ 8–12

EXCEL OM Data File **Ch02Ex1.xls** can be found at **www.pearsonhighered.com/heizer**.

A. Ramey/PhotoEdit Inc.

Most U.S. toy companies now outsource their production to Chinese manufacturers. Cost savings are significant, but there are several downsides, including loss of control over such issues as quality. A few years ago, Mattel had to recall 10.5 million Elmos, Big Birds, and SpongeBobs. These made-in-China toys contained excessive levels of lead in their paint. More recently, quality issues have dealt with poisonous pet food, tainted milk products, and contaminated sheetrock.

Global Operations Strategy Options

As we suggested early, many operations strategies now require an international dimension. An international business is any firm that engages in international trade or investment. A multinational corporation (MNC) is a firm with *extensive* international business involvement. MNCs buy resources, create goods or services, and sell goods or services in a variety of countries. The term *multinational corporation* applies to most of the world's large, well-known businesses. Certainly IBM is a good example of an MNC. It imports electronics components to the U.S. from over 50 countries, exports to over 130 countries, has facilities in 45 countries, and earns more than half its sales and profits abroad.

International business
A firm that engages in cross-border transactions.

Multinational corporation (MNC)
A firm that has extensive involvement in international business, owning or controlling facilities in more than one country.

Operations managers of international and multinational firms approach global opportunities with one of four strategies: *international*, *multidomestic*, *global*, or *transnational* (see Figure 9). The matrix of Figure 9 has a vertical axis of cost reduction and a horizontal axis of local responsiveness. Local responsiveness implies quick response and/or the differentiation necessary for the local market. The operations manager must know how to position the firm in this matrix. Let us briefly examine each of the four strategies.

An international strategy uses exports and licenses to penetrate the global arena. This strategy is the least advantageous, with little local responsiveness and little cost advantage. But an international strategy is often the easiest, as exports can require little change in existing operations, and licensing agreements often leave much of the risk to the licensee.

International strategy
A strategy in which global markets are penetrated using exports and licenses.

The multidomestic strategy has decentralized authority with substantial autonomy at each business. These are typically subsidiaries, franchises, or joint ventures with substantial independence. The advantage of this strategy is maximizing a competitive response for the local market; however, the strategy has little or no cost advantage. Many food producers, such as Heinz, use a multidomestic strategy to accommodate local tastes because global integration of the production process is not critical. The concept is one of "we were successful in the home market; let's export the management talent and processes, not necessarily the product, to accommodate another market."

Multidomestic strategy
A strategy in which operating decisions are decentralized to each country to enhance local responsiveness.

A global strategy has a high degree of centralization, with headquarters coordinating the organization to seek out standardization and learning between plants, thus generating economies of scale. This strategy is appropriate when the strategic focus is cost reduction but has little to recommend it when the demand for local responsiveness is high. Caterpillar, the world leader in earth-moving equipment, and Texas Instruments, a world leader in semiconductors, pursue global strategies. Caterpillar and Texas Instruments find this strategy advantageous because the end products are similar throughout the world. Earth-moving equipment is the same in Nigeria as in Iowa.

Global strategy
A strategy in which operating decisions are centralized and headquarters coordinates the standardization and learning between facilities.

LO5 *Identify* and explain four global operations strategy options

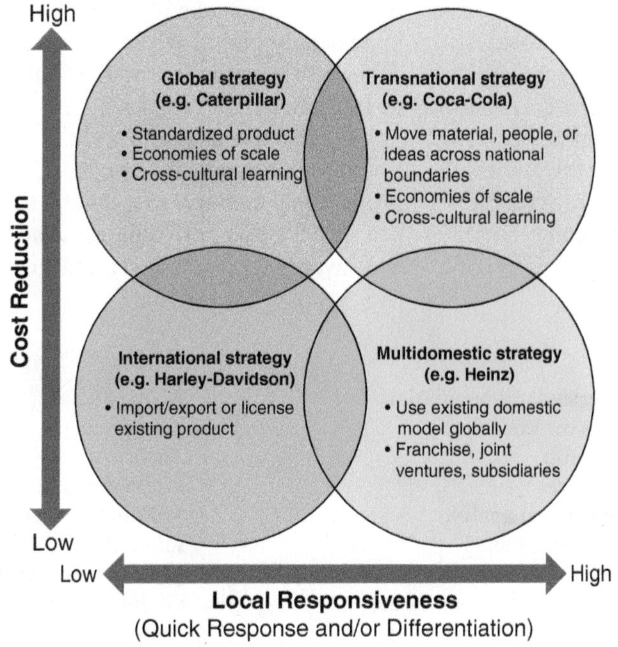

Figure 9
Four International Operations Strategies
Source: See a similar presentation in M. Hitt, R. D. Ireland, and R. E. Hoskisson, *Strategic Management: Concepts, Competitiveness, and Globalization*, 8th ed. (Cincinnati: Southwestern College Publishing).

© Washington Imaging/Alamy

ERIC LALMAND/AFP/Getty Images/Newscom

In a continuing fierce worldwide battle, both Komatsu and Caterpillar seek global advantage in the heavy equipment market. As Komatsu (left) moved west to the UK, Caterpillar (right) moved east, with 13 facilities and joint ventures in China. Both firms are building equipment throughout the world as cost and logistics dictate. Their global strategies allow production to move as markets, risk, and exchange rates dictate.

Transnational strategy
A strategy that combines the benefits of global-scale efficiencies with the benefits of local responsiveness.

A **transnational strategy** exploits the economies of scale and learning, as well as pressure for responsiveness, by recognizing that core competence does not reside in just the "home" country but can exist anywhere in the organization. *Transnational* describes a condition in which material, people, and ideas cross—or *transgress*—national boundaries. These firms have the potential to pursue all three operations strategies (i.e., differentiation, low cost, and response). Such firms can be thought of as "world companies" whose country identity is not as important as their interdependent network of worldwide operations. Nestlé is a good example of such a company. Although it is legally Swiss, 95% of its assets are held and 98% of its sales are made outside Switzerland. Fewer than 10% of its workers are Swiss.

Summary

Global operations provide an increase in both the challenges and opportunities for operations managers. Although the task is difficult, operations managers can and do improve productivity. They build and manage global OM functions and supply chains that contribute in a significant way to competitiveness. Organizations identify their strengths and weaknesses. They then develop effective missions and strategies that account for these strengths and weaknesses and complement the opportunities and threats in the environment. If this procedure is performed well, the organization can have competitive advantage through some combination of product differentiation, low cost, and response.

Increasing specialization provides economic pressure to build organizations that focus on core competencies and to outsource the rest. But there is also a need for planning outsourcing to make it beneficial to all participants. In this increasingly global world, competitive advantage is often achieved via a move to international, multidomestic, global, or transnational strategies.

Effective use of resources, whether domestic or international, is the responsibility of the professional manager, and professional managers are among the few in our society who *can* achieve this performance. The challenge is great, and the rewards to the manager and to society are substantial.

Key Terms

Maquiladoras
World Trade Organization (WTO)
North American Free Trade Agreement (NAFTA)
European Union (EU)
Mission
Strategy
Competitive advantage
Differentiation
Experience differentiation
Low-cost leadership
Response
Resources view
Value-chain analysis
Five forces model
SWOT analysis
Key success factors (KSFs)
Core competencies
Activity map
Outsourcing
Theory of comparative advantage
International business
Multinational corporation (MNC)
International strategy
Multidomestic strategy
Global strategy
Transnational strategy

Ethical Dilemma

As a manufacturer of athletic shoes whose image—indeed performance—is widely regarded as socially responsible, you find your costs increasing. Traditionally, your athletic shoes have been made in Indonesia and South Korea. Although the ease of doing business in those countries has been improving, wage rates have also been increasing. The labor-cost differential between your current suppliers and a contractor who will get the shoes made in China now exceeds $1 per pair. Your sales next year are projected to be 10 million pairs, and your analysis suggests that this cost differential is not offset by any other tangible costs; you face only the political risk and potential damage to your commitment to social responsibility. Thus, this $1 per pair savings should flow directly to your bottom line. There is no doubt that the Chinese government engages in censorship, remains repressive, and is a long way from a democracy. Moreover, you will have little or no control over working conditions, sexual harassment, and pollution. What do you do and on what basis do you make your decision?

Michael Yamashita/CORBIS-NY

Discussion Questions

1. Based on the descriptions and analyses in this text, would Boeing be better described as a global firm or a transnational firm? Discuss.
2. List six reasons to internationalize operations.
3. Coca-Cola is called a global product. Does this mean that Coca-Cola is formulated in the same way throughout the world? Discuss.
4. Define *mission*.
5. Define *strategy*.
6. Describe how an organization's *mission* and *strategy* have different purposes.
7. Identify the mission and strategy of your automobile repair garage. What are the manifestations of the 10 strategic OM decisions at the garage? That is, how is each of the 10 decisions accomplished?
8. As a library or Internet assignment, identify the mission of a firm and the strategy that supports that mission.
9. How does an OM strategy change during a product's life cycle?
10. There are three primary ways to achieve competitive advantage. Provide an example, not included in the text, of each. Support your choices.
11. Given the discussion of Southwest Airlines in the text, define an *operations* strategy for that firm now that it has purchased AirTran.
12. How must an operations strategy integrate with marketing and accounting?
13. How would you summarize outsourcing trends?
14. What potential cost-saving advantages might firms experience by using outsourcing?
15. What internal issues must managers address when outsourcing?
16. How should a company select an outsourcing provider?
17. What are some of the possible consequences of poor outsourcing?
18. What global operations strategy is most descriptive of McDonald's?

Using Software to Solve Outsourcing Problems

Excel, Excel OM, and POM for Windows may be used to solve many of the problems in this text.

X USING EXCEL OM

Excel OM (free with your text and found at our companion website) may be used to solve Example 1 (with the Factor Rating module). Program 1 provides the data inputs for seven important factors, including their weights (0.0–1.0) and ratings (1–5 scale where 5 is the highest rating) for each country. As we see, BIM is most highly rated, with a 3.9 score, versus 3.3 for SPC and 3.8 for Telco.

P USING POM FOR WINDOWS

POM for Windows also includes a factor rating module. POM for Windows is also found at our companion website, **www.pearsonhighered.com/heizer** and can solve all problems labelled with a P.

Program 1

Excel OM's Factor Rating Module, Including Inputs, Selected Formulas, and Outputs Using National Architects, Inc., Data from Example 1

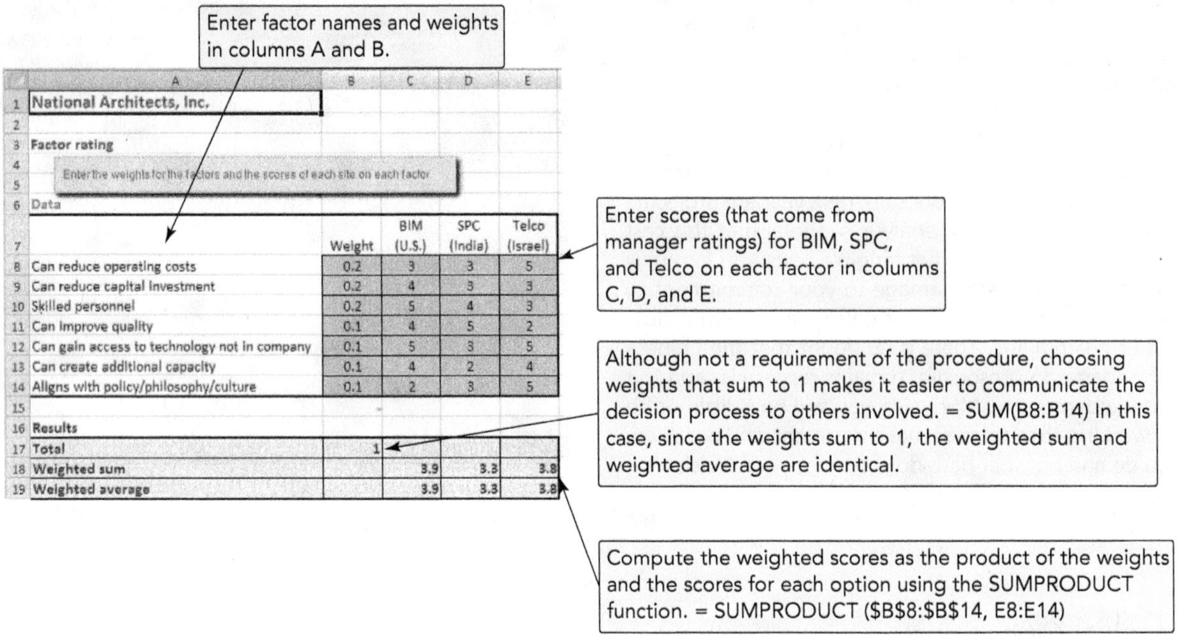
Enter factor names and weights in columns A and B.
Enter scores (that come from manager ratings) for BIM, SPC, and Telco on each factor in columns C, D, and E.
Although not a requirement of the procedure, choosing weights that sum to 1 makes it easier to communicate the decision process to others involved. = SUM(B8:B14) In this case, since the weights sum to 1, the weighted sum and weighted average are identical.
Compute the weighted scores as the product of the weights and the scores for each option using the SUMPRODUCT function. = SUMPRODUCT ($B$8:$B$14, E8:E14)
National Architects, Inc.
Factor rating
Enter the weights for the factors and the scores of each site on each factor
Data

	A	B	C	D	E
7		Weight	BIM (U.S.)	SPC (India)	Telco (Israel)
8	Can reduce operating costs	0.2	3	3	5
9	Can reduce capital investment	0.2	4	3	3
10	Skilled personnel	0.2	5	4	3
11	Can improve quality	0.1	4	5	2
12	Can gain access to technology not in company	0.1	5	3	5
13	Can create additional capacity	0.1	4	2	4
14	Aligns with policy/philosophy/culture	0.1	2	3	5
15					
16	Results				
17	Total	1			
18	Weighted sum		3.9	3.3	3.8
19	Weighted average		3.9	3.3	3.8

Solved Problems

Virtual Office Hours help is available at www.myomlab.com.

SOLVED PROBLEM 1

The global tire industry continues to consolidate. Michelin buys Goodrich and Uniroyal and builds plants throughout the world. Bridgestone buys Firestone, expands its research budget, and focuses on world markets. Goodyear spends almost 4% of its sales revenue on research. These three aggressive firms have come to dominate the world tire market, with total market share approaching 60%. And the German tire maker Continental AG has strengthened its position as fourth in the world, with a dominant presence in Germany. Against this formidable array, the old-line Italian tire company Pirelli SpA found it difficult to respond effectively. Although Pirelli still had 5% of the market, it is a relatively small player in a tough, competitive business. And although the business is reliable even in recessions, as motorists still need replacement tires, the competition is getting stronger. The business rewards companies that have large market shares and long production runs. Pirelli, with its small market share and specialty tires, has neither. However, Pirelli has some strengths: an outstanding reputation for tire research and excellent high-performance tires, including supplying specially engineered tires for Ducati motorcycles and Formula 1 racing teams. In addition, Pirelli's operations managers complement the creative engineering with world-class innovative manufacturing processes that allow rapid changeover to different models and sizes of tires.

Use a SWOT analysis to establish a feasible strategy for Pirelli.

SOLUTION

First, find an opportunity in the world tire market that avoids the threat of the mass-market onslaught by the big-three tire makers. Second, use the internal marketing strength represented by Pirelli's strong brand name supplying Formula 1 racing and a history of winning World Rally Championships. Third, maximize the innovative capabilities of an outstanding operations function. This is a classic differentiation strategy, supported by activity mapping that ties Pirelli's marketing strength to research and its innovative operations function.

To implement this strategy, Pirelli is differentiating itself with a focus on higher-margin performance tires and away from the low-margin standard tire business. Pirelli has established deals with luxury brands Jaguar, BMW, Maserati, Ferrari, Bentley, and Lotus Elise and established itself as a provider of a large share of the tires on new Porsches and S-class Mercedes. Pirelli also made a strategic decision to divest itself of other businesses. As a result, the vast majority of the company's tire production is now high-performance tires. People are willing to pay a premium for Pirellis.

The operations function continued to focus its design efforts on performance tires and developing a system of modular tire manufacture that allows much faster switching between models. This modular system, combined with billions of dollars in new manufacturing investment, has driven batch sizes down to as small as 150 to 200, making small-lot performance tires economically feasible. Manufacturing innovations at Pirelli have streamlined the production process, moving it from a 14-step process to a 3-step process.

Pirelli still faces a threat from the big three going after the performance market, but the company has bypassed its weakness of having a small market share with a substantial research budget and an innovative operations function. The firm now has 20 plants in 12 countries and a presence in more than 160 countries, with sales approaching $5 billion.

Sources: Based on *The Economist* (January 8, 2011): 65; *Just Auto* (February 2009): 14–15 and (December 2008): 14–15; and **www.pirelli.com**.

SOLVED PROBLEM 2

DeHoratius Electronics, Inc., is evaluating several options for sourcing a critical processor for its new modem. Three sources are being considered: Hi-Tech in Canada, Zia in Hong Kong, and Zaragoza in Spain. The owner, Nicole DeHoratius, has determined that only three criteria are critical. She has rated each firm on a 1–5 scale (with 5 being highest) and has also placed an importance weight on each of the factors, as shown below:

FACTOR (CRITERION)	IMPORTANCE WEIGHT	OUTSOURCE PROVIDERS					
		HI-TECH (CANADA)		ZIA (HONG KONG)		ZARAGOZA (SPAIN)	
		Rating	Wtd. Score	Rating	Wtd.Score	Rating	Wtd. Score
1. Cost	.5	3	1.5	3	1.5	5	2.5
2. Reliability	.2	4	.8	3	.6	3	.6
3. Competence	.3	5	1.5	4	1.2	3	.9
Totals	1.0		3.8		3.3		4.0

SOLUTION

Nicole multiplies each rating by the weight and sums the products in each column to generate a total score for each outsourcing provider. For example the weighted score for Hi-Tech equals $(.5 \times 3) + (.2 \times 4) + (.3 \times 5) = 1.5 + .8 + 1.5 = 3.8$. She selects Zaragoza, which has the highest overall rating.

Problems

Note: Px means the problem may be solved with POM for Windows and/or Excel OM.

• **1** The text provides three primary strategic approaches (differentiation, cost, and response) for achieving competitive advantage. Provide an example of each not given in the text. Support your choices. (*Hint:* Note the examples provided in the text.)

•• **2** Within the food service industry (restaurants that serve meals to customers, but not just fast food), find examples of firms that have sustained competitive advantage by competing on the basis of (1) cost leadership, (2) response, and (3) differentiation. Cite one example in each category; provide a sentence or two in support of each choice. Do not use fast-food chains for all categories. (*Hint:* A "99¢ menu" is very easily copied and is not a good source of sustained advantage.)

•• **3** Match the product with the proper parent company and country in the table below:

PRODUCT	PARENT COMPANY	COUNTRY
Arrow Shirts	a. Volkswagen	1. France
Braun Household Appliances	b. Bidermann International	2. Great Britain
Volvo Autos	c. Bridgestone	3. Germany
Firestone Tires	d. Campbell Soup	4. Japan
Godiva Chocolate	e. Credit Lyonnais	5. U.S.
Häagen-Dazs Ice Cream (USA)	f. Tata	6. Switzerland
Jaguar Autos	g. Procter & Gamble	7. China
MGM Movies	h. Michelin	8. India
Lamborghini Autos	i. Nestlé	
Goodrich Tires	j. Geely	
Alpo Pet Foods		

••• **4** Identify how changes within an organization affect the OM strategy for a company. For instance, discuss what impact the following internal factors might have on OM strategy:

a) Maturing of a product.
b) Technology innovation in the manufacturing process.
c) Changes in laptop computer design that builds in wireless technology.

••• **5** Identify how changes in the external environment affect the OM strategy for a company. For instance, discuss what impact the following external factors might have on OM strategy:

a) Major increases in oil prices.
b) Water- and air-quality legislation.
c) Fewer young prospective employees entering the labor market.
d) Inflation versus stable prices.
e) Legislation moving health insurance from a pretax benefit to taxable income.

•• **6** Develop a ranking for *corruption* in the following countries: Mexico, Turkey, Denmark, the U.S., Taiwan, Brazil, and another country of your choice. (*Hint:* See sources such as *Transparency International*, *Asia Pacific Management News*, and *The Economist*.)

•• **7** Develop a ranking for *competitiveness* and/or business environment for Britain, Singapore, the U.S., Hong Kong, and Italy. (*Hint:* See the *Global Competitive Report*, *World Economic Forum*, and *The Economist*.)

•• **8** Claudia Pragram Technologies, Inc., has narrowed its choice of outsourcing provider to two firms located in different countries. Pragram wants to decide which one of the two countries is the better choice, based on risk-avoidance criteria. She has polled her executives and established four criteria. The resulting ratings for the two countries are presented in the table on the next page, where 1 is a lower risk and 3 is a higher risk.

SELECTION CRITERION	ENGLAND	CANADA
Price of service from outsourcer	2	3
Nearness of facilities to client	3	1
Level of technology	1	3
History of successful outsourcing	1	2

The executives have determined four criteria weightings: Price, with a weight of 0.1; Nearness, with 0.6; Technology, with 0.2; and History, with 0.1.

a) Using the factor-rating method, which country would you select?
b) Double each of the weights used in part (a) (to 0.2, 1.2, 0.4, and 0.2, respectively). What effect does this have on your answer? Why? PX

•• **9** Ranga Ramasesh is the operations manager for a firm that is trying to decide which one of four countries it should research for possible outsourcing providers. The first step is to select a country based on cultural risk factors, which are critical to eventual business success with the provider. Ranga has reviewed outsourcing provider directories and found that the four countries in the table that follows have an ample number of providers from which they can choose. To aid in the country selection step, he has enlisted the aid of a cultural expert, John Wang, who has provided ratings of the various criteria in the table. The resulting ratings are on a 1 to 10 scale, where 1 is a low risk and 10 is a high risk.

John has also determined six criteria weightings: Trust, with a weight of 0.4; Quality, with 0.2; Religious, with 0.1; Individualism, with 0.1; Time, with 0.1; and Uncertainty, with 0.1. Using the factor-rating method, which country should Ranga select? PX

CULTURE SELECTION CRITERION	MEXICO	PANAMA	COSTA RICA	PERU
Trust	1	2	2	1
Society value of quality work	7	10	9	10
Religious attitudes	3	3	3	5
Individualism attitudes	5	2	4	8
Time orientation attitudes	4	6	7	3
Uncertainty avoidance attitudes	3	2	4	2

•• **10** Fernando Garza's firm wishes to use factor rating to help select an outsourcing provider of logistics services.

a) With weights from 1–5 (5 highest) and ratings 1–100 (100 highest), use the following table to help Garza make his decision:

		RATING OF LOGISTICS PROVIDERS		
CRITERION	WEIGHT	OVERNIGHT SHIPPING	WORLDWIDE DELIVERY	UNITED FREIGHT
Quality	5	90	80	75
Delivery	3	70	85	70
Cost	2	70	80	95

b) Garza decides to increase the weights for quality, delivery, and cost to 10, 6, and 4, respectively. How does this change your conclusions? Why?
c) If Overnight Shipping's ratings for each of the factors increase by 10%, what are the new results? PX

••• **11** Walker Accounting Software is marketed to small accounting firms throughout the U.S. and Canada. Owner George Walker has decided to outsource the company's help desk and is considering three providers: Manila Call Center (Philippines), Delhi Services (India), and Moscow Bell (Russia). The following table summarizes the data Walker has assembled. Which outsourcing firm has the best rating? (Higher weights imply higher importance and higher ratings imply more desirable providers.) PX

		PROVIDER RATINGS		
CRITERION	IMPORTANCE WEIGHT	MANILA	DELHI	MOSCOW
Flexibility	0.5	5	1	9
Trustworthiness	0.1	5	5	2
Price	0.2	4	3	6
Delivery	0.2	5	6	6

•••• **12** Rao Technologies, a California-based high-tech manufacturer, is considering outsourcing some of its electronics production. Four firms have responded to its request for bids, and CEO Mohan Rao has started to perform an analysis on the scores his OM team has entered in the table below.

		RATINGS OF OUTSOURCE PROVIDERS			
FACTOR	WEIGHT	A	B	C	D
Labor	w	5	4	3	5
Quality procedures	30	2	3	5	1
Logistics system	5	3	4	3	5
Price	25	5	3	4	4
Trustworthiness	5	3	2	3	5
Technology in place	15	2	5	4	4
Management team	15	5	4	2	1

Weights are on a scale from 1 through 30, and the outsourcing provider scores are on a scale of 1 through 5. The weight for the labor factor is shown as a w because Rao's OM team cannot agree on a value for this weight. For what range of values of w, if any, is company C a recommended outsourcing provider, according to the factor-rating method?

Refer to MyOMLab for this additional homework problem: 13.

CASE STUDIES

Minit-Lube

A substantial market exists for automobile tune-ups, oil changes, and lubrication service for more than 250 million vehicles on U.S. roads. Some of this demand is filled by full-service auto dealerships, some by Walmart and Firestone, and some by other tire/service dealers. However, Minit-Lube, Mobil-Lube, Jiffy-Lube and others have also developed strategies to accommodate this opportunity.

Minit-Lube stations perform oil changes, lubrication, and interior cleaning in a spotless environment. The buildings are clean, painted white, and often surrounded by neatly trimmed landscaping. To facilitate fast service, cars can be driven through three abreast. At Minit-Lube, the customer is greeted by service representatives who are graduates of Minit-Lube U. The Minit-Lube school is not unlike McDonald's Hamburger University near Chicago or Holiday Inn's training school in Memphis. The greeter takes the order, which typically includes fluid checks (oil, water, brake fluid, transmission fluid, differential grease) and the necessary lubrication, as well as filter changes for air and oil. Service personnel in neat uniforms then move into action. The standard three-person team has one person checking fluid levels under the hood, another assigned interior vacuuming and window cleaning, and the third in the garage pit, removing the oil filter, draining the oil, checking the differential and transmission, and lubricating as necessary. Precise task assignments and good training are designed to move the car into and out of the bay in 10 minutes. The idea is to charge no more, and hopefully less, than gas stations, automotive repair chains, and auto dealers, while providing better service.

Discussion Questions

1. What constitutes the mission of Minit-Lube?
2. How does the Minit-Lube operations strategy provide competitive advantage? (*Hint:* Evaluate how Minit-Lube's traditional competitors perform the 10 decisions of operations management vs. how Minit-Lube performs them.)
3. Is it likely that Minit-Lube has increased productivity over its more traditional competitors? Why? How would we measure productivity in this industry?

Strategy at Regal Marine

Video Case

Regal Marine, one of the U.S.'s 10 largest power-boat manufacturers, achieves its mission—providing luxury performance boats to customers worldwide—using the strategy of differentiation. It differentiates its products through constant innovation, unique features, and high quality. Increasing sales at the Orlando, Florida, family-owned firm suggest that the strategy is working.

As a quality boat manufacturer, Regal Marine starts with continuous innovation, as reflected in computer-aided design (CAD), high-quality molds, and close tolerances that are controlled through both defect charts and rigorous visual inspection. In-house quality is not enough, however. Because a product is only as good as the parts put into it, Regal has established close ties with a large number of its suppliers to ensure both flexibility and perfect parts. With the help of these suppliers, Regal can profitably produce a product line of 22 boats, ranging from the $14,000 19-foot boat to the $500,000 44-foot Commodore yacht.

"We build boats," says VP Tim Kuck, "but we're really in the 'fun' business. Our competition includes not only 300 other boat, canoe, and yacht manufacturers in our $17 billion industry, but home theaters, the Internet, and all kinds of alternative family entertainment." Fortunately Regal has been paying down debt and increasing market share.

Regal has also joined with scores of other independent boat makers in the American Boat Builders Association. Through economies of scale in procurement, Regal is able to navigate against billion-dollar competitor Brunswick (makers of the Sea Ray and Bayliner brands).

Discussion Questions*

1. State Regal Marine's mission in your own words.
2. Identify the strengths, weaknesses, opportunities, and threats that are relevant to the strategy of Regal Marine.
3. How would you define Regal's strategy?
4. How would each of the 10 operations management decisions apply to operations decision making at Regal Marine?

*You may wish to view the video that accompanies the case before addressing these questions.

Source: Pearson video.

Hard Rock Cafe's Global Strategy

Video Case

Hard Rock brings the concept of the "experience economy" to its cafe operation. The strategy incorporates a unique "experience" into its operations. This innovation is somewhat akin to mass customization in manufacturing. At Hard Rock, the experience concept is to provide not only a custom meal from the menu but a dining event that includes a unique visual and sound experience not duplicated anywhere else in the world. This strategy is succeeding. Other theme restaurants have come and gone while Hard Rock continues to grow. As Professor C. Markides of the London Business School says, "The trick is not to play the game better than the competition, but to develop and play an altogether different game."* At Hard Rock, the different game is the experience game.

From the opening of its first cafe in London in 1971, during the British rock music explosion, Hard Rock has been serving food and rock music with equal enthusiasm. Hard Rock Cafe has 40 U.S. locations, about a dozen in Europe, and the remainder scattered throughout the world, from Bangkok and Beijing to Beirut. New construction, leases, and investment in remodeling are long term; so a global

*Constantinos Markides, "Strategic Innovation," *MIT Sloan Management Review* 38, no. 3 (Spring 1997): 9.

strategy means special consideration of political risk, currency risk, and social norms in a context of a brand fit. Although Hard Rock is one of the most recognized brands in the world, this does not mean its cafe is a natural everywhere. Special consideration must be given to the supply chain for the restaurant and its accompanying retail store. About 48% of a typical cafe's sales are from merchandise.

The Hard Rock Cafe business model is well defined, but because of various risk factors and differences in business practices and employment law, Hard Rock elects to franchise about half of its cafes. Social norms and preferences often suggest some tweaking of menus for local taste. For instance, Hard Rock focuses less on hamburgers and beef and more on fish and lobster in its British cafes.

Because 70% of Hard Rock's guests are tourists, recent years have found it expanding to "destination" cities. While this has been a winning strategy for decades, allowing the firm to grow from one London cafe to 162 facilities in 57 countries, it has made Hard Rock susceptible to economic fluctuations that hit the tourist business hardest. So Hard Rock is signing a long-term lease for a new location in Nottingham, England, to join recently opened cafes in Manchester and Birmingham—cities that are not standard tourist destinations. At the same time, menus are being upgraded. Hopefully, repeat business from locals in these cities will smooth demand and make Hard Rock less dependent on tourists.

Discussion Questions*

1. Identify the strategy changes that have taken place at Hard Rock Cafe since its founding in 1971.
2. As Hard Rock Cafe has changed its strategy, how has its responses to some of the 10 decisions of OM changed?
3. Where does Hard Rock fit in the four international operations strategies outlined in Figure 9? Explain your answer.

*You may wish to view the video that accompanies this case before addressing these questions.

Outsourcing Offshore at Darden

Video Case

Darden Restaurants, owner of popular brands such as Olive Garden and Red Lobster, serves more than 300 million meals annually in over 1,700 restaurants across the U.S. and Canada. To achieve competitive advantage via its supply chain, Darden must achieve excellence at each step. With purchases from 35 countries, and seafood products with a shelf life as short as 4 days, this is a complex and challenging task.

Those 300 million meals annually mean 40 million pounds of shrimp and huge quantities of tilapia, swordfish, and other fresh purchases. Fresh seafood is typically flown to the U.S. and monitored each step of the way to ensure that 34°F is maintained.

Darden's purchasing agents travel the world to find competitive advantage in the supply chain. Darden personnel from supply chain and development, quality assurance, and environmental relations contribute to developing, evaluating, and checking suppliers. Darden also has seven native-speaking representatives living on other continents to provide continuing support and evaluation of suppliers. All suppliers must abide by Darden's food standards, which typically exceed FDA and other industry standards. Darden expects continuous improvement in durable relationships that increase quality and reduce cost.

Darden's aggressiveness and development of a sophisticated supply chain provide an opportunity for outsourcing. Much food preparation is labor intensive and is often more efficient when handled in bulk. This is particularly true where large volumes may justify capital investment. For instance, Tyson and Iowa Beef prepare meats to Darden's specifications much more economically than can individual restaurants. Similarly, Darden has found that it can outsource both the cutting of salmon to the proper portion size and the cracking/peeling of shrimp more cost-effectively offshore than in U.S. distribution centers or individual restaurants.

Discussion Questions*

1. What are some outsourcing opportunities in a restaurant?
2. What supply chain issues are unique to a firm sourcing from 35 countries?
3. Examine how other firms or industries develop international supply chains as compared to Darden.
4. Why does Darden outsource harvesting and preparation of much of its seafood?

*You may wish to view the video that accompanies this case study before answering these questions.

• **Additional Case Study:** Visit **www.myomlab.com** or **www.pearsonhighered.com/heizer** for this free case study:
Outsourcing to Tata: The Indian outsourcing firm is hired by New Mexico.

Bibliography

Beckman, S. L., and D. B. Rosenfield. *Operations Strategy: Competing in the 21st Century*. New York: McGraw-Hill, 2008.

Bravard, J., and R. Morgan. *Smarter Outsourcing*. Upper Saddle River, NJ: Pearson, 2006.

Crotts, J. C., D. R. Dickson, and R. C. Ford. "Aligning Organizational Processes with Mission." *Academy of Management Executive* 19, no. 3 (August 2005): 54–68.

Flynn, B. B., R. G. Schroeder, and E. J. Flynn. "World Class Manufacturing." *Journal of Operations Management* 17, no. 3 (March 1999): 249–269.

Greenwald, Bruce C., and Judd Kahn. *Globalization: The Irrational Fear That Someone in China Will Take Your Job*. New York: Wiley, 2009.

Hirschheim, R., A. Heinzl, and J. Dibbern. *Information Systems Outsourcing*. Secaucus, NJ: Springer, 2009.

Lee, Hau L., and Chung-Yee Lee. *Building Supply Chain Excellence in Emerging Economies*. Secaucus, NJ: Springer, 2007.

Kaplan, Robert S., and David P. Norton. *Strategy Maps*. Boston: Harvard Business School Publishing, 2003.

Kathuria, R., M. P. Joshi, and S. Dellande. "International Growth Strategies of Service and Manufacturing Firms." *International Journal of Operations and Production Management* 28, no. 10 (2008): 968.

Midler, Paul. *Poorly Made in China: An Insider's Account of the Tactics Behind China's Production Game*. New York: Wiley, 2009.

Porter, Michael, and Nicolaj Siggelkow. "Contextuality within Activity Systems and Sustainability of Competitive Advantage." *Academy of Management Perspectives* 22, no. 2 (May 2008): 34–36.

Rudberg, Martin, and B. M. West. "Global Operations Strategy." *Omega* 36, no. 1 (February 2008): 91.

Skinner, Wickham. "Manufacturing Strategy: The Story of Its Evolution." *Journal of Operations Management* 25, no. 2 (March 2007): 328–334.

Slack, Nigel, and Mike Lewis. *Operation Strategy*, 3rd ed. Upper Saddle River, NJ: Prentice Hall, 2011.

Wolf, Martin. *Why Globalization Works*. London: Yale University Press, 2004.

APPENDIX

SOLUTIONS TO EVEN-NUMBERED PROBLEMS

2 Cost leadership: Sodexho
Response: a catering firm
Differentiation: a fine-dining restaurant

4 **(a)** Focus more on standardization, make fewer product changes, find optimum capacity, and stabilize manufacturing process are a few possibilities
(b) New human resource skills, added capital investment for new equipment/processes
(c) Same as (b)

6 See www.transparency.org or www.apmforum.com

8 **(a)** Canada, 1.7
(b) No change

10 **(a)** Worldwide, 81.5 weighted *average*, 815 weighted *total*
(b) No change
(c) Overnight Shipping now preferred, weighted total = 880

12 Company C, $1.0 \leq w \leq 25.0$

Rapid Review

Main Heading	Review Material	MyOMLab
A GLOBAL VIEW OF OPERATIONS AND SUPPLY CHAINS	Domestic business operations decide to change to some form of international operations for six main reasons: 1. Improve supply chain 2. Reduce costs (labor, taxes, tariffs, etc.) 3. Improve operations 4. Understand markets 5. Improve products 6. Attract and retain global talent ▪ **Maquiladoras**—Mexican factories located along the U.S.–Mexico border that receive preferential tariff treatment. ▪ **World Trade Organization (WTO)**—An international organization that promotes world trade by lowering barriers to the free flow of goods across borders. ▪ **NAFTA**—A free trade agreement between Canada, Mexico, and the United States. ▪ **European Union (EU)**—A European trade group that has 27 member states.	
DEVELOPING MISSIONS AND STRATEGIES	An effective operations management effort must have a *mission* so it knows where it is going and a *strategy* so it knows how to get there. ▪ **Mission**—The purpose or rationale for an organization's existence. ▪ **Strategy**—How an organization expects to achieve its missions and goals. The three strategic approaches to competitive advantage are: 1. Differentiation 2. Cost leadership 3. Response	**VIDEO 1** Operations Strategy at Regal Marine
ACHIEVING COMPETITIVE ADVANTAGE THROUGH OPERATIONS	▪ **Competitive advantage**—The creation of a unique advantage over competitors. ▪ **Differentiation**—Distinguishing the offerings of an organization in a way that the customer perceives as adding value. ▪ **Experience differentiation**—Engaging the customer with a product through imaginative use of the five senses, so the customer "experiences" the product. ▪ **Low-cost leadership**—Achieving maximum value, as perceived by the customer. ▪ **Response**—A set of values related to rapid, flexible, and reliable performance.	**VIDEO 2** Hard Rock's Global Strategy
ISSUES IN OPERATIONS STRATEGY	▪ **Resources view**—A view in which managers evaluate the resources at their disposal and manage or alter them to achieve competitive advantage. ▪ **Value-chain analysis**—A way to identify the elements in the product/service chain that uniquely add value. ▪ **Five forces model**—A way to analyze the five forces in the competitive environment. Forces in Porter's five forces model are (1) immediate rivals, (2) potential entrants, (3) customers, (4) suppliers, and (5) substitute products. Different issues are emphasized during different stages of the product life cycle: ▪ ***Introduction***—Company strategy: Best period to increase market share, R&D engineering is critical. OM strategy: Product design and development critical, frequent product and process design changes, short production runs, high production costs, limited models, attention to quality. ▪ ***Growth***—Company strategy: Practical to change price or quality image, strengthen niche. OM strategy: Forecasting critical, product and process reliability, competitive product improvements and options, increase capacity, shift toward product focus, enhance distribution. ▪ ***Maturity***—Company strategy: Poor time to change image or price or quality, competitive costs become critical, defend market position. OM strategy: Standardization, less rapid product changes (more minor changes), optimum capacity, increasing stability of process, long production runs, product improvement and cost cutting. ▪ ***Decline***—Company strategy: Cost control critical. OM strategy: Little product differentiation, cost minimization, overcapacity in the industry, prune line to eliminate items not returning good margin, reduce capacity.	

Rapid Review continued

Main Heading	Review Material	MyOMLab
STRATEGY DEVELOPMENT AND IMPLEMENTATION	■ **SWOT analysis**—A method of determining internal strengths and weaknesses and external opportunities and threats. ■ **Key success factors (KSFs)**—Activities or factors that are key to achieving competitive advantage. ■ **Core competencies**—A set of unique skills, talents, and activities that a firm does particularly well. A core competence may be a combination of KSFs. ■ **Activity map**—A graphical link of competitive advantage, KSFs, and supporting activities.	Virtual Office Hours for Solved Problem: 1
STRATEGIC PLANNING, CORE COMPETENCIES, AND OUTSOURCING	■ **Outsourcing**—Procuring from external sources services or products that are normally part of an organization. ■ **Theory of comparative advantage**—The theory which states that countries benefit from specializing in (and exporting) products and services in which they have relative advantage and importing goods in which they have a relative disadvantage. Perhaps half of all outsourcing agreements fail because of inappropriate planning and analysis. Potential risks of outsourcing include: ■ A drop in quality or customer service ■ Political backlash that results from outsourcing to foreign countries ■ Negative impact on employees ■ Potential future competition ■ Increased logistics and inventory costs The most common reason given for outsourcing failure is that the decision was made without sufficient understanding and analysis. The factor-rating method is an excellent tool for dealing with both country risk assessment and provider selection problems.	**VIDEO 3** Outsourcing Offshore at Darden Virtual Office Hours for Solved Problem: 2 Problems: 3–12
GLOBAL OPERATIONS STRATEGY OPTIONS	■ **International business**—A firm that engages in cross-border transactions. ■ **Multinational corporation (MNC)**—A firm that has extensive involvement in international business, owning or controlling facilities in more than one country. The four operations strategies for approaching global opportunities can be classified according to local responsiveness and cost reduction: ■ **International strategy**—A strategy in which global markets are penetrated using exports and licenses with little local responsiveness. ■ **Multidomestic strategy**—A strategy in which operating decisions are decentralized to each country to enhance local responsiveness. ■ **Global strategy**—A strategy in which operating decisions are centralized and headquarters coordinates the standardization and learning between facilities. ■ **Transnational strategy**—A strategy that combines the benefits of global-scale efficiencies with the benefits of local responsiveness. These firms transgress national boundaries.	

Self Test

■ **Before taking the self-test,** refer to the learning objectives listed at the beginning of the text and the key terms listed at the end of the text.

LO1. A mission statement is beneficial to an organization because it:
- **a)** is a statement of the organization's purpose.
- **b)** provides a basis for the organization's culture.
- **c)** identifies important constituencies.
- **d)** details specific income goals.
- **e)** ensures profitability.

LO2. The three strategic approaches to competitive advantage are ____, ____, and ____.

LO3. Core competencies are those strengths in a firm that include:
- **a)** specialized skills.
- **b)** unique production methods.
- **c)** proprietary information/knowledge.
- **d)** things a company does better than others.
- **e)** all of the above.

LO4. Evaluating outsourcing providers by comparing their weighted average scores involves:
- **a)** factor-rating analysis.
- **b)** cost-volume analysis.
- **c)** transportation model analysis.
- **d)** linear regression analysis.
- **e)** crossover analysis.

LO5. A company that is organized across international boundaries, with decentralized authority and substantial autonomy at each business via subsidiaries, franchises, or joint ventures, has:
- **a)** a global strategy.
- **b)** a transnational strategy.
- **c)** an international strategy.
- **d)** a multidomestic strategy.

Answers: LO1. a; LO2. differentiation, cost leadership, response; LO3. e; LO4. a; LO5. c.

APPENDIX: SOLUTIONS TO EVEN-NUMBERED PROBLEMS

APPENDIX
SOLUTIONS TO EVEN-NUMBERED PROBLEMS

Operations and Productivity

2 **(a)** 2 valves/hr
(b) 2.25 valves/hr
(c) 12.5%
4 Varies by site and source.
6 Productivity of labor: 9.3%
Productivity of resin: 11.1%
Productivity of capital: –10.0%
Productivity of energy: 6.1%
8 **(a)** .0096 rugs/labor-dollar
(b) .00787 rugs/dollar
10 Productivity of capital dropped; labor and energy productivity increased.
12 **(a)** Before: 25 boxes/hr
After: 27.08 boxes/hr
(b) Increase: 8.3%
(c) 29.167 boxes/hr
14 **(a)** .293 loaves/dollar
(b) .359 loaves/dollar
(c) Labor change: 0%; Investment change: 22.5%
16 **(a)** 220 hours per laborer; 66,000 labor hours
(b) 200 hours per laborer

Operations Strategy in a Global Environment

2 Cost leadership: Sodexho
Response: a catering firm
Differentiation: a fine-dining restaurant
4 **(a)** Focus more on standardization, make fewer product changes, find optimum capacity, and stabilize manufacturing process are a few possibilities
(b) New human resource skills, added capital investment for new equipment/processes
(c) Same as (b)
6 See www.transparency.org or www.apmforum.com
8 **(a)** Canada, 1.7
(b) No change
10 **(a)** Worldwide, 81.5 weighted *average*, 815 weighted *total*
(b) No change
(c) Overnight Shipping now preferred, weighted total = 880
12 Company C, $1.0 \leq w \leq 25.0$

Project Management

2 Here are some detailed activities for the first two activities for Day's WBS:
1.11 Set initial goals for fundraising.
1.12 Set strategy, including identifying sources and solicitation.
1.13 Raise the funds.
1.21 Identify voters' concerns.
1.22 Analyze competitor's voting record.
1.23 Establish position on issues.
4

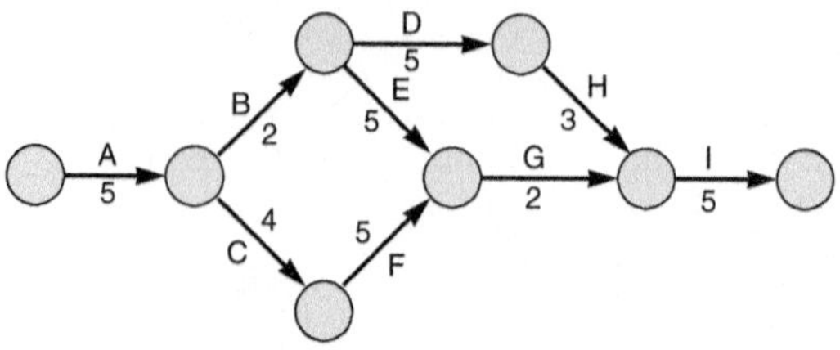

A–C–F–G–I is critical path; 21 days.
This is an AOA network.

6 **(a)**

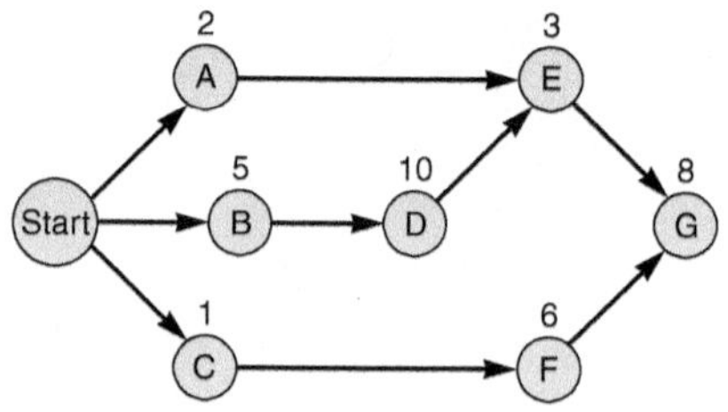

(b) B–D–E–G
(c) 26 days
(d)

Activity	Slack
A	13
B	0
C	11
D	0
E	0
F	11
G	0

8

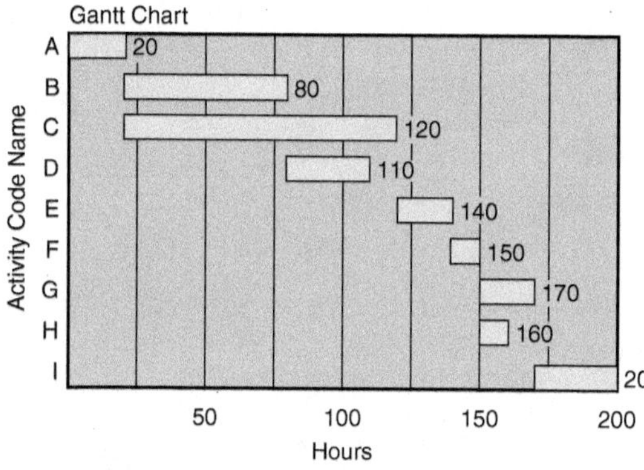

10

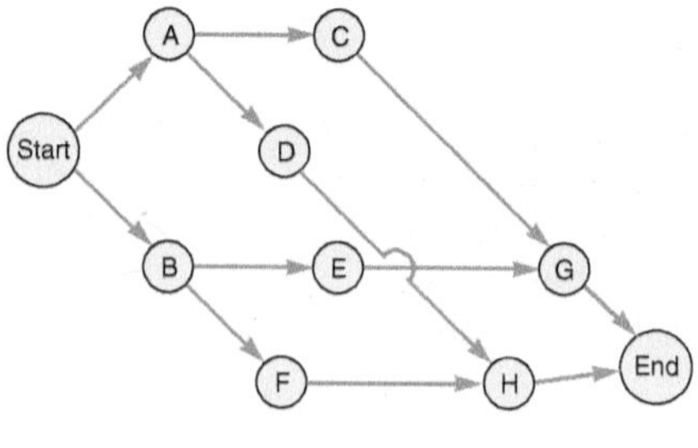

12 **(a)**

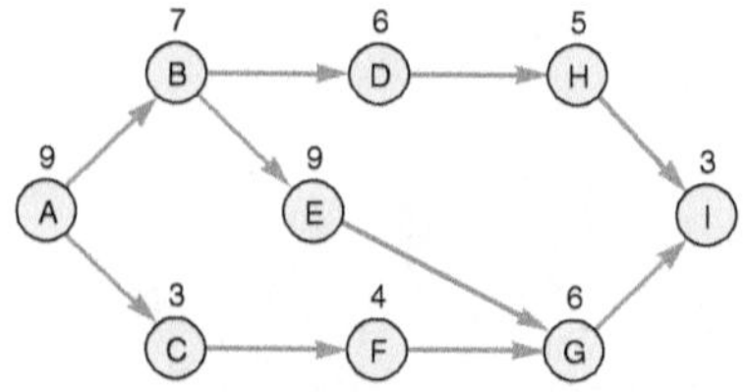

(b) A–B–E–G–I is critical path.
(c) 34

14 **(a)** A, 5.83, 0.69 | G, 2.17, 0.25
B, 3.67, 0.11 | H, 6.00, 1.00
C, 2.00, 0.11 | I, 11.00, 0.11
D, 7.00, 0.11 | J, 16.33, 1.00
E, 4.00, 0.44 | K, 7.33, 1.78
F, 10.00, 1.78
(b) Critical path is C–D–E–F–H–K. Time = 36.33 days.
(c) Slacks are 7.17, 5.33, 0, 0, 0, 0, 2.83, 0, 2.83, 18, and 0, respectively, for A through K.
(d) $P = .946$

16 Crash C to 3 weeks at $200 total for one week. Now both paths are critical. Not worth it to crash further.

18 Critical path currently is C–E for 12 days. $1,100 to crash by 4 days. Watch for parallel critical paths as you crash.

20 **(a)** 16 (A–D–G)
(b) $12,300
(c) D; 1 wk. for $75
(d) 7 wk.; $1,600

22 **(a)** A–C–E–H–I–K–M–N; 50 days
(b) 82.1%
(c) 58 days

24 **(a)** .0228
(b) .3085
(c) .8413
(d) .97725
(e) 24 mo.

26 **(a)**

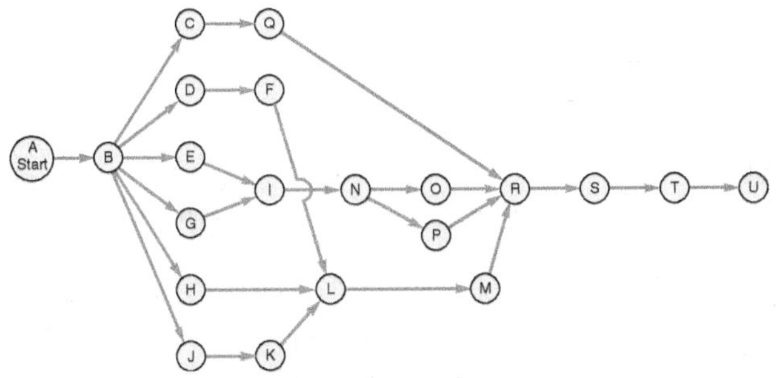

(b) Critical path is A–B–J–K–L–M–R–S–T–U for 18 days.
(c) **i.** No, transmissions and drivetrains are not on the critical path.
ii. No, halving engine-building time will reduce the critical path by only 1 day.
iii. No, it is not on the critical path.
(d) Reallocating workers not involved with critical-path activities to activities along the critical path will reduce the critical path length.

Forecasting

2 **(a)** None obvious.
(b) 7, 7.67, 9, 10, 11, 11, 11.33, 11, 9
(c) 6.4, 7.8, 11, 9.6, 10.9, 12.2, 10.5, 10.6, 8.4
(d) The 3-yr. moving average.

4 **(a)** 41.6
(b) 42.3
(c) Banking industry's seasonality.

6 **(b)** Naive = 23; 3-mo. moving = 21.33; 6-mo. weighted = 20.6; trend = 20.67
(c) Trend projection.

8 **(a)** 91.3
(b) 89
(c) MAD = 2.7
(d) MSE = 13.35
(e) MAPE = 2.99%

10 **(a)** 4.67, 5.00, 6.33, 7.67, 8.33, 8.00, 9.33, 11.67, 13.7
(b) 4.50, 5.00, 7.25, 7.75, 8.00, 8.25, 10.00, 12.25, 14.0
(c) Forecasts are about the same.

12 72

14 Method 1: MAD = .125; MSE = .021
Method 2: MAD = .1275; MSE = .018

16 **(a)** $y = 421 + 33.6x$. When $x = 6$, $y = 622.8$.
(b) 5.6
(c) 32.88

18 49

20 $\alpha = .1$, $\beta = .8$, August forecast = $71,303; MSE = 12.7 for $\beta = .8$ vs. MSE = 18.87 for $\beta = .2$ in Problem 19.

22 Confirm that you match the numbers in Table 1.

24 **(a)** Observations do not form a straight line but do cluster about one.
(b) $y = .676 + 1.03x$
(c) 10 guitars
(d) $r^2 = .68$; $r = .825$

26 270, 390, 189, 351 for fall, winter, spring, and summer, respectively.

28 Index is 0.709, winter; 1.037, spring; 1.553, summer; 0.700, fall.

30 **(a)** 337 **(b)** 380 **(c)** 423

32 **(a)** $y = 50 + 18x$
(b) $410

34 **(a)** 28 **(b)** 43 **(c)** 58

36 **(a)** $452.50
(b) Request is higher than predicted, so seek additional documentation.
(c) Include other variables (such as a destination cost index) to try to increase r and r^2.

38 **(a)** $y = -.158 + .1308x$
(b) 2.719
(c) $r = .966$; $r^2 = .934$

40 131.2 → 72.7 patients; 90.6 → 50.6 patients

42 **(a)** They need more data and must be able to address seasonal *and* trend factors.
(b) Try to create your own naive model because seasonality is strong.
(c) Compute and graph your forecast.

44 Trend adjustment does not appear to give any significant improvement.

46 **(a)** $y = 1.03 + .0034x$, $r^2 = .479$
(b) For $x = 350$; $y = 2.22$
(c) For $x = 800$; $y = 3.75$
(Some rounding may occur, depending on software.)

48 **(a)** Sales (y) = −9.349 + .1121 (contracts)
(b) $r = .8963$; $S_{xy} = 1.3408$

Design of Goods and Services

2 House of quality for a lunch:

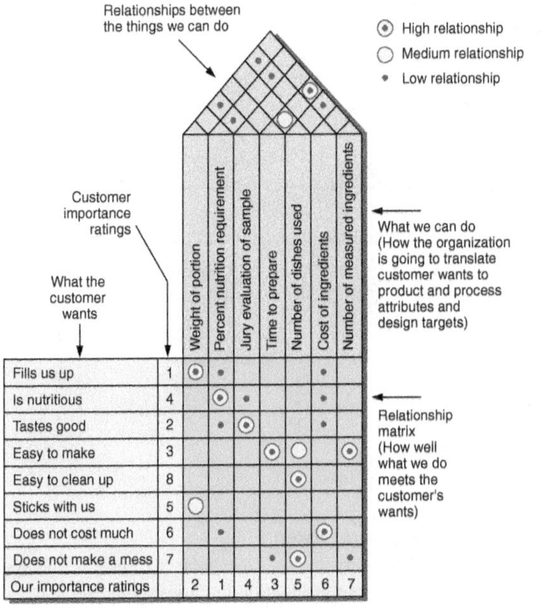

4 Individual answer. Build a house of quality similar to the one shown in Problem 2, entering the *wants* on the left and entering the *hows* at the top.

6 An assembly chart for the eyeglasses is shown below:

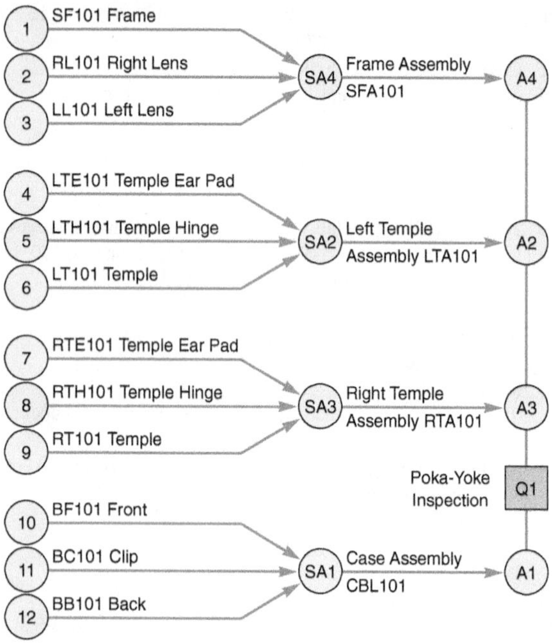

8 Assembly chart for a table lamp:

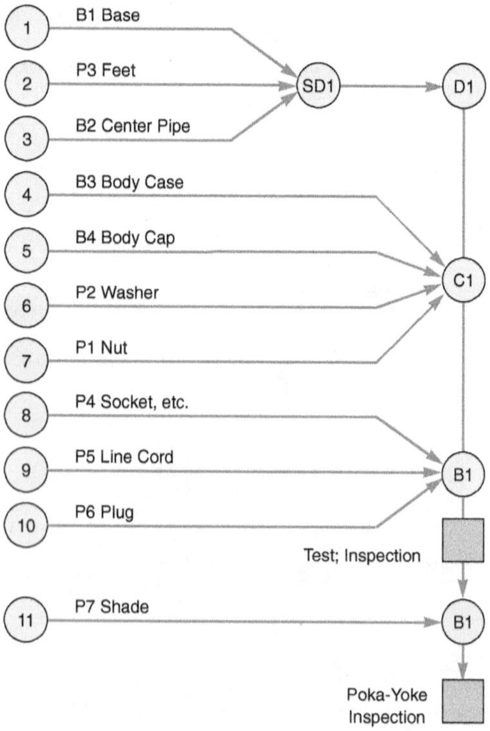

10 *Possible strategies:*

Kindle Fire (growth phase):

Increase capacity and improve balance of production system.
Attempt to make production facilities more efficient.

Netbook (introductory phase):

Increase R&D to better define required product characteristics.
Modify and improve production process.
Develop supplier and distribution systems.

Hand calculator (decline phase):

Concentrate on production and distribution cost reduction.

12 All 10 strategic OM decisions are impacted by their position in the PCN diagram. Comparing just one of these 10 decisions, *product design*:

(a) *Manufacturing*: Must commit to product decisions based on historical data of user preferences (e.g., more risk, no direct interaction)

(b) *Direct interaction*: The sandwich maker must build a system and hire personnel capable of making sandwiches for an end user who may literally be coaching the sandwich maker (e.g., "more mustard, no onions") as the sandwiches are made

(c) *Sandwich buffet*: Commit to purchase, prepare, and sanitarily display the sandwich components which may (or may not) be selected by the end user

14 Low technology, cost = $145,000

16 Deluxe version, EMV = $4,000

18 Joint design, EMV is lowest at $109,8000

20 House of Quality Sequence for Ice Cream

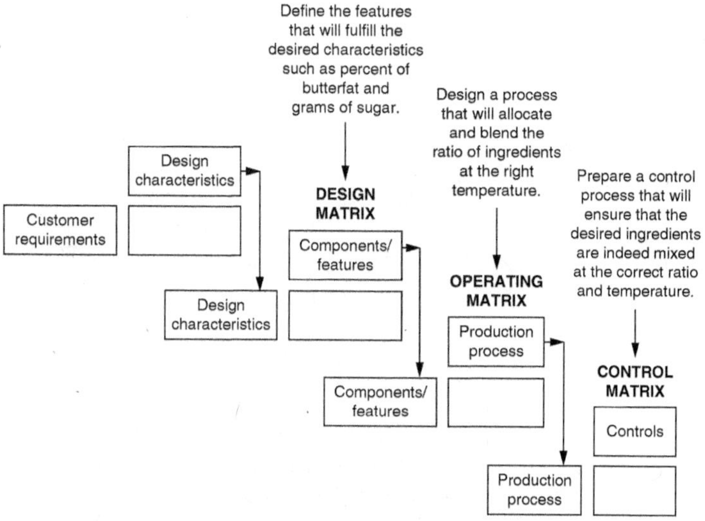

Sustainability in the Supply Chain

S2 Brew Master revenue retrieval = $5.31 provides higher opportunity.

S4 $66,809

S6 3.57 years

S8 3.48 years

Managing Quality

2 Individual answer, in the style of Figure 6(b).

4 Individual answer, in the style of Figure 6(f).

6 Partial flowchart for planning a party:

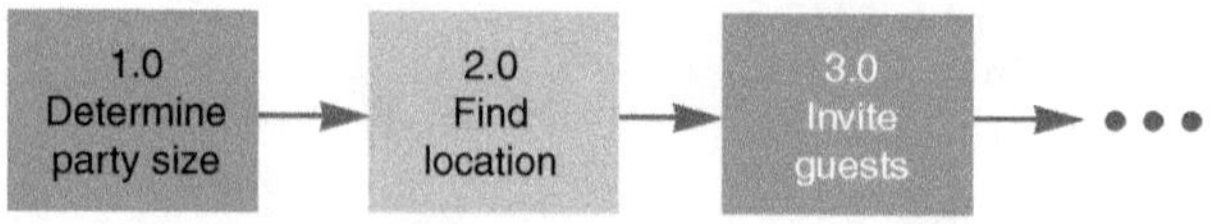

8 See figure on next page for a partial fish-bone. Individual answer in the style of Figure 7.

10 Individual answer, in the style of Figure 7 in the chapter.

12 Pareto chart, in the style of Example 1 with parking/drives most frequent, pool second, etc.

14 See figure below.
Issues: Materials: 4, 12, 14; Methods: 3, 7, 15, 16; Manpower: 1, 5, 6, 11; Machines: 2, 8, 9, 10, 13.

16 **(a)** A scatter diagram in the style of Figure 6(b) that shows a strong positive relationship between shipments and defects
(b) A scatter diagram in the style of Figure 6(b) that shows a mild relationship between shipments and turnover
(c) A Pareto chart in the style of Figure 6(d) that shows frequency of each type of defect
(d) A fishbone chart in the style of Figure 6(c) with the 4 *Ms* showing possible causes of increasing defects in shipments

▼ *Figure for Problem 8.*

Partial Fish-Bone Chart for Dissatisfied Airline Customer

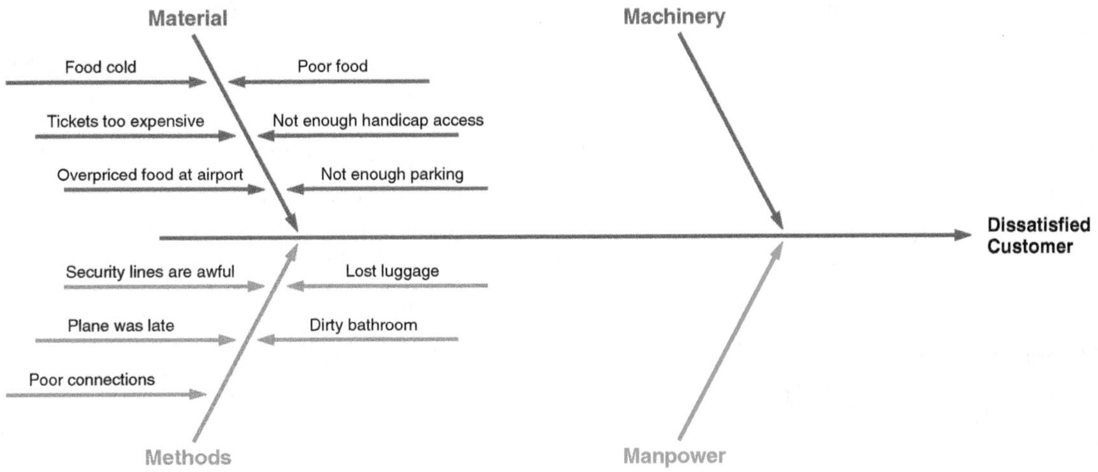

▼ *Figure for Problem 14.*

Partial Fish-Bone for Incorrect Formulation

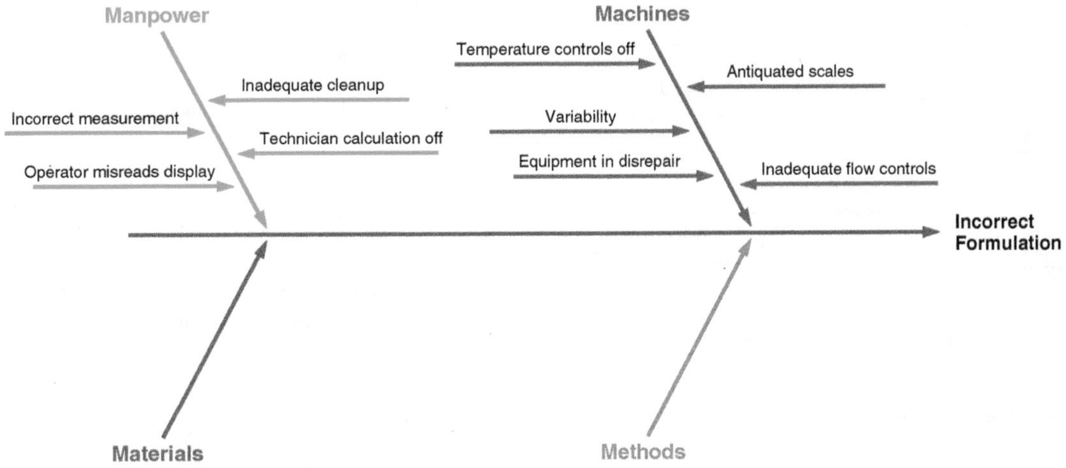

Statistical Process Control

S2 **(a)** $UCL_{\bar{x}} = 52.31$
$LCL_{\bar{x}} = 47.69$
(b) $UCL_{\bar{x}} = 51.54$
$LCL_{\bar{x}} = 48.46$

S4 **(a)** $UCL_{\bar{x}} = 440$ calories
$LCL_{\bar{x}} = 400$ calories
(b) $UCL_{\bar{x}} = 435$ calories
$LCL_{\bar{x}} = 405$ calories

S6 $UCL_{\bar{x}} = 3.728$
$LCL_{\bar{x}} = 2.236$
$UCL_R = 2.336$
$LCL_R = 0.0$
The process is in control.

S8 **(a)** $UCL_{\bar{x}} = 16.08$
$LCL_{\bar{x}} = 15.92$
(b) $UCL_{\bar{x}} = 16.12$
$LCL_{\bar{x}} = 15.88$

S10 **(a)** $\sigma_{\bar{x}} = 0.61$
(b) Using $\sigma_{\bar{x}}$, $UCL_{\bar{x}} = 11.83$, and $LCL_{\bar{x}} = 8.17$.
(c) Using A_2, $UCL_{\bar{x}} = 11.90$, and $LCL_{\bar{x}} = 8.10$.
(c) $UCL_R = 6.98$; $LCL_R = 0$
(d) Yes

S12 $UCL_R = 6.058$; $LCL_R = 0.442$
Averages are increasing.

S14

UCL	LCL
.062	0
.099	0
.132	0
.161	0
.190	.01

S16 $UCL_p = .0313$; $LCL_p = 0$
S18 **(a)** $UCL_p = 0.076$; $LCL_p = 0.002$
S20 **(a)** $UCL_p = .0581$
$LCL_p = 0$
(b) in control
(c) $UCL_p = .1154$
$LCL_p = 0$
S22 **(a)** *c*-chart
(b) $UCL_c = 13.35$
$LCL_c = 0$
(c) in control
(d) not in control
S24 **(a)** $UCL_c = 26.063$
$LCL_c = 3.137$
(b) No point out of control.
S26 $C_p = 1.0$. The process is barely capable.
S28 $C_{pk} = 1.125$. Process *is* centered and will produce within tolerance.
S30 $C_{pk} = .1667$
S32 AOQ = 2.2%
S34 **(a)** $UCL_{\bar{x}} = 61.131, LCL_{\bar{x}} = 38.421, UCL_R = 41.62, LCL_R = 0$
(b) Yes, the process is in control for both $\bar{x}$- and *R*-charts.
(c) They support West's claim. But variance from the mean needs to be reduced and controlled.

Process Strategy

2

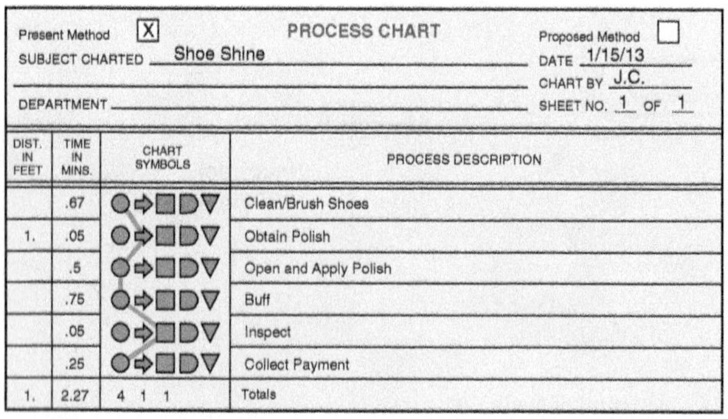

4

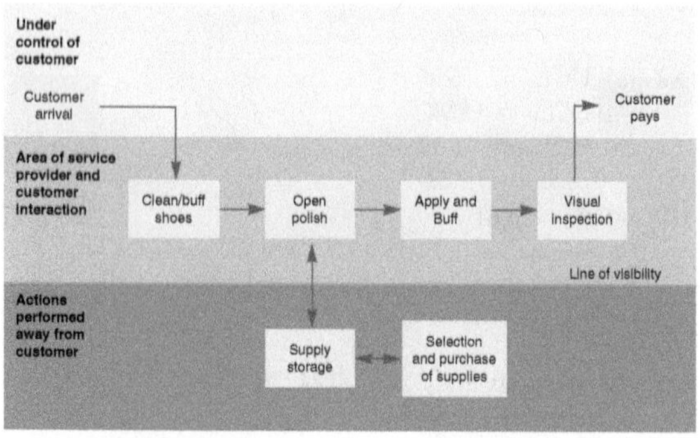

6 GPE is best below 100,000.
FMS is best between 100,000 and 300,000.
DM is best over 300,000.

8 Optimal process will change at 100,000 and 300,000.
10 **(a)**

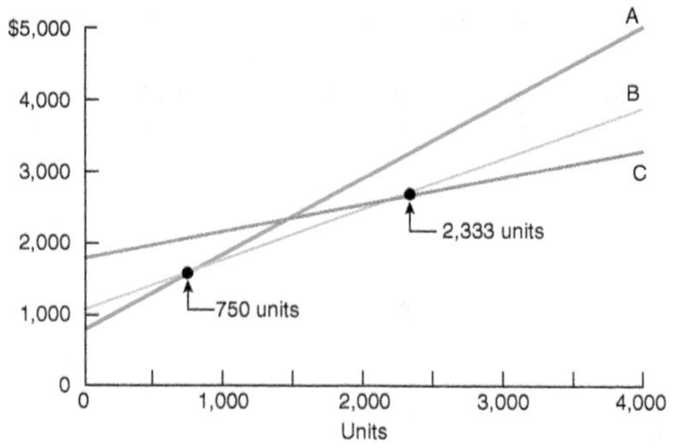

(b) Plan c
(c) Plan b
12 Rent HP software since projected volume of 80 is above the crossover point of 75.
14 **(a)** Intermittent
(b) $200,000

Capacity and Constraint Management

S2 69.2%
S4 88.9%
S6 Design = 88,920
Fabrication = 160,680
Finishing = 65,520
S8 5.17 (or 6) bays
S10 15 min/unit
S12 **(a)** Throughput time = 40 min
(b) Bottleneck time = 12 min.
(c) Station 2
(d) Weekly capacity = 240 units
S14 **(a)** Work station C at 20 min/unit
(b) 3 units/hr
S16 **(a)** 2,000 units
(b) $1,500
S18 **(a)** $150,000
(b) $160,000
S20 **(a)** $BEP_A = 1,667$;
$BEP_B = 2,353$
(b, c) Oven A slightly more profitable
(d) 13,333 pizzas
S22 **(a)** $18,750
(b) 375,000
S24 Yes, purchase new equipment and raise price. Profit = $2,500
S26 $BEP_\$ = \$7,584.83$ per mo
Daily meals = 9
S28 Option B; $74,000
S30 $4,590
S32 NPV = $1,764
S34 **(a)** Purchase two large ovens.
(b) Equal quality, equal capacity.
(c) Payments are made at end of each time period. And future interest rates are known.

Location Strategies

2 China, $1.44
4 India is $.05 less than elsewhere.
6 **(a)** Mobile = 53; Jackson = 60; select Jackson.
(b) Jackson now = 66.
8 **(a)** Hyde Park, with 54.5 points.
(b) Present location = 51 points.

10 **(a)** Location C, with a total *weighted* score of 1,530.
(b) Location B = 1,360
(c) B can never be in first place.

12 **(a)** Great Britain, at 36;
(b) Great Britain is now 31; Holland is 30.

14 **(a)** Italy is highest.
(b) Spain always lowest.

16 **(a)** Site 1 up to 125, site 2 from 125 to 233, site 3 above 233
(b) Site 2

18 **(a)** Above 10,000 cars, site C is lowest cost
(b) Site A optimal from 0–10,000 cars.
(c) Site B is never optimal.

20 **(a)** (5.15, 7.31)
(b) (5.13, 7.67)

22 **(a)** (6.23, 6.08);
(b) safety, etc.

24 **(a)** Site C is best, with a score of 374
(b) For all positive values of w_7 such that $w_7 \leq 14$

Layout Strategies

2 **(a)** $23,400
(b) $20,600
(c) $22,000
(d) Plan B

4 Benders to area 1; Materials to 2; Welders to 3; Drills to 4; Grinder to 5; and Lathes to 6; Trips × Distance = 13,000 ft.

6 Layout #1, distance = 600 with areas fixed
Layout #2, distance = 602 with areas fixed

8 Layout #4, distance = 609
Layout #5, distance = 478

10 **(a)** 1.68 minutes
(b) 4.76 ≈ 5
(c) cleaning

12 **(b)** Cycle time = 9.6 min.;
(e) Idle time/cycle = 15 min.
(f) 15 hours/day idle.
(g) 8 workstations with 76.6% efficiency is possible.

14 **(a)**

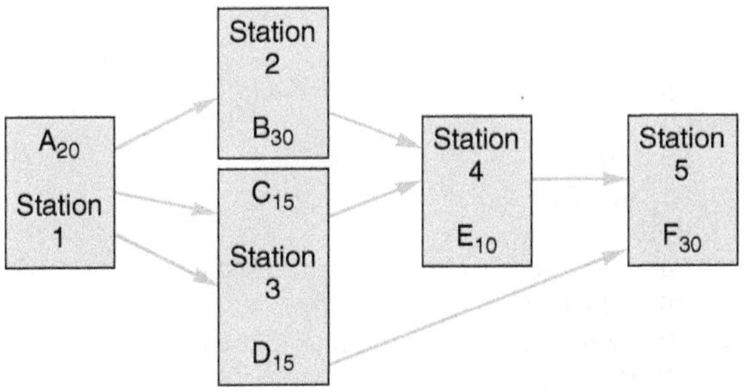

(b) cycle time = 30 sec./unit
(c) 4 stations = *theoretical* minimum, but 5 are needed
(d) Station 1–Task A; 2–B; 3–C, D; 4–E; 5–F
(e) Total idle = 30 sec.
(f) E = 80% with 5 stations; E = 66.6% with 6 stations

16 **(a, b)** Cycle time = 6.67 min/unit. Multiple solutions with 5 stations. Here is a sample: A, F, G to station 1; B, C to station 2; D, E to station 3; H to station 4; and I, J to station 5. **(c)** Actual efficiency with 5 stations = 83% **(d)** Idle time = 5 min/cycle.

18 **(a)** Minimum no. of workstations = 2.6 (or 3).
(b) Efficiency = 86.7%.
(c) Cycle time = 6.67 min/unit with 400 min/day; minimum no. of workstations = 1.95 (or 2).

20 Minimum (theoretical) = 4 stations. Efficiency = 93.3% with 5 stations and 6 min. cycle time. Several assignments with 5 are possible.

22 **(a)** Theoretical min. no. workstations = 5
(b) There are several possibilities. For example, Station 1–Task A; 2–C; 3–B and F; 4–D and G; 5–E, H, and I; 6–J. Or 1–A; 2–C; 3–B and F; 4–D and G; 5–E, H and I; 6–J.
(c) $n = 6$
(d) Efficiency = .7611

Human Resources, Job Design, and Work Measurement

2

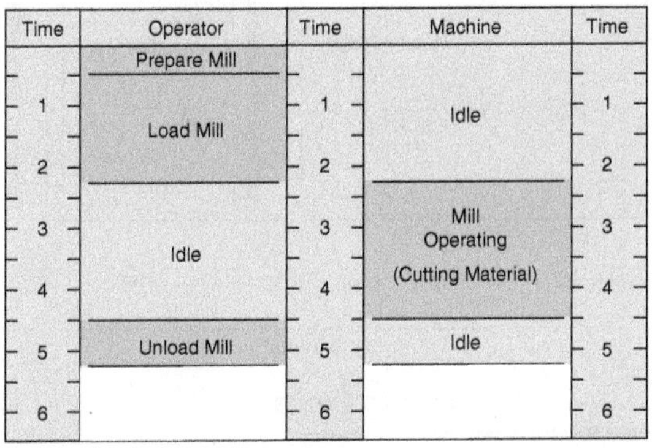

4 The first 10 steps of 4(a) are shown below. The remaining 10 steps are similar.

OPERATIONS CHART	SUMMARY						
PROCESS: CHANGE ERASER	SYMBOL	PRESENT				DIFF.	
ANALYST: ______		LH	RH	LH	RH	LH	RH
DATE: ______	○ OPERATIONS	1	8				
SHEET: 1 of 2	⇨ TRANSPORTS	3	8				
METHOD: (PRESENT) PROPOSED	□ INSPECTIONS	1					
REMARKS:	D DELAYS	15	4				
	▽ STORAGE						
	TOTALS	20	20				

LEFT HAND	DIST.	SYMBOL	SYMBOL	DIST.	RIGHT HAND
1 Reach for pencil		⇨	D		Idle
2 Grasp pencil		○	D		Idle
3 Move to work area		⇨	⇨		Move to pencil top
4 Hold pencil		D	○		Grasp pencil top
5 Hold pencil		D	○		Remove pencil top
6 Hold pencil		D	⇨		Set top aside
7 Hold pencil		D	⇨		Reach for old eraser
8 Hold pencil		D	○		Grasp old eraser
9 Hold pencil		D	○		Remove old eraser
10 Hold pencil		D	⇨		Set aside old eraser

6 Individual solution.

8

Process Chart
Charted by *H. Molano*
Date ______ Sheet *1* of *1*
Problem *Pit crew jack man*

Summary	
○ Operation	2
⇨ Transport	3
□ Inspect	
D Delay	2
▽ Store	
Vert. Dist.	
Hor. Dist.	
Time (seconds)	12.5

Distance (feet)	Time (seconds)	Chart Symbols	Process Description
15	2.0	○ ⇨ □ D ▽	*Move to right side of car*
	2.0	○ ⇨ □ D ▽	*Raise car*
	1.0	○ ⇨ □ D ▽	*Wait for tire exchange to finish*
10	1.8	○ ⇨ □ D ▽	*Move to left side of car*
	2.0	○ ⇨ □ D ▽	*Raise car*
	1.2	○ ⇨ □ D ▽	*Wait for tire exchange to finish*
5	2.5	○ ⇨ □ D ▽	*Move back over wall from left side*

10 The first portion of the activity chart is shown below.

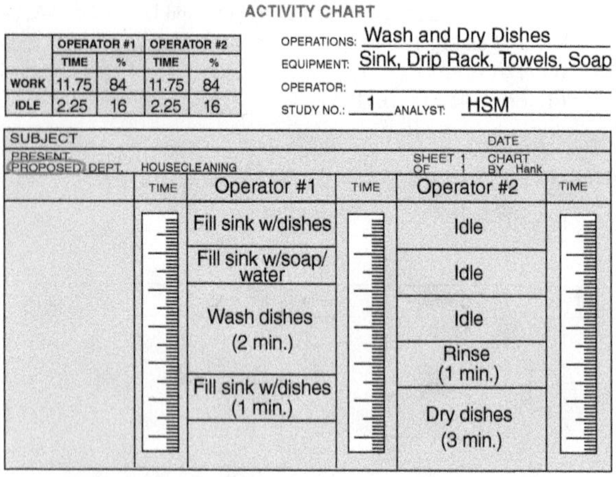

12 The first portion of the process chart is shown below.

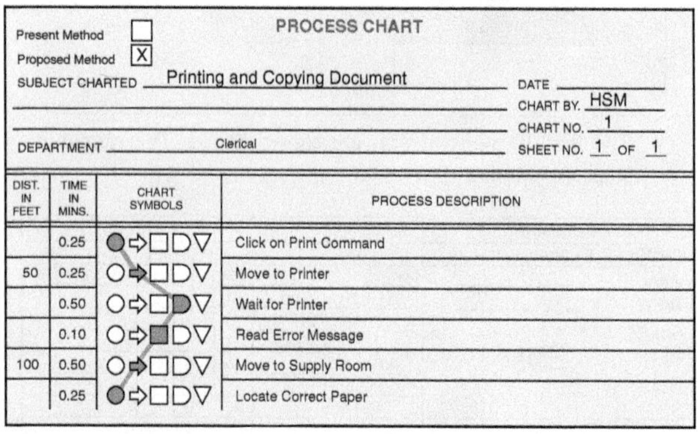

14 NT = 7.65 sec; slower than normal
16 (a) 6.525 sec
(b) 6.2 sec
(c) 6.739 sec
18 (a) 12.6 min
(b) 15 min
20 (a) 12.0 sec
(b) 14.12 sec
22 10.12 min
24 (a) 3.24 min
(b) 4.208 min
26 n = 14.13, or 15 observations
28 (a) 45.36, 13.75, 3.6, 15.09
(b) 91.53 min
(c) 96 samples
30 (a) 47.6 min
(b) 75 samples
32 n = 348
34 73.8%
36 6.55 sec
38 (a) 240 min
(b) 150 hr
(c) Clean 8 rooms; refresh 16 rooms; 38 housekeepers
(d) 50 employees

Supply Chain Management

2 Problems include communication, product valuation, selecting virtual partners
4 (a) Only a 5.7% decrease in material (supply chain) costs are required to yield a profit of $25,000, but (b) a 22.2% increase in sales is necessary for a $25,000 profit.
6 (a) Weeks of supply = 3.85
(b) % of assets in inventory = 11.63%
(c) Turnover = 13.5
(d) No, but note they are in different industries
8 (a) Last year = 10.4
(b) This year = 9.67
(c) Yes

Supply Chain Management Analytics

S2 Two supplies best, $42,970
S4 (a) $P(2)$ = 0.017463
(b) $P(2)$ = 0.018866
(c) Option 1 (2 local suppliers) has lower risk.
S6 (a) 2.5
(b) 1.2
(c) 1.25
(d) 1.8
(e) Retailer
S8 (a) 1.20
(b) Bullwhip = 0 if order sizes all the same.
S10 Donna Inc., 8.2; Kay Corp., 9.8
S12 Individual responses. Issues might include academics, location, financial support, size, facilities, etc.
S14 Use faster shipping, option a, since daily holding cost is more than daily cost of faster shipping.
S16 $20.34

Inventory Management

2 (a) A items are G2 and F3; B items are A2, C7, and D1; all others are C.
4 108 items
6 (a) 600 units
(b) 424.26 units
(c) 848.53 units
8 (a) 80 units
(b) 73 units
10 (a) 2,100 units
(b) 4,200 units
(c) 1,050 units
12 (a) 189.74 units
(b) 94.87
(c) 31.62
(d) 7.91
(e) $1,897.30
(f) $601,897
14 (a) Order quantity variations have limited impact on total cost.
(b) EOQ = 50
16 (a) 671 units
(b) 18.63
(c) 559 = max. inventory
(d) 16.7%
(e) $1,117.90
18 (a) 1,217 units
(b) 1,095 = max. inventory
(c) 8.22 production runs
(e) $657.30
20 (a) EOQ = 200, total cost = $1,446,380
(b) EOQ = 200, total cost = $1,445,880
22 (a) 16,971 units
(b) $530.33
(c) $530.33
(d) $56,250
(e) $57,310.66
24 (a) EOQ = 410
(b) Vendor Allen has slightly lower cost.
(c) Optimal order quantity = 1,000 @ total cost of $128,920

26 **(a)** EOQ (1) = 336; EOQ (2) = 335
(b) Order 1,200 from Vendor 2.
(c) At 1,200 lb., total cost = $161,275.
(d) Storage space and perishability.
28 **(a)** Z = 1.88
(b) Safety stock = $Z\sigma$ = 1.88(5) = 9.4 drives
(c) ROP = 59.4 drives
30 100 kilos of safety stock
32 **(a)** 291 towels
(b) 2,291 towels
34 **(a)** ROP = 1,718 cigars
(b) 1,868 cigars
(c) A higher service level means a lower probability of stocking out.
36 103 pounds
38 **(a)** $3
(b) $.90
(c) 63,675 programs
(d) 23.1%
40 **(a)** Q = 400 lb.
(b) $600
(c) $600
(d) ROP = 369.99
(e) 69.99
(f) $209.97
(g) Safety stock = 61.61

Aggregate Planning and S&OP

2 **(a)** $109,120 = total cost
(b) $106,640 = total cost
(c) No, plan 2 is better at $105,152.
4 Cost = $214,000 for plan B
6 **(a)** Plan D, $122,000
(b) Plan E is $129,000
8 Extra total cost = $2,960.
10 **(a)** Plan C, $104,000; **(b)** plan D, $93,800, assuming initial inventory = 0
12 **(a)** Cost is $314,000.
(b) Cost is $329,000 (but an alternative approach yields $259,500).
(c) Cost is $222,000.
(d) Plan C.
(e) Plan C, with lowest cost and steady employment.
14 $1,186,810
16 $100,750
18 $90,850
20 **(a)** Cost using O.T. and Forrester = $195,625.
(b) A case could be made for either position.
22 Current model = $9,200 in sales; proposed model yields $9,350, which is only slightly better.

Material Requirements Planning (MRP) and ERP

2 The time-phased plan for the gift bags is:

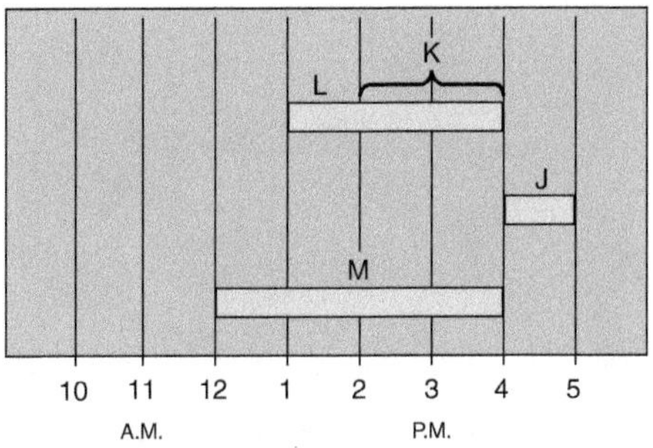

Someone should start on item M by noon.

4 Gross material requirements plan:

Item		Week 1	2	3	4	5	6	7	8	Lead Time (wk)
S	Gross req.							100		
	Order release					100				2
T	Gross req.					100				
	Order release				100					1
U	Gross req.					200				
	Order release			200						2
V	Gross req.				100					
	Order release		100							2
W	Gross req.				200					
	Order release	200								3
X	Gross req.				100					
	Order release			100						1
Y	Gross req.			400						
	Order release	400								2
Z	Gross req.			600						
	Order release		600							1

6 Gross material requirements plan, modified to include the 20 units of U required for maintenance purposes:

Item		Week 1	2	3	4	5	6	7	8	Lead Time (wk)
S	Gross req.							100		
	Order release					100				2
T	Gross req.					100				
	Order release				100					1
U	Gross req.					200	20			
	Order release			200	20					2
V	Gross req.				100					
	Order release		100							2
W	Gross req.				200					
	Order release	200								3
X	Gross req.				100					
	Order release			100						1
Y	Gross req.			400	40					
	Order release	400	40							2
Z	Gross req.			600	60					
	Order release		600	60						1

8 **(a)**

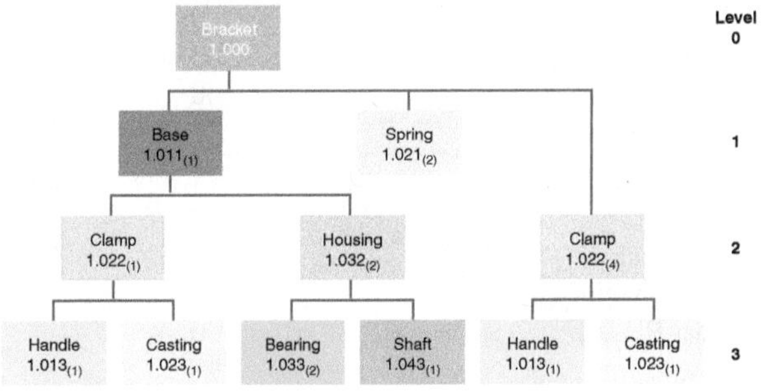

(b) For 50 brackets, the gross requirements are for 50 bases, 100 springs, 250 clamps, 250 handles, 250 castings, 100 housings, 200 bearings, and 100 shafts.

(c) For 50 brackets, net requirements are 25 bases, 100 springs, 125 clamps, 125 handles, 125 castings, 50 housings, 100 bearings, and 50 shafts.

10 (a) Gross material requirements plan for the first three items:

Item		Week 1	2	3	4	5	6	7	8	9	10	11	12
X1	Gross req.								50		20		100
	Order release							50		20		100	
B1	Gross req.							50		20		100	
	Order release					50		20		100			
B2	Gross req.							100		40		200	
	Order release					100		40		200			

(b) The net materials requirement plan for the first two items:

Level: 0 **Parent:** **Quantity:**
Item: X1 **Lead Time:** **Lot Size: L4L**

Week No.	1	2	3	4	5	6	7	8	9	10	11	12
Gross Requirement								50		20		100
Scheduled Receipt												
On-hand Inventory								50		0		0
Net Requirement								0		20		100
Planned Order Receipt										20		100
Planned Order Release									20		100	

Level: 1 **Parent: X1** **Quantity: 1X**
Item: B1 **Lead Time: 2** **Lot Size: L4L**

Week No.	1	2	3	4	5	6	7	8	9	10	11	12
Gross Requirement									20		100	
Scheduled Receipt												
On-hand Inventory									20		0	
Net Requirement									0		100	
Planned Order Receipt											100	
Planned Order Release									100			

12 (a) Net material requirements schedule (only items A and H are shown):

	Week 1	2	3	4	5	6	7	8	9	10	11	12
A Gross Required								100		50		150
On Hand								0		0		0
Net Required								100		50		150
Order Receipt								100		50		150
Order Release							100		50		150	
H Gross Required									100		50	
On Hand									0		0	
Net Required									100		50	
Order Receipt									100		50	
Order Release								100		50		

(b) Net material requirements schedule (only items B and C are shown; schedule for items A and H remains the same as in part a).

		Week 1	2	3	4	5	6	7	8	9	10	11	12	13
B Gross Requirements								200		100		300		
Scheduled Receipts														
Projected on Hand	100							100		0		0		
Net Requirements								100		100		300		
Planned Order Receipts								100		100		300		
Planned Order Releases						100		100		300				
C Gross Requirements								200	200	100	100	300		
Scheduled Receipts														
Projected on Hand	50							50		0		0		
Net Requirements								150	200	100	100	300		
Planned Order Receipts								150	200	100	100	300		
Planned Order Releases						150	200	100	100	300				

14 (a)

Level	Description	Qty
0	A	1
1	B	1
2	C	1
2	D	1
3	E	1
1	F	1
2	G	1
2	H	1
3	E	1
3	C	1

Note: with low-level coding "C" would be a level-3 code

(b) Solution for Items A, B, F (on next page):

14 **(b)**

Lot Size	Lead Time	On Hand	Safety Stock	Allo-cated	Low-Level Code	Item ID		1	2	3	4	5	6	7	8
								Period (week)							
Lot	1	0	—	—	0	A	Gross Requirement								10
for							Scheduled Receipt								
Lot							Projected on Hand								0
							Net Requirement								10
							Planned Receipt								10
							Planned Release							10	
Lot	1	2	—	—	1	B	Gross Requirement							10	
for							Scheduled Receipt								
Lot							Projected on Hand	2	2	2	2	2	2	2	0
							Net Requirement							8	
							Planned Receipt							8	
							Planned Release						8		
Lot	1	5	—	—	1	F	Gross Requirement							10	
for							Scheduled Receipt								
Lot							Projected on Hand	5	5	5	5	5	5	5	0
							Net Requirement							5	
							Planned Receipt							5	
							Planned Release						5		

16 **(a)** Only item G changes.
(b) Component F and 4 units of A will be delayed one week.
(c) Options include: delaying 4 units of A for 1 week; asking supplier of G to expedite production.

18 EOQ = 57; Total cost $ = $1,660

20 Lot-for-lot can be considered best; it has the lowest cost.

22 **(a)** $1,200
(b) $2,370
(c) $1,100
(d) Periodic order quantity is lowest.

24 Selection for first 5 weeks:

Week	Units	Capacity Required (time)	Capacity Available (time)	Over/ (Under)	Production Scheduler's Action
1	60	3,900	2,250	1,650	Lot split. Move 300 minutes (4.3 units) to week 2 and 1,350 minutes to week 3.
2	30	1,950	2,250	(300)	
3	10	650	2,250	(1,600)	
4	40	2,600	2,250	350	Lot split. Move 250 minutes to week 3. Operations split. Move 100 minutes to another machine, overtime, or subcontract.
5	70	4,550	2,250	2,300	Lot split. Move 1,600 minutes to week 6. Overlap operations to get product out door. Operations split. Move 700 minutes to another machine, overtime, or subcontract.

26 Here are the order releases for the table and the top:

Lot Size	Lead Time (# of periods)	On Hand	Safety Stock	Allo-cated	Low-Level Code	Item ID		Period (day) 1	2	3	4	5	6	7	8
Lot for Lot	1	—	—	—	0	Table	Gross Requirements					640	640	128	128
							Scheduled Receipts								
							Projected on Hand								
							Net Requirements					640	640	128	128
							Planned Order Receipts					640	640	128	128
							Planned Order Releases				640	640	128	128	
Lot for Lot	1	—	—	—	1	Top	Gross Requirements				640	640	128	128	
							Scheduled Receipts								
							Projected on Hand								
							Net Requirements				640	640	128	128	
							Planned Order Receipts				640	640	128	128	
							Planned Order Releases			640	640	128	128		

Short-Term Scheduling

2

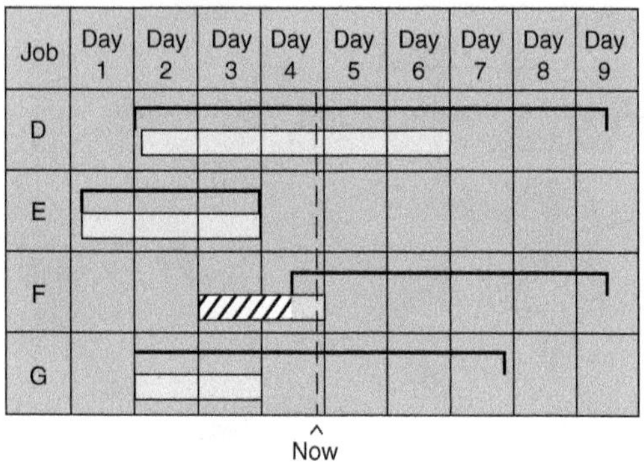

4 **(a)** 1–D, 2–A, 3–C, 4–B
(b) 40

6 Chris–Finance, Steve–Marketing, Juana–H.R., Rebecca–Operations, $210

8 Ajay–Jackie, Jack–Barbara, Gray–Stella, Raul–Dona, 230

10 **(a)** A, B, C, D, E
(b) B, A, D, E, C
(c) E, D, A, B, C
(d) C, B, A, D, E
(e) SPT is best.

12 **(a)** A, B, C, D
(b) B, C, A, D
(c) D, A, C, B
(d) C, B, D, A
(e) D, C, A, B
SPT is best on all measures.

14 **(a)** A, B, C, D, E
(b) C, A, B, E, D
(c) C, D, E, A, B
(d) B, A, E, D, C
EDD, then FCFS are best on lateness; SPT on other two measures.

16 1, 3, 4, 2, 5

18 E, D, C, A, B, F

20 7 employees needed; 6 have two consecutive days off. The 7th works only 3 days/week.

JIT, TPS, and Lean Operations

2 3.75, or 4 kanbans

4 Size of kanban = 66; number of kanbans = 5.9, or 6

6 **(a)** EOQ = 10 lamps
(b) 200 orders/yr
(c) $200

8 7.26 min.

10 **(a)** Setup cost = $5.74
(b) Setup time = 8.61 min

Maintenance and Reliability

2 From Figure 2, about 13% overall reliability.

4 Expected daily breakdowns = 2.0
Expected cost = $100 daily

6 **(a)** 5.0%
(b) .00001026 failures/unit-hr.
(c) .08985
(d) 98.83

8 R_s = .9941

10 R_p = .99925

12 **(a)** R_p = .984
(b) Increase by 11.1%.

14 R = .7918

16 **(a)** .972
(b) .980

18 System B is slightly higher, at .9397.

Decision-Making Tools

2 **(a)**

Size of First Station	Good Market ($)	Fair Market ($)	Poor Market ($)	EV Under Equally Likely
Small	50,000	20,000	—10,000	20,000
Medium	80,000	30,000	—20,000	30,000
Large	100,000	30,000	— 40,000	30,000
Very large	300,000	25,000	—160,000	55,000

(b) Maximax: Build a very large station.
(c) Maximin: Build a small station.
(d) Equally likely: Build a very large station.

(e)

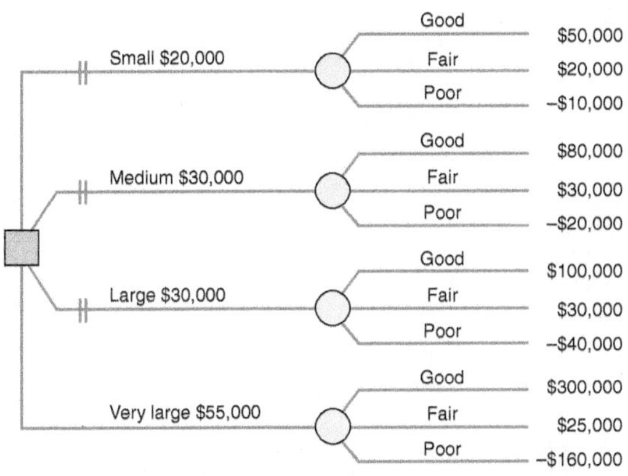

4 **(a)** Alternatives: N, M, L, D. States of nature: Fixed, Slight Increase, Major Increase
(b) Use maximin criterion. No floor space (N).
6 Buying equipment at $733,333
8 **(a)** E(cost full-time) = $520
(b) E(cost part-timers) = $475
10 Alternative B; 74
12 8 cases; EMV = $352.50
14 **(a)**

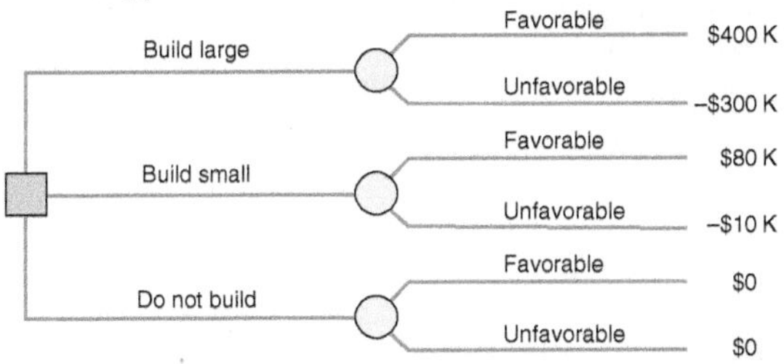

(b) Small plant with EMV = $26,000
(c) EVPI = $134,000
16 **(a)** Max EMV = $11,700
(b) EVPI = $13,200 − $11,700 = $1,500
18

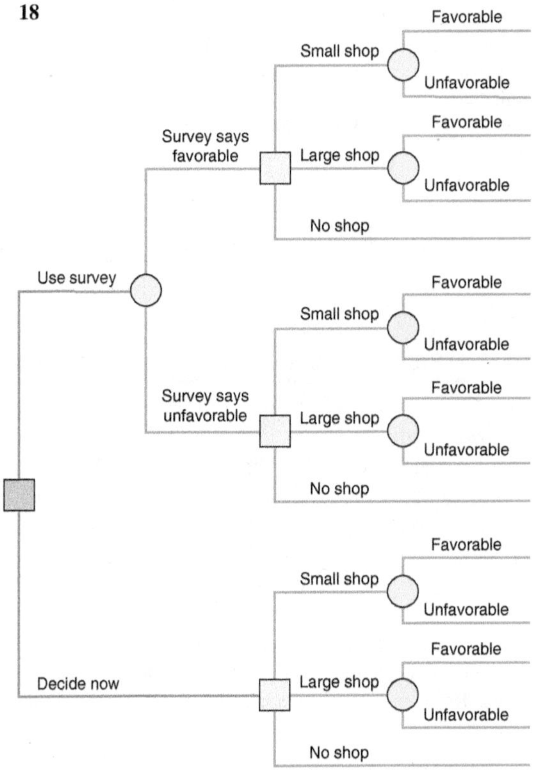

20 No information and build large; $4,500.
22 **(b)** EMV(Y) = 4.2, which is best

Linear Programming

2 Profit = $100 at $X = 0, Y = 10$
4 **(b)** Yes; $P = \$3{,}000$ at (75, 75) and (50, 150)
6 **(a)** Min $X_1 + 2X_2$
Subject to: $X_1 + X_2 \geq 40$
$2X_1 + 4X_2 \geq 60$
$x_1 \leq 15$
(b) Cost = $.65 at (15, 25)
(c) 65¢
8 $x_1 = 200, x_2 = 0$, profit = $18,000
10 10 Alpha 1s, 24 Beta 2s, profit = $55,200
12 **(a)** $x_1 = 25.71, x_2 = 21.43$
(b) Cost = $68.57
14 **(a)** $x_1 = 7.95, x_2 = 5.95, x_3 = 12.6, P = \$143.76$
(b) No unused time
(c) 26¢
(d) $7.86
16 **(a)** Let X_{ij} = number of students bused from sector i to school j.
Objective: minimize total travel miles =
$5X_{AB} + 8X_{AC} + 6X_{AE}$
$+ 0X_{BB} + 4X_{BC} + 12X_{BE}$
$+ 4x_{CB} + 0X_{CC} + 7X_{CE}$
$+ 7X_{DB} + 2X_{DC} + 5x_{DE}$
$+ 12X_{EB} + 7X_{EC} + 0X_{EE}$
Subject to:
$X_{AB} + X_{AC} + X_{AE} = 700$ (number of students in sector A)
$X_{BB} + X_{BC} + X_{BE} = 500$ (number students in sector B)
$X_{CB} + X_{CC} + X_{CE} = 100$ (number students in sector C)
$X_{DB} + X_{DC} + X_{DE} = 800$ (number students in sector D)
$X_{EB} + X_{EC} + X_{EE} = 400$ (number of students in sector E)
$X_{AB} + X_{BB} + X_{CB} + X_{DB} + X_{EB} \leq 900$ (school B capacity)
$X_{AC} + X_{BC} + X_{CC} + X_{DC} + X_{EC} \leq 900$ (school C capacity)
$X_{AE} + X_{BE} + X_{CE} + X_{DE} + X_{EE} \leq 900$ (school E capacity)
(b) Solution: $X_{AB} = 400$
$X_{AE} = 300$
$X_{BB} = 500$
$X_{CC} = 100$
$X_{DC} = 800$
$X_{EE} = 400$
Distance = 5,400 "student miles"
18 Hire 30 workers; three solutions are feasible; two of these are:
16 begin at 7 A.M.
9 begin at 3 P.M.
2 begin at 7 P.M.
3 begin at 11 P.M.
An alternate optimum is:
3 begin at 3 A.M.
9 begin at 7 A.M.
7 begin at 11 A.M.
2 begin at 3 P.M.
9 begin at 7 P.M.
0 begin at 11 P.M.
20 Max $P = 9x_1 + 12x_2$
Subject to:
$x_1 + x_2 \leq 10$
$x_1 + 2x_2 \leq 12$
$x_1 = 8, x_2 = 2$; profit = $96
22 $x_1 = 14, x_2 = 33$, cost = 221
24 5 corner points
26 **(a)** Minimize = $6X_{1A} + 5X_{1B} + 3X_{1C} + 8X_{2A} + 10X_{2B} + 8X_{2C} + 11X_{3A} + 14X_{3B} + 18X_{3C}$

Subject to:

$X_{1A} + X_{2A} + X_{3A} = 7$
$X_{1B} + X_{2B} + X_{3B} = 12$
$X_{1C} + X_{2C} + X_{3C} = 5$
$X_{1A} + X_{1B} + X_{1C} \leq 6$
$X_{2A} + X_{2B} + X_{2C} \leq 8$
$X_{3A} + X_{3B} + X_{3C} \leq 10$

(b) Minimum cost = $219,000

28 One approach results in 2,790 medical patients and 2,104 surgical patients, with a revenue of $9,551,659 per year (which can change slightly to $9,548,760 with rounding). This yields 61 integer medical beds and 29 integer surgical beds.

30 Apple sauce = 0, Canned corn = 1.33, Fried chicken = 0.46, French fries = 0, Mac & Cheese = 1.13, Turkey = 0, Garden salad = 0, Cost = $1.51.

Transportation Models

2 $208
4 $170
6 **(a)** A–1, 10; B–1, 30; C–2, 60; A–3, 40; C–3, 15
(b) $1,775
8 Houston, $19,500
10 Total cost = $505
12 Optimal site is St. Louis, at $17,250

Waiting-Line Models

2 **(a)** 44%
(b) .36 people
(c) .8 people
(d) .53 min
(e) 1.2 min
4 **(a)** .5
(b) .5
(c) 1
(d) .5
(e) .05 hr
(f) .1 hr
6 **(a)** .667
(b) .667 min
(c) 1.33
8 **(a)** .375
(b) 1.6 hr (or .2 days)
(c) .225
(d) 0.141, 0.053, 0.020, 0.007
10 **(a)** 2.25
(b) .75
(c) .857 min. (.014 hr)
(d) .64 min. (.011 hr)
(e) 42%, 32%, 24%
12 **(a)** 6 trucks
(b) 12 min
(c) .857
(d) .54
(e) $1,728/day
(f) Yes, save $3,096 in the first year.
14 **(a)** .075 hrs (4.5 min)
(b) 1.125 people
(c) .0083 hrs (0.5 min), 0.083 people
16 **(a)** .113 hr. = 6.8 min
(b) 1.13 cars
18 **(a)** .05
(b) .743
(c) .793
20 **(a)** 3, 2, 4 MDs, respectively
(b) Because $\lambda > \mu$, an indefinite queue buildup can occur.

22 **(a)** 4 servers
(b) 6 servers
(c) $109
(d) 83.33%
24 2 salespeople ($340)

Learning Curves

2 **(a)** 507 min
(b) 456 min
(c) 410 min
(d) 369 min
4 **(a)** 1,546 min
(b) 2,872 min
(c) 3,701 min
(d) 6,779 min
6 **(a)** 14.31 hr
(b) $71,550
(c) $947,250
8 **(a)** 80%
(b) 3.51
(c) 3.2, 2.98, 2.81
(d) 21.5
10 **(a)** 72.2 hr
(b) 60.55 hr
(c) 41.47 hr
12 Susan will take 3.67 hr and Julie 2.43 hr. Neither trainee will reach 1 hr by the 10th unit.
14 $748,240 for fourth, $709,960 for fifth, $679,960 for sixth
16 **(a)** 70 millicents/bit
(b) 8.2 millicents/bit
18 26,755 hr
20 **(a)** 32.98 hr, 49.61 hr
(b) Initial quote is high.
22 **(a)** Four boats can be completed.
(b) Five boats can be completed.
24 .227 hr
26 Just above 85% learning rate

Simulation

2 0, 0, 0, 0, 0, 0, 0, 2, 0, 2
4 Profits = 20, −15, 20, 17.50, 20; average equals $12.50.
6 At the end of 5 min, two checkouts are still busy and one is available.
8

Arrivals	*Arrival Time*	*Service Time*	*Departure Time*
1	11:01	3	11:04
2	11:04	2	11:06
3	11:06	2	11:08
4	11:07	1	11:09

10 **(a, b)**

No. Cars	Prob.	Cum. Prob.	R.N. Interval
3 or fewer	0	0	—
4	.10	.10	01 through 10
5	.15	.25	11 through 25
6	.25	.50	26 through 50
7	.30	.80	51 through 80
8	.20	1.00	81 through 00
9 or more	0	—	—

(c) Average no arrivals/hr = 105/15 = 7 cars

12 Here are the random-number intervals for the first two departments. Random number intervals correspond to probability of occurrence.

From	To	R.N. Interval
Initial exam	X-ray	01 through 45
	OR	46 through 60
	Observ.	61 through 70
	Out	71 through 00

From	To	R.N. Interval
X-ray	OR	01 through 10
	Cast	11 through 35
	Observ.	36 through 70
	Out	71 through 00

Each simulation could produce different results. Some will indeed show a person entering X-ray twice.

14 **(a)** 5 times
(b) 6.95 times; yes
(c) 7.16 heaters

16 **(a)** Expected average demand is about 8.75, average lead time is 1.86, average end inventory = 6.50, average lost sales = 4.04. Values and costs will vary with different sets of random numbers. Random numbers were selected from right-hand column of Appendix III (07, 60, 77, 49, etc).
(b) $520,110, or $21,671 per month

18 Total stockout cost = $80; total holding cost = $40; so total cost = $120 with ROP = 4 vs. total cost = $223 with ROP = 2 in Problem 17. Weekly costs are found by dividing by 10.

Online Tutorial 1

T1.2 5.45; 4.06
T1.4 **(a)** .2743
(b) 0.5
T1.6 .1587; .2347; .1587
T1.8 **(a)** .0548
(b) .6554
(c) .6554
(d) .2119

Online Tutorial 2

T2.2 (selected values)

Fraction Defective	Mean of Poisson	$P(x \le 1)$
.01	.05	.999
.05	.25	.974
.10	.50	.910
.30	1.50	.558
.60	3.00	.199
1.00	5.00	.040

T2.4 The plan meets neither the producer's nor the consumer's requirement.

Online Tutorial 3

T3.2 **(a)** Max $3x_1 + 9x_2$
$x_1 + 4x_2 + s_1 = 24$
$x_1 + 2x_2 + s_2 = 16$
(b) See the steps in the tutorial.
(c) Second tableau:

c_j	Mix	x_1	x_2	s_1	s_2	Qty.
9	x_2	.25	1	.25	0	6
0	s_2	.50	0	−.50	1	4
	z_j	2.25	9	2.25	0	54
	$c_j - z_j$	.75	0	−2.25	0	

(d) $x_1 = 8, x_2 = 4$, Profit = $60

T3.4 Basis for 1st tableau:
$A_1 = 80$
$A_2 = 75$
Basis for 2nd tableau:
$A_1 = 55$
$X_1 = 25$
Basis for 3rd tableau:
$X_1 = 14$
$X_2 = 33$
Cost = $221 at optimal solution

T3.6 **(a)** x_1
(b) A_1

Online Tutorial 4

T4.2 Cost = $980; 1–A = 20; 1–B = 50; 2–C = 20; 2–Dummy = 30; 3–A = 20; 3–C = 40

T4.4 Total = 3,100 mi; Morgantown–Coaltown = 35; Youngstown–Coal Valley = 30; Youngstown–Coaltown = 5; Youngstown–Coal Junction = 25; Pittsburgh–Coaltown = 5; Pittsburgh–Coalsburg = 20

T4.6 **(a)** Using VAM, cost = $635; A–Y = 35; A–Z = 20; B–W = 10; B–X = 20; B–Y = 15; C–W = 30
(b) Using MODI, cost is also $635 (i.e., initial solution was optimal). An alternative optimal solution is A–X = 20; A–Y = 15; A–Z = 20; B–W = 10; B–Y = 35; C–W = 30

Online Tutorial 5

T5.2 **(a)** $I_{13} = 12$
(b) $I_{35} = 7$
(c) $I_{51} = 4$

T5.4 **(a)** Tour: 1–2–4–5–7–6–8–3–1; 37.9 mi
(b) Tour: 4–5–7–1–2–3–6–8–4; 39.1 mi

T5.6 **(a)** Vehicle 1: Tour 1–2–4–3–5–1 = $134
(b) Vehicle 2: Tour 1–6–10–9–8–7–1 = $188

T5.8 The cost matrix is shown below:

	1	2	3	4	5	6	7	8
1	—	107.26	118.11	113.20	116.50	123.50	111.88	111.88
2		—	113.53	111.88	118.10	125.30	116.50	118.10
3			—	110.56	118.70	120.50	119.90	124.90
4				—	109.90	119.10	111.88	117.90
5					—	111.88	106.60	118.50
6						—	111.88	123.50
7							—	113.20
8								—

APPENDIX

USING EXCEL OM AND POM FOR WINDOWS

Two approaches to computer-aided decision making are provided with this text: **Excel OM** and **POM** (Production and Operations Management) **for Windows**. These are the two most user-friendly software packages available to help you learn and understand operations management. Both programs can be used either to solve homework problems identified with an icon or to check answers you have developed by hand. Both software packages use the standard Windows interface and run on any IBM-compatible PC operating Windows XP or newer. Excel OM is also available for the Mac.

EXCEL OM

Excel OM has been designed to help you to better learn and understand both OM and Excel. Even though the software contains 24 modules and more than 60 submodules, the screens for every module are consistent and easy to use. Modules can be accessed through either of two menus that are added to Excel. The Chapter menu (Excel 2007/2012) or the Heizer menu (Excel 2003, Excel for Macs) lists the modules in *chapter* order, as illustrated for Excel 2007/2010 in Program IV.1(a). The Alphabetical menu (Excel 2007/2010) or Excel OM menu (Excel 2003, Excel for Macs) lists the modules in alphabetical order, as illustrated for Excel OM for Macs in Program 1(b). This software is provided at no cost to users of myomlab (www.myomlab.com) or purchasers of a new copy of this textbook. The software can also be purchased at www.pearsonhighered.com/heizer. Excel 2003 or newer must be on your PC or Office 11 or greater must be on your Mac.

To install Excel OM, after the web page opens, click on the Software option on the left side, click on the Download link, and follow the instructions. Default values have been assigned in the setup program, but you may change them if you like. For Windows, the default folder into which a program will be

▼ **PROGRAM 1(a) Excel OM Modules Menu in Add-In Tab in Excel 2007/2010**

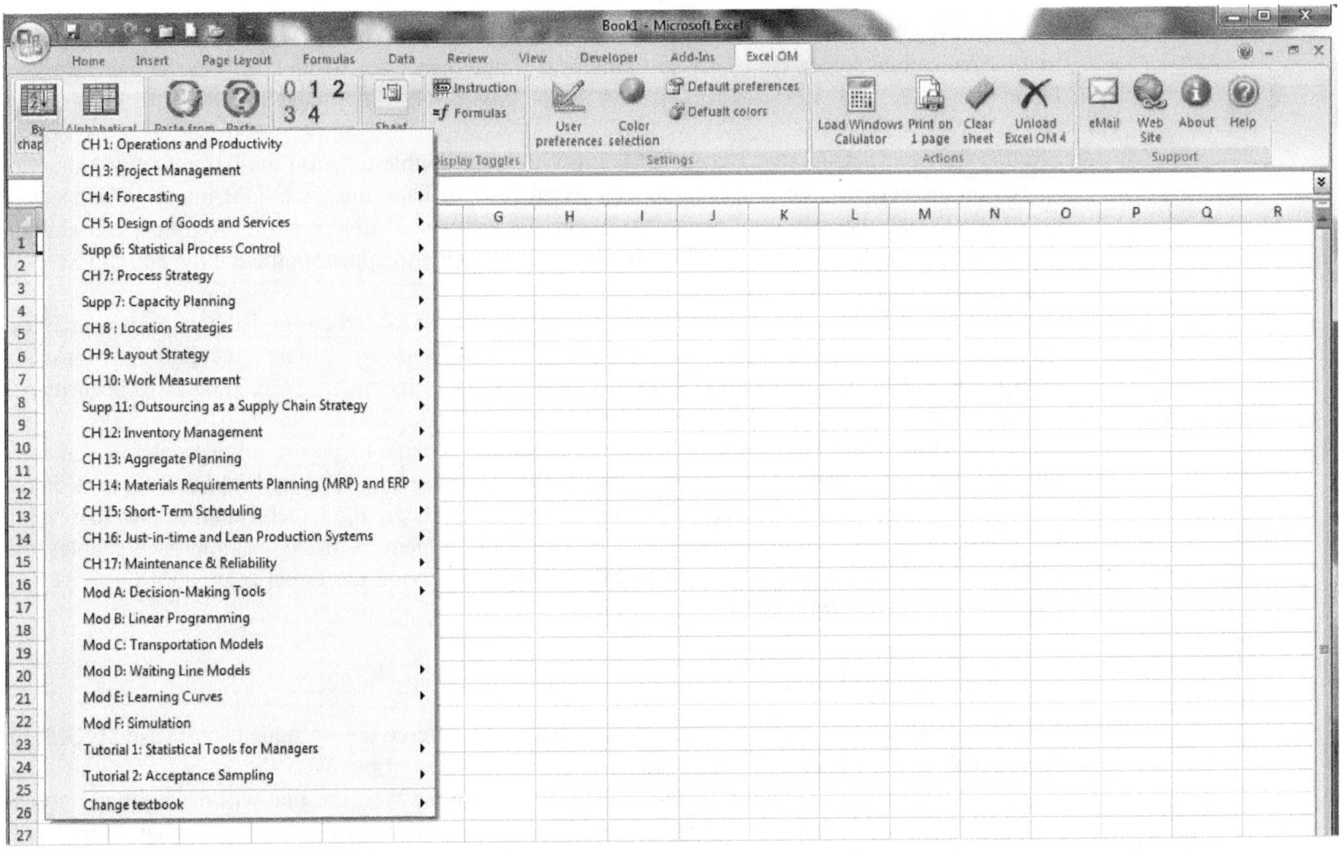

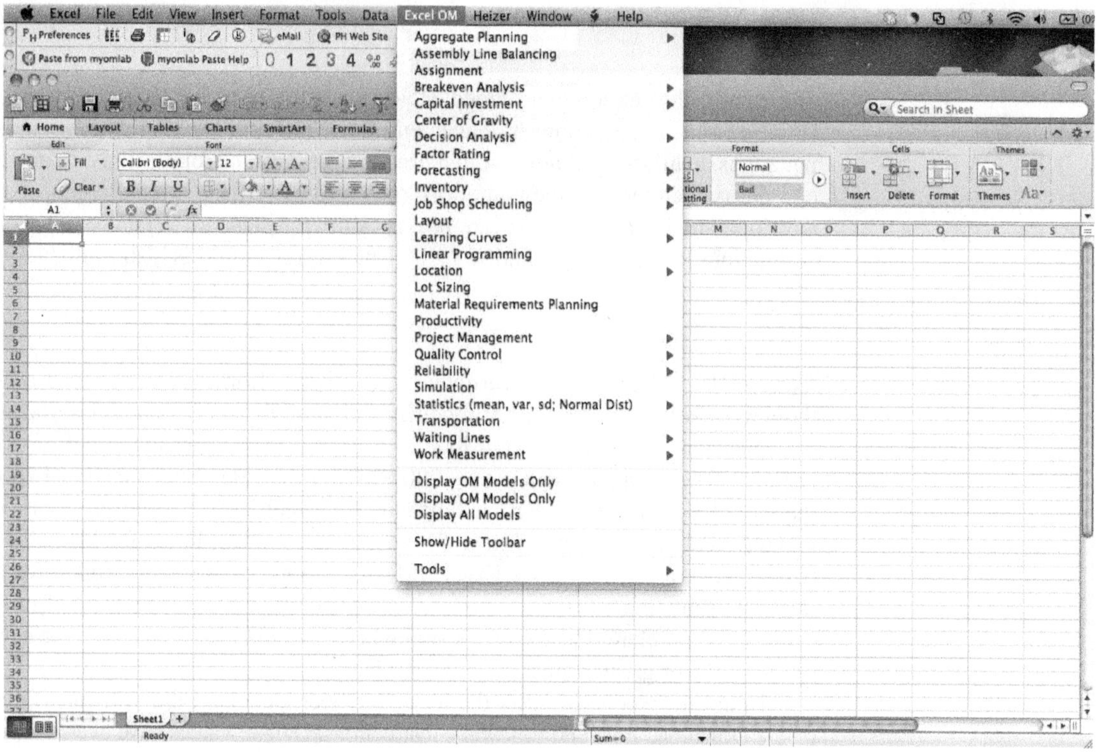

▲ **PROGRAM 1(b)** **Excel OM Modules Menu in OM for Macs Version**

installed is named C:\Program Files(x86)\ExcelOMQMv4. For the Mac, the Excel OM folder is placed in the Applications folder. Generally speaking, it is simply necessary to click *Next* each time the installation asks a question.

Starting the Program To start Excel OM using Windows, double-click on the Excel OM V4 shortcut placed on the desktop during installation. In Excel 2007 or later, the Excel OM menu will appear in an Excel OM tab that will be added to the Excel 2007 ribbon, as displayed in Program 1(a), while in earlier versions of Excel or on the Mac, the Excel OM menu will appear in the main menu of Excel, as displayed in Program 1(b).

If you have Excel 2007 or later and do not see an Excel OM tab on the Ribbon, then your Excel security settings need to be revised to enable Excel OM V4. Please consult the Excel 2007/2010 instructions at the support site, www.prenhall.com/weiss, or see the document Excel 2007.2010.Security.pdf that has been installed in the default directory.

Excel OM serves two purposes in the learning process. First, it helps you solve problems. You enter the appropriate data, and the program provides numerical solutions. POM for Windows operates on the same principle. However, Excel OM allows for a second approach: the Excel *formulas* used to develop solutions can be modified to deal with a wider variety of problems. This "open" approach enables you to observe, understand, and even change the formulas underlying the Excel calculations—conveying Excel's power as an OM analysis tool.

POM FOR WINDOWS

POM for Windows is decision support software that is also offered free to students who use MyOMLab or who purchased this as a new text. It can also be purchased at our Web site www.pearsonhighered.com/heizer. Program 2 shows a list of 24 OM modules on the Web site that will be installed on your hard drive. Once you follow the standard setup instructions, a POM for Windows program icon will be added to your desktop, and a program group will be added to your Start, All Programs menu. The program may be accessed by double-clicking on the desktop icon.

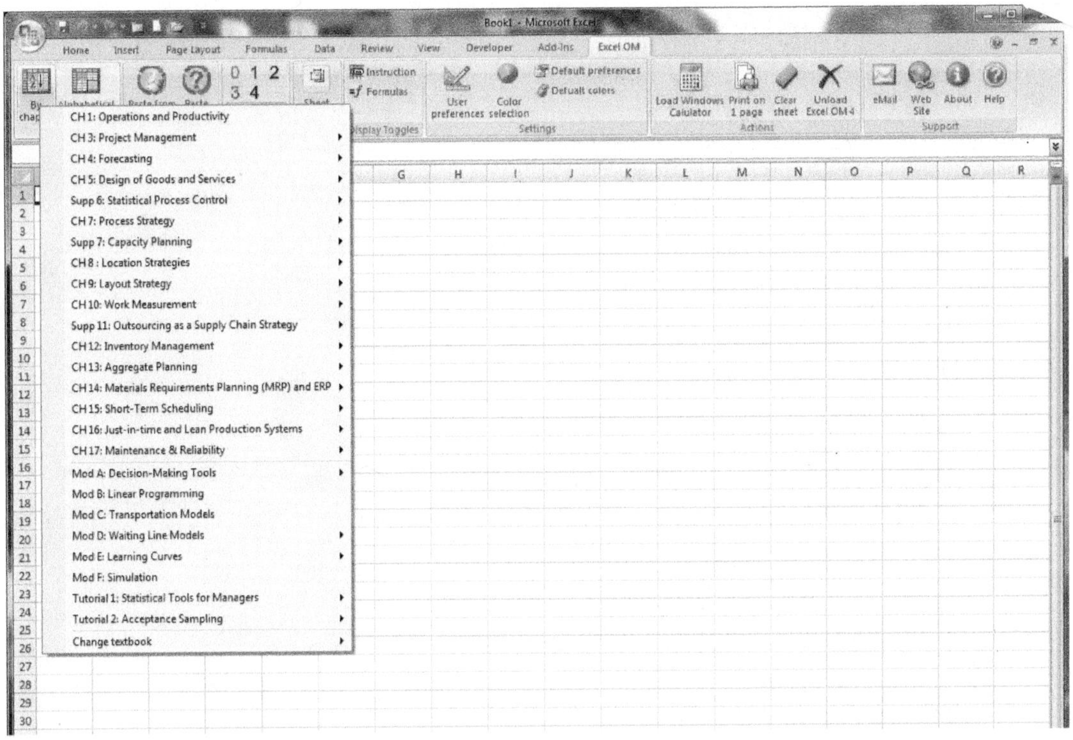

▲ **PROGRAM 2 POM for Windows Module List**

USING EXCEL OM AND POM FOR WINDOWS WITH MYOMLAB

It is very easy to copy data from myomlab and paste the data into either Excel OM or POM for Windows. After creating a model in Excel OM or POM, go to MyOMLab and click on the Copy icon. Then, in POM or in Excel OM, click on **Paste** from MyOMLab icon on the toolbar or in the right-click menu.

Updates to POM for Windows and Excel OM are available on the internet through the Downloads and Support links at *www.prenhall.com/weiss*.

Index